THE CAMBRIDGE COMPARATIVE HISTORY
OF ANCIENT LAW

The Cambridge Comparative History of Ancient Law is the first of its kind in the field of comparative ancient legal history. Written collaboratively by a dedicated team of international experts, each chapter offers a new framing and understanding of key legal concepts, practices and historical contexts across five major legal traditions of the ancient world. Stretching chronologically across more than three and a half millennia, from the earliest, very fragmentary, proto-cuneiform tablets (3200–3000 BCE) to the Tang Code of 652 CE, the volume challenges earlier comparative histories of ancient law/societies, at the same time as opening up new areas for future scholarship across a wealth of surviving ancient Near Eastern, Indian, Chinese, Greek and Roman primary source evidence. Topics covered include 'law as text', legal science, inter-polity relations, law and the state, law and religion, legal procedure, personal status and the family, crime, property and contract.

CAROLINE HUMFRESS is Professor of History and Co-Director of the Institute of Legal and Constitutional Research at the University of St Andrews, and L. Bates Lea Global Professor of Law at the University of Michigan Law School. She is a Philip Leverhulme Prize winner and recipient of *Il Premio della Corte Costituzionale della Reppublica Italiana* (awarded by the Gérard Boulvert Society for the Study of European Civilization). She has published widely on ancient and early medieval law, rhetoric and forensic practice, and their intersections with modern scholarship.

DAVID IBBETSON is Regius Professor Emeritus of Civil Law at the University of Cambridge and an Honorary Fellow of Clare Hall, where he was President from 2013 to 2020. He has published widely on the ways in which Roman law influenced (and continues to influence) English law, as well as on the ways in which Roman law related to other early legal systems.

PATRICK OLIVELLE has been Chair of both the Department of Religious Studies at Indiana University, Bloomington, and of the Department of Asian Studies at the University of Texas. He has edited and translated seven early treatises on Indian law, including the Laws of Manu and the legal treatise of Yājñavalkya. As the author of over thirty books, his works have won awards from the Association for Asian Studies and the American Academy of Religion.

THE CAMBRIDGE COMPARATIVE HISTORY OF
ANCIENT LAW

*

Edited by

CAROLINE HUMFRESS
University of St Andrews, Scotland

DAVID IBBETSON
University of Cambridge

PATRICK OLIVELLE
University of Texas, Austin

Shaftesbury Road, Cambridge CB2 8EA, United Kingdom

One Liberty Plaza, 20th Floor, New York, NY 10006, USA

477 Williamstown Road, Port Melbourne, VIC 3207, Australia

314–321, 3rd Floor, Plot 3, Splendor Forum, Jasola District Centre,
New Delhi – 110025, India

103 Penang Road, #05–06/07, Visioncrest Commercial, Singapore 238467

Cambridge University Press is part of Cambridge University Press &
Assessment, a department of the University of Cambridge.

We share the University's mission to contribute to society through the pursuit of
education, learning and research at the highest international levels of excellence.

www.cambridge.org
Information on this title: www.cambridge.org/9781107035164

DOI: 10.1017/9781009452243

© Cambridge University Press & Assessment 2024

This publication is in copyright. Subject to statutory exception and to the provisions
of relevant collective licensing agreements, no reproduction of any part may take
place without the written permission of Cambridge University Press & Assessment.

When citing this work, please include a reference to the DOI 10.1017/9781009452243

First published 2024

Printed in the United Kingdom by TJ Books Limited, Padstow Cornwall

A catalogue record for this publication is available from the British Library.

Library of Congress Cataloging-in-Publication Data
NAMES: Humfress, Caroline, editor. | Ibbetson, D. J. (David J.), editor. | Olivelle,
Patrick, editor.
TITLE: The Cambridge comparative history of ancient law / edited by Caroline Humfress,
University of St Andrews, Scotland; David Ibbetson, University of Cambridge; Patrick Olivelle,
University of Texas, Austin.
DESCRIPTION: Cambridge, United Kingdom ; New York, NY : Cambridge University Press,
2024. | Includes bibliographical references and index.
IDENTIFIERS: LCCN 2023053473 | ISBN 9781107035164 (hardback) | ISBN 9781009452250
(paperback) | ISBN 9781009452243 (ebook)
SUBJECTS: LCSH: Law, Ancient. | Law, Ancient – History.
CLASSIFICATION: LCC KL147 .C36 2024 | DDC 340.5/3–dc23/eng/20231117
LC record available at https://lccn.loc.gov/2023053473

ISBN 978-1-107-03516-4 Hardback

Cambridge University Press & Assessment has no responsibility for the persistence
or accuracy of URLs for external or third-party internet websites referred to in this
publication and does not guarantee that any content on such websites is, or will remain,
accurate or appropriate.

Contents

List of Figures   page vii
List of Maps   viii
List of Contributors   ix
Preface   xi
1 Comparative Timeline (BCE)   xvi
2 Comparative Timeline (CE)   xvii
List of Abbreviations   xviii

1 · Orientation   1
DAVID IBBETSON

2 · Law as Text   20
MICHAEL GAGARIN, WITH ERNEST CALDWELL, DAVID IBBETSON, TIMOTHY LUBIN, GEOFFREY MACCORMACK, JOSEPH G. MANNING AND MARTHA T. ROTH

3 · Legal Science   73
DARIO MANTOVANI, WITH ERNEST CALDWELL, SOPHIE DÉMARE-LAFONT, CAROLINE HUMFRESS, DAVID IBBETSON, GEOFFREY MACCORMACK, PATRICK OLIVELLE, ROBIN OSBORNE, WILLIAM TOOMAN AND BRUCE WELLS

4 · War, Peace and Interstate Relations   146
KATELIJN VANDORPE, WITH SOPHIE DÉMARE-LAFONT, GEOFFREY MACCORMACK, MARK MCCLISH, PATRICK OLIVELLE AND NICOLAS WIATER

5 · Law and the State   181
MARK MCCLISH, WITH ARI BRYEN, SOPHIE DÉMARE-LAFONT, GEOFFREY MACCORMACK AND ROBIN OSBORNE

Contents

6 · Law and Religion 231
BRUCE WELLS, WITH NOAH BICKART, DONALD DAVIS, EDWARD HARRIS, CAROLINE HUMFRESS, GEOFFREY MACCORMACK, ROBIN OSBORNE AND KATELIJN VANDORPE

7 · Legal Procedure 303
PATRICK OLIVELLE, WITH MICHAEL GAGARIN, CAROLINE HUMFRESS, GEOFFREY MACCORMACK, JOSEPH G. MANNING AND BRUCE WELLS

8 · Status and Family 376
TIMOTHY LUBIN, WITH ARI BRYEN, SOPHIE DÉMARE-LAFONT, MICHAEL GAGARIN, CAROLINE HUMFRESS, GEOFFREY MACCORMACK AND JOSEPH G. MANNING

9 · Crime, Redress and Social Control 446
ARI Z. BRYEN, WITH TIMOTHY LUBIN, GEOFFREY MACCORMACK AND ROBIN OSBORNE

10 · Property 512
JOSEPH G. MANNING, WITH EDWARD HARRIS, DAVID IBBETSON, TIMOTHY LUBIN AND GEOFFREY MACCORMACK

11 · Commerce and Contracts 565
DAVID IBBETSON, WITH ERNEST CALDWELL, EDWARD HARRIS, GEOFFREY MACCORMACK, JOSEPH G. MANNING AND PATRICK OLIVELLE

12 · Conclusion 598
CAROLINE HUMFRESS

Bibliography 615
Index 670

Figures

2.1	Stele of Ḥammurabi, found at Susa, c. 1750 BCE (basalt), Paris, Musée du Louvre (© Bridgeman Images).	*page* 31
2.2	Chinese script. Tang dynasty (618–907 CE) calligraphy attributed to Lee Yang-bing (Li Yangbing), a high-ranking Tang dynasty Chinese government official (imperial magistrate), important literary figure and noted calligrapher (© Pictures from History / Bridgeman Images).	39
2.3	Babylonian clay tablet with legal text written in cuneiform script, from Ugarit or Ras Shamra, Syria, 13th century BCE (A. Dagli Orti, © NPL – DeA Picture Library / Bridgeman Images).	46
3.1	Gortyn code, inscription on stone slabs in Doric dialect, Gortyn, Crete, Greece, 5th century BCE (A. Dagli Orti, © NPL – DeA Picture Library / Bridgeman Images).	115
3.2	Relief portraying a magistrate sitting on a 'bisellium' and surrounded by lictors and figures, 3rd century CE, Baths of Diocletian, Rome, Museo Nazionale Romano (A. Dagli Orti, © NPL – DeA Picture Library / Bridgeman Images).	118
6.1	Ancient Egyptian Ma'at, goddess of cosmic order, shown wearing her feather crown. Tomb of Seti I (KV 17), 19th Dynasty (c. 1292–1187 BCE), Luxor, Egypt (© Luisa Ricciarini / Bridgeman Images).	244
6.2	Section of the Community Rule scroll, c. 100–75 BCE (parchment), deals with community property legislation possibly for a Jewish Essene sect at Qumran (© Israel Museum, Jerusalem / Bridgeman Images).	247
6.3	Interior of Cave no 26, Gupta period (6th century CE), Ajanta, Maharashtra India (© Bridgeman Images).	250
6.4	Relief depicting Nemesis, the goddess of justice and revenge, 2nd–3rd century CE, from Laiiqie, Syria. Musée National de Damas, Syria (G. Dagli Orti, © NPL – DeA Picture Library / Bridgeman Images).	252
6.5	Jesus Christ before Pilate, who washes his hands. Cast of a sarcophagus with 'traditio legis' in the Vatican Grottoes, 350–70 CE. Vatican Museum, Rome (© Frank Buffetrille. All rights reserved 2023 / Bridgeman Images).	267
7.1	A page from one of the earliest manuscripts of Manu's law code (© Patrick Olivelle).	305
9.1	Depiction of democracy crowning Demos, with Athenian 'law against tyranny' (337 BCE), Athens, Agora Museum (© Luisa Ricciarini / Bridgeman Images).	461

Maps

1	Eurasian developments, 3000 BCE to 800 CE (© Cambridge University Press)	*page* xxv
2	The ancient Near East (© Cambridge University Press)	xxvi
3	Map of lower Mesopotamia with location of Uruk – triangles represent site names and circles are modern cities (© Cambridge University Press)	xxvii
4	Ancient Israel and surrounding regions in the Iron Age (© Shane Kelley / Kelley Graphics and Tracy Lemos, reproduced with permission)	xxviii
5	The world in 1 CE (© Cambridge University Press)	xxix
6	Ancient central Eurasia (© Cambridge University Press)	xxx
7	India, 600 BCE (© Cambridge University Press)	xxxi
8	Magadha kingdom, Mauryan Empire and Gupta Empire, India, 322 BCE–550 CE (© Cambridge University Press)	xxxii
9	Greek poleis, eighth–fifth centuries BCE (© Cambridge University Press)	xxxiii
10	Roman Republic, 500–44 BCE (© Cambridge University Press)	xxxiv
11	Europe and Mediterranean in the third century CE (© Cambridge University Press)	xxxv
12	East Asia, 650 CE (© Cambridge University Press)	xxxvi
13	Trade Routes of the Phoenicians, 1200–800 BCE (© Cambridge University Press)	xxxvii
14	The 'Silk Roads', c. 206 BCE–220 CE (© Cambridge University Press)	xxxviii

Contributors

NOAH BICKART, Joseph and Morton Mandel Chair in Jewish Studies, John Carroll University

ARI BRYEN, Associate Professor of History, Classical and Mediterranean Studies and Law, Vanderbilt University

ERNEST CALDWELL, Senior Lecturer in Premodern Chinese Studies, SOAS

DONALD R. DAVIS, Jr, Professor, Department of Asian Studies, University of Texas at Austin

SOPHIE DÉMARE-LAFONT, Professor of Legal History, University Panthéon-Assas and Directeur d'études, École Pratique des Hautes Études

MICHAEL GAGARIN, James R. Dougherty, Jr, Centennial Professor Emeritus, University of Texas at Austin

EDWARD HARRIS, Emeritus Professor (Classics and Ancient History), Durham University

CAROLINE HUMFRESS, Professor of Medieval History, University of St Andrews and L. Bates Lea Global Professor of Law, University of Michigan

DAVID IBBETSON, Emeritus Regius Professor of Civil Law, University of Cambridge

TIMOTHY LUBIN, Jessie Ball duPont Professor of Religion and Adjunct Professor of Law, Washington and Lee University

GEOFFREY MACCORMACK, Emeritus Professor of Jurisprudence, University of Aberdeen

JOSEPH G. MANNING, William K. and Marilyn Milton Simpson Professor of Classics and History and Senior Research Scholar in Law, Yale University

DARIO MANTOVANI, Professor of Law, Culture and Society of Ancient Rome, Collège de France

MARK MCCLISH, Associate Professor of Religious Studies, Northwestern University

List of Contributors

PATRICK OLIVELLE, Jacob and Frances Sanger Mossiker Chair Emeritus in the Humanities, University of Texas at Austin

ROBIN OSBORNE, Professor of Ancient History, University of Cambridge

MARTHA T. ROTH, Chauncey S. Boucher Distinguished Service Professor of Assyriology in Near Eastern Languages and Civilizations, University of Chicago

WILLIAM TOOMAN, Senior Lecturer in Old Testament / Hebrew Bible, University of St Andrews

KATELIJN VANDORPE, Professor of Papyrology and Ancient History, KU Leuven

BRUCE WELLS, Associate Professor of Middle Eastern Studies, University of Texas at Austin

NICOLAS WIATER, Senior Lecturer in Classics, University of St Andrews

Preface

'A straight question deserves a straight answer, so here goes. What is the use of comparison? Quite simply, I have joined the camp of those who prefer a history that is open to all human societies across both space and time.'[1]

An aeon ago, lost in the mists of time (c. 2010 CE), two Romanists and an Indologist had a dream: to fashion a properly comparative history of ancient law which would showcase the complexity of legal thought and practice across ancient Eurasian societies and traditions. That dream has taken a lot longer to realize than anyone – with the exception perhaps of Michael Crawford – originally anticipated. The fact that it has been realized at all is a testimony, first, to the international team of specialists who have generously dedicated their time, expertise and resources to the *Cambridge Comparative History of Ancient Law* (*CCHAL*) project for well over a decade, and second, to the unwavering support of Dr Michael Sharp at Cambridge University Press.

The shape of the *CCHAL* project and its distinctive working methodology were developed collaboratively over the course of four international project meetings. The first and second project meetings were hosted by the Faculty of Law at the University of Cambridge in May 2011 and June 2012, with funding support from The Maitland Trust. The third project meeting took place in July 2014 at Yale Law School, generously funded by the same, with the support of Professor Jim Whitman. The fourth and final meeting was held at the University of St Andrews in May 2017, with funding support from The Leverhulme Trust, the University of St Andrews and Cambridge University Press.

The initial goal of the *CCHAL* project was to redefine the mainstream study of ancient law, by placing ancient Near Eastern, Hellenistic, Greek, Egyptian, Roman, Chinese and Indian source material in conversation with each other.

---

1 Detienne 2008: 37.

The formidable linguistic, technical, legal, historical and comparative skills needed to achieve this goal could only be met by assembling a relatively large team of experts into five, roughly area-specific, working groups: 'Near Eastern', including a specialist 'Egypt' sub-group; 'Greek' / 'Hellenistic'; 'Roman'; specialists in ancient 'Chinese' material; and specialists in ancient 'Indian' sources.[2] At the second project meeting in 2012, the decision was taken that every chapter in *CCHAL* would be written collaboratively by a designated team, with a working methodology that was more in line with that of the social sciences, than with the usual working practices of ancient lawyers and historians.

Every *CCHAL* chapter is, accordingly, the product of collaborative work undertaken by a discrete team of experts – as far as possible corresponding to one specialist from each major ancient legal tradition – working under the direction of a lead chapter writer. Early in the project, a further crucial decision was taken that the basic structure and framework for each chapter would be decided by that chapter's lead author: for example, Chapter 7 'Legal Procedure' is structured according to the categories and typologies found in relevant ancient Indian material (as proposed by Patrick Olivelle, its lead author). Once a lead author had circulated their initial plan for their respective chapter, that chapter's team of experts was asked to comment on the categories, assumptions and typologies that underpinned the proposed plan – in addition to providing the lead chapter author with specific information and scholarly detail from their own fields of expertise. Each and every *CCHAL* chapter has thus been repeatedly planned, written, rewritten and refined over time. This challenging and labour-intensive working method had two self-conscious aims: first, to develop a genuinely comparative perspective for each and every topic covered, and second, to remove any temptation to centre 'Rome' as a default category against which all other ancient legal traditions could (... should ... would) be compared.[3]

The *CCHAL* is thus as much an experiment in collaborative working and thinking, as it is a set of comparative essays on discrete themes relating to

2 Contributors to the *CCHAL* project have included Simon Corcoran, Michael Crawford, Caroline Humfress, David Ibbetson, Andrew Lewis, Dario Mantovani, Benet Salway, Boudewijn Sirks, Jim Whitman (Roman); Donald Davis, Ethan Kroll, Timothy Lubin Mark McClish, Patrick Olivelle (Indian); Michael Gagarin, Edward Harris, Robin Osborne, Nicolas Wiater (Greek and Hellenistic); Ernest Caldwell, Geoffrey MacCormack, Robin Yates (China); Noah Bickart, Ari Bryen, Sophie Démare-Lafont, Joseph G. Manning, Rachel Neis, Martha Roth, William Tooman, Katelijn Vandorpe, Bruce Wells (Near Eastern and Egypt). And Michael Sharp (Cambridge University Press).

3 See Chapter 12, this volume, for further discussion.

ancient law. As discussed in Chapters 1 and 12, nineteenth- and early twentieth-century scholars compared ancient laws and legal systems but from within progressivist and teleological frameworks of development, more usually than not connecting ancient legal traditions with modern processes of nation-state construction. The *CCHAL* project, in contrast, is aligned with a twenty-first-century movement away from a 'national legal history' trend, towards the more cosmopolitan – if not global – impetus that animates much legal history today. We hope that our readers will take away a sense of what is distinctive about the various ancient legal traditions identified, rather than assuming that all 'ancient law' was the same – in addition to an appreciation of ancient legal traditions as dynamic and complex in various, contrasting and similar, ways.

Our concentration throughout has been on comparative legal history, rather than comparative law with a historical focus. In other words, we write as ancient historians who work on law and legal institutions, rather than as ancient lawyers who are interested primarily in doctrinal law. Chapter 1 lays out the basic parameters of our ancient source material and evidence, but it is perhaps worth stating at the outset what we mean by the term 'legal tradition'. We adopt the working definition of Duve:

> 'Legal traditions' are now increasingly understood as a product of a long-standing diachronic process of communication – isolated from the chaotic mass of historical normativity by later observers, but by no means pure and clearly delimited from each other. They say more about those who construct them than about the historical path-dependencies, which are much more complex evolutionary processes ... it should be the permanent task of legal historians to point out the complexity of the evolution of law, the manifold processes of exchange, and thus also the constructed character of 'legal traditions'.[4]

The *CCHAL* project did not set out to produce a taxonomy of five, or so, major ancient legal traditions. We intend 'legal tradition' as a heuristic labelling device, not as a description of a set of realities on the ground. Our five ancient legal traditions should not be thought of as internally coherent units or 'systems'. There are 'no stable historical or geographical referents' that correspond to our five (or so) ancient legal traditions.[5] As discussed in Chapter 12, we have been all too aware of the dangers of seemingly

---

[4] Duve 2022: 362–63.   [5] To adapt a phrase from Ruskola 2012: 258.

compressing vast swathes of historical time and space into a single designation: 'Near Eastern', for example. We were forced to take a number of other pragmatic decisions too, for example excluding *shar'ia* despite the fact that early Islamic legal material is best understood as part of the (late) antique world.

As Chapter 2 outlines, what each of our five (or so) ancient legal traditions share is the existence of written evidence for their early history. We did not set out with the aim of tracing legal genealogies or causal connections, though of course these exist and merit much more detailed study (for example, in terms of transregional connectivity through trade networks; political and/or sociocultural contact, such as the Achaemenid expansion into the Indus Valley; imperial conquest and other military action, etc.). A fundamental and on-going challenge has been how to compare where we seemingly lack (evidence for) both structure and system, especially when our understanding of 'law' in a given ancient context may lie through a rejection of modern categories such as 'system of laws', 'administration of justice', 'criminal law', etc. Would a distinction between 'law' and 'custom', for example, have had (the same) meaning across all the ancient times and places referred to within these chapters?

In the end, after much discussion, we arrived at ten substantive topics for comparison: 'law as text' (Chapter 2, lead author Michael Gagarin, Greek); 'legal science' (Chapter 3, lead author Dario Mantovani, Roman); 'war, peace and interstate relations' (Chapter 4, lead author Katelijn Vandorpe, Near Eastern / Egyptian); 'law and the state' (Chapter 5, lead author Mark McClish, Indian); 'law and religion' (Chapter 6, lead author Bruce Wells, Near Eastern); 'legal procedure' (Chapter 7, lead author Patrick Olivelle, Indian); 'status and family' (Chapter 8, lead author Timothy Lubin, Indian); 'crime, redress and social control' (Chapter 9, lead author Ari Bryen, Roman / Egyptian); 'property' (Chapter 10, lead author Joseph G. Manning, Near Eastern / Egyptian); and 'contract' (Chapter 11, lead author David Ibbetson, Roman). All categories are 'generic enough to allow the beginnings of a comparison but neither [are] too general nor too specific to any particular culture'.[6] Chapter 12 concludes with a set of broader frameworks and observations, and an invitation to future comparative research.

A project that has been this long in the making does not come to fruition without incurring innumerable debts, scholarly and otherwise. First and

---

6 Detienne 2008: 25.

foremost, we thank our fellow project contributors and Michael Sharp and his team at Cambridge University for keeping faith with us (and at times it really did seem like an act of faith!). We owe an immense debt of gratitude to our respective academic institutions: Birkbeck College, University of London; University of Cambridge; University of St Andrews; and the University of Texas at Austin, in addition to the funders who made our four international project meetings possible: The Maitland Trust, The Leverhulme Trust, Cambridge University Press and the Law School, Yale University. We also acknowledge the additional bibliographical research undertaken by Glenn Mills and Freja Stamper in their roles as Undergraduate Research Assistants to Caroline Humfress, at the University of St Andrews (2018 to 2019).

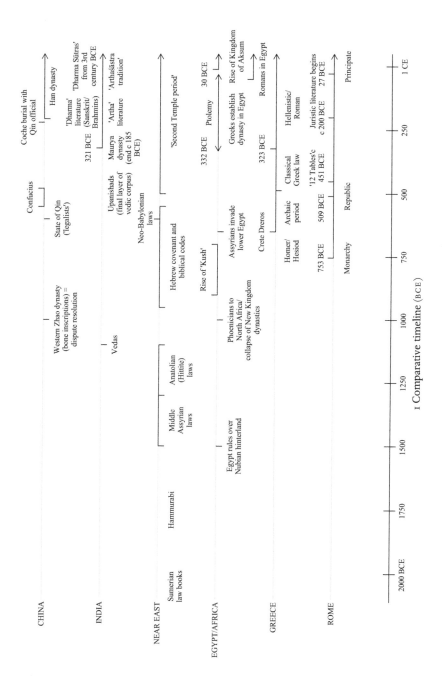

1 Comparative timeline (BCE)

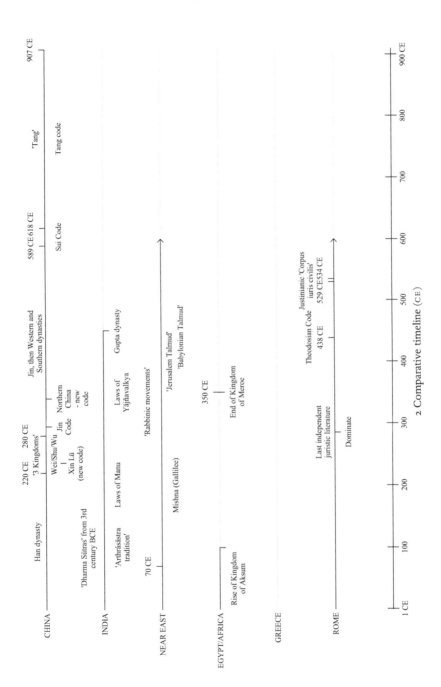

2 Comparative timeline (CE)

Abbreviations

AE	*L'Année Épigraphique*
Aes.	Aeschylus
Aeschin.	Aeschines, *Speeches*
Andoc.	Andocides, *Speeches*
ĀpDh	*Āpastamba Dharmaśāstra*
Arist.	Aristotle
ARM	*Archives royales de Mari* (1950–). Paris
Aulus Gellius	Aulus Gellius, *Attic Nights*
AT	Wiseman, D. J. (1953) *The Alalakh Tablets*. Ankara
Ath. pol.	*Athenaion politeia* [Constitution of the Athenians]
b. B. Bat.	*Baba Batra*, Babylonian Talmud [Tractate]
b. B.K.	*Baba Kamma*, Babylonian Talmud [Tractate]
b. Git.	*Gittin*, Babylonian Talmud [Tractate]
b. Hul.	*Hullin*, Babylonian Talmud [Tractate]
b. Ket.	*Kethuboth*, Babylonian Talmud [Tractate]
b. Kidd.	*Kiddushin*, Babylonian Talmud [Tractate]
b. Ned.	*Nedarim*, Babylonian Talmud [Tractate]
b. Pes.	*Pesachim*, Babylonian Talmud [Tractate]
b. Qam.	*Baba Qama*, Babylonian Talmud [Tractate]
b. Qidd.	*Qiddushin*, Babylonian Talmud [Tractate]
b. Sanh.	*Sanhedrin*, Babylonian Talmud [Tractate]
b. Shabb.	*Shabbat*, Babylonian Talmud [Tractate]
b. Shavu.	*Shavu'ot*, Babylonian Talmud [Tractate]
b. Sotah	*Sotah*, Babylonian Talmud [Tractate]
b. Yeb.	*Yebhamoth*, Babylonian Talmud [Tractate]
b. Yoma	*Yoma*, Babylonian Talmud [Tractate]
BDh	*Baudhāyana Dharmaśāstra*

List of Abbreviations

BM	British Museum
BṛSm	*Bṛhaspati Smṛti*
Bruns, *Fontes*	Bruns, C. G., Mommsen, T. and Gradenwitz, O. (1909–12) *Fontes*
Chr	Chronicles (Hebrew Bible)
Cic. *Att.*	Cicero, *Epistulae ad Atticum*
Cic. *Balb.*	Cicero, *Pro Balbo*
Cic. *Brut.*	Cicero, *Brutus*
Cic. *Cat. or.*	Cicero, *In Catilinam*
Cic. *De off.*	Cicero, *De officiis*
Cic. *De orat.*	Cicero, *De oratore*
Cic. *De rep.*	Cicero, *De republica*
Cic. *Verr.*	Cicero, *In Verrem*
Cic. *Part. or.*	Cicero, *Partitiones oratoriae*
Cic. *Top.*	Cicero, *Topica*
CIG	*Corpus Inscriptionum Graecarum* (1825–60)
CIL	*Corpus Inscriptionum Latinarum* (1863–)
CSEL	*Corpus Scriptorum Ecclesiasticorum Latinorum* (1864–)
CT	*Cuneiform Texts from Babylonian Tablets in the British Museum* (1896–). London
CTH	Laroche, L. (1966/1971 repr.), *Catalogue des textes hittites*. Paris
Dem.	Demosthenes, *Speeches*
[Dem.]	Pseudo-Demosthenes, *Speeches*
DHal	Dionysius of Halicarnassus, *Rhōmaïke archaiologia (Roman Antiquities)*
Deut	Deuteronomy (Hebrew Bible)
Dio	Dio Chrysostomus, *Speeches*
Diod.	Diodorus Siculus, *Bibliotheca Historica*
EA	Knudtzon, J. (1914), *Die El-Amarna Tafeln*. Leipzig
Exod	Exodus (Hebrew Bible)
Ezra	Ezra (Hebrew Bible)
GDh	*Gautama Dharmasūtra*
Gen	Genesis (Hebrew Bible)
Herodotus	Herodotus, *Histories*
Hesiod, *Works*	Hesiod, *Works and Days*
Hesiod, *Theog.*	Hesiod, *Theogony*

List of Abbreviations

IC	Guarducci, M. (ed.) (1935–1950), *Inscriptiones Creticae*. 4 vols. Rome
IG	*Inscriptiones Graecae* (1873–)
ILAlg	[Volume I] Gsell, S. (ed.,) (1922), *Inscriptions Latines de l'Algérie*. 2 vols. Paris; [Volume II] Pflaum, H.-G. (ed.) (1957 and 1976), *Inscriptions Latines de l'Algérie*. 2 vols. Algiers
ILAfr	Cagnat, R. and Merlin, A. with the collaboration of Chatelain, M. L. (1923), *Inscriptions latines d'Afrique (Tripolitaine, Tunisie, Maroc)*. Paris
Iliad	Homer, *Iliad*
Iscrizioni di Cos	Segre, M. (ed.) (1993), *Iscrizioni di Cos*. Rome
Isaeus	Isaeus, *Speeches*
Isocrates	Isocrates, *Speeches*
JEN	Chiera, E. (ed.) (1927–39), *Joint Expedition with the Iraq Museum at Nuzi*. 6 vols. Paris
Jer	Jeremiah (Hebrew Bible)
Justinian, *Digest*	Justinian, *Digest*: Watson, A. et al. (eds. and trans.) (1985), *The Digest of Justinian*. 4 vols. Philadelphia, PA
Justinian, *Cod*.	Justinian, *Codex repetitae praelectionis*: Frier, Bruce W. et al. (2016) (eds. and trans.), *The Codex of Justinian: A New Annotated Translation with Parallel Latin and Greek Text*. 2 vols. Cambridge
Justinian, *Inst*.	Justinian, *Institutes*: Birks, P. and McLeod, G. (1987) (eds. and trans.) *Justinian's Institutes*. London
Juvenal	*Satires*
KAŚ	*Kauṭilya Arthaśāstra*
KātSm.	*Kātyāyana Smṛti*
KātyDh	*Kātyāyana Dharmaśāstra*
Kbo	Figulla, H. (1916–21) *Keilschrifttexte aus Boghazköl*. Leipzig/Berlin
Kgs	Kings (Hebrew Bible)
Lev	Leviticus (Hebrew Bible)
	Lex Irnitana Crawford, M. H. and González, J. (eds. and trans.) (1986), 'The *lex Irnitana*: A

	New Copy of the Flavian Municipal Law', *Journal of Roman Studies* 76: 147–253
Liban. *Ep.*	Libanius, *Letters*
Liv.	Livy, *Ab urbe condita* [History of Rome]
LSAM	Sokolowski, F. (ed.) (1955), *Lois sacrées d'Asie Mineure*. Paris
LSCG	Sokolowski, F. (ed.) (1969), *Lois sacrées des cités grecques*. Paris
LSS	Sokolowski, F. (ed.) (1962), *Lois sacrées des cités grecques: supplément*. Paris
Lys.	Lysias, *Speeches*
M.Chr.	Mitteis, L. and Wilcken, U. (1912) *Grundzüge und Chrestomathie der Papyruskunde*. 2 vols. Leipzig/Berlin
MDh	*Mānava Dharmaśāstra* [Manu, Law Code]
m. 'Ar.	'Arakin, Mishnah (Tractate)
m. 'Avot	Avot, Mishnah (Tractate)
m. Baba Batra	Baba Batra, Mishnah (Tractate)
m. Hag.	Hagigah, Mishnah (Tractate)
m. Pe'ah	Pe'ah, Mishnah (Tractate)
m. Pesah.	Pesahim, Mishnah (Tractate)
m. Qidd.	Qiddushin, Mishnah (Tractate)
m. Sanh.	Sanhedrin, Mishnah (Tractate)
m. Shabb.	Shabbat, Mishnah (Tractate)
m. Sukkah	Sukkah, Mishnah (Tractate)
m. Yeba.	Yebamot, Mishnah (Tractate)
m. Yoma	Yoma, Mishnah (Tractate)
Menander	Menander, *Fragments*
ML	Meiggs, R. and Lewis, D. (eds.) (1989), *A Selection of Greek Historical Inscriptions to the End of the Fifth Century BC*. Rev. ed. Oxford
NārDh	*Nārada Dharmaśāstra*
NSm	*Nārada Smṛti*
NRSV	New Revised Standard Version
Num	Numbers (Hebrew Bible)
Od.	Homer, *Odyssey*
OGIS	Dittenberger, W. (1903 and 1905), *Orientis Graeci Inscriptiones Selectae. Supplementum*

List of Abbreviations

	sylloges inscriptionum graecarum. 2 vols. Leipzig
P. BM	*Catalogue of the Demotic Papyri in the British Museum (1939–1990)*. 4 vols. London
P. BM Andrews	Andrews, C. A. R. (ed.) (1990), *Ptolemaic Legal Texts from the Theban Area*. London
P. BM Glanville	Glanville, S. R. K. (ed.) (1939), *A Theban Archive of the Reign of Ptolemy I Soter*. London
P. Coll. Youtie	Hanson, A. E., et al. (eds.) (1976), *Collectanea Papyrologica: Texts Published in Honor of H.C. Youtie*. Bonn
P. Fam. Tebt.	van Groningen, B. A. (ed.) (1950), *A Family Archive from Tebtunis*. Leiden
P. Flor.	Comparetti, D. and Vitelli, G. (eds.) (1906–15, repr. 1962), *Papiri greco-egizii, papiri fiorentini*. 3 vols. Milan
P. Hal.	*Dikaiomata: Auszüge aus alexandrinischen Gesetzen und Verordnungen in einem Papyrus des Philologischen Seminars der Universität Halle (Pap.Hal. 1), von der Graeca Halensis* (1913). Berlin
P. Hausw. Manning	Manning, J. (ed.) (1997), *The Hauswaldt Papyri* (Demotic Studies XII). Nos. 1–25. Sommerhausen
P. Mattha	Donker van Heel, K. (ed. and trans.) (1990), *The Legal Manual of Hermopolis (P. Mattha)*. Leiden
P. Mich.	*Michigan Papyri* (1931–). Ann Arbor
P. Oslo	*Papyri Osloenses* (1925–36). 3 vols. Oslo
P. Oxy.	*Oxyrhynchus Papyri* (1898–). London
P. Petra	*The Petra Papyri* (2002–18). 5 vols. Amman
P. Rein.	[Volume I] Reinach, T., Spiegelberg, W. and de Ricci, S. (eds.) (1905), *Papyrus grecs et démotiques recueillis en Égypte*. Paris; [Volume II] Collart, P. (ed.) (1940), *Les Papyrus Théodore Reinach*. Cairo
P. Tebt.	*The Tebtunis Papyri* (1902–2005). 5 vols. Berkeley, Los Angeles, Leiden and Boston

P. Tsenhor	Pestman, P. W. (ed.) (1994), *Les papyrus démotiques de Tsenhor (P. Tsenhor)*. Leuven
Philostr. *VA*	Philostratus, *Life of Apollonius*
Pind. *Ol.*	Pindar, *Olympian Odes*
Pl. *Apol.*	Plato, *Apology*
Pl. *Euthyphro*	Plato, *Euthyphro*
Pl. *Laws*	Plato, *Laws*
Pl. *Symp.*	Plato, *Symposium*
Pliny *Ep.*	Pliny the Younger, *Letters*
Plut. *Vit. Caes.*	Plutarch, *Life of Caesar*
Plut. *Vit. Lyk*	Plutarch, *Life of Lykourgos*
Plut. *Vit. Pyrrh.*	Plutarch, *Life of Pyrrhus*
Plut. *Vit. Ti. Gracch.*	Plutarch, *Life of Tiberius Gracchus*
Plut. *Vit. Sol.*	Plutarch, *Life of Solon*
Pollux	Julius Pollux, *Onomasticon*
Polybius	Polybius, *Histories*
Prov	Proverbs (Hebrew Bible)
Psalm	Book of Psalms (Hebrew Bible)
Ps. Asc. *Verr.*	Ps-Asconius, *Commentary on the Verrines*
	Pūrva-Mīmāṃsā-Sūtra Mimamsa sutra of Rishi Jaimini
Res Gestae	Caesar Augustus, *Res Gestae Divi Augusti*
Ṛgveda	The RigVeda
Rhet. Her.	*Rhetorica ad Herennium*
RO	Rhodes, P. J. and Osborne, R. (eds.) (2007), *Greek Historical Inscriptions 404–323 BC*. 2nd ed. Oxford
	Śabara-Bhāṣya Commentary by Sabarasvāmin on the *Pūrva-Mīmāṃsā-Sūtra* of Jaimini
Sam	Samuel (Hebrew Bible)
SB	Preisigke, F. et al. (1963 repr. –) *Sammelbuch griechischen Urkunden aus Ägypten*. Wiesbaden
SEG	*Supplementum Epigraphicum Graecum* (1923–) [references are to volume and inscription number]
Sifre Deut.	*Sifre Deuteronomy*
Soph. *OT*	Sophocles, *Oedipus Tyrannus*

Soph. *Ant.*	Sophocles, *Antigone*
Strabo	*Geography*
Tab.	Twelve Tables, in S. Riccobono, *Fontes juris romani antejustiniani, I: Leges.* Florentiae 1940–42 (2nd ed.)
tabl. A	Tablet A: Driver, G. R. and Miles, J. C. (eds. and trans.) (1935), *The Assyrian Laws, Edited with Translation and Commentary.* Oxford
Tac. *Ann.*	Tacitus, *Annales*
T. Berakhot	Tractate Berakhot
Theod. Cod.	*Codex Theodosianus* (Theodosian Code)
Theoph. *Char.*	Theophrastus, *Characteres*
Theoph. *fr.*	Theophrastus, fragment (trans. Szegedy-Maszak)
Thgn.	Theognis, *Elegaic Poems*
Thuc.	Thucydides, *History of the Peloponnesian War*
T. Shabbat	Tractate Shabbat
UPZ	Wilcken, U. (ed.) (1977), *Urkunden der Ptolemäerzeit (ältere Funde).* 2 vols. Berlin.
Val. Max.	Valerius Maximus, *Facta et dicta memorabilia*
VDh	*Vasiṣṭha Dharmaśāstra*
ViDh	*Viṣṇu Dharmaśāstra*
Xen. *Hell.*	Xenophon, *Hellenica*
Xen. *Mem.*	Xenophon, *Memorabilia*
YDh	*Yājñavakya Dharmaśāstra*
YOS	Yale Oriental Series

Maps

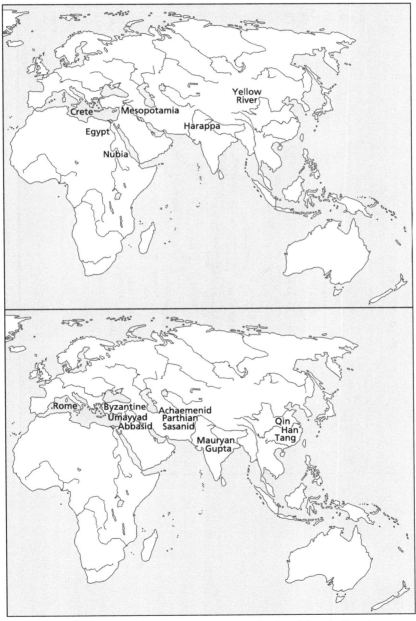

1 Eurasian developments, 3000 BCE to 800 CE (© Cambridge University Press)

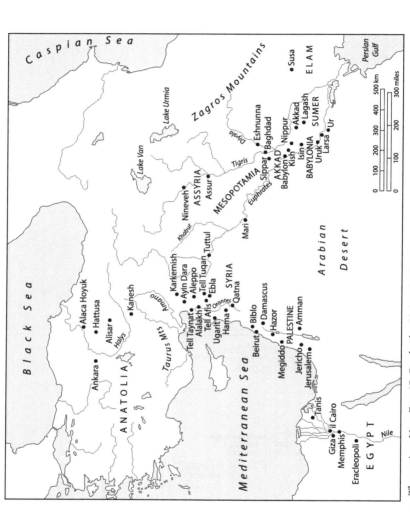
2 The ancient Near East (© Cambridge University Press)

3 Map of lower Mesopotamia with location of Uruk – triangles represent site names and circles are modern cities (© Cambridge University Press)

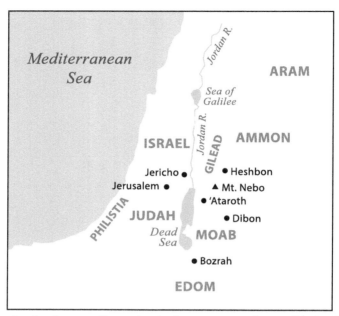

4 Ancient Israel and surrounding regions in the Iron Age (© Shane Kelley / Kelley Graphics and Tracy Lemos, reproduced with permission)

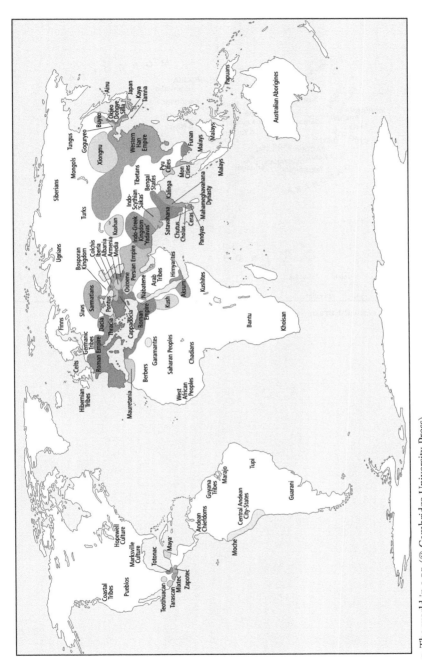

5 The world in 1 CE (© Cambridge University Press)

6 Ancient central Eurasia (© Cambridge University Press)

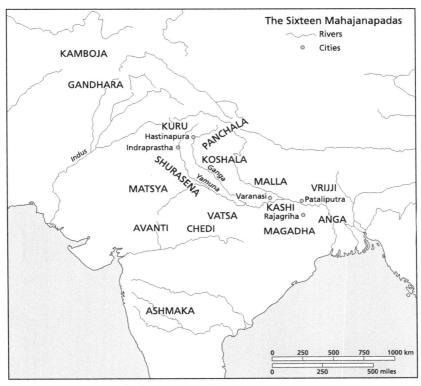

7 India, 600 BCE (© Cambridge University Press)

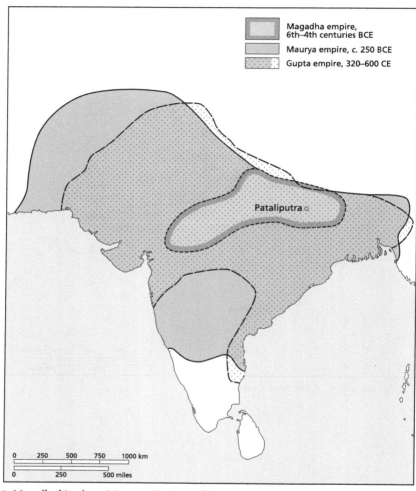

8 Magadha kingdom, Mauryan Empire and Gupta Empire, India, 322 BCE–550 CE
(© Cambridge University Press)

9 Greek poleis, eighth–fifth centuries BCE (© Cambridge University Press)

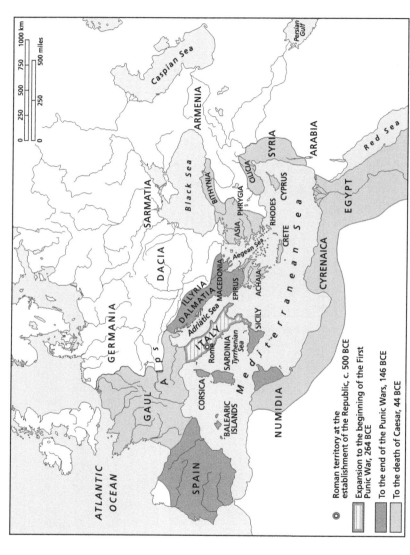

10 Roman Republic, 500–44 BCE (© Cambridge University Press)

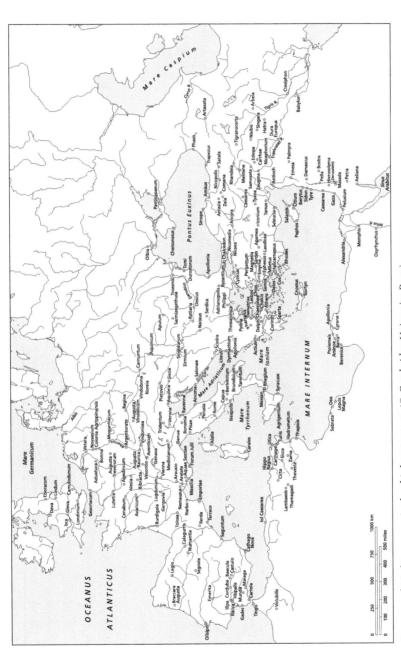

11 Europe and Mediterranean in the third century CE (© Cambridge University Press)

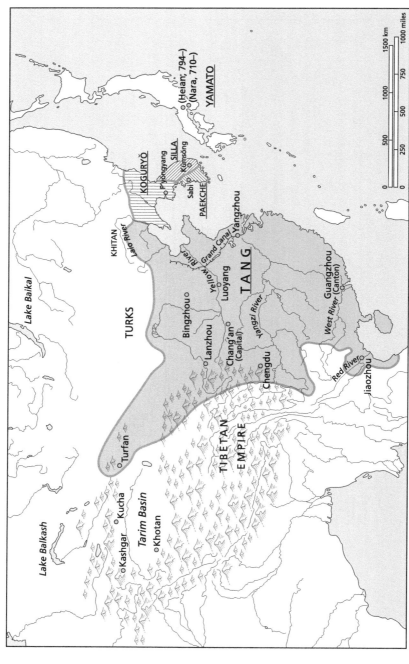
12 East Asia, 650 CE (© Cambridge University Press)

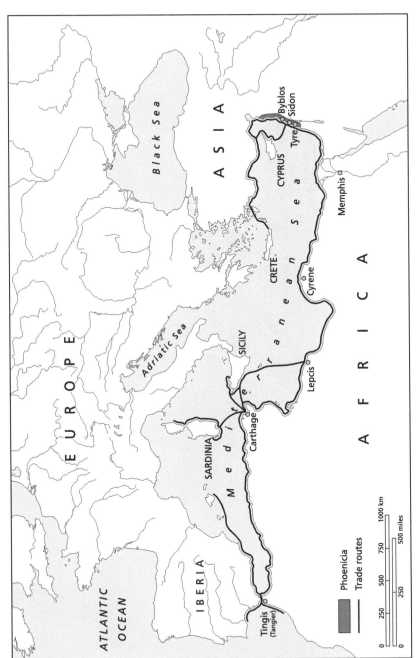

13 Trade Routes of the Phoenicians, 1200–800 BCE (© Cambridge University Press)

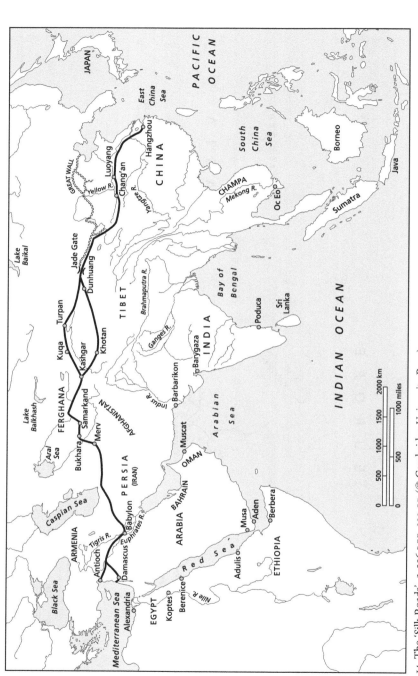

14 The 'Silk Roads', c. 206 BCE–220 CE (© Cambridge University Press)

Orientation

Lead Author: DAVID IBBETSON

Introduction

Over the last two decades or so, comparative lawyers and legal theorists have begun to look more globally at legal phenomena, moving away from the almost exclusively 'Western' focus of most work in the subjects.[1] Legal historians have started to follow.[2] All are still feeling their way.

The quest for a definition of law adequate to encompass the phenomena we might wish to call 'law' in diverse societies and cultures has thus far proved fruitless. Most contemporary legal theories, explicitly or implicitly, adopt a top-down state-based model which might be appropriate to modern 'Western' societies but which does not fit easily with, say, Micronesia.[3] Typical is the influential theory of H. L. A. Hart's *Concept of Law*, seeing law as a union of primary and secondary rules, a system of norms identified and enforced by officials. Systems consisting solely of primary rules are described as 'primitive' or 'pre-law'; more accurately, perhaps, they are seen as operating in societies without the same problems of co-ordination found in modern 'western' states.[4] It may be said that such societies do not have law, but that does no more than solve the problem by defining it out of existence. Analogously, Thomas Duve has pointed to the need to avoid Eurocentric – or Sinocentric – assumptions about the nature of law when attempting to understand legal history globally.[5]

The comparative history of ancient law raises yet bigger problems. We cannot go along the path trodden by Sir Henry Maine, whose *Ancient Law*

---

[1] For example, Donlan and Heckendorn Urscheler 2014; Twining 2009; and Menski 2006.
[2] Tate, de Lima Lopes and Botero-Bernal 2019 and Duve 2020.
[3] Tamanaha 2001: xi–xii, 91. [4] Hart 1961: 91–97, with xlix–li. [5] Duve 2020: 88.

looked only at the law of 'progressive' societies, that is, Roman law (together with early English law) with only passing references to Greece and India.[6] Nor can we comfortably follow Louis Gernet, whose 'Law and Prelaw in Ancient Greece' draws a dividing line between irrational and rational modes of dispute settlement.[7] If we are to try to get to grips with law in early societies, we cannot arbitrarily exclude those societies which were not 'progressive'; nor can we exclude those which allow the resolution of disputes by oath-taking (formally abolished in England, we might note, only in 1833, and a practical reality until the end of the sixteenth century) or other non-rational means, nor those reliant on custom, nor those where we cannot draw a sharp line between legal, moral and social norms.

The problem of ancient law is not dissimilar to the problem of identifying a conception of law appropriate to modern transnational regulatory regimes, a range of mechanisms with different characteristics.[8] In connection with these, Cotterrell has written: 'A concept of law will need to be adequate to structure a project as an inquiry related to law, but not so fully elaborated as to close off inquiry in advance about diverse phenomena that it might be illuminating to treat as legal in some sense.'[9] All the more is this so with ancient legal systems. With these we have the problem that not only might the frameworks be different, which they almost certainly were, but the surviving evidence too is very patchy. In these volumes, therefore, we adopt no fixed model of law but recognize that boundaries may be fuzzy. Some chapters look at institutions which would commonly fall within a functional approach to law:[10] for example, courts and other mechanisms for the resolution of disputes, 'state' or community bodies exercising social control, experts having or claiming to have knowledge of the way things ought to be. Some chapters look at features which may, or may not, be dealt with by law: such things as property, personal status, contracts. Yet others look at factors which may have conduced to the emergence of phenomena falling within the idea(s) of 'law': the formation of states, the use of writing. We hope through this method to shed some light on the 'legal' in the ancient world.

What follows in the present chapter is, first, a description of the type of evidence that survives and of which we make use, and secondly, a brief chronological orientation into the principal geographical regions we examine.

---

6 Maine 1861.   7 Gernet 1981.   8 On which see Cotterrell 2014.
9 Cotterrell 2014: 194.   10 Twining 2009: 88–121.

Types of Source Material

When dealing with ancient law, we are inevitably constrained by the surviving source material; in practice, that means written sources. Each type of written evidence raises its own problems of interpretation, especially when we are reliant on evidence considerably later in date than the source it purports to reproduce: the Roman Twelve Tables, for example, probably date from around 450 BCE, but the evidence we have of the contents comes from four or more centuries later.[11] Moreover, written sources exist against a background of non-written contexts which we cannot know. This is a necessary limitation of the work.

The types of written material that we use fall into seven rough categories with somewhat fluid boundaries.

Normative Texts

Normative texts typically take the form of rules laid down by some higher authority, including the community or an assembly representing the community. The rules might be mandatory, directed towards 'subjects', indicating how they were to act in some circumstance, without any necessary assumption that there existed any mechanism equivalent to a court or other executive agent which would (or could or should) enforce the rules. They might presuppose the existence of some such mechanism, where the enactment of the rule both obliged the 'subject' to act in a particular way and also authorized the court or executive agent to intervene where there was an infraction. Without having independent evidence of the social context, it can be difficult, or impossible, to distinguish between these.

A particular type of legislation is a code or collection of precepts. These may claim divine authority (for example, the Hebrew Decalogue, the Babylonian Laws of Hammurabi); they might have a religious source and include provisions applicable to the secular ruler (for example, the Hindu Manavadharmasastra); they might be purely secular (for example, the Cretan Laws of Gortyn, the Roman Twelve Tables). Such texts might serve a variety of functions: they can contain mandatory precepts; they can be aspirational; they can be fundamentally symbolic, showing the power and authority of the lawmaker.

---

11 Crawford 1996: 356–57.

Commentaries

A normative system could consist of nothing more than a set of rules or procedures, written or oral, but alongside these rules there may also be writings about the system by people recognized as having (or claiming to have) some special expertise; these may be isolated individuals (for example, Zhang Fei, collector of the Jin Code, in China) or substantial groups (as the Roman jurists, or the Jewish rabbis, or the Indian Brahmins). Where the system they are commenting on is clearly a legal system, we can call these commentaries 'juristic writings', but it may well be better to avoid that terminology in general so as not to force a particular definition of 'law' onto the evidence and so as not to ignore any relationship that might exist between 'legal' commentaries and commentaries on 'religious' texts and the like. The ancient (Indian) Dharmaśāstra tradition, for example, produced scholastic commentaries from around 700 CE to around 1800 CE.

The status of these commentaries will depend to some extent on the status of those writing them, but the fact that they exist at all is an indication that the system has reached a sufficient level of sophistication that there can be experts. Slightly paradoxically, this is clearer where the authors of the commentaries do not have any particular position which gives them a power to interpret authoritatively. Equally, the status of commentaries depends on the weight which is given to them, and this is something that might change over time.

Although we would probably not naturally call them commentaries, alongside these we need to take into account writings on ethics, whether seen from a religious or secular standpoint (the ethical works of Aristotle or Confucius are prime examples). These share an important characteristic with commentaries, in that they purport to identify (rather than create) norms of behaviour. However, even more than is the case with commentaries, they can only be seen as indications of norms which might have been more generally recognized. Similar considerations apply to what might be called political or constitutional writings: on the one hand these might reflect existing structures, but on the other they could merely be statements of what some individual thought an ideal structure would be.

Documentary Records

Any normative system may come to involve the production of written records, especially in a society with widespread literacy. These may take many forms: formal records of the result of lawsuits or of evidence presented as part of a lawsuit; contracts; transfers of property; wills; and, in an international context, treaties. They may be on stone, such as boundary markers; on bronze, as the Chinese oracle bones; on wood, for example the triptychs preserved by the eruption of Vesuvius; clay, as in Mesopotamia and Anatolia; or papyrus and paper where climatic conditions allowed their preservation (Egypt, western China).

Documents such as these testify to a legal system in action, though we must always be alert to the risk of forgeries. Moreover, they raise their own problems of interpretation. First of all, these documents presuppose the rules and practices of the system in which they operate, without describing them. In order to get beyond the bare bones of the documents themselves, we need texts of a different type to provide the context for them, or imagination to provide a hypothetical reconstruction of that context. Moreover, even a large sample will rarely shed light on anything more than a small part of any system. Secondly, documentary forms may be conservative, repeating formulae that are known (or expected) to achieve the desired end. Hence, there may be cases when their wording cannot be interpreted literally with any degree of confidence. Thirdly, we cannot assume the typicality of the documentary forms: the very fact that they have been put in writing may mark them out from more typical transactions which were carried out orally but which have left no record.

'Reports' or 'Records' of 'Cases'

As well as formal documents recording their outcome, lawsuits might generate a variety of informal documents. A litigant or other person might record a decision privately as a memorial for the future. Alternatively, or additionally, they could be recording the reasons for decisions, perhaps reflecting a framework within which at any rate some decisions were seen as generating more abstract rules, whether these were seen primarily as ways of regulating behaviour or as the basis of future decisions in similar cases. Distinct from these are descriptions of trials, in which we can read what was being said and done, especially when we can read the speeches of advocates (Cicero, Demosthenes and so forth), as well perhaps as what was decided; though it may not be easy, and is perhaps not important, to discern real trials from fictitious ones.

These texts have inherent limitations. A record of a decision in a boundary dispute, for example, will rarely if ever tell us how the decision was reached, though (assuming it is genuine) it will tell us that there existed a process for resolving such cases. A record of a reasoned decision will point to the result of the instant case; the way in which the decision is justified will give some indication of the type of reasoning that is acceptable; and the fact that the reason is recorded may suggest that the reasoning and decision in one case is expected to have some influence on future cases. 'Reports' and 'records' of actual cases may be valuable in confirming, or questioning, the status of normative texts, if they reveal that the formal norms were or were not applied. However, it is important to bear in mind that the recorded case may be untypical – that it is recorded at all may make it so by definition – or may have contained features which we cannot now know; there may have been a purpose behind the text, such as the desire to portray a person in a good or bad light, which has influenced its writing; and there may have been conventions as to how the text should be written which mean that it cannot be taken be taken as a straightforward description of what was said or done. No less importantly, what is not said may be as important as what is, and there will all too frequently be assumptions obvious at the time but unknowable today.

Portrayals of Legal Processes, and Model Forensic Speeches

Fictional texts, which do not even purport to portray genuine events, may nonetheless be of considerable value. Descriptions of trials, or more generally of legal process, in plays, myths, or other literary genres, cast light on actual legal processes and expectations. A trial scene in a dramatic work, for example, is perhaps unlikely to misrepresent too radically what went on in a real trial, though it may not reflect details with any degree of precision; and it is always possible that in the particular context a departure from normal practice might have been exactly what was being described.

The use of technical legal language in non-legal contexts may similarly be illuminating. In a comedy, for example, the humour may depend on words or phrases being used outside the legal context, but the fact that they are used at all may reveal facets of their legal meaning. In particular, they may assist in dating the introduction of the terminology into the law.

A particularly valuable source may be model forensic speeches such as those of the Greek Antiphon and Isaeus. These provide illustrations of legal rhetoric and so give information about forms of legal reasoning; they can also be a source of knowledge about substantive law. As with other sources, however, care is needed in their interpretation. We cannot simply assume that exercises in a school of rhetoric are necessarily wholly accurate reflections of genuine legal argument, either as to their form or as to their substance. However, that said, in so far as their function depends on forensic plausibility they can hardly have strayed too far from reality.

Ritual Forms

Law is not merely about the resolution of disputes. It also has an important part to play in achieving results such as the transfer of property, the restructuring and creation of family relationships, the formalization of contracts or treaties. These may involve the use of ritualized forms of language, gesture or ceremonial, and where we have evidence of such rituals they can enable us to penetrate beneath the bare facts of the transactions themselves. They may carry on their face some meaning as well as the explicit legal one. If the same ritual is used to achieve what appear to be different ends, such as the adoption of a child and the transfer of property in early Roman law, it might reasonably be supposed that the transactions were (at least at some time) seen to be related to each other, and any common feature so identified may help to reveal something about the perceived nature of the transactions concerned. Some systems, such as that of ancient China, placed enormous reliance on correct ritual forms.

These ritual forms may be immensely conservative, and may continue to be used as ways of doing things and to employ language to describe what is being done long after those ways and that language have ceased to be current. On the one hand, this means that later evidence can sometimes be read back to a much earlier period, but on the other hand, it means that we cannot assume that the use of some ritual at a particular time should be interpreted in the way that it might have been in an earlier period.

A further feature of this type of evidence is that it may be provided in non-written forms. Rituals, because of the importance in them of visual elements, may be commemorated in painted or sculpted images; they may also create distinctive artefacts. It may, perhaps, enable us to draw links between different systems, and with cultures which have not themselves left any written evidence.

'Law' in Other Forms of Text

Finally, we may be able to find material of relevance to law in other forms of text: political, ethical, religious, works of grammar and lexicography, etc. Such texts may be especially valuable in revealing ways in which law split off from other forms of normative discourse. All such evidence, of course, needs to be carefully evaluated.

The Principal Legal Traditions: An Overview

The Ancient Near East

'Ancient Near Eastern Law' encompasses all of those legal systems of Mesopotamia, Anatolia, Egypt and Syro-Palestine between the middle of the third millennium BCE and the end of the fourth century BCE. Although each of these systems had an independent existence, there are sufficient similarities among them that they can fairly be treated as representative of a broadly unitary legal culture. Moreover, as well as jurisprudential similarities it is possible to find detailed parallels which point to direct borrowings between systems, as when identical clauses are found in contractual documents emanating from very different times and places.

Although a substantial amount of evidence survives, it is very patchy. Hence, even in Mesopotamia, whose baked clay tablets were very durable, there are a few periods about which we know a great deal and long periods about which we know very little: much depends on the chance of excavations. The Hittites, too, used clay tablets, but we know rather less about their law since practically all of our information comes from a single site in central Anatolia. Information about Egypt at this time is very sparse, and what we know about the law of the Hebrews is largely derived from the Hebrew Bible.

The most important surviving texts are 'law codes', i.e. unitary texts which deal with a variety of legal materials. In Mesopotamia these are represented by two relatively brief Sumerian texts, the earliest dating from around 2100 BCE, followed by the very substantial codes of Eshnunna and Hammurabi dating from 1770 and 1750 BCE, respectively. After this, we have the Middle Assyrian Laws (fourteenth century BCE) and the Neo-Babylonian Laws (seventh century BCE). The Anatolian Hittite Laws date from between the sixteenth and twelfth century, showing signs of development over this period, while the Hebrew Covenant and Deuteronomic Codes date from between 1000 and 600 BCE. Nothing comparable survives from Egypt. It is probable, though not undisputed, that these codes were designed to regulate individuals' behaviour and in all probability to provide a framework within which disputes could be resolved; whether disputes were in fact generally resolved by reference to them is unprovable, though we do find some explicit references to cases having been decided according to the words of a text, and provisions specifying that in some circumstance a person might exonerate himself by swearing an oath are focused more on the trial process than on the substantive rule of liability or norm of behaviour. It may be that some of the codes, in particular the Babylonian ones, had a dual existence, beginning as bodies of rules regulating behaviour but then mutating into texts used as exercises in scribal schools, preserving the wording of the original codes at the same time as allowing the practical law to develop.

A common feature of the codes is their casuistic form, specifying what the result would (or should) be in a specific situation, as, for example, where the Hittite Laws deal successively with sexual activity with pigs, dogs, oxen, horses and so on; that said, there is occasional evidence of some generalization taking place, as where the circumstances which would mitigate liability for killing another person could be stated at an abstract level.

Alongside these codes, we find a handful of specific acts of legislation, the earliest being the twenty-sixth-century BCE Edict of the Sumerian King Irikagina, as well as occasional instructions to royal officials. Some records of trials survive, created either as records of decisions or as aides-mémoire of evidence, and glimpses of trial process can be caught from a small number of descriptions of trials, either genuine or hypothetical.

By far and away the largest amount of surviving material evidence is in the form of documents recording legal transactions of many different types. These presuppose legal ideas rather than stating them directly, though the sheer number of surviving texts makes it possible to get some sense of the fundamental ideas found in the different legal systems. More importantly, the mere fact of their existence in such quantities means that we can be reasonably sure that writing played an important part in these systems, though we cannot, of course, know how common were transactions which were not made or recorded by the use of writing.

Several features of the law of the Ancient Near East point to the existence of some form of intellectual tradition: the use of writing to record transactions only makes sense in a world in which the outcome of future disputes was to a substantial extent predictable; the use of the casuistic form in the codes presupposes a process whereby the proper result in a *casus omissus* could be found; the indications in some texts of a process of generalization of rules or adaptation of earlier forms to new circumstances indicate a degree of reflection on the relationship between legal forms and social rules; and structural parallels between legal texts and other forms of specialist literature suggest that there might have been some individuals who were regarded as having a special legal expertise. However, we do not have any evidence that these legal experts, assuming they existed, generated any form of literature of their own, identifying common abstract features lying behind apparently disparate rules, drawing analogies between clear rules and ambiguous situations, or using any 'scientific' method to develop the law.

Similarly, although it is possible to see elements of secularization in the Ancient Near Eastern texts and in their legal processes, we should not be too quick to conclude that the law in these systems was divorced from religious values. This was clearly not the case with the Hebrew codes, and a millennium earlier the Babylonian Code of Hammurabi referred expressly to the divine origin of the text. It is probably better to see the law as a set of normative rules for behaviour existing against a background of religious beliefs and taking a good deal of their colour from them.

As the first five books of the Hebrew Bible (the Pentateuch) came to be treated as the actual words of God in orthodox Jewish thought, the Covenant and Deuteronomic Codes obtained something like statutory force. From around 70 CE they attracted substantial exegetical commentaries, *midrashim*, from rabbinic scholars. The biblical basis of these commentaries, and hence their religious nature, was transparent. By contrast, the Mishnah, a form of Jewish law perhaps with a primarily educational function, was not so explicitly tied to the biblical texts; it was intensively studied in Babylonian academies and attracted its own learned commentaries.

India

Historical sources in India date back to approximately 1200 BCE in the form of the Vedas, hymns and poems of praise to the deities of the Vedic pantheon, which shares figures with other Indo-European mythologies. Later texts, extensions of the early Vedic collections, focus primarily on the details of sacrificial rituals at the centre of religious life for Brahmins and kings of the Ārya communities of northern India. The final layer of the Vedic corpus, the Upaniṣads, was composed beginning in the sixth century BCE as philosophical and religious speculations on the inner nature of the ritual. Like the Upaniṣads, competing religious ideals focused on liberation from transmigratory bondage and contributed to the founding of both Buddhism and Jainism also in the fifth century BCE, the canonical sources for which claim contemporary antiquity. Along with archaeological evidence from early historic India, the Vedic corpus in Sanskrit and the suggestive canonical texts in Pāli (Buddhist) and Ardhamāgadhī (Jain) provide the basis for all that we know of India prior to the foundation of the first large political formation in Indian history, the Maurya dynasty, in c. 321 BCE; though the dating of individual texts is highly uncertain, some almost certainly dating to periods after the Mauryas.

The Principal Legal Traditions: An Overview

It is really after this time that the textual sources of law in ancient India become clearer and more numerous. In what is often called the classical period of India's history (between the Maurya and Gupta dynasties, fourth century BCE–fifth century CE), a new genre of Sanskrit literature focused on *dharma*, and especially the social, legal and religious duties of Brahmins and otherwise Brahminized groups. This literature includes prescriptively stated rules for legal matters such as marriage, inheritance, adoption, crime, procedure and statecraft, in addition to ritual practices, penances, dietary restrictions and the like. The oldest of these Dharmasūtras, aphoristic treatises on *dharma*, may have been composed in the third century BCE. In perhaps the first century CE, an apparently independent tradition of Sanskrit learning also appeared concerning *artha*, politics and statecraft, but including extensive descriptions of courts, legal procedure and titles of substantive law. In spite of the secular nature of this Arthaśāstra tradition, its substance was already by the second century CE co-opted and incorporated into the religious scheme of *dharma* in the paragon text of ancient Indian law, the Laws of Manu, or *Mānava-Dharmaśāstra*. Over the next three centuries or so, several other important Dharmaśāstras, treatises on *dharma*, were composed that refined and elaborated on the style and the substance of the Laws of Manu. Throughout this classical period, monastic codes in Buddhist and Jain communities also developed. For Buddhists, ascetic discipline was detailed in the Vinaya, a separate branch of learning that prescribes the daily regimens for monks and nuns. For Jains, ascetic rules are woven into several scriptural sources. Together, these texts constitute the major sources for legal history in ancient India because dated inscriptional sources from the period yield only indirect information about law or legal practice. The same is true of other literature including the famous epics of India, the *Mahābhārata* and *Rāmāyaṇa*, grammatical texts, and early literary works.

Law in ancient India was not conceptualized apart from its interconnections with religion, morality, social duty and politics; yet, it is wrong to think that Indians confused natural boundaries between these ideas. Rather, social life and human experience were categorized along different lines. Speaking very broadly, Vedic Brahmins, the authors of Dharmaśāstra, looked to ritual as a central metaphor for understanding human experience, with law, religion, morality, etc. seen as conforming to *dharma*, the complex pattern of highly normative human actions that lead to positive earthly and transcendental results. In other traditions, asceticism and monasticism formed the backdrop against which legal matters were handled, with correspondingly less attention paid to the legal concerns of laypeople. What is very clear from the extant sources is that our current knowledge of ancient Indian law is distorted both by the theological underpinnings of the law as given in the texts and by the fact that the authors were experts in a sophisticated intellectual milieu that prided itself on timelessness and systematization. Even major historical ruptures are impossible to discern from the legal materials alone. In contrast to some ancient laws, therefore, Indian law as we know it is primarily a scholars' law. Evidence of actual cases, settled disputes, trial procedures, or promulgation – if they occurred formally at all – is almost completely missing from the historical record. It is possible to read the Indian texts against the grain for indications about practical matters, and we do so where possible. The process in this case is nearly the opposite of what must be done for areas such as Mesopotamia and Greece, where practice-oriented sources abound and systematic rules and principles must be inferred. In general, however, we present the evidence of the texts, with regular reminders about the limitations of taking this textual information as a complete history.

Within Dharmaśāstra, by far the most elaborate and influential tradition of legal thought in ancient India, *dharma* refers primarily to *varṇāśramadharma*, the *dharma*s of caste (*varṇa*) and life-stage (*āśrama*), a synchronic and a diachronic way to categorize human beings into broad contextual frameworks of proper legal, moral and religious behaviour. The contextuality of *dharma* is extremely important in order to avoid any idea of equality before the law, which the authors of our ancient texts would have regarded as absurdly blind to social reality; or of universal applicability, which would have been seen as contrary to social order. Instead, both the determination of what is legal and the adjudication of conflicts about the law must begin from a frank assessment of the complete status of the parties involved. The epistemology of law, the authoritative determination of law's proper sources and substance in particular contexts, was an overarching concern of Dharmaśāstra authors, a near obsession that distinguishes ancient Indian law to some extent from other traditions.

If we ask what ancient Indian brahmins held the law to be, we may look to a classification of the substance of *dharma* found in the Laws of Yājñavalkya (c. fourth century CE). The text is divided into three sections: *ācāra*, *vyavahāra* and *prāyaścitta*. *Ācāra* refers generally to the customary laws observed in various social groups, but more specifically to the paradigmatic ritual, dietary and marital practices of Brahmins and Kṣatriyas (the highest two *varṇa*s) that constitute the distinctive social status of those castes. *Vyavahāra* in this context comes closest to a narrow domain of law in that it deals with legal procedure (evidence, witnesses, judicial decision, etc.) and the (eighteen) titles of substantive law ranging from the Non-payment of Debts, Partnerships and Inheritance to Theft, Sexual Assault and Slander. The responsibility for supervision of this legal domain and the punishments it entails rest with the king. Finally, *prāyaścitta* signifies a complex array of penances or expiations, most involving fasting, that are prescribed for various offences in either of the legal domains above. Ideally, penances were voluntarily accepted on the advice of a Brahmin council as a means to be restored to community. In short, while law as *dharma* incorporates wide-ranging legal rules, intricate legal procedures and severe punishments, the system overall is aspirational, a framework for achieving and maintaining both a respectable social status and positive religious benefits. Practical actions underlie the system, but always in the service of a theoretical result to be gained through observance of the law.

China

Although our earliest direct evidence of law in China comes from the middle of the Western Zhou dynasty in the tenth century BCE, it may be possible to trace the beginnings of later legal institutions back to the late Shang dynasty in the twelfth century, from when there survive substantial numbers of descriptions on bone of ritual punishments. As well as inscriptions of this sort from which we may infer a system of punishments, by the tenth century we have evidence from both inscriptions and literary texts of the existence of a regular system for the resolution of disputes. From this time onwards we have a steady stream of contemporary inscriptions as well as received texts describing earlier history.

From the seventh century BCE, first from the state of Qin, there is evidence of legislative activity, though most of this is known only from later texts. This legislation had two principal foci: the regulation of officials, and the organization of crimes and punishments as a means of controlling the populace. Earlier legislation was sometimes reformed or recast, indicating that these enactments were designed to be followed and were not merely rhetorical aspirations of a ruling elite. Neither here nor in later texts was there any suggestion of a divine origin for the rules; they were explicitly state regulation.

Caches of documents dating from the late fourth century BCE onwards, seemingly buried with legal officials, cast a great deal of light on the working of the legal system before the creation of the Han dynasty (206 BCE); the most significant of these is from Qin and can be dated to about 217 BCE. These caches contain a variety of material: legislation regulating land use, the distribution of food, state officials, workers and many other topics; books for the guidance of local officials responsible for drafting of legal cases for consideration by others; and discussions of controverted points of law and their resolution.

This practical legal system existed against the background of philosophical writings. These may have begun with Confucius (551–479 BCE), though he may have built on earlier thinkers' work. In tension with his ethical philosophy and concern with appropriate rituals was the approach of the so-called legalists of the following generations, stressing the obligation of subjects to obey the law strictly and the need for the law to further the interests of the state; particularly important among these legalists was a chief minister of the state of Qin in the middle of the fourth century BCE, whose work had some part to play in the development of Qin law.

The coming of the Han empire (206 BCE to 220 CE) marked a change, in so far as it extended the former penal law; it was said that the Han law contained 490 articles dealing with the death penalty, framing 1882 offences, and with thousands of case-law precedents, so that there were cupboards full of documents whose contents were far too large to be assimilated. This code remained in force, probably with occasional amendments, until the end of the dynasty. Fragments of other enactments are found in tombs and in rubbish heaps of forts, showing that the process of legislation continued alongside the code. Linguistic differentiation between statutes (*lü*) and ordinances (*ling*) suggests that there were different types of legislation, perhaps approximating to penal law and administrative regulation, and in the later Han period there was a further subdivision of ordinances into three types. Another type of legal text was the collection of 'precedent', i.e. descriptions of customary practices which were treated as having legal force, especially in the management of officials. Related to this were collections of rulings or decisions in matters of ritual, infliction of penalties and the like which were similarly treated as being authoritative statements of the law.

A small number of documents witnessing private transactions have survived from this period, and these give us a glimpse of private law. It is likely that this was normally not a concern of the state, except where wills were concerned (explicitly regulated in the Han laws of 186 BCE) or where land transactions might have had implication for the levying of taxes, though the very existence of documents suggests that some regular system for the resolution of private disputes existed, and it is very probable that state officials were involved with this. However, there is as yet very little evidence of legislation on matters of private law, and it is thought likely that these continued to be governed primarily by customary norms.

Shortly after the fall of the Han dynasty, the Wei dynasty promulgated a code, the *Xin Lü* (New Code), perhaps the first collection of statutes that can properly be termed a 'code'. Then, in the late third century there appeared another code, the Jin. As with the Han Code, the Jin Code dealt with criminal law, but it was accompanied by a preface which reveals a degree of intellectual sophistication in the understanding of the law, distinguishing, for example, between different degrees of criminal culpability and providing examples of the way in which the code was to operate. The practical function of this preface is brought out by its advice to magistrates on how to interpret the body language of those appearing before them and hence reach conclusions about their innocence or guilt. Although the Jin Code was to be displaced in a further period of political unrest, a new code was promulgated by Mongol ancestors in the north of China at the end of the fourth century. This code was repeatedly amended in the fifth and sixth centuries, culminating in the Heqing Code of 564 CE.

It was with the Sui (589–618 CE) and Tang (619–907 CE) dynasties that ancient Chinese law reached its major watershed. Of great importance was the Tang Code of 652 CE, building on a Sui code which is no longer extant but which in its turn brought together elements from the earlier Jin and Heqing codes. By this time, too, it is known that there was a law school, and the Tang Code itself sprouted both commentary and discursive sub-commentary. Moreover, surviving documents from western China enable us to see more clearly the working of the civil law – which was still absent from the codes except in so far as penal law impacted on it – and later texts also preserve decisions on matters of private law. Under the Tang, too, there was a resurgence of Confucianism in both criminal and family law, providing the basis for the later development of law in China and also in Japan, Korea and Vietnam.

Greece

The earliest surviving written law from Greece dates to the seventh century BCE, but the works of Homer and Hesiod (late eighth century BCE) testify to systems for the settlement of disputes. In the case described as portrayed on the shield that the god Hephaistos makes for Achilles in *Iliad* 18, the parties state their case in public before a group of elders, who offer their individual views as to what settlement is just and are themselves judged by the onlooking community which rewards the elder giving the best judgement. Hesiod, who complains about an unjust settlement of his dispute with his brother, and of 'bribe-devouring kings', inserts dispute settlement in his community into an overall scheme of divine justice, finally enforced by Zeus.

The earliest law inscribed on stone comes from the Cretan city of Dreros and can be dated to approximately 650 BCE. The evidence for written laws is strongest in Crete, but examples are found all over the Greek world. Distinct from traditional customs, and sometimes expressly stating that they had been approved by the polis, these laws were displayed in public places, ensuring that they could be generally known; whether popular literacy was sufficient to exclude these being simply manifestations of the power of an elite group is disputed.

From the fifth century onwards, such inscribed laws are supplemented by literary evidence – descriptions of legal systems, writings directly reflecting action in court, and philosophical discussions of the nature of law. By far the best evidence of the latter comes from Athens. Historical writings cast light on the operation of the law; the *Athenian Constitution* attributed to Aristotle describes in detail the powers and duties of Athenian magistrates towards the end of the fourth century BCE; and in particular a corpus of approximately 100 forensic speeches prepared for real Athenian cases enables us to reconstruct substantial parts of substantive Athenian law, as well as legal procedure.

Although evidence from outside Athens principally illuminates individual laws, it is sufficient to reveal such variation as to make it impossible to speak of a unitary 'Greek law'. We can, however, discern a Greek legal culture which had as one of its characteristic features that communities recognized their (normally written) laws as containing the rules which constituted the framework of their political and legal relations.

Given the volume of surviving evidence, it is worth stating what we do not find. First, it appears that the classical Greeks did not develop a specifically 'legal' science, in the sense of ways of identifying legal rules by a process of reason. Philosophical works, most notably Aristotle's *Ethics* and *Rhetoric*, show the use of reason to formulate ethical norms, but there is no hint of anything to parallel this in the law. Rather, legislation provided the fixed set of rules within which legal argument took place, with litigants or their representatives making use of ethical principles alongside other forms of argument to frame their case in the most favourable way. Secondly, outside Egypt, we do not find much direct evidence of written transactions, although we do know that writing was used to make contracts and the like. It is probable that this is just a trick of survival, since they would have been written on perishable material rather than inscribed on stone; and it is telling that the evidence which does survive is *horoi*: inscriptions inscribed on stone recording mortgages of land.

The expansion of Greek political control across the eastern Mediterranean and Near East following the conquests of Alexander the Great brought Greeks into contact with already sophisticated legal systems. In Egypt what the Macedonian dynasty of Ptolemies did was to establish a Greek legal system alongside the pre-existing Egyptian legal system. Egyptians were able to choose to use the Greek courts if they wanted to, and (at least in principle) Greeks were able to choose to use the Egyptian courts. The Greek law used was not the law of any particular polis, but rather a 'legal *koine*' in which different Greek traditions were intermingled. Some royal legislation was written, though it is not clear that it was displayed in public according to the Greek model, but in general the laws remained unwritten, functioning as a form of created custom. That said, written documents were in very common use, and it is from these that we gain much of our understanding of the law.

The Greek world fell under the dominance of Rome from the second century BCE onwards. Now, parallelling what had happened in Ptolemaic Egypt, forms of Greek law and Roman law existed side by side. Papyri, which continue to survive in large numbers from Greco-Roman Egypt, reveal an intermingling of Greek and Roman legal traditions, though by the beginning of the third century CE Roman law was very clearly the principal element. Nonetheless, although Greek law disappeared as an independent system, Greek practices such as the use of documents had a significant influence on the way in which post-classical Roman law was to develop.

Rome

Although there may have been earlier legislation, our knowledge of Roman law begins with the Twelve Tables, dated by later tradition to 451–449 BCE. It is possible that this might have been influenced by models from outside Rome, though there is no scholarly agreement on this. Although no original text survives, later references allow us to reconstruct its contents. In some places the reconstruction is so fragmentary that we can do little more than guess as to its meaning, while in others it is sufficiently precise that we can interpret it with fair confidence. Although treated in later times as a foundational text, it was not in any sense a total statement of the law; rather, it presupposes an existing regime in which details needed to be specified. There is clear evidence of legislation after the Twelve Tables, though much is concerned with the making of war and peace rather than the creation of rules of general application. Very little of this survives epigraphically.

Later sources describe the early form of legal procedure, *per legis actionem*. We cannot be certain that these descriptions are accurate, but there is little reason to reject them out of hand. This procedure involved the swearing of oaths; it is likely that in its earliest stages disputes were resolved by supernatural means to identify where a false oath had been sworn. In addition, we have descriptions of formal procedures for transferring important items of property and creating family relationships.

Later tradition had it that the repositories of legal knowledge at this early stage of Roman law were the pontiffs, priests. This does not mean that the law was indistinguishable from religion but does suggest that there was a religious dimension to legal procedure. Except where there was specific legislation on matters of substance, it is likely that substantive norms were based on custom or social practice.

In formal terms there was no discontinuity between the first and second (traditional) phases of Roman law, but the characteristic features of the latter, by contrast with the former, were the use of a more sharply defined legal procedure and the secularization of legal knowledge. The new form of procedure, known as the formulary system, was introduced by the praetors. It almost certainly originated in the third century BCE to deal with disputes involving foreigners, and in the middle of the second century BCE it was extended to disputes between citizens. Instead of involving a very general claim to a remedy, supported by an oath, the claim was more precisely delineated by reference to the basis of the claim, the cause of action. Gradually the praetors built up a list of available formulae and defences, their Edict, a list which had become more or less ossified by the beginning of the Empire (conventionally dated as 27 BCE). In the second century BCE, the pontifical monopoly of legal knowledge was lost, and there grew up a body of secular jurists. These jurists did not speak with a single voice, nor with authority attaching to a particular status. They might disagree with each other and gave reasons for their conclusions, so that others could evaluate their different points of view. A substantial amount of the work of these men survives; this is largely in the *Digest* of Justinian (533 CE), though there are fragmentary papyri containing small sections of these works. In addition, a codex of the fifth century CE gives us most of the text of the *Institutes* of Gaius, an important writer of the second century CE.

From this phase, in addition, there is some surviving evidence of transactions contained in documents, and also of decisions reached by emperors sitting as judges; but this evidence is very thin indeed. More useful are the texts of *leges datae*, procedural rules governing Roman provinces, especially communities in Iberia. These provide much information from which we can reconstruct the mechanics of legal processes, complementing what we can learn about substantive law from the writings of jurists.

The flowering of juristic thinking came to an end after the first quarter of the third century CE. By this time jurists had been sucked into the imperial civil service – the process had begun under Hadrian a century earlier – and their legal work largely consisted of responding to questions and giving legal advice in the name of the emperor. Since by this time the word of the emperor was law, these responses were by definition authoritative statements of what the law was. They could be seen as a form of legislation, alongside the formal legislation of imperial edicts, and from the end of the third century CE collections began to be made of these, the most important of which was the *Codex Theodosianus* (438 CE). The proliferation of 'legislation' did not supplant the earlier juristic writings, and in this third phase we find short collections of these being made, such as the *Pauli Sententiae*. These works have some use in confirming the texts of earlier jurists, but they tell us little of the law of their own time except in so far as they uncover a form of, what has been termed, 'vulgar law' in the Western Empire.

Unlike in the previous phases of Roman law, now we do have a very substantial number of transactional texts, especially contracts and land transfers. Most of these are papyri from Egypt and hence reflect what might be a provincial form of Roman law. These can be read alongside both the contemporary imperial constitutions and the earlier juristic writings, allowing us to trace developments in the law in this latest phase.

The most important work of this phase, marking its end, was the *Corpus Iuris Civilis* of Justinian, compiled in the 530s CE and updated until the 560s. The two main parts of the *Corpus* were the *Digest* or *Pandects*, containing almost a million words of extracts from the jurists writing between the first century BCE and the third century CE, very heavily concentrated towards the end of the period, and the *Codex*, a collection of imperial constitutions dating from the second century CE to the time of Justinian himself. In addition to these there were the *Institutes*, an introductory teaching manual, and the *Novels*, later legislation of Justinian himself.

2

Law as Text

Lead Author: MICHAEL GAGARIN

Contributors: ERNEST CALDWELL, DAVID IBBETSON,
TIMOTHY LUBIN, GEOFFREY MACCORMACK, JOSEPH G.
MANNING AND MARTHA T. ROTH

Introduction

At a relatively early stage of their development, all the societies included in our study, located on the Eurasian continent, developed both some form of law and some form of writing, enabling them to produce written legal texts. This achievement distinguishes them from early societies in other parts of the world.[1] In comparing the various manifestations of legal texts in these societies, however, we must be aware that both 'law' and 'text' have complex ranges of meanings and that these may be different in the different societies we are examining. Thus, while we look for similarities among societies, at the same time we must be aware of significant differences.

Despite the impossibility of giving an adequate definition of either 'law' or 'text', we must begin with a tentative working definition. For the purposes of this chapter, we define law as a society's formal procedures for the regulation of conduct, the punishment of offences and the resolution of disputes, together with the personnel authorized to adjudicate disputes and impose punishments, and with authoritative rules governing these procedures and designating right and wrong conduct that is subject to these procedures. The procedures may or may not be formally stated or explicitly required, as long as they are clearly established in practice. The rules of law may be recorded separately from other sorts of rules (as in the Twelve Tables), or they may be intertwined with rules governing many other aspects of life (as in the Laws of Manu).[2]

---

[1] As Huxley 2006: 163 states, 'most parts of Eurasia share a commitment to written law that was rarely matched in Africa or the Americas and never in Oceania or Antarctica'.
[2] This definition raises many further questions, such as what constitutes a society, that cannot be considered here.

Introduction

A further complication is that the terminology used by different societies in speaking of law varies. Rome, China and Egypt each have two terms roughly equivalent to 'law' and 'justice'. In Roman texts, *lex* denotes a statute, whereas *ius* denotes law more broadly as an institution and overlapping to some extent with 'justice', and this use has carried over into most civil law societies today (*loi/droit, legge/diritto, Gesetz/Recht*). China similarly uses two words: *fa*, which not unlike *lex* denoted specific statutes, and *li*, denoting the customary norms of order and proper conduct. China also has a third word, *xing*, which denotes punishments; it is closely connected to *fa*, in part because most Chinese statutes prescribed punishments for those who disobeyed the rules. Egypt also used two different words, *hp*, 'law' or 'rule', normally occurring in the plural, and *ma'at*, variously translated in English as 'justice', 'social order' or 'connective justice' (a concept that bound the king to society). In Mesopotamia, the phrase *kittum u mīšarum* 'justice and correct procedure' (both words derived from roots connoting security or reliability and widely used outside of legal contexts) is commonly used, while collections of laws, individual legal provisions, legal judgments and court cases may all be designated by the term *dīnum*, a term more closely associated with judicial and legal matters.

India and Athens, on the other hand, each have one word broadly meaning 'law'. In India, *dharma* designates rules of law but also matters that modern Western societies would tend to categorize as justice or righteousness; it also designates customary practices of all sorts that have nothing to do with law as we think of it. The scope of *dharma* matches that of Greek *eusebeia* (which was used to translate *dharma* in an inscription of Aśoka from the mid-third century BCE) and Latin *pietas*. But India also had several terms more narrowly associated with law: *vyavahāra* (law and legal procedure); *maryādā* (usually 'local law'); *nyāya* (law as embodied in a ruling or judgment); *sthiti* (a fixed rule or statute); *samaya* (agreed-upon rule); and *vyavasthā* (established norm). *Dharma* used in the plural also denoted particular norms with legal force. The Greek term *nomos* (generally translated as 'customary rule') is almost as broad: in classical Athens it designates a law or statute, but it also includes general principles and customary practices. Elsewhere, however, other terms are used to designate a statute in ancient Greek texts: some cities, including Athens in the archaic period, use *thesmos* ('what is set down or established'); Gortyn uses *graphos* ('writing') or variations like *ta gegrammena* ('what has been written'); and Sparta and a few other cities use *rhētra* ('what is spoken').

As for text we define it as anything written, even if it was originally composed orally and only later written down. We do not treat purely oral material as text, however, since we have no direct access to it. To be sure, (unwritten) principles, customs and traditions of any society, no matter how literate, inevitably affect the law of that society in many ways; but in this chapter, at least, we will not be considering any features of 'oral law' that are not manifest in written texts. For our purposes, then, law and text are inextricably connected. Some theories of law, such as natural law, disconnect law from text, but this chapter presupposes a positivist view of law in which writing is almost always necessary for recognizing that a rule is in fact a law.[3]

Our insistence on texts, however, raises the question, who read these texts? It is very difficult to determine literacy rates in antiquity, and there is considerable disagreement about levels and kinds of literacy in different areas. In recent years scholars have tended to ascribe higher levels of literacy to ancient societies than they did previously, but even so, literacy was certainly low everywhere in comparison with modern developed countries, but it probably was higher in Greece and Rome, with their simple alphabetic scripts, than in other areas. Literacy undoubtedly differed for different groups in most areas.

Within the limits of literacy, texts were important for communicating the laws to a larger audience, in addition to communicating them to those in more distant places and fixing the law so that it was and remained the same everywhere across the society. Only by using written texts could the central authorities in two great empires of antiquity, China and Rome, attempt to impose a consistent, detailed order on all parts of their territories, though traditional non-textual community norms continued to supplement the written laws.

Texts were sometimes preserved publicly in archives or by officials, or privately by families.[4] Our evidence for archives varies widely and leaves many unanswered questions, so that general patterns are impossible to discern. The existence of archives can be inferred from the discovery of a depository (though care must be taken to distinguish between an archive and a rubbish heap of discarded documents), or from literary references or even artistic representation. In Egypt, in the tomb of Rekh-mi-rē at Thebes,

---

3 It is not impossible that a community's laws could be 'recognized' (in the sense of Hart's 'rule of recognition' (see footnote 24 below)) without writing. Some would argue that the early Icelandic 'lawspeaker's' annual recital of the community's laws, which was considered authoritative, served as a means of recognizing this set of rules as authoritative; it is possible, however, that he used writing to aid memory (see, for example, Sigurdsson 2004: 55–60, Jones 1984: 347 and Hansen 2018).

4 For more on ancient archives, see Posner 1972 and the chapters in Brosius 2003 and Faraguna 2013. None of these includes material on China or India.

Introduction

there is a court scene in which forty rolls of laws are spread out before the vizier, the main court official, which seems to indicate that all legislation was preserved.[5]

In the Near East, large groups of clay tablets have been found in secure archaeological contexts; some of these groups (or 'archives') include functional legal documents as well as copies or extracts of law collections. Everywhere in Greece, laws were inscribed, usually on stone, and displayed in public places, and in Athens copies of these were made on papyrus and stored in the central archive, the Metroon, which probably originated around 400 BCE and primarily served as a repository for proceedings of the Council and Assembly.[6] Legal documents may also have been preserved by individual officials or by family members in the classical and Hellenistic periods. During the Roman empire records were kept in various archives of legal transactions and court decisions, but the preservation of laws is more problematic. The compilers of the later Roman law codes, such as that of Justinian, must have consulted copies of earlier legislation, but it is not clear whether these were systematically ordered in a central archive (for example, in Constantinople) or even whether they were complete. In India, on the other hand, legal texts were preserved in expert communities, especially the Brahmins, where they were copied and studied.

We have organized this chapter according to the following main categories of legal texts:

Laws: authoritative rules, whether issued by a public authority (including statutes, edicts, and proclamations), or established by tradition (and written down)

Documents: includes contracts, deeds, wills, receipts and other written texts with legal effect

Procedural Records: formal accusations, petitions, rescripts, transcripts of trials (if these are for use in further legal proceedings), forensic speeches and verdicts, if these are officially recorded

Judicial Opinions: written judicial opinions that have the authority and force of law, and the opinions and commentaries of jurists that have become authoritative statements of the law as applied in practice

Secondary Legal Texts: texts produced or consumed outside the institution of law but that have significance for or provide evidence for law (i.e. evidence that can be used by legal historians in reconstructing the law of

---

5 Posner 1972: 72–74.   6 See Sickinger 1999.

the past).[7] These include historical accounts and reports, literary representations, instructional texts, documents with information about law (treaties, letters, etc.) and visual 'texts'.

For each of these categories except the last, we will examine when, how and why the texts emerged in each society; who wrote, produced or enacted the texts and under what circumstances; who constituted the audience for them; and finally (in most sections) other features of the texts that may shed light on the different societies' view of and use of these texts. The last group, however, contains so many different kinds of texts, each with its own history, that it seems best to treat these differently and examine each kind of secondary text separately.

Laws

Emergence of Laws

Like all societies, those being considered here first developed without the knowledge of writing. For Greece and the Near East during this preliterate period we have evidence of what we may call 'oral law': that is of traditional rules of proper conduct, preserved and transmitted in oral form, together with established procedures for settling disputes. Our knowledge of this stage is indirect as it depends on reports in secondary texts that were probably preserved orally at first but were eventually put in writing. The main secondary texts that shed light on oral law are early poetry, especially the epics of Homer in Greece and the Hebrew Bible in the Near East. Both sources portray scenes of dispute settlement, most famously the trial scene on Achilles' shield in the *Iliad* (18.497–510), and the judgments of Solomon in the Hebrew Bible (1 Kgs 3.16–28), both of which probably reflect traditional practice. The Hebrew Bible also has several collections of rules that reflect the oral law of earlier times, and similar rules are scattered haphazardly throughout the Homeric poems. 'Secondary' texts provide some, limited, information about preliterate rules and procedures in Rome, India and China.

A different kind of evidence for preliterate law comes from the laws and law codes that were first enacted in these societies. In ancient Greece, Draco's seventh-century BCE homicide law, for example, is clearly building on oral rules and procedures that are portrayed in Homer.[8] Similarly, in some of the

---

7 Note that this use of 'secondary' is not the same as Hart's well-known legal distinction between primary and secondary rules (see footnote 24 below).
8 See Gagarin 2008a: 30–31, 96–97.

Hittite laws or royal edicts from the Near East there are clear statements about old practices and new revisions. Presumably the earliest written laws of these and other societies were not created *de nihilo* but reflect, perhaps with substantial modification, the traditional rules and procedures of the earlier period.

As societies passed out of the oral stage with the discovery of writing, they began to write texts with legal import. These texts were created for different purposes and took different forms in different societies. Judging from the primary texts that have survived to the present – which of course present a selective and incomplete picture – in most areas, laws were the first legal texts to be written (Rome, Greece and perhaps China). In the Near East, however, functional administrative documents such as land transfers appear to predate laws, and likewise in China, documents are the earliest texts that have survived (though laws may have been written earlier). Some secondary texts were created before the earliest legal texts, but these generally portray law in the preliterate period and do not inform us about later legal texts.

Laws began to emerge for different reasons across the ancient societies discussed here. The most important distinction affecting the enactment of legislation appears to have been between small communities which were mostly confined to a single city, as in Greece and early Rome, and societies which, by the time they began to enact laws, had been organized into larger territories with larger populations ruled by a single monarch. The earliest laws by far come from societies that were governed by a single ruler at the time of the earliest legislation. As the sole authority, the ruler was responsible for issuing laws, primarily in the form of decrees or edicts, which were generally intended to be publicized widely, usually by governors or other members of the ruler's administration. These edicts took various forms. Some explicitly state rules that apply in their community. Others take a more indirect route and describe judgments the ruler has given in resolving disputes or other actions he has taken in the recent past. By writing down these past acts and publicizing them, the ruler is in effect prescribing rules that apply to the present and future.

In the Near East, evidence for royal decrees dates back to the Old Kingdom of Egypt, c. 2650–2135; most such decrees, recorded on stelae in Hieroglyphic and erected in temple precincts, concern royal revenue. They may be copies of texts first written on papyrus and then rewritten on stone for the purpose of publicity and security. Only slightly later, edicts were issued by Sumerian ('Mesopotamian') rulers in the twenty-sixth to twenty-fourth centuries BCE. They were written on stelae and displayed in public or copied onto clay tablets for use by legal scribes and authorities. They list reforms and other measures the ruler has taken to improve the kingdom and correct injustices.[9] In this way, the Sumerian edicts foreshadow a similar concern with promoting the image of the ruler that we find in later 'law collections', the earliest example of which are the (again Sumerian) Laws of Ur-Namma (c. 2100 BCE).

In China it was not until around 1500 BCE during the Shang dynasty (c. sixteenth to eleventh centuries) that edicts and legal decisions issued by the ruler were recorded in writing, though none of these survive.[10] At this time writing may have been used for evidentiary or recording purposes only. In the Western Zhou period (c. 1045–771 BCE), laws were probably communicated through participation in meetings of the princes of independent states or through proclamation by the ruler at assemblies of the people or mustering of the troops, but they might also be displayed on boards outside the palace gates. There are reports of varying reliability in the early histories of laws or collections of laws, issued by Shang and Western Zhou rulers, from the twelfth to the eighth centuries BCE. It is generally accepted that, after the collapse of the Western Zhou, various states produced collections of penal or other laws during the seventh and sixth centuries.

The earliest Chinese laws that have survived to the present-day come from the fourth and third centuries BCE. These were engraved on metal vessels and displayed in the royal palace; they might also be written on bamboo slips kept in the royal archives, and possibly also put on public display in the form of inscribed boards. Bamboo strips from the state of Qin (second half of the third century BCE) contain a variety of procedural regulations.[11] Some of these give rules for official conduct, guidelines for keeping accounts and procedures for the inspection of officials. Others define terms and stipulate procedures in order to ensure that officials interpret and execute items of the Qin code in the manner intended by the Qin royal court. Another section of texts instructs officials on how to conduct investigations (including, for example, the detailed examination of the body) and interrogations (of litigants and witnesses) so as to secure and transmit accurate results. Note that earlier texts on bamboo strips contain procedural reports; these are discussed in 'Procedural Records' below.

> Within the population, my rajuka officers take care of many hundreds of thousands of living beings. I have given them independent authority to grant rewards and to impose punishments, in order that rajuka officers may carry

---

9 Wilcke 2003: 141–43.   10 On the emergence of laws in China, see Caldwell 2014 and 2018.
11 See Hulsewé 1985a: esp. 183–207.

out their tasks with confidence and without fear, and bestow welfare and wellbeing on and grant favours to the people of the countryside. They will know how to bestow wellbeing and how to inflict pain. . . .

Just as one feels confident in entrusting one's child to a proficient nurse, knowing, 'She is a proficient nurse. She is able to take good care of my child', so I have appointed the rajuka officers for the welfare and wellbeing of the people of the countryside.

That the rajuka officers, being fearless and confident, may carry out their tasks unperturbed – for this reason I have given them independent authority to grant rewards and to impose punishments. For this is what is to be desired: there should be impartiality in judicial proceedings and impartiality in imposing punishments.

My practice, moreover, has extended as far as this: for men who are confined in prison, on whom the sentence has been passed, and who have received the death penalty, a stay of three days is granted. Their relatives will make them reflect on what provides protection for their lives. Having been made to reflect on the fact that their lives end in death, they will give gifts for the sake of the world beyond, or they will perform fasts.[12]

Aśoka's inscriptions were unprecedented and remain exceptional in Indian history. It would be more than five centuries before another king used an inscription to set policy or propound an ordinance, and none would ever again have multiple copies of a set of edicts inscribed in many places. The later texts are local ordinances contained in copperplate records of the Pallava and Gupta kings, though these refer to earlier orders that have not survived, and to what are apparently already well-established rules, such as 'the eighteen exemptions' mentioned by King Śivaskandavarman in the Mayidavolu copperplates.[13] Gupta and later inscriptions also make allusion to procedural matters, noting the probative value of written documents and witnesses in the case of disputes, and referring to the responsibility of the king and his officer to enforce decrees.

With the spread of Buddhism, what can be termed 'South Asian culture', including elements of legal thought and practice, were carried into central Asia. For example, a Kharoṣṭhi document from Niya in Xinjian, on the southern edge of the Takla Makan Desert, records a royal order that 'the king's law' (*rajadhaṁa*) should not be applied 'unlawfully' (*adhaṁena*), and seeks to clarify the status and tax rate of a particular individual.[14]

Circumstances were quite different in ancient Greece and early Rome, where after an era of semi-legendary kings, a relatively large share of the

---

12 Translation by Tim Lubin from the French version in Bloch 1950: 164–65.
13 Olivelle 2023: 312–13.   14 Salomon 1998: 273.

population had some role in the governance of the community. As a result the earliest laws were enacted with some input from the community and were displayed in public spaces, where they could be seen and read by members of the community. To be sure, literacy rates in these early societies were probably not high, and many residents may have been content with visual confirmation of the laws' existence. Nonetheless, literacy was probably higher in Greece and Rome, with their relatively simple alphabetic scripts, than in other societies with more complex writing systems. Thus, in Greece and Rome at least some members beyond the ruling elite would have been able to read these laws.

In ancient Greece, the earliest extant law comes from the Cretan city of Dreros (c. 650 BCE); it was written on stone on the side of a temple.[15] The law limits the term of office of the *kosmos* (the highest official in the city) and begins with the words: 'this was pleasing to the polis (city)', a common expression in Greek for the enactment of legislation. We do not know the exact composition of the political community designated by the term 'polis' at this time, but it very likely included a fairly large segment of the community. Laws were also enacted in many other Greek cities in the period 650–600 BCE, notably in Athens, where the laws of Draco (c. 620) and Solon (c. 590) formed the basis of classical Athenian law. Draco may have written many laws, but only one survived: a homicide law written perhaps on bronze and displayed in public. Solon wrote a large set of laws on many different topics; they were inscribed on revolving wooden *axones* (axles), which readers apparently turned while reading the text; these were displayed in the agora, or communal gathering area.[16] Both of these legislators were given some sort of authority to write laws by the community. Laws were also enacted in this period in many other Greek cities, and were written on stone or other materials and displayed in similar ways.[17]

In Rome, the earliest laws we know of were the Twelve Tables (451–449 BCE), a large collection of laws inscribed on twelve tablets probably made of bronze (though some reports say ivory) and set up in the marketplace. According to tradition, they were enacted to meet the demands of the people to know for themselves what the law was. Legislation of this sort, however, did not dominate in Rome as it did in Greece. In Rome, two other forms of legislation emerged. The more important of these, the praetor's

---

15 Gagarin and Perlman 2016: 197–221.
16 Leão and Rhodes 2015 has texts, translations and commentaries on all of Solon's laws.
17 See Gagarin 2008a, which also covers much of the other Greek material in the 'Law' of this chapter.

edict, was an annual declaration by one of the highest officials in the city stating which actions he would enforce during his term of office; these were put in writing and displayed in the forum from perhaps as early as the third century BCE. Laws were also enacted by popular assemblies throughout the period of the Republic. In addition, the opinions of jurists, which could sometimes take on the authority and force of law, began to be put in writing probably during the second century BCE. These, however, will be treated separately below.

In later periods, Greece and Rome continued to write laws in the same way as earlier, with input from the people, until Rome became an empire in the late first century BCE. In Greece, different cities continued to enact their own laws and display them publicly even after Philip and his son Alexander (the Great) established Macedonian control over them. Alexander also established Macedonian control over other, non-Greek parts of the world, bringing a rather different form of 'Greek law' to these areas. Egypt is the only part of this new Greek world about which we know very much, and it may not have been typical. It was ruled (332–30 BCE) by a Greek-Macedonian dynasty, the Ptolemies, who issued edicts concerning the operation of their administration (especially tax collection) but enacted little or no legislation of the sort found in the earlier Greek cities. Matters that did not concern the royal administration came under a complex combination of Greek and Egyptian (demotic) law.

During the early Roman empire, laws continued to be enacted by the Roman Senate, but other forms of legislation also became common.[18] For example, law was sometimes stated in rescripts (the emperor's responses to petitions), which were usually written not by the emperor himself but by officials in his administration. These rescripts served to clarify points of law rather than make new law, and could be addressed to either officials or private individuals. Some rescripts were copied and preserved in collections (or 'codes' – see below), such as the Gregorian and Hermogenian Codes in the 290s CE. Rescripts were also included in the Justinianic *Code* (c. 535 CE), a work that capped a tradition of written collections of laws in both Greece and Rome that stretched back, as we have seen, to the laws of Draco, Solon and the Twelve Tables.

In single-ruler states new forms of legislation sometimes supplemented rulers' edicts. It was also common to create written collections or 'codes' of

18 Corcoran 2014.

laws. In China and Egypt it appears that these collections were intended for lower-level officials in the royal administration who would be in charge of enforcing the law in the kingdom; in India and the rest of the Near East, however, the relationship of these collections to actual practice is more problematic.

In China, with the development of the bureaucratic state from the fourth century BCE onwards, laws as enactments of the ruler proliferated – although these were certainly distributed to officials, the extent of their availability to the general public is unclear. It does seem clear, however, that an essential requirement for the framing of a law was its redaction in writing. In Egypt, we have evidence for laws, though not the laws themselves, in the New Kingdom, in the form of an 'instruction text' from the tombs of the two Viziers (c. 1450 BCE), who were the officials in charge of the administration of law. This text gives detailed instructions about how the law is organized; how disputes should be handled; what conduct is criminal; and how contracts and other matters are organized. It is questionable, however, whether there was a written 'code' or collection of laws.

In the Near East outside of Egypt, after the Laws of Ur-Namma (c. 2100 BCE), eight other ancient collections of laws have survived, six on clay tablets inscribed in cuneiform and two from the Hebrew Bible.[19] Most or all of these cuneiform collections were originally written on stone monuments set up in temples throughout the kingdom, but with the notable exception of the Laws (or 'Code') of Ḥammurabi (c. 1750 BCE), which survives both in contemporary monuments – including the famous stone stele now in the Louvre – and in later copies and extracts on clay (Figure 2.1), all that survives of the other collections are later copies on clay tablets.[20] These collections were meant to be communicated to the larger public, both through the proliferation of inscribed copies throughout the territory and by (oral) proclamation. Most scholars, however, do not think they were intended as direct guides for actual legal practice but rather to promote the image of the king as wise and just.[21]

Finally, we see a different pattern across the extant ancient Indian material. Collections of normative texts, the Dharmasūtras and Dharmaśāstras, were produced by 'religious' professionals – the Brahmins – probably beginning in the third century BCE. They may have first been composed orally but were then written down in sacred books and frequently copied and recopied. They were meant to be read by other scholars and were taught in the Brahmin communities. These collections of normative texts were not cited as law in

19 Milstein 2021: 156.   20 Lafont and Westbrook 2003: 183.   21 Wells 2020.

Figure 2.1 Stele of Ḥammurabi, found at Susa, c. 1750 BCE (basalt), Paris, Musée du Louvre. © Bridgeman Images: number DGA5519845 (www.bridgemanimages.com/en/mesopotamian/code-of-hammurabi-the-god-shamash-dictating-his-laws-to-hammurabi-king-of-babylon-found-at-susa-iran/basalt/asset/5519845)

lawsuits and trials but provided the ethical and theoretical framework for legal practice. They are sometimes designated 'religious laws', as they combine the modern Western categories of 'religious' and 'legal' rules.[22] The 'legal' material in them includes procedural rules, formal substantive rules, regulations for forensic institutions and remedies for misconduct. The Dharmaśāstras provide elaborated rules of legal procedure, including the earliest procedural precepts (mostly dealing with fact-finding, witnesses and

---

22 For further discussion see Chapter 6, this volume.

conflicting evidence). The topic is developed considerably in the *Arthaśāstra* and the eighth chapter of *Manu* (both from around the second century CE), prefacing the description of eighteen grounds of litigation. The topic is presented much more systematically in the *Yājñavalkya* (fourth to fifth century CE) and *Nārada* (fifth to sixth century CE) 'codes'.[23]

The wide diversity of legal texts in antiquity raises the question of recognition: how did people at the time determine that a certain text had the authority of law? To be sure, not all the texts discussed above did have the authority of law – if by that we mean that they could be enforced by the state. Many rules of the Dharmaśāstras, for example, were not applied to most members of the society; their legal force was probably limited to the internal regulation of Brahmin communities, although these texts enjoined even kings to ensure compliance. As for laws in the stricter sense of rules enforceable by means of a legal process, there was, to our knowledge, no explicit (written) 'rule of recognition' anywhere in the ancient world.[24] Rather, it was simply understood that, for example, this rule (or these rules, or this set of rules) is a valid law.[25]

Rules that were understood to be laws generally included some combination of three factors: rules that were explicitly authored by a ruler ('these are the laws of King X') or by the community ('the following was pleasing to the polis'); rules that were preserved in a certain way or in a certain place; and rules that were communicated directly to the officials charged with overseeing and enforcing the law, or to the wider community, or to both at the same time. In the last case, communication could either take an oral form, such as by being read out to a public gathering, or could involve the written law being displayed or deposited somewhere where it could be read by those for whom it was intended. In whatever way the rule was recognized as a law, however, it would presumably have to be preserved in some place where it would be available to its intended audience.

23 For further discussion, see Chapter 7, this volume.
24 As used here, a 'rule of recognition' is, in Hart's words, a rule that specifies 'some feature or features possession of which by a suggested rule is taken as a conclusive affirmative indication that it is a rule of the group to be supported by the social pressure it exerts' (1961: 94). In other words, a rule of recognition tells you how to determine which ones of the many rules in a community are laws, rather than some other kind of rules.
25 The so-called 'law of citations' (426 CE), included in the *Code* of the Roman Emperor Theodosius II (*Theod. Cod* 1.4.3, 438 CE), is perhaps the earliest ancient antecedent to Hart's 'rule of recognition'. This 426 CE imperial ruling restricted citations of juristic literature in Roman court proceedings to the works of five (authoritative) Roman jurists: Papinian, Paul, Gaius, Ulpian and Modestinus. It was finally superseded in 533 CE by the promulgation of Justinian's *Digest*.

In sum, written laws emerged in ancient societies in various ways and for various reasons. Most early laws lack features that generally characterize oral compositions and thus were probably not simply written transcriptions of rules that were previously oral. These societies would have remained largely oral during and long after the period when people first began to write, and hence many of the orally preserved rules that had not been superseded by written laws would have remained in effect, as they do even in today's highly literate cultures. Moreover, the earliest written laws almost certainly bore a close relation, at least in terms of content, to previous oral rules. Specific details might change or, more likely, additionally details would be included, but a written law that directly contradicted traditional practice would not likely be enforceable, at least not without severe disruption.

Laws were written down for several purposes, including to give a degree of permanence to them and to ensure consistent enforcement and adjudication throughout the society. Laws were also written down for various other purposes, as we have seen. In Greece and Rome it appears that an important purpose was to communicate rules to those affected, either to those in charge of enforcing the law, or to those required to live by it, or both. When the purpose of writing laws was to communicate them more broadly, the written texts might be made widely available to the entire community by being displayed in a public place, or copies might be made available to a smaller number of officials, who might or might not communicate them to others. In some cases it seems to have been important to create a more or less permanent text by using durable materials; at other times more perishable materials were used. It is also possible that writing, especially writing on more permanent materials, could be seen as a way to lend greater authority to the laws. And another common purpose, especially in single-ruler societies was the ruler's desire for publicity, which was probably a factor even in some Greek and Roman legislation.

Other written laws seem to be intended as a record of actions taken in the past, either in order that those actions could be enforced in the future, or just to give them a high degree of durability. Yet another reason for writing laws can be seen in India, in the spread of Indian legal traditions along with other features of Indian culture and religion to Southeast Asia during the high-classical Gupta era (fourth to sixth centuries CE). This included the Brahmanical conceptions of *dharma* as well as many practices including the use of inscriptions to convey property rights, and sometimes to record the outcome of disputes. This spread of ancient Indian legal traditions, which began in the fifth century CE, was particularly important in Cambodia and Indonesia. These regions did not use writing at all before their 'Indianization', but the adoption of Indian models mostly involved the articulation of local norms and legal practices within an imported overarching conceptual framework. Many early records were composed in Sanskrit, but very quickly there was a shift to the use of the local language, amply augmented by Sanskrit loanwords for terms of art. In inscriptions from Borneo, Java, and Sumatra, the influence of concepts from Dharmaśāstra is even more pronounced than in India. Javanese 'Dharmaśāstras' (only superficially Indian in content) came to be composed locally, something that happened in Burma and Thailand as well. This suggests that the notion of the 'lawbook' was taken much more literally in these emulative settings than it ever was in India proper.[26]

Production of Laws

Laws in ancient societies were enacted by different kinds of authority, depending primarily – but not solely – on the system of government at the time. Whatever the governance form, laws and decrees were often said to have been sanctioned by a god or gods, which would give them divine authority and protection. Where there was a single monarch (king or emperor) the ruler issued laws himself, though his exact role in the enactment is often not clear. He may have had other officials draft laws and then issue them in his name; he may have suggested the general features of the laws he wanted to enact but left the details in the hands of others; or he may have drafted some of the laws himself. In any case, the actual writers of laws were often scribes, trained and educated professionals who may have composed, or helped to compose, the text as well as writing it down.

Across the ancient Mesopotamian evidence, the proposal of legislation would in some cases be equivalent to its ratification; the issuance of a decree by a monarch, for instance, in itself completed the enactment process. Although literary texts suggest that assemblies of citizens might be asked to ratify laws, no such process is known from the historical records that survive. Similarly, in ancient Indian texts it seems to be taken for granted that – besides the Dharmaśāstras themselves – local laws would be for the most part

---

26 Olivelle and Davis 2017.

formulated orally; offences and disputes were also expected to be adjudicated in local or group-specific forums and appeals to state authorities are envisaged only in the gravest or most irresolvable cases. In rare cases, we have evidence for local rulers being petitioned to endorse local rules by decree. The earliest such decree to survive within the ancient Indian tradition is the Charter of Viṣṇuṣeṇa (592 CE western India), which lays down some seventy-two statutes (*sthiti*), most of which concern the rights and privileges of a guild of traders vis-à-vis the state and other groups.[27] At least some of these seventy-two rules run counter to rules found in the Brahmanical rule-books of *dharma*.

In non-monarchical societies the community generally had a role in legislation. In Greece, each city legislated in its own way, but in most cases some sort of popular body seems to have worked together with one or more officials to enact legislation. This could sometimes take the form of the community authorizing a single individual, like Solon, to produce legislation, or an assembly or other body may have enacted laws themselves, perhaps in consultation with officials. In Dreros, the earliest preserved law was enacted by 'the polis'. In Athens in the fifth century BCE, the Assembly alone enacted laws; during the fourth century, however, this process was modified so that a committee of lawgivers (*nomothetai*) first had to approve a law before it could be voted on by the Assembly. After an individual proposed a law, the text was written down on a temporary wooden tablet and posted in public so that all concerned could read it. After approval by the Assembly, the law was then written on some more durable material for public display.

In the city(-state) of Rome, the overthrow of the monarchy in 509 BCE led to rule by annually elected officials who, as tradition has it, issued and put their names on various laws. One or more of these officials may have been the author(s) of the Twelve Tables (c. 451–449 BCE), but we cannot be certain. Later legislation was enacted either by various Republican assemblies or occasional plebiscites of the Roman people, usually on the initiative of a consul, whose name attached to the legislation, or by means of the praetor's edict, or by advisory resolutions of the senate, which if not vetoed by a magistrate, became *senatus consulta* ('decrees of the senate'). During the Roman empire, ratification by the Senate of Rome (or later by the Senate of Constantinople) of a law proposed by the emperor was a mere formality, but

---

27 Wiese and Das 2019.

the pretence of independent ratification was nonetheless sometimes maintained.

Audience and Use

Written laws were intended to be read by (or read out to) various audiences ranging in size from the population at large to – in extreme cases where they were buried or entombed (see below) – no one, except perhaps the gods. The most important factor in determining who read ancient laws was probably literacy. As noted above, scholars tend to disagree widely about the level and kind of literacy in different areas, but as already noted above it was probably higher across ancient Greek and Roman cultures, with their simple alphabetic scripts, than in other traditions.

In the absence of direct evidence, conditions surrounding the writing of laws can be suggestive of their audience. In general, laws that were prominently displayed in public spaces were probably intended to be read by many people, often in connection with actual or potential litigation. Some scholars think that levels of literacy were so low that laws could not have been inscribed and displayed in public in order to be read by many members of the community. The purpose of the laws would thus lie primarily in their visual impact, which may have conveyed a sense of the power and authority of the ruler or ruling elite. This explanation of public display as a kind of propaganda is more plausible for a one-off set of laws. like the Near Eastern Laws of Ḥammurabi, which most contemporary scholars think was not used in actual litigation, or for the Roman Twelve Tables than for the laws of most Greek cities, hundreds of which were written and displayed in different cities, many of them relatively short texts addressing a single issue. In such cases, any propaganda effect stemming from public display would almost certainly diminish over time, and inscription on stone would no longer be worth the resources it required.[28]

In Greece and in early China (770–445 BCE), all laws were displayed in public, as were Egyptian royal decrees and many Near Eastern royal promulgations. Later in China, laws became too numerous to display in public and so copies were made and distributed to the officials who applied the laws. However, ordinary people seem to have been able to submit enquiries about the laws to the officials in charge and receive written replies. The authorities might take steps to draw the public's attention to

---

28 See further Gagarin 2008a: 67–71.

laws that concerned them by setting up the text in a public place.[29] Whatever the level of literacy, publicly displayed laws would have been available for consultation by the general public, even if most would need help from friends or, depending on the complexity of the text in question, from legal experts.

In practice, in most societies, even publicly displayed laws may have been read by only a small number of people, such as scribes, notaries and advocates, who could then give advice to their clients, literate and illiterate, just as lawyers generally do today, even though their literate clients could if they wished consult the texts of statutes on their own. Laws intended for this professional audience may have been kept in less accessible places, where even though anyone who wished could consult them, they would normally be read only by a relatively small number. Or, multiple official copies may have been made for distribution to public officials or by individuals for their own use. For example, a third-century BCE papyrus (P. Hal. 1), apparently compiled by a lawyer from various sources, contains excerpts from a variety of laws in Alexandria in Egypt – but this may have been a private copy and as such not available to the general public.

Highly specialized legal texts, such as rules for conduct in a particular place, may have been displayed only in the relevant place, where only the limited audience for whom these rules were relevant would have read them. For example, a law concerning conduct in a sacred precinct may have been displayed only at the entrance to the precinct. Finally, in China, some legal texts have been found in tombs, but the purpose of these is unclear and controversial; they may simply have been the prized property of the official buried in the tomb.[30]

Special Features of Laws

Codification.[31] From time to time, different cultures produced collections of laws that are often referred to as 'codes'. The term 'code' – derived from the Latin term *codex* ('book'), a specific form of material production that was used for the great late antique law codes (*codices*) of the Roman emperors Theodosius II and Justinian – has evoked much debate and has been applied to many different kinds of collections. Probably no ancient collection meets

---

29 In China the legalists insisted on the wide dissemination of laws, see Duyvendak 1963: 327–29.
30 See the discussion in Barbieri-Law and Yates 2015, vol. I: 107–9.
31 See Lévy 2000 for studies of codification in Greece, Rome and the ancient Near East.

the strict modern standard of systematic organization, first displayed by the French Napoleonic *Code Civil* of 1804 (though even that code is not and could never be complete in the sense of covering every possible situation). Some ancient collections of laws were clearly intended to form a more or less complete, unified, and systematically organized set. Which of these, if any, should be designated a 'code' in the modern sense is largely a matter of definition, and any firm dividing line between a code and a collection more generally is to some extent arbitrary. For our purpose, therefore, it seems more useful to indicate the degree of completeness and organization on a continuous scale than to establish the precise dividing line between codes and other collections of laws.

Several of the later Chinese collections probably come closest to modern standards of codification.[32] Beginning in the sixth century BCE, a large number of penal laws were engraved on vessels or written on bamboo slips so that they could be used by officials throughout the kingdom who were charged with enforcing the laws. With the rise of the bureaucratic state in the fourth century BCE, such collections greatly increased in scope so as to cover administrative as well as penal matters. From the establishment of the Qin state (c. 350 BCE)[33], all succeeding empires and dynasties made a point of issuing a comprehensive collection of administrative and penal rules. An important change in the nature of these collections occurred in the third and fourth centuries CE, when the state of Wei (220–265 CE) and the Jin dynasty (265–420 CE) produced collections of rules that had a structural unity not found in the earlier collections. The Jin collections of laws were carefully crafted documents in which general principles were systematically combined with specific articles. The former not only explained terms used in the specific articles but also set out rules for the way in which those articles were to be applied by the officials entrusted with the determination and the sentencing of offences. The section with specific articles was organized not just according to subject matter, but in such a way that the sentencing of offences was related not only to the particular article defining the offence and prescribing the punishment but also to other articles deemed by the legislators to be relevant. This form of organization provided the model for all later Chinese collections, including the highly influential Tang code of criminal law (the

---

32 For what follows see MacCormack 2004 and Caldwell 2018.
33 Although the Qin empire itself lasted a short time, the Qin state dates from c. 350 BCE, and the extant laws were produced by the state rather than the empire. Thus, we can have a composite date of c. 350–206 BCE for the Qin state and empire.

Tanglüshuyi) produced in the seventh century CE, though the earliest surviving version is from 737 (Figure 2.2).

In the strictest sense, only the *Tang Penal Code* with Commentary met the standard of systematic organization found in the *Napoleonic Codes*. For example, article 53 of the *Tang Penal Code*, from the 'General Principles' section, defines certain technical expressions used throughout the code to specify the way in which an offender was to be sentenced. Where the phrase 'X is to be sentenced to the same punishment (*yu tong zui*)' occurs, X is to be sentenced to the same punishment as that prescribed for the comparable offence, with the exception that should the punishment for the latter offence be capital, the punishment in the present offence was to be limited to strangulation, thus excluding beheading. But should the phrase 'treat as (another offence) and sentence (*zhun ... lun*)' occur, the punishment to be applied in the present case was not to exceed exile, even if the punishment for the comparable offence was capital. These definitions illustrate the 'principle of economy of means' that characterized the drafting of the *Tanglüshuyi*.

No other ancient civilization achieved the same degree of codification as these later Chinese codes. In the Near East, several large collections of laws attributed to the authority of particular rulers have survived but none is

Figure 2.2 Chinese script. Tang dynasty (618–907 CE) calligraphy attributed to Lee Yangbing (Li Yangbing), a high-ranking Tang dynasty Chinese government official (imperial magistrate), important literary figure and noted calligrapher, c. 8th century CE. © Pictures from History / Bridgeman Images: number PFH1164265 (www.bridgemanimages.com/en/noartistknown/china-chinese-script-tang-dynasty-618-907-calligraphy-attributed-to-lee-yang-bing-li-yangbing-c-8th/nomedium/asset/1164265)

comprehensive. Even as large a collection as the Laws of Hammurabi (c. 1750 BCE), with over 300 provisions, is clearly not complete; there must have been enforceable laws on matters not covered in this collection that were recognized by some other means. Rules concerning ritual behaviours, for example, are not included in Hammurabi's laws nor in any of the surviving Akkadian or Sumerian law collections, though ritual norms for sacrifices, priestly installations, etc., are recorded outside of the 'legal' corpus. Some of these collections have a specific limited focus, such as the Middle Assyrian Laws (about 1100 BCE) with about sixty provisions devoted to behaviours and restrictions of royal women, which may have been but one 'chapter' of a larger series of collected rules covering an array of circumstances.

In Egypt we have no direct evidence of codification processes, though a comprehensive code may have existed. The 'Duties of the Vizier' (c. 1450 BCE), which lays out in detail how law was organized; how private disputes were adjudicated; what was 'criminal' and so on, perhaps comes closest to a codification. A later collection, the so-called Hermopolis Legal Code from the third century BCE, is a kind of manual of forms or types of contracts and procedures. A later collection of forms of contracts from the first millennium CE also in many ways resembles a law code.[34]

In Rome, the great compilations of imperial constitutions promulgated in the names of the emperors Theodosius II and Justinian during the later (Eastern Roman) empire were fairly comprehensive collections; nonetheless, compared with the Tang Penal Code at least, they are relatively loosely organized. During the earlier Roman empire, informal yet still authoritative collections were made, for example the late third-century CE Gregorian and Hermogenian Codes; however, these also fall considerably short of full codification.

In Greece, Solon's early sixth-century legislation appears to have been fairly comprehensive, but we know nothing of its organization. The fifth-century Gortyn Law 'code' resembles Hammurabi's laws in being a loosely organized and only partial collection of laws. In Athens, a collection of laws was made at the end of the fifth century BCE; most of these were older laws that were simply republished. This Athenian collection aimed at being complete, but it does not appear to have been conceived as a systematic and unified collection and it is not clear what principles of organization, if any, it followed.

---

34 For more on ancient Egyptian law codes, see Lippert 2004.

From the extant evidence, India seems to have been the least concerned with legislation – and thus with codification. Apart from Aśoka's edicts (mid third century BCE), discussed above, which include occasional decrees systematically published in multiple inscriptions across his empire, written statutes are rarely encountered. The few rare examples that survive of charters or statutes are presented as the conventions of a particular group that have been endorsed by a local ruler to establish their validity and to ensure compliance. The 'Charter of Viṣṇuṣeṇa' (592 CE), discussed above, is the earliest known example; again, it does not appear that this charter was intended to be comprehensive.

Language. Laws are normally written in the main language of the community to which they apply, but complexities arise when more than one language was used by significant parts of that community. Communities that spoke a single language or dialect, like the individual Greek cities, generally wrote laws only in one language; as did those communities with a centralized bureaucracy, such as Rome and China, and those with a ruling class which enacted laws primarily for its own use, as in India Although the earliest laws from Mesopotamia are written in Sumerian, by the early second millennium BCE Akkadian (that is, Babylonian and Assyrian dialects) was used as the language of commerce, diplomacy and scholarship for more than two millennia – despite much cultural and linguistic change in the society and even as Aramaic increasingly came to predominate.

Communities with mixed populations managed their language differences in various ways. They might enact a single set of laws but circulate these in multiple versions in more than one language, as in the Eastern part of the later Roman empire where laws circulated officially in both Latin and Greek.[35] Or they might use different laws, in different languages, for different language groups, as in Ptolemaic Egypt where the population was a mixture of Egyptian, Greek, Jewish and other peoples. Each of these groups apparently had their own law, written in their own language: the 'laws of the country' for use in Egyptian courts; the 'laws of the cities' for use in Greek courts; and some form of Jewish law for Jewish communities. As Egyptians and Greeks mingled together and intermarried, however, the use of one or the other sets of laws became more flexible. With the Roman conquest in 31 BCE, Roman laws, written in Latin, began to be used by the administration, but many individuals continued to use Greek (and to a lesser extent Demotic) laws.

35 Millar 2006.

Syntax. Many laws take a casuistic or conditional form: 'If X happens, the consequence is Y.' The condition may be introduced by 'if', 'when', 'whoever', 'in case' or other such words. The law may specify a violation by someone ('if X kills Y'), or simply an event ('if X dies'). The consequence may be a penalty, physical or monetary ('he is to be put to death or pay a certain fine'); a prescribed action ('his sons are to divide his estate in equal shares'); or a procedure to be followed ('he is to be subjected to the river ordeal' or 'the judge is to swear an oath and decide the case himself').

Sometimes the law begins with a command or a prohibition, followed by a conditional sentence stating the consequences for not complying with the command or violating the prohibition: 'X is (is not) to do Y; if he does (does not do) Y, the consequence is Z.' Other laws may simply state a rule of conduct ('a goat is to be sacrificed to Apollo on the first day of the festival'); or a rule of procedure ('the judge is to decide within fifteen days'); or a definition or clarification of a term ('a son is either a natural son or an adopted son'). In these cases, nothing explicit is said about the consequences for violating the rules, though in many cases implicit but unstated consequences would probably follow, such as a suit against the violator; or dismissal of the case if a judge does not decide in time; or if another claimant tries to prevent an adopted son from inheriting.

In China, from at least the Han dynasty (206 BCE–221 CE), all laws were issued in casuistic form. They consisted of the *lü* (statutes), understood to be the old laws handed down from ruler to ruler or even from dynasty to dynasty, and the *ling* (orders), new rules designed by the ruler to cover the contingencies of the moment. Either *lü* or *ling* might have a penal or administrative content, and they might be issued together in the same collection of laws. After the Han, the distinction was different: *lü* were penal rules, whereas *ling* were administrative rules. Collections of these types of laws were issued separately. *Lü* always had a casuistic form, except for a section on general principles in collections of penal laws, which define terms or set out general rules for the administration of penal law, which lack the element of punishment. *Ling* were administrative rules that lacked any statement of punishment. By the time of the Tang (618–907 CE) we have four clearly distinguished kinds of legal rule, each issued in separate 'collections': the penal code consisting of articles defining offences and imposing punishments (*lü*); the administrative statutes (*ling*) regulating the conduct of the administration, yet without imposing punishments for specific derelictions of duty on the part of officials; the ordinances (*shi*), being rules derived from imperial edicts designed to supplement the general administrative provisions of the *ling* by setting out in detail the way in which they were to be applied in specific localities or for specific purposes; and the regulations (*ge*), being rules, either penal or administrative in content, extracted from imperial edicts addressing urgent issues of the day. Of these various collections of laws only the *lü* stand out as a code in the strict sense. The other collections of laws merely assemble rules according to subject matter.

Precision. Almost all laws, with the exception of the Dharmaśāstras (which are not poetic works but rather prose set in verse), were written in prose so that they are generally more precise than the rules found in poetic works. Laws vary widely in the degree of precision and amount of technical language they contain. Some early laws, especially those written for small cohesive communities, are fairly elliptical, making them often difficult for modern scholars to understand – though their meaning was presumably clear to those for whom they were intended. The first law on the Twelve Tables, for instance reads, *si in ius vocat, ito*, which literally means, 'if he summons to trial, may he go'. We might express this more clearly as 'if X summons Y to court, Y must appear'. This style continues to be used for laws in the praetor's edict. Later Roman laws, however, including (it appears) statutes passed by assemblies, are much more precise and detailed. For example, the *Lex Quinctia* (9 BCE), aimed at protecting Rome's water sources, begins:

> Whoever after the (successful) proposal of this statute shall knowingly with wrongful deceit have holed or fractured, or shall have seen to the holing of fracture of, the underground conduits, the covered channels, the arches, pipes, tubes, reservoirs, pools of the public aqueducts, which are (or shall be) brought to the city, or shall have damaged them, to the effect that those aqueducts or any aqueduct of them not (be able) to come to, descend to, flow to, reach, be brought to the city of Rome, or to the effect that in the city of Rome and in those places where there are or shall be buildings continuous with the city it should not rise, be distributed or be divided, or be brought into reservoirs or pools, in those gardens, properties, places, to the owners, possessors or usufructuaries of which gardens, properties, places water has been or shall have been granted or attributed, he is to be condemned to pay etc.[36]

Athenian laws, on the other hand, tended to be written with somewhat less precision. The grain-tax law (374/3 BCE), for example, begins:

> In order that there the people may have grain publicly available, sell the tax of one-twelfth at Lemnos, Imbros, and Skyros, and the tax of one-fiftieth in grain. Each share will be five hundred *medimnoi*, one hundred of wheat and

---

36 Translation by Crawford 1996, vol. II: 793–800.

four hundred of barley. The buyer will convey the grain to Piraeus at his own risk and will transport the grain up to the city at his own expense and will heap up the grain in the Aiakeion. The city will make available the Aiakeion covered and with a door, etc.[37]

In these texts, the Romans appear concerned to define precisely and without any ambiguity what constituted damage to the water supply. The Athenians, on the other hand, laid out in a simple narrative what they wished to see happen. In each case, the language of the law may be indicative of the attitude each culture has towards its legal system: an emphasis on precision and completeness in Rome versus clarity and simplicity in Athens. The Laws of Ḥammurabi, which may not be intended for practical or precedential use, resemble Athenian laws more than Roman. That is, while seemingly precise at first glance, the provisions are brief and elliptical, leaving open possibilities of application.

Documents

Documents have a very different place than laws in a society's legal system but are just as important, if not more important, in most areas. Presumably in the beginning transactions were oral: a transaction was simply remembered by those involved or, if necessary, it occurred in the presence of witnesses who could testify to it later. Written documents began to be used by most ancient societies as soon as they developed written formats, and continued to be used, often with very little change, throughout their history. Even if not legally required, the continual recurrence of similar situations meant that most types of documents were more or less formulaic. In some societies, however, transactions remained oral long after the society formalized written recording practices.

In this section we discuss documents that can and often do exist apart from any litigation (though they are also sometimes used in litigation) such as contracts (or agreements); receipts; property records (including deeds and records of sales); wills; and status records (for example, manumission records). Below we will turn to procedural records: documents that were created and existed only in the context of litigation.

Emergence of Documents

Most documents were created by individuals to meet various immediate needs. In many cases the need was commercial. Their use in court was

---

37 Translation from RO: 121.

usually not consciously envisioned at the time of their creation, but almost all documents could potentially be used in court if necessary. Documents were also needed in those parts of the ancient world (though not, especially, in early Greece and Rome) when governments began to control large territories. The administration of these territories often required the use of written instruments in order to record systematically such things as land ownership or population distribution for various purposes, including most importantly taxation.

Before writing people relied on human memory. A will or a contract took the form of one or more individuals expressing their wishes or confirming a transaction, usually in front of witnesses, who could be called on later to recall the details of the will or contract, perhaps prompted by physical aids such as, for example, boundary stones (for land transactions) or branding or tattooing (for slave or cattle sales). Other matters would simply be remembered by those involved. Buyer and seller remembered the sale, a landowner and his neighbours remembered his ownership and so on. Writing brought a degree of certainty to such matters but was not infallible and forgeries certainly existed.

Ancient societies differed with regard to the ease of writing and the availability of materials for writing, and these factors undoubtedly affected the creation of documents. Because these conditions could vary widely, it is less easy to systematize or give general rules for the use of documents than it is for laws. The survival rates of documents, moreover, also vary considerably. Our present-day knowledge about the use of written documents is substantially diminished because most ancient societies used relatively perishable materials for the bulk of their documents. Whereas the authors of laws would often have wanted to create a fairly permanent copy for use by future generations, the creators of documents would often have seen no need for the document to last longer than their lifetimes, or at most for a generation or two after that.

When the size of communities and the number of tradesmen were relatively small, traditional, oral forms of transaction would be sufficient. As communities grew larger, as commerce became more extensive and complex, and as personal ties among merchants weakened, however, people began to find written documents a convenient tool for remembering the often complex details of transactions and providing a clear and lasting record which later would be difficult to dispute.[38] The more complex the society, the

---

38 See Chapter 11, this volume, on commerce and contracts.

larger the community; and the more diverse the population that engaged in commerce, the more likely it would be that written documents would be desired and used.

The earliest written documents that have survived to the present day are probably those from Mesopotamia, where the normal medium for documents was the cuneiform clay tablet (Figure 2.3). Clay was readily available and easy to write on by impressing a stylus into the damp clay. After drying or baking (intentionally in a kiln or unintentionally in a conflagration), it became quite durable. The earliest documentary records include some very fragmentary 'proto-cunieform' tablets from Uruk III (3200–3000 BCE) – these appear to record land sales.[39] They may also suggest the existence of a central land register. Sales of moveable property are recorded in cuneiform clay tablets dating to the early twenty-fourth century BCE; written contracts and

Figure 2.3 Babylonian clay tablet with legal text written in cuneiform script, from Ugarit or Ras Shamra, Syria (13th century BCE). A. Dagli Orti, © NPL – DeA Picture Library / Bridgeman Images: number DGA507918 (www.bridgemanimages.com/en/a-dagli-orti/babylonian-clay-tablet-with-legal-text-written-in-cuneiform-script-artefact-from-ugarit-or-ras/nomedium/asset/507918)

39 Gelb et al. 1991: 27–32.

accounts of litigation begin to be put in writing later in the same century. The form of these was probably based on that of binding oral agreements that were made earlier. Marriages were concluded by customary activity (rites, gift exchanges, etc.), but marital property (bride wealth, dowries) and marital rights and obligations (inheritance, residency, secondary wives, divorce options) would be recorded in documents that also included statements of status. Inheritance generally followed accepted local custom (sons sharing equally or with eldest receiving preferential share); only when unusual heirs (brother, wife, adoptee, daughter, nephew, unmarried son), an unusual testator (widow, priestess, adoptive parent), or potentially contestable properties (purchased land, slaves) were involved was resort made to written documents. Later, in the last centuries of the Achaemenid and then Seleucid periods (fifth to first centuries BCE), we find that as Aramaic and writing on parchment began to supplant Akkadian and writing on clay tablets, certain types of transactions began to be recorded exclusively in the new medium. Since parchment is perishable and far less durable than (baked) clay, almost none of these latter transactions survive.

Outside of ancient Mesopotamia, the normal materials for writing documents were considerably more perishable than the clay tablets. In Egypt, the primary writing material was papyrus which under the right conditions – buried in very dry sand – can last for millennia, but in most other environments is quite perishable. Ostraka (fragments of broken clay pottery) were cheaper than papyri and thus they were commonly used for short texts; however, their relatively small size and erratic shape were unsuitable for legal documents, which are generally longer. Written documents are relatively scarce before the New Kingdom (1550 BCE), but from this time on they increase significantly until they become abundant in the Ptolemaic period (after 332 BCE). Most of the surviving documents from earlier periods were found in tombs, going back to the late third dynasty (c. 2600 BCE), and most of these deal with mortuary practices and estates.[40] In the Middle Kingdom (2125–1550 BCE), some archives containing documents survive; these can be supplemented by letters, stories and reports about documents.[41] Documents that survive from the New Kingdom (1550–1069 BCE) and afterwards include a few public records, such as the investigation and trial of various officials, and many more private documents, including 'archives' with documents attesting to all the business of a family or an estate, including sale, loan, lease, litigation, marriage, adoption, partnership and inheritance documents.[42] Temples and tombs were

40 Jasnow 2003a: 96.   41 Jasnow 2003b: 256.   42 Jasnow 2003c: 291–94.

important locations for publicizing the final resolutions of private disputes of elites. The so-called Stèle juridique, erected at the temple of Karnak, for example, records the resolution of a loan dispute involving high officials and a large amount of gold. From about 650 BCE we begin to have documents written in Demotic, a newer form of the Egyptian language. These are joined by many Greek documents in the Ptolemaic period (332–30 BCE) and also Latin documents in the Roman period after 30 BCE. Both Demotic and Greek documents from this period often come from private or public archives. Among them are marriage contracts, divisions of inheritance, loans, leases and cessions of property rights.

Taken as a whole, the evidence overwhelmingly suggests that in Egypt and the rest of the Near East written documents were far more numerous and more important than written laws. The discovery of more evidence is very unlikely to change this picture. The high status of scribes in both areas was the result of this situation and also a partial cause of its perpetuation. In other parts of the ancient world, however, documents were less important; they existed everywhere, but were often less important than oral agreements.

In China, the materials on which most documents were written – bamboo and wood – were also relatively perishable, but we have excerpts from such documents (not the documents themselves) inscribed on bronze vessels from the period of the Western Zhou (1045–771 BCE). These record details of contracts, property transactions and lawsuits. The documents themselves, as preserved in family or official archives, are first found in the late fourth century BCE when bamboo strips from a tomb preserve accounts of trials and other legal matters involving the state, such as government loans, but not records of private transactions between individuals.[43] Later, in the Han dynasty (206 BCE–220/1 CE), excavated specimens of contracts and even a will written on bamboo or wood have been found in tombs or wells, probably put there by people fleeing their homes as these were considered good places to hide important property. Marriage agreements were usually concluded orally, but they might also be concluded in writing; no written marriage agreements from early China have survived, but later documents suggest that these existed.[44]

Written contracts were useful in case of dispute, but writing does not seem to have been a requirement for the validity of a contract; however, contracts for which no written version existed might be the subject of litigation. For example, we do not know the exact sequence of the development of

---

43 Loewe and Shaughnessy 1999: 590.   44 For Han contracts, see Scogin 1990.

formalities for certain kinds of contracts recorded in ancient Chinese documents, but in the Tang codes (seventh century CE) we have important rules for the conclusion of contracts relating to land and those relating to the sale of slaves and animals in the markets. At this time the disposition of land was severely restricted, but, where it was transferable, the purchaser was under an obligation to register the transaction with the authorities. This implies that contracts for the sale of land were required to be in writing: for the sale of slaves, cattle or horses in the market, the drawing up of a market certificate was necessary under which the buyer acquired certain rights should the slave or animal sold prove to have a defect.[45] In the case of written wills, on the other hand, we learn from the Han laws (186 BCE) that the head of a family was freely allowed to make a will: he simply told his wishes to a local official, who recorded these in writing in a three-part document and registered one part with the district court.[46] Later, however (according to the Tang Code), a will could no longer be made except in the absence of male heirs – apparently there was no longer a requirement that it be written or registered.[47]

In ancient Indian communities most documents were probably first written on palm leaves or other perishable material, but no doubt a durable copy from these was sometimes made at a later date. Thus, the earliest records that survive are inscribed on stone (from the first century CE) and copper plates (from the third century). These records become progressively more common through the centuries, especially in south India. The most common sort of legal documents here take the form of inscriptions recording the granting of land and specific privileges to Brahmins or other religious groups. Legal documents for evidentiary purposes in court became significantly more important during the Gupta empire (around the fourth and fifth centuries CE).[48] Dharmaśāstras provide rather explicit models for such documents, prescribing many elements of their form. Inscriptions on copperplates (or exceptionally other metals) were typical for land-grants to Brahmins individually or collectively (and later for other property transactions), or to record rights and privileges conferred by authority. These functioned as deeds and were held privately, to be produced in court in the case of a legal challenge. Records on stone were common for gifts to institutions of various religions (Hindu, Buddhist, Jain) and were usually integrated into temple precincts. Besides providing the circumstances and stipulations of the

---

45 For Tang contracts see Hansen 1995: chapter 2 and Johnson 1997: 485 (article 422).
46 Text and translation in Barbieri-Law and Yates 2015, vol. II: 801 (par. 17).
47 MacCormack 2008: 421–24.   48 Lubin 2023; see Chapter 7, this volume.

endowment, they might regulate certain aspects of temple administration. In these cases, the reason for displaying the record in the temple itself would have been to have a public record of the terms of the transaction to ensure that they continued to be observed. However, one might also judge that, especially in cases where the inscription was placed in an inaccessible position, the inscription was a sort of speech act directed to the deity itself, to elicit blessings for the pious donor. In a few cases, the deity is invoked as a divine witness. There is no evidence for written wills in ancient India.

In Greece documents probably began to be written down in the sixth century BCE. In direct contrast to ancient India, wills were perhaps the earliest form of written legal documentation: the legislation of Solon (c. 590 BCE) explicitly allowed Athenians to make wills if they did not have a natural son. A natural son would inherit automatically, but in the absence of one, Solon seems to have wanted to allow a posthumous adoption. Wills were presumably written on papyrus but none survive. This may be because in Athens written wills were always rather suspect.[49] Litigants in inheritance disputes, for instance, commonly argued that the written will either was forged or did not represent the testator's true intentions, and that witnesses, who were present at the time and knew the testator and his family, could testify more accurately to his intentions.

Contracts may also have been written in Greece around the time of Solon, especially in connection with maritime commerce, but written contracts only became the norm in the fourth century BCE. Maritime contracts were probably written earlier than others because the contracting parties often came from different cities or from countries other than Greece; they thus did not necessarily have common customs as a basis for oral understanding. Agreements between two Athenians, however, were traditionally made orally in the presence of witnesses, who could later be called to testify in case of a dispute – though this too began to change in the fourth century BCE. Many Greek contracts written on papyrus survive from the third century BCE and later, but most of these come from Egypt after Alexander's conquests resulted in large numbers of Greeks settling there and in other parts of the Near East, where papyrus could be well preserved in the dry sands. Greek settlers in these territories also made much more use of written documents than Greeks in the traditional poleis, because the settlers, many of them former mercenaries, often came from different cities and thus lacked a common legal tradition. In fourth-century BCE Athens, for instance,

---

49 Cohen 2003.

marriage contracts were not normally written, but as soon as Greeks settled in Egypt, written marriage contracts become very common.[50]

At Rome, certain oral forms of transactions such as wills and contracts (or agreements) were valid, so that written versions served only an evidentiary purpose as 'documents of record'. Whether oral or written, many kinds of documents were subject to formulary requirements; that is, in order to be valid they had to adhere to certain prescribed words and phrases. In classical Roman law definite forms of phrasing were required for contracts, but it seems that it was not until the Roman empire that some transactions were formally required to be recorded in writing in order to be valid, and even in these cases the recording may have been primarily intended to establish prima facie evidence of the recorded transaction. Sale of land and donations, however, seem to have had stricter requirements for the execution of written documents.[51]

Production of Documents

Most documents either served the private needs of individuals and were created by a single person (for example, wills) or by agreement between two people (contracts); or they served the state and were created by an official, often one who managed a public archive for documents (such as a land registry), or who oversaw a public project (such as a construction project). The document would have been written either by the person or persons who created it, or by a scribe or secretary. The latter practice was more common in antiquity because most ancient societies had low levels of literacy and thus depended on scribes, but in Greece scribes for this purpose do not appear to have existed before the Hellenistic period (after 323 BCE). Those who could not write well probably had help from friends or patrons. In Rome, notaries could gather information from the parties to a contract, but only special professionals, the *tabelliones*, had the authority to write a final, binding version. In Egypt in the Ptolemaic period and later, documents were often formally notarized, giving them a greater degree of authority, and were then registered and deposited in public records offices.

Documents were written on readily available materials. As noted above they were usually written on papyri (or ostraca) in Rome, Greece and Egypt; on clay tablets in Mesopotamia; on palm leaves in India; and on bamboo or wood in China. The written document would commonly be deposited for

---

50 See Gagarin 2008a: 235–37.
51 For further discussion of these complex issues with respect to ancient Rome, see Meyer 2004.

safekeeping with a third party, or sometimes with an official, and copies would often be kept by all concerned parties. Some public documents, such as property deeds or contracts for public works, were recorded on more durable materials and were deposited in official depositories or archives.

Documents may have served primarily as evidence of transactions, allowing the parties to recollect precise details whether for formal citation in a lawsuit or perhaps more often for informal reference. Over time, however, some written documents also came to constitute the transaction in themselves; that is, the act of writing the document constituted the transaction. In many ancient contexts, documents were subject to formal requirements that determined their validity, such as the requirement of a certain number or kind of witnesses. Witnesses were often present at the creation of documents, and their names were often included in the document. In Ptolemaic Egypt, for example, we often find an extraordinarily high number of witnesses in documents – sixteen for most sales, twelve for leases. In all periods in Mesopotamia, contracts recorded the parties, the transaction, the agreement, the names of witnesses, the name of the scribe and the date.

Similarly for the evidence from ancient China, certain oral documents such as contracts (which were recorded in writing for evidentiary purposes) often followed required formats – though the oral original may not have had similar requirements. For example, sales of slaves or animals required long documents, whereas other commodities required short documents. The uniformity of wording in sales contracts throughout the empire suggests the availability of models. The formal requirements for contracts meant that they probably were often drafted by scribes, who knew the standard terms for various kinds of contract and specialized in helping people draft them, but other non-professionals may also have drafted contracts following a model. Before the fourth century BCE, contracts were signed by both parties and the witnesses or guarantors; later the scribe (but not the parties) and the witnesses or guarantors signed them, and in the Tang period only the party soliciting the transaction together with witnesses or guarantors signed. For the Tang, the sale of certain kinds of property in the markets (slaves, horses, cattle) required the production by the market officials of a certificate showing the details of the transaction. Only if the purchaser had obtained a market certificate could he seek to have the contract cancelled on the ground of a defect in the slave, horse, or animal bought. Some certificates for the sale of slaves have been found in excavations.

Once written documents begin to be produced, it appears that they continued to be written with relatively little change in content or form.

Over the course of more than two millennia of Sumerian and Akkadian documentation in Mesopotamia, for example, changes took place in such things as formulation and expression, and the number of witnesses, but the basic document remained the same.

Audience and Use

Documents had a more limited and immediate audience than laws, and because similar documents were generally used in similar ways in all ancient societies, there was less variation in their audience and use among these societies than there was with most other legal texts. Copies of documents would normally be given to the relevant party or parties (in the case of contracts, receipts and the like), and a copy would often also be given to a third party, who could be a private individual or a notary, or to a public official, who may have deposited the document in an official archive or repository; however, most documents did not circulate more widely than this. Wills must often have existed only in a single copy, kept by the testator or entrusted to a friend, or at most a second copy would be made by the notary or whoever drew up the will. Contracts and the like would have been made available to the contracting parties and would also often be deposited with a third party for safekeeping, but probably not given to many others. In some cases one copy would serve for all – and would prevent potential fraud in copying.

In India, there is evidence to suggest that a loan document should be torn up when the loan was repaid, or another document created to record the repayment. Instalment payments could be noted on the back of the original loan document. In Ptolemaic Egypt each party received a copy of the sales contract and another copy was deposited in a local records office. Notaries sometimes made copies or abstracts of these for their own use. All the documents pertaining to the property being sold were conveyed to the new owner. Deeds and receipts probably existed in a single, or at most two, copies. In Mesopotamia, copies of contracts would be held by all parties or by the party who acquired the new right (e.g. the new owner of a property, the husband in a marriage, the heir in an adoption or inheritance, etc.) and could be kept by families for generations.

Special Features of Documents

Since documents are generally produced for specific purposes, different types of documents tend to have similar features. A contract, for example, will almost always contain the names of the contracting parties at or near the beginning and will then state the substance of the agreement followed by further details and contingencies. Additional information, such as the date, the names of witnesses, the name of the scribe, the location where it was written or the place of deposit of the contract are regularly mentioned in some cultures but not in others. In fourth-century BCE Athens, contracts were not dated but the names of witnesses were normally added at the end. In Ptolemaic Egypt, on the other hand, dates were normally included, as were the names of witnesses. The language could be either Demotic or Greek, perhaps depending on which courts would adjudicate any dispute arising out of the contract (see 'Law' section, above).

The degree of formalism or standardization of language varies considerably in the documents of different ancient 'legal systems'. Even in societies without strict formal requirements, it was often conventional to include certain standard facts (such as date, place or names of witnesses) and to use certain standard ('boilerplate') language. Societies in which professionals – scribes, notaries, lawyers – write most or all documents generally show greater uniformity of language and factual information. Even in classical Greece, however, where to our knowledge documents were often written by ordinary individuals and there were no formal requirements as to content or wording, similar types of documents tend to include similar types of information and to use similar language in many places. For example, there was no legal requirement that witnesses be present in order for a will or a contract to be legally valid, but even so, witnesses were almost always present and their names were generally recorded on the document in question.

Strict formalism is often seen as a hallmark of earlier Roman law, especially that of the period of the Roman Republic (509–27 BCE). Yet written documents seem to have been relatively rare in early Rome. In China, as noted above, contracts were especially detailed and generally included the date, the names of the parties, and in cases of sale, certain standard clauses regarding description of the object sold, payment of price and right to undisturbed possession. The practice of signatures varied: in the Han period (206 BCE–220 CE), contracts were signed by both parties and by the witnesses or guarantors; in the pre-Tang period, the scribe and witnesses or guarantors signed, but not the two parties; and in the Tang period (618–907 CE), only the party soliciting the transaction together with witnesses or guarantors sign. Most documents were written in two parts; each party retained half of the document, which might then be matched with the other should a dispute arise. The similarity of language in documents found across the Chinese empires and dynasties suggests that parties employed scribes, who followed standard models for written contracts.

The most formulaic of ancient documents are probably to be found in an Indian context. These develop a form of 'legalese' that has roots in Aśoka's edicts (mid third century BCE) and gets carried over from language to language in the form of loanwords and calques (loan translations), as the language of expression shifts from Prakrit to Sanskrit to various regional languages. Aśoka's edicts, unique as they are in many ways, exhibit certain features that are retained across a gap of hundreds of years; this indicates a continuity in the drafting of official documents, since it is doubtful that anyone in the second century CE could have read Aśoka's letters from 400 years earlier in order to copy his conventions. These conventions include the use of the Prakrit verb *āṇapayati* ('command, issue an order') to authorize the contents of the record as the will of the king. Later legal inscriptions distinguish the king's authorization (*vijñāpana*) from the actual executing (*ājñāpana*) of the order when the king performs the latter himself. Among other conventions of these documents are the inclusion of the date (and sometimes, the place) of the order; an exhortation to ensure that the validity of the order will last 'as long as the moon and sun'; and direct reference to the efficacy of the written record itself.

Documentary legalese is also exhibited in ancient formulas from India that begin to appear in the early fourth century CE. Grants during the Pallava dynasty (from the second century CE onwards), for example, may contain a simple verb in Prakrit coupled with its causative to specify both direct and indirect forms of action ('exempt, and cause others to exempt'). A century later, the same formula occurs in Sanskrit. This latter example and others like it presume a well-known set of standard exemptions applying to Brahmin endowments. Donative grant decrees, which doubled as deeds to the rights and properties granted, also adopted a 'boilerplate' pattern that remained very stable over the centuries. The more elaborate of these decrees were commonly prefaced by a verse portion that praised the donor; the 'business portion' tended to be cast in something close to a vernacular (in Prakrit in the classical period, and later in a formal, 'Sanskritized' register of the regional vernacular), though some records are entirely in Sanskrit. The structure of this section included: a preamble (invocation, place of issue, grantor's name, titles and genealogy, and the officials addressed); the notification (specification of the grant, identifying lands by name, administrative division, physical boundaries; terms of the grant, including rights and exemptions; names of the recipients and their respective shares; and the occasion, purpose or intended function of the grant); and the conclusion (exhortation to respect the terms of the grant in perpetuity; date; names of officers and functionaries; and authentication by signatures). Copperplate grants issued by a king were commonly bound by a ring bearing the royal insignia. This documentary structure was standardized through the production of formulary 'blanks' that provided a generic text with variable terms and names to be supplied.[52]

Procedural Records

In this section we discuss procedural records: that is documents that were created and existed only in the context of litigation, such as the texts of pleadings or records of trials.[53]

Emergence of Procedural Records

Procedural records were documents that were produced explicitly for use in litigation (or in appeals), or that arose directly out of litigation. They include the initial complaint, the litigants' pleadings, depositions of witnesses, verdicts, and records of trials and other procedures. Before writing, and even after writing was used for other matters, all of these kinds of texts existed or could have existed in oral form. Even records of trials could have had an earlier oral form. In the fifth-century BCE Cretan city of Gortyn, for example, there was an official known as a 'rememberer' (*mnamon*), who apparently attended all trials. He could be required to testify in a later case about what had happened at an earlier trial, if, for example, one of the litigants in the earlier case had died in the meantime. His testimony would have amounted to an oral account of at least the main issues of the earlier trial and the verdict.

Because many stages of procedure like the pleading functioned well without any need for writing, written procedural texts generally emerge later than laws or documents. The reasons why these, or other aspects of procedure, were recorded in writing varied. In private cases writing may have satisfied a desire for clarity, fairness, or certainty. A simple accusation such as "X killed my goat" was unproblematic and could be easily remembered without needing to be written down; but the addition of details concerning time, place, method and other circumstances could make remembering more difficult, at which point it might be advantageous to all involved, especially the accused, to have a written account of the accusation.

---

52 Olivelle and Davis 2017.
53 On legal procedure more generally, see Chapter 7, this volume.

A requirement to submit evidence, such as witness depositions in writing before a trial, might also make the process fairer for the accused, and in some cases for the accuser too. Written copies of these and other aspects of litigation would also serve the needs of any litigant who wished to appeal the verdict or engage in subsequent litigation, for example by indicting a witness for perjury.

Another factor affecting the desire for procedural records in private (and public) cases was the complexity of legal process. A process with many procedural rules or strict formal requirements, such as existed in classical era Rome, could feel a greater need to use writing in order to ensure that the rules had been correctly followed. At first, witnesses may have attended all such proceedings, and these could then testify that the litigants had (or had not) correctly followed the rules; however, a written record would eliminate any uncertainty about whether, say, the accusation had followed the required format.

Other factors that may have motivated the creation of a written record include publicity. A written record of the accusation and the verdict could serve as a reminder and deterrent to others, especially if displayed in public. The texts of pleadings may also have been written down to help the litigant remember his arguments, and they may have been preserved in order to promote a political agenda or advertise the author's ability as a speechwriter (or both). In cases involving taxation, administrators may have wanted to have a written record, especially of the verdict for future use. And where the same legal processes held sway across a fairly large area, so that litigation was handled by separate courts or officials, written records of trials could help standardize procedures and promote consistency.

Ancient Chinese empires saw, perhaps, the most widespread use of written procedural records, which became a significant feature of legal procedure very early. In the complex Chinese imperial bureaucracy, higher authorities regularly supervised the handling of cases by lower officials; they might provide models for the conduct of legal proceedings, or issue orders in particular cases. In this connection we find written records of dates for hearing cases and other instructions issued to those hearing a case. In return, a lower official hearing a case would sometimes send a complete written record of the hearing to his superiors in order to receive direction on how to proceed. These documents might record all stages of a case, including the accusation, the defendant's response (which could be a confession) and witness testimony, though by their very nature they did not include the final action. Private inscriptions on bronze vessels from the period of the Western Zhou (1045–771 BCE) record excerpts of trials – generally when the verdict favoured the recorder – which were almost certainly taken from official accounts of trials that had been deposited in the royal archives.[54] Records of cases continue to be produced in later centuries, primarily because in the centralized bureaucracy that administered the legal system, in which one code of (a specific kind of) laws held sway over the entire empire, these records were needed to train the officials charged with administering the law and to ensure consistency throughout the empire. The earliest official procedural records to survive are written on bamboo strips discovered in a tomb at Baoshan in the state of Chu (dated to 316 BCE).[55] Because the deceased was the highest administrator of law in the Chu court, the legal documents consist primarily of actual case reports and decisions; they deal not only with offences like homicide or assault, but also with disputes over property. Some of them establish dates for the progress of cases, and require officials to hold hearings and make recommendations within a fixed time. These documents suggest a fairly complex procedure for trials, in which written transcriptions of the interrogations and findings were to be submitted from the district originally hearing the case to higher authorities. Some of these bamboo strips contain instructions from the ruler to a subordinate specifying how certain judicial cases should be handled (though these seem not always to have been obeyed).

Written accounts of judicial cases continued to be produced during the Chinese Qin and Han periods.[56] One extraordinary document from 28 CE is a virtually complete legal transcript, written on wooden strips, of two hearings in which a military officer sued a person he had commissioned to sell fish at a certain price; interestingly, this litigation proceeded on the basis of an oral contract that had not been reduced to writing.[57] Still later, bamboo strips from the archives of the state of Wu (222–280 CE) also contain records of litigation.

In Rome, even in early times before the city implemented its rule over a wide territory, the formalism of Roman law seems to have encouraged the production of procedural norms. By the time of the Twelve Tables (c. 450 BCE), a Roman plaintiff was required to specify the precise form of action (*legis actio*) to which his case belonged, and his complaint had to conform strictly to one of the few allowable *actiones*: a single wrong word could

---

54 Skosey 1996.   55 Weld 1999.
56 For the Qin, see Lau and Staak 2016; for the Han, see Barbieri-Low and Yates 2015, vol. II: 1171–416.
57 See Hulsewé 1979.

invalidate the case. In the famous example cited by Gaius (second century CE), a man lost his case about the cutting down of vines because he used the word 'vines' in the action instead of calling them 'trees', as required by the Twelve Tables.[58] Often the accused also had to respond with specific words. It appears that a list of the acceptable *actiones* was put in writing at an early date, perhaps the third or second century BCE, and accusations too might then be written to ensure adherence to the rules. Moreover, the two-stage Roman formulary process, which developed in the late Republic as an alternative to the *legis actiones*, required a magistrate, after hearing the initial pleading of the litigant and defendant, to issue his formal charge, a statement of the precise issue to be decided by the judge. At first, this may have been a simple oral statement, but as these charges became more complex, they had to be written down.

The rise of a professional 'class' of Roman jurists, probably from the late second century BCE onwards, also meant that verdicts began to be written down and collected. To the extent that the writings of these jurists became authoritative, written verdicts gained official legal status. Another group of procedural texts we find being written toward the end of the Roman Republic (first century BCE) are the pleadings of advocates. Only those of Cicero (106–43 BCE) survive complete, and many of these are thought to be heavily revised for publication. They seem to have been intended to promote their author and keep his views (and his name) in the public light. Finally, we have approximately two hundred and fifty mostly fragmentary transcripts of court proceedings from the late first century BCE. Later, during the Roman empire, written petitions to the emperor and other officials seem to have become increasingly popular.

In Egypt, as in some other societies with a single authority, accusations could be conveyed by a written petition to said authority, who could act on the petition himself or refer it to the legal system for action. Petitions are known since the Old Kingdom as a form of private redress and continue to be a major medium of addressing private wrongs, through the Roman period and well beyond. In addition, official trial transcripts are found in Egypt as early as the 'tomb robbery papyri' (c. 1070 BCE), which record the official state investigation of royal tomb robberies in Thebes. Both Greek and Demotic records of trials survive from the second century BCE; these were official copies issued to one of the parties in the dispute, and they give us a detailed picture of this administrative procedure. Imperial era case transcripts from Egypt, some of which are

---

58 Gaius, *Institutes* 4.11. See further in Chapter 3, this volume.

bilingual, do not seem to have been formally compiled as a single document but were rather recorded as an entry in the official minutes (*commentarii*), which every public officer in Roman Egypt kept. In the later Roman period, we do find individual transcripts of specific cases being recorded: a petition to the prefect from 186 CE (P. Oxy. 2.237) preserves an extensive record of a dispute between father and daughter which, in turn, also preserves a diverse array of other legal texts and procedures.

Although traditional Athenian procedure did not require a written accusation, one of the earliest Athenian legislators, Solon (c. 590 BCE), instituted a new form of procedure that, at least in classical times, was called a 'writing' (*graphē*). It is likely, therefore, that already in the early sixth century BCE this type of indictment had to be put in writing. By the early fourth century BCE, it appears that all formal accusations at Athens had to be written. In the classical period, some verdicts, but probably not all, were recorded in writing. For example, convictions of major public figures would be recorded, as would convictions resulting in a debt to the city or the public confiscation of property. Official lists were kept of public debtors, which could be modified as debts were paid or further debts incurred. Finally, towards the end of the fifth century BCE (c. 430) the practice arose of hiring a speechwriter (logographer) to compose a litigant's plea. The logographer would write out a speech, which the litigant would memorize and deliver as his own. About a hundred of these speeches survive, perhaps deriving from copies that the logographers kept for themselves.[59]

Evidence for procedural texts is less common across the extant evidence from ancient Mesopotamia, where charges might be brought by either the wronged party or the local authorities, but there was no clearly required process of charge, counter-charge, etc., that demanded written forms. Rather, the written document was formulated from the perspective of the conclusion and thus records the outcome rather than details of the process. The earliest records, from the period of Ur III (twenty-first to twentieth century BCE), are brief summaries of trials; some give no verdict, perhaps because a settlement was reached.[60] Other trial records survive from almost all periods and sites, almost always recording only one stage of what could be protracted proceedings, most often witness testimony or the judges' final decision.

A number of laws have survived that regulated procedure in India, but no procedural records have yet been found. The legal treatises, however, require

---

59 For a selection of these pleadings, see Gagarin 2011.
60 Lafont and Westbrook 2003: 184.

the issuance of a court document called *jayapatra* (document of victory) to the party that wins a lawsuit.

Production of Procedural Records

Across our extant evidence, accusations were generally written by the person bringing the legal action (or a scribe or notary paid by him), or by the official who took charge of the case for the trial. Accusations generally had a short life and were written on cheap, easily available materials, such as scraps of papyri or bamboo strips; in Athens they were written on reusable wax tablets. General information about the forms of accusation, however, was probably written on more durable materials. We are told that at Rome, a collection of allowable *actiones* was published around 300 BCE, and they may have been available to magistrates in writing earlier than this.

If a written record was made of a trial, it was normally created by a clerk or other court official specifically charged with this task. This record could be used on appeal and would usually include the verdict in the case. In the Near East, where many trial records contain only verdicts, they are often written tersely and reveal little about Near-Eastern procedural practice. Sometimes, especially in public cases where conviction resulted in a fine owed to the state, the verdict alone may have been recorded, probably on some fairly durable material, though these could usually be erased when the debt was paid. In some cases, the verdict might be written and displayed in public, so that all could see the strict justice handed out to criminals.

Forensic speeches in Athens could be delivered extemporaneously, but many were composed and written beforehand, either by the litigant himself or by a logographer employed by him. Written speeches were often preserved, almost certainly on papyrus, by either the litigant or his logographer (or his family), or perhaps by booksellers or others who sold or circulated copies. They may have served as examples of effective arguments that could be studied by others. Scholars disagree whether or not these were revised for publication after the trial.

With respect to evidence from ancient Chinese contexts, there seems to have been a flourishing profession of legal scribes and copyists entrusted with the making of official administrative and judicial records in the states of Chu and Qin. The practice of using scribes to record laws and legal documents would have accelerated during the Qin and early Han empires (from 221 BCE), when such scribes would have acted as officials within the imperial administration.[61]

---

61 Yates 2014a.

Audience and Use

Like documents, procedural texts were generally used in similar ways in all ancient societies, and most of them thus show little variation in their use and audience among the different societies. Most procedural texts were created for a specific trial or other procedure and would have been made available to the participants in the trial, namely litigants (and perhaps their advocates), judges and jurors, or to officials overseeing the case.

Accusations would have been read by (or perhaps communicated orally to) the defendant and the judge or jury; however, they may have been posted outside (or inside) the courtroom or building so they could also be read by others attending the trial, and in cases of broad public interest, they may have been more widely circulated. Transcripts of a trial would have been written for and used to appeal the result or in further proceedings arising from the earlier case, or they might have been made and kept by individuals for their own records. Petitions were intended to be read by kings, emperors or more likely members of their staff. Official responses or answers to petitions (for example, in the Roman context, 'rescripts') were intended to be read by petitioners and anyone else who had occasion to consult them where they had been publicly posted; they may also have been more widely circulated as persuasive precedents for future cases. Forensic speeches in Athens were written for use by the litigant in the case for which it was written; in some cases the litigant or his family may have kept a copy, just for their own interest.

Occasionally procedural texts achieved wider circulation. In Mesopotamia, in the second millennium BCE, model court cases may have represented actual trials that then attained new use as didactic tools for use in schools. Other types of procedural texts may have been circulated because they were of great public interest: including, for example, indictments from ancient Athens such as the trial of Antiphon for treason in 411 BCE, or of Socrates for impiety in 399 BCE. Verdicts that were of great public interest could also be published for a wider audience. And in Athens, forensic speeches were often preserved and circulated more widely, either for use by others who wished to study them, or as political pamphlets if the case had significant public interest. The speech of Antiphon at his trial for treason, for example, was widely read (and admired) even though he was convicted in the case. Cicero may have published versions of his forensic speeches to further his political career.

In China, a procedural text might circulate between the various levels of the administration. For example, a recommendation for the decision to be made by a local official had to be sent upwards through a series of levels for confirmation. The reply was sent downwards through the same layers.

Special Features of Procedural Records

Like documents some kinds of procedural texts tend to follow standard patterns, while others show considerable variation. An accusation, whether in court or in the form of a petition to the ruler, names the accuser (except sometimes when the first person is used) and the accused, and specifies the complaint – when, where, how, why, etc. – with varying amounts of detail. A verdict, which is more rarely recorded if the accused was acquitted, generally states the name of the defendant who has lost the case together with the penalty or compensation that was assessed by the court. Less often, other details are supplied or an explanation is given as to why the judge ruled in this way. Other procedural texts often show more variation.

Transcripts of trials, for example, normally include the complaint; the name of the court (and sometimes of the judge or judges); the pleadings, and the verdict – though within these categories there is room for considerable variation. There may also be some indication of why the transcript was made (often for the purpose of appeal). Across the extant evidence from ancient China, great importance is attached to the presiding official's preliminary written report of the circumstances of the crime, as best he could determine them, and his interrogations of the parties and witnesses. This detailed account could then be reviewed by his superiors, who might, if necessary, propose a legally appropriate solution. Ancient Mesopotamian court documents (like contracts and other legal texts) were also written from the perspective of the concluded process; in this sense, a 'court case' or 'trial' record will provide only selective and partial evidence of stages of accusation, process and verdict.

Forensic pleadings are exceptional in that they show an almost unlimited degree of variation. In late Republican Rome, for example, Cicero seems to have been unrestrained in developing arguments on behalf of his client. And in classical Athens, litigants – often together with their logographers – developed the argumentative strategy they felt would best serve their case. Plaintiffs would, of course, state their complaint and would normally include a narrative account of the relevant events (as they saw them) together with a plea for justice, but they could also include much else depending on their case. Defendants had even more leeway; they might give a different narrative or add new facts, and they would normally assert their innocence, but beyond this almost anything was possible. Litigants could call witnesses and introduce documents; in classical Athens these were not normally included in the text of the speech but were indicated by the brief notation 'witness', 'contract' and the like.

Judicial Opinions and Commentaries

Emergence of Judicial Opinions and Commentaries

Authoritative judicial opinions and commentaries were relatively rare in ancient societies, being known only from China and Rome, the two societies in which a single legal system served an especially large territory (at least in theory). In such circumstances, the recording and distribution of authoritative rulings and opinions helped to ensure uniformity throughout the territory. In addition, different kinds of commentaries were developed in Mesopotamia and Greece (see below).

In the City of Rome, by the time of the Twelve Tables, a college of *pontifices*, who were apparently not judicial officials but priests of some sort, issued interpretations of the law to magistrates and individuals. These were issued orally at first, but by c. 300 BCE some were probably being written down and preserved. 'Jurists' (*iuris consulti.* or *iurisperiti* 'those learned in the law') gradually began to replace the *pontifices* as those whose opinions were most valued. These jurists had no official position, but the opinions of some of them were held to be authoritative. Leading jurists also began to produce commentaries on parts of the law, and by the first century CE these had become legally authoritative texts. Jurists used cases, real and hypothetical, and often cited the opinions of their predecessors, sometimes quoting from them at length before delivering their own opinions. Over time, these opinions refined the law, adding rules for various contingencies not addressed in the original statute or text. Collections of these opinions were sometimes published for convenience. The largest of the (extant) juristic collections, the *Digest*, promulgated as imperial statute by Justinian in the sixth century CE, continues to be a major source of our knowledge of Roman law.

In China, authoritative commentaries on laws, written by jurists, are known from at least the third century BCE.[62] The earliest, from the state of Qin, takes the form of questions and answers; it is unclear whether its author was an official or a private person. Later under the Han (206 BCE–220/1 CE),

---

62 On what follows see for the Qin, Hulsewé 1979: 120–82; for the Han, Hulsewé 1955: 55; for Du Yu, Heyde 1981; and for the Tang *shuyi* commentary, Johnson 1997: 39–41.

many private commentaries on the law were written, although only fragments have survived. Some of these no doubt were regarded as more authoritative than others. The important code in force under the Jin dynasty (265–420 CE) also gave rise to influential commentaries, including one by the official Du Yu, paper fragments of which have recently been excavated. The most important early commentary is the *shuyi* commentary, which was incorporated into the Tang penal code. Each article of the code is followed by an elucidating passage from the commentary. Sometimes there is an added section in the form of 'question' and 'answer', reminiscent of the much earlier Qin commentary. The Han dynasty also produced a number of authoritative collections of legal decisions, some ascribed to individual jurists, others to the highest legal authorities. Historical sources refer to various collections of *bi* ('comparisons') as well as to 'decisions' of the principal law officer in the government.[63] These constituted an authoritative model for officials trying future cases, as did a recently excavated collection of cases, recorded on bamboo slips, which were decided by the highest legal authorities in the early Han (before 186 BCE). The Tang dynasty is also known to have produced collections of judicial decisions.

On a smaller scale, Mesopotamian scribes produced limited commentaries on legal materials concerning lexical items, but not legal opinions; and Greek scholars under the Roman empire also produced lexica of legal terms, often as an aid to reading the forensic speeches from classical Athens. The grammarian Harpocration (second century CE) wrote a *Lexicon of the Ten Orators*, explaining legal and other kinds of terms used by the ten main logographers. Most of these works sought to explain terms used centuries earlier that were no longer in current use and were thus incomprehensible to most people. Thus, they had no legal authority in their own time and should perhaps be treated as 'secondary legal texts' (see 'Secondary Legal Texts' below).

Production of Judicial Opinions and Commentaries

In antiquity, opinions and commentaries were produced by scholars who had no formal legal credentials, unlike the trained judges who write opinions in common law today or the civil-law jurists today who generally have academic credentials. At first, opinions were given orally in response to specific enquiries, often for an actual case, but it was soon realized that an opinion might be of (persuasive) use in other cases and could achieve wider circulation if written down. This led to the further step that jurists and other

---

[63] For *bi*, see Hulsewé 1955: 48–49.

scholars began to issue collections of opinions, sometimes focused on a single area of law. In China these could become full commentaries; in Rome, extracts from the most important of these were incorporated into the *Digest* of Justinian.

In addition to jurists, during the later Roman empire, particularly in the Eastern empire, we find legal experts who taught in law schools, the most famous of which was founded in Beirut in the third century (before 289 CE). These postclassical law teachers also advised judges with their opinions, and some of their opinions were just as highly regarded as those of the leading (classical era) jurists.

Audience and Use

Although at first some opinions were produced for litigants or their advocates, as the opinions grew in number and scope a significant part of their audience came to be other specialists in the law. The opinions of Roman jurists, for example, were probably intended to be read primarily by other jurists or would-be jurists, as well as perhaps by advocates. Earlier opinions were often copied by later jurists, sometimes repeatedly, often with further comments or other modifications. These would not necessarily have circulated among the general public but may have been used in legal education as a supplement to works like Gaius' *Institutes*.

Across the material from ancient China, the views of officials on legal matters often seem to be intended for a much broader audience and could even be recorded in the 'Standard Histories' of the period (see below). In contrast, the legal commentaries produced in ancient Mesopotamia and Greece seem to have been primarily intended for non-legal audiences, probably including students.[64]

Secondary Legal Texts

'Secondary legal texts' are those texts that were produced outside the institutions of law or were intended primarily for audiences outside these institutions, but that shed light on points of law and may even affect the law in various ways. For scholars, these secondary texts are often an important source of information about ancient legal systems. Secondary legal texts include historical accounts and other reports of legal proceedings; literary

---

64 For the 'Special Features of Judicial Opinions and Commentaries', see Chapter 3, this volume.

Secondary Legal Texts

portrayals; philosophical and religious works; non-legal documents like letters, treaties or honorary decrees that may allude to or provide information about legal matters; and textbooks, school exercises, non-authoritative commentaries and other instructional materials. We also include a few visual 'texts' that may instruct or shed light on the law.

Secondary legal texts do not just inform modern scholars; they also informed members of those societies who heard, or read or viewed them at the time, by conveying not just facts about what the law was or how litigation worked, but also values, including the importance of law and of obedience to the law. Many, perhaps most, members of the community probably acquired their information about law in their community primarily from these kinds of 'secondary texts'.

Historical Accounts and Reports

Most ancient societies produced histories that included some information about law. These could be official histories, produced by the country's rulers, but more commonly they were written by individuals with no official position. Among the best known of these, the Roman historians Livy (59/64BCE–17 CE) and Tacitus (56–c.120 CE) describe a variety of legal matters in their works, as do the Greek historians Herodotus (d. c. 430–420 BCE) and Thucydides (c. 460 BCE?–d. after 404BCE?), and the later biographer Plutarch (46–d. after 119 CE) who wrote a very popular collection of lives of famous Greeks and Romans which often include legal episodes. A lesser-known Greek historian, Diodorus Siculus (first century BCE) includes a description of law in Ptolemaic Egypt which has elements that appear to be accurate descriptions of the administration of law.[65] In Egypt, a late Old Kingdom official biography, recorded in the tomb of Weni, provides important information about the organization of the courts in the Old Kingdom.[66] For early China, many surviving histories of the period contain details about laws and other legal matters. These include the official histories of each dynasty, sponsored by the state, which normally contain one or more chapters on law and punishment; these provide an important source of information for the law and legal institutions of the relevant periods.[67]

---

65 Diod. 1.94.   66 Richards 2002.
67 Many of these histories have been published: see the Legal Treatise of the *Hanshu* (Hulsewé 1979: 321–455); the Legal Treatise of the *Jinshu* (Heuser 1987); the Legal Treatise of the *Suishu* (Balazs 1954); the Legal Treatise of the *JiuTangshu* and that of the *XinTangshu* (Bünger 1996).

A rather different work is the *Constitution of the Athenians*, attributed to Aristotle but likely written by a member of his school (late fourth century BCE).[68] This is the only work from an original group of 158 *Constitutions* of different Greek cities that survives in full, not just in scattered fragments. It first gives an account of Athenian constitutional history up to the end of the fifth century BCE. This contains some useful historical information, especially about Solon's laws. More information, however, can be found in the second part of the work, which is a description of Athenian government in the late fourth century BCE (*Ath. pol.*, chapters 42–69). This contains descriptions of the judicial system, including the duties of various officials involved in the administration of justice (52–53, 56–59) and the composition of the jury courts (63–66) and finally an overview of trial procedure.[69]

Literature

The creative literature of most societies contains works that present various aspects of the law. These cannot, of course, be taken for objective accounts, but when used carefully they can give useful information about actual legal conditions.

In Rome, the comedies of Plautus (third to second century BCE) give information about law, though it can be difficult to separate elements of Roman law in these plays from the legal context of the Greek originals on which they were based. In early Greece, the Homeric poems (eighth or seventh century BCE) contain much information about law, including a well-known 'trial scene' in the *Iliad* (18.497–508), in which two litigants plead their case before a group of judges. In the fifth century BCE, dramatic works representing law include Aeschylus's tragedy, *Eumenides*, in which Orestes is tried by the court of the Areopagus and acquitted (on a tie vote) on the charge of killing his mother, and Aristophanes' comedy *Wasps*, whose protagonist is addicted to serving on juries, and whose chorus consists of jurymen represented as wasps with sharp stingers. Characters in Menander's comedies of the late fourth century BCE and other literary texts also confront many legal problems, especially in connection with marriage and inheritance.

In the Middle Kingdom in Egypt (c. 1900 BCE), a literary text known as *The Tale of the Eloquent Peasant* is valuable for its picture of the legal procedure

---

68 Conveniently translated with notes by Rhodes 1984. For a full study of the work, see Rhodes 1981.
69 For a full study of Athenian governmental institutions including judicial officials and the law courts, see Hansen 1991.

involved in the redress of a private wrong, in this case the misbehaviour of an official. It also sheds light on the official state structure and emphasizes the oral eloquence required before state officials.[70] From the Ptolemaic period (third century BCE), *The Tale of Setne* is extremely important for the concept of property bound to family groups, for expectations about inheritance, and for several other legal matters.[71]

Mesopotamian literary texts from all periods include plot motifs and allusions to trials, assemblies, etc., although it is unclear whether such information reflects or is informed by legal norms or ideals, or is intended as parody. There are a number of depictions of courtroom procedure in the story literature and courtly drama of ancient India: a massive exposition of *dharma* is incorporated as one character's instruction of another in the twelfth book of the Sanskrit epic *Mahābhārata* (which probably acquired its final form in the fourth century CE, but which was first composed much earlier, perhaps in the ninth or eighth century BCE), AND a Sanskrit play, *Mṛcchakaṭikā* (c. fifth century CE), has a full scene of a court procedure, including the writing of the plaint and the plea. In China, from the Han period we have *The Contract for a Youth* (59 BCE) about a slave under contract.[72]

Philosophical, Religious and Other Intellectual Works

For our purposes the philosophical and rhetorical works of Greece and Rome can be considered together as part of a single tradition. As noted above, of the original 158 *Constitutions* of Greek states compiled by Aristotle's school only that of Athens survives. But Aristotle (384–322 BCE) drew on the material gathered for this project in writing his *Politics*, which sometimes cites specific laws from various cities. Also useful is his *Rhetoric*, which contains much advice about forensic rhetoric. Aristotle's influence is clear throughout the later rhetorical tradition, notably in the rhetorical works of the Roman authors Cicero and Quintilian (c. 35–d. after 96 CE).

Aristotle's teacher Plato (c. 429?–c. 347 BCE) devoted his last major work to law. Plato's *Laws*, however, is not a description of law in Greece or Athens but contains an ideal set of laws for an imaginary city. Many of these clearly resemble actual Athenian laws, but they also clearly differ significantly from Athenian laws in many respects; thus, it cannot be used for the most part in reconstructing actual Athenian law. Cicero's *De legibus* (*On Laws*) is clearly modelled on Plato's work and is similarly of little use in understanding what Roman law was actually like in his day. Potentially more useful is the work

70 Parkinson 1991 and 2012.   71 Vinson 2018.   72 Wilbur 1967: 383–92.

Laws by Aristotle's student Theophrastus (c. 37 –c. 287 BCE), a collection of laws from different Greek cities; regrettably, only fragments of this work survive.

For ancient China, the most instructive literature are philosophical discussions of the role of law in essays on good government and the like, books on ritual and morality which often contain references either to laws or to moral prescriptions which came to be incorporated in the law, and encyclopaedias which have sections on laws and punishments.[73] With respect to the material from ancient India – in addition to the Dharmaśāstras which are 'religious' and 'legal' texts through and through (see 'Law' section above) – many *Purāṇas* (scriptural compilations) contain didactic chapters on the rules of *dharma*. Most famously, the *Bṛhad-Āraṇyaka-Upaniṣad* (probably composed c. 700 BCE) offers a famous maxim on the meaning of *dharma*: 'It is by *dharma* that the weaker gains satisfaction over the stronger.' This suggests a general ideal of equity and social justice, promoted in a standard that is internalized in any rightly instructed person. The most significant legal text comes from Kauṭilya's *Arthaśāstra*, the treatise on political science composed around the turn of the millennium – an entire book of the treatise is devoted to law and legal procedure.[74]

Evidence from ancient Egypt gives us a further source of evidence, which was undoubtedly more widespread across the Near East: oracles.[75] Oracles were sometimes used to resolve disputes in the New Kingdom and elites also used oracles to publicize that property conveyances were free and clear. Texts of oracles were recorded on stelae or on temple walls.

Non-Legal Documents

Legal documents like contracts and wills have been treated above ('Law' section), but many kinds of non-legal documents provide information about law. Letters, for instance, have been discovered from many ancient societies that report on or discuss litigation (existing or potential) and other sorts of legal transactions. From Rome, the best-known are collections of Cicero and Pliny the Younger (61/62–c. 113 CE), but the large collection of letters of the fourth-century CE author Symmachus also gives information about law. Letters from Ptolemaic or Roman Egypt may provide similar information.

Decrees that are not specifically legal may also provide information about legal matters. Honours granted to some civic benefactors, for example, may include protections or exemptions involving legal matters. Another kind of

---

73 Caldwell 2018.   74 McClish 2019b; see also Chapter 7, this volume.   75 Ray 1981.

decree found in Greek cities beginning in the late fourth century BCE records the city's thanks for a group of foreign judges who have recently settled internal conflicts within the host city; some of these provide legal information about the dispute or its resolution.[76]

Treaties, too, may provide information about, say, legal procedures that were previously being violated or that one or the other party agree to follow. In the fifth century BCE, for example, Athens concluded treaties with many of its 'allies', in which they agreed to refer serious criminal cases to Athens and abide by Athenian justice.

Instructional Materials

Instructional materials, especially materials for legal instruction, may provide as much information (or more) as any other source about the legal system of any ancient society that developed them. The scribal schools of Mesopotamia transmitted the standard formulary and terminology for contracts to generations of students. Model court cases and model contracts illustrated the norms of recording such events. The form of the legal provision was transmitted through the copying of extracts from the laws of Ḫammurabi, for example, for over a thousand years.[77]

Evidence for various sorts of instructional texts is plentiful for Rome. These include materials for rhetorical instruction, which typically prepared students by rehearsing forensic pleadings in hypothetical court cases; but the most useful texts were those prepared by jurists with the aim of instructing prospective lawyers. Of these, the best-known today is the *Institutes* of Gaius (second century CE), which can still be used as an introductory textbook for Roman law.[78]

Finally, as noted above, a text from Egypt known as the 'Duties of the Vizier' also seems to be instructional and is of great importance for understanding the organization of law in the Middle and New Kingdoms. It outlines the responsibilities of the highest legal official in the state. The extant copies of the text come from the New Kingdom tombs of these officials.

Visual 'Texts'

Leaving aside any potential visual effects of written texts, pictorial representation can provide information about law. The cartoon on the top of the Ḫammurabi stele now in the Louvre, for example, depicts the king receiving

---

76 See the texts collected in Ager 1996.   77 Roth 1995, see also Roth 1979.
78 For further discussion, see Chapter 3, this volume.

from the sun god the emblems of authority, from which the viewer understands that the king and the laws inscribed on the stele enjoy divine approval. In Egypt, the images of Ma'at on temples are particularly important as a statement of the relationship of the king to law and order. The ceremony associated with the image of the king offering to Ma'at makes one think of an explicit contract between king and the gods, and by extension between the king and society. We also noted above ('Introduction') the court scene in the tomb of Rekh-mi-rē at Thebes, in which forty rolls of laws are spread out before the vizier.

'Visual' information of a different sort comes from excavated skeletons from Han and pre-Han cemeteries in China, which show the way in which persons were shackled and mutilated for offences. Particularly important are skeletons in Han cemeteries which suggest that the practice of mutilation of the foot continued for some time after the supposed abolition of this punishment in 167 BCE.[79] These Han skeletons serve as an important reminder that 'visual' information about law and punishment – like the textual information discussed in this chapter – can present itself to scholars of ancient law in many different forms and contexts.

Conclusion

Perhaps the most difficult question raised by this chapter is the exact relationship between law and text. In a 2008 publication I suggested several different ways of defining 'law', the first of which is the most relevant to this chapter: namely that law is a body of rules written down in such a way that they can be 'recognized' as laws.[80] In this sense we see that ancient laws can be written in different kinds of places and on different materials and still be recognizable as laws. We have also observed that a wide variety of other sorts of ancient texts, though not themselves laws, shed light on the actual operation of a society's legal system and on the way in which legal statutes are implemented in practice.

---

79 See Barbieri-Low 2007: 238–39.
80 Gagarin 2008a: 3–4. 'Recognized' is meant here in the positivist sense set forth by Hart 1961: 94–97 (see above n.24).

3
Legal Science

Lead Author: DARIO MANTOVANI

Contributors: ERNEST CALDWELL, SOPHIE DÉMARE-LAFONT, CAROLINE HUMFRESS, DAVID IBBETSON, GEOFFREY MACCORMACK, PATRICK OLIVELLE, ROBIN OSBORNE, WILLIAM TOOMAN AND BRUCE WELLS

Introduction

Any comparative description of a social and cultural phenomenon, such as 'law' and its practice, requires a definition in order to identify the parallel elements in different traditions and societies which are to be compared.[1] An indiscriminate application of the concept of 'legal science', however, would deprive our exploration of its cross-cultural character and hinder comparison. This is especially the case if we define 'legal science' in its strictest sense: the study of the content of legal norms and of their systematic order (a definition mainly elaborated in the nineteenth and twentieth centuries under the influence of Roman law and of codification, which is also indebted to a positivistic concept of science). Instead, throughout this chapter, an effort has been made to characterize 'legal science', as far as possible, from the internal point of view of each tradition and society. In this perspective, we will refer to both the set of activities carried out by 'legal experts', in the whole domain of law (legislation, adjudication, legal counselling and education), and the legal experts themselves, as far as they were regarded as such by their own societies.

The chapter thus starts from a sociological approach, focusing on the identification of legal experts: people who, in each given society and according to its standards, were deemed to possess legal knowledge to such a degree that it characterized their social position and/or function. Special attention

---

With thanks to Edward Harris for useful comments.
[1] See Chapters 1 and 2, this volume.

will be given to the distinction of different subcategories and functions of legal experts, where there might be significant differences among traditions. This, in turn, implies the question of whether or not, in each given society, law was considered to be a specific field of knowledge, distinguishable from others.

Whatever their role might be in each given society, these experts built an epistemic community, that is a network of individuals with recognized expertise, suitable for enabling cohesion of the legal discourse. They were linked by a set of shared notions of validity, i.e. intersubjective criteria for weighing and validating legal knowledge. They also shared a set of normative and principled beliefs, which provided a value-based rationale for their decisions.[2] After identifying the experts, the chapter shifts its attention to their working habits and focuses on legal knowledge itself, that is on the notions of validity and values they shared. This is what might be called 'legal method': a pool of methodological guidelines used by legal experts involved in determining the content of law.[3] Once again, our approach does not prejudge any answer to questions about what legal experts did. Legal science, in this perspective, is in the first place the method(s) followed by those engaged in declaring 'what is law' (i.e. in declaring the qualification that corresponds to a behaviour according to a given legal system, and whose activity was deemed to be the product of a specialized expertise, irrespective of whether their opinion was binding or not). Examples of this role include the Chinese officials appointed to be in charge of the administration of justice (some of whom also wrote authoritative legal commentaries) and Roman jurists. But this focus on the function of declaring 'what is law' does not exclude other activities that are relevant.

In fact, legal expertise lies behind many operations whose authors are sometimes anonymous but nonetheless were necessary: the drafting of statutes requires legal knowledge no less than learned commentaries on those statutes, as does the application of statutes by a judge, or the drafting of a valid contract. In comparing ancient societies, one has also to bear in mind that legal expertise is to be searched for where documents allow us to seek for it, and that the type of documentation at hand may change substantially from one culture to another. Therefore, in our historical-comparative perspective, 'legal science' or 'method' must be understood as an expression of convenience to indicate an area of expertise that – in its contents and in the

---

2 On the concept of epistemic communities, see Cross 2013.   3 Núñez Vaquero 2013.

allocation between the agents and institutions of the legal system – can also differentiate profoundly from that designated by the same words today.

Legal Knowledge as a Specialized Field of Knowledge

Do jurists make the law, or does the law make jurists? If it is possible in a society for some people to develop legal expertise, then that society must consider law as a phenomenon that is (more or less) distinct from other cultural phenomena with which it has points of contact, such as religion, politics, ethics and oratory. An important indication of this distinctiveness is the existence of a textual tradition that separates law from other spheres. In particular, rules (i.e. prescriptive provisions, comparable in form – if not in validity – with today's statutes) function as a catalyst for societies to reflect specifically on the law, and they encourage the rise of experts.

Most available sources on traditional (imperial) Chinese law – to start our outline from East to West – depict a formal system primarily concerned with penal and administrative, not private, law. Law took the form of complex sets of directives issued by the rulers (emperors), on the one hand as prescriptions for the way in which their officials were to carry out their duties, and on the other as prohibitions governing the behaviour of the people. Broadly speaking, the administrative regulations defined the duties of officials but did not define offences and impose punishments, whereas the penal statutes defined offences (which might relate to the behaviour of officials as well as ordinary people) and established punishments for infraction.[4] Judicial rulings created law only in a secondary sense; the decisions of the highest court in doubtful cases were regarded as 'precedents' that provided guidance for the resolution of similar difficulties in the future. The major role possessed by enacted law strengthened the perception of law as a specialized field of knowledge. The collection of laws was complex; those who mastered its intricacies were officials, who at various levels were concerned with the implementation of legal rules, and, occasionally, other persons, not necessarily serving officials, who write elucidations of, or commentaries on, the law. Of course, in ancient China, as in any developed society, political considerations and struggles for power at court could influence the content of particular pieces of legislation. Equally, fear of the displeasure of 'Heaven', manifested in the form of omens or prodigies, could influence the administration of justice through the grant

---

4 See Chapter 5, this volume.

of amnesties and the like. But these were tangential considerations. They did not affect the intrinsic nature of law as a discrete set of specialized rules.

In ancient India, if we take *dharma* to refer (among other things) to law, we see its intimate connection to – what we refer to in modern terms as – 'religion'. In many jurisprudential texts dealing with the epistemology of *dharma*, we see primacy given to the Veda, sacred scripture par excellence within the Brahmanical tradition, as the source of *dharma*. Yet, as it will be shown later, *dharma* as law was also viewed as a special area of expertise distinct from other areas, especially in lists of experts in various sciences that we encounter in these texts. The specialized knowledge in the field of law is referred to as *Dharmaśāstra*, with the term *śāstra* having the meaning of both 'science' and 'text'. Political science was called *Arthaśāstra* and it had its own textual tradition. The main text is Kauṭilya's *Arthaśāstra* written probably in the first century CE. This science, however, was incorporated into the Dharmaśāstra tradition by Manu in the second century CE and gradually lost its independent status. Law proper was understood as an integral part of political science: Book 3 of Kauṭilya's work, for example, was devoted to it. Yet, at the same time, legal science was clearly distinguished from political science. There was no separate branch of knowledge devoted to oratory or rhetoric.

The earliest reference to legal science in extant ancient Indian material occurs in the writings of two early grammarians: Kātyāyana (late third – early second century BCE) and Patañjali (mid-second century BCE), both of whom use the term *dharmaśāstra* to refer to legal science and to legal texts. The earliest extant text from the tradition of legal science is the *Dharmaśāstra* of Āpastamba (third to early second centuries BCE), although he himself refers to earlier authors of such treatises. Texts in this genre continue to be produced until the second half of the first millennium CE. These texts contain not only legal science per se, but also material we would today consider religious, such as rites of passage, daily rituals, ancestral rites and expiations for sins.[5] The close relation between religion and law in ancient India is partly dependent on the fact that Brahmins, the priestly class within the hierarchical ordering of Indian society, were both religious/ritual experts and legal experts. The two fields, therefore, bled into each other. Much of the reasoning and theory within legal science were borrowed from the Vedic exegetical tradition of Mīmāṃsā; rules of textual interpretation became rules of legal thinking.

---

5 Further discussion in Olivelle and Davis 2017.

With respect to ancient Near Eastern material, the so-called law codes, or law collections, present scholars with two particular problems: the question of their origins and the question of their judicial use. One view interprets these collections as having been commissioned by kings for the purpose of recording important laws; in some cases, laws that might not have been part of well-known customary rules or that needed clarification. This view, therefore, sees the collections as legislation or statutory law that would have been used by courts to determine verdicts.[6] A second view considers many of the laws to have derived from royal rescripts.[7] We know that kings, Hammurabi (c. 1792–1750 BCE) but others as well, issued rulings on a variety of disputes that were brought to their attention. According to this view, these royal pronouncements were depersonalized and incorporated into the law collections to give them broader applicability and force; scribes, possibly under the king's direction, likely expanded on these rulings and created additional provisions. Like the first view, this approach accepts that the collections would have been consulted by judicial personnel. A third view claims that the collections should be understood as containing academic or scribal literature as opposed to binding ordinances.[8] This literature may have sought to describe some of the laws that were already being practised, or it may represent mostly scenarios that the scribes producing the collections thought posed interesting or important legal problems. In similar fashion to the previous view, this school of thought maintains that some of the provisions may well derive from actual disputes decided by the king or lower officials.[9] Whether or not judges would have consulted any of these provisions is debated among scholars who hold this view. Most of the provisions in the collections sound like laws that could have been enforced, although there are few clear indications that the codes were specifically applied in juridical practice.[10]

If one accepts either of the last two views, then one could conclude that much of the process underlying the codes' compilation was based on inductive reasoning. The king or the scribes – or perhaps both – were drawing inferences about what rules should be broadly applied across society based on specific instances and the decisions issued in those instances. At the very least, scribes were considering a range of specific legal problems and deciding which ones should be included in their collections for future study, reflection and/or instruction. This inductive approach is reflected in the casuistic

---

6 Neumann 2003: 85–88.   7 Démare-Lafont 2000a; 2007.   8 Roth 2000.
9 Westbrook 1989.   10 Wells 2008a; but see Charpin 2005, with some important evidence.

formulation that characterizes most of the provisions in the law collections. In contrast, proponents of the first view might argue that deductive reasoning drove the process. Important rules had already been established, and they were written down so that all future problems and disputes would be subject to their authority. Regardless of one's view, it is evident that rational thought guided thinking about law in the ancient Near East. In fact, apart from the law collections, some extant letters, which deal with disputes arising in cases of successions or family law, refer to principles and rules and also show careful reflection on law. We are thus dealing with what may be called legal thinking. The law collections themselves show that law was becoming, or had already become, a field with clear boundaries and distinctives that separated it from other fields of knowledge and practical activity.[11]

Law certainly bore a close relationship with 'religion' at some points.[12] In official state rhetoric, law was often spoken of as a way of carrying out proper religion. Ḥammurabi, for example, refers to the mandate given to him by the gods to establish justice in his land, and he presents his extensive collection of laws as the principal means by which he fulfilled this mandate. In ancient Israel, law was closely connected to the worship of the god Yahweh, based on what is known from the texts of the Hebrew Bible. Nevertheless, our evidence shows that ancient Near Eastern societies could treat law as a separate area of culture. In Babylonia, those referred to as 'judges' were usually identified by that term only when performing a judicial function and were identified in alternative ways when acting in other capacities.[13] Later, during the Neo-Babylonian period (625–539 BCE), we know that scribes trained to fulfil a variety of roles could go on to have a career specifically in the law as a judge.[14] Even from the Hebrew Bible, we learn that there could be experts 'in the law'. This may have indicated expertise in both religious and civil law, but sometimes a clear distinction was made between the two with responsibility and authority granted to an individual only in one of these areas.[15]

The 'rabbinic movement' (c. 70–550 CE) emerged between the first and third centuries CE in Roman Palestine. It was a movement of self-appointed 'sages' (the *ḥakhamim*) and their disciples who collected, preserved, and expanded the religious (esp. legal) traditions of the Second Temple and Tannaitic periods (c. 400 BCE–220 CE). As a social movement, it endeavoured to direct the activities of everyday life for Palestinian Jews to correspond with

11 Démare-Lafont 2007.   12 For more detailed discussion see Chapter 6, this volume.
13 Westbrook 2005.   14 Holtz 2008.
15 As, for example, at 2 Chronicles 19:11 (on which see further below).

rabbinic law.[16] How widely accepted their authority might have been in the first centuries CE is unknown. The movement spread to Jewish communities in Babylon, possibly as early as 225 CE. By the early Middle Ages, the rabbinic movement was the most prominent expression of Judaism in Palestine, Babylon and beyond. The time of the rabbinic sages is conventionally divided into two periods, the Tannaitic (*tanna'*, 'teacher'; c. 70–220 CE) and the Amoraic (*'amora*, 'speaker'; c. 220–550 CE). Classical rabbinic legal literature was produced in these two periods and locations: Palestine and Babylon. Legal training, the status of sages and roles that sages played in their communities sometimes differed between the two places and evolved in both.

The domain of the rabbinic sages was religious law (*halakha*). Both terms, 'religious' and 'law,' can be misleading. Rabbinic law was not state law and was not enforced by political authorities. It was the law of a recognized ethnic-religious community: 'Judaism'. It only had force and effect within that community. The extent of rabbinic and, hence, halakhic authority differed according to time and place. In many places the community was divided, some recognizing rabbinic authority and others not (for example, Karaites). Also, because it was the law of a community and because its roots go back to the laws of the Torah, rabbinic law includes many topics that in some other cultures would not be considered 'religious' but 'civil' or 'criminal' law: marriage law, contract law, laws regarding damages and so forth.

Each of the ancient Greek poleis also possessed and administered its own set of laws. In many, if not most, of the cities the law was laid down in written statutes (from the seventh century BCE in Athens), some of them being more or less complete codes setting forth procedural methods and substantive rules for the administration of justice. Nevertheless, three ancient Greek literary texts illustrate the limits of human expertise in law, at the same time as commenting on relations between the human and the divine. Within the extant ancient Greek material, the earliest piece of dispute settlement that may be likened to a court hearing is the scene portrayed on the Shield of Achilles (Homer, *Iliad* 18). Here a picture is given of a man who has killed another having his recompense rejected by the man's relatives and needing to get a ruling from 'one who knows [what is right]'. The way of deciding 'who knows [what is right]' is to have a number of elders give their view, and for the people to decide which of them 'spoke justice most straightly' (*Iliad* 18.501–8). The straightness of the justice is decided by the people on

---

16 Schwartz 2001: 103–5.

hearing the judgment, not in advance on the basis of some prior expertise. In Aeschylus' *Eumenides* the hung verdict on the matricide Orestes is settled, however, by the goddess Athena herself. Here the expert judgment might seem to belong to the gods. But in fact Aeschylus has Athena give reasons for her voting for acquittal that are distinctly personal – she approves the male principle because she herself was not born from a mother but from the head of Zeus (Aes. *Eumenides* 734–53). This seems at the very opposite end of the scale from legal expertise. The third revealing text from the ancient Greek material is Plato's *Euthyphro*, where Euthyphro's father consults the Exegetes about what to do with a labourer who had killed a man, and while the Exegetes are being consulted the labourer, who had been bound and left in a ditch, dies of exposure (Pl. *Euthyphro* 4 C, 9A). Here the *Exegetai*, who are shadowy officials who make just one appearance in Athenian forensic oratory, having been consulted about the murder of an old woman, rule on the ritual to be followed with regard to the funeral and also advise on legal procedure (Dem. 47.68–70).

It is important that each of these three cases involves homicide. It is over the shedding of blood, in particular, that law and religion most obviously met. Death and bloodshed, like birth, sex and disease, were occasions when individuals were reckoned in danger of incurring pollution and to require the purification of those involved if they were to be in good standing with the gods. Law took no interest in birth (except with regard to status and inheritance), sex or disease (unless inflicted by a human agent), but bloodshed and death were its proper concern too.[17] The clear distinction set out by the Exegetes in Demosthenes *Oration* 47 reflects this fact: they had no special authority over matters of (legal) procedure and could only give advice, whereas they were authoritative on matters of ritual.

Outside areas in which there were relevant religious considerations – across the relevant evidence from ancient Greek cities – those who judged a legal case effectively acted as their own legal experts, although plaintiffs offered them plenty of legal advice. In Athens, aside from homicide cases which involved a court made up of former holders of the office of archon, cases were judged by mass 'juries' who operated as judges rather than being under the direction of a judge and could be expected to be familiar with the laws as inscribed.[18] The citizens who served on these mass 'juries' could thus acquire significant familiarity with legal argument through their involvement

---

17 Osborne 2011: 158–84.
18 cf. Dem. 47.71, cited above: after consulting the *Exegetai*, the litigant then goes and reads the text of the law itself on the stele.

Legal Knowledge as a Specialized Field of Knowledge

over the course of a year, or of successive years, in many cases.[19] As members of the assembly, some members of the jury panel would have had experience in approving new laws (see below), as well as of interpreting old ones.

In the city of Rome at the end of the archaic age, 'law' (*ius*) likewise appears as a 'system of expectations' sufficiently separate from other societal structures, and in particular from religion. In order to appreciate law's distinctness from the religious sphere, the Twelve Tables (451–449 BCE) are instructive. Although their textual tradition is uncertain, they are illuminating simply for the subject matters they include: civil procedure, structured as a rational and even confrontation between the parties; succession; several aspects of family relationships; property and its transmission, especially with regard to agricultural land and relations among neighbours; torts and crimes.[20] These are the subjects that in Roman legal life, in every epoch, are typically regulated by private and criminal law (public law is only marginally present in the Twelve Tables). The points of contact with religious life are few and circumscribed. Perhaps most noteworthy is the use of *sacramentum* in civil procedure. Both parties challenged each other to confirm their respective positions through an oath that implied the consecration of an object; the consecrated object of the losing party would then be given over as a dedication to the gods.[21] This religious institution was only a framework, since the resolution of the conflict itself was based on the empirical verification of the facts of the case and on the application of legal norms and arguments that could be checked rationally. The Twelve Tables also contain several norms about funerary rites (*Tab.* X), which confirms all the more the distinction between law and religion: they are in fact limited to certain (so to say) 'civilian' aspects, pertaining to banning burial and cremation within the city and to limitations on spending and luxury. As for prescribing how funerary rites were to be carried out, this was subject to a separate order that fell within the competence of a college of priests, the pontiffs (*pontifices*). This order was itself also called *ius* (distinguished through the adjective *pontificium* or *sacrum*): thus, here the same term (*ius*) was employed that was also in use for 'the law of the city' (*ius civile*). Moreover, as we will see, at least until the end of the third century BCE not only the *ius pontificium* but also the *ius civile* was controlled by the *pontifices*. Every year, one of the pontiffs would respond to questions submitted by private individuals.[22]

---

19 On the legal knowledge of the average Athenian [male], see Harris 2010.
20 Crawford 1996, vol. II; Humbert 2018.   21 See Chapter 7, this volume.
22 Justinian, *Digest* 1.2.2.6 (Pomponius *l.s. enchiridii*); this statement, although contested, is confirmed by other sources, such as Cic. *De orat.* 1.186; DHal. 10.1.4; Liv. 9.46.5.

The concentration of expertise in the hands of the pontiffs in both the *ius pontificium* and the *ius civile*, between the fifth and third centuries BCE, has parallels in other societies where we can observe the accumulation of diverse types of knowledge in a single group of 'experts' (as in ancient India and the Near Eastern material). As for Rome, it would not be accurate to think that this caused law and religion to blend. The Roman *pontifices* – also in their capacity as chief operators in the sacred sphere – were not charismatic figures, and they were not considered to be in direct communication with the divine. Rather, the *ius pontificium* worked as a rational technique: it sought to understand and control the relationship between the world of man and the world of the gods through repeatable and repeated acts. For the Romans to conduct the rites (i.e. to 'do') was to 'believe'.[23]

Along the same lines, Roman jurisprudence was also clearly distinct from oratory: the skill of persuasive discourse. In Rome, the separation between the two was both cultural and functional. In cultural terms, law evolved before Greek rhetoric was introduced to Rome (which became known systematically over the course of the second century BCE). In functional terms, both in civil and in criminal procedure, the person who had the task to persuade the judges of the good reasons of his client was an orator/advocate (*patronus, orator*): an individual educated in rhetoric (from when such education was available in Rome).[24] The 'jurist' (*iuris consultus, iuris peritus*) played a different role: namely to give advice to whom would consult him (private party, advocate, judge, magistrate) without intervening directly in the lawsuit. Just as in the case of religion, so with oratory the distinctness from law does not exclude crossover: on the one hand, the ideal orator (as developed, for example, by Cicero and Quintilian) was to possess good knowledge of the law. That this was indeed the case is shown by the declamations, forensic speeches composed in the rhetorical schools for practice or for entertainment. Legal knowledge is clear in particular for those declamations attributed to Quintilian (*Declamationes maiores* and *minores*). They often contain arguments that were drawn from the Roman jurists, even when the legal norms set at the basis of the fictional case scenario do not correspond to Roman law but are a deformation of it.[25]

On the other hand, Roman jurists almost always had a rhetorical education, which was a shared characteristic of elite education. As such, over time (at least from the second century BCE) the jurists also refined techniques of argumentation and demonstration that derived from rhetoric: for example,

23 Scheid 2005. 24 Gunderson 2009. 25 Mantovani 2007.

they perfected the technique of definition, and they accepted strategies for interpreting laws that had been exploited in the *status negotialis* of the judicial rhetoric. These interrelationships explain why the same person could fulfil two functions, those of jurist and orator, privileging the one or the other.[26] At the end of the day, these roles are, culturally and functionally, clearly distinct. The distinction is epitomized by the dictum attributed to the late Roman Republican jurist Aquilius Gallus: 'This is not a matter for the law but for Cicero' when any one brought to Aquilius a case which turned on a question of fact.[27]

Legal Experts

In ancient China, India, the Near East, Greece and Rome, legal knowledge was considered a specific field of knowledge: law was considered a topic more or less distinct from other facets of society and embodied in specific texts. This, in turn, implies that the production (or, at least, collection) of such regulations and their application were deemed to be specialized intellectual activities. This does not necessarily imply, however, that jurists as such were a distinct group of persons, in the sense of individuals who were exclusively devoted to legal science. In fact, it seems a special group of people named after their profession only arose (eventually) in Rome: 'jurists' (*iuris periti* or *iuris consulti*). In Rome too, as we have already seen, legal knowledge was in the hands of the pontiffs, the most important Roman priesthood, over a long period of time. In all ancient societies law thus acquired autonomy while developing in close connection to other social spheres, and such connection was in many societies reflected in the exercise of legal activities by people who also engaged in other intellectual tasks. The Roman case might therefore be considered the one which has gone the longest way towards specialization. A sketch of the sociological profile of people engaged in law in different societies is the best way to draw out a set of comparisons.

In traditional China a class of legal experts comparable to the Roman jurists in their most developed phase never arose (and there was certainly no class comparable to the modern solicitor, barrister or judge of the common law). The underlying reason was probably the desire of the

---

26 Typical examples are L. Licinius Crassus and Q. Mucius Scaevola, both consuls 95 BCE: *eloquentium iuris peritissimus Crassus, iuris peritorum eloquentissimus Scaevola* (Cic. *Brut.* 145).

27 Cic. *Top.* 51: *'nihil ad ius; ad Ciceronem,' inquiebat Gallus noster, si quis ad eum quid tale rettulerat, ut de facto quaereretur.*

ruler and the government to keep the implementation and interpretation, though not necessarily the knowledge, of the law entirely in their own hands. Hence private legal experts were discouraged and in later dynasties even persecuted. Nevertheless, we can distinguish several groups of persons who, from different points of view and with different levels of specialized knowledge, had a particular interest in the law.

Our first group consists of persons concerned primarily, on a highly theoretical level, with the origin of law and its role in government (these two issues might be closely related). Such persons are customarily treated as belonging to schools of thought which developed during the Warring States and flourished in that period and that of the early Han, probably up to the end of the second century BCE. We may distinguish three such schools, beginning with the so-called legalists or members of the Legalist school (*fajia*).[28] The legalists were philosophers or statesman who advocated a prominent place for law in government and society. Their fundamental aim, driven originally by the political and social conditions of the Warring States, was to devise and recommend to the ruler of the state in which they served policies that would strengthen his economic and military position vis-à-vis other states. The essential measure for achieving this purpose was the operation of a centralized authority concentrating power in the hands of the ruler through a bureaucratic structure staffed by officials appointed by and strictly accountable to the ruler. Neither the ruler nor his officials were to administer the state according to their own constantly changing perceptions of what was good, desirable, or expedient. They were to govern in accordance with fixed laws, impartially implemented, and comprehensible to all. Hence the interest of the legalists lays in promoting the utility of law as an effective means for the control of the population (including officials), so that all subjects of the ruler might work in ways that were advantageous to the state. Particular prominence was given to the use of punishments, and to a lesser extent rewards, as motivations for the people to behave in the ways prescribed by the laws.

The legalists insisted that laws should be clear, not contradictory, and published widely, so that the people might be aware of their duties. Overall, these principles had an enduring effect in the crafting and even publicizing of legislation. In other respects, legalist doctrines had less success. The goal of equality before the law, under which all persons alike irrespective of status were to be treated in the same way, was never achieved, even in the state and

---

28 The term 'legalist' is a matter of controversy; see Goldin 2011.

empire of Qin, much less so in later dynasties. Nor was law even strictly separated from morality as the legalists advised. For them the only standard of right was that constituted by the law. One much noted phenomenon, often wrongly described as the 'Confucianization of the law', was the incorporation into the law of many principles of conduct derived from the spheres of morality or etiquette during the Han and later periods. The best-known legalists are Shang Yang and Han Fei. Shang Yang was first minister in the middle of the fourth century BCE to the ruler of the state of Qin. He was responsible for the inauguration of a legislative programme that sought to implement a strict regime of offences and punishments, even applicable to aristocrats. Writings attributed to him are collected in the *Shangjunshu* (*Book of Lord Shang*).[29] Han Fei was a philosopher of the third century BCE, related to the royal house of the state of Han, who never held high office but wrote the most comprehensive account of legalist doctrines now extant.[30]

The second 'school of thought' which can be said to have arisen during the Warring States are those philosophers who subscribed to the Huang-Lao (Yellow Emperor and Laozi) school of thought, who became particularly influential in court circles during the early Han period. The doctrines of this school, now known in some detail from texts excavated in 1973, such as the *Jingfa* (*Canon of Law*), derived law (*fa*) from the Way (*Dao*), where *Dao* expressed the total phenomena making up the human and non-human worlds. The term points to the fact that all phenomena have their predetermined modes of behaviour and their regularities of movement, with human regularities of behaviour being determined by hierarchies fixed in nature. It is these hierarchies fixed in nature that were understood to structure human institutions including the family and society (basically according to a distinction between 'superiors' and 'inferiors').[31]

The dominant impression one receives from the *Jingfa* and other Huang-Lao texts is that the authors were particularly concerned to exhibit the regularities of the four seasons, as well as the constancy in the movements of other natural phenomena like the sun and moon, as the models established by the *Dao* for the ruler to follow. The elements of regularity and constancy in nature showed that the ruler must not act in an arbitrary or partial fashion. He must follow the (correct) laws which he had enacted for the regulation of the people. He must also maintain the hierarchical distinctions given in nature between the 'noble and the base', 'superior and inferior', 'ruler and

---

29 Duyvendak 1963.   30 Liao 1939 and 1958; MacCormack 2006a.
31 Turner 1989; Peerenboom 1993; Yates 1997.

minister' and 'father and son'. One of the most important functions of the ruler was the infliction of punishment upon those who had transgressed the laws. Only the guilty should be punished, and punishment should be administered at the appropriate time. According to the rhythms of nature, autumn and winter were the seasons of decay and death and hence punishment should be reserved for this period. Such views played a part in the adoption of legal rules requiring the infliction of the death penalty in the winter.

Our third 'school' is the Confucian cosmological school, again with its roots in the Warring States but also flourishing during the early Han. Its best-known representative is Dong Zhongshu (c. 179–104 BCE). This school has obvious affinities with Huang-Lao thought, but there are differences, the most important of which concern the roles of *Dao* (the Way) and *Tian* (Heaven). For Confucians, the *Dao* does not occupy the forefront of their cosmic scheme. The creation and ordering of the universe are ascribed to *Tian*, which itself produces the *Dao*. Further, *Tian* is conceived by early Confucians not as an impersonal force, but as an anthropomorphic agency endowed with characteristics of consciousness and intention. Heaven will be aware of human misdeeds and form the intention of warning and punishing the ruler. The interaction between Heaven and human behaviour is sometimes described in early Confucian writings as mediated through the release of a 'breath' or 'vapour' termed *qi*, which can affect the balance between the two component principles of the universe (*yin* and *yang*). If the ruler misgoverns, a bad *qi* arises from his acts, disturbing the correct balance between *yin* and *yang*. Such disturbance leads to the occurrence of calamities and abnormalities in nature.

Views of this kind undoubtedly influenced the Han government (and even later governments) in their response to disturbances in nature manifested through excessive rainfall or drought. A frequently stated theme on the part of rulers and ministers was that such disturbances indicated that punishments were not being applied justly and therefore that amnesties should be issued. Furthermore, there is some evidence that the Han government took seriously the argument that the rhythms of nature provided a model for the enactment of specific rules for the conduct of affairs. A wall excavated in 1992 has an inscription entitled 'Document of the Edict of Monthly Ordinances for the Four Seasons'. The inscription refers to an imperial edict issued in 5 CE, which prescribed in detail the activities for each month of the year to be performed by the people.[32]

---

32 Sanft 2008–9. On the early Confucian cosmological school in general, see Wang 2000.

Quite a different class of legal experts is constituted by officials who either presided over or worked in the various administrative bodies concerned with judicial matters. These officials can be subdivided into three groups: high-ranking officials who presided over agencies of the central government concerned with the administration of justice or over local courts; low-ranking officials operating in the townships and villages; and the scribes or clerks who staffed the judicial agencies and local courts. We shall take each in turn.

High-ranking officials include those who operated at the head of the ministry of justice or (in later dynasties) the supreme court in the central government, the governors of commanderies and the magistrates of districts. These officials, drawn from the upper ranks of society, received no legal training as such but might, through the course of their work, become knowledgeable about legal matters and the way in which the statutory criminal and administrative rules should be applied. This is especially true of the officials appointed to be in charge of the administration of justice, such as the Han commandant of the court (*tingwei*) or the president and vice-presidents of the supreme court (as under the Tang). Sometimes officials wrote important commentaries on the law. At the beginning of the Jin dynasty (265–420 CE), a high official, Du You, wrote a commentary on the Jin Code regarded as one of the two most important, the other being written by Zhang Fei about whom nothing else is known. The most famous and authoritative legal commentary in the period we are considering was produced for the Tang Code by Changsun Wuji (died 659 CE), brother-in-law of Tang emperor Taizong (reigned 627–49 CE). Known as the *shuyi*, it was incorporated into the text of the penal code and was regarded as possessing the same force as the articles of the code. Although high-ranking officials at an early stage of their career might have passed examinations, these examinations were confined to non-legal topics. The only exception occurred in the Tang. In this dynasty one avenue through which an individual might secure an appointment was passing the state examination. The examinations covered a wide range of topics, one, unusually, being law. The examination in law was instituted in 632 and was probably intended for persons from ordinary families who intended careers as legal specialists in the offices of the central government.

Turning now to low-ranking officials, these operated in villages and townships and could thereby acquire considerable legal knowledge. An example is supplied by the bailiffs (*sefu*) of the Qin and Han dynasties, who adjudicated disputes in civil matters, were required to be present at the drawing up of wills and may have advised people on the drafting of contracts and the like.[33]

---

33 Zhang 2008: 124–26.

Finally, we have the scribes or clerks (*shi*). The newly discovered documents relating to administration in the Qin and early Han show that this hereditary class of official staffed all the administrative units of the state. Among their multifarious duties was the compilation, including the recording in writing, of the decisions of the units to which they were attached. They were also responsible for the writing down of the penal and administrative statutes associated with their roles and for preparing transcripts of the evidence given in judicial proceedings. In addition, they acted as coroners with responsibility for determining the cause of death or serious injury. They necessarily had to have considerable knowledge of the law. It is probable that one such scribe compiled the commentary on the Qin laws of the third century BCE known as 'Questions and Answers on Points of Law' (*Falü dawen*).[34] Written in a dialogic form, the text contains numerous questions and detailed answers on topics such as proper sentencing and statutory interpretation. The Tang examination in law (noted above) may have been designed to produce this particular type of official.

A further group of individuals who are portrayed in ancient Chinese material as having a specific interest in legal knowledge can be termed 'private legal experts'. For example, some scholars who had specialized in the study of the classics or in particular writings from the classical canon also became well known for their knowledge of the law. Two such persons from the Han were Dong Zhongshu and Zheng Xuan (127–200 CE). Dong, often regarded as the founder of Han Confucianism, had held relatively minor official positions but was regarded as a pre-eminent authority on the classics, especially the *Zuo zhuan* (a commentary to the Annals of the Spring and Autumn, *Chun qiu*). He was consulted by Emperor Wu (reigned 140–86 BCE) on major matters of state, but also as a private individual gave rulings on difficult legal points when requested by the government.[35] Zheng, another famous classical scholar, who held no official position, wrote a commentary on the Han laws, deemed so excellent that in the succeeding (Three Kingdoms) Wei dynasty (220–65 CE), the emperor ordered that it alone should be consulted for the elucidation of the law. Perhaps we should also include under this head Zai Fadu, who was placed in charge of the drafting of the code of the Liang dynasty (502–57 CE), since he could recite the text of the lost code of the preceding dynasty, the Southern Qi (479–501 CE), memory of which had been preserved in his family.[36]

---

34 On scribes see Yates 2014a: 144–45. 35 Loewe 2009. 36 Balazs 1954: 34.

No equivalent to modern lawyers ('solicitors' or 'barristers') appears in the evidence from ancient India: there were no legal experts who would plead cases on behalf of their clients in courts of law. Nor were there any ancient Indian equivalents of Roman orators: a professional trained to plead for a cause. There was no legal representation in ancient Indian court settings, even though it remains a possibility that individuals consulted legal experts in preparing their cases. Substitutes for the litigants were permitted when the principals were unable or incapable of representing themselves, but these substitutes were not lawyers but generally relatives of the litigants. There were, however, legal experts and the extant evidence gives specific technical terms for such individuals. On the whole we can distinguish between legal experts who served in some capacity within the courts and those who worked outside the court; for example, as legal experts writing texts on jurisprudence or as legal experts sitting in legal assemblies called *pariṣad* that decided matters of law when the law was unclear or did not address the issue at hand.

Let us take the second kind of expert first. The institution of *pariṣad* is quite ancient, and the term may have first referred to royal advisory councils. But we find the term used with reference to an assembly of experts within the context of law already in the oldest legal text, that of Āpastamba (third to early second century BCE) when he says that for matters he has not discussed people should follow the directives of legal assemblies (*pariṣad*).[37] The next oldest text, that of Gautama (late second to early first century BCE), also refers to an assembly consisting of ten members with different expertise, including three who are experts in *dharma* (*dharmavid*, literally 'one who knows *dharma*') used here probably as a technical term. The texts of Baudhāyana and Manu, on the other hand, used the term *dharmapāṭhaka* (preceptor of *dharma*) in this context.[38] The other term used, *dharmapravaktṛ* (expounder of *dharma*), probably is a synonym, although it emphasizes the teaching and promulgating of *dharma*.

Outside the institution of *pariṣad*, we have the authors of legal treatises, clearly viewed as legal experts and referred to as *dharmaśāstrakāra* ('composers of legal treatises'). In all likelihood, these texts had a didactic function; used in legal education, which was probably carried out along with other subjects – such as Vedic scripture, grammar, exegesis and logic – in traditional Brahmanical venues of instruction, normally the house of a teacher with

---

37 *ĀpDh* 1.11.38. On the development of legal procedure more generally, see Chapter 7, this volume.
38 *BDh* 1.1.8 and *MDh* 12.111; cf. *MDh* 8.20.

whom the students resided. More organized forms of education appear to have arisen with royal grants being made to Brahmin communities to foster learning. From early medieval sources, however, we get information about a special institution called *ghaṭikāsthāna*. These appear to have been public educational institutions receiving royal patronage. They had a teaching faculty and a set curriculum, with legal science or Dharmaśāstra occupying a prominent place. It is, of course, difficult to say whether similar institutions of learning devoted to legal science existed in the ancient period as well.

Donald Davis has written about the significance of *responsa*, or legal consultation, in ancient India, similar to that exerted by jurists in Rome: 'The evidence for legal consultation in Hindu law includes direct and indirect historical records of responsa, depictions of legal inquiry and response in narrative texts, and key passages in the religious-legal texts called Dharmaśāstra.'[39] A principal task of the institution of the *pariṣad*, noted above, included responding to legal questions. Indeed, the frame-stories of several Indian legal treatises show that the texts were composed in response to questions posed to an authoritative figure. Here is the opening of Manu's treatise: 'Manu was seated, absorbed in contemplation, when the great seers came up to him, paid homage to him in the appropriate manner, and addressed him in these words: "Please, Lord, tell us precisely and in the proper order the laws (*dharma*) of all the social classes"' (MDh 1.1–2). And the treatise of Yājñavalkya begins: 'Having paid home to Yogīśvara (Yājñavalkya), the sages said: "Tell us completely the laws of social classes, of orders of life, and of the rest"' (YDh 1.1).

Within courts of law themselves, we have evidence for officials who were charged with executing the law faithfully and observing the rules of legal procedure. The judge (*prāḍvivāka*), who substituted for the king, was no doubt expected to be a wise and learned person, but sources do not clearly state that he was a legal expert. In cases of miscarriage of justice, for example, he is not mentioned as one who is subject to punishment; it is a group (generally three) called *sabhya* (comparable to an 'assessor' in the Roman tradition) that is subject to such punishment. These were legal experts who advised the judge and who probably arrived at the final verdict after reviewing the evidence. We find confirmation of this in a statement of the *Nārada Smṛti*: 'Only after dismissing the litigating parties, however, should the assessors make a decision regarding the case. The assessors alone declare

---

39 Davis 2010: 1.

a man to be defeated, and thereafter the king punishes him in accordance with his legal treatises.'[40]

Finally, in the tradition of Arthaśāstra, or political science, there is an official called *dharmastha*. This official had administrative duties relating to law even outside the courtroom. For example, people are required to seek his permission before doing certain things that have legal implications. A bench of three *dharmasthas* also presided over lawsuits brought by private individuals. In the Dharmaśāstra tradition of jurisprudence, the institution of *dharmastha* disappears, but it is probable that the three *sabhyas* within the court represent the old institution of *dharmastha*. The Arthaśāstra tradition also has an official named *pradeṣṭṛ*, who was the counterpart of *dharmastha*, but whose duties pertained to criminal matters and public order. There is some information about such criminal courts, especially in the context of the evaluation of evidence of criminal acts, autopsies and forensic investigations.[41]

There is no role equivalent to that of a Roman jurist in the evidence from the ancient Near East. The closest that one might come to finding a group of legal experts would be with judges or scribes. Those who were granted judicial authority and even referred to by the term 'judge' (not all who adjudicated cases were referred to by that term), however, typically held other positions; they served as government officials at the royal, provincial or local level; as businessmen; as city elders; as temple officials; or were respected members of their communities.[42] The production of law collections, however, speaks to law as a specialized field. For example, the Middle Assyrian laws would have required a good deal of specialized knowledge, given that they consist of thirteen tablets very carefully arranged by topic and containing a large number of details that the average scribe would be unlikely to know. We also have lexical lists and other texts that appear to have been training materials for scribes learning how to record legal documents. In later periods, additional evidence for the law being a special area of knowledge turns up. In southern Mesopotamia during the Neo-Babylonian (625–539 BCE) and early Persian periods (539–484 BCE), there appears to have been a group of judges who served in that role as their primary occupation and thus could be considered professional judges, although some may have been appointed more for their family connections than for their legal knowledge. Even for members of prominent families, though, there was a training period during

---

40 *NSm Mātṛkā* 2.42 (trans. Patrick Olivelle).   41 See Chapter 7, this volume.
42 Westbrook 2005.

which they served as court clerks, as it were, performing scribal duties for the sitting judges.[43]

Mention is made of judges in the Hebrew Bible as well. Part of the Deuteronomic Code often associated with the reign of the Judean king Josiah (640–609 BCE) contains the divine command to appoint judges in every town (Deut. 16:18–20). An earlier Judean king, Jehoshaphat (early to mid-ninth century BCE), is said to have carried out this very action, but the report comes from a much later text (2 Chr 19:4–11) and is likely unhistorical. It does, however, refer to a legal distinction between the 'things of Yahweh' and the 'things of the king'. The text says that the high priest was given legal authority over the former, while the governor (*nāgîd*) of Judah had authority over the latter. Presumably, these men were considered to possess special competence in these areas. Other biblical texts, on the other hand, only require judicial officials to be men of piety, wisdom and integrity (Exod. 18:21–23; Deut. 1:13–17). There is one scribe, though, who is identified as 'expert in the law (*tôrâ*) of Moses' and 'devoted to studying the law (*tôrâ*) of Yahweh' (Ezra 7:6, 10). The narrative in which he figures accords him a judicial function in that he is commissioned by the Persian king to appoint 'magistrates and judges' in the province on the west side of the Euphrates River (Ezra 7:25).

As noted in the 'Introduction' above, rabbis constituted a social subgroup consciously characterized as legal experts. Much of the information included in rabbinic sources regarding the rabbinic legal profession, training and science, however, must be treated with caution. Rabbinic literature itself is our main source of information about the rabbis, but it seldom provides details about legal education or the daily duties of sages.[44] What information it does provide must also be carefully considered. Legal training and practice evolved through the centuries and the rabbinic texts that are the main sources of information about the rabbis and their practices did as well. The greatest rabbinic legal source, the *Bavli* (or 'Babylonian Talmud'), incorporates laws and discussions spanning at least five centuries, many of which cannot be dated with accuracy. Because the *Bavli* is a synthesis, any account which treats it as a straightforward historical source will include many anachronisms.[45]

As far as their functions are concerned, in the Tannaitic period (c. 70–220 CE), rabbis sometimes served as judges, though not in a capacity authorized by the

---

43 Holtz 2008.   44 Cohen 1981a.
45 These cautions and others are detailed in Fonrobert and Jaffee 2007: 1–14; Lapin 1995: 1–19; Lapin 2008: 206–12; and Kalmin 2001: 187–200.

state. In Palestine, the state courts were those of the Roman provincial governors and were convened under their authority. For those individuals and communities that respected rabbinic training and authority, a sage might be asked to arbitrate a dispute or to rule on an aspect of religious practice. Such a legal proceeding was occasionally called a 'court', but the make-up and procedures of such a court – or even if legal procedures were yet codified – is unknown. The authority of the rabbinic court rested entirely on the reputation of the sage and the disputants' or community's willingness to submit to his judgment.[46] In Palestine of the Amoraic period, rabbis begin to appear in municipal positions like tax-collector or as permanent judges appointed to religious courts by the patriarch.[47] Almost nothing is known about social history in the Parthian empire, a silence that extends to the Babylonian amoraim.[48] There are accounts of court judgments being discussed with disciples or disputed by other sages who seem to be in attendance (for example, b. B.K. 84a). In this way, the court could serve an educational function too.

From a sociological standpoint, in the tannaitic period, there are examples of tradesmen and lower-class people becoming rabbis (for example, R. Yochanan), and many rabbis had to maintain a profession to support themselves.[49] However, there are also examples of dynastic families within which rabbinic positions were handed down through the generations.[50] The number of rabbis in Palestine appears to have been quite small. A catalogue of the names of rabbis cited in rabbinic sources shows how small a group it was. The number of named rabbis barely exceeds one hundred in any generation and usually is half that number.[51] For both Palestine and Babylon, by the amoraic period most sages were urban, even if they lived in tension with their context.[52]

At least as important as the relationship of the sages to (Roman and Parthian / Sasanian) political authorities was their relationship to other religious authorities. In Palestine of the Tannaitic period, synagogues were often under the influence if not the direct control of wealthy elites. The influence of the rabbis over synagogue practices appears to rise very gradually.[53] In Babylon the process was the same but began later. Tradition claims that disciples of rabbi Yehuda Ha-Nasi (Judah the Prince) brought the Mishna to Babylon c. 220 CE and began to disseminate rabbinic tradition in

---

46 Schwartz 2001: 103–28.   47 Rubenstein 2007: 64–65.   48 Schwartz 2007: 89–93.
49 Urbach 1968: 123; Hezser 1997: 257–66.   50 Hezser 1997: 96–100; Goodman 1983: 93.
51 Levine 1989: 66–69.
52 Lapin 1999: 187–201; Halbertal 1998: 159–72; Schwartz 2001: 162–76.
53 Levine 2008: 466–98.

Babylonian communities. How quickly the rabbinic tradition became the dominant expression of Judaism in Palestine or in Babylon is a matter of debate. Much modern scholarship has assumed that rabbinic control was essentially accomplished by the middle of the Amoraic period. Recent scholarship disputes this point of view and argues that rabbinic power and rabbinic influence was limited throughout the Tannaitic and Amoraic periods.[54] Hartmut Lapin has argued that the process of establishing a rabbinic-defined 'orthodoxy' occurred in parallel to the movement to establish 'orthohodoxy' within Christianity.[55]

In no ancient Greek city, to our knowledge, was any legal specialist recognized, except in as far as individuals were understood to have skills as lawgivers. But specialists in matters religious and specialists in the arts of verbal persuasion both effectively acquired legal authority, in at least some circumstances. Most Greek cities seem to have traced the laws which they used in the classical period back to some individual lawgiver or to a sequence of lawgivers, each adding to or revising the work of earlier lawgivers.[56] Some of these lawgivers were in essence mythical figures, like Lycurgus at Sparta (Herodotus 1.65), but of others there is no doubt of their existence. Exactly how they were chosen for their role is often, as with Solon of Athens, obscure, but oral tradition held that some of them were appointed after consultation with the Delphic oracle – an indication of the close involvement of the gods with the sphere of law. A good example of such a lawgiver is Demonax of Mantineia, who is appointed to revise the laws at Cyrene after an incident of civil strife.[57] When cities were formed afresh in the classical period, individuals were appointed to be their lawgivers; Protagoras, for example, is reputed to have formulated the laws for the new city of Thurii, in southern Italy, in the 440s BCE. No distinction is made in these stories, however, between constitutional law (which seems often to be at the centre of attention) and the rest of the law code.

Whether lawgivers were reckoned legal experts with regard to their own laws is a moot point. The lawgiver getting caught by his own law was something of a topos (Diod. 13.33.2–3), and lawgivers were often reckoned to have moved out of the community after setting up the laws so as not to be tempted to change them (*Ath. pol.* 11 on Solon). But interpretation of law in the courts made much of the lawgiver's intention. Athenian orators in the fourth century ascribe not just individual laws but views about the matters on

---

54 See especially Schwartz 2001.   55 Lapin 1996.
56 Szegedy-Maszak 1978; Hölkeskamp 1999.   57 Herodotus 4.161; Arist. *Politics* 1319b19ff.

which he legislates to Solon.[58] But Athenians were well aware of the difficulty of making law and of the limitations to the lawgiver's foresight (cf. *Ath. pol.* 9.2).

In classical Athens the lawmakers were the people themselves. In the fifth century laws could be made by bringing a proposal to the Athenian Assembly and having it agreed by a simple majority. In this sense all Athenian citizens were legal experts. In the fourth century law had to be made by a special session of the Assembly at which the 6,000 citizen males attending turned themselves into *nomothetai* (lawgivers), but although the advice that they received was now more systematic, in as far as a group was appointed to think seriously about the issues, this again made ordinary Athenians experts in the law.[59] Speakers in Athenian courts occasionally take advantage of the conceptual unity between Athenians as lawmakers and Athenians as judges/ jurors (*dikastai* in Greek, a function that implied judging both questions of fact and questions of law, and thus a certain expertise) by talking of the intention of the lawmaker (see below) as the intention of the *dikastai*.[60]

In the end, the real expert witnesses were the laws themselves (which of course in turn implied that litigants had a good knowledge thereof). Laws were not only quoted in court to make arguments – and not simply the law under which the case was being heard, but others whose force was merely persuasive – but were invoked as if living witnesses.[61] Perhaps the most famous case of this comes outside the law court, in Plato's dialogue *Crito*, in which Socrates imagines the laws objecting to his escaping prison in order to escape (just) execution (*Crito* 50a6–54d1). Similar tropes, however, were played in the law courts themselves, as when Euphiletos in Lysias 1 quotes himself as invoking the laws as the executioner before he kills Eratosthenes (Lysias 1.26).

Plaintiffs in law courts in the Greek city conducted their own prosecutions and defences, except in the very few cases so serious that the city itself took on the prosecution. But plaintiffs could consult others in drafting their case, have their case written for them by others or be supported by fellow-speakers (*synegoroi*).[62] From the end of the fifth century BCE onwards, law-court speeches survive from Athens that were written by professional

---

58 Dem. 18.6–7, 22.25ff.; [Dem.] 43.62), using the general tenor of the laws to illustrate an attitude to morality (cf. Aeschin. 1.6–32). See Thomas 1994; Yunis 2005: 201–8; Harris 2006: 3–28.
59 Canevaro 2013.   60 So Aeschin. 3.14, cf. Lysias 14.4.
61 Dem. 54.24 is a good example of invoking laws other than that on which the case is based.
62 Rubinstein 2000.

speechwriters for others to read. In these writers, known as *logographoi* ('writers of words'), it is hard to separate rhetorical from legal expertise in these writers. Certainly, the way in which different orators seem to have got reputations for taking on different sorts of cases – most notably Antiphon and homicide cases (noted by Hermogenes, *Peri Ideon* 2.11) and Isaeus and inheritance cases – suggests that command of the relevant area of law was important.

Certainly, it is important for the speaker to pretend to an understanding of the law. They may be explicit about having done research: 'examining and studying the laws day and night' (Hypereides, *Against Athenogenes* 13), but more usually they simply assume command through the trope of reference to the lawgiver's intentions. One infamous case is in Lysias' Speech 1, in which Euphiletos defends himself over the killing of Eratosthenes whom he claims to have caught committing adultery with his wife. At one point he quotes a law (not preserved), and then comments:

> Clearly the lawgiver believed that those who commit rape deserve a lighter penalty than those who seduce ... He believed that those who act by violence are hated by those who have been assaulted, whereas those who act by seduction corrupt the minds of their victims ... The victim's whole household becomes the adulterer's ... Because of this the lawgiver laid down the death-penalty for adulterers.[63]

Such confident claims to legal knowledge both rely on the thought that the lawgiver or lawgivers were legal experts and ask the jury to regard the speaker as a legal expert.[64]

Classical Athens operated with mass juries – 201, 501, etc. – selected by lot from a panel of 6,000 that was re-formed annually (*Ath. pol.* 63–66).[65] There was undoubtedly some continuity from year to year, and Aristophanes' satire on Athenians who were addicted to serving on juries, *Wasps*, implies that some, and in particular the elderly, may have sought every opportunity to serve. Given the notorious Athenian litigiousness, which is also satirized by Aristophanes, such addicts will have acquired considerable experience. The same applies even more strongly to the court of the Areopagus, which dealt with homicide cases, which was made up of ex-archons (Athens allotted nine archons each year); in the Areopagus the same men will have heard cases of the same sort over a long period. It is notable that homicide cases before the

---

63 Lysias 1.32–3 (trans. Todd).
64 For other cases in Lysias, see 3.42 with Todd's commentary ad loc., 26.9; Dem. 33.1–2, 45.44.
65 See also Chapter 5, this volume.

Areopagus never cite the homicide laws: there was no need. There are some allusions to the Areopagus having particular rules over irrelevance and the possibility of enforcing these must have depended on the experience of the Areopagite jury.[66] It is notable that arguments before the Areopagus focus more closely on the legal issue in question than cases before the popular courts (see below). Such a pattern of a more or less consistent body of men hearing similar cases over a long period was probably common in other Greek cities too. But in no Athenian court, and as far as we know in no court anywhere in Greece, was discussion among the jurors possible before the decision was taken for condemnation or acquittal. Any expertise acquired was therefore of rather limited impact and although speakers in Athenian courts variously treat the jury as a third party, sorting out a dispute between plaintiffs, or as the injured party in an offence against the city,[67] they never treat them as legal experts.

None of this meant that there was no interest in the theory of law. Although many of the lawgivers that we know of in archaic Greece are associated with only a small number of particular laws, there was clearly some theorizing behind much archaic law-making and this was embodied in the form of the laws themselves. One example of this is Solon's decision to arrange his law code by magistrate. But the indications are that such theorizing was as much political and sociological as it was in any sense 'legal'. Philosophical discussion of the nature of law was clearly prominent among the sophists of the fifth century BCE and is reflected in various ways in surviving works. Ancient Athenian Tragedy variously engages with issues of law and its enforcement (most particularly in Sophocles *Antigone*). The question of the citizen's 'legal contract' with his city is also at the core of Plato's *Crito*. Furthermore, the relationship between law and political authority is debated between Alcibiades and Pericles in Xenophon's *Memorabilia* (1.2.40–46); Plato attempts to legislate himself for the 'second-best city' in *Laws*; Aristotle discusses constitutional law at length in *Politics* (esp. book 2) and the principles of law in *Rhetoric*; and Theophrastus wrote a treatise *On Laws*. All this in addition to discussions by speakers in the courts about the principles of law. When democracy was restored to Athens in 403 BCE, following the 'rule of the Thirty [tyrants]', there was clearly a discussion about the difference between one-off decisions and the setting of permanent rules, which led to the Athenian Assembly restricting its own role to one-off

---

66 Lys. 3.46; Lycurgos 1.11–13; Pollux 8.117; and Antiphon 5.11, 6.9. Further discussion in Harris 2019a.

67 Rubinstein 2005: 145.

decisions and distinguishing meetings of the Assembly as lawgivers (*nomothe-othetai*), responsible for making and revising the law, from ordinary meetings of the Assembly.[68]

As already argued, law's separation from other social domains – present as we have seen in various degrees in the ancient societies discussed here – is particularly clear in Rome. This is the case not only for law as a phenomenon (the *ius civile* as a social practice with marked boundaries), but also for the people who are experts in the law. The internal point of view is worth considering: the existence of a 'group' that is formally or at least culturally distinct is revealed by the name whereby these experts present themselves (*iuris consultus*; *iuris peritus*; *iuris auctor*; νομικός). In the epigraphical record the term *iuris consultus* (and its variants) is used as an addition to, and as a qualifying element in, the *cursus honorum* – as becomes clear from for example of the eulogy of P. Pactumeius Clemens, suffect consul of 138 CE.[69] The same emerges, though on a more modest scale, in the case of Ann[i]us Namptoius fl(a)m(en) [p(er)]p(etuus) / iuris consultus magister st[udiorum] cur(ator) rei p(ublicae).[70] In addition to terminology, there are other clear signs of a collective self-awareness: most notably, the jurist Sextus Pomponius in the second century CE drew up a list of important jurists who were considered the ones who had 'laid the foundation' of the law and who had 'passed it on' (*l.s. ench.*, Justinian *Digest*. 1.2.2.35).

In Rome, as we will see in detail, the *iuris consulti* were involved directly or indirectly in every phase of legal life.[71] In addition to this pervasiveness, the role of the jurists was particularly important from a qualitative perspective: although they did not possess a direct power to 'create' law (at least until some of them acquired the so-called *ius respondendi* under Augustus and later emperors), the jurists through their reasonings determined how the sources of law were to be construed (i.e. statutes, senate decrees, edicts, imperial constitutions); formulated general rules; and found the best solution for individual cases. The Roman jurists thus constituted an epistemic community whose discourse organized and shaped Roman private law.

Since a large number of jurists (second century BCE – late third century CE) wrote down their responses and their commentaries on statutes and on other norms, legal literature in Rome formed a sort of restatement-in-progress of the

---

68 cf. Aeschin. 3.39 and see further below.
69 CIL VIII, 7060 = ILAlg II.1, 646 = AE 2007, 106: Numidia, Cirta.
70 *ILAfr* 273 a, b = AE 1916, 87, 88: Africa Proconsularis (Afr. procons., Roman province), Thuburbo Maius; 361 CE (1997, 314 nr. 103).
71 Cic. *Top.* 65; Ps. Asc. *Verr.* II 1.129, with Lehne 2016.

law and gave access to it.[72] The high-level rationality that characterizes this literature is what determined its success as the basis of medieval and modern law in Europe, which it reached in the compact form of Justinian's *Digest*, an anthology promulgated as imperial statute in the year 533 CE.

Sociologically, from the end of the pontifical monopoly on the knowledge of the *ius* until the end of the Republican age (first century BCE), the figure of the jurist par excellence coincides with that of the aristocrat: that is, the descendant of magistrates, often himself engaged in a political career. Turning to the activities of *iuris consulti*, we can distinguish between them according to whether they were solicited by a private party (or by a public body), or a body otherwise invested with a public task (such as judges). We shall examine each in turn.

Regarding the responses (*responsa*) to private individuals, jurists were consulted at their homes or in public places by people seeking legal advice, either about planned legal transactions or to obtain opinions about disputes with other individuals. These activities most characterized their role in the eyes of public opinion, to the point that according to Cicero 'the house of the jurist was the oracle of the whole city' (Cic. *De orat.* 1.200). They also gave advice to orators, that is to experts in public speaking who represented the parties in a proceeding, by providing them with legal arguments (*hastae*, i.e. weapons) (Cic. *Top.* 65). Even when responding to private queries, the jurists assumed an impartial position, they responded according to the law and their prestige was linked to this impartiality, as shown by P. Mucius Scaevola when he (reportedly) said that he would not hesitate to displease a client (Cic. *De orat.* 1.239–240).

Jurists also played an important role as counsellors of magistrates who exercised jurisdiction, in that they had influence over both the drafting and the applications of the edict: a publicly displayed text that announced the norms governing the administration of justice; particularly important were the edicts of the urban and peregrine praetors in Rome, which may have constituted a model for the edicts of provincial governors. They also assisted judges, who in the Republican age were private individuals, often without much legal knowledge.[73] It remains moot whether this assistance to judges took the form of a group of advisers (*consilium*) or of individual assistants (*adsessores*).[74] Although direct evidence is lacking, it is likely that in the Republic 'private' jurists, who were often members of the Senate, also assisted magistrates in presenting to the people legislative bills (*rogationes*),

72 Mantovani 2016.   73 Gagliardi 2008.   74 Lehne 2014: 271–90.

which were technically very refined. Moreover, lower-rank magistrates' assistants probably also possessed legal knowledge (*apparitores, scribae, praecones,* see below), but they were certainly not qualified as *iuris periti*.[75]

The figure of the Roman jurist par excellence – of great prestige, capable of producing law through his *interpretatio* put down in *responsa* and diffused in writing – reached its climax between the first decades of the second century and the first half of the third century CE. This is the age of men such as Salvius Iulianus, Gaius, Cervidius Scaevola, Aemilius Papinianus, Iulius Paulus and Domitius Ulpianus. In this period, *equites* ('horsemen') filled some of the senior administrative and military posts of the imperial government and the jurists likewise mainly belonged to this equestrian order. This continues until the beginning of the fourth century CE. The last jurists to whom written works are attributed date to the time of the emperor Diocletian: Aurelius Hermogenianus and Aurelius Arcadius Charisius. From the age of Augustus, as we shall see, some jurists were given the responsibility to give responses to the public *ex auctoritate principis*, that is, with a kind of increased authority as a reflection of the authority of the emperor; this contributed to make 'the jurist' a well-defined role, since highly prestigious figures formed a sort of model that contributed to giving the group its own identity.

The picture so far concerns the functioning of jurists of an aristocratic or equestrian background, whose activities were recorded in written works. On the other hand, no clear traces survive for the Republic of lower-key jurists who provided assistance in minor affairs.[76] Even in the absence of evidence, we must presuppose their existence. Otherwise, it is difficult to explain how Roman law could spread among Italic municipalities after the extension of citizenship during the first century BCE. These jurists, who for convenience's sake (but improperly) can be called 'minor', are in turn documented with certainty for the Principate. Their most distinctive feature is that they have not left literary evidence of their work and are also not cited by literary jurists for their opinions. Yet in the evidence from the empire they are attested in inscriptions and papyri almost everywhere, up to the fifth and sixth centuries CE.[77]

In terms of geography, such 'minor' jurists could be found in Rome but also sometimes came from the provinces, such as Praetextatus, *iuris peritus nobilissimus ex Africa* (CIL VI 33867) and T. Oclatius Athenagoras *iuris studiosus*

---

[75] David 2019.
[76] The Cascellius mentioned as an expert in public auctions at Cic. *Balb.* 45 and Val. Max. 8.12.1 may represent a 'minor' jurist, yet he was still an equestrian and hence upscale.
[77] So already Mitteis 1891: 198, albeit within a devaluation of late antique legal culture.

around the middle of the third century (CIL VI 33868), who moved to Rome from Nicomedia. These jurists can also be found in Italy, Spain, Narbonensis, Dalmatia, Africa, Asia Minor: for example, Aelius Aurelius Ammianos Papias, honoured in Aphrodisias in Caria in the second–third century as νομικὸς ἄριστος (CIG 2787). The names of νομικοί appear naturally with particular abundance in Egyptian papyri, which should, however, not be interpreted as a sign of greater frequency there than in the other provinces.[78] Assessing their social positions is made difficult by the scarcity of evidence, often limited to short funeral inscriptions. However, it is likely that even these 'minor' jurists were not from lower strata; among them we certainly find members of the local elites: for example, *Marinus eq(ues) R(omanus) iuris peritissimus* was of equestrian rank (CIL VIII 8489: Mauretania Sitif., Sitifis). Of slightly lower class was Q. Vetidius Iuvenalis (*ILAlg.* I 1362: Afr. Proc., Thubursicu Numidarum), whose children were sent to study Latin and Greek in Carthage and became equestrians (AE 1903, 320; 321). M'. Cornelius Carpus, *iuris studiosus* (CIL III 2936: Iader), came from a family of freedmen who had made their fortune with the oil trade in Dalmatia. An inscription listing four generations of a certainly high-rank family attests to a true lineage of jurists at Colybrassus in Cilicia between the third and fourth centuries CE (SEG 26, 1456).[79]

Moreover, even though these jurists did not leave any written works, we should not imagine that they found themselves in complete cultural isolation. There is evidence that they were in epistolary contact with 'major' jurists. Here the text excerpted at Justinian, *Digest* 3.5.33 is significant: the great jurist Iulius Paulus (Severan Age) reproduces a letter sent to him by L. Nessenius Apollinaris: the latter's activity as a jurist in Ephesus is now known thanks to epigraphic evidence (AE 1975, 793).

Among these 'non-literary' but far from despicable jurists, we may find those functioning as *consiliarius* or *assessor*. These lawyers lent their experience to advise on all aspects of the administrative and judicial activities carried out by magistrates or officials: 'The tasks of the assessor, carried out by jurists, consist roughly of the following things: proceedings, petitions, writs, edicts, decrees, official correspondence' (Justinian *Digest* 1.22.1; Paulus, *liber singularis de officio adsessorum*). These jurists thus constituted a sort of neural network for the transmission of Roman law throughout the empire. It is in reference to this phenomenon that the *Expositio totius mundi*, a

[78] The list in Kunkel 1967 is to be supplemented: see Liebs 1987, 2002a, especially 2002b, 2005; Humfress 2007b; Jones 2007; and Laes and Strubbe 2014: 186–89.
[79] Liebs 2002b: 17.

mid-fourth-century CE text from the reign of Constantius, mentions Berytus (modern Beirut); we hear that from this town, the seat of an important law school, 'men [spread] to all the earth who sit alongside judges, and who knowing the laws protect the provinces'.[80] We must therefore avoid a mistake of perspective: the most famous jurists are those who have left literary works through which we know them. However, we must not let them eclipse the existence of a widespread, far larger network of jurists with good expertise and probably of good social backgrounds.

As already stated, the production of juristic literature ceased towards the end of the third century CE during the age of Diocletian. The extension of citizenship and hence of the applicability of Roman law to (almost) all free inhabitants of the empire in 212 CE led to the need of having access to a uniform rule of law. This was provided by the works of late second- and third-century jurists who produced wide restatements of law. Their writings quickly became a sort of closed 'canon'. No new books were written, whereas the most authoritative older ones continued to be copied and circulated in Late Antiquity, being studied in schools as part of the education of new jurists. In addition, quotations from these works were cited in court proceedings (*recitatio*). Legal innovation was reserved for emperors. Nevertheless, even after the age of Diocletian, jurists continued to give *responsa*, although they were not collected in books.[81] For example, contrary to what had long been thought, the newly found letters of St Augustine show that at the beginning of the fifth century CE jurists were still asked for counsel.[82]

The transformation of the role of the jurist in Late Antiquity also depended on another phenomenon. From the first century CE, requests for legal advice were addressed increasingly to the *princeps*. As such, we can observe the existence of a 'double channel': rescripts from the emperor, *responsa* from the jurists. Jurists were also getting more involved in government. Three main aspects of this involvement can be discerned: first, the function as counsellors of the *principes*; second, membership of the imperial chancery (especially in the role of *procuratores a libellis*, agents in charge of responses to petitions addressed to the emperor); and finally, the recruitment of jurists into the

---

80 *Expositio totius mundi*, 25 (trans. Dario Mantovani).   81 Liebs 2019.
82 Eustochius, in Africa: *Ep.* 24, CSEL 88, 1981: 126–27 = *Bibliothèque Augustinienne*, 46B: 386–87. See also *Consultatio veteris cuiusdam iurisconsulti* and, for the East, *Scholia Sinaitica* 4 and the texts associated with the sixth-century CE figure Dioskoros of Aphrodito (MacCoull 1988).

major imperial offices (including the praetorian prefecture). We will examine each in turn.

Given the magnitude of the problems facing the empire's administration, it is no surprise that emperors shared with many advisers the weight of the many political, administrative, judicial and regulatory decisions they were to take on a daily basis. Augustus already asked a few *prudentes*, including Trebatius, about the validity of *codicilli* confirmed by will (Justinian, *Inst.* 2.25 pr.). However, the presence of jurists among the emperor's counsellors became more prominent and more constant only in the second century CE. Just like the emperors, so the urban magistrates, provincial governors, great prefects and officials in general – and also local magistrates and minor judges – all had advisers on their side, properly called *adsessores*.[83]

In addition to acting as advisers at various levels, jurists were also in demand to fulfil delicate offices within the palace secretariats. Particularly influential were the offices of *procurator a libellis* and *ab epistulis*: imperial agents responsible for the issuing of rescripts, i.e. of furnishing written answers to petitions (of all sorts) in the form respectively of a subscription to the petition booklet or of an epistle. This type of correspondence was such an important phenomenon that nowadays it is considered emblematic – though not exhaustive – of the princeps' 'style' of governing.[84] While at first petitions were mostly requests for benefits and privileges, with Hadrian questions of a legal nature acquired markedly more weight. Such questions would previously have been submitted to private jurists (and continued to be, sometimes cumulatively: see above on Justinian, *Cod.* 3.42.5 of 239 CE). At the same time, the office of *procurator a libellis* was often entrusted to eminent jurists of equestrian background. The career of Lucius Volusius Maecianus is significant: initially *a libellis* of Antoninus Pius (when the latter was not yet an emperor), he took up this task again from about 150 CE, after his protector had taken on imperial power. From Constantine onwards, the *quaestor sacri palatii*, who in Late Antiquity assumed essential functions in the administration of justice, was often a jurist.[85]

Finally, the influence of jurists can be seen emerging more generally from the growing importance of legal knowledge in pursuit of a career in the imperial bureaucracy. More general careers in the imperial bureaucracy need to be distinguished from the specific role of editor of normative rules (in particular the office *a libellis*), even though both phenomena have the same

---

83 Wieling 2000; Lehne 2014: 275–90.
84 Millar 1992, cf. Connolly 2010; Mantovani 2020.
85 Honoré 1998.

root. In other words, the career of a jurist such as the aforementioned Lucius Volusius Maecianus did not stop at the role of *a libellis* but led to the highest equestrian office (*praefectus Aegypti*, around 160–62 CE); having then been granted senatorial rank, Maecianus held the prefecture of state treasury and eventually the (suffect) consulate in 166 (CIL XIV 5347; AE 1955, 179: Ostia). Such promotions are also attested by the careers of other later jurists (of whom Domitius Ulpianus, who became *praefectus praetorio*, is probably the best-known example). Even though not all offices directly entailed legal activities, the link between knowledge of the law and career advancement suggests that the imperial administration became increasingly characterized by being subjected to legal forms.[86] The importance of knowledge of the law for an imperial career continues in the fourth and fifth centuries CE, as is well known from the correspondence of Libanius. As far as the East is concerned, this rhetor attests that legal education, principally through the schools of Rome and Berytus in Syria, was considered essential for practising as an advocate, as well as for access to public offices.[87] A notable example of such a figure is Oecumenius, the governor of Asia (about 400 CE), for whom the city of Aphrodisias raised a (recently discovered) robed statue, holding a scroll in his right hand while having a bunch of other scrolls beside his left foot. In the inscription, Oecumenius is defined as an expert jurist, bilingual, in Latin ('the Italian Muse') and Greek ('Attic of the golden voice'), and as having literary pretensions ('he has stirred Muses'). He is also said to be incorruptible: 'pure of mind, pure of hands'. The mouth of Oecumenius' statue gives a slight smile: this benevolent expression, along with the inscription and scrolls that form a contrast with his military clothing, conveys the idea that the *militia* of these imperial officials was exercised in legal forms.[88]

Legal Training

We turn now to legal training. Although there probably were no jurists in the strict sense of the term in ancient India, as we have seen there were experts in law who presided over courts and wrote texts dealing with *dharma* (which includes law). Consequently, there must have been institutions that transmitted this knowledge from one generation to another. We do not have contemporary accounts of such institutions – with the exception of the Vedic education of a young boy, after his Vedic initiation imparted by a teacher

---

86 History of historiography in Humfress 2007a.
87 Liban. *Ep.* 2.154; 234; 2.44–46; 11.187; 18.288; 31.26–28; 43.4–5; 62.21–23.   88 Smith 2002.

(generally done at the teacher's home, where the pupil also resided).[89] There is evidence that students would seek out teachers who specialized in particular subjects, such as grammar or poetry, and it is likely that legal education was also transmitted by such specialists. Inscriptional evidence suggests that schools or colleges called *ghaṭikāsthāna*, established and endowed by kings, were in existence by at least the fifth century CE.[90] Some of these were large with several thousand members. Sources do not give a clear picture of the curriculum of studies at these educational institutions, and instruction may have varied from place to place. Inscriptions show that at least some of these colleges taught Dharmaśāstra, which was the major textual means of discussing legal issues.

In comparison with the ancient Indian material, it is clear that rabbinic law (*halakha*) was produced by those sages who taught and studied in rabbinic educational institutions. Yet regarding these institutions, often grandly called 'academies', much remains unknown before the Gaonic period (700–1100 CE). The information on formal legal training is anecdotal and sparse. Despite the claims of rabbinic literature – that it was the founding rabbis of the 'academies' who not only preserved *halakha* but composed much of it and taught it – very little attention has been directed to the question of the pedagogic purposes for which rabbinic *halakha* itself might be suitable.[91]

There is a long-standing tradition that R. Yichanan ben Zakkai founded the first rabbinic academy (a *yeshiva* or *metivta*) in 70 CE after Jerusalem fell to the Romans in the First Jewish War. This proposal has now been thoroughly disproven.[92] The usual term for a rabbinic school in the Tannaitic period (c. 70–225 CE) is *bet midrash*, 'house of study'. From anecdotes in the *Mishna* and *Talmudim*, it seems that any building could serve as a *bet midrash* (*T. Shabbat* 2:5; *T. Berakhot* 4:18), though archaeological evidence suggests that, mostly, instruction occurred at the teacher's domicile.[93] It may be that rabbinic training in the Tannaitic period was less like formal education and more like Greek philosophical training of the classical age: no dedicated building, no books, no formal curriculum, just a teacher and a circle of students learning discursively.[94] At least some disciples lived with their masters and served as domestic help, and disciples had the freedom to choose to leave their master at any time.[95]

---

89 Scharfe 2002. 90 Minakshi 1938: 186–212.
91 Samely 2017: 147–200; Schofer 2005: 23–64.
92 Goodblatt 1994: 232–76; Jacobs 1995: 115–23.
93 Levine 1989: 25–29; Hezser 1997: 191–209.   94 Goodblatt 1975: 268–71; Cohen 1981b.
95 Hezser 1997: 339–47.

In Palestine of the Amoraic period (c. 220–550 CE), the *bet midrash* continued to be the location for instruction. In the *Yarushalmi* (sometimes referred to as the 'Palestinian' or 'Jerusalem' Talmud), the names *bet va 'ad* (Hebrew) or *be va 'ada* (Aramaic) for 'assembly house' and *sidrah* (Hebrew) or *sidra '* (Aramaic) for 'hall of studies', both appear on occasion, but they seem to be synonyms for *bet midrash*.[96] In Babylonian sources of the amoraic period, the names *be rav* 'master's house' or *be rav* X 'house of master so-and-so' are common and appear as equivalents to *bet midrash*, as the name itself suggests.[97] Although tradition claims that two great academies (*yeshivot*) of rabbinic learning were established in Babylon at Sura and Pumbedita early in the third century, these are the names of academies from medieval Baghdad.[98]

In addition to the private education offered to disciples by individual rabbis, the Bavli refers to *pirka '*, which seems to have been a teaching forum in which rabbis offered lectures to lay audiences. Some topics were not deemed suitable for such an audience and were reserved for the *bet midrash* (b. Ned. 23b; b. Ḥul. 15a). Although it is unknown how often a *pirka '* was convened, where one might have taken place or how well attended they might have been, there are intimations that other rabbis did attend them (B. Kid. 28b). In addition the *Bavli* (the 'Babylonian Talmud') refers to the *kallah*, possibly meaning 'assembly' or 'cell': a periodic closed gathering of rabbinic sages and their disciples.[99] It is not entirely clear if these were already formal gatherings in the amoraic period.

In Rome, during the Republican age, legal knowledge – in line with its elite nature – was mainly transmitted within families. This happened either from father to son, or by securing an internship through aristocratic family connections with a reputable jurist, who admitted the young man in his home. Already in the last century BCE, individuals seem to have arisen who attracted and were willing to be surrounded by a greater circle of 'auditors' (*auditores*), namely young people who learned by listening-in while the jurist was giving *responsa* and who might occasionally have been involved in discussions of cases of particular interest. Servius Sulpicius Rufus (consul 51 BCE), for example, had numerous auditors. This figure of the jurist-intellectual with his own circle appears to have consolidated itself in the Principate: M. Antistius Labeo is said to have devoted six months a year to his disciples, retiring for the other six to write. Masurius Sabinus (floruit under the

---

96 Rubenstein 2007: 62–64.
97 Urman 1995: 232–55; Rubenstein 2001; Goodblatt 2008: 830–35.
98 Goodblatt 1975: 77–79, 162–65; 2008: 821–30.   99 Goodblatt 2008: 835–36.

emperor Tiberius) marks, as far as we know, a turning point. Of a modest social background, Sabinus never embarked on a political career; rather, he is depicted as a teacher supported by the contributions of his law students, as rhetoric or philosophy teachers used to be (Justinian, *Digest* 1.2.2.52, Pomponius *l.s. ench.*). The prestige acquired by Sabinus, both culturally – his *libri iuris civilis* became the main book of reference up until Ulpian – and publicly – he became part of the equestrian order and received from Tiberius the right to publicly give legal advice (a benefit whose contours remain nevertheless unclear) – demonstrate that he established a new model of jurist-teacher-intellectual.

It is perhaps in light of the relation between this new type of jurist and his auditors that the *sectae* or *scholae* of Cassiani (or Sabiniani) and Proculiani should be seen. These were two 'schools' that for about a century-and-a-half catalysed juristic teaching and antagonism. The two movements are named after Gaius Cassius Longinus, consul 30 CE (successor of Sabinus), and Proculus, consul in 37? CE. No attempt to explain the difference between these two legal schools in terms of methods or values has been fully persuasive.[100]

The increasing circulation of legal works facilitated access to Roman law by new social strata in search of a profitable profession. Petronius, writing in the late first century CE, reports a merchant's intention to buy legal books so that his son might study the law (*Satyricon* 46). One result of this push towards divulging legal instruction was the birth of a true isagogic literature. Around the middle of the second century CE, Gaius wrote the first manual – the *Institutiones* – that, thanks to a careful organization of the material, occupied for law the space that the *artes* already had in many other fields: a systematic exposition of a discipline.[101] As a further result of the growing demand for legal education, the middle of the second century CE saw the establishment of a new teaching model, in addition to the one practised by the leading jurists. Lawyers of minor appeal apparently stopped giving *responsa* and devoted themselves professionally to teaching. The fact that in the second and third centuries CE some of the major jurists came from the provinces (such as Julian from Africa, and Ulpian from Syria) strongly suggests that they received at least some legal education in their respective provinces, where there were teachers already active.[102] Such teachers are referred to in the third century CE by Modestinus (Justinian, *Digest* 27.1.6.12, *De excus.*). The *Constitutio Antoniniana* (212 CE) further extended Roman law

---

[100] For further discussion see Stein 1995. [101] Fuhrmann 1960. [102] Liebs 2002b: 5–6.

directly, or in dialectic with local law and practices.[103] Knowledge of Roman law subsequently became the most important viaticum for young people with great hopes, to recall the expression of Gregory Thaumaturgus' master (*In Origenem* 5.57–62). It was an indispensable skill to qualify for various attractive professions.[104] Traces of Roman law teaching are attested for Salona (third century CE); Smyrna (third century); Augustodunum (fourth century); Carthage (fourth century); Narbonne (fifth century); Lugdunum (fifth century); Caesarea in Palaestina (sixth century); and Alexandria (fifth to sixth century).[105] In addition to professors teaching individually, true centres of legal education were established: the main ones were in Berytus in Syria and of course in Rome. Though not so prestigious to its teachers, Constantinople was also home to a school that under Justinian became the other official educational centre in the Eastern Roman empire. We are informed about the contents of the fifth-century CE study plan in the East by the *Constitutio Omnem* of Justinian (533 CE).[106] It is notable that the bulk of the fifth-century legal instruction plan was still constituted by the writings of jurists from the second and third centuries CE.

Legal Literature

Across all the cultures considered here, legal practice was (more or less extensively) related to writing.[107] This is the case both for legal rules and for private legal documents. At the beginning of this chapter, we pointed out that the presence of written rules (statutes), in particular, is a key factor in the emergence of legal knowledge as a separate area of expertise. Documents of legal practice, especially contracts and testaments, also reveal knowledge of the law (when they are in accordance with the law in force). However, in what follows, we focus on a special category of texts: legal literature, texts produced by individuals who comment on laws, or gather precedents or express legal opinions. In these works, we might expect that reflection on law reached its highest level.

Beginning with the extant evidence from ancient China, we can identify two specific types of legal literature in the period from the Qin/Han to the

103 Humfress 2013.
104 The age at which studies were supposed to end was twenty-five years (Justinian, *Cod.* 10.50.1, 287 CE).
105 Liebs 2002b: 24.
106 See also Justinian, *Cod.* 2.7.22.4 (505 CE) and Justinian, *Cod.* 2.7.24.4 (517 CE) on the five-year study programme.
107 See also Chapter 2, this volume.

Tang: commentaries on the law and collections of cases (precedents). The earliest known authoritative legal commentary, in the form of 'questions and answers' on points of difficulty, forms part of the Qin laws of the third century BCE. It was possibly written by a scribe who was required to have a detailed knowledge of the law for the performance of his duties (see above). During the later Han dynasty (25–220 CE), numerous and conflicting commentaries appear to have been written on the statutes, but no details survive.[108] In order to prevent uncertainty in the application of the law, only the commentary of Zheng Xuan was permitted to be used during the (Three Kingdoms) Wei dynasty. However, new commentaries appeared in the succeeding Jin dynasty. Two particularly important commentaries were written as explanations of the Jin Code, one by Du You (see above) and the other by Zhang Fei, part of which was incorporated in the Treatise on Punishments contained in the *Jinshu* (History of the Jin dynasty).[109] These commentaries, although composed on imperial orders and so especially authoritative, do not seem to have possessed the same legal force as the code (*lü*) itself. In fact they might give diametrically opposed interpretations of the one legal rule. Officials applying the law were in a position to choose which interpretation they preferred. The same element of uncertainty that had characterised the Han interpretation and application of the law through the citation of divergent commentaries was reintroduced under the Jin. The Jin commentaries remained in use during the succeeding dynasties in the south. The edict of 502 CE, which ordered the drafting of the code for the Liang dynasty (502–57) specified inter alia that, if versions of the same rule were found in different commentaries, only one version was to be preserved. Commentaries here refer to those written during the Jin and even perhaps to Han ones.[110]

Private commentaries were discouraged under the Tang (for the officially sponsored *Shuyi* commentary see above). At the beginning of the dynasty, the vice president of the Supreme Court, Zhao Renben, wrote a small work for the benefit of officials applying the law, entitled *Fali* (Law and Precedents), which may also have included references to leading cases. The emperor, when his attention was drawn to this work, prohibited its continued use on the ground that, since the rules contained in the code had been inherited from the past and been deliberated upon many times by officials, there was no need for further commentary. However, it seems that, despite

---

108 Hulsewé 1955: 55. For the commentary written by Zheng Xuan, see above.
109 Heyde 1981; Wallacker 1986; and Bourgon 1999.   110 Balázs 1954: 35.

discouragement from the authorities, a few private works, including collections of cases, were in use during the Tang.[111] Finally, we should distinguish legal commentaries written with the specific purpose of elucidating the law from historical and ritual classics which might, at times, be utilized for the resolution of difficult legal cases. Dong Zhongshu, for example, was known for basing his decisions upon passages from the *Zuo zhuan* (Annals of the Spring and Autumn).[112]

We turn now to our second type of legal literature from the Qin/Han to the Tang periods: collections of cases (legal precedents). During the four centuries of the Han dynasty a number of collections of cases on doubtful points were compiled, probably with the expectation that they could be used as guides for future decisions. As with the legal commentaries, these collections might be officially sponsored or produced on their own authority by officials or scholars interested in the law. During excavations, the text of the laws of 186 BCE was found alongside the text of one such collection of cases entitled *Zouyanshu* (Referral of Doubtful Cases).[113] The collection comprises decisions on doubtful cases submitted to the highest legal authorities during the first years of the Han dynasty together with a few decisions from the pre-Han period. These precedents were not 'binding' in the sense that judges were bound by law to follow them in future cases, but they provided guidelines for the treatment of difficult cases that might arise later. The language of some cases from the *Zouyanshu* collection has led some scholars, however, to question whether these were truly officially authorized 'precedents' or perhaps were intended as more literary versions of legal texts which became increasingly popular during the later Tang and Song dynasties. Regardless of their intended function, recently published manuscript collections contain additional collections of legal cases and thus confirm that such collections circulated among officials at least as early as the second century BCE.[114]

We also have references in the sources to a number of other collections of various kinds of decisions compiled during the Han. Some, like the *Zouyanshu*, may have been officially authorized; others may have been compiled by officials acting in a private capacity.[115] We know that the high official Bao Yu in the latter part of the first century CE sponsored the publication of a collection of civil cases compiled by his subordinate Cheng Chung. Later, Bao Yu's own decisions were collected and published.[116]

[111] Bünger 1996: 58–61.   [112] Wallacker 1985: 59–72; Queen 1996.
[113] Lau and Lüdke 2012.   [114] Korolkov 2017.
[115] Hulsewé 1955: 55–56 gives a list of such collections.   [116] de Crespigny 2007: 14.

Legal Literature

Collections of cases on different aspects of the law were also probably published during the Tang.[117]

In the evidence for ancient India, the earliest literature to incorporate discussions of substantive and adjectival law are the treatises devoted to *dharma* called *Dharmaśāstra* (as already noted above). Written in aphoristic prose calle *sūtra,* the earliest of the extant texts of this genre, the *Dharmasūtra* of Āpastamba, is dated to about the middle of the third century BCE. Three other texts of the *sūtra* type date to the last couple of centuries BCE. The literary tradition of political science also had a strong interest in law. Kauṭilya's *Arthaśāstra* (first century CE) devotes its entire third book to substantive law and legal procedure.[118] In it we have the beginnings of the titles of law (*vyavahārapada*): namely, grounds under which a civil lawsuit can be filed with the court. It was the lawbook (*dharmaśāstra*) of Manu (second century CE), however, that incorporated both substantive and adjectival law into his treatise, borrowing heavily from the *Arthaśāstra*. It devotes two long chapters to legal procedure (*MDh* 8–9), and from that time the focus of legal science in India was legal procedure rather than substantive law. Within the context of legal procedure, Manu presents an eighteen-fold classification of the titles of law, or grounds under which a person is permitted to file a lawsuit. These eighteen will remain standard in later texts.

The next treatise is that of Yājñavalkya assigned to the fifth century CE. He devotes the second of his three chapters to legal procedure and develops a complex technical vocabulary. He is also the first to have a long section on documents, especially contracts for loans. This is the first time that we see clearly spelled out the elements required for a document to be legally valid, including the signatures of the parties, witnesses and the scribe. From the middle of the first millennium CE, we have at least three texts (*Nārada, Bṛhaspati* and *Kātyāyana*) that are totally devoted to legal procedure and take the discussions of this topic to a new level of sophistication. As Barth observed as early as 1876: 'If we except the monuments of Roman legislation, antiquity has not perhaps left us anything which is so strictly juridical.'[119]

Legal documents from the ancient Near East include contracts, trial records, boundary inscriptions, debt-release decrees, treaties and letters, but the most important literature for understanding the legal reasoning of the region comes in the law collections. Very few trial records disclose the reasoning of a court; two records: the so-called Nippur Homicide Trial and

---

[117] Bünger 1996.
[118] Olivelle 2013; McClish 2019b. Further discussion in Chapter 7, this volume.
[119] Cited in Lingat 1973: 102.

the trial of Jeremiah in the Hebrew Bible (Jer 26) appear to reflect debate among the members serving on judicial panels, but we have little else in this regard.[120] The law collections provide the best insight into how scribes thought about the law and how to organize it. They possess both a legal and a literary nature. Scholars have demonstrated that certain sequences of provisions in the Laws of Hammurabi, for example, follow literary considerations more than legal ones.[121] In contrast, however, three manuscripts of the Laws of Hammurabi, copied in the century following its initial publication, contain rubrics or headings that are more concerned with legal categories than literary features.[122]

The sources underlying the provisions in the law collections have provoked a great deal of scholarly discussion (see 'Introduction' above). The range of possible sources is diverse; royal pronouncements and judicial verdicts, for example, could well have given rise to some of the provisions. Provisions in earlier law compilations could have been adopted by scribes into later collections; the Laws of Hammurabi, for instance, may have drawn on parts of the Laws of Ur-Namma (c. 2100 BCE), the Laws of Lipit-Ishtar (c. 1930 BCE) and the Laws of Eshnunna (c. 1770 BCE). In addition, the scribes compiling these collections probably produced new provisions in various ways, possibly in an attempt to identify how their society's legal system could deal with new and unusual situations. The method and reasoning by which they produced such provisions are discussed further below. Other sources (including customary law, traditional lore, etc.) may have been influential as well.

As we have already seen, classical rabbinic literature is vast – no part more so than *halakha*. Much remains unknown about the transmission and preservation of *halakha*. Rabbinic sources claim that ancient legal traditions were handed down orally and by memorization to the Tannaim who recorded them in texts like the Mishnah. Later, this body of tradition was progressively expanded, resulting in the whole body of rabbinic *halakha*: Mishnah, *Tosefta*, Talmud and *Baraita*. *Halakhic* texts are composed in a number of languages and dialects, which speaks to the high literacy of the sages. Mishnaic Hebrew (the Hebrew dialect of the late antique rabbis), Amoraic Hebrew, Babylonian Aramaic and Galilean Aramaic are all represented extensively. In addition, rabbinic literature deploys a multitude of loanwords from still other languages, especially Greek and Latin.

---

[120] See Roth 1998 on the so-called Nippur Homicide Trial and Westbrook 2007 on the trial of Jeremiah.
[121] Bottéro 1992a: 156–84.   [122] Roth 2000: 19.

The Mishnah and *Tosefta* (plural = *Toseftot*) originated in Palestine of the tannaitic period and are written in Hebrew. The Mishnah (from Hebrew *shana* 'repeat' or 'learn'; *m. Avot* 3:7) is a legal compendium, produced in the second and third centuries CE, in Galilee, and ascribed by tradition to Yehuda ha-Nasi (*m. Avot* 2:2). It is called Mishnah because it is the 'second' law, in relation to the law of Moses recorded in the written Torah. The Mishnah is divided into six orders (*sĕdārîm*) that deal (roughly speaking) with gifts, sacred times, marriage, damages, holy items and purity. It is an anthology of legal traditions interposed with differing rabbinic opinions on their interpretation and application, opinions that are never reconciled. It is important to stress that the *Mishnah* of Yehuda ha-Nasi is the *Mishnah* promoted by the rabbinic sages. It seems likely that other collections of tannaitic law once existed.[123] Production of the Mishnah marks the end of the Tannaitic period and the dawn of the Amoraic. The *Toseftot* ('additions') are supplements to Mishnah. They include additional proofs for laws, interpretations, justifications, implications or applications and so forth. There is some dispute about the relationship of the *Toseftot* to the Mishnah; some think they predate the Mishnah and were deliberately omitted from it, whilst others think they are supplements to it. The *Tosefta* was redacted as a collection in the third century CE and is organized according to the structure of the Mishnah.[124]

The greatest works of rabbinic *halakha* are the Talmudim (singular *talmud*, 'study'). The Talmudim are compilations: Mishnah with *gemara* (Aramaic 'complete' or 'learn' – early sources sometimes use the terms *talmud* and *gemara* as synonyms). *Gemara* is interpretation and justification of Mishnaic *halakha* by the Amoraim, collected and edited by later anonymous redactors.[125] There are two Talmudim: the *Yarushalmi* ('Jerusalem' or 'Palestinian' Talmud) and the *Bavli* ('Babylonian' Talmud). Some portions of the Talmudim are written in Hebrew while others are in Aramaic. The Aramaic *sugyot* (sing. *sugya*), a pericope of *gemara*, are generally thought to be younger than the Hebrew. Like Mishnah, *gemara* record dissenting opinions and alternative applications of laws without reconciling them. The editors of the Talmudim are unknown.

The *Yarushalmi* follows the structure of the Mishnah, but it is incomplete. The *Yarushalmi* includes *gemara* for only thirty-nine of the Mishnah's sixty-three tractates (that is, the first four orders and part of the fifth). The reasons

---

123 Epstein 1964; Liebermann 1968.
124 Levine 1989, 23–42; Strack and Stemberger 1996: 150–63.   125 Halivni 1986: 76–92.

for these gaps are disputed. Some attribute the absence to editorial intent, some to accidents of transmission, and some think they never existed.[126] The *Yarushalmi's gemara* include much that is not *halakhic*: narrative extracts (*aggadah*), biblical interpretation and the like, and the work is less unified in its contents and arrangement than the *Bavli*. The *Bavli* is not complete either. It includes *gemara* for thirty-six-and-a-half of the sixty-three tractates of the Mishnah. The reasons that it is not complete are similarly disputed.[127] The *Bavli*, though, is more than twice the length of the *Yarushalmi*: some 2,700 folio pages in the Bomberg edition (dating to 1520–23). Both Talmudim include *baraitot*. A *baraita* (Aramaic 'outside') is a teaching that appears in one of the Talmudim and that is ascribed to a rabbi from the time of the Mishna (a *tanna*), but does not appear in the Mishnah. They are distinguished from the rest of *gemara* by their alleged antiquity.

The final category of *halakhic* literature is *midrash halakha*. The *midrashim* (from *darash* 'to seek') are commentaries on biblical texts, mostly from Palestine. They were written up to the eleventh century CE but have precursors as old as the Second Temple period (c. 400 BCE–70 CE).[128] *Midrash halakha* refers to the composite midrashic commentaries on the legal portions of the Torah of Moses. Though it comments on law, *midrash halakha* is not, properly speaking, legal literature in its own right. An interpretation from a midrash is not cited as an authoritative legal ruling, though it can be cited as a precedent. Also, the distinction between *halakhic* and *aggadic midrashim* is not a clean one. The *halakhic midrashim* are continuous commentaries: they comment on all portions of biblical books, not just the laws.[129]

As discussed in the 'Legal Experts' section above, ancient Greek cities – especially Athens – fostered 'a literary tradition of political science' that included systematic thought on law – comparable in some respects at least to the later ancient Indian tradition of Arthaśāstra. Given the fact, however, that legal specialists (beyond 'the lawgivers') were not recognized, to our knowledge, in any ancient Greek city – we cannot really speak of a separate category of what we might term ancient Greek 'legal literature' comparable to ancient Chinese, Indian, Rabbinic or Roman 'legal literature'. Nonetheless, as argued in the 'Introduction' above, the presence of written rules (statutes) is a key factor in the emergence of legal knowledge as a separate area of expertise. Whilst not developing a separate category of what we might term

---

126 Wewers 1984.   127 Kalmin 1989.   128 Fraade 1991: 1–23.
129 Kasher 1990: 547–94; Strack and Stemberger 1996: 247–75.

'legal literature', it nevertheless seems to have been normal for ancient Greek cities to inscribe laws and display them in locations accessible to people in general.[130] Solon's laws were displayed on the Athenian Acropolis or on the Areopagus hill, and when the Athenian law-code was revised at the end of the fifth century BCE the laws were written up in the Stoa Basileios in the Agora. What is probably the earliest surviving Greek law was written up on the wall of the Temple of Apollo at Dreros.[131] Our knowledge of the Gortyn laws derives entirely from their survival as inscribed documents, with the so-called Great Code, dating from the middle of the fifth century BCE, covering twelve full columns of text inscribed on a wall (Figure 3.1). If laws were displayed in public, did people in general read them? One fifth-century BCE law from Thasos explicitly rules out pleas of ignorance of the law from either citizens or foreigners – so certainly there is an expectation that the residents in a city

Figure 3.1 Gortyn code, inscription on stone slabs in Doric dialect, Gortyn, Crete, Greece, 5th century BCE. A. Dagli Orti, © NPL – DeA Picture Library / Bridgeman Images: number DGA2825551 (www.bridgemanimages.com/en/noartistknown/gortyn-code-inscription-on-stone-slabs-in-doric-dialect-gortyn-crete-greece-greek-civilization-5th/photo/asset/2825551)

---

130 Further discussion in Chapter 2, this volume.
131 Gagarin and Perlman 2016: 197–221.

make sure they know the local rules (unfortunately in this case we are not sure what the rule is about, but it is likely to be related to trade).[132] Athenian orators occasionally claim that they have gone and looked up a text (as in [Dem.] 47.71), or ask for a law to be read out 'from the stele'.[133]

As we have already argued, there can be no doubt that ancient Rome developed a separate category of legal literature. Yet it is worth stressing again, at the outset, that the activities of the Roman *iuris consultus* were in principle oral: a client submitted his case to the jurist and expected his *responsum*. Perhaps at the end of the fourth century BCE (with Justinian, *Digest* 1.2.2.36, Ap. Claudius Caecus) and certainly at the beginning of the second century BCE, Roman jurists began collecting and disseminating their intellectual work in writing. With the spread of territories under Roman rule, moreover, oral consultations and responses gradually turned to written form.[134]

The first written work, the *Tripertita* of Sextus Aelius Paetus (consul 198 BCE), was a commentary on the law of the Twelve Tables, accompanied by *formulae* of actions and transactions. The genre of the commentary runs through the entire history of Roman legal literature and takes on different subject matters, encompassing the marriage statutes of Augustus and various other *leges publicae* of private and criminal law; Roman Senate resolutions with normative force (*senatusconsulta*); and the edict of the praetor. The first to write a commentary on the edict of the praetor was Servius Sulpicius Rufus, consul 51 BCE, and the last, Iulius Paulus, prefect of the provisions in 223 CE.[135] Commentaries on writings by other jurists are also a characteristic of Roman legal literature: the same Servius Sulpicius Rufus can be considered a harbinger, who criticized the work of the most important jurist of the previous generation, Quintus Mucius Scaevola (*Reprehensa Scaevolae capita*). Commentaries on works of previous jurists grew in importance during the Roman Principate. We find, for example, commentaries again on the work of Quintus Mucius by Gaius and Sextus Pomponius in the second century CE, and on the work of Masurius Sabinus (first century CE) by Sextus Pomponius (second century CE), Domitius Ulpianus (died 223) and Iulius Paulus (third century CE). This attention to works of previous jurists indicates that they had become 'classics'. The same is the case for Papinian's writings (died 212), to whose works the jurists of the next generation – Ulpian and Paul – added annotations.

---

132 Osborne and Rhodes 2018: no.103A, line 9.
133 Andoc. 1.95, Lys. 1.30. Further discussion in Sickinger 1999: 160–76.
134 Mantovani 2018a.   135 Wibier 2014.

When not taking the form of commentaries, juristic works were primarily collections of resolved cases; each entry involved a brief description of the facts followed by the legal doctrine that the jurist considered appropriate, sometimes with a shorter or longer motivation. We will return to the method followed by jurists in resolving cases in more detail later, but for now we can note that jurists relied on the one hand on laws: *senatusconsulta*, edicts, imperial constitutions, and on the other hand on widely shared principles and rules, not issued by public powers, elaborated over the centuries by jurists themselves. One point needs to be clarified: in part, jurists recorded in their written work the answers they had given to clients. However, in many cases jurists took up cases from the book of another jurist, for which they also accepted that jurist's solution or for which they proposed a different solution (the practice of jurists handing down almost literally the same arguments is noted by Cicero, *De orat.* 1.192). The interrelation between jurisprudence and juristic literature is therefore indissoluble: the progress of the *ius* unfolded through a slow, but incessant, selective accumulation along the thread of written memory. Thanks to the literary record, discussions could take place in a distended present, from the second century BCE to the third century CE – a process comparable, in some respects, especially to our discussion of ancient Indian and rabbinic legal literature above. Obviously, the very fact that legal literature was a sort of colossal cross-temporal dialogue allowed the emergence of diverging views on how to resolve individual cases (*iura controversa*); when this happened within the Roman tradition, it was up to the judge to choose between the opinions on the table – sometimes freely, sometimes following criteria dictated by political power.

Between the second and third centuries CE, manuals arose that were addressed to magistrates and officials and intended to clarify their tasks (Figure 3.2). This genre developed from Republican-era forerunners: Varro, for example, instructed Pompey as a consul on the method of conducting meetings of the Senate and Lucius Cincius Alimentus wrote on the duties of jurists. The ten books on the duties of the provincial governor by Ulpian (*De officio proconsulis*) were particularly rich and successful. In certain cases, this literature was developed out of instructions that emperors issued to officials (and certain magistrates) at the beginning of their assignments (*mandata*).

As noted above, law was the last of the disciplines at Rome to have systematic manuals, organized according to the expository strategies of Hellenistic *technai*. Such handbooks only came into being in the time of the Antonines (138–193 CE), namely with Gaius' *Institutiones*, followed by other similar manuals up until the Severan Age (193–235 CE). The *Institutiones* of Aelius Marcianus, dating from the middle of the third century CE, are particularly important here: a fragment of

Legal Science

Figure 3.2 Relief portraying a magistrate sitting on a 'bisellium' and surrounded by lictors and figures, 3rd century CE, Baths of Diocletian. Rome, Museo Nazionale Romano.
A. Dagli Orti, © NPL – DeA Picture Library / Bridgeman Images: number DGA501225 (www.bridgemanimages.com/en/noartistknown/roman-civilization-relief-portraying-magistrate-sitting-on-bisellium-and-surrounded-by-lictors-and/nomedium/asset/501225)

a fourth-century copy on papyrus has recently been found.[136] However, while for the other disciplines the road to handbooks was a sort of ascension, as if such manuals embodied complete mastery of the subject matter, in the case of Roman law the systematic manual not only came late but also remained a product with the limited purposes of elementary and divulgatory didactics.

Having reached its maximum expansion at the beginning of the third century CE, due to multiple factors Roman juristic literature became exhausted and came to a standstill with Diocletian at the beginning of the fourth century (see above). However, this does not mean that the books of jurists or their contents disappeared. The jurists' writings continued to be copied and kept circulating in Late Antiquity, as is shown by numerous papyri and parchments, recently collected and edited.[137] The jurists' writings were also studied in schools and they were cited in the courts. When Justinian decided to reorganize the law in the sixth century, he devoted the largest of his three legal collections, the *Digest*, to the ancient literature of the jurists – a sign that it remained the fundamental structure of law even after the production of new works had ceased. To get an idea of the vastness of juristic literature, a catalogue put in front of the *Digest* lists thirty-eight 'ancient authors' and their works that were mined for the compilation of the *Digest* itself, which Justinian reckons amounted to almost two thousand books.

---

136 Fressura and Mantovani 2018.
137 *Redhis* project: see 'Digital Corpus of Literary Papyri online'.

Turning now to imperial constitutions, imperial pronouncements with normative value began with Augustus and increased dramatically in number from the age of Hadrian (second century CE). the imperial chancery itself circulated these constitutions in various forms: sometimes in epistolary form, if addressed to individual recipients; sometimes posted in public, as is the case for edicts. In the second century CE, jurists began to incorporate imperial constitutions into their books. As such they acquired a relatively wide circulation, even in cases where the constitutions were originally meant to apply to a specific case, such as for rescripts (that is responses given by the emperor to an individual or a community or a magistrate who had addressed him with a specific question). The growing importance of constitutions and their increasing number created a need for collections. Already under Marcus Aurelius we find the use of 'semestral' collections (Justinian *Digest*, 29.2.12 and Justinian, *Inst.* 1.25.1), on which the jurist Papirius Iustus may have based a collection in twenty books. Two collections made under Diocletian had great success: the *Codex Gregorianus* (perhaps 291–4 CE), and the *Codex Hermogenianus* (perhaps 293–4), which assembled rescripts from Hadrian onward. 'General laws' (*generales leges*) were officially collected by the emperor Theodosius II (438 CE) and by Justinian (529; second edition 534 CE).

Legal Reasoning

Any legal operation requires reasoning: writing a law, issuing a judgment, drafting a contract or a will, commenting on a law, giving an opinion on how to resolve a case, even considering how to change the law in force. A comparison between ancient legal traditions in this respect must take into account the differences of roles highlighted above and the varying availability of sources. Thus, for example, whilst in Rome private legal experts (jurists) played a crucial role in the functioning of the legal system, this does not mean that reflections on law only developed in Rome – as we have seen already across the ancient Chinese, Indian, rabbinic and to a lesser extent earlier Near Eastern and Greek textual evidence. Any comparison must then take into account the state of the documentation: the work of jurists is richly documented for China and Rome; for the ancient Near East we have extensive documentation of legal transactions (e.g. contracts), which instead is rather poor for Rome. The law collections that are extant for the ancient Near East could, in turn, be seen as the product of a reflection based on law in action. It is therefore always necessary to be aware that different evidential records may suggest differences between different cultures, and (vast) time periods, that historically did not exist.

Chinese law as a system of penal statutes and administrative regulations was essentially 'statute based' and not 'case based'. This meant that when a magistrate or other official with the responsibility for hearing a case was faced with a person accused of an offence, he went through the following steps in his investigation: first, through a series of interrogations of the relevant parties and witnesses, the magistrate gradually ascertained the facts of the case. In order to obtain what he suspected to be the truth, when confronted with inconsistencies in the statements of the parties, he might as a last resort use torture to compel a confession. For the Qin/Han period and later, there is no evidence of the use of oaths in the evaluation of the evidence or ordeals in the determination of guilt. During the Warring States some states, such as Chu, are known to have required parties and witnesses to confirm the truth of their statements by means of a meng oath, in which the gods were called upon to punish a perjurer.[138] Second, the ascertainment of the facts permitted the judge to identify the statutes which might be relevant to the determination of the case. The final stage was the identification of which of the possibly relevant statutes precisely covered the facts as disclosed by the interrogation, followed by the application of the punishments prescribed by these statutes. More than one offence may have been committed by the accused, or others involved in the trial may have been found to have committed offences. Punishments again were assigned according to the statutory rules.[139]

The technical term used to express the application of the relevant statute(s) to the facts of the case is *dang*. Prima facie *dang* means 'ought' and carries the implication that the facts of the case 'match' the statutory description of the offence and therefore entail the application of the punishment prescribed for that offence. However, it has also been argued that in Qin/Han law *dang* bears a more technical sense in situations where the facts did not disclose a straightforward commission of an offence. Where complicating factors were involved, the court had to weigh up the various factors and then calculate the punishment according to the appropriate tariffs. This process of weighing up and calculating fell within the meaning of *dang*.[140]

The resolution of 'civil cases', those involving disputes over inheritances, marriages, debts, etc., proceeded on a different basis, though even here,

---

138 Weld 2003: 160–67.
139 For the process of decision making in the Han, see Brown and Sanft 2011.
140 Liu 1998: 268, 279–84.

where a statute was in point, it was identified and applied. What was crucial in such cases was the production of the written instrument, such as the will or contract, upon which the plaintiff relied. Without the production of this kind of written evidence, the case could not be heard. What controlled the final resolution of the case by the 'presiding' official was the precise terms of the will or contract.

The use of analogy deserves a special mention. The Tang Code in its general principles has an article (50) designed to deal with the case in which the judge is faced with an offence for which no formal law can be found. In such cases punishment is to be imposed by analogy. Article 50 states: 'All cases involving sentencing of crimes that have no formal article bring up a heavier offence in order to make clear a lighter punishment if the punishment should be decreased. If the punishment should be increased, then a lighter offence is brought up to make a heavier punishment.'[141] The *shuyi* commentary illustrates the first proposition with the example of theft. Theft between relatives was punished specifically under the code less severely than theft committed between ordinary persons, but nothing is said about fraud or cheating between relatives. By analogy the obtaining of property in this way from a relative is also to receive a decreased punishment. The second proposition is illustrated from the law of *mousha* (plotting to kill). A mere plot to kill a close senior relative was punished by decapitation. Although nothing was said in the law about the case in which the relative was actually killed or just wounded, the same punishment (by analogy) was to apply.

An explanation of legal reasoning must take into account also the way in which the drafters of statutes did employ technical legal language in the construction of laws (see also the note on *dang* above). A good example is supplied by the phrase *tongfa* ('same law as').[142] This phrase was used as a kind of shorthand to indicate that the offence in question should be treated and punished in the same way as another (stipulated) offence. An illustration is supplied by the early rules on theft contained in the Qin laws of the third century BCE. The Qin legal texts on the liability of a person, whether an official or a private individual, who had wrongfully appropriated government property reveal two approaches. One is to hold that the offence is to be punished 'by the same law as theft' (*yu dao tong fa*), the other is to treat the offence as 'being theft' (*wei dao*). Thus, the appropriation (consumption) of military rations to which one was not entitled constituted theft (*wei dao*).[143]

---

141 Johnson 1979 : 254–56.
142 Brown and Sanft 2011 prefer to translate *fa* in this context as 'legal category'.
143 Hulsewé 1955: 163 (D132).

Ordinary persons who absconded with tools or arms that had been lent to them by the government, when subsequently caught, were to be made liable on the ground of theft (*wei dao*) according to the value of the property.[144] On the other hand, the statutes provided that, where the official in charge of a government storehouse concealed shortages in the grain or other goods stored there, the case was to be treated in the same way as theft (*yu dao tong fa*). The same formula is used to describe the liability of officials who privately borrow money stored in the treasury of a commandery.[145] One can see the difference between the two classes of case. Where the offence is denominated *wei dao*, we have a case of direct and unlawful appropriation of property belonging to the government, even though, as in the example of the borrowed arms or tools, the thief might initially have had a right to the possession of the property. But to conceal shortages of grain in a warehouse under one's jurisdiction or to borrow money from the treasury, which one intends to return, is to commit an act falling short of direct and unlawful appropriation of government property. Hence, these offences are punished not as theft but as offences analogous to theft. The law of theft is to apply in the sense that the offender is punished according to the value of what he has concealed or borrowed.

    Another point that may be relevant here is the construction of the ancient codes themselves, before the issuing of the Tang Code (and its revisions). This shows a gradual evolution in two important respects. In the first place, the administrative rules, initially included in the same collection of statutes as the penal rules, come to be separated and published independently as collections of ordinances (*ling*). The principal distinction is that, unlike the penal statutes, they did not specify punishments for offences but simply defined the duties of officials or other persons. In the second place, the combination in the collections of laws of 'general principles' and 'specific offences' was refined. In the Han collection of laws from 186 BCE, for example, some rules which set out the general criteria governing or qualifying the application of the specific rules detailing punishments for offences (such as the rules on the privileges or collective liability of officials) are contained in a section which follows the two sections of specific rules dealing with violence and theft. By contrast, in the Tang Code (seventh century CE) we have a much more fully worked out set of 'general principles' placed at the head of the code before the various sections detailing the specific offences.

---

144 Hulsewé 1955: 157 (D109).   145 Hulsewé 1955: 129 (D26).

In the absence of jurists acting as experts – at least in the strict sense defined in relation to the Roman jurists above – Indian legal reasoning can be grasped from the activity, instructions and self-representation of judges. The Indian judge was not viewed simply as a referee between the two litigating parties but also as a magistrate who was seeking the truth in the case brought before the court. Manu uses the metaphor of a hunt to elucidate the function of a judge: 'As a hunter traces the location of an animal by the trail of blood, so a king should trace the location of justice by deductive reasoning. When he is conducting a judicial proceeding, he should pay close attention to the truth, the object of the suit, himself, the witnesses, the place, the time, and the appearance' (MDh 8.44–45). Prior to the presentation of evidence, the court thus has to decide which party has the burden of proof. It depends on the kind of plea entered by the defendant. In the case of denial, the burden falls on the plaintiff. If other kinds of pleas are entered, such as a special plea (for example, an acknowledgement of the plaint – such as 'they took out the loan' – but pointing to the special fact that the loan has already been paid back), then the burden may fall on the defendant (in our example, this would be to prove that the loan has been paid back).

The phase of court proceedings when evidence is presented is followed by the court's assessment of the testimony and other evidence.[146] If different kinds of evidence referring to different time periods are produced, the texts give a rule with regard to which has great force. Yājñavalkya states: 'In all litigations, evidence relating to a later transaction has greater force; in the case of a pledge, gift, or purchase, however, evidence relating to an earlier transaction has greater force.'[147] Judicial deliberation is often called by the technical term *yukti*. Texts present clues that indicate whether witnesses are telling truth or documents are authentic or forged. Manu notes with regard to witnesses: 'He [the judge] should discover the internal disposition of men by external signs – voice, colour, expression, bearing, eyes, and gestures. Inner thoughts are discerned by the bearing, expressions, gait, gestures, and manner of speaking, and by changes in the eyes and face' (MDh 8.25–26). Documents can be forged: 'In order to authenticate a dubious point, one should look at a writing sample from the man's own hand or resort to reasoning, implication, evidence, peculiar marks, connection, title, and inference' (YDh, 2.95). 'Marks' refers to unique symbols that may be on the document, and 'connection' to the previous dealings that the creditor and debtor may have had. The court deliberations were conducted by the chief

---

146 See Chapter 7, this volume.   147 YDh 2.23 (trans. Patrick Olivelle).

judge (or king) and his three legal experts or assessors (*sabhya*). The legal reasoning behind the deliberations was intended to lead to a just verdict, which was then announced in open court.

As noted above, it is difficult to identify the precise nature of the extant law collections from the ancient Near East.[148] The provisions in the collections may well have derived from a variety of sources, and the codes, as we have them today, certainly contain legal content but – as for all our comparable ancient evidence, albeit to differing extents – they exhibit literary features as well. Hence the way in which this literature was produced and the methods utilized by scribes to organize and expand on the law at their disposal constitute the main focus of discussions concerning legal science and reasoning in the ancient Near East.

The major law codes or collections are essentially lists of legal problems or issues and their corresponding resolutions: for example, the Laws of Ḥammurabi state: 'If a man [*awīlu*] should blind the eye of another man [*awīlu*], they shall blind his eye' (196).[149] These lists are similar in structure and format to lists that collected, organized and expanded on other types of knowledge, such as lists of omens and their interpretations and lists of medical symptoms and their diagnoses.[150] There are also important differences, but these lists appear to be the result of scribal efforts (perhaps initiated by a ruling king) to collect and organize important knowledge within particular areas of culture. The exact methods behind these efforts are never discussed in the extant texts; we can, though, infer aspects of them. The omen lists may be illustrative in this regard. A provision in such a list was likely derived and then put to use as follows: (1) some phenomenon takes place that is interpreted by a divination expert; (2) the phenomenon is recorded in writing, but all names of those involved are removed – i.e. the event is depersonalized; (3) the occurrence and its interpretation are placed into the format of a casuistic statement; (4) this and other occurrences, along with some hypothesized variations on them (for example, if the phenomenon had occurred under slightly different circumstances), are compiled together into a list of casuistic statements; (5) the list is maintained for future reference by divination experts and supplemented as necessary.[151]

It is likely that many, though certainly not all, of the provisions in the ancient Near Eastern law codes or collections developed in a comparable manner. Legal problems arose that were resolved by kings and others

---

148 See Roth 1997.   149 Trans. Roth 1997.
150 Bottéro 1992a; Van De Mieroop 2015: 143–81.   151 Magdalene 2011: 44–45.

granted judicial authority (judges, local officials, town elders, etc.). The problems and their solutions were depersonalized, written down in casuistic form, and then compiled into lists. The evidence for the law collections developing in this way is much less clear than that for the omen lists. Nevertheless, narratives from the Hebrew Bible appear to depict just this sort of process for the creation of legal provisions.[152] In Numbers 9:6–14, for example, a problem arises that involves individuals who want to observe a holy feast but are unable to because of the ritual impurity that they have contracted. Moses consults the deity, Yahweh, who issues a depersonalized, casuistically formulated ruling, which becomes part of a short list that contains variations on the original problem. In Leviticus 24:10–22, a similar process is described, with the additional indication that a pre-existing law code (that of Exod 21:23–25) seems to have been consulted, excerpted and included as part of the resulting list. While kings and other authorities in the ancient Near East may have put these lists into use for legal purposes, they also employed them in other ways. With the Laws of Ur-Namma, the Laws of Lipit-Ishtar and the Laws of Ḥammurabi, for example, their publication was to extol the king and demonstrate to the gods and all others the justice of his rule.[153]

It is fairly evident that the scribes who compiled the lists composed provisions in addition to those that derived from rulings in specific situations. To begin with, the status of the central figure in a provision might be altered to create a new provision. What should the solution be, for example, if the person injured is not a citizen but a slave (Laws of Eshnunna 55; Laws of Ḥammurabi 252; Exod 21:32)? What should be done if the woman involved in the tryst was neither married nor betrothed (Middle Assyrian Laws 55; Deut 22:28–29)? Scribes also incorporated boundary cases. These were cases that formed the opposite ends of a given scenario as a way of implying how all of the situations that fall within these two extremes might be handled, for example consensual adultery involving a fully married woman in one case and forced sex with a betrothed woman in another (Laws of Ḥammurabi 129–30). There are also cases that show up in multiple law collections (for example, goring bulls, pregnant women who are struck and miscarry) and may have been part of the standard scribal curriculum.[154] Scribes may well have created other provisions to explore how the law would handle new and unusual situations.

The law collections in the Hebrew Bible present a further insight into the nature and development of legal literature. There are indications that the

---

152 Westbrook 1985.   153 Finkelstein 1961.   154 Westbrook 1985.

authors of later biblical collections knew and were, in some measure, responding to (not simply duplicating) earlier collections. The authors of the Deuteronomic Code in Deuteronomy 12–26, for instance, seem to have reworked parts of the Covenant Code from Exodus 20:2–23:33.[155] Biblical scholars disagree as to whether the goal was to overturn and supersede the older collection or to adapt it to a new set of circumstances. What stands out about some biblical provisions is the inclusion of second-person forms, an unusual feature among ancient Near Eastern law collections. Some provisions combine both second-person and third-person grammatical forms, and, in certain cases, it appears to be the use of the second person that marks free composition on the part of the scribal author, while the third-person forms signal the utilization of material from a previous collection.[156]

Rabbinic and Second Temple legal argumentation is critically concerned with the expansion of the laws of the written Torah to accommodate any legal question or circumstance. The fact that the laws in the Torah of Moses are selective did not pose an insurmountable problem. *Halakhic* argumentation is predicated on a belief that the laws of the Torah, being divine, are not limited by their explicit content, that they possess a certain plasticity, a capacity to speak to issues that lie outside the sphere of their explicit content.[157] Note the importance placed on the idea that the Torah is eternal and heavenly in, for example, *m. Sanh.* 10:1 and *b. Sanh.* 99a. From this, it is easy to see why rabbis did not create a uniquely 'legal' form of argumentation or reasoning. Instead, they developed a hermeneutic that both permitted and controlled the (re-)application of Torah to new legal questions. These same principles were then employed in the creation of new law, based on previous rabbinic precedents. Four important clarifications, however, are required here. First, although the rabbis at times employed a protean hermeneutical vocabulary in the form of the *middot* (interpretative principles), this quasi-technical language was not used systematically or consistently, nor was it employed exclusively for legal texts or legal arguments.[158] Second, at times medieval rabbis did enquire about the 'essence of halakhic and legal principles', including questions concerning human nature and social relationships, but this operated only peripherally: the conduit through which a rule entered the rabbinic legal system was interpretation.[159] Third, it is important to recognize that the application of rabbinic hermeneutics was not limited to

---

[155] Levinson 1997.   [156] Stackert 2007: 38–47.
[157] M. 'Avot 5:22 and m. 'Avot 3:14. Kasher 1990: 548–50.
[158] Bacher 1905; Strack and Stemberger 1996: 16–30; Samely 2002: 26–28.
[159] Elon 1994: 137–41, 987–1014.

the legal sphere but is evident whenever the rabbis engage with religious texts. Finally, rabbinic hermeneutical procedures are not uniquely or exclusively rabbinic. They have important precursors in Second Temple period literature, in the Hebrew Bible and in ancient Near Eastern literature more generally.[160]

Rabbinic hermeneutical assumptions were never fully articulated (for example, b. Sanh. 34a, b. Sotah 3a). They must be inferred from examples of rabbinic exegesis.[161] The most important inference is that rabbinic hermeneutics is co-extensive with rabbinic claims about the nature of scripture, including the assumption, described above, that the written Torah possesses the power to speak to any legal question. Because every *halakhic* ruling, particularly in the Mishnah and Talmudim, must ultimately be based on some scriptural warrant, rabbinic interpretation was committed to the notion that scripture is full of meaning. That is, the substance of a scriptural locution cannot be reduced to the semantic cargo of its individual words. Individual words, phrases and clauses may be freighted with implications, with referential deixis and with hidden meaning (in the form of codes like *atbash, haphak, gematria* and *notarikon*). At the same time, the rabbis also believed scripture to be cohesive and coherent. Contradictions, tensions and inconsistencies are not admitted: in the eyes of the rabbis, scripture is perfect in its design and its content (whereas human interpretation is not).[162] Applying these principles to legal interpretation was a complex affair.

Rabbinic legal interpretation was neither unchanging nor uniform. Since, it was not mechanical, no summary could be sufficient. We can highlight six features of rabbinic legal interpretation that we take to be common, but they are neither universal nor comprehensive. Neither are they exclusive of one another. Rather, they impinge on one another in important ways:

(1) Every grapheme in scripture was taken to be meaningful and not just in a particular syntactic configuration. The configuration evident in scripture – as paragraphs, verses, clauses, phrases and words – was not the only possible or permitted configuration. The rabbis granted themselves license to re-divide syntactic units and individual words into smaller ones, and to treat them as if they stood alone, apart from the syntactic or literary context in which they were first encountered.[163]

---

160 Fraade 1998; Bernstein and Koyfman 2005.   161 Alexander 1984.
162 Goldberg 1987; Samely 1991; 1992; Fraenkel 1991: 11–12; Gvaryahu 2017.
163 Samely 1999; 2002: 31–58.

(2) Naturally, the rabbis did not follow the canons of modern philology and semantics when assigning meaning to words. Assigning meaning to a word in a specific literary context was not constrained by that context (based on feature 1). The interpreter could choose from the full range of semantic possibilities for any word, regulated only by its employment elsewhere in scripture. This was true even if the word happened to be part of a collocation or a bound syntactic unit (e.g. a construct phrase). In addition, new meanings could be suggested based on the word's similarity to other words (e.g. two out of three root letters being the same; exchange of letters of similar sound; exchange of letters of similar shape; reversing the order of the letters). In addition, the choice of a particular word in scripture could be interpreted as excluding other words.[164]

(3) Analogy is a basic principle of rabbinic legal interpretation and key to the power of interpretation to both expand scriptural law and create new law. A specific case could be associated by analogy with another specific case. The cases do not need to be linked by shared topics or vocabulary, though they often are. They might be linked by a similar reward or punishment, by a greater-to-lesser relationship (if x is true for greater person y, x must be true lesser person z), by a lesser-to-greater relationship, by a common-status relationship (e.g. what is true of a woman is true of a child), by the equal consequence of two infractions, or by the proximity of two laws in scripture, to name a few possibilities.[165]

(4) Rabbinic legal interpretation often moves from a specific biblical law (or a portion of a law) to more general application of that law. A host of techniques are employed to accomplish this, some of which are also employed in analogical arguments. The following are a few examples. Biblical laws that appear to be unrelated to one another can be brought into a new configuration based on shared vocabulary or synonyms or topics. Laws might be treated as metaphors (e.g. Deut 22:9–11) or as exemplary of a wider category which can then be defined by the interpreter. Terms like 'all' and distributives like 'each man' legitimated widening a law's application to additional persons or situations. Negatives could be interpreted similarly. Lists as short as two items were seen as tolerant of additions.[166]

(5) One of the most obvious poetic features of the Hebrew Bible is its relentless use of repetition. It is not just sounds and words that are

---

164 Yadin 2004; Teeter 2014; Samely 1990; 1995; 1999; 2000.
165 Alexander 1984; Hirschfeld 1840.
166 Strack and Stemberger 1996: 18–20; Samely 2002: 226–52.

repeated. So too are laws, stories, poems, oracles, arguments and plotlines. Small-scale repetitions (individual words, phrases and clauses) are a particular focus of rabbinic interpretation. Under the principle that nothing in scripture is superfluous, repeated words were assumed to provide new information of one kind or another. Usually, any iteration of a word or phrase after the first was interpreted as referring to a different topic, referent, event or action (though techniques noted in feature 2 above could also be used to eliminate any apparent redundancy).[167]

(6) Most of the Hebrew Bible is not law, and the rabbis do draw *halakha* from narrative texts. This is authorized, in their view, by the close connection between laws and many of the stories in the Hebrew Bible (e.g. Gen 38 and Levirate, Nehemiah and Sabbath law). Some characters are viewed in an idealized way, and all their actions – divorced from the situational context of the biblical storyline – are treated as normative (e.g. Abraham). For others, only specific actions establish a precedent (e.g. David). This is just one reading-consequence of the rabbinic assumption that all scripture possesses abiding relevance.

In one way or another, each of these six features was an important rabbinical technique for expanding the capacity of a scriptural law to speak to new situations or circumstances.

We can uncover broadly comparable complexities in reasoning relating to legal matters within ancient Athenian political and rhetorical literature in particular. Aristotle's *Rhetoric*, for example, divides proofs in court between 'artful' and 'artless'; the former depend on argument alone, the latter on external documents – evidence from witnesses, challenges to torture, contracts and (mentioned in a later passage) laws and oaths.[168] In fact 'artless' proofs were far from 'artless' since witness statements and challenges to torture were open to being carefully phrased to yield the sense required, and speakers could order the claims they made in such a way as to ensure that it was the claim that was supported by artless proofs that came last and appeared to substantiate the whole case.[169] There seems to be a general story to be told of the way in which legal arguments developed in late fifth-century BCE Athens from relying on 'artless proofs' to relying on 'artful proofs', in particular arguments from probability.[170] Scholars have also proposed other types of ancient Athenian shifts from 'the irrational' to 'the rational': for example, the earliest homicide trials tend to display pre-rational,

---

[167] Heinemann 1970; Samely 2002: 328–58. [168] Janko 1987: 170. [169] Carey 1994.
[170] So Carey 1994: 96.

formalistic argument, whereas homicide cases heard by the Areopagus, in particular, display a close attention to the central legal requirement to prove that the homicide was intentional.[171] Arguments in other courts may be less closely focused on the case in hand and may cite laws other than the law under which the case is brought (so Dem. 54.24, a case of 'battery', *aikeia*, which cites the laws on hubris and on clothes-stealing, but not the law on battery). The argument here is not irrational, but it is not closely focused on the (statute) law.

This kind of relatively undeveloped legal argumentation seems to be linked to the unwillingness of juries to concentrate solely on issues of breaches of the law. Even in cases which were introduced to show that the lawsuit being brought against the speaker was illegal, the discussion ranges well beyond the issue of legality to raise the issues in the original dispute.[172] Other speeches frequently point out breaches of legal technicalities but do not use them to insist that a case is thrown out, merely as more evidence against the opponent (cf. [Dem.] 42.1–4, Dem. 36.25). Aristotle's *Rhetoric* discusses the potential clash between fairness and following the letter of the law, and suggests that 'the arbitrator sees what is fair, but the jury looks to the law', while at the same time stating that it is fair 'to look not to the law but to the legislator, and not to the word but to the intent of the legislator' (Arist. *Rhetoric* 1.13.13–19). Lysias urged a jury to 'have the same mind in passing judgement as in legislating' (fr. 87).[173]

As a confirmation of the assessment often repeated in the present chapter, that legal reasoning can be detected in a variety of legal operations, it is worth reviewing ancient Athenian procedures involved in replacing a law. As laid out in Demosthenes 24 *Against Timocrates*, which is itself a speech brought under the procedure for objecting to laws – the 'writ against an inexpedient law' (*graphe nomon mê epitêdeion theinai*) – the Assembly had to start the process by agreeing to allow a new proposal and then the new proposal had to be displayed in public and any existing contradictory law had to be repealed.[174] The Assembly constituted themselves as *nomothetai* and appointed champions to argue the case for the existing law. In the two relevant Demosthenes cases that we have, Demosthenes both claims technical breaches in procedure in the ways the laws in question have been brought and tries to show inconsistency between the new law and existing laws.[175] There are some signs that, as well as providing a potential field day for

---

171 Lanni 2006: 87–96.   172 Lanni 2006: 67. For a different view, see Harris 2018a.
173 On fairness see further Harris 2013b.   174 Canevaro 2013; see also Canevaro 2016.
175 Dem. 24 *Against Timocrates* 17–19.24–5 and Dem. 20 *Against Leptines* 89–94.

those who wished to oppose a new law, the idea that laws should contain no contradictions was repeatedly espoused by the Athenians in the fourth century.[176] None of those involved in this procedure was a legal expert – those proposing laws were self-appointed, those responsible for defending old laws had no special qualification.

The modus operandi of the Roman jurists is often called 'casuistic': they expressed their opinions as responses to consultations by private individuals or by magistrates (whom the jurists were counselling). Those seeking the consultation were expected to lay out a set of facts, i.e. 'the case', and they expected, in turn, to hear from the expert 'what is the law'. If the adjective 'casuistic' adequately describes juristic activity when viewed 'from the outside', it is a rather empty term in relation to its methodology. Hence, it is necessary to explore how the Roman jurists came to the solutions for the cases that were put before them.

Before offering a detailed description of juristic reasoning, it is instructive to read by way of example a response by Quintus Cervidius Scaevola. In the second half of the second century CE, this jurist was practising intensely as a private consultant (with queries reaching him from all the provinces). At the same time, he was also engaged in the service of the empire: he was counsellor to Marcus Aurelius and a *praefectus vigilum*, i.e. chief of firemen and city police in Rome. For this specific case, the question and the response are preserved in his *libri responsorum*, a sort of repertory, probably edited by a student after his death[177]:

> Someone has purchased a house from the guardian of a ward and, for the purpose of renovation, has brought in a carpenter. This one found money there. It is asked to whom the money belongs. I answered: if it was not treasure-trove, but it was for example money that was lost or mistakenly not removed by the one to whom it belonged, then it was still the property of the erstwhile owner.[178]

Scaevola formulates his solution at the end of an argumentative chain; though only partially explicit, it can be fully reconstructed, helping us understand the juristic method 'from within'. First of all, there is a need to qualify the money that was found in the house, whether or not it is 'treasure-trove'. In order to do so, Scaevola tacitly refers to a long-established

---

176 Dem. 20.91, Aeschin. 3.38–40.   177 Talamanca 2000–2001.
178 Justinian, *Digest* 6.1.67 (Scaevola, 1 resp.): *A tutore pupilli domum mercatus ad eius refectionem fabrum induxit: is pecuniam invenit: quaeritur ad quem pertineat. respondi, si non thensauri fuerunt, sed pecunia forte perdita vel per errorem ab eo ad quem pertinebat non ablata, nihilo minus eius eam esse, cuius fuerat* (trans. Dario Mantovani).

definition of treasure, that jurists themselves had drafted: 'an ancient deposit of money, of which no memory exists, so that it has no present owner'.[179] At this point, the answer takes two alternatives into consideration. On the one hand, it is possible that, in light of the definition, the rediscovered money should be considered as 'treasure trove' – for example, a coin hoard hidden decades ago by an unknown person inside a wall now torn down by the craftsman. If this is so, the money belongs to the new owner of the house (and the workman, depending on the circumstances, may claim half of it). We should note that Scaevola does not say all this; it would have been redundant. It was enough to evoke the word *thesaurus*: the legal regulations that governed it were well known, and they were not controversial having set by a constitution of the emperor Hadrian: if treasure was found on a person's own land, he was entitled to keep it; if found on another person's land, half went to the finder and half to the owner of the land (see Justinian, *Inst.* 2.1.39). Therefore, according to this first alternative, the Roman jurist found himself in a situation not very different from a system of codified law.

Scaevola developed the second alternative in more detail, namely that the money is not 'treasure trove', but simply money lost by one of the house's inhabitants who had either forgotten its location or had forgotten to take it away when they vacated the house (of course, whoever claims to have left money in their home must give evidence for that in court: this also is a fundamental principle of Roman procedure that Scaevola does not have to stress explicitly). Unlike for 'treasure trove', no rules set by a legislator existed for lost money. It is therefore worth considering how Scaevola comes to his solution, namely that the money is the property of the person who forgot it in the house, not of the buyer. Apart from taking the definition of *thesaurus* as a (negative) starting point, his response is based on a series of undisputed legal principles, which are brought up by jurists in very diverse contexts. These were indeed veritable 'rules' (*regulae*), felt as binding, even if not established by statutes or by other enacted laws. First of all, movable goods (such as money) do not become part of real property (such as a house), i.e. such goods do not automatically become the property of the owner of the real property (to give a further example, a wild animal sitting in a tree does not become the property of the landowner). Next, for a found object to become the property of the person who takes possession – in our case here, the workman – the thing must have been voluntarily abandoned by its owner. Since in Scaevola's examples this had not happened, there was no

---

179 Justinian, *Digest* 41.1.31.1 (Paulus, 31 *ad edictum*).

legal basis for the workman to become the owner. Another line of reasoning in Scaevola is as follows: in addition to the main object (the house), the sale contract may sometimes include other things contained in the property (for example, furnishings) if the parties agree on this. In this case, the jurist (implicitly) excludes that the parties intended, though tacitly, that the money was part of the sale. Finally, it should be noted that in the question submitted to Scaevola the house had been sold by the guardian of a ward. The jurist does not mention this aspect in his response. This was superfluous, since the sale of urban property by a guardian was allowed (in principle). Scaevola's response is therefore the result of an argumentative chain that makes his 'opinion' rational, open to review and reproducible, and as such applicable to other, similar cases.

Scaevola's narration of the facts in the passage quoted above also requires some additional observations: 'Someone has purchased a house from the guardian of a ward and, for the purpose of renovation, has brought in a carpenter. This one found money there.' The narration only contains the bare essence, without any superfluous details or literary intentions. Yet we are dealing with a definite, specific situation. Applying Scaevola's response to another case of finding money in a sold house thus requires prudence. In fact, even slight differences in the facts may require rethinking the argumentative pathway and may produce a different solution. In short, case and response are, so to say, inseparable, forged by the jurist as perfectly matching parts. Therefore, it is very difficult to use Roman juristic texts to resolve a problem arising from facts that they did not explicitly take into consideration (these were difficulties that faced, for example, medieval jurists and still face students of Roman law today who are asked by their professor to find the solution that a Roman jurist would have given to cases elaborated ex novo).

Another aspect of the jurist's relationship with facts must be emphasized. As can be seen from the text, Scaevola does not take a stand on the actual nature of the found money, whether or not it is 'treasure trove' (according to the legal definition). It was the task of the judge to ascertain that. Scaevola's response is made purely about the law and proposes both alternatives. It was the task of the parties to prove to the judge that the facts were in their favour. Similarly, note that Scaevola does not state that (in the case of lost money) the money belongs 'to the ward', as we might expect, but uses a wider periphrasis ('belongs to him who already owned it'). In fact, the money could belong to someone else who had visited the house and left it there (for example, the guardian). The anatomy of Scaevola's response shows in what sense one can speak of a 'method of the Roman jurists', that is, a procedure that follows argumentative rules and is based on shared values.

There is no modern, encompassing and formal, description of the method of the Roman jurists based on a systematic study of their decisions. There are studies on individual texts and (especially from the twentieth century) on the *rationes decidendi*. However, there is no coherent scholarly analysis, and so the idea is still prevalent that the jurists employed an intuitive or empirical method.[180] In order to understand the method of the jurists, it is necessary to make a distinction between 'argumentative patterns' and 'values'. Argumentative patterns are, for example, the syllogism (a form of deductive reasoning which arrives at a logical consequence based on two or more propositions that are asserted or assumed to be true); the *reductio ad absurdum* (a form of inductive argument which attempts to disprove a statement by showing it inevitably leads to an absurd or impractical conclusion); and analogy (because two things are similar, what is true of one is also true of the other). Values are broad preferences concerning appropriate courses of action or outcomes. Such preferences may be determined by, for example, statutes or imperial constitutions; or they may be contained in rules formulated by jurists to embody the undeclared law (as opposed to rules enacted by popular assemblies or senate or emperors); or they may be found embodied in concepts such as equity (*aequitas*) or expediency (*utilitas*). Patterns of inference and values are best shown by this example from Cicero's *Topica*: 'If a slave has not been declared free either by the censor, or by the praetor's rod, or by the will of his master, he is not free: but none of those things is the case: therefore he is not free' (Cic. *Top*. 10). The pattern of inference here is a conditional syllogism whose major premise states that Q (= freedom) is true 'if and only if' P (= manumission) is true. As no manumission has been performed, the slave is not freed. As for the content, the major premise embodies an undisputed legal institution (*manumissio*), which was partly defined by statutes partly by juristic construction. If someone asked a jurist about a man's status, he could thus give a rational *responsum*.

A remark is on point. The jurists' reasoning included in general both deductive and inductive inferences. In some cases – more than often believed – their decision was reached by deduction from a rule (*apodeixis*, demonstration), as in the example above – deduction from statutes was also more widespread than often believed. In other instances, the decision was reached by a process of induction (*epagôgê*), as in the case of analogy.

---

180 For a fine critical panorama, see Thomas 2014.

A deductive, top-down approach, leads to a conclusion which 'results of necessity' (Arist. *Prior Analytics* I.2, 24b18–20). Induction – that is a 'bottom up' approach, 'argument from the particular to the universal' – is a non-necessary inference, and so it leaves open alternative solutions. Although the conclusions bear different degrees of probability, both procedures are rational and the path that leads to the conclusion can be retraced and tested.

One of the most characteristic features of Roman legal thinking is the *fictio*.[181] Fiction involves extending (or, in rare cases, excluding the extension of) the legal treatment of one case to another, 'pretending' that factual elements existed that were absent in reality. *Fictio* was used by the legislator, for example, during the first century CE to extend the procedural law that had been established for the city of Rome and Roman citizens to Latin *municipia*.[182] Jurists used *fictio* as well, especially to solve 'logically perplexing' cases, for example when an impossible testamentary condition, if taken to the letter, might threaten the will's invalidation: 'an impossible condition has to be considered as if it had been not written'(ἀδύνατος *condicio pro non scripta accipienda* est).[183] *Fictio* is not a pattern of argumentation, nor is it a value. It is a way to fabricate reality in order to extend it to a regulation that would not fit it. The decision to mould reality, however, depends on inductive reasoning and on values: in the first case mentioned, the guiding principle is the legislator's will (for the purposes of expediency and political integration) to unify the private procedures in Rome and in the Latin municipalities; in the second, the guiding principle is to preserve the effectiveness of the will.

The normative values, that is claims about how things ought to be, are of diverse types and importance. In the reasoning of the Roman jurists (as well as among the 'artless proofs' of the rhetors: see above), the most important place is assigned to statutory law: *lex publica* or *plebiscitum*, depending on whether it was passed by the whole people or the plebeians. As Cicero states: 'in arguing controversies there ought to be nothing that has more weight than the statutory law itself' (*lege firmius in controversiis disceptandis esse nihil debet*. Cic. *Top*. 95). The pre-eminence of statutes is enshrined in the lists of sources written by the *iuris consulti*. The list at Gaius, *Institutes* 1.3–7 is paradigmatic: it opens with *lex* and measures the importance of other sources

---

181 Ando 2011; Thomas 2011.
182 For example, *Lex Irnitana*. LXI: *adque uti esset si eam rem in urbe Roma praetor p(opuli) R(omani) inter ciues Romanos iudicari iussisset*; 'as it would be if a praetor of the Roman people in the city of Rome had ordered that matter to be judged between Roman citizens' (trans. Michael Crawford).
183 Justinian, *Digest* 8.7.20 pr. (Labeo *posteriorum a Iavoleno epitomatorum*, 2).

in proportion to *lex*. According to a view heavily influenced by the nineteenth-century discussion for and against the use of legislation, Rome would only have known a few private-law statutes after the Twelve Tables.[184] This erroneous impression is due to the systematic deletion by the Justinianic compilers of references to *leges publicae* in the *Digest*. Such statutes were numerous, even in the field of private law, and they had accumulated over the years so as to form 'the present endless multiplicity and variety of our statutes' lamented by Tacitus (*Ann*. 3.25).[185] In Rome, the *leges publicae* were fundamental not only for the specific rules they set, but also because they enshrined general principles that jurists applied also in cases not expressly anticipated: for example, the freedom to dispose of property by will and the *favor libertatis* (the principle that, in case of doubt, the solution must be adopted that favours the attribution of freedom rather than slavery).

In the context of normative rules and in addition to the *leges publicae*, it should be noted that the Senate also produced an intense body of norms (which was recognized in the early Principate as having the same force of statutory law). We should also mention the growing importance of imperial constitutions from the time of Augustus, with their production intensifying exponentially (Gaius, *Institutes* 1.5–6). In a somewhat different way, the edicts of the praetor and the other magistrates, which announced to the public the directives governing the administration of justice, also functioned as normative texts that had an impact on jurists in deciding cases. It was not by chance that the praetor's edict was called by some *lex annua* – 'a yearly statute' – referencing the duration of office of the issuing magistrate and also, metaphorically, its binding force (Cic. *Verr*. 2.1.109). In their responses, the Roman jurists thus had to keep in mind the provisions of the *leges* and the other normative texts listed above. In doing so, they had to apply to the normative texts the interpretative techniques that were precisely defined in rhetorical treatises in Rome, starting from the second century BCE. The interpretation of a statute was carried out by the jurist – as by rhetoricians – according to the duality *ex verbo* / *ex sententia*, i.e. according to the literal tenor of the law / in line with the intention of the legislator (see, for example Justinian, *Digest* 1.3.19 (Celsus, 33 *digestorum*)).

Along with the *leges* (and other positive statutory sources), Roman jurists, when stating what legal doctrine governed a particular situation, had to keep in mind a constellation of legal institutions. Only part of these were established by statutes, but all were equally binding and at the forefront of their

---

184 See Whitman 1990.   185 Mantovani 2018b.

legal consciousness. An example is the position of *pater familias*, the oldest living male in a household, the only subject with a full legal capacity, whose role came with a series of corollaries.[186] For example, a child, whether male or female (while a free Roman citizen), did not have an estate. All legal transactions s/he carried out benefited the father's estate; and through her/his legal acts s/he could not diminish the father's estate.

Likewise, certain legal acts in certain epochs of Roman history were characterized by remarkably rigid forms: verbal, gestural and symbolic. The legal acts performed *per aes et libram* are a good example: these involved the weighing of bronze so as to function as counter-value (for example, the sale of slaves, draft animals, land; the testament 'by scales and bronze'; the subjugation and release of the debtor in the form of the *nexum*). The rigidity of the forms – although not always set out in statutory law – had a normative effect in the sense that it required Roman jurists to give more importance to fulfilling the rite than to the parties' actual will. On the other hand, it was easier for them to attach importance to the parties' intent when the legal institution was not dominated by the external form (for example, the more recent type of contract of sale, based on mere consensus and inspired by the principle of *bona fides*).

The jurists were therefore constrained by principles, rules and guidelines set by normative sources and fundamental legal institutions. Even when respecting this perimeter (something modern commentators often tend to underestimate), their activities were not at all free. Such additional norms were sometimes definition (as in the case of 'treasure trove' seen above), sometimes veritable 'rules' (*regulae*), in the sense that they possessed explicit content formulated by the legal tradition in the form of a prescriptive statement, in a pragmatic-linguistic sense; to give just one further example, 'the surface yields to the ground' (*superficies solo cedit*).[187]

After examining some normative principles with explicit content (from laws to rules) that underlie Roman legal reasoning, let us consider some of the principles incorporated in value terms (or 'principle terms'). Their content is not directly formulated in the form of a prescriptive statement, and we must therefore derive it from the semantic and argumentative use of these words by the jurists. Among these principle terms, the most productive is *aequitas*, 'equity'. *Aequitas*, as a normative principle, in addition to expressing the equal treatment of similar cases, requires restoring the equilibrium of wealth between two subjects that come into contact, preventing one from

---

186 See Chapter 8, this volume.   187 Gaius, *Institutes* 2.73 (trans. Dario Mantovani).

taking advantage of the other. More generally, *aequitas* means that those who benefit from a situation must also bear the disadvantages. *Aequum* means precisely 'flat, balanced'. The jurists did not conceive of *aequitas* as the 'justice of the concrete case' in the sense that it corresponds to the Aristotelian ἐπιείκεια, but rather as a precise norm for resolving conflicts, an inspiration precisely to 'equalling it out'. In Roman juristic thinking, *aequum* is the constitutive principle of law itself. From another point of view, we can say that the value term of *aequitas* was used by Roman jurists as the lexical synthesis of a series of explicit normative rules, some of which have been presented above.

Utilitas – another word with normative value – solves situations where other arguments are not decisive; it may even overrule ordinary rules for the sake of expediency. For example, in a case where logic does not allow a choice from various possible solutions – more people have injured one person, but no one knows who gave the deadly blow (Justinian, *Digest* 9.2.51 (Iulianus, 86 *digestorum*)) – *utilitas publica* suggests that everyone should be punished as a murderer. From a modern perspective, *utilitas* may appear to be a change-oriented value that can accommodate the pressures of economic or social interest into the reasoning of jurists. However, as can be seen from the example just quoted, *utilitas* expresses (often) fundamental values of community living, such as punishment for the crimes. *Utilitas* thus functioned as a stabilizing factor, to a greater extent than it inspired reforms.

In summary, the Roman jurists' method must without a doubt be labelled as 'rational', although this is often disputed by modern scholars. In fact, Cicero explicitly theorized this in a treaty written in 44 BCE for the jurist C. Trebatius Testa (*Topica*), a work which offers a partial but accurate classification of the reasonings of the *iuris consulti* within the framework of Aristotelian logic. As we have seen, the Roman juristic method made use of both inductive inferences and deductive arguments; the fact that the roman jurists searched for arguments (as Cicero himself stated in his *Topica*) may convey the impression that 'thinking like a jurist' means that virtually any solution can be argued for in an acceptable manner. This does not hold true, however, for Roman jurists for two reasons. First, their position was not that of the advocate, trying to make the best of their client's case; the jurist stood as an impartial adviser above the parties, and they were implicated in a discussion with jurists of their own age and prospectively with jurists of future generations. Crucially, the only points at stake for the jurists was their own justifications. Second, and most important, what distinguishes the topical reasoning of jurists from that of orators is that jurists felt themselves bound by values that lay inside the law or at least that were widely recognized as acceptable.

Law and Nature

The relationship between law and nature cuts across many of the aspects examined so far: the possibility of distinguishing law from other fields in each given society; the possibility of distinguishing jurists from other experts; finally, and above all, legal reasoning.

In early China there were two distinct strands of thinking that may be subsumed under the heading of 'natural law'. The first can be termed the cosmological approach: that is, an approach to a 'higher law' governing the universe (cosmos) and its constituent parts, human and non-human. The constituent parts of the cosmos are interrelated in complex ways. When all the parts are working in a way that accords with the law, there is 'harmony' in the universe. Hence, we often find invoked in modern writing the notion of 'cosmic harmony' as characteristic of a properly functioning universe. When any part is not working as it should, the effects of its malfunctioning are felt in other parts of the universe. Significantly, a failure on the part of humans, especially the ruler, to behave in the way ordained for the universe can have adverse consequences for the physical world (the appearance of abnormal phenomena, floods, droughts, and so on). Such a cosmological approach to natural law appears to have developed first in the third century BCE and reached its apogee in the early Han (second century BCE), although we see traces of its influence throughout the imperial period. The second strand of thinking in early Chinese texts referable to natural law is what may be termed the moral approach. The term 'moral' adverts to a conception of higher law founded on the principles, derived from human nature itself, which govern the way humans should behave in their dealings with each other. The most important such principles are those defining the status within the family or society which individuals hold vis-à-vis each other, such as that of father and son or ruler and subject. These principles, constituting an absolute morality, formed the core of the ethical thinking of Confucianism (and later of neo-Confucianism) and played a crucial part in the formulation of the rules on family relationships and the duties of a subject to the ruler found in Han (206 BCE–220 CE), Tang (618–907 CE) and later law. One should perhaps not insist upon too great a divide between these 'cosmological' and 'moral' approaches to natural law. The moral approach itself may well import some aspect of cosmology, such as the invocation of Heaven, as the ultimate authority for the correct principles of human conduct. The point, however, is that, whereas this approach places the emphasis upon the content of the rules constituting the absolute morality, the cosmological approach places the emphasis upon the nature of the universe and its constituent elements.

Both the 'cosmological' and the 'moral' approaches have some resemblance to what is understood by natural law in the Western (European) tradition. Thus, in early China we have located in the cosmos a super-human agency as the ultimate authority for the 'right way' to behave on the part of humans. This agency may be understood abstractly as the Way (*Dao*) conceived as the impersonal patterns of nature or Heaven (*Tian*) conceived as an impersonal power. Or it may be identified with Heaven conceived as an anthropomorphic being equipped with the faculties of understanding and intention. In this latter case we can see a parallel with God invoked in Western natural law thinking. An even closer analogue to modern Western natural law thinking is offered by the 'moral' approach. We are able here to speak of a higher law constructed, through the application of reason, on the basis of man's own nature. While such higher law might be cited as the ground for the criticism of the actions of a particular ruler, no argument seems to have been advanced in early China that a statute enacted by the ruler should be invalid on the ground that its content conflicted with the higher law. Generally speaking, the differences between modern Western (European) ideas of natural law and those worked out within the various Chinese traditions are perhaps more important than the similarities.[188]

As we have already noted, the term *dharma* served as the point of connection between law and nature in ancient Indian literature. In its uses in the earliest Vedic collections (prior to eighth century BCE), *dharma* refers to both ritual and cosmic foundations or supports. Sacrificial rites, life-giving rains and the nourishing sun are all called *dharmas*.[189] By the third century BCE, however, the cosmic and natural connotations of *dharma* gave way to an ethical and juridical sense that comes to dominate other meanings, especially in Brahmanical or Hindu traditions. In the legal literature called Dharmaśāstra from this period on, *dharma* means ethics and law in society. In spite of earlier links with cosmic and natural phenomenon, the jurists declared that the sources of *dharma* were the Veda, primordial scripture, the legal texts (*smṛti*) authored by the sages and the normative conduct (*ācāra*) of

---

188 For further comparative discussion see MacCormack 2013b.
189 Horsch 2004 (1967): 428–29, 435.

people who adhered closely to both of these (see, for example, *GDh* 1.1–2 and *MDh* 2.6).

In the minds of the *dharma* experts, the Veda occupied the uncreated, fixed starting point for justification of the law's foundations. It was this theological commitment to the Veda that encouraged the idea that people, animals and natural phenomena have inherent dispositions, actions and roles. In the classical (post-Vedic) tradition, the role of the Veda became primarily symbolic rather than substantive: 'In actual fact, the Vedic texts contain little enough in the way of rules of *dharma*. Strictly speaking, the Vedas (*saṃhitās*) do not even include a single positive precept which could be used directly as a rule of conduct.'[190] As Sankararama Sastri put it, this idea of the Veda is the 'fundamental fiction on which the entire edifice of Hindu theology and philosophy rests'.[191] As a result, the Veda supplies a patina of natural law, but never a real, substantive grounding in a transcendent source such as God, Nature or Reason.[192] Rather than the observation of regularities in nature leading to an idea of social rules and regularities, the fixity of the Veda supplies the presumption that nature must also be regular or ruled as an extension of *dharma*. With only a nod to revelation, therefore, the experts of the *dharma* traditions compiled the legal texts with an eye first to customary laws and then to internal scholastic debates and concerns for systematization. To this extent, legal science may be said to have created the law itself in ancient India.

An analysis of the relationship between law and nature in relation to the ancient Near Eastern evidence has to rely on inferences, since we lack extended treatises that comment on this matter. It could be argued, for example, that the claims made by Ḫammurabi of Babylon, in the prologue to his famous law collection, are an attempt to align law with the proper natural order. He maintains that the gods have endowed him with the special wisdom needed to render the correct judgment for each of the legal situations presented in the code. If his wisdom is indeed divine, then perhaps his decisions correspond to what the gods have ordained as right and 'natural' for human relations. On the other hand, Ḫammurabi's boast that his laws are implementing the wisdom and will of the gods may simply be a means of declaring the legitimacy of the king's authority when it comes to ruling over the legal affairs of Babylonian society. The king sat at the pinnacle of the justice system, such as it was, and could intervene in any case referred to him.

---

190 Lingat 1973: 7–8.   191 Sankararama Sastri 1926: 46.   192 Davis 2006.

No one would have questioned his authority, but the theoretical grounding of his power seems to have required an appeal to the gods.

Some scholars have sought to identify a more substantial allusion to natural law in the Hebrew Bible. Christine Hayes argues that portions of Deuteronomy may point in this direction.[193] At Deut 4:6–8, Moses says: 'This will show your wisdom and discernment to the peoples, who, when they hear all these statutes, will say, "Surely this great nation is a wise and discerning people!" ... What other great nation has statutes and ordinances as just as this entire law that I am setting before you today?' If other societies can recognize the justice and beneficence of Israelite law, then the implication may be that they are doing so based on criteria that determine what is right and proper and that are universally acknowledged. If so, then the author of this text seems to be suggesting that Israelite rules correspond to what could be called natural law. But, according to Hayes, a very different approach to law tends to predominate throughout biblical literature.[194] This other approach equates the good with the will of the deity Yahweh, regardless of whether or not other nations can recognize his will as good. The law may appear to be – or even genuinely be – arbitrary and subjective, but it is the deity and not a universally applicable set of criteria that determines what is right and wrong. She contrasts the two approaches by describing the latter as grounded in divine will rather than in divine reason, which seems to be the basis of the former. In the end, it is difficult to tease out any explicit attitudes from ancient Near Eastern material, whether biblical or otherwise, on the precise relationship between law and the natural order.

Law (*nomos*) and nature (*physis*) were frequently opposed in ancient Greek thought. *Nomos* was about cultural practices (so most famously Herodotus 3.38), and it was held that it was the fact that they were long customary cultural practices that gave *nomoi* authority (Arist. *Politics* 1269a20). Yet the regularity of nature was recognized: for Aristotle nature had its reasons ('nature does nothing in vain'), and so what is natural happens 'always or for the most part'– but note the second part of the formula 'for the most part' (Arist. *Physics* 198b35). Plato too recognizes the existence of 'laws of nature' precisely in noting something occurring 'contrary to the laws of nature' (*Timaeus* 83e4–5).[195] But Plato also suggests in *Laws* that since laws are the products of intelligence they should be defended as 'either natural or not inferior to nature' (*Laws* 890d).

---

193 Hayes 2015: 24–41.   194 Hayes 2015: 15–24.   195 Long 2005: 422.

Famously, from time to time Greek writers acknowledge 'unwritten law' or 'common law'.[196] The most famous example comes in Sophocles' *Antigone*, where Antigone invokes 'unwritten law' to justify her burial of her traitorous brother Polyneices in defiance of the law of the state (*Antigone* 453–57). Aristotle refers to this example at *Rhetoric* 1.13.2 where he suggests that there are some natural laws that exist without there having to be any association which has formally legislated. Various Greek writers refer to such common laws or unwritten laws, and they cover matters such as honouring parents, incest, violence towards a wife, killing in self-defence, returning a deposit, which the gods may be thought to enforce in their own ways.[197] Such unwritten laws are regarded as guiding the behaviour of individuals through the operation of shame (Thuc. 2.37.3, Pl. *Laws* 841B, cf. 838B).

Whether natural law played any part in judicial decisions is disputed. We are told that in 403 the Athenians explicitly banned magistrates from resorting to 'unwritten law' (Andoc. 1.85), but it appears that there was a clause in the Athenian dikastic oath which obliged jurors to decide according to the law and where there was no law according to justice, hence introducing an idea of universal justice. Such uses as we have of appeals to natural law in ancient Athenian literature do so to reinforce rather than to undermine the law (cf. Dem. 45.53).

Finally, Romans absorbed their ideas about the law of nature from Greek and Hellenistic thought. In this case too, Cicero was an especially effective mediator; particularly elaborate examples of this reception are found in his treaty *On Laws* (*De legibus*) for philosophy and, as regards rhetoric, in the manual *On invention* (*De inventione*). These ideas soon became familiar to jurists as well. The first assured references go back to Labeo, in the Augustan age, who speaks of *naturalis aequitas* (i.e. natural justice). Gaius, in the second century CE, qualified the *naturalis ratio* as the source of laws observed among all peoples (*ius gentium*).[198] The couple *ius civile* and *ius naturale*, previously only sporadically attested, becomes common among jurists of the late second and third century CE. Although the terminology underwent several changes, the underlying concepts seem quite stable. The 'law of nature' constituted a set of principles derived from a political anthropology largely inspired by Stoic doctrine and embedded in jurists' reasoning – the following principles

---

196 Jones 1956: 61–64.
197 Dem. 25.65; Xen. *Hell*. 4.4.19–24; (Ps-)Arist. *Oikonomika* 1344a; Sophocles *Philoktetes* 1230–34, 1250 with Herodotus 6.86.
198 Gaius, *Institutes* 1.1.

clearly fall into this category: the principle of self-preservation:[199] the principle of the normative relevance of blood relations:[200] and the principle of respect for a word given.[201] When referring to this political anthropology, Roman jurists resorted to the concept of natural law (*ius naturale*) or natural equity (*naturalis aequitas*) and made clear that sharing these principles was contingent on some innate reason common to all men (and in some cases to all animals as well).[202]

The jurists deemed some of these principles as inherent to Roman civil law itself, and, therefore, they used them as criteria for their decisions. On other points, they were aware that Roman law had departed from natural principles: this is the case of slavery, recognized as legal, despite the fact that, by nature, all men are born free (as Ulpian himself states). Nevertheless, the reference to the natural condition of freedom did not lead to a critique of slavery. Jurists used it instrumentally, to widen the range of action of enslaved persons in the interest of their master (and of society as a whole). Enslaved persons were awarded a 'natural' (not civil) 'legal capacity'; they were able, for example, to conclude contracts in the interests of the master. The enslaved person's natural capacity was thus made to coexist with their legal subjection (by analogy with property) to the power of their owner.

Therefore, beyond the ideological superstructure and the appeal to nature, the crucial point is that, in Roman legal thought, these are perfectly functioning and 'testable' norms for reaching decisions. This is not without consequences. As the Romans inherited from the Greeks their reflection on law and nature, so the Romans left it to Western medieval and modern thought. Through the reinterpretations made from the sixteenth to the eighteenth century, from Grotius to Locke, all the way down to today's doctrines of human rights, the works of Roman jurists collected in the *Digest* were the basis of 'jusnaturalism'. Some of the theoretical and practical difficulties of modern conceptions arise from the fact that they generalize ideas which, as seen above, had a specific role in the reasoning of Roman jurists.

---

199 Justinian, *Digest* 43.16.1.27 (Ulpianus, 69 *ad edictum*): 'one may repel force with force, Cassius writes, and this right exists from nature'.
200 Justinian, *Digest* 38.8.2 (Gaius, 16 *ad edictum provinciale*).
201 Justinian, *Digest* 2.14.1 pr. (Ulpianus, 4 *ad edictum*): 'this edict rests on natural equity: for what is so much in accord with human faith as to observe that which men have agreed upon among themselves?'
202 For example, the instinct to perpetuate the species: Justinian, *Digest* 1.1.1.1 (Ulpianus): 'hence come the union of male and female ... the generation and the rising of offspring'.

Conclusion

The ancient world saw the development of epistemic communities, centred on the articulation of rules and principles that we might consider as pertaining to 'law'. The presence of written rules (statutes) seems to be a key factor in the emergence of such communities, and of legal knowledge as a separate area of expertise. Nevertheless, the expression of the law in each of the ancient societies analysed in the present chapter (China, India, Near East, Greece, Rome and rabbinic) diverged in rather fundamental ways, in content and form. These divergences can be explained: the actors of the epistemic communities themselves had different functions in the societies in which they arose. The scribes of the Near East, or the near-priest expounders of the *dharma* in India, the bureaucrats of China, the citizens of Greek city states or the aristocrats of Rome all had different social standing which, in turn shaped their relationships to the law. But thinking about the law was a multidimensional affair, where legal experts were in conversation not only with contemporary or near-contemporary norms and opinions, but also with their predecessors, so that an entire legal literature arose from the rationale of experts: legal literature, therefore, seems to be – beyond the differences in shape and depth – a feature shared by all societies examined. The rabbis of Second Temple Judaism engaged with previous decisions much like the Romans jurists engaged with one another. If the scribes of the ancient Near East emphasized the royal statutes, later generations were keened to circumscribe or define their applications and Chinese thinkers collected precedents to provide guidelines for the treatment of cases that might arise later.

This chapter shows that, at its core, legal expertise in the ancient world was a transversal phenomenon whose dynamics were defined primarily by the positions of its practitioners within their contemporary society, and historically as part of a chain of other thinkers. So, legal reasoning was not unique to one particular ancient civilization, nor were its tenets uniform throughout the ancient world. Considering the law from a socio-intellectual perspective explains the numerous divergences, which belong to the social dynamics, but also highlights the various similarities. This is nowhere clearer than in the fact that most of these societies took 'the law of nature' as a central idea.

4

War, Peace and Interstate Relations

Lead Author: KATELIJN VANDORPE

Contributors: SOPHIE DÉMARE-LAFONT, GEOFFREY MACCORMACK, MARK MCCLISH, PATRICK OLIVELLE AND NICOLAS WIATER

Introduction

This chapter discusses a wide range of friendly and hostile interstate relations in the ancient Near East, ancient India and China, archaic and classical Greece, the Hellenistic states, Republican and Imperial Rome. 'State' is a concept under debate, as it may encompass empires built not only by conquest, but also by 'invitation' (such as the position of classical Athens in the Delian League) or by a combination of both systems (for example, the early Ptolemaic empire).[1] Furthermore, when reading this chapter one should keep in mind that 'state' or 'polity' is a dynamic concept in the sense that many 'states' have been formed as a result of hostile or even friendly relations before entering into new types of relationships.

The title of this chapter starts with 'War', not 'Peace', which is not coincidental.[2] The ordinary state of affairs in many ancient polities may have been war, not peace, and war itself may have been considered in some premodern societies as a legal way of proving rights. The Egyptian pharaoh had to guarantee Maat, order and justice, and had to protect the Nile country against the chaos coming from abroad. The ordinary state of affairs in classical India is 'contest' or 'competition'; war is only one means of carrying this out. War as a 'contest' is also a common theme in the ancient

---

[1] For this approach, see Scheidel 2013. See also Chapter 5, 'Law and the State', this volume.
[2] See the proceedings *War and Peace in the Ancient World*, edited by K. A. Raaflaub (2007), which have, contrary to this chapter, a strong focus on peace (ideologies of peace, intellectual concern with peace, efforts to restore or stabilize peace). Except for the contribution by M. Van De Mieroop, we were not able to consult *Making Peace in the Ancient World* (Lanfranchi, Ponchia and Rollinger 2022), which came out when this chapter was in print.

Greek world, although at the same time wartime was considered detestable. In China, at least in the Spring and Autumn period (771–464 BCE), the warrior aristocracy regarded warfare as a religious activity connected with the worship of the ancestors and considered it a duty owed to the ancestors both to consolidate and to enlarge upon what had been achieved by them in the acquisition of territory. In Rome, war was a frequent occurrence but should not simply be considered (and was not considered by the Romans) the 'normal' state of affairs. Neither, however, was peace, at least not before the very late Republic and the early Empire when the *pax Augusta* or *Romana* was introduced. But war and peace are closely intertwined; even the warlike Assyrians wanted peace and it was war that led to peace: 'Peace does not come without a battle. There will be no friendly relations without fighting', leading ultimately to a *pax Assyriaca*.[3] This chapter will show that notwithstanding the numerous conflicts and wars fought in antiquity, all polities, even the dominant ones, tried, through all kinds of alliances and diplomatic relations, to establish peaceful relations in view of political stability and economic prosperity. Hence, the third component of this chapter's title, 'interstate relations', may be the most promising from a comparative perspective. The Greeks in particular have experimented with alternative forms of conflict management.

Comparing different societies is hampered by the different forms of government, such as monarchy, aristocracy, oligarchy, tyranny, dictatorship, democracy, and by the differences between large empire-structures (for example, the Great Powers' club in the ancient Near East, the Western Zhou dynasty or the Qin/Han empires in China, the Hellenistic states or imperial Rome) and conglomerations of small states (such as the city states of classical Greece or the regional polities – the *mahājanapadas* – across north and central India in the second urbanization period, c. 700–320 BCE). Another problem in approaching this topic from a comparative point of view is that, for some regions, our understanding of the issues at stake is strongly coloured by the theoretical or literary character of the sources rather than historical documents. As such, the study of ancient India in respect of war, peace and interstate relations is typically the study of various theories and classificatory schemes; the most important and most representative is by far the *Arthaśāstra*, the only treatise on statecraft in India dealing extensively with relations between polities.[4]

---

3 Quotation from the Epic of Tukulti-Ninurta, translated in Van De Mierop 2022: 20.
4 All translations from the *Arthaśāstra* are from Olivelle 2013.

Hospitality Rules and Customs

Before moving on to higher-level cooperation between states, we examine here how individuals were protected or received in a private or official context 'abroad', be they private persons, merchants or people travelling in an official capacity.[5] Today these visitors are (or should be) protected by human rights or international laws. In antiquity there were hardly notions of human rights,[6] but there were concepts of basic rights that may have led to a kind of natural or 'international' law protecting foreign nationals.

The ancient Near East was characterized by constant conflicts and warfare between city states or larger territorial states. Owing to the unstable political situation, the protection of travellers or foreigners received a lot of attention in interstate relations. Commercial agreements protected the merchants' interests in the host country and transit zones, and sometimes even in enemy territory, as long as these respected customs obligations. If they traded royal merchandise, they could be exempt from taxes. Bad treatment of merchants had a negative impact on interstate relations.[7]

Diplomacy played an important role in ancient Near Eastern societies, and since the Old Babylonian period there was a protocol on how diplomats or envoys should be treated. The receiving state had to guarantee their safety and provide accommodation, food, sometimes clothing; on the other hand, diplomatic immunity as such is hardly attested; the archives from the palace of Mari seem to testify to such an immunity.[8] Envoys could, nevertheless, be mistreated and even detained for extended periods, to somehow gain an advantage from their presence. But such behaviour was disapproved of, as evidenced by diplomatic correspondence from the Late Bronze Age: 'to treat a messenger badly is against the acceptable custom'.[9] Diplomats or envoys needed a letter of accreditation and a pass, which they had to present in the transit zones and which entitled them, for example, to food supplies for themselves and their horses. The message

---

5 In what follows, foreigners who travel in an official capacity are termed more generally 'envoys' or 'delegates', more specifically 'messengers' or 'heralds' when they just convey a message, or 'diplomats', 'emissaries' and 'ambassadors' when also appointed to conduct diplomacy. It is, however, not always easy to make a neat distinction between these categories and much depends on the common practice of the respective disciplines.
6 See in general, e.g., Amunátegui Perelló 2014, who traces the roots of human rights in the Greek world.
7 Charpin and Durand 1997; Altman 2012: 67, 75–78, 96.
8 Durand 1997: 591–94 ('Les ambassades').
9 KBo 7.11: obv. 6', complaint by the Hittite king Hattusili III as one of his messengers was arrested by Ramesses II; see Edel 1994, I: no. 37, and Altman 2012: 165.

from their king, kept in a sealed envelope, was to be read by them upon arrival. For security reasons, messengers travelled in convoys of twenty people or more. On their return, they could be accompanied by envoys of the host state, so that the latter could check whether their king's message was being passed on correctly.[10]

When foreign nationals (especially 'authorized' merchants[11]) were mistreated, the host nation had to provide compensation. When in the Phoenician port of Dor goods were stolen from the ship of the Egyptian Wenamun, the prince of Dor was expected to compensate; however, the latter ultimately refused, as someone from Wenamun's own crew turned out to be the culprit.[12]

The unstable political situation led to a specific group of 'travellers' in the ancient Near East, which received peculiar attention in treaties.[13] These 'travellers' encompassed a large group of runaway people, including slaves who fled their master; deserting soldiers; people in debt; political refugees; and free people who ran away from war, blood feud or hunger. There is very little evidence that such people could turn to a sanctuary that offered protection (religious asylum). States were not obliged to extradite fugitives unless a treaty had been concluded providing for the extradition of these people to their country of origin; such treaties were common and failure to adhere to this agreement could be grounds for going to war, underlining the importance of the procedure. On the other hand, free people, who for other reasons chose to reside abroad, were not to be enslaved in the host country according to the treaties, and were allowed to return to their homeland at any time.

From the New Kingdom onwards, when Egypt started to maintain more intense contacts with foreign polities, Egypt became part of the ancient Near Eastern system of diplomacy, despite the general Egyptian attitude towards foreigners: this attitude was strongly determined by the world-view in which the pharaoh had to ensure order and justice and protect Egypt from the outside world where chaos reigned (see Chapter 3, this volume). Thus, the Egyptians considered all foreigners in principle as enemies, but a distinction must be made between foreigners as a group, who were the enemy, and foreigners as individuals, who could be useful to Pharaonic society as

---

10 Westbrook 2000: 33–34; Altman 2012: passim; Pfoh 2019.
11 For problems encountered by 'non-authorized' merchants according to the archives of the palace of Mari, see Durand 2000: 60–61 (esp. nos. 928–29).
12 Green 1979; Westbrook 2000.   13 Westbrook 2000: 36; Altman 2012: passim; Hipp 2021.

workmen, soldiers or diplomats, and towards whom a more positive attitude could be adopted, even in the case of deportees.[14]

In ancient India 'international' travel was thought of as normal for only certain kinds of individuals such as kings (and their retinues), ambassadors, long-distance merchants and wandering ascetics. Sealed passes were needed to enter or to exit the countryside.[15] Persons from other territories could enter the countryside only when they had obtained such an entry permit or when vouched for by the caravan. Any specific rules regarding the treatment of one or another type of person must be understood against the backdrop of a society greatly concerned with hospitality and the formalities of courtly culture. According to Megasthenes, ambassador of Seleucus Nikator at the court of Candragupta Maurya (r. 320–298 BCE), an administrative body of five persons was set up for foreigners in the cities; the duties of this administrative body were to see that no foreigner was wronged, that physicians were sent when they were ill and, after death, that they were buried and their property was returned to their family.[16] At the same time, however, 'strangers' were treated with suspicion in certain contexts:

> Secret agents deployed on roads and in roadless tracts should arrest anyone with a wound, carrying harmful tools, hiding behind a package, agitated, overcome by intense sleep, or tired from travel, or any stranger within or outside the city, in temples, holy places, woods, and cemeteries. Likewise, inside the city they should carry out searches in empty houses, workshops, taverns, places for selling boiled rice and cooked meat, gambling halls, and residences of religious orders.[17]

According to the 'Law of envoys' (*dūtadharma*) they were immune from capital punishment: 'Even when weapons are raised, envoys say exactly what they were instructed to say. Even the lowest-born among them are exempt from being killed.'[18] Nevertheless, the position of the envoy, particularly one delivering disagreeable news, was delicate and flight was recommended when under threat of imprisonment or death.[19]

Special dispensations were offered by the king to foreign traders, including boat and caravan operators, thus facilitating the import of commodities. Local officials were responsible for protecting caravan traders and reimbursing the value of any merchandise stolen from them.[20] Likely provision of

---

14 Valerio 2019.   15 KAŚ 2.34.1–4.
16 See Megasthenes' work *Indika*, fragments of which are recorded in Diod. (2.42) and Strabo (15.1.50).
17 KAŚ 2.36.13–14.   18 KAŚ 1.16.14–15.   19 KAŚ 1.16.32.   20 KAŚ 4.13.7–12.

areas for the housing of foreign traders in the capital indicates a similar responsibility for foreign traders on the part of the City Manager.[21]

Sealed passes for travel were needed for persons from other territories to enter, issued by several officers employed by the state. Forgeries were punished. The kingdom's borders, especially the river crossings, were controlled by the Frontier Commander and the Superintendent of Shipping.[22]

For ancient China, evidence on hospitality mainly stems from the later period of the Tang dynasty (619–907 CE). Tang China was a hugely cosmopolitan state with large numbers of foreigners from many different countries travelling or staying in the country. Most were merchants or traders, but there were also many Buddhist monks visiting Tang monasteries. However, the basic policy of the laws seems to have been 'segregation' not 'hospitality'. The authorities assigned a special quarter of the city for resident foreign traders or merchants. They elected their own leader or headman to deal with disputes, but the Chinese authorities maintained control over these enclaves in the sense that all crimes were tried by a Chinese court. According to the Tang code (article 88), the general policy of the government was to discourage intercourse between the Chinese and travelling (as distinct from resident) foreigners. Trade with them was forbidden and no commoner or official, unless he had specific business, was to approach them. This contrasts with the position accorded foreigners who had permission to live in China. They might conduct trade with Chinese and even marry a Chinese woman, although they were not permitted to take such a wife with them when they returned to their own country.[23]

The Chinese Tang government established a special department (the *Honglu si*) with responsibility inter alia for foreign envoys. It established a protocol for the paying of homage and the presentation of tribute by emissaries of foreign powers visiting the Tang court. On their appearance at court, the emissaries were ranked according to the importance of the state which they represented. They wore national dress and presented objects typical of their country. Special rules governed the acceptance of horses and other animals offered by the envoys. Other rules governed the way in which envoys were lodged and fed, the duration of their stay and their treatment should they become ill or die. Emissaries arriving by sea were required to wait at the port of disembarkation until permission had been obtained from the court to proceed to the capital for an audience. Emissaries arriving by

---

21 KAŚ 2.4.16.   22 KAŚ 2.34.1–4, 2.21.26 and 2.28.18.
23 For the rules in the Tang code, see Schafer 1963: 14–25; Johnson 1979: 252 and 1997: 54–56; Benn 2002: 40–43. See also Chapter 8, this volume.

land were required to bear half a tally in the form of a bronze or wooden fish to match the other half retained by the Tang court. Such tallies were sent to the foreign state in advance of the visit and served as credentials of the envoy subsequently sent.[24]

In the ancient Greek world, the individuals outside their own city state could always rely on personal relationships of friendship, known as 'guest friendship' (*xenia*), which already surfaces in Homer's epics as a rule-based Greek tradition.[25] The more formal institution of the proxeny (*proxenia*) provided all citizens of a given city with state protection and hospitality in a foreign city: the *proxenos* was a prominent figure who acted in his own polity as a kind of patron for citizens of another city state, similar to the diplomatic office of 'honorary consul' today. For private persons, the *proxenos* arranged accommodation, introduced them to magistrates who were of interest to the visitors, or stood surety for those who wanted to borrow money. He also entertained envoys from the city which he represented, negotiated the release of prisoners and so on. Because sometimes difficult tasks were involved, more than one *proxenos* might be appointed; often the *proxenos* belonged to the same family over several generations, which ensured continuity. The *proxenos* was rewarded with honours in the city that had appointed him. This institution became an honorary function when new types of agreements emerged. The asylum right was another typical Greek phenomenon: a visitor who was at risk of being arrested or whose belongings were to be seized could be protected by the *asylia*-right, which had been granted to him personally or to all citizens of his city. In the Hellenistic period, visitors to cities with regional or panhellenic sanctuaries saw themselves protected for the duration of the religious festivals associated with those sanctuaries.[26]

Heralds of ancient Greek city states, who came to declare war or an ultimatum, were inviolable as protégés of the god Hermes and were rarely maltreated. Envoys were received with respect after presenting credentials, but they did not enjoy diplomatic immunity: they could be arrested for violations or had to leave enemy territory in the event of an imminent conflict. For official delegations which attended festivals or games at the invitation of the organizing city state, accommodation was provided: in Olympia the delegations were housed in the large guest house known as

---

24 In general, see des Retours 1947, I: 408–17; Benn 2002: 189; Abromson 2008: 72, 94; Lewis 2009: 163–64.
25 Alonso 2007: 212–13.
26 Marek 1984; Lonis 2007: 241–46, 256–62; Giovannini 2007: 92–93.

the Leonidaion, funded by Leonidas of Naxos around 330 BCE. Moreover, the delegates, athletes, artists and merchants could count on a safe journey and stay: a sacred truce, interrupting all hostilities for a longer period (three months in case of the Olympic games), was proclaimed to guarantee the safe travelling of these delegations, at least within the territories of the participating cities.[27] Thus, the panhellenic games took place on a regular basis, contrary to the modern Olympic Games which were not organized during the world wars. In 420 BCE, the Spartans were fined and excluded from the Olympic games because they had invaded the territory of the organizing community of Elis during the truce.[28] When in 348 BCE an Athenian who travelled to the Olympic games, was intercepted by soldiers of Philip II of Macedonia, the latter attributed the incident to the ignorance of his men and compensated the victim.[29]

As across the Greek city states, in Rome hospitality could be granted on a personal level (*hospitium privatum*) and guest friends could exchange tokens as symbols of their relationship: the so-called *tesserae hospitales* (in ivory, clay, metal, representing the handshake). The reception of foreign traders rather relied on conventions and established practices, although some provisions were established in treaties such as the Roman-Carthaginian Treaties (509 and 348 BCE), obliging the presence of a herald or town clerk when business was conducted, and guaranteeing the price, presumably to avoid conflict.[30] The treaties also show that local rules and regulations applied and that provisions could be different in, for instance, Sardinia and Sicily.[31] From 242 BCE, a special praetor, the *praetor peregrinus*, was probably responsible for dealing with foreigners in Rome in legal conflicts.[32]

Since there was no professional diplomatic service, communities would usually appoint particularly suitable individuals as envoys, either because they already had friendship relationships, because they were famous (philosophers, etc.) or because of their rhetorical abilities. In Latin, in fact, *orator* is also used in the sense of 'ambassador'/ 'envoy'. The power of the state in sending them was an important factor in the protection of envoys. Several instances are recorded where the Romans began a war because Roman

---

27 Mosley 1973; Lonis 2007: 246–55; Giovannini 2007: 54–55, 93–97, 201–2.
28 Thuc. 5.49–50.
29 Dem. 19 (*De falsa legatione*) pr. 2.3; Aeschin. 2 (*De falsa legatione*) 12–13; see Giovannini 2007: 202 for this and the previous example.
30 Polybius 3.22.8–10; 24.
31 For example, Polybius 3.24.11–13 on the Second Roman-Carthaginian Treaty of (probably) 348 BCE.
32 Corey Brennan 2000: 603–9.

envoys' rights had been violated, for example against Tarentum in 282 BCE or against the Illyrian queen Teuta in 230 BCE. Moreover, the peace negotiations with Carthage in 203 BCE, after the end of the Second Roman-Carthaginian War, were interrupted because the Carthaginian fleet had attacked Roman envoys.

Delegates (*legati*) who came to Rome in an official capacity, for example as representatives of their respective communities, were protected by the *ius gentium* for the duration of their mission, including the journey to and from Rome.[33] They received provisions, housing and gifts at state expense; also special honours such as a sacrifice in Rome's political and religious centre, the Capitol, or special seats in the theatre (the latter also known from special honours accorded to envoys by Greek communities). In the imperial period in particular, delegates from faraway peoples were seen as an acknowledgement of Rome's power and influence. Augustus considered delegations from many different foreign peoples as a sign of prestige.[34]

Whenever war was concerned (see further below), the priests called *fetiales* could function as envoys especially in the early Roman period. The larger Rome's sphere of influence grew, the less practicable that became and often prominent members of Roman society, especially former consuls or the consuls themselves, were appointed envoys. Envoys from the enemy might carry special signs to make them recognizable, especially olive branches or white ribbons or both. These were fairly common throughout the Mediterranean world as code for peaceful intentions: the Gauls in the Alps carried them when they (falsely) offered their help to Hannibal, and the Carthaginian envoys carried them when coming to negotiate with Scipio at the end of the Second Punic War.[35]

Hospitality was customary in all societies from the earliest times; concrete rules could be laid down in treaties or through formalization of processes and practices such as those protecting envoys the existence of which is presupposed as early as Homer.[36] The treaties focused mainly on merchants and on messengers and diplomats, groups that were of importance from a political and economic point of view. We can speak of a natural law concerning the treatment of diplomats in ancient times, as hospitality towards this group

---

33 Cf. Justinian, *Digest* 50.7.18: *Si quis legatum hostium pulsasset, contra ius gentium id commissum esse existimatur, quia sancti habentur legati*. The term *ius gentium* occurs first in a philosophical, rather than strictly legal sense, at the end of the second century BCE and, according to Wieacker 1988: 444, only becomes a juridical technical term in the second and third centuries CE.
34 *Res Gestae* 31.   35 Polybius, 3.52.3; 28.20.2, 10; cf. Justinian, *Digest* 1.8.8.
36 Piccirilli 2002.

shows many similarities across societies: credentials were needed, accommodation and protection had to be provided by the host country, and specific institutions were introduced to receive the diplomats appropriately (such as the proxeny in Greece, administrative bodies in India and special departments in China). General diplomatic immunity apparently did not exist, except for immunity from capital punishment for envoys who had to deliver disagreeable news.

The situation is different with regard to hospitality towards persons who travelled in a private capacity, which seems to be better attested for the Greek and Roman world where safer conditions could have given impetus to travel; among the Greeks, the awareness that there was an ethnic bond undoubtedly played a role as well. Across other ancient communities, including those in India, China and the ancient Near East, international travel for private individuals was less evident, except for ascetics (India) or monks (China). In the ancient Near East, evidence relating to the large group of fugitives shows that travelling abroad was mainly a matter of fleeing bad conditions at home.

States Forming Alliances and Pursuing Diplomacy

Both smaller city states and more powerful territorial states, whether they were monarchical, aristocratic or democratic in nature, sought political stability through alliances and diplomacy more generally. This section focuses on the types and goals of alliances and the establishment and role of diplomatic relations.

In the ancient Near East, interstate treaties were primarily oral agreements, which were not required to be written down but often were. The binding element was the oath sworn by the parties to their respective gods; at the same time the gods acted as witnesses. Ceremonies could frame the oath taking, including the offering of sacrifices and the sharing of a meal.[37] The main types of agreements were commercial and political treaties. Among the latter category, we can distinguish between 'parity' and 'subordination' treaties.[38] Parity treaties were concluded between equal partners, such as the treaty between the Hittite king Hattusili III and the Egyptian pharaoh Ramesses II.[39] The main subjects of the parity treaties were the extradition of runaways and defensive alliances. The subordination treaties were unilateral

---

37 Westbrook 2000: 36–39; Charpin 2019 and 2022; Lafont 2022.
38 Westbrook 2000: 39–40; Altman 2012: 111–45 and passim; Charpin 2019; for the subcategory of peace treaties, see Van de Mieroop 2022.
39 Beckman 1999: no. 15; Van de Mieroop 2022: 24.

agreements concluded with vassals. They were not so much dictated by the dominant monarch, but rather the result of negotiation. The vassals had to supply troops, pay tribute and pay annual homage. They had to respect their lord's friends and consider his enemy an enemy too. A vassal could count on the protection by the suzerain.[40] The texts could contain an 'escape' clause, which ensured that a certain commitment had not to be fulfilled if it conflicted with a commitment promised in a previously concluded treaty with another party. An example of this is the treaty between Niqmepa of Alalakh and the king of Tunip: '[The king] of the Hurrian people is my (over) lord! If <the words of the treaty> would conflict with (the interests) of the king of the Hurrian people, I would not break (my former) oath to the Hurrian king, my (over)lord, (and) these terms (of the treaty) would be exempted from the (present) oath.'[41] Treaties could be limited in time but were usually concluded for the lifetime of the parties (*in casu* the rulers), until the Amarna age, when they included the following generations.[42] If one of the parties died without a legitimate successor or had been dethroned, or if one of the parties violated the terms, the treaty could be terminated.

Egyptian society, unlike the rest of the ancient Near East, was for a long time a relatively closed society, with only few contacts with foreign polities.[43] In the late Middle Kingdom and the Second Intermediate Period, West Asian immigrants crowded into the eastern Delta and much of the country came under foreign rule. After the Hyksos were eventually expelled by Pharaoh Ahmose I, founder of the eighteenth dynasty, Egypt fundamentally changed in terms of foreign policy and more intense interstate relations were established, leading to international diplomacy.[44] This peculiar period of the Late Bronze Age is known as the 'beginning of international diplomacy',[45] when 'a real, rational, methodical and complete diplomatic system developed throughout the Near East, with a whole series of shared institutions, procedures and rituals'.[46] The Amarna correspondence between the Egyptian court of the eighteenth dynasty and other ancient Near Eastern states in the mid-fourteenth century BCE shows the diplomatic relations between, on the one

---

40 Ragionieri 2000: 48.   41 *AT* 2: 73–75, trans. Altman 2012: 118.   42 Charpin 2019.
43 Nevertheless, one of the greatest literary works of Pharaonic Egypt, the history of Sinouhe, is about a foreign journey: the hero fled to the Syro-Palestinian area at the beginning of the Middle Kingdom because of political turmoil, but in the end he returned, relieved, to his homeland, see Lichtheim 2006: 222–35.
44 Zangani 2019.
45 See Cohen and Westbrook 2000, with an introduction on the Amarna correspondence by the editors at 2–12; also Liverani 2001 and Zangani 2019.
46 Lafont 2001b: 39.

hand, the Great Powers' Club[47] (Egypt, the Mittani, Babylonia, the Hatti and Assyria), and, on the other hand, Egypt and its vassal states in the region of Syria-Palestine. Most of the letters are written in the lingua franca of the time: Akkadian. Through diplomacy, a balance of power was sought that led to political stability, peace and a safe environment for caravan routes, in a region previously characterized by constant warfare. As the Great Powers lay relatively far from each other, the constant exchange of messengers was crucial to maintain contacts; furthermore, great importance was attached to the exchange of gifts, including luxury goods such as gold, but also of all kinds of experts such as physicians (the Egyptian doctors had a great reputation).[48] The bond was also strengthened through dynastic marriages, a practice already known in Mesopotamia in Ur III and Mari.[49] In these marriage alliances between the major players, the bride's parents could demand that their daughter be the king's chief wife, so that their grandson would become the legitimate successor. The Babylonian king, whose sister had been given in marriage by their father to the Egyptian pharaoh Amenhotep III (who married several foreign princesses), tried to check through messengers he sent to his sister whether that promise was kept by the pharaoh but was unsuccessful.[50] The great kings considered themselves brothers,[51] and notions such as 'friendndship' (atterutu, râmuttu, lit. 'love') or 'concord' (salimu) are regularly found in their letters.[52] Despite these fraternal and familial relations, there was distrust, and polities kept an eye on each other through a well-developed intelligence service.[53] The diplomatic system was successful, no major wars were fought and it lasted for more than 200 years – only to be destroyed by external factors. But diplomacy also remained on the agenda of the major players later on, only to disappear 'with the advent of empires with a "universal" claim and then with the hellenization of the East and the vanishing of the "cuneiform culture"'.[54]

The ancient Indian theory of interstate relations (as represented by the Arthaśāstra) views foreign relations from the perspective of strategies available to the home state, whose ruler is styled a vijigīṣu ('he who desires to conquer'). This attunes us to what amounts to an axiom of South Asian statecraft: all states seek to dominate their rivals (both allies and enemies).

---

47 Liverani 2000.   48 Zaccagnini 2000.
49 Meier 2000; Altman 2012: 46, 142–45; Charpin 2019.
50 EA 1 :10– 61; Altman 2012: 143, note 237. See also Liverani 2001: 189–195 on equal vs. unequal marriages.
51 The vocabulary of the family in diplomacy and international relations goes back to the beginning of the second millennium. See Lafont 2001a: 232–38.
52 Zaccagnini 2000: 144–45.   53 Cohen 2000; Altman 2012: 134, 138.
54 Lafont 2001b: 39.

Conquest (whether military or diplomatic) is the goal that organizes all reflection on relations between states, including alliances. According to this theory, states have available 'Six Stratagems' (*ṣāḍguṇya*) to use against their rivals: a non-aggression pact; declaration of hostilities; remaining stationary (i.e. doing nothing); marching to battle (whether as threat, to fight or both); seeking shelter (i.e. submitting to another state for protection); and the 'double policy' of pursuing a pact with one state and conflict with another (used when a king is too weak to successfully engage in hostilities with an opponent with whom he must nevertheless fight). Only the first and the last stratagem leave room for alliances. The last strategy of the 'double policy' is apparently related to a second kind of pact: the strategic partnership (*samavāya*).

There are, however, other ways of thinking about relations between states in India. Often in the source material, foreign powers (*para*) are conceptualized as various types of allies (*mitra, sāmanta*) and enemies (*ari, śatru, amitra*). Interstate relations can be conceived geographically in terms of a *maṇḍala* ('circle') with the home state at the centre, ringed by a circle of enemies. Beyond this is a concentric circle of allies, and, beyond that, further concentric circles of enemies and allies.[55] The *maṇḍala* theory, therefore, examines interstate relations in general and alliances in particular as structured by strategic geographical considerations.

Still other ways of thinking about alliances can be found. We read in the *Arthaśāstra* of different kinds of allies: 'One with a territory once removed [as in the *maṇḍala* theory] is a natural ally; one related to the mother or father is an innate ally; and one who has sought refuge for [i.e., by giving] money or life is a contingent ally.'[56] Overall, four basic kinds of alliances seem to be presented in the *Arthaśāstra* – grouped in terms of the structure and goals of the partnership:

(1) Non-aggression: Such non-aggression pacts were a minimal kind of 'alliance' as two states agreed not to aggress against one another and nothing more (which only establishes the absence of hostilities between states). Typically, such treaties were sought by weaker states to forestall inevitable aggression by stronger states. Because stronger states sought concessions for such treaties, whether in the form of wealth, soldiers, land or hostages, the cost of such pacts for the weaker state could easily amount to long-term subordination.

---

55 See further McClish 2019b: 32.   56 KAŚ 6.2.20.

(2) Alliance: This is a long-term relationship characterized by peaceful relations, cooperation and, ideally, pliancy and subordination. The ideal ally is described as: 'Bequeathed by the father and grandfather; consistent; submissive; not prone to duplicity; eminent; and able to mobilize quickly'.[57] Such relations were apparently based on the presence of mutual enemies, familial ties or recognized dependency. The relationship between these kinds of 'alliances' and the other types discussed here is not entirely clear.

(3) 'Consociation' (samavāya): This is a structured, strategic partnership among two or more states. Such partnerships were generally understood to be organized around the achievement of a specific goal, whether to gain something or to forestall aggression. They could, as such, be relatively short-term partnerships or longer more durable political formations. The bond in these cases was based on pacts stipulating the goals of the consociation as well as the shares falling to each member. We should imagine these consociations as dynamic political formations, often possessed of many members, and themselves an arena for contest between states.

(4) Confederacy (saṅghāta): Saṅghas are stable political formations not characterized by the uniform sovereignty of a single king or by alliances between such sovereigns, but by a single territory ruled by 'leaders' or 'principals' who share sovereignty in some way. They were held together both by mutual understandings and by marriage ties. In some instances, the confederacy had a chief.[58] The Arthaśāstra describes two types of saṅgha: those living 'by using the title of king' and those living 'by commerce and the use of weapons' ('commercial' confederacies).[59] Trade agreements themselves do not seem to constitute separate kinds of alliances, that is apart from the 'commercial' confederacies.

Historical instances of these kinds of formations are harder to come by, except for the saṅghas-confederations, which may be identified with specific, well-known, historical confederations. In general, disputes or contention could be resolved without recourse to war by the giving and receiving of gifts or other gestures of conciliation.[60]

For ancient China, one may distinguish between equal and unequal alliances between states, but in both cases an unequal relationship is involved between a superior and inferior state(s). The difference between both types

---

57 KAŚ 6.1.12.   58 KAŚ 11.2.56.   59 KAŚ 11.1.4–5.   60 KAŚ 9.6.14ff.

lies rather in the level of subordination, the unequal alliances also being treaties with non-Chinese states or tribes. An unequal alliance might develop into a marriage treaty system, as was the case in the Han period.

Taking 'equal' alliances first: early Chinese treaties of 'equal' alliance are illustrated only from the period of the Spring and Autumn (771–464 BCE), when the ruler of the polity that was in the strongest position – known as the hegemon (*ba*) – might summon conferences of the other states to make agreements as to the principles of conduct they were to follow and the general need to support the Zhou royal house. These agreements were solemnised in the form of an oath termed *meng* (blood covenant), in which the participants performed a sacrifice, smeared their lips with the blood of the sacrificial victim, invoked the gods as witnesses and enforcers, and swore to uphold the terms of the agreement. Such interstate conferences might be held to establish a peace after one polity with its allies had defeated another, thus the *meng* were designed to demonstrate loyalty to a new hegemon as acts of subservience. One example given in the writings of the Confucian philosopher Mencius (372–289 BCE) is that of a conference in 651 BCE summoned at the instance of the ruler of the state of Qi, then the most powerful of the states. At the conference the participating states agreed upon the following principles of conduct: the unfilial should be slain, a family's heir should not be displaced, a concubine should not be taken as a wife, the old should be honoured and the young treated with kindness. These were all principles designed to reinforce the fundamental hierarchical family relationships. In addition, the states swore to maintain friendly relations among themselves and to support the Zhou royal house.[61]

Turning now to the 'unequal alliance' and marriage treaty system: Some of the earliest evidence suggests the Shang dynasty interacted with neighbouring polities and that the rulers of the Western Zhou acknowledged peripheral groups with which they traded a measure of autonomy, but if these groups broke the agreement they made, then the Zhou believed they had the right to attack. The acceptance of tribute from inferior states, as found from Han onwards, has its antecedents in the Spring and Autumn (771–464 BCE). During the sixth century BCE, the stronger states would make agreements with smaller states within their sphere of influence under which the latter were under an obligation to pay court visits and make gifts.[62] From the Han empire (206 BCE–220 CE) onwards, China regulated its relationship with non-Chinese states or tribes according to two basic patterns: one characterized by the

---

61 Legge 1960: 437–38.   62 Hsu 1999: 562–63.

periodic payment of tribute from the inferior state to China and the other by the semi-incorporation of the foreign people (regarded as 'inner vassals') within the administrative framework of the Chinese empire. The latter status entailed not just the obligation to send tribute and even hostages but also that of supplying the Han with soldiers and labourers and contributing to the defence of the borders. A considerable degree of administrative control was exercised by the Han government over the activities of such 'inner subjects', monitored through the creation of special offices.[63] The peculiar relationship with the tribes of the Xiongnu, organized into a confederacy at least as powerful as the Han, developed – after the Han founder was defeated – initially into a 'marriage treaty system', in which the Han court was to send a princess to the Xiongnu ruler (*shanyu*) as well as gifts several times each year. But the positions of the Han and Xiongnu reversed after the successes under Han emperor Wudi (r. 141–87 BCE) when the marriage treaty system was replaced by a new tributary system according to which a Xiongnu prince and tribute (*gong*) were to be sent as hostage to the Han court, and the *shanyu* was to attend the Han court to pay homage in person.

During the Tang (619–907 CE) the dual system under which foreign states either just paid tribute or were subject to a degree of administrative control continued. The Korean kingdoms, for example, were regarded as vassal states, sending tribute to the Tang court but not subject to interference. On the other hand, the peoples in the area that later became Vietnam were under the administrative control of the Tang government.[64]

Archaic and classical Greece became a patchwork of sovereign micro-states: poleis or city states, and *ethne* or tribal communities (having no urban centre unlike the *poleis*). Their pursuit of autonomy resulted in a far-reaching particularism. The micro-states, however, often sought rapprochement, partly for economic or security reasons, partly because they gradually realized that they shared a common ethnic identity (*ethnogenesis*) based on a shared language, religion, mythology, etc. The latter tendency may explain why certain alliances were strongly focused on peacekeeping rather than control of foreign regions – although there were exceptions, especially in relation to military alliances. There were various forms of alliances which were intended to be permanent, and as such were sealed by oaths and other symbolic practices, but they ultimately failed. The Greeks were never united, even in the face of looming threats from abroad, until Philip II of Macedonia, an outsider, realized Greek political unity with the establishment of the

[63] Yü 1986: 379–81; Lewis 2007: 145–49.   [64] Lewis 2009: 154–55.

league of Corinth, a hegemonic alliance of which he was the leader. The subsequent Hellenistic era led on the one hand to the formation of the Hellenistic kingdoms of which city states became part, and on the other hand to alliances such as the Achaian and the Aetolian confederations, in the northern Peloponnese and central Greece respectively, uniting large areas that did not end up as part of a monarchy. Rapprochements are attested between the Hellenistic realms and these leagues: for example, the early Ptolemies, the Hellenistic monarchs ruling Egypt, sought to intervene in Greek politics by financially supporting the Achaian confederation in their common struggle against Macedonian hegemony. Ptolemy III even became the leader of the Achaian confederation and also concluded a military pact with the Aetolian league.[65] The Achaian and the Aetolian confederations were the last attempts to transcend the fragmentation of the Greek polis-system, but they were ultimately absorbed by the Roman empire.

The following four types of alliances are found in the ancient Greek world.[66] First, 'equal citizenship' (*isopoliteia*), a simple form, well-attested in the Hellenistic period: an agreement whereby a city state granted citizenship rights to all members of another city state (for example, a mother city granting citizenship to a colony). Citizens could exercise their civil rights in the foreign city state only if they took up residence there. Secondly, the amphictyony.[67] This was a cultic league of neighbouring, but politically independent states clustered around a religious centre; the member states were those who 'dwelt around (the temple)' (*amphiktyones*). Its aim was to protect collectively a transregional sanctuary, that is a sanctuary of importance to a wider area (and not just to one city state). But at the same time, the cultic league created a neutral platform where there was room for non-violent interstate communication and settling conflicts in a peaceful way. The amphictyony of the Panionium included twelve Ionian cities of Asia Minor from around the Poseidon temple on the Mycale peninsula. The best-known amphictyonic league is that of Delphi protecting the oracle temple of Apollo (originally centred around the temple of Demeter of Anthela near the Thermopylai). The membership was confirmed by an oath, promising to protect the sanctuary against violators, punishing them with 'hand and foot and voice' and thus allowing sacred wars.[68] The oath also arranged the war between the amphictyony's members: one could not, for example, cut a member's city from water supply. Each member sent two representatives

---

65 Hölbl 2001: 45, 51–52.   66 Lonis 2007: 267–87; Giovannini 2007: 222–89.
67 Funke 2013.   68 Aeschin. 2.115.

to the meetings, one held in spring and one in the fall. As a consequence of its strong reputation and success, Apollo's Delphian temple became an international oracle, dealing with problems also from outside the amphictyons' territory. Thirdly, the military alliance (symmachy).[69] Comparable to NATO or the former Warsaw Pact, this was in its purest form an alliance on a voluntary and equal basis between two or more Greek states to combat a common enemy, such as the Hellenic league that attempted to avoid the invasion of the Persians in 481 BCE. But most symmachies were hegemonic alliances, established for security reasons with a single and strong state as its leader (*hegemon*). The authority rested with the council (*synedrion*) where decisions were taken according to the principle of equality of votes, but the influence of the leading state was predominant. The members were bound by an oath, not among themselves but with the leading state. In the event of war, the command was left to the *hegemon*. The danger, however, was that the *hegemon* could affect the autonomy of the members in the political, judicial or financial spheres and that the alliance degenerated into a dominion (*archè*). The Delian League, established in 478 BCE to withstand the Persians after these failed to conquer the Greek mainland, held its meetings on the small island of Delos, where initially the league's treasury was kept. The members contributed to build a substantial fleet. The league, under the leadership of democratic Athens, ensured economic prosperity and safety at sea, but evolved into an instrument of dominance in which Athens behaved imperialistically and punished members who wanted to leave the union. One of Athens' politicians, Cleon, denounced this imperialist behaviour, observing that 'a democracy is incapable of governing others'.[70] The fourth type of alliance found in the ancient Greek world is the confederation (*koinon*).[71] This was a new state, formed by a number of micro-states with a common ethnic affiliation and having its own institutions, officials, coinage and a federal army. Citizens henceforth possessed a double citizenship: that of the *koinon* and that of their city state or tribe (reminiscent of a modern-era federal state such as the European Union). A transregional sanctuary usually served as meeting place.[72] One of the communities could be dominant, such as Thebes in the Boiotian league, but in general powerful members preferred to negotiate compromises. As we learn from the *Hellenika Oxyrhynchia*, the constitution of the Boiotian league divided Boiotia into eleven districts, each providing one federal magistrate; Thebes controlled four of these districts.

69 Cartledge 2002b; Ma, Papazarkadas and Parker 2009; Figueira and Jensen 2013.
70 Thuc. 2.14.   71 Larsen 1968; Beck 1997; McInerney 2013.   72 Funke 2012.

Treaties in the Greek world were confirmed by an oath, which was protected by the gods. Breaking oaths could bring the wrath of the gods and could clash with public opinion.[73] Another possible guarantee for the implementation of treaties was the exchange of hostages, but such a phenomenon has only been attested among the Greeks in agreements with 'barbarians' (that is, non-Greeks). A stronger state (such as Athens, Sparta, Thebes or the Hellenistic monarchs), however, could unilaterally demand hostages to enforce obedience and loyalty.[74]

Owing to the patchwork of small states, which even as part of a Hellenistic empire still enjoyed a certain degree of independence, a supranational authority was lacking that could impose sanctions. Yet the city states wanted to prevent or settle conflicts diplomatically and experimented with all kinds of interstate dispute resolution.[75] These experiments often settled minor disagreements, such as discussions about the ownership of border lands. The alliances described above already demonstrate that consultation took place within their context, but a typical phenomenon of the Greek world was arbitration and mediation by a third party, discussed in the next section.

During the Republic (and earlier), the Romans used a range of different forms to formalize relationships with other polities, the specific nature of which are often heavily contested. One of the problems is that many treaties and alliances are attested only in later historical narratives such as Livy's *History of Rome* (*Ab urbe condita*) and Dionysius of Halicarnassus' *Early Roman History* (*Antiquitates Romanae*), both first century BCE. The key core concepts are *foedus* ('treaty'), *amicitia* ('friendship') and *societas* ('partnership'). The old distinction between a formal category of 'equal' and 'unequal' treaties (*foedera aequa* and *iniqua*) is no longer widely used. The relationship between the Romans and their treaty partners varied according to the real-life power and influence of those partners; often the Romans set themselves up as the 'senior' partners even in agreements that at first sight seem to be among equals. Only in rare cases was there a real relationship of equality – for example, in the agreements with the Parthians in the late Republic and early Empire. Even those agreements were represented by Augustus as military and political successes on the part of the Romans, for example, after the Roman defeat at Carrhae in 53 BCE, one of the most traumatic events for the Romans: large numbers of Roman soldiers were lost with the Roman standards falling into the hands of the Parthians. Augustus negotiated the return of the standards, which had haunted the Roman collective

---

73 Chaniotis 2004.   74 Giovannini 2007: 151–55.   75 Giovannini 2007: 143.

consciousness as a symbol of this humiliating defeat. He did not, however, dare take on the powerful Parthian empire militarily. And yet, the breastplate of the famous Prima Porta statue portrays the hand-over of the standards from the 'barbarian' in a clearly triumphant light: it looks like an acknowledgement of Parthian defeat and an assertion of Roman superiority.

The *foedus* was a 'ceremonial treaty of peace and friendship between Rome and another state which is placed under the protection of the gods'.[76] The well-known *foedus Cassianum*, called after the consul who represented Rome, was concluded in 493 BCE after the first serious military conflict between the Romans and allied Latin towns. Both sides wanted a lasting peace and promised each other help when warred upon. The text was inscribed on a column behind the speakers' tribune on the *Forum Romanum*. The highly prominent and symbolically charged location gives an idea of the importance that continued to be attributed to this foundational document of Roman power in Italy. The text is found, in Greek, in Dionysius of Halicarnassus (first century BCE):

> Let there be peace between the Romans and all the Latin cities as long as the heavens and the earth shall remain where they are. Let them neither make war upon another themselves nor bring in foreign enemies nor grant a safe passage to those who shall make war upon either. Let them assist one another, when warred upon, with all their forces, and let each have an equal share of the spoils and booty taken in their common wars. Let suits relating to private contracts be determined within ten days, and in the nation where the contract was made. And let it not be permitted to add anything to, or take anything away from these treaties except by the consent both of the Romans and of all the Latins.[77]

The various conflicts between Rome and other Italian communities led to more agreements; many of these resulted from Roman victories after military conflicts and were thus concluded between a superior Rome and a subordinated party. Rome obliged the subject Italian territories to denounce the existing treaties and operated a differentiated system of integrating, or partially integrating, other communities into their sphere of influence by (initially, selectively) granting citizen rights (with or without voting rights).

During the early Republic, the granting of citizenship was a means of political control for the Romans and was therefore not desirable for the defeated. The right to vote, when you had it, required travelling to Rome,

---

76 Galsterer 1998/2006.   77 DHal 6.95.2–3 (trans. Cary).

sometimes over long distances, to exert that right, which was not feasible for owners of small holdings or farms. But by the time of the 'Social Wars' at the beginning of the first century BCE, citizenship might have become something desirable.[78] A strong testimony to the fact that the Republican system of treaties was working, and not based simply on fear and/or military oppression, is provided by an episode of the Hannibal war: when Hannibal was active in Italy after his invasion in 218 BCE, he did not manage, contrary to his intentions, to split the Roman system of alliances. The Italians remained, for the most part, on Rome's side. Many other factors, however, contributed to the success of the Roman expansion in Italy, such as elite groups that wanted to be associated with Rome for political and economic reasons and for prestige.[79] Rome's relationship with peoples and communities in Italy needs to be distinguished from that with peoples and communities outside of Italy.[80] In particular, Rome did not quickly extend citizenship via agreements to people outside Italy. Here, the Romans also often used pre-existing Hellenistic Greek diplomatic 'infrastructure', such as the role of arbiters in interstate conflicts and of 'benefactors' to Greek communities, in order to gain influence.

Generally, the strength of Roman interstate relations was that they offered concrete advantages (at least to key individuals, if not to entire communities) alongside the demand for services, especially military support. If the treaties of the Republic are considered from the perspective of empire building, they clearly show that the Romans – while generally not being very interventionist – did expect their treaty partners to provide military assistance when required. Those troops under Roman influence gave Rome extraordinary military power. This is seen today as one of the key factors in the successful creation by the Romans of an empire of unprecedented scale.

---

78 But note that the aims of the 'Social War' are controversially debated in scholarship, and the war has variously been seen as a fight for citizenship and greater involvement in Roman power or, indeed, as a rebellion against Rome. On the pros and cons of citizenship in Rome's development, see Rosenstein 2007: 233–34: 'In the short run, therefore, enrolment among the Roman citizenry would not have seemed a terribly desirable outcome to the Latins or any of the other peoples in central Italy who over the course of the fourth and third centuries suffered this fate when they, too, met defeat. But citizenship laid the foundations over the long run for reconciliation between Rome and the limited number of its vanquished enemies upon whom it chose to impose this status', namely by offering especially members of the higher social strata good career options. See also Terrenato 2019.
79 This has recently led scholars like Terrenato to propose a revisionist view of how Roman expansion happened in Italy (see Terrenato 2019).
80 Cf. Rosenstein 2007: 241–42.

Amicitia and *societas* could result from a formal document or treaty, as already shown by the *foedus Cassianum*. The three treaties between Romans and Carthaginians concluded before the outbreak of the First Roman–Carthaginian War (264 BCE) can be considered commercial treaties, as they define the spheres of influence of the trading partners. Nevertheless, they conceptualize the relationship between Romans and Carthaginians in terms of *philia-amicitia*, 'friendship'. Oaths had to be sworn to confirm the treaty, pointing to the strongly religious character of those and other treaties, at least in early times. Friendly relationships did not, however, always require a formal document or treaty, as in the case, for example, of the *amicitia* between Rome and Saguntum which played a key role in the outbreak of the Second Roman–Carthaginian War in 218 BCE (the famous Hannibalic War). There is no official record of this *amicitia*-relationship, however, which had led some scholars to argue that later references to such a relationship are an ex-post construction of the Romans claiming there had been an agreement only in order to justify their war against Carthage.[81]

Amicitia became a prominent tool of international relations in the later Roman Republic and (early) Empire. Foreign rulers all over the world became keen to receive the title of *amicus populi Romani*, an endorsement from the Romans of their position of power, which gave them prestige through 'official' Roman backing. Badian concisely sums up the nature of these *amicitia* agreements: 'At first often seen as a connection between "equals", this *amicitia* became, with the increasing power of Rome, more like a client–patron relationship, where unlimited demands were made upon the "client", while Rome as "patron" was obligated to nothing.'[82] Using client kings as a way of demonstrating the extent of Roman power was also popular with Augustus, who mentions how many ambassadors from different peoples came to pay their respects to him (see above).

The large group of alliances entered into by ancient polities can be classified according to the principles of equality or subordination. Subordination treaties regulated the payment of tribute by the weaker police and/or the supply of troops or labourers; in ancient China the inferior, non-Chinese, states could also partly be incorporated into the administrative framework of the Chinese empire as 'inner vassals'. Many of the so-called equal treaties had in practice

---

81 Cf. Hoyos 1998: 175–78, esp. 176.
82 Badian 1996/2006. See also Hardwick 2000: 345, who speaks with respect of Augustus' presentation of Roman power of 'the association between setting new frontiers, pacification and the claim of justice, as well as the exploitation of quasi-diplomatic mechanisms such as client-kingship'.

a dominant partner, such as the 'equal' alliances in the Chinese Spring and Autumn period, the hegemonic leagues of the Greek world, or most treaties concluded with Rome being the 'senior' partner. Alliances with some degree of equality between the partners range from commercial agreements, treaties on the extradition of refugees or non-aggression alliances and military collaborations to face a common enemy to confederations in which the participating states cooperated closely and shared citizenship. Treaties were an essential part of diplomacy, which emerged as an international system in the ancient Near East in the mid-fourteenth century BCE. In more distant states, such as the ancient Near Eastern polities, envoys and the exchange of gifts played a crucial role, while in smaller, neighbouring states, such as the Greek city states, consultation took place on the occasion of leagues' meetings. Arbitration or mediation through the intervention of a third party to settle conflicts seems to be a typically Greek phenomenon (see next section).

In ancient times no international court was available to settle legal disputes if diplomacy failed, so the question is how the agreements laid down in a treaty could be enforced? Alliances in almost all ancient societies (India was an exception) were sealed by an oath to the gods, who were considered witnesses and enforcers. The oath taking could be accompanied by sacrificial ceremonies or shared meals. Public opinion also played a role especially in democratic regions, which disapproved of breaking agreements. Sometimes treaties could be enforced by exchanging or unilaterally demanding hostages, or a broken oath could be punished by military intervention.

Arbitration, Mediation and a 'Common-Peace' Experiment

In this section we briefly consider an alternative to diplomacy in conflict management: arbitration and mediation with the help of a third party in whom both parties put their trust.[83] These phenomena, which are a kind of early precursor of an international court, are typical of the Greek world and are hardly attested elsewhere.[84]

Mediation brought parties together to confer without loss of face, but involved no judicial authority; unlike arbitration, which entailed a judicial process in which the parties accepted the arbitrator's authority. The arbitrator, who conducted a trial and pronounced a verdict, was typically

---

83 Giovannini 2007: 177–84; Ager 2013; Magnetto 2015.
84 For the ancient Near East, for example, one instance is found in Herodotus 1.74 relating to the year 585 BCE; Altman 2012: 202–3.

a prestigious private person, a group of people with an established reputation or another community (*ekkletos polis*). Such interstate arbitration could take a lot of time: the settlement of a dispute between two Cretan poleis initially took six months and was even extended to one year.[85] Either the trial was held in the arbitrating city, in the presence of delegations of both parties, or the court could be mobile (for example, because it wanted to inspect disputed borders). Such forms of dispute resolution were not only used in conflicts between smaller states, but also in response to imperialist actions by Hellenistic monarchs, where the third party was rather a dominant power, such as the Roman Senate. The initiative for arbitration could come either from the litigants or from the third party, as was the case when the Roman Senate, through its envoy Popillius Laenas, ordered the monarch Antiochus IV to abort his attack on Egypt in 168 BCE, albeit mainly because Rome feared a too powerful Seleucid kingdom.[86] The interstate arbitration should not be confused with the summoning of foreign judges, who were involved in trials between private citizens of the same city. The initiative for this was taken by the city state of the litigants. The ad hoc court of foreign judges had to restore 'concord' (*homonoia*), especially in disputes arising from commercial and economic matters or from crimes.[87]

An unusual Greek experiment from the fourth century BCE, which also exceeded the national borders of the parties involved, were the 'common peace' (*koine eirene*) treaties.[88] All Greek cities, whether they had participated in the conflict or not, were asked to abide by the terms of the 'common peace'; the treaty was not limited in time, unlike other peace treaties. Smaller, more vulnerable states in particular had an interest in such a general peace, but powerful states did not always feel the need to keep to the terms of such treaties and often chose to impose their will through military actions.

States Declaring War and Fighting 'Just' Wars

This section gives an overview of how states started a war procedurally and whether (and how) they legally justified recourse to armed conflicts – in other words, was there such a thing as a 'just war'? Justifications of war should be distinguished from factors that drove wars, such as a competition culture or economic considerations; these underlying factors are not discussed here. Furthermore, the question is answered whether certain rules in

---

85 Chaniotis 1996: nos. 54–56.   86 Ager 2013.   87 Crowther 2007; Magnetto 2015.
88 Jehne 1994; Tritle 2007: 180–81; Ager 2013.

wartime applied regarding the handling of captives and enemy property, as established nowadays in the Geneva conventions. Finally, we briefly consider the concept of neutrality.

Attitudes to war in the ancient Near East are different depending on whether tribal groups were involved, who saw war as the normal course of events, or city states and larger territorial states, which preferred peace with a view to smooth trade relations and economic prosperity. If it did come to a war,[89] divine approval was required. Because many conflicts were about territorial issues, the judgment of the gods was important because they had set the boundaries and changing these borders was considered sacrilege. Eventually, the outcome of the battle was regarded as a divine ordeal (an 'ordeal by battle'). In addition, a declaration of war addressed to the enemy was necessary. The lack of such a declaration was regarded as unethical, as is apparent from, for example, 'The Instruction of King Merikare' which refers to an Asiatic nomad who ' does not announce the day of combat, like a thief who darts about a group'.[90]

A war had to be justified in the ancient Near East, and the declaration of war often contained the actual reason for the attack. In addition to territorial claims, many other issues (often religiously inspired) could give rise to a war, as we find, albeit post factum, in the Assyrian royal inscriptions and in 'Letters to the Gods': 'by the command of the god', to punish wrongdoers, usurpers or rebels, protect allies or enforce peace, etc.[91]

The treatment of the enemy when defeated could differ depending on whether they were rebels (who were dealt with harshly) or enemies who surrendered quickly (who could be treated mercifully). The cruelty of the Assyrians is notorious. One of the most striking practices in the ancient Near East, including Egypt, and rarely attested in the Greek or Roman world, is the deportation of all or part of the inhabitants of conquered communities, even though it was not an imperial policy until under the Assyrian Tiglat-Pileser III (744– 727 BCE).[92] Also the (statues of the) patron gods of the enemy could be taken captive.[93]

Egyptian society occupies a somewhat special place in the just war debate, partly because of the ideology that the pharaoh was the only one in the world

---

89 For the rules of war in the ancient Near East, see Liverani 2001: 108–115.
90 'The Instruction of King Merikare', lines 91–94 (trans. Lichtheim 1980: 104); Altman 2012: 52.
91 Oded 1992; Altman 2012: 174. See also Gerardi 1986 and Liverani 2001.
92 Oded 1979; Altman 2012: 108–11, 180–84, 187–89.   93 Altman 2012: 65–66, 110–11, 185–87.

who could guarantee Maat: order and justice. As a figure who ran a divine office, he had to protect Egypt from the outside world, full of chaos. Consequently, any threat to the Egyptian monarchy was seen as a violation of Maat, triggering just war as a form of self-defence. 'No man can settle down, being despoiled by the imposts of the Asiatics. I will grapple with him, that I may cut open his belly! My wish is to save Egypt and to smite the Asiatics!' was the justification of war by Pharaoh Kamose against the Hyksos who invaded the Delta.[94] When New Kingdom Egypt became part of the international community, that community paid little attention to the Egyptian world-view and the pharaoh continued to propagate the ideology mainly in his own country. Slaying the enemy, be it foreign groups or rebellious subjects, was a popular ritual on the temple walls, where the pharaoh, in front of the god, holds one or more enemies by the hair or raised arm to strike them down with a sword, axe or mace, 'expressing the complete and utter annihilation of the forces of chaos'; slaying the enemy on temple walls remained a popular motif, even among the Greco-Macedonian (Ptolemaic) kings, when in addition a variant of this ritual surfaced where the king spears inimical forces, the spear being the soldier's fundamental weapon in the Greek-Macedonian context.[95]

The ancient Indian *Arthaśāstra* conceived interstate relations in competitive terms, even among states that were considered 'allies'. In this respect, the concept of *dharma* is important: when the world is properly ordered, there is peace and prosperity. Hostility and war could be both the result of the loss of *dharma* and a righteous response to it. Whether a king resorted to war or another means of engagement was a matter of strategy (for the six stratagems, see above). Among the six strategies, *vigraha* can be considered a declaration of war insofar as it publicly inaugurated a state of open conflict but was not itself the act of marching to battle.[96] Such decisions were undoubtedly preceded by diplomatic efforts, as shown by instances of emissaries delivering such messages in the epics. Certain symbolic acts, such as the lighting of beacon fires, could be used to signal the commencement of hostilities.[97] There is a distinction between *vigraha* as a state of hostilities and battle (*yuddha*) itself. The *Arthaśāstra* distinguishes between 'open war' in which the location and timing of the attack is announced; 'covert war' 'causing fright, surprise attack'; and 'secret war' which includes 'secret measures' and the use of secret agents.[98]

---

94 Pritchard 1969: 232; Cox 2017, translation from 373.
95 Coppens 2021, quotation from 437.   96 See Olivelle 2011 for further discussion.
97 Viswanatha 1925: 129.   98 KAŚ 7.6.40–41.

The *Arthaśāstra* further declares: 'War at a pre-announced time and place, however, is the most righteous (*dharmiṣṭa*).'[99]

There was no notion of an international order that enforced the sovereignty of states. It is held as a truth in the *Arthaśāstra* that stronger states attack weaker states and that all states seek to subordinate or 'outwit' their rivals (friend and foe). Although no 'legal' justification need be given for an attack, our sources demonstrate the necessity of typifying such contests as 'righteous battle'. While subordination of one's rivals may have been a given, unrestrained war was strongly censured. In general, attacks against 'unrighteous kings' were seen in the *Arthaśāstra* as more legitimate interventions than against 'righteous' kings. Also the legal literature of Dharmaśāstra, as well as Buddhist and Jain literature, tends to be decidedly against unrighteous forms of fighting. One formulation of laws of war are given in the *Baudhāyana Dharmasūtra* (c. third century BCE): 'The king should not turn back in battle or strike with barbed or poisoned weapons. He should not engage in battle with people who are afraid, intoxicated, mad or delirious, or who have lost their armour; as also women, children, old people, and Brahmins, unless they are trying to kill him.'[100] The tradition expounds greatly on such rules, and issues of righteous battle are central to both of the great epics.

For early China, the historical sources of the Western Zhou and the Spring and Autumn periods (c. 1045–464 BCE) contain several examples of a 'solemn declaration' or 'oath' (*shi*) made by the ruler, or commanding general, to his troops before the opening of a campaign. For example, the *Shang shu* (Book of Documents) attributes to a Zhou prince a speech to his soldiers (the 'Speech at Fe or *Feishi*', thought to have been written in the Spring and Autumn period) in preparation for an attack on some rebellious tribes (c. 1000 BCE), in which he orders them to have their equipment in good order, not to leave the ranks to pursue escaping animals or servants, not to commit robbery and to prepare provisions for the day on which the 'punishment' of the rebellious tribes is to commence.[101] Lewis, dealing with 'solemn declarations' recorded in the *Zuozhuan* (Annals of the Spring and Autumn period, 771–464 BCE), emphasizes their religious nature. He sees war in Zhou China as a religious activity by the warrior aristocracy (constituting the ruling class in the various states), marked by invocations to the gods and sacrifices to the ancestors, especially those of the reigning house.[102] The aristocrats felt obliged to defend and improve upon the achievements of the ancestors, including the acquisition of territory. At the same time, there were important chivalrous aspects to warfare deriving from

99 KAŚ 10.4.1.   100 BDh 1.18.9–12.   101 Legge 1960: 621–25.   102 Lewis 1990: 22–25.

the acute sense of honour possessed by the participants. There was a readiness to take offence and resort to war to expunge the shame. Lewis concludes 'it was through its role in defending the state's or the lineage's honour that warfare became a fundamental part of the ancestral cult'.[103]

The 'Speech at Fe or *Feishi*' of the Zhou prince had referred already to the idea of the justification for war, in the notion that the enemy deserved to be 'punished'. In another document contained in the *Shang shu*, the 'Speech at Mu' or *Mushi* (thought to have been written in the Spring and Autumn or Warring States periods), the Zhou king, preparing for the conquest of the Shang state (middle of the eleventh century BCE), justified the campaign in an address to his army as the punishment of a ruler who has listened only to the words of his wife, has abandoned the sacrifices to the gods and has mistreated his relatives.[104] He is now to receive the punishment of Heaven, inflicted by Heaven's agent: the Zhou king. The above-mentioned warrior aristocracy's sense of honour also embraced, however, the acceptance of certain rules under which campaigns should be waged (to be distinguished from the rules of just wars developed later in the Warring States). Thus, it was considered dishonourable to meet the enemy and not engage with him by fixing a date and place for battle. Furthermore, advantage should not be taken of any special difficulty affecting the opposed state. Thus, should the ruler of the enemy state die during the course of the campaign, the honourable course of conduct was to withdraw.

Things changed with the onset of the Warring States period (464–221 BCE), marked by the dissolution of the old aristocratic lineages, the disengagement of war from the ancestral cult and concepts of honour, and the formation of armies composed of peasants and commanded by professional generals. According to theoretical discussions of warfare written during the Warring States, recourse to violence had to be legitimate, in the sense that it should be justifiable and its application governed by rules.[105] Violence should, however, not be exercised in an indiscriminate or unrestricted fashion. Hence, war should be waged only during the autumn, not in the spring and summer, when the farmers are busy in the fields. The *Lüshi chunqiu* (Annals of Lü Buwei), compiled in 239 BCE, in its 'calendar for the four seasons' notes that in the first month of autumn the ruler should make ready his army and proceed to punish the wicked. In addition, a war should be conducted without excessive use of force and with proper regard for the welfare of the ordinary people in the state under attack, as well as for such enemy soldiers as should

---

103 Lewis 1990: 36.   104 Legge 1960: 300–305.
105 See Sawyer 1993: 126; Turner 1993; McNeal 2012: 237.

be captured. The same section of the *Lüshi chunqiu* specifies that 'when it reaches the outskirts of the capital [of the enemy state], the army does not destroy the Five Foods, plunder graves, cut down trees, burn stores and supplies, torch houses, or confiscate livestock'.[106] How far these ideals were implemented in practice is another matter.[107]

Greek society seems to have been permeated with warfare between the smaller city states, the larger hegemonic alliances or the Hellenistic monarchs. Not only are the Greeks thought to be belligerent, also the notion of war as an *agon*, a 'contest', the main aim of which was to assert one's superiority over the adversary, is a common theme in scholarship.[108] But the Greeks did not see war simply as a game. Already Homer, even if he is regarded as a 'war singer', considered war a detestable scourge and described the blessings of peace.[109] Although the notion of a just war is not as formalized as it was with the Romans, there is clear evidence that the Greeks believed that war should be legitimate.[110] In the dialogue between the Athenian invaders and their Melian victims, Thucydides writes: 'There should be such a thing as fair play and just dealing [...] we are standing for what is right against what is wrong.'[111]

Starting a war in the Greek world was not so easy due to the numerous peace and alliance treaties, the provisions of which prohibited the taking up of arms against each other and/or made arbitration mandatory in case of emerging conflicts. The Thirty Years' Peace treaty between Athens, Sparta and their allies, concluded in 446/445 BCE, stipulated that differences had to be settled by arbitration – a problematic clause for Sparta and its league when they wanted to start the Peloponnesian War against Athens fifteen years later; Athens emphasized that clause on the eve of the war.[112] Furthermore, sacred truces had to be respected in the context of festivals or games. When Sparta wanted to launch a campaign against its eternal enemy Argos, the latter immediately introduced such a truce for one of its festivals, but at an unusual time of the year. Only after the oracles of Zeus in Olympia and Apollo in Delphi indicated that it was not sacrilege to break an illegitimate truce, did Sparta dare to act.[113]

This last example already indicates that before a war was started, the will of the gods had to be taken into account. Omens such as thunder and lightning

---

106 Knoblock and Riegel 2000: 173, 178, 185.
107 Generally see McNeal 2012: chapter 2; Turner 1993: 296–305.
108 E.g. Lonis 1979 : 25–29. Further examples in Giovannini 2007: 141–42, 146.
109 Tritle 2007: 172–73.   110 Giovannini 2007: 147, 150; Ager 2013.
111 Thuc. 5.90.104, trans. Warner 1954; Ager 2013: 498.   112 Thuc. 1.78.4; Ager 2013.
113 Bonnechere 2010 and 2013.

were carefully observed: the battle of Leuktra is said to have been preceded by several omens.[114] Oracles were consulted.[115] Although there are hardly any examples among the so-called historical oracles on stone, in general the oracles tended to be 'peacemakers' rather than 'warmongers'.[116] The Delphic oracle consulted by the Spartans before the start of the Peloponnesian War was in favour of the latter, as the Athenians realized when the plague broke out in their city during the war.[117] Sacrifices were made before the start of the war: Alexander sacrificed in honour of Zeus in Dion before his campaigns, but also immediately before an encounter when the troops were lined up.[118] After a victory, the god who provided support was honoured with a monument or the donation of booty, as the Athenians did in honour of Apollo at Delphi after their Marathon victory over the Persians.[119] Not only divine goodwill was pursued: a declaration of war, like all foreign decisions, had to be approved in the popular assembly of a city state. In the case of an alliance, the decision had to be approved by the alliance's council.[120] The Peloponnesian War was even approved on two levels: by the Spartan people's assembly and by the alliance council.[121]

Little is known about how the declaration of war was communicated to the enemy.[122] In some cases a letter was delivered to the adversary by a herald, such as the letter of Philip II, Alexander's father, to the Athenians.[123] The arrestation of envoys could also be seen as a war declaration, or arms could be taken up if one of the parties refused peace proposals. During the war, the rules of normal life no longer applied, as Diodorus of Sicily points out.[124] The parties were obliged, however, to observe truces and to respect the inviolability of temples and of the goods or people under the protection of the gods (asylum seekers); the combatants had to behave correctly towards the enemy who surrendered.[125] Not everyone adhered to these rules; in 274 BCE Pyrrhus, king of western Greek Epirus, had his Gallic mercenaries plunder the royal tombs of Macedonia at Aigai (modern Vergina).[126]

The core of the Roman ideology of 'just war' was that the Romans or their allies had been wronged in some way. The first step in the declaration of war would therefore have been the opportunity that the wrongdoer make

---

114 Tuplin 1987; Bonnechere 2013.   115 Lonis 1979: 69–87.
116 Parker 2000; Bonnechere 2013: 380.   117 Thuc. 1.118.3 and 2.54.4–5.
118 Lonis 1979: 95–110.   119 Lonis 1979: 129–72.   120 Giovannini 2007: 185–92.
121 Thuc. 1.67–72.1, 79–87.6.   122 Giovannini 2007: 143.   123 Dem. 12.
124 Diod. 30.18.2.   125 Phillipson 1911: 302–3; Giovannini 2007: 143–44; 197–203.
126 Plut. *Vit. Pyrrh.* 26.12–13.

restitution. That was built into the earliest ritual of declaring war which was the domain of a priesthood called the *fetiales*. The ritual goes back to the period when Rome was a small city state and was mostly involved in conflicts with its neighbours, such as disputes about boundaries. The priest would go to the frontier and request restitution of the wrongdoer, who had thirty days to respond. If he did not respond or refused, the Senate drew up a resolution for war, the people were called to ratify it and then war was solemnly declared by the head of the *fetiales*, the *pater patratus*, by throwing a spear, dipped into blood, into the enemy's territory. That changed as Rome's sphere of power grew; it was now the Roman envoys (*legati*) who demanded restitution. Moreover, in the event of a declaration of war the spear was now thrown symbolically into enemy territory by throwing it over a column: the 'war column' (*columna bellica*) at the temple of the war goddess, Bellona, in the Circus Maximus. At first, however, the declaration itself, the *indictio belli*, would remain with the *fetiales*. That, too, changed with time, perhaps in the early 230s BCE: first the Senate drew up a resolution which was then ratified by the people and could be enacted or not by the *legati*. The *legati* would then go to the enemy to demand 'restitution'. That happened in the famous declaration of the Second Roman Carthaginian War, where the Roman envoys demanded that Hannibal, the 'aggressor', be handed over or else the Romans would declare war. It was only under Augustus, as part of the large-scale restitution of 'traditional' institutions, that the *fetiales* were re-instituted as a priesthood. In the time in between, the *fetiales* probably provided advice on formalities at the beginning and end of wars and were involved in the surrender of Roman officials who had violated the law protecting envoys, or had ratified a treaty without prior authorization by the Roman people (*iniussu populi*).

The theory of the 'just war' (*bellum iustum*) was formulated systematically only in the late first century BCE by Cicero, and presumably under the influence of Stoic philosophy. Cicero states that the reasons for the war were 'in defence of the allies' (*pro sociis*) or 'in defence of the Roman sphere of influence' (*pro imperio*).[127] An example is Augustus' statement in his *Res Gestae* that 'I made peaceful the Alps . . . but attacked no people unjustly.'[128] In practice, however, the idea of the 'just war' had existed for a long time. Fabius Pictor for example, the first Roman historian (end of the third century BCE), gives as one of the causes of the war against Hannibal the 'injustice' (Greek *adikema*) committed against the Saguntines. Contemporaries realized,

---

127 Cic. *De off.* 2.26.   128 *Res Gestae*. 26.3 (trans. Cooley 2009); cf. Hardwick 2000: 345.

however, that not every war that was 'just' by the Roman criteria was really a just war. So Caesar, who presented his war in Gaul as the defence of an ally, was criticized by his adversary Cato the Younger in the Senate in 55 BCE that his war was actually 'unjust' (*iniustum*) and that Caesar ought to be handed over to the enemy lest the gods' wrath fall upon Rome.[129] Often, therefore, there was a tension between the actual causes of wars and their representation in public. Generally, however, the dominance of the ideology of the just war meant that, unlike in modern imperialist discourse, one would hardly find an open acknowledgement from a Roman that war was being waged to subdue 'the barbarian' or gain new territory. Greek authors, by contrast, had no such qualms, and Strabo describes Augustus' conquest of the Alps as a successful and much-needed fight against uncivilized 'barbarians' and brigands.[130]

According to the *ius belli*, suffering material and physical damage, including destruction of houses and property, enslavement, burning of crops, etc., was simply a normal aspect of warfare, as they were seen also in the Greek world. Reports of excessive violence and wanton destruction are rare for the Romans, but that is certainly, at least in part, due to 'whitewashing' in later narratives. It was quite normal in Roman warfare to plunder, destroy, kill and enslave civilians, especially if they had not accepted Roman superiority, and were not willing to subject themselves to Roman rule voluntarily or when prompted to do so (*deditio*; see below) and threatened with siege by the Romans. The column of Marcus Aurelius (late second century CE) depicts scenes of aggression against the defeated, including women, and visual allusions to rape. Already Polybius saw this as a strategy.[131] The idea that inspiring fear was part of Roman foreign policy has been emphasized also by modern scholars.[132] There was no equivalent to the Geneva convention, and the defeated were at the victor's mercy. To an extent, that was mitigated by an ideology of *clementia*, the idea that if the enemy surrendered, they could (but had no right to) expect to be treated with leniency. The most concise expression of this idea is a phrase in Vergil's *Aeneid*: the Roman habit is 'to spare those who subject themselves and to destroy the arrogant (*parcere subiectis et debellare superbos*)'.[133] The *parcere*, 'sparing', however, applies only to those that have surrendered or voluntary accepted Roman supremacy. If the enemy did not surrender, the Romans would fight until they had won,

---

129 Suetonius, *Life of Julius Caesar* 24.3; Plut. *Vit. Caes.* 22.3, with discussion in Hardwick 2000: 346.
130 Strabo 4.6.6–7; cf. Cooley 2009: 223 on *Res Gestae* 26.3.   131 Polybius 10.15.4–5.
132 E.g. Rosenstein 2007.   133 Vergil *Aeneid* 6.853.

that is, until the enemy sent an embassy to ask for peace negotiations. The Romans expected a *deditio in fidem*, which meant that the defeated community relinquished any claim to decide their own fate. The Roman general was then free to do whatever he saw fit: in many cases, he would re-establish the community's integrity, but a *deditio* implied no guarantees for leniency: the Roman commander could also decide to raze the city to the ground, kill the men, sell everybody else into slavery and loot the place.[134]

'Peace' was thus intrinsically connected with military success. As Rosenstein put it well: 'Peace on any terms other than victory was not only repugnant to the majesty of Rome in the senators' view but a threat to its very existence.'[135] Those times that the Romans were themselves defeated or in highly unfavourable situations, they would nevertheless refuse peace negotiations: 'The Roman tradition was to impose rather to seek peace.'[136]

Except for India, where we have to rely largely on the secular tradition as found in the *Arthaśāstra*, in all ancient societies divine approval or at least invocation of the gods was required to start a war. In the ancient Near East, the gods could even decide the war via 'ordeal by battle', while in the Greek world omens were observed, oracles were consulted and sacrifices were made in different phases of the war. Rome installed a special priestly college (the *fetiales*) for the rituals involving war. In China's Spring and Autumn period, warfare was also part of the ancestral cult. A second important condition for starting a war in antiquity was the declaration of war to the enemy, providing information among other things about time and place, unless it was a 'secret' or 'surprise' war (as mentioned in the Indian *Arthaśāstra*).

Although from a legal perspective wars did not always need to be justified, all ancient societies sought to fight only 'righteous' wars (or what was righteous in their eyes), whether they saw war as normal behaviour of the stronger state or king; as the execution of a divine command; as a kind of self-defence protecting the state and its allies; or as a way to punish rebellious or misbehaving people. Notions of a just war are extant in all societies, but as noted above the concept of a 'just war' (*bellum iustum*) is elaborated upon systematically only in late Republican Rome, probably under the influence of Stoic philosophy.

When we turn to the aspect of basic humanitarian rights in wartime, we see that violence towards the enemy in wartime was, to a greater or lesser degree, the order of the day in antiquity. Ancient societies were well aware

---

134 On *deditio* see Dahlheim 1968: 66–67; Hölkeskamp 2000: 244–47; also, Gruen 1982.
135 Rosenstein 2007: 236.   136 Thus Barton 2007: 248.

that they used savage treatments, among other things, to inspire fear, especially the ancient Near Eastern deportations (the Assyrians, in particular, had a strikingly bad reputation). If polities envisaged avoiding excessive violence, treating captives correctly or showing leniency, then it mainly concerned enemies who had surrendered. But even such good intentions were not always put into practice.

Neutrality is a concept that is hardly found in ancient times. The reason may be that, across many societies, polities were or felt obliged by alliances or bloodline affiliations to support an ally or benefactor. Some expressions may, though, point to a notion of neutrality: in classical Indian political theory, some cognate concepts, such as 'remaining stationary' (*āsana*) and being 'uninvolved' (*udāsīna*), can refer to neutrality.[137] The Greek city states, having a certain degree of autonomy, could choose to remain neutral in conflicts as denoted by 'keep quiet; be at rest' (*hesuchian agein*); even though, again, there was no well-defined legal procedure for such neutrality.[138] The Romans were not particularly favourable towards claims of neutrality. As Baltrusch puts it concisely: 'The concept of neutrality as a status did not exist for the Romans.'[139]

Conclusion

Some researchers studying war, peace or interstate relations refer to the possible existence of an international law; they approach the subject, however, with a focus on only one of the ancient civilizations discussed in this chapter.[140] For centuries, the ancient Near East, classical India, ancient China, and the Greek and Roman worlds show a remarkably high degree of uniformity of principles and customs between states that had regular contact but were mutually independent. If such an international law existed within those regions, then it might have had its origins in international consent and agreements which are now untraceable. To speak of an international law, in the sense of a set of normative rules defining obligations between states, however, is undoubtedly a step too far. Nonetheless, similar principles and customs are found even between societies of classical and Asiatic antiquity

---

137 McClish 2014: 253–54.
138 Thuc. 5.84; Bauslaugh 1991; Giovannini 2007: 192–97; one way of escaping participation in a war in the Greek world was to claim that an oracle had disapproved of participation: see Lonis 1979: 76.
139 Baltrusch 2008: 126, 'Für die Römer gab es das Institut der Neutralität überhaupt nicht'; see also Phillipson 1911, vol. II: 303–12.
140 For example Altman 2012 on the ancient Near East; Chaniotis 2004 on the Greek world.

that had little or no contact and, therefore, could hardly make agreements or exert influence (although contacts intensified in later, Hellenistic and Roman times): for example, in the treatment of envoys, the use of oaths, the start of a war or the need to justify warfare. These similarities may rather point to a kind of 'natural' law, based on values intrinsic to human nature.[141]

International bodies where consultation was possible, such as the Delphic amphictyony, were scarce. International diplomacy, on the other hand, played a crucial role in the ancient world, and all ancient societies could rely on a well-developed framework for such contacts. An international body that could act as an arbiter in disputes over the violation of customs, laws or territorial agreements between states, similar to today's International Court of Justice (one of the organs of the United Nations), was almost non-existent in the ancient world; the exception is the Greek world, where arbitration by a third party was common. The ancients (except for India) rather relied on the gods, who were the object of 'peace' oaths and other treaties, or were consulted when a war was to be started. The gods were the ultimate, supranational authority who ensured that lawlessness would be punished. 'The fear of the gods was not necessarily or always less effective than the fear of United Nations sanctions in modern international law.'[142]

---

141 For further discussion of 'natural law', see section 'Law and Nature', Chapter 3, this volume.
142 Chaniotis 2004: 207.

5
Law and the State

Lead Author: MARK MCCLISH

Contributors: ARI BRYEN, SOPHIE DÉMARE-LAFONT,
GEOFFREY MACCORMACK AND ROBIN OSBORNE

Introduction

Much modern legal thought assumes that 'law' and the 'state' are exclusively related to one another, so that only states can make law and that law is, therefore, always 'state law'. This position, which Griffiths has named 'legal centralism', holds that: 'law is and should be the law of the state, uniform for all persons, exclusive of all other law, and administered by a single set of state institutions'.[1] There is, as Griffiths and others have identified, a strongly ideological dimension to such thinking, which mixes 'assertions about how the world ought to be' with '*a priori* assumptions about how it actually and even necessarily is'.[2] In order that such assumptions do not hinder our analysis of law in the ancient world, we must remain open to the possibility that 'not all the phenomena related to law and not all that are law-like have their source in government'.[3] Indeed, we find in the ancient world complex legal environments in which much of law has its source beyond the state. This does not mean, however, that we must label as 'law' every normative order or rule set that we encounter in the ancient world.[4]

Forms of governance varied considerably across ancient societies. Monarchy based on a dynastic principle was the basic pattern of governance in China, classical India, Mesopotamia, and arguably also Rome after 14 CE, although it took different forms. Representative forms of government prevailed at times in ancient Rome and Greece. In ancient Greece, the

---

1 Griffiths 1986: 3.
2 Griffiths 1986: 3. The prevalence of this view reflects the success of historical efforts by states to naturalize this relationship (see Tamanaha 2008: 379).
3 Moore 1986: 15. 4 Twining 2010.

fundamental political unit was the polis, conceived of as the community of *politai* ('citizens'). Even so, there was no particular privileged form of government in the polis, and different cities at different times were governed by sole rulers, by a select minority of the native adult free-born residents, or by the majority of those residents. Even after the advent of monarchy, Romans continued to recognize the ideological value of portraying their monarch, when possible, as a civilian 'first-among-equals'.

There was considerable variability in the degree of centralization both between and within polities in different societies. After the Western Zhou / Spring and Autumn period (c. 1045–464 BCE), for instance, states in China became highly centralized. What is more, political power in ancient monarchies was commonly characterized by fluidity, as in the ancient Near East, where the king held supreme authority but had to negotiate with other constituencies, such as local powers and tribal groups. Stanley Tambiah has suggested for South and Southeast Asia the model of the 'galactic polity': 'a kind of galaxy-type structure with lesser political replicas revolving around the central entity in perpetual motion of fission or incorporation'.[5] Larger political formations, of course, increase the complexity of state systems. The Roman imperial monarchy, for example, presided over a complicated system of government, at the bottom of which there is evidence for significant self-determination by urban communities governed by property-owners. Empires and independent city states are quite different legal environment, and issues of scale, centralization and complexity undoubtedly lie behind some of the differences between state legal systems explored in this chapter.

Whatever its form, the ancient state was only one player, albeit a dominant one, within legal worlds characterized by integration and fragmentation as well as by contest and cooperation. The purpose of this chapter is to compare how states in different cultures interacted with their respective legal environments. For reasons discussed in Chapter 1 (above), a direct comparison between state systems is not feasible, not least as the scholarly traditions which have developed around each area neither bring the same assumptions nor use the same analytical frameworks. A focus on five general areas – constitutional norms, legislative power, jurisdiction, the structure of the state legal system and legitimacy – allows us to see some of what is distinctive and what is common between cultures and more generally to isolate issues deserving more focused scrutiny. In all of this, however, we must remain attuned to the fact that, regardless of tradition, concepts related to law were

5 Tambiah 1976: 102.

often developed to legitimize and empower various actors.[6] Exploring 'law and the state' is as much about understanding suasion as it is about understanding structure.

Constitutional Frameworks and Norms: Shaping State Power

All states exist within normative frameworks that, however formalized or implicit, structure expectations about the origin, use and goals of political power. These frameworks are often informal, embedded in myth, religion, ritual, ethics and moral law. In some cases, however, ancient states codified positive rules meant to authorize and delimit the power of the state, approaching forms of 'constitutional law'. Here, we examine both informal and formal normative frameworks that help us to understand how law did and did not help to shape the state's use of political power.

According to the extant evidence from Mesopotamia, the gods determined the order of the world and human beings were to shape their lives according to divine principles. The king was considered to be the best interpreter and performer of divine will. He was 'capable' (*le'û*) and, in this sense, omniscient.[7] In theory, this made him sovereign: the ultimate holder of power. The legal provisions gathered in the Near Eastern law collections also contributed to this understanding of the cosmic order.[8] The prologues or epilogues of these law collections refer constantly to the gods, who appointed the king in order to make justice and equity prevail in the land. They further explain that the king has complied with the order of the gods in issuing the law collection. His justice had been established in accordance with divine expectations. Kingship, however, was not the only political authority in Mesopotamia. Collective powers were also active in some cities where the king did not play a prominent role, such as in Emar and Aššur at the beginning of the second millennium BCE.[9] There is a distinction, however, as collective bodies, such as local assemblies, are never called *le'û*, even though they were in practice endowed with the power of decision. Finally,

---

6 Tamanaha 2008: 396.
7 Up to the point that the king was sometimes worshipped like a god. About divine kingship, see Brisch 2012.
8 Roth 1997.
9 Dercksen 2004; Fleming 1992. The situation became quite different later, with the territorial expansion of the Assyrians and the formation of the kingdom and then of the empire.

the 'divine will' on which legal rules were based was also to be found within custom and tradition.

Law itself was not the source of the king's power in ancient Mesopotamia, nor did it limit his authority formally in any way. There was nothing like a constitution, whether written or oral, that framed the definition and exercise of political power. The only manner in which law did constrain political power at all was in the form of covenant treaties, between vassals and suzerains. Royal authority derived instead from the gods through a ceremony of investiture and from tradition: keeping the ways of the predecessors, acting along the lines of the fathers, and observing the commands of the gods. The weight of these practices was felt more compelling than any legal sanction. In this sense, one could consider these practices as 'constitutional', in the same vein as the French *lois fondamentales*. In periods of crisis, however, the dynastic principle did not prevent making an appeal to the gods so as to determine which prince might be the best candidate to succeed his father.

In ancient India, state power was symbolized by the *daṇḍa* ('staff'; 'sceptre'), which represented the king's capacity for violence put to constructive ends. Within the realist tradition of statecraft, the king's capacity for violence was the source of his power and was constrained only by practical limits.[10] Jurists of the mainstream Brahmanical tradition, however, characterized *daṇḍa* as a divine force, generated by the gods to be used in keeping with the cosmic principle of *dharma*. As it is written in the epochal Laws of Manu:

> For the king's sake, the Lord formerly created Punishment, his son – the Law (*dharma*) and protector of all beings – made from the energy of Brahman ... For punishment (*daṇḍa*) is immense energy, and it cannot be wielded by those with uncultivated selves. It assuredly slays a king who deviates from the Law (*dharma*), along with his relatives.[11]

This position – that state power was ultimately subject to the cosmic law of *dharma* – eventually triumphs in Indian legal thought, even if it remains aspirational. For, we find signs in many places of an ongoing negotiation between state power and law.[12] In addition, we find the recognition that acts against *dharma* were sometimes necessary to save *dharma* itself – a major

---

10 See McClish 2019b.
11 MDh 7.14 and 7.28. In this passage punishment (*daṇḍa*) is both equated with *dharma* and subject to *dharma*. The idea seems to be that true punishment, i.e. not merely violence, is that which conforms to *dharma*.
12 Compare, for example, KAŚ 3.1.39 with 3.1.45, as discussed in Olivelle and McClish 2015 and McClish 2019a.

theme of the great Sanskrit epic, the *Mahābhārata*.[13] The great legal codes of the orthodox jurists – considered a form of secondary scriptural revelation[14] – are themselves expressions of *dharma*, and jurists such as Manu and Yājñavalkya include sections on statecraft as *rājadharma*: the 'sacred law for kings'.

No formal legal sanction, however, could be brought against a king who violated *rājadharma*. Despite detailing substantive rules for kings, *rājadharma* remained a moral law serving only rhetorical purposes in the political sphere by bolstering or diminishing the legitimacy of a ruler aspiring to be seen as 'righteous'. As elsewhere, this may have been particularly important to new kings, usurpers and conquerors. In this way, the Brahmanical priesthood possessed in *(rāja)dharma* a potentially powerful restraint on the king. A king's legitimacy could suffer if he was perceived to be acting improperly (*anyāyena*).[15] The rhetoric of *rājadharma* appears simply to be a particular interpretation of that more general sentiment.

Whether understood in terms of *rājadharma* or not, however, there were strong customary expectations regarding the proper use of royal ruling power. The realist tradition expresses these in general terms and regards them rather as a matter of staving off discontent among the subjects.[16] However articulated, such expectations were never formalized into anything like constitutional law. Texts of the statecraft tradition, in particular, do provide regulations (*pracāra*), and rules are given for various state officials.[17] Certain mid- to low-level state functionaries appear to have been subject to investigation and trial for misconduct in the course of their official duties. It is not clear, however, whether or how royal courts dealt with such matters.

Of significance within the ancient Chinese evidence, in a similar context, is the concept of the 'Mandate of Heaven', evidenced from the time of the Western Zhou (c. 1045–771 BCE). Rendered as a principle of government, this doctrine enshrines the belief, constantly propagated by emperors and their officials, that the ruler is responsible to Heaven for his governing of the people. In both pre-Confucian and Confucian thinking, the Mandate refers first of all, and indeed primarily, to correct moral behaviour on the part of the ruler. Particularly in the Han (206 BCE–220 CE) and later dynasties, failure by

---

13 See Fitzgerald 2004: 128–42.
14 These are the so-called *smṛti*s, teachings that were 'remembered' by the great sages, as opposed to the original revelation of the Vedas, which were 'heard' (*śruti*).
15 *KAŚ* 7.5.16-27.   16 *KAŚ* 7.5.16-27.
17 See, e.g., *KAŚ* 2.6.14; 2.7.2, 3, 9, 10, 24; 2.8.3. Many of these procedures are given at *KAŚ* 2.11-34.

the emperor to observe the correct ritual behaviour in his family relationships might also be construed as a sign of lack of virtue that called for an adverse response from Heaven. Lack of virtue in government might manifest in other ways, such as the undue influence of improper persons on policy-making or government decisions, harsh or improper use of punishments and flagrant cases of corruption and injustice, especially in the context of homicide.

That said, we should perhaps not over-emphasize the role of the Mandate. For example, under the influence of the 'legalists', a school of thought that flourished in the fourth and third centuries BCE (see Chapter 3, this volume), the Qin rulers in particular established a system of government under which the ruler's legitimacy and authority were not open to question. The Mandate, instead, seems to have served rather specific rhetorical purposes and was strictly applicable to the extreme situation in which a ruler had been so wicked or even negligent in his care for his people that Heaven had withdrawn its Mandate from his rule and transferred it to another. As such, it was typically invoked by the founder of a new dynasty to explain the reasons for his success and procure legitimacy for his government. One also finds, however, individual rulers invoking the Mandate of Heaven as a principle by which they are guided in the conduct of government. They may accept the blame for some failure on the part of the government and express the fear that, unless things were put right, Heaven might withdraw its Mandate from their dynasty, or they might assert that they are striving to govern in order to justify Heaven's trust in them.[18]

There is a widely held view, particularly associated with the teachings of Confucius, that there existed a higher moral law, codified in the ancient ritual classics such as the *Liji* (*Book of Rites*), which imposed a stronger and superior obligation on humans than human positive law (*fa*), which could refer specifically to the directives of the ruler. In this context *fa* is contrasted with *li* (rites or propriety). *Li* expressed a fundamental set of moral values making up the true imperatives for human conduct. Should there be a conflict between the principles of conduct demanded by *fa* and those enjoined by *li*, then the latter should prevail.[19] There is, however, no clear evidence that the latter always prevailed over the former. If ambiguous, *fa* might be interpreted in a manner that accorded with 'higher law'.[20] *Li* does

---

18 Gaurier 1992: 27–54; Loewe 1994: 88–93.   19 Chang 2000: vii–xii.
20 Chang 2000: vii–xii.

come gradually to be integrated into penal codes from the time of the Han, or earlier.

Across the ancient Chinese evidence, there are recognized limits placed upon the ruler's power, limits recognized by prudent rulers themselves. Even the 'legalists' – renowned as a school of philosophy and statecraft that focused upon the importance of the ruler as the source of law – advocated that the country should be governed by the law itself as distinct from the personal wishes of the ruler.[21] We do have important statements by ministers of constitutional principles that militated against arbitrary acts on the part of the emperor, though they did not always prevent them. An example comes from the early Han. The emperor, contrary to the law, wished to order the execution of an individual who had displeased him. On this occasion the commandant of justice enunciated the following principle: if the emperor, acting on the spur of the moment, had ordered the execution immediately, then no objection could be made in law, since the emperor was exercising his prerogative as supreme legislator and judge (in effect making new law). But if (as in the present case) he had first handed over the offender for examination and sentence by the proper authorities (the commandant of justice), then the matter should take its course in accordance with the established law without imperial interference. The emperor, in fact, accepted this principle.[22]

One could also look beyond constraints on the emperor or ruler and view the administrative legal system as a rather functional constitutional system defining and limiting the actions of the vast majority of Chinese government(s). Rulers, though not accountable to any human agency, do generally seem to have observed a 'functional constitution system', although they tended to ignore it or act in an absolute or arbitrary fashion only where they felt personally threatened.

Turning now to evidence from ancient Greece, issues of the nature and extent of the power of the ruler are explored with regard both to humans and to the gods in the *Iliad* and *Odyssey*. Not only does the *Iliad* stage a dispute related to the power of single ruler, but the issue of the power of Zeus, the 'king' of the gods, is explicitly raised. The consciousness that there may be constraints on what a ruler can do that come from outside written law is figured in later Greek discussion of the relation of the laws of states to what are referred to as 'unwritten laws'. These are sometimes considered to be moral/religious imperatives that can override, but which more normally

---

[21] Chang 2000: vii, ix.   [22] Watson 1961: 536–37.

reinforce, state law.[23] Sometimes they are thought of as filling in gaps and they are effectively extrapolated from state law. A widely accepted premise of fourth-century Athenian democratic ideology, however, was that their rigorous procedure for enacting a law ensured that all their laws were just.[24]

In the most general sense, the actions taken by a city had to be commensurate with the values established by its law code, but the exercise of state power was not itself explicitly constrained by law. In the Athenian democracy of the fourth century BCE, a distinction was made between *nomoi* (rules that apply to all) and mere *psephismata* (decisions that affect only individuals). Individual *psephismata* were not allowed to be passed in violation of any existing decrees or laws, and a procedure existed (the *graphe paranomōn*) to punish people who proposed such things. At the same time, the state could pass additional laws or repeal existing laws, and law could, potentially, order anything.

Early Greek laws are, however, marked by an interest in defining the powers of political offices, particularly magistracies, and terms of office, but also the powers of the people as a whole.[25] One particularly famous instance comes from Sparta, from which Plutarch preserves what appears to be a seventh-century BCE constitutional law which, as well as recognizing various divisions into which the Spartans are divided (tribes, 'obes'), establishes a council of elders working together with the two kings and grants powers to an assembly, while specifying that that popular assembly can be over-ruled by the elders and kings.[26] Here, we approach something like constitutional law.

We can also trace ways in which law limited state power in practice. From as early as the picture of the 'city at peace' on the Shield of Achilles in *Iliad* 18, procedural rules governed how legal decisions were to be made. Further, the legality of any decision could be challenged, often explicitly before a body representing 'the people', although this did not represent a limitation based on law per se.[27] More directly, we find challenges to the legitimacy of monarchs, and insistence that courts scrutinize the actions of magistrates

---

23 Moral/religious imperatives in Sophocles' *Antigone*; Cf. Thuc. 2.37.3 and Dem. 23.61.
24 See, for example, Aeschin. 1.178; Dem. 20.93–94; further discussion in 'Jurisdiction' section below.
25 As in the Dreros law: Gagarin and Perlman, 2016: 197–221.
26 Plut. *Vit. Lyk.* 6, the seventh-century BCE date appears to be guaranteed by an allusion to this arrangement in the work of the poet Tyrtaeus (fragment. 4).
27 For appeal to a popular council, see ML 8 (Chios, sixth century BCE). Appeal to a popular court was also a key element of Solon's laws, as emphasized by *Ath. pol* 9.1. There was no appeal, however, from the verdict of a popular court.

regularly.[28] A magistrate might be tasked to confirm whether another magistrate had done his duty.

As elsewhere, law and state power clashed most often in relations between states. It is sometimes claimed in political debates that the actions of a state were in contravention of the 'common laws of the Greeks' or even 'the common laws of mankind', meaning what would generally be accepted as just.[29] We find this invoked, for instance, with respect to the treatment of ambassadors or the defeated.[30] Between states, but also within states, one of the crucial issues was whether laws could constrain the strong.[31] States could likewise be constrained by laws relating to two or more self-governing communities.[32]

In Republican Rome the relationship between law-making, the 'constitutional' structure of the state and non-legal frameworks was highly complex. To begin with, the Roman state (*res publica*) was structured by numerous priesthoods and its activities were deeply intertwined with religious observance. Scrupulous ritual observance supported the *pax deorum* (the mutually beneficial relationship between the gods and citizens of Rome). Magistrates collaborated with colleges of priests (*augures*) to consult auspices before major political decisions to determine whether or not the gods were in favour.[33] Other colleges of priests interpreted divine wishes to determine state obligations at a particular moment. According to one tradition, Roman jurisprudence itself emerged from such priestly authorities.[34] Rome was no theocracy, however, and a guiding assumption of Roman religion was that the gods themselves were parts of the civic community; relations with them ought to be conducted 'under the sign of reason ... in the same way as they were conducted between one citizen and another, or rather between clients and their patrons, but never between slaves and their masters'.[35] Other important guides to political practice included history and tradition. This could be framed in different ways, such as 'the custom of the ancestors' (*mos maiorum*). Some imagined these as set parameters for acceptable political action, although deciding what specifically constituted the *mos maiorum* was far from straightforward. The category of 'the lawful' (*ius*) might, in theory, shape expectations of what sorts of actions were acceptable and even

28 For Athens see *Ath. pol.* 45.3, 48.4, 54.2. For Gortyn see, e.g., *IC* iv.15.p-g1: '"The *kosmos* in charge, if he does not exact payment [of a fine], is to owe it himself.'
29 Polybius 2.58.6–7.   30 Ambassadors: [Dem.] 12.3; 'the defeated': Isocrates 4.123.
31 Plut. *Vit. Sol.* 5.2; Dem. 15.29.   32 For further discussion see Chapter 4, this volume.
33 If the auspices proved or were deemed unfavourable, the magistrates could decide to either cancel the vote or declare its results void. Linderski 1986.
34 For more detailed discussion see Chapters 3 and 6, this volume.   35 Scheid 2003: 28.

constitute a check on supposedly unconstitutional legislation. In practice, however, there was relatively little agreement on such principles. What 'constitutional' principles were articulated come almost entirely at the end of the Republic, amidst a situation of remarkable political chaos. Constitutional thinking, in other words, seems to have been a reaction to political chaos and was never actualized in practice.[36]

Romans of the Republic did, however, seek to regulate the operation of many state institutions. The writings of jurists on public law and legislation shaped legal procedures, conduct in state institutions and the qualifications and activities of officials.[37] A preference for regulating offices can also be seen in the rules Romans wrote for other communities.

The status of Rome's emperors was only partially captured by formal law. Imperial power itself was framed, in Roman constitutional language, as something conferred by the sorts of political organs that pre-existed the monarchy.[38] But the insistence on the formal continuity of institutions like the Republican magistracies belied more complex realities. The founder of the Principate, Augustus, claimed that he 'accepted no office contrary to established tradition'.[39] Yet Augustus and later emperors possessed powers that, regardless of similar titles, bore little resemblance to earlier institutions.[40] 'Constitutionality' or legality was essential to legitimacy and could be performed scrupulously when circumstances dictated. Despite this commitment to constitutionality, there was very little in ancient Rome that might be analogous to 'constitutional law'. Categories of 'public law' developed in the pre-monarchical phase and, later, there emerged a relatively inchoate body of second-order constitutional thinking.[41] A system emerged wherein the emperor was conceived to be subject to all laws from which he was not formally exempted, but in which emperors were given a grant of *imperium* (the right to issue a lawful order) by the Senate which could confer extensive powers.[42] By the Severan age, the emperors might often declare

---

36 Straumann 2016.
37 Those who violated rules of this kind were sometimes held to account through a system of courts and fines, although state actors could and did act outside of the normal order. Straumann 2016: 63–117.
38 Emperors insisted that they were continuing a pre-existing Republican tradition that went back to the expulsion of Rome's kings in the late sixth century BCE.
39 *Res Gestae* 6.   40 Tac. *Ann.* 1.3.   41 Straumann 2016.
42 One example comes from partially preserved legislation granting imperium to Vespasian in the following form: 'whatever he considers to be in accordance with the public advantage and the dignity of divine and human and public and private interests he shall have the right and the power to do and to execute' (trans. Johnson, Coleman-Norton and Bourne 1961).

that although they were formally exempted (*soluti*) from the laws, they nevertheless preferred to live by them.[43] In contrast, other organs of government, such as the Senate, the Roman magistrates, senatorial positions and the great equestrian commands, were governed by a fair amount of law, and productive of a relatively robust public law discourse – if not a constitutional one.

The power of emperors was defined by individual provisions in different pieces of legislation, although often so capaciously so as not to function as much of a constitutional limit. The origin of particular powers – such as the emperor's jurisdiction – remains something of a mystery.[44] It would not be until the early third century CE that we have a clear statement of principles concerning the nature and boundaries of the emperor's power.[45] All the same, over the last century, scholars have questioned the degree to which the 'constitutional' status of emperors mattered. Other factors supported an emperor's power, such as wealth, friendships and networks of reciprocity, conspicuous displays of generosity, patronage of the military and reputation as a victorious general (*imperator*). Likewise, the stability of imperial rule also depended on strategic use of resources such as coercive violence, control of armed soldiers near the city of Rome, encouragement of and periodic participation in the self-immolation of problematic members of the aristocracy and the conspicuous punishment of dissenters. The importance of these factors notwithstanding, the deep commitment of Romans to the enactment of constitutional rituals, titles and forms should not be discounted. Even the legal decisions of vicious emperors carried legal force until formally overturned.[46] The idea of a constitutional monarchy may have been a fiction, but it was a fiction to which large numbers of people were committed, even in the face of countervailing evidence.

Certain of the Roman (imperial) provinces in the eastern Mediterranean, such as Roman Egypt, were populated by a large number of pre-existing communities that had traditionally had some – if widely varying – degrees of autonomy. In such contexts the use of ruling power was strongly shaped by a particularly complex set of normative systems, some of which were broadly 'legal'; whether as custom, moral law, procedural restraints or the ability to challenge the legality of sovereign decisions. Alongside these, and exclusively

---

43 Justinian, *Inst.* 2.17.8(7).   44 Tuori 2016.
45 See Justinian, *Digest* 1.4.1 (= Ulpian, *Institutes* 1).
46 As shown in Nerva's confirmation of the acts of prior emperors (Pliny, *Ep.* 10.58), extensive legal change between emperors – or even between dynasties – was in general to be avoided.

in some cultures, normative frameworks were embedded in myth, religion and ethics.

In the Egyptian countryside of the Roman period, Roman officials claimed the right to intervene in the legal sphere but rarely claimed a monopoly over the entire scope of law. Provincial officials claimed that they would 'hear cases' on particular topics.[47] Their activities might, by turn, allow or prohibit specific actions; assign remedies or responsibilities in others; claim jurisdiction or delegate it to specific actors; and tolerate certain, pre-existing, practices. Even when exercising the right to issue edicts for their provinces as a whole, state officials confined themselves almost exclusively to discrete legal questions: procedures at the governor's assizes, where one is obligated to register documents, and so forth.[48] Their edicts, in other words, tend to react to particular circumstances in the province, rather than attempting to encompass or define 'law' in its entirety. Roman governors also sent letters to subordinate administrators detailing how they should act in certain circumstances.

In Egypt different types of legal documents flowed from the office of the governor in Alexandria or were generated during the governor's annual assize (*conventus, dialogismos*) in which he travelled through Egypt and heard cases. Any of these could serve as a source of law, setting more or less specific precedents in intention and application. But it seems that there was not, in the first four centuries of Roman rule, any attempt to provide complex municipal 'charters' or constitutions for individual communities on the model of those of the Latin-speaking West.[49]

Overall, one is struck by the general sufficiency of non-legal constitutional frameworks in shaping stable state regimes over long periods of time. Those operant in a given culture are too complex for analysis in this context, much less a full comparison, but high among them in all cultures must certainly be counted both lineage and the traditional expectations adhering to monarchy as an inherited cultural institution. Moreover, these non-legal frameworks are important even in cultures where ruling power is conceived as subject, in different ways, to legal constraints. It is interesting to consider under what circumstances they were seen as more effective than positive rules and vice versa. Here, too, we must consider the role of (traditional) administrative

---

47 SB XII 10929, Edict of governor M. Petronius Mamertinus, c. 133 CE.
48 Governor's assizes: P. Oxy. VI 2754, III CE; documents: P. Oxy. I 34 = M.Chr. 188, 127 CE.
49 Cf. Abbott and Johnson 1926.

practices and procedures as de facto constitutional constraints on the exercise of political power.

In whatever form, constitutional legal frameworks appear to have served as one among many resources for buttressing or challenging the authority of the ruler. From this perspective, constitutional law is as much, or indeed more, about legitimacy as about substantively delimiting the exercise of state power. At the same time, we must account for the distinctiveness of specifically legal remedies as a means of limiting or shaping ruling power. Here we must distinguish between limitations on ruling power itself and rules governing the competencies of political offices, which are more in evidence across cultures and sometimes enforced by legal institutions. The present analysis is limited, however, by a lack of detail regarding scale, governmental types and the material dimensions of governance, including the centralization of ruling power and the organization of state bureaucracy.

Legislative Power and State Authority over Law

Although all states acted through law, their power over law (or typical legal practice) varied considerably. States were not universally understood as the source of law, or at least the source of all law. Most commonly, states' participation in the greater legal environment was more restricted. In this section and the next, we examine their practices and/or the jurisprudential concepts that shaped shared understandings of states' powers with respect to law. The focus will be on two areas in particular: legislation and jurisdiction. To what extent could and did states create, amend or repeal laws, and how did they shape or engage with the various normative domains constituting the greater legal order? The former question, discussed here, expands upon the previous analysis of constitutional limitations on state power. The second question is reserved for the next section.

With respect to ancient India, it seems that the greater part of state law was always concerned with dispute resolution and always had its main source in custom, tradition and convention.[50] The first comprehensive legal 'code' that we possess, found in the third book of *The Arthaśāstra of Kauṭilya* (c. first century BCE – CE, with revisions in the third century CE), gives rules for public transactions between private parties able to be litigated in royal courts.[51] This body of law is referred to as *vyavahāra*,

---

[50] See Lariviere 2004; Wezler 2004.
[51] On the dating of the text, see especially Olivelle 2013; McClish 2019b.

meaning in origin 'commerce' or 'transaction' and carrying the strong sense of 'how things are actually done in the world'. Rules governing *vyavahāra* were first systematized into 18 'feet' or 'grounds', called *vyavahārapadas*, in the Laws of Manu (c. second century CE):

1. *ṛṇādāna*: non-payment of debt
2. *nikṣepa*: deposit
3. *asvāmivikraya*: sale by non-owner
4. *sambhūya samutthāna*: partnership
5. *dattasya anapakarman*: non-fulfilment of gift
6. *vetanasya adāna*: non-payment of wage
7. *saṃvidaḥ vyatikrama*: violation of contract
8. *krayavikrayānuśayo*: cancelling purchase or sale
9. *svāmipālayoḥ vivāda*: dispute between owner and herdsman
10. *sīmāvivādadharma*: law of boundary disputes
11. *daṇḍapāruṣya*: physical assault
12. *vācikapāruṣya*: verbal assault
13. *steya*: theft
14. *sāhasa*: violence
15. *strīsaṃgrahaṇa*: sexual crimes against women
16. *strīpuṃdharma*: law of husband and wife
17. *vibhāga*: inheritance
18. *dyūtāhvaya*: gambling and betting

The rules of such *vyavahāra* codes, however, were never treated as statutes. They derived their authority neither from the king, nor from their formalization as a code of laws by a legal authority per se; rather, it was the rules themselves, as conventions accepted by people, that were authoritative (to the extent that they were). Certainly, the treatises (*śāstras*) in which such 'codes' were recorded and developed provided influential guidance in court cases, but justice did not derive simply from the application of their rules to the case at hand.

Ancient Indic jurisprudence focused on *vyavahāra* and private litigation rather than on criminal law, and the latter is much less well attested in the extant literature of the ancient period.[52] The *Arthaśāstra* does describe a system of criminal law under the more general rubric of *kaṇṭakaśodhana*: 'the Clearing of Thorns'. Olivelle argues that this system of criminal law operated in 'parallel and similar to the civilian court system' and more

---

52 See Chapter 3, this volume.

specifically that 'its rules of procedure were similar to, or identical with, those followed in the civilian courts', but such criminal courts 'became obsolete in the early centuries of the common era', essentially becoming absorbed into the *vyavahārapadas*.[53]

In general, according to ancient Indic evidence, the king was expected to enforce or overturn the decisions reached in his courts and to personally render decisions in some disputes, but his legislative power was limited to decrees and edicts (*śāsana*; *ājñā*). Such decrees were typically restricted in scope, usually only granting favours to specific parties or prohibiting certain practices deemed unrighteous. They could, on occasion, be somewhat more comprehensive, as we find in the edicts of Aśoka (third century BCE) or the Charter of Viṣṇuṣeṇa (sixth century CE). The latter recognizes the validity of a set of special customary rules for a private community, some of which infringe upon the king's ruling power beyond the standards espoused in the legal codes.[54] Particularly, later in the ancient period, it seems that kings claimed the right to recognize the validity of such 'local' laws, which might otherwise not be considered authoritative in royal courts.[55] Even here, however, we see that although royal pronouncements could inflect existing norms, kings did not generate new bodies of law.

Mainstream Brahmanical jurists took a somewhat different view on these matters, and their perspective came to dominate the expert legal tradition. Most rules in the Dharmaśāstra likely have their origin in authoritative customs.[56] Nevertheless, these same rules are ascribed superlative sacred status by virtue of the legal fiction that all rules of *dharma* have their ultimate source in divinely revealed scriptures called the Vedas, even though few rules from the legal codes can be traced in the Vedic corpus.[57] As *dharma*, much customary law, including rules governing civil disputes, came to be treated as part of a greater, divine normative order. The assimilation of bodies of customary law within this normative framework, as concretized in their own legal texts, helped establish learned members of the priestly Brahmin class, experts in *dharma*, as themselves proximate sources of law in the sense that they are best equipped to know, interpret and declare law of all kinds.[58]

---

53 Olivelle 2012b: 632, 635, 638. 54 Lubin 2015; Wiese and Das 2019. 55 Rocher 1989.
56 See Lariviere 2004. 57 See, for example, *ApDh* 1.1.1–3; *GDh* 1.1; *MDh* 2.6, etc.
58 As should be clear from this brief overview, the relationship between Dharmaśāstra and custom is complex. In addition to Lariviere 2004, see also Lingat 1973. We find, for instance, the principle that when a recognized custom conflicts with the teaching of a *dharma* text, it is 'common sense' that the former should prevail (*NSm Mātṛkā* 1.34). This does not cancel out, though, the intrinsic capacity to critique customs that offend the sensibilities of Dharmaśāstra as unrighteous. Even the *Arthaśāstra* allows for the

The establishment of Brahmanical jurists as proximate sources of law, primarily through the activity of adjudicating civil disputes, is accompanied by the commensurate tendency in these texts to reduce the king's already limited legal authority to the enunciation and enforcement of legal decisions, shorn of their deliberative element. Hence, some mainstream Brahmanical texts even argue that a king's edicts are not valid unless they agree with *dharma* as expounded in their own codes, although other sources disagree on this point.[59]

We can reasonably doubt whether rules such as these ever functioned in any formal way to nullify the king's limited power to legislate through edicts and, to that extent, may have served as structural limits on the royal power of edict. They likely had rather more influence as kings and their advisers deliberated the implications or consequences of a proposed edict or as communities articulated criticisms thereof. In fact, mainstream Brahmanical texts implicitly recognize royal legal authority and express anxiety over it. Thus, while it is clear that not everyone agreed with the claims found in the mainstream Brahmanical legal literature, it is also evident that law became a tradition of Brahmanical expertise and was structured around and infused with their jurisprudential and theological perspectives. Brāhmaṇical influence on the theory and practice of state law, including the king's limited power to legislate, was probably in some cases quite substantial, even if claims to such authority in their texts are best treated as aspirational.

The term usually translated as 'law' in written evidence from ancient China is *fa* 法. Semantically, *fa* meant 'norm'. In early imperial China *fa* consisted of the statutes (*lü*), administrative regulations (*ling*) and penal elements, such as imperial edicts, enacted by the state. It seems *lü* in early China were probably predominantly penal in character, defining offences and prescribing punishments. *Ling* defined the duties of officials without stipulating punishments for infraction (offences committed by officials being contained in the *lü*). There never developed in China a 'formal' or 'official' system of what we today might term 'private law' governing transactions between individuals involving property, debt, inheritance, marriage and the like – such transactions were, however, addressed in the penal codes themselves insofar as to ensure the proper use of land and to maintain the behaviour appropriate to the hierarchical relationships within the family.

king to annul existing customs deemed 'unrighteous' and establish a righteous practice (*KAŚ* 13.5.14).
59 McClish 2017c: 310–11; Olivelle and McClish 2015.

This does not mean that lawsuits concerning contract, property and the like were uncommon in early China; they regularly came before the courts and were decided in accordance with either the relevant norms contained in the statutory penal rules or other rules well understood in the community.[60] People regulated their daily lives and transactions through customary practices, but they were never treated systematically as a separate, 'official', sphere of law. From the public perspective, law was seen as predominantly concerned with 'punishments', a view reflected in the most common early term for law: *xing* (punishments). Hence, law in China has essentially to be considered as 'state law', at least from the rise of the bureaucratic state during the period of the Warring States (c. 480–221 BCE) in which power came to be centralized in the hands of the ruler.

In general then, in the written evidence from ancient Chinese states, law expresses the intention of the ruler and hence might emanate only from him, even if in practice rulers were advised by their ministers on the content of the laws that they issued. The objective of the ruler was to exercise detailed control over the lives of his subjects through the enactment of laws that defined the manifold ways in which they were to behave. The laws were administered and implemented by officials appointed by and responsible to the ruler, the state being divided for this purpose into a number of administrative districts. Judicial decisions as such did not constitute a source of law, though those decided by the highest court might constitute authoritative guidelines for the resolution of future cases. Different understandings prevailed, however, as to the origin of the ruler's authority to issue legitimate law. For example, the Zhou ruler could legitimately issue law by virtue of his holding of the Mandate of Heaven (天命). The legalists, on the other hand, took legitimacy for granted and merely constructed a legal order that would not call into question the authority of the rulers (c. 350–206 BCE) to legislate (and set norms). The Mandate of Heaven re-emerges with Han Confucianism, and the picture becomes more complex insofar as it became necessary to maintain the authority and legitimacy to govern and establish norms publicly. Disputes were routinely settled privately, but there is clear evidence – within relatively recently excavated legal texts in particular – that disputes might also be submitted to the authorities, especially the bailiff (*sefu*), a local official appointed by the governor or county magistrate, with the

---

60 That some kind of system did exist is demonstrated by the texts edited and translated in Barbieri-Low and Yates 2015. Generally, see Zhang 2010.

responsibility inter alia of hearing lawsuits.[61] Disputes arising from such matters appear often to have been submitted to the state judicial agencies for resolution. None of this, however, was conceptualized as *fa* per se.[62]

Ancient Greek legal culture(s) recognized two sources of law: law as something absolute and imposed by supernatural powers (*dikê*) and law as produced through human efforts from corporate or community contexts (*thesmos, nomos*). *Dikê* referred to normative behaviour, effectively the whole system of justice (and in early Greek philosophy the order of the cosmos), and is commonly translated 'justice'. The same term can be used to refer to a particular lawsuit. Of laws resulting from human efforts, *thesmos* emphasized the rules emerging from decisions made by self-governing bodies, while *nomos* emphasized law as custom, tending at the extreme towards 'habit' or 'habitus'. In its more general sense, *nomos* belongs to cultural groups, rather than political groups.[63] In its specific sense, however, *nomos* is also used to refer to particular rules established by particular political bodies.[64]

As in other ancient political and legal traditions, human-made law had its own legitimacy within the cities of ancient Greece, but there remained a sense that behind particular laws was a background of general agreement over at least some norms – an agreement that might be ascribed to the gods.[65] So, some Greeks talked in terms of 'unwritten laws' (*nomoi*) originating from the gods, and such laws still maintained some hold on popular conceptions of what was right.[66] Greek states in general traced their law to particular

---

61 The legal texts excavated at Zhangjiashan in 1985 contained a number of statutory rules on inheritance, contract, debt and property. Barbieri-Low and Yates 2015.
62 See Zhang 2010: vii.   63 Best illustrated by Herodotus 3.38.
64 Cf. RO no. 26, line 3. In some circumstances a distinction is made between the written results of human judicial activity and the 'unwritten law' of custom and tradition, but the written results of human decisions are themselves frequently associated with the gods through consultation of oracles, etc. So Herodotos 1.65 on Lycurgus at Sparta, or the presentation of the purification law at Cyrene (RO 97) as delivered by an Apolline oracle. The source of unwritten law is sometimes identified not as the gods but as 'nature' (Dem. 18. 275). Although there is no consistent belief that the gods take the side of justice, Greek poets do from time to time insist that justice is of Zeus (cf. Hesiod, *Works* 9, 36).
65 Cf. Xen. *Mem.* 4.4.19–23 and Pl. *Laws* 838ab on incest.
66 Soph. *Ant.* 454–55 and Thuc. 2.37.3 for the force of unwritten law. One Athenian litigant even concedes that if the law does not support his opponent, the opponent should win the case if his case is just (Dem. 44.8). But the oath taken by jurors in Athens is recorded as having begun 'I will vote according to the laws and the decrees of the Athenian people and of the Council of 500' (Dem. 24.149) and Dem. 20.118 tells a court that they have sworn 'to pass judgment according to the laws, . . . and on matters concerning which there are no laws to make as just a decision as you can' – with no allusion to unwritten laws, and when unwritten laws are referred to in Athenian courts it is always to support the written law despite Arist. *Rhetoric* 1375a26–34. See Gagarin 2008a: 204.

lawgivers rather than to the gods, and those lawgivers acquired a status sufficient to ensure that later laws were also ascribed to them.[67] What seems to have been emphasized, however, is not the status of *thesmos* over against *nomos* or *dikê*, but the power of self-governing bodies to *decide* based on what were considered the most salient or authoritative rules.

Ancient Greek city states thus tended to claim broad powers of legislation. The state could create, amend or strike down law, subject to certain procedural restraints, and law could, potentially, order anything. Such claims varied with different political formations, but in Athens, disputes over the origins of such authority centred on whether the people had the right to do whatever they pleased. From one perspective, law was no different from state power, or, at least, it was a framework within which state power was expressed.[68] It was a mark of the tyrant that state power operated in an illegal way.[69]

There was some sensitivity to the problems that might arise from law's broad reach.[70] Any form of normativity, however, could be treated as law. Additionally, there was an expectation that laws should be mutually consistent. Because they were sometimes created piecemeal, laws could come to contradict one another and the Athenians, in particular, put some effort into weeding out contradictory laws. At the end of the fifth century BCE, the Athenians introduced a new board of 'lawmakers' (*nomothetai*), whose job it was to examine all proposed legal changes. Individuals were appointed to subject the proposed new laws to scrutiny and to report on their relationship to existing law and the lawmakers agreed only once they were satisfied that the proposed change did not contradict existing law. As stated above, even once a change in the law had been agreed, it was possible to have judicial scrutiny through the prosecution for bringing an unsuitable law.[71]

Modern scholars have disputed the extent to which any ancient Greek state attempted to provide a complete set of rules for all aspects of community life. Many early laws survive only as isolated enactments, and even when we have extensive legislation, as in the great fifth-century BCE 'code' from the Greek city of Gortyn, we find some topics treated carefully and systematically

---

67 One important consequence of this was that lawgivers, as opposed to gods, could not be expected to give signs, and so law was interpreted on the basis of arguments about the lawgiver's intention without possibility of decisive contradiction.

68 This is explored by Xenophon in a dialogue which he creates between Alcibiades and Pericles, in which Pericles straightforwardly identifies law with state power, to have Alcibiades object that states can do things wrong, and that their exercising power wrongly can hardly be law (Xen. *Mem.* 1.2.40–46).

69 Herodotus 3.80.   70 Cf. Xen. *Mem.* 1.2.40–46.

71 Canevaro 2013: 139–60. See also Chapters 2 and 7, this volume.

and others not so.[72] However, there is no doubt that a 'complete code' became an aspirational target for some, as is most completely visible in Plato's own attempt to formulate such a code in his *Laws*. Plato's originality in this code shows up in the way in which he prefaces his laws with explanations, designed to reveal explicitly what the lawgiver's intention was, and hence to secure that the law operated in accordance with that intention. Plato's law-code differs significantly from the laws of actual Greek cities in not concerning itself with laying down every regular activity, and so separating law off from, for instance, the religious calendar.[73]

As for the evidence from ancient Greece, so too, broadly speaking, for the evidence from ancient Mesopotamia: laws were issued by human authority not by the gods, though the source of their legitimacy lay among transcendent powers. The authority of the Near Eastern king to produce collections of legal provisions is most often related to his identity as the 'king of justice', which included the duty to protect the widow and the orphan – two representatives of the weak people in Mesopotamian society. If, as might be assumed, royal legislation was subsidiary, in the sense that laws were enforced on demand by aggrieved parties, and addressed primarily to citizens of the capital city, especially those living outside their political community, then the law collections could have been a means of encouraging mobility among elites, as well as a means of spreading the political influence of the centre towards conquered areas.[74] In the Hittite kingdom we have examples of laws being amended, as some provisions of the Hittite laws mention both the former sanction and the new one.[75] There is no evidence, however, for repealing laws in the ancient Near East.

It is assumed by many scholars of the ancient Near East that the content of the law collections derived from the scribal curriculum and not from the king, who published them just as a medium for his propaganda.[76] It is even debated whether the king had the ability to intervene with respect to the content of law, although substantial variation in the legal collections over time might be seen to point to such interventions. One exception to this is the rescript in Old Babylonian times, which was practised by King Samsu-iluna of Babylon (1749–1712 BCE).[77] It is highly probable, however, that this is what

---

72 Gagarin 2008a: chs. 6–7; Gagarin and Perlman 2016: G72.
73 Morrow 1960; Saunders 1994.
74 Royal legislation as subsidiary: Démare-Lafont 2000a. For an initial presentation of the broader argument here, see Démare-Lafont 2015a.
75 See the edition by Hoffner 1997.   76 Kraus 1960; Bottéro 1987: 191–223.
77 Janssen 1991.

Ḫammurabi calls his *dīnat mīšarim*, 'just judgments', which is to say a process by which legal provisions were created based on a consultation of the king upon request of the local judges (note the similarity with Roman rescripts). This could be the key to understanding how legal provisions were issued in Mesopotamia, in a manner similar to how the rescript eventually became one of the most important tools for clarifying rules of law in the Roman empire. The Mesopotamian process of 'codification' could be analogized to this practice. If so, the 'codes' would be, at least in part, collections of royal rescripts, like their Roman counterparts, the Gregorian and the Hermogenian Codes (late third century CE).

Legislation was only one source of law in the Roman world, one that sat alongside, in the words of Cicero: 'decrees of the Senate, judicial decisions, opinions of those learned in the law, edicts of magistrates, custom (*mos*), and equity'.[78] The relative balance of these various sources were contested during the Republic, though the advent of monarchy would bring them into a more stable relationship.[79] In the Roman Republic, legislation (*lex*, pl. *leges*) was passed by the assembled people voting in one of several assemblies. In archaic Rome, assemblies of the plebeians, called by tribunes, could pass legislation ('statutes'). The power of these plebian assemblies proved formidable: eventually patricians were forced to concede that votes of the people would count as binding upon the entire community. Subsequent laws superseded earlier ones, so that legislation could occasionally oscillate violently between particular positions. Nevertheless, Roman legislation had a strong tendency towards repetition, seeking only marginal corrections to earlier laws.

As we have already seen for the ancient Greek cities, little was out of bounds for legislation. Roman assemblies passed laws on both public and private matters, on topics that ranged from the competence of the Roman Senate to compensation required in cases of damage. Legislation invested magistrates with their powers: being chosen in an election was not sufficient. Once elected, powers had to be conveyed to magistrates by a *lex curiata*, a vote of the 'curiate' assembly (different from the assemblies that elected the magistrates). Legislation similarly was necessary for particular religious acts.[80]

---

78 Cic. *Top.* 28.   79 See Chapter 3, this volume.
80 A robust example comes from 217 BCE when the Romans were threatened by the Carthaginian invasion during the Second Punic War, after they had a major battle. The dictator (a temporary magistrate), Q. Fabius Maximus, urged the Senate to investigate the loss, which they determined occurred in response to the previous consul's defective performance of religious rites. Accordingly, they sought to repair their relationship

The question of inherent limits on the power of legislation was raised often in the final years of the Roman Republic, a period which saw an acceleration of popular initiatives to grant so-called 'extraordinary commands' to particular, charismatic individuals. The question was never given a proper answer. A variety of practical checks existed, however, on the power of the assemblies. For instance, assemblies could not meet *sua sponte* – the people had to be summoned by a magistrate or a tribune to engage in their power to legislate. Legislation, moreover, could be vetoed by even a single tribune, prohibiting a law from being carried. Magistrates could intervene in other ways: they could decide that the auspices were unfavourable and prevent meetings, or declare unfavourable auspices after the fact. Similarly, the Senate could declare that the necessary procedures for passing legislation had not been observed, and the citizens were not bound by the acts of the assembly. As one might imagine, such notionally elevated concerns were often put in the service of political agendas.

Under the Roman empire, the primary source of legislation was the emperor himself. Claiming for themselves the power of tribunes, the emperors – starting with Augustus – were able to call meetings of the Senate or of the people. The Roman Senate continued to issue decrees (*senatus consulta*) under the early Empire, but none that impinged on imperial wishes, while the assembled people quickly vanished from view. The jurist Ulpian (second to third century CE) claimed that people had passed a *lex* bestowing all of their powers upon the emperor, and this became the official view. The question remained, however, as to whether the emperor's legislative power was limited. He was not bound by the rules that had governed the passage of legislation under the Republic, but there were questions as to how far he could go.[81] It seems that most of the limits placed on the emperors were customary and engaged in voluntarily.[82] Ultimately, the weight of

---

with the gods. To do this, the *pontifex maximus*, the chief priest of the Roman state, urged the vow of a *ver sacrum*, a 'sacred spring' – the sacrifice of one year's entire harvest of animals, if the gods would preserve them for five years against the Carthaginians. The *pontifex maximus*, however, could only prescribe the proper remedy; in order to make the vow legal, it had to be voted on by the people, taking the form of legislation. The legislation passed, and the gods held up their end of the bargain; the people, in point of fact, delayed the sacrifice to 195 BCE. Perhaps more interestingly, in voting for the *ver sacrum*, the people also decided that certain defects in the sacrifice were nonetheless to be considered acceptable to the gods (Liv. 22.10).

81 Claudius famously declared that he was permitted to wed his niece in violation of traditional prohibitions on incest (though only a brother's daughter, by the emperor's example, not a sister's daughter): Gaius, *Institutes* 1.62.

82 A particularly unusual example comes from Justinian's *Digest*, which records the response of the emperor Antoninus, in Greek, to a petition from a certain

precedent, the legitimating force of tradition and the capacity to forget certain particularly ugly decisions provided the only boundaries on the content of imperial legislation. Over the course of years, imperial legislation covered an increasing amount of social life.

In theory Romans imagined that they preserved a sharp distinction between the metropole and the rest of the empire. The rest of the empire was considered to be largely populated by cities that possessed the power to make rules for their own citizens. In practice, however, legislation from Rome involved itself deeply in these communities' internal affairs. Even the claim that other cities ought to be free was legislated, as seen in a plebiscite from around 70 BCE in which the Roman people legislated the freedom of the people of Termessus in Pisidia.[83] It should be quickly added that the remaining clauses in the plebiscite cover relatively few issues of substance.

Such 'constitutional' legislation, written primarily in Rome, tends to default to the position that non-Roman communities ought to organize themselves in ways that are collegial to those communities, all the while respecting the *maiestas* ('superiority') of the Roman people. This, despite the fact that the contents of such legislation itself often undermined that position.[84] These subordinated political communities did, in fact, produce legislation, some of it preserved on stone inscriptions.[85] The legislation that has been preserved is not extensive, and it does tend to exhibit a conformity to Roman expectations of what constitutes good policy. The role of Roman governors and imperial officials, operating between the metropole and the community, helps to explain this state of affairs. Romans were sent abroad to govern territories directly (not including cities or territories declared to be

'Eudaemon of Nicomedia': '"Antoninus, King and Lord, we were shipwrecked in Icaria and robbed by the people of the Cyclades". Antoninus replied to Eudaemon: "I am master of the world, but the law of the sea must be judged by the sea law of the Rhodians where our own law does not conflict with it". Augustus, now deified, decided likewise.' (Justinian, *Digest* 14.2.9). The claims of the emperor get precisely to the problem: he is not in fact bound to observe the law of the Rhodians. The 'Rhodian law' was probably neither Rhodian nor law, but it was part of a long tradition through which Romans handled the question of property jettisoned at sea, and anyway, the emperor Augustus had originally decided to apply it to cases such as these.

83 Johnson, Coleman-Norton, and Bourne 1961, no.79: 'Whoever have been Termessians and whoever by the laws of these Termessians have become Termessians before April 1, when Lucius Gellius and Gnaeus Lentulus were consuls, and whoever have been and were born from them: all these and their descendants, being Termessian citizens, shall be free, friends, and allies of the Roman people, and these thus shall enjoy their own laws, and it shall be lawful for them, being Termessian citizens, to enjoy their own laws in a such a way as shall not be contrary to this law.'

84 Ando 2011.   85 Kantor 2015.

independent) and produced legislation in the form of edicts relevant to the province itself. Such legislation tended to be both reactive and practical, but could prove important in adjudicating disputes at the provincial level and influenced the legislative activity of subordinated communities, whom Rome recognized as 'self-governing' units within its territory.

Across these ancient cultures we find that the state was not the sole source of rules. Even in cultures where state bodies could pass binding legislation, like those of China, Greece and Rome, we have nothing like the wide-ranging scope of legal codes of the modern period. This suggests that we might be able to view state law in the ancient world as existing at the intersection of 'sovereign' decree and inherited customary rules. The example of India is particularly instructive here. In all cases it seems that much law was unwritten, i.e. 'traditional', even if discoverable or 'codifiable'. Identifying the salient rule from among a heterogeneous body of norms appears to have been a regular feature of ancient courts, and many ancient legal 'codes' served to identify rules for various reasons rather than to give them the authority of legislation.

To be certain, wherever formal legislative processes existed the laws produced therefrom would have possessed a special status and could be considered different in kind from other kinds of norms. But nowhere do we see a fully comprehensive state legal code emerge that, as in modern states, tends to efface all other sources of law. Even in states with robust legislative traditions, state law seems analysable as a limited set or pattern of interventions into a more complex normative order.

One thing we have not been able to compare directly in this chapter is the characteristic uses to which law was put by states. Why did state law in China focus primarily on punishment of offences, while in India the focus was private disputes? And how did these foci shape not only legislative efforts, but reflection on law more generally?

Jurisdiction: The State within the Greater Legal Environment

Closely related to the topics just discussed, states claimed different kinds of jurisdictional authority, conceived here generally as the state's power to decide who had the authority to declare law or make legal decisions. States did so in a number of different ways: by claiming ultimate authority in dispute resolution; by recognizing or nullifying the rules of non-state groups; by restricting or accepting the scope of their powers; by recognizing hierarchy among them; and so forth. An analysis of the jurisdictional powers claimed and practices used by states provides us with the opportunity to explore the dynamics of contest and cooperation between various legal authorities in ancient societies.

There was no single and specific concept analogous to 'law' in ancient Mesopotamia, although notions of justice permeated social life. The absence of such a conception complicates any theoretical discussion of legal pluralism: everything could potentially be considered 'legal,' even if our sources tend to paint a different picture. There are thousands of documents enforcing local norms, which tells us that law was basically a practical activity. Even though it was felt to differ from other occupations, law was never isolated from the rest of everyday life. This might help to explain the lack of true jurists and the paucity of professional judges in the cuneiform/Mesopotamian sources. As to bodies of law or legal domains, alongside the various oral customary laws echoed in the numerous legal deeds, there were written rules of law issued by kings. The latter includes law collections, edicts of debt cancellation, rescripts and administrative regulations. In addition, possibly, there are also rules of law issued by assemblies of merchants such as those in the city of Aššur at the beginning of the second millennium.[86]

Ancient Near Eastern states engaged a number of areas of social life through law, both civil and criminal. In the realm of civil law, family law (regarding, for example, marriage, filiation and inheritance) are particularly well documented. We also find provisions about property, contracts and responsibility. Personal status is dealt with only incidentally. In the realm of criminal law, family law is again prominent, particularly adultery, incest and rape. Theft is also mentioned, as well as other types of offenses, such as abortion, homicide, false accusation and fraud.[87]

Interestingly, however, the law collections from ancient Mesopotamia and Asia Minor are more interested in areas only poorly represented among available deeds and contracts. For instance, there are not very many extant marriage contracts and very few criminal trials. The reasons for this remain unclear. Restoration edicts deal mainly with the cancellation of debt in specific cities or states.[88] The rescript of Samsu-iluna addresses two issues related to a type of nun living in Sippar: requiring them to have income before entering the cloister and protecting their property from their father's

---

[86] Veenhof 1995.   [87] See the edition of the law collections by Roth 1997.
[88] Kraus 1984; Charpin 1990 and 2000.

creditors.[89] Finally, administrative regulations deal with rules to be observed by the Assyrian palace staff.[90] These are the key areas of social life to which state law spoke.

The impression we get from the ancient Near Eastern legal deeds and contracts is that those who used the law were ultimately free to decide the type of rule they would use.[91] State law was only one option among others for addressing concerns, and not necessarily the best one. The clauses of a contract could be more severe or more lenient than the average practice, if the parties wished to do so. If, as might be concluded, state law was subsidiary, in the sense that it was only activated when invoked by aggrieved parties, then we see why it appears to have had left very little visible impact on the legal life of ancient Mesopotamians. The legal control, if any, would be a posteriori, in front of a judge, if one party broke the agreement. We perceive no a priori intervention of the public authorities.

Legal requirements, both state and customary, that were felt to be inadequate or onerous were circumvented through the creative use of legal categories.[92] For instance, a man could resort to adoption to cover up the purchase of a family property (especially a plot of land), which was probably forbidden by the law though we have no direct evidence of such a prohibition. In such cases, the adopter/seller received an annual or monthly income from the adoptee/buyer, like a life annuity sale. Public authorities were aware of such dissimulation, but they did not prevent it, nor did they change the rule of law in order to adapt its content to social practices. Ultimately, state law collections must be understood against the background of customary law. The gaps found in the state codes are understood to have been filled by non-state rules. In this sense, state law was not only subsidiary, but also complementary.

In general, across the ancient Indian material, the concept of *dharma* speaks to all of the duties and obligations incumbent on individuals based on their particular life circumstances. Aspects of this *dharma* were manifest not only in the law codes, but also in the traditional rules of private communities, familial obligations and ethics generally. While *dharma* always invoked a diffuse sense of righteousness, specific norms could be considered *dharma* if they were judged to be in agreement with it.[93] We have the term *caritra* to

---

89 This rescript, issued in the second half of the eighteenth century BCE, is known from several copies found in a private house in Sippar (close to Baghdad); Janssen 1991.
90 Roth 1997: 195–209.
91 For an overview of the various topics addressed in relation to legal deeds and contracts, see Westbrook 2003b: 62–66.
92 Boyer 1954.   93 Lingat 1973: 176ff.

cover customary law, which was also conceptualized as the 'law of regions,' 'the law of castes,' 'the law of families' and so forth.[94] We can compare here also the concept of *ācāra*, usually translated as 'conduct', often in relation to specific communities, but which also had clear normative force. As such, it is clear that private bodies had their own sets of rules, and we can presume they were formalized to varying degrees. The best-documented examples from the ancient period are Buddhist monastic law and Brahmanical customary law, which, however, became the framework for expressions of universal law and to that extent lost its purely private character. Moreover, it is clear that royal courts sought to decide cases first based on the customary law of the litigants.[95] It is only failing this that the state legal code, called *vyavahāra*, came into force. By the time of the *Arthaśāstra*, it is clear that the state took efforts to record the laws of such private groups both for administrative purposes (such as taxation) as well as legal purposes.[96] Eventually *caritra* comes to refer to 'documentary evidence', indicating that the state had official processes for recognizing or sanctioning the law of private groups as part of the larger body of state law, as discussed above.[97] It appears that the establishment of private law often involved negotiation between the private group and the king. As such, we find the practice of *sthitipatra*: a document wherein private groups not only recorded their own laws in royal archives but were able to enshrine preferential treatment from the king in respect of their taxation, legal treatment and so forth.[98] What seems to have mattered in all of this is the official recognition by the state of both the peculiarities as well as special privileges recorded in private law.

The state undertook to articulate the relationship between various legal traditions by establishing a hierarchy of legal authority prevailing in state courts.[99] The early Indic legal tradition divided the greater normative order into four hierarchical legal domains of diminishing power: royal edict (*śāsana*); custom (*cāritra*); transactional law (*vyavahāra*); and justice or righteousness (*dharma*).[100] Royal edicts, as mentioned, were narrow proclamations and, as enunciations of the king, were paramount. If no edict existed bearing on the matter in dispute, the customs of private groups were considered authoritative, but probably only in cases where the litigants recognized a common customary law. When that was not the case or customary law was insufficient to provide guidance, the state's codification of transactional

---

94 Lingat 1973: 200.
95 *KAŚ* 3.1.39; *NSm Mātṛkā* 1.10, etc. See Lingat 1962 and Olivelle and McClish 2015.
96 See *KAŚ* 2.7. 97 Rocher 1989. 98 Lubin 2015. 99 Olivelle and McClish 2015.
100 Olivelle and McClish 2015.

law (*vyavahāra*) was authoritative. If none of these legal domains provided rules or guidance on the resolution of a dispute, the judge could rule based on *dharma*, here, in a generic sense, of what is generally 'just' or 'righteous'. As mentioned above, the norms provided by these authorities were not interpreted as statutes, although one might reasonably assume that royal edicts were most likely to be treated as such.

The law code of Yājñavalkya (c. fourth – fifth centuries CE) articulates a hierarchy of five legal venues: the family (*kula*), guild (*śreṇi*), association (*pūga*), royal judges appointed by the king (*arthādhikṛta*) and the king (*nṛpa*) himself.[101] Each of these, we are told, is more authoritative than the one before. In theory, therefore, the decision reached in a (probably extended) family tribunal could be appealed to the guild, and so forth. We have evidence, particularly from the medieval period, that litigants typically preferred to have their disputes resolved in such 'private' courts and tribunals rather than state courts.[102] State courts would have served either as courts of appeals to these lower courts or as courts of first resort for individuals not recognizing a common customary law (i.e. not belonging to the same community). In this sense, it is important to recognize the extent to which state law here served to 'manage' a legal system that was largely private in practice, by affirming or annulling lower rulings as well as ordering (or recognizing the traditional ordering) of private jurisdictions.

Lastly, we must make note of another phenomenon evident in later, medieval texts, but likely of greater antiquity: the independent operation of Brahmanical tribunals.[103] In certain instances, private litigants could take their disputes to learned Brahmins who would rule on the case. This was in keeping with broader practices of resorting to Brahmins for rulings on a variety of questions, such as marriage or purity; such rulings seemed to have a kind of ultimacy to them, at least in practice, although the Brahmins themselves had no power to enforce the ruling.[104] They simply had the authority to proclaim what was *dharma*. It can be presumed that the state had a complex relationship with such rulings, sometimes agreeing, sometimes disagreeing, mostly paying no attention.

---

101 *YDh* 2.31. Note Olivelle's critical edition records *nṛpo 'rthādhikṛtāḥ* ('the king and those appointed to legal matters (i.e. state justices)') rather than *nṛpenādhikṛtāḥ* ('those appointed by the king'), which is also attested. The former reflects a system of five rather than four legal venues, as at *NSm Mātṛkā* 1.7, although the king would have been presumed to represent the fifth, and highest, venue, even in the case of the latter.
102 Jha 1924: 7.   103 Davis 2014: 5–13.   104 Davis 2014:10. See McClish 2017b: 278–79.

All of this suggests, although we cannot precisely confirm, a greater legal system operating largely outside of the purview of the ancient state, where state law pertained to specific groups probably in relatively close proximity to the king's administration, but capable of intervening elsewhere in the system as needed. Ultimately, however, it is certain that for most people the laws of their non-state communities, including their religious groups, were far more salient than the law of the state, which, for most, was probably not only distant, but perhaps often substantively indistinct.

Ancient Greek thought, as noted earlier, recognized 'unwritten laws'. These may have had persuasive force for an individual in making them act in a particular way, but they were never put 'in force' by a particular legal authority. There was a strong sense of justice (*dikê*) as a universal value, however, and this could support ad hoc judicial forums. The earliest of Greek hexameter poems, Hesiod's *Works and Days* and Homer's *Iliad*, are both in their different ways discussions of justice intended for listeners drawn from many different cities. *Works and Days* discusses justice against the background of a supposed real-life dispute over inheritance between Hesiod and his brother, Perses, set against a city which has some mechanisms for deciding disputes, but mechanisms that Hesiod holds to be corrupt – such as 'bribe-devouring kings'. The *Iliad* discusses justice in the context of a fictional quarrel over human 'war-booty' between Agamemnon and Achilles, set against an ad hoc political unit of troops from a whole catalogue of Greek cities united by an oath made by their leaders to defend Agamemnon's brother Menelaos against any who might steal his beautiful wife, Helen. The ad hoc nature of this political community means that any normal means of dispute settlement, such as are described in the context of the picture of the city at peace shown on the shield made for Achilles by the god Hephaistos, are absent. Justice has to be created from first principles and in the face of individuals with strong personalities.

One also finds more or less formal legal domains distinct from the state in ancient Greek material, for example the 'law of the Brytidai' (an Athenian phratry), as well as the law practised by subgroups of the polis and religious bodies. The state is expected to enforce their rules. In Athens we find a law that specifically imbues the decisions of subgroups of the city state with the force of law. It could be argued that non-state law picked up a variety of local behaviours (in various senses of local) that state law did not have to involve itself with. These are, in essence, separate spheres of activity. The state sought to establish standards of conduct in the areas of property, homicide and interpersonal violence, other interpersonal relations (familial and sexual), proper relations to the gods, duties to the state and obedience to state authority. But, the division between state and non-state law arguably arose in the first place because state law was not thought appropriate when a given set of circumstances involved only restricted groups. For these reasons, the relationship between state law and non-state law was relatively organic. Except in unusual circumstances, there seems to have been very little competition or conflict between state and non-state law. For instance, Sophocles' *Antigone* enacts one possible area where such competition meant conflict. But, although that conflict may have in fact occurred in real life, it would only do so under remarkable circumstances. While Antigone and Creon clash, the more normal route is for the dictates of non-state law – that is to say overriding religious or moral concerns – to be used to influence the interpretation or enforcement of state law.[105] The only potential rival to state law, in this respect, is supernatural intervention. Guidance on what was required in relation to the gods might be sought in relation to legal actions.[106] Alternatively such guidance could be sought independently, by consultation of oracles.[107] Divine intervention to settle disputes, quite outside the field of law, might be invoked by curses, and curses could also be invoked in relation to cases in court, to affect or determine the result of a court case.[108]

The use of volunteer prosecutors in many ancient Greek cities would suggest that state law itself was more relevant to the lives of their citizens and subjects than in other contexts examined here. That is, state law provided the framework within which it was expected that all disputes were settled, although here we must keep in mind the difference in scale between a Greek polis and the transregional polities typical of other cultures under consideration here. The frequency with which state law was resorted to in ancient Greece can be inferred also from the image that (state) law was subject to abuse.[109] There was some sense in classical Athens, in fact, that the Athenians were over litigious, both in general and in as far as there was a problem with 'vexatious litigation'. There is some debate about the relationship between the image and the reality of 'vexatious litigation'.[110] It is

---

105 See, for example, Dem. 45.53.
106 Cf. the consultation of *exegetai* (discussed in Chapter 3, this volume) who are in one case reckoned to work on the basis of 'unwritten law' (Lys. 6.10).
107 But there was an expectation that no one consulting an oracle would ask permission to act illegally/immorally: the locus classicus is the story of Glaukon at Herodotus 6.86.
108 On curses see Eidinow 2007.
109 Note, for example, Menander, 545: 'The laws are a splendid thing, but a man who looks too closely to the laws is clearly a vexatious litigant."
110 Osborne 1990 and Harvey 1990.

clear, however, that (state) law was perceived as being vulnerable to abuse. This opened the way to law being seen as what arguably it was: a means of prolonging rather than of settling disputes.[111]

While law is equated with the directives of the ruler in ancient Chinese sources, officials acting on his behalf, such as the governors of the major administrative areas into which the country was divided, might issue executive directions for the conduct of the people under their jurisdiction. These did not count as formal laws across the periods that we are considering, but some exceptions occurred occasionally, and this allows us possibly to speak of pluralist systems of law within single states. Such exceptions were more characteristic of the Western Zhou than of the later imperial period. The Zhou king accepted the principle that newly conquered people should be permitted to retain their own laws, no doubt with certain qualifications. At the beginning of Western Zhou the prince who was granted as a fief the central portion of the territory previously ruled by the conquered Shang king was urged by the Zhou king to respect and apply the just laws that had obtained under the Shang (sixteenth–eleventh centuries BCE).[112] The late Western Zhou and Spring and Autumn periods (770–464 BCE) demonstrate increased plurality within the Zhou cultural sphere, as individual kingdoms exhibit different laws.[113]

Even during the Warring States, some latitude was allowed to the people of a newly conquered area. The state of Qin in the third century BCE, in its progressive series of conquests, tolerated at least initially the continued operation of existing laws in newly annexed areas.[114] As the Qin progressed through the southwest and then moved east, however, the dominant strategy of cultural homogenization prevailed. The Letter of Governor Teng from the Shuihudi tomb 11 clearly demonstrates the frustration of a regional governor over his subordinates' inability to stamp out local practices.[115] In his letter, he threatens such officials with punishments.

In the first fifty years of the Han dynasty we have a phenomenon, never again found in imperial China, resembling the Western Zhou practice of enfeoffing royal princes as rulers of territories. Liu Bang, emperor Gaozi, the founder of the dynasty entrusted large portions of the country to the government of members of his own family who took the title of king,

---

111 So Osborne 1985 and Cohen 1995; for a contrasting view, Harris 2006a and 2013b. See most recently Lanni 2016. For Athenian litigiousness see Christ 1998.
112 As recorded in the *Kanggao*, see Karlgren 1950: 40.13.
113 References to *Jin law* or *Chu law*, etc. can be found in Zuo zhuan, Zhanguo ce, etc.
114 Liu 1998: 210, 237–38, 324.   115 See Hulsewe 1978a: 182–85; and Caldwell 2018: 63–67.

appointed their own officials and had very extensive powers – including, it seems, the power of introducing new laws in their kingdoms. In the middle of the second century BCE, these powers were drastically reduced. The officials appointed by the king were replaced with ones appointed by the emperor, and the administration was then conducted along the lines of normal administrative divisions of the country. Within another thirty years the kingdoms as such had all been abolished, so ending finally what may have been another example of pluralist legal systems.[116]

The Roman state exerted a great deal of energy in selecting officials and procedures for deciding cases but never sought to monopolize options for settling disputes, as opposed to judging cases. Issues arising within the family were to be dealt with by an ad hoc tribunal run by the senior male ascendant (the *paterfamilias*). Evidence for this practice is hard to come by, but it seems safe to suppose that punishments dispensed to slaves and children were frequently carried out at the discretion of the *paterfamilias*.[117] Such procedures reinforced the patriarchal structures of control and deference on which the Roman state was imagined to be founded. Whether this should be understood as a 'jurisdiction' in a formal sense is perhaps interesting mostly to jurists, but domestic justice did emulate some of the formal elements of a courtroom: the *paterfamilias* provided himself with a group of advisers (*consilium*), was supposed to give the accused the opportunity to defend himself and announced something of a formal 'verdict'. Significantly, his decision could include disherison, exile or even death. In important cases the public paid attention.[118]

The 'jurisdiction' of the father and the jurisdiction of the state were also complementary in other ways, particularly regarding civil disputes within lineages. Roman private law operated from the patriarchal assumption that the father, by virtue of his *patria potestas*, owned all the property within

---

116 See Loewe 2004, chapter 11.
117 Similarly, the Vestal Virgins were subject to the jurisdiction of the Pontifex Maximus.
118 Fathers might be praised for their decisions or criticized. Seneca reports that in one case a father was deemed to have acted so far out of bounds that he was assaulted in public, and only barely saved by the intervention of the emperor (Seneca, *On Clemency*, 1.15). In some cases the power of the patriarch was not only unpopular but imagined to have exceeded its boundaries entirely: thus, Justinian, *Digest* 48.9.5 records the case of a man who had killed his son, who was having an affair with his stepmother, while together on a hunt. The father subsequently tried to hide behind his household 'jurisdiction' to defend his actions, but the emperor Hadrian nonetheless had him exiled to an island, claiming that he 'killed his son less by the right of a father, than by the right of a bandit' (*quod latronis magis quam patris iure eum interfecit*). See, in general, Saller 1999.

a family unit.[119] Dependants and slaves might be granted quasi-ownership of some property by their fathers (*peculium*), but the grant was revocable. Accordingly, since children did not own property, they would have no standing to sue their fathers, nor fathers their children: by strict civil law, the same person would end up as both plaintiff and defendant in the same case. Similarly, all those under the father's *potestas* were barred from suing him in cases of degrading or insulting behaviour (*iniuria*). The Roman jurists even specify that children who have been emancipated from such power may only sue their fathers under aggravated circumstances.[120] Slaves were in a similar position, and the state took no cognizance of their complaints against their masters until late in the monarchy. Even then it would have been difficult for slaves to take advantage of provisions protecting them from abuse. Freedmen might find themselves subject to the jurisdiction of their former masters or patrons.[121] The father was 'sovereign', in a sense, and his discipline was normatively understood to prevail.

Outside of the family, the Roman city state encouraged civil disputes to be settled by means other than formal adjudication.[122] Arbitration, whereby the disputing parties entrusted settlement of their dispute to a mutually trusted party, was encouraged. It could be done informally but was considered to be non-binding in such cases. One imagines, nonetheless, that such arbitration was often effective. If there was little trust between parties, arbitration could be carried out by means of a *compromissum*: an agreement that the results of the arbitration would be treated as a contract binding upon the parties and enforceable in a state courtroom. If they preferred, the parties could bring formal charges, for example in the court of the Urban Praetor in Rome or in the courts of *municipia* if the amount under dispute was not too significant.

A similar system prevailed in the provinces. Disputants were welcome to settle informally, but they might also appeal to local authorities.[123] It is difficult to assess the actual use of formal and informal processes. They are perhaps best imagined as packages of tactics that disputants might avail themselves of, even at the same time. In the provincial landscape, the penetration of state and imperial law was never complete and certain social

---

[119] Saller 1999. See also Chapter 8, this volume.   [120] Justinian, *Digest* 47.10.7.3.
[121] According to Justinian, *Digest* 47.10.7.2: 'We allow a patron a restricted right of punishment of his freedman, and the praetor will not listen to the latter complaining of contumely unless there be an element of aggravation; for the praetor does not have to tolerate the slave, now a freedman, complaining against his master that the latter abused him verbally or moderately chastised or corrected him.'
[122] A helpful overview can be found in Bablitz 2016, to which this account owes a debt.
[123] Kelly 2010.

groups were given relative autonomy to organize themselves and set their own ground rules. For instance, comparable to some extent with evidence from ancient India, we have a number of papyrological examples of 'charters' or 'regulations' of guilds and organizations; these would appear to have been generated by the members of the groups themselves, though they show some broad similarities.[124] Among loci for mediation of disputes we find a range: from the highly informal gathering of relatives to sign private agreements regulating the conduct of members of their families to more formal and binding arrangements for settling more complex disputes, arrangements which also take place with various levels of state sanction.[125] There remains controversy as to the extent to which Christian ecclesiastics were able to exercise formal and informal jurisdiction.[126] There were also sub-state or private legal practices that co-existed with official practice or in some ways overlapped or echoed state practices.[127] Although such practices were not necessarily recognized as 'lawful' according to the norms and rules of the Roman state, it is striking, nonetheless, that in at least some of these situations the actors considered themselves to be acting lawfully.

In all cases, we observe states recognizing or even encouraging the use of non-state legal forums for dispute resolution. The family, even extended family, clan or caste, would likely have been one of the most important such non-state institutions, but so too, in different contexts, were guilds, cities and other collectives. What we must imagine in all cases is a complex normative order in which the state might sometimes be a remote player. Certainly, the engagement of the state would have been most intensive and structuring in urban centres where the government housed its primary institutions. Farther afield, access to royal adjudication may have been infrequent or non-existent. Finally, what counts as 'law,' and what is visible from this point of view, depends on culturally specific interpretations of the normative order and the state's place within it.

What is not clear from this comparison is the relative size of the different polities and the attendant complexity of their legal environments. Certainly, the question of jurisdiction was one thing in Greek city states and another in imperial polities in China. In all cases, however, we must assume that many communities and their legal systems are nearly or entirely obscured in our extant sources. To that extent we do not get a particularly clear sense overall

---

124 P. Mich. V 243, 244, 245 (all first century CE).
125 Informal: P. Oxy. L 3581, fourth or fifth century CE; more formal: Gagos & Van Minnen 1994.
126 See Humfress 2011.   127 See Chaniotis 1995 for the case of Lycia.

of the communities for whom state law was most salient or for whom it was not. State claims to supreme legal authority were not accompanied by the effacement of other legal authorities, which undoubtedly made for a degree of variability in the different legal systems.

State Legal Systems

The previous sections have emphasized the ideational aspects of the relationship between law in the state. In this section, we turn to consideration of the state legal system itself. We will focus on both the structure and operation of the system, particularly its use by various parties.

In ancient Greece we see the legal system most fully at work in classical Athens by virtue of the survival from the late fifth and the fourth century BCE of more than one hundred speeches written for delivery in Athenian courts. Official investigations of wrongdoing were rare, but possible (the most famous example followed the systematic vandalism of statues of the god Hermes on the eve of the departure of a large military expedition from Athens to Sicily).[128] Some officials had responsibility for arresting wrongdoers if they caught them in the act, but the vast majority of prosecutions, including criminal prosecutions, were brought by private individuals. Legal procedure, particularly consequences for both unsuccessful prosecution or the condemned defendant, were affected by whether the case was brought by the injured party (or by a close relative) or by a third party if the injured party were incapacitated by the crime. Both prosecutors and defendants were expected to speak in their own cause, but either or both parties could also bring in supporting speakers.[129] These supporting speakers might in fact take up most of the time in the court. The courts themselves were manned by mass juries, which could comprise several hundred, chosen by lot – there were allotment machines for the purpose – from a panel of 6,000 *dikastai* who were selected annually from male citizens, over the age of thirty, who had sworn a formal oath. The *dikastai* heard time-limited speeches from prosecutor and defendant, supported by witness statements, but the witnesses were not cross-examined and the *dikastai* had no possibility for discussion before they cast their vote with tokens which allow each individual to keep his vote secret.[130]

---

128 See Esu 2021.   129 Todd 1993: 91–97; Rubinstein 2000.
130 Todd 1993: 82–91, with *Ath. pol.* 63–69. Whether the text of the oath of the *dikastai* which appears in texts of Dem. 24.149–51 is reliable is uncertain.

Arbitration was a common feature of Greek dispute settlement from the earliest time, as when Nestor tries (but fails) to arbitrate the dispute between Agamemnon and Achilles at the beginning of the *Iliad*. In classical Athens arbitration was required in most private suits before they could go to trial. Citizens who were sixty years old were assigned as arbitrators; they heard from both sides and rendered a decision, but if either side rejected it, the case went to trial. Private arbitration was also common, with family members or friends often acting to settle disputes. Disputants could also agree to formal, binding arbitration; most often each party selected one arbitrator and then they agreed on a third, neutral figure. We hear of many such arbitrations, both successful and unsuccessful.

All magistrates were audited at the end of their term (normally a year) in office, and financial officials had their accounts examined before a law-court monthly.[131] Once a prytany (i.e. ten times a year), there was a designated opportunity to denounce officials in the assembly for major offences against the state, such as treason, attempting to overthrow democracy, taking bribes to speak against the interests of Athens, deceiving the people with false promises.[132] Such cases might be dealt with by the assembly or referred to a law court. Summary jurisdiction by the assembly occurred on a notorious occasion in 406 BCE when the generals who had failed to rescue Athenian sailors wrecked in the naval battle at Arginousai, in which they had been victorious, were condemned to death, but this action by the assembly caused an outcry and was clearly considered by many Athenians to be a case of the assembly exceeding its proper powers.[133]

Across ancient Indian polities the king himself was by long tradition the chief judge, in keeping with his possession of *kṣatra* ('dominion'), as the final authority in the realm obligated to punish with his *daṇḍa*.[134] Our texts typically address legal instructions to the king himself in reference to his personal role as judge at his court (*sabhā*).[135] Even as the judiciary grew larger and more complex, the king's court remained the central node within the legal system, serving as the source of judicial authority and the supreme appellate court.[136] It was also a venue for specific cases, such as those through which the king could demonstrate his care for the poor and the sacred. The king was to be assisted by court three assessors (*sabhyas*) and could (perhaps routinely) designate a high official to hear cases in his stead.[137] The *Arthaśāstra* represents a variation to this paradigm by discussing legal procedure in the

---

131 *Ath. pol.* 48.   132 *Ath. pol.* 43.4.   133 Xen. *Hell* 1.7.   134 Lingat 1973: 211–15.
135 See, e.g., GDh 11.19–26; MDh 8.1–3.   136 YDh 2.31.   137 See, e.g., MDh 8.9.

context, not of the king at his court, but of panels of three 'justices' (*dharmasthas*) working at courts throughout the realm. Other terms for these officials appear to be *prādvivāka* and *sabhya*. Such courts are what the later legal tradition will call *adhikṛta*: 'appointed [by the king]'.[138] This term came to represent a layer of courts 'beneath' the king's court and probably the bulk of the state judiciary. According to the *Arthaśāstra*, such courts were to operate in the provincial capital as well as the larger cities and towns throughout the realm.[139] Cases that had been heard in lower, private courts and tribunals could be appealed to these state courts. Whether they were permanent institutions situated in purpose-made structures is at present not known.

It is less clear how law worked in larger states and across imperial formations. Our best evidence comes from the Mauryan empire during the reign of Aśoka (r. 269–232 BCE). It seems that, while the central territory of Māgadha was directly governed by Aśoka, various regions (such as Ujjayinī and Takṣaśilā) were controlled by princes or governors. Laws were administered locally by officials called *nagalaviyohālakas* and *lajūkas*, with a degree of guidance and oversight coming from the imperial center. In his fourth pillar edict, Aśoka addresses the duties and responsibilities of the *lajūkas*, 'provincial officers' (also *rajūka* or *rājūka*). He tells us there that he has left to their discretion the assigning of honors and infliction of punishments.[140] In what is probably an example of the kinds of instructions rendered to the *lajūkas*, Aśoka says: 'For, I desire this: there should be uniformity (*samatā*[141]) in litigation and punishment.' He continues:

> My practice, moreover, has extended as far as this: for men who are confined in prison, on whom the sentence has been passed, and who have received the death penalty, a stay of three days is granted. Their relatives will make them reflect on what provides protection for their lives. Having been made to reflect on the fact that their lives end in death, they will give gifts for the sake of the world beyond, or they will perform fasts. For this is my wish, that when the time has expired, they may gain the world beyond, and that the manifold practice of dharma, self-control, and distribution of gifts may increase among the people.[142]

---

138 *YDh* 2.30.   139 *KAŚ* 3.1.1.   140 Fourth Pillar Edict (Topra); trans. Olivelle (2023).
141 This term means literally, 'sameness,' and has been interpreted by Hultzsch (1925: 125) and Olivelle (2023) as 'impartiality'. I do not exclude this sense when I render the term, more ambiguously, as 'uniformity'.
142 Fourth Pillar Edict (Topra); trans. Olivelle (2023).

Another instance of imperial instruction to justices comes from the first Kaliṅga edict, where Aśoka instructs his *nagalaviyohālakas* ('judicial officers of the city') at Tosalī as follows:

> At the direction of the Beloved of Gods, the mahamatras of Tosali, who are the judicial officers of the city, are to be so instructed.
>
> Whatever I set my eyes on, that I seek to carry out through action and to realize through appropriate means. And I consider this to be the principal means in this matter – to give you instruction. For, you take care of many thousands of living beings with the thought 'Would that we gain the affection of men.'
>
> All men are my children. Now, what I desire for my children, namely, that they be provided with complete welfare and wellbeing in this world and the next, the same do I desire for all men. But you do not realize how far reaching this matter is. Perhaps one officer may realize it, and he too only partially, not fully.
>
> For, you must look into this – 'Are they well cared for?' – constantly. If a single officer learns of someone's imprisonment or torture, the result is that for no reason his imprisonment happens to be terminated, whereas many others continue to suffer. In such cases, you must aspire: 'We will keep to the middle way.' One fails to act in this manner due to these proclivities: envy, quick temper, cruelty, haste, lack of zeal, laziness, and lethargy. So, you must aspire: 'May these proclivities not develop in us.' The root of all this is being always free of quick temper and haste. Anyone who is lethargic should pull himself up and get going, proceed and advance.

Whoever among you looks at it the same way should tell each other:

> Look, such and such are the instructions of the Beloved of Gods. Carrying them out fully yields great reward, while failure to carry them out fully brings great misfortune. For, by carrying them out improperly one gets neither heavenly favors nor royal favors.
>
> The average performance of this task brings a double reward; how much more, then, when it is carried out to an exceptional degree! If you carry it out fully, however, you will attain heaven and you will be freed from your debt to me.
>
> This writing, furthermore, should be listened to on the day of the Tishya constellation. Even in between the days of the Tishya, when an opportunity presents itself, even a single individual may listen to it. And acting in this way, you will be able to carry it out fully.
>
> For this purpose, has this writing been inscribed here, so that judicial officers of the city may at all times see to it that the people are not shackled or subjected to torture without reason. And also for this purpose I will dispatch every five years a Mahamatra who is neither harsh nor fierce, and who is

gentle in his actions in order to find out whether they are acting according to my instructions.

From Ujjain also, furthermore, the Prince should dispatch for this purpose an individual of the same type – and he should not let three years pass without doing this. Likewise, also from Taxila. When these Mahamatras set out on a tour without neglecting their own tasks, they should find out also whether they are acting according to the king's instructions.[143]

In both of these edicts – Aśoka's fourth pillar edict and the first Kaliṅga edict we find no evidence of an imperial code but witness rather the exercising of the emperor's supreme legal authority through both specific and systematic interventions. Moreover, there should be *samatā*, whatever that may mean precisely ('sameness', 'uniformity' or 'impartiality') in judicial activities. Otherwise, regional administrators are granted broad judicial powers. In order to enforce conformity to these commands, a judicial officer's activities are subject to review on a quinquennial basis by powerful officials dispatched by the emperor himself and on at least a triennial basis by the regional governor.

Formal litigation in Republican and early imperial Rome over civil matters bore some resemblance to processes of arbitration.[144] In the Republic, civil litigation was theoretically a voluntary process. Both parties had to agree to go to court and to submit themselves to the court's authority. Unlike arbitration, however, the praetor had the power to appoint someone from a list of high-ranking judges. It is striking that the Romans understood this judge – both the finder of facts in the case and the person empowered to declare a verdict – to be a private person, rather than a public official invested with state power.[145] The state officials involved in handling cases in the city state of (Republican) Rome were the praetors, who would craft an account of their dispute that fit within one of the model *formulae* that he proposed for litigation. The phase of the trial taken up with crafting the *formula* (the '*in iure*' phase) was imagined to be something of an interactive process between the praetor, who was advised by jurists, and litigants. A large number of such *formulae* are preserved or can be reconstructed. *Formulae* could be adapted to meet the needs of the case, to include counter-pleas (*exceptiones*), counter-counter-pleas, and so forth. Once the formula was crafted, it was left to the judge to find whether the facts fitted the legal definition of the case (the '*apud iudicem*' phase). Unlike arbitration, a decision was required, and it was

---

143 Separate Edict I. Trans. Olivelle (2023).   144 Riggsby 2010: 116.
145 The similarity between private arbitration and litigation, however, might lead to some erroneous conclusions. For an overview, see Kaser 1967.

essentially all-or-nothing. Eventually, in a broad variety of transactions known as 'good faith' actions, the judge was empowered to award damages only up to the amount of 'what is good and fair'.[146]

Romans themselves made a sharp distinction between arbitration and litigation. Litigation involved jurisdiction, and only select magistrates were given the authority to 'declare what is law' (*ius dicere*): in the Republic, the praetors (and sometimes the consuls) themselves alone possessed this power. It eventually extended to the emperor as well.[147] The *in iure* phase of litigation, presided over by a praetor with the power of jurisdiction, had important consequences for the course of litigation more generally: agreeing on the formula during the *in iure* phase is said to have 'consumed the action' – meaning that the same question could not subsequently be re-litigated[148] Notionally independent communities (such as municipalities) were similarly understood to have elected their own equivalents of praetors and consuls (normally *duumviri iure dicundo*).[149] Despite gestures towards consensus, Roman litigation operated on a presumption that the state played a unique role in defining what the law was and who was to decide it. Disputes could be settled in other ways, but the act of ruling upon a dispute *as a case* was fundamentally a prerogative of the state.

This development continues into the Roman empire after the advent of monarchy. Cases began to be heard not just in the praetor's court, with its two-part procedure, but increasingly by magistrates who also served as judges. The most important of these was the emperor, who could serve as a judge in the first instance. More often he served as a court of appeal for litigants from throughout the empire. The development of an appellate procedure, still poorly understood, eventually led to the 'hierarchicalization' of Roman courts.[150]

---

146 In practice, most litigation was messy, expensive and coercive. The emphasis on consent between the parties in determining the legal issue *in iure*, for instance, was surely an ideological gesture. The parties had little choice but to 'consent' to appear in court, as they might lose by default if they refused to appear. The process for executing judgments was similarly unpleasant, probably by design.
147 Peachin 2015; Tuori 2016.   148 On consular jurisdiction, see Pina Polo 2011: 122–34.
149 In a preserved charter (written at Rome for a colony in Spain), the privilege of jurisdiction is specified to belong only to specific individuals: 'No person in this colony shall adjudicate or have jurisdiction, save the *duumviri*, or a prefect left in charge by a *duumvir* or an aedile, as provided by this law. Nor shall anyone cause by virtue of such imperium or authority any person to adjudicate in the said colony, except those persons who properly adjudicate by this law' (*Lex Coloniae Genetivae* 94, trans. Johnson, Coleman-Norton and Bourne 1961 (No. 114)).
150 Not only could the emperor correct errors and find reasons to treat particular litigants more equitably, but he (and his court) could also be asked to decide more complex questions of law by issuing rescripts – answers to particular legal questions. Many such

Outside of communities notionally recognized as independent, Roman governors, like praetors in Rome, sat at the apex of the judicial system. They could hear cases themselves or delegate to others the task of hearing cases, on analogy with the formulary procedure (and in some provinces, at least, the formulary procedure may have been used).[151] In Roman Egypt, where we can see provincial litigation with a high degree of granularity, legal complaints might be sent a variety of individuals: some of them Roman administrators; some locals appointed by Romans to govern *nomes* ('counties'); and some (such as centurions) whose official status was rather more ambiguous. Those sent to the prefect – especially legal complaints of important individuals – were either passed for judgment to select judges (*iudices pedanei*) or, quite often, to one of two *epistrategoi*, who were Roman officials subordinate to the prefect. Cases might also be sent for judgment to the *strategoi*, the chief administrators of the *nomes*, who were not Roman officials, but rather recruited from the local elites of the province. In some limited cases the governor might serve as judge, though the precise means by which he chose to take cognizance of particular cases is hard to reconstruct. Traditionally, Roman governors reserved for themselves the right to dole out capital punishment: the *ius gladii*. We know less than we would like concerning criminal and capital cases in Egypt, which is perhaps surprising given the extent of the documentation. In their imaginative literature of the provinces, justice was always conceived as being meted out by Roman governors and emperors.[152]

The organization of early Chinese states centred on the ruler (emperor) who in law constituted the sole source of all legislative, judicial and executive authority.[153] The ruler was personally involved in acts of legislation at least to the extent of ordering that rules on particular matters be compiled and then providing formal ratification. He might on occasion act as judge, but normally his judicial function was performed by ministers and officials on his behalf, though he retained a final veto. Again, the ruler might, and frequently did, issue executive decisions on any matters that concerned him. Normally, however, the administration of the state was conducted by a complex hierarchy of officials, appointed by and responsible to the ruler. These officials staffed the central organs of government as well as fulfilling the roles of governors and magistrates, administering the territories into which the

---

rescripts are preserved, each likely the work of a skilled jurist operating as part of the imperial administration. See Chapter 3, this volume.
151 See Rüfner 2016: 261.   152 Musurillo 1954; Harker 2008; Rodriguez 2010.
153 See Olberding 2022.

empire was divided. Within their spheres of jurisdiction, they exercised delegated judicial and executive, though not legislative, functions. The system was highly centralized and tightly controlled with magistrates regularly reporting to governors and governors to the central ministries or the throne. The only exception occurred at the beginning of the Han (206 BCE–220 CE) when relatives of the emperor were enfeoffed as hereditary kings with extensive independent powers over large portions of the country.[154] Delegation of authority of this kind had been completely abandoned by the end of the second century BCE.

Professional judges (Sum. *di-ku₅*, Akk. *dajānu*) are attested in Mesopotamia at least since the beginning of the second millennium.[155] The qualification and training of these professional judges, however, is still poorly understood.[156] They sat not only in the capital city, but travelled throughout the kingdom, giving verdicts either on their own or in conjunction with local judges. The king, however, was the ultimate judge: he intervened ex officio in all trials, through various procedures. Some cases were reserved exclusively for the king, such as crimes ('matter of life' *dīn napištim*) and disputes related to the domain, and certain people fell under his direct protection by virtue of their status. Various methods existed for parties to appeal to the king for justice. Although the king is omnipresent in judicial life according to official inscriptions of various period, it seems that his actual interventions would have, in practice, been limited. His principled jurisdiction focuses primarily on administrative law, blood crimes and political issues. At all times, moreover, administrative officers possessed judicial powers. The governor of a province, for example, might settle important disputes arising within his domain, usually alongside other dignitaries or local notables, and always upon authorization of the ruler.[157] Heads of families had domestic jurisdiction over their dependents, mostly in matters regarding family law, although they were not empowered to carry out capital punishment. Elders could also

---

154 Lewis 2007: 60–68.
155 See § 5 of the Laws of Ḥammurabi: as a result of his misconduct, the judge is dismissed from his 'judicial seat' (*kussī dajānūtišu*).
156 There was perhaps a centre for the further training of future lawyers in Nippur in the second millennium. In Babylonia, the function tends to concentrate in the hands of several families (sixth–fifth century BCE), still based on their professional skills. About the Mesopotamian judges, see Neumann 2006–2008.
157 Judicial powers were distributed among various officials, according to a cascading delegation of powers scheme. The network seems to be more extensive in the empires of the first millennium, particularly in Assyria where qualified staff, such as the 'verdict clerk' appeared. See Jas 1996.

State Legal Systems

intervene to solve public or private law disputes.[158] They served as guardians of customary traditions, recalling previous jurisprudence, political practices or tribal customs.[159] Commercial litigation was settled by specific courts composed of traders responsible for investigating the cases of their peers.[160] No judges, regardless of professional qualifications, were remunerated for their judicial activities.[161]

There is no word for a 'court' in Akkadian or Sumerian. Forums for judicial activity were temporary, occurring within an assembly of magistrates, whether professional or not. The local assembly, composed of citizens, sometimes decided on civil and criminal, but also political and administrative cases, but it was not a court in the narrow sense. Hence, there were no specific buildings dedicated to judicial activities. There seems to be no hierarchical order among the various legal forums; although the royal court was obviously at the summit, there is no evidence of appeal. When the location of judicial activity is mentioned, it is usually 'the gate' of the city; an administrative or a religious building; or an open space with the population in attendance. Apart from the king, who renders justice alone, all the courts are composed of a plurality of judges, often in odd numbers. Regardless of the status of the personnel, whether religious or lay authorities, the sentence was pronounced by the lay authority.[162]

A type of public prosecutor's office may have functioned during the first half of the second millennium, with an officer (*qaqqā'um*) whose role was to inform political authorities of any misdeeds of which he was aware.[163] During the Assyrian empire, a public prosecutor (*bātiqu*) was responsible for prosecuting offences against the Crown and possibly calling for a punishment.[164] Judges sometimes requested the assistance of experts – for instance a graphologist or a land surveyor – before making their decision. In Nuzi

---

158 Lion 2012. The role of elders is well illustrated in the Mari sources (Syria, eighteenth century BCE), and in the Bible.
159 On previous jurisprudence see, for instance, Jeremiah's trial in the Bible, Jer 26:17–19.
160 Veenhof 1991. This is well documented esp. in Assyria at the beginning of the second millennium.
161 Instead, they receive gifts (*šulmānu*) from the litigants, who sometimes complain of various abuses, such as denial of justice, abuse of rights and racketeering. Only Shamash, the god of justice, can punish the corrupt judge: public authorities were powerless to control their probity. See Démare-Lafont 1999a.
162 The frequent references to the temple or its staff in the Mesopotamian trials point to procedural requirements (oath taking) or to cases involving the interests of the temple (for instance, offences committed by an oblate who stole assets belonging to the temple), in which case the investigation is carried out by a mixed court involving lay and religious dignitaries, but the sentence is pronounced by the secular or temporal authority.
163 Charpin 1993a.   164 Villard 2023: nos. 139 and 155.

(Mossul area, fourteenth–thirteenth century BCE), bailiffs were responsible for recording the refusal of a party's appearance or the proper taking of an oath. A report from a single bailiff could cancel the whole procedure.[165] The Sumerian court reports from the end of the third millennium BCE mention a court officer (*maškim*) who acted as a kind of 'institutional witness', reminding the court of sentences rendered in earlier trials.[166]

Two chief comparative questions emerge from the discussion in this section, regarding state legal systems generally. The first concerns the areas in which states used law most intensively, whether private disputes, criminal punishments or both. All states can be seen to engage both domains, although China and its close association of law with punishment seems to be exceptional in a number of interesting respects. The second comparative question has to do with what aspects of dispute resolution and/or punishment the state formally took to itself and what aspects were left to private actors. As no state sought to completely efface the role of private actors in the resolution of disputes altogether, we might proceed by thinking about state legal systems as the results of varying strategies to exercise state power through law in complex legal environments populated by numerous and heterogeneous 'private' legal authorities. In comparing traditions, however, we continue to be bedevilled in both areas by differences in the scale, purposes and ambition of state activity.

Law and Legitimacy

In all cases examined, law is used to enhance the legitimacy of state power. In Mesopotamia, it is usually argued that the law collections were used for this purpose because they served primarily as opportunities for an official eulogy of his own qualities in the prologue and epilogue of the work. In India, the king's primary obligation to preserve harmony and social order was seen as

---

165 Démare-Lafont 1999b: 384 and 499. Although lawyers are not attested as a rule, the nineteenth–eighteenth century BCE Assyrian merchants could resort to attorneys in their commercial trials. They perform procedural acts on behalf of their clients and are appointed by the public authorities or recruited by an individual, who drafts a contract specifying the amount of the salary to be paid. The attorney has a performance obligation: if he loses the trial, he will have to reimburse the sums already received. The temptation is great then to lengthen the procedure, as the bickering allows an unscrupulous attorney to live at the expense of his client. See the examples gathered by Michel 2023: nos. 84–86. A similar institution may have existed in the mid-third millennium; several texts mention an individual who apparently carries out procedural acts on behalf of a party residing outside the jurisdiction of the court.
166 Lafont 1997.

accomplished through a few archetypal activities, one of which was resolving disputes and 'protecting *dharma*'. This is given expression through various myths on the origin of kings, such as when the king is crowned by society to forestall the 'law of the fishes', wherein the weak are devoured by the strong. Hence, courts and the king's practice of law were seen as efforts towards fulfilling his primary obligations to the people. In Mesopotamia, the cancellation of debts through the promulgation of *mīšarum* or *andurāru* edicts – acts emblematic of 'social justice' – were archetypal activities of the legitimate king. Across the extant evidence for ancient Greek city states, the close relationship between the two meant that law and legitimacy were nearly coterminous. In general, cities courted reputations for being law-abiding rather than anarchic – there was a preference for dealing with people who recognize law.[167]

The relationship between law and legitimacy is seen particularly when a perceived disrespect for law undermines the legitimacy of states. It is a favourite commonplace about tyrants in ancient Greece that their downfall follows their transgression of the law, particularly with regard to proper behaviour towards women, and the same trope is seen in the story of the last of the kings of Rome and his rape of Lucretia. In India, where the symbol of *dharma* was broader than 'law', a king might conceivably have greater latitude in claiming adherence to or protection of *dharma* as 'the good'. For instance, the *Arthaśāstra* argues that seeking political advantage through amoral or immoral means is necessary if *dharma* is to be supported.[168]

Within both the realist and mainstream Brahmanical perspectives on the Indian state, law played an important role. The archetypal duty of the king was the protection of his subjects from thieves and raiders. Even realists such as Kauṭilya recognized that the king was responsible for securing an ordered society by resolving disputes among his subjects. The commitment to law for realists, however, is likely to have been commensurately pragmatic: as a means to control markets, punish enemies of the state and nuisances, prevent bloodshed between individuals and groups, and promote the king's image as a just, fatherly ruler. Even so, realists recognized that a king failing to punish those deserving would lose the support of the people.[169]

---

[167] Cf. Xen. *Mem.* 4.4.17.
[168] This is the purport of the claim that governance (*daṇḍanīti*), which is focused exclusively on efficacy, ensures the enterprise and security (*yogakṣema*) of the Vedic scriptures (*KAŚ* 1.4.3).
[169] *KAŚ* 7.5.25.

The mainstream Brahmanical tradition, however, takes this further, by making of *dharma* an unseen cosmic force that, when unprotected, strikes down kings.[170] Because, as we have seen, adherence to *dharma* is understood as a necessary condition for effective rule, Brahmanical sources of different kinds idealize the *dharmarāja* ('*dharma*-king') who piously observes his personal *dharma*. All of the king's duties, in this perspective, were subject to *rājadharma*, whose successful performance had both worldly and soteriological consequences.[171] For mainstream jurists the king's obligation to *dharma* exceeded litigation and punishment, manifesting particularly in his obligation to enforce strict caste segregation and the Brahmanical privilege of receiving gifts and officiating at rituals.[172] Beyond simply being seen as a just and fatherly ruler, the *dharmarāja* also supported Brahmins and enforced caste society. Kings could be thought of as either *dhārmika* or *adhārmika*, righteous or unrighteous, and this affected the way they were dealt with by rivals and foreign states.[173] Adherence to righteous custom, law and conduct, often including patronage of Brahmanical cultural institutions, was the determining factor in this regard.[174] A good king was one in whose kingdom there was no crime or threat to his subjects, and kings were felt to accomplish this by cultivating strength and pursuing *dharma* justly and earnestly.[175] This was also felt to endear the king to the people.

Within democratic constitutions in the ancient Greek world, breaches of legitimacy were excluded almost by definition. Any democratic magistrate who acted illegitimately would be acting illegally and even when the assembly as a whole acted in a way that breached its own established procedures, individuals would be blamed for misleading the people, rather than the regime as a whole losing legitimacy. Issues of legitimacy therefore arise almost entirely in non-democratic regimes or at levels above or below that of the Greek city. Within monarchical regimes legal legitimacy and legitimate descent often go together. In Sparta the most common way to undermine a king's authority was to question his descent, a tactic employed by Cleomenes to secure the banishment of his fellow king Demaratus, who had earlier used a similar tactic against Cleomenes.[176] The main situation in which breaches of law undermine legitimacy comes when cities assume power over others and then act in ways that are seen as improper, if not strictly illegal. This was the case with the Spartan occupation of the acropolis of Thebes in 381 and with the various excessive actions taken against other

170 E.g. MDh 8.15.   171 Lingat 1973: 211–12.   172 E.g. MDh 7.24, 7.35.
173 E.g. KAŚ 7.13.11–12; 9.6.21.   174 KAŚ 7.5.20.   175 See Scharfe 1989: 44–51.
176 Herodotus 6.51, 65–70.

Greeks by the Athenians.[177] But in both these cases, what was breached was 'international law', a set of expectations lacking any authority to compel their observation.[178]

For ancient China, it probably helps to distinguish between, on the one hand, the Western Zhou and the Han and later dynasties, and, on the other, the state and empire of Qin. For the former we have the notion of a 'higher law' that might be associated with the ancestors, the gods, and particularly with Heaven (as expressed in the formulation 'the mandate of Heaven'). The legitimacy of the ruler is determined by the extent to which his behaviour accords with that demanded by the 'higher law'. In this context what may be termed positive law is only one of the aspects of the ruler's behaviour relevant to the satisfaction of the 'higher law'. The historical and ritual sources tend to emphasize as even more important the need for the ruler to exhibit in his own person and conduct the fundamental moral values of the elite class, or even those that transcended class such as filial piety. Positive law (the enactments of the ruler for the government of the country) came to be seen, especially from the Han dynasty onwards, as an important means for securing the maintenance of these values in society, as well as the means for securing order and obedience to the ruler.

The state and empire of Qin (c. 350–206 BCE) – considered the societies which exhibited par excellence the influence of legalist thinking – dispensed with the need for the ruler either to comply with the dictates of a 'higher law' or to manifest a particular kind of moral behaviour (though some values such as filial piety were still important even under the Qin). Thus, we can say that for the Qin the very existence and maintenance of the law, especially in the form of penal rules prescribing the behaviour to be shown by the ruler's subjects, was the essential factor in securing the legitimacy of the state. It might not be going too far in this context to identify the state with the (positive) law.[179]

To a certain extent, the Romans shared with other societies the belief that lawful behaviour is productive of legitimacy. Accordingly, as noted above, numerous rules guided the passage of legislation, regulated the conduct of magistrates and governed the 'constitutional' structure of the Republic. On the other hand, the Republic was marked by a strongly aristocratic element that at times refused to be bound by law for some sort of higher purpose. To be certain, not all people shared this view, or that the requirements of law

---

177 Spartan occupation: Xen. *Hell.* 5.4.1, 6.3.9–10; Athenians: Xen. *Hell.* 2.2.3, Isocrates 4.100.
178 Low 2007.   179 For detailed debate see Su Li 2018.

could be evaded when a problem was simply too important for a scrupulous application of legal rules. Provincial communities, Christians in particular, complained vigorously about perceived violations of procedure.[180] More generally, provincial litigants insisted that administrators were legitimate to the extent that they behaved in rational and predictable ways.

There was always the threat that an emperor might turn out to be mad, or evil or unpredictable. But the opposite desire remained as well: for a leader who could transcend the demands of law and determine who *truly* was right and who was feigning it. Thus, when a learned Greek of the third century CE narrated the life of the holy man Apollonius of Tyana, one of the things on which he remarked was Apollonius' ability to see through artifice and to discern guilt and innocence.[181] Emperors were supposed to do the same: to use their powers to decide who was truly innocent and who truly awful. But they had to do more than search for the truth and apply the law dispassionately. They might also at times have to display pity and sadness, even anger. Perhaps the culmination of this tradition is crystallized in an edict of the emperor Constantine, who authorizes 'all the provincials' to defy the normal legal order and bring him directly evidence of bureaucratic malfeasance:

> If there is anyone, of any station, order, or rank, who is certain that he can show, truly and clearly, that anyone, be they judge or companion or friend or palatine official, has proven to have acted without justice and integrity, let him come safely and without fear and call upon me. I myself shall hear all these things, I myself shall judge them and, if the charge shall be proven, I myself shall avenge myself. Let him speak, and let him speak safely and with candour; if he shall prove it, as I said, I shall avenge myself against whomever has deceived me with a false show of integrity up until this time. I shall reward the man who reveals and proves this, both with rank and materially. So shall the highest divinity always be propitious to me and keep me safe, as I hope, and keep the state blessed and prosperous.[182]

The righteous anger of emperors against malefactors helps us to understand the underpinnings of the imperial theory of legitimacy. For emperors, legitimacy comes precisely from the fact that they can transcend the law as currently constructed. They do so by aligning or justifying their legal pronouncements with authentic feelings of anger. On such logic, law's legitimacy derives not from its alignment to higher principles, but from the fact of its

---

180 Often, in their case, committed by officials too bored or malicious to be bothered with such things: Bryen 2014.
181 Philostr. *VA* 5.24. A trope that also appears in early Christian 'holy' life-writing.
182 *Codex Theodosianus* 9.1.4, trans. Pharr et al.

original alignment to the most visceral feelings of the head of the political and, eventually, the 'religious' order.

In Mesopotamia, the king claimed that he provided 'just ways for the people of the land' (*ana šutēšur nišī mātim ūsim*; Laws of Ḥammurabi, prologue col. v ll. 14–17) which seems to be a key reference in royal rhetoric but also a way to assert its legitimacy. However, because of the subsidiary nature of the laws issued by the king, the local rules remained available as long as the parties agreed. Debt-cancellation edicts, moreover, could be circumvented by inserting a renunciation clause in the contract or by disguising the loan as a work lease, two practices that apparently did not affect the legitimacy of the king.[183] The essential notion of 'king of justice' rather refers to the possibility for any of his subjects, at least in theory, to appeal to his jurisdiction. Any failure to this duty would probably have jeopardized his legitimacy or at least tarnished his public image. Naram-Sin (2254–2218 BCE), for instance, the grandson of Sargon of Agade, remained in the collective memory as a brutal and warlike ruler who was more dedicated to quelling rebellions than to delivering justice.

Across ancient traditions, acting lawfully is bound up with legitimacy – often to the point that the two are equated. Where notions of righteousness encompass those of law, however, law can become symbolic of a ruler's adherence to righteousness. Conversely in such situations, a ruler might express his or her legitimacy by acting above or beyond the law, when the adherence to law is seen as an impediment to some good. Given sometimes capacious notions of law and justice operating in a system, we should expect a variety of perspectives, though one imagines recurring debates across the system between the necessity, even righteousness, of sometimes acting outside the law.

Conclusion

The main purpose of this chapter has been to aggregate analyses of different ancient legal cultures with respect to several key areas related to 'law and the state'. Divergence of conceptualizations of law-related categories, differences in source material, complexities attending their respective interpretation, and variations between the scholarly attitudes and practices among those studying each tradition have meant that any attempt at an even minimally

---

183 Circumvention: Démare-Lafont 2000a: 61–62 and disguised as a work lease: Charpin 1993b.

comprehensive comparison must avoid the strict definition of key comparative categories and be destined to remain both somewhat abstract and uneven. Nevertheless, we get glimpses in this comparative study of features and dynamics shared across traditions as well as areas of apparent disjuncture that call for more vigorous explication.

We might end, then, with a few promising avenues for further inquiry. First, under what circumstances was positive law felt or empowered to provide effective constitutional restraints on ruling power or, at least, to provide a useful means of shaping expectations about its use? And, in those cultures where forms of constitutional law can be found, how did they operate alongside other cultural forms that also shaped the exercise of ruling power? Second, can legislative power and practices in ancient societies be understood on a continuum if we see them all as various strategies for negotiating the relationship(s) between a ruler's power and customary norms? And, again, under what circumstances were state bodies empowered to or inclined to use legislation as a means of creating or formalizing law? Third, how intensive was state involvement in the greater legal order? Another way of asking this is to pose the fundamental questions: to what extent was law central to governance? What aspects of social life were addressed and what other legal authorities were tolerated, empowered or ignored?[184]

---

184 See Chapters 8 and 9, this volume.

6

Law and Religion

Lead Author: BRUCE WELLS

Contributors: NOAH BICKART, DONALD DAVIS, EDWARD HARRIS, CAROLINE HUMFRESS, GEOFFREY MACCORMACK, ROBIN OSBORNE AND KATELIJN VANDORPE

Introduction

An examination of the relationship between law and religion in ancient societies encounters a range of complexities. The main reason for this is that the two concepts were not distinguished from each other as they are today. In the study of the ancient world, it is difficult to separate religion from other facets of civilization. Ancient languages generally had no specific word for religion, and, for many ancient societies, what we call religion was not a discrete cultural phenomenon but something that permeated the whole of life and society. Religious beliefs and practices were part and parcel of daily living, family structures, business transactions and political administration; they formed the foundation for the vast majority of personal and social activities. According to Émile Durkheim, virtually all aspects of culture, including law, issued forth from what modern scholars label as religion.[1] In several of the societies examined here, maintaining law and order had a distinctly religious purpose: to retain the favour and beneficent presence of the gods and to avoid their wrath and punishment. For example, Ḥammurabi, the great king of Babylonia (1792–1750 BCE), claimed that his extensive list of laws fulfilled the divine mandate that he had received to establish justice in his land. While some may be sceptical of Ḥammurabi's sincerity and wonder what ulterior motives he may have had in his use of such rhetoric, the basic claim was that, without the laws and the just social order they created, he would lose the favour of the gods, the land would descend into chaos and the entire population would suffer. In short, enacting

---

[1] See the discussion of Durkheim's views in Allan 2012: 123–25.

and enforcing law was one way of doing religion. For Ḥammurabi and the Babylonians, without religion, there was no need for law, and without law, religion could not be properly carried out.

One of the most well-known instances of the intertwining of what modern discourse labels 'law and religion' comes from the special agreement recorded in the Hebrew Bible known as the covenant.[2] The biblical descriptions present the creation of the covenant as taking place prior to the establishment of the monarchy in ancient Israel and Judah. Nevertheless, the majority of scholars believe that these descriptions were mostly composed during the latter half of the monarchic period (c. 750–586 BCE) or within a century or so thereafter.[3] What is striking about this particular agreement is that it is established between a god (Yahweh) and a group of people (the Israelites).[4] We know of agreements from elsewhere between a group of people and a monarch or between a monarch and a god, but the king is particularly conspicuous in the Israelite covenant by virtue of his absence and his replacement by a deity. Certain biblical texts (e.g. 2 Kgs 11:17) afford the king a minimal role in similar covenants, but the descriptions of the principal covenant in the Pentateuch give the king no role whatsoever. The only Pentateuchal text to mention him in connection with the covenant (Deut 17:14–20) requires him to write out a copy of the law (tôrâ), which contains the covenant's obligations, to read it regularly and to obey it.

The word for covenant in the Hebrew Bible, bərît, can identify contracts between individuals (e.g. Gen 21:27, 1 Sam 18:3) and treaties between political entities (e.g. Gen 14:13, 1 Kgs 20:34). The notion of a treaty is especially important for understanding the covenant between Israel and Yahweh because the biblical descriptions thereof imbue it with all the markings of what scholars of the ancient Near East call a vassal treaty. A vassal treaty was typically concluded between a powerful king and a much less powerful ruler, who became, for all intents and purposes, the vassal of the former.[5] A group of people, rather than an individual ruler, could take on the role of vassal.

---

2 The Hebrew Bible contains most of the surviving literature, prior to the Greek period, of ancient Israel and Judah. Israel occupied the northern half of Palestine, Judah the southern half; 'Israel' can also be used to identify both kingdoms together.
3 Koch 2008: 264.
4 The inscription on an amulet (seventh century BCE) found at Arslan Tash in northern Syria says that the god 'Assur made an eternal covenant with us'; see Pardee 1998. The statement seems to be part of an incantation to ward off evil beings, and the amulet was likely displayed in a private house. Its context remains obscure, as does the referent of the pronoun 'us', but it may offer a curious parallel of sorts to the biblical notion of a covenant between a deity and a group of people.
5 See Chapter 4, this volume.

Evidence for these agreements comes from multiple ancient Near Eastern societies (e.g. Syrian, Hittite, Assyrian, Babylonian), and they typically contain the same basic elements, which included a commitment of allegiance on the part of the vassal and a (sometimes very lengthy) set of stipulations that he (or they, as the case may be) must obey.[6] The Israelite covenant incorporates these and other common elements, including linguistic markers that characterized such treaties, and puts the Israelite people into the place of the vassal. The so-called laws in the Hebrew Bible are actually presented as the covenantal stipulations or duties that the Israelites are now required to obey as the vassal of the god Yahweh. Thus, this covenant manifests the features of a legal document – a treaty – and yet seems to consist of distinctly 'religious' content when viewed from a modern perspective.

Admittedly, the biblical authors may not have conceived of it in these terms. That is, they may not have thought of their literary product as containing both legal and religious dimensions because that distinction was not part of their cognitive environment. The biblical authors most probably modelled their covenant on the vassal treaties of neighbouring societies with which they were familiar; and these, too, contained both 'legal' and 'religious' characteristics. Thus, the biblical authors may not have thought of themselves as producing something that was somehow more religious than the vassal treaties that they had drawn upon. Rather, the substitution of a god for the emperor or king may well have been a political move on their part – an act of resistance against an oppressive monarchy or empire. Nevertheless, it is phenomena like that of the Israelite covenant – moments where law and religion appear to merge or interact in significant ways – that are the focus of this chapter. Throughout many of its sections, the chapter foregrounds the discussion of the data from ancient Israel – and, to a lesser degree, Mesopotamia – partly because it is the religious ideas of ancient Israel that readers may be most familiar with and where the intersection of law and religion, in many cases, stands out most prominently.

One difficulty in approaching this topic is delineating what we mean by the concept of religion. Many would argue that attempting to define religion is an exercise in futility.[7] But it seems important to provide a provisional definition in order to establish a basis for identifying the cultural elements within the ancient societies under analysis here. In his book, *Religion in Human Evolution*, Robert Bellah adapts a definition from the work of Clifford Geertz that is useful for this discussion. For Bellah, religion is 'a system of symbols that,

6 Most of these treaties can be found in Kitchen and Lawrence 2012.   7 Martin 2012: 1–6.

when enacted by human beings, establishes powerful, pervasive, and long-lasting moods and motivations that make sense in terms of an idea of a general order of existence'.[8] To paraphrase and – undoubtedly – oversimplify, one might say that religion is a system of symbols that creates a sense of cosmic order. Religion in the ancient world, as we will see, had a great deal to do with creating and maintaining what was believed to be cosmic order, and law was an integral part of this effort. Bellah goes on to argue that human existence entails what he calls multiple realities, the dominant reality being that of the 'world of daily life'.[9] One could also think of these as forms of life (à la Wittgenstein). People enter other forms of life or realities – Bellah asserts that all realities, including that of daily life, are socially constructed – when they leave the world of daily life by engaging in activities such as sleep, play, art, entertainment and most of all religion.[10] Each reality comes with its own parlance, boundaries, priorities and rules. Very often, of course, our multiple realities overlap with each other, and we can find ourselves inhabiting or trying to inhabit more than one reality at a time.

From this perspective, law could be considered its own reality or form of life, with its own symbols, rules, language, sense of time and space, ways of making things happen and so forth. Regardless of whether one thinks of it as a part of daily life or as a separate reality, however, what is of interest in this chapter are those moments at which law reaches over into the set of symbols that, for the inhabitants of the ancient world, created their religious reality and draws upon those symbols and that reality to achieve legal ends. These symbols include divine beings, cultic officials, cultic rituals, religious texts and even religious terminology, among other things. What we will also find is that moments occur when the reverse of this process takes place: when religion draws upon law. Various religious practices appear to have relied on law in the sense that they made use of concepts and formulations that likely originated in legal practice or that became associated more with the reality of law than with that of religion. Thus, one of the main goals of this chapter is to identify instances where the sources at our disposal are more or less explicit about – or, at least, give us strong grounds for inferring – either type of manoeuvre: law making use of religious symbols or vice versa.

The following discussion is divided according to five major, analytical, categories that can be identified across ancient cultures: the establishment of the legitimacy and authority of law; public law and state governance; the use of religious rituals in legal contexts; the interaction of religious officials and

---

8 Bellah 2011: xiv.   9 Bellah 2011: 2.   10 Bellah 2011: 2–4.

the legal system; and the relationship between religion and acts of wrongdoing. In the first and third areas, it is mostly law that needs religion to achieve its goals. In the second area, one finds religion utilizing legal mechanisms in order to ensure its continued influence on and pre-eminence in most of the ancient societies being studied here. With the final two sections, the matter of which reality is borrowing from which becomes much less clear: both areas appear to draw on and support each other in what is often a mutually beneficial relationship, but one that is not always tidy or straightforward. In the end, the chapter aims to provide greater breadth in our understanding of the relationship between law and religion and also greater specificity in our descriptions of how the two interacted within these ancient cultures.

Religion and Legal Authority

Religious Legitimation of Law

Sociologist Peter Berger has argued that the behavioural norms of most societies develop to the point where they acquire a life of their own and start to be taken for granted.[11] The societies that created them come to believe – or, perhaps, those in charge begin to claim – that these norms are somehow coextensive with the cosmos and originated in something much greater than the efforts and activities of human beings. When the source of the norms takes on the aura of having a mysterious and awesome power, they become associated with the sacred and thereby acquire divine legitimacy. While this description may not necessarily apply to human societies across the board, it points to the frequent connection that one finds in ancient societies between law and what people perceived as divine will.

The grounding of the legitimacy of law in religious terms prevailed throughout much of the ancient world. That is, most of the cultures under consideration left behind a variety of evidence for their belief that right and proper laws ultimately find their origin in the will of the gods or in the great cosmic order established at or near the beginning of time. Occasionally, this is expressed indirectly, such as when a human lawgiver is hailed as the source of the laws but either he or his laws receive divine approval (e.g., Ḥammurabi of Babylon, Clisthenes of Athens). In some cases, the belief weakens over time, and the authority of law receives a more exclusively political, as opposed to religious, grounding. Some ancient cultures certainly set forth their religious

[11] Berger 1967.

claims about law more explicitly than others, and a few appear to have accepted only a rather tenuous connection between law and divine will. Still, whether an ancient society maintained that law originated with the gods, was approved by them or was necessary only to appease them, it was often a religious orientation to the world and to perceived reality that undergirded the authority and effectiveness of law in the ancient world.

Perhaps the clearest example of attributing the origins of law directly to a deity comes from ancient Israel and Judah. Biblical texts describe how the god Yahweh spoke laws directly to Moses who, in turn, transmitted them to the people of Israel. In fact, a few texts refer to Yahweh as having inscribed some of the laws with his own hand (Exod 31:18; Deut 4:13; 5:22; 10:4); others describe Moses as the copyist (Exod 24:4; 34:28; Deut 31:9) or the one who instructs the Israelite people in the laws (Deut 1:5; 4:44). While these texts come from different authors (c. 800–400 BCE) whose perspectives were often at odds, there is uniform consensus among them that Yahweh is the ultimate source and author of the law – the *tôrâ*. As noted above, the figure most conspicuous by his absence in these portrayals of the *tôrâ*'s origins is the king.[12] He is neither lawmaker nor lawgiver – nor even the mediator between Yahweh and the people. The creation and transmission of the law have been placed into the mythic past before either Judah or Israel was ruled by a monarch. According to other biblical texts, kings are responsible for administering the law, but, for the *establishment* of law, they are unnecessary. This strategy on the part of the biblical authors may have been a subtle or even not so subtle attempt to diminish the importance of their own society's royal administration or, perhaps, that of a foreign imperial power (e.g. Assyria) that had come to dominate the area.[13] Their elevation of *tôrâ* was simultaneously a diminishment of the crown.

In the neighbouring societies of Mesopotamia, the gods play a crucial role, but the law finds its immediate source in the king.[14] Instead of the laws having divine authorship, as in Israel, the king in Mesopotamia has a divine commission to establish justice in the land. Fulfilling this mandate includes the creation and enforcement of law.[15] Good laws please the gods. Moreover, much of the rhetoric describing the king's actions in this regard points to the gods as the source of the king's wisdom, which enables him to construct fair and effective laws. The best evidence for this comes from Babylonia when it rose to prominence during the Middle Bronze Age (c. 1800–1600 BCE),

---

12 Levinson 2008: 22–29.   13 Otto 2002: 176–86; Wright 2009: 343–46.
14 Van De Mieroop 2015: 175.   15 Hurowitz 2011: 91–92.

especially under the reign of its most famous king, Ḥammurabi. The collection known as the Laws of Ḥammurabi (c. 1750 BCE) comes with an extensive prologue and epilogue, extolling the virtues and just legal enactments of Ḥammurabi. The king, speaking in the first person, claims that the chief gods of the pantheon appointed him 'to make justice prevail in the land' and that, when the patron god of Babylon, 'commanded me to provide just ways for the people . . . I established truth and justice as the declaration of the land'.[16] He did this, he claims, through the rules that he instituted. He identifies these rules as the 'just decisions which Ḥammurabi . . . has established', but he also signals the source of his ability to arrive at such decisions: 'I am Ḥammurabi, king of justice, to whom the god Shamash has granted (insight into) the truth.'[17] The gods bestowed on him a wisdom without precedent or parallel: 'my pronouncements are choice; my ability is unrivalled'.[18] To hear Ḥammurabi tell it, one would think that no prior kings had ever attempted this task or hardly know they had even existed. But there were predecessors. At least two earlier kings produced extensive written collections of laws and spoke of themselves in much the same way: Ur-Namma of the city of Ur (c. 2100 BCE) and Lipit-Ishtar of the city of Isin (c. 1930 BCE) both claim to have 'established justice in the land' in keeping with the divine mandate issued to them and in accord with the gods' standard of justice and truth. One can add to this the abundant claims that each ruler was appointed by the gods, ruled by the will of the gods and, therefore, possessed divine legitimacy. At the level of rhetoric, the law's authority was founded in religious claims and went hand in hand with claims about the authority of the human promulgator of the law.[19]

The legitimacy of law is also inextricably linked with religion in ancient Egypt, where one finds an important similarity to the situation in India (discussed directly below). Right and proper order is built into the fabric of the universe; it does not emanate from the gods but encompasses the gods. This fundamental concept of Egyptian thought – a grand cosmic order – was identified as *ma'at*, the first known reference to which comes in the Pyramid Texts of the twenty-fourth century BCE king, Unas. In ancient Egypt, this idea embraced more than simply justice and order. Rather, it covered all of life and nature, since the Egyptians made no distinction between science and theology, cosmos and society, religion and state. We will return to the concept of *ma'at* in more detail below.

16 Roth 1997: 76 and 80–81. For a recent and comprehensive edition of the Laws of Hammurabi, see Oelsner 2022.
17 Roth 1997: 133 and 135.   18 Roth 1997: 134.   19 Neumann 2003: 61–63.

In turning to ancient India, one finds that the ultimate source of law in classical Hindu tradition is said to be found in the Vedas. They are known by the Sanskrit term *śruti* – literally, 'what is heard', because the texts were transmitted orally from generation to generation by religious specialists. The specific rules of classical Hindu law are not found in these texts, however, but in the other two main sources of Hindu law: *smṛti* and *ācāra*. The former, *smṛti*, includes the Dharmaśāstras: texts that set forth the rules and traditions according to which righteous people conduct their lives. The latter, *ācāra*, contains the standards and norms of particular social groups and is often designated as customary law. Although these two sets of texts – and the *ācāra* in particular – formed the basis for legal practice and decision-making during the classical period, they were said (by some) to derive from the principles found in the Vedas, which, in turn, could be seen as having divine origins or, at least, origins beyond the human realm. According to the tradition, the Veda is *apauruṣeya*: 'not of human origin' and *nitya*: 'eternal'. In other words, for the Hindu tradition, law in its purest, original form is unauthored and simply part of the universe itself. No god actually wrote it. Thus, law emanates from a transcendental source that we can, quite legitimately, call religious. It should be noted, though, that this represents the standard view. The Arthaśāstra tradition, which was eventually more or less co-opted by Dharmaśāstra after the first century CE, was wholly secular and based legal authority on the authority of the state. The two views continued to coexist in India for some time with a productive tension existing between a religiously grounded view of *dharma* ('law' in this context), on the one hand, and an acknowledgement that huge areas of *dharma* had little or nothing to do with the Vedas and, thus, with religion as such, on the other.

Earlier scholarship on traditional Chinese law held that there was no evidence for the belief in ancient China that law had divine origins.[20] The subsequent discovery of a collection of texts from the Warring States period (c. 480–221 BCE), associated with what is called Yellow Emperor or *Huang-Lao* thought, changed this view. In these texts, law (*fa*) is said to have originated in the Way (*dao*). The *dao*, of course, is not a divine being as such. Nevertheless, law is seen as part of the order of nature and is derived from and sustained by the 'force' or 'power' that gives rise to all that exists. The texts invoke a myth in which law appears at creation when the world first emerges from chaos.[21] As in India, law is not said to have been written or authored by the gods, but it is part of the cosmic order – part of the way that things are supposed to be.

20 Bodde and Morris 1967: 10. 21 MacCormack 2001.

While law in ancient China may have originated simply in the need for state regulations, a religious (or, at least, quasi-religious) dimension to law seems to have developed – in specific contexts – over time.

The situation in Greece was somewhat different.[22] The famous lawgivers there – Lycurgus of Sparta; Drakon, Solon and Clisthenes of Athens – do not claim to have been the recipients of divine revelation or a divine mandate to create laws. Instead, they typically received a commission to write laws from their respective communities. They could, then, receive a divine endorsement of the commission (e.g. Solon) from the oracle at Delphi; they might also receive divine approval (e.g. Clisthenes), again at Delphi, of the laws after they had written them down.[23] According to Herodotus (1.65), Lycurgus received both an endorsement of his commission and divine approval of his newly written laws. Moreover, the governing bodies that created secular laws in Greece were generally also involved in establishing religious laws, such as those concerning priestly positions, religious festivals and the like.[24] In the late fifth century BCE, for example, it was the Athenian assembly that passed legislation calling for an additional shrine to be built for Athena and for a new priestess to be appointed for service there.[25] Crucially, the Athenian assembly made these decisions according to the procedures that it ordinarily followed. Unlike some other ancient societies, there was no separate body that issued religious laws.[26]

The gods could be credited with responsibility for 'unwritten laws', just as they could be held responsible for seeing justice done.[27] Such laws were deemed to contain the 'fundamental principles of justice on which the laws of the city were based'.[28] It was assumed that one would already know the gods' views on a variety of issues and could legislate without consulting them directly. With respect to other matters, occasional consultations of the gods regarding new laws or changes to existing ones were necessary. But this consultation was more for the purpose of obtaining the support of the gods rather than as a genuine quest for their advice.

---

22 See also Chapter 2, this volume.
23 Harris 2006a: 51–56; Naiden 2013: 84–87. For a recent edition of Solon's laws, see Leão and Rhodes 2015.
24 Parker 2004.   25 Meiggs and Lewis 1969: no. 44.
26 Gagarin 2013: 60 argues that written collections of Greek law do not contain strictly religious laws; those that appear to be religious, according to this view, are included because the polis had a financial interest in the matter.
27 Soph. Ant.: 454–55; Hesiod, Works: 36.
28 Harris 2012a: 289. See also Harris 2006a: 53–57.

The story of Roman law has sometimes been told as one of emancipation from 'priestly control' (e.g. Justinian, *Digest* 1.2.2, Pomponius, *Enchiridion*). Prior to the fifth century BCE, the early guardians and interpreters of legal *formulae*, the precise sets of words and actions needed to accomplish legal acts, were also religious state officials: the *pontifices*, members of the pontifical college in Rome. Most of the law resided in unwritten traditions, known primarily to the priests, and no definite distinction seems to have been maintained between what we might term 'religious' and ordinary legal rules. According to one version of the story, the people became dissatisfied with the control of the law being in the hands of the priests, who were appointed from the aristocratic (patrician) class. There was sufficient popular protest, so the story goes, to force the creation of the Twelve Tables, in which a number of the traditional laws were spelled out for everyone to see. Still, the content and details of a number of laws remained hidden (Liv. 9.46). 'This may account for the existence of the popular tale of Appius Claudius, a clerk to one of these pontiffs, who stole a document containing details of the actions-at-law and published it. This broke the pontifical monopoly over the law (and presumably over legal practice).'[29]

If law had once been under the control of a priestly association and other state officials with religious functions, these sorts of developments ultimately led to the opposite state of affairs. By the later Roman empire, certain religious matters – concerning both belief and practice – came under the control of imperial law. Roman jurists, most famously the third-century CE jurist Ulpian, had divided the part of law that governed relations between gods and humans from the part that governed relations among humans. Thus, during the late Republic and throughout the time of the empire, matters concerning religion were classified as part of the Roman *ius civile*, specifically under the branch of Roman public law: 'Public law is concerned with the Roman 'state', while private law is concerned with the interests of individuals, for some matters are of public and others of private interest. Public law comprises religion, priesthoods, and magistracies.'[30] Although Ulpian's definition demonstrates a connection between sacred and temporal matters within the sphere of public law, some aspects of Roman religion were not subject to political bodies (e.g. relocation of shrines, method of ritual performance).[31] What was important was that correct relationships between men and gods were part of the *utilitas publica*, the public weal or common good.[32] But the classical Roman jurists

---

29 du Plessis 2012: 18.   30 Justinian, *Digest* 1.1.1.2 (Ulpian, *Institutes* bk 1).
31 Rüpke 2007: 4.   32 See Chapter 3, this volume.

seem not to have been particularly interested in working this branch of Roman law out for themselves. There is some evidence that books of Roman sacral law existed and that certain important jurists wrote commentaries on them, but Justinian's *Digest* excerpted none of this material. By the time of Justinian himself, in the mid-sixth century CE, the process seems to have completed a full circle, when the religious grounding of law was once again in vogue. The emperor ascribed his authority to rule to the Christian God and believed 'knowledge of God' (Justinian, *Digest* 1.1.1) was essential to understanding law.

Scholars vary in how they have sought to explain the underlying reasons for the different relationships that one can observe between the gods and law in these societies. One recent study suggests that, for Israel, Mesopotamia and Greece, the key distinction resides in these societies' different attitudes towards kingship.[33] In Israel, kings were largely held in disdain by the scribes who produced our extant texts; they ascribed to their god instead many of the duties that would typically have been performed by the king (e.g., the establishment of law, decisions concerning the timing and nature of debt-cancellation decrees – on which see below). In Mesopotamia, the king was commissioned by the gods and endowed with divine wisdom, but he was the author of the law. In Greece, by contrast, the lawgiver is human but not royal, and the laws, though endorsed at times by the gods, needed popular consent, which appears to have been the main goal towards which any divine endorsement or approval was directed. Thus, in Naiden's view, the law was the god's in Israel; it was the king's in Mesopotamia; and it was the people's in Greece. Another important examination of this issue focuses on the disagreements in ancient Israelite and Greek society concerning what ultimately makes law 'divine' – what makes it worthy of obedience and respect. In ancient Israel, the emphasis was on law's origins such that, for laws to be divine, it is not necessary that they align with reason or universally applicable principles; it matters only that they are established by virtue of divine revelation. The Greek understanding, in contrast, maintained that law was divine when it did indeed align with human reason, was universally applicable and rang true to one's life experience. According to Hayes, the heirs of these traditions, early Jewish and Christian writers, struggled either to bridge the gap or to prioritize one approach over the other, while the rabbis formulated their own understanding of the relationship between their god and law.[34] In any event, law requires a story that affords it authority and

---

33 Naiden 2013.   34 Hayes 2015.

legitimacy, and in the ancient world the gods were an important part of that story.

Religious Concepts of Law, Order and Justice

Most of the cultures under discussion promoted religiously oriented concepts about justice and proper order in society that they believed their legal systems were meant to embody. Moreover, it was the divinely mandated duty of the ruler to see that these concepts were implemented throughout the society at large. The two principal concepts in Mesopotamia were *kittu(m)*, often translated as 'truth', and *mīšaru(m)*, often translated as 'justice'.[35] The latter was perhaps the more accentuated of the two. It included better conditions for the poor and those who were considered weak in political and legal terms. Hammurabi refers to himself as the *šar mīšarim* (king of justice) and claims that the gods appointed him 'to make justice (*mīšarum*) prevail in the land, to abolish the wicked and the evil, to prevent the strong from oppressing the weak'.[36] An important way in which Mesopotamian kings claimed to have established justice in their lands was through the proclamation of particular decrees, often referred to as *mīšaru*-edicts. The text of one of the most well-known, the Edict of Ammisaduqa (c. 1600 BCE), who was the great-grandson of Hammurabi, refers to itself as 'the tablet of the decree which the land was ordered to hear at the time that the king invoked a *mīšarum* for the land'.[37] The usual goal of such decrees was to cancel debts and other private obligations in order to give ordinary citizens a chance to start afresh financially and to recover any property that had been confiscated by creditors.[38] They functioned as a type of economic stimulus package and are discussed in more detail below.

In ancient Israel, a pair of terms captured this concept: *mišpāṭ* and *ṣedek/ ṣədākâ* ('justice and righteousness'; sometimes the order of the terms is reversed). They included the establishment and maintenance of legal justice.[39] One text says of King David that he 'administered justice and righteousness to all his people' (2 Sam 8:15). Another extols an unnamed Israelite king: 'The king in his might loves justice. You have established equity; you have executed justice and righteousness in Jacob [Israel].(Psalm 99:4). The word for 'equity' in the previous text is *mêšārîm*, the Hebrew cognate to Akkadian *mīšaru(m)*. These terms also encompassed the idea that

---

35 Neumann 2003: 61–63. 36 Roth 1997: 134 and 76.
37 Pritchard 1969: 184. On the distinction between these edicts and law collections, see Barmash 2020: 49–86.
38 Westbrook 1995: 154–59. 39 Weinfeld 1982.

the ruler would enact policies and render decisions that would improve the plight of the poor and marginalized – usually symbolized by the widow and orphan. A prayer that is said to have been offered on behalf of King Solomon asks: 'Give the king your justice, O God, and your righteousness to a king's son. May he judge your people with righteousness, and your poor with justice' (Psalm 72:2).

As noted above, *ma'at* was the fundamental concept in ancient Egyptian society for cosmic order. The notion encompasses truth, nature, harmony, morality, law, politics, culture and a religious world view. Assmann identifies it as the 'basic concept underlying all commitments and obligations ... and ... all thought and action'.[40] Gods, kings, people and forces of nature have a fixed place in the world of *ma'at*. If people do not act according to *ma'at*, nature becomes unbalanced and catastrophe (e.g. famine, plague) ensues. The ideas of law, truth and a just social order are closely linked to *ma'at*. Doing *ma'at* is acting justly, and speaking *ma'at* is speaking truth. All of this comes to be personified in the goddess Ma'at, depicted with a feather on her head that stands for truth (Figure 6.1). In the hall where the dead are judged, the heart of the deceased is weighed against the feather of Ma'at. If the heart does not prove to be heavier than the feather, the deceased may pass into the afterlife. The king, who bears the title 'He who loves *ma'at*', plays a special role in preserving cosmic order. Chaos can be avoided and order can be maintained by placating the gods through cult practices such as the daily rituals in which the cult statues are clothed. As high priest and chief intermediary between the gods and the people, the king is responsible for the proper performance of these rituals. The classical concept of *ma'at* gradually changes with the emergence of a kind of personal piety in later periods. A more direct path to the gods is now available, without mediation by the king. People can address their prayers to the gods and, through oracles, obtain justice directly from the gods.

The meaning and interpretation of *dharma* in the Hindu tradition are highly disputed. It cannot be reduced simply to law or justice or even proper order. In general, *dharma* in Dharmaśāstra almost always identifies *varnasramadharma*, the duties required because of one's caste and life-stage, which come out of a particular vision of social life structured both synchronically (*varna* 'caste') and diachronically (*asrama* 'life-stage'). In some contexts, it can also mean justice, order or even merit. The term, however, is unlikely to have been an important one in early Vedic literature. It seems to have come

---

40 Assmann 2001: 18.

Figure 6.1 Ancient Egyptian Ma'at, goddess of cosmic order, shown wearing her feather crown. Tomb of Seti I (KV 17), 19th Dynasty (c. 1292–1187 BCE), Valley of the Kings, Egypt. © Luisa Ricciarini / Bridgeman Images: number LRI4640749 (www.bridgemanimages .com/en/egyptian-19th-dynasty-c-1292-1187-bc/tomb-of-seti-i-kv-17-maat-goddess-of-truth-and-justice-and-hieroglyphs-19th-dynasty-fresco/fresco/asset/4640749)

to conceptual prominence during the reign of the Buddhist ruler Aśoka, in the third century BCE.[41] As described further below, Aśoka vigorously promoted Buddhism and the Buddhist concept of *dharma*; consequently, the political influence of the Brahmins was markedly reduced. The threat posed to Hinduism by this growth in Buddhism required a response on the part of the Brahmins. They appear to have expanded the scope of their writing about ritual to all social forms; this was their way of protecting *dharma* from its degradation as the 'teaching' of the Buddha. As part of this expansion of the purview of *dharma*, they incorporated into *dharma* the concept of *artha* – statecraft and polity. In this way, law was brought into the domain of religion. The modern conception of law in India corresponds most closely to what started out as *artha*. With the aforementioned expansion, this was folded into *dharma* and later reconceived as *rajadharma*, the *dharma* of the

41 Olivelle 2004b and 2005b.

king. This included legal procedure as well as substantive laws of inheritance, debt, contract, partnership, theft, assault and other areas of law. A similar distinction appears in the story about the Judean king, Jehoshaphat, in the Hebrew Bible (2 Chr 19). In the story, most likely apocryphal but meant to advocate a particular policy, Jehoshaphat distinguishes between 'things of Yahweh' and 'things of the king', the latter category encompassing most of the same legal issues as the *dharma* of the king. As we have seen, the movement in Rome was more in the direction of religion being subsumed under the area of law. By Late Antiquity, Roman emperors issued enactments that aimed to regulate religious belief and practice, at the same time as the institutional Christian church began to carve out its own legal space. In India, however, it is noteworthy that what started out as a religious concept, *dharma*, tended to incorporate other concepts, such as *artha*, and give them a distinctly religious orientation.

In early China a basic idea prevailed that the universe, comprising both natural and human phenomena, was governed by fixed principles, described collectively as the Way (*dao*) or Heaven's principles (*tianli*). The Way established how natural elements, such as the moon, sun and stars, should behave and, in the human world, how individuals should relate with others. One of the components of this view was that human behaviour should reflect the hierarchies, implicit in the natural world, that form part of the Way. In particular this meant that persons should respect and obey any other person towards whom they stood in a junior relationship. This included children vis-à-vis their parents, junior relatives vis-à-vis older family members, wives vis-à-vis their husbands and subjects vis-à-vis their ruler. The more senior member in the relationship, on the other hand, should protect and look after the junior. Maintaining the proper behaviour, especially through the personal example set by the ruler and the instruction and guidance given by him, meant that the harmony of the universe remained undisturbed. To some extent at least, although some scholars may exaggerate the significance of this point, an offence against the law disturbed cosmic harmony. According to certain strands of ancient Chinese thought, part of the emperor's responsibility to maintain the Way was to impose the proper punishment. The matching of offence and punishment was thought to restore the disturbed harmony. Equally, a failure on the part of the emperor and his officials to make a just apportionment of punishment between the guilty and the innocent would also lead to a disturbance.[42]

---

42 Bodde and Morris 1967: 43–48; MacCormack 1989.

The key term in ancient Greek is *dikē*. One of its basic meanings was 'trial' or 'court case' (this is true of Hebrew *mišpāṭ* as well), but it also signified justice, fairness, retribution and what is right.[43] It was used to represent a stable world, a sense of moral order and impartiality in judgment. *Dikē* was personified. According to Hesiod, she was the daughter of Zeus and Themis: the most powerful of the gods and of 'Law' or 'Statute' or 'Right'.[44] In his *Works and Days*, Hesiod opposes justice to *hubris* (violence, outrage) and says that in the end justice prevails and that, when she is dragged away by those who devour bribes and give crooked judgments, she brings evil to that city.[45] Hesiod's image here builds on the driving out of *Dikē* by those who judge crookedly at *Iliad* 16.387–8. In a vignette which later poets picked up, Hesiod lays out some of the basis for this: the maiden Justice (Dikē), whenever she is hurt, tells her father Zeus about it and he makes the people pay for the wanton behaviour of their rulers.[46] Theognis, writing in the sixth century BCE, reckons that possessions that come from Zeus and with justice will last, while those obtained unjustly do not; he acknowledges, though, that wrongdoing is not punished at the moment it is committed, but in the gods' own time.[47] The elegies of Solon refer to the city in which citizens 'have no regard for the august foundations of Justice' and where Lawlessness (*dusnomia*, bad law or a bad attitude towards law) is contrasted with Lawfulness (*eunomia*, good law or a good attitude towards law); the latter 'reveals all that is orderly and fitting', weakens *hubris* and straightens crooked judgments.[48] *Eunomia* is here essentially the same as *Dikē*, and it is not surprising that Pindar gives Dikē two sisters: 'Eunomia (order) and that unsullied fountain *Dikē*, her sister, sure support of cities; and *Eirene* (peace) of the same kin, who are the stewards of wealth for mankind – three glorious daughters of wise-counselled Themis'.[49] Once again, the forces of law and justice are opposed to *hubris*. What is notable about these later poets is that Justice acquires more force in her own right and is less dependent on the protection of Zeus.[50]

With all of these concepts, the belief seems to have been that what is right, just and orderly originated in and was assured by the power of the divine realm. The key terms discussed above represent, among other things, the system of order that was required within the human realm to keep chaos and

---

43 See also Chapter 3, this volume.
44 Hesiod, *Theog.*, 901–2. Zeus is associated with Themis in other circumstances too in early Greek literature, as at *Iliad* 2.68.
45 Hesiod, *Works*, 213–24.   46 Hesiod, *Works*, 256–64; Aes. fragment 530.
47 Thgn. 197–208.
48 On Solon's *Elegy* 4.14 and its relationship to Hesiod, see Irwin 2005: 155–98.
49 Pind. *Ol.* 13.6–9.   50 Irwin 2005: 174–5.

Religion and the State

Figure 6.2 Section of the Community Rule scroll, c. 100–75 BCE (parchment), deals with community property legislation possibly for a Jewish Essene sect at Qumran. © Israel Museum, Jerusalem / Bridgeman Images: number IMJ386186 (www.bridgemanimages.com/en/noartistknown/section-of-the-community-rule-scroll-c-100-75-bc-parchment/parchment/asset/386186)

disorder in check. Some communities believed that the latter were perpetually seeking re-entry back into the ordered sphere (Figure 6.2).

In any case, it was imperative for rulers to establish order in their land and to maintain it through a variety of means, including law. A number of kings – and tyrants in the Greek context – made use of the rhetoric of justice and order for the sake of legitimating reforms enacted during their rule. These reforms may have been motivated by the desire to curry favour with the populace or to diminish the power of those elites who might be in competition with the ruler. Nevertheless, it is largely the ideology of justice and correct order to which the rulers appealed and on which they claimed to base their actions.

Religion and the State

Enforcement of Religious Practice

In the ancient Near East, it is the literature of ancient Israel and Judah that most prominently speaks of the imposition of the state religion: the worship of the god Yahweh. It is difficult to know at exactly what points in time Yahwism was considered the state religion in Judah (we know less about Israel in this regard), but a number of biblical texts certainly portray it as such. Portions of the book of Deuteronomy stipulate the death penalty for apostates; they also require individuals to report family members who practise non-Yahwistic worship and to participate in their execution. Laws commanding exclusive allegiance to Yahweh on the part of the entire citizenry appear in all the major legal collections of the Hebrew Bible and are formulated largely as non-religious laws would be. The basic ideology in Judah is that the god established a special relationship with the kingdom's founder, David; and that David's descendants, who occupy the throne, ought to enforce the exclusive worship of Yahweh throughout their realm. In the book of Kings, stories are told that exalt the monarchs who purge the land of all non-Yahwistic worship and especially those who eliminate worship at sites outside of Jerusalem, so that all religious donations and activities support the main temple there. Although ancient Judah is known for the concept of monotheism, this is a rather late development in its history (probably late sixth century BCE) and was not a belief enforced by law. The overriding concern was exclusive allegiance to the Yahwistic cult.

It is unclear, though, to what extent the kings of Israel and Judah enforced the exclusive worship of Yahweh. Some archaeological evidence suggests that two kings – Hezekiah (late eighth to early seventh century BCE) and Josiah (late seventh century BCE) – attempted to limit religious activities outside of Jerusalem; while others, such as Hezekiah's son Manasseh, evidently did not. Many scholars accept that much of the biblical literature calling for such exclusive worship comes from the time of Josiah.[51] Even if it is later, the literature praises Josiah as the greatest Judean king for his efforts to quash alternative forms of worship and perhaps preserves some accurate memories of his reign. During the so-called post-exilic period, in the fifth and fourth centuries BCE, the Persian empire held sway. In lieu of enforcing Judean religion as a matter of state governance, strict Yahwists sought to impose both religious and ethnic purity on the Judean community, going so far as to force their men to send away any wives, along with their children, whose ethnic purity was in doubt (Ezra 9–10). This action was to be done 'according to the law (*tôrâ*)' (Ezra 10:3), although the specific identity of this law is open to question.

Arriving at a definition for state religion in ancient Egypt is problematic. Two main complications exist. First, because of the mediating role of the Egyptian king, official religion and the royal administration were tightly interwoven. The state and the temple functioned together as a single entity rather than two separate institutions. This would change in the Greco-Roman period, when the civil functions of the temple administration were

---

51 Levinson 2008: 82–83; Na'aman 2008: 243–48.

gradually taken on by state officials unaffiliated with a temple, and when ancient Egyptian religion was strongly Hellenized, surviving only in a syncretized form. Second, apart from their devotion to the Egyptian king, ancient Egyptians worshipped a variety of gods, and some cities promoted the worship of certain deities over others. Atum was considered to be the sun god and the creator god at Heliopolis, whereas the priests of Thebes hailed Amun as the sun god and, later, the combination of Amun and Re (Amun-Re). At Memphis, in contrast, Ptah was worshipped and credited with creation. Only twice in ancient Egypt was a particular kind of cult enforced. In the fourteenth century BCE, Akhenaten (Amenhotep IV) attempted to replace all gods with the sun god and tried to *impose* this religion throughout much of the land. He deposed a number of priests, erased inscriptions with the name of the god Amun and destroyed Amun's temple in Karnak. Most other temples, however, were probably not closed, given the crucial role that temples played in the Egyptian economy. His son (Tutankhamun) restored the cults abolished by Akhenaten shortly after the latter's death. Turning briefly to the Roman period, Christians came under persecution at times, as in other parts of the empire. Many were forced to choose between participating in pagan sacrifices or face arrest and even death. Several *libelli* from mid-third-century CE Egypt, the time of the persecutions under Decius, certify that the holder participated in a pagan sacrifice. The concepts of religious syncretism and 'local worlds', however, continue to be important into Late Antiquity and beyond.[52]

It is probably not accurate to claim that in ancient India there was a state religion as such. Instead, rulers often used religious motivations, practices and institutions as means to expand, consolidate and legitimate their power. It is true that rulers could proclaim their allegiance to particular religious traditions and promote certain religious identities, institutions and practices. Nevertheless, the forcible practice of religion throughout the state seems absent, except perhaps by those closest to a particular ruler. Two examples are illustrative. First, Aśoka, an emperor from the third century BCE, famously espoused a form of Buddhism, especially after he had a change of heart due to the massacre of tens of thousands of people in Kalinga. He publicly inscribed his penitence and directed his functionaries to take up non-violent practices and follow the Buddha-*dharma*. He strongly promoted and supported Buddhism, but, as far as we can tell, did not seek to have Buddhism supplant Hinduism throughout the empire. In one of his inscriptions, Aśoka

---

52 Frankfurter 2018.

claims that 'it is conquest by Dharma that Beloved-of-the-Gods [an epithet of Aśoka] considers to be the best conquest ... Here in the king's domain among the Greeks, the Kambojas, the Nabhakas, the Nabhapamkits, the Bhojas, the Pitinikas, the Andhras and the Palidas – people everywhere are following Beloved-of-the-Gods' instructions in Dharma.'[53] While his promotion of Buddhism may have certainly increased its adherents, there is no evidence that he forced the religion on the populace. Second, the Gupta dynasty in the fourth–sixth centuries CE invented what we now know as the Hindu temple, as part of its effort to use the worship of Visnu to help with state consolidation (Figure 6.3). This appears to be a very significant moment in Indian history, for it shows the interconnection of the state and the temple directly from the beginning of the creation of the institution of the temple.[54] Law continued to be transmitted, studied and administered in ways that kept it largely sheltered from the state and temple administrations, but it also came into regular contact and, at times, conflict with both institutions. Still, even with the establishment of the Hindu temple and all that went along with

Figure 6.3 Interior of Cave no 26, Gupta period (6th century CE), Ajanta, Maharashtra India. © Bridgeman Images: number EAM162620 (www.bridgemanimages.com/en/indian-school/interior-of-cave-26-photo/nomedium/asset/162620)

---

53 Translation adapted from Dhammika 1993.
54 Willis 2009: 3–4. Compare Canepa 2018 on the late antique development of a specific 'topography of power' in Sasanian Iran.

it, there does not seem to have been a regular, ongoing effort to maintain a uniform and state-wide religious tradition on the part of India's rulers.

In China, evidence for the doctrine commonly described in Western literature as 'the Mandate of Heaven' stretches from the earliest period of the Zhou dynasty (c. 1045–256 BCE) to the fall of the Qing in 1911/12 CE. One ancient form of this doctrine held that the ruler, as the representative of Heaven (a deity known as *Tiān* in Chinese) on earth (the 'Son of Heaven'), is responsible to Heaven for the proper governing of his people and, in particular, for ensuring that they observe the principles of behaviour enjoined by Heaven. Failure by the ruler to maintain proper behaviour either in his personal example or in the laws which he established, as well as any failure on his part to see that only the guilty were punished, disturbed the harmony and proper functioning of the universe. Thus, the ruler was expected to enforce proper behaviour, and this included religious behaviour. Any negligence in this regard would elicit signs of Heaven's displeasure, typically manifested in the form of natural disasters. Especially under the Han (206 BCE–220 CE), there developed a 'science' for the interpretation of such manifestations of Heaven's will. Various events were interpreted in a political context as criticisms, or sometimes as endorsements, of the decisions of the government or emperor. For example, in 166 CE the private scholar Xiang Kai submitted a memorial (a formal and official written communication) to the king arguing that the unseasonable weather of that spring and summer was a divine sign that punishments were excessively harsh and cruel.[55] Although the doctrine of the 'Mandate of Heaven' undoubtedly played an important role in political rhetoric, it is difficult to determine whether it had much bearing on the day-to-day administration of the law, on the enforcement of religious practice, or as a determinant of the content of the legal codes.

Defining state religion in Greece is also difficult, if not impossible.[56] Ancient Greeks certainly believed in the gods and took seriously the religious practices that they understood were necessary to keep the gods appeased (Figure 6.4). The Athenians certainly acknowledged that the crime of impiety (*asebeia*) was a grave offence. The various trials that we know of for impiety, however, suggest that judges could be persuaded to accept a number of rather different views about what constituted impiety. The particular view adopted in a case might depend upon its broader context. In cases of impiety, the court decided on a penalty by choosing between the punishments proposed by the

---

55 de Crespigny 2018: 147–48 (= ch. 55, Yanxi 9: 166).   56 Papazarkadas 2011: 16–17.

Law and Religion

Figure 6.4 Relief depicting Nemesis, the goddess of justice and revenge, 2nd–3rd century CE, from Laiiqie, Syria. Damascus, Musée National de Damas. G. Dagli Orti, © NPL – DeA Picture Library / Bridgeman Images: number DGA519297 (www.bridgemanimages .com/en/g-dagli-orti/relief-depicting-nemesis-goddess-of-justice-and-revenge-from-con cepts-revenge-1-laiiqie-syria-2nd/nomedium/asset/519297)

prosecution and those by the defence. The notorious, but unusual, case in this regard is that of Socrates, where the court chose the death penalty. The charge against him read: 'Socrates does wrong by not acknowledging the gods the city acknowledges, and introducing other, new powers. He also does wrong by corrupting the young.'[57] Exactly why Socrates was condemned has been very much debated. Already in the fourth century BCE, there are indications that people considered the condemnation to have been for political reasons, given that Socrates was associated with some men who were part of the regime of the Thirty Tyrants. This indicates something of the complex interplay of religion and politics and the difficulty of separating them.[58]

In some respects, there was a fair degree of religious 'open-mindedness' at Athens. Tragedies explored the moral limitations of the gods (e.g. in Euripides' *Hippolytos*), and Greek literature more generally, and Homeric epic most notoriously, displayed the gods as petty, squabbling and cheating on each other. Plato worried about this and wanted to respond by censoring

[57] Parker 2005: 67.   [58] Todd 1993: 309–10.

the poets (*Republic*, Book 10), but there is no evidence for widespread sensitivity over this issue in classical Athens. One should be careful, however, not to deduce from the theatrical portrayal of the gods as possible inventions to dupe men into good behaviour that the Athenians tolerated the kind of full freedom of thought that allowed for the disregard of the gods and religion in general. In *Laws*, Book 10, Plato, Socrates' own pupil, gives extensive arguments against atheism and thinks that atheism must be ruled out.[59] Various festivals at Athens were prescribed in the law code, and the magistrates responsible probably had to ensure that they took place. But some of the pressure on other citizens to take part in these and other religious activities was social in nature. Participation in religious festivals offered both the main source of meat to eat and one of the few contexts in which there was opportunity for men and women to socialize together.

As elsewhere, religious practices marked much of Roman life, including daily home life, gatherings of local associations, military campaigns and the meetings of the Senate. Failure to observe the necessary rites passed down from the ancestors could lead to social, political and military disaster. With some religious performances, however, such as communal festivals, it can be difficult to discern the degree to which such activities were important in their own right or whether they served mainly to promote what it meant to be Roman. As Beard has argued: 'One of the functions of the Roman ritual calendar – the sequence of religious festivals as they occurred throughout the year – was to define and delineate Roman power, Roman history and Roman identity.'[60] From a modern perspective, Roman religion can appear to be an ill-defined, amorphous collection of beliefs and practices. It was ever expanding by the inclusion of more and more gods, the worship of which could be introduced in Rome by generous benefactors, victorious generals and even immigrants. Even though the Romans typically did not impose their own religion on conquered people groups, this does not necessarily mean that they were tolerant of all religious practices, especially those that they perceived to threaten their system of law and order, as the eventual tensions with Judaism and Christianity bear out.

Generally, though, the state did not interfere for good or ill with the practice of private religion – the performance of rites related to personal and family deities. Cults that were officially recognized by the state received state funding, and it was possible for individual persons or associations to

---

59 On atheism and the ancient world more generally, see Whitmarsh 2015.
60 Beard 1987: 1.

provide additional funding to the cults of state deities as well. For the state, what was important was the consistent execution of the sacrifices and honours that were owed to the state gods so that the prosperity and order of Rome might be ensured.

To ignore or neglect the required rituals was to deny the gods their rightful due and invite divine wrath (*ira deorum*) upon Rome and its people. Romans from all strata of society were encouraged to show proper esteem for the gods and were expected to participate in public rituals in order to show not only their respect for the gods but also their support of Roman society and its values.[61] The advent of emperor deification with Augustus complicated the relationship of the state to the gods. Augustus actually claimed to be the son of a god but was deified by the Senate upon his death. Others, such as Nero, held that they were actually living gods. One of the implications of this was the expansion of the law of *maiestas* under Tiberius. Previously, acts considered to constitute treason were usually limited to those involved in military action waged against Rome. Subsequently, other acts could be included that might be construed as 'against the Roman people and their security'.[62] It seems to be the case that, with a divine emperor, acts against the state were deemed to be the near equivalent of sacrilege.

The Calendar: Holy Days and Festivals

In Mesopotamia, one of the most important rituals was the autumn New Year festival in Babylon; most of our information concerning this festival comes from the first millennium BCE.[63] While the festival may have originated as a celebration of the moon god, at Babylon it came to be a celebration of the patron deity of the city, Marduk. It commemorated his supremacy among the gods and his installation as the god of Babylon. During one of the days of the festival, the high priest of Marduk's temple would strip the king of his royal adornments and have him kneel before Marduk like a servant. The king was required to swear to the god that he had not sinned against the city and that he had carried out the duties assigned to him by the gods. The high priest would then strike the king on the cheek. If the king cried, then Marduk approved of him, but, if not, the king would soon be overthrown. Retaining the presence and favour of Marduk was vital to ensuring proper order and justice in the land, and the king's participation in this ritual was indispensable.

Numerous texts from the Hebrew Bible attest to the importance of the seventh day of the week for ancient Israelite cultic observance, though

---

61 Gradel 2004: 15. 62 Fahrner 2020: 84. 63 See Debourse 2022.

exactly when Sabbath-keeping was introduced into ancient Israelite culture remains a conundrum. For the later rabbis, the Sabbath was the most important Jewish holiday; an entire tractate (*m. Shabb.*) of the Mishnah is devoted to this topic. Several biblical laws command that no *məlā'kâ* ('work, business') be performed on the Sabbath because it is a 'holy' (*qādôš*) day and not to be 'defiled'. Whoever does work on that day is to be put to death. But the Bible does not define the notion of 'work' with any precision; other than the specific prohibition on the lighting of fires (Exod 35:3), it does not define the term. The rabbis (*m. Shabb.* 7:2) noted that the same word (*məlā'kâ*) for prohibited work on the Sabbath is one of the words used to describe the work involved in constructing the tabernacle (e.g. Exod 35:29). Thus, the rabbis inferred that it is those kinds of activities, which were associated with building the tabernacle, that are forbidden.

Other biblical texts mention three major pilgrimage festivals to be observed annually: the festival of unleavened bread, the festival of weeks and the festival of booths.[64] All three were in honour of the god Yahweh and corresponded both to important times in the agricultural cycle and to significant points in the story concerning the Israelites' journey out of Egypt and through the wilderness of Sinai. Moreover, the texts give the impression that all three were carefully regulated by law and that the populace was compelled to participate in their observance. There are some discrepancies, however, in the legal texts detailing their observance. It seems clear that many Israelites accepted their importance, but different groups may have disagreed concerning exactly how to observe them. The first festival, that of unleavened bread (*maṣṣôt*), began on the fifteenth day of the first month of the new year that was celebrated in the spring (eventually, under the influence of the Babylonian calendar, the new year began to be observed only in the fall), and lasted for seven days. It was ushered in by the holiday of Passover (*pesaḥ*), which took place the day before when each family sacrificed a one-year-old sheep or goat and ate it that same evening. The two observances may well have originated separately as seasonal or agricultural celebrations, but they are joined in nearly all the biblical texts referring to them. The biblical aetiology is that they commemorate the Israelites' escape from slavery in Egypt. Some extra-biblical confirmation of their observance comes from the Judean colony of soldiers at the island of Elephantine in Egypt. A letter from there dated to 419 BCE appears to refer to the two festivals and attests to the observance of Passover on the fourteenth

---

64 Gesundheit 2012.

of the month and that of *maṣṣôt* from the fifteenth through the twenty-first. The second, the festival of weeks (*šābuʿôt*), coincided with the spring harvest season. Only one text specifies an exact time and explains the origin of the festival's name: 'You shall count seven weeks (*šābuʿôt*). You shall begin to count the seven weeks from the time when the sickle is put to the standing grain. Then you shall observe the Festival of Weeks to Yahweh your God.'[65] The festival of 'booths' (*sukkôt*) was the third major festival and began on the fifteenth day of the seventh month, lasting for seven days. During this time, all people were to live in a temporary shelter (*sukkâ* 'booth') as another commemoration of the deliverance from Egypt. Various offerings were to be made on a daily basis to Yahweh during the festival.

Rabbinic literature also takes these festivals seriously. An entire tractate in the Mishnah, for example, deals with the festival of unleavened bread (*m. Pesah*) and another with the festival of booths (*m. Sukkah*). The rabbis delineated how these festivals should be celebrated by Jews in their local settings. They established how unleavened bread should be made and eaten on Passover, how and when booths ought to be constructed and lived in, and how a collection of plants should be gathered on *sukkôt*. The discussions of these festivals explain how all of this should be done as if the temple cult were still functioning, but they also mandate the performance of the festivals in a post-temple world.[66] In addition to the Pentateuchal festivals, the rabbis expounded on the holiday of Purim, which is first described in the biblical book of Esther, and the post-biblical holiday of *ḥănukkâ*, or Hanukkah, which celebrated the Jewish rebellion of 167–160 BCE against the Seleucid empire (*b. Shabb.* 21b). They also added a series of fast days, most of which are connected to the destruction of the temple, most importantly the ninth day of the month Av (Tisha B'Av), which marks the day on which the First Temple fell to the Babylonians and the Second Temple to the Romans.

Texts from the so-called Priestly Writings, found mainly in Leviticus and Numbers, specify additional observances.[67] One of these was a 'day of remembrance' (Lev 23:24) on the first day of the seventh month of the year, which the rabbis would transform into the Jewish New Year (*Rosh Hashana*). Another was the 'day of atonement' on the tenth day of the seventh month, when the shrine and the populace were cleansed of all pollution and sin through a set of sacrifices and other rituals (Lev 16). Rabbinic literature describes how, in a post-temple world, Jews are to ask

---

65 Deut 16:9–10.   66 Tabory 2006.
67 On the Priestly Writings, see Schwartz 2009 and Wöhrle 2021.

forgiveness from others on this day and to confess their sins to God as part of an elaborate prayer ritual (*b. Yoma* 9). Finally, there was the year of jubilee, which was to be observed every fifty years, when debts were cancelled and confiscated property and persons returned to their original owners and families (Lev 25). Noting how the cancellation of debts led to pressure on the flow of capital, the rabbis instituted a legal fiction known as the *prozbul* (from Greek *prosbolē*). This allowed poorer individuals still to receive loans as the year of debt-cancellation approached, and it provided protections for lenders so that they could continue to collect these debts (*b. Git.* 34b–37b).

We know more about religious festivals in ancient Egypt than state or politically oriented celebrations. As with other societies, it is unclear to what extent these festivals were governed by law, but it stands to reason that rules were in place to ensure their proper observance. Celebrations of the king included the *Sed* or *Heb-sed* festival during the pharaonic period; the *basileia* of the Ptolemaic period, royal festivals celebrated on the twelfth day of Dystros, when Alexander had been crowned in Memphis; and the 'Augustan days' (*hemerai sebastai*), celebrated according to the Roman cultic calendar.[68] Particular priests and rituals were required for each. Some religious festivals, such as the 'feasts of heaven' (*ḥb.w n pt*), were tied to astronomical events, such as the heliacal rise of Sirius, but most were seasonal feasts (*ḥb.w tp trw*) and based on the civil calendar. This calendar consisted of three seasons – flood, sowing and harvest – each four months long. In the first month of the flood season, the festival of the god Thoth was celebrated; in the second month, 'the beautiful feast of Opet' took place during which the god Amun of Karnak visited the sanctuary of Luxor on a portable bark-shrine, accompanied by Mut and Chonsu, the other members of the Theban triad. For most of these festivals, the king was nominally the principal officiant, though he attended the Opet-feast more regularly than others.

Many astrological and calendrical events necessitated the performance of specific rituals in ancient India. The full and new moon sacrifices, for instance, were central to the Vedic cult. Also important were the five great sacrifices or practices (*yajnas*) that were to be performed daily. These were the *Brahm-yajna* (the study of scriptural texts, learning, teaching others), the *Deva-yajna* (the worship of the gods with the offering of oblations), the *Pitri-yajna* (the offering of oblations and thanksgiving to one's ancestors), the *Manushya-yajna* (helping to feed others) and the *Bhuta-yajna* (the feeding of all living creatures). In addition, there were the thrice-annual ancestral

---

68 See Teeter 2020.

offerings.[69] More offerings and sacrifices were made as needed. There were, in fact, a large number of such rites, but there is no particularly good evidence that the performance of these sacrifices and rituals was enforced by law or by sanction. Failure to perform them would have been seen as shirking in orthodox Brahmin communities and might have attracted censure or even worse, but records indicating punishments for not performing them are lacking. It is rewards that are held out to motivate observance of the rites. Omitting them is usually cause for a penance at most, and descriptions of such penances are vague, leaving their exact nature and severity open to question.

Less is known from ancient China about regular observances related to special days in the calendar. Most of our information relates to the calendars and almanacs prepared under the supervision of the government departments concerned with sacrifices. Those from the Qin and Han dynasties contain notes on which days were auspicious for certain activities and those that were not. Consulting such almanacs were a routine part of an official's life. An almanac would indicate, for example, the days on which it was auspicious for an official to take up his appointment or to seek an interview with a superior. For example, a day book excavated from a Qin tomb lists the days on which it was auspicious for a bailiff (*sefu*) to carry out his duties. The bailiff was a local official with significant legal duties. In the early Han dynasty, bailiffs were required to take part in the making of wills and in the settlement of disputes over property, debt and the like.[70]

The calendar and the observance of festivals and other sacred days varied from city to city in ancient Greece. The calendar at Athens was part of the law code. This is because the performance of particular rituals on particular days was something that the state (or polis) had enjoined as a rule, since at least the beginning of the sixth century BCE. Religious celebrations were not limited, however, to those required by the state. Every *deme* (village / ward) and every *phratry* (fictive kin-group) had its own additional calendar of sacrifices, but those enjoined by the state can be understood as required by law. For example, a man who revised the law to add some sacrifices and leave out others found himself in court as a result.[71] Athens' extensive calendar of festivals was looked after by boards of officials appointed by the state. A very significant part of the state budget was spent on festivals, largely on the basis of enforced contributions – known as 'liturgies' – from those over a certain

---

69 Olivelle 2019b: 135.   70 Poo 2014; Yates 1994: 107; Yates 1995: 339; Yates 2012–13.
71 See Lys. 30, with Todd 1996.

wealth threshold. Although the contributions were not voluntary, exactly how much one contributed was voluntary and political capital could be gained from particularly generous donations.

Ancient Greek cities named the months of their calendars after festivals that were celebrated in honour of their respective gods. These and other important festivals were called *heortai*. At Athens, more than thirty-five *heortai* were celebrated annually, some of which marked key agricultural events. Processions and sacrifices to one or more gods, usually followed by a banquet, formed the core of a festival, though the combination of gods, stories, ritual performances, plays, games, parades and other components that constituted a festival could differ dramatically from place to place and from time to time, as could who was allowed to take part, with evidence for exclusions by sex, citizenship and status. There is no indication that any Greek city worried about ritual niceties, in the way that is known to have happened at Rome, though breaches of stated rules might be grist to an opponent in court.[72] In addition to satisfying the gods, an important role of festivals in Greek society seems to have been for the enjoyment and entertainment of the general populace.[73] This may help to explain the variations one finds in how the festivals were observed. It is important to realize that, from Homer onwards, the Greek gods had a sense of humour and were treated as such. Greek plays could joke about gods being deprived of the smoke from sacrifices (as in Aristophanes' *Birds*), and gods were put on stage and made fun of in various comedies (e.g. Dionysus in Aristophanes' *Frogs*).

For the Romans, a universal religious calendar did not exist. Each city was responsible for establishing its own, and this applied to colonies as well. For example, the charter of the Roman colony at Urso in Spain reads:

> Whoever shall be *duumvirs* after the foundation of the colony, they ... are to raise with the decurions, when not less than two thirds shall be present, which and how many days it may be agreed shall be festivals, which sacrifices shall be publicly performed, and who shall perform those sacrifices.[74]

Thus, the calendar did not have to follow that of the capital, Rome. Once created, the calendar was managed by religious officials, but only the local assembly or senate could introduce new festivals. The calendars that have survived in stone inscriptions refer only to the regular and major festivals; undoubtedly, a wide range of other rituals and important cultic days also had to be observed.

---

72 As in Apollodorus' case against Neaira: [Dem.] 59.   73 Scullion 2007: 201–3.
74 Rüpke 2006: 40.

The calendar of the city of Rome had 109 days devoted to honouring the gods and about 60 of these were also marked as public festival days. Courts and assemblies could not convene on such days, and other types of business could not be transacted. Rulers such as Caesar and Augustus increased the number of holy days (*dies nefasti*) and festivals in order to honour themselves and their military victories. The regular and fixed festivals, which did not include the so-called moveable feasts (*feriae conceptiuae*), began with the Kalends – the first of each month – when sacrifices were made to the god Juno on the Capitol. A number of feasts celebrating agrarian events (e.g. the growth of grains and other crops, the beginning of the grape harvest) were observed, as were more civically oriented festivals, which included several related to the spirits of the dead and two celebrations of the end of the year. The Romans had a civic and religious year that began on March 15, but, starting in about 152 BCE, the consuls began assuming their annual duties on January 1. In addition, there were private rites and festivals related to families, guilds of merchants or artisans and other groups that were not recorded in official calendars. The genesis of many Roman festivals remains unclear, and the multifaceted discourse concerning their origins suggests that their meaning lay not so much in whatever original purpose they may have had but in their ability to portray and promote Roman identity and the cultural power inherent therein.[75]

Religion in Governance

In the ancient Near East, the king was considered to be the highest religious authority in the land. He was the ultimate head of household and all of his subjects were said to be his 'slaves'. His special status was sanctioned by the gods, and, even though very few Near Eastern rulers, outside of Egypt, claimed divinity for themselves (for example, Naram-Sin at Akkad in the twenty-third century BCE and Shulgi and his successors at Ur during the first sixty years or so of the second millennium BCE), the special relationship between the king and the gods gave him a more-than-human status. He was, at the very least, an intermediary between the human and the divine realms. On the stela that preserves the Laws of Ḥammurabi, the relief on the upper portion shows Ḥammurabi receiving the sceptre of justice from the god Shamash. Ḥammurabi's head is slightly higher than that of the god, a feature that may be intended to show in what high esteem the gods held the king. In Assyria, the body of the king Tukulti-Ninurta I is referred to as the flesh of the

---

75 Beard 1987.

gods, and Assyrian kings are often depicted with a divine radiance – the *melammu*. Another Assyrian king, Esarhaddon, is described as the 'perfect likeness of the god'.[76] All of this supported an ideology that gave divine sanction to the king, his authority and his legal decisions. He was not, however, above the law. According to political discourse at least, a king was required to uphold his duties to his gods and to his land just as other citizens were. These included establishing justice and order in his realm, supporting the temples so that regular daily offerings could be made to the gods on his behalf, and participating in the rituals required to honor and appease the gods.

Divination played an important role in an array of governmental decisions, especially at the royal court. Perhaps the most common form of divination used by royal administrations in the ancient Near East was extispicy: the examination of the entrails of a sacrificial sheep. Evidence for this practice comes from early in the second millennium BCE and continues through the first half of the first millennium BCE. Divination experts who carried out the procedure generated reports on their findings. Unusual features in the entrails were thought to be omens from the gods and were treated as predictive. The experts developed systems for determining what predictions were indicated by particular abnormalities, and they recorded the correlations between specific phenomena and specific predictions in writing for consultation by future diviners. Fairly extensive records of omen reports have been preserved from the reigns of two Assyrian kings, Esarhaddon and his son Ashurbanipal, who reigned during much of the seventh century BCE. It was at this time that a new genre seems to have emerged, namely, queries to the sun-god Shamash, the patron deity of divination. Astrological omens were also deemed important and subjected to scrutiny during this period in Assyria. Scribes whose specialty was the study and interpretation of the written collections of such omens rose in importance within the Assyrian royal administration and became influential advisers to the king. Their chief role was to determine how the king could avoid any coming disasters portended by evil omens. One way that was devised has been called the substitute-king ritual. Some hapless citizen would be forced to take the throne as the official king of the land, even though he was king only in name. Once the danger predicted by the omen was believed to have passed, the substitute king would be executed, and the real king would once again become the official head of state.

76 Schneider 2011: 120.

As discussed previously, Mesopotamian kings would, when circumstances warranted or they simply wished to do so, issue *mīšarum*-edicts to free many of their subjects of burdensome debt and other obligations. This was an important royal duty and part of a ruler's divine mandate to create a just society. The earliest known edicts, those of Enmetena and Irikagina (from the twenty-fourth and twenty-second centuries BCE, respectively), claim to be reforms in the sense that they curbed abuses of power by government officials and rectified economic inequalities in society. If a family had lost their house or slave or child due to default on a debt, these edicts allowed them to reclaim what had been forfeited. Whether or not the reforms were as far-reaching or as enthusiastically supported by the populace as advertised is open to debate. Eventually, lenders and other business owners created contractual language designed to remove a transaction from the purview of such edicts.

In ancient Israel and Judah, some groups judged their kings to be remiss in this regard, and they sought to remove the prerogative to proclaim debt remissions from royal hands. They demanded the issuance of such an edict according to a regularized schedule. A text from Deuteronomy requires it every seven years, and a text from Leviticus every fifty years, in the so-called jubilee year.[77] It is difficult to determine whether such systematic decrees were ever implemented. It appears that Judean kings enacted them on an ad hoc basis, as kings did elsewhere in the Near East. According to one biblical narrative, Zedekiah, the last king of Judah, issued a *dərôr* edict and all the debt-slaves in Jerusalem were released.[78] Then the text says that the creditors turned around and reclaimed all of the slaves they had just freed, though no reason for this is given. The text's message is that divine punishment will ensue specifically for the failure to obey the command to release debt-slaves every seven years.

In ancient Egypt, the king bore five royal names, several of which referred to his special relation with the gods, Horus in particular (e.g. 'Young Horus'). But it is not quite right to say that the king, at this time, was exactly the same as a god. He only had a divine *Ka*, a spirit, which passed from one pharaoh to the next. During the coronation ceremony, the king was invested with the crowns of Upper and Lower Egypt, goddesses in their own right; it was at this moment that he received the divine spirit which gave him supernatural powers and he became the 'god of the living'. These rites were necessary

---

77 Deut 15:1–6 and Lev 25.
78 Jer 34. Hebrew *dərôr* is cognate to *andurāru*, a term that was also used in Assyria and Babylonia to describe debt-remission edicts.

for legitimate kingship. Those who were usurpers or took the throne in some other non-traditional way often had themselves chosen publicly by a god during a religious festival. Although the royal office was considered sacred, the pharaoh himself was not an object of cultic worship during his lifetime. This changed in the Hellenistic period.[79] The second Ptolemaic king and his wife laid the foundation for a successful royal and dynastic cult, where deceased and living kings were worshipped as gods and served by their own priests.

The king in India was also idealized in the Dharmaśāstra as the paragon or model householder.[80] Thus, all of the usual household (*grhya*) rites required of a householder were expected of the king as well. These included numerous daily rites (mostly offerings into the three household fires) and the five 'great sacrifices' (see above). Along with these, kings were exhorted to undertake and patronize large-scale, 'public' rites (*srauta*), including famously the *rajasuya* and the *asvamedha* sacrifices. The latter, for example, involved consecrating a horse and setting it loose to run free for a year. The king was then supposed to conquer any hostile area entered by the horse. At the end of the year, elaborate additional rites were performed, and the horse was sacrificed. Certain rites, including these two in particular, were the special obligation of a ruler and were held to be crucial for good governance. It appears unlikely, however, that many kings actually performed some or all of these. It may have been that there was little social pressure and few expectations concerning them on the part of the supporting elites and the general populace.

In ancient China, the state took a great interest in the proper performance of the necessary sacrifices to Heaven, the imperial ancestors and numerous other spirits. Both the Han (206 BCE–220 CE) and the Tang (618–907 CE) – and we may assume the same was true of other dynasties – had elaborate government departments concerned with the maintenance of proper sacrificial rituals at both the central and the local levels. The Han had a senior minister, the 'superintendent of ceremonial' (*taichang*), who oversaw all state sacrifices. His department included officials responsible for drawing up the annual calendar and identifying auspicious and inauspicious days for offering sacrifices, for intoning prayers and for performing divination. Commanderies and prefectures also had officials attached to them whose duty it was to oversee the sacrifices to local deities.[81] The Han law of 186 BCE contained

79 Manning 2010.   80 McClish 2019b.
81 Bielenstein 1980: 17–19; Loewe 2006: 24–25; Yates 2012–13: 35–36; and Kalinowski 2010: 339–66.

rules for the training of religious specialists who were to become 'invocators' (*zhu*); they were the officials who recited the prayers at state sacrifices.[82] The Tang also had a government department concerned with the supervision of state sacrifices called the court of imperial sacrifices (*taichangsi*). It included a range of officials and duties corresponding to those of the Han department for 'ceremonial'.[83] The Tang code prescribed punishments for officials who made mistakes in the preparations for, or the conduct of, the state sacrifices.[84] Earlier dynasties certainly had similar rules. It is important to note, however, that, with limited exceptions such as the Han 'invocators' and certain specialist diviners, the officials staffing the departments concerned with sacrifices were not religious specialists. They were ordinary career officials who had been given responsibility for matters involving religion. They might in the course of their careers be transferred to other duties.

In Greece, the Athenian assembly opened with a purificatory sacrifice and with prayers and curses (Aeschin. 1.23), as parodied in Aristophanes' *Thesmophoriazousai*. The nine archons, traditionally the chief magistrates in Athens, had a variety of religious roles.[85] Moreover, the Council of the Areopagus, which was made up of ex-archons, was the court that heard charges related to most types of religious offences. If offences concerned the Eleusinian Mysteries, then standard law-court procedure was followed, but only those who had themselves been initiated in the Mysteries were allowed to take part. In addition, a great many Athenian magistrates might be called on to perform religious duties.[86]

Omens play an important part in Homeric epic, and the consultation of the liver of the sacrificial animal before battle remained standard and could affect military decisions. Armies had a 'seer' with them in order that the liver-inspection might be properly carried out. But already at Troy, Hector dismisses omens: 'One omen is good, to fight for the city'; omens are debated, too, in the assemblies held on Ithaca in the *Odyssey*.[87] In the classical period, however, we have no evidence for omens being used to manipulate assembly meetings or contribute to a particular line of persuasion. Speakers in the assembly certainly made reference to oracles, and indeed the Athenian assembly might decide to consult an oracle when its business concerned the gods. Notable cases include the appropriate behaviour in the face of the Persian invasion; the question of whether to ask Greek cities to contribute

---

82 Yates 2014a: 147–48.   83 des Retours 1947: 315–24.   84 Johnson 1997: art. 67, 70.
85 See *Ath. pol.* 57.1–2, 58.1.
86 For example, see *Ath. pol.* 54.6–7; Dem. 21.114–15; and Theophr. *Char.* 21.11.
87 *Iliad* 12.243; *Od.* 2.146–207, also 24.443–71.

first fruits to Eleusis; and what to do about an area of sacred land between Attica and Megara which was subject to dispute.[88] In the case of the Eleusis first-fruits decree, it is clear from an amendment that one of the people who was most active in the discussion was a man who was a seer (*mantis*) and who seems to have tried to use his status as a religious expert. Traces of religious experts being listened to by the Athenian assembly are not common, although we do have one decree proposed in response to statements made by someone explicitly identified as the priest of Asclepios, but this is because the decree itself concerned the finances of the sanctuary of Asclepios.[89]

In 426/5 BCE the Athenians, responding to an oracle, carried out a purification of Delos and established a new festival there.[90] Whether the Athenians had decided to consult an oracle or whether someone pointed out an item from an oracular book is not known. There had been a purification of Delos in the sixth century by the Athenian tyrant Peisistratus, and that seems to have been in accordance with an oracle in a book. One factor here is likely to have been their responding to the outbreak of plague.[91] A few years later the Athenians decided that the purification had not been complete and removed the people of Delos from the island, only to have an oracle from Delphi subsequently require that the people of Delos be restored to their homes.[92] Like the attempt to collect first fruits from the other Greeks, the purification of Delos was far from being a purely religious matter: these were ways of extending the reach of the Athenian empire. The Athenian empire was also made to contribute to the gods, however. One sixtieth of the tribute paid by the allies to Athens was given to Athena – it is from the records of the payments to Athena that we are able to reconstruct the history of tribute payment within the Athenian empire. When the Athenians took over territory from allies in a punitive move following a revolt, they set aside a tenth of the land taken for the gods; Athenian shareholders rented out the remaining plots.[93] Allies were also obliged to contribute a cow (for sacrifice) and a full set of armour to the festival of the Panathenaea.

Divination and the taking of auspices played a fundamental role in governance at Rome. The practice of augury was important for a wide range of matters related to governmental administration. At the beginning of the Republic, only patricians functioned as augurs, but plebeians began to hold the office by 300 BCE. They divined the will of the gods, often from the

---

88 Persian invasion: Herodotus 7.141–42; first-fruits to Eleusis: ML, no. 73; and sacred land under dispute: RO 58.
89 IG ii² 47. 90 Thuc. 3.104. 91 As stated by Diod. 12.58.6. 92 Thuc. 5.1; 5.32.1.
93 As with the territory of Mytilene; Thuc. 3.50.2.

observation of birds – the direction of their flight, aspects of their singing, their manner of eating – but other phenomena were relevant as well: thunder and lightning, the entrails of sacrificial animals and foreboding events in general. The convening of the senate, the establishment of new colonies, the assumption of official duties by a new magistrate, military decisions – all of these could require an augural ceremony. The point was to consult the gods concerning any significant action that might affect the *pax* or well-being of Rome.

One might conclude from this that, when it came to governmental affairs, the sacred took precedence over the secular or political, but the reverse was often the case. Under the Roman Republic and into the early Empire:

> ... the senate controlled internal politics by issuing written recommendations as if they were decrees (*senatus consulta*) and by using magistrates as the executive arm of its decisions. The senators managed policy as regards religion, concerning both the construction of temples and the acceptance of new gods in the Roman pantheon .... In addition, the senators were the juries of the permanent courts since the last half of the second century BCE, as well as the priests of the Roman civic religion. In short, the senate was effectively the governing body of the Roman Republic.[94]

Under the empire, however, the development of the imperial cult, in addition to the rise of 'freelance religious experts', complicated the picture considerably.[95]

In the early fourth century CE, the emperor Constantine's promotion of Christianity as a religion of empire led to a fundamental shift in the relationship between Roman government and religion (Figure 6.5). The rise of the institutional Christian church also created an alternative focus for governance – one that created specific challenges and opportunities for late Roman emperors and imperial bureaucrats.[96]

Religious Rituals in Legal Contexts

Promissory Oaths

In most of the cultures under analysis, there were legal transactions or events that were facilitated by the use of religious procedures or rituals.[97] One of the most common procedures utilized in the Near East in this way was the

---

94 Pina Polo 2016: 89.   95 Wendt 2016.   96 Humfress 2007b.
97 For this and the following section, 'Judicial Oaths, Ordeals and Oracles', see also Chapter 7, this volume.

Figure 6.5 Jesus Christ before Pilate, who washes his hands. Cast of a sarcophagus with 'traditio legis' in the vatican Grottoes, 350–70 CE. Vatican Museum, Rome. © Frank Buffetrille. All rights reserved 2023 / Bridgeman Images: number FBU7287238 (www.bridgemanimages.com/en/frank-buffetrille/christ-before-pilate/marble/asset/7287238)

promissory oath, especially in the formation of contracts. Although not every contract was secured by an oath invoking one or more gods, many contracts were. Throughout the region and across its historical time periods, there were essentially two ways to ensure that the obligations of a contract could be enforced.[98] First, one party could perform its obligations and thereby create an enforceable obligation on the other party to fulfil its obligations (this situation – where one party has performed and is now waiting for the other party to do so – is sometimes referred to as a 'real contract'). If, for example, one party paid the required purchase price for an item, it was now incumbent on the other party to transfer ownership and possession of the item to the first. Second, both parties could swear promissory oaths to perform their obligations. These oaths could be used to secure the entire contractual agreement, or they could be directed towards subsidiary issues within the agreement. International treaties were a type of contract secured by oaths before the gods. In the case of parity treaties, the parties swore reciprocal oaths, agreeing to provide the same type of political and military

---

98 Westbrook 2003b: €6–67.

support for each other. When the parties were of unequal status, the weaker party (or vassal) swore allegiance to the more powerful party (or suzerain).

Promissory oaths could also be utilized in other contexts. A number of Near Eastern litigation records disclose that, at the conclusion of a trial, one or both parties could be made to swear that they would not enter into litigation over the same matter again. It was typically the losing party that took this type of oath, but both parties could be involved, especially if the winning party happened to be the plaintiff. Evidence for similar declarations at the end of a trial comes from ancient China. At least three records from the Western Chou reveal that the losing parties swore an oath (*shih*) to perform what the court required of them or else be subject to specific punishments.[99] In the Near East, one finds promissory oaths in legal-administrative contexts as well. A number of records from Neo-Babylonian temple archives show that individuals, who were not directly under the authority of temple officials, swore promissory oaths that they would carry out the administrative duties assigned to them by the officials.[100] Should they fail, according to these texts, they would have to answer to – and likely be punished by – the royal administration. With promissory oaths that are sworn within a legal context, it seems that punishment for failure to make good on the oath was not left entirely to the gods but that human authorities would intervene and punish those who did not keep their word.[101]

Rabbinic literature, following biblical law, delineates two categories of promissory oaths, the *neder* and the *shevuah*. They differ from one another in that the former is an oath based on an object and the latter on an individual. In other words, a *shevuah* is something that one declares about oneself – a declaration about the past or a promise about the future. A *neder*, on the other hand, generally forbids the benefit of some object to the speaker (e.g. 'let wine be forbidden to me'). Given that violations of both kinds of oaths require a sacrifice to be brought to the temple, and given the destruction of the temple, both are discouraged by the rabbis. One who takes such an oath is described as 'evil' (*b. Ned.* 21a). One major power that the rabbis grant themselves is the power to annul the *neder* (*m. Hag.* 1:8). Jews famously annul all vows made each year on the eve of the Day of Atonement through a publicly recited litany, *kol nidrei,* which is recited in synagogues all over the world to this day.

---

99 MacCormack 2007: 17–18.   100 Magdalene, Wells and Wunsch 2019: 90–111.
101 Ries 1999.

Judicial Oaths, Ordeals and Oracles

Other religiously oriented procedures could be used towards the end of a trial, not to ensure adherence to the verdict, but actually to establish a verdict in the first place. These procedures fall into three basic categories: the oath, the ordeal and the oracle.[102] The oath was employed in slightly different ways throughout these cultures, as detailed below. As a decisive procedure, however, it came most often near the end of a trial when the judges of the case at hand would require one of the litigants to swear by the gods to the veracity of his or her claims. Across certain cultures (e.g. ancient Mesopotamia), if the litigant went through with the court-ordered oath, the case was decided in that litigant's favour: that is, the oath was considered dispositive. The ordeal typically involved the performance of some physical action on the part of one or both litigants. Whoever successfully performed the action won the case, and it was believed that the outcome was ultimately controlled by the gods. The river ordeal in the Near East, for example, required litigants to submit themselves to judgment by the river's god. Details are scant, but those who entered the river likely had to travel a prescribed distance without sinking, though failing the ordeal did not always mean death. An individual could be hauled out of the water and punished in some other way (including monetary fine or confiscation of property).[103] In an oracle, a question about the trial was submitted directly to a god who returned an answer that revealed who should win the case.

In most periods of Near Eastern history, the dispositive oath was fairly common and used mostly to resolve cases where the evidence was insufficient, ambiguous or otherwise problematic. When judges decided to employ the oath, they imposed the responsibility to swear on one of the parties at trial or, occasionally, on the witnesses who testified on behalf of one of the parties. The court would then often move to a cultic site where the oath was performed. In some instances, a divine statue or emblem was transferred to the current site. Should the party swear as instructed by the court, that party won the trial.[104] At times, parties might promise to swear an oath in the hopes that the other party would acquiesce in the face of such bravado or that the judges might be convinced by this willingness to risk the wrath of the gods. The Babylonian record of a proceeding from around 1700 BCE is illustrative, in

---

102 Scholars of ancient Greece also use the phrase 'judicial oath' to refer to the annual event when '6,000 Athenian citizens over the age of 30 were selected to decide cases in court and they swore the judicial oath to vote in accordance with the laws and decrees of the Athenian people' (Harris 2012a: 287).
103 Paulus 2015.   104 Lafont 1997.

part because it exhibits similarities to what we find in a speech written by the Greek orator Lysias (c. 445–c. 380 BCE). In what is best described as a pre-trial hearing, an Old Babylonian military general responds to an accusation as follows: 'I will kiss the lips of my child and, before the emblem of the god Shamash, I will swear to you that your barley, oil and tablets were not brought into my house nor were they broken.'[105] The general is denying any complicity in the alleged theft of the plaintiff's goods. He is even willing it seems, to subject his own children to possible divine revenge by incorporating them into his oath of innocence. Whether or not he will be allowed to swear would be for the court to decide. In the speech from Lysias, the widow of the man whose estate is in question is quoted as having asserted to her sons' guardians:

> When [my husband Diodotos] sailed out, you received five talents as a deposit for safe keeping from him. About this I am willing to bring both my children by Diodotos and those borne to me later wherever you say and to swear. But I am not so desperate or so mad for money as to commit perjury by my children before I die.[106]

Here, the speaker discloses what remains unspoken in the Old Babylonian texts: that the willingness to involve one's children should be enough to persuade the court. It is important to note that, in Greece, an oath was one of the few sorts of evidence from women that were accepted in court. A woman's oath was needed to give her testimony evidentiary value.

River ordeals also occurred throughout various periods of Near Eastern history. One early text (c. 2500 BCE) contains a summary of multiple cases decided in this way.[107] From the first half of the second millennium BCE, we have legal provisions in which a woman accused of promiscuity by someone other than her husband must undergo the river ordeal.[108] Because the matter has become public, it must now be resolved in public, presumably for the sake of her husband's honour. If it had been only the husband who suspected his wife, an oath by the woman before a priest would have sufficed – a much less public resolution.[109] In the Middle Assyrian Laws (c. 1200 BCE), men who are suspected of having slept with another man's wife may be required to

---

105 The text is Feigin 1979 (= YOS 12): no. 325. The tablets, referenced by the general, were probably state-issued and certified that the plaintiff in the case had rights to the commodities listed. To break a tablet meant to make the agreement it recorded null and void.
106 Lys. 32.13; see Parker 2005: 70.   107 Wilcke 2007: 46.
108 Laws of Ur-Namma, art. 14; Laws of Ḥammurabi, art. 132.
109 Laws of Ḥammurabi, art. 131; Num 5:11–31.

undergo the river ordeal, usually if the wife has so accused them. There is ample evidence for the use of the ordeal in cases related to property disputes, which would not have been considered capital cases.[110] In a Late Bronze Age case from the city of Nuzi, a plaintiff in a dispute over the ownership of a field tells the judges that he does not have written proof of his claim but is willing to undergo the river ordeal.[111]

A notable development takes place in the ancient Near East in the mid-first millennium BCE. Recourse to the dispositive oath undergoes a noticeable decrease, and the use of the river ordeal disappears altogether from the extant evidence. In contrast, the occurrence of non-dispositive oaths increases. Prior to the Neo-Babylonian period, it appears that any party or witness could take such an oath, which, while not resolving the suit, might increase the weight and efficacy of the proffered testimony. It was typically not court-ordered but voluntary on the part of the individuals before the court, and it generally invoked only the king and not the gods.[112] In the Neo-Babylonian period, the dominant position of the dispositive oath was challenged by a form of the non-dispositive oath. Unlike its earlier usage, it invoked the gods as well as the king, but it still remained non-dispositive. Litigants could now swear by the gods to the truth of their position and still lose the case.[113] Interestingly enough, much of the Neo-Babylonian evidence concerning trials derives from temple archives. Given the temple's frequent involvement in administering dispositive oaths, it is in a temple context where one would expect the dominance of the formal, dispositive oath to be retained – but that is not the case. The temple courts were as prone as any at the time to disregard sworn statements and seek to resolve cases on the basis of ordinary evidence.[114]

According to rabbinic law, judicial oaths could be mandated only in civil cases in which insufficient evidence could be produced.[115] For example, if a plaintiff could produce only one witness, in place of the requisite two (as required at Deut 19:15), the defendant is allowed to swear an oath and be exempted from paying anything to the plaintiff (b. Kettubot 87b). Similarly, if a defendant acknowledges partial debt, that defendant may swear an oath and be exempted from paying the full amount claimed by the plaintiff (b. Git. 51b). The oath described here is thus best understood as a kind of rebuttal of the claim of the plaintiff by the defendant, as if to call in God as a witness in the

---

110 Frymer-Kensky 1977: 505; Durand 1988: 515.   111 Wilhelm 1995.
112 Dombradi 1996, vol. I: 331; Wells, Magdalene and Wunsch 2010.
113 Magdalene 2007: 78–84; Wells, Magdalene and Wunsch 2010: 18–20.
114 Joannès 1997: 169–70; Wells 2008b.   115 b. Shavu. 42b, 45a, 48b.

absence of a human one. This is actualized by use of the divine name, which is not to be mentioned 'in vain'.[116]

The judicial oath is known from ancient Egypt, as well, and became much more prevalent in later periods. It began as an oath invoking both the king and the gods and evolved in the Late Period (712–323 BCE) into one that invoked only the gods. It survived into the Hellenistic period in hundreds of Demotic temple oaths; some Greek temple oaths are also attested. As in other ancient cultures, such temple oaths could end a dispute when the judges did not have convincing evidence; this procedure is also found in Greek courts, notably those of the 'chrematists' – judges who represented the king. The dispositive temple oath was usually imposed on the defendant, and the legal consequences of taking or refusing the oath were laid down beforehand. The oath, starting with the invocation of a local god, was sworn in the presence of both parties, a representative of the court and a priest. Since only the higher priests were allowed to enter the temples, the oath was taken in a place open to all people, such as a stone niche or a shrine dedicated to the god, or at a temple gate.

There is ample evidence for judicial oracles, in addition to judicial oaths, in ancient Egypt. One procedure involved oracles that are sometimes referred to as 'ticket' oracles. Two alternative decisions were formulated on a papyrus or ostracon, usually one positive and one negative. The god would then choose one of the alternatives, though the details are unclear.[117] This basic procedure continued from the New Kingdom well into the Roman period. So-called *Sortes* books developed from this procedure.[118] The earliest known exemplars come from the third century CE and are attributed to the legendary Egyptian sage Astrampsychos. They contained 100 questions that people of that time might inquire about, along with ten possible answers to each question. A priest would assign a number to a petitioner's question and the petitioner would say a number between one and ten, which would be added to the question's number. The result would direct the priest to the correct answer in the *Sortes* book. In later versions, biblical patriarchs or Christian saints took the place of Astrampsychos.[119]

Another oracle procedure was especially popular in Egypt during the New Kingdom. Priests would carry a god outside the temple and individuals could then consult the god for a verdict in a case. The god, possibly manipulated by the priests, could 'nod' or not: when the answer was affirmative, the statue

---

116 Exod 20:7; Deut 5:17.   117 See the discussion in chapter 4 of McDowell 1990.
118 Browne 1987.   119 Frankfurter 1998: 179–96.

moved forward; when negative, it moved backward. The divine answer and the names of witnesses were recorded. If the defendants in these cases did not wish to accept the verdict, they could initiate the procedure again before another oracle god. Popular oracle gods were Amun of Thebes, Chnum of Elephantine and the deified kings Ahmose and Amenophis I. These oracles may have taken place during annual festivals, when the god left the temple, or it may have been that the processions were organized for this judicial purpose. Both ticket and procession oracles were, probably unsuccessfully, prohibited by the prefect of Egypt in 199 CE after the Roman emperor Septimius Severus visited the Nile country.[120]

In India there is some mention of oaths and ordeals in older literature such as the Law Code of Manu. According to this code, 'when two persons are litigating matters for which there are no witnesses and the judge is unable to discern the truth', judges may make use of an oath or an ordeal.[121] Oaths were allowed when 'made in connection with lovers, marriages, fodder for cows, or firewood, or to protect a Brahmin'.[122] They may have been allowed in other cases, although this is less clear. Instead of an oath, judges could also require an ordeal, such as carrying a hot iron ball for a prescribed distance or staying submerged in water while a runner retrieved a shot arrow.[123] 'When the blazing fire does not burn a man, the water does not push him up to the surface ... he should be judged innocent.'[124] Oaths and ordeals do not appear in actual legal texts, however, until the fourth century CE. By that time, these two procedures were reserved only for particular trials, usually those concerning matters of great import. Still, the impulse to rely in some measure on the divine, for the sake of reaching a verdict, is clearly in evidence.

With limited exceptions, oaths and ordeals seem to have had very little place in early Chinese judicial practice. We do know of the so-called blood covenant (*meng*): an oath involving a sacrifice in the legal procedure of the state of Chu in the fourth century BCE. The evidence comes from the *Chou li* and from texts found in a Chu tomb. The *Chou li* says that litigants should perform the *meng* prior to beginning the actual trial: each litigant is to bring a sacrifice and take an oath in support of his or her position. This would put each litigant under the threat of punishment by the spirits should they swear falsely. Thus, those who are thinking of making a false claim would be afraid to take the oath, 'with the result that there is a decrease in lawsuits'.[125] Texts taken from the tomb show that the *meng* could be imposed by judges later in

120 P. Coll. Youtie I 30.   121 *MDh* 8.109 (Olivelle 2004a: 131).
122 *MDh* 8.112 (Olivelle 2004a: 131).   123 See Olivelle 2004a: 270.
124 *MDh* 8.115 (Olivelle 2004a: 131).   125 MacCormack 2007: 13.

a trial. In a case where both litigants accused the other of homicide, 'the witnesses on each side were called upon to take the *meng* oath in support of the accuracy of the allegations made by their principals'.[126] It may have been the party with the most witnesses at the oath ceremony who won the case, or possibly the party with the most eminent witnesses. What is of note is that ancient Chinese law allowed both parties (or their witnesses) to take the oath, while in the Near East, Egypt and, as we will see, Greece, the oath was typically allowed to only one party at trial. That party held an advantage since victory could be secured by taking the oath.

Ancient Greece also had its own form of the dispositive oath, though it appears rarely to have occurred.[127] The evidence that most clearly attests to it comes in the mid fifth-century BCE Laws of Gortyn, found at Crete. The code envisions three possible ways by which cases are decided: 'by witnesses, by oath of denial, and by judgment'.[128] The second means appears to be a dispositive oath. The code refers to the one who is *horkiôtera*, 'more oath-worthy' or 'more entitled to the oath', as the one who should swear: for example, one section refers to a raped female slave as the one 'more entitled to the oath'.[129] We are not privy to exactly what she would swear, but it seems clear that her oath would prove decisive in the case. This might suggest that the judge ordinarily directed the one making the complaint to swear the oath (as also at Laws of Gortyn IV.6–8), but, when a judge or official (*mnamon*) is accused, it is the defendant who is 'more worthy of the oath' (*IC* iv.42 B 3–9). The content and form of these oaths were not decided by the oath-takers but, apparently, by the judge. In some cases, a party's witnesses were required to swear together with the party, as, for instance, when a man catches another having sex with his wife; he along with four witnesses are to swear that they genuinely caught the other man and did not entrap him (*IC* ii.36–45). More remarkable is the procedure set up in the case of a boundary dispute, where the case seems to be decided by whichever side has the greater number of witnesses who swear (*IC* iv.81 11–16). The goal may have been to favour the party that had more individuals who were willing to submit themselves to the threat of divine punishment.

---

126 MacCormack 2007: 14.
127 See, in general, Sommerstein 2013; and Sommerstein and Torrance 2014.
128 Parker 2005: 70, referring to Laws of Gortyn XI.26–31 (the column and line numberings follow the edition in Gagarin and Perlman 2016).
129 Parker 2005: 71; Laws of Gortyn II.15–16, see also Gagarin and Perlman 2016: 345 whose translation differs slightly: 'And the slave woman is to be the one who swears.'

A more common use of the oath, especially at Athens, was the oath-challenge: a strategy whereby a litigant 'asks his opponent to swear a specific oath or offers to swear one himself ... If the opponent refuses to accept the proposed oath (as he almost always does), the proposer may cite this refusal as evidence of his opponent's guilt.'[130] Aeschylus deploys the oath challenge in his tragedy *Eumenides*, when the Furies protest Orestes' refusal to swear the oath (that he did not kill his mother) with which they have challenged him and when Athena objects that 'an unjust cause should not gain victory because of oaths' – that is, a case may be more complex than a simple oath can reveal.[131] Extant law-court speeches from Athens contain mention of twenty-three oath-challenges, of which only two are accepted and only one is ever actually sworn. In seventeen of the twenty-three oath-challenges, litigants or their supporters offer to swear an oath; all are rejected, not surprisingly, since acceptance of the challenge would be tantamount to acceptance of the challenger's position in the case. Four other cases entail offers by litigants of an oath to their opponents, and here the oaths tend to be conditional or narrowly worded. In the case where the oath is sworn, the oath-taker is a woman named Plangon who swears to the effect that Boeotus and his brother were the sons of Mantias, in consequence of which Mantias is forced to register them in his phratry.[132] The speaker claims that in swearing this oath Plangon double-crossed him, since she had agreed that he would pay her 30 minas and she would refuse the proposed oath. The oath she swears here puts an end to any possibility of litigation on the question of paternity. But whether an oath was decisive in a trial depended on whether the wording of the oath was such as to address the central issue of the case.

Various kinds of oaths are also found in operation in numerous legal contexts under the Roman Republic and Empire. These contexts include the settlement of litigation, as shown in a wax tablet from Puteoli dated to 49 CE (*TPSulp* 28). Oaths could also be tendered as a mode of property acquisition, especially in provincial practice. They were also required from magistrates and other officials with legal responsibilities. Finally, there is evidence for oaths being used in order to establish evidence from at least the Late Republic. By the time we reach the later Roman empire, there are examples from provincial practice of legal disputes being concluded by processes that include the swearing of oaths before the shrines of local martyrs and

---

130 Gagarin 2005b: 88–89; see also Gagarin 2007.   131 Aes. *Eumenides*, 429–32.
132 Dem. 39.3–4, 40.8–11; a case notorious enough to be mentioned by Arist. *Rhetoric* 2.23.11.

(Christian) saints (P. Petra IV.39). We should assume that these practices were more prevalent than the extant documentation would suggest.

The widespread use of these procedures – the oath, ordeal and oracle – reflects their inherent appeal. In the case of the oath, for example, its benefits seem to have been twofold. First, when judges resorted to the dispositive oath, they were able to rely on the gods as a kind of anti-perjury enforcement mechanism. They trusted that the gods would eventually reveal the truth of the matter and impose whatever punishment they deemed appropriate. Second, the oath allowed the judges to see which verdict should, for the time being, be rendered – with the only delay being the time required for performance of the oath itself. A third motivation may have played a role as well. In certain cases, judges may have wished to force the litigants to settle. One way to do this was to impose the oath on one of the parties at trial. Trial records from the Near East show that it was not uncommon for the one required to swear, instead, to propose a settlement with the other party or even to capitulate in the case.[133] Oath-swearing was a grave matter, and many litigants preferred not to subject themselves to the potential of divine retribution. In a Babylonian case from around 1800 BCE, for example, a man sues a priestess over a field; the judges require the priestess to take an oath, but at the temple gate where she is to swear, she opts to settle with the plaintiff, though we are not told the details of the agreement.[134]

One can see in these cultures the coming together of religious belief, on the one hand, and the desire to render an appropriate legal verdict, on the other. One of the classic works on this facet of ancient law is that of Kurt Latte, who, over one hundred years ago, sought to explain a court's reliance on cultic procedures as one of the results of a weak central political authority that lacked the necessary enforcement mechanisms to see that its judges' decisions were carried out.[135] Similar explanations have been offered for the prevalence of such procedures in the Near East, but the evidence on enforcement capabilities is disputed. Scholars have varied in their assessment of trial verdicts, deeming them to be as weak as mere suggestions and as strong as decisions backed by the full authority and might of the royal administration.

It is unlikely that any one explanation will suffice. A combination of multiple factors, such as the strong religious orientation of the cultures, the nature of the judiciary (including, at times perhaps, the lack of a police force at its disposal) and the exigencies of timely resolutions, would seem to provide the most reasonable account. The oath, in particular, would not

---

133 Lafont 1997.   134 Figulla 1967 [= CT 47]: no. 12.   135 Latte 1920.

have been effective outside a culture that took the gods and their intervention in human affairs most seriously. The ordeal is somewhat different in this respect. Its effectiveness does not necessarily hinge on the beliefs of the one undergoing the ordeal. Moreover, there is no expectation that the gods will impose punishment in the future; the verdict is immediate, as is any divine punishment imposed during the ordeal, even up to death. Nevertheless, in some cases, it appears that individuals ordered to submit to an ordeal could seek to reach a settlement with the other party in the case and thereby avoid whatever pain or difficulty they would otherwise risk in the ordeal.

Religious Officials and the Law

Throughout much of the ancient world, religious officials were subject to the authority of the legal system and often exercised judicial authority within that system to varying degrees.[136] It is not always clear to what extent their activities were bound by law or in what contexts they had jurisdiction to resolve disputes. In the Hebrew Bible, priestly offices are considered hereditary, but different texts invest them with different levels of authority. Two main strands of thought are preserved: one reserves judicial authority mainly for state and local officials (e.g. judges, town elders, etc.), while allowing priests a partial role in the process; the other grants judicial authority almost entirely to priests. Most texts in Deuteronomy reflect the former but grant priests a kind of supervisory role alongside certain judges. In cases that are too difficult for local courts to decide, for example, the trial moves to the central court (in Jerusalem) to be adjudicated by the priests and judges who preside over that court (Deut 19:17). A few texts from Deuteronomy, however, which appear to stem from one particular editorial stage in the book's development, promote priestly authority above all else.[137] In similar fashion, the Priestly Writings, which likely post-date most of Deuteronomy, reserve judicial decision-making entirely for the priests and the ʿēdâ ('congregation' or 'assembly'), the exact make-up of which is unclear but which would have been under priestly control. Later texts from the post-exilic period (post 500 BCE) split judicial duties between state and religious officials. The text of 2 Chronicles 19:11, which advocates for a particular policy through a revisionist description of a past event, assigns authority over religious disputes ('every

---

136 Carbon and Harris 2024.
137 For example, Deut 21:5: 'Every dispute and every assault shall be settled according to their [the priests'] decision.'

matter of Yahweh') to the high priest and over other disputes ('every matter of the king') to the state.

In terms of rabbinic law, although the rabbis granted themselves certain powers, such as the annulment of oaths, and certain economic benefits, such as the rights to the best spots in the marketplace (b. B. Bat. 22a), they are considered to be subject to the law as all other citizens. Rabbinic law, despite its focus on the reality of a post-temple world, continued to apply biblical law to the priestly caste in some areas – such as the prohibition against coming into contact with death and the prohibition against marrying women with prior sexual experience.[138] In addition, both Talmuds contain numerous examples of rabbis serving as judges not only in matters of ritual law but also in matters regarding civil disputes; they could also serve as mediators (b. Sanh. 6a).

In ancient Mesopotamia, temple personnel were typically divided into prebendaries and temple dependents or oblates. The latter consisted of those who were essentially bound to the temple for life. The former consisted of individuals who held prebends – that is, they were entitled to shares in the temple income in return for services provided to the temple. These services could include the performance of cultic rituals, but only a designated group of prebendaries were allowed to administer rituals or even to enter the sacred areas within the temple compound. Such an individual was referred to as a 'temple enterer' (ērib bīti) and can be referred to by the term 'priest'. Other prebendaries were involved in the provision of foodstuffs (bakers, brewers, herdsmen, gardeners), craft professions (goldsmiths, builders), or basic administrative activities (scribes, measurers, gate-keepers).[139] Although the king was considered each temple's highest authority and chief prebendary and could appoint officials to prebend-holding administrative positions, most prebendaries were drawn from the elite families of a given temple's urban area. A prebend was heritable, though subject to the legal rules governing inheritance, and prebendary families retained their privileges for generations. In the Neo-Babylonian period, prebends also became alienable: they could be sold, pledged for debt and confiscated on default.[140] The ownership of the prebend and the performance of the duties associated with it became bifurcated. Prebendaries could now hire substitutes to perform the duties or have their slaves do the work, so long as the status of a 'temple enterer' was not required. The ownership of prebends could also be the subject of lawsuits.

---

138 Lev 21:1–2 and Lev 21:14 respectively.   139 Jursa 2010: 158.   140 Jursa 2010: 163–64.

The more that prebend-holding became a business, the more it became subject to the legal system.

Overall, a distinction between religious and royal jurisdiction seems to have prevailed in Mesopotamia. In the Neo-Babylonian period, for instance, in addition to courts presided over by state-appointed officials, there was a collection of temple courts where temple officials heard cases and rendered verdicts.[141] These officials, who served both as priests with cultic privileges and responsibilities and as administrators, had full judicial authority in the matters under their jurisdiction. Such matters included disputes among and wrongs committed by temple personnel. Temple officials did not handle disputes unrelated to temple concerns. In some cases, one finds a combination of state judges and temple officials. These typically involved persons outside the temple's direct authority who had wronged the temple in some way, often by stealing temple property. The role of priests in earlier periods is not as well-defined. They can preside over certain disputes, but the texts reveal too few details to identify the relationship between the subject matter of the trial and temple interests. Priests could become involved when procedures such as the oath were required by the judges. They produced the divine statue or emblem before which the oath was sworn and were generally responsible for administering the oath procedure.

We have no clear evidence that priests or temple officials regularly served as judicial authorities in Hittite society, but there are a few texts demonstrating that their actions were subject to legal regulations. The most well-known text is CTH 264, often entitled 'Instructions for Priests and Temple Personnel'.[142] The stipulations in the document seek to control all manner of priestly behaviour, from their observance of festivals to their sexual activities. Other topics covered in the text include the manner in which sacrifices are to be made, protocols for dealing with theft of temple property, keeping watch over the temple grounds at night, maintaining purity, handling gifts from the king, and the behaviour of shepherds managing temple herds. Punishments for disobedience range from public humiliation to death, and sometimes the execution of the offender occurs together with his wife and children.

The combining of the religious and the judicial was common in ancient Egypt. The place where verdicts were rendered was often of a religious nature. Judicial oaths and oracles typically occurred at temples, and tribunals of Egyptian priests or even Greek officials (e.g., the *strategos*) in the Hellenistic

---

[141] Holtz 2009: 296–99.   [142] Miller 2013: 244.

period presided over cases there. Temple gates were sometimes explicitly called the gate 'where justice (*ma'at*) is performed' (*rw.t-dỉ.t-mꜣʿ.t*) or 'where *ma'at* is satisfied'. State officials could be vested with both political and judicial authority. In addition to being the supreme political figure, the king was the highest priest in the land and the supreme judge. These functions find their unifying core in the king's mandate to ensure stability and peace throughout the land. The king could issue *hp.w* (laws), including religious obligations, which were meant to be expressions of *ma'at*. He could also rule on individual cases, although this was uncommon. The pharaoh was assisted by a kind of prime minister, the vizier (there were two viziers from the New Kingdom onward), who had a variety of responsibilities but whose principal area was jurisdiction. While the pharaoh was in practice the legislator, the vizier fulfilled executive and judicial functions, presiding over the great court (*qnb.t ʿꜣ.t*) at Memphis and at Thebes. The vizier also held religious responsibilities, supervising the temples and thus ensuring the continuation of proper sacrifices. The king could assign him additional religious duties such as organizing cultic festivals. At lower levels of jurisdiction, priests (along with mayors, local prophets and others) could function as judges, and as noted above temple courts are attested. Most priests held civil or military positions, as well, and benefited financially from both vocations. In the later period, the great courts disappear, and in Hellenistic times, the local and temple courts partly survive in the court of the *laokritai*, priests-judges from the local temple supervised by the crown in the person of an *eisagogeus* or 'introducer'. The Egyptian *laokritai*-courts were eventually superseded by the Greek ones, which generally operated outside a religious context. In late antique Egypt there is evidence for Christian clerics, holy men and monastics performing roles associated with both legal and judicial practice.

Prior to the introduction of the Hindu temple in the fourth century CE, there were priests who presided over Vedic rites, which used temporary altars and lacked permanent structures, but they had essentially no legal authority or power, at least according to the extant texts. These priests were Brahmins – it is important to note, though, that not all Brahmins were priests – and may have been scholars as well. The two roles diverged around the early centuries CE. Prior to this, the specifically legal role of priests was limited to consultative and scholarly modes. A king may have turned to them for advice on legal matters or a group/council (*parisad*) may have been formed to deal with ritual and legal infractions in some cases. A specifically judicial role for Brahmins comes after the divergence of roles. It is after this point that, according to the Dharmaśāstra tradition, scholarly Brahmins were specifically identified as suitable judges and could thus be appointed by the king. In practice, it seems that others became involved in judicial decision-making as well. Some Dharmaśāstra texts from the early medieval period reveal that older and respected businessmen could also sit on judicial panels, perhaps to provide counsel when commercial matters were brought before the court. Eventually, priests became second-class citizens, those willing to perform rites in temples for ordinary people. It was the elite Brahmins, scholars supported by royal patrons, who were the authors of the legal texts, not the priests who then began to administer the newly emerging temples. Over an extensive period of time, as temples became more and more powerful, the temple Brahmins gained political power and also became important as legal figures, but this is primarily a change of what is more properly called the medieval period in India.[143]

Individuals who performed religious rituals and engaged in other religious activities were certainly widespread in ancient China, and their relationship with the state's legal authorities was not always harmonious. But ancient China provides us with no clear evidence that priests, or other religious functionaries, held judicial or other types of legal authority. As mentioned above, those who oversaw the performance of sacrifices and other necessary religious rituals were state officials who could be reassigned to other duties if their superiors saw fit. While religious officials did not enact or enforce the law, they were subject to it. The policies from the Northern Wei (386–534 CE) and later periods towards Buddhism illustrate this point. At times, the religion was discouraged and strictly controlled. A decree of 444 CE, for example, required, under pain of death, persons privately supporting Buddhist monks in their homes to surrender the monks to the authorities; another decree from 472 CE was directed against persons who harboured travelling Buddhist monks; it also forbade the creation of new Buddhist monasteries. In some later decades, greater toleration was shown; and a decree of 508 provided that monks (whether Buddhist or Daoist) who committed homicide or any serious offence were to be handed over to the secular authorities for trial and punishment, whereas for all other offences monks might be judged by their own superiors according to the rules of their order.[144] The Tang code itself merely stated, in the context of theft of or damage to Buddhist or Daoist statutes, that an offence committed by a Buddhist or Daoist monk in stealing or damaging the statues of their own

---

143 Further discussion in Olivelle and Davis 2017.
144 Hurvitz 1956: 65–66, 76–77 and 84.

faith was to be punished more severely than the same offence committed by a layperson.[145]

From ancient Greece, official instructions and rules for priests and other officials involved in cultic activities come in two forms. On the one hand, there are decisions made by the assembly or another sovereign body that may establish the existence and conditions of a priesthood. In this way, the Athenians in the 430s BCE established a new priesthood of Athena Nike and determined that the priestess should be selected by lot from all Athenian women (who offered their names); they also established what the payment and privileges should be. On the other hand, there are the regulations put up in sanctuaries themselves, which do not invoke a specific source of authority but lay down the rules that operate in the sanctuary. Modern scholarship refers to these as 'sacred laws', but they are laws only insofar as they may be policed and enforced within the sanctuary that displays them. These rules variously concern general behaviour in the sanctuary, details of ritual and who may take part, and they can also determine the share of the sacrifices that the priests and priestesses receive. The parts of the animal and the exact amount of certain parts are often delineated, and in one case a penalty is specified for priests who take more than their share.[146] In the Hellenistic period, when priesthoods are regularly sold, we have cases of families accepting priesthoods in exchange for substantial privileges, including exemption from taxes; tax exemption was one of the incentives offered to attract buyers of a priesthood.[147] Some regulations include more detail than others when it comes to the privileges and responsibilities of cultic offices. At the city of Cos, for instance, inscriptions not only grant the priests the front seats at celebrations but also prescribe precisely what they are to wear. Most of what is granted to and also required of priests, however, seems to relate strictly to the life of the sanctuary.[148] Thus, when *LSCG* 154 A (from Cos) requires that 'the purity and purification ... be accomplished according to the ancestral and sacred laws', it would probably be a mistake to confuse these sanctuary regulations with the laws of the city in question.[149] There could certainly, however, be some overlap between these sanctuary regulations and matters that the state felt free to determine.

Priesthoods in ancient Greece fell into two groups: those that were hereditary and those acquired through sale, election or allotment. It appears that some priesthoods were deemed hereditary based on tradition and that

---

145 Johnson 1997: art. 285–86.   146 *LSS* 113, fifth-century BCE from Axos.
147 *LSAM* 13.19 from Pergamum and *LSAM* 71 from Cassosus.
148 See, for example, *Iscrizioni di Cos* ED 89, 177, 180, 215.   149 Lupu 2009: 42.

this right to inherit the office was, eventually, given legal recognition.[150] The two groups of priesthoods, however, cannot always be cleanly divided. The decree from Pergamum mentioned above (*LSAM* 13, dated to 133 BCE) grants hereditary rights to the family of the founder of the priesthood of Asclepius there, but the basis of this grant is not clear. In the case of the priesthood of Apollo at Gytheum, a first-century BCE decree (*LSCG* 61), which grants the priesthood of a sanctuary of Apollo to the family of Philemon son of Theoxenos, makes it clear that this privilege has effectively been bought by his having paid for the sanctuary's restoration. Philemon's descendants are to serve as the sanctuary's priests for eternity. Because the decision relates not just to one tenure of the priesthood but is to apply permanently, the document, published by the city, calls the decree a *nomos*. The sale of priesthoods extends as far back as the fifth century BCE, although the practice was not widespread and is best attested in Asia Minor.[151] Most of the relevant documents follow the structure and formula of a contract and grant the purchaser the office for life. They also typically contain the rules of the priesthood. One such record, *LSAM* 52 from the reign of the Roman emperor Trajan, records a sale conducted by the college of *strategoi* (generals), who refer to the conditions that the buyer agrees to as a *nomos* and describe how the sale of a priesthood of Asclepius should work. Elected priests were ordinarily limited to a specific term in office – generally either one year or the lifetime of the elected priest. A decree from Heraclea under Latmus, from around the turn of the eras (SEG 40.956), indicates that, after debate, the consultation of an oracle resulted in annual elections for the priesthood of Athena Latmia being chosen as the means of selecting priests rather than putting the priesthood up for sale. A priesthood could also simply be granted or allotted to an individual, though the evidence for this is not as abundant. One text (*LSAM* 79, from the first century BCE; location unclear) appoints a priestess for life and states that, after her death, the city will hold a lottery to select her successor.

As discussed previously classical Roman jurists placed priests, like magistrates, within the category of public law. According to Ulpian, such law consisted of '*sacra*, priests and magistrates', with *sacra* having to do with objects that belonged to the gods and rituals that were performed on their behalf or in their honour. There were plenty of rituals, however, carried out by private individuals, who could be thought of as religious officiants, and it is not always clear how Roman law distinguished between the public and

---

[150] Lupu 2009: 45.   [151] Lupu 2009: 48; see also Dignas 2002: 150–53, 251–71.

private sphere when it came to religious activities. Several distinctions had to be maintained simultaneously. These included distinctions between space for public rituals and space for those deemed private; between those who presided over what occurred in each type of space; between deities themselves, in terms of which deities were associated with the state; and between cultic acts for the public sphere and those acts utilized in the private sphere.[152] Although the Romans may often be touted for their religious 'tolerance', this tolerance did not apply simply to anything that might be done in private: 'Tolerance extended to those private observances that did not infringe upon public cult – cult acts undertaken by magistrates, performed in public spaces, directed to the gods of the community, and expressive of a shared zeal for the common good.'[153] This characterization of the 'public' as benefiting the common good shows up in the fifth century CE in the arguments of Augustine, Bishop of Hippo, where he relies on the legal distinction between public and private for the sake of distinguishing between the miracles of Moses in the book of Exodus and those of the Egyptian magicians.[154] What Moses did served the weal of the whole community and was, therefore, fully legitimate. The actions of the magicians served only themselves and were rendered suspect. In short, by serving the state, priests served the public good. What was done in private was only of interest to the 'state' if the public good, as understood by the political authorities, was threatened.

Religion and Wrongdoing

Crimes against the Gods and the Sacred

Crimes against the gods in the ancient Near East were part of a larger category that entailed crimes against a superior: kings and officials, as well as gods.[155] The death penalty was the most common punishment. The texts of the Hebrew Bible indicate that wrongs against the deity included witchcraft, apostasy, blasphemy and violation of the Sabbath law. In addition, there are laws in the Priestly Writings (mainly in Lev 18 and 20) that describe certain illicit sexual acts, such as incest, bestiality and what appears to be male homosexual intercourse as affronts to Yahweh. Death is required for most of these. One unusual wrong has to do with the so-called *molek*-offering; individuals are not to offer their children as sacrifices in such an offering. Scholars disagree as to whether the term *molek* identifies a type of sacrifice,

---

152 Ando 2006: 10.   153 Ando 2006: 10.   154 Ando 2006: 11–12.
155 On 'crime' see Chapter 9, this volume.

the god to whom the sacrifice is made or something else. In any case, the punishment is to be death by stoning, according to Lev 20:2–3. In that same text, however, the god Yahweh says that he will also 'cut him [the perpetrator] off from his people'. Since a punishment additional to death seems to make little sense, the idea may be that the god will prevent the sacrificer's line of descent from continuing.

Rabbinic law sees violations of law as being divided into two categories – violations against another human being and sins against God (*m. Yoma* 8:9). With regard to each, the rabbis argue that the process of *teshuva* (literally 'return') or repentance, alongside the acceptance of punishment and the experiencing of the Day of Atonement, can allow for forgiveness. In a sense, however, all crimes are seen as crimes against God in rabbinic law, since the legal system is conceived of as one transmitted by God to Moses. Even rabbinic injunctions are seen as quasi-divine.[156] Further, when the rabbis saw themselves as unable to rule on capital cases – in part because some governmental authorities would not allow them to and probably also in part because, with the destruction of the temple, the Sanhedrin ceased to operate and could no longer extend its authority to other Jewish courts – they state that anyone guilty of a capital offence, not executed by an earthly court, would nonetheless die in a manner befitting the crime committed.[157] Again, such offences were seen as crimes against God and, therefore, certain to be punished by God.

In Egypt, those who opposed the authority of the king, mediator between gods and men, were deemed to have insulted the gods and the world order. They were considered impious and sentenced to death. The punishment could be executed in a religious context, as suggested by the *Chronicle of Osorkon*, where rebels in Thebes were put to death by the high priest and prince Osorkon, and then burnt as an animal sacrifice.[158] In order to discredit them in future generations or in the afterlife, the rebels' names were banned in official documents and replaced by a negative epithet such as 'impious' or a negative version of their real name: 'Re hates him' instead of 'Re loves him'. In Greek propaganda from Egypt, state rebels were called the 'enemies of the gods' (*theoisin echthros*).

In ancient India, the Vedic rites were observed in a somewhat erratic manner and not, for the most part, under the compulsion or direction of

---

156 For example, Deut 19:17 is read so as to imbue rabbinic enactments with divine sanction (*Sifrei Deut* 190).
157 *b. Sanh.* 37b. On the authority of the Sanhedrin, see *b. Sanh.* 88b.
158 On the *Chronicle of Osorkon*, see Broekman 20c8.

a state or ruler. Nevertheless, intricate rules existed for the consecration and sanctity of the sacrificial space. Any violation of these rules had to be rectified ritually, or else one ran the risk of ruining the sacrifice itself. Following proper protocol in this regard, however, seems to have been mostly a matter of self-policing rather than legal enforcement. With the rise of temples in the fourth century CE, states and rulers became more invested in the patronage and preservation of specific cults at the temples they endowed. Laws governing offences against the temples, though, are uncommon. The Dharmaśāstra seems to have developed against a cultic background of Vedic ritual and evolved only slightly to make space for the different religious practices that arose in the early centuries CE. There are hints of change in some places, but it is really only in the medieval texts that temple rites are more explicitly accepted and temple-related religious practices discussed at length.

Some evidence from India points to certain individual offences having both secular and spiritual punishments, administered by the state and by the gods, respectively. Punishment from the latter would come in a spiritual fashion such as in the form of karmic retribution. For example, in a decree granting tax-free income to a group of Brahmins, a Pallava king from the fourth century CE threatens anyone who interferes in the agreement with state-imposed punishment and with being 'the lowest of men, tainted with five mortal sins'.[159] This combination of politically and religiously grounded law is also seen in the Dharmaśāstra. Even though the Dharmaśāstra may still be understood as essentially presenting a religious system, a distinction can be observed in how it handles particular legal issues, due primarily to the fact that many of its provisions derive from the more secular Arthaśāstra tradition. The latter attributes to the king a significant role 'in determining, applying and enforcing the principles of Dharma'.[160] There are times when the religious orientation of the one tradition and the more political orientation of the other appear to come into conflict. A text in the *Nārads Smṛti* states that individuals should not speak at a trial unless they are appointed to do so by the king, but as Lubin explains, 'the commentator cites a verse arguing just the opposite': 'One who knows the Sastra ought to speak whether or not he has been appointed. One who lives by the Sastra speaks with divine authority.'[161] According to Lubin, Asahaya, an early commentator on the *Nārads Smṛti*, harmonizes the two verses by imagining that a situation might arise in which court officials forget what the Sastra really means and render a verdict contrary to it. If there is a Brahmin present who recognizes the

---

159 Lubin 2007: 94.   160 Lubin 2007: 98.   161 *NSm* 3.1; Lubin 2007: 102.

error, he should speak up and support what he says with statements in the Sastra, 'because Sastra is indeed the speech of the gods'.

The understanding represented by Asahaya may reflect a line of reasoning found in aspects of ancient Near Eastern thought as well, although the two societies differed in actual practice. The desire embedded in each culture is that justice be done, and the belief in each is that the gods and the truth they reveal can be relied upon to ensure that just decisions are rendered. In the Near East, when courts had recourse to the oath or ordeal, they were in essence passing the cases before them on to the gods for ultimate resolution. The Hindu tradition, while still looking for truth from the gods, has built divine truth into the Sastra such that direct consultation of the divine realm is unnecessary. In the scenario envisioned by Asahaya, it is the Brahmins' responsibility to remind the courts of this divine truth and the role it can play in safeguarding justice within the process of resolving judicial disputes.

Various religious offences were prohibited in ancient Chinese law. We know, for example, from the Tang Code that officials could be punished for making mistakes in preparing for or performing sacrifices.[162] The theft of objects such as food offered to the gods in the sacrifices was, in all dynasties, an offence that could be committed by anyone, not only state officials. The Qin laws of the third century BCE punish any theft from the offerings made in official sacrifices, even though the theft should be of a single kidney worth one cash.[163] Another Qin law punished the digging up and appropriation of offerings used in royal sacrifices after they had been buried.[164] For the Han we have references in the sources suggesting that the theft of objects used in the state sacrifices or the imperial ancestral temple was a capital offence.[165] The Tang Code treats the theft of objects dedicated to the spirits in the great sacrifices as one of the 'ten abominations', calling it a 'great irreverence' (*bujing*). Although this classification shows that such theft was viewed as one of the most serious offences in the code, the punishment was exile, not death.[166]

Other practices are also forbidden in the extant evidence from ancient China. Certain types of magic and sorcery were punishable offences (discussed further below). The possession of particular books was prohibited in all dynasties. The reason for these prohibitions was the concern that such works might encourage dissatisfaction with the ruling dynasty. By the end of the Han period, the writing or possession of books concerned with divination

---

162 Johnson 1997: art. 67 and 70.   163 Hulsewé 1985a: 127 [D21].
164 Hulsewé 1985a: 128 [D23].   165 Watson 1961: 537; Hulsewé 1988: 172.
166 Johnson 1979: art. 70.

and the interpretation of prodigies or the like was proscribed.[167] This proscription was followed by later dynasties. For example, a Northern Wei decree of 485 CE declared that books of charts (of the heavens) and prophecies should be burned; any failure to do so would be a capital offence.[168] The Tang Code prohibited private individuals from possessing books dealing with the calendar, the sun, the moon or the stars, and those describing methods for the prognostication of good and evil.[169] The practice of astronomy was also prohibited. Again, this was motivated by the fear that astronomical readings of the movements of the planets could give credence to criticisms of the government or to the pretensions of usurpers. The Tang Code, following a tradition that seems to have started in the Jin dynasty (265–420 CE), imposed two years of penal servitude for the possession of astronomical instruments and the private study of the heavens.[170]

One other interesting prohibition from ancient China was that directed at the keeping of *gu* poison. Made from venomous insects and snakes, it was believed to have a particular (magical) potency in causing harm, its victims being certain to die. The poison was regarded as a species of illicit magic. The association between *gu* and magic makes its use sometimes difficult to distinguish from the practice of witchcraft, referred to as *wu gu*. Yet it seems that, from the time of the Han, the law distinguished between two offences, one termed *wu gu*, and the other the making or keeping of *gu* poison. The Han commentator Zheng Xuan (127–200 CE) cited a rule from the Han statutes on banditry (*zei lü*), according to which anyone who dared to employ *gu* against another, or taught or instructed another to use it, was to be beheaded.[171] The Northern Wei code of 431 CE contained two rules with a fairly clear distinction between the offences of making or using *gu* poison and witchcraft (*wu ku*). The code provided that, in cases of making *gu* poison, those responsible, both men and women, were to be beheaded and their houses burned. This case was distinguished from that of *wu gu*, for which the punishment was very different: drowning after a goat had been placed on the offender's back and a dog in his or her arms.[172] The Tang Code punished the making or keeping of *gu* poison with strangulation and required exile for those who lived in the same house as the principal offenders.[173]

Greek law, at least at Athens, dealt in different ways with different sorts of religious offences. In the case of misbehaviour at a religious festival, the offence could be prosecuted by a procedure known as *probolê*. The *probolê* was

---

167 Dull 1966: 400–407.   168 Jenner 1981: 30.   169 Johnson 1997: art. 78–79.
170 Johnson 1997: art. 78.   171 Hulsewé 1985a: 33 [2k].   172 Tongzu 1980: 223.
173 Johnson 1997: art. 262.

a vote of censure on the part of the assembly and did not bring with it the automatic imposition of a penalty. If the person who brought the *probolê* was successful in eliciting a vote of censure, he could then choose to bring a private action or public action.[174] This is the procedure invoked by Demosthenes in his prosecution, *Against Meidias*; Demosthenes charges Meidias with hitting him during the Dionysia festival and lists similar offences that have occurred in the past.[175] A second kind of offence concerned abuses of the god's property, and this was dealt with in a normal court. 'Theft of sacred things' (*hierosylia*) is known from various cases (e.g. Dem. 19.293). Those found guilty of *hierosylia* could be executed and, according to Xenophon were treated like traitors: death or exile, confiscation of property and denial of burial in Attica.[176] Finally, there is impiety (*asebeia*) which variously encompassed what people did (for example, violence against religious officials and breaches of sanctuary rules); what they did not do (omissions of sacrifices); and what they thought. This included vandalizing divine statues; interfering with sacred olive trees; assaulting religious officials; the performance of a sacrifice on the wrong day or by the wrong official; and not recognizing the gods that the city recognized but recognizing new gods.[177]

There were also laws in ancient Greek cities (so-called 'sacred laws', discussed above) relating to issues such as sacrifices, temple property, religious personnel, and the care and protection of sacred space. These laws could come from various levels of authority including federal leagues (controlling panhellenic sanctuaries); an individual polis; tribes and demes; and even private associations.[178] Legal jurisdiction to enforce the rules and punish violators was typically granted to officials of local sanctuaries. These individuals, in turn, were accountable to higher state or local officials.[179] For example, in a lengthy set of rules from the Amphiareion at Oropos, the priest of the sanctuary there is 'to compel the *neokoros* (sanctuary attendant) to take care of the sanctuary and of the visitors to the sanctuary according to the law'.[180] This 'law' would have included the other rules listed which dealt with potential offences (for example, theft of or damage to donated objects and sanctuary property, failure to pay required fees and violent acts); the role of the priest to judge these offences; the fines to assess; as well as regulations for

---

174 Dem. 21.23–28, 176–77.   175 Dem. 21.175–80.
176 Isocrates 20.6, compare RO 36. 13–14; Xen. *Hell.* 1 7.22.
177 Divine statues: Thuc. 6.27–29, 60–61; Andoc. 1 passim; sacred olive trees: Lys. 7; religious officials: RO 28B 24–30; sacrifice: Dem 59.116; the gods: Pl. *Apol.* (on the political dimensions of this charge against Socrates, see Gagarin 2013: 73–76).
178 Harris 2015b.   179 Aeschin. 3.18 with Harris 2015b: 57.
180 RO 27 and *LSCG* 69; Lupu 2009: 10.

the performance of incubation and the offering of sacrifices. Another fourth-century BCE inscription from Peiraieus, *LSCG* 36, instructs the demarch to fine those who violate certain religious rules according to 'the laws governing such matters' (*khromenon tois nomois*). The sanctuary officials in these cases would have been responsible to the city of Oropos in the case of the Amphareum and the deme of Peiraieus in the case of *LSCG* 36.

Sanctuary land was protected in particular ways in ancient Greek cities.[181] Boundary markers set forth rules prohibiting any private construction. A second-century BCE inscription lists imprecations and penalties for those who feed their cattle or cut wood on sanctuary land. Another states: 'Whoever leads ... or pigs or cattle within the lustral basins not for the purpose of sacrifice, they shall be liable to imprecations and shall be fined by the *hieropoioi*, the council, or the rest of the magistrates whatever fine each office is authorized to fine.'[182] Recurring issues include damage from fire; littering; unauthorized lodging and camping; and protection of 'trees and vegetation, water sources, movables, and animals'.[183]

According to Roman law there were essentially two types of sacred 'things' or objects; once considered sacred, an object could not be sold, given as a gift or even owned in the ordinary sense.[184] The first type (*sacer*) consists of those 'things' dedicated to specific deities: temples, land, statues and other objects. Such donations were usually made by the state or had to be approved by the state. A dispute concerning dedicated land relates to the famed orator, Cicero. After his exile, Cicero's house was burned and his chief opponent, P. Clodius Pulcher, had a temple dedicated to the gods there, presumably to prevent Cicero from ever reclaiming his former estate. When Cicero returned, he was able to reclaim most of his moveable property but not the land. He took his case to court, where he argued – not against the basic principle that land so dedicated cannot be reclaimed – but that the dedication was improperly performed.[185] The second type of sacred 'thing' (*res religiosa*) is land used for burial, which becomes sacred when the body is placed in its grave and is performed by a person approved for this task. Interestingly, there is ample evidence that tombs were still bought, sold and inherited, and scholars are undecided on how to explain these transactions. It may be that it was not the ownership of the actual tomb or land that was being sold but something else.

---

[181] Papazarkadas 2011.
[182] *LSS* 51 / SEG XLVIII 1037, Delia 180–166 BCE; Lupu 2009: 23.
[183] Lupu 2009: 25.   [184] Riggsby 2010: 207.   [185] See Stroh 2004.

Across at least three of the cultures discussed here – Greece, India, the Near East – we find beliefs that certain religious ideas were to be kept secret from the uninitiated and violations of this restriction were to be punished.[186] In Greece, one form of impious behaviour was to reveal 'the Mysteries', something that involved mock performance.[187] This was on par with other important cultic wrongs, including those that occurred when the wrong people carried out a ritual at the wrong time and in the wrong place. A provision in the Law Code of Manu from India states that Sudras, members of the lowest caste, were not to listen to recitations of the Vedas. Those caught doing so were to have molten lead poured into their ears – mostly likely a highly exaggerated punishment for the purpose of making a point. If Sudras did, in some way, come to understand something of Vedic teachings, they were not to tell anyone else, at the risk of having to drink boiling oil (*MDh* 8.272). According to the *Rgveda*, c. 1200 BCE, study of the Vedas, even the sounds of which were deemed to carry power, was reserved for members of the Brahman, Kshatriya and Vaisya castes who had been properly initiated.

We also have evidence from Mesopotamia for the secrecy of certain kinds of knowledge. For example, experts in cult rituals, omen interpretation, astrology, exorcism and other areas recorded aspects of their craft in written form and ascribed both secrecy and divine origins to these corpora.[188] Such knowledge could be described as the 'secret of the gods' and was protected through a variety of measures: 'placing admonishments on tablets that warned users not to show them to anyone, making users of a tablet take an oath not to disclose the contents, inscribing secrecy labels on tablets ... and finally attaching *Geheimwissen* colophons to restricted tablets'.[189] A Neo-Babylonian text mentions a similar restriction: 'The chief administrator of the Eanna temple said to Bēl-kāṣir, "Do not have the temple oblates recite tablets." If he has an oblate recite tablets, he will bear the guilt of an offence against the king."[190] Some scholars interpret the text to mean that Bēl-kāṣir, presumably a scribe, is to keep the contents of the tablets secret from temple oblates (a lower class of temple personnel who worked for the temple and

---

186 Egypt may also have had legal restrictions on secret religious knowledge, although the situation there is less clear; see Rossi 2004: 87–95. There is also some evidence for Rome in relation to the so-called 'mystery' or 'elective' cults.
187 Parker 2005: 65.   188 Lenzi 2008: 77–122.
189 Lenzi 2008: 379–83 adduces evidence from the Hebrew Bible for secret divine revelations in ancient Israel as well. The difference there, as he notes, is that a revelation's secret origins did not require it to be preserved from general dissemination. Such revelations were typically understood as needing to be proclaimed to all who would listen.
190 YOS 19 110; Beaulieu 1992; the text is published in Beaulieu 2000.

were entirely dependent on it for their sustenance). Others argue that the scribe is not to allow oblates to do the recitations that accompanied particular ritual performances, most likely because they were not considered ritually fit or pure.[191] In any event, the restriction of particular religious knowledge and texts to a few privileged specialists is evident.

Purity and Pollution

The concepts of purity and pollution may be best known from Greece, but they were also important in ancient Israel, India, Egypt and perhaps to a lesser extent Rome.[192] They were categories that were regulated by law in each culture and that could exert a powerful influence on the lives and world view of the members of these societies. Only those who were 'pure' or 'clean' could interact with the divine and, thus, participate in certain rituals, prayers and other activities. Each culture also had rites that allowed individuals to be ritually cleansed and moved from a polluted state to one of purity or cleanness.

In ancient Greece, the terms most commonly associated with purity were *hagnos* and *kartharos*, while pollution was usually termed *miasma* or *musos*. Polluted individuals would bring the wrath of the gods upon themselves and their community. In some cases, it was possible for such individuals to undergo purification rituals in order to rid themselves of the pollution and thereby forestall the imposition of divine punishment.[193] Rituals could also be required when one wished to enter sacred space in order to protect that space from pollution. Activities that could bring pollution within the confines of a shrine included birth, death, sex, defecation and business transactions. A number of inscriptions disclose additional measures that could be taken to protect the purity of sacred areas by forbidding entry with pack animals, footwear, goods produced from pigs and even women on occasion.[194] There is also evidence for multiple other causes of *miasma*, which could preclude entrance to a shrine: childbirth or miscarriage, along with any contact with the fluids and tissue that accompany them; abortion; menstruation; sexual

---

191 Magdalene, Wells and Wunsch 2019: 88–89.
192 The concepts of purity and pollution are not as well known from other cultures. In China, for example, the Tang Code exhibits only some sense of these ideas: it requires officials concerned with the preparations for some sacrifices to observe periods of abstinence for a certain number of days. Abstinence always involved refraining from sexual relations, but, in the case of the great sacrifices, it also involved not performing a number of official duties such as the signing of documents or participation in legal trials (Johnson 1997: arts. 67–70).
193 Bendlin 2007: 178.   194 *LSCG* 82.5–6; *LSCG* 109; and *LSCG* 124.18–20.

intercourse, even with one's own spouse; eating particular animal products; contact with a corpse; and bloodshed.[195] The necessary purification for each typically required individuals to wait a prescribed amount of time and, in some cases, wash themselves, before attempting to enter sacred space.[196] The basic principles seem to have applied across the sources, although the specific requirements and punishments could vary from place to place.[197]

The act that could result in the worst type of pollution was homicide. The ancient Athenians recognized three different types of homicide, and each had different consequences in terms of pollution.[198] Intentional homicide brought on permanent and ineradicable pollution; the only remedies for the community were to execute or exile the wrongdoer.[199] Some scholars have claimed that views along these lines, such as Plato's, hark back to an earlier time and that concerns about pollution were actually fading in the fourth century BCE as Athens' legal institutions grew in strength and stability.[200] But pollution continued to be invoked, especially in relation to many acts that were not even deemed illegal (for example, having sexual relations, giving birth and having contact with relatives who had died naturally), as the long purification law from fourth-century Cyrene shows.[201] In light of this, there seems to be little reason to deny that beliefs about pollution continued to influence reactions to homicide in a legal context into the fourth century BCE and beyond and that they helped to articulate and support 'the state's attempt to monopolize the use of legitimate force'.[202]

The second type, involuntary homicide, resulted in pollution that could be purified, should the one who committed the act be pardoned by the victim's family and undergo the necessary purification rituals; otherwise, the wrongdoer had to remain in exile.[203] Justified homicide did not result in any ritual pollution whatsoever.[204] In sum, there were clearly concerns about pollution resulting from homicide in Athens and efforts to curtail its spread: those accused of homicide were banned from shrines and sacrifices; homicide trials

195 See the text from Thyateira in Malay and Petzl 2017: 25–26.
196 The amount of time varies between inscriptions. In SEG XXVIII 421 (Arcadia, Megalopolis, c. 200 BCE), for example, the times are nine days after childbirth, forty-four days after an abortion, seven days after menstruation, three days after eating the meat of goats or sheep; after sexual intercourse, a person must bathe but is not required to wait beyond that (Lupu 2009: 205–13). See Lupu 2009: 15 for a list of inscriptions.
197 For more on the differences among these rules in ancient Greece, see Osborne 2011.
198 Harris 2012a: 293.
199 Dem. 23.22; Pl. *Laws*, Book 9; *Ath. pol.* 57.3; and Antiphon 5.13. Discussion in Parker 1983: 112–14 and Harris 2015a: 15–19.
200 Parker 1983: 125–30.   201 RO no. 97.   202 Harris 2015a: 14.
203 Dem. 23.72 and 37.59.   204 Dem. 23.74 and *Ath. pol.* 57.3.

took place in the open air; and defendants in exile for involuntary homicide 'stood in a boat offshore and delivered [their] reply to the charges without setting foot in Attica'.[205]

Extensive regulations on purity and pollution from ancient Israel come in the Priestly Writings. As noted above, it is unclear if and when these rules were put into widespread practice; at the time of their initial composition, they may have functioned more as priestly ideals than enforceable law. Instead of purity and pollution, biblical scholars usually speak of the concepts of 'clean' (*ṭāhôr*) and 'unclean' (*ṭāmē'*). The former concept is similar to the Greek idea of normality, while the latter designates what in the Greek world would be considered polluted. A third concept has to do with what is 'holy' (*qādôš*). This referred primarily to the divine sphere, but humans could also be considered holy including priests (by means of divine appointment and ritual inauguration); Israelite citizens (by means of obedience to Yahweh's dictates); those who took special vows; and Levites who served the cult but not as priests. A variety of objects could be made holy as well. That which was polluted could not come into contact with the holy without consequences. All forms of pollution could affect the shrine, Yahweh's dwelling place, arousing his anger and leading to his departure from the community. It was this eventuality that most of the purity regulations seem designed to prevent.[206]

Cases of pollution (or uncleanness or impurity) in the Hebrew Bible may be divided into those that were permitted, because they arose in the course of natural and necessary life activities, and those that were not, because they were deemed preventable.[207] Permitted pollution came from contact with a human corpse; eating the meat of certain animals; touching the carcass of certain animals; contracting certain skin lesions; touching a house or item with certain types of fungal growths; a seminal emission; menstruation; childbirth (specifically the discharge that accompanies childbirth); and abnormal genital secretions in both men and women. In some cases, those polluted in this way could contaminate others: menstruating women passed the pollution to objects, which, in turn, contaminated those who touched them; individuals polluted by semen, however, did not contaminate others. All those affected by permitted pollution could pollute sacred space and sacred objects. The typical remedy was to remain in the polluted state either

---

205 Bans from shines and sacrifices: Dem. 2c.158; Antiphon 6.35–36; see also *Ath. pol.* 57.4 and Soph. *OT* 236–42; open-air homicide trials: Antiphon 5.11; exile for involuntary homicide: Dem. 23.78; Pollux 8.120, quotation from Harris 2015a: 12.
206 Klawans 2001 and Hundley 2011: 35. 207 Klawans 2001.

one day (e.g. seminal emission); seven days (e.g. touching a human corpse, birthing a male child); or fourteen days (e.g. birthing a female child) – then bathe oneself and wash one's clothes. Other ritual acts, including sacrifices, could be required as well. Prohibited pollution affected those who delayed the necessary purifications required for permitted pollution; priests contaminated by contact with the corpse of a non-relative; and those who committed particular sins such as adultery, incest, bestiality, homosexuality, wrongful worship and homicide. In some texts, this type of pollution contaminated the land. No remedy for this existed; once the land's allowance for pollution was full, Yahweh would punish the people and force them to live in exile. In other texts, removing the transgressor was sufficient to abate the pollution. In the event of an accidental homicide, the perpetrator lived in a city of asylum until the death of the high priest, after which the pollution was believed to have been purged. In the case of unsolved murder, the elders of the town closest to the site where the victim was discovered had to break the neck of a heifer (perhaps the meaning is to decapitate it) by a flowing brook and wash their hands over the heifer while proclaiming their innocence; this was to ensure the purification of the community (Deut 21:1–9).

In rabbinic law, *ṭumah* and *ṭohorah* (the nominal forms of *ṭāmē'* and *ṭāhôr* mentioned above) are used to connote the state of being ritually 'impure' and 'pure' respectively. A person or object that contracts *ṭumah* is said to be, 'ritually impure' and thereby unsuited for certain holy activities until undergoing purificatory actions, which usually include the elapse of a specified time period and immersion in a ritual bath. The noun *ṭohorah* describes a state of ritual purity that qualifies the person or object in that state to be suitable for holy purposes. Whereas biblical law confines much of this system to the temple and the priests who operated there, rabbinic law, following the Pharisees of the Second Temple period, encouraged all Jews to maintain the distinction between these states.[208] Moreover, the rabbis (following Pharisaic precedent, as can be seen in Matthew 15:2 and Luke 11:38) instituted additional categories of impurity. This included the well-known 'impurity of the hands', for which a ritual of hand washing was developed before eating and prayer (b. Ḥul. 33b).

One finds some similar purity concerns in other ancient Near Eastern societies, especially that of the Hittites. In the Hittite kingdom, those who served as priests and worked in any way with the food destined for the gods were required to be 'pure'; they were to have washed themselves, be

---

208 Cohen 1987: 159.

'trimmed' with respect to their hair and nails and be dressed in 'pure garments' (CTH 264 art. 2).[209] Pigs and dogs are singled out as animals that should not be allowed to enter the room where the gods' food was being prepared. The rationale given in the text is that gods and men think alike. A servant who goes to his master will have bathed and put on clean clothes, and, just as a human master will be aggravated by a servant who fails in this regard, so too will the gods. Temple personnel must also bathe following sexual activity and before returning to temple service (CTH 264 art. 14). As for life outside the temple, the Hittite Laws recognized pollution as coming from bestiality and incest, and there were varying levels of seriousness within each category. For example, a person could be put to death for having sex with a cow, sheep, pig or dog (Hittite Laws 187, 188 and 199) but not with a horse or mule (Hittite Laws 200a). Those guilty of bestiality were not to come into the king's presence, nor could they ever become a priest. Illicit relations with family members included those with one's mother and daughter (Hittite Laws 189); others were allowed under certain circumstances. Purification rituals could be performed for animals (Hittite Laws 163), although the reasons for requiring such rituals are not clear.

According to the Indian Law Code of Manu, there are twelve bodily substances that can cause impurity or pollution: 'body oil, semen, blood, marrow, urine, faeces, ear-wax, nails, phlegm, tears, discharge of the eyes, and sweat'.[210] The rules apply mainly to Brahmin householders, and various means of purification are provided. At *MDh* 5.106 the 'agents of purification' are listed as 'knowledge, austerity, fire, food, earth, mind, water, smearing with cow dung, wind, rites, sun, time'.[211] For example, after urination or defecation, a man is to put earth on the penis and the anus, sip water and then apply water to those same body parts. Touching or carrying a human corpse can require a purification period from a half day to three days, depending on one's relation to the person who had died. The pollution acquired through sexual intercourse or through touching a menstruating woman or a woman who has just given birth can be cleansed by means of bathing. Biblical texts (Lev 15:18–23) also require bathing following these actions. Another point of similarity between Manu and the Hebrew Bible has to do with involuntary emissions of semen at night. In the case of a Brahmin student, he is to 'bathe, worship the sun, and softly recite three times the verse: "May the virile strength return again to me".'[212] A combination of time and water is

209 Edition in Miller 2013: 244–65.   210 *MDh* 5.135 (Olivelle 2004a: 95).
211 Olivelle 2004a: 93.   212 *MDh* 2.181 (Olivelle 2004a: 37).

necessary in the case of an Israelite man: he is to wait until the evening and then bathe in order to cleanse himself.[213]

Ancient Indian law also specified particular actions ('sins') that could require individuals to purify themselves. These are actions that, according to the Law Code of Manu, had to be atoned for through prescribed penance. In some cases, the language of purification is used to describe the beneficial result of the penance. For example, the penances for all of the following are described as having purifying effects: the killing of a Brahmin unintentionally (*MDh* 11.90); sex with an elder's wife (*MDh* 11.104); a Vedic student who breaks his vow of chastity (*MDh* 11.124); and the killing of certain animals (*MDh* 11.142).

In Egypt, temple staff had to observe certain rules and execute purification rituals prior to service and before entering holy places. The 'Book of the Temple' is a recently discovered (but not yet fully published) text written in Middle Egyptian and probably dating to the Middle Kingdom; it describes vows of priestly purity, which are also extant in Greek translation. The handbook remained popular even in Roman times. The *Gnomon of the Idios Logos*, a set of rules from Emperor Augustus that were later revised, contains several instructions for priests taken over unchanged from an older Egyptian compilation of temple laws.[214] These include rules about cultic purity, including the prohibition on wearing woollen garments, having long hair, sacrificing heifers that have not been inspected and branded and allowing priests who are sick to perform cultic service. Failure to follow the regulations concerning priestly purification was punishable. With the advent of Christianity, priestly purity rules were adapted in various ways. In Coptic extra-biblical literature, for instance, priests were prohibited from spitting in the sanctuary; in pharaonic Egypt, on the other hand, spitting was part of magical rites used to curse, heal or bless.

Magic and Sorcery

Several ancient societies (especially the Near East and Egypt) accepted the idea that one could invoke divine powers through ritual words or actions for either harmful or beneficial effects. Beneficial magic was typically used to counter the power of harmful magic, to appease angry gods, or to curse those who were perceived as the legitimate enemies of a city or state. The ideas underlying beneficial magic and the procedures accompanying its practice generally differed little from the basic religious conceptions and practices of

---

213 Lev 15:16 and Deut 23:11–12.   214 Sippel 2022.

a given society.²¹⁵ Terms that refer to harmful magic are often translated as 'sorcery' or 'witchcraft'. Such magic was deemed harmful to society and could be dealt with through the legal system. Its practitioners could be brought to court, charged with crimes and punished, often with death. The rituals involved in beneficial magic were usually similar to those of harmful magic. One of the crucial distinctions was whether the magic was viewed as benefiting society or not. If those in power deemed the actions to be detrimental to their rule or to what they believed was good for society, the practitioners could be charged and punished.

In the ancient Near East, anyone, even slaves, could attempt to perform magic; the most basic act was that of a curse.²¹⁶ The Laws of Ur-Namma (art. 25), for example, punish a female slave who curses someone acting in the name of her mistress. A proverb from the Hebrew Bible also assumes slaves can curse: 'Do not slander a male slave to his master, lest he curse you and you become guilty' (Prov 30:10). According to the 'Great Hymn of Shamash', known mainly from Neo-Assyrian copies, 'the curse of the people' will catch a merchant who defrauds his customers. A curse was essentially a petition to the gods to punish someone. They could act on the curse or ignore it, but once spoken, the curse was active and could be executed by the gods at any time. Ordinary folks who attempted magical acts often appealed to their family gods.²¹⁷

Professionals had additional means available to them. A number of Mesopotamian texts distinguish between the *āšipu* and the *kaššāpu/kaššaptu*.²¹⁸ The former was a priest (the term is often translated 'exorcist') who received advanced training and was usually part of a temple cult. The latter is consistently employed as a pejorative term, whether of men (*kaššāpu*) or of women (*kaššaptu*). It typically identifies someone who is acting outside the accepted priestly groups and who might receive payment for performing magic. The *kaššāpu* and *kaššaptu* are the ones who are most often sanctioned in legal texts. Both types of professionals were believed to have special knowledge about the divine world and special relationships with particular deities and thus to have real power. The *āšipu* and the *kaššāpu/kaššaptu* used the exact same techniques.²¹⁹ Particular differences, however, stand out. First, the *āšipu* practised defensive magic, to protect or clear someone from the effects of sorcery, while the *kaššāpu/kaššaptu* practised harmful magic. Second, the latter performed magic in secrecy, but the *āšipu* performed his

---

215 Beaulieu 2007.   216 Kitz 2014: 349–69.   217 Kitz 2014: 369.
218 Kitz 2014: 370–426.
219 Farber 1995: 1898.

rituals in public and with the imprimatur of the cult. Third, an *āšipu*-priest was always a man, whereas the one practising harmful sorcery was most often depicted as a woman. The male term *kaššāpu* is only attested in combination with its female counterpart, and all references to those accused of practising sorcery are to women.[220]

When it seemed that an individual had been the object of sorcery (presumably at the hands of a *kaššāpu/kaššaptu*), there were several avenues of recourse: one could seek protection through apotropaic objects; ask directly for divine aid; or take the *kaššāpu/kaššaptu*, if known, to court.[221] One could also gain the assistance of a professional, such as an *āšipu*. The textual evidence shows that Mesopotamians sought out such help for various problems including illnesses and ghosts.[222] To counter harmful magic, an *āšipu* could help one recite an incantation in an attempt to reverse the ill effects of the magic and punish the *kaššāpu/kaššaptu*. The incantation series *Maqlû*, a set of eight tablets from the early first millennium with dozens of incantations, contains some recitations that take the form of legal claims made before the divine court: 'I have called upon you Gods of the Night ... because a witch has bewitched me ... I am unable to rest day or night ... Stand by me Great Gods and give heed to my suit. Judge my case and grant me a decision' (*Maqlû* I 1–14). It also includes spells that one could recite, apparently over a figurine of one's tormenter, for the sake of inducing the gods to kill the *kaššāpu/kaššaptu*: 'May she (the *kaššaptu*) die! May I live! (*Maqlû* I 19).[223]

Harmful magic is dealt with in several legal texts. According to the Laws of Hammurabi (art. 2), if one man accuses another of sorcery but is unable to substantiate the claim with evidence, the defendant in the case must undergo the river ordeal. Such accusations were, therefore, taken very seriously. Several law collections single out sorcery for special sanction and stipulate the death penalty.[224] The Middle Assyrian Laws (art. 47) present a situation in which someone has heard, from an eyewitness, about an act of sorcery performed by either a man or a woman. The text says that the one who has heard about it must inform the king, who will then summon the eyewitness and – along with an *āšipu*-priest – interrogate him; the practitioner, if found guilty, will be put to death. Sorcery was seen as a menace to society,

---

220 Abusch and Schweber 2011: 5 and 7.   221 Westbrook 2006.
222 Geller 2016 (on illnesses) and Scurlock 2006 (on ghosts).
223 Translations adapted from Abusch 2015. Although there are some letters that refer to accusations of sorcery, the only surviving trial record where the defendant is charged with sorcery is badly broken (see Westbrook 2006: 50 n. 13).
224 Neo-Babylonian Laws ch. 1; Exod 22:17; Deut 18:10–11; see also Hittite Laws 44b and 111 and Telepinu Edict art. 50.

especially to those in power, and kings and their administrations were intent on using all means at their disposal, including the legal system, to keep it at bay.

Ancient Egyptians resorted to magical practices in a variety of legal contexts. When a victim was not able to prove his right in civil courts and had gone to the authorities in vain, he could seek divine help. From the Old Kingdom onwards, people wrote letters to the dead, invoking their help in all kinds of matters including health problems but also in cases of injustice. These letters affirm a belief in the power of the dead (considered an 'effective spirit', *3ḥ*) to influence the course of events and, in Greco-Roman times, even to destroy humans or to intervene on behalf of the supplicant with the infernal tribunal. The letters were left behind in tombs, which, for that purpose, were called the 'noble mail box of Osiris' in Egyptian, or the 'deposit box (*puxis*)' in Greek. An alternative practice developed in Late Period and Ptolemaic Egypt, when letters were sent to the gods, in particular to Thoth, 'the Lord of law' (*p3 nb ḥp*), who was considered the chief judge of the Egyptian pantheon. Through these letters people ask to be saved or express hope that the offender will be punished. Such letters were probably hidden in a safe or sacred place. These letters remind one of Greek prayers for justice found in Egypt, such as the famous 'curse' of Artemisia, which is in fact a prayer to Oserapis found in the Memphite Serapeum, asking for the punishment of her husband because he has not given a proper burial to their child (*UPZ* I 1). These letters and prayers are to be distinguished from Greek and Roman curse tablets in that they mention the name of the supplicant, contain additional notions of supplication and provide some grounds for appeal.[225]

Magic and magical practices are an inherent part of Egyptian religion: for the Egyptians there is no fundamental distinction between religion and magic; they are compatible terms. 'Official' magical rites, notably execration rites, are performed by priests for the benefit of the gods, the country and the king. Heka was the Egyptian force representing magic and was at the same time deified, being the patron of magic and medicine. Heka was part of the natural cosmic order (not of the mundane order): a generative force or a kind of energy that, in order to preserve the cosmic order (*ma'at*), had to be channelled through magical rituals and recitations. Hence, magical practices were not prohibited in Egyptian society. The only trial for sorcery is related to the harem conspiracy under Ramesses III, where magical spells had been

---

[225] On curse tablets more generally, see Tomlin 2010.

pronounced and inscribed figurines and potions had been used by the conspirators. They were condemned for sorcery against the king, not for sorcery as such, and were executed or forced to commit suicide. The traditional magical practices were continued during the Roman and Christian centuries, despite imperial sanctions (e.g. the aforementioned official ban under Septimius Severus) and despite Christian condemnation of 'pagan' practices.

Conclusion

At the outset of this chapter, law and religion were described as separate realities or forms of life, and this overview has identified a wide range of areas where the extant evidence shows fairly extensive interaction between the two throughout the ancient world. Given the important role of religion in ancient societies' world views, one might expect to find a significant amount of overlap with these realities. Practices such as the use of oaths to secure contracts or decide trials and the patterning of religious rules after legal formulations bear this expectation out. We also find, however, important points of separation. Several societies exhibit concurrent but separate lines of jurisdiction, with cultic officials presiding over cases related to offences that affected temple or other religious affairs, and state officials handling other situations. Even conceptually, some ancient societies distinguished, at least at certain times, between what might be considered state law and more religiously oriented law: *dharma* vs *artha*, or 'things of the king' vs 'things of Yahweh'. It is not always clear why there is overlap in certain circumstances and separation in others. In the area of judicial decision-making, it seems evident that most of these cultures wished to have some version of a lie-detector test, and the notion of the divine court (via rituals, such as the oath or oracle) presented itself as a ready-made solution. With other matters, though, one senses a tension between law and religion (for example, when secular and religious punishments are both imposed) and a mix of competing priorities. Which should take precedence? There is a begrudging acknowledgment by each reality of the need for and influence of the other. Even certain anti-monarchical biblical authors were willing to recognize political-legal authority in the form of a king but sought to subject it to the authority of what they perceived as authentic religion (Deut 17:14–20).

Within the interactions described above, law appears to have drawn on the religious form of life principally for the sake of authority and legitimacy. In a number of ancient societies, law either comes from, or is mandated by, the gods. Even Greek rulers and officials, including those in classical Athens, sought divine endorsement for new laws at times. The use of religious rituals to ensure the enforceability of contracts or to identify the proper verdict in a trial constitutes another appeal for authority. This was a way to throw the weight of the gods behind the law and to coerce legal actors into obedience. In contrast, religion borrowed from legal reality for the sake of effectiveness. It needed the apparatus of the state to ensure that important rituals were carried out, and it relied on legal language and categories (e.g. *nomos*) to enforce its norms. Thus, one can observe mutual reliance between these two forms of life, but the relationship shifted over time and in different ways. Changes occurred in southern Mesopotamia such that certain aspects of the legal system began to rely less frequently on cultic procedures and to give greater weight to what we would consider ordinary legal mechanisms; nevertheless, the legitimation that was necessary for political and legal authority still appealed to the gods. At Rome, law was separated from religion for a time but developed an especially complex relationship during the Christian (and particularly the sixth-century CE Justinianic) era. Despite these developments, though, it remains manifestly the case that across the ancient world law and religion persisted as closely connected social realities, betraying little of the stark separation that characterizes these two facets of culture in many modern societies today.

7
Legal Procedure

Lead Author: PATRICK OLIVELLE

Contributors: MICHAEL GAGARIN, CAROLINE HUMFRESS,
GEOFFREY MACCORMACK, JOSEPH G. MANNING
AND BRUCE WELLS

Introduction

In modern Western jurisprudence, laws are generally classified into 'substantive' and 'adjectival'. Substantive laws govern the everyday life and transactions of individuals and groups; whereas adjectival laws deal with matters related to substantive law, such as how violations of substantive laws are to be adjudicated and punished. In *The Concept of Law*, H. L. A. Hart calls the former 'primary rules' and the latter 'secondary rules' and subdivides 'secondary rules' into three: rules of recognition (how laws are enacted and come to be known); rules of change (how laws are emended or abrogated); and rules of adjudication.[1] This chapter deals with the third kind of secondary rules dealing with the procedures to be followed in adjudicating disputes and lawsuits arising from the breach, or the perceived breach, of primary rules.

When there is a dispute between private individuals or groups, or when an individual is accused of a crime by the state, a legal system requires a process by which a just resolution or verdict can be reached. Justice must be seen to be done. At an anthropological level, once we move away from face-to-face small-scale communities, where the leader's wisdom and judgment would always be sufficient and respected, a system of justice requires transparent and accepted rules for adjudicating disputes and accusations. These rules of adjudication are what we mean by legal procedure. First, these rules confer on certain individuals the power to adjudicate, constituting them as judges. Second, they constrain the way judges and other court personnel conduct a court case, prescribe the kinds of evidence that are valid and acceptable, and

---

[1] Hart 1961: 91–99.

point out how evidence should be assessed and the manner in which decisions are reached. In the ancient world, especially in preliterate societies, these rules were rarely formalized or written down, and thus it is difficult to identify specific rules of procedure, except when these are reflected in later written material. In many of the societies under consideration, moreover, there were no specialized treatises dealing purely with legal procedure. It has to be deduced from existing records of court cases, legal codes, jurisprudential texts and other material. India and China are exceptions.

Legal procedure (*vyavahāra*) is the most developed aspect of ancient Indian jurisprudence. Legal codes from the last three centuries before the common era deal with some aspects of procedure, such as witnesses. From at least the first century CE, we have sections of legal codes and from about the sixth century CE we find specialized codes exclusively devoted to the examination of legal procedure. Here, the entire court procedure is said to have four feet: plaint, plea, evidence and verdict. Each of these feet is subjected to minute description and further classification.[2] Texts from about the middle of the first millennium CE, such as those ascribed to Yājñavalkya, Nārada, Bṛhaspati and Kātyāyana, develop a technical and scholastic vocabulary with regard to the various elements of court procedure.[3] For example, the plaint has several terms depending on what aspect is highlighted: the initial charge is *āvedana*; when revised by the plaintiff and written down, it is *bhāṣā*; when it is viewed within the context of logic as the probandum, it is *sādhya*; when it is viewed within a system of debate and argumentation, it is *pūrvapakṣa*.[4] A central feature of legal procedure was the 'titles of law' (*vyavahārapada* or *vivādapada*), enumerated in Manu's law code to be eighteen in number (Figure 7.1).[5]

The Chinese legal system of the Qin dynasty (third century BCE) paid particular attention to the conduct of criminal investigations and trials, as opposed to civil disputes among private individuals. There were detailed rules for the examination of the 'crime scene', for the making of accusations and for the way in which the trial should be conducted. The judge was expected be careful to extract the truth from the accused and witnesses in successive examinations and cross-examinations and resort to torture, in the

---

2 Olivelle and McClish 2015.
3 For the texts, see *YDh*, *NSm*, *BṛSm* and *KātSm*, and more generally, Olivelle, Brick and McClish 2015.
4 There is a detailed discussion of legal procedure in India, including translations of major primary sources, in Olivelle 2016a.
5 As discussed in Chapter 5, this volume.

Figure 7.1 A page from one of the earliest manuscripts of Manu's law code (© Patrick Olivelle)

form of beatings with the stick, only if the person under interrogation proved recalcitrant, was found to be lying or obdurately refused to confess. Rules further provided a mechanism for appeal.[6] The Qin procedural system was essentially inherited and operated by the succeeding Han dynasty (206 BCE–220 CE), as we know from the laws of 186 BCE, which placed a similar emphasis upon the requirements for careful interrogation and the eliciting of the truth.[7] Much later, the Tang Code of the seventh century CE drew upon and refined the procedural system of the earlier dynasties. Matters such as the jurisdiction of the courts, false accusations, the conduct of a trial and the application of torture, the treatment of doubtful cases and the determination of punishment were regulated in detail.[8]

Although we do not have a specific collection of written laws governing legal procedure from the ancient Near East, its judicial systems followed particular rules and were not subject to the whims of their respective monarchs. Ample evidence reveals that government officials were subject to the rule of law: including, for example, the Edict of Irikagina from the twenty-fourth century BCE and the prosecution of public officials – such as Kuššiharbe, the mayor of Nuzi in the Late Bronze Age – for abuse of power. Even kings were considered subject to the law, given that their mandate from

6 Hulsewé 1955: 6–7.   7 Barbieri-Low and Yates 2015, vol. I: 111–86.
8 See Johnson and Twitchett 1993.

the gods was to enact justice throughout their lands. In practice, kings could become highly involved in judicial affairs, if they chose to do so and were able, therefore, to manipulate certain outcomes in favour of their own interests. There were limits, however: serious manipulation had to be carried out at least under the guise of legality. In addition, all human judicial authorities were believed to be subject to the divine court. There is evidence from nearly all regions and time periods of courts putting the final decision of a trial in the hands of the gods through the use of various procedures, including oaths, ordeals and oracles.

Egypt has a long documented history of written law and of legal procedure, although no systematic 'code' of rules of procedure survives until the so-called Hermopolis Legal Code: a document of forms and procedural rules written in the third century BCE, some of which, however, goes back to the early first millennium BCE.[9] It is clear that written complaints and promissory and assertory oaths were an important part of legal procedure since the times of the Old Kingdom. The process is outlined in literary texts of the Middle Kingdom (c. 2000 BCE). But there are two broad periods in Egyptian history where the evidence allows us to reconstruct procedure and legal institutions with some certainty: the New Kingdom (c. 1550–1069 BCE) and the Hellenistic (Ptolemaic), Roman and 'Byzantine' eras (c. 332 BCE–400 CE). This does not mean that there was uniformity in procedure during this time, but simply that we have good evidence to outline the institutions in these periods. The workmen's village at Deir el-Medina, western Thebes, during the New kingdom (especially between c. 1295 and 1065 BCE) provides an abundance of material to study how private disputes were resolved.[10] The use of oracles to identify a thief, for example, is a common procedure at Deir el-Medina and presumably in other places as well.

In Greece, an informal legal procedure is portrayed in the poems of Homer and Hesiod: litigants can bring their disputes to a public hearing in the *agora* (central public space) presided over by respected members of the community, variously identified as elders, kings, leaders, etc. Community members also were present and made their views known. In most cases a decision was reached in the end which had the support of the community; though it was not binding, the loser's only alternative to accepting it was to leave the community. In the classical period, law and procedure varied among city states. For most, we have no evidence, but in Sparta, judicial duties were divided among the two kings, twenty-eight elders and five ephors. The kings

---

9 See Jasnow 2003a, 2003b and 2003c; Manning 2010.   10 McDowell 1990.

judged some family matters and cases involving public roads, the elders judged the most serious cases where the penalty was death, exile or disenfranchisement, and the ephors apparently had authority over all other cases.[11] At Gortyn in Crete, a judge heard cases. For a few cases the law prescribed a specific decision according to the testimony of a witness (in a dispute whether a man was free or a slave, a witness testifying that he was free automatically decided the case) or a sworn oath (in a dispute over property in a divorce, if the wife swears that the property is hers, then it is hers). For all other cases, the judge listened to the pleadings of the two litigants and then decided on his own.[12]

In classical Athens a group of 'jurors', usually numbering between 200 and 500, decided cases.[13] Litigants pleaded their own cases, though they could pay a speechwriter to write their speech for them, and in some cases, one or more friends might share the allotted time. Litigants could present depositions from witnesses and almost any other sort of evidence they wanted, except for hearsay testimony, which was banned in most circumstances; but they had to present all their evidence first at a preliminary hearing, so that their opponent would know it before the trial. The jury voted right after hearing the two pleadings and whoever received the most votes won the case.[14]

In the city state of Rome, the administration of justice was based on the principle that individuals with a 'right' (*ius*) should have a remedy: the ability to pursue their claims through some kind of formalized process.[15] The provisions of the Twelve Tables (c. 451–449 BCE) – the first written and authoritative collection of law at Rome – were focused on legal procedure in the sense of defining when, how, and under what circumstances Roman citizens could activate the system in order to seek formal legal redress. Under the Republic and early Empire, the praetor's edict, published annually by successive urban praetors in Rome until c. 130 CE, was structured for the main part according to a specific type of civil trial procedure: beginning with the summoning of a defendant, then covering various available remedies, before turning, alongside other matters, to the enforcement of judgments after trial. An emphasis on procedure is in fact a fundamental characteristic of Roman legal science.[16] As Peter Stein notes, however: 'The Romans themselves did not separate procedure from substantive law and the relevant texts were

---

11 See MacDowell 1986: 123–50.   12 See Gagarin and Perlman 2016: 136–39.
13 Scholars are in disagreement whether to call these jurors or judges. In this chapter both terms are used.
14 See Todd 1993: 77–163.   15 See Gaius, *Institutes*, Book 4, written mid-second century CE.
16 See Capogrossi Colognesi 2015: 137.

scattered through the whole *corpus iuris civilis*.'[17] Extra-legal sources, such as the speeches of Cicero (106–43 BCE) and the writings of Pliny the Younger (61/2–c. 113 CE), in addition to documentary and epigraphic material, provide crucial information that has been used to reconstruct broad Roman frameworks, as well as detailed procedural rules.

The history of Roman legal procedure has conventionally been divided into three somewhat overlapping periods. The first, the *legis actiones* (actions in law), is the oldest type of (formal) Roman civil procedure; the trial was divided into two stages, the first taking placing before a magistrate and the second before a lay judge (*iudex*) who may have been selected by the (citizen-) litigants themselves. Cases had to be brought according to a fixed set of words and actions. If a case could not be expressed according to the relevant fixed set of words, then it could not be heard; conversely, if the fixed set of words were spoken incorrectly, or formalized gestures and actions performed incorrectly, then even a legitimate case would collapse. The second type of Roman civil procedure is known as 'the formulary system', and it probably began to develop in the late third or early second century BCE. It is usually associated with the courts of the urban praetor (*praetor urbanus*) and the praetor for cases involving 'foreigners' (*praetor peregrinus*) at Rome. It was formalized c. 17 BCE by a series of Augustan imperial enactments: the so-called *leges Iuliae iudiciariae*, alongside another statute known as the *lex Aebutia* (Gaius, *Institutes* 4.30). Under the formulary system, the Roman praetors did not decide legal cases themselves; rather, they clarified the exact nature of any given dispute so that the citizen-judge who was subsequently appointed to hear a given case – in a second phase of the proceedings – could do so according to a written formula (a 'statement of the issue to be tried'). To give a relatively simple example of a formula issued by the urban praetor: 'Let Titius be judge. If it appears that the defendant ought to give ten thousand sesterces to the plaintiff, let the judge condemn the defendant to the plaintiff in that sum; if it does not so appear, let him acquit.'[18] The Roman formulary system was thus based on a two-phase, remedy-based, procedure. Unlike the *legis actiones*, however, the written *formulae* provided by the praetors at Rome were designed to be flexible and responsive.[19] The formulary system thus assumed access to a high level of

---

17 Stein 1999: 57.   18 Crook 1967: 77.
19 As Crook 1967: 77 notes: 'probably the plaintiff, with expert advice, chose the one most appropriate and if necessary asked for modifications to it that would more precisely meet his contentions, and the defendant would make objections and ask for other modifications'.

Introduction

legal expertise on the part of both the praetors at Rome and the parties to the suit. It effectively gave rise to the development of a new branch of Roman civil law, known as the *ius honorarium*, as well as new forms of legal protection such as the praetorian interdict.[20] The third type of Roman civil procedure rose to prominence under the later Empire and is known as *cognitio*: an 'inquiry' or 'inquisition' handled entirely by the emperor or a government official, or individuals delegated under imperial authority, and as such capable of bureaucratic review via appeal.

The periodization of these three distinct phases within Roman civil procedure to some extent mirrors the political and administrative history of the city of Rome itself: 'The *ordo iudiciorum* or "way the courts worked" of the Republic and earliest Principate gave way, though gradually, in Rome to the legal procedure of the *cognitio extra ordinem*, whose judges were the emperor and his delegates.'[21]

In the specific area of Roman 'criminal law' (public offences that were held to affect the community as a whole), the first separate court was established in the city of Rome in 149 BCE.[22] Before this, public offences were mainly heard by assembles of the whole (voting) population.[23] The establishment, by statute, of a distinctive 'criminal' court structure in Rome, the so-called *quaestiones perpetuae* (standing inquiries), was thus a relatively late development in Roman legal history. In the Roman provinces the relationship between state and local jurisdiction was complex: for example, the newly discovered *lex Irnitana*, 'a copy of a model "town charter" prepared for *municipia* in Spain', records numerous and detailed rules on procedures for litigation, many of which seem to be direct reflections of the practice at Rome.[24] By the later Empire, the vaguely defined contours of the *cognitio* ('*extra ordinem*') had developed into a specific set of rules and bureaucratic procedures that spanned the empire as a whole and covered both 'civil' and 'criminal' spheres.

As we explore the legal systems of the ancient world, some comparative questions and themes will be significant. These include, but are not limited to, the following:

---

20 Nonetheless, despite the relative sophistication of the formulary procedure: 'The system as a whole seems to have been designed to work best as a state-sponsored form of arbitration. That is, it assumes a certain level of cooperation from both parties to resolve their dispute and a basic agreement that the mechanism is a legitimate one' (Riggsby 2010: 116).
21 Crook 1995: 56.
22 For further discussion of the complexities in referring to 'criminal law' in ancient contexts, see Chapter 9, this volume.
23 Riggsby 2010: 196–97.   24 Metzger 2015: 274.

- Impartiality of judges.
- Right of defendant to know the charges before trial.
- That no punishment can be assessed without a governing law.
- Equality before the law, even though there are distinctions made between equal treatment in terms of procedure and equal treatment in terms of punishment.
- General distinction in lawsuits between 'public' and 'private'.
- Delays permitted for pleading and trial.
- Retrial of cases and the appeal process.
- Discouragement of frivolous lawsuits.

Constitution of the Court

By 'court' we understand both the constitution of the personnel, including the judge(s), who have jurisdictional authority to adjudicate lawsuits and the physical location or the legal space where those proceedings take place. In all likelihood, however, dispute resolutions on the ground by private individuals were most often carried out by leaders of local communities or arbitrators agreed to by the parties to a dispute; few of these would have reached the courts. The legal procedures followed in these informal settings and the physical locations of such proceedings do not tend to be captured by the extant material. Most of our sources deal with cases brought before state officials, and these probably represent only a small fraction of the disputes between individuals and groups within those societies.

Courts, Judges and Court Personnel

In complex societies, such as those we are examining, disputes and accusations of misconduct would have been resolved in different fora, including informal ones constituted by family groups, villages and religious elders. Not all legal orderings of the ancient world, however, formally recognized these legal fora or assigned them (various) gradations of authority. As already noted, much of the information we get concerns the state courts administered by central authorities.[25]

In the ancient societies we are surveying, there was no strict separation of executive/administrative and judicial functions or personnel. In most, such as the Near Eastern, Chinese, Indian and imperial Roman, the ultimate

---

25 See Chapter 5, this volume.

judicial power rested with the king or ruler, who normally delegated this authority to other officials acting in the capacity of judges. Many of these judges probably had other administrative and/or military functions, besides adjudicating lawsuits. The exception is Athens where a jury system prevailed: in classical Athens, as in most cases for the Republican and early imperial city of Rome, 'judges' in civil (private) and criminal (public) cases were not necessarily individuals with legal expertise. The Indian, ancient Near Eastern, Egyptian and Chinese systems provide for a distinct judiciary at least at the highest levels, with distinctive titles given to those who presided over courts; this was also the case in (the city state of) Gortyn. Yet, in most of these systems, with the possible exception of the Indian, those wielding judicial authority also carried out other administrative functions. Under the Roman empire, judicial powers were exercised by civil and military administrators, acting within their specific spheres of jurisdiction. An imperial magistrate's judicial powers could also be delegated to others, whether lay or professional (as in the case of a *iudex datus* or *iudex pedaneus*). A papyrus dated 124 CE, for example, refers to a former *strategos* (a regional official) being delegated by the Prefect of Egypt to judge a case concerning the performance of state liturgies (P. Fam. Tebt. 24).

Indian jurisprudence, however, recognized various venues where lawsuits and disputes could be resolved and assigned them increasing levels of authority, thus permitting appeals from lower (technically called *pūrvasabhā*) to higher venues (*uttarasabhā*). Sources point to as many as fifteen such venues, such as villages, professional or mercantile groups, and cities. The standard number, however, is five: family; guild; company or association; appointed official; and the king. Only the last two are formally constituted courts, and the information provided by the extant sources pertain only to them. Sources do not give any information as to the constitution of the lower venues for dispute resolution, or to the procedures followed by them – but in all likelihood they were presided over by leaders of the various groups.

We have two distinct but overlapping traditions in the ancient Indian jurisprudence with regard to the constitution of royal courts. The one connected with the tradition of political science and governance represented by Kauṭilya's *Arthaśāstra* (first century CE) envisages a separate bureaucracy of justices called *dharmastha* with broad authority to adjudicate lawsuits initiated by private individuals and groups.[26] A bench consisted of three such justices, who were assisted by several court officials and employees.

26 Olivelle 2016a: 200, comparing Kauṭilya's vocabulary with that of Manu.

It appears that these justices also had a limited number of other bureaucratic functions outside the courtroom; their permission, for example, was required before a man becomes an ascetic or a widow gets remarried. The second tradition is connected with the deeply Brahmanical legal system of Dharmaśāstra, a textual tradition encoding religious, civil, and criminal laws and rules of legal procedure. In it, judicial authority is explicitly placed in the king, an authority he could – and in practice usually did – delegate to professional judges. The latter are expected to be Brāhmaṇas: the social class associated with ritual and religious authority. Judges are frequently referred to as *prāḍvivāka* (interrogator) perhaps indicating that originally this official was responsible for interrogating the litigants and the witnesses. Sources give the qualities that a judge should possess: learned in a variety of disciplines, born in a good family, impartial, honest, kind, even-tempered, energetic and without greed. If a Brāhmaṇa with these qualities cannot be found, the king is advised to appoint even a Kṣatriya or a Vaiśya possessing such qualities. The court officials include a scribe (*lekhaka*); bailiff (*sādhyapāla*), who also acted as a marshal to carry out court orders such as summons; an accountant (*gaṇaka*) useful in cases involving financial matters; and at least three assessors called *sabhya*. The assessors were trained in law and assisted the judges in evaluating the evidence, especially the testimony of witnesses, reviewing the applicable laws and arriving at a just verdict. It is likely that the assessors had legal training; they are, for example, held responsible for any miscarriage of justice in a court case and not the judge, who probably lacked legal training and depended on the assessors for advice on the law and the proper evaluation of evidence. We hear of assessors being punished for malfeasance including bribery. Dharmaśāstras from about the middle of the first millennium CE, however, show that elderly and experienced merchants and traders also participated in court proceedings to give advice on commercial matters coming before the court. Indian sources divide courts into stationary and mobile. The former are the main courts in major population centres presided over by state-appointed judges. The mobile ones usually travelled to remote locations and villages. The transportation costs incurred by court personnel had to be borne by the litigants.[27]

From the earliest times in China – as in India and the ancient Near East – the authority to decide lawsuits was deemed to be part of the general authority to govern vested in the ruler. That authority, however, was delegated by him to officials who exercised it in the discharge of their general

---

27 See KAŚ 3.1.17–33.

administrative duties. For the first period under consideration, that extending from the beginning of the Western Zhou to the end of the Spring and Autumn (twelfth to fifth centuries BCE), the practice appears to have been for the ruler, when appointing a minister or official, to specify his duties in the document of appointment. Among these duties might be the power to hear lawsuits and apply punishments within the general area of the appointee's jurisdiction. Such judicial authority was simply an aspect of the minister or official's general executive authority. Even in the later period, no clear separation between judicial and administrative functions developed. During the Warring States (c. 480–221 BCE), with the increasing centralization and bureaucratization that marked political development in individual states, the territory under the control of the ruler became subdivided into administrative districts, each governed by an official appointed by and accountable to the ruler. This official, as part of his general duty of administration and responsibility for the maintenance of law and order, judged criminal and civil lawsuits that arose within the area under his jurisdiction. Even before the establishment of the Qin empire (221–206 BCE) and the Han empire (206 BCE–220 CE), we know from judicial records excavated from tombs that in the states of Chu and Qin the minister in the central government with judicial responsibilities operated an office staffed by a large number of minor officials, such as scribes and clerks, who had the double function of alerting the minister to the cases that should be tried and then organizing court proceedings. For the Han we have considerable information on the complex layers of authorities concerned with judicial investigation. In the post-Han period, there is little information on the judicial powers and duties of officials responsible for local administrations, though it is likely that the basic pattern established under the Han continued. We do know, however, that at the level of the central government a more complex and sophisticated system for the administration of justice evolved.

In both the Southern (317–589 CE) and Northern (386–589 CE) dynasties, a gradual change occurred in the way the judicial powers of the emperor came to be exercised by officials of the central government. Three distinct agencies concerned with judicial matters developed in this period: the ministry of justice or board of punishments (*xingbu*); the censorate (*youshitai*); and the supreme court (*dalisi*). Among the duties of the ministry of justice was that of inquiring into offences committed by officials in the capital and cooperating with the other judicial agencies in the investigation of serious offences. The censorate was responsible for the impeachment of officials who had committed offences. The supreme court, an elaboration of the judicial function of the Han official termed *tingwei*, was responsible for the hearing of 'doubtful' cases (cases involving offences committed by officials or other high-ranking persons, in many instances referred from the local authorities) and for the review of capital cases. Local authorities no longer had the final decision in cases that required the imposition of the death penalty. Implementation of capital punishment required ratification by the throne after confirmation of the correct interpretation of the law by the supreme court. The court had experts on its staff trained in the law. The same system, based on the Northern Qi (550–577 CE) model, was followed by the Sui (581–618 CE) and Tang (618–907 CE) dynasties. The ministry of justice (or board of punishments) checked the accuracy of cases referred to it by the supreme court or other administrative organs in the empire. It also cooperated with the censorate and the supreme court in the investigation and sentencing of the most important criminal cases. The censorate, apart from impeaching delinquent officials, also undertook, in cooperation with other departments of the central government, the prosecution and hearing of cases brought by disadvantaged persons alleging an injustice. The Supreme Court was the final court of review for cases referred to it from district and provincial administrations. These cases included those in which the offender had been sentenced to exile or death. After consideration by the court, they were forwarded again to the board of punishments, which, in conjunction with other departments, considered the proposed sentences and, if necessary, revised them, submitting death sentences to the throne for final ratification.[28]

In the ancient Near East, judicial systems, like administrative systems, had three basic levels of authority: royal/central, provincial and local. Officials at all three levels were authorized to hear and decide a wide range of legal disputes.[29] Cases could be sent to higher courts, with the king as the pinnacle of human justice. Over all levels of judicial decision-making, including that of the king, stood the divine court. In Egypt also documentary evidence suggests that a hierarchy of courts developed over time, but we are ill informed about how they interrelated. There certainly were local courts centred around temples, but in smaller places disputes were probably resolved by village headmen.[30]

As in India, the systems of the ancient Near East also take the king to be the ultimate judge over the entire judicial system; he could intervene in any case he wished. Most cases, however, were presided over by other officials.

---

28 Johnson and Twitchett 1993: 133–34, 138.   29 Westbrook 2005.
30 For developments during the Ptolemaic era, see Manning 2010: 165–201.

A court could be constituted by a single government official, but the common practice was for judicial panels to consist of more than one individual. We do not know the precise qualifications necessary to wield judicial authority other than that a person had been granted, at least in theory, such authority by the king. There are, however, instances of government officials (military, administrative – at all major levels of the hierarchy); local councils or 'assemblies' (made up of city elders or a collection of free men); religious officials; other temple administrative personnel; merchants' associations and men who carry the title 'judge' deciding legal disputes. Various combinations of these personnel often served together on a judicial panel. 'Judges' can be identified simply by that title or by a longer title such as 'judges of the king', 'judges of (city name)' or 'judges of (temple name)'. It appears that, in most periods, those labelled as 'judge' held other positions as well; serving as a judge, therefore, was not their sole occupation.

Scholars of the ancient Near East still debate whether the term 'judge' identifies primarily a profession or simply a function. In general, because there was no clear separation between the administrative and judicial branches of government, part of the regular duties of administrative officials was to hear and decide legal disputes when cases were brought before them.[31] In the Neo-Assyrian period (tenth-seventh centuries BCE), for example, we do not have information about even a single case being adjudicated by a 'judge'; those who decide cases are administrative officials of assorted ranks. For the most part, the evidence leaves us in the dark as to the precise distinction between officials granted the title 'judge' and those identified by their administrative title (e.g. 'governor'). A clearer distinction seems to be evident in the Neo-Babylonian period (seventh–sixth centuries BCE) when those who achieve the status of royal judge ('judge of the king') appear to be professional judges who held their position permanently. Several, in fact, retain their position as royal judge despite changes in king and even changes in imperial power (e.g., from the Babylonians to the Persians). There is no evidence of formal legal training for becoming a judge. Some scribes who worked on behalf of judges are eventually promoted to the position of judge. This sort of rise within the administrative/judicial hierarchy was not due entirely to merit, since these individuals typically came from prominent families, some of whose members held the position of judge previously. Qualifications for judges, apart from those whose administrative positions that brought with them judicial responsibilities, are unclear but likely included social respect

---

31 Wells 2020.

due to the individual's perceived wisdom and positive moral standing. Temple officials and temple-related bodies were typically involved in judicial matters only when temple interests were somehow at stake in the dispute.

Across the Near Eastern material, evidence for other court officials does not come in every historical period and, when it does, it offers little specificity.[32] Neo-Sumerian (twenty-first–twentieth centuries BCE) records refer to the *maškim*, probably a function like that of a court recorder. Other periods attest to individuals, probably administrative officials (such as the Old Babylonian *qabbā'um* and the Neo-Assyrian *bātiqu* or *bātiqānu*) whose responsibilities included investigating government officials for misconduct. It is unclear whether these individuals were an official part of the judiciary. Other officials (the Old Babylonian *redûm* and the *manzatuḫlu* from Nuzi) are associated with helping the court carry out certain orders, such as the summoning of defendants. Scribes must have worked on a regular basis for courts of all periods, but they are only rarely given formal titles related to their judicial work. The *ša pān dēnāni* ('the one present at court cases') from the Neo-Assyrian period may be the best example of such a scribe. Finally, both the Neo-Assyrian and the Neo-Babylonian periods attest to the *sartennu* and *sukkallu*. In the Neo-Assyrian period, these officials were two of the king's closest advisers and the ones most often attested as deciding cases in this period. Officials with these titles served, during the Neo-Babylonian period, as the supervisors or chief judges of the royal court ('judges of the king'). Some court officers collected fees, such as the *maškim* in the Neo-Sumerian period. These fees probably went towards the revenue of the royal administration. They are not attested in all periods.

In the Old and Middle Kingdom periods of Egypt (third – second millennium BCE), a court known as the 'Six Great Houses' existed, about which we know very little. The term for court during the Old and Middle Kingdoms was *djadjat*, but it appears to have gone out of use. During the New Kingdom (sixteenth – eleventh centuries BCE) the 'Great Courts' were located in urban centres. Occasionally the court is called 'the Thirty', whose members were high-ranking state officials or priests. Some places, such as the important and well-documented workmen's village at Deir el-Medina in western Thebes, had their own local courts, known as the *qenbet* (council) and made up of eight to fourteen important persons from the village.[33] Court sessions were probably public, usually held in front of the main temple gate of the town.[34] Judges were not 'professionally' trained in law. Men with the title 'Royal

---

32 See Démare-Lafont 2000b.　　33 McDowell 1990.　　34 Van den Boorn 1985.

Scribe' were the key to the technicalities of the law, including the format of legal documents, and they played a key role in representing the state in trials and in maintaining written records. The trial record of a case conducted at the end of the second century BCE, from Asyut Middle Egypt, specifies that the court was composed of three priests from the local temple and a state official known as the *eisgogeus* (introducer) in Greek.[35] He probably functioned as a representative of the state in the trial.

The Greek data from Gortyn (Crete) indicates that a single judge (*dikastas*) presided over cases. In classical Athens, in contrast, there were between two hundred and five hundred – or more in certain high-profile cases – *dikastai* who acted as judges/jurors and decided an entire case, with no separate presiding judge. The jury system is specific to Athens, and we see no evidence that is comparable in scope in other legal systems of the ancient world – although a selective jury-system was used at Rome in the standing criminal ('public') inquiries of the late Republic and Principate. In Athens various officials supervised court cases but were not directly involved in the trial. There were probably one or more clerks and a few other assistants. In the first stage of Athenian private cases after 403 BCE, the dispute was first sent to a public arbitrator. There was also a specialized court, the Areopagus, which heard cases of homicide and certain religious crimes, and several other special courts for homicide. We find the term *dikasterion* in many inscriptions, and there is no need to doubt that these courts also had many judges. There is some evidence for large courts in Greek city states outside Athens. In Athens, private cases for less than ten drachmas were tried by the 'Forty' and not subject to transfer (*ephesis*) to another court.[36]

The judges in Athens took a judicial oath.[37] It contained four main clauses. The first is the one most frequently mentioned by Attic orators: 'I will vote according to the laws and decrees of the Athenian people.' The second clause was to hear both sides, accuser and defendant impartially. The third clause was a promise to vote with one's most just judgment. This was interpreted two ways: on the one hand, to make an honest vote, that is one that was not influenced by favour or enmity towards either party, and on the other hand, to use one's most just judgment in cases where the law did not give clear

---

35 BM EA10508,2 www.britishmuseum.org/collection/object/Y_EA10508-2; accessed 06/09/2022). Further discussion in Manning 2012: 113–14; Allam 2008; and Manning 2003b: esp. 823 and 831.
36 The 'Forty' was a board of administrative officials, four from each of the ten tribes (*Ath. pol.* 53.2).
37 Dem. 21.34, 42, 177, 188, 211–12. Further discussion in Harris 2006b.

guidance. The fourth clause was the second most frequently cited: 'I will vote only about the charges in the indictment.' The indictment (*engklema*) was the document submitted by the accuser when he initiated proceedings. He had to give his full name: name, patronymic and name of deme; the full name of the defendant; the name of the procedure he selected (this was important for the official who received the charge so he could determine whether the case fell within his jurisdiction or not); and the specific charges expressed in the language of the substantive part of the relevant law he was following. The court did not make a general judgment about the character of the defendant.

The Roman civil procedural system is complicated both by the three distinct periods of its legal history and by the fact that both archaic and classical procedures consisted of two stages. As already noted, the first stage of the 'ordinary' procedure of the late Republic was conducted *in iure* before a magistrate who was a state functionary; while the second stage, *apud iudicem*, took place relatively informally before a 'judge'. Although the individual who presided over the second stage is called 'judge' (*iudex*), he was actually a private and lay individual often without any legal knowledge or experience, possibly chosen from an 'album' of names by the parties to the dispute themselves, specifically for that trial, but authorized by the magistrate. The extent to which the formulary system extended beyond Rome to the provinces is controversial. In any case, under the Roman Principate and later Empire it is the so-called *cognitio* ('*extra ordinem*') procedure that dominates in the extant sources. This creates a corresponding focus on the imperial official who oversaw the proceedings. Those who acted as imperial magistrates, such as the provincial governors, did not necessarily have any kind of legal education or expertise, but they were assisted by advisers (*adsessores*). These advisers were also sometimes referred to as *consiliarii* and may have been grouped into small advisory councils that formed part of the magistrate's (personal) office staff. Under the *conventus* system of the earlier imperial period, provincial governors and their staff were expected to travel throughout their provinces, administering justice in larger cities on specific days fixed by the governor in advance. A famous bilingual – Latin and Greek – inscription, dated 216 CE, records the emperor Caracalla acting in a similar capacity: deciding on a local legal case 'on circuit' at Antioch, supported by a team of *consiliarii*.[38] During the later Empire, however, a Roman magistrate's office staff was fixed to the locality (and the 'office') rather than to the individual. A late Roman magistrate's legal advisers,

---

38 SEG XVII 759; see further Crook 1995: 91–95.

moreover, were appointed by the state and were salaried. Thus, when a given magistrate's term of service ended and he moved on, the office staff would remain in place, thereby providing continuity and institutional memory.

In ancient systems such as those of China and the ancient Near East, where judicial functions were part of the normal administrative duties of officials, the court costs were borne by the state. In other systems, such as we see in the Indian material, the cost of running a court was borne by the litigants themselves, thus encouraging most litigants to settle their disputes in informal settings or by private arbitration. Court costs and fines levied against losing parties must have been a source of considerable income to the state. Indian sources indicate that travel costs of court officials and wages for court employees had to be paid by the party that loses the case: 'Wages for the men are one-eighth. Provisions for travel are assessed according to the prevailing prices. The losing party has to pay both these' (KAŚ 3.1.17–33). It is unclear whether this applies to all courts or only the mobile ones that travelled to villages. It appears, however, that the fines and penalties imposed on the litigants, especially on those who lose their cases, were used to defray court expenses. In classical Athens, both sides paid a small court fee in private cases, but the loser had to reimburse the winner for his share. There was no fee for cases valued at up to 100 drachmas; up to 1,000 drachmas, the fee was three drachmas; and over 1,000, thirty drachmas. In certain public cases the plaintiff had to pay a fee, although the amount of the fee is not stated. There was, however, a penalty for bringing frivolous lawsuits. If an accuser brought a public case and either did not gain one-fifth of the votes or did not bring the case to court after it was approved at the *anakrisis*, the accuser had to pay a fine of 1,000 drachmas and lost the right to bring public cases in the future.[39]

Legal Space

Today the term 'courtroom' probably brings to mind the image of an imposing building in which judges, court officials and lawyers work on criminal and civil lawsuits. Law is physically located within the formal legal space of the courthouse. In the ancient societies we are surveying, however, there is limited evidence of separate structures set aside solely and specifically for the purpose of adjudicating lawsuits. In all likelihood, legal proceedings were generally carried out in public spaces, whether they were temples, city gates, central fora or public buildings. There is some evidence that such

---

39 See Harris 2006a: 405–22.

spaces were publicly identifiable, so that people could go to the 'court' to seek redress.

In India the most common term used for the location of a high court sanctioned by the king is *sabhā,* which is the same term used for the formal audience hall of the king, and which may have doubled as a court when it was not used for other purposes. Another term for a court is *adhikaraṇa* or *dharmādhikaraṇa,* which may indicate any administrative building used to hear cases rather than one dedicated specifically for this purpose. Yet it appears that some of these buildings may have been identified as courthouses, because we hear of people 'going' to a *sabhā* or *adhikaraṇa* to present a case or to request judicial intervention. Unlike in other ancient societies, temples or other religious structures are not mentioned as locations for court proceedings, perhaps because public temples became widespread only well into the common era. Some sources, however, indicate that a building meant specifically for court proceedings was built within the fort: 'In the middle of the fort he should construct a separate building provided with water and trees and in its eastern section prepare a courthouse (*sabhā*) facing the east and endowed with all the proper attributes' (*BṛSm* 1.45–46).

We have some (later medieval) sources for physical courtrooms in ancient China. During the Tang dynasty (618–906 CE) and probably earlier too, the setting of the court was designed to be as intimidating as possible to the offender. Situated in the magistrate's official compound, probably next to the prison, the courtroom consisted of a raised section on which was placed the tables of the magistrate and his assistants, around which was the area the attendants and constables stood. The offender (in criminal cases) was brought in from the prison, made to kneel before the magistrate's dais and then interrogated under the threat of beatings from the constables standing over or near him.[40]

For most periods of the ancient Near East, in contrast, we have no references to actual buildings where those with judicial authority heard cases. The extant documents typically indicate that one or more of the litigants simply went or appeared 'before' judges or other officials. When a location is designated, it is usually a temple or a temple gate, although such a location did not necessarily mean the involvement of priests or temple officials. This changes, however, in the Neo-Babylonian period, when occasional texts begin to mention the 'house of judgment' (*bīt dīni*), the first reference coming in a text from the 27th year of Nebuchadnezzar II (578 BC). In a literary composition extolling the virtues of that king, for example, he is

---

40 van Gulik 1956: 50–58.

said to have 'built anew the house of judgment' in Babylon. It cannot be completely ruled out, however, that, at times, the phrase connotes whatever location the judges handling a given case may happen to be. In ancient Egypt also, trials were held in public and usually in the forecourt of a temple or in front of a gate often called 'the place of giving justice'.[41]

There is likewise limited evidence for physical courthouses (*dikastērion*) in ancient Greece, although archaeologists have identified several structures in the Athenian *agora* as court buildings, dating to different periods. The main one is a square portico, open in the middle. It had a raised platform from which litigants would speak and seating, probably benches, for the several hundred judges/jurors (*dikastai*). Buildings that served as the offices of officials who were involved in litigation could function as courts. This would include the Athenian Stoa Basileios for the *Basileus*, which has been securely identified.[42] The building where the Council of 500 met has been identified, as has the Metroon (the record office).

The Roman case, again, is complex not least because of the three distinct – but overlapping – periods with regard to civil procedure. As noted above under both the *legis actiones* and the formulary procedure, proceedings were carried out in two stages. With respect to the formulary procedure, the first stage before the *praetor* probably took place in an audience hall in his residence, but the second stage could be held anywhere with the plaintiff summoning the defendant to meet at a specific place and time.[43] By the late Empire (i.e. from the late third century CE), most civil and criminal trials were heard before a magistrate – either a civil or a military official – probably in an audience hall or room within his official residence. In 331 CE the emperor Constantine ordered that legal proceedings before magistrates had to be heard in public; intended as part of an imperial ideology of 'transparent' (provincial) government, Constantine's 331 edict can also be read as implicit evidence that closed civil hearings – held within the magistrate's 'private chambers' – were the norm in practice.[44] Criminal cases under the classical and postclassical periods alike, however, were frequently held outdoors with large crowds in attendance. As Brent Shaw argues:

> The Roman state consciously intended its punishments to be public and strikingly visual precisely in order to achieve the terror-effect that was to provide the desired deterrent. The public trials staged by Roman governors

---

41 See Van den Boorn 1988; Manning 2012.   42 See Shear 1971.
43 See Bablitz 2007; de Angelis 2010.
44 *Theod. Cod.*1.16.6 (Constantine, addressed 'to the Provincials' and posted 1 November 331 CE). See also *Theod. Cod.* 1.12.1 (Constantine).

were calculated to be preventative spectacles, visual sights that were meant to startle: an ekphrasis of administrative power and of undisguised coercion so riveting that it was further developed in internal pictures of the mind.[45]

Roman criminal hearings were effectively a kind of public theatre and entertainment, designed to project a specific ideology of state power.

Jurisdiction

Given the different levels of courts recognized by many of the legal traditions of the ancient world, we can expect their jurisdictional authority to vary. In all the systems we are examining, with the exception of non-monarchical polities such as Athens and republican Rome, the king is the highest judicial authority with the widest jurisdiction.[46] All appeals to higher authorities end with the decision of the king or his court. Broadly speaking, the king's jurisdiction was limited to the territory he controlled – even though within that territory he might (in ideological, if not practical, terms) exercise total jurisdiction with regard to all disputes, persons and locations. The jurisdiction of lower courts was limited either to a designated geographical area or to particular individuals or groups.

In ancient India the case is mixed. Some lower courts, such as family, by which is probably meant an extended family unit, and guild, exercised jurisdiction over its own members, irrespective of the region where they resided. The jurisdiction of others, such as village and city courts, were geographically limited; they exercised jurisdiction only over people residing within demarcated geographical areas. Related to jurisdiction is another issue central to the Indian legal system: the court and the litigants have to identify the laws under which the trial is to take place – the rule of recognition in Hart's scheme. This is significant in India because the system recognized different laws applicable in different regions and in different social groups. There was no single law code applicable everywhere and to everyone. We have an interesting example recorded in a medieval text, but which probably attests to a long-standing legal custom. A man from a tribe called Ābhīra is brought to court accused of adultery. He admits all the evidence provided to the court but tells that he should not be punished because the law in his own tribe permitted sex with someone else's wife. He is acquitted.[47]

The limitation as to geography is clearly evident in ancient China, where the state bureaucracy was divided into territorial units. We have seen that the three lower levels of courts – commanderies (*jun*), districts and towns/

---

45 Shaw 2003: 534.   46 See also Chapters 5 and 6, this volume.
47 Further discussion in Lubin 2015.

villages – had jurisdiction over increasingly smaller areas. Courts with more limited jurisdiction were overseen by the higher court, for example, district courts by the administrator of the commandry to which they belonged.

For an ancient Near Eastern court to have jurisdiction over a dispute, it typically had to have subject matter jurisdiction over the issue at stake and in person jurisdiction over at least one of the parties involved in the dispute.[48] This meant that the secular (non-temple) courts handled most matters, with higher levels of authority becoming involved when a matter went beyond the borders of local officials. Temple officials could hear disputes that involved only temple personnel and temple concerns (e.g. theft of temple property). Non-temple and temple officials presided together over cases connected with both temple and non-temple personnel or interests.

Classical Roman jurists, writing under the Principate, derived the Roman legal concept of jurisdiction (*iurisdictio*) from *ius dicere*: the power to speak law (*ius*), in other words to administer justice. This specific power could only be held by magistrates with *imperium*. *Imperium* (from the Latin *imperare*, to command) was the central concept in Roman public law and was ranked by degrees: 'so that a consul had greater *imperium* than a praetor, and the emperor (*imperator*) had *imperium* greater than that of any magistrate'.[49] In classical and postclassical Roman jurisprudence, *iurisdictio* – the power to administer justice – was understood to be conceptually subordinate to *imperium*; there could be no *iurisdictio* without some degree of *imperium* but both, subject to certain limitations, could be delegated. Any given magistrate's *imperium* and hence their *iurisdictio* could also be subject to specific financial and territorial restrictions. The *imperium* of a provincial governor, for example, could only be exercised within their given province. Hence their *iurisdictio* could normally extend only over those persons who had the appropriate domicile – a question that the governor himself was expected to decide upon. By the later Roman empire, the jurisdictional authority of imperial officials could be exercised in numerous different settings: from the summary hearings of military officers, financial officials and other kinds of imperial bureaucrats to the various audiences and courtroom tribunals presided over by imperial magistrates and their delegates.

48 Démare-Lafont 2000b.   49 Johnston 1997 93–94.

Preliminary Court Proceedings

Civil and Criminal Cases

In modern jurisprudence the distinction between civil and criminal cases is basic to how cases are filed and litigated. This modern distinction does not hold good for the legal systems of the ancient world. The very meanings of 'civil' and 'criminal' may be inapplicable in many contexts. In India, for example, cases such as assault and rape, which would be considered criminal in contemporary legal systems, are subject to private litigation; the state filed no charges and acted simply as an impartial judge.

Although the modern distinction between civil and criminal cases may not be applicable to the ancient world, many systems, nevertheless, recognized with varying degrees of specificity the distinction between private litigation and public ('state') prosecution of certain types of conduct. For example, in the ancient Near East the difference between private/civil and state/criminal procedures appears to consist only in the penalty: corporal punishment is allowed in criminal cases but only fines in civil cases. The state and government officials have a vested interest in the former, for suppression of crime is one of their major concerns. The procedures of the two forms of litigation generally parallel each other, even though some legal systems take the one or the other as the paradigm for describing rules of legal procedure. In India and Rome, for example, legal procedure is described in the context of private litigation, while in China criminal prosecution by the state appears as the locus for discussing procedure. There are also differences among the systems on the scope of private litigation. In India, as we have seen, offences such as assault and rape are subject to private litigation, even though they could hardly be called civil cases – while the same offences are treated as 'criminal' cases, prosecuted by the state, in other systems. Within the context of the ancient world, therefore, it may be more appropriate to consider the distinction as one between litigations initiated by private individuals or groups for resolving disputes or to redress a grievance and those initiated by the state for offences that it considers significant for the functioning of the state and society.[50]

Plaintiff and Access to Justice

A primary issue with regard to a private individual filing a lawsuit that initiates a court proceeding relates to access to justice. Who is eligible to

---

50 There is a similar distinction in Greek law between 'private' cases in which there is only payment of damages and 'public' cases which may involve execution or exile. See Gagarin 2020: especially 10–33.

move a court? This is not as simple or straightforward in the legal systems of the ancient world as it is (in theory) in contemporary societies. Many of the ancient systems distinguish human beings living within a particular jurisdiction in a variety of overlapping ways: male and female; adults, children, and the aged; head of household and dependents; free people and slaves; citizens and foreigners; people belonging to different classes or castes of society and the like.[51] All these distinctions play a part in an individual's access to justice.

In all systems there were minimum eligibility requirements for filing a lawsuit, although they are not always explicitly spelled out. 'Minors' were universally viewed as incompetent, although the age of majority varied widely. There were also other categories of people considered incompetent. In India, for example, the age of majority was twelve years for girls and sixteen for boys, although it is not always clear whether this was intended only for legal transactions, such as marriage, or also for becoming a plaintiff; more generally, people who were considered dependents (*asvatantra*), such as sons in an undivided household, women and slaves, could not file independent lawsuits. Roman law, classical and postclassical, also placed restrictions on competency to file a suit: these included age and gender restrictions, in addition to those with certain physical disabilities such as the deaf and the dumb. In classical Athens suits could be filed by adult male citizens and *metics* or quasi-permanent residents.[52] Some types of maritime cases could perhaps be filed by foreigners.[53] Athenian cases involving women and children were conducted by their spouses, parents, or other relatives. The age of majority at Athens was eighteen, and once a year those who had turned eighteen during the past year were enrolled as citizens all together, and hence their exact ages would vary; some who looked especially old or young may have been enrolled at an earlier or later age. There is no indication in ancient Near Eastern sources, however, that restrictions were placed on who could file lawsuits. There are instances in which women and even slaves, when suing for their freedom, bring cases to court.

Almost all cases in classical Athens were tried in the popular courts. Homicide cases and some religious cases were heard by the Areopagus, a body consisting of all former archons, nine of whom served each year.

---

51 On legal definitions of status, see Chapter 8, this volume.
52 The access to courts by non-citizens in Athens is a complex topic involving also treaties concluded between states providing access to each other's courts for their respective citizens. See Gauthier 1972.
53 At Gortyn we hear of a 'citizens' court' and a 'foreigners' court'; presumably the first was open only to citizens, the second to foreigners.

In some systems, however, the plaintiff had to choose the forum in which to file his suit. The Indian system, as we saw, recognized several fora for litigation, including family, guild, village and the royal court, with the king himself given sometimes as the ultimate court. The first three have limited jurisdiction with respect only to individuals belonging to those groups. The royal courts, about whose procedures we have the most information, were probably accessed in serious cases or when cases could not be satisfactorily resolved at a lower level. Given the court costs and fines levied by the high court, most litigants would have preferred to settle matters elsewhere. Roman law developed complex rules governing the determination of the competent fora in which specific cases should be heard. Roman plaintiffs did not have the right to choose the jurisdiction in which to file suit – nonetheless, both legal and extra-legal sources reveal various procedural customs and practices that could be exploited by litigants in order to place or bar hearings before a particular forum, or to move a case between fora. The general principle under the Roman *cognitio* (*'extra ordinem'*) procedure was that an accuser or plaintiff would usually proceed in the forum that had jurisdiction over the accused or defendant: in ordinary cases this could mean a bureaucratic court within whose area the accused or defendant was domiciled. There were, however, numerous exceptions, including criminal cases in which an accuser could proceed in a court within whose jurisdiction the alleged crime had been committed.

For criminal proceedings in China, once information had been presented concerning the possible commission of an offence, the state ensured the arrest of the alleged offender and brought him to trial. For civil cases, the law at different times imposed restrictions on the class of persons who might lodge accusations with the authorities. The Qin laws of the third and second centuries BCE prohibited children or slaves from bringing accusations against their parents or masters with respect to offences committed by the latter against them. This prohibition did not extend to serious offences committed by parents or masters against persons who were not members of the household.[54] The Han laws of 186 BCE extended this prohibition to any offence committed by the parent or master irrespective of whether the victim was a member of the household or not, making such accusations a capital offence.[55] The Han laws also provided that accusations against anyone brought by children under the age of ten, or by certain categories of convict,

---

54 See Hulsewé (1985a): 147–48, D 87–88 (Ch'in law).
55 *Ernian lüling*, slip 133; see Lau 2005, 343–45.

should not be heard (*Ernian lüling*, slip 134). The Tang Code subsumed the bringing of accusations by a child, or grandchild, against a parent or patrilineal grandparent under the head of *buxiao* (lack of filial piety): one of the most serious offences known to the code, classified under the title 'ten abominations'. Such accusations, as in Han law, were punished.[56] The only exceptions were plotting rebellion and the like. Slaves and personal retainers were under a similar restraint with respect to their masters. Outside of these exceptions, anyone was able – and in the case of the most serious offences against the state was obliged – to report a criminal offence. The relevant statute makes an exception in the case of persons convicted of a capital offence unless, again, the crime was something akin to plotting rebellion.[57] For civil litigation, we have little specific information. It appears that any head of household might bring a civil complaint against another head. Normally, since all household property was deemed to be under the control, if not the ownership, of the head, disputes over such property would arise only after his or her death and be a matter for litigation between the heirs. Records surviving from the Han show that even convicts, serving their period of labour in the border garrisons, might sue ordinary persons with respect to debt.[58] We know from contracts recovered from the desert in Turfan that women in eighth-century China were able to bring civil actions if they were single or widowed, or if their husbands were absent.[59] Equally, we can reasonably assume that Han women who were heads of household were able to engage in civil litigation.

The Plaint and Summons

In the earliest periods and in informal settings for dispute resolution, the plaint may not have followed a strict legal format and probably consisted of an oral petition. Within a formal court system, however, the tendency was to have the plaint properly drafted and set in writing. It was important that both the court and the defendant knew exactly what the accusation was, and that the plaintiff could not modify his plaint at a later point in the court proceedings. Writing down the plaint (and the plea) let the court have the exact wording, especially in cases where a considerable time may elapse before a verdict was rendered. In some contexts, including proceedings described in extant Indian material, the plaintiff was given the opportunity to emend his initial charges before the final wording of

---

56 MacCormack 2006b: 64–65. 57 Johnson and Twitchett 1993: 116, 140.
58 Zhang 2010: 10–11. 59 Deng 2012: 462.

the plaint was committed to writing. In Republican Rome, on the other hand, under the formulary procedure, plaintiffs were bound by the relevant 'formulae'.

An important step in ancient court proceedings is summoning the defendant. Within the context of dispute resolution, and in informal settings of a local court, it is likely that both litigants were present from the very start of the proceeding. In more formal settings, however, the initial charge was filed independently by the plaintiff or, in criminal cases, by a state official and subsequently the court had to summon the defendant or to issue an arrest warrant. The systems differ as to who was responsible for enforcing the summons: some, including Roman, Greek and Near Eastern, tended to depend on the resources of the plaintiff to bring the defendant to court in private litigation; while others, such as the Indian, also authorized court personnel to enforce the summons.

Indian texts, showing a scholastic tendency, give complex and detailed rules regarding the plaint and develop a highly technical vocabulary. The first stage consists of the initial accusation, given the technical designation *āvedana*, filed with the competent authority. This accusation is written down on a temporary surface (*pāṇḍulekhya*) such as the ground (on sand) or a wooden board with chalk. The plaintiff is then given a chance to emend this initial charge (without, however, substantially altering the initial plaint), which must be completed before the defendant enters his plea. When the corrections are completed, the formal plaint, now with the technical designation *bhāṣā*, is written down on paper (most likely, palm leaf). After this the plaintiff is not permitted to alter the plaint under the penalty of losing the case (*hīnavādin*). A valid plaint is required to have certain characteristics. These include containing the full charge; being complete, using words with clear and literal meanings, without contradictions, capable of proof, concise; stating the year, season, month, fortnight, day, time, region, house and so on; containing the description of the articles listed in the charge; and giving the names of the plaintiff and defendant and their ancestors. If any is missing, a plaint becomes specious (technically called *pakṣābhāsa*). Another requirement of a valid plaint is that the charge should fall within the pre-set titles of law or grounds for litigation (*vyavahārapada*), generally given as eighteen.[60] Although the list differs slightly in different sources, they are given by Manu as: non-payment of debts; deposits; sale without ownership; partnerships; non-delivery of gifts; non-payment of wages; breach of contract; cancellation of a sale or purchase; disputes between owners and herdsmen; boundary

---

60 Olivelle 2010: 41.

disputes; verbal assault; physical assault; theft; violence; sexual crimes against women; issues concerning husband and wife; partition of inheritance; and gambling and betting (*MDh* 8.4–7).

In the Indian system, before summons could be executed, the court officials had to ascertain that there was a prima facie case that the defendant had to answer. If the plaint was implausible, fell outside the recognized titles of law or had flaws that made it a specious plaint (*pakṣābhāsa*), the case was dismissed (*KātSm* 87–88). The burden of enforcing the summons fell principally on the plaintiff, even though in later texts we find a greater involvement of the court. Summoning was done by either dispatching the royal seal, probably through the plaintiff or a messenger, or through a court official such as the bailiff (*sādhyapāla*). Children, the sick, women who have just given birth and so on were exempted from appearing in person. If the plaintiff feared that the defendant may abscond or flee, he was authorized to put the man in legal detention (*āsedha*). It was forbidden to arrest or to require the presence in court of anyone when it entailed an unreasonable burden, such as farmers during sowing and harvest seasons. A reasonable amount of time was given to the defendant to appear in court and enter a plea. A substitute (*prativādin*) was permitted except in serious cases such as murder and adultery.

In China, once again, we have to distinguish between criminal and civil proceedings. Although most of our information relates to the former, we can infer from bronze inscriptions and historical sources some details of the way in which civil litigation was conducted during the Western Zhou (1045–771 BCE) and Spring and Autumn periods (770–464 BCE). Bronze inscriptions show that in the Western Zhou a party initiating a claim against another and seeking redress in a royal court would make a statement of the facts upon which he relied before the judge appointed to hear the case, possibly in the form of a solemn declaration or 'oath' (*shi*). The other party (defendant) then made a statement accepting or denying the claim. For the Spring and Autumn period, we have details of a litigation in 563 BCE between two nobles, each claiming the right to be chief minister at the royal court. The case was heard by an envoy sent from the state of Jin. He heard oral submissions from the representatives of the parties and then ordered them to submit written summaries of their respective claims. One party was unable to produce a summary and fled, leaving his rival the victor.[61] In all these cases it seems that scribes attached to the court would make a written record of the statements of the parties and witnesses.

---

61 Zuozhuan, Xiang 10; Legge 1887: 448–49; see Creel 1970: 177–78.

The submission of written pleadings was important under the Han. Once the original plaint, whether written or oral, was made to the *sefu* (the bailiff), the district official, who at this time had the jurisdiction to hear civil complaints, interrogated the plaintiff and the defendant, made a written record of their evidence and his findings, and then submitted the complete dossier to the district magistrate.[62] In the post-Han period, civil proceedings appear to have been conducted initially before the district magistrate, but the procedure of successive examination of the statements of the plaintiff and the defendant and the production of a written record remained constant. For criminal proceedings, information is available from the Qin and Han laws. Once an accusation relating to an offence has been made by a competent individual and recorded in writing, the magistrate ordered the arrest and detention of the suspect. The Qin *Fengzhenshi* (models for sealing and investigating), issued by the central government to local officials and providing guidelines for the conduct of a trial, specify that the plaintiff and defendant should be carefully interrogated, the questions and answers being recorded in writing.[63] The Han laws of 186 BCE specify that the investigating officer must base his examination on the original report of the accusation. He is to confine himself to an investigation of the specific offence charged and not conduct a 'fishing expedition'.[64] More detail with respect to accusations is contained in the Tang Code: article 355 states that an accusation of an offence made to the court must specify the year and month in which the alleged offence took place and, further, must set out the true facts without incorporating material on which there was dispute. Submission of an improper accusation was to be punished with a beating of fifty strokes with the light stick.[65]

Evidence concerning ancient Near Eastern procedures reveals little about the attributes of a valid plaint. There are particular clauses in the trial records from some periods (e.g. *dīnam šūḥuzu* in the Old Babylonian period, a literal translation of which is 'to cause [the parties] to seize justice'), indicating that judges (or other officials) granted the case a hearing, but no information is given concerning whether certain criteria had to be satisfied to obtain a hearing. The impression given by the texts is that, if one went before the judges, one received a hearing. In some periods, initial confrontations between the plaintiff and the defendant took place prior to the actual trial. Evidence for such pre-trial confrontations comes from the Old Babylonian

---

62 See Zhang 2008: 124–25.   63 Hulsewé 1985a: 184, E2 (Ch'in laws); Korolkov 2011, 48–49.
64 *Ernain lüling*, slip 113; Barbieri-Low and Yates 2015: 509 (19).
65 Johnson and Twitchett 1993, 119–20, 139.

and Neo-Babylonian periods, as well as from the Hebrew Bible.[66] Witnesses were typically present, and the plaintiff/accuser would address the defendant directly in the second person. If no settlement of the dispute could be reached at this point, the parties went before a court, where the accusation was repeated, this time in the third person. In the earliest period in Egypt a trial began with an oral petition, but in later periods the plaint was required to be written down. The procedure during the New Kingdom is fairly well established. The religious text known as 'The Book of the Dead', in which the deceased person went through a trial of their life before the gods of Egypt, mirrors well a civil proceeding. In the Ptolemaic period, the trial originated in a written petition to a Ptolemaic official which could be referred subsequently for resolution to a local Egyptian court.

In the ancient Near East also, generally speaking, it was necessary that defendants appear before the court. Some trial documents record the initial accusation but then state that the defendant must be brought and that, once this is done, the accusation must be repeated. It seems that plaintiffs often bore the burden of bringing the defendant to court. In some cases, though, there is evidence that the courts had some power in this regard. For example, the *manzatuḫlu* official is known from the city of Nuzi.[67] His duties included summoning and bringing defendants to court; when a defendant refused the *manzatuḫlu*'s summons, the court found in the plaintiff's favour.

In ancient Athens, the accuser filed a written plaint with the appropriate official, who then set a date for the preliminary hearing. It contained the name, patronymic and demotic (or deme of residence for metics) for the accuser and defendant, the name of the procedure followed, a statement of the charges following the key terms of the substantive part of the statute, and the names of the two witnesses to the summons made to the defendant. If the charges did not follow the key terms of the statute, the official would reject the plaint, and the case would not go forward. The plaint would then be discussed at the preliminary hearing (*anakrisis*), and the presiding magistrate might insist that changes be made to the wording.[68] The defendant had to be formally summoned prior to the presentation of the plaint, usually by the plaintiff himself accompanied by witnesses. If the defendant did not show up, he could be convicted in absentia, but certain excuses (illness, absence from the city) were allowed.

---

66 Wells 2020.   67 Zaccagnini 2003: 572.
68 On the plaint, see Harris 2013a. The litigant swore to 'keep to the point', that is, to discuss only the charges made in the plaint: see Rhodes 2004.

In Rome, as we have seen, the earlier *legis actiones* procedure depended on a few preordained and inflexible verbal and gestural formulas that effectively restricted the type of claims and situations for which legal redress would be granted. The Roman formulary procedure was also based on predetermined formulas, but these were granted on the basis of the praetors' own jurisdictional authority hence:

> The structure of such formulas and their prescriptive content could vary endlessly, depending on how the rigid and abstract ancient rules were adapted [by the praetor and his jurists] to the diverse array of new cases, and according to the jurists' own ability to think forward and innovate. This rich variety of formulas thus gave the praetor much greater freedom to frame a case in terms more closely matched to the substance of the dispute and actual content of the parties' claims.[69]

In Roman 'criminal' cases, both the *quaestio* and the *cognitio* procedures required that a named accuser had to commit to pursuing the case to its end.[70] The accuser was expected to lodge the details of the accusation, in writing, before a competent tribunal; once formally submitted, the case could not be abandoned without the accuser being punished with the exception of unavoidable circumstances, such as the death of the accused.

It was essential to both the *legis actiones* and the formulary procedures in Rome that the defendant or someone representing the defendant was present for both stages of the hearing. A magistrate could issue a summons compelling the defendant to attend, but ultimately it was up to the plaintiff to attempt to enforce this order. The praetors at Rome developed some measures against reluctant litigants, but 'the law simply gave "cover" to a plaintiff who used force against a refusing defendant'.[71] This is generally the case throughout Roman procedure: enforcement is usually left to private means. Under the later bureaucratic *cognitio* procedure, however, the issuing and enforcement of the summons was supported by some, though limited, administrative mechanisms: for example, the issuing of a public notice (*edictum*) summoning a defendant who could otherwise not be reached. If an individual formally summoned to a hearing under the *cognitio* procedure repeatedly failed to appear, then the court could find for the other party (treating the non-appearance of the summoned individual as a form of 'contempt of court', *contumacia*).[72]

---

69 Capogrossi Colognesi 2015: 134.   70 For 'criminal law' in Rome, see Harries 2007.
71 Metzger 2015: 282.   72 Bellodi Ansaloni 1998.

Plea

The ancient legal systems diverge remarkably in dealing with the defendant's plea. In some, such as the Athenian, the plea (or 'counter-plaint') was a simple admission of guilt or, in most cases, the denial of the charges. There does not appear to have been a complex classification of pleas in the ancient Near East either, although defendants could countersue if they believed that the plaintiff was in the wrong. Depending on the situation, they might claim that the plaintiff actually owed them money, had brought a false suit, or the like. Defendants could also accuse third parties for being guilty of the wrong in question by means of what could be called an impleader accusation. Courts would then often pursue a trial against the third party or join the two defendants (the original defendant plus the third party who now stands accused by the original defendant) in the same case.

In Rome, under the formulary system, the praetor's formula covered both the plaint and the plea – as part of his instructions to the *iudex* who would preside over the second phase of the hearing. After specifying the identity of the parties and the basic question to be decided (the *intentio*), a given formula could then go on to state relevant defences (*exceptiones*), followed by the plaintiff responses to these defences, followed in turn by the defendant's responses to the plaintiff responses and so on. The final stage of this first phase of civil proceedings in Rome was known as *litis contestatio* ('joinder of issue'). It was at this point that the plaintiff formally instigated the claim (the action) and the defendant, the defence (the repudiation of the action), before witnesses. Under the single-phase Roman *cognitio* procedure, the structure of the trial was at the discretion of the presiding magistrate, although detailed procedural rules developed over time; *litis contestatio*, for example, remained a central part of the proceedings (although the event itself lost its technical function of constituting a 'novated obligation'). Strictly speaking, the order of the trial was at the command of the presiding magistrate, although late Greco-Roman rhetorical handbooks suggest that standard patterns of pleading evolved, including templates for pleas (and plaints) for courtroom use.

The Indian jurisprudence stands out as containing long and elaborate discussions and scholastic classifications of pleas (*uttara*) with an elaborate technical vocabulary. A valid plea, just like the plaint, must contain certain characteristics: it must answer all the elements in the plaint and should be easily understandable without explanations and not ambiguous. If these traits are absent, then it is called a specious plea (*uttarābhāsa*). There are four kinds of valid pleas, each with technical terms attached: admission (*sampratipatti* or *satya*); denial (*mithyottara* or *mithyā*); special plea (*pratyavaskanda* or *kāraṇa*); and prior judgment (*prāṅnyāya*). The first two are easily understood. In a special plea the defendant admits the truth of the plaint but presents a reason why he is not guilty. For example, if the charge is that he took a loan, a special plea would admit that he took the loan but assert that he has already paid it back. The plea of prior judgment (*prāṅnyāya*) is when a defendant asserts that the charge contained in the plaint has been the subject of a prior lawsuit, which the defendant won. As we will see, the burden of proof will shift to the defendant in the last two kinds of plea. When the plea has been edited and corrected, it is also written down. The defendant was protected against any further lawsuits by a third party before the original suit against him has been disposed of. He was also given time to construct their plea, and in some circumstances the court proceedings may be adjourned until the defendant could present himself in court.

Sureties and Wagers

Many ancient legal procedures required the litigants, at the very beginning of the trial, to present to the court sureties who were capable of satisfying the various requirements placed on the parties by the litigation. In India the rule was that a surety (*pratibhū*) capable of satisfying the verdict in the case should be secured from each party. Sources present lists of individuals who cannot be sureties: such as family members; paupers; ascetics; those without adequate resources to pay the required penalties and fines; an enemy; and anyone who has a criminal record. If a litigant cannot provide a surety, he is remanded until the end of the proceedings. Several kinds of sureties are recognized, but for purposes of litigation two are significant: surety for appearance (*darśanapratibhū*) and surety for payment (*dānapratibhū*). The former is only responsible for making sure that the litigant appears in court at the appointed time. The second is responsible for any payments resulting from the verdict when the litigant fails to do so. We have little information on this topic in Chinese sources, although the Tang Code has certain rules on guarantors. Where an accusation of a criminal offence was made, both accuser and accused (except for officials) were to be kept in detention. However, the accuser was usually allowed to furnish a guarantor (*bao*) with respect to his future appearance.[73]

The main type of surety known from ancient Near Eastern records is the surety for appearance. It is especially prominent in Neo-Babylonian texts.

---

73 Johnson and Twitchett 1993: 122, 143.

Litigants – and sometimes even witnesses – who are required to appear before the authorities at a future date will often have their appearance guaranteed by one or more third parties. Family members could serve in this capacity. At times, the guarantors are required to deliver the litigant to a particular venue by a particular date. In other cases, the guarantors are responsible for bringing the litigant at whatever time the latter is summoned. In a proceeding dating to 543 BCE, for example, the guarantor is given a deadline and threatened with a stiff fine:

> Nabû-bān-aḫi guarantees for Nergal-ina-tēši-ēṭer to Zēria, chief administrator of the Eanna temple and to the priests of the Eanna temple. On the tenth day of Addaru (month 12), Nabû-bān-aḫi shall bring Nergal-ina-tēši-ēṭer and hand him over to Zēria and the priests. If he does not bring him, he will pay five minas of silver to the temple.[74]

A variety of penalties are listed for guarantors who fail in their assigned duty. Only in some cases are they required to pay the penalty at stake in the case. In classical Athens, sureties were used to guarantee that a defendant showed up in court, in which case the defendant would avoid being placed in jail until the trial – this parallels the Indian 'surety for appearance'. Similarly, in the early Roman *legis actio* defendants had to provide 'guarantors' (*vades*) during the first part of the proceeding. These guarantors were responsible for enforcing the appearance of defendants during the second phase of the proceedings before a judge, and thus are comparable to the surety for appearance in the Indian texts. Later Roman practice included the use of a personal surety (*vadimonium*), agreed through *stipulatio* (a formal, but simple, form of Roman oral contract).

Another feature of some legal systems is the wager or stake. One or both parties to a dispute may tell the court that they would bet a certain sum that they would win the case. This appears to have been voluntary, but when one party dared the other in this manner, it may have been difficult for the other not to respond with his own wager. The whole exercise was probably intended to influence the court with regard to one's own confidence in the strength of one's case. Thus, in the Indian system, lawsuits were classified into those without a wager (*apaṇa*) and those with a wager (*sapaṇa*).[75] A few scholars have speculated that a wager may lie behind the trial scene on the shield of Achilles in Book 18 of the *Iliad* (mid-eighth century BCE), but most doubt this. There is no historical evidence for wagers in Greek law, as also for other systems.

---

74 YOS 6 165; Dougherty 1923: 81.   75 For the Indian wager see Lariviere 1981b.

Assigning the Burden of Proof and Disclosing the Evidence to the Court

It is a general principle of modern jurisprudence that the accuser has the burden of proving the case, not the defendant. This is true also in most ancient legal systems. In Roman civil trials, for example, the base principle was: 'he who affirms has to prove, not he who denies' (Justinian, *Digest* 22.3.2). This principle, however, was based on the assumption that the defendant entered a plea of denial (not guilty). If the plea was one of admission (guilty), then no evidentiary proof was needed and the court proceedings came to a close at this stage. Hence, in the Indian tradition, it is said that a plea of admission results in a lawsuit with just two feet: plaint and plea. But we have seen that pleas could be complex, and in some cases the burden of proof could shift to the defendant.

In ancient Indian jurisprudence, after the plea had been entered the judge and assessors had to consider in a formal way which of the litigants had the burden of proving their case – this is a judicial deliberation given the technical designations *parāmarśa* and *pratyākalana*. The basic principle is articulated thus: 'In a single lawsuit, however, the burden of proof cannot fall on both the litigants' (*KātSm* 190). The litigant on whom this burden falls is determined by which of the four pleas is entered by the defendant. In the first, admission, the issue is moot. In the second, denial, the burden of proof falls clearly on the plaintiff. If the plea is of the third kind, called special plea, then the burden of proof falls on the defendant. In this plea, the defendant admits the veracity of the plaint but denies his guilt. So, when he says: 'Yes, I borrowed 1,000, but I paid it back a month later', he has the burden of proving that he actually paid the amount back to the creditor. The same is true if the fourth kind of plea is entered, that is, 'prior judgment'. In this case, the defendant has to provide evidence that such a judgment was made in his favour in a prior trial on the same charge. This may consist of witnesses, but also the production of the 'victory-document' (*jayapatra*) given after a judgment in a state court.

Ancient Near Eastern evidence suggests that when someone was accused in court of wrongdoing, whether it be for breach of contract or for a more serious offence such as theft or assault, the initial burden (which is somewhat similar to what the US system calls 'the burden of going forward') was transferred to the defendant. Should the defendant fail to appear and answer the charges, the defendant would lose the case. What we ordinarily understand as the burden of proof can also be called the burden of persuasion. In US criminal cases, this burden requires the prosecution to establish guilt beyond a reasonable doubt. In the ancient Near East, it seems that establishing a prima facie case was sufficient to meet this type of burden. This can be seen in those cases where judges issue conditional verdicts, in which they say that one party is required to bring additional witness testimony or that party will lose the case.[76] The task of bringing this additional evidence is placed on the defendants when the accusing parties have evidence in their favour that is either circumstantial (e.g. the defendant was present at the scene of the crime); physical (e.g. the stolen goods were seized in the possession of the defendant); documentary (e.g. a debt note attests to the fact that the defendant owes the plaintiff money); or testimonial (e.g. one or more witnesses testify for the plaintiff's position). When no such evidence exists, this task is placed on the plaintiff/accuser. In ancient China there seems to have been no specific rules on assigning the burden of proof. In Greece also there was no formal burden of proof, but at Athens some litigants attempted to assign one, telling the jury in a capital case, for example, that they must be absolutely certain before convicting because any mistake can never be corrected.[77] In Rome plaintiffs normally had to prove the facts on which their claim was founded, and defendants, those facts which served as a basis for the denial/exception of the plaintiff's claim.

If the defendant has not admitted guilt, then the case moves to the evidentiary stage. Before that starts, in some ancient systems the litigants are required to give to the court details of the evidence they will use in the case. The extent and form of this presentation, however, differ in different systems. In India the evidence to be used by the litigants had to be submitted in writing at the beginning of the trial, but this consisted, it appears, of only the list of witnesses and documents; these 'appointed' witnesses are called *niyukta*. Under special circumstances and with the approval of the judge, further witnesses (*aniyukta*) could be called upon to give testimony even if their names were not in the lists provided. Classical Athens, however, had the most elaborate presentation: in public cases, every bit of evidence had to be presented in writing at the preliminary hearing. This included not just the names of the witnesses, but also the full text of their depositions. The litigants also had to submit the texts of contracts, laws, challenges, letters and the like, and any document of any sort that a litigant intended to use in the trial. These documents were sealed up until the trial, when the witnesses simply had to

---

76 Wells, Magdalene and Wunsch 2010.
77 On the 'topos of the irrevocability of capital verdicts' in classical Athenian oratory, see Usher 1999: 39, fn. 47.

assent to the text they had already submitted in writing. No new evidence could be introduced at the trial, so each side knew beforehand all the evidence the other side would present. In private cases, however, all the evidence presented to the arbitrator was placed in a sealed box (*echinos*). It was submitted to the judge only if one of the litigants did not accept the judgment of the public arbitrator (*Ath. pol.* 53.2).

The ancient Near Eastern material is silent about any evidentiary stage in proceedings. In Rome, again, the two-stage procedures of the *legis actiones* and the formulary system assigned the evidentiary stage of the proceedings to the second phase ('before the judge'). Under *cognitio* procedure, the disclosing of evidence was handled by direct order of the imperial magistrate or his delegate. Detailed rules for the disclosure of evidence were elaborated under later Roman bureaucratic procedure, as demonstrated by imperial constitutions excerpted in the Codes of Theodosius II (438 CE) and Justinian I (534 CE).

Legal Representation

The issue of legal representation is complex. There can be different kinds of representation, from a substitute or stand-in when a litigant is unable to attend court proceedings to a modern-style legal representation by an attorney. Representation can also include the provisions of legal advice, consultation and assistance in drafting the litigants' presentations to court. Most ancient systems permitted substitutes – generally family members or relatives – even though the expectation was that the litigants themselves would be present in court. This must have been the norm in the earliest periods when 'litigation' probably resembled some form of mediation or arbitration and the disputants had to present their side of the story to the mediator(s) or arbitrator(s). Across all ancient contexts, however, representation by a professionally trained lawyer or attorney (in the modern sense of an individual with expert legal knowledge) was probably relatively unusual.

The available evidence from ancient India does not show any kind of legal representation by an attorney; there were no lawyers in the modern sense of the term.[78] Nevertheless, substitutes or representatives (*niyukta*, *pratinidhi* or *prativādin*) were permitted when the plaintiff or defendant was prevented from being present in person. A substitute could also be used when a litigant was timid, an imbecile, insane, aged, a woman, a child, or sick, or when their work prevented them from appearing in person. The substitute generally was the father, mother, relative, friend, servant and so on, a person, in other

---

78 Rocher 1968/1969 (= Rocher 2012: 417–34).

words, who was connected to the litigant and who knew the circumstances of the case. There are cases, however, when substitutes were not allowed and these involved charges of serious crimes such as murder, theft, adultery, eating forbidden food, abducting or deflowering a virgin, assault, counterfeiting, and treason against the king. One of the reasons why a tradition of legal representation did not develop in India may have been the very structure and expectations of a legal case. The king or the judge did not act simply as a referee to decide who won the argument; he was an investigative magistrate who was expected to get at the truth. Thus, rhetoric, although not absent, was not as significant an element in the proceedings as, for example, in Greece or Rome.

From the time of the Warring States (464–221 BCE) and through the epoch of imperial China, legal representation in court was not allowed. Both the accuser and the accused, plaintiff and defendant, were required to appear in person before the court and be subjected to interrogation. During the Western Zhou and Spring and Autumn periods, however, legal representation in cases involving nobles or high-ranking persons appears to have been common. The bronze inscriptions of the Western Zhou show nobles using subordinates to appear in court in their place.[79] For the Spring and Autumn, we have a statement in the *Lüshi chunqiu* (*Annals of Lü Buwei*) to the effect that Deng Xi of the state of Zheng in the middle of the sixth century BCE was a famous advocate much sought after for his ability as a persuader, his fees being articles of clothing. He is presented as a main reason for the failure of the law in Zheng to function properly at that time. Ultimately, he was put to death, with, it is said, a resultant beneficial effect on the administration of justice.[80]

In all periods of ancient Near Eastern history, litigants most often represented themselves. There probably was nothing like an attorney in the modern sense. Occasional references to representatives or substitutes can be found, such as the *rābiṣu* from the Old Assyrian period and the *puḫu* from the city of Nuzi, but these were likely used when the litigant themself could not be present at the trial. Trial lawyers do not appear in the extant evidence from ancient Egypt until mid-Ptolemaic times, but by the mid-second century BCE advocates are recognized and appear in trials providing technical advice on legal matters such as rules of evidence before a court.

In ancient Greek city states litigants generally had to conduct their own cases. At times, though, they could have a friend present either the whole

---

79 Skosey 1996: 119.   80 See Knoblock and Riegel 2000: 454–55.

case or part of a case, on their behalf – or a supporting speaker could be selected for their legal expertise.[81] A speaker, for example, might state that he is speaking for a friend whose Greek is not very good. Demosthenes, however, claims that he presented the case 'On the Crown' for a different reason: he, not the actual defendant (Ctesiphon), was the real target of the prosecution.

There is no mention of advocates in any of the laws from Gortyn. In Athens, however, where rhetorical expertise was a significant element in persuading the members of the jury, a litigant could hire a speechwriter ('logographer') to write the speech that the litigant would deliver. Presumably he and the logographer would also confer on strategy. Logographers had no formal legal training but were expected to have considerable practical experience in various aspects of the law and of forensic rhetoric. The importance of rhetoric and persuasion within the court proceedings is highlighted by numerous curse tablets that have been excavated, curses that attempt to make the opponent tongue-tied and inarticulate in court.[82]

The origins of advocacy in Rome probably lie in the relationship between patron (*patronus*, later used in the sense of 'advocate') and client (*cliens*), thus marking it out from other ancient legal traditions:

> The Romans, at any rate, were from early times accustomed to the representation in court of one citizen by another of greater *auctoritas*. The mentality of classical Athens was profoundly populist and that entailed adherence, at least as an ideal, to the concept that a citizen ought to say his own say before his peers. That of the Romans was oligarchic and characterized, at best, by a vast sense of noblesse oblige that inculcated the protection of the lower in status by the higher.[83]

By the time of the early Principate, however, there is a marked development towards the professionalization of Roman advocacy, with advocates themselves rising up from humbler and provincial backgrounds. According to the poet Juvenal (died c. 127 CE): 'it's the citizen from the lower plebs whom you'll find eloquent: he's the one who regularly defends the cases of the unlettered noble' (Juvenal, VIII 47–49). In the late Republican period in Rome, there is evidence for regular representation by advocates in civil, criminal and administrative cases. In particular, proceedings before the

---

81 See, e.g., Dem. 59.15.
82 Gager 1992. On the use of writing in Athenian trials, Pébarthe 2006.
83 Crook 1995: 32.

standing 'criminal' inquiries (*quaestiones*) provide a wealth of information about the practice of advocacy. These include speeches given by Cicero (106–43 BCE), who was acknowledged in his own lifetime as a leading advocate.[84] A Roman 'advocate', just as the Greek logographer, was primarily an expert in rhetoric, rather than legal science, although some were trained in both. This was especially true in the higher bureaucratic courts of the later Empire, where some advocates were organized into corporate bodies and attached to the court's office staff. In the later fifth century CE, moreover, advocates attached to the high-ranking imperial courts were expected to prove their knowledge of substantive law.[85] Set tariffs for payment also developed, whereas in the earlier periods advocates were not supposed to receive any (monetary) remuneration.

Evidence

As already noted, the litigant on whom the burden of proof falls has to prove his case and this requires legally valid and acceptable evidence. In the ancient legal systems, there were four broad genres of evidence, although not all of them were present in every system or in every historical period of any single system. The four are: witnesses; documents; oaths/ordeals; and possession or enjoyment (as proof of ownership of a property).

Indian legal texts classify evidence into human (witnesses, documents, possession) and divine (oaths and ordeals). In preliterate societies and even in societies where writing was limited to a small and elite segment of the population, live witnesses provided the most common form of evidence, even though recourse to divine means, such as oaths and ordeals, may have been present from a very ancient period. The importance given to possession or enjoyment (*bhukti*) in Indian jurisprudence is quite unique among ancient legal systems. Possession of a property for a certain period of time as proof of ownership became an important element of evidence in the Indian legal system. Indeed, this must have been the most common indicator of ownership in human societies: if someone has lived in this house, milked this cow or worn these clothes for a period of time, it constitutes prima facie evidence for his ownership of them. Even in India, however, possession was associated with a narrow range of disputes, mostly relating to ownership of real estate and moveable property such as slaves and farm animals.[86]

---

84 See Powell and Paterson 2004.   85 See Humfress 2007b.
86 For a more extended discussion of possession, see Chapter 10, this volume.

The weight given to various forms of evidence differed depending on the system and the period. In classical Roman law, for example, both parties effectively had free choice over means of proof: the value of documents, witnesses, oaths and so forth was supposed to be treated a priori 'equal', although obviously it could differ in practice. In so far as classical Roman law had a theory of proof – 'a system for the admission or exclusion of what was relevant or irrelevant, proper or improper for the consideration of a *iudex*' – this was developed initially by forensic advocates, to the extent that some modern scholars argue that 'proof' was intended to persuade, not to convince.[87] There seems to have been a move in the later Empire towards valuing documentary evidence more greatly as proof; under Justinian, for example, testimonies and oaths sworn on Christian gospels were considered inviolate. In India also greater weight tended to be placed on documentary evidence after the Gupta period, roughly from the fourth century CE. Given that at its execution a document had to be witnessed and signed by the witnesses – as well as by the parties to the transaction – it thereby acquired an added weight which was not subject to the vagaries of memory.

Witnesses

Witnesses clearly constitute the most ancient and the most common type of evidence in a court of law. This was especially so in preliterate societies. Many ancient legal systems specify qualifications and criteria of eligibility for witnesses, as well as a minimum number. There is, moreover, some overlap between live witness testimony in a court and the requirements of witnesses for legal transactions (e.g. loans and pledges) and legal documents.

Detailed prescriptions are given about the qualifications and eligibility of witnesses (*sākṣin*) in ancient Indian sources.[88] Witnesses should come from good families and be upright, honest and intelligent. People belonging to various social groups and professional guilds can be witnesses in lawsuits filed by individuals within those groups: women for women and outcasts for other outcasts. The principle seems to have been that people within a particular group become witnesses for others in that group, although there were numerous exceptions. Various kinds of people are said to be ineligible (*asākṣin*): women; children; old people; gamblers; drunkards; the insane; public sinners; actors; heretical ascetics; forgers; people with impaired organs, fallen from caste, close to the litigants, or with a stake in the suit; associates and enemies of the litigants; thieves; and individuals who are violent or with

---

[87] Crook 1995. [88] See especially *YDh*: 121–40.

a criminal record. In general, a minimum of three witnesses were required, even though this is waived under some circumstances. Further, the qualifications needed to be a witness are waived in cases involving adultery, theft, assault, and violence. A special case in India is that 'hearsay' was accepted and thus witnesses who had heard others testify to certain facts may testify to that in court. These secondary witnesses are called *uttarasākṣin*.

Witnesses also constituted the crucial form of evidence in ancient Chinese criminal trials and were subject to the same process of interrogation as the accuser and accused. In some cases, at least according to the Tang law code, concordant testimony by a certain number of witnesses was necessary for a conviction. Article 474 of the code provided that high-ranking officials, or persons aged seventy and above, or fifteen and under, or who were disabled, might be convicted only on the testimony of at least three witnesses.[89]

The ancient Near East presents two kinds of witnesses: testifying witnesses, who actually presented live testimony at a trial, and observing witnesses, who were present at trials simply to observe and attest to the proceedings that took place.[90] Testifying witnesses were the preferred form of evidence and were often favoured over even documentary evidence, since forged documents were not unknown.[91] Children seem to have been entirely excluded as witnesses, since they are not attested as testifying in extant trial records. Women were generally allowed to testify, and even slave testimony was accepted in certain instances. There is no definitive statement in most of the law codes as to the number of witnesses required, but having two witnesses was often enough to win at trial. Such a statement does appear in the Hebrew Bible.[92] Trial records from the Neo-Babylonian period, moreover, show courts asking for a second witness (usually from the accusing party but sometimes from the defendant) in order to lock in a conditional verdict that the courts has issued. A case dating to 586 BCE provides an example: 'When a witness for Bēlšunu has come and has testified against Tabnea that he (Tabnea) took a ram from the possession of Bēlšunu, the temple shepherd, then Tabnea will pay 30 times (what was taken) to the temple' (YOS 17 32). All witnesses, as well as the parties to the litigation, could be interrogated by those adjudicating the trial. In Egypt, rules of evidence developed gradually and by the time of the trial document in the Archive of Tefhape (around 170 BCE) clear rules were in place.[93] Witnesses were an

---

89 See Johnson 1997, 543.   90 Wells 2004: 21–22.   91 Wells 2004: 108–9.
92 Num 35:30; Deut 17:6, 19:15.
93 Thompson 1934. Further discussion in Manning 2010: 207–16 and Appendix.

important part of trials. Torture of witnesses is documented especially in criminal cases.

In the case of ancient Greek city states, qualifications are specified for 'formal witnesses': witnesses who are specifically summoned to witness a document or a procedure of some sort.[94] A certain number of these may be required (one, two, three, or more), and there may be age (adult, adult for fifteen years, etc.) and status (e.g. 'free') requirements. A land dispute, however, calls for the nine neighbours to testify, which is also the case in India for all kinds of boundary disputes. In Athens, witnesses generally had to be adult male citizens. Witnesses and those speaking on behalf of a litigant (*sunegoroi*) in Athens could be non-Athenians.[95]

At Rome, a document made in the presence of and signed by witnesses for the purpose of evidence was known as a *testatio*. Late Roman imperial constitutions also refer to *testimoniales*, written official certificates or witness statements. In Roman law, the validity of certain legal acts or transactions depended on them having been officially witnessed (e.g. a testament or last will). Witnesses to solemn legal acts had to be above the age of fourteen. The deaf, dumb, lunatics and the like, and individuals convicted of a crime were disqualified. There were especially detailed rules concerning the legal capacity to act as a witness to a last will or testament.[96] Solemn legal acts usually required seven witnesses; for other acts where the presence of witnesses was evidentiary, rather than required by law, two usually sufficed. Some restrictions existed with regard to near kinship with a person involved in the act or transaction, having a close friendship, being sworn enemies and the like. Witnesses in trials testified with respect to facts; for example, if you witnessed a legal act or transaction, then you were legally obligated to testify in court concerning that fact. In a Roman judge's eyes, and perhaps in other parts of the ancient world as well, the worth of witnesses was dependent on their social status, financial condition, moral uprightness and other such perceived qualities. Justinian's *Digest*, for example, instructs judges to explore exactly whether a witness is worthy of confidence (Justinian, *Digest* 22.5.3 pr.).

Documents

In all the ancient legal systems, with the advent of literacy, documents recording the transaction, that is the basis of litigation, came into prominence

---

94 Gagarin 1984.   95 On the function of witnesses in Athens, see Rubinstein 2007.
96 Champlin 1991.

as a major, if not the major, form of evidence – especially with regard to land and commercial transactions. Documents, of course, had the advantage of being able to testify to transactions that had taken place in the distant past, such as the purchase or sale of land. They also had the disadvantage of being subject to forgery and surreptitious emendations. Documents, therefore, had to be further validated by the presence of the scribe who executed them and/ or the witnesses who signed them.

In India, legal documents in the form of contracts and deeds became commonplace only around the fourth century CE, possibly due to the spread of literacy to a broader segment of the population. It is also during this period that professional scribes (*kāyastha, lekhaka*) come into prominence. Prior to this, the major and often the sole form of evidence was live witnesses. But the Indian legal tradition quickly developed detailed rules with regard to the execution of legally valid documents as seen in the fifth-century legal code of Yājñavalkya. A document may be written by one of the parties to the contract or, more likely, by a professional scribe. The nature of the transaction, as well as the year, month, fortnight, and day and the names of the parties, their lineages and the names of their fathers must be written down. The document must be signed by the parties, by the scribe and by the witnesses. A document is valid without witnesses if it was executed by one of the parties in his own hand, as long as no force or fraud was involved in its execution. In the case of loans, which in India constituted the paradigmatic transaction, the document remained with the creditor. When an instalment was paid, the amount was written on the back of the document or in a separate receipt. When the entire amount has been paid the document is either destroyed, or a new one attesting to the payment is made.

In early China, documents were essential for the conduct of legal proceedings, whether criminal or civil. All proceedings in criminal cases were conducted in the form of written accusations, written records of interrogations, written judgments and written reports to superiors.[97] Equally, civil cases proceeded on the basis of a written complaint, with a written record being made of the evidence and the decision, though the procedural formalities were not as strict as in the case of criminal accusations.[98] In addition, documents of another kind, that is, other than records of proceedings, had an essential evidentiary role in civil cases. In the event of a dispute over a land transfer, debt, sale, inheritance and the like, no legal action could be taken

---

97 See Barbieri-Low and Yates 2015, vol. I: 111–86. 98 See Zhang 2010: 34–36.

unless a document recording the transfer, contract, debt or will could be produced to the court.

Forged documents were known in the ancient Near East and were produced in court, sometimes with disastrous consequences.[99] Although documents could be introduced as evidence in the ancient Near East, because of the suspicion that they might be forged the scribe of the document, or one or more of the witnesses listed in the document, were typically summoned to testify. In the case of classical Athens, on the other hand, documents were regularly relied upon and can be divided into two broad types: those that were created specifically for use in court (such as witness testimony) and those that existed for other purposes and were later used in court. Litigants might also introduce written evidence of decrees or tax records from ports.[100] Wills and contracts would in most cases probably have been drafted by the party or parties involved. There were no formal requirements, but such documents were normally witnessed, with the names of the witnesses sometimes being included in the document. Witness testimony in Athens was in many cases probably written by the litigants (or their logographers), who specified exactly what they wanted the witness to say. Oaths and the evidence of slaves could only be admitted into court if both parties agreed. Since this almost never happened, the usual way of introducing such testimony is by issuing a challenge to the other side to accept the oath or slave testimony. The document that is then introduced in court is not, strictly speaking, the oath or the slave testimony but the challenge, which would include the oath or testimony that would have been given had the challenge been accepted. These documents are sometimes designated as the 'challenge', but at other times are simply called the 'oath' or the 'slave testimony.'

In Roman law, a written document could be drafted by a private professional who might draw it up for an individual using 'formula-books', or patterns, of specific document types: testaments, contracts, loans, petitions and the like there is evidence from Egyptian papyri that such specialists resided in villages, as well as in towns and major cities. These *tabelliones* would be stationed in public fora or marketplaces, as well as in offices with their own clerks and secretaries (*scribae, notarii*). Under the later Empire, Justinian ruled that every *tabellio* had to seek official authorization (Justinian, *Cod.* 4.21.17) and could be compelled to testify in court regarding the documents he had drawn up. Notaries and scribes were also attached to

---

99 See text no. 169 in Joannès 2000a.
100 Written evidence of decrees: Dem. 19 and Aeschin. 2; tax records from ports: Dem. 32.18, 34.34.

the offices of imperial magistrates and later sources imply that there were set tariffs for having legal documents copied (in part or whole). Other documents (contracts, wills, laws, oaths and so on) would have had other kinds of authorship.

Oaths and Ordeals

Oaths and ordeals share the common feature that an unseen divine or cosmic force is expected to intervene to establish the truth. As we have seen, Indian jurisprudence classifies evidence into human and divine. An oath is made by the litigants as a guarantee of their truthfulness; it is expected that some calamity will befall the individual who takes an oath falsely. An ordeal is a more structured event in which the subject has to perform or to undergo some activity through which his or her innocence or guilt is established. These kinds of evidence require a cultural setting in which the belief in such supernatural forces is prevalent, and it is presupposed that no litigant would take an oath or undergo an ordeal lightly.

Even though early Indian texts indicate the existence of ordeals, such as that by fire, the legal literature does not speak clearly about ordeals until about the fourth century CE. The literature prior to this time uses the term *śapatha*, which refers specifically to oaths but appears to have been used occasionally with a broader meaning to include ordeals as well. Texts from the fourth century onward use the technical term *divya* for an ordeal; the term literally means divine and indicates that in an ordeal it is the divinity that guarantees the truth. The number of ordeal types becomes large in medieval sources, but documents from the fourth to sixth centuries CE give five: balance, fire, water, poison, and holy water – with detailed descriptions of how and to whom each ordeal is administered.[101] Some of these ordeals are reserved for certain individuals, such as Brahmins and women. Ordeals are permitted to establish guilt or innocence only in certain kind of lawsuits, and they can be employed only in cases involving serious matters or large sums of money. Further, they can be used only in cases where no human evidence is available, or when there is conflicting evidence. One source says: 'If the one party presents human evidence and the other party divine evidence, the king should accept the human evidence and not the divine' (*KātSm* 218). Ordeals are also not permitted in cases involving corporate bodies, such as guilds, where only human evidence is permitted. It is likely that at least in the case of some ordeals, court proceedings would have to be halted and the court moved to a different location where the ordeal would

---

[101] Lariviere 1981a gives a detailed description of Indian ordeals.

take place. The balance ordeal, for example, required the subject to be weighted in a particular balance specially erected for the purpose. After invoking the balance, the subject is weighed again, and if they weigh less they are considered innocent. The ordeal of fire required a person to carry a red-hot ball of iron on the joint palms covered with some leaves through eight circles before depositing the ball on the ninth. If the hands are not burnt, the subject is considered innocent. In the water ordeal the subject remains submerged in a body of water until an arrow shot by an archer is retrieved and brought back by a runner. If he is able to remain under water during the process, he is considered innocent. Poison and holy water share a common feature in that after consuming the substance the subject must not suffer either sickness or death in the case of poison, or they or their household should not experience a disaster during a specific period of time in the case of holy water.

For early China we have to distinguish two kinds of oath: the *meng* (covenenant) and the *shi* (solemn declaration). The *meng* was a ritual involving a sacrifice to the spirits, the smearing of the lips of the participants with the blood of the victim, the recording of the terms of the covenant in a document and the inclusion of a term that called upon the spirits to punish any of the oath takers who failed to honour his undertaking. The *shi* was a solemn affirmation of the truth of a statement for which the person making the statement pledged his own faith. It is disputed whether the *shi* also involved an invocation of the gods or spirits as witnesses. Excavated texts show that the *meng* was used in legal proceedings in the state of Chu during the fourth century BCE. Judges had recourse to a *meng* to determine the reliability of the accusations made by parties. In one case involving cross-allegations of homicide, the witnesses on each side were called upon to take the *meng* oath in support of the accuracy of the allegations made by their principals. We do not know whether the outcome depended upon which party could produce the greater number of oath-swearing witnesses or upon which could muster witnesses of a higher status.[102] The use of the *meng* did not occur in the legal procedures of the rival state of Qin, which in the end imposed its rules throughout China. The Western Zhou bronze inscriptions evidence the use of *shi* in lawsuits; the loser is required to make a solemn declaration (*shi*) that he would carry out the terms of the judgment. Neither the *meng* nor the *shi* appear in the legal procedures of the Qin/Han or later periods.

There is no firm evidence that ordeals were widely used in ancient China. We have only one instance (and its interpretation is controversial) in which

---

102 See Weld 2003: 160–67.

an ordeal appears to have been used to resolve a protracted lawsuit between two ministers in the state of Chi in the eighth century BCE. The ruler ordered that the two disputants bring one goat (a one-horned animal) and that they then make a sacrifice and swear to the truth of their respective claims through a *meng*. While one party was speaking, the goat butted him so demonstrating his guilt. We possibly have here an example of an ordeal in which the 'judgment of god' is manifested, but no certain conclusion can be drawn.[103]

Courts in the ancient Near East had recourse to oaths and ordeals when they did not believe that they could render a verdict based on the evidence before them. At times, it appears as if they had sufficient evidence but still chose to decide the case through an oath or ordeal. For example, in one text from Nuzi in the Late Bronze Age, although the defendant had five witnesses and the plaintiff none, the judges resorted to an oath ritual to decide the case.[104] The court would decide at the end of the trial which party – or, in some cases, which party's witnesses – should take the oath. Those involved would then often move to a temple or some other sacred site. The oath was dispositive: if the party required to swear did indeed take the oath, that party won the case. Such oaths almost always invoked one or more deities. Occasionally, oaths that invoked only the name of the king were sworn at earlier stages of a trial but served merely to add weight to a party's testimony. Judicial oaths functioned in this way for most of ancient Near Eastern history. In the Neo-Babylonian period, oaths sworn by the gods are no longer consistently dispositive. They are commonly taken on a voluntary basis, and those who swear them can lose their case at court. They carry a diminished importance at this point.

The primary ordeal utilized in the ancient Near East was the river ordeal. Some claim that there was also a drinking ordeal, but the evidence for this is obscure. Like the judicial oath, courts made use of the river ordeal at the end of a trial. One of the parties (or a substitute, perhaps the party's witness) entered a river – it is always said to be of their own accord – in order to have the river god determine that party's guilt or innocence. What signalled guilt or innocence is unclear. It may have been that floating meant innocence and sinking meant guilt, although guilty parties could be pulled from the river and punished by means other than death. There is some indication that individuals undergoing the ordeal had to make it across the width of the river, possibly while carrying some sort of weight or other object. The river ordeal

---

103 See MacCormack 1995.   104 Pfeiffer 1932, text 108.

was employed from the mid-third millennium through the Neo-Assyrian period. It is entirely lacking from legal texts of the Neo-Babylonian period and does not appear to have been practised in ancient Israel.[105]

We have no evidence for ordeals in Greece. Oaths, as we have seen, are regularly sworn by judges and jurors, and sometimes by witnesses and litigants. Exculpatory oaths are specified in a few cases at Gortyn. For example, in a divorce the woman can take her own property with her; if she is accused (presumably by her husband) of taking more than that, she is allowed to swear an oath at the temple of Artemis and if she does, she can take the disputed property.[106] In classical Athens, litigants sometimes say that they or some other person is ready to swear to something, or sometimes challenge the opponent to swear an oath, but such 'oath-offers' or challenges have no formal legal validity.

Oaths played a crucially important role during all phases of Roman procedural law, although who or what was sworn by changed in practice: Jove; the genius of the emperor; Christ and other Christian saints and figures; and so forth. According to Gaius, who probably taught Roman law during the mid-second century CE, one of the forms under which the ancient *legis actiones* could be raised included 'by oath' (Gaius, *Institutes* 4.13–14). Under the formulary system at Rome, the praetor further developed the existing system of procedural oath-taking (*iusiurandum in iure*), according to which both parties to a suit could place any fact or legal point beyond contention. Oaths were also used as sureties during judicial trials: for example, the Roman oath known as the *iusiurandum calumniae* could be demanded by either the defendant or plaintiff to a trial, as a guarantee against legal chicanery and trickery. Traditionally Roman law left the punishment of a broken oath to Jove himself: oaths, like curses, were bound by transcendental norms. Similarly, the evidence for Roman practices that invoke supernatural intervention in mundane affairs is mainly extra-legal. In the early fifth century CE, Augustine, Bishop of Hippo, suggested sending two recalcitrant members of his congregation to the shrine of St Felix at Nola in Italy 'where the dreadful works of God open up the guilty conscience and compel it to confess by punishment or fear'.[107]

---

105 Wells 2008b.   106 Gagarin 2013: 69–70.   107 Bartlett 2013: 312.

Evidence

Forensic Investigation

By forensic investigation we mean the examination of evidence or the crime scene by law enforcement or judicial officials in order to determine the guilt or innocence of the accused, or as a means of discovering the perpetrator(s) of a crime. This would most commonly take place in criminal cases and long before an actual case is filed. The investigation of a crime or crime scene would take place soon after the report of a crime has been received by the appropriate authority. As we shall see, not all ancient systems of justice appear to have placed as much emphasis on forensic evidence as the Indian Arthaśāstric tradition.

The Indian system of justice as presented in the Dharmaśāstras generally focus on private disputes brought before a court, not crimes that the state itself may have investigated. Within this context, there was some, limited, room for forensic investigations. The points raised sometimes pertain to theft and claims of ownership. Thus, a man found in possession of stolen goods would be deemed a thief, unless he is able to prove how he acquired them. Judges, however, are warned that appearances often can be deceptive, and different articles and animals may have very similar characteristics and markings. Stolen goods may be stashed in someone's property without his knowledge. In private lawsuits, attention is paid to the forging of documents or changing the wording of authentic documents to given an advantage to a litigant. The truly forensic investigations, however, are carried out in criminal cases and these are described only in Kauṭilya's *Arthaśāstra* (first century CE).

Kauṭilya's *Arthaśāstra* gives detailed descriptions of crime scene investigations in the case of thefts and burglaries, alongside information about autopsies when there has been a sudden death. With respect to crime scenes, the investigator is advised how to tell whether a burglary was committed by an insider or someone coming from the outside. Some of these clues are physical: how the burglar entered the house; the possession of burglar's tools by the accused; and even a footprint left at the scene matching that of the accused. Other 'clues' are social: for example, possible suspects to be considered by the investigator include a man close to the burgled household who is known to have fallen on hard times; or a poor woman; or a domestic servant in the house who has fallen in love with another man. As already noted, Kauṭilya's text gives a detailed description of autopsies and how to tell the cause of death: if the anus and eyes are closed, and the teeth have bitten into the tongue, then the deceased has drowned; whereas if there are marks on the throat and the eyes are open wide, they were strangulated. It appears from the evidence of the *Arthaśāstra* that there was a separate court system for criminal cases, where defendants could defend themselves from charges filed by a state official.[108] We have an interesting piece of advice given to judges in criminal cases:

> In the presence of the victim of the theft, as well as internal and external witnesses, he should question the accused about his country, caste, lineage, name, occupation, wealth, associates, and residence. He should check these against affidavits made by others. Then he should question him about what he did the previous day and where he spent the night until his arrest. If he is corroborated by the person providing his defense, he is to be considered innocent; otherwise, he is to undergo torture. A suspect should not be arrested after the lapse of three days, because his interrogation is inadmissible, except when he is found with incriminating tools.[109]

Officials are also warned that murderers often try to disguise their crime by making the death look like a suicide.

The Qin legal documents of China preserve evidence of the importance attached, already in the third century BCE, to an examination of the scene of a crime and, in cases of unexplained death, of the body. For example, a detailed examination of the corpse was made, with an investigation of its exact physical state, the number and nature of wounds, if any, the state of the clothing and the proximity of any weapons. In cases of alleged theft, a detailed examination was made of the place in which the theft was said to have taken place.[110] Forensic investigation is seldom mentioned, on the other hand, in ancient Near Eastern trial-related documents – but it does occur, especially in the Neo-Babylonian period. Usually, a piece of physical evidence is brought before the court and 'inspected'. Items examined in this way include two duck carcasses, the carcass of a cow, a live cow, a container of dates, inscribed tablets, iron shears, an iron dagger and a person's brand or tattoo. We do not know the precise details of any of these inspections. The investigation of a crime scene may also have been carried out. Paragraphs 36–37 of the Old Babylonian Laws of Eshnunna suggest that the lodgings of a bailee should be inspected for evidence of a thief's breaking and entering the lodgings to steal the goods that have gone missing and are the subject of a dispute.

---

108 Olivelle 2012b.   109 *KAŚ* 4.8.1–5.
110 Hulsewé 1985a: 198–200 (Ch'in laws); Bodde 1982.

There are lurid reconstructions of 'crime scenes' in the rhetorical speeches of advocates in Rome, as well as a host of rhetorical rules governing how you place an action for maximum desired rhetorical effect. An action involving criminal intent, for example, should be said to have taken place, or to have been plotted, in secret and at night. But beyond its use in the rhetoric of arguments within the court, we do not have evidence of an examination of the crime scene or autopsies within either the Roman or the Greek legal system.

Torture for Evidentiary Purposes

In many ancient legal systems, some form of mental or bodily violence – what would be termed torture today – was frequently used as part of the investigative process and collection of evidence. Torture was used primarily in 'criminal' cases, or at least in cases in which the state had a direct interest. Most ancient systems restricted the use of torture to certain kinds of individuals, especially those from the lower levels of society, including enslaved persons.

In India, there is no indication that torture was used in civil disputes brought before a court by individuals or groups. The evidence we have comes from Kauṭilya's *Arthaśāstra*, pointing to its use by the judiciary in criminal cases brought by the state.[111] There is also evidence in Kauṭilya's *Arthaśāstra* for the use of torture in police investigations where there is likelihood that a person has committed a crime, for example burglary or murder. Kauṭilya enumerates that:

> Someone who has previously committed a crime, someone who confesses and then retracts, someone in whose possession a portion of the loot is found, someone who has been arrested by reason of the act or the stolen goods, someone who embezzles from the king's treasury, or someone subject to death by torture on the king's orders – he should subject these to torture administered collectively, individually, or repeatedly.[112]

Among those exempt from torture are Brahmins, women, children, the elderly, those who are sick, intoxicated, insane, hungry or thirsty, and weak individuals. The text also lists several kinds of torture, as well as an ancient text, now lost, dealing with the administration of torture called *Kharapaṭṭa*. A distinguishing feature of the ancient Indian tradition is that, unlike others

---

111 See Olivelle 2012b.   112 KAŚ 4.8.26.

where witnesses also may be subjected to torture, only the accused is subject to torture.

The Legal Treatise of the *Hanshu* (History of the Former Han Dynasty) as well as earlier sources from ancient China emphasize that the best way for an interrogator to elicit the truth was through the 'five types of scrutiny (*wu ting*)'. These were examination of the statements of the accused; consideration of his facial expressions and his breathing; of the way in which he reacted to the questions of the judge; and of his eyes. The same point was made in the Tang Code of the seventh century CE.[113] If a judge is convinced, however, that a party, especially the accused, was lying, he might have recourse to torture to force the individual to state the truth. The crucial point here is that the legislators all recognize that torture should be a last resort, given the propensity of persons in pain to say whatever their questioner desires, even though this may not in fact be the truth. The type of torture, the amount, and the number of occasions on which it might be administered were all strictly controlled by the law, although abuses clearly occurred. Details vary under different dynasties. Tang article 476 gives a very clear conspectus of the procedure to be adopted by the Tang magistrate and is worth quoting:

> In all cases where a prisoner is to be interrogated, the circumstances must first be considered. Then the documentary statement and the reasoning must be examined. This must be done repeatedly. If a decision still has not been reached, then the prisoner may be interrogated under torture.

The *shuyi* commentary adds:

> According to the statutes on Judicial Officials: 'All investigating officials trying a case should first carry out the five types of scrutiny (*wuting*), and investigate thoroughly all the testimony. If there is anything doubtful in the statement of the facts of the case, and the accused will still not make his confession of guilt, only then may judicial torture be applied.'

The Tang legislated comprehensively on the use of torture, confined to beatings. Torture was to be applied only in cases of doubt, where the accused refused to confess. Beatings were to be administered by a stick of specified dimensions, the blows to be evenly distributed between back, buttocks and upper thighs. They might not be inflicted on more than three occasions, each separated by twenty days, and the total number of blows should not exceed two hundred. Despite the detailed rules of the Tang and earlier dynasties on

---

113 See Hulsewé 1985a: 342; Johnson 1997: 545.

the use of torture, abuses seem to have been endemic. Given the requirement that an accused could not be convicted and sentenced unless he acknowledged his guilt, magistrates frequently resorted to the unauthorized use of torture to force a confession. Consequently, one of the most common problems faced in the appeal process was the allegation that the conviction was unsound because the confession had been improperly secured through excessive beating or other illegal methods.

In the Near Eastern material, there is little clear evidence of torture during interrogations, although some of it is quite suggestive. In the Neo-Babylonian period, for instance, a procedure known as *maš'altu* (lit. 'questioning' or 'interrogation') is attested and whenever it is implemented, it results in a conviction (or confession) of guilt. Hence several scholars have inferred the use of torture underlying this procedure. In the later Hellenistic period, a device known as 'the ladder of interrogation' (also *maš'altu*) is referred to, though the precise way in which it was used is unclear.[114] In ancient Egypt, as noted above, rules of evidence had developed by at least 170 BCE governing the use of witnesses in trials, and the torture of witnesses was apparently permitted, especially in criminal cases.

In relation to ancient Greece, we have evidence for the use of torture only from Athens where it could be used against slaves alone. Masters had almost complete control over their slaves and if they thought it necessary, they could torture one of their own slaves to acquire information about a crime. This information could be cited in court, but it was not equated to formal documentary evidence. In addition, if the testimony of a slave was needed to help resolve a dispute, the slave could be interrogated under torture only if both sides agreed. In almost all the cases we know of, one of the two parties refused the other's proposed interrogation. Occasionally the proposal to interrogate under torture was accepted by both, but even then, the agreement always broke down before the interrogation was completed. Thus, we have no actual examples of a slave being interrogated under torture in order to obtain evidence for a trial. Greek orators sometimes question the reliability of evidence gained by torture. Some scholars think the whole institution was a fiction and was only used for rhetorical purposes (for instance, to be able to accuse one's opponent of not wishing to learn the truth); others think torture was used, though rarely, and that it's simply chance that no actual cases survive.[115] In Athens torture could also be used against metics and foreigners.[116]

---

114 See Joannès 2000b.   115 See Gagarin 1996; Mirhady 1996.
116 See Dem. 18.132. Also Harris 1995: 172 and Bushala 1968.

As John Crook explains, classical Roman law viewed torture as a means to uncover truth:

> To the Romans [torture] was not a category of punishment but a method of interrogation of witnesses. In the case of slaves, their evidence was not admissible except under torture. Numerous rules were evolved about this, such as that of Augustus that 'you cannot begin with torture,' i.e., that there must be a prima facie case of some kind before slaves could be interrogated, some prior evidence for them to refute or corroborate. Augustus, indeed, seems to have wanted to confine slave torture to evidence in 'capital and atrocious' crimes and Antoninus Pius laid down that in pecuniary suits torture was only to be used if the truth could not be reached otherwise.[117]

Roman citizens could appeal against being tortured and evidence suggests that free individuals were not tortured for evidentiary purposes under the late Republic. Under the Principate, however, torture was extended beyond slaves to *humiliores* (free individuals of a low status). The emperor Marcus Aurelius apparently ruled that those of the highest status and their families were exempt from torture, but the so-called 'magic and treason trials' that took place in the late fourth century CE at Rome and Antioch prove that those of senatorial rank were not necessarily immune.[118]

Presentation and Evaluation of Evidence

In the previous section we dealt with the kinds of evidence permitted under different ancient systems of law, as well as the rules governing each kind of evidence – especially witnesses and documents. Here we deal with the actual presentation of evidence within a trial. In the Indian division of legal procedure, this is called the third foot. It is also the most important, because the evidence and the way it is presented will be a deciding factor in the verdict of the court. It is most significant in those systems, such as the Greek, where persuasion and rhetoric play a central role in swaying the decisions of the court or members of the jury. As we have already noted, litigants in Athens would often employ speechwriters to help them in their rhetorical presentation.

In India there was a formal swearing-in of witnesses (*sākṣyanuyojana*) by the interrogating judge. They were told of the dire consequences awaiting

---

[117] Crook 1967: 275. On Roman legal punishment, see Robinson 2007 and for the late antique period Hillner 2015.
[118] On the Antiochene treason trials c. 372 CE, see Kelly 2018.

a witness who testifies falsely. Sources give examples of these sermons by the judge. Here is one directly related to the theology of karma and rebirth: 'Naked, shaven-headed, wretched, and racked with hunger and thirst, a man will have to go to his enemy's house carrying a skull-bowl to beg for alms food – should he give false testimony. Barred from the city and remaining famished outside the gate, a man will see mostly his enemies – should he give false testimony' (NSm 1.183–84). Different modes of swearing-in are used depending on a witness's social class. A Brāhmaṇa, for example, is required to swear by the truth; a Kṣatriya, by his weapons and vehicles; and a Vaiśya by his cattle, seeds and gold. The witnesses are questioned by the judge separately, unless a particular event was witnessed collectively by a group of witnesses. The interrogation of the witnesses is done in open court and in the presence of the parties to the dispute. Unlike in Greece and Rome, rhetoric appears to have played only a minor role in Indian judicial proceedings.

There were two competing factors in an Indian trial. On the one hand, the case was viewed as a debate or as a form of logical inference. Thus, the plaint is called *sādhya*, the demonstrandum; the evidence is called *sādhana*, the means of arriving at the knowledge of the truth, that is, the minor premise in a syllogism; and the verdict is called *sādhyasiddhi*, the demonstration of the demonstrandum. Within this framework, the onus of proving the case falls on the plaintiff, or on the defendant if the burden of proof has fallen on him because of the kind of plea he entered. On the other hand, the court officials had the obligation to make sure that justice is done, and they were expected to find out the truth. One text advises the judge to trace the location of truth by deductive reasoning, as a hunter traces the location of an animal he has shot by the trail of blood (MDh 8.44). Thus, rhetorical persuasion by the litigants must be tempered by the judge's own assessment of the evidence and the honesty of the witnesses and the litigants. When both litigants have witnesses, those of the plaintiff are questioned first, unless the burden of proof has fallen on the defendant in which case his witnesses take priority. There does not appear to have been cross-examination of witnesses by the litigants or their representatives; the interrogation was done by the judge. The demeanour and the manner of speaking of the witnesses are viewed as keys to the court's determination of their veracity.

In the ancient Near East witnesses were not sworn in. They might be required to take an oath later in the trial, but only if the judges were to decide that they cannot reach a verdict based on the evidence (including witness testimony). Witnesses also testified orally in fifth-century BCE Athens, but from the fourth century BCE their depositions were written down beforehand and sealed up in a jar before the trial. At the trial, a clerk read out the testimony and the witnesses merely stated their assent. Witnesses were never cross-examined. If a witness did not want to testify when asked, he could swear an oath of disclaimer saying that he did not have the knowledge that was requested of him.[119]

It is also at this stage that documents and evidence relating to possession are to be presented to the court. Indian sources advise the court officials about ways to detect forged or altered documents. The authorship of a document can be authenticated both by witnesses and by comparing the handwriting of the litigant or the scribe who executed the document. In Greece, courts played no role in examining or evaluating evidence; rather, this was done by the litigants themselves. In Athens in the time between the preliminary hearing and the trial each side could examine and evaluate the other side's evidence, confirming, for example, that a law had been correctly cited. In court litigants could discuss the evidence (e.g. 'his witnesses will lie') but could not introduce new evidence.

As we have already seen, in Rome torture was not simply a category of punishment but a method of interrogating witnesses. In the case of some witnesses, such as enslaved persons, for example, their testimony was admissible only after torture had been administered. With regard to other types of evidentiary practice, Roman disputes over ownership could involve the presentation of some corporeal thing before the magistrate. For example, under earlier procedure, when land was involved the two parties were directed to go to the land in question, 'lay on hands according to law' and come back with a symbolic part of the object: for example, a tile for a house, a clod of earth for a farm.[120]

Punishment for Perjury

As documents can be forged, so witnesses can lie. This is an ever-present problem for ancient courts, as it is for contemporary ones. Perjury can result in a miscarriage of justice. In all ancient legal systems, therefore, perjury was considered a very serious crime, and in some also a grave sin with serious consequences after death. We saw the oration given by an Indian judge to prospective witnesses containing some of these consequences. Although *sensu stricto* perjury is lying under oath, we consider here any kind of false testimony that a witness may render in court.

[119] Rubinstein 2005.   [120] See Aulus Gellius XX.10.10.

Indian law functioned under the belief that witnesses, who were all normally placed under oath, will suffer karmic retribution in the next life when they give false testimony. But the law also has provisions for this-worldly punishment of such witnesses. Punishments for perjury depended on the underlying reason ranging from delusion and fear to greed and anger. The punishments range from different levels of fines to execution. One source prescribes a fine that is double the amount under litigation on the perjured witness. Suborning perjury is also a punishable crime, as also any kind of collusion between litigants and witnesses. One fifth-century CE Indian text says: 'The person who suborned perjury, as well as the witnesses, should be fined individually twice the amount under litigation' (*YDh* 2.83). When perjured testimony is detected, a mistrial is declared; and if a verdict has already been rendered, it is annulled, and a new trial is ordered. Manu even recommends the death penalty for giving false testimony (*MDh* 8.119–23). Ancient Indian jurisprudence also recognized, however, that under certain circumstances a person may be excused or even required to give false testimony. The main reason for such testimony is the fear that telling the truth would subject a person to the death penalty. These sources also give religious expiations that would erase the sin incurred through that kind of excusable false testimony.

While there was no law of perjury in the strict sense in China, since (after the Qin conquest of China) neither the statements of the parties nor the evidence of witnesses was given under oath, the principal sanction for incorrect statements or evidence was supplied by the law of false accusation. The Han laws of 186 BCE contain two relevant statutes, probably derived from equivalent Qin laws. One specifies that a person who brings a false accusation against another on a capital charge is to be sentenced to the most serious form of penal servitude; for non-capital charges he is to be sentenced to the difference between the punishment prescribed for the offence of which accusation was made and that for the offence (if any) of which the accused was actually guilty.[121] The other deals with witnesses who do not speak the truth and specifies that, where the accused as a result of the false testimony has been sentenced to death, the witness is to be condemned to the most serious form of penal servitude. When the sentence is not capital, the witness is to be sentenced to the difference between the punishment actually imposed and that (if any) which should have been imposed in the absence of the false testimony. The official in charge of proceedings is to explain the law to the

---

121 *Ernian lüling*, slip 126 (Barbieri-Low and Yates 2015: 547 (1)).

witness prior to his giving evidence.¹²² The Tang Code provides generally that the accuser is to receive the punishment for the offence which is the subject of the false accusation, but that in cases of plotting rebellion and the like he is to be punished with decapitation (article 342). The code has a separate article on witnesses who give false evidence with the result that the accused is sentenced to either a greater or a lesser punishment than he should have received (article 347). The lying witness is to be sentenced to a punishment two degrees less than that which has been imposed or remitted in consequence of his testimony. However, crucially, the *shuyi* commentary explains that this rule applies only where evidence has been given in a case involving high-ranking officials, the old, the young or the disabled, that is, in cases where the evidence of witnesses is an essential requirement for conviction.¹²³

While what has been said above relates to criminal prosecutions in China, it seems that a similar rule on false accusation governed civil suits too, at least in Han times. Before investigating a civil complaint, the bailiff (*sefu*) explained to the parties, particularly, it seems, the defendant, that under the statutes there was reciprocal liability in respect of false statements.¹²⁴ It is not easy to see how the rule worked in practice where the matter under investigation did not involve a crime but, for example, theft or the dishonest acquisition of another's property. If no crime was involved, there was no statutory punishment and therefore no base upon which the doctrine of 'reversed punishment' could operate.

It is unclear whether there is any evidence for the punishment of perjury per se in the ancient Near East, if perjury is strictly defined as lying under oath. Typically, any oath taken in a trial would end that trial and it would be left to the gods to deal with the oath-taker, if he or she had sworn falsely. There is evidence for the imposition of punishment for false accusation and for false testimony, both of which would have been unsworn. The first two paragraphs of the Laws of Hammurabi (as well as Laws of Lipit-Ishtar, chapter 17) deal with false accusation and the next two with false testimony by non-party witnesses. All four penalize false accusers/witnesses by imposing on them whatever punishment or fine is at stake in the case in which they are testifying, a principle we find also in Indian law. In theory, then, false testimony in a capital case could lead to the execution of the false witness. A few Old Babylonian trial records confirm punishment for false accusers and

---

122 *Ernian lüling*, slip 110 (Barbieri-Low and Yates 2015: 509 (16)).
123 See Johnson and Twitchett 1993: 126, 141–42.   124 Examples given in Zhang 2010: 1–3, 16.

witnesses, though it does not occur exactly as stipulated in the Laws of Hammurabi in every case. By the Neo-Babylonian period, there is evidence only for the punishment of false accusers, and this is the crime that is singled out for special emphasis in the legal texts of the Hebrew Bible, including in the Decalogue. The expression 'you shall not bear false witness' refers to false accusation or wrongful prosecution, and the false accuser is to receive the same punishment that the falsely accused was being threatened with.[125] Some have suggested that in the Neo-Babylonian period an actual punishment for perjury had been instituted, but this is disputed.

In the case of Greece we know nothing about perjury in Gortyn, but in Athens there was a specific procedure (a *dikē*) for false testimony. The case was normally brought by the losing litigant against one of his opponent's witnesses, and in some cases (we are not sure exactly under what circumstances) it could lead to a retrial of the original case before a different jury. Someone convicted three times of false testimony lost his civic rights, meaning among other things that he could not testify in court. The penalty of partial *atimia* (lit. 'dishonour') for perjury refers to the loss of civic rights and could include confiscation of property of the person and his descendants. Partial *atimia* is any lesser version; here there is the loss of rights (to vote in the assembly, bring suit in court, etc.) but not the confiscation of property. Under Roman law perjury was considered an offence against the gods (Jove in particular) and thus it was generally left to the gods to take their revenge. There were, however, some circumstances in which false testimony aimed at gaining a profit could qualify as a crime. Perjury committed under an oath sworn by the genius of the emperors could also be classified and punished as *crimen maiestatis* (treason).

Evaluation of the Evidence and Court Deliberations

Once the litigants have presented their evidence and arguments, it is the responsibility of the judge and court officials to evaluate the evidence and to deliberate among themselves with regard to which litigant has provided the most convincing evidence and the strongest argument. The exception is Athens with its jury system where no formal deliberation took place before the jurors cast their votes.

In Indian legal procedure there was time allotted after the evidentiary phase for the court to undertake a formal deliberation and to evaluate the evidence presented by the litigants. This phase of the judicial proceedings is

---

125 Exod 20:16; Deut 5:20 and Deut 19:16–21.

called *anumāna* (that is, judicial inference as to the veracity of the case presented by the litigants) or *pratyākalita*, although this term is also used with regard to the court deliberation regarding the burden of proof. Those taking part include the king or judge and the assessors (*sabhya*). During this phase of the proceeding, the litigants, witnesses and others within the court are asked to leave. The assessors are expected to advise the judge regarding points of law, as well as the evidence presented. It appears that there were also other experts who served the court in an advisory capacity, including experienced and elderly merchants and traders who could offer advice on commercial matters. The veracity of the witnesses is judged by the manner in which they presented their testimony; if they act agitated, if their voice and complexion change, if they perspire, then their testimony will be discounted. If the witnesses give differing testimony, in general the majority view is accepted. If they are more or less equally divided, then the view of those the court considers to be better qualified because of learning and virtue prevails. When the outcome is decided through an ordeal, however, the manner in which innocence or guilt is established by the various ordeals is clearly laid down. In criminal cases, as in China, there was the possibility of applying torture to extract a confession – in addition to forensic investigations and interrogation of the accused and witnesses.

Throughout the period under consideration, we find statements in ancient Chinese sources that show the need for those entrusted with judicial responsibilities to carry out their investigation with the utmost care and probe the case to the bottom. At the beginning of Western Zhou, the ruler when enfeoffing a young prince urges him to use great care in the application of the punishments and in particular to consider the evidence in criminal cases for several days, even months, should that be necessary to determine the truth. The Qin Models for the conduct of legal proceedings (*Fengzhenshi*) stipulate that the judge should listen fully to the words of the person being questioned, while the Han laws of 186 BCE make it an offence for a judge in his investigation to go beyond the charge actually stated in the indictment.[126] The Han laws further specify that a judge who does not hear the case with proper diligence is to be punished.[127] The Tang statutes required the investigating officer, when an accusation was lodged, to subject the accuser to interrogation on three different days, making clear to him each time the punishment for false accusation. The primary purpose of the judicial inquiry

---

126 *Ernian lüling*, slip 113 (Barbieri-Low and Yates 2015: 509 (19)).
127 *Ernian lüling*, slip 93 (Barbieri-Low and Yates 2015: 501 (9)). Generally, see Zhang 2011 and Korolokov 2011.

was to establish the true facts of the case. In order to do this, the judge had to be able to identify lies told by the parties or witnesses. The laws establish certain methods that the judge is to adopt. First, he is to identify from his successive interrogations of the parties and witnesses any discrepant statements and then confront (*qie*) the persons in question with these discrepancies in order to obtain a resolution. Further, he is not only to listen to what the parties and witnesses say, but at the same time observe their demeanour, their expression, breathing and eyes, an advice to the judges also given in Indian legal texts. If through the application of these techniques the judge was still convinced that a party, especially the accused, was lying, he might have recourse to torture to force the individual to state the truth (as discussed above).

Doubtful cases were those in which there was uncertainty as to whether, on the proven and admitted facts, an offence had been committed, or as to the appropriate rule to be applied for the sentencing of the offender. The material on torture and confession shows that there was a strong reluctance on the part of the investigating authorities to accept that there might be a doubt as to the facts themselves. For example, a clear procedure for the handling of doubtful cases was established at the very beginning of the Han dynasty. An imperial edict of 200 BCE established a system of referral for cases in which persons had committed crimes, but the investigating authorities were in doubt as to which punishment should be imposed. Doubtful cases arising in the prefectures or districts were to be referred to the grand administrator of the commandery to which they belonged. Should the grand administrator not be able to resolve the matter, or should a doubtful case for the first time arise before him, referral was to be made to the commandant of justice in the capital. Should the commandant of justice still be in doubt, he was to submit the matter to the emperor in a memorial stating the relevant statutes, ordinances and precedents.[128] Good examples of the process of referral are contained in a recently excavated document entitled *Zouyanshu* (Referral of Doubtful Cases).[129]

In essence the principle of referral of doubtful cases established under the Han was maintained in later dynasties. For example, the Tang statutes provided that 'doubtful' cases arising at a local level should be referred to the supreme court for decision. Should the supreme court still be in doubt, the case was to be referred to the ministry of justice. We might note that

---

[128] Hulsewé 1987.
[129] This document has been translated in Barbieri-Low and Yates 2015 and by Lau and Lüdke 2012.

article 502 of the Tang Code dealing with 'doubtful cases' was concerned with cases in which there was at the end of the investigation still a genuine doubt as to whether the accused had committed the offence with which they were charged.[130] In such cases the article provided that they might pay a sum of money to redeem the punishment stipulated for the offence. The reason for the system of referral is not made explicit in the sources. Almost certainly it lay in the desire of the emperor and central government to retain control of the law-making power. There was a danger that, should provincial officials be left with a discretion to decide doubtful cases on their own authority, not only would decisions be made contrary to the policy of the government, but also the law would come to be applied in markedly different ways in the various provinces of the empire. Hence the government perceived and stressed a need for uniformity in decision-making.

Coming to the ancient Near East, we know that courts deliberated. The standard term for this in the Neo-Babylonian period is the reciprocal form of the verb *malāku* ('to confer, discuss'). But we have very little insight into the nature of these deliberations. Only two texts seem to provide much insight in terms of how a court might discuss what the legal grounds for its decision should be, and both are literary compositions as opposed to actual trial records. They are the Nippur Homicide Trial from Old Babylonian Mesopotamia and Jeremiah 26 in the Hebrew Bible. Both show that factions could develop within a judicial panel and disagreements could occur between the panel's members.

At Athens the large juries did not deliberate formally, but in the time it took for all of the several hundred jurors to cast their vote, presumably some of them discussed the case. We have seen the centrality of rhetoric and oratory within the Greek legal system. Some of these speeches were written for the litigants by professional writers or logographers. These were meant to influence the judgment of the jurors. As noted above, Roman magistrates under the late Republic and Empire did not necessarily have any kind of legal education or expertise but were served by legal advisers (*adsessores*). In any given province, a magistrates' advisory council would probably include local 'big men' and other influential persons, as well as Roman legal experts and the like.

Verdict

The final stage of the legal proceeding, flowing directly from evaluation of the evidence, is the verdict rendered by the court. Most frequently, a verdict

130 Johnson 1987.

included not only the decision as to the victor in the dispute but also any fines or penalties to be imposed on the losing party. In most systems the verdict is final and unconditional, but the ancient Near East provides a counter-example. There the (final) verdict takes the form of a conditional statement that pronounces the victor 'if' certain conditions that are spelled out are fulfilled.

The verdict (*nirṇaya*) within the Indian system is the fourth and final foot of the four feet of legal procedure (*vyavahāra*). Even though it was the chief judge who pronounced the verdict, it appears that the three assessors were the ones responsible for it: 'The *sabhya*s [assessors] really decided the suit, the presiding judge merely conducting the trial and the king delivering and carrying out the judgement.'[131] Thus, when there was a miscarriage of justice, it was the assessors who were punished and not the chief judge. The verdict may be a simple guilty/innocent decision in cases such as rape or assault. In monetary disputes, on the other hand, the judge may have to hand down a more complex decision. The issue arises when a plaint has several points (e.g. that the defendant has borrowed money and a cow) and the evidence supports only some of them (e.g. money); or when a larger amount is claimed, while only a portion of that is supported by the evidence. According to one opinion, if the defendant has denied all the points in the claim, then even when only a few of them have been proven the defendant becomes liable for all. The other opinion holds that the plaintiff can obtain only the portion he has proved through evidence. In this case the defendant is required to pay the rest to the state. There were also further fines imposed on the losing party. As one text puts it: 'The amount that one man falsely denies and the amount that the other falsely claims – the king should impose a fine equal to double those amounts on those two men who are proficient in unrighteous conduct' (*MDh* 8.59). In a plea of denial, the entire claim, if proven, was paid to the creditor and an equal sum to the state. If the suit included a stake or wager, then the losing party has to pay the wager plus the fine. As in most ancient – and modern – contexts, litigation was a profitable business for the state.

Criminal proceedings in ancient Chinese sources stand out from those recorded for other ancient systems by the fact that for there to be a conviction, it was necessary that the accused acknowledge that he had committed the offence in question. Such confession was a vital part of the evidence for his guilt. It is this fact that underlies both the need for recourse to

---

131 Aiyangar: 91–92. See also *NSm Mātṛkā* 2.42.

torture and the danger of its application, in that there was a likelihood that persons subjected to torture would make false confessions, which they would later recant. The ancient Near Eastern courts, on the other hand, had a unique practice of rendering what are best described as conditional verdicts. These state what verdict will take effect if a particular condition is met. The condition is typically either the performance of a ritual (oath, ordeal) or the production of further evidence by one of the parties. Oaths or pledges that the parties will abide by the verdict and not sue again were required in some periods. They show up especially in documents from the Old Babylonian period and those from the Late Bronze Age, including from Nuzi and Emar. They are not very prevalent in other periods (e.g. the Neo-Sumerian period or the Neo-Babylonian period).

In contrast the verdict in ancient Egypt was clearly declared by the court: 'A is in the right and B is in the wrong', but it was not always unanimous. Occasionally the losing party was required to take an oath to fulfil any duties to the winning party required from the judgment. The second-century BCE Asyut trial document, discussed above, records the legal reasoning behind the judges' decision, concluding with the signatures of the judges and the scribe who recorded the text.[132] In Athens the verdict was simply in favour of one side or the other. Some verdicts may have been written down, mainly those in public prosecutions, or when a convicted person owed money to the polis. Not all verdicts in private cases, however, were written down. Fines and damages or some other remedy were sometimes specified beforehand by law or by the accuser, for example by naming the damages he was seeking. In certain cases where no penalty was specified (made famous in Plato's fourth-century BCE recreation of the trial of Socrates in the *Apology*), after a guilty verdict each side proposed a single penalty and the jury then had to choose one of them.

In Rome, the verdict given by a *iudex* under the second stage of the formulary procedure or a decision given by a formal arbitrator was final. In the case of a *iudex* under the formulary procedure, no reasons have to be given for the judgment. The judgment was effectively a determination of whether the plaintiff had proved the necessary facts as set out in the formula: 'yes' or 'no'. The only judgments that the *iudex* could pronounce under the formulary procedure were monetary; that is, the judge could only award a sum of money, not the return of property, etc. There were, however, various legal devices available for encouraging a defendant to 'perform rather than pay'.[133]

---

132 See footnote 35 above; see also the detailed discussion in Allam 2008.
133 Johnston 2022: 141.

Verdict

Document Recording the Verdict

The Indian system seems to have been unique in requiring the court to give a victory document (*jayapatra*) to the winning party, stating the gist of the case, including the plaint, plea and evidence, and the final verdict. It is to be signed by the judge and bear the royal seal. Some sources give the technical term *paścātkāra* to a document containing the above features, while restricting the term *jayapatra* to verdicts reached without a full court trial, as when the plaint has been thrown out and the plaintiff loses in a summary judgment, or when the defendant presents a plea of admission. It is this kind of document that a defendant pleading 'prior judgment' (*prāṅnyāya*) has to produce to prove his case. In contrast, in classical Athens verdicts were probably not written down unless it was a major public case or involved a fine payable to the city.

Evidence from other ancient traditions suggests a varied involvement of different types of court officials in issuing documents recording the verdict. In China the sentence was recorded by the court in writing and read to the accused, who was required to accept it; frequently the written record of the verdict, which had to contain a reference to the statutory provision upon which the sentence was based, was reported to a superior authority for confirmation. Similarly in Ptolemaic Egypt, according to the trial record from Asyut, Middle Egypt, discussed above, the pleadings of plaintiff and defendant were read out by a scribe in front of the parties. The three judges asked each party if they agreed to what they had said in their oral statement at the trial. Then documents were produced that supported each party's claims. The judges found for the defendant on this basis, affirmed their decision with their signatures at the end of the document, along with the signature of the scribe of the judges – perhaps the author of the large trial document itself.[134]

In Rome there were various practices relating to recording the verdict, including entry of the verdict into the relevant magistrate's 'daybook'. Under the *cognitio* procedure, litigants could request the issuing of a written document on payment of a fee; imperial constitutions specify that the sentences themselves had to be written down by the magistrate and could not just be pronounced orally. We also have some evidence for the exact costs associated with litigants requesting written copies of Roman imperial magistrates' sentences.[135]

---

134 See the discussion in Allam 2008.
135 On imperial Roman court costs and fees, see Haensch 2015.

Enforcement of the Verdict

In 'criminal' cases, the state obviously had an interest that a court's verdict be carried out against the criminal, or, in the case of an acquittal, the accused be set free. The situation is more complex in private or civil lawsuits. If the court proceedings are viewed as some kind of arbitration, then the litigants themselves would be responsible for the enforcement of the verdict. In some systems, prior to the trial the litigants would undertake to abide by the court's verdict, sometimes under oath. In others, the court itself or other state agencies would enforce the verdict, especially if it also involves fines payable to the state.

In Indian jurisprudence, the court was responsible for making sure that the settlement contained in the verdict was enforced. This was facilitated by the fact that the litigants had to present sureties to the court. In the case of financial disputes, it was expected that the losing party would give the amount claimed to the victor. If this was not done, the state would enforce it, claiming a further fine. If the losing party was unable or unwilling to settle the claims and fines, the court could force his surety to pay up. In cases requiring physical punishment or execution, these were always carried out by the king; lower courts were not permitted to impose these penalties. Similarly, in criminal proceedings – which is the traditional paradigm for legal procedure in China – the state saw to the enforcement of a sentence: whether it was inflicting a beating, sending the offender into penal servitude or exile, or carrying out the execution in the event of a death sentence. For civil cases there was no state mechanism available for the enforcement of the judgment; it appears that the Chinese system considered these trials as forms of arbitration.[136] Persons who failed to pay their debts or compensation due under a contract were not imprisoned. The only help afforded by the state for which we have evidence from the Han dynasty is the garnishing of wages (for the benefit of the plaintiff) where the defendant was a soldier employed in a frontier garrison.

There are documents from the ancient Near East that record the enforcement of verdicts, but we have very little information on how that enforcement was carried out. Some scholars have questioned whether ancient Near Eastern courts had coercive power to enforce their decisions.[137] While the evidence in this regard is not entirely clear, most trial records show that the process of adjudication was more than mere arbitration. Government officials at the central and provincial levels could rely on the power of the state to enforce their decisions, and even local officials probably had the backing of the royal administration in serious cases (cases involving what we would

---

136 See Zhang 2010: 8–9.   137 Démare-Lafont (2000).

consider criminal matters). When decisions were rendered in private disputes, courts often required both litigants to swear that they would not challenge the verdict in the future. This has been interpreted as a sign of the court's weakness in the area of enforcement. On the other hand, some documents record the actual execution of judgment. Even though verdicts were occasionally disputed, outright disobedience in the face of a judicial verdict is extremely rare in the extant documentation.

In classical Athens execution was carried out by the city. Other sorts of punishment, besides fines, are rarely attested in the extant evidence. Fines or damages assessed by the court were collected by the individual affected, or by the city if the fine was to go to it. If a winning litigant could not collect, he could come back to court to get a summary judgment that might allow him to seize property up to the value of the fine. Court fees were probably collected ahead of time. Out-of-court settlements would normally prevent further litigation. If one of the parties to the settlement brought a case about matters resolved in the settlement, the other party would bring a *paragraphe* to block the action on the grounds the case had been settled (e.g. Dem. 37).[138] In a *diadikasia* – used in inheritances and some other cases – there might be more than two litigants, and the court would have to vote for one of the claimants. The phase of the trial in which each side proposed a penalty was the *timesis*. Penalties could include a fine, permanent exile and confiscation of property and death – though they were not specified in some types of public actions (*graphai*). Time in prison was not normally used as a penalty in Athens; nor was it specified, probably, in other Greek city states.

As noted above, under the (private or civil) formulary procedure in Rome only monetary damages were awarded. If the convicted defendant failed to pay damages, then enforcement would require a second, separate proceeding. Similarly, if disputants made a joint formal agreement under Roman law to abide by an arbitrator's award – termed a *compromissum* – then they could reasonably expect a Roman magistrate, such as the Urban Praetor of Rome or a provincial governor, to enforce that award through a separate proceeding if certain other conditions had also been met. In general, under Roman law, it fell to the successful plaintiff to execute the judgment of the court; although there is also evidence for some forms of official state intervention, as happened, for example, in the execution of a rescript of the emperor Pius (Justinian, *Digest* 42.1.15 pr). State intervention also undoubtedly took place 'unofficially', as in the famous case mentioned by Cicero where an individual

---

138 Harris 2015c.

named Scaptius used troops given by a provincial official to exact a debt owed from Salamis in Cyprus (Cic. *Att.* 5.21.10ff.)

Appeals

The litigants do not always have to accept the verdict of a court; they can appeal. This was as true in ancient legal systems as it is in contemporary law. But the possibility of an appeal implies, as we have already noted, a gradation of courts, where higher courts could review lower-court decisions and, if warranted, reverse them.

The notion of appeal and retrial in the Indian system is laid down clearly in this text from the middle of the first millennium CE: 'When someone is not satisfied, however, even after a decision has been reached by a family and the like, the king should investigate how it was carried out and take up again for review one that has been badly conducted' (*BṛSm* 1.9.23). Here 'family' refers to the lowest of the five fora given above for settling disputes: family, guild, association and appointed judges, each succeeding ones having greater authority, with the king himself given sometimes as the fifth and ultimate court. If the higher courts (*uttarasabhā*) or the king finds malfeasance on the part of court officials, they are subject to a fine. Some sources call for fines equal to twice the amount in dispute also on the victorious party, assuming that they also had a hand in the corruption. Even a judgment of the royal court could be appealed to the king himself, who is instructed to set aside verdicts that were wrongly reached (*durdṛṣṭa*) or where bribery or other malfeasance has taken place.

As noted above, according to Roman law the verdict rendered by a *iudex* under the second stage of the formulary procedure or a sentence given by a formal arbitrator was final and could not be appealed, unless some impropriety or irregularity was alleged against the judge or arbitrator himself. Nor was there any appeal from the 'criminal' *quaestiones perpetuae* at Rome. Under the Roman empire the fact that the judge was an imperial magistrate opened the way for the formalization of a bureaucratic appeals system, where an appeal against a magistrate's judgment could be lodged with his superior, all the way up to the emperor himself. In fact 'much the most important innovation in the machinery of justice made by the Principate was appeal'.[139] The volume of civil appeals under the early and late Empire seems to have been relatively high. An appeal from a sentence given by

---

139 Crook 1967: 73.

a lower Roman magistrate or official to a higher court could, in general, be made – although there were no appeals from praetorian prefects, who judged in the place of the emperor, or from the emperors themselves. Under the later Empire, rules were established governing how and when appeals may be made, and fines were laid down against making frivolous appeals. The development of an appeals system must have had an impact on substantive Roman law during the classical and postclassical periods, providing a (relatively) systematic means of integrating and unifying case-specific legal decisions and principles.

There were no appeals at Athens or, as far as we know, at Gortyn. Yet losing litigants could and often did bring another suit on a related matter, such as a suit for false testimony against the witnesses. This could open up the dispute to a new trial. The Athenian Assembly could nullify the verdict of a court, but this was rare.[140] There is evidence, however, for appeals from various periods in the ancient Near East, but there is no sense of a clear mechanism for making appeals and no clear rules by which they operated: the king had the authority to overturn previous verdicts, though this was rare, and his decision was final. Appeals seem to have been made by means of a petition to an official higher in authority than those who adjudicated the initial case. In periods where they are attested, appeals are almost never successful, and some appellants are punished for having brought a case a second time without justification. Laws of Ḫammurabi, chapter 5 states that, if a judge renders a final verdict but later changes that decision, he will be fined an amount that is equal to twelve times the amount that was at issue in the case. We do not have any records across the extant Near Eastern material recording the actual prosecution of judges. There seems to have been no formalized procedure for appeals in Egypt before the Greco-Roman period, although there was a hierarchy and appeals to higher courts are documented.

For China we have to distinguish two different processes: review and appeal. On the one hand, we have the administrative review of the judicial performance of lower-level administrators conducted by their immediate superiors of the kind illustrated in the Han by the supervision of the commandery with respect to the prefectures under its jurisdiction. On the other hand, the emperor was always concerned with the way higher-ranking local officials carried out their judicial duties. To ensure that local authorities properly carried out their duties, the central government adopted a practice of periodic review of performance,

---

140 See Pecorella Longo 2004 and Harris 2016a: 80–81.

with particular reference to the handling of criminal cases. For the pre-Tang period, this is best documented for the Han and Northern Wei dynasties. The effectiveness of supervision by the government undoubtedly varied according to the relative power positions of the central and local governments. Sometimes, as in the last decades of the Han or during most of the Southern Dynasties, proper and constant supervision by the central government of the activities of local authorities appears to have fallen into abeyance. Various mechanisms of review were adopted by the central government. Sometimes we have the dispatch of special envoys to ensure that justice was administered properly throughout the empire, but sometimes we have more regular procedures. This is the case with the creation of regional inspectors (*cishi*, later called *mu* or shepherds) by Emperor Wu (reigned 140–86 BCE) of the former Han (206 BCE–25 CE) in 106 BCE. Each year the inspectors were to examine the way in which the grand administrators of commanderies carried out their duties. The remit of the inspectors was defined by 'six articles', the third of which specified that they were to inquire inter alia into 'whether the grand administrators and chancellors (of kingdoms) have failed to give proper attention to difficult law cases or have put people to death too harshly'. This system was also adopted by the Later Han (25–220 CE), although then the inspectors were classified as part of the local administration and not as officers of the central government. A contemporary source notes that in the course of their annual review the inspectors were to examine the cases of persons detained in prison, in order to ensure that convictions had been sound, and were to correct any injustice.[141] The Northern Wei adopted the Han system of dispatching special envoys to scrutinise the way in which local authorities were performing their duties. We first hear of this kind of inspection in 455 CE when the emperor sent an imperial secretary and other officials to tour the country in order to receive complaints about wrongdoing (including judicial malpractices) on the part of the local administrations (Cheng Shude: 379). This system of review carried out by emissaries of the local government was followed by the Sui and Tang dynasties, though this did not amount to the establishment of an institution, an inspectorate, resembling that created by Emperor Wu of the Han.

Remaining with the ancient Chinese source material, the automatic review of judgments in criminal cases conducted within the official hierarchy itself has to be distinguished from the kind of intermittent review discussed above. There developed a practice under which all serious cases were required to be reviewed by a higher authority. We can no longer trace

---

141 Generally see Bielenstein 1980: 90–92; de Crespigny 1981: 40–79.

Appeals

how this practice came to be enshrined in the law codes of the pre-Tang period, but we can observe the final result as detailed in the Tang Code itself. The Tang administrative statutes (*ling*) provided that offences entailing beating with the heavy stick or less might be finally decided by the county, but that in cases of offences entailing penal servitude or more, the decision of the county must be referred to the next highest level (the prefecture). The prefecture might make a final decision in cases entailing penal servitude, but those entailing exile for life or death had to be referred to the Supreme Court of Justice. Capital cases were to be submitted by the supreme court to the emperor for a final ruling.[142]

Appeals, as distinguished from reviews, refer to the process by which a person convicted of an offence or members of his family might request a rehearing on the ground of an injustice. Such right to appeal was already enshrined in the early Han laws of 186 BCE. The flood of appeals proved an embarrassment to the government, and the right to appeal was later qualified in various ways, and even abolished altogether by (Three Kingdoms) Wei, though revived under the Jin (265–420 CE). Apart from specific rules permitting appeal, there was always the recognition that the emperor as the ultimate source of justice might be invoked where any of his subjects complained of a manifest injustice that had not been corrected by the imperial officials. Such exceptional recourse to the throne came to be regulated through an institution known as 'striking the drum'. A special drum was placed outside the palace. Anyone alleging an injustice that required the emperor's personal intervention might strike it to bring the matter to the attention of the government.[143] We first hear of 'striking the drum' in the Jin dynasty (265–316 CE) and also have examples from the Southern Dynasties (317–589 CE). The Northern Wei code of 431 CE provided that a drum should be placed outside the palace gates. Any person alleging an injustice might strike the drum. Thereupon it was the duty of the appropriate officials to report the matter to the emperor. An imperial decree during the Sui provided that as a last resort persons suffering an injustice might 'strike the drum' and submit their petition to the appropriate officials who would then report directly to the emperor. The Tang Code and statutes introduced quite detailed rules concerning one special case of recourse to the drum. Should an offender have been sentenced to penal servitude, exile or death, he was required to accept the sentence. If he refused, the court was to hear his

---

142 Johnson and Twitchett 1993: 133, 139, 145–46.
143 For this kind of direct recourse to the throne, see Qiang Fang 2013: 15–22.

reasons and, on their basis, order a further investigation. Even after reinvestigation, should the offender still refuse to accept the sentence, the matter was to be referred to a succession of higher authorities and ultimately, in the event of continued refusal by the offender, to the emperor. Should the responsible official not be prepared to forward the case, the offender might strike the petitioner's drum, thus ensuring imperial attention. This regulation for a special case did not exclude a petitioner's right to 'strike the drum' for other kinds of alleged injustice.

Conclusion

All legal systems of the ancient world present well-structured procedures for the resolution of both private and public legal disputes, whether they are of a civil or a 'criminal' nature – notwithstanding the substantial differences that we have also noted. This underscores the anthropological necessity we noted at the outset: a system of justice requires transparent and accepted rules for adjudicating disputes and accusations. There are certain fundamental features of legal procedure, clearly with sharp differences, that are present in all. All empower certain individuals to function as judges. In some systems, such as the Indian, the judges are professionals without other functions within the state bureaucracy. In the majority of systems, however, bureaucrats and military officers also acted as judges. In classical Athens, the judges or jurors were selected from the public. But they all were empowered by the state to administer justice within the legal system. All systems placed some kind of restriction on access to the justice system and on the qualification to act as witnesses in a court of law. Some restrictions are based on citizenship (native versus foreign), on gender and age, and on social class (free versus enslaved persons and caste distinction in India).

The procedure of the trial itself shows considerable variations especially in the kinds of admissible plaints and pleas; the relative weight given to various types of evidence; the manner in which arguments are presented; and legal representation. There is also considerable variation in the use of torture for legal purposes, including who is subject to torture (plaintiff, defendant or witnesses; slaves or freemen; men or women; lower or higher social class; and the like). It was important for all systems that whoever comes before the court, especially the witnesses, speak the truth. Perjury was considered a serious crime, although the remedies and punishments vary. The legal procedure followed in a court is aimed at ensuring that the truth behind the accusations, claims and counterclaims is discovered and the court can render an impartial and fair verdict. Many systems tell the judges how to interpret evidence, how to detect false testimony and forged documents. It is never possible to be 100 per cent sure that the verdict is correct; evidence cannot give absolute certainty. One Indian source tells us that the only result that is absolutely correct is when the defendant pleads guilty. But even there, the sources warn, an innocent person may plead guilty because of the fear of torture.

Some systems, as we have seen, had a gradation of courts and permitted appeals of decisions of lower courts to upper one and finally to the ruler himself. Once a final verdict had been reached, there was the question of enforcement. Some systems, moreover, like the Indian and the Chinese, empowered the court to enforce its verdicts: including both compensation to the victim and any fines or penalties to the state. In others, private litigations were considered a kind of judicial arbitration that the parties promised to abide by. Often the judges themselves were not involved in enforcing the verdict.

8

Status and Family

Lead Author: TIMOTHY LUBIN

Contributors: ARI BRYEN, SOPHIE DÉMARE-LAFONT, MICHAEL GAGARIN, CAROLINE HUMFRESS, GEOFFREY MACCORMACK AND JOSEPH G. MANNING

Introduction

Law's subjects are not generic persons; they come encoded with overlapping distinctions that determine how they will be treated – what capacities they have or limitations they face – before the law. These are distinctions of personal status, that is, an individual's position before the law with respect to particular social groupings and institutions, including the state. Statuses have normative implications: any given status may entail particular rights, duties, capacities and incapacities. Some sorts of status are ascriptive and lie beyond the legal subject's control (although legal means can sometimes be found to get around limitations posed by such status); others sorts of status are achieved in consequence of legally defined acts. Henry Sumner Maine, the nineteenth-century comparative legal historian, famously concluded that the history of law since antiquity discloses that 'the movement of the progressive societies has hitherto been a movement *from Status to Contract*'.[1] This pattern, which he deemed a 'law of progress', entailed a corresponding diminution in the authority of the family, since, in his view ascriptive status in ancient law was primarily an extension of family: 'All the forms of Status taken notice of in the Law of Persons were derived from, and to some extent are still coloured by, the powers and privileges anciently residing in the Family.'[2] This chapter will revisit the topic of personal status and its bearing on other aspects of ancient law, including much material that Maine did not or could not consider.

---

1 Maine 1861: 170. 2 Maine 1861: 170.

Introduction

Of all the traditions of ancient law, Roman law has loomed largest in Western legal history because European and Anglo-American legal systems continue to employ categories derived from that tradition. In Roman jurisprudence the 'law of persons' (*ius personarum*) distinguished several forms of status (*caput*) formally recognized by law, but in fact we cannot understand any legal system without taking into account other sorts of personal status, recognized in the society of which they are a part, insofar as the norms connected with them impinge on the actual working of law.[3] Like many other legal concepts, legal statuses are a special application of social categories that have other roles in human affairs. But juridical understandings of status tend to diverge from common perceptions and cultural representations.[4] Divergences of this sort may be difficult to pin down where we must rely mainly on normative works because of the absence or paucity of documents. Nevertheless, any comparison of the notion of status in ancient legal traditions must look beyond the formal status categories of any one system, in order to consider their relation to social structures and institutions and the interplay between diverse forms of status in the actual working of law.

In Roman law, for example, personal status at law was conceptually defined at three levels: free vs unfree (*status libertatis*); citizen vs alien (*status civitatis*); and age and relation within the family (*status familiae*). Although only these sorts of status were defined in legal terms, other status considerations had an impact on legal status. In the Roman world, ranks (*ordines*) conferred social privileges as well as legal status (such as citizenship). Holding public office 'allowed the elite to infuse the system with their own values . . . creating distinctions between the advantaged and disadvantaged beyond those categories enumerated in Roman law of persons'.[5] As already noted, at base the conceptualization of status in Anglo-American and European legal discourse partakes of the legacy of Roman law; nonetheless personal statuses – both those that are formulated in legal terms and those that are not – were an important factor in all known ancient legal systems. The first problem for comparing them is to establish where the structural analogies and disparities lie.

---

3 'Legal procedures cannot be studied in isolation from the social environment which engendered them', so said Garnsey 1970: 7 in his 'study of discrimination based on status in the administration of law' (p. 2).
4 Saller 1994 (especially Parts II and III) demonstrates this in the case of the Roman family.
5 Taylor 2016: 359.

From the perspective of modern liberal, individualistic conceptions of justice, the very notion of a status hierarchy as a factor determining legal rights, duties, capacities and incapacities might seem to be incompatible with ideals of equality before the law and especially with a notion of universal human rights. In fact, ancient societies, though in many cases intensely hierarchical and riven with status distinctions, could formulate principles of justice and equity that accommodated and indeed depended upon such distinctions.[6] Even today, analogues of the Roman ancient categories persist: citizenship or other status vis-à-vis the state; marital and family status; and (despite the abolition of 'legal' slavery) penal forms of degraded or unfree civic status.[7] Likewise, modern systems continue to mandate legal disabilities, concessions or protections on the basis of age, cognitive or physical impairments and race. George Letsas makes a useful distinction between 'rank-status' (reflecting 'the position one occupies within a social ordering of esteem or prestige') and 'role-status' ('the position one occupies within a pattern of social interaction'), arguing that the latter remains useful in egalitarian legal frameworks as a way of conceptualizing offences that 'regulate asymmetrical relations in which one of the parties suffers from background vulnerabilities and dependencies' and can be used to 'restore moral equality between the parties'. In ancient legal orders, rank-status and role-status frequently coincided, and status offences often concerned matters of esteem or privilege, but it will be clear in what follows that many statuses in ancient law can be understood as role-statuses, which served as a basis for assigning particular obligations, rights, privileges and powers not necessarily based on esteem or prestige.[8]

With these comparative reflections in mind, I propose to survey the terrain with an eye to the most commonly encountered distinctions that provide the context and rationale for status: kin units and larger clan or class distinctions defined by birth; political divisions and bodies; and corporate groups of a voluntary nature. Cutting across all of these are ascriptive individual statuses ostensibly determined by biological features: race, gender, age and mental or physical disabilities.[9] Most types of personal status, however, are

---

6 For a discussion with examples from India, see Lubin 2022.
7 Gustav Radbruch sought to show in 1938 that modern German criminal penalties had their roots in the unfree status of the medieval serf (English translation in Dubber 2014: 407–13).
8 Letsas 2023: especially 1 and 7–15.
9 Bond 2003, for example, applies this concept to contemporary debate on international human rights. The deleterious social consequences of this cross-cutting phenomenon (e.g. the intersection of racial and gender status) has in recent decades been described by legal theorists since Kimberlé Crenshaw as 'intersectionality' (1989).

subject to modification in accordance with customary norms, ritual acts or formal legal mechanisms. Hence, our analysis will necessarily require that we attend not only to statuses formally recognized as legal statuses within a given legal system, but also to other social statuses within the broader plural normative environment that affect how an individual is treated under the law in practice. Legal statuses endow individuals on principle with particular rights and obligations, but other statuses on which the law is theoretically neutral may nevertheless correlate with differential access to remedies or differential treatment by officials and institutions.

Moreover, the family looms large in most ancient polities as a microcosm of the larger polity, as well as its smallest corporate unit. Whatever the merit of Maine's claim that 'primitive law' derives all forms of legal status ultimately from the family, it is certainly the case that several important forms of personal status in ancient legal systems were defined in relation to family. 'Family' in this context refers not to a set of social relations (let alone mere biological relations) but to the relations regulating a household, which may include servants and other dependents: the *familia* of the Romans; the *oikos* of the Greeks; the *gṛha* or *kuṭumba* in India. The authority and power of the male head of household was often seen as analogous in some respects with that of the sovereign over the subject or the master over the enslaved person. For these reasons, personal status in ancient law cannot be adequately treated without giving particular attention to the family as a legal entity. On the other hand, the statuses associated with the larger institutions in society tend to inflect those of the family, so we will begin with those.

Status within the Polity

Legal orders, both civil and 'religious', recognized various distinctions of personal status, often in a hierarchy: from free to bondsman or slave; from citizen to resident alien or foreigner.[10] Broad distinctions used in some systems classify people in terms of caste, tribe or other forms of fictive macro-level kinship; even when these are not legal distinctions in a formal sense, they can have implications in legal practice. The legal apparatus in place may in turn be seen to mould and even redefine statuses, for example, through regulatory reforms or decisions in family law. Status could provide the basis for deciding which laws applied or which forum had jurisdiction and in assigning privileges or special consideration before the law. Individuals and

---

10 On 'religion' and legal orders, see Chapter 6, this volume.

groups, moreover, sometimes found ways to 'game the system' by changing their social status.

There seem to be fundamental differences in how ancient legal systems defined legal subjects at the level of polity. Civil status (e.g. that of a 'citizen' or a free subject) is often at the heart of ancient legal systems promulgated by civil authorities. In the Greco-Roman sphere – especially in Athens and in Rome – a clearly distinct status of citizen was defined, along with the specific appertaining rights. Elsewhere, formal legal criteria of citizenship were not formalized to the same extent; instead, legal sources adopt and give legal force to an originally more 'vernacular' distinction between native and foreigner, often framed partly in geographic and partly in ethnic terms.

By contrast, there exist comprehensive legal systems codified by religious authorities: for example, members of a class of ritual or scriptural experts.[11] These comprehensive legal systems are conceived as defining and regulating a community framed in terms of membership in what may be called an 'ecclesial polity' – that is, a geographically dispersed, trans-state, but formally delimited community that is constituted and regulated by a complex legal apparatus, with membership signalled by codified ritual markers and observance of norms of piety.[12] The major ancient examples of this are the Brahmanical *dharmaśāstra* law of India and the rabbinic law (*halakhah*) of the Talmud, but these were joined in the late antique / early medieval era by Islamic law (*shariah*) and Christian ecclesiastical ('canon') law.[13] Legal systems of this sort persist in the modern world as transnational legal systems, which can be and sometimes are established in some form by particular states – usually in a localized (nationalized) or hybrid form – but which also exist alongside the official law of individual states, often in tension with such state law.

In the case of both Talmud and Dharmaśāstra, however, we are dealing mainly with scholastic traditions and the normative texts produced by them. Especially for the ancient period, it is almost impossible to determine to what extent and in what manner these elaborate legal systems regulated the lives of

---

11 'Comprehensive' in the sense of applying to a broad range of social relations, practices and institutions beyond those applicable only to ordained clergy or ritual precincts. This leaves aside religious legal systems whose jurisdiction did not extend beyond the internal governance of a body of religious professionals, for example, Buddhist monastic law (*vinaya*).

12 Further work needs to be done to clarify the concept of a non-state religious polity overlapping with state polities. Legal pluralists and sociologists have taken some steps in this direction; see, for example, Cotterrell 2008.

13 Buddhist monastic law, by contrast, claimed no jurisdiction beyond the order of formally ordained religious professionals.

people. It is likely that some section of the respective target audiences (the 'observant') were subject to – and more importantly, subjected themselves to – such law. It is also likely that, however much both systems present themselves as extrapolating from a scriptural basis and learned interpretations thereof, their strictures actually represent a textualization of customary norms observed within the sections of society to which the authors belonged. The few documentary records that do survive of legal dealings of Hindus and Jews in antiquity mainly reflect the laws of the civil polity. In any case, it is clear that members of such groups operated in a legally plural environment and the law of these 'ecclesial polities' – as defined above – likely relied on ostracism and other social sanctions for recalcitrant offenders.

The rabbis could not avoid addressing the question of Jews' obligations to the (non-Jewish) state. Dharmaśāstra, because it seems often to have elicited at least token support from kings, had wider influence on legal practice, at least through providing a jurisprudential framework that helped spread a distinctive legal culture across South and parts of Southeast Asia. In Dharmaśāstric law, the primary distinction was between those dignified by the high-status label Ārya, with gradations justified by social function, and those excluded from that category (non-Ārya). In Talmud, Jews were the full parties to the Covenants with God that constituted the basis of Jewish law; non-Jews (Gentiles, 'the [other] nations') had attenuated rights. In both cases, however, internal gradations assigned certain special privileges to priestly lineages defined by birth. This was a systemic feature of Dharmaśāstric law, which prescribed gradations by caste-category for many forms of legal capacity. The gravity of offences and the severity of punishments likewise varied according to the relative caste status of the offender and the person harmed.

Free versus unfree status appears in both types of legal system. All Greek city states recognized a basic division between free and slave. In addition, Athens had a legally defined status of citizen (*politēs*), which was distinguished from that of *metic* (resident alien) and foreigner.[14] Athenian citizens could be disenfranchised – lose the right to vote in the Assembly or be a juror in court – temporarily, for being a public debtor; or permanently, if convicted of treason or other serious public crimes. Social class distinctions beyond these were not formally recognized, but in practice rights might be differentially distributed according to wealth. So, for example, in Athens the four census classes established by Solon enjoyed differential access to magistracies.

14 Hunter 2000.

Sparta was 'arguably, a pioneer in implementing the idea of citizenship as connoting deep membership in a strong corporate body, and thereby instantiating a thoroughly Greek notion of *politeia*'.[15] As in Athens, Spartans could apparently become disenfranchised if they were too poor to pay their obligations to the city. Sparta also had a special servile group, the helots, who were original inhabitants of the country and who worked the land for free citizens. The lexicographer Pollux classed the helots, along with the *penestae* of Thessaly, as occupying a status 'between free and slave'. There probably were ordinary slaves at Sparta too, but this is not certain. Among the free, a group of 'Spartiates' had an elite status amounting to that of a 'citizen'. The rest of the territory was inhabited by *perioikoi* (neighbours) living in surrounding villages, free but subject to Spartan domination. As Cartledge explains:

> the idea implemented by Sparta was not of a citizenship of equals, but instead of peers, citizens who were only comparatively equal; that is, they were accounted equal in some but not all respects to each other, and, no less importantly, equal with other in comparison and in contrast to all the many other categories of unequals, the very existence of which was such a marked feature of inegalitarian, hierarchical Spartan society as a whole.[16]

'Citizens' (*politai*) are mentioned twice in the extant evidence from Gortyn in connection with adoption, which they may perhaps be required to approve – but we do not know what distinguished a 'citizen' from others. More common is 'Gortynian', often in the plural, designating what appears to be the body politic; we also do not know what distinguished members of this group, but it may have been residency in the city. In one text 'the Gortynians' enact a law protecting a certain group in the city.[17] Citizens were divided into groups called *hetaireiai*; a smaller number, those who had been expelled from their *hetaireia* (and maybe some others, such as freed slaves), belonged to the little-understood class of *apetairoi* who were free but of lower status; they are mentioned only in laws on sexual offences.

In classical Roman jurisprudence, the law of personal status was elaborated in great detail. Three basic criteria determined legal status: freedom, citizenship and household (*familia*). John Crook, paraphrasing the second-century CE *Institutes* of Gaius, sums up the permutations of Roman status thus:

1. People (male and female) are either slaves, or they are free.
2. Free people are either free by birth, *ingenui*, or free by grant of freedom from slavery, 'freedmen', *libertini*.

---

15 Cartledge 2018: 186.   16 Cartledge 2018: 186.   17 Gagarin and Perlman 2016: 436–39.

3. Free people are also either Roman citizens; or 'Latins' (and if Latins either coloniary Latins or, under the Principate, Junian Latins); or peregrines (and if peregrines either citizens of some particular peregrine community or of none).
4. Roman citizens are either independent – 'in their own power', *sui iuris, suae potestatis* – or in the power of someone else, *alieni iuris*.
5. Persons *sui iuris* are either under guardianship, *tutela* or caretakership, *cura, curatio*, or under neither of these.[18]

Free citizens also belonged to classes that were socially and politically consequential, but which were not directly taken account of in Roman law (with some exceptions noted below). These classes include the patrician and equestrian orders, which were hereditary; and senatorial status, which was not; as well as local town orders. Ownership of a specified amount of property was a requirement, except for patrician status.

Besides these overlapping elite statuses, the Roman curial class, a class of wealthy provincials, were responsible for paying for public services and received privileges in exchange. These had to be free citizens of means and under the early Empire came to be regarded at law as *honestiores* (honourable men), which entailed privileges such as exemption from being subject to torture during a trial.[19] In the later Empire, as the financial obligations of decurions exceeded the revenue they could collect, many managed to evade their curial responsibilities by taking on other prestige roles that superseded those obligations, including positions in the army, the government and the Christian church. In practice 'the criteria for legal privilege were social and dependent upon status', particularly as manifested in the discretion exercised by judges in deciding whether to apply 'legal' penalties (normally reserved for upper classes) or the more degrading administrative sanctions to which the lower orders were subject.[20] In fact Cicero, writing under the late Roman Republic, citing the example of Athens when the Areopagus council was stripped of its legal authority, saw it as a defect of unalloyed democracy that 'equality itself is unequal when it does not recognize grades of dignity' (*tamen*

---

18 Crook 1967: 36. Crook goes on to note many other status categories dealt with in the present chapter, 'which involved partial differences of rights and duties which could nevertheless be quite important, such as age and sex (the special position of infants and of women), being married with a stated number of children, married without children, or unmarried, being a soldier, being a senator or member of the equestrian order or neither, and in the provinces being a magistrate or councillor of your city or neither'.
19 The curial class might be compared with the local and regional assemblies of India and the group status of their members as *mahājanas* ('great men' of the community).
20 Thus argues Garnsey 1970: 6–7 and Part IV, on the increasing application of the *cognitio* procedure.

ipsa aequabilitas est iniqua, cum habet nullos gradus dignitatis) (Cic. *De rep.* 1.43).[21] Legislation similarly prevented 'degraded' people from taking magistracies in Italian municipalities (*lex coloniae genetivae*).

Early Roman jurisprudence did not often deal with questions of moral worth (though it certainly asked about, say, whether a slave was known to be good or vile for the purpose of certain questions). But one legally consequential social status beginning in the Roman Republic was the stigma of *infamia* (disrepute); an individual deemed *infamis* was stripped of the right to bring a 'popular action' (*actio popularis*, an action brought in the interest of public order); to serve as an assessor or witness; and to be eligible for public office. Conversely, in 326 CE Constantine declared that the proprietress of a tavern, unlike her barmaids, was 'respectable' and thus could be tried for adultery.[22] From 380 CE, *infamia* was applied more expansively to marginalize heretics, apostates and pagans, which may have encouraged violence against such groups. Yet despite the loss of protections and social dignity entailed by the status of *infamia*, it might be utilized as a loophole for avoiding other legal consequences. During the reign of Tiberius, a senatorial woman named Vistilia attempted (albeit unsuccessfully) to avoid prosecution for adultery by registering as a prostitute, which would have rendered her *infamis*. Similarly, heresy may even have been used at times as a means for avoiding the increasingly heavy burden of curial service during Late Antiquity. This may be one of the reasons why Diocletian, Theodosius II and Justinian all issued rescripts affirming that religious deviants were in fact eligible for civic service, albeit without the usual legal privileges pertaining

---

21 As cited in Garnsey 1970: 3 (modified). This idea has its origins in Aristotle's discussion of fairness as treating equals equally and unequals unequally (*Politics* 1280a, 1281a, 1282b, 1301a–1302a, 1307a, 1308a). It is echoed even more emphatically by Pliny the Younger (*Ep.* 9 5) as he cautions a provincial governor to balance his solicitude for the local people with due recognition for the 'the most respectable citizens': 'so as to preserve the distinctions of rank and dignity; for, if these are confounded, disordered, and intermingled, nothing is more unequal than this very equality' (*ut discrimina ordinum dignitatumque custodias; quae si confusa turbata permixta sunt, nihil est ipsa aequalitate inaequalius*).

22 'If any woman had committed adultery, it ought to be inquired whether she was the mistress of a tavern or a servant woman, and thus in the performance of her servile duty she herself frequently proffered the wines of intemperance. If she were the mistress of a tavern, she shall not be exempt from the bonds of the law. But if she has given service to those who drink, then, in consideration of the mean status of the women who is brought to trial, the prosecution shall be blocked and the men who are accused shall go free. The reason is that respect for chastity (*pudicitia*) is required (only) of those women who are held by the constraints of the law and who enjoy the status of a respectable woman (*materfamilias*), while those whose mean status in life has not been deemed worthy of compliance with the laws shall be rendered immune from judicial severity' (Justinian, *Cod.* 9.9.28).

thereto.²³ Similar loss of legal status through disrepute can be identified in sources for ancient India. Kauṭilya lists the 'heinous sinner' (*abhiśasta*) among those ineligible to be party to a legal transaction (*KAŚ* 3.1.12). This status had earlier been applied to those guilty of killing a Brahmin (*ĀpDh* 1.24.6–9, third century BCE), but Kauṭilya probably had a wider range of infamy in mind. Elsewhere it seems to denote someone with a prior record of sexual misconduct (*MDh* 8.373) or a suicide, who should be deprived of funeral rites (*VDh* 23.14).

The formally defined conception of citizenship developed by the Greeks and Romans – which lives on as a distant model for full civic status in nation-states today – seems to have been particular to the Greco-Roman approach to law. Most other ancient law traditions seem not to have framed their laws so explicitly in terms of belonging to a particular civic or imperial polity. Instead, status categories of a broader social or ethnic character were adopted to serve legal functions.

Thus in early second-millennium Babylon – though the specific import of the labels are hard to pin down – the salient distinctions were between privileged elites ('nobility'), free non-elites ('commoners') and slaves or servile groups, with some references to others denoted by a geographic label. For instance, Sumerian lu₂ and Akkadian *awīlu*/*amīlu*, though attested in a wide range of meanings, often connote respectability and may precede a name or title in the sense of 'gentleman'.²⁴ Grades of dignity even within that class were recognized by law: the Laws of Ḥammurabi (chapter 202; c. 1750 BCE) decrees that an *awīlum* who slaps the face of another freeman (*awīlum*) 'who is higher than him' (*ša elišu rabû*) is sentenced to a public whipping. Such references point to an aristocracy, the composition of which seems to have shifted, during the neo-Assyrian empire (ninth–eighth centuries BCE), from a landed nobility defined by birth or skills to a class defined by personal privileges that were granted and revoked at the king's pleasure. Babylonian commoners were called maš.en.kak (Sumerian) and *muškēnu* (Akkadian), and in the Laws of Ḥammurabi the *muškēnum* (previously understood as a half-free villein attached to the land he was cultivating without owning) appears to be inferior to the *awīlum* 'free/noble man' but superior to the *wardum* 'slave'. But the tablets from Mari in Syria (from the eighteenth century BCE) have shown that the word refers to a commoner who has no personal assets but depends on an institution (e.g. a temple or palace) or a wealthy landowner for his sustenance.²⁵ According to others, he would be a 'subject' in contrast to the awīlum, 'man of authority',²⁶ or a kind of peregrinus who lives in another city than his own.²⁷

---

23 Bond 2014. 24 Westbrook 2003c 377. 25 Charpin 2012. 26 Von Dassow 2014.
27 Démare-Lafont 2015a: 87.

Figures called 'Assyrian man/woman' (*aššuraju/aššura'ītu*) appear in Middle Assyrian (fourteenth–eleventh centuries) laws and in several legal deeds. Though earlier interpreted as being on a par with the *muškēnu*, the term most likely refers to the geographical origin of a person and their relevant personal law. Being an 'Assyrian' meant living under the law of the city of Aššur. By means of privilege, Assyrians could probably carry their personal status with them even when travelling abroad – maybe as an extension of the privileges of the merchants, who were very active in this city from the nineteenth century BCE onward.[28] More generally, any free person given as a pledge in a forfeiting clause (by which the creditor gets the complete ownership of the pledge if the debtor does not repay by the stipulated date), they lost their status and were considered enslaved.

In Pharaonic Egypt the state distinguished between Egyptians and outsiders and between elite and non-elite, although it is not clear that Egyptian law formally made such distinctions beyond free vs slave. What survives in the private sphere are mostly texts generated by elites: the priestly scribal class and especially for the Middle and New Kingdoms, the military, some of which address the concept of *ma'at* (justice, social order), an ideal to be realized through the behaviour of kings towards the gods as well as to all men.[29] The tension between expectations of justice for all and the norms of a hierarchical society is evoked in an important Middle Kingdom text (c. 1900 BCE) known as the *Tale of the Eloquent Peasant*, which tells of a peasant seeking justice after being abused by a low-level official.[30] The right for all to petition the state to redress wrongs was always apparently a part of Egyptian law and was manifest in important texts such as the *Duties of the Vizier* of the New Kingdom.[31] In Ptolemaic Egypt, in addition to political status expressed as citizenship, there were a few other political statuses. Male parties to private contracts written in Greek or Egyptian generally have status titles of some kind, either as soldiers, priests or others who served within a temple estate. Women in contracts usually have the simple title 'woman' or 'married woman'. It is not entirely clear if the male titles were associated with the census or if the use of such titles had particular ramifications for social status within Ptolemaic law. At the very least, it certainly reflects the fact that those who were engaged in contracting for property rights by using written contracts were

---

28 See Michel 2020.   29 Assman 2001; see also Chapter 6, this volume.
30 Parkinson 1991.   31 van den Boorn 1988.

indeed those individuals who had status within the royal or temple domain.[32]

Disentangling ethnicity and citizenship can be hard. Both Ptolemaic and Roman Egypt recognized the ethnic diversity of its populace by developing a legal-pluralist scenario in which each of the major groups was governed by its own laws.[33] The 'national laws' (*politikoi nomoi*) of ethnic groups were recognized by Ptolemaic courts: '*ethnika* (ethnic labels) were recorded in all legal documents, alongside personal names and patronymics'.[34] A legal *koine* of Greek traditions became the governing law of the Greek population, adjudicated by Greek-speaking judges, while Egyptian law was normally determined by the *laokritai*, the Egyptian court held at temples. The sizeable Jewish population was generally governed by the Torah.[35] The most significant change came in the state's recognition of Greek citizens in the three Greek poleis, Alexandria, Naukratis and Ptolemais. Military rank, status differences between those recognized as Greek and Egyptians, and claims of ethnic origin were closely monitored, at least at first. The Ptolemaic state forbade on penalty of death any claimed change in status or ethnic origin. By contrast, P. Tebt. I 5 (118 BCE) redrew jurisdictional boundaries of lawsuits based not on the ethnicity of the parties, as in the early Ptolemaic period, but on the language in which the disputed contract was drafted.[36]

In Roman Egypt, citizens of Alexandria appear to have had extra privileges compared to the rest of the population; those who were citizens of other 'Greek' cities seem to have had rights over and above those who lived in the towns or the countryside. Pliny attests that citizenships themselves were ranked: he asks to have his doctor granted Roman citizenship and Trajan replies that such a citizenship is privileged and that under normal circumstances the doctor must first obtain Alexandrian citizenship (Pliny *Ep.* 10.6). The most important privileges of citizenship seem to have been: first, exemption from compulsory public services in an area outside of one's region (i.e. citizens of Antinoopolis only had to perform public services in Antinoopolis, even if they were living in a different community); and second, the ability to have cases that involved a conflict of laws transferred to one's home venue (again, if an Antinoopolite got into a dispute in a village somewhere, he could have the case moved to Antinoopolis).[37] It also

---

32 On property rights see Chapter 10, this volume.   33 Clarysse 2019.
34 Honigman 2019: 315.   35 For detailed discussion see Honigman 2016 and Kugler 2022.
36 Pestman 1985b.
37 P. Mich. VI 365 records the decision of an *epistrategos* to move a trial to Antinoopolis in a case of violence and extortion.

appears that people with a particular privileged citizenship would more rapidly get a response when they submitted a petition and were dealt with more frequently by higher-ranked officials.[38]

There were – to a Roman administrator at least – four main 'ethnic' groups in Egypt: Egyptians, Greeks, Romans and, for a certain time, Jews. Everyone who was not a member of the 'Greek' cities – Alexandria, Naukratis, Antinoopolis, Ptolemais – was classed an 'Egyptian' and were subject to certain types of taxation. An early Roman administrative document, the *Gnomon of the Idios Logos*, circulated among officials, describes a number of disabilities in the form of penalties to the state that attached to individuals (especially Egyptians) who put themselves in positions where these discrete 'ethnic' groups might be mixed (by, for example, marrying outside of one's status group). To what extent such provisions were capable of enforcement is a harder question; certainly, cities kept census rolls and used a process called *epikrisis* to verify the (high) status and privileges (e.g. a lower rate of poll tax) of new registrants.[39] How this would have worked in the countryside is a harder question. At the very least, the Roman government may have thought of itself as administering a province whose populace was divided into discrete ethnic classes, though there is no agreement on what such a policy would have entailed.

The extension of Roman citizenship to the free population of the empire in 212 CE wiped out a lot of the local distinctions, at least formally and juridically.[40] Scholars tend to think that a lot of these classifications were already obsolete and that the system was instead tending to privilege status distinctions based not on citizenship, but on formal rank: the *honestiores / humiliores* distinction, wherein councilmen, senators and the equestrian order were counted among the *honestiores* and everyone else was counted among the *humiliores*.[41] Can we conclude from this that the expanded legal horizon implicit in the 212 CE decision effectively drained the traditional, Roman, political status of citizenship of particularity and thus its utility, reinforcing trans-local distinctions of social rank?

This development in the third-century CE Roman empire in fact moves in the direction of the legal order reflected in classical Sanskrit texts and early epigraphy from India, where we find little indication of a formal status precisely corresponding to 'the citizen'. All these sources look to the transregional macro-statuses, such as the four 'estates' (*varṇas*). This distinctive

---

38 Lewis 2000. 39 Scheuble-Reiter and Bussi 2019.
40 On these complex issues see Kantor 2021; Ando 2023. 41 Garnsey 1970.

aspect of Indic law reflects the pervasive influence of Brahmins, who developed an elaborate religious legal system of their own (Dharmaśāstra) but also seem to have insinuated themselves into many state-based juridical administrations as well, both as judges or assessors and as advisers, with the result that most of the extant textual sources bear a strong Brahmanical imprint.[42] The social divisions that appear to have been most widely recognized in practice were called *jāti* (lit. 'birth-group', cognate with Latin *gens*), the term rendered today by 'caste'. The Brahmanical legal texts imposed over this *jāti* structure its idealized model of four *varṇas*. The three upper *varṇas* were further called *Ārya* ('worthy, noble'); the *Śūdra* label was intended to cover all others, at least at first.

According to Dharmaśāstra, the precepts of *dharma* (comprising legal, ethical and religious obligations) pertain mainly to those who belong to one of the upper *varṇas*; the *dharma* of Śūdras (when it was put in those terms) was to provide obedient service to Āryas (in spite of which a 'slave status' was not envisioned). Marginal groups included tribal peoples (*aṭavika*) and various despised groups (e.g. *caṇḍālas*, 'dog-cookers', 'carrion-eaters' or more generally *antyaja*, 'lowest-born'). The legal status of such groups is nebulous, but the Dharmaśāstras are apt to declare that they are 'excluded from all *dharmas*' (YDh 1.93). Indian sources also distinguish foreigners, sometimes by name as *Yona* ('Ionian', i.e. Greek); *Pahlava* (Persian); *Bāhlika* (Bactrian); *Śaka* (Scythian); or more generically *mleccha*, a category that comprehends much more than simply people from a different country and carries the implications of Greek *barbaros*.

On the other hand, although distinctions of class (*varṇa*) are invoked at various points in Kauṭilya's *Arthaśāstra*, the relevant categories for purposes of administrative law are: occupation, age, sex; or they classify people by place of settled residence, ethnicity or other social divisions. For instance, according to Kauṭilya, whether for administrative and revenue purposes (KAŚ 2.36.3) or in registering a lawsuit (KAŚ 3.1.17), individuals are to be identified by place, caste (*jāti*), lineage, name and occupation. Kauṭilya speaks of the subjects of the king as city-folk (*paura*) or country-folk (*jānapada*), usually as a pair; both groups are subject to policing and surveillance (KAŚ 4.5.13, 1.13.1); have to pay fines and taxes (KAŚ 1.13.3); and have the right to have their lawsuits heard (KAŚ 1.19.10). These appear, however, to be more sociological categories than legal ones (see, e.g., KAŚ 8.1.24–32). It may be that in the older stratum of his work (first or early second century CE), Kauṭilya gave less

---

42 See also Chapters 3, 6 and 7, this volume.

attention to class (*varṇa*) as a systematic determinant of legal status, but the final redactor (late third or fourth century) amplified this aspect to reflect the influence of the ascendant Dharmaśāstra tradition. Class distinctions are invoked in specifying acceptable marriage alliances; revocation of marriage; the length of time a husband may stay away before a wife can remarry; inheritance; village seniority; exhortation of witnesses; verbal assault and Śūdra-on-Brahmin physical assault; and penalties for selling Ārya children into slavery.

Leaving aside such explicit consideration of class in defining rights or penalties, one of the most common legal ramifications of class distinctions was jurisdictional: that is, the determination of which law or which forum was appropriate. It appears that apart from the most serious or prominent cases, most offences and disputes in ancient India were dealt with at a local level by civic, caste, lineage or guild councils. Records of the work of such councils survive only from medieval periods, but even the earliest Dharmaśāstras refer to them and enjoin the king to recognize their rules and their decisions as legitimate. The *Arthaśāstra* shields foreign merchants (not called *mleccha*) from commercial lawsuits unless they are affiliated with or belong to a local corporate body. This indicates some legal status for economically important aliens, while also affirming the prerogatives of trade organizations. When the king himself is called upon to decide cases, he is supposed to do so only after ascertaining the laws peculiar to the groups involved. An unusual inscription, the so-called Charter of Viṣṇuṣeṇa (592 CE) records and endorses a long roster of laws specific to a guild of merchants in a particular locality in western India.[43] The ruler explicitly states that he was petitioned by the merchants to provide this written endorsement; it is notable that much Dharmaśāstric technical terminology appears in the charter, including a common formula used to recognize the validity of other customary rules not explicitly mentioned.

Many crimes and violations of ritual purity rules could lead to loss of caste status and thus exclusion from society. Punishment resulting from legal process did not necessarily remove this stigma and the attendant social sanctions; for this, specific expiations were proposed, and the ruler or a Brahmin assembly might be called upon to attest to their having been duly performed, whereupon the guilty party could be readmitted to full social status.

In early China, the major status groups besides the royal family were officials and the general free populace (on bonded servile groups and slaves,

---

[43] Lubin 2015.

see 'Slavery and Servitude' below). In the early Tang period, as in India, Islamic (Arab) or other foreign groups resident in the main cities were to some extent considered to be outside Chinese law; the Tang Code provided that, where a crime was committed by a member of a foreign group against another member of the same group, jurisdiction was to be left to that group.[44] Only if the offender and victim belonged to different foreign groups would the matter be decided by Chinese law.

Public or Military Office

Official statuses conferred by authority commonly entailed rights (often but not always including special immunities) and responsibilities. Such offices might be revocable or contingent, but in some cases they could be passed down hereditarily – thus blurring the distinction between conferred status and status by birth.

Perhaps nowhere else did public offices constitute such a prominent feature of a legal system as in early China. Before the rise of the bureaucratic state in China in the fourth century BCE, the hereditary aristocrats of the Western Zhou kingdom (c. 1045–771 BCE) and the states into which it subsequently became divided constituted a privileged group, treated differently by the criminal law, though details are sparse. Once the centralized, bureaucratic, state arose, the governing class came to be constituted by officials appointed by the ruler, who might also confer on them noble rank if they did not already possess it (e.g. as a relative of the ruler). Rank entailed privileges: in the Qin and Han dynasties (221 BCE–220 CE), the lowest noble rank was sometimes granted wholesale to all heads of families. Officials as a class were 'superior' to the rest of the population, deriving their status from their connection with the ruler. This 'superiority' was marked by entitlement to special kinds of clothing, ornaments, transport and – at least in the Tang (618–907 CE) – houses. Under the Tang, sumptuary laws regulated these matters in detail, with variations corresponding to the rank of the official or noble. Breach of the sumptuary laws was itself a punishable offence. Officials were entitled to respect from persons under their jurisdiction. Offences committed against them by such persons were punished more severely than if they had been committed against commoners.

More important were the privileges enjoyed by officials and nobles under the criminal law. Early books that set out proper principles of morality and

---

44 Hansen 2021: 24–25.

government – *Liji* (*Book of Rites*) and *Zhouli* (*Rites of Zhou*) – already show that even prior to the bureaucratic state nobles were entitled to lenient treatment in prison, execution in private and exemption from enslavement. The Qin/Han laws also permit persons of rank more lenient punishments than the commoner, such as exemption in some cases from the infliction of a mutilating punishment. We find the privileges of nobles and officials (and their relatives) most completely defined in the Tang Code (from the seventh century CE) which already drew on laws from the preceding centuries.[45] The general principle applied was the higher the rank the greater the extent of privilege. The highest-ranking nobles and officials could not be sentenced or punished for a capital offence without special permission from the emperor. For most non-capital offences, they were entitled to a reduction of the regular punishment. Slightly lower-ranking officials and nobles, together with relatives of the highest-ranking officials and nobles, were entitled to special consideration from the emperor should they be convicted of a capital offence, and to reduced punishment for non-capital offences. Officials of the lowest rank, together with relatives of nobles and officials of the second group, were entitled merely to a reduction of punishment in non-capital cases. In addition, there were the important privileges constituted by 'surrender of rank or office' and 'redemption by payment of copper', both conceptions going back at least to the Han. In the Tang period, officials of any rank sentenced for a non-capital offence might obtain total or partial exemption from the prescribed punishment by surrendering their office. Should surrender not entitle them to complete exemption, the balance of the punishment might be redeemed by payment of copper.

In India rules on appointment to public office probably varied from state to state, but the Brahmanical texts propose many guidelines. The Dharmaśāstras emphasized the propriety of appointing Brahmins to certain positions, but Kauṭilya's *Arthaśāstra* (although the text was subjected to Brahmin revision and expansion) is much less insistent on this. For example, prospective officers were supposed to be subjected to various tests, but *varṇa* is not mentioned as a requirement for any office. Similarly, the caste or other social status of individuals named as officials in inscriptions is rarely mentioned, though in a few cases it may be inferred from their names. Certain offices were especially likely to be filled by a Brahmin: for example, royal chaplain (*purohita*), judges (*dharmādhikārin*), and offices dealing with records

---

45 See also Ng 2020 on the *Tang Liu Dian* (The Six Rules [Statutes / Codes] of the Tang): 'the earliest complete Chinese administrative law code that has survived to the present day' (compiled 738–39 CE).

and documents, and the Śāstras give explicit justifications for this. However, as in early medieval inscriptions, it is likely that other economically or politically influential castes supplied many officers of the state in practice. Officials were given stipends, land rights and other benefices. Though ultimately officers served at the ruler's pleasure, cases can be found of individuals holding office across successive reigns, which suggests at least the possibility of some sort of professional bureaucracy. Some positions may have become hereditary, as suggested by references to 'the son of a minister' in the *Pañcatantra* (a collection of edifying tales for young princes).[46]

Our best evidence for the official statuses of an actual state comes from the edicts of King Aśoka (mid-third century BCE), complemented by the descriptions of Megasthenes, Seleucus Nicator's ambassador to Aśoka's grandfather's court in Pāṭaliputra. These depict the mature Maurya imperial formation, almost never acknowledging any internal regional or social divisions, though neighbouring peoples are enumerated. The only social group regularly singled out for special mention is the composite grouping of *samaṇa-brāhmaṇa* (or *brāhmaṇa-samaṇa*), referring collectively – it seems – to Brahmanical and non-Brahmanical mendicants as equally suitable recipients of honour and financial and material support. Aśoka also refers to the Buddhist Sangha (mendicant order) and to some other religious groups. He also discusses various types of royal official: *yukta, rajuka* and *prādeśika* (of uncertain functions, Rock Edict 3); *mahāmātras* (ministers) in charge of various matters,[47] including *dhaṃma-mahāmātras* ('ministers of dharma', responsible for public morality and the regulation of religious groups, Rock Edicts 5 and 12); and *paṭivedakas* ('informers', to report on public affairs, Rock Edict 6). Aśoka makes a point of sending round another set of officers to check up on the others. Nothing is said of private or family law, or of any special treatment of his officials in legal matters.

Kauṭilya's administrative structure, which may have been modelled to some degree on an actual (but unidentified) kingdom, has at the top a group of high officials: the counsellor-chaplain (*mantri-purohita*, of necessity a Brahmin); treasurer (*saṃnidhātṛ*); and the 'collector' (*samāhartṛ*, actually responsible for managing domestic affairs). Although the Brahmanical notion of *varṇa* (class) is not invoked, ministers (*amātya*) should be high-born (*abhijāta*); otherwise, however, they are ranked according to the degree to which they embody a list of ideal personal qualities (*KAŚ* 1.9.1–3).

---

46 Though see Olivelle 1997: xlvii.
47 The *mahāmātras* may not have been merely ministers but individuals with their own power bases; see Scharfe 1993.

Accordingly, he envisioned 'a meritocracy within the strictures of a traditionally hierarchical society'.[48] Below these ministers there was an array of departmental chief officers (adhyakṣa). Kauṭilya further gives rules generally prohibiting the king's men from being witnesses in a civil suit (some exceptions apply) and from being held to recover debt when they are engaged in the king's work. They may also stay away longer before their wives can remarry. It is not clear whether they could be party to a civil suit, but it might be assumed that they could. Also, there are specific investigative procedures to root out corruption among them. More generally, the king's punishment of his own people is carried out without reference to (and probably outside of) courts. If a state employee was corrupt or troublesome, the king could simply punish him. Investigative and judicial mechanisms are not mentioned. Likewise, the king could use secret means if public action was undesirable for some reason.

By contrast, far from having special status under the law, officials in ancient Greek city states were generally subject to all the same laws as others and in practice were often punished quite harshly for dereliction of duty. The only special privilege, it would seem, is that at Gortyn the leading official, the *kosmos*, was immune from prosecution (and also could not himself prosecute) while in office; but once his (probably one-year) term was over, any case brought by or against him would be tried and any fines levied by the court would be calculated from the time of the original complaint.[49] In Ptolemaic Egypt, by contrast, an important part of Alexandrian city law governing social status is preserved in a significant text dated to the middle of the third century BCE: P. Hal. 1 (we may presume that similar statutes existed in the other two Greek cities of Egypt, Naukratis and Ptolemais). According to this text, those in the service of the king (e.g. military personnel) were exempt from being brought into court; the wives and children of soldiers were also exempt from being brought until the soldier returned home. Such exemptions probably did not survive the transition to Roman rule. Various Roman governors' edicts seek to rein in misconduct by officials, and petitions for redress similarly complain that officials abused their position. We have little knowledge of how effective such edicts and complaints were, but they certainly had strong ideological value.

In Roman public/administrative law, the holding of office was subject to varying property, residence and age qualifications. For example, under the later Roman Republic the minimum age for election to the praetorship was

---

48 McClish and Olivelle 2012: 40.   49 Gagarin and Perlman 2016: 66–76.

thirty-nine and to the consulship, forty-two. Holding public office was, however, not restricted to independent (*sui iuris*) heads of household: a Roman praetor who was still under 'paternal power' (*patria potestas*, on which see below), for example, did not have to obey the will of his *paterfamilias* in relation to his official duties (Justinian, *Digest* 1.6.9, Pomponius).[50] In the Roman provinces, membership of the city/town council (*boulē*) was expected to shield a person from subjection to degrading punishments, especially corporal punishments. With the exception of Antinoopolis, formally recognized councils of this sort were absent in Egypt, at least until the visit of Severus in the early third century.

Slavery or Servitude

Despite important local differences, one broad commonality across ancient societies is the positing of unfree statuses of various sorts: statuses which called for legal definition and regulation of the relations between free and unfree. First, there was very commonly a spectrum from unfree to what have been called 'half-free' servile statuses. The latter included a wide range of arrangements, often voluntary or contractual in origin but entailing loss of personal autonomy on the part of the servant such that the condition verged on slavery. These could include servants of the royal court or state; labourers bound to the land as dependents of a landlord; and personal retainers whose service was remunerated but could not be terminated freely. On the basis of (sometimes misleading) analogies with similar patterns in medieval and colonial Europe, they are frequently referred to for convenience as serfs, villeins or bonded labourers.

The broad range of traditional practices seen in antiquity contrasts with the increasing preponderance of a race-defined conception of slavery during and after the period of European colonial expansion, which Orlando Patterson called an example of 'intrusive' forms of slavery: those in which the slave, captured or purchased, is conceived of as an unassimilable alien, often identified as an inferior race – in contrast to 'extrusive' forms (in which full members of society lose free status for one of a variety of reasons).[51] A partly similar classification was proposed by the anthropologist J. L. Watson: 'two major types – or modes – of slavery', open and closed, corresponding to whether slaves could be assimilated into the dominant kinship or social order (as was common in some African societies)

50 Johnston 2022: 38–39.   51 Patterson 1982.

or were permanently excluded from any such assimilation (very commonly so in Asia).[52]

Watson proposes two general features of slave status that seem to apply cross-culturally and trans-historically: first, 'the property aspect of slavery must be accepted as primary – this is what distinguishes slavery from all other forms of dependency and involuntary labour'; second, 'all slaves are, in the final analysis, subject to the will of their owners'.[53] He further notes that coercion involved more than policing and physical abuse; an owner could resort to 'more subtle means of control . . . incentives and "liberties", such as the freedom to travel or to contract one's own marriage'. Slave status was distinguished by the convention that enslaved people constituted a form of living property, commonly subject to sale and purchase, by analogy with cattle (hence the term 'chattel slave'). This dehumanization ranged from severely attenuated rights and agency to total loss of legal personhood. This posed vexing legal conundrums: if a slave was in some sense a person and in some sense an object, how were these senses to be balanced or reconciled? Did slaves' residual personhood place limits on how they might be treated by a master? How much personal legal agency did they enjoy? Could they act as witnesses in a trial? Enter into contracts? Bring a case in court? Convey inheritance to their offspring? If they committed a crime or tort, who was legally responsible? What protection, if any, did the law offer them against harm and mistreatment? If they were assaulted, what penalties did the perpetrator face? Who was deemed the victim in such a case (the slave or the master)?

Often independently, disparate societies exhibit a very similar range of scenarios for the creation of slaves. The most common were enslavement through capture in war; as a criminal penalty; or as a consequence of unpaid debt or other financial straits. Once established, slave status (as also many sorts of half-free status) would be inherited by offspring, creating a slave 'caste', and slave families were in many cases at risk of being split up at the whim of the owner. Manumission was possible as a reward for exemplary service – or in the case of debt-slaves, for satisfying the terms of the debt – though for most enslaved people freedom remained out of reach. The Roman 'freedman' (*libertus*), for example: 'occupied a complex and often problematic place in Roman society between slaves on the one hand and freeborn citizens on the other'.[54] In several traditions, however, the children

---

52 Watson 1980: 15–16. Reid 1983 develops this model.   53 Watson 1980: 8–9.
54 Mouritsen 2011.

begotten of a slave-woman by her master or her free husband would be deemed free and in some cases might entail freedom for the mother or even other family members. Another important distinction often encountered – including in classical Athens, Rome and China – was that between 'private slaves' (those who belonged to a household) and 'public' or 'government' slaves (those owned by the commonwealth or imperial state).

Socially and legally, the condition of slaves in Mesopotamia – called ir_3 'male-slave' and $geme_2$ 'female-slave' in Sumerian, and $(w)ardu/(w)ardātu$ in Akkadian – depended on the nature of their enslavement. Permanent chattel slaves – whether by birth, by booty or by purchase – were considered objects and could be sold, but not killed, by their master. In the Neo-Sumerian period (c. 2100–2000 BCE), freed slaves, commonly termed $dumu$-gir_{15} (or $dumu$-gi_7, lit. 'native son') in documents, were said to have been rendered 'like a son of a man/a city', namely like a free person. There were also temporary slaves, mainly by reason of debt, but also prisoners of war who could be redeemed with a ransom. Debt-slaves usually lived with and worked for the creditor; they were theoretically protected against ill-treatment. A distinctive sign of slavery during the Old Babylonian period, the *abbūtum/appūtum*-mark (maybe a hairstyle associated with a metal object) seems to have been inflicted as a punishment and was not permanent. Even permanent slaves had various rights and protections. Temple slaves of the first millennium, though often of the low *širku* ('oblate') status and marked with a brand in the hand, could own goods and enjoyed the right to marry without permission of the temple. Some were able to attain high positions. Slaves belonging to families of notables could play an important economic role, especially in the first millennium: they could run a tavern, make business transactions in the name of their owners and earn money.[55]

Slaves in the Greek world could be bought and sold freely. Most belonged to individuals, but in Athens the city also owned slaves, some of whom carried significant responsibilities. In addition to ordinary slaves (*douloi*), Gortyn also had a second servile category often described as 'serfs' (*woikeis*) but who appear to have gradually become assimilated to the status of ordinary slaves; *woikeis* were in some sense tied to the land.[56] Both groups could own property (though probably not real property). Individual owners

---

55 Richardson 2019 argues, on the basis of 'letters from the Old Babylonian period (2004–1595 BC, the age of Hammurabi)', that 'the primary economic functions of slaves had to do with information and credit in an economic environment of mercantilism, rather than with labour in the agricultural sector'.
56 Gagarin 2010.

also sometimes entrusted their slaves with significant responsibilities; bankers, for example, sometimes let a slave run their bank and keep part of the profits. We know of two slaves in Athens who became very rich in this way, bought their freedom and because of their generous donations to the city were later given citizenship.[57] At Sparta the helots worked for individual Spartiates but may have belonged to the city.[58] It is not clear whether Cretan cities owned slaves.

At Gortyn serfs (*woikeis*) could probably only be sold in connection with the sale of the land to which they were attached. Helots could not be sold. Greek slaves could be freed by their owners (or in the case of the helots, in Sparta, by the city). In Athens, freed slaves became metics if they continued to reside at Athens – that is, as resident non-Athenians; as such, they were obliged to pay the *metoikion* poll tax.[59]

Harm to slaves was treated differently from violence against free people.[60] Even so, violence against a Greek slave fell into the category of *bia*, normally denoting harm to a person ('injury'), and at Gortyn the law explicitly prohibited the rape of a slave. Likewise, the Athenian law on *hybris* (arrogant assault) explicitly applied to slaves: 'if anyone commits *hybris* against anyone, either a child or a woman or a man, whether slave or free'.[61] Scholars disagree about why this is so, or just what the effect was. In any case, although in some ways slaves were mere property, in many cases their humanity was recognized if only at a basic level. For example, in Athens a slave could be subject to judicial torture and in fact generally had to be, in order for the testimony to be admissible, apparently on the mistaken assumption that this would ensure truthfulness; this was not the case in Gortyn, however, where we have records of the testimony of slaves prevailing over that of free citizens.[62] David Lewis argues forcefully against the idea that slaves in the Greek world could be said to enjoy rights at all, even at Gortyn, where records have suggested to many that slaves had 'certain enforceable rights' to property and marriage that were unknown elsewhere.[63] In fact, 'these rules did not grant or acknowledge rights for slaves, but were chiefly aimed at clarifying the property rights of free citizens in complex scenarios where disputes over "who owns what" might have led to conflict and litigation. . . . [It was] a matter of rights, but rights for slaveowners, not slaves.'[64]

The widespread lack of protections of the slave body vis-à-vis the state can also be seen in the Roman legal system's tendency, in the provinces

---

57 See Vlassopoulos 2009 for further discussion. 58 Hodkinson 2000: 119–21.
59 See Hunt 2018; Meyer 2023. 60 See Chapter 9, this volume. 61 Gagarin 2020: 99.
62 Lewis 2013: 415. 63 Finley 1981: 137. 64 Lewis 2013: 415–16.

especially, to define rank or status or citizenship as a system of marking off who can legitimately be touched or violated, where, how and by whom. Slaves had no such protections. Romans had (in theory) full protection from violation by all but the governor or other Roman officials; others were in between. Thus, Philo of Alexandria recounts how Alexandrian nobles were punished with a certain kind of lashing, Jewish elders with the same sort and 'Egyptians' with another sort (Philo, *In Flaccum* 78–80). Similarly, the prefect of Egypt declared in the fourth century CE that a certain punishment was grave even when applied to slaves, but constituted a violation when applied to free men (P. Oxy. IX 1186).

Although the quality of life as a slave could differ widely depending on rural versus urban context and the educational level of the slave, the Roman legal system tended to treat all enslaved people alike. Manumission was possible, but freed slaves faced certain constraints: they owed their manumitting patron public deference (*obsequium*, which limited legal action against the patron) and agreed to stipulated labour (*operae*). Especially in the east, instead of *operae* they were often contracted to perform general service, often of unlimited duration (a contract called *paramonē*). Thus, slaves and freedmen remained legally distinct from the groups of semi-autonomous farmers who had agreed to be 'tied' to the land in Late Antiquity: the *coloni*, or, in parts of Egypt, the *enapographoi georgoi*. If one of these farmers (or anyone else who had agreed to permanent employment through *paramonē*) broke that agreement, then, no matter to what extent the subject's position was curtailed, the dispute would be treated, in law at least, as a contractual matter – rather than falling under the heading of a right *in rem*. However, Harper points out that in cases where freedmen who were bound by *paramonē* agreements to their patron violated those agreements, the resolution was not contractual, but rather the revocation of manumission.[65]

In the late Roman empire, a large part of the population came to occupy a grey zone between free and unfree, partly because of efforts to enforce compulsory hereditary occupations on many classes of people, which has been described as a 'levelling of position between free persons and slaves'.[66] *Coloni* (tenant cultivators) listed in the landlords' tax records were bound to the land; similarly grain shippers, butchers, bakers and others were 'bound' to their trades. Constantine had decreed in 332 that *coloni* could be punished by the landowner just like slaves. Though distinguished from *servi rustici*, they amounted to 'slaves of the land itself to which they were born' (Justinian,

---

65 Harper 2016: 373–74.   66 Westermann 1955: 139–49.

Cod. 11:52.1). This status gave them a usufructuary right. Similarly, sons of soldiers were obliged to serve as well, and sons of government factory workers had to follow work in the factory.[67] Although this was the situation envisioned in the texts, modern scholars have raised questions about the degree to which such laws were actually enforced.[68]

In China, the hereditary classes of servile persons and slaves constituted groups strictly delimited from the ordinary, free population.[69] Servile groups ('bondsmen'), occupying a status regarded as intermediate between 'free' and 'slave' (especially during the fifth to the seventh centuries CE) included 'service households' attached to the government and performing various kinds of labour and 'personal retainers' who were attached to private persons, often to work the land. As elsewhere, servile status could come about (in practice) as a consequence of capture in war; via the 'unauthorized' sale of children, or even of oneself, in times of poverty; or as a result of conviction for a serious offence, where relatives of the principal offender were subject to enslavement: 'an established deterrent rooted in the powerful concept of collective liability within the household or even beyond'.[70] According to Qin laws of the third century BCE, private slaves could be bought and sold like cattle, whereas personal retainers worked at the direction of their masters but might not be bought or sold. Both statuses (bonded servant and slave) once established were hereditary, though manumission was possible. Class separation was maintained by laws prohibiting marriage between free persons and slaves or members of servile households attached to the government, but not between free persons and 'personal retainers'. During the post-Han, pre-Tang, period in the south there were also important marriage prohibitions between different classes of the free population. Upper-class families (*shi*) were not permitted to marry members of the lower class (*shu*).[71]

Ancient India offers the notable case of an entire social class that on principle was regarded – by Brahmanical authorities at least – as inherently destined to serve the higher classes. Brahmanical scriptures offered as a rationale for the Śūdra class (*varṇa*) that they were created from a primordial cosmic being's feet to serve the three higher Ārya classes. It is not definitely known to whom the Śūdra label was originally applied, what sort of deference was expected and whether it was obtained. From the early historical period, it seems that groups classed as Śūdra included a wide range of social groups, from common labourers to farmers and artisans.

---

67 Wacher 2013: 466.
68 Bodnaruk 2022 surveys legal sources and relevant epigraphic evidence.
69 Yates 2001.   70 Scheidel (2017): 134.   71 Barbieri-Low (2007): 36.

Meanwhile, other groups were deemed lower than Śūdra, and when being exhorted to tell the truth in court, Śūdras should be threatened with the guilt of 'sins causing loss of caste status' (*pātaka*), which implies that they have status to lose (*MDh* 8.88). The *Mānava Dharmaśāstra* includes some maxims that seem to call into question the full free status of Śūdras. For instance, it asserts that a Brahmin may expropriate anything from a Śūdra, since Śūdras, like women and sons with a living father, cannot really own anything independently (*MDh* 8.416–17). Yet this is belied by many other passages that show that Śūdras were (at least in principle) accorded most of the same basic civic rights to property, security of person and access to law as higher classes, albeit with some gradations. Even a son begotten by a Śūdra on a slave woman could, with his permission, be allotted a share in the inheritance (*MDh* 9.179). This, of course, presupposes that Śūdras actually could have property to be inherited. More telling still is the maxim that 'even a capable Śūdra must not accumulate wealth, for when a Śūdra becomes wealthy, he harasses Brahmins' (*MDh* 10.129) – rueful wisdom offered to a Brahmin audience, not in any sense a law. All authorities agree that Śūdras could serve as witnesses, and Kauṭilya in fact seems to include Śūdras within the privileged Ārya category (*KAŚ* 3.13.1).

Even in the midst of asserting rhetorically the Śūdra's intrinsic servility, the rules implicitly acknowledge a real distinction between Śūdra and slave (*dāsa*). Śūdra status in the oldest Dharmaśāstras may have been similar to that of the helots in Sparta. In one case, scholastic authorities note that a Śūdra may not be given away like ordinary property and, although a Śūdra has a duty to serve, he may choose not to (*Pūrva-Mīmāṃsā-Sūtra* 6.7.6). Slaves may belong to other classes besides Śūdra (and still 'lower' groups), and the full range of ways of becoming a slave are seen: being born to a slave; capture in war; debt-bondage and other types of penal enslavement; and voluntary enslavement for sustenance. In many respects, slaves were mere chattel. A slave may also be obtained through purchase, gift or inheritance (*MDh* 8.415). Making off with someone else's slave entails the same liability as theft (*MDh* 8.324). On the other hand, slaves would appear to have retained substantial legal protections and recognition of their personhood. Slaves may be punished by beating them only on the back with a rope or bamboo strip, which is the same method allowed for punishing a son, pupil, wife or brother; any other mode of beating entails a penalty (*MDh* 8.299). Rape of a female slave incurs a fine, and gang-rape entails a much higher fine, assessed on each perpetrator (*YDh* 2.295 (291)). Kauṭilya affirmed that slaves could own property, which would be inherited by their own relatives; the owner of the slave would have only residual claim (KAŚ 3.13.22). By contrast, the Dharmaśāstras were more inclined to deny that slaves (or even women) could own property (e.g. NSm 5.39). However, even the Mānava Dharmaśāstra concedes that 'when there is no one else, even a woman, a child, an old man, a pupil, a relative, a slave, or a servant may give testimony' (MDh 8.70).

Kauṭilya provides detailed rules regarding slaves, distinguishing between slavery proper and serving as a pledge (ādhi) (KAŚ 3.13.1–25). Persons serving as pledges are protected from being made to perform particularly degrading or polluting tasks and from corporal punishments. People might sell themselves into slavery for cash; their children are counted as having their pre-slavery social rank and they can redeem themselves. Such servitude can also be a way of working off a fine. The king is charged with enforcing discipline on slaves and pledges (KAŚ 2.1.25). The Arthaśāstra includes a rule specifying that although it is not wrong for barbarians to sell or pledge their offspring, 'an Ārya cannot become a slave' (KAŚ 3.13.3–4), yet there are other passages that may indicate that it could happen – not least the immediately preceding sentences, at the start of the chapter, which criminalize the purchase or pledging of a minor of any of the four classes but thus implies that purchase or pledge of an adult of these classes is acceptable.[72] In any case, even an Ārya in distress may become a 'belly-slave' (udara-dāsa) to avoid starvation. In such cases, minors must be redeemed first – the slavery of Ārya minors particularly agitated Kauṭilya.

Provision is made for a ceremony of manumission in Dharmaśāstra (NSm 5.40–42). Kauṭilya provides specific rules for buying one's way out of slavery or pledge status, as well as rules protecting slaves and pledges against specific forms of maltreatment. A woman who bears the child of her owner should cease to be a slave on that account, along with her child, and even her siblings, if she looks after the household affairs (KAŚ 3.13.23). A slave once redeemed cannot be sold on again into slavery unwillingly by the redeemer (KAŚ 3.13.24–25).

The rabbis discussed slaves as property, comparing them to land in the manner of their acquisition (money, deed, possession), but in most other respects they were treated as moveable property.[73] Somewhat as Dharmaśāstra sought to set limits on the enslavement of those with Ārya status, the rabbinic jurists also drew

---

[72] Olivelle 2013: 614–15 is inclined to interpret the term ārya in these cases as meaning only 'free', rather than designating class affiliation. This is awkward, however, considering that the term is so loaded elsewhere. I rather see statements like KAŚ 3.13.15 as interventions of a Brahmanical redactor uncomfortable with the notion of an Ārya slave.

[73] Comparison with land: b. Kid. 22b; moveable property: b. B.K.12a; b. B. Bat. 68a, 150a; b. Yeb. 99a; and b. Giṭ. 38b.

a fundamental distinction between the Jewish slave and the Gentile slave. Enslaved Jews should be released debt-free and even with a gift after six years of labour and every jubilee year signalled the liberation of all Jewish slaves no matter how long they had served. In addition, Jewish female slaves' bondage was said to end at the onset of puberty, or upon the death of her master (*b. Kidd.* 17b). These general limitations could be evaded by a biblical legal device: if, by the slave's wish, the master pierces the slave's ear with an awl, the bondage becomes permanent (Exod 21:5–6; Deut 15:16–17). But in the Second Temple period, the jubilee years having ceased, it was argued that there could be no more Jewish slaves at all.[74] Non-Jewish slaves served with no time limit (on the basis of Lev 25:46), but they could be freed by payment of money by a third party or by deed of release made by the master (*b. Qidd.* 22b). Many disfiguring bodily injuries – expanding on the examples of loss of an eye and a tooth in Exod 21:26–27 – were listed as grounds for ordering the freeing of a slave (*b. Qidd.* 24b–25b). Marriage to a free woman (including the master's daughter) would result in release from slave status, as would being heir to the master's entire estate, on the grounds that one thus comes to own oneself.[75]

According to late antique rabbinic literature, slaves could act on behalf of their masters (except in matters of divorce: *b. Gitt.* 23b) and were entitled to hold property on their own account, although some ownership rights were limited. Slaves were not considered personally liable for torts, but once freed could be required to pay damages for harms committed during their servitude (*b. B.K.* 8:4). Acknowledgement of basic 'civil rights' of enslaved Jews may be seen in various Talmudic passages: they have the right to remain in the land of Israel; cannot be sold for export (*b. Gitt.* 4:6); if taken abroad by the master, they may demand repatriation (*b. Ket.* 110b) or flee to Israel without fear of extradition (*b. Gitt.* 45a, invoking Deut 23:16). The rabbis regarded sale of a Jewish slave to non-Jew as illegal and as terminating slave status if it occurred; the seller could be ordered to reimburse the buyer tenfold as a penalty (*b. Gitt.* 44a–45a). Bodily injuries inflicted on Jewish slaves were supposed to be treated just as injuries to free Jews (*b. B.K.* 8:3). All slaves in a Jewish household should be circumcized.[76]

Several ancient legal systems dealt explicitly with the legal questions posed by sexual alliances and marriages between slaves, as well as those between an enslaved person and a free person – and the ambiguous status of the offspring of such unions – with widely differing results. Examples from Talmud and

---

[74] *B. Git.* 65a; *b. Kidd.* 69a; and *m. 'Ar.* 29a.
[75] *M. Pe'ah* 3; *b. Gitt.* 8b–9a and 39b–40a; and *b. Pes.* 113a.   [76] Hezser 2022: 134–37.

from the *Arthaśāstra* have already been noted. At Gortyn free women and probably free men too could marry slaves (and presumably *woikeis* as well).[77] Where the couple resided determined the status of the children; residence in the free person's house meant free children, while residence in the slave's meant slave children.[78] But such intermarriages were not recognized in the city states of Athens or Sparta.

Marriage between slaves is treated in great detail in the Mesopotamian law collections, though we have no clear example thereof in practice. The reason why marriage was preferred to concubinage was sociological: in most cases, it is to be assumed that the husband was enslaved for a debt, which meant a temporary period of enslavement, while his wife was probably a slave by birth. It is against this background that chapter 4 of the Laws of Ur-Namma (c. 2100 BCE) should be understood: it states that the manumission of the slave-husband does not entail freedom for the slave-wife.[79] The children born to a slave couple are slaves themselves (*wilid bītim* 'born in the house') – a status label seen in other ancient law traditions (e.g. India's MDh 8.415). Mixed unions, which are well attested, entail interesting complexities in the status arrangements. They usually involve a free man with a slave-woman. She is sometimes given as a secondary wife to a married man in cases of cultic or biological sterility of the wife: her owner is her mistress, whose rights are reduced once the slave has given birth to child(ren); such a situation could create tensions between the two women (as one sees also in Genesis accounts of Sarai, Rachel and Leah). In such cases, 'the legal personality of the slave was split. As the Old Babylonian contracts express it: "To H, W2 is a wife; to W1, she is a slave".'.[80] Under the Babylonian law, the mistress could punish her by marking her and reducing her social position within the household, but she could not sell her (Laws of Ḫammurabi, chapters 146–47). By contrast, Assyrian contracts maintain the right of the wife to sell the slave even after she has produced a child. Children born in such conditions are fictitiously assigned to the wife; the slave woman acts as a surrogate mother.

Some Mesopotamian law collections also specify that married men could have sex with their female slaves without making them concubines: according to the Laws of Lipit-Ishtar (c. 1930 BCE, chapter 25), any resulting offspring was not servile, the slave-woman and the child were free, but the child was not recognized as the heir of the master. If, however, the widowed master married the slave-woman, the child would inherit (Laws of Lipit-Ishtar, chapter 26). The

---

77 For distinctions among servile groups, see 'Slavery or Servitude' section above.
78 Gagarin 2010 and Lewis 2013.   79 Westbrook 1998: Civil 2011: 246.
80 Westbrook 1998a: 228.

Laws of Ḫammurabi share the same view, except that freedom was granted upon the master's death and inheritance required an adoption by the master.

Marriage of a free man with a slave-woman, though rarely attested, is mentioned in the second-millennium Hittite Laws (chapter 31). Such a marriage could be broken very easily by both spouses, by estrangement or remarriage; the assets were shared equally but the children followed their father, with the exception of one for the mother. A special case concerns the marriage of a slave to her own master. Westbrook has shown that the statuses of wife and slave were incompatible mainly in view of the law of inheritance: either the children were slaves and thus incapable of inheriting their father's estate (which frustrates the purpose of Mesopotamian marriage), or they were free while their mother remained a slave, which means that they would inherit their own mother when their father died.[81] In order to avoid such absurd legal consequences, marriage nullified or at least suspended the slave status of the wife with regards to her husband.

Marriage of a free woman with a male slave is also dealt with by Mesopotamian law collections: for example, according to the Laws of Ḫammurabi, the wife remains free and the children are equally free; upon death of the slave-husband, the assets are shared equally between the owner of the deceased and the wife, on behalf of her children; the widow keeps her dowry, if she had one (Laws of Ḫammurabi, chapters 175–76). Contemporary documents show a different picture: in one contract from Sippar,[82] written some years after the Laws of Ḫammurabi, a man marries his slave with a free woman and decides that the children and the assets of the couple will belong to him. A still more complicated case is described in the Laws of Ur-Namma: 'If a male slave marries a freed woman, and presents his master with one heir, the son who had to be presented to his master [will share] one-half of the goods of his father's house (and) his father's building. No son of a freed woman will become a slave without the acquiescence of the master' (Laws of Ur-Namma, chapter 5).[83] It would seem that this was a case of a slave marrying a freed woman (dumu-gir$_{15}$), who has been manumitted probably because she has borne a child to the owner of her husband (cf. Laws of Lipit-Ishtar, chapter 25). The male child placed at the disposal of the master would be the latter's own son; he inherits half the goods of 'his father', namely the master of the slave. Thus, the situation here is not about a freeborn woman

---

81 Westbrook 1998a. See also Démare-Lafont 2015a.
82 Westbrook 1988: 123 (text CT 48 53).   83 Translation by Civil in George 2011: 246.

marrying a slave, but rather about a former slave-woman who became free by bearing the child of her husband's master.[84]

In sum, slavery was a complex feature of the legal landscape in all the ancient cultures surveyed here. The complexity lay in the fact that nearly every other aspect of law was involved, sometimes multiple aspects simultaneously: apart from the laws governing slave status per se, the laws on marriage, inheritance, contracts, physical violence, and testimony in court, among others, were regularly brought into play.

Despite the serious vulnerabilities and hardships entailed by slave status, the evidence from most traditions indicates that, formally at least, the law tended to affirm at least minimally that slaves were people and thus could not (or at least should not) be treated altogether as mere objects. Where circumstances produced ambiguities of status (e.g. through marriage or children), the law could be responsive to those ambiguities by altering or mitigating slave status and all systems included mechanisms for cancelling that status and conferring on the freed individual some or all of the rights of free citizens. Many of the same considerations apply to the diverse forms of half-free status that existed in ancient worlds. The fact that the various gradations of slave status were normally transmitted to offspring at birth, however, acted as a check on social mobility (except in some cases of mixed free–unfree unions) and served to reinforce the stigma and legal impotence of those at the bottom of the social hierarchy.

Putatively 'Natural' Ascriptive Statuses

Besides status in relation to the polity or ethnos and free or servile status, another set of status distinctions with thoroughgoing legal implications were those ascribed on the basis of physical or psychological factors: those based on sex, age and physical or mental conditions. These attributes tend to be treated in our sources as 'given' by nature or biology; however, they are all in fact culturally constructed categories – not least in the sphere of law. Moreover, although in certain systems some of these may not constitute formal legal classifications, they have legal consequences that can cut across other aspects of legal status.

---

84 This is S. Démare-Lafont's view of the case (personal communication), noting that the text uses the unexpected verb gub 'to stand, to be assigned to', rather than 'to give' (šum$_2$) or 'to place' (gar) because the biological father has not recognized the child. For a different interpretation, see Westbrook 1998a.

In all known ancient systems, the default legal subject was male. That is to say, laws of general applicability envisioned a male (gendered) subject, except where women were specifically concerned. This reflects the fact that the ancient societies represented in the record of legal history were patriarchal in various respects. Accordingly, the salient sex-based status distinction in ancient law was that of 'woman'. Usually, the most important status distinction in terms of age is between minor and major (adult), although some legal traditions make special provisions for the aged as well. Age-related status rules, especially the 'age of majority' (see below), may differ depending on gender. Those with physical or mental impairments may face the same limitations and/or protections as minors. In India (and in varying contexts elsewhere too) other gender statuses are sometimes recognized: the hermaphrodite, the eunuch and other effeminate men (*klība*). In Brahmanical discourse these other gender statuses seem not to have been acknowledged so much as a 'third gender', in any modern sense of the term, but rather as bodily impairment. For example, according to Dharmaśāstra, such individuals cannot inherit, and brothers have a duty to maintain them.

Women

Women's legal agency in some places required some sort of male intermediary, not unlike the guardian of a minor. Even where women had full legal agency, their rights of inheritance or other rights tended not to be as favourable as those of men of comparable status, and almost everywhere their eligibility for civic roles was limited at best.

That said, however, the legal statuses and rights of women in antiquity were extremely diverse. In Mesopotamia, women who depended economically on a man (a father, husband, brother, etc.) were considered dependent, while widows and prostitutes were considered independent.[85] But this was a social distinction; all (free) women enjoyed full legal capacity, even those who lived in the shadow of a husband or a father.[86] Moreover, though considered independent, prostitutes' lower social status entailed legal restrictions. The Laws of Lipit-Ištar forbade divorcing a wife to marry a prostitute (chapter 30) or maintaining in the marital home a prostitute who has borne children (chapter 27).[87] The status of daughter was not very different from that of son, except in inheritance rights (see below). It was expected that the daughter of a good family would get married and have children. The honourable status of wife was signalled by her wearing a veil, which was

---

85 See Gelb 1979 and Roth 2013b.   86 Démare-Lafont 2011.   87 Roth 2013b: 150.

forbidden to slaves and prostitutes.[88] Despite their full civil capacity, women faced particularly harsh criminal penalties, mainly due to the fact that the offences were seen as threats to the family (adultery, abortion, incest, rape), including the risk of bringing in foreign blood.[89] Widows were deprived of any male support in their family. Their economic situation was precarious, especially when their deceased husband did not grant them any gift; they could only rely on their dowry. One creative legal remedy to prevent a widow being expelled from the family house (at least in Syria and Assyria, where wills are attested) was for the wife to be declared the 'father and mother' of the estate in her husband's will; this legal fiction aimed at creating mandatory joint ownership between the surviving wife and her children during her lifetime.[90]

In Pharaonic Egypt, women – or at least elite women for whom there is some good documentation – had legal standing in law to bring their own cases, own and control property in their own name, make wills and other types of legal agreements and so on. Ptolemaic law recognized the Egyptian tradition of the independence of women with respect to contract making and the control of property in their own name. In sum, according to VerSteeg, the legal status and rights of (elite) women in ancient Egyptian law 'were superior to those found in many other ancient civilizations': 'Women served as judges on the court at Deir el-Medina. They testified as witnesses during trials. Women had legal authority to own, buy, and sell property. Records show that women paid taxes.'[91]

In broadly similar terms women in classical Athens had the status of citizen – but they had no 'political' roles. They could not, for example, vote in the Athenian Assembly or serve as jurors. Until 450 BCE citizenship by birth descended only through the male line, but a decree of Pericles in that year made the citizenship of the mother a requirement as well. In financial and legal matters, women had to be represented by a male 'lord' or 'guardian' (*kyrios*): the father or other male family member prior to marriage, succeeded by the husband, and by a son following the demise of the husband. It is not clear whether they could own real property, but in any case even their other property was controlled and administered by the guardian in all but trivial transactions. In a speech, Isaeus (10.10) mentions that 'the law explicitly forbids a child or a woman from contracting for the disposal of anything of a value above one *medimnos* of barley', a rule satirized in Aristophanes' play, *Women at the Assembly* (1024–25), in which women,

---

88 See, for example, *Middle Assyrian Laws tablet A* (c. 1050 BCE, Assur), chapter 40 (Roth 2013b: 165–66).
89 Démare-Lafont 1999b.   90 Westbrook 2001; Stol 2016: 283.   91 VerSteeg 2021.

having come to power, pass a law imposing the same limit on men. In practice, women seem sometimes to have had more economic autonomy; it may be that transactions that violated the law were only deemed invalid if a guardian challenged them in court.[92] By contrast, Gortyn women could own property, including real property in their own right and could buy, sell or mortgage it, without the need for a guardian; women also participated in litigation themselves. At Sparta women apparently could also own property in their own right. In the Hellenistic period (after 323 BCE), it appears that women everywhere generally owned more property and participated more in public affairs than they did in classical Athens.

Roman law, too, seems to have given women not under paternal power a high level of legal and financial independence, although as Cantarella states: 'During the long centuries between the date of the mythical founding of Rome (753 BC) and the first decades of the sixth century AD, when Justinian's *Corpus Iuris Civilis* was enacted, the legal condition of women underwent substantial transformation.'[93] In general, wives could own property while adult children still 'under the power' (*in potestate*) of the *paterfamilias* could not.[94] In practice, women had the same rights of succession as men. Women aged twelve years and above who were *sui iuris* did need a tutor to 'authorize', to give legal effect to, some of their actions under Roman private law – although in almost all cases a woman could compel a tutor to give his authorization. From the emperor Augustus onwards, women could be exempted from (some of) the legal restrictions normally imposed on their female sex if they gave birth to a specific number of legitimate, surviving, children (Gaius, *Institutes* 1.194 on the *ius liberorum*). Despite some indications of a more general 'period of emancipation' for (elite) women under the early Roman empire, late Roman legislators attempted to restore 'old values and virtues' at the same time as negotiating 'the profound effects of Christian ideology on the relationship between genders'.[95]

The position of women in Roman Egypt is complicated by the legal pluralism that begins to characterize the province from the Ptolemaic period onwards, to which more factors become added with the Roman takeover in 30 BCE. In theory, each of the 'ethnic' communities in Egypt was regulated by its 'own' laws, and the position of women in each of these communities would be structured accordingly. Thus, the autonomy of Greek women would have been curtailed relative to their Egyptian counterparts; Roman

---

92 Schaps 1979: 52–56; see more generally Cantarella 2005.   93 Cantarella 2016: 419.
94 Saller 1994: 155.   95 Cantarella 2016: 428 and 429.

women would have been subject to *patria potestas*; and so forth. The situation would, again theoretically, have been simplified after the extension of citizenship in 212 CE, when in theory the different practices would have been subsumed within Roman law and treated essentially as custom, though always subject to a repugnancy clause. The realities were more complex, and papyrus documentation shows the kinds of cross-pollinations typical of colonial encounters. The tendency of the documentation seems to be that (a) individuals tended to be creative in picking which legal regime would serve them best in which circumstances and (b) women ended up having more leeway than the law might have granted them *stricto sensu*. That is, insofar as 'female' status goes – in spite of all the relatively common papyrological evidence concerning guardianship, etc. – it doesn't appear from petitions at least that being female in Roman / Byzantine Egypt was a major disadvantage in relation to justice and adjudication.

The relatively 'tighter' Athenian laws on the guardianship of women have a close parallel in the Dharmaśāstra maxim that women should be dependent on male authority at every stage of their lives:

> Even in their own homes, a female – whether she is a child, a young woman, or an old lady – should never carry out any task independently. As a child, she must remain under her father's control; as a young woman, under her husband's; and when her husband is dead, under her sons'. She must never seek to live independently.[96]

This is an ethical norm, likely applicable more to women in Brahmin or other high-status groups, however, with violations entailing social rather than legal consequences (e.g. disgrace: *MDh* 5.149). There is ample inscriptional evidence of women making religious endowments on their own authority, which at least suggests that in many places and social contexts they had control of their own property. Note that the norm for widows in early Dharmaśāstra was chaste celibacy, not the putatively self-sacrificial act of 'suttee', which begins to appear as a controversial option in medieval works – the earliest mention in a code being the *Vaiṣṇava Dharmaśāstra* of c. seventh century CE. The earliest commentators reject the idea, but it becomes increasingly approved in later Dharmaśāstric works.[97]

On the whole, across the ancient Indian material, there is a trend over time from women's relative parity of status with men in several respects to increasing dependency – at least in principle. Stephanie Jamison has recently

---

96 *MDh* 5.147–48; cf. 9.3   97 Brick 2012, 2023.

noted that 'their status in the eyes of the law seems to have changed over time – with their visibility to the law paradoxically increasing even as the assertions of their nonindependence becomes more strident'.[98] *Āpastamba* carries over the old Vedic conception of ritual partnership of husband and wife to matters of property: 'the household couple has dominion over the property' (*kuṭumbhinau dhanasyeśāte*; *ĀpDh* 2.29.3). But later normative works restrict the wife's own resources to 'women's wealth' (*strīdhana*). Manu's code oscillates between declaring that women, like sons and slaves, have no property at all (*MDh* 8.416), to affirming the opposite by enjoining the king to protect the property of virtuous women (*MDh* 8.28–29). Women's wealth can comprise assets from a bride's natal family either at the wedding or later, as well as gifts of affection from the husband (*MDh* 9.195). She may not dispose of this property, however, except in adversity, such as extended absence of her husband, or abandonment by him. He too may draw on it in adversity. In contrast with the Dharmaśāstras, Kauṭilya's *Arthaśāstra* offers women somewhat more control of resources (*KAŚ* 3.2.19–34). Kauṭilya allowed a woman sole control over an endowment up to a set limit, and bride wealth (ornaments) of unlimited value (*KAŚ* 3.2.14). Conversely, Kauṭilya subjects a woman to half the fine that a man would face for the same offence (*KAŚ* 3.3.1–2). Dharmaśāstras sometimes cast doubt on the value of a woman's testimony as a witness in court (e.g. *MDh* 8.77), but the consensus seems to be that it is acceptable when better evidence is lacking, or for certain types of crime.

In China, the limitations imposed on women in the public sphere were broad: once married, they were not supposed to leave the marital home except under extraordinary circumstances. Legally, they were granted some privileges, not as extensive as those granted the old, young or disabled, on the ground that they were by nature weaker than men. This perception entailed that they were not subject to quite the same sort of convict labour as men. If confined in prison, they were treated more leniently than men. In Tang law they might not be sent into exile alone. Should a woman commit a crime punishable by exile, she was to be beaten and sentenced to forced labour instead of exile. Pregnant women who had committed a capital offence were not to be executed until 100 days after they had given birth. Women also enjoyed privileges, as did the old and young, in the context of 'collective prosecution', where their punishment might be less severe than those of male relatives also collectively prosecuted.[99]

---

98 Jamison 2017: 139.   99 MacCormack 1996: 134.

Age

The main age distinction was between minor and adult, the latter being the status conferring legal competency before the law. The particular definition of that competency, however, varied widely from culture to culture. Extreme old age, for example, was in some cases cited as entailing certain protections akin to those afforded minors.

Majority was attained at age eighteen for males in Athens and probably elsewhere in ancient Greece too. The distinction was not applied to females in Athens; but at Gortyn, twelve was the age at which girls could marry. Ancient Greek city states did not grant any special privileges to either young or old, except insofar as various political and religious offices were available only to those over a certain age; some positions with responsibilities for care or education also required a man to be of a certain age (e.g. forty years). A possible exception is an Athenian law that required (presumably adult) children to care for their elderly parents.[100] It is worth stressing here, as Gagarin notes, that '[f]rom earliest times, the Greeks took for granted certain basic rules concerning the treatment of people in general or of certain groups of people ... But such rules were not generally expressed in terms of these people's rights but in terms of the obligations others have to treat these people in certain ways.'[101] In other words, children had an obligation to care for their aged parents, rather than the aged parents having 'a right' to be cared for.

Under Roman private law, children whose *paterfamilias* died were classed as *sui iuris*, but they could not exercise full legal capacity due to their age. They thus needed a 'guardian' (*tutor*) to supplement their legal capacity and to secure any patrimony/property. A child legally became an adult at the onset of puberty, but Roman jurists differed on when and how exactly this should be determined, especially in the case of boys (usually age twelve for girls). There gradually developed provisions for 'curators' and legal protection via legal remedies for minors under twenty-five years old. Twenty-five was also the minimum age for appointment to a curial assembly. One major status marker in Roman Egypt involved the 'gymnasial' class. Membership in the gymnasium and participation in the *ephebia* marked one out as a citizen of one of the 'Greek' cities. This was achieved through a process of formal scrutiny of one's status called *epikrisis*, which took place at or around age fourteen. Old age did not present any disabilities, legally speaking, but did come to include a few privileges. Thus, the emperors Septimius Severus and

---

100 Gagarin 2020: 151.   101 Gagarin 2020: 151.

Caracalla exempted those over seventy years from compulsory public services; Constantine appears to have lowered the age to sixty. Interestingly, the papyrus that preserves the edicts of Severus and Caracalla (P. Flor. III 382) is a petition asking to be relieved of such services and as proof of his age (since Egyptians often were not very exact about their ages) the petitioner attaches a copy of his certificate of *epikrisis*.

Kauṭilya's *Arthaśāstra* specifies the age of legal competency for entering into transactions to be twelve for a woman (*dvādaśavarṣā strī*) and sixteen for a man; these correspond to ideal ages commonly prescribed in ancient Indian sources for a marriageable women and a man's completion of childhood studies (*KAŚ* 3.3.1). Kauṭilya exempted young and old (seventy years and older) from interrogation with torture and recognized 'elders' as authorities in certain cases (boundary disputes). 'Elders' can decide certain cases themselves; they are also teachers of the king. Unrecovered debt can be sought after the usual ten-year expiry by minors and elders inter alia. Finally, according to Kauṭilya, kings are obligated to look after the affairs of minors and elders.

The young (persons aged fifteen and under) and the old (persons aged seventy and over) were granted significant privileges in traditional Chinese law, with respect to the commission of offences, but they could also be subject to certain legal disabilities.[102] The ritual classics stipulate that the young and old should be treated leniently by the criminal law. In the case of the former, the ground was compassion for their weakness, and in the case of the latter it was respect for their years. This approach was adopted by the law which came to develop distinctions between different age groups. Han law already provided that persons aged seventy and above or sixteen and under, who committed offences entailing mutilation, were to be beaten instead of mutilated. Persons aged nine and under, who committed homicide, were to be reprieved from death. Neither the young nor the old were to be manacled or fettered while in prison. In the Han the old (age uncertain) were also granted 'royal staffs' as a sign of honour.[103] Possessors of such staffs obtained additional privileges. For example, an insult was treated as a serious offence. By Tang times an elaborate system of legal privileges had been contrived for the old and the young. The older or younger one was, the greater the extent of privilege: those aged between seventy and seventy-nine or between eleven and fifteen could avoid punishment for non-capital offences by payment of copper; those aged between eighty and eighty-nine or eight and ten were

---

102 MacCormack 1990: 113–15.   103 Guozhong 2016: 31.

exempt from liability for non-capital offences, with special consideration by the throne in case of a capital offence; those aged ninety and above or seven and below were to be immune from prosecution altogether. In addition, the laws mitigated punishment of the young and old in 'collective prosecution': that is, where relatives of the offender were involved in liability, as in the most serious offences such as rebellion.

Mesopotamian sources are an exception in that they do not specify an age of majority. From the legal point of view, it was probably the shift from dependency to legal and economic autonomy, marked by residence outside the parents' house, that was diagnostic. For instance, the virgin wife who dwells in her father's house (Laws of Ḫammurabi, chapter 30) is certainly considered a minor because she lives under the authority of the head of the household. The transfer into the house of her husband ended that dependency. Younger children appear in the Mesopotamian records as objects rather than persons; their social condition seems to be close to that of slaves, except that, when they are born free, they are expected to become persons, though it is not clear exactly at what point that change takes place.[104] First-millennium sources babies and small children by size rather than by age; 'tall' children are those ranging from six to twenty-five years old.[105] Abandonment and abduction of children were common. The Laws of Ḫammurabi imposed the death penalty for abduction (chapter 14), but it was not effective as a deterrent, to judge by Old Babylonian letters telling of long quests of parents to find and retrieve their children. Abandoned children could be adopted, unless they were still looking for their biological parents (Laws of Hammurabi, chapter 189); if the biological parents could prove their rights over the child, they took it back even if it had been legally adopted or sold.

The elderly tended to be marginalized, mainly because of their decreasing economic contributions. Children could expect support from their parents, but the reverse was also true, as stated in the prologue of the Laws of Lipit-Ištar (c. 1930 BCE): 'I (Lipit-Ištar) made the father support his children; I made the child support his father.'[106] Apart from this, Mesopotamian law offered only contractual arrangements for the support of the elderly; these could include adoption; *paramoneē* (immediate or delayed manumission of a slave in return for care of his owner); or antichretic loan (in which the interest of the loan is replaced by care for the creditor).[107] Contracts stipulated the allocation of food rations on an annual basis, sometimes combined with

---

104 Detailed discussion in Flynn 2018.   105 Joannès 1997.
106 Cited from Stol 1998: 60 (trans. M. Roth).   107 Westbrook 1998b.

cultic obligations (funerals, prayers). Within the family, sustenance duty probably entailed the hosting of the old parent in the house of the child. Fulfilment of these obligations conditioned inheritance rights. Thus, a son could be disinherited if he ran away from his sick and old father, who could in turn choose another heir (including a daughter or even someone outside the family). Finally, joint ownership between father and children could provide a means of support – as suggested by several Anatolian contracts dating from the nineteenth to eighteenth centuries BCE.[108]

Disability

Physical defects disqualified people from many statuses and functions according to Dharmaśāstra: those who are impotent, blind, deaf, mute, insane or mentally deficient could not inherit and were excluded from most legal transactions; the mentally impaired were prevented from giving testimony in court; a blind man could not become king. But – like elders, children and women – those with disabilities were also sometimes granted special protections. In classical Athens where the disabled and the poor were provided a small monthly stipend, a speech survives from a trial in which a man who apparently needs two walking sticks is claiming to be poor enough to deserve this payment (Lys. 24).

Various Roman rules prescribed 'curators' – appointed primarily out of concern to safeguard the patrimony – for the insane. Curators were also appointed for 'the spendthrift' (*prodigus*) 'on the analogy of an insane person' as Ulpian said (Justinian, *Digest* 27.10.1). Other individuals were also deemed incapable of managing their own affairs.[109] Roman jurists understood that the blind were subject to particular disabilities. For example, they could not make applications to the praetor, on the grounds that they 'cannot see and respect the magistrate's insignia' (Justinian, *Digest* 3.1.1.5). Though the blind could be judges, they could not serve in magistracies; similar rules, it seems, applied to the deaf. We also find discussions in Roman juristic texts of whether disease or physical/mental impairment of a slave amounted to a 'defect' in the goods and thus a breach of specific (sale, etc.) contract.[110]

In China the disabled, following recommendations in the ritual classics and here too on the analogy of provisions for the old and young, were also granted privileges by the law. Tang law included the disabled within the categories of the old and young.[111] Those 'disabled', in the sense that they had

---

108 Veenhof 1998.   109 Frier and McGinn 2004: 445–47.
110 On contracts see Chapter 11, this volume.   111 Johnson 1979: 29–31.

lost the use of one limb, were dumb, were blind in one eye or were dwarfs, were treated in the same way as persons aged seventy and above, or fifteen and under. Those who were 'incapacitated', in the sense that they lacked the use of two limbs, were blind in both eyes, or were insane, were to be treated in the same way as persons aged eighty and above, or ten and under. Of particular note is the recognition given to mental, as well as physical, disability.

Although not all traditions addressed this topic (the Mesopotamian sources are silent), we find a striking tendency across cultures to give legal recognition to both physical and mental forms of disability and to assign to those affected some of the legal limitations and privileges otherwise applicable to the very young or the very old.

Family Status

Jeremy Bentham once observed that 'it is in the bosom of a family that men serve an apprenticeship to government'.[112] Although broad status distinctions such as those treated in the preceding sections may determine which set of laws apply, or how they apply to a given individual, in the public domain, it is rather the family or household that has often been seen as constituting the core of the system. In part, this is because households, as the smallest social units, are the primary constituents of the larger polity. This relation of parts to whole also takes on symbolic and metaphoric value insofar as the polity is often represented to be a household writ large, with the ruler as patriarch and the subjects as children and dependents. The salience of the family in ancient law no doubt also arises from the fact that so many basic social and economic relationships – relations that give rise to disputes and offences requiring legal remedies – are created within and between households. Unfree groups and aliens thus tend to figure as special cases, rather than central concerns, in the body politic. The same may even be said of large classes meriting special privileges: their distinctiveness has legal implications but is peripheral to the core legal distinctions – inflecting or supplementing the core categories without determining them. Rather, the core categories of law were modelled on those of the family, to the extent of resorting to legal fictions, often through contracts, to create or alter relations between non-kin.

In most systems of ancient private law, the categories of family (a unit of kinship relation) and household (a unit of shared residence and property)

---

112 Quoted from Lobban 2016: 156–57.

were so tightly entwined as to be inseparable.[113] Power over the household generally lay with the senior male, known in Roman law as the *paterfamilias*. Although there were variations across places and periods, the most widespread pattern was for children (see 'marriage' below) and all descendants related to the senior male through the agnatic (male) line to be subject to the authority of the head of household. The Roman version was a particularly strong form of the system.

In Roman law the authority of the head of the household was referred to as the *patria potestas* – 'paternal power' – from which dependents could be released through emancipation or the death of the *paterfamilias* himself. The second-century CE jurist Gaius famously claimed that *patria potestas* was 'unique to Roman citizens, for virtually no other peoples have power over their children that is as great as ours' (Gaius, *Institutes* 1.55). On the other hand, the Roman system was unusual in the degree to which married women remained under their own father's power and retained separate property rights. The *paterfamilias* owned all family property, and hence anything acquired by those under his *patria potestas* accrued to him. Also by private law (although slavery itself was defined by Roman jurists as part of the *ius gentium*), slaves owned by a *paterfamilias* were his property and thus part of his *familia*. In sum, 'the overriding concern of Roman family law is not with setting standards for a family's life and internal governance but rather with the implications of family structure for the holding and disposition of property'.[114] Roman private law enabled funds of property to be made available to dependent sons, daughters and slaves through the institution of the *peculium*. From at least the fourth century CE, by the rule of *bona materna*, property could be inherited by a child from the maternal side.[115]

In China and India, as well as in the Near East including Jewish communities, most authority over the household theoretically lay in the hands of the (normally male) head of household, though certain limitations might be set on his authority and power. The key differences emerge when we consider the particular terms of the marital union, the roles of children and other dependents, and the disposition of family property.

Marriage and Its Dissolution

Although often depicted as the most natural of relations, marriage is in some ways the legal fiction at the heart of many traditions of ancient law: in many

---

113 Gelb 1979, citing the distinction made by Bender 1967: 493, 'the referent of the family is kinship, the referent of the household is propinquity or residence'.
114 Frier and McGinn 2004: 4.   115 Lewis 2015: 158.

systems (though not that of Rome), the bride leaves her birth-lineage and is 'naturalized' into that of her husband, such that their children count only in his line and their union creates new affinal relations between others in their families. Marriage provided a crucial legal mechanism for creating several personal statuses recognized as central to the ideal household under law: husband, wife, son, etc. The ancient marriage is pre-eminently a contractual relation (often arranged between families), whose purposes include creating and securing property and social status and transmitting them to heirs. It is a potentially unstable enterprise in that multiple interests must be taken into consideration and adequately protected including those of the bride and groom, their respective kin and their eventual offspring and their spouses. The family (and household) thereby created was fundamentally hierarchical, with the (male) head of household having the most prerogatives. For this very reason, however, the rights of the dependent parties – of the wife or wives above all – were spelled out and various legal means, contractual or statutory, were developed to define and safeguard their position. Insofar as the act of marriage was accompanied or effected by rites, it could have ethical or religious – and in the Brahmanical case, sacramental – aspects. Nevertheless, in spite of the Brahmin jurists' scruples, all ancient societies provided legal mechanisms for dissolving a marriage; indeed, marital arrangements often built in elements that anticipated this contingency, even if they differed in how far they disapproved and stigmatized divorce. We find a range of approaches to the issue, from liberal to restrictive, and from fairly egalitarian to highly male-biased, with many examples of institutional change over time.

In the ancient Near East, marriage had two stages, labelled by modern scholars as 'inchoate' and 'perfect' marriage.[116] The first stage was optional and corresponded with the agreement between the two families, realized with the delivery of the bridal gift (*terḥatu*) by the groom or his father. At this point, the marriage was created only towards third parties – hence the denominations *mutu* 'husband' and *aššatu* 'wife' for the protagonists – but was not yet completed between the spouses. This second stage, which completed the marriage, was ritualized in various ways and legally described with the verb *aḫāzu* 'to take'.[117] The action(s) covered by this technical term are not clear: *verba solemnia*; transfer of the bride to the house of the groom; sexual relations; or celebration and wedding banquet, are all good candidates,

---

116 Thus Driver and Miles 1935, after the terminology of Canon law, *matrimonium initiatum* and *perfectum*.
117 Westbrook 1988.

according to regions, periods and contexts. Probably a combination of all or some of these actions was required. In any case, this final step usually involved property consequences: restitution of the bridal gift to the groom and delivery of the dowry to the bride by her own family. The wife sometimes also received a dower (*nudunnû*) from her husband, the amount of which was either customary or conventional, designed to support her in case of widowhood. These exchanges probably took place when an offspring was expected or already born.

The correlation between matrimonial allowance and procreation is explicit in Neo-Babylonian documentation and very likely in second-millennium Babylonia.[118] It appears as a logical consequence of the legal nature of the dowry and the dower. Both were separate properties of the married woman, administered by her husband; they were designed to pass down to the children of the couple or to return to their original owners if the marriage dissolved without heirs. Such a restitution was not easy to obtain, as shown by several Old Babylonian trials, hence the wish of the families to postpone the settlement of the property aspects of marriage until the birth of progeny. The whole process depended on a contract (*riksu*), oral or written, determining the forms and effects of the marriage. Without such a contract, the marriage was deemed not to exist. It has been suggested that this agreement was a preliminary contract: in other words, that betrothal was legally binding and not merely informal (on the basis of a distinction between the formation of marriage itself, involving the bride and the groom, and the marriage contract, made by the groom and the parents of the bride).[119]

In addition to this dominant pattern, other (probably less formal) ways of getting married are attested, described with derivative forms of *aḫāzu* or with other verbs such as *erēbu* 'to enter' or *pussumu* 'to veil'. Law collections resort to this alternative vocabulary when marriage was agreed, for instance, with a raped girl, a widow or a concubine. It has been suggested that this specific terminology, especially the *aḫāzu* derivations, reflected situations where the woman was no longer a virgin when she married her husband.[120] But this conclusion inserts into the field of law a purely cultural criterion. Virginity was probably expected by the groom and claimed by the bride primarily as a sign of personal and family worthiness and probity. Thus, an inchoate wife accused of pre-marital intercourse in a letter from Mari asserted her innocence by stating: 'He (the seducer) has kissed my lips (and) touched my sex (but) his penis has not penetrated my sex. I have not done what should not be

118 Démare-Lafont 2012.   119 Westbrook 1988: 53–58   120 Driver and Miles 1935.

done to my husband' (ARM 26 488). As a matter of fact, the chances of making an honourable marriage diminished if the bride had been deflowered, not so much because of the economic depreciation of the woman but rather in consideration of moral convenances. Therefore, the standard *aḫāzu*-marriage was perhaps intended primarily for the first legitimate union of a daughter from a good family, not necessarily a virgin, though this condition was probably a social – and not a legal – requirement.

Marriage was monogamous as a rule. Although, by way of exception, a man could marry two women in case of natural or cultic sterility or of illness. Old Assyrian merchants also had two wives because of their specific way of life, spending months either in Aššur or in Kaneš for their business activities.[121] In such cases, a hierarchical relationship was created between the two wives, the second being subordinated to the first in terms of sisterhood or slavery according to Old Babylonian and Old Assyrian contracts. The legal difference between the two women does not lie in their mutual relationship or in modes of divorce, but in the status of their offspring: children were deemed born of the two wives when they were 'sisters', but were attached to the first-ranking wife alone if a maid had borne them.[122] In case of misbehaviour of the first-ranking wife, she was demoted and the secondary wife took her place. In Assyria, an infertile primary wife (*aššatum*) had the right to buy a slave who would bear a child for her mistress and be sold after the birth; but if she had the status of secondary wife (*amtum*), this right belonged to the husband.[123] Assyrian contracts also make clear that both wives should never meet, in order to keep both families apart. The situation was thus closer to 'double monogamy' than to real bigamy. Moreover, special clauses sometimes stated that secondary wives living in Anatolia ought to travel with their husbands. As Michel goes on to argue, it is difficult to determine whether such statements were intended to prevent married men from committing adultery or to provide them with potential itinerant pledges always available to secure their loans.

Babylonian law collections speak of divorce with the verb *ezēbu* 'to leave' and sometimes a combination of *zêru* 'to hate' and *aḫāzu* 'to take' (in marriage) in a negative form, while contracts resort to the standard formula: 'You are not my husband/wife', sometimes preceded by the verbs *zêru* 'to hate' or *muššuru* 'to release'. As a symbolic gesture, a husband could 'cut the hem' (*sissikta batāqu*) of his wife's garment. Legally, husbands and wives both enjoyed the same right to divorce, with or without grounds. Thus Assyrian,

121 Michel 2020.   122 Westbrook 1988; Veenhof 2007.   123 Michel 2006.

Syrian and, less frequently, Babylonian contracts from the second millennium make provisions for an equal compensation for both spouses in case of breach of marriage. More commonly, however, the wife's right was precluded by imposing severe contractual penalties. Northern Old Babylonian deeds threaten her with enslavement or death by drowning or defenestration, while Neo-Babylonian tablets sometimes refer to the 'iron dagger'.[124] This last penalty was incurred if the woman was 'seen' (*amāru*) or 'found' (*kašādu*) with another man. It has been argued that this formulation was intended to worsen the situation of the wife, whose compromising behaviour would be assimilated to actual adultery. But this aggravation of her situation should be considered in light of the large quantity of silver owed by a husband who wished to divorce. Both deterrent provisions would thus aim at preventing the parties from breaking the contract.[125] The major goal was to protect a poor bride, who got married with no dowry, from being repudiated almost for free by a cynical husband; the harsh presumption placed on her appears to result from some sort of bargaining between the spouses.[126]

In the rabbinic conception, too, marriage was explicitly a contractual arrangement, constituted through two acts: 'betrothal' (*erusin*; *qiddushin*) by means of money, contract or sexual intercourse (*Midrash Qiddushin* 1:1). The first (and ideal) option involved 'acquiring' the woman by a payment to her, which should be accepted before witnesses. The couple were considered married once the object had been accepted. The marriage was formalized with a written contract (*ketubah*) between the groom and the bride's father (or other male representative) stipulating the financial obligations and rights of the partners. The name of the contract alludes to the pledge to the bride of an endowment in case of death or divorce. Fathers could betroth a daughter without her consent, even as a minor. The second act, called *huppah*, was the consummation of the marriage, frequently occurring long after the 'betrothal'. Divorce was envisioned to be a unilateral act normally available only to the husband, without the need for the wife's consent (*m. Yeba.* 14:1).

Rabbinic literature enshrined an ideal of male control over his own and his wife's property, but documents on papyrus suggest that in practice women had legal means to protect their own interests by keeping their property separate.[127] It is not clear how far Jewish practice in post-Exile antiquity conformed to the rabbinic model. Michael Satlow proposes that 'the first purpose of rabbinic marital legislation was to create a legal entity that could

---

124 Roth 1988. 125 Roth 1988. 126 Wunsch 2020; Waerzeggers 2020.
127 Satlow 2001: 217.

be called "Jewish marriage". This entity was, in part, a vehicle for establishing identity.'[128] In other words, 'Jewish marriage' was a vehicle for establishing membership in the Jewish community. It has been noticed that semi-autonomous Jewish communities (*politeumata*) in Egypt, which may have been able to adhere to their own civil laws, did not appear to follow anything like rabbinic law and in fact tended to give the wife much more autonomy. One papyrus document from 218 BCE records how a Jewish women married according to the 'civil law (*politikon*) of the Jews' was able to divorce her husband.[129]

Another corpus of Aramaic and Greek legal papyri from Judean caves, dating to the first and second centuries CE, include marriage contracts explicitly described as having been made 'according to the law/custom of the Jews' (echoing the use of the term *politikon* in the divorce document from Egypt), yet show little sign of rabbinic marriage norms.[130] Scholars of Jewish law in antiquity have struggled to explain what relation these documents might bear to 'Jewish law'. Cotton regarded them as the elements of a 'still-to-be-codified halacha'.[131]

Laws surviving from ancient Greece recognize both marriage and divorce, with the latter being initiated by either spouse. Marriage in Athens was arranged by a girl's father, brother or other male relative. It was usually accompanied by the payment of a dowry to the future husband by the male relative. The dowry was not a legal requirement but was normal for all but the poor; the wealthier the family the larger the expected dowry. The dowry did not belong to the husband but was managed by him and would then be inherited by their children. In a divorce, he would have to return the dowry. A large dowry could thus give a woman some protection against divorce.[132] At Gortyn, a girl may have had more say in determining the marriage; dowries were not given but male relatives sometimes, perhaps often, gave girls gifts when they married. These were the girl's own property, however, not just held in trust (so to speak) for her children, as at Athens. In a divorce, a Gortynian woman took her own property with her together with half the produce of that property – the same rules for marriage and divorce applied to serfs and probably also slaves.[133] At Sparta, in line with the policy of maximizing the population of Spartiates, marriage was strongly encouraged for men;

---

128 Satlow 2001: 68.   129 Tcherikover 1957–64, vol. I: 238, n. 2.
130 For example Cotton and Yardeni 1997.
131 Cotton 1998: 179. For further discussion see Czajkowski 2017.
132 On dowry practices in classical Athens, see Foxhall 1989: 32–39.
133 Gagarin 2008b; Gagarin 2012.

there were penalties for celibacy and rewards for having children. Most marriages were arranged between families, but it appears dowries were forbidden. Divorce was possible, though we hear of it primarily in connection with wishing to take a new wife to replace one who had not borne children.[134]

Evidence for marriage laws and practices in pharaonic Egypt is relatively scare, hence 'the question of marriage patterns in ancient [pharaonic] Egypt is a thorny issue that is difficult to ascertain from the sources. Instead of attempting an encompassing approach, most works discuss only a few aspects that are related to marriage, such as inheritance and succession ... polygamy ... or divorce.'[135] There is, however, a range of relevant source material on marriage, divorce and widowhood for Ptolemaic Egypt (332–30 BCE). There is no Ptolemaic-era normative law that governed the age of marriage, but the standard for men was about twenty years of age and for women about fourteen. Ptolemaic marriage contracts establish very clearly the rights of the woman's maintenance during the marriage and protect her with respect to this and to her property brought into the marriage in the case of divorce. The 'eldest son' had special obligations with respect to the burial of his parents and was recognized in the law. The status of divorced women was probably very low. Widows were, on the other hand, protected by the community. In the case of intestacy, neither Greek nor Egyptian law recognized the right of the surviving spouse.

In classical Roman law, the *familia* (household) was constituted by a set of legally defined relationships and not merely by kinship.[136] Marriage, moreover, was not necessarily a key component in the legal creation and dissolution of the *familia*: a wife did not automatically join the 'household' of her husband, but under certain, legal, forms could remain under the power of her *paterfamilias* if she had one surviving. Roman law recognized two types of legal marriage (*conubium, justae nuptiae*). In the early Republic, elites practised marriage *cum manu* whereby the bride was transferred from the 'hand' (*manus*) of her father (that is, from *patria potestas*) into that of her husband, such that she entered into his family as agnate and as cognate, as if in the position of a daughter (*in familiam viri transibat, filiaeque locum obtinebat*, Gaius, *Institutes* I.3). Among patricians, this was normally accomplished through the rite of *confarreatio*, which involved sharing a loaf of spelt bread;

---

134 Hodkinson 2009: especially 436–39.
135 Olabarria 2020: 174 (with references to further literature).
136 See Treggiari 1991 (late Republic to early Empire); Treggiari 2019 (late Republic); and Kuefler 2007 (late Empire).

among plebeians, marriage took place via *coemptio* (fictive 'purchase', a legal device not actually involving money, used also for adoption and emancipation of children; Gaius, *Institutes* I.113) and *usus* (a sort of common law marriage, recognized after one year of continuous cohabitation, though the woman could avoid coming under the husband's *manus* by dwelling apart at least three nights in a year[137]). However, by the end of the Republic, *manus* marriage had been supplanted by marriage *sine manu*, in which the wife remained under the guardianship of her father until his death and then became autonomous (*sui iuris*). Social class was at first important in another way: in the early Republic, *conubium* was not allowed between patricians and plebeians, though this impediment was removed by the *Lex Canuleia* (445 BCE).

In classical Roman jurisprudence marriage tends to be conceptualized as a continuing contract entered into by consent. In the absence of any other specific restrictions (age, degree of relationship, etc.), the capacity to enter into a legally recognized marriage extended to Roman citizens and also, under certain circumstances, to freedmen, *peregrini* ('foreigners') and others. It did not extend to slaves. The main legal effect was that children born into marriage were legitimate and subject to paternal power. For a marriage to be valid, both parties had to have legal capacity (usually twelve years for girls and fourteen for boys) and not be within a degree of family relationship prohibited by Roman law; consent had to be given by the parties themselves, or for an individual 'in power' by his or her *paterfamilias*. In the standard classical form of marriage, the wife did not fall under her husband's power and the spouses' property also remained separate; 'gifts' between spouses were prohibited. The exception was dowry: 'property provided by or on behalf of the wife, for example by her *paterfamilias*, relatives or friends'.[138] The dowry was owned by the husband during the marriage, but with restrictions on what he could and could not do with it. According to Johnston, the Roman legal rules relating to dowry should be understood as 'residual': they only took effect in the absence of specific agreements between the parties. Rome further recognized concubinage as a sort of quasi-legal relationship, for example, as a means of redefining the relationship away from a criminal charge of 'debauchery' (*stuprum*).

Rome (and Greco-Roman Egypt) had very liberal divorce laws and divorce was widely accepted. From early times, men could divorce unilaterally, especially if the wife had 'misbehaved', and by the last century BCE women

---

137 Aulus Gellius III.2; Gaius, *Institutes* I.111.   138 Johnston 2022: 42.

too had acquired a unilateral right to divorce a husband (though this came later for women married by *manus*). Eventually divorce came to lose much of whatever shame did attach to it; there is even a famous instance of a noble woman remarrying whilst pregnant with the child of her first husband – who also attended the couple's wedding feast.[139] Contractual penalties for future divorce of the sort employed in Assyrian and Babylonian marriages were firmly rejected by Alexander Augustus in 233 CE: 'From ancient times it has been determined that marriages are unrestricted. Therefore, it is agreed that pacts not to permit divorce are not valid, and stipulations by which penalties were imposed on the person who had effected a divorce are considered invalid' (Justinian, *Cod.* 8.38.2). Unilateral divorce appears to have been allowed until the later Roman – Christian – empire.

The legal rules on marriage in China fundamentally followed the prescriptions laid down in the ritual classics: marriage of a son or daughter was to be arranged by the parents through a go-between, with an exchange of presents on betrothal. In Tang law a marriage might be constituted by a written or a private agreement between the families of the boy and girl; the giving of betrothal presents by the groom's family was deemed to constitute an agreement to marry.[140] The law had to deal with the consequences of promises to marry which were broken, a not uncommon event since promises might be made by a family when the boy and girl involved were very young, and later come to be regretted. Some variation occurred in the evaluation of the relationship between 'agreement' and 'betrothal gift'. The first legal rule of which we have knowledge comes from the Jin dynasty (265–420 CE). This provided that no mere private agreement of marriage was to be enforceable unless the betrothal gifts had been sent from the groom's to the bride's family. Later the law with respect to private agreements was changed. The Tang code provided that, whether there had been a written agreement to marry or merely a private understanding between the families (in both cases arranged through a go-between), failure to honour the betrothal was a punishable offence, even though no property had yet passed between the families. Under the Northern Wei dynasty (386–534 CE), a law was introduced to prohibit marriage between persons of the same surname – a generalization of the prohibition against incest. From the Northern Wei code, the prohibition passed into Tang law, but it was probably often disregarded in practice.

---

139 Tac. *Ann.* 1.10.5 and Dio 49.44.1–2 on Octavian, Livia and Tiberius Nero. See Cantarella 2002: 278, however, on restrictive Roman rules relating to pregnancy, divorce and widowhood.
140 On marriage and divorce during the Tang era, see Benn 2002: 243–48.

The legal position of a concubine vis-à-vis the wife seems to have gradually worsened in the post-Han period. In the Han it does not seem unusual for a concubine to have been promoted to the status of wife. However, a Jin decree of 274 CE stated that a concubine was not to be allowed to occupy the position of legal wife, a stipulation that appears to have entered the statutory law of the Northern Wei from which it, too, passed into Tang law. The Tang Code made it a punishable offence for a husband either to reduce his wife to the status of concubine or to elevate a concubine to the status of wife.

Qin laws from the third century BCE had made it a punishable offence for a husband to beat and wound an obstreperous wife, but under the Han law of 186 BCE a husband faced no liability for beating and wounding a wife (unless a sharp weapon were used), while a wife who beat her husband was to be punished. The Tang adopted a middle ground: the wife was treated as 'junior' in relation to her husband, such that a husband who assaulted or even killed his wife was punished less severely than a wife who assaulted or killed her husband. In Han China, divorce was less strictly regulated by the law than it came to be in the Tang period. Husbands might divorce a wife for a wide range of reasons. Equally wives appear to have been free to divorce their husbands or leave them to marry someone else. Specific rules on divorce in the law codes appear to have been introduced first in the Northern Wei. The Tang Code, building on Northern Wei law, provided for divorce unilaterally on the part of the husband (though not on the part of the wife) on one of 'seven grounds': lack of sons, immoral behaviour, disobeying husband's parents, talking too much, committing theft, jealousy and an incurable disease. The Tang Code also provided for mutual divorce by consent of both husband and wife.

In contrast with the discussion above, India's Dharmaśāstras – the product of a priestly tradition – regarded marriage as a sacrament. It was conventional to classify marriage arrangements in a hierarchy from pure to impure. The lower end of the spectrum, included (albeit with disapproval) elopement and 'demonic' forms of union such as kidnap and rape, but the ideal was the 'gift of a virgin' (*kanyādāna*). The Dharmaśāstric model of marriage resembled the archaic Roman *manus* marriage: a bride was integrated into her husband's lineage, under his authority. It was the marital union that rendered the husband competent (*adhikārin*) to fulfil most of his ritual obligations, besides providing him with legitimate heirs. The sacral authority and doctrinal priorities of the Brahmin class probably encouraged the notion that marriage was not merely a contract. A maxim affirms that marriage serves two functions: the fulfilment of ritual obligations (possible only for married householders according to doctrine) and the procreation of offspring (which, in turn, fulfilled a 'debt' said to be owed to one's ancestors; ensured that one's own rites would be performed; and provided an heir and continuance of the patriline). Kauṭilya, as usual, emphasizes legal (contractual) concerns over sacral ones: 'Transactions presuppose marriage' (KAŚ 3.2.1), which means that marriage is the transaction (vyavahāra) that renders someone legally competent for other transactions.

Precisely because of the sacramental character of marriage, Dharmaśāstra jurists tended to find reasons to discourage or circumscribe divorce – not unlike the direction in which Christian ecclesiastical or 'canon' law would turn the late antique Roman legal tradition. While Indian men might marry more than one woman, concurrently or not, a wife's union to her husband was ideally to be unique and permanent. In spite of this, there are numerous maxims expressing disapproval of women remarrying, implying that this in fact must have been fairly common. The question whether a widow might remarry was a matter of controversy. Two Dharmasūtras and Manu (MDh 9.76) prescribed specific waiting periods for women whose husbands have gone away, depending on the reason for their absence, but the option to remarry tended to be limited to childless women. Most authorities recommended a life of austere celibacy for widows; Nārada Smṛti (12.97–102) is the only Dharmaśāstra to endorse widow remarriage. The notion that a truly virtuous woman, a satī, should heroically immolate herself on her husband's funeral pyre, in a rite called sahagamana ('accompanying' in Sanskrit and 'suttee' in English) is not found at all in sources before the seventh century CE. From that period, as widows' rights to inherit household property expended, Dharmaśāstrins increasingly favoured suttee.[141]

Although the Arthaśāstra likewise affirms the ideal of a widow who 'dedicates herself to Dharma' by remaining chaste, it also details the financial arrangements in the event that she chooses to remarry. Moreover, it recognizes divorce (mokṣa, 'release') on the grounds of 'mutual hatred' and seems to allow it at the instance of either spouse so long as the other consents. Where a woman sues for divorce on the grounds that her husband is at fault (guilty of some offence), she may even keep her bride wealth, but she must return it if she is at fault (KAŚ 3.3.15–19).[142]

---

[141] Brick 2014, 2023.
[142] The final sentence of this passage from Kauṭilya's Arthaśāstra, which states that all of this does not apply in the case of pure forms of marriage, looks to be an addition to reconcile this work with Dharmaśāstric dogma on the sacramental character of the union.

Adoption

Adoption and other types of fictive family status were accomplished through legal means for a variety of purposes. The most common purpose was to compensate for a lack of biological offspring needed to safeguard family property or to perform ritual functions. Since in most cases these aims both depended upon preserving the patriline, some systems envisioned only the adoption of boys, but we find several alternative scenarios as well.

Adoption was a very highly developed family institution in the ancient Near East, perhaps because it was put to such a wide array of uses. The most important of these, as elsewhere, was to provide descendants to the childless (including to a priestess under a ritual rule of chastity). The adoptee was usually a baby, either a foundling or one given by his biological parents under contract. Less well understood is a case in the Laws of Hammurabi in which a child was adopted 'in its water' (*ina mêšu*, chapter 185) and then reared by the adopter, whose rights were henceforth irrevocable. The implication seems to be that a contract was made with the biological parents even before birth and was fulfilled by the adoptive father's subsequent performance of parental obligations.[143] A few Sippar tablets from the reigns of Hammurabi and Samsu-iluna speak of an adopted child as 'pulled from the womb' (*šilip rēmim*), perhaps pointing to a child injured during delivery, or illegitimate or unwanted, but the purpose of such an adoption is unclear.[144] An unusual type of documentation included the imprint of a baby's foot on a clay tablet, with just eight examples surviving, spanning the third to first millennia BCE. These may have served as temporary placeholders for an actual child during a period when a foundling's parents were sought or a newborn was being suckled; such records may normally have been destroyed after transfer of the child or finalization of the adoption.[145]

In Athens, the adopted son was often a relative; if a man had a daughter but no son, the adopted son was commonly the man chosen to be the daughter's husband. Adoption could be either *inter vivos* or (as a result of Solon's legislation) testamentary. In the latter, a man directed in his will that someone be adopted as his son (and sometimes also marry his daughter) after his death.[146] This may have happened when a man without a son made his will at the last minute and did not have time to go through adoption proceedings. At Gortyn, and probably also at Sparta, adoption was possible only *inter vivos*. In

---

143 Démare-Lafont 2016–17.   144 Stol 2000.   145 Démare-Lafont 2016–17.
146 Further details in Rubinstein 1993. On adoption across the ancient Eastern Mediterranean, see Huebner 2013.

Ptolemaic Egypt, besides records of adoption to establish an heir, one could, by legal process, create an heir outside of the family line. In India, where the sons were responsible not only for producing further offspring but also for sustaining their deceased forebears through the performance of ancestor rites, the Dharmaśāstra tradition placed strict limitations on candidacy for adoption, to avoid depriving a biological father of his only heir. Accordingly, an only child could not be adopted, and the adoption of girls is not envisioned.

Similarly, in China, both the ritual classics and the law consider the adoption of a son primarily from the standpoint of the need of the family which lacked male descendants to continue its line and the making of sacrifices to the ancestors. Hence it was desirable that the boy adopted belong to the same family (preferably being the son of a brother of the adopting father), or at least bear the same surname as that of the adopting family. Han and later law in fact prohibited the adoption of a child with a different surname. In practice, however, children bearing different surnames, especially from relatives in the female line, might be adopted. Examples of different surname adoption are known from the Han and immediate post-Han periods. One exception to the rule against different surname adoption was permitted by the law. Should a boy aged three or under have been abandoned by his natural parents, he might be reared and adopted by another family (not necessarily as heir), whose surname the child then took. Once adopted, the boy acquired the same status in the family as a natural born son.

Of course the availability of legal mechanisms to create fictive kinship and all that such kinship might entail opened the door to various forms of indirection. Although like instrumentalist uses of law more generally, these may have been found widely in antiquity, recorded instances cluster in particular milieux. For instance, in middle-period Babylonia ostensible adoptions could mask a sale. A Nuzi squire named Teḥip-tilla built up a large estate by gradually acquiring adjoining plots of otherwise inalienable land through inheritance from more than a hundred adoptive fathers.[147] Sources from eighteenth-century BCE Elam and thirteenth-century BCE Ugarit and Nuzi record instances of two adults aiming to create a partnership or to regulate family matters through a fictitious link of brotherhood.[148]

Levirate

Another such remedy for the case of a man dying sonless was the so-called 'levirate marriage' by which a widow unites with her brother-in-law (*levir*, in

---

147 Müller 2012.   148 Zaccagnini 2003.

Latin), with a son born of the union being treated as the son of the deceased. This old Israelite custom is illustrated in Deuteronomy 25.5–10 but appears to have fallen out of usage in the wake of the destruction of the Temple.[149] The alternative to levirate marriage was the 'release' (*halitzah*) of the widow.[150] Satlow observes that: 'Jewish writers from Roman Palestine understood the biblical levirate marriage as a Jewish equivalent of the Greek *epiklarate* – i.e., the claim that a man has on the property and widow of an heirless male relative – in which the disposition of the family's estate was the primary concern. This might relate to why Palestinian amoraim prefer that a man release the widow from the obligation of levirate marriage.'[151]

In India, several Dharmaśāstras (with the notable exception of the oldest lawbook, *ĀpDh* 2.27.2–7) endorsed the similar practice of 'appointment' (*niyoga*), by which a male relation of the deceased (preferably a brother) is designated to beget upon the widow a male child, to be treated as the heir of the deceased for all intents and purposes. The practice appears to be alluded to already in *Ṛgveda* 10.40.2. However the lawbooks were usually careful to specify that the relation was not one of marriage; copulation was restricted to the woman's fertile period and was to cease as soon as she delivered a male child. Several authorities approve it contingent also on the willingness of the wife.

All these levirate-type arrangements share the character of legal fictions devised to posthumously endow a man who died sonless with an heir. In the Eastern Roman empire, the custom of a brother marrying his brother's still-virgin widow – called an 'Egyptian' practice – was banned by law in 475 CE (Justinian, *Cod.* 5.5.8).[152] Levirate-type arrangements, however, continue to be attested in late Sasanian (Persian) legal sources.

The 'Female Son'

Another legal fiction sometimes encountered, serving a purpose similar to that of levirate, is the act of turning a daughter into an ersatz son for the sake of passing down family property in the absence of a male heir. In Babylon, this was done by means of testament or adoption, in order to control the fate of the family estate by attaching the property to the direct masculine line and excluding other male relatives. Beyond the preservation of material interests in the family, the concern was also of religious nature in that the masculinized daughter was in charge with the ancestor's cult.[153]

---

149 Ilan 1995: 152–57.   150 Friedman 1996; Satlow 2001: 186–89.   151 Satlow 2010: 355.
152 Cohen 2018: 342.   153 Westbrook 2003d: 680.

A similar arrangement is found in India's Dharmaśāstra texts, which speak of the *putrikā*, the 'female son'. This is a daughter designated to produce heirs in her own father's line, rather than in her spouse's. There is some ambiguity in the sources whether a 'female son' is considered an heir, but she was authorized to perform the ancestor rites for her father – as in the Babylonian case. For this very reason, some Indian sources recommend against marrying a woman without brothers, lest her progeny be alienated from the husband's patriline.

Apprenticeship

In the ancient Near East at least, adoption was sometimes used as a legal framework for apprenticeship. This fact may explain the scarcity of apprenticeship contracts in Mesopotamia – most of which, dating mainly from the Neo-Babylonian period (seventh and sixth centuries BCE), involve slaves entrusted to a craftsman by a wealthy family, especially the Egibi family of Babylon.[154] A distinctive feature of these adoptions meant for professional training is that, contrary to normal adoption contracts, they include a clause stipulating that the adoptee should remain the elder son, regardless of any previous or future children, natural or adopted. This convergence of adoption and apprenticeship is clearer in several provisions of law collections (Laws of Lipit-Ishtar, chapter 20b; Laws of Ḫammurabi, chapters 188–89; Hittite Laws, chapters 200b), where it says that a young man who has been living at his master's home for several years should stay with him if fully trained, or go back to his parents if not. In such an adoption, the 'father' had an obligation to provide training or else lose the child.

This rule is exemplified in a fourteenth-century BCE Nuzi contract whereby a man gave his son in adoption to a slave-weaver, who was to teach him his craft and to marry him off; so long as he performed his duties, the adopter enjoyed all the prerogatives of a father, including domestic jurisdiction (JEN 572).[155] A contract from the reign of Cyrus was cancelled (*pasāsu*) by the natural mother several years later without explicit reason, but using an expression: '[he] has returned to his father's house' (found also in the Laws of Ḫammurabi, chapter 189) which implies an uneducated apprentice; similarly, a Nuzi contract records that a biological father took back his son and compensated the adopter.[156] In this respect, apprenticeships created

---

154 Further discussion in Cohen and Kedar 2011: 238–41.   155 Démare-Lafont 2016–17: 46.
156 Démare-Lafont 2016–17: 48, fn. 17.

a parent–child relationship, yet were simultaneously contracts, giving them a hybrid character close to that of modern guardianship.

Status as a Factor in Succession or Inheritance

The major distinctions in laws of inheritance and succession in the ancient world lay in whether or not they made use of written wills (or other sorts of documents); whether, when and how family property could be divided among heirs; and the degree to which women had a share in inheritance, whether as testator or heir. In most societies, women could inherit, but sons, especially the eldest son, received preferential terms in some way. For example, in Mesopotamia, sons received a larger portion of the estate than daughters. Several inheritance laws (e.g. in southern cities during Old Babylonian times) allot to the eldest son an extra share or a double share of the estate. The exclusion of daughters from succession was mitigated to some extent, insofar as daughters received a share of their paternal estate in the form of a dowry (Babylonian *nudunnû*; Assyrian *šerku*). In practice, this dowry worked as an anticipated inheritance share. The connection is clear in Neo-Babylonian laws, where the amount of the dowry could be scaled down proportionately if her father's assets had declined by the time of delivery, though the terms of the agreement otherwise remained unchanged (Neo-Babylonian Laws, chapter 9).

However, the Mesopotamian dowry differed from regular inheritance mechanisms on two major points. First its assignment was by no means mandatory and the father could refrain from giving it to his daughter, while on the other hand, he was not allowed to disinherit his sons except in case of serious and repeated filial offences (Laws of Ḥammurabi, chapters 168–69). Second, even if the woman were legally the owner of her dowry, her ability to settle these goods was limited both by her husband's management and by legal restrictions preventing her, for instance, from bequeathing it to her husband in the absence of children. In such a case, the dowry was to be returned in full to the 'house of her father' (*bīt abiša*), which effectively meant to her brothers. Sometimes, the consumable part of the dowry was removed from the initial amount, or the husband tried to negotiate its content.[157] In Neo-Babylonian times, a small portion of the dowry (*mulūgu*) could be given directly to the woman for her personal use.[158] During the same period, specific deeds concerning the reinvestment of the dowry were drafted

---

157 For Old Babylonian examples: Westbrook 1988; Jursa 1997.
158 Oelsner, Wells and Wunsch 2003.

when the husband had sold part of his wife's goods. There was a dual goal: to replace the missing item in value, and to maintain its nature as separate property, thus putting it beyond reach of the husband's creditors. All in all, the purpose of many of these legal rules was to make the dowry inalienable, while rendering it unavailable to the woman to hand over as a separate estate to her children or to return to her brothers.

Inheritance rules of the elite (generally coming from the temple milieu) are well known in Egypt at least for Greco-Roman times, but we assume such rules were traditional. Partible inheritance was the norm: all children were understood to have a right to inherit property from parents. Rights to inherit father's property are stipulated in the so-called marriage contracts that are preserved from the ninth century BCE onward.

The Hebrew biblical tradition dictated that the firstborn son should succeed his deceased father as head of the family, including control of the family property. As in Indian jurisprudence, the firstborn son is assigned a double share (Deut 21.17). Sons of concubines were also eligible, even when there were legitimate sons, although the Hebrew Bible includes narratives of them being sent away at the wife's request. When petitioned by the daughters of Zelophehad, Moses ordained by divine decree (in the manner of a 'responsum') the hierarchy of heirs for a man who dies sonless, beginning with daughters, followed by brothers and father's brothers (Num 27.6–11); in response to a subsequent appeal by clan elders, however, Moses further ordained that the heiresses must then marry 'anyone they please' so long as it be from among their father's clan, in order to avoid alienating the family property (Num 36: 6–9). Michael Fishbane observes:

> The remarkable fact from a legal standpoint is that this second responsum, requiring the daughters to marry a paternal relative, produces a veritable legal fiction. For if the daughters of Zelophehad must marry into their father's family ... the inheritance would necessarily revert to precisely those males who would be next in line if the father had no children whatsoever (per *Num.* 27: 9–11). Accordingly, the ruling in favour of female inheritance provided by the first adjudication (*Num.* 27:8) is functionally subverted by the responsum in *Num.* 36:6–9 – even though its specific provisions remain valid (27:9–10).[159]

On the other hand, according to the Hebrew Bible, testators had the capacity to name an heir of their choice. The childless might name someone else – not necessarily a relative – as heir, as Abraham considered appointing his slave

---

159 Fishbane 1985: 105; about this episode see also Johnson 2020: 217–65.

Eliezer, passing over his nephew Lot (Gen 15.3). Even when there were children, it was within the right of the father to prefer one child to another in the disposition of his property.

Under rabbinic law daughters appear in the listed hierarchy of heirs, but a wife has no statutory inheritance rights to their husband's estate under most circumstances (m. *Baba Batra* 8:2), although the husband inherits from his wife. However, the *ketubah*, the agreement made between a groom and his bride's male legal guardian, was meant to provide for the widow's support until she remarries.

Women in classical Athens, having little direct control of property, could not make a will. Only a man's sons (or sons of sons) inherited directly; daughters inherited only if there were no equally close male relative, by being named in a will. If a man died leaving only a daughter she became an *epiklēros*: '[one] with the estate' (often translated 'heiress' but in a sense quite different from the modern one) – the estate would be in her name and would pass to her male children, but she could not manage it directly.[160] Rules provided that a relative marry the 'heiress', which could require her to divorce a prior husband. To avoid the uncertainty that this might occasion, a man might adopt a son (who might often be a relative) and direct him to marry the 'heiress'. If a man died childless, complicated rules governed the distribution of the estate; we have many speeches from litigation that resulted from this situation. Otherwise, as in Mesopotamia, dowry usually constituted the daughter's only share of family property (even in some cases including land); its value ranged from 5 to 25 per cent of paternal property.[161] But such property was controlled and administered by the husband, or returned to the woman's father or other former guardian (*kyrios*) in case of divorce.

In Gortyn, women were in a better position with regard to property and inheritance; something similar seems to have been true of Sparta (Herodotus VI.57.4). Both sons and daughters inherited directly, though a daughter's share was half that of a son's. Women were not subject to a guardian and could thus control their own property, retain it if divorced and pass it on to heirs. As in Athens, if there was an 'heiress' – called *patrōiōkos* at Gortyn, *patroukos* at Sparta: 'holder of the patrimony' – there were complex rules about who should marry her, beginning with father's brother or other close relatives. There were other complex rules about the distribution of the

---

160 Kamen 2013: 92.　　161 Leduc 1991: 302ff.

property in this case, but it appears that the 'heiress' received some of it herself.

Any Roman citizen with full legal capacity could make a will (and legal capacity could be supplemented by a tutor, curator, etc.). Roman law had detailed requirements that varied over time with respect to the formal requirements that had to be met for a will – and crucially the appointment of an heir – to be considered valid. 'What is important is that all these requirements were requirements of form and not content. Provided the testator succeeded in complying with the form, which with legal advice need not have been difficult, the will could leave property to anyone the testator wanted.'[162] Nevertheless there were certain technical restrictions. For example, from the late Republic descendants or ascendants might challenge a will on the grounds that they had been 'unduly' passed over. Property could also be assigned as a 'trust' (*fideicommissum*), which sometimes served as a means of circumventing the limitations of testation (e.g. the requirement that heirs be citizens). There were also complex rules governing intestate succession. In the developed Roman law, the *gens* (clan, extended family) played no part in the rules that governed distribution of an estate on intestacy; this is not the case, however for earlier pre-classical ('archaic') Roman law. In general, developed Roman law operated a system of partible inheritance: male and female children were treated equally, without distinction between elder and younger. According to the edict(s) of the urban praetor (the *ius honorarium*), the priority of claims to intestate succession went first to children, then to agnatic relations, then to cognatic relations and finally to spouses.

The head of the household in ancient China, normally the most senior male, but possibly a senior woman, was responsible to the government, in the bureaucratic state, for the obligations placed on the family with respect to corvée, payment of taxes and registration of members of the household and land. The head controlled the use of the family property but did not own it. Pre-Han law discouraged the building of large, extended families living in the same household and therefore required the head to divide the family property between the adult sons who thereupon formed separate households and functioned as heads of their own families. In Han law division of the property between sons and the formation of separate households was a matter for the head of the family's judgment. He was not compelled by law to make the division. The trend in the post-Han law was against the separation of

---

162 Johnston 2022: 53.

households in the lifetime of the family head. The Tang Code made it an offence for sons or grandsons to establish separate households in the lifetime of parents or grandparents. Upon the death of the latter, after completion of the appropriate period of mourning, separate households with division of property might be achieved. On the death of the head, the headship together with any title he possessed normally passed to his eldest son by his wife (not a concubine). The Han law of 186 BCE established the following order of succession in the absence of sons: father or mother, widow, daughter, other descendants, grandparents, sons of brothers (brothers probably should come in this list towards the top). There are problems in understanding exactly the way the law of succession worked. It is, however, clear not only that women might assume the position of head of the household, but that the deceased's widow (not a relation by blood) was given a certain priority in the order of succession.[163] This flexible position, which allowed women to become head of the household, changed in the later law. Under the Tang a stricter patrilineal model was followed. Only the male descendants of the deceased (in the appropriate order, elder being preferred to younger) might take his place as head of the household. Sons of concubines might succeed, but only if there were no sons by the wife. In the absence of a male successor, the household became 'extinct'.

Where there was no will, ancient Chinese legal sources expect that control of the family property will pass to the new head. In the Han, the head might, if the circumstances were appropriate, proceed to the establishment of separate households and a division of the property. In Tang law, on the death of the family head, followed by the establishment of separate households by the sons, the property was to be divided equally between them. Should there be no male descendants, the property was to be divided equally between daughters, whether married or not (account being taken of property previously assigned to married daughters as dowry), or, if there were no daughters, between other close relatives. Both Han and Tang law provided that the head of the household might dispose of property by will, but the head's discretion in the matter was far greater in the Han than the Tang. The Han law, while laying down formal conditions for the making of a will, did not specify how the property was to be divided. Tang law, by contrast, contemplated the making of a will only in circumstances where the family lacked male descendants. Excavated deeds suggest in fact that wills were made even where the

---

163 Further discussion in Yates 2021: 173ff.

testator had sons, but merely to confirm an equal division of property between them. Otherwise, property was left to other relatives or monasteries.

India stands apart from all other ancient legal cultures in that it did not have anything like a testamentary will, either in theory (Dharmaśāstra) or in practice. It was simply taken for granted that family property would pass down to heirs at the death of the parent, if it had not already been partitioned among the offspring. Estates were divided between surviving sons, with the eldest having a pre-emptive claim to the best piece of personal property and a double share of the rest; according to the code of Manu, sons should in turn give a quarter share to each unmarried sister (*MDh* 9.111–18). Manu engages in a complex calculus to determine the relative inheritance due to the sons of multiple wives of different social statuses: what if the most senior son was born of an inferior-status wife, etc.? In the absence of any male descendants, a widow should inherit; otherwise, she should receive a lifelong maintenance. In any case, daughters inherit the personal property of their mother. Manu further declares the following not to be heirs: a son born to an unmarried woman, a son acquired with marriage, a purchased son, a son born to a remarried woman, a son given away in adoption and a son by a Śūdra wife (*MDh* 9.160). These types of sons could not inherit despite their filial relation to their father, which goes to show that their legal status trumps any 'natural' or 'biological' connection.

Voluntary or Professional Associations

Status defined by one's voluntary membership in a corporate group, whether commercial, professional, educational or religious, in some legal systems had particular legal implications, de jure or de facto, quite apart from the fact that members were subject to the internal regulations of the group. In some cases there were mechanisms for those internal regulations to be recognized and enforced by a wider public authority, though disputes between members of different groups called for mediation or adjudication by a wider authority. It is evident that the degree of formalization of regulatory norms differed widely, although being unwritten and customary did not necessarily mean they were vague or ineffective.

India's Dharmaśāstra jurisprudence explicitly provides for resolving disputes among members of an occupational group (such as traders, herdsmen, money-lenders or craftsmen) to be settled by members of their own group (*GDh* 11.21), on the same principle as the one by which regions, villages, castes and even individual families were empowered to regulate their internal affairs in accordance with their own customary norms. Scholastic sources sometimes propose that witnesses called in court should preferably belong to the same class as the parties to the dispute, women for women, low-caste for low-caste (*MDh* 8.68, *KātSm*.348), but this seems to be merely a gesture to the caste doctrine. The *Arthaśāstra* (3.11.25–50) and many Dharmaśāstra texts take it as the general rule that members of almost any status may serve as witness provided they are legally competent; personally trustworthy (members of disreputable professions are sometimes cast in doubt); have knowledge of the matter under contention and are disinterested parties (*MDh* 8.62–70). Nārada calls for members of guilds (*śreṇi*), associations (*pūga*) and other groups (*varga*) to be so identified by some sign in legal disputes (*NSm* 4.155). Each such group established agreed-upon rules (*samaya*) to govern its own affairs; such rules were sometimes formally recognized and enforceable by state authorities. The Charter of Viṣṇuṣeṇa (592 CE, western India) provides an almost unique ancient Indian example of actual guild laws, surviving in this case because they were recognized and endorsed by a king petitioned to do so by the guild itself.[164] But the Dharmaśāstras frequently refer to the existence of such rules and enjoin kings to recognize and, if necessary, enforce the rules of these and other self-governing groups.

Religious professional groups – the Buddhist, Jaina and Ājīvika mendicant orders as well as Brahmin priestly and scholastic communities – developed elaborate legal codes and apparatus for internal self-governance and discipline (with expulsion or ostracism as the highest sanction), but in disputes involving laypeople (as well as serious criminal conduct) they were subject to the generally prevailing law.

In India and Southeast Asia, there was a widespread practice of rulers (and later other elites) establishing religious endowments to ascetics of various orders (Buddhist, Jaina, etc.) as well as to groups of Brahmins with their families (for priestly functions and/or scriptural expertise). These endowments early on came to include tax exemptions (reallocating those funds to support the beneficiaries) and encompassed an expanding set of immunities from interference by agents of the state. This included giving the beneficiaries jurisdiction to hear local disputes and to collect fines. Surviving inscriptions recording such grants date from the beginning of the Common Era (a practice that spread to Southeast Asia by the seventh century at the latest), but the basic principle of religious exemption involved in such documents can be traced back to an edict whereby the emperor Aśoka Maurya (third

---

164 Wiese and Das 2019.

century BCE) granted tax relief to a village because it was the Buddha's birthplace.[165]

We have evidence for a number of professional associations in Roman Egypt, and imperial legislation seems to regulate membership in such organizations unless they have official government approval. The questions are essentially: how voluntary were they? Were they tightly regulated, or could they be assembled and disbanded at will? Venticinque considers that they were not obligated to register with or be approved by the government, but that under certain circumstances they could be disbanded.[166] Copies of 'associational charters' (*nomoi*) survive on papyrus, which contractually bound members to a set of standards and prescribed monetary penalties for violations. So it seems that their 'status' allowed them to self-regulate with state blessings, provided they did nothing seditious. There were, however, imperial edicts regulating certain professions that were valuable to the state: bakers, purple-dyers, weapons manufacturers, ship-builders, etc. It seems likely, however, that these regulations were not concerned with all 'valued' professions (e.g. salt-merchants).

Members of religious orders were one of the most visible and important examples of a status of this type. Buddhism was introduced to China sometime during the Han period (206 BCE–220 CE) and by at least the third century CE persons ordained as Buddhist or Daoist priests constituted a separate social group marked by their distinctive lifestyle. Under the Tang dynasty Buddhism was fostered by the central government (up to 843 CE), contributing to the establishment of affluent Buddhist monasteries with relatively extensive landholdings and business interests. From the sixth century CE, there is a tendency in the law to permit a Buddhist or Daoist priest who had committed one of the less serious offences (not rebellion or homicide) to be tried and sentenced by the authorities of his own order. Tang law specifically allowed Buddhist or Daoist clergy who had committed offences to be tried in accordance with the procedures established by their own orders and not by the state courts.[167]

'Religious' voluntary associations were also well known in Greco-Roman Egypt. Priesthoods were generally inherited from father to son although the state did attempt to regulate this; occasional sales of priesthoods are known in the Ptolemaic period. In first-century CE Egypt, examples survive of people writing petitions as the 'tax-exempt priest' of such and such a temple. An

---

165 Lubin 2018b, 2023. 166 Venticinque 2016.
167 The late Roman principle of *privilegium fori* for Christian clerics provides a direct comparison.

inscription of 54 CE (OGIS 2.664) frees the priests of Soknopaiou Nesos from being compelled to farm public land. According to Bagnall, ('pagan') priestly status started declining in importance probably in the late first or second centuries – though more recent scholarship challenges this narrative.[168] In Late Antiquity, Christian monastic organizations could inherit property, for instance, and in one case, we have a petition from a woman against a monk which is addressed to a bishop, which suggests that this particular group came to occupy something of a legal carve-out. Christian monks seem to be otherwise largely integrated into society in other ways, such as, for instance, in continuing to be responsible for compulsory public services.[169]

A partly similar situation is that of individuals or groups endowed by public or state authority with special privileges with regard to royal or public property. Such privileges could be granted for a variety of reasons including recognition of past official or military service, economic development, and/or religious function. These privileges might take the form of tax exemption or relief, legal immunity or internal autonomy. For example, in Ptolemaic Egypt 'royal farmers' (those who farmed royal land) were immune from lawsuits during critical periods of the agricultural year (e.g. P. Rein. 18, Akoris, 108 BCE), similar to comparable military exemptions. Members of private associations also benefited from similar privileges as the result of membership.

These admittedly diverse sets of evidence suggest, in any case, that voluntary associations and public servants sought and were often granted particular forms of special status and exemptions from otherwise applicable prerogatives of the state. These might be negotiated or petitioned for, and given legal force through a decree or grant document. 'Religious' groups seem to have been particularly successful in securing immunities and substantial jurisdictional autonomy, which may have been seen as a way for states to signal – to their subjects as well as to the god(s) – their magnanimity, their piety and their deference to an even higher law.

Status as a Factor in Legal Penalties

A striking area of difference in the laws of antiquity is the matter of whether individuals of different statuses were assigned different penalties for the same offences. Ancient Egyptian law appears unique in that 'neither the status of the thief nor the status of the victim appears to have been relevant in fixing penalties for theft. Thieves received the same punishments regardless of their

---

168 Bagnall 1993: 267; Sippel 2020.   169 For further analysis see Doerfler 2013.

Status as a Factor in Legal Penalties

social standing.'[170] From the Ptolemaic period, though, we have a legal ordinance from Alexandria (P. Hal.) that details different treatment of slaves and freemen in penalties for assault.

In general, personal status was not formally a factor in determining penalties in the Greek world, though male and female adulterers were treated differently. In fifth-century BCE Athens, although an adulterer might be killed with impunity, the law prescribed no specific penalty, but specified that the adulteress must be repudiated by her husband and excluded from public sacrifices.[171] The main exception was Gortyn, where the laws on rape and adultery (and only these) set different fines according to the status of both the violator and the victim. The woman faced no penalty, though social sanctions were likely; but the guilty man must pay a fine, on a sliding scale depending on the status of both the man and the woman (free, *apetairos*, or slave). Fines for rape varied in a similar fashion, with slaves paying double the fines assessed for free men. The fine for raping a free man or woman was ten times the fine for raping an *apetairos* and forty times that for raping a 'serf' (*woikeus*). The sex of the victim made no difference in most cases.[172]

In Mesopotamian criminal law, on the other hand, social status had a great bearing on many sorts of penalties. Law collections show that social status could have legal discriminatory consequences. In the Laws of Ḫammurabi, some physical injuries are punished differently according to the relative status of the persons involved. In many cases an injury caused to a peer incurred a talionic penalty; if the victim was of inferior status, a fine in silver was prescribed; or if a monetary penalty was the norm for injuring a peer, the penalty for an inferior was less (Laws of Ḫammurabi, chapters 196–201). Offences against a superior called for special humiliation: for example, flogging for an *awīlum* who slaps a superior or cutting off of an ear of a slave who slaps an *awīlum* (Laws of Ḫammurabi, chapters 202–5). Likewise, abortion by blows was punished by a fine of ten shekels if the victim were the daughter of an *awīlum*; of five shekels for the daughter of a *muškēnum*; and of two shekels if the victim were a slave (Laws of Ḫammurabi, chapters 209, 211, 213). Death of the mother gave rise to a talionic punishment if the victim were the daughter of an *awīlum* and was punished by a fine of thirty or twenty shekels if the victim were the daughter of a *muškēnum* or a slave (Laws of Ḫammurabi, chapters 210, 212,

---

170 VerSteeg 2002: 163.   171 Dem. 59.87 [*Against Neaira*]; Dem. 23.53; and Lys. 1.
172 *IC* iv.72 col. II 2–45; cf. Lys. 1.32; Pl. *Laws* 874e; and Plut. *Vit. Sol.* 2.

214).[173] The Assyrian laws also deal with abortion by blows against the 'daughter of an *amēlu*' (tabl. A, chapter 21), against a married woman (tabl. A, chapters 50–51) or against a prostitute (chapter 52). The first offence is liable to be a heavy fine and corporal punishment; others are punished with talion (the wife of the culprit is beaten) and a compensation for the lost life; the death penalty is incurred in case of death of the pregnant woman, or if the couple had no sons; the sanction for the loss suffered by the prostitute is also talionic (blow for blow) and financial (compensation for the lost life). Similar distinctions between free and slave women are attested in the Laws of Lipit-Ištar and in the Hittite Laws.

In China the respective statuses of offender and victim were one of the most important factors determining the severity of punishment. Imperial China was a strictly hierarchical society divided at the broadest level into 'superiors' and 'inferiors'. Thus, officials were 'superior' in relation to commoners; senior officials were 'superior' in relation to subordinates; free persons were 'superior' in relation to persons of servile status; and, very importantly, relatives of a higher generation, or of the same generation but older, were 'superior' in relation to relatives of a lower generation, or of the same generation but younger. The general principle can be summarized thus: where a person classified as 'inferior' committed an offence against a person classified as 'superior', the punishment was more severe than that imposed in the reverse case.

The most elaborate status-wise distinctions are seen in India's lawbooks. The Dharmaśāstras (and under their influence, Kauṭilya's *Arthaśāstra*) frequently – though not in all cases – recommended calibrated penalties based on the social rank of both the perpetrator and the victim. According to these, Brahmins are never supposed to be subjected to capital punishment and can only be sentenced to banishment for capital crimes. Whether this immunity was recognized in practice we have little way of knowing. Many monetary penalties for injuries were likewise subject to calibration by rank. As noted above, Kauṭilya viewed youth, old age and frailty as mitigating factors in assigning punishments prescribed.

---

173 The expression 'daughter of an *awīlum/muškēnum*' is usually understood as 'member of the social group of the *awīlū/muškēnū*', but this view has been challenged (Westbrook 2006; Roth 2013) in favour of a literal meaning 'daughter of an *awīlum/muškēnum*'. This would mean that the law either considers the case of a woman being pregnant without being married, or focuses on the social rank of the victim rather than on her matrimonial condition.

In short, there appears to have been great variety across the ancient world in the degree to which status factored into penalties. Egypt and the more democratic ancient polities seem to have avoided making statutory status distinctions in this respect, apart from distinctions of sex. But part of the differences across legal cultures lies in whether status distinctions are taken into account on a 'statutory' basis or rather as a matter of unwritten convention or judicial discretion (as we saw above in the case of Roman law).

Conclusion

The evidence reviewed here casts considerable doubt on evolutionary or teleological accounts such as that of Henry Sumner Maine.[174] Even if it is accepted that in modern legal cultures family status no longer constrains the general rights and legal actions open to individuals, forms of personal status before the law long continued – and arguably continue today – to inflect all but the most basic human rights and legal capacities. Meanwhile, we see that contract developed very early in ancient legal history (see Chapter 11 below). Ascertaining the status of parties to contracts, moreover, remained central to construction and legal viability long after antiquity, indeed up to and including the present day.

Personal status appears in ancient legal arenas in a wide variety of ways. Some types of status, insofar as they were defined by law, determined the way individuals related to legal authorities and to each other. Beyond legal status, the legal consequences of social status came about through differences in application of the law based on the prejudices and discretion of judges and officials, or in the terms and conventions of contractual arrangement. Finally, occupational or official statuses entailed legal consequences specific to each: special rules and norms that applied either as a feature within the larger system, or as a separate body of regulations applied within a plural legal environment.

---

174 Maine has been criticized on the grounds that his argument boils down to a paean for the 'unrestrained and unrestricted freedom of contract' (VerSteeg 1988– 1989; though he sees this as misconstruing Maine's argument). The last decades have seen Maine's dictum taken up in the form 'from status to contract to status' by legal scholars who use it to lament a supposed modern shift away from liberal individualism and back to state paternalism and legal protections of status prerogatives via identity politics (as discussed in Schmidt 2017). The critique offered in that case focuses rather on how Maine's argument underappreciates the way forms of personal status retained their salience, as well as the vigour and variety of ancient contracts.

Another conclusion to be drawn from our comparison is that it cannot be sufficient to distinguish between legal status and (mere) social status and then to bracket social status as irrelevant (at worst) or merely contextual (at best). Legal categories and social categories are interconnected and the boundaries between them can be blurry, with social status getting invoked in the penumbra of law. In any case, comparison across cultures requires an inclusive policy: to exclude social statuses from consideration would miss the opportunity to observe how different systems construct legal personhood differently, and risks conveying a misleadingly idealized picture of law as actually being blind to social factors outside its formal parameters – that is, it risks presenting a normative model as a description of practice.

Athens and Rome stand to one side in propounding a nominally egalitarian standard for free citizens, though in both cases the citizen status was itself a position of privilege and lacked gender parity.[175] At the other end of the spectrum, Indian Dharmaśāstra and Chinese legal sources made systematic legal distinctions between classes. Other traditions steered between these poles (e.g.: Gortyn; Kauṭilya's *Arthaśāstra*; and Indian law in practice). However even the most explicitly hierarchical of these traditions can articulate a notion of relative or scaled equity on the grounds that differences of status are themselves legitimate and justifiable.

Those systems formulated by 'religious' authorities more or less distinct from and independent of a particular sovereign, state, or civic apparatus, represent the polity in terms of statuses that transcend the state and may be in tension with the law of a given state. Beyond this distinction, however, 'religious' and state-based legal systems otherwise tend to organize themselves around a common set of status distinctions, especially those pertaining to family relations and those distinguishing free from unfree statuses.

Since the efficacy of law depends upon the support of political and economic power and/or some other embodiment of authority, it is not a matter of wonder that even a putatively egalitarian system, such as classical Roman law, was largely geared to the protection of elite interests, including property rights. Under Roman law 'the have-nots, the vast majority of citizens, were right out of it', as David Daube observed.[176] Even if this is

---

[175] 'Although Roman private law itself was nominally egalitarian and seldom based upon overt differentiations of social class and wealth ... nonetheless there are solid reasons to believe that the outlook, values and interests of the upper classes (from whose ranks the Roman jurists were overwhelmingly drawn) were crucially important in shaping both the overall texture and the specific rules of classical Roman family law' (Frier and McGinn 2004: 6).

[176] Daube 1969: 72.

true in general, it may come through more clearly in legal traditions that produced law collections and jurisprudence, for these are most likely to be thoroughly imprinted with the vision of elites than those individual laws that have come down to us, for these more directly address the needs of social harmony and the negotiation that went into attaining and preserving it. This at least may be true of laws created by collective governing bodies, rather than by royal fiat.

In any case, cross-cultural comparison of ancient laws reaffirms the intrinsically constructed character of personal status (both legal and social), even in the case of types of status (such as age and sex) which putatively hinge on biological facts; they become statuses only when they are defined normatively or codified legally. We may also observe that this constructed character of status sometimes allows one status to stand in for another in a figurative or fictive way when the business of law suggests a procedural analogy. Thus, as we have seen, the disabled could be treated like the very young or very old due to their (perceived) shared trait of dependency. In Roman law a slave was sometimes treated like a son and vice versa. A foreigner could be treated like a Roman for particular procedural purposes; and a prisoner of war, though living, could be deemed 'dead' for legal purposes such as property transfers and upon ransom brought back to the status of the living (through the Roman legal fiction of *postliminium*). An Indian daughter could count as a son; and in Mesopotamia, a widow could have authority as both 'father and mother of the estate' through a clause inserted into her husband's will. Transpositions of this sort should remind us that however 'natural' a status may seem, they are all culturally and institutionally defined and within the legal sphere, to varying degrees, subject to the shifting concerns of authority and the negotiations and contestations of legal process.

9
Crime, Redress and Social Control

Lead Author: ARI Z. BRYEN

Contributors: TIMOTHY LUBIN, GEOFFREY MACCORMACK AND ROBIN OSBORNE

Introduction: Prohibitions and Incentives

Legal systems offer both positive and negative incentives to those who will be held accountable to their requirements. Positive incentives might include protecting someone's private property (or authorizing a category of 'private property' in the first place); protecting the agreements of willing parties; providing speedy mediation of grievances through transparent processes; or backstopping individuals who protect their own interests. Negative incentives are generally more coercive: forbidding particular behaviours; authorizing violence against particular members of a community (slaves, in particular, feature prominently in ancient Mediterranean law); and creating formal means of severing ties with individual community members (through modes of capital punishment or exile, for example). The distinction is not absolute. Frequently positive incentives have negative components: for instance, certain status-designations may be monopolized by a group and protected by the threat of harm against those who might usurp them. This is the case with citizenship in Roman law, where citizens were encouraged to marry and trade with other citizens through state protections of *conubium* and *commercium*, while at the same time punishing those who usurped citizen status with expulsion from Rome (through a 'statute', the *lex Papia* of 65 BCE).[1] What is more, negative incentives need not be articulated, for they are often implicit in the structure of positive incentives by a sort of *inclusio unius, exclusio alterius*. Though these incentive structures are really parts of a whole, they can be disentangled for analytical purposes.

[1] Gardiner 1993.

Introduction: Prohibitions and Incentives

Ancient states created explicit incentives (both positive and negative) with some frequency through statutory pronouncements; ancient societies likewise developed institutions that created incentive structures for the people who interacted with them, even if these incentives were not always articulated in the language of legislation or jurisprudence. The universe of negative incentives tends to map most closely onto the categories that scholars working in a contemporary legal tradition would group under the heading 'criminal law', which might be distinguished, for analytical purposes, from 'private law' (the body of law regulating property, transactions and family status).[2]

This chapter will focus on the world of negative incentives in ancient law and in particular, on the ways in which state authority (be it royal, religious, juristic, communal or bureaucratic) defines particular acts as problematic or illegitimate. In other words, this chapter will focus on the moments in which the state says 'no' and marks certain actions (or certain elements of an action) as out of bounds and requiring correction, restitution or even the deployment of violence. These are moments in which state power attempts to deploy negative incentives to cause subjects to conform to the state's understanding of normative behaviour. States could do this either by enforcing such prohibitions themselves (through, for example, police or magistrates) or by incentivizing subjects to bring particular transgressors to state-sponsored fora for the purposes of sanction, correction or dispute resolution. Since in no ancient society was 'the state' coterminous with 'the community' (or even 'the aristocracy' or 'the powerful' more generally), these state prohibitions cannot be understood as the mere codification of pre-existing communal norms; they should rather be understood as attempts at state*craft* – attempts to secure recognition that membership in some particular community required conformity to certain behavioural norms and hence recognition of state power and the importance of obedience among subjects or community members.

---

2 The distinction is, of course, highly imperfect. The universe of what is usually termed 'torts' (in the Anglo-American tradition); 'delicts' (in the continental tradition); or more generally 'civil wrongs' (harms that require compensation but which are not necessarily marked as particularly socially deleterious) tends to fit poorly within, for example, the private/criminal distinction – as do 'religious' regulations which, I will suggest, might plausibly be characterized as branches of criminal law. The point is not to be anachronistic, but rather to emphasize that 'criminal law' and 'tort law' are ultimately parts of broader processes that cannot be accounted for simply by enumerating prohibitions and punishments.

By the same token, however, it is important to remember that, precisely because of the lack of identity between 'the state' and 'those wielding (social) power', most ancient states were substantially lacking in their ability to make their claims felt across their territories (such as they were) or throughout the communities subject to them. In the words of Seth Richardson, they were 'presumptive states' whose sovereignty was tenuous.[3] They lacked robust powers of enforcement, and they relied in large measure on their subjects' bringing problems to a state venue – and, a fortiori, their subjects' at least contingent acknowledgement of the legitimacy of state institutions – for redress.

What is more, in all ancient societies (as in modern ones) there were numerous other social organs – in the form of private groups, corporations, neighbours and families – who made and enforced prohibitions on 'antisocial' conduct, frequently to much greater effect than states. Accordingly, historians err if they take the state's understanding of normative behaviour as more than a state claim – an *attempt* by the state to articulate and provide institutional sanction to its vision of its ideal instantiation and, by turn, its ideal subject. States were not always successful in turning their visions into practice and usually the practices that emerged was rather more a *translation* or *reinterpretation* of the state's claims. Accordingly, the degree to which state sanctions actually resulted in 'social control' (the probability that people will internalize the systems of value outlined by the state legal system and limit their behaviours accordingly) can never be assumed. I return to this question in the section 'Punishment' below.

Crime and Statecraft: Processes of 'Marking Off'

Writing sometime between 426 and 415 BCE, Herodotus, a Greek from Halicarnassus in Asia Minor, told the following story in his *Histories* as part of his explanation of the origins of the empire of the Medes. Regardless of its historicity, it is a sophisticated meditation on the nature of statecraft in ancient societies:

> Everyone was full of praise for Deioces and wholeheartedly endorsed his nomination, until at length they agreed that he should be their king. He ordered them to build him a palace fit for a king and to assign him personal guards for his protection, and the Medes did so: they built him a large, secure residence in a part of the country he designated, and they let him pick his

---

3 Richardson 2012. See further Ando and Richardson 2017.

personal guards from among the whole Median population. Once power was in his hands, Deioces insisted that the Medes build a single city and maintain this one place, which involved caring less for their other communities. The Medes obeyed him in this too; they built the place which is now known as Ecbatana – a huge, impregnable stronghold consisting of concentric circles of defensive walls. This stronghold is designed so that each successive circle is higher than the one below it just by the height of its bastions ... There are seven circles altogether, and the innermost one contains the royal palace and the treasuries. The largest of the walls is approximately the same size as the wall around Athens. The bastions of the outer five circles have all been painted various colours – first white, then black, red, blue, and orange. But as for the bastions of the last two circles, the first are covered in silver and the second in gold. So Deioces had this stronghold built for himself, surrounding his own residence, but he told the whole population to build their houses outside the stronghold. Once the building programme was completed, Deioces was the first to establish the following rules: no one was to enter into the king's presence, but all business was to be conducted through messengers; the king was to be seen by no one; and furthermore absolutely no one was to commit the offence of laughing or spitting in the king's presence. The reason he instituted this grandiose system of how to behave in relation to him was to prevent any of his peers seeing him. They had been brought up with him, their lineage was no worse than his, and they were just as brave as he was, so he worried that if they saw him they might get irritated and conspire against him; on the other hand, if they could not see him, they might think that he had changed. Once he had established this system and had used his position as tyrant to protect himself, he became a harsh champion of justice. People used to write their suits down and send them in to him, and then he would assess them and send his verdicts back out. That was how he dealt with lawsuits. Another system he instituted was that if he heard that an offence had been committed, he would have the perpetrator brought to him and then inflict on him the punishment the crime deserved. And he had people spying and listening for him throughout his kingdom.[4]

According to Herodotus, Deioces' power comes initially from popular agreement that he is a righteous man, but popular agreement is highly unstable. Stability (and the eventual transmissibility of rule) comes from the particular institutional configuration he designs. For Herodotus' Medes, institutions were not metaphors; they were embodied in architectural arrangements. Deioces insists that, as a monarch, he is to be insulated from his subjects and that those subjects be further divided into more- and less-privileged strata

---

4 Herodotus 1.98–100 (trans. Waterfield).

(those living 'around the walls' and those within the palace itself). Accordingly, he divided the palace into a series of colour-coded concentric circles, which had at their architectural (and, one might add, cosmological) centre both the person of the king and his property. This process of separation of the ruler from his subjects is built on the logic of prohibition which operates as the foundational act of criminal law: subjects were not to see the king – those who were granted a dispensation to see him were to have their behaviour in his presence regulated by further prohibitions against otherwise quotidian practices. The act of ruling is equated to the act of policing: the king's 'watchmen' were to go out through the kingdom to ensure that his dictates were being followed; in circumstances where they were not, Deioces would exact punishment personally. Deioces' subjects, in turn, were imagined to respond to this new institutional configuration by submitting their grievances to him: jurisdiction and physical separation being, in Herodotus' account, merely two sides of the same coin.

While ostensibly about the origins of Medean power, Herodotus' account of statecraft would have been something of a parable for his fifth-century BCE Greek audience. They too were interested in the nature of ancient state power and, in particular, in the ways that individuals came to hold such power. They told stories about usurpations by 'tyrants' – popular individuals, usually from elite families, who overcame local aristocracies to take sole control of cities – stories that always sought to explain their own politics as well. Through these stories, they reckoned that state power was something easily taken through control of public spaces and their affiliated institutions (downplaying a variety of other ways in which archaic elites used monumental civic and religious dedications both at home and abroad, the veneration of 'heroic' ancestors and systems of guest friendship to secure their power).[5] As Herodotus' narrative shows, they were especially interested in the process by which one individual marked himself off as different from others.

Herodotus' narrative demonstrates that he took this process of statecraft to be something that extended across cultures. He was not naïve in so thinking. In spite of their radically varied forms of government, density of institutions and reach over their own (and other) territories, ancient states, like their modern counterparts, placed a high value on stability – or, to put it in somewhat more materialist terms, on the perpetuation of their own rule. To achieve this, states needed both resources and the means to perpetuate their control of resources, both material and symbolic. What this meant, as

5 Anderson 2005.

a practical matter, was that for certain purposes ruling officials (or those acting in the name of ruling officials) attempted to carve out a legal space in which they could act in ways that might otherwise be off limits to private parties: for example, by taking private property from another, equal party, or by physically violating a social equal in the name of righting a wrong. Put slightly differently, these arguments over criminal law were similarly arguments over the nature, composition and perquisites of the ruling class.

This quest to control resources involved two forms of marking: the marking of people and the marking of things. In both cases, the person or thing 'marked' was distinguished as being somehow special, different from those otherwise subject to regulation. This marking could be defended in a number of registers (say, as being of a privileged religious or moral status) and the violation of a privileged person or thing could be redressed in a variety of ways as well. It ought finally to be added that this 'materialist' approach to the ancient state makes no claims about whether these were *conscious* – that is cynical – attempts to gain control of resources for the purpose of ensuring political stability and self-perpetuation. My claim, rather, will stand to the extent that the evidence patterns in a particular sort of way, towards achieving and maintaining control over their subject population, irrespective of their various technologies or ideologies of rule.

In order properly to understand the context of these individual prohibitions, one must look first to the practices of statecraft and the search for political stability that underwrite them. This means both looking to the ways that ancient states defined certain groups of people as somehow distinct or off-limits to others and thinking of this logic of prohibition as in large measure designed to capture resources, whether material or symbolic. The particular logic by which people are marked-off will of course vary cross-culturally, as will the rationales by which these prohibitions are defended as natural, necessary, moral, historical, etc. There will be similar variation in the kinds of resources that these prohibitions secure: particular priesthoods, for example, which place their holders in a position of mediating between the gods and the political community; extraction of taxes and labour; rights to jurisdiction; control over urban space; or, by contrast, ability to define territorial boundaries. The list could be extended and variations mapped, but I will not attempt that here.

The 'Marking Off' of Officials

Aulus Hostilius Mancinus was a curule aedile. He brought suit before the people against a courtesan called Manilia, because he said that he had been struck with a stone thrown from her apartment by night and he exhibited the wound made by the stone. Manilia appealed to the tribunes of the people. Before them she declared that Mancinus had come to her house in the garb of a reveller; that it would not have been her business to admit him and that when he tried to break in by force, he had been driven off with stones. The tribunes decided that the aedile had rightly been refused admission to a place to which it had not been seemly for him to go with a garland on his head; therefore they forbade the aedile to bring an action before the people.[6]

The story in question comes down to us from Aulus Gellius' second-century CE *Attic Nights*, a learned florilegium of earlier texts. In this case, the text is probably a paraphrase from a jurist writing at the turn of the millennium, Gaius Ateius Capito, who in turn is referring to a case from what was possibly the year 151 BCE.[7] The story turns on a basic problem of the nature of political authority in a state run by an oligarchy: Mancinus was that year's curule aedile, that is, he was the magistrate in charge of the regulation of city commerce and the giving of games, a position that involved the regulation of markets and, a fortiori, the regulation of the city's prostitution industry. But Mancinus' status, we might surmise, also gave him a sense of entitlement. Even after this embarrassing incident, he would go on to have a modestly successful political career. He was similarly a senator. So when he appeared at Manilia's door, he would have expected that she let him in, drunk or not. Clearly she disagreed and fended him off with a shower of rocks. His pride wounded, he sought to treat her as a criminal by haling her in front of the popular assembly for conviction and punishment. She would manage to save herself, however, by attempting to draw a distinction: Mancinus, because he appeared drunk, garlanded and at night, was not acting in an *official* capacity (that is, as an aedile). Hence his behaviour – and her body – was out of bounds. The tribunes, however, reasoned out their verdict in a different way: it was not that Mancinus was only an aedile at specific times during the day and not an aedile at others, but rather that it was inappropriate that *as* an aedile – that is, a magistrate of aristocratic status – he should be drunk and wearing a reveller's garland. Hence Manilia was right to deny him entry.

This rather sophisticated story about official authority and its boundaries at Rome dramatizes a constellation of problems inherent in ancient criminal law. Key to criminal law's operation is the creation of a set of people who

---

6 Aulus Gellius IV.14 (trans. Rolfe 1927: 355 with modifications).
7 Dates from Broughton 1951–60.

were to be understood as somehow inviolable and who, in turn, were permitted to engage in acts that might otherwise be off-limits to others. In this case, because of his official position, Mancinus reckoned that he was entitled to enter Manilia's home and inspect her; whereas a random, rowdy, passer-by would not be. The creation of people with this distinct status is both a mechanism of enforcement (because some, though not all, state actors who were inviolable were thereby enabled to punish) and a source of substantive criminal law (because the violation of such individuals created a reason to punish). It is also a source of tension, because there might be an unclear overlap between a person's actual power and their legal/official status.

In this instance, legal office and social status overlap: Mancinus, as aedile, is an enforcer of laws and therefore people must clear out of his way. Likewise, as a person of elevated social status, Mancinus is a person not to be violated, much less violated by his social inferiors. The debate, in this case (and the reason why such a story was of interest to a jurist), is over how far those privileges extend, and where to draw the line between privileges inherent in status and those inherent in office. There are three positions offered in Mancinus' case: that he was simply privileged; that he was privileged only at the times in which he was acting in an official capacity; and that he was privileged at all times during his term of office subject to good behaviour. These three alternatives illustrate something of the ancient Roman debate on the matter.

In Rome, this debate played out at the broader level of institutions. Each of the various answers to the question above, of when an official was capable of invading the space of another citizen or subject, manifested themselves in distinct ways. At the most formal level, the Roman state conceded to its agents the ability to act in more-or-less whatever way the agent deemed necessary to carry out state business. Roman magistrates, for example, were given the power to punish (to apply *coercitio*). This power was eventually rolled back in the case of Roman citizens (by a *lex Porcia* of the early second century BCE), in no small measure because, by this time, the Roman people as a whole considered themselves as collective sovereigns who presided over a vast array of cities and territories whose populations and rulers were bound to respect Roman *maiestas* (superiority).[8] But the power to use violence to punish was limited only in the case of citizens. Governors of provinces – where the majority of the inhabitants were not citizens – could use their

---

8 Cic. *Verr.* 2.5.149; see Lavan 2013: 91–93.

power to violate subjects whom they deemed difficult or obstreperous. State officials in charge of Roman armies could likewise violate soldiers in vicious ways when on campaign, in the name of military discipline.[9] Similarly, the Roman state was content to allow its provincial tax collectors leeway to extract resources from subject populations, and had no qualms about authorizing the sorts of coercion and muscle that such a process necessarily entailed.[10]

By contrast, other members of the Roman state were marked by their sociopolitical status more generally, rather than just their particular office at a given moment. Senators were marked off by special clothing, the production of which was eventually made into a state monopoly and its usurpation criminalized.[11] These same Roman senators were protected from degrading conduct by heightened penalties for their assailants.[12] When accused of criminal misconduct, especially conduct related to state business, they had the privilege of defending themselves before a jury of their peers (a matter of some contention in the turbulent politics of the first century BCE, which at times involved senators having to submit to being judged by their lesser-ranked, though still aristocratic peers, the equestrians).[13] But these privileges were not only extended to male members of the ruling class: analogous privileges were extended, for instance, to the Vestal Virgins, whose religious duties were necessary to statecraft.

The deference extended to aristocrats – in particular to *nobiles*: those whose ancestors had held high political office – and to representatives of state authority (often identical, in the Roman Republic) was wide and not always adequately captured in the language of legislation and jurisprudence. Still, there were conflicts between these two sources of authority.[14] Thus, when, in the midst of second-century BCE political upheavals, the Roman Senate had declared a public crisis, the aristocrat and Pontifex Maximus P. Scipio Nasica insisted that the consuls put the politician Tiberius Gracchus to death, but the consul replied that he would do no violence against Roman citizens. Nasica, in turn, simply led a group of followers out to lynch the potential tyrant himself.[15] This assumption of the power to do violence, despite his status as a *privatus* (someone not holding a magisterial office), was later remembered by Cicero as being not only the right thing to

---

9 Phang 2008. 10 Cic. *Verr.* 2.5.22.
11 *Theod. Cod.* 10.21.1 (Valentinian and Valens to Archelaus, Count of the Sacred Imperial Largesses, 382 CE).
12 Gaius, *Institutes* 3.225. 13 Lintott 1999: 157–61. 14 See Lendon 1997: esp. 1–29.
15 Plut. *Vit. Ti. Gracch.* 19.

do, but also precedent-setting.[16] The claim that Nasica's action set a precedent would turn out to be controversial: Cicero's own use of crisis powers to execute the Catilinarian conspirators without trial later led to Cicero's own exile.

Such 'marking off' of rulers was not uniquely Roman, though the particular tension between status and office dramatized in the story of Mancinus or the actions of Nasica might have been. In the case of Tang China (618–907 CE), particular crimes were grouped in the category of 'abominations', which included offences like incest and murder, but also destroying state stability:

moufan: plotting rebellion;

moudani: plotting great sedition, that is, plotting to destroy the ancestral temples, tombs or palaces of the reigning house;

oni: 'contumacy', that is, plotting to kill or killing various categories of senior relatives;

budao: 'depravity', that is, killing three persons in one family, dismembering a person or engaging in magical practices;

dabujing: 'great irreverence', that is, stealing the property of the emperor or otherwise behaving in an improper manner towards him;

buxiao: 'lack of filial piety', that is, accusing to the court or cursing one's paternal grandparents or parents, maintaining a separate household in their lifetime or committing other acts of disrespect to this class of relative;

bumu: 'discord', that is, plotting to kill or sell close relatives;

buyi: 'unrighteousness', that is, killing one's departmental head, magistrate or teacher, certain acts of disrespect on the part of the wife towards her husband;

neilun: 'incest', that is, illicit sexual intercourse between certain categories of relative (Tang Code, article 6).[17]

In the case of the Tang Code, we are looking at the end of a more complex process of legal redaction. The Tang Code, an expanded version of a code of the preceding Sui dynasty (589–618 CE), was first promulgated in 624 CE, but the earliest complete version dates from 737. The Tang Code derived the concept of the 'ten abominations' from the codes of the later Northern Dynasties, such as that of the Northern Qi (550 577 CE), but an embryo concept of the most serious offences was already present in Han law (206 BCE–220 CE). Still, it was estimated by a contemporary legal expert that at one point the earlier Han penal statutes provided for 610 capital offences, 1,698

---

16 Cic. *Cat. or.* 1.2   17 Johnson 1979: 61–83.

penal servitude offences and 2,681 other offences.[18] By contrast, the Tang Code contained in all 502 articles, distributed between the section on 'general principles' and that on 'specific offences'. In that context, the distinction between the 'ten abominations' and other offences is particularly salient. The 'ten abominations' concerned behaviour that contravened the fundamental duties owed by the individual to the emperor or to senior relatives, or which otherwise exhibited great wickedness. In essence they were regarded as unpardonable and so excluded from regular amnesties. Not all the abominations attracted the death penalty, but they were all regarded as particularly damaging to the structure of the family and the state.

The guiding metaphors of family and state are key: on the logic of the 'abominations', violence against the emperor was imagined to be of a kind with violence against close kin.[19] This is particularly telling in an empire that, in contrast to the Roman empire, exhibited a high degree of bureaucratic rationalization. Indeed, a significant number of the offences in the code concerned misbehaviour or errors of officials. One of the most important objectives of Tang legislation, whether in the penal statutes or administrative regulations, was to ensure that officials acted within the limits established by the law and did not exercise personal discretion or commit arbitrary acts that impaired the efficiency of the government and brought it and the emperor into disrepute. What is more, Tang officials were held to be strictly liable for failures to carry out his duties – a standard inherited from the Qin state and empire (c. 350–206 BCE) and the Han period (206 BCE–220 CE).[20] By contrast, the emperor himself was imagined, by a different logic, to stand fundamentally apart from the hierarchy of bureaucrats; he was marked off as a being that occupied a moral position analogous to one's closest kin.

Of course, this did not exhaust the list of ways by which the emperor was deemed distinct. Apart from the various offences falling within the first three of the abominations (rebellion and the like), the Tang Code had a number of other offences relating to the emperor personally or the conduct of the government: cursing or putting spells on the emperor; possessing prohibited books dealing with military tactics or the interpretation of omens and prodigies; pursuing astronomical studies; making use of magical writings or incantations to delude the masses and promote dissent; slandering or

---

18 *The Legal History of the Jinshu* (History of the Western Jin Dynasty) attributes this numerical categorization of offences to the reforming official Chen Chong, appointed minister of justice in 94 CE: Heuser 1987: 68. For a short biography of Chen Chong, see de Crespigny 2007: 61–62.
19 MacCormack 1996: 55–56.   20 Barbieri-Low and Yates 2015, for example, vol. II: 509.

criticizing the government; deceiving the throne through falsifying documents or making improper recommendations; counterfeiting or forging imperial of official seals and documents; disclosing military or state secrets; showing disrespect to the emperor (manifested in numerous ways such as resisting the bearer of an imperial edict, making mistakes in the preparation of the imperial food or the construction of the imperial chariots); entering the precincts of the palace without authority; and stealing imperial property, including objects used in the state sacrifice.[21]

The Indian case shows an analogous process, though the nature of the evidence means that its contours are of course different. The normative texts, such as Manu's Dharmaśāstra, were composed by a Brahmin class whose relations to actual political power were complex, to say the least.[22] In these texts we see a process by which kingship is acknowledged and kings are recognized as distinct in political rank and subject to protections, but the texts additionally claim that their legitimacy is contingent on extending similar – and sometimes even greater – protections to the Brahmins themselves. In other words, Brahmins, who tenuously held an aristocratic/expert status, continually sought to define their protections in relationship to state officials who were protected in an analogous way. In a number of cases this was framed as a problem of criminal law. Thus, in Manu's Dharmaśāstra we read that 'Manu, the son of the Self-existent one, has proclaimed ten places upon which punishment may be inflicted. They are applicable to the three classes; a Brahmin shall depart unscathed. They are: genitals, stomach, tongue, and hands; feet are the fifth; and then eyes, nose, ears, wealth, and body' (*MDh* 8.124–25). By contrast, in the later Laws of Nārada we read that 'In this world there are only two persons who are exempt from accusation and punishment – the brāhmaṇa and the king – for these two support the world.'[23] There were prohibitions on the killing of Brahmins as well, and the equation between the killing of Brahmins and the act of regicide. Thus, the Laws of Nārada state that 'If an evil-minded man assails a king, even a sinful king, it is worse than murdering one-hundred brāhmaṇas. He should be skewered and roasted in a fire.'[24] As Ludo Rocher explains, the passage is not to be understood as a literal prohibition from which we might elaborate a doctrine of sovereign immunity, but rather as an exaltation; nonetheless, the comparison between the killing of a Brahmin and the killing of a king

---

21 Tang Code, articles 59, 103, 109–10, 264, 268, 270–74, and 362–63 (Johnson 1979: 17, 71, 77–78, 267, 274, 278–82 and 419–20).
22 See Lubin 2005; McClish 2019b.   23 *NSm* 15–16.21 (Lariviere 1989: 190).
24 *NSm* 15–16.30 (Lariviere 1989: 191–92).

(both absolutely prohibited) is important precisely in that it is an apples-to-apples comparison, one that differs only by degree rather than by kind. Such courtesy is emphatically not extended to other status groups, who abide by differing *dharmas*.[25] This competition, in a sense, between Brahmins and kings to be protected and distinguished seems to have produced an interesting political dynamic, at least in the imagination of the Brahmins. This competition over status was articulated by reference to criminal law – that is, by reference to who was prohibited from infringing upon whose person, and with what effects, or by reference to whose person was immune from degrading acts of punishment. What is more, this competitive dynamic was not distinctly Indian: a similar competition, in the Roman Republic, is evident between senators and equestrians, who jockeyed with one another for the privilege of not being judged by others in capital cases.

This arrogation of protections to Brahmins had a further effect: other groups lower down on the imagined hierarchy similarly competed for inclusion among the ruling classes. Such competition might be especially threatening. Again, in Manu's Dharmaśāstra we read:

> Let a king, if he so wishes, get someone who is a Brahmin only by name to interpret the law, or even someone who simply uses his birth to make a living, but under no circumstances a Śūdra. When a Śūdra interprets the law for a king, his realm sinks like a cow in mud, as he looks on helplessly. The entire realm, stricken with famine and pestilence, quickly perishes, when it is teeming with Śūdras, overrun by infidels, and devoid of twice-born people".[26]

Within this pattern of jockeying for status and protection, democratic Athens might seem to be exceptional. Certainly, Athens had some policing or quasi-policing institutions, such as the 'Eleven', a group of annual magistrates tasked with taking summary action against *kakourgoi*, 'scoundrels,' an amorphous group of wrongdoers which seems to have included, at the least, 'thieves, kidnappers and clothes-stealers'.[27] To curb this undesirable behaviour, this set of eleven annually allotted magistrates was made responsible for taking action against *kakourgoi*. Specifically, they were empowered summarily to arrest *kakourgoi* who were – in theory at least – 'caught red handed' in a procedure known as *apagogē* (lit. 'leading away'). If those caught confessed, they could be summarily executed; if they denied, they were brought to trial.[28] The Eleven were similarly empowered in the related procedures in which a third party either took the Eleven to the accused

25 Rocher 2012: 352–53. 26 *MDh* 8.20–22 (trans. Olivelle 2005a).
27 *Ath. pol.* 52.1; Isocrates 15.90; and Antiphon 5.9. 28 Hansen 1976a.

and required them to arrest him, or himself made the indictment to the court over which the Eleven presided. Still, this authorization of others to use force does appear to be different in kind from the ways in which other, normally larger state entities such as Rome or China dealt with the marking off of the ruling class. Overall, much more in Athens was left to the initiative of the individual citizen, who was supposed to act independently – though always in accordance with the laws – to stop crime.[29] In other words, the processes of marking off enforcers of rules that was evident in the Roman, Indian or Chinese worlds world might seem, at first glance, radically different from the ways that rules were enforced in classical Athens.

Such differences are in fact only of degree, not of kind. To understand why this is the case, some background is necessary. Athenian democracy was structurally engineered precisely in response to the processes of 'marking off' a ruling class that I outlined above. Mass voting, sortition to fill public offices, popular juries (paid, no less), and the institution of ostracism (exiling an individual for ten years, without loss of property, on the basis of a popular vote) all were designed to ensure that within the citizen body there could be no stable 'ruling class' that could mark itself off as distinct. Even those aristocrats who styled themselves 'the beautiful and best' (*kaloi k'agathoi*) were reduced, as democratic rule was strengthened, to presenting themselves before the courts and the assemblies as acting in the interest of 'the people' (*ho dêmos*).[30] The goal was to try to ensure an identity between the voting (that is, male) citizenry as a whole and the 'state'.

This identification between the ruling class and the citizenry as a whole, however, was most assuredly a fiction – an ideological claim that helped to sustain the institutional make-up of the democracy. The result of this identification was the construction of a fictitious person, 'Demos' ('The Assembled People'), in whose interest the individual citizen was supposed to act.[31] Crucially, the ways that 'Demos' was to be treated mirrored the processes of marking off that were evident in the case of the Roman aristocracy, the Roman Emperor, or the Emperor of China. Thus 'Demos' was entitled to make laws protecting himself (as in the prefaces on Athenian inscriptions, 'It seemed good to the Council and to Demos'), such as the laws that prohibited anyone from overthrowing the democracy (see below) or

---

29 The consequences of this devolution of power and authority nonetheless remain controversial: see Cohen 1995, Lanni 2016, with Herman 2006, Harris 2013b.
30 Ober 1990.   31 Anderson 2009.

serving in an anti-democratic regime.[32] 'Demos' was similarly allowed, as a collectivity, to rule over others, as was the case in the Athenian empire, and along with this privilege to collect tribute from allies and to treat parts of such tribute as its personal property. 'Demos' was similarly able to be satirized, in the able hands of the playwright Aristophanes, as a fat blob responsive primarily to blandishments – precisely, that is, the way one might represent a degenerate oligarch who had marked himself off as distinct from his subjects.

This metaphorical extension of the personhood of 'Demos' is best captured in the 337/336 BCE 'Law against tyranny', discovered in the Athenian Agora. The relief at the top of the law depicts a female figure placing a crown on the head of a seated, bearded male figure, normally interpreted as Democracy crowning Demos (Figure 9.1).

The law, in part, reads:

> If anyone rise up against the people for a tyranny or joins in setting up the tyranny or overthrow the people (*dêmos*) of Athens or the democracy at Athens, whoever kills the man who has done any of these things shall be undefiled.
>
> And it shall not be permitted to any of the councillors of the Council of the Areopagus, if the people or the democracy at Athens is overthrown, to go up to the Areopagus or sit together in the meeting or to deliberate about anything at all; and if when the people or the democracy at Athens has been overthrown any of the councillors of the Areopagus do go up to the Areopagus or sit together in the meeting or deliberate about anything, he shall be without rights, both himself and his descendants, and his property shall be made public and the tithe given to the Goddess.[33]

Three conclusions might be drawn from this inscription: first, the insistence on the personification of Demos – with his crown and the corresponding protections of his person from harm – fit comfortably within the scheme described above by which state actors marked themselves off from others. In this sense, Athens is exceptional only insofar as it reached into a differing ontological space to create, and then protect, its leadership – that is, the Athenians moved from marking off actual people to marking off a corporate person.[34] Second, as the law on tyranny alludes (and as Athens' periodic

---

32 For example, Andoc. 1.96–98. See further Ma 2009: 129, who understands this democratic pronouncement as part of a broader tradition deriving from the Achaemenid empire. Harris 2013–14 has expressed doubt about the authenticity of this citation.
33 RO 2007: no. 79, lines 7–22.
34 Anderson 2009. On the iconography of this relief, see Blanshard 2004.

460

Crime and Statecraft: Processes of 'Marking Off'

Figure 9.1 Depiction of democracy crowning Demos, with Athenian 'law against tyranny' (337 BCE), Athens, Agora Museum. © Luisa Ricciarini / Bridgeman Images: number LRI4625962 (www.bridgemanimages.com/en/greek-school/birth-of-democracy-freedom-crowning-the-athenian-people-low-relief-of-the-stele-of-the-law-voted/bas-relief/asset/4625962)

spasms of internal violence demonstrate), this collective representation of the assembled male voting populace was always vulnerable to individuals who would defect from social consensus regarding the importance of democracy. The problem with ranging protections around a fictitious corporate person is that, in contrast to a material person who is vulnerable only in a single place and at a single time, a corporate person could be 'damaged' in many ways and at many times simultaneously. Thus the vehemence with which the Athenians protected their democracy and the amount of intellectual energy that they spent thinking about its possible subversion: from the passage in Herodotus that opened this section, itself a meditation on the seductiveness of tyranny, to the satires of Aristophanes. Third, in this process of marking off particular individuals as sacrosanct, there was an analogous process, namely, that of using criminal law to mark *others* as subject to violence.

The 'Marking Off' of Subjects

> You place Christians on crosses and stakes. What statue is not first shaped by clay moulded on a cross or stake? It is on a gibbet that the bodies of your gods are first dedicated. You tear with hooks at the sides of Christians. But all the parts of your gods are even more vigorously worked with axes, planes and rasps. We place our heads on the block; your gods are without heads until lead and glue and wedges are applied. We are driven to face the beasts – those indeed which you place beside Liber, Cybele and Caelestis. We are burned with fire; so too are they, as they leave the crude ore. We are condemned to the *metalla* (mines); these are the origins of your gods. We are relegated to islands; by custom your gods are born and die on some island.[35]

The above passage comes from the late second- to early third-century CE North African, Christian polemicist Tertullian. Tertullian's point was to underscore the irony of the ways in which the Roman government punished Christians, but the means by which he achieves his goal are telling. He equates the punishments of Christians to the process by which Romans themselves constructed idols: just as the statues of the gods are moulded into shape, so too are the bodies of the Christians. The logic underpinning Tertullian's polemic seems to be that there is a double futility at work in the punishment of Christians: first, the punishment is not being done in the name of anything greater than a material, constructed being (the deities themselves); second, the very means of punishing the Christians fails to deliver their intended meaning, for the means of punishment are identical to the means of constructing and sanctifying the Roman deities themselves.

Regardless of how persuasive this logic may have been to his intended audience, what is important here is how Tertullian links punishment to broader attempts at consecration and resource protection. Tertullian understands this process as literal and material: in precisely the same ways that the statues of the gods are crafted, so too are Christians 'crafted' in the government's attempt to force them either to recant their 'misanthropic' beliefs or to die for their obstreperousness. In making these links Tertullian, ever the legalist, might have been reaching back to the archaic Roman Twelve Tables in which punishment and consecration were inextricably linked:

---

35 Tertullian, *Apology* 12.3–5 (trans. Millar 2004).

8.5: If he has grazed or cut a crop by night, he is to be hanged for Ceres. If he is below puberty, he (the magistrate) is to flog (him) and he (the culprit) is to settle for a penalty at double.

8.10: If a patron shall have done harm to a client, he is to be *sacer*.[36]

Inherent in the Latin word *sacer* are two senses: that of being the property of a god, or of the Roman people, and therefore inviolable; and that of being execrable, being forfeit to the god because of a particular wrongdoing. This is the sense of the 'punishments' in the Twelve Tables.[37]

The process of marking people and things as sacred or accursed was a central part of ancient Mediterranean statecraft. It took a variety of forms. As just noted, individuals could be declared sacred because of particular crimes, such as the patron who defrauded his client. In this sense, the marking off is most akin to a process of punishment. As shown above, insisting that certain people were to be considered inviolable because of their elevated status is akin to this. But there were other modes of marking people as well. Thus, the Greeks developed, in the late archaic and classical periods, a language of 'pollution', by which cities asserted that certain acts rendered a person somehow unclean or offensive to a deity, which in turn required them either to undergo purification or to avoid the area in question. Thus, those who were polluted by homicide were expected to self-exile and would only in theory be granted re-admission to Athenian territory if they proved their innocence by undergoing a particular form of trial in which the accused defended himself from a boat anchored off the shore (*Ath. pol.* 57). Here the line between pollution and punishment is particularly blurry – the state does assume that the polluted person should take it upon themselves to leave, and does try to create incentives (religious, in this case) for others to avoid said person. But it is also likely that in the Greek world pollution worked to regulate behaviour which law was unable to regulate otherwise.[38] In this sense, it served state purposes by attempting to impose incentives upon its subjects but was always ultimately an *attempt* at social control, rather than something in which the state itself invested its own resources.

By an analogous logic, Mediterranean states could mark certain subjects as somehow unfit to receive certain privileges. These provisions were largely attempts at regulating the composition of the aristocracy, and ensuring that

---

36 Ed. and trans. Crawford 1996.
37 A different Roman concept of punishment, *poena* (penalty), seems to have meant rather 'compensation', and was given to an injured party
38 Osborne 2011: 170–81. For a different perspective on pollution, see Harris 2015a. See also Chapter 6, this volume.

their moral and religious claims to dominance were not undermined. Thus, in the Roman world members of the aristocracy who had degraded themselves (by appearing on stage or engaging in 'shameful' trades) were prohibited from holding particular offices. Some Greek cities took a similar path. Aristotle reports that: 'In Thebes there used to be a law that one who had not abstained from the market for ten years could not take part in office' (Arist. *Politics* 3.5.7). In Athens, by contrast, those who had prostituted themselves were banned from political participation.[39] The link between the 'shameful' trades of commerce and prostitution was not accidental.

But aristocracies, as Tertullian suggests, were not the only groups whom the state marked off and thus regulated. There was also interest in regulation of the lowest classes. In the Roman case, much of this revolved around the question of slavery. Slaves were understood, in the Roman empire, as always capable of posing an incipient threat to public order, but in Republican Rome there was relatively little interest in marking off slaves as a class. In their capacity as private property, enslaved people were of course subject to the wills – and violence – of their owners. But they remained off-limits to the violence of others, guarded (if this is the right word) by a *lex Aquilia* which forced a party who wrongly harmed or killed another's slave to pay compensation to that slave's owner. During the Empire the situation begins to shift: In the mid-first century CE, the Roman Senate entertained a proposal to force slaves to wear easily identifiable clothing. The result, we are told, was abortive, as senators worried that this would end up promoting a sense of unity among slaves, and hence, rebellion (Seneca, *On Clemency* 1.24). But the anxieties about slaves persisted. Over the course of the Empire, it was transmuted into a broader fear of the lower classes more generally, such that there emerges, in the fourth century CE, a 'dual penalty' system: slaves and lower-class people (previously sharply distinguished from slaves) both came to be punished in especially harsh ways.[40] The binary of freedom/slavery, moreover, served across the Mediterranean world as a hermeneutic for organizing a number of relationships, such as that between Greeks and 'barbarians'.[41] The same binary also served as a way of theorizing relationships of domination even between free people (such as Roman emperor and senatorial aristocrat).[42] As such, the creation of a 'marked-off' class of subjects came to be productive of a vast body of political thinking that, in turn, served

---

39 On the Athenian laws concerning prostitution, see, with further references, Lanni 2010: 55–57. On 'disreputable' professions in the Roman world, see now Bond 2016.
40 Garnsey 1970; Rilinger 1988.   41 Cartledge 2002a: chapter 7.
42 Roller 2001: chapter 4.

to stabilize the state. It is this tradition, according to some, that serves as the foundation for much contemporary thought today.[43]

While ancient Mediterranean societies at times sought to mark off particular groups of subjects, the case in China is more complicated. Officials, as noted above, were often held to a standard of strict liability in their dealings, and as such, might find themselves liable on even more counts than a non-official. As Geoffrey MacCormack has noted, Confucian philosophy took status hierarchy as a given fact and distinguished between 'superior' and 'inferior' men, reserving punishment (often equated, in the Chinese system, with law itself) for the 'inferior' men. But this central Confucian principle was in tension with the more general programme of the so-called 'legalists'. The legalists emphasized the even application of punishments across all levels of society, as part of a broader strategy of ordering the state for maximum efficiency in war.[44] While the influence of the legalists was important in crafting the codes, ultimately officials received a variety of privileges covering all offences except the ten abominations, the extent of which depended upon their rank. The highest officials in cases entailing the death penalty could neither be prosecuted nor sentenced without the express approval of the emperor. Middle-ranking officials might submit a petition to the throne for special consideration in capital cases. All officials were entitled to a reduction in punishment of one degree for offences entailing the punishment of exile or less as well as the privilege of redeeming the finally assessed punishment by payment of copper. Redemption seems to have worked in this way. Officials might redeem their punishment by surrendering their office. A tariff matched the punishment with the grade of office surrendered. Should the surrendered office not be sufficient to redeem the whole punishment, the balance was redeemable by payment of copper.

The 'marking off' of officials does not mean, of course, that in Chinese society there was no attempt to control the subject population; in fact, the scope of control seems far greater when the entire population, rather than just a subsection thereof, was treated as susceptible to special regulation. The practice of household registration is a case in point. The registration of the people of the empire was one of the principal bases for the control exercised by the ruler. The entire population was subject to the requirement to register. Registration had been introduced during the Warring States period (c. 480–221 BCE) but continued by the Qin, Han and succeeding dynasties. Each head of household was required to register with the local authorities

43 Patterson 2008.   44 MacCormack 1990: 26–40.

a full list of the members of his household, including servants and slaves, the number of cattle/horses it possessed and the amount of it held. Failure to register, or an inaccurate registration, was an offence. On the basis of the information so obtained the government then assessed the taxes due from the household as well as the compulsory labour duties – for military service or the construction of public works – for which it was liable. The system of household registration was probably the administrative basis for the organization of the population into groups of five families (*wujia*), a form of mutual responsibility established by the state of Qin in the fourth century BCE. This kind of organization of the population became an enduring feature of the government of the country in the imperial age, even if at times it may have functioned only spasmodically. Excavated household registers from the early second century BCE list an individual denominated as *wuzhang* (Head of the unit of five families). This shows that the county to which the registers applied was organized into units of five families under a head who was specifically listed as such in the census returns to the government.[45]

The registration of the population was more than just an administrative or fiscal measure; it was also about distributing responsibility for criminal offences. In a number of situations, Chinese law imposed punishment for the same offence not just on the individual who had committed the wrongful act but upon other persons as well. A characteristic feature of the penal law throughout the imperial period was the principle of 'collective liability' applied to the most serious offences. This meant that not just the individual who had committed the offence but also his relatives were to be held liable, though the latter may (not necessarily) attract a lesser punishment than the former. The extent to which relatives were drawn into the net of liability differed according to the gravity of the offence. For the most serious offences, such as plotting rebellion, large numbers of relatives might be put to death or otherwise severely punished. For less serious offences, collective liability might be restricted to the offender's wife and children. In Tang law, for example, where an individual rebelled, their father and any son aged sixteen or above were to be strangled (instead of decapitated, the fate of the principal offender); younger sons, as well as their wife, mother, brothers and sisters, daughters and grandsons in the male line were to be enslaved; while their father's brothers and their sons were to be exiled.[46] By contrast, where

---

45 Hsing 2014: 157–63. For the 'five families' in the Sui (581–618 CE), see Wright 1979: 96.
46 Tang Code, article 248 (Johnson 1979: 239).

a person had killed three members in one family, only their wife and children were involved in liability and subject to the punishment of exile.[47]

Biological families were not the only groups punished collectively. The units of five families (*wujia*) previously mentioned similarly were placed under obligation with regard to criminal law. Their head was obliged to denounce to the authorities any offence committed by a member of the unit, and to provide help where a member was threatened with attack or theft. He also shared an obligation in the event of offences committed by a member. The laws of the Qin empire from the third century BCE, for example, provided that where a member of the group of five neighbouring families committed an offence, all members of the group together with the village chief were liable to punishment.[48] Further, should a commoner give false particulars as to his age when registering, and the village chief and elders failed to denounce the deceit, they and the members of the commoners group of five families (*wu*) were all to be fined.[49] The system of mutual liability of neighbours passed into the Han and later dynasties, though we have only sporadic references in the historical sources to instances of liability.

Finally, not only were families collectively liable, officials were as well. The general principle governing the liability of officials was that of strict liability. An official was liable for failure to carry out his duties irrespective of whether the failure had been deliberate or inadvertent, although the level of punishment might reflect the degree of fault shown. The principle of strict liability helps explain the liability placed upon superiors for errors committed by subordinates. Just as the official who made the mistake or failed to perform a duty satisfactorily was liable irrespective of proof of personal fault, so also his superiors might be involved in liability irrespective of fault. For example, one Qin law provided that, where an overseer of an office was to be fined two suits of armour, his superiors, the prefect and his assistant, were to be each fined one suit.[50] Under the Han the strict Qin rules of liability were modified. The general position appears to have been that, if the superior had condoned the wrongful act of his subordinate, he was liable to the same punishment; if he had intended to report the offence but through error had failed to do so, he might redeem the punishment; but if he was not aware of his subordinate's offence, where no fault could be imputed to him personally, he was not liable.[51]

---

47 Tang Code, article 259 (Johnson 1979: 257).
48 Hulsewé 1985a: 125 (D18), 145–46 (D81, 82).   49 Hulsewé 1985a: 145–46 (C20).
50 Hulsewé 1985a: 98–99 (B25).   51 Heuser 1987: 95.

Although the Chinese state may have hoped to control the population more broadly, on the ground things looked somewhat different. Large numbers of documents from the official registration of households – relating to the Qin, Han and later periods – have now been excavated. Some show how, despite the penalties for false registration, deliberately false returns were made to obtain a reduction in the tax or labour burden imposed on the household. For example, documents from the early Han show a surprisingly large number of elderly persons and children registered in households. Since both these classes of person were exempt from taxation, it is likely that the heads of households were fabricating the numbers of elderly and children in the family.[52] Conversely, these excavated documents may also provide confirmation of the application throughout the empire of government policy on the allocation of resources. For example, household registers from the early Tang confirm that the complicated system of allocation of land by the government to individual households, known as the 'equal fields' system, whose actual application had been doubted by scholars, was in fact put into practice and effectively operated in the early Tang.[53]

Overall, then, there is a surprising degree of commonality across otherwise varied ancient societies, at least so far as the basics of criminal law go. Though there was some variation because of institutional capacity and ideological underpinnings, most ancient states participated in processes of marking off a separate class of state officials. To one degree or another, they similarly sought to mark particular groups of subjects off from the community as a whole. In the case of Athens and Rome, this might be a relatively restricted process, such as marking off a group of people as subject to high levels of violence and degradation (such as slaves in Athens and Rome) or as polluted. The marking off of slaves sustained the identities of the free and naturalized other sorts of domination. But the ambitions of the state might similarly have been vast, as in the case of China, where, at least in theory, entire populations might be registered and recorded, taxed and punished collectively.

Punishment

> Punishment (*xing*) produces force, force produces strength, strength produces awe, awe produces virtue. Virtue has its origin in punishments. For the more punishments there are, the more valued are rewards, and the fewer rewards there are, the more heed is paid to punishments, by virtue of the fact that people have desires and dislikes. What they desire are the six

---

52 Hsing 2014: 182–83.   53 On 1973: 123.

kinds of license [care for old age, living on others, beauty, love, ambition and virtuous conduct], and what they dislike are the four kinds of hardship [shame, disgrace, labor and hardship]. Indulgence in these six kinds of license will make the country weak; but the practice of these four kinds of hardship will make the army strong. Therefore, in a country which has attained supremacy, punishments are applied in nine cases and rewards in one. If in nine cases, punishments are applied, the six kinds of license will stop, and if in one case rewards are given, the four kinds of hardship will be practiced. If the six kinds of license are stopped, the country will be without crime; and if the four kinds of hardship are practiced, the army will be without equal.[54]

The preceding passage, drawn from the third-century BCE *Book of Lord Shang* (purporting to report the opinions of the Legalist Lord Shang himself, of the fourth century BCE) is more forthright than many other texts in making clear the linkages between punishment and subject-craft. Lord Shang's point is simple: punishment is critical in creating docile subjects, forcing them away from things that they might naturally take to be social goods – filial piety, beauty, love – by application of a harsh set of negative incentives. Subjects have 'desires and dislikes', local calculations of utility that, on Lord Shang's account, weaken the state precisely because they impede processes of control. The challenge of a strong state is to invert the local system of utility by accustoming the people to practise hardship. The end result of the process is a people made docile by exhaustion. In the meantime, they will have produced the material necessary to achieve domination and even virtue.

This account of the rationale for punishment is by any measure harsh, even dehumanizing. It was not popular even when Lord Shang himself proposed it. (Lord Shang met his end for urging that the ruler's son and heir be punished as a commoner; when the son in turn became ruler, he charged Lord Shang with treason, and exterminated him along with his family.) His account is nonetheless important, if only as an ideal-type by which states claim their authority. Crucially, Lord Shang explains the value of punishment only as a mode of supporting the state by simple pacification of the people, who can be treated as mechanistically responding to incentives. Concerns about legitimacy – a subjective category – are not entertained. To a degree, of course, Lord Shang was correct: legitimacy does not come from punishment, or at least, from the fact of punishment itself. Legitimacy, it might rather be said, comes from the *style* of punishment, that is, how well a particular sovereign performs any given punishment at a particular time,

---

54 *Book of Lord Shang*, trans. Duyvendak 1963: 210–11.

and on a particular victim. It is an aesthetic category, one that persuades onlookers (and at times victims). Naturally, it was in practice nearly impossible to separate the two.

Thus, the importance of Lord Shang's ideal type: most ancient states could not operate from the presumption – or even the workable fiction – that they presided over subjects who could be reduced to mere seekers of pleasure and avoiders of pain. This was not even true in China, thus the legal codes map out a continual process by which punishments were mollified. Mutilation was replaced by the 'five punishments': beating with the light stick, beating with the heavy stick, penal servitude (forced labor), exile and death. The individual number of strokes given in a beating and the distance to which people were exiled were both regulated, and possibilities for commutation were introduced.[55] To what would have been Lord Shang's consternation, punishment was indeed linked to legitimacy.

To be sure, amelioration of punishment is not the only avenue towards legitimation. Spectacular punishment can both strengthen and legitimate state authority in the eyes of subjects. As Maud Gleason explains, the nature of punishment as a spectacle is that, when carried out with the proper theatrics and the proper degree of horror, it can realign the subjectivities of those who view the event, causing them to identify with the state, rather than the person punished.[56] Whether harshness will be tolerated, rewarded or recoiled from, is linked to a society's history, the target of the harshness and the semiotic field that enables viewers (and punishers, and the punished) to make sense of the act itself. To render sense of these diverse variables across time and space is a task that shall not be attempted here. But the existence of these variables may serve as a methodological warning: namely, that we ought not equate punishment or proscribed acts with a given 'society's' values more broadly, or even with a given state's attempt to reify those values into a system of redress.

We might instead seek to distinguish between the 'why' and the 'how' of punishment. The matter of how ancient states punished is more straightforward. The creation of a list of acts that incur punishment (rather than merely require restitution) is a common act of ancient statecraft, though the lists vary substantially from culture to culture and have been subject to varying levels of jurisprudential rationalization. The targets of punishment likewise show cultural variation. In Chinese penal law, family members might be punished for the crimes of a relative, whereas this was largely not true in the Roman

---

55 MacCormack 1990: 100–18.   56 Gleason 1999: 300.

empire. These cultural variations are indeed important: in order to make sense *as punishment* (rather than something else), punishment had to operate within the confines of a local symbolic system – or attempt to create a symbolic system of its own. Thus, in any particular society punishments will 'make sense' at an emic level only in relation to other punishments, or in relation to other systems of symbols that people use to make sense of their world. In some cases 'punishments' may have strong traces of sympathetic magic: for example, removing the hand of a thief in India, or burning an arsonist in early Republican Rome. In other contexts, 'punishments' may make sense only within a dense system of local meaning: for example, stripping two young Christian women and forcing them to fight a savage cow.[57] Such a list might be easily extended. For the purposes of comparison, however, it is sometimes salutary to treat individual punishments outside of these contexts, and that is what I shall do in what follows.

The How of Punishing

We can distinguish four main sub-types of punishment: execution and social exclusion; corporal punishment; degradation of rank; and monetary punishments, such as fines, confiscations and punitive damages.[58] These categories obviously are not mutually exclusive: one might be beaten and fined, for example, or exile might be accompanied by the confiscation of one's goods. All ancient states engaged in practices of execution and social exclusion, such as forced exile, denaturalization or sale into slavery. A brief list will suffice to illustrate variety.

In the Roman Republic death was prescribed for a variety of criminals: for parricides (who were to be sewn into a sack and thrown into the Tiber river); for 'manifest' thieves (who were thrown from the Tarpeian rock – though theft was later treated as a private tort); others were strangled and dragged down the Gemonian Stairs.[59] Later in the Republic, where formally codified criminal law tended to focus on elites, (self-imposed) exile, usually in advance of a judgment of guilt, was the most common method by which elites were punished. We know frustratingly little about how everyday crimes by non-elites were punished. In the developed Roman empire, guilty parties could be

---

[57] On the symbols that made such a punishment particularly humiliating, see Shaw 1993: 7–8.
[58] Note that the category of 'punitive damages' begins to shade into what, in modern typology, would be grouped under the law of torts. The distinction in antiquity, however, was unstable.
[59] In general, see Cantarella 1991 on both Rome and Athens.

tortured to reveal collaborators and then crucified, burned alive or sent to be worked to death in mines or quarries. Most famously, they could be condemned to fight in the arena (*ad bestias*), which was likewise usually a death sentence. Higher-status offenders were beheaded, a punishment understood to preserve their dignity. The practice of punishing, however, was always subject to particular whims: thus Tacitus claims that when Nero punished the Christians in Rome, they were covered with animal skins and torn by dogs, affixed to stakes and burned as torches to illuminate his gardens (Tac. *Ann.* 15.44). The emperor Constantine, in the fourth century CE, ordered handmaidens who suborned adultery to be punished by having molten lead poured down their throats (*Theod. Cod.* 9.24.1.1, Constantine to the people, 320/326). But these were mostly ad hoc bursts of imperial wrath.

In classical Athens two forms of death penalty seem to have been used: *apotympanismos* (a form of crucifixion leading to death from exposure) and drinking hemlock. There has been some speculation that the latter was introduced by the regime of the Thirty in 404–403 BCE because it gave a non-spectacular form of death.[60] *Kakourgia* (see above) which rendered a person liable to summary arrest by the Eleven also rendered a person liable to *apotympanismos*. Though cities other than Athens doubtlessly executed criminals, overall we know rather less about the details. Even in the case of Athens the details of *apotympanismos* have to be reconstructed from a single source.[61] Athens and other Greek cities also used practices of exile, sometimes as an alternative to capital punishment, and sometimes as a punishment in itself.[62]

Chinese law used two forms of death penalty: beheading and strangulation. Strangulation appears to have been introduced as a regular punishment first under the Northern Wei (386–534 CE). Beheading was deemed the more serious since the offender passed into the afterlife to his ancestors with his body incomplete. There were three degrees of life exile determined by the distance from his home to which the offender was sent. Unlike in the Athenian and Roman cases, however, the Chinese system of punishment was highly rationalized. In addition to the various degrees of execution and exile, there were also five degrees of penal servitude determined by the number of years and months for which the offender was required to labour (ranging from one year to three years). The same was true for corporal punishments: each form of beating was also divided into five degrees accorded to the number of strokes administered, the maximum for the

60 Todd 2000.   61 Allen 2000: 200–201.   62 Gray 2015.

light stick being fifty blows and the maximum for the heavy stick being one hundred blows.[63]

Many ancient states similarly used violence against the body, stopping short of death as a punishment. This could take a variety of forms: as in later Chinese law (with its rationalized system of blows with a stick), so too in early Chinese law there existed a rationalized system of mutilations. Thus, in the Warring States period sources speak of the *wuxing* (five punishments) applied under the Western Zhou (c. 1045–771 BCE). These were all of a corporal nature: death, castration, amputation of the foot, amputation of the nose and tattooing. These were still employed in the Spring and Autumn periods (770–464 BCE). The chronology of their eventual abolition remains a matter of dispute. The Qin laws of the third century BCE deployed the following punishments: death, hard labour of varying degrees of severity and fines. Mutilation (amputation of the foot or nose, or branding) was imposed on persons sentenced to the more serious forms of hard labour, while fines were typically (though not exclusively) employed as sanctions for errors committed by officials in the course of their duties. The early Han largely maintained this system until 167 BCE in the reign of Emperor Wen when the mutilating punishments were altogether abolished, being replaced with beatings. Still, castration continued to be imposed after 167 BCE, possibly as an alternative to the death penalty.[64]

Mutilation, with its rich visual component, was not exclusively Chinese. Both Greeks and Romans used tattooing as a form of punishment. Greeks restricted this practice to slaves, though Romans extended it to free people who were convicted of crimes as well. Branding, however, was extremely rare: it appears to be non-existent in Greece and the evidence for its use in Rome is frequently ambiguous.[65] To this we might add that plenty of violence was improvised by officials, meted out merely because of wrath or annoyance. Thus we find, in a letter preserved on papyrus from second-century CE Roman Egypt, a case of what appears to be improvised violence:

> [Writer's name lost,] to the gathering, greetings. First of all we wish you health. We want you to know, that on the sixth our case was heard through, and we won. Petseis was flogged, while a herald cried 'do not cause trouble, but abide by the judgment (of the court)'. Therefore we write to you, so that you can rejoice and be merry and conduct a wreath-wearing (festival),

---

63 Tang Code, articles 1–5 (Johnson 1979: 55–61).
64 On Emperor Wen and the mutilating punishments, see Sanft 2005.   65 Jones 1987.

together with the whole gathering, both of ... and of children. We (?) pray for your health. Thoth 6.[66]

Such brutality surely left traces upon the body, and even if their precise significance would have escaped an onlooker, scars from whips and rods were richly evocative of having been treated slavishly.

To this list of punishments we might add that a number of ancient societies also kept official places of confinement. Athens had a public prison near the marketplace. It was administered by public officials and used to house those who had been arrested or condemned to death. It similarly held debtors and those who had failed to pay fines.[67] A similar situation prevailed in Rome. Technically, at least according to Roman jurists, prisons were designed primarily for detention rather than punishment. In point of fact, people languished within them; similarly, those condemned to 'work' (*opus*) in the mines were housed in quarters indistinguishable from prisons.[68] Over the course of Late Antiquity, moreover, confinement in a Christian monastery (a form of imprisonment) came to be used as part of a sentence.[69] A similar pattern prevailed in China, where imprisonment was not a punishment as such. Still, both the central government and the agencies of local government were equipped with prisons in which were detained persons accused of offences (even witnesses); persons sentenced to penal servitude, exile or death (pending execution of the sentence); and persons sentenced to penal servitude when not at work building roads and the like. The Tang Code, and no doubt earlier codes, contained detailed rules for the treatment and care of prisoners.[70]

In addition to punishments directed primarily at the physical person – through violence to his life, manipulation of his body or his formal exclusion from a community – ancient states similarly punished by directing their attention to the social person (by taking away his rank or status). Offences against the state were regularly punished by loss of civic rights (*atimia*) at Athens, as well as in other Greek cities.[71] This was a penalty that did not enforce exile nor remove citizenship as such, but did remove the right to vote and speak in the assembly and take any public office, along with the right to

---

66 P. Oxy. 73.4960.   67 Hunter 1997.
68 I look forward to the publication of Letteney and Larsen (forthcoming), which should put the study of Roman-era imprisonment on a new empirical footing.
69 Hillner 2015; Krause 1996.
70 Benn 2002: 198–201, 205–6; Dutton 1992: 119–22; Johnson 1979: 542 (Tang Code, article 473).
71 Cf. Dem. 21 (*Against Meidias*), 95–99.

prosecute or appear as a witness in court (any attempt to do so would make him liable to summary arrest and execution). *Metics* (resident foreigners) who attempted to usurp citizen rights were similarly liable to penalties that caused them to revert to their original status or worse – metics might be punished by being sold into slavery as citizens never were. Greek cities in the Hellenistic period also sentenced people to exile, either as the individual sentence for a particular crime, or collectively, against groups perceived to threaten or to have violated the civic peace.[72] Analogously, in China convicts were prohibited from serving as officials; their status, in this respect, was thus made analogous to slaves, merchants, artisans and people from 'base' groups.

In the Roman empire individuals could be deprived of the ability to hold a certain rank if convicted of certain behaviours. Thus senators who had engaged in certain acts, appearing on stage for instance, might be prohibited from serving in the senate. Similarly, particular crimes (and some private delicts) were classified as *actiones famosae*: cases in which a guilty verdict carried *infamia*, a condition of partial civic disenfranchisement. *Infames* were barred from serving in civic office, as well as suffering other disabilities.[73] Similarly, the Romans punished by degradation of status. This might range from the archaic declaration, noted above, that a particular individual be stripped of his rights and declared *sacer*, to more finely graduated degradations of status in later periods – alongside penalties of death, exile and confiscation of goods. The process of status loss – called *capitis deminutio* – came in degrees: *capitis deminutio maxima* involved loss of one's freedom; *capitis deminutio media* involved the loss of one's civil status; while *capitis deminutio minima* merely entailed the change of one's family and was not a category used in criminal law. As the practice of *capitis deminutio maxima* suggests, certain acts were punished with enslavement, permanent or temporary, in mines, quarries or on the building and maintenance of public works. It is worth stressing that across the ancient traditions surveyed here, most of the punishments directed against rank are primarily directed against elites (the exception is classical Athens which operated by treating all citizens formally as political elites). This is not surprising. It is hard to use degradation of rank effectively against people with little (or no) rank to speak of.

Lastly, we might note the use of money in systems of punishment. This could take two main forms: payment of a fine to the state (or to a god), and

---

72 Gray 2015: 117–19. Emily Mackil's forthcoming book (*Property Power: The Politics of Ownership in the Ancient Greek World*) on property in the classical and Hellenistic periods will surely shed much-needed light on the subject of confiscation.
73 Greenidge 1894.

payment to an injured party. The two were not mutually exclusive. I will focus briefly here only on *fines*, that is, money used as a penalty (*compensation* is discussed below).

In China – as in the 'post-Roman', 'Germanic', codes of the so-called Western successor kingdoms – physical injury was punished according to a tariff.[74] The severity of the punishment differed according to the part of the body which had been injured and the nature of the object (hand/foot or knife) used to inflict the injury. Similarly, Roman procedure knew a category of 'penal actions', wherein a person sought from an offender a penalty for that person's conduct. In some cases that penalty might be some multiple of the value of the object: so in cases of theft, either twice or four times the object's value; in cases of wrongful damage to slaves or chattel, the value of the compensation for the ruined or damaged object was doubled if the offender denied that he was responsible and subsequently lost the case. Some actions could *only* be for punitive damages, in cases such as interpersonal violence when it would be politically inconvenient to price those damages to market (for to do so would be to treat a free person as an object, or a slave). Interestingly, though in South Asia fines were used, there was not a system of paying punitive damages to the victim. Such compensation could be determined by reference to a schedule of prices, such as the one found on the Charter of Viṣṇuṣeṇa 32–47, where fines (in silver coins) were assigned for various degrees of assault: thus, verbal or minor physical abuse was priced at 6¼ coins; *ullambana* (?) or mutilation of the ear, 27 coins; visible injury, 48 coins and so on.[75] Similarly, in Athens we see fines used in several cases. Hence the law on theft quoted by Demosthenes:

> Whatever someone loses, if he receives it back, the penalty to be a double fine, but if he does not receive it back, the double fine to be in addition to the additional penalty. The thief to be bound in the stocks by his feet for five days and as many nights if the Heliaia orders the additional penalty. Anyone who wants to can propose the additional penalty when the discussion of penalties comes up.[76]

In a whole range of Athenian laws, there was no fixed penalty, and the penalty was decided by a process of *timesis* ('evaluation') with the prosecutor and defendant making proposals as to the relevant penalty. Broadly speaking,

---

74 On the 'body legal' in the law collections of the post-Roman successor kingdoms, see Oliver 2011.
75 For text and translation see Lubin 2015: 232–38.
76 Dem. 24.105. See also Dem. 114 and Lysias 3.15–16 for the stocks.

in all suits arising from contractual obligations the penalties seem to have been decided by *timesis*, as also most suits where the damage was immaterial (e.g. for false witness).

The Why of Punishing

This rather brutal set of lists gives a fairly good overview of the 'how' of punishment across ancient cultures. To be sure it could be extended, the typologies fiddled with in the details, and the individual punishments subdivided in differing ways. But even if we improved the typologies, we will make little progress in explaining the 'why' of punishment. This 'why?' might be asked in several different registers: why did ancient states attend to punishment in such detail? What were they hoping to achieve not only by punishing, but by talking so much about punishing? Why did punishment serve as such a fertile area for statecraft?

A venerable school of thought answers this question by turning to an explanation rooted in legal evolutionism. Ancient states, the theory goes, were inherently fragile and were under constant threat from private violence and self-help. Punishment and criminal law are always delicate matters, and ancient states (especially early states) were always weak and ultimately reactive. Thus, the elements that make it into criminal law are precisely those matters that command consensus: prohibitions on murder and theft, prohibitions protecting the family, matters of religion concerning which there is strong consensus among the leading classes or even society as a whole.[77] The goal of law, on this reading, is maximally effective dispute *processing*; if the rules are clear and the incentives (even negative incentives) calibrated to tolerable levels, potential litigants will choose to avail themselves of legal processes rather than fighting it out in the street. This mode of explanation has great merits. Not least, it resembles some ancient accounts of statecraft, such as Aeschylus' *Oresteia*, wherein the state, Athens, under the aegis of Athena, creates a court to bring under control a multi-generational blood feud.

But this account, while usable in particular ways, is nonetheless inadequate. It is best suited to archaic state law, rather than the more developed and rationalized law-making of post-Qin China, for example. But even in its application to archaic states, it is incomplete. It makes some headway in explaining laws on murder and the setting of prices for compensation. It explains rather more poorly, however, a practice such as the making of

[77] See Weber 1978 (1922): 547–52.

a religious prohibition.[78] Similarly, insofar as this mode of explanation makes sense of archaic law, it fails to explain why similar tactics of punishment continue to receive attention and elaboration in later, more developed, ancient legal systems – why, that is, the discourse of punishment persisted. It makes little sense to use this mode of explanation to describe the interests of the state in classical Athens, for example, where we have no evidence of formal (or informal) blood-feuding, but a continued interest in punishing.[79] The same can be said of the developed Roman Republic and of the later Roman empire.[80]

We might similarly return to Lord Shang: punishment mattered to ancient states because it was linked to the exercise of power and to the moulding of subjects. If we are uncomfortable with the idea that punishment was fundamentally conservative, or if the motivation behind prohibition was fundamentally the processing of disputes, Lord Shang's account may give us some traction. It has the advantage of reminding us that states, even archaic states, do more than just 'react' to external stimuli; in fact, on Lord Shang's telling, the state is capable of projecting its power to great distances. Such a claim, in turn, reminds us that states – even early states – did indeed work from a set of priorities that did not necessarily align with those of their subjects.

But Lord Shang's approach is not without problems. In addition to his failure to account for the historical phenomenon of legitimacy (already noted, and to which I will return momentarily), Lord Shang's account fails theoretically. He is correct that *violence* is linked to the exercise of power; he leaves unanswered the harder question: namely, why a particular subset of ancient state violence was defined *as punishment*. Ancient states had no problems using violence. They attacked other states, for example. Being great at making war was very much to a leader's credit. Royal rituals of hunting might similarly be placed in this category, as might the occasional instances by which state leaders (normally in aristocracies) commemorated their achievements in athletics. Conquest, of nature or of other men, was a violent process, but it would be strange indeed to think of these violent rituals as somehow a *punishment* of their victims. War-making might be the exception here, though I would argue that when war-making was explained as the result of needing to punish another state, this represents the subsuming of the language of war within the language of punishment and criminal law.

---

78 On the reactive state in legal historiography, see Whitman 1995–96.
79 Harris 2013b. The interest in punishment receives its most extensive and sophisticated theorization in Plato's *Laws*; see Saunders 1994.
80 Lendon 1997.

War, as James Q. Whitman has recently reminded us, is most normally at home within the realm of property law.[81]

Some headway might be made by remembering that the process of punishing was not simply an act of violence, but an act of violence that claimed to be linked to broader ideas about justice. In other words, punishing is not just about using state violence, but about using state violence *justly*. This may seem, at first blush, like a crude attempt to give ideological cover to violent practices. But here the comparison to other forms of state violence, royal hunting for example, is telling. Royal hunting, like punishing, is intimately connected to statecraft. Hunting can be glorious, macho, intimidating, beautiful and violent, sometimes even simultaneously. Hunting – especially the hunting of dangerous animals for sport – can mark the difference between a king and a commoner, a privileged agent of the state and one who must obey (for instance, by the prohibition on entering royal hunting lands). The killing of animals can reveal one's character – whether one is mean and vicious, crafty and resourceful, or brave and magnanimous. The killing of animals might similarly be reckoned as a form of public service, a means by which the land becomes pacified.[82] One can triumph over animals just as one can triumph over an adversary kingdom, and with no hint of dissonance or irony. But while fraught with tremendous symbolic and political weight, hunting an animal – doing violence to it – is a matter utterly unconcerned with justice. Kings and their attendants visited violence on wild animals because they were beautiful, rare, dangerous, or particularly tasty, not because they were disobedient. In other words, such hunters may kill animals, but they do not punish them.[83]

It should be added that this is not because animals were held to be incapable of learning. As Thomas Allsen has argued, throughout the Eurasian landmass animals were understood to have intelligence and to organize themselves as hierarchical communities. They were capable of respecting royal sovereignty, and also capable of undermining it – by sensing that a particular ruler was defective and seeking to harm him. Pliny would go so far as to claim that certain animals, elephants in his case, were capable of understanding religious prohibitions and seeking divine sanction for

---

[81] Whitman 2012. The difference between war and punishment/justice was already articulated by Thuc. 5.89.
[82] This understanding is part of the Greek mythological tradition, i.e. in the stories of the Calydonian boar.
[83] Allsen 2006.

particular actions.[84] In other words, one does not, when hunting, refrain from punishing animals because they lack the ability to be deterred (a common rationale for the 'why' of punishment and something anyone with a pet dog knows), nor because they lack moral character. It is rather that hunting and punishing are simply different modes of doing violence.

One might suggest that the reason for this difference is epistemological. To be recognizable as punishment, one must have more than mere state violence. There must be a communication of the rationale for that violence, and the option of avoiding it. In other words, there must be something of a communication, a drama which sets up a give-and-take between subject and ruler. Punishment is not just *when* the state hurts you, or even the grudging recognition *that* the state gets to hurt you (that is, the recognition of legitimacy). It is rather that you know – or you are treated as though you had ought to know – *why* the state is hurting you. The state, in other words, has made a claim, even if offered in bad faith, that the infliction of pain is ultimately your decision. Hence the need to publish and to publicize criminal prohibitions, something that ancient states did with great frequency. It may be that this is a meagre form of justice, and one that consists primarily in the formality of offer and acceptance, but it is a claim about justice and its relation to statecraft nonetheless.

Making Sense of Crime

> Particular Justice on the other hand, and that which is just in the sense corresponding to it, is divided into two kinds. One kind is exercised in the distribution of honour, wealth, and the other divisible assets of the community, which may be allotted among its members in equal or unequal shares. The other kind is that which supplies a corrective principle in private transactions. This Corrective Justice again has two sub-divisions, corresponding to the two classes of private transactions, those which are voluntary and those which are involuntary. Examples of voluntary transactions are selling, buying, lending at interest, pledging, lending without interest, depositing, letting for hire; these transactions being termed voluntary because they are voluntarily entered upon. Of involuntary transactions some are furtive, for instance, theft, adultery, poisoning, procuring, enticement of slaves, assassination, false witness; others are violent, for instance, assault, imprisonment, murder, robbery with violence, maiming, abusive language, contumelious treatment (*hybris*).[85]

---

84 Pliny, *Natural History* 8.3; cf. Jerome, *Life of Paul of Thebes* 16. Allsen 2006: chs. 8–9.
85 Arist., *Nicomachean Ethics* 5.2.12–13 (trans. Rackham 1934: 267).

As the foregoing text illustrates, there was some sort of connection between ideas of justice generally and the day-to-day practice of criminal law. In the typology advanced by Aristotle, criminal wrongdoing comes under the broader heading of 'corrective justice' – which can further be divided into voluntary and involuntary actions. Involuntary actions, moreover, can be divided into the secret and the violent. These lists of wrongs, he asserts, are not random groups of unpleasant acts that are deemed, by positive law, as deserving of punishment; they are instead 'crimes' because they fall under the broader pattern of 'involuntary' transactions – they constitute the opposite of buying and selling and leasing. The duty of the judge, in this schema, is fundamentally restorative: the judge, Aristotle asserts, has a duty of correcting the imbalances caused by a violation. When he does this, he is justice embodied (*dikaion empsychon*).

What is interesting about the account of Aristotle (or that of Plato, or that of many others) for thinking comparatively about the interaction between criminal law and the ancient state more generally is not the content of his account. It is rather the fact of his social position in giving an account. Thinking systematically about criminal law in the ancient world is precisely not the task of those who make and enforce it. It is a job for philosophers and commentators, not, generally, for those who have a formal role in government. In keeping with the line of reasoning laid out above, one might think of the division of labour between the state (which defined punishable offences), and the subjects (who undertook to figure out a theory of punishable offences) as something of a technique of statecraft itself. Ancient states were by and large happy to mark off rulers from subjects, to prohibit certain acts or even thoughts (to the extent that they could) without offering much reason for so doing. Unpacking the framework or logic behind these prohibitions was an attempt at making sense of the state, and, a fortiori, the position of the subject within it. It was also a mode of creating social control, for, by thinking about the nature and authority of the state, many (though not all) of its interpreters came to interpellate themselves as subjects of it. The logic of punishment (as explained in the previous section) might also extend to the process of making rational sense of criminal law. I will circle back, at the end of this section, to the thorny question of social control.

To treat in detail the many registers of jurisprudence, both formal and informal, that sought to apply rational structures to criminal law, and to treat them in all of their diachronic and geographic complexity, is a task that far exceeds the space available, and I shall not attempt to do so here. I should like to suggest, however, that when people sought to make sense of criminal law, they did so according to two broad patterns. Either they interpreted criminal prohibitions as having their source in something cosmic or transcendent (as Aristotle did, in trying to link criminal prohibitions to a transcendent category: justice), or they thought of criminal prohibitions as pragmatically tied to promoting order within the civic community itself. These two ways of imagining criminal law are not, of course, mutually exclusive: one can imagine that the thing one prohibits for the pragmatic purpose of promoting civic order within a community *also* is the type of prohibition that should be universal (such thinking is typical, for instance, of certain types of religious militancy).[86] But this is not always the case in ancient societies, and this particular sort of move in thinking about criminal law deserves to be explained, rather than taken for granted.

Before proceeding to the analysis, however, a preliminary point deserves to be made. Criminal law, and its associated processes of state- and subject-craft, can and usually does exist independently of attempts to make sense of it. There is no necessary relationship between the act of prohibition and its rationalization. Acts may be prohibited because there is a high degree of social consensus that they are awful or terrible. In some cases, common consensus on the disgustingness of acts may be so strong that certain types of prohibited actions may escape legislation altogether. When one sees legislation emerging on such matters, one may be tempted to conclude that the legislative prohibition is an index of the frailty of consensus, evidence of its recent breach, or an index of a change in procedures for dealing with it. This might be the case for Rome of the Twelve Tables, where legislation touched on only a few key items where, given their immediate political context, there might have been a recent rupture in normative expectations – such as the relationship between patron and client. The Twelve Tables nonetheless left a vast sweep of activities unregulated. Such a default position in criminal law may apply to archaic law more broadly. But positing high degrees of consensus is not necessary for explaining why some criminal prohibitions remain unrationalized. The criminal law of the Roman provinces, for instance, was not, in the first three centuries CE, subjected to rationalization. Particular bad acts were prohibited, and those prohibitions were publicized. To the extent that those making prohibitions rationalized them, it was largely by reason of

---

[86] Cf. Sizgorich 2009 for Christian and Islamic contexts. The pre-Christian Romans vacillated on this question: Roman law was at once normatively radically particularistic, being tied to the city of Rome and its citizens alone, and potentially also capable of generalization to other, non-analogous civic groups: Ando 2014. Compare Rüpke 2014 on a similar move in Roman religion.

state. An edict of the prefect of Egypt, probably Quintus Aemilius Saturninus, dating to 197/98 CE and prohibiting divination may be taken as exemplary:

> Encountering many who believed themselves to be deceived by the practices of divination I quickly considered it necessary, in order that no danger should ensue upon their foolishness, clearly herein to enjoin all people to abstain from this hazardous inquisitiveness. Therefore, let no man through oracles, that is, by means of written documents supposedly granted under divine influence, nor by means of the parade of images or suchlike charlatanry, pretend to know things beyond human ken and profess (to know) the obscurity of things to come, neither let any man put himself at the disposal of those who enquire about this or answer in any way whatsoever. If any person is detected adhering to this profession, let him be persuaded that he will be handed over to the extreme penalty ... Nor will you be free from risk, if I should learn again of such persons being overlooked in the districts in your charge, but you will undergo the same punishment as those who are being protected. For each of those, even though he dares deeds contrary to the prohibitions, is only one, whereas he who does not everywhere suppress them has himself become the cause of risk to many.[87]

At some level, such reasoning is circular: the government arrogates to itself the ability to decide what constitutes a threat to the stability of its own power. Saturninus takes the position that he acts because he is only reacting to cases that he has seen on the ground. But this insistence is rhetorical: Roman governors were approached by all manner of people, with all manner of complaints, and they reacted by legislating/prohibiting only when it seemed reasonable to them. To the extent, then, that there is a theory of problematic acts, it is a thin one indeed: an act is problematic when the state decides it is. The point here is to emphasize that there is no necessary relationship between prohibition and its rationalization, or even between rationalization and broader social consensus: an empire could function perfectly well (it could maintain political control and extract resources) without a rationalized account of its own law, criminal or otherwise, and without a strong consensus on what acts ought, and what ought not, to be prohibited.

Similarly, just as criminal law can function effectively without careful rationalization, so also can criminal procedure. The classification of legal actions at Athens, for instance, seems to be organized on the principle that some offences were more in need of outside intervention than others. It was based on a division between those where the injured party was expected to seek redress himself, if redress was required, and those where the nature of

---

[87] SB 14.12144 (trans. Rea 1977: 153–54).

the offence was such as to require third-party intervention. Cases that required third-party intervention themselves divided between those that by their nature prevented the injured party from action ('being wrongly shut up as an adulterer') and those where the injured party was not obviously an individual. These last included offences against the gods (e.g. temple robbery) and offences against the collectivity (e.g. trade laws). In some cases prosecution of these latter offences was not merely open to third parties, but third parties were encouraged to take up the state's interest by the promise of a share of the monetary penalty imposed. In the case of offences against the gods, slaves may be offered freedom in return for giving evidence, though more normally slave evidence was valid only if taken under torture. But the hierarchy of actions implied by these classifications is not in every respect obvious – so homicide is not an action that third parties can bring, because the offence is taken to be not against the city as a whole but against the family of the victim, who are left responsible for following it up. In some cases very similar offences could be classified in a variety of ways – so if someone was beaten up they could prosecute for 'battery' or they or someone else could prosecute for *hybris* ('outrage'). The risks incurred by prosecutors varied according to the class of actions involved – a prosecution in a *graphê* or *apographê* that failed to get a fifth of the jury's votes brought a fine to the prosecutor of 1,000 drachmas.[88]

Similarly, the earliest acts formally made 'crimes' in the Roman Republic were distinguished by procedural elements in the modes by which accusations were made and then the accused was tried; eventually crimes came to be tried in permanent tribunals, or *quaestiones perpetuae*. A leitmotiv that unites most of the things that became subject to trial in a *quaestio perpetua* was that the issue at hand often posed a harm that was dispersed across society in a way that made it hard to identify a specific victim according to the normal procedures of praetorian law: things such as provincial extortion (*res repetundae*), electoral bribery (*ambitus*), political violence (*vis publica*) and harming the superiority of the Roman people (*maiestas*). But at the same time the Romans also created a permanent court on injury committed by violence set up by the *lex Cornelia de iniuriis*; this would appear to be an exception to the broader pattern. Later legislation attempted to preserve these categories by adding new offences to them, while preserving their basic structure: thus attacks on the emperor would come to be absorbed by the category of

---

[88] Dem. 22.26–7, 53.1. For a general account of Athenian procedure, see Todd 1993: chapter 7. For freeing slaves see Osborne 2000.

maiestas, while the misconduct of a magistrate (through violating a Roman citizen) would become *vis publica*. The first attempts to make sense of this system would emerge only relatively late in Roman history: it would be the jurists of the Severan period (late second to early third centuries CE) who first sought to articulate a broad structure through which to make sense of the massive diversity of criminal prohibitions.[89]

The fact that individual subjects or groups sought to explain the nature of their world of criminal prohibitions is of historical interest. In each case, the specific circumstances that led to them doing so deserve specific explanations. It would be rash to postulate some sort of trans-historical urge to explain such features of society. Nevertheless, it is telling that even if the reasons why ancient societies started to rationalize their own criminal law are difficult to understand, when they did so they tended to follow one of two broad explanatory paths: the cosmic or the civic.

Cosmic Justifications

The most historically consequential 'cosmic' justification of prohibitions in the Western tradition is encapsulated in the Christian idea of 'sin' – a violation of the laws of god and a sign of the violator's moral turpitude. Importantly, however, the idea of sin is neither especially ancient nor especially primordial. This does not mean that there were no attempts to think of certain rules as taking their form in nature (rather than in culture or in convenience) – there were. But it suggests that we must be careful to mark the difference between late antique or medieval Western 'cosmic' justifications of prohibitions and those more commonly in use in the pre-Christian world.

In South Asia particular acts of harm could be understood, if done intentionally, to have karmic consequences and require particular forms of expiation.[90] In fact, there was controversy over whether deliberate 'sinful' acts could be expiated at all. Some authorities argued that since the penance does not destroy the karma itself, the karmic consequences will have to be experienced. For others, it depends on the gravity of the 'sin'. Considerations of 'sin' and expiation are pertinent to the question of legal status to the extent that a state of unexpiated 'sin' entails social sanctions, namely shunning or banishment, which the king was sometimes expected or even called upon to enforce, if necessary. Others, while recognizing that view, also note the view

---

[89] Ulpian's *de Officio Proconsulis* and Callistratus' *de Cognitionibus* (early third century CE) are important moments in this process.

[90] For example, *MDh* 11.46.

that such sins may be expiated.[91] Yājñavalkya takes the view that although the penance cannot wipe away a deliberate sin, it does restore the sinner to social competency (*YDh* 3.220–26). This emphasis on sin, however, did not mean that all bad acts were subsumed within the realm of the cosmic. At least in the system of the *Arthaśāstra*, there was a fairly sharp distinction between 'dispute' (*vivāda*) and crime. Civil disputes (provoked by one of the sixteen-odd 'grounds for litigation') were heard by a civil court judge, or a *dharmastha* (lit. one who 'stands in or for dharma'). By contrast, crime was dealt with through punishment (*daṇḍa*, 'the staff'), an aspect of government referred to as 'the cleansing of thorns' (*kaṇṭhaka-śodhana*). But not all crime was thereby sinful. Crime could be punished with *daṇḍa* (which was also the symbol of political authority), but it could also incur the need for private, spiritual correction, or 'penance' (*prāyaścitta*). The two concepts – the political and the cosmic – were never, in the actual practice of criminal law, blended into one.[92]

The relation between crime and the cosmos in Chinese law is similarly a matter of controversy. A well-known view is that the commission of an offence disturbed the harmony or balance of nature, which might be restored only by the appropriate punishment of the offender. This line of thinking, however, is found among educated Confucians, rather than being an innate feature of Chinese society more generally. More importantly, perhaps, the view that ordinary human crimes (rather than shocking instances of injustice or brutality) affect the harmony of the universe is largely absent from the legal sources, which instead stress balance and retribution. Nonetheless, the idea seems to have remained important at the level of political theory, namely, in urging that the ruler must rule in a style that promoted natural harmony.[93]

In most of its history, the Roman world lacked a concept of sin (at least with respect to law). But there are some tantalizing hints that cosmic justifications played a role in early Roman law. For example, the earliest Roman legal procedure (the *legis actio* procedure) involved both parties placing a sort of wager on the outcome of the proceedings, with the losing party sacrificing the wager to the gods.[94] The procedure, as preserved, relates to claims of real property, and the theory behind the wager appears to be that since both parties cannot be right about their ownership, one must

---

91 *GDh* 19.3–6 and *VDh* 22.1–5. 92 Lubin 2007. 93 MacCormack 1990: 40–45.
94 Gaius, *Institutes* 4.13–17. See also Chapter 8, his volume.

necessarily be lying, which requires an expiation. However, by the time we learn of this method of settling disputes it had long since gone out of use.

In later times, however, there was an unarticulated link between criminal prohibition and the maintenance of order more generally. This idea eventually came to have cosmic consequences. In the middle of the third century CE, for example, the emperor Decius might mandate that all inhabitants of the Roman world (which would mean, by this period, all Roman citizens) make a sacrifice to ensure the health of the empire, or be punished. This move might be taken as the beginning of a process. The period from the fourth century CE on would involve a more developed theory of wrongdoing which did indeed have religious overtones, and which featured increasingly sophisticated attempts to rationalize the list of criminal acts – a move towards rationalization that took place *pari passu* with the increasing number of state officials.

Ancient Greece also lacked any notion of 'sin' but allowed for punishment over and above restitution of damage and for additional punishments for failure to act. Failure to act is a frequent concern in early law, particularly in relation to offences which are themselves matters of failure to act, and some communities listed a whole chain of responsible bodies, each supposed to check that the other had done their job (so, notably, the law from seventh-century BCE Tiryns).[95] But the idea of sin was not the only way to connect criminal justice to cosmic order more generally. We have already seen that Aristotle's account of justice relied on positing a transcendent category (justice) to which individual acts of positive law were to conform. We may also include under this heading understandings of criminal law that were rooted in natural law theories, such as Cicero's (which took inspiration from Plato).

Civic Justifications

The emphasis on transcendent principles is no surprise to those comfortable with contemporary jurisprudence, which has largely naturalized the idea that prohibitions are legitimate to the extent that they are in accordance with some sort of broader, metaphysical principle (be it justice or something else, such as economic rationality). Even lines of thinking that distinguish between *mala in se* and *mala prohibita* take this as a starting point. But there is a further rationale for thinking about what unites the prohibitions of criminal law, namely, that prohibitions are not based on some sort of universal,

---

95 SEG 30.380.

generalizable principle, but rather on what is necessary to achieve or preserve some sort of local, civic community. This can be taken also as being the kind of law that preserves a local, civic community such that it can be distinguished from other communities.

What we might call the 'civic' justification of prohibitions is common, for instance, in certain Jewish traditions. In describing the rules of Passover, for instance, the instructions for the Passover feast are justified by a historical explanation that precludes transcendence: 'Seven days you shall eat unleavened bread, and on the seventh day there shall be a festival for the Lord. Unleavened bread shall be eaten for seven days; no leavened bread shall be seen among you in all your territory. You shall tell your children on that day, "It is because of what the Lord did for me when I came out of Egypt."'[96] This combination of positive commands and legal prohibitions, in its (fictional) historical specificity, precludes universalization; the commands are relevant to the community insofar as it inscribes itself within a particular historical and civic genealogy. The same logic is at work in the rules pertaining to the Passover offering itself:

> This is the ordinance for the Passover: no foreigner shall eat of it, but any slave who has been purchased may eat of it after he has been circumcised ... If an alien who resides with you wants to celebrate the Passover to the Lord, all his males shall be circumcised; then he may draw near to celebrate it; he shall be regarded as a native of the land. But no uncircumcised person shall eat of it; there shall be one law for the native and for the alien who resides among you.[97]

Later, post-exilic Jewish thought takes up similar themes; a particularly salient collection of thinking in this vein is most apparent in the Mishnah tractate *Avodah Zarah*, and the later Talmudic explications of these rules designed to keep Jews distinct from Gentiles. This produces oddities of political theory: the rabbis of the Talmud insist that the rules designed to solidify the civic community are relevant only to Jews, *and* that they are necessary to enjoy eternal paradise (hence imbuing them with both civic and cosmic justification simultaneously). This tension between the cosmic and the civic endures as a problem in contemporary Jewish thinking about how to justify legal prohibitions.[98]

But this mode of thinking is not unique to Judaism, nor even to communities that think of themselves as having a genealogical relationship to

---

96 Lev. 13: 6–8 (trans. NRSV).   97 Lev. 12: 43–49 (trans. NRSV).
98 Cf. Walzer, Lorberbaum and Zohar 2003: 20–29, citing *BT Avodah Zarah* 2a-3b.

it (such as the prohibitions incumbent upon Muslims, for instance). A similar sort of civic justification for criminal prohibitions can be seen, inter alia, in texts that come from Athens. The decree prohibiting tyranny and the overthrow of the Athenian democracy, discussed above, might operate according to a similarly 'civic' logic, although it does not make its logic obvious. More direct and to the point is the explanation given by Demosthenes concerning the Athenian law prohibiting the use of violence (*hybris*):

> The reason is that the legislator thought all offenses that a person commits when using violence are public wrongs that threaten even those who are not directly involved. Although few possess physical strength, the laws belong to all people; the man who has given his consent needs protection suitable for an individual, but the victim of violence requires the protection of the community. For this reason, the lawgiver has granted to anyone who wishes the right to bring a public action for outrage and has made the entire penalty payable to the state: he thought that the man who attempts to outrage harms not only the victim but the city and that punishment of the offender was a sufficient amount of justice for the victim, but that he should not receive money for his own benefit as a result of such crimes.[99]

For Demosthenes, the prohibition on the use of violence is justifiable not according to universal principles, but rather because it serves to bind the community together, and to preserve democratic institutions in the face of actually existing differences in wealth. One might object by saying that this is just a universal principle that pretends to be a civic principle, but this is incorrect: Demosthenes continues by quoting the Athenian law against *hybris*, and then, in praising it, says: 'If the barbarians should hear and understand this law, don't you think that they would collectively choose you to protect their interests?' Not, that is, that they would adopt it because it was good according to some universalizable standard; but that it would give the Athenians a privileged position with respect to others.

Social Control

The preceding discussion might leave the impression that ancient states acted largely without limitation on what they could do, or who could act in their name with impunity, or what they could prohibit to retain their hold on material and symbolic resources. It similarly suggested that some part of their operation was founded in punishment, and, by a similar impulse, in pushing others to interpellate themselves as subjects. In other words, the preceding

---

99 Dem. 21 (*Against Meidias*) 21.45 (trans. Harris 2008: 102–3).

discussion suggests that ancient states were, on balance, quite good at achieving their objectives. Such a picture would, however, be misleading.

Ancient states could not wall themselves off from all the kinds of limitations usually placed on less-privileged actors. This is so for two reasons. Ancient states are rarely monolithic, especially when those states are oligarchic; competition between important power brokers will at times lead them to create institutional limitations to the power of other members of the state. Thus in the highly competitive Roman Republic, tribunes passed legislation to limit the initiative of imperial agents or of commanders in the field who were starting wars outside of their own provinces.[100] In a similar context of political instability, the emperor Constantine sought, in consolidating his power, to create institutional mechanisms of appeal and supervision to rein in the acts of what he perceived to be errant governors and managers of imperial properties.[101] In the context of South Asian statecraft, Aśoka instituted a group of *dhamma-mahāmāta*s to check official abuse of the poor and the weak, in particular, to secure the release of deserving prisoners. Similarly, since ancient state power was always fragile and porous, the need to legitimize some state intrusions led to petitions, complaints and strikes, which could in turn lead to state concessions limiting officials in their duties. Rock-cut inscriptions featured in both South Asian and Roman contexts as visual cues indicating the long-term commitment of authority to acting in a responsible fashion, reining in particular officials, extending special concessions to privileged constituencies, such as the exemptions from corvée labour for 'blacksmiths, chariot-makers, barbers, potters, and the like', in the Charter of Viṣṇuṣeṇa.[102]

Even in the context of a democratic city like Athens, the power of the people themselves became an issue. We see this both in a law of uncertain date, republished in the late fifth century BCE, which strictly limits the circumstances in which the Council can pass a death sentence or other serious penalty, and in the furore which followed the Athenian Assembly's decision to execute the generals who had failed to pick up survivors after the sea battle at Arginoussai. The doctrine on which the Assembly had acted – that it is a terrible thing if the people cannot do what they want to do – was effectively repudiated, and the powers of the Assembly limited in various ways – partly by removing law-making from the Assembly, partly by insisting that significant rewards for named individuals could be granted only after

---

[100] E.g. the *lex de praetoriis provinciis* (Crawford 1996: no. 12). [101] Dillon 2012: 156–89.
[102] Wiese and Das 2019. Compare, for example, Roman inscriptions regulating the use of requisitioned transport: Mitchell 1976.

a vote of at least 6,000 people (the conventional number for the full assembly in the fourth century BCE, at least).[103]

But states did not often self-limit. More commonly, in developing systems of criminal law, ancient states attempted in various ways to control their populations and to bolster their power and legitimacy. It is important to remember, of course, that these were only *claims* to how states would attempt to solve problems, and that the use of legal language was, in this as in all other legal contexts, a branch of rhetoric (in the sense of a system of practical reasoning about what one *should* do), rather than a definitive statement of fact or history (i.e. that in all cases of type X, we (have) solve(d) the problem by procedure Y). Historians would do well to be cautious about inferring, from the universe of criminal law or the world of tort, what values any particular ancient society *actually* held most dear. A better option would be to think about the kinds of positive and negative incentives that states offered to their subjects as attempts at normative intervention in the world where they could potentially exercise control: what I have referred to above as 'subject-craft'. The South Asian king Aśoka seemed particularly aware of this when he conceded, in his seventh Rock Edict, that 'progress among the people through *Dhamma* has been done by two means, by *Dhamma* regulations and by persuasion. Of these, *Dhamma* regulation is of little effect, while persuasion has much more effect.'[104] It was something of an unusual moment of candour among the vast catalogue of negative incentives produced by ancient states.

So did it work, and if it did, under what sort of circumstances? That is, did these attempts by state power to intervene in the world of their subjects result in the probability that their subjects would have internalized these imperatives to the degree that they would have modelled their behaviour accordingly – that is, that they avoided particular forms of proscribed conduct, or, when faced with such conduct, would in turn submit it to the state for judgment and punishment?

Here extreme caution is necessary, since the answer will vary according to the historical particulars of any given society. Even then, no one answer will be possible, since all societies have their various subcultures, their outsiders, their insiders who are non-conformists and their insiders who grumble but obey (not to mention their teacher's pets). So no general claims about the degree to which ancient states were able to actualize their policies will follow

103 Hansen 1976b.   104 Olivelle 2023.

herein. What will follow, instead, are some broader methodological claims about how we might try to answer the question itself.

First, we should be looking, in our evaluations of the capacities of ancient states to promote social control, not just at legal documents, but rather at the entire range of behaviours, rhetorics and documentary practices that might constitute *either* a direct engagement with state laws, *or* an alternative way of modelling behaviour. Like fossil hunters, in other words, we might find the impression of a state practice in something that is otherwise dirt or mud, in something that is literature or religion, or in a practice like informal community mediation. To continue the metaphor: we err substantially when we look for only the fossilized thing itself. This means that in evaluating the 'impression' made by ancient law we must also look for traces of law-avoidance, the construction of alternative systems of value in reference to or in conversation with legal categories, and in the animation of 'legal' categories in strange or surprising places (such as the schoolroom, the temple or the theatre).

Second, and relatedly, historians should use extreme caution when they find such traces of state law and must not uncritically assume that the existence of a 'trace' or this or that legal term meant that subjects 'knew the rules' or were replicating state assumptions about a particular rule or term when they used it. By this I mean that we ought not assume that law is somehow hegemonically implanted in the consciousness of ancient subjects, or that, if it is, that this process is friction-free or otherwise unproblematic. To take just a single example: in the possibly fifth-century CE Sanskrit play *The Little Clay Cart* (*Mṛcchakaṭika*), the mother of a putative murder victim suggests that the case should not be heard if she does not make a complaint, implying a recognition that this is the rule of a civil dispute (though disregarding the fact that it is a criminal matter in the king's eyes). The judge scoffs at this notion and carries on with the trial. Similarly, the Brahmin defendant in the play claims exemption from capital punishment, on the basis of Dharmaśāstra principles. Interestingly, the king also feels free to disregard this principle and send the Brahmin for execution.[105] These narrative reversals are not just evidence that 'law' made it into 'literature', but that in the process of narrating a story to a particular community, this author played on, or commented on, a world of legal expectations that, when reversed, served to promote justice – even at the expense of a high-status person.

---

105 Ed. and trans. Acharya 2009: Act 9.

Crimes and Torts

> If a slave is said to have been contumeliously killed, why is it that the praetor should not allow the matter to be resolved by a private action to the prejudice of the *lex Cornelia* (concerning assassins and poisoners)? The same issue would arise if the plaintiff wished to bring an action 'because you administered poison to kill a slave'. And so the praetor acts more correctly if he does not allow such an action. Now, we normally say that in those cases where public proceedings are possible, we should not be prevented instead from bringing a private action. This is true, but in those cases where the issue is not one which chiefly has public consequences. What, then, do we say of the *lex Aquilia* (concerning wrongful damage of slaves and chattels)? Now that action is not chiefly concerned with whether the slave has been killed; in the Aquilian action, the main issue is with the loss which the owner has suffered; but in the Cornelian action it is that the death or poisoning should be punished, not that the loss be made good. What, then, if someone wishes to bring the private action for insult because his head has been struck by a sword? Labeo says that there is no objection because, he says, there is nothing here which has public overtones. This is not true; for who can doubt that it should be said that the assailant can be proceeded against under the *lex Cornelia* (concerning assassins and poisoners)?[106]

The text above, drawn from Justinian's *Digest*, juxtaposes the opinions of two Roman jurists, each writing in a different political context: Labeo, writing at the turn of the millennium, and Ulpian, writing in the early third century CE. The question turns on the best way to deal with malefactors whose bad acts might be dealt with either through private means of compensation, such as a lawsuit or 'action' in the praetor's court, or through public or criminal courts: in this case, an indictment under the *lex Cornelia* concerning assassins and poisoners, a criminal statute. In theory, there were certain circumstances in which both avenues would have been open to a litigant. But in practice, the jurists crafted a rule: in cases that had 'chiefly public consequences' (*publicam exsecutionem*), one had to use the public, criminal procedure. At first glance this is a straightforward rule, but in fact it only kicks the can down the road: for how does one determine whether something has chiefly public consequences? The jurists proffer two examples. In the case of a slave that has been killed, according to the jurists, we deal only with the loss (*damnum*) suffered by the owner; this is private. What, then, about violent wounding to a free man? Here the jurists disagree. If the wounded man interprets it as *iniuria* (degrading violence), according to Labeo, he certainly can sue privately.

---

106 Justinian, *Digest* 47.10.7.1 (Ulpian, *Edict* 57).

Not so, Ulpian replies: wounds by swords to the heads of free men are certainly public, and can – and must – be pursued criminally, through the *lex Cornelia*.

The divergent opinions of the Roman jurists on this relatively technical question pose, *in nuce*, some of the problems raised by the problem of distinguishing crime from tort. Both acts are problematic; only one is publicly so. The logic that distinguishes the private from the public is slippery, if not circular. There is a choice between the two procedures, except when there isn't, and though there might originally, that is in Labeo's day, have been room for thinking that some bad acts were merely private, three centuries later the state (and the jurists who advised it) decided that a particular act (malicious wounding) might jeopardize social order more generally, though they failed to articulate specifically why. Nonetheless, the wounded man would have to forgo his right to private compensation and bring the public action instead.

It may seem odd, at this juncture, to turn away (at least momentarily) from the state and its claims about punishment and prohibition, and their attendant civic and cosmic consequences, and turn instead to the world of purely civil compensation – the world of 'tort' or 'delict' or, more generally, private wrongs.[107] While it is a fairly straightforward matter to understand the processes through which the state claims and constructs its own authority through its language of crime, it is less straightforward to do so by looking at its attempts to regulate private transactions and force the righting of wrongs. Nonetheless, some account of tort has played a feature role in many early comparative attempts to explain the origins of states and of state-based law as distinct from custom. A number of the earliest, that is, nineteenth-century, accounts of comparative law were concerned in particular with the question of harm and the emergence of systems of regulated compensation out of primitive systems of revenge.[108] These accounts of private revenge becoming state-managed torts were, in turn, framed as responses to Enlightenment accounts that located the origins of government in a moment of contract.[109]

Though the history of tort has indeed done some heavy lifting, historiographically speaking, it is nonetheless far from clear why states would have chosen to extend themselves to rectify private wrongs in the first place. And indeed, in some cases ancient states simply chose not to make a category of

---

107 In what follows I shall use the word *tort* for the sake of economy.
108 For an overview, see Whitman 1995–96; for a contemporary version of such a comparative account, see Miller 2006.
109 Whitman 2002.

torts at all. China here is a case in point. Before the establishment of the bureaucratic state, there is evidence from Western Zhou bronze inscriptions that one noble might sue another for theft before the court of the Zhou king. But this kind of 'private prosecution' is not found once the Qin had established control over China. After the rise of the bureaucratic state, rather than constructing parallel systems of criminal law and tort law, Chinese law codes instead categorized wrongs such as theft and property damage (*tsang*) as crimes, although they also stipulated that the wrongdoer pay over compensation to the victim – unless the wrongdoer had been sentenced to death or exile and had consumed the goods in question.[110] Although there was no distinction between tort and crime, there was still a difference in procedure for the handling of criminal or civil cases such as those dealing with breach of contract.[111] But China is in this regard exceptional; most other ancient states did promise, for one reason or another, to compel provision of remedies to private persons who had been harmed by other private persons.

In what follows, I shall make no attempt to answer the question of why ancient states might have initially chosen to protect people from the acts of others, nor to hypothesize why they might protect behaviour X but not behaviour Y. Similarly, I shall leave to others the work of comparing the vast number of individual provisions of ancient tort law, and to explaining their variation.[112] I shall instead confine myself, in what follows, to understanding the ways that tort and crime provisions intersect from the view of state claims, and to the ways that ancient states sought to create for themselves order and stability. In this respect, at least, crime and tort in ancient societies move along broadly similar paths, even if in some ancient societies they were understood to be somehow different.

The creation of these parallel systems of punishment and private compensation was not exclusively Roman. A similar structure operated in classical Athens. Litigants might choose, in certain cases, between seeking private compensation and public punishment. The choice would determine the procedure that they used for bringing the case. In the case of assault, for example, a litigant could choose between a *dikê aikeias*, a private suit for

---

110 MacCormack 1990: 222–23.   111 See Chapter 7, this volume.
112 Older evolutionary accounts, as noted above, relied on accounts which began in private revenge and ended in state sanctions; these have been called into question but not necessarily replaced. The more recent trend, though still far from an orthodoxy, is to adapt the language of 'New Institutional Economics' to explain state roles in creating the conditions for transactions, including, ultimately, the rectification of wrongs (though this has rarely been treated explicitly): for example, Frier and Kehoe 2007 and Bresson 2016a. See also Chapter 10, this volume.

compensation and a *graphê hybreos*, a public/criminal suit for punishment. Only the injured party could bring a *dikê*, but any concerned citizen could bring a *graphê*. Still, as in the Roman case, there might be slippage between the two categories: a litigant might claim, in a private suit for compensation, that the reason he deserved such compensation was precisely because the failure to compensate him might have negative *public* consequences for the polis as a whole.[113] Such is the logic, for example, in Demosthenes' prosecution of Meidias: Demosthenes argues to the popular jury that when Meidias slapped him while Demosthenes was a chorus-master, Meidias was essentially assaulting not just Demosthenes himself, but the entire polis. Meidias, at least on Demosthenes' account, defended himself by saying that he was merely, and privately, 'at war' with Demosthenes. In other words, Meidias argued that the slap was a private transaction, essentially one between two prominent and high-status individuals (for it is such people who tend to be privately 'at war' with one another).[114]

Viewed from the perspective of statecraft, both the Athenian and the Roman systems have an important similarity to the processes of 'marking off' outlined in the section 'Crime and Statecraft' above. In both cases it is actions, rather than subjects or officials, that are marked as being particularly problematic. This is not in itself surprising, but what is interesting in these cases is that these problematic actions are further inscribed within a dichotomy of public/private. It matters that this dichotomy is also a hierarchy: public issues take precedence over private ones. The creation of the category of tort, then, might be said to contribute to statecraft by the way that it frames – and then encourages citizens to reframe – particular bad acts according to state logic. That Athenian litigants, for example, might try to convince juries that a private/tortious bad act had public consequences was, then, a way of politicizing the private and inviting its regulation. The 'response' of someone like Meidias – that there were some affairs that were strictly the private matters of elites – would have been looked on askance in the context of the radical democracy (which is why Demosthenes attributes this argument to him) where the polis might claim to take an interest in even especially intimate aspects of its members' existence.[115]

Still, not all systems of tort operated through the logic of public vs. private. In Roman Egypt, for example, the Roman state advertised its purpose as the

---

[113] Cohen 2005: 215–19.   [114] See Cohen 1995, chapter 5.
[115] On portrayals of elite character in the radical democracy, and the careful balancing act that such portrayals required, see Ober 1990. On the politics of intimate acts in the democracy, see Davidson 1997.

promotion of justice in general, and encouraged its subjects to send in petitions that presented narratives of some complexity, from which a magistrate or his staff would distil a legally actionable issue, such as breach of contract, interpersonal violence, theft or damages. While the legal system was theoretically open to all manner of complaint, certain transactions required specific forms of documentation to be valid. Thus complaints revolving around the ownership of land required that the land be formally registered in an official archive. Certain contracts likewise were subject to registration. Legally complex matters, as well as matters that involved a privileged disputant, were generally heard by the higher levels of the provincial administration; more mundane problems, and the problems of low-status people, were generally passed to local magistrates for adjudication. The governor also heard cases that related to more serious breaches of social order. One governor's edict of the second century gives a list: murder, banditry and poisoning are joined to interpersonal violence and complaints by patrons against freedmen and parents against children, among others.[116] The edict is of particular interest to Roman historians because, although the edict is published in Greek, the categories seem to be direct translations of terms from Roman criminal law. This list did not, of course, exhaust the universe of matters in which the governor might choose to intervene, and this kind of discretion was key to maintaining his power over his province. An important effect of this system of justice, however, was key to the practice of statecraft more generally. To litigate matters, subjects would have to present themselves as abject, while addressing state representatives as all-powerful and beneficent:

> To Herodes, also called Tiberius, strategos of the division of Themistos in the Arsinoite nome, from Sarapous, daughter of The–, from the town of Theadelphia. (Okymenes), son of (?), was made my guardian by you, though he is wretched in character and in his actions. Using his customary nastiness and daring, he continually assaults me. Now in my own home, he does aggravated violence to me, not only by verbally abusing me, but also by abusing me with blows. Therefore, since I am not able to be passive and since for a long time, every day, I have daily been in danger of my life, I flee to you, weak and defenseless, and ask that he be brought before you for fitting punishment, so that I can obtain your help and relief, live peacefully in my property, and receive your benefaction. Farewell. Year twelve of Imperator Caesar Traianus Hadrianus Augustus. Hathyr 7.[117]

---

116 SB 12.10929 (133–37 CE).   117 P. Oslo 2.22 (127 CE).

By contrast, in the city of Rome itself the kinds of matters which would lead to the urban praetor giving an 'action' were more sharply circumscribed.

The urban praetor was an annually elected magistrate who would publish an edict listing the kinds of matters in which he would provide legal relief, along with sample *formulae*: set statements framing the standards by which an issue would be adjudicated, which would be then given to a judge who was appointed to hear the case. The praetor was largely bound by the contents of his annual edict (which changed relatively little year-to-year). The difference between the praetor and the provincial governor, with respect to their amounts of discretion, seems most easily explained by the difference in the political structures in which they operated: the metropolitan Roman system originated in a largely oligarchic society with high degrees of elite competition. This made it reasonable to place limits on magisterial power, especially vis-à-vis the magistrate's ability to dominate citizens; the other was a system in which there was a substantial power differential, and in which the vast majority of the population were not Roman citizens (whom the governor was likely to treat favourably). Nonetheless, starting in the late second century BCE, and expanding rapidly after the transition to one-man rule, the number of prohibited actions grew exponentially, even as the categories through which a remedy might be sought remained roughly the same (that is, more transactions were treated under each individual heading).[118] In other words, as the fierce oligarchic competition of Rome's earlier, Republican phase subsided, the need to control the scope of magistrates was reduced; in a world where a single sovereign (the emperor) was broadly responsible for the well-being of all his subjects, there was less need to worry about limiting the number of things for which one could sue, and a greater need for the state to present itself as generally beneficent. This was not, however, without consequence for the way that citizens were in turn understood. Whereas in the Roman Republic citizens were important members of a political collectivity who voted and carried arms, under the Principate they were, by contrast, mere civilians, subject to a monarch who unified, in his person, all critical organs of power and politics.[119] So far as litigation about harms was

---

118 For example, the number of things that might be treated as *iniuria* expanded radically in the second and third centuries CE and came to include not just the original idea of degrading interpersonal violence, but also offered remedies to someone who was prevented from fishing on the public seashore, or whose son was taken into a tavern, or someone who was insulted that a third party were filthy clothes to their detriment. On the nature of this relatively capacious category, see Daube 1991 (1951). In general see Bryen 2018.

119 Ando 2012: 11.

concerned, this had the result of encouraging subjects in the monarchy to emphasize their abjectness and vulnerability as well, just as provincials did.[120] Once again, we see an analogous process whereby the offer of relief from harm or injury becomes a process by which the state came to induce performances of obedience.

This is in contrast to the ways that South Asian jurists dealt with lists of actions, or 'grounds of litigation' (*vyavahāra-pada*), of which two are preserved: book three of the *Arthaśāstra* gives sixteen specific grounds: marriage, inheritance, immovable property, breach of contract, non-payment of debts, deposits, slaves and labourers, partnerships, cancellation of sale or purchase, sale without ownership, relation between owner and property, forcible seizure, verbal assault, physical assault, gambling and betting. A miscellaneous category is appended. Manu says they are eighteen in number: non-payment of debts, deposits, sale without ownership, partnerships, non-delivery of gifts, non-payment of wages, breach of contract, cancellation of a sale or purchase, disputes between owners and herdsmen, boundary disputes, verbal assault, physical assault, theft, violence, sexual crimes against women, marriage, partition of inheritance and gambling and betting (*MDh* 8.4–8). These lists of actions were explained in the Dharmaśāstra as transactions gone awry. Such transactions, furthermore, were required to be done in public, during the daytime, and willingly (*KAŚ* 3.1.2–12). The lists attempted to be comprehensive. As Manu argues, 'These are the areas in which, for the most part, disputes among the people arise; and the king should decide their cases based on the eternal Law' (*MDh* 8.8).

I should like to note one further way in which the law of tort is similarly imagined as a practice of statecraft, that is, as a practice of 'marking off'. If one of the promises of tort law is that subjects will be protected, the other side of that claim is that subjects are vulnerable. Yet not all subjects are vulnerable in precisely the same ways. Consider the following provisions from the Laws of Hammurabi:

§197 If an *awīlu* should knock out the tooth of another *awīlu* of his own rank, they shall knock out his tooth.
§198 If he should knock out the tooth of a commoner (*muškēnim*), he shall weigh and deliver 20 shekels of silver.

---

120 Ando 2011.

§209 If an *awīlu* strikes a woman of the *awīlu*-class and thereby causes her to miscarry her fetus, he shall weigh and deliver 20 shekels of silver for her fetus.
§210 If that woman should die, they shall kill his daughter.
§211 If he should cause a woman of the commoner-class to miscarry her fetus by the beating, he shall weigh and deliver 5 shekels of silver.
§212 If that woman should die, he shall weigh and deliver 30 shekels of silver.[121]

Though they feature prominently in the passages of Hammurabi's Laws that deal with personal injury and insult (chapters 198–223), the distinction between *awīlu* and commoner cannot be said to animate the entirety of the law collection.[122] It seems to be of especial importance in setting the rates for injury and insult. A similar set of assumptions seems to structure the biblical material as well, and analogies can be found in the Dharmaśāstra.[123]

The ancient Near Eastern pattern, however, is not easily generalizable to the ancient Mediterranean. Athens, as noted above, prohibited the commission of *hybris* even against slaves. In developed Roman law penalties for interpersonal violence were increased when inflicted across status lines: thus, says the second-century jurist Gaius, *iniuria* is considered aggravated (*atrox*) when inflicted on a high-status person such as a senator 'by a person of low social status' (Gaius, *Institutes* 3.225). In other words, the most basic case of tort (one person hitting/touching another) was generative of a particular sort of map of the social landscape and the political community as the state wished to divide and rank it. At times this produced interesting results. The Roman case is in this regard instructive: not only did the Roman jurists regard violence as in some cases less serious if done across certain status gaps, they regarded it as no issue at all. Thus they would refuse, as a matter of course, to allow a child to sue a parent, or a freedman to sue a patron, in cases that might bring the latter party into disrepute. What is more, they were open about the fact that certain types of violence by high-status persons against low-status persons was natural and normal, so long as it served a paideutic function.[124] What is more, even if subordinated people (people under the power of the father) were violated, it was normally the father himself (not his

---

121 Ed. and trans. Roth 1997.
122 Other relevant sections in the Laws of Hammurabi distinguishing an *awīlu* from a commoner: 8 (theft of animals), 138–40 (divorce settlements), 175 (marriage with slaves of the respective classes). Passages mentioning commoners but not distinguishing one from an *awīlu*: 15–16 (harbouring fugitive slaves), gap h (sale of a house). See the index of Roth 1997: *s.v.* commoners (*muškēnu*).
123 Westbrook and Wells 2009: 69–73; MDh 8.9.
124 Justinian, *Digest* 47.10.11.7 (Ulpian, *Edict* 57).

subordinates) who was given the right to sue – unless, that is, he was considered to be a base person, incapable of protecting his family. From the world of personal violation, a whole map of social hierarchy was drawn.[125]

The Roman case is, perhaps, extreme and likely reflects its political context: the period between the very late first century BCE and the second century CE when old concepts of honour were reimagined and made to animate certain highly symbolic bodies of law (the law of injury, in this period, was betimes a place for thinking through the law of *maiestas*, which was increasingly equated with violence against the sovereign).[126] But it is instructive with respect to the ways in which the law of torts and criminal law fit together more broadly. Both are modes of marking particular members of the population, and placing them in hierarchical relationships with other parts of the population. In theory, of course, so far as tort law goes, they are equal in one respect: namely, that they must seek to have these statuses validated by state authorities.

Statecraft, Social Control and the 'Monopoly on Violence'

> If a king desires to obtain the seat of Indra and inexhaustible and imperishable fame, he should never ignore even for a moment a man who perpetrates violence. A man who perpetrates violence should be considered far more evil than someone who is offensive in speech, who steals, or who assaults with a rod. A king who condones a man who engages in violence is quickly brought to ruin and becomes the object of hatred.[127]

As the above passage from Manu's *Dharmaśāstra* suggests, 'violence' was very much on the minds of ancient legislators. A legitimate king, on Manu's telling, is one who keeps alert at all times for the man who perpetrates 'violence'. The definition of 'violence', however, raises questions. The passage itself comes from the section of the *Dharmaśāstra* dealing with the 'dharma of the king' and in particular, that section which outlines the eighteen 'grounds for litigation' (see above). 'Violence' (*sāhasa*) is neither the first nor the last on this list; it is fourteenth, sandwiched between theft and adultery. It is distinguished from offensive speech, theft and physical assault. The text, moreover, turns quickly from the question of the content of

---

125 Bryen 2016. 126 Bryen 2018. 127 *MDh* 8.344–46 (trans. Olivelle 2005a).

prohibited violence to acts of permitted violence, though tellingly *not* discussing *sāhasa* at all: 'Twice-born men may take up arms when the law is thwarted or when the vicissitudes of time bring calamity upon the twice-born classes.' It similarly allows for cases of self-defence. In other words, here we seem to have an especially broad category, one that mirrors the English 'violence', that begins by defining it as a fundamental social problem, one linked to legitimacy, prohibited by the king except in very particular circumstances (to defend oneself or when social disorder has emerged such that class hierarchy is threatened).

Critically, however, the definition remains somewhat intractable. Manu, it seems, has blurred the category of *sāhasa*, which was quite clear in the *Arthaśāstra*, where it referred to robbery in the sense of mugging: forcible seizure of property. Here, however, Manu is content to be quite imprecise about what is being referred to, simply saying that it is very bad. The linking factor is that the word *sāhasa* is based on the noun *sahas*, meaning 'force'; *sāhasa* then meaning 'forcible' and hence 'forcible [seizure]', but the digression on other, legitimate uses of force confused the later tradition. Manu's brevity on this matter seems to indicate that one will know violence when one sees it, or even, that the ability to see it is an element of the ruler's esoteric knowledge which in turn enables his rule.

Manu's discussion of violence invites at least two sets of questions. At one level, we might ask for greater precision in the conceptual terminology: what, that is, should we take to be included under the rubric of 'violence'? How ought we to define it (for analytical purposes), and how does that definition map (or fail to map) onto ancient distinctions? At another level, we might ask about the explanatory role of violence in our accounts of statecraft and criminal law: specifically, we might try to place criminal law within an account of state power in the modern theoretical tradition, namely, the definition proffered by Max Weber of the state as the entity which (successfully) claims a monopoly on legitimate physical force/violence (*Gewaltsamkeit*) within a given territory.[128] In other words, when crafting criminal prohibitions and

---

128 Weber 1992 (1919): 6–7: 'Heute dagegen werden wir sagen müssen: Staat ist diejenige menschliche Gemeinschaft, welche innerhalb eines bestimmten Gebietes – dies: das "Gebiet", gehört zum Merkmal – das *Monopol legitimer physischer Gewaltsamkeit* für sich (mit Erfolg) beansprucht. Denn das der Gegenwart Spezifische ist: daß man allen anderen Verbänden oder Einzelpersonen das Recht zur physischen Gewaltsamkeit nur so weit zuschreibt, als der *Staat* sie von ihrer Seite zuläßt: er gilt als alleinige Quelle des "Rechts" auf Gewaltsamkeit.' In the English translation of Gerth and Mills (Weber 1946: 78): 'Today, however, we must say that a state is a human community that (successfully) claims the *monopoly of the legitimate use of physical force* within a given territory. Note that "territory" is one of the characteristics of the state.

systems of compensation and then holding subjects accountable to them, were ancient states seeking to 'monopolize' 'violence'?

We shall not settle the ancient definitional problem here, but some hint of its complexity might be taken from the difficulty of pinning down the phenomenon of violence in English. The semantic range of the English violence is rather large (and, probably unfortunately, continually expanding); what kinds of things ought to count as 'violence' is similarly a matter of great controversy, at least in the Anglophone world. Violence might range from physical assault to emotional and sexual mistreatment, at an individual level, to broader social dysfunction at another. Sometimes violence refers to a real or perceived concentration of criminal behaviour ('that's a violent neighbourhood'), at other times to state (or even non-state) behaviours that are perfectly legal but nonetheless ethically questionable ('police use too much violence in apprehending suspects'), or even to fully subjective reactions to the acts of others. The ambiguity inherent in the word makes it both frustratingly imprecise to a lawyer and of especial advantage to governance.[129]

But even if we accept that terminological precision in English will be hard to come by, might some headway be made in thinking about ancient statecraft as fitting within a Weberian model? We might begin by noting three things: first, that Weber insisted that the 'monopoly' be on *physical force*, and that this force be *legitimate*. We should note, thirdly, that Weber's use of *Gewaltsamkeit* is difficult to translate precisely into English: depending on the moral valence, we might consider it 'violence' or 'force'; it is in either case an abstraction (lit. 'violent-ness'), which, at first blush, seems to fit uncomfortably with the concreteness of physical acts (which take place within a given territory, no less).

Still, so far as criminal law in the abstract or as an ideal goes, Weber's model is tempting. What is criminal law except the attempt to reign in various undesirable practices whereby an individual might be violated? The provision of safety for one's subjects was certainly an ideal broadly shared by rulers throughout the ancient world. Moreover the image of the monarch stamping out injustice – including violent practices (such as theft or

---

Specifically, at the present time the right to use physical force is ascribed to other institutions and individuals only to the extent to which the state permits it. The state is considered the sole source of the "right" to use violence.' Weber's definition was unabashedly modern ('*heute* dagegen . . .'), but his formulation drew on the earlier attempts of von Jhering 1919 (1893) to understand the *ancient* state: Whitman 2002. On the persistence of Weber's thought in modern accounts of the state, see Novak 2015.

129 See further Bryen 2013: chapter 3.

murder) – was not hard to encounter, even as far back as the boasts of Hammurabi: 'The gods Anu and Enlil, for the enhancement of the well-being of the people, named me by my name: Hammurabi, the pious prince, who venerates the gods, to make justice prevail in the land, to abolish the wicked and the evil, to prevent the strong from oppressing the weak, to rise like the sun-god Shamash over all humankind, to illuminate the land' (Laws of Hammurabi, prologue).[130] Subjects echoed the ideology. To take just one fawning and verbose example (one also wilfully ignorant of history), we might point to Aelius Aristides' second-century panegyric directed at the city of Rome:

> And now, indeed, there is no need to write a description of the world, nor to enumerate the laws of each people, but you [i.e., the city of Rome] have become universal geographers for all men by opening up all the gates of the inhabited world and by giving to all who wish it the power to be observers of everything and by assigning universal laws for all men and by stopping practices which formerly were pleasant to read about, but were intolerable if one should actually consider them and by making marriage legal between all peoples and by organizing the whole inhabited world like a single household. Indeed, the poets say that before the rule of Zeus everything was filled with faction, uproar, and disorder, but that when Zeus came to rule, everything was put in order and the Titans were banished to the deepest corners of the earth, driven there by him and the gods who aided him. So too, in view of the situation before you and under you, one would suppose that before your empire everything was in confusion, topsy-turvy, and completely disorganized, but that when you took charge, the confusion and faction ceased and there entered in universal order and a glorious light in life and government and the laws came to the fore and the altars of the gods were believed in. Formerly as it were emasculating their fathers, men ravaged the earth. And they did not swallow their children, but in the strife of faction they slew those of one another and their own even at the temples. But now total security, universal and clear to all, has been given to the earth itself and those who inhabit it. And men seem to me to have found many means for being completely free from suffering evil and for being well governed.[131]

The basic principle is a constant, though subject to countless variations: a just state is one that protects its subjects (and their property), either by eliminating or co-opting potentially threatening sub-state actors (such as nasty landlords or local bandits – a distinction at times hard to make).[132] It similarly

---

130 Trans. Roth 1997: 76–77.   131 Aristides, *Oration* 26.102–4 (trans. Behr 1981: 95–96).
132 Shaw 1984.

ensures that any pesky friends or neighbours cannot take advantage of an innocent. Reining in these forces of defection ought surely to be described as a process of statecraft, and quite likely a process of statecraft by which violence is reined-in, even eventually 'monopolized'.[133]

But while this model may fit well with an ideal of criminal law, it must be admitted that the totality of actually existing criminal law fits into it rather less well. We can take as an example the case of revenge killing in China. Chinese officials had at best an ambivalent relation to the practice of revenge killing. On the one hand, a strong moral obligation rested on family members to seek out and kill an outsider who had killed one of their number. This obligation was particularly potent in the case of a son whose father had been killed. A passage in the *Liji* (*Book of Rites*) attributes to Confucius the statement that the son should not live under the same sky as the slayer of his father (I: 92, 140). To kill a person who had killed your father, even at the risk of inaugurating a feud, was regarded as an imperative duty derived from the twin concepts of family honour and filial piety. Although the law never formally permitted killing in revenge and indeed on occasion explicitly prohibited it (from the standpoint of the law killing in revenge constituted premeditated homicide), in fact the officials responsible for trying cases of revenge killing and often the emperor himself either imposed a non-capital sentence or even granted a complete reprieve.

Under the Han, revenge killing was relatively frequent. Formal Han law did not specifically provide that 'revenge' might constitute a defence to a charge of homicide. Yet judicial officials on the whole were tolerant and recommended non-capital sentences, the ruler himself sometimes granting a reprieve. At times though after the Han, some rulers considered that revenge killings posed too great a threat to peace and social stability and attempted to stop them by means of draconian laws that prescribed the execution not just of the revenge killer but also of members of his family, as, for example, laws enacted in 223 CE under (Three Kingdoms) Wei and 435 CE (under the Northern Wei).[134] Nevertheless, the general approach of the authorities remained uncertain.

The same oscillation between the law punishing revenge killings as premeditated homicide and the moral consensus that persons who killed in revenge had a 'private right' which should permit mercy also characterized the Tang approach. The Tang Code itself, following a precedent established under the Jin dynasty, attempted to minimize the risk of revenge by

133 For example Riggsby 1999: 113.   134 See Ch'ü 1980: 81.

providing that, where a killer had been pardoned by an amnesty, he was to be sent with his family to a place around 700 miles distant from the victim's family, should that family contain a close relative of the victim.[135]

The question, then, is whether this alternation between periodic neglect, prohibition and leniency ought to be described as part of the monopolization of violence. On a charitable reading, we might imagine that the monopolization of violence is a process that has a telos (the nineteenth-century state) and that what we see in the Chinese case is a stage in the process by which the state *eventually* came to monopolize violence, albeit a stage at which the process is as yet incomplete. Though there is a certain elegance to this, teleological assumptions about the development and eventual perfection of the state (leading to the nineteenth century) are at best out of fashion. Perhaps more problematically, the teleological explanation does little to aid in understanding the Chinese case on its own terms. It will not do to declare that China either did not have a state or had only an incipient quasi-state because it did not monopolize violence in the case of revenge killing; aside from becoming an exercise in question-begging, such an argument ignores empirical reality: the tiered bureaucracy, the elaborate systems of control and extraction, the standardization of weights and measures – all state practices. Moreover, it does little to explain the tense give-and-take between state priorities and local moral imperatives – a give-and-take that would have revolved around debates about justice and ultimately, legitimacy.

The mention of legitimacy leads to another consideration: the second way to read Weber is with a shift in emphasis, focusing less on the fact of 'monopoly' and whether one existed or not, and more on the practice of legitimation of violence. On this reading, the state does not need to monopolize *all* violence, it need only successfully claim to monopolize the means of declaring certain violence legitimate or not.[136] In Weber's explanation, to be a state is to be the sole source of the *right* to use violence. This perhaps makes better sense of the Chinese case. Thus, while it is clear that the ruler of the Qin state and empire arrogated to himself the right to control the behaviour of his subjects and to punish those who disobeyed the rules which he established, in a limited number of cases jurisdiction for wrongful behaviour remained within the family. The Qin laws prohibited children or slaves from bringing accusations against their parents or masters with respect to offences committed by the latter against them. The Han laws of 186 BCE extended this

---

135 Tang Code, article 265 (Johnson 1979: 269–70). Generally on 'revenge killing', see Dalby 1981: 267–88.
136 This is closer to Weber's later formulation of the issue: 1978 [1922]: 901–9.

prohibition on the part of children or slaves to any offence committed by the parent or master irrespective of whether the victim was a member of the household or not, though other persons, such as relatives of the victim, might bring an accusation.[137] Later, in a process commencing with a decree of Emperor Xuan in 66 BCE, this jurisdictional bar became transmuted into a general principle of 'mutual concealment' under which relatives were entitled, without incurring liability, to conceal and not report to the authorities offences committed by one of their number.[138] Certain particularly grave offences (plotting rebellion etc.) were excluded from the scope of this immunity.

Still, the fit remains somewhat imperfect. If we hew closely to Weber's original formulation, we will have to ask whether or not it makes sense to say that the state is the *sole source* (*alleinige Quelle*) of the right to use violence. This seems to reflect better the practice of allowing parents and masters to punish children and slaves, while barring children and slaves from bringing accusations against their parents and masters (a similar practice prevailed in the Roman world as well); it seems to be less of a fit with the practice of revenge killing. We similarly have to ask whether the state has to be the 'sole source' of the right to use violence from an emic or etic perspective. That is, would it matter if in Chinese society those punishing their children did so because *they* thought that the state gave them this right, or is the fact that modern scholars might explain this practice as resulting from the state's having given it to them? This may seem picayune, but it is actually essential: if it is only an etic matter, that is, only a question of the way *we* recognize a state, then the 'monopoly on violence' boils down to a triviality, if not an illogicality: the feature of a state is that a state says that in circumstance X it will punish violence (or even that in circumstance X violence is wrong), but in circumstance Y it will not. We must then be dealing with an emic question, a matter of local belief and understanding: the feature of a state is that when it says it will punish violence of type X but not of type Y, people listen and act accordingly. Otherwise, the 'legitimate' part of the equation makes no sense. But does that mean that they then understood the state to be the actual source of the right to use violence?

From here we move from the theoretical matter of Weber's ideal type to an empirical matter that requires verification in each case. In some cases, it was surely true that people thought that the state granted the right to use violence. We can consider an Athenian example. In classical Athens it

---

137 See Lau 2005: 343–45.   138 Dubs 1954: 24.

counted as 'involuntary homicide' for a man to take the life of another man whom he caught in the act of adultery with his wife, daughter or concubine kept for the procreation of children; involuntary homicide was nevertheless subject to law. We possess a courtroom speech, in which a person availed themselves of the defence that, in killing an adulterer, their homicide was involuntary:

> But first I wish to relate what took place on the last day. I had an intimate friend named Sostratus. After sunset I met him coming from the country. As I knew that, arriving at that hour, he would find none of his circle at home, I invited him to dine with me; we came to my house, mounted to the upper room, and had dinner. When he had made a good meal, he left me and departed; then I went to bed. Eratosthenes, sirs, entered, and the maidservant roused me at once, and told me that he was in the house. Bidding her look after the door, I descended and went out in silence; I called on one friend and another, and found some of them at home, while others were out of town. I took with me as many as I could among those who were there, and so came along. Then we got torches from the nearest shop, and went in; the door was open, as the girl had it in readiness. We pushed open the door of the bedroom, and the first of us to enter were in time to see him lying down by my wife; those who followed saw him standing naked on the bed. I gave him a blow, sirs, which knocked him down, and pulling round his two hands behind his back, and tying them, I asked him why he had the insolence to enter my house. He admitted his guilt; then he besought and implored me not to kill him, but to exact a sum of money. To this I replied, 'It is not I who am going to kill you, but our city's law, which you have transgressed and regarded as of less account than your pleasures, choosing rather to commit this foul offence against my wife and my children than to obey the laws like a decent person.'[139]

To be sure, the speech – written by the professional speechwriter Lysias – is an excellent example of rhetoric and was designed to be persuasive and appeal to the jury. Since the Athenian democracy, as noted above, functioned on the myth that there was an identity between the state and the male citizenry, this kind of appeal made especial sense (though we do not know if it worked). But the idea that in the great majority of cases people thought that they derived their right to use violence from the state alone seems empirically problematic. Is it really likely that Chinese parents understood that the right to beat their children came from the state? Or is it more likely

---

139 Lysias, 1.22–26 (trans. Lamb 1930: 15–16).

that they imagined that the right to use violence was tolerated by the state, whereas the source of the right was something different?

We might raise one final concern about the monopoly on violence, this one having to do with the problem of anachronism. Like the issues raised above, this concern has to do with the fit between actually existing criminal law and the theoretical schema by which we explain it. In particular, my concern is with what we might term 'religious criminal law'. To give just a single example, this one drawn from a sixth-century BCE inscription from Dyme in Arkadia (Greece):

> If a woman wears a garment made of animal skin, it is to be consecrated to Demeter Thesmophoros. If she does not consecrate it, may she die a bad death for her conduct unfavourable to the cult, and may the person who at that moment holds the office of *dêmiourgos* pay a fine of 30 drachmas. If he does not pay, he is to be convicted of impiety. This law is to be in place for ten years. This bronze plaque is to be sacred.[140]

By my logic, this 'religious' prohibition should surely count as a piece of criminal law. In addition to containing a prohibition (on the woman and on the *dêmiourgos*), it provides a negative incentive: the woman is to be treated as cursed, and the *dêmiourgos* is fined and subject to punishment for impiety. As Robin Osborne has explained, laws such as these are extremely hard to enforce, and the emphasis on the polluting nature of the act (the wearing of a leather garment) serves to 'bring the offender into the public gaze and justify treating him or her as needing to be separated from and then reintegrated into society'.[141] On this logic we might identify this prohibition as undertaking a process of 'marking off' similar to the one outlined in the section 'Crime and Statecraft' above. We might even emphasize that the difficulty of enforcement is no bar to the publication of a criminal prohibition (compare anti-sodomy regulations in contemporary society), remembering that this goal of this discourse of prohibiting is in no small part to make transparent state *claims* about the content of a well-ordered society, rather than to actualize those claims in practice.[142]

But can we then say that this prohibition relates to the monopolization of violence? One would search in vain (or engage in unwarranted speculation) to find a rationale for such a prohibition that justifies it as an attempt to crack down on illegitimate violence. We might instead follow James Q. Whitman, who similarly casts doubt on the adequacy of the 'monopolization of

---

140 *LSS* 32 (trans. Osborne 2011: 173).   141 Osborne 2011: 174–75.   142 Richardson 2017.

violence' for explaining (especially archaic) law. To begin with, he argues, there is the matter of anachronistically projecting modern concerns back on to ancient law: the better solution is to emphasize that 'the codes that have come down to us were produced not in the course of a typically nineteenth-century campaign to clamp down on violence, but in a much more alien archaic effort to control the marketplace and to deal with the problems of body mutilation in a world of sympathetic magic and ritually-ordered social hierarchy'.[143] In other words, we should accept the existence of a distinct ancient psychology that did not differentiate religion from statecraft and sought to order society in a particular sort of way. Again, according to Whitman: '[the] hypothesis that lies nearest to hand ... is that our sources were created by authorities that aimed first and foremost to bring ritual and social order to societies that set great store by the intactness of the human body'.[144]

This is broadly right, and the emphasis on the different psychology of ancient peoples is important. Whitman wishes primarily to make sense of archaic law; but what do we do with later periods, which show similar tendencies? After all, the Dyme law is just the earliest of a series of laws, some of which extend into the first century CE, that is, into a world marked by a radically different social structure, a more professionalized administration (indeed, these cities had been incorporated into the Roman empire), a shift in the ruling class and a shift in the structures of Greco-Roman religion. Should we then just think of these prohibitions as atavisms?

Conclusion

This set of questions leads me back to where I began: with the emphasis on the control of material and symbolic resources. Whitman is certainly correct that these prohibitions speak to an interest on the part of ruling groups to maintain cosmic harmony and social purity; they also speak to the need of ruling groups to maintain power. And here there is no need to deal in the thorny metaphysical problem of how someone monopolizes an abstraction like violence. Ancient states monopolized practically nothing; this does not mean that they did not have large *shares* of things.[145] The possession of a large share of something is frequently sufficient to achieve a significant measure of control over the important aspects of the organization of political power in

---

[143] Whitman 1995–96: 82.   [144] Whitman 1995–96: 80.
[145] For a survey of bibliography on the character of ancient states, see Scheidel 2013.

society.[146] What is more, achieving a large share of resources means getting one's hands on both tangible things, for example money, land and animals, but also on symbolically critical intangibles: for example, the right to determine the purpose of urban space; the ability to consecrate temples; the right to create calendars and set measurements; and the right to set the terms by which someone will be violated. As I said at the outset, this does not have to be a conscious process, and indeed it probably was not. It sufficed that state actors could think of it as their right, and then vindicate that right because they managed, however tenuously, to structure the flow of resources – and hence power – in a given society. When it worked – and often it only worked for so long – it secured itself through a system of incentives designed to replicate the structures that the rulers held dear. This set of incentives is the criminal law.

---

146 On the dynamics of power in so-called 'natural states', see North, Wallis and Weingast 2009.

10

Property

Lead Author: JOSEPH G. MANNING

Contributors: EDWARD HARRIS, DAVID IBBETSON, TIMOTHY LUBIN AND GEOFFREY MACCORMACK

Introduction: General Orientation to the History of Property and Property Rights

The concept of property predates civilization. Indeed, as Bowles and Choi have persuasively argued, the concept of private property and agriculture co-evolved during the 'Neolithic Revolution'.[1] In other words, private property existed before states or formal legal institutions. The so-called 'endowment effect' (a 'natural respect' for property even in the absence of formal legal institutions) has been observed in animals as well.[2] This extends the classical narrative of Blackstone about the origins of property much further back in the history of human cooperation.[3] By the time we get to our first written legal documentation discussed in this volume, the concept of property, of ownership and of property rights had evolved, therefore, for more than 7,000 years. But we cannot tell a single, linear story of development, say from agriculture to civilization to the Roman codes, about either the history of property or of conceptions of ownership. In some places, Egypt and the ancient Near East, for example, legal institutions evolved for millennia.[4] Although the basic forms of sale and lease are documented in Egypt by at least as early as the New Kingdom, c. 1500 BCE (intra-family conveyance of

---

We are grateful to Bob Ellickson, Yale Law School, Cary Martin, University College London, Henry Smith, Harvard Law School, and F. Scott Kieff, George Washington University Law School, for their comments on earlier drafts of this chapter.
1 Bowles and Choi 2013.   2 Gintis 2007. Thanks to Bob Ellickson for the reference.
3 Cf. Rose 1990.
4 For a survey of ancient Near Eastern property law, see Westbrook 2003a. Some exceptions: Neo-Sumerian (Ur III) period in the Near East, c. 2100 BCE, with more than 1,000 published contracts as of 2003, see Lafont and Westbrook 2003: 185.

property occurs much earlier), extensive records only begin to survive in the Persian period (seventh century BCE). Early Chinese law has in recent years been bolstered by major new archaeological finds yielding substantial new material.[5] For Roman legal history, the formation of the empire, of provincial administration and changing citizenship boundaries had significant impacts on the conception and the enforcement of property rights.[6]

Formal rules of ownership and inheritance formed the basis of all premodern legal regimes and undergirded economic performance (for instance, growth), as has been frequently stressed by New Institutional Economists, although quantifying outcomes is less than straightforward.[7] Beyond this, the enforcement of property rights reveals a good deal about the diverse economies and cultures of premodern societies. The sources for property rights are rich and varied, and the control and use of resources occupy a considerable part of private legal documentation in all premodern systems that have yielded written material. For Egypt and the ancient Near East, these records extend back into the middle of the third millennium BCE.[8]

The legal systems discussed here, those of ancient Greece, Egypt, the Near East, Rome, India and China, differed radically in size, political configuration, labour organization and agrarian system. Each system evolved considerably over time, although we cannot trace details over the more than one thousand years covered in detail on this chapter. Our knowledge of demographic trends is sketchy at best, and property relations would have been different in the large urban centres of Babylon, Alexandria, Rome and Chang'an than in their hinterlands.

The basic distinction in the premodern world regarding land was between, on the one hand, private or individualized property embedded within family / kinship groups; and on the other hand, public property or property embedded within state organizations. 'All land belongs to the king' – something frequently referred to with respect to Egyptian and ancient Near Eastern property rules – was essentially an ideological claim on the central position of the ruler rather than an absolute claim to owning the soil. In the ancient Near East and Egypt, land was commonly controlled by either the ruler or by temple estates in which various personnel were attached, including tenants who worked the land. Earlier social theories centred around concepts of an

---

5 Barbieri-Low and Yates 2015.
6 For a history of the development of property rights in Roman law, see du Plessis 2015.
7 North (1990). For a comparative perspective, see Ma and Van Zanden 2011. On New Institutional Economics and North's legacy, see Galiani and Sened 2014.
8 Westbrook 2003b.

'Asiatic Mode of Production' and 'oriental despotism' have drawn a strong contrast between property systems in the Near East and Egypt and the systems of the classical Greek and Roman worlds. The contrast has been too sharply drawn and considerable recent work on Egypt and the Near East has nuanced our understanding.[9]

For example, the extensive private family archives from Ptolemaic Egypt (305–30 BCE) preserve, to a large extent, more ancient legal traditions and provide details of the actual complexities of Egyptian land tenure. Persons attached to temples could hold, work, lease and sell the land by private contract.[10] In part such an institutional structure of family holding embedded within a large, perpetual foundation (in this case, a temple estate) was the outcome of an environment in which irrigation basins were managed in cooperative groups. The regulation and management of water was controlled not by the king, as the theory of 'Oriental Despotism' implies, but by local and regional communities centred around these temples that could control very large amounts of land across an extended area. Individualized boundary marking would have been less efficient in many cases.[11] Where there was less of an imperative for the coordination of irrigation, as in China or Rome, there was greater scope for individual allocation of plots.

The distribution of land in Greece varied widely by region and over time. Estimates, as in all cases in the ancient world, must be reduced to educated guesses given our lack of hard demographic figures. In the region of Athens, where land was more equitably distributed than elsewhere, by the end of the fourth century BCE it is estimated that 12,000 citizens owned at least 2.7 hectares of land and 9,000 citizens more than that, out of a total citizen population of roughly 30,000.[12] As we shall see, the classical Roman legal system developed elaborate rules and legal categories. Egypt as a Roman province provides an excellent case study of how these property rules were adapted and elaborated in a pre-existing ancient system.[13]

Ancient Thought on Property and Its Historical Context

Classical sources are the usual point of departure for a discussion of ancient thought on property. In classical Athens, abstract thinking about the role of property in society was a feature of the intellectual tradition that was highly

---

9 Manning 2010; Jursa 2010.
10 Manning 2003a. See examples in Keenan, Manning and Yiftach-Firanko 2014.
11 Ellickson 1993: 1328–30.   12 Bresson 2016: 143–44.   13 Jördens 2010.

developed later by the Roman jurists and codified in several great codes of law.[14] Plato and Aristotle are the two major sources for ancient Greek thought about property and its role in society. In *The Republic* (462b–c) Plato argued that common ownership was necessary to promote the optimum political equilibrium. Aristotle, conversely, thought that private property brought about public benefits: '[W]hen everyone has a distinct interest, men will not complain of one another, and they will make more progress, because everyone will be attending to his own business.'[15] Old Testament sources and Chinese thinkers had much to say as well.[16] In Egypt and the ancient Near East, there was a tradition of 'wisdom literature' that informs us of some aspects of property, particularly as it concerned inheritance. But in both broad contexts, it is the primary sources documenting legal practice that have uniquely survived.

There was a vagueness in the general vocabulary of 'ownership' and 'possession' that in some cases has obscured the modern analysis of property rights in ancient Egypt.[17] Even in Ptolemaic and Roman times, ownership and possession could be interchangeable concepts – an owner was someone who possessed the object. Land was often described as 'in the possession of' (*n ḥr*) someone. Egyptian law, however, did distinguish between simple possession and ownership. But for those who purchased property, their rights were well defined in private sale contracts mentioned in the previous section. The Hermopolis legal compendium emphasizes the role of a 'public protest' and the leasing of the land for three years to demonstrate ownership of land/property. The demotic Egyptian contracts literally say that property rights were based on 'exercising control' (*ir shy*) of property to the exclusion of others. Already in the Old Kingdom, c. 2500 BCE, land could be privately conveyed between parties. As in southern Mesopotamia, temples were critical institutions that controlled and managed large portfolios of land over an infinite time horizon. This was an important way of managing risk in highly variable irrigated environments. Within this long-term framework, individuals in Egypt in state service (soldiers, or servants who were attached to a temple estate) were given land that often was privately conveyable. The same, broadly, applies to the ancient Near East at least by Neo-Babylonian times and is well documented in the Achaemenid period.[18]

---

14 Schiavone 2012.
15 Arist. *Politics*, 1263a. For the views of Plato and Aristotle on property, see Garnsey 2007. See further Waldron 2020.
16 On Old Testament sources see, for example, Wright 1990. 17 Manning 1995.
18 Oelsner, Wells and Wunsch 2003: 938. For a major synthesis of the first millennium near eastern material, see Jursa 2009, 2010.

China, like Egypt, provides us with a long history of the development of property law. Mencius, like Aristotle. and writing at roughly the same time in the fourth century BCE, thought that private property promoted virtuous behaviour and better economic performance.[19] During the Western Zhou dynasty (c. 1045–771 BCE), in theory, there is some evidence for the proposition that all land was regarded as being at the disposition of the king.[20] In practice bronze inscriptions show that numerous grants of land were made by the king to the heads of the aristocratic lineages. At the beginning of the period, these grants tended to cover large tracts of land; later grants of smaller parcels known as 'fields' were more common. The recipient lineages acquired the right to use the land so granted for their own purposes. To judge from a number of inscriptions from the middle of the period, the right to use included the right to sell, give or exchange land, as well as the right that the land should pass to the heir of the recipient. Nevertheless, there is again some evidence that the king retained a residual right of control in the sense that his consent might be needed for any transfer to another lineage. It is even possible that, under some circumstances, the land could be reclaimed by the king and given to another lineage head. The great lineages in turn are likely to have granted land from lineage holdings to the heads of sub-lineages as they split from the main body, though we have no direct evidence. We do not know what rights, if any, to the land were acquired by the individual households assigned particular portions to cultivate under the direction of the lineage.

While the pattern of landholding established under the Western Zhou basically continued, there is evidence of the beginning of the system under which grants of land were made by rulers to individual heads of families as a reward for military service or to facilitate production and therefore tax revenue. But there is no evidence that recipients had the right to alienate the land, which was inheritable, as distinct from the right to cultivate it for their own profit subject to the payment of tax.

In Indian scholastic sources, land constituted a primary form of 'substance' or 'material good' (*dravya*), which, as 'property' (*sva*) constituted 'wealth, assets' (*dhana*). The relation of owner (*svāmin*) and owned (*sva*) appears already in Pāṇini's c. 400 BCE grammar (*Aṣṭādhyāyī* 6.2.17). In actuality there was private land and rights to convey. The ruler's rights were mainly residual rights, seen, for example, when land that had been abandoned or in tax arrears could be reclaimed. In Ptolemaic Egypt a public auction was used

---

19 Ho 2016.   20 Li 1996: 121–29.

to sell such land. In India, property lacking clear title or heir was likely to escheat to the ruler. The independence (*svātantrya*) of private owners in occupying or using their property, alienating it or passing it to their heirs was otherwise limited only by conventional obligations to the state. These obvligations, including, for example, taxes and levies, were justified by the state's obligation to protect the substance and rights of owners (for example, *MDh* 8.304–5), an idea invoked in epigraphy as well. Kauṭilya's *Arthaśāstra* as well as the Dharmaśāstras arrogate to the king most claims to any treasure or natural resources underground (and thus a monopoly on mining).

India also developed a theory of ownership; mostly again in works of grammar (from c. 400 BCE, to explain the possessive case relation), but also in works of ritual theory and logic.[21] Kauṭilya provides the first legal reference to the 'connection between property and owner' (*sva-svāmi-sambandha*, KAŚ 3.16.29), but its theoretical refinement was the province of the Mīmāṃsā school of Vedic exegesis, which was concerned with the correct observance of Vedic ritual injunctions. For Śabara (fourth century CE), transfer of ownership meant renouncing a prior relation between owner and owned and creating a new one created through the acceptance by the recipient (*Śabara-Bhāṣya* 3.3.15.44, 4.2.13.28, 10.3.12.50). Medieval theorists would engage in much subtle reasoning over the cognitive aspects of being an owner, or a state of *yatheṣṭa-viniyoga-yogyatva* ('fitness to be used as one wishes') that was thought to inhere in the thing owned.[22]

Possession or, as the Indians called it, enjoyment (*bhukti*) – deriving from customary law (adjudicated in local assemblies without any written record) that was then formalized in scholastic/normative texts – became an important element of evidence in the Indian legal system. The same held true for demotic Egyptian law that prescribes a three-year process of proving ownership (described below), in addition to the Roman *usucapio* and *longi temporis praescriptio*. Indeed, this must have been the most common indicator of ownership in human societies: if someone has lived in this house, milked this cow or worn these clothes for a period of time, it constitutes prima facie evidence for his ownership of them. Even in India, however, possession was associated with a narrow range of disputes, mostly relating to ownership of real estate and moveable property such as slaves and livestock. Normally, possession provided proof of ownership when the current owner did not have title in the form of a document. Title was always thought to have greater legal force than enjoyment, although it was also admitted that title

---

21 Kroll 2010: 24–29.   22 See Kroll 2010 for fuller discussion.

alone without even a modicum of enjoyment does not prove ownership. Thus, a person with simply a deed to a property will have trouble establishing ownership if he has never occupied and enjoyed that property; an assumption could be made that the document was forged. In general, when someone has enjoyed a property for a period of time (generally twenty years for immovable property and ten years for moveable) in the presence of and without objection from the person who is now claiming ownership, he establishes ownership.

Some kinds of property, however, such as pledges, deposits and the property of minors, were not lost through enjoyment by someone else. It is most likely that in India possession was a more significant proof of ownership, especially with regard to real estate, in the earlier period when titles consisting of written documents were rare. In the texts from the middle of the first millennium CE onwards, sources are more sceptical about proof of ownership based solely on possession. Yet, even later sources assert that in the case of land or house in the possession of a single family for three generations, possession is stronger than a document.

Greek law generally distinguished between possession and ownership.[23] Our sources are overwhelmingly from Athens. Ownership of land and houses was restricted to citizens unless an explicit right was granted.[24] Both city states and temples could also own real property. Public roads, the public marketplace (*agora*) and public buildings could also be owned by the city state.[25]

Private law, the law of things, was of paramount importance in developed Roman law, forming two of the four books of Gaius' *Institutes* (mid-second century CE). The law of things was divided into property, succession and obligations (contract and 'delict'). So far as the law of property was concerned, the focal idea was *dominium ex iure quiritium*, which can be defined as 'full ownership' by a Roman citizen. This was an exclusive power relationship between a person and a thing, structurally identical to the relationship between a *paterfamilias* and a subordinate family member; just as a child could have only one father, a thing could have only one owner.[26] Conceptually speaking, ownership was indivisible. Not all property, however, was capable of private ownership. Some things were subject to divine law and not ownable by humans; an example is *res religiosa*, land in which

---

23 Kränzlein 1963.
24 MacDowell 1978: 133–54; Maffi 2005: 259. On the evolution of property rights in Greece from an institutional economics perspective, see Economou and Kyriazis 2017.
25 Harris 2021.   26 Birks 1985.

a corpse was buried. Some things, like the walls of a city, could not be owned by an individual, nor could things like the air and the sea. There were other sub-classifications of things, such as that between *res mancipi* (essentially Italic land, slaves and livestock) and other things, the former requiring, at least in theory, a formal mode of conveyance, and perhaps representing the core items of family property in early Rome. Roman law also recognized incorporeal property: rights which could be given protection against the world. It is with the idea of incorporeal property that we see the coming together of 'legal' ideas of property and 'economic' ideas of calculable assets.

The 'absolute' idea of dominium did not represent the totality of property rights in Roman law and a plethora of subordinate rights were recognized. Most important was possession, given independent protection from around 200 BCE, whose core idea was actual enjoyment. It may be that in practice, in contrast to theory, claims to possession were more important than claims to ownership. Life interests, usufructs, gave the holder (commonly a widow) the right to the use and fruits of property; if vested in non-natural persons, such as the Christian church in late Roman law, their maximum length was 100 years.

All property rights in the Roman family were vested in the oldest living male ancestor: the *paterfamilias*. It followed that subordinate family members, unless emancipated and so liberated from paternal authority, could own or possess nothing. In practice, though, they would commonly be given a fund which they could administer as if it were their own, a *peculium*.[27] In later law, gains from military service became a form of *peculium*: *peculium castrense*, with practically all the incidents of ownership; but the holders were never described as owners. Slaves too could be granted a *peculium*; this remained the property of their master in law, though in practice it may have been seen as the slave's. The slave might build up his *peculium* and buy his freedom from his master. The reconciliation of legal theory with practical reality generated a fiendishly complex body of law.

Rights *in rem*: the right to exclude and the right to convey were the key concepts in Egyptian law (see the comments in the 'Introduction' above). Property sale contracts written in demotic Egyptian show that the conception of private property rights was well developed in private contracts. A typical demotic Egyptian land sale contract from the third century BCE was structured as follows:

27 Micolier 1932.

- Dating protocol – Regnal year, month, of King Ptolemy; the names of eponymous priests in the Ptolemaic dynastic cult who served that year.
- Statement of satisfactory price – Vendor has declared to buyer: 'I am paid in full (not a universal clause). You have satisfied my heart with the purchase price of my land.'
- Specification and location of property – 'Located within the temple estate of god so-and-so ... (or within the royal fields)'.
- Specification of the neighbours, or a landmark (the desert edge, a canal, etc.) – Neighbouring property, normally in the order south, north, east, west.
- Conveyance of the property in exchange for money – 'I have given the plots to you in exchange for money. You have given me the value of the plots in money.'
- Acknowledgement of receipt of price – 'I have received the money, it is complete, there is no balance. I am satisfied.'
- Statement of clear title – 'This is your property, no one else has any claim to it.'
- Declaration of guarantee by seller – 'Anyone who comes against you about the property I will remove him from you'; 'You have a right to all documents pertaining to the property'; 'I will swear an oath in court that I will defend your title to this property against the world.'
- Signature of scribe.
- The names of witnesses, usually sixteen, on the verso.[28]

These documents, plural (a real sale consisted of two documents: one acknowledging the acceptance of the price and the other, a quitclaim), were an important aspect of proving title, and all such texts relating to the object of sale were conveyed to the purchaser at the time of sale. It is important to note that such documents placed the emphasis on the seller's defence of the title against any claimants. In particular circumstances, separate documents, a 'deed of division' to assign particular shares to more than one party, or

---

28 There are documents of very similar structure (albeit much later in date) from fifth- to eighth-century CE Bengal (India):

The petition (*vijñapti*) of the applicant, to purchase a parcel.
the purpose and terms of the purchase, according to the 'local customary rate'.
the list of relevant 'government record-keepers' whose approval is needed.
the order (*ājñapti*) sanctioning the purchase, with description of the boundaries; the gifting of the parcel thus purchased; and the formula of perpetuity and provisions for enforcement (or imprecations against violators).
For the parallel Indian framework, see Lubin 2018a: 53–61.

a 'document of non-interference' could be written to further define and to protect rights.[29]

Modern Theories about Property

The 'fundamental jural relations' approach, as outlined in the classic studies by Hohfeld, with his emphasis on property as a 'bundle of rights', has been a dominant framework for understanding property law.[30] In this analysis of property rights, the 'owner' possesses merely 'better rights' than others – rather than absolute rights. Some legal theorists have rejected this approach as excluding much subtlety in property rights regimes by dis-embedding 'property' from its various economic functions in particular societies.[31] A right to property may be defined as follows:

> A property right is an enforceable authority to undertake particular actions in specific domains. The rights of access, withdrawal, management, exclusion and alienation can be separately assigned to different individuals as well as being viewed as a cumulative scale moving from the minimal right of access through possessing full ownership rights. All of these rights may be held by single individuals or by collectivities. Some attributes of common-pool resources are conducive to the use of communal proprietorship or ownership and others are conducive to individual rights to withdrawal, management, exclusion and alienation.[32]

Ellickson's and Thorland's 1995 article provides a good theoretical overview of the 'Blackstonian' bundle of land entitlements in their pure form, which of course was based heavily on Roman legal conceptions: (1) ownership by a single individual; (2) in perpetuity; (3) of a territory demarcated horizontally by boundaries drawn upon the land, and extending vertically down to the depths and up to the heavens (*cujus est solum, ejus est usque ad coelum et ad inferos*);[33] (4) with absolute rights to exclude entrants; (5) with absolute privileges to use and/or abuse the land and (6) absolute powers to transfer the whole, or any part, by sale, gift, devise, descent or otherwise. The basis of defining private property rights is hence the ability to exclude, to use and to pass on interest in the land to successors.[34] These rights are well described in

---

29 See, for example, El-Aguizy 1989 with a money penalty for non-performance of the promise to not interfere with property that had been sold.
30 Hohfeld 1913 and Hohfeld 1917.   31 Baron 2014. See also Glackin 2014.
32 Ostrom and Hess 2007.
33 Epstein 2016 (quoting Blackstone, *Commentaries*, Book 2, chapter 2).
34 Ellickson and Thorland 1995: 336, n. 77.

ancient Near Eastern and in Egyptian sale documents. There was a special procedure for prohibiting an individual from enjoying property rights that were disputed.[35] In Greece, owners exercised exclusive physical control over their property. Athenian law recognized an action for ejectment with respect to land and also provided a remedy by which a rightful owner of moveable property could assert their claim when the illegal possession was 'obvious' (*ep'autophoro*).[36]

Modern philosophical debates about the definition of property have tended to be divided between 'essentialists' and 'sceptics'.[37] The former, seeking 'to uncover the single true definition of property as a legal concept', is represented by Honoré whose classic 1961 essay identified eleven 'standard incidents' of 'the liberal concept of ownership' as follows: (1) the right to possess: the 'exclusive physical control' of a thing, 'the right to be put in exclusive control and the right to remain in control', an *in rem* right – there are attendant remedies to maintain or to regain possession; (2) the right to use; (3) the right to manage, related to two further factors: power of access, power to contract for use; (4) the right to income; (5) the right to the capital: the power to alienate, the power 'to consume, waste or destroy'; (6) the right to security, an indefinite time horizon, an 'immunity from expropriation' except in limited cases when a state can take with 'adequate compensation'; (7) the incident of transmissibility (both this and the next contain an element of time); (8) the incident of absence of term: life interest except in cases where transmission across generations is allowed; (9) the prohibition of harmful use (many cases here in premodern law: buildings that obscure neighbour's light in Egypt; animals that cause harm to others; noxal liability in Roman law whereby the *paterfamilias* was responsible for delicts committed by a son or a slave; or the several actions allowed under Roman law for harm caused by a domesticated animal); (10) liability to execution: property could be seized for debt, for example, an important mechanism in the growth of credit and

---

35 Baetens and Depauw 2015: 210–11. The known example of legally 'blocking' a party from use of property concerns a building plot. The example from the Asyut trial discussed by Baetens and Depauw, and below, suggests that blocking the sale of produce from vineyards whose ownership was disputed might be another example of the procedure.
36 See Harris 2016b, who cites for this procedure Harpocration *s.v. exoulês*, and Harrison 1968: 218, 311–12 following earlier studies by Rabel in believing that this action could only be brought against those who excluded someone who was entitled to enter into land for the purposes of execution, but the Harpocration passage indicates that its application was broader than this. Todd 1993: 144–45 follows Harrison. On the meaning of the phrase *ep'autophoro*, see Harris 2006a: 373–90.
37 Merrill and Smith 2012: 16.

(11) residuary character.[38] Not all of these incidents, of course, need be present.

Honoré outlined three areas in which rules about property may vary: first, what can be owned? Second, who can own? And third, what restrictions are placed on the rights of owners? The answers to Honoré's three questions vary considerably across the premodern world. One could add that environmental factors such as access to water (irrigation or rainfall) and annual changes in fields caused by flooding or the lack thereof, often not considered in previous analyses, also played important roles in property relations. The River Nile, for example, provided sufficient flood waters in most regions to adequately produce grain crops roughly 70 per cent of the time.[39] Disastrously high, or insufficient, floods required relying on storage and redistribution networks. In irrigated agrarian systems, therefore, it was common to design land tenure arrangements that included large, regional institutional (i.e. temple) management of land embedded in which were family-held land portfolios.

Consider Saite – Persian, Ptolemaic and Roman era Egypt, for example, which offers an abundance of material from the papyri (land surveys, tax receipts, private sales and leases).[40] There, agricultural land was generally located in irrigation basins surrounded by dykes and irrigation channels. Water access depended on the maintenance of dikes and canals and of course the annual flood of the Nile, which varied, occasionally considerably, year to year. As we will see there was a well-developed concept of private ownership of land, but usually land was held as family portfolios and perhaps should be considered an early form of a semi-commons.[41] The state (in taxation claims) and local temples, which were responsible for managing land in their regions, retained interests in the land as well.

In certain cases, one can observe expansion in private property rights. The Hellenistic period (c. 323–30 BCE) in Egypt is one such case. Indeed, in the Near East and in Egypt, there appears to have been an expansion of private property in land, probably as a means to incentivize land productivity in the context of growing populations, especially in new urban centres.[42] In Ptolemaic Egypt, military allotments, known as *kleruchies*, were originally life tenancies and were taken back by the state but by the later second century

---

38 Honoré 1961; see further Harris 2020, 2021.   39 Said 1993: 96.
40 A land survey from the Persian period has recently been published by Martin 2019.
41 Smith 2000.
42 For example in the Fayyum depression in Egypt, where a major land reclamation project took places in the middle of the third century BCE (Thompson 1999).

BCE, at least in some documented cases, such plots could be inherited and could be held by women.

Anglo-American legal theory developed during the seventeenth and eighteenth centuries by Hobbes, Locke, Hume and Mill has generally dominated theoretical treatments of property in pursuit of a 'scientific basis for the study of "political economy"'.[43] Henry Maine, in chapter 8 of his *Ancient Law*, treated the early history of property but was almost exclusively concerned with Roman law and the 'Natural Modes of Acquiring Property' (and above all *occupation*), possibly because Egyptian, Near Eastern and Chinese sources were unavailable to him. We should not assume, however, that Roman categories fit equally well into other premodern or non-Western societies. Much theorizing even in more recent treatments has missed out on the rich material from the pre-Roman world in particular, although strong connections between the ancient written traditions of Egypt and the Near East and the later Roman system are indirect at best.

Sources

Sources that document property and ownership in the premodern world vary considerably in both time and place.[44] For Egypt, it is the documentary papyri dating from the seventh century BCE onward – from the Saite-Persian, Ptolemaic, Roman and Byzantine periods – written mainly in Greek or demotic Egyptian, which offer the legal scholar very rich sources of primary evidence for state recording, contracting, inheritance rules and procedures and disputes related to private property.[45] We can trace private property back to the third millennium BCE, but it is with the Iron Age c. 1000 BCE that we can observe significant changes in economic and political structures globally. While there was a long history of writing and the recording of property rights in Egypt and the Near East, substantial (extant) documentary evidence begins in Egypt and Babylon from the seventh century BCE, in Greece from the fifth century BCE and in China from the fourth century BCE.

Nevertheless, even here, the survival of our documents means that it is only a few places: the southern Fayyum and the Theban region in Egypt and Babylon in the Near East, for example, where we have sufficient evidence to have details of legal practice relating to property and ownership. For Greece,

---

43 Rose 1990: 37. See the survey by West 2003.
44 For a more general discussion of primary sources, see Chapters 1 and 2, this volume.
45 Keenan, Manning and Yiftach-Firanko 2014; Bagnall 2009. For Aramaic legal sources from Egypt, see Porten 1996.

it is Athens that dominates legal history, but there are many epigraphic sources for the wider Greek world particularly for the Hellenistic period.[46] For Athenian law, the forensic court speeches of Demosthenes and Lysias, among others, are of particular importance.[47] Of especial note here are the so-called leagues (*koinon*/pl. *koina*), agglomerations of usually small city states of the Greek mainland that became a common feature of the Hellenistic period.[48] In certain cases – including the Chalcidian League in the fourth century BCE – citizens of a member state could own property throughout the territory of the *koinon*.[49] For Roman law it is the province of Egypt that has left us the most extensive information, but the documentation of property rights reflects a hybridization of many centuries of scribal practice, rather than a distinctive Roman legal tradition per se. Gaius' *Institutes* (mid-second century CE) and the later Roman imperial codes are invaluable for Roman abstract thinking about property rules, but there was much development and great diversity of legal experience in the provinces. Diversity of legal experience is also the case more generally: disputes over ownership of land are known in Egypt from the New Kingdom c. 1250 BCE, but very little 'legislation' and nothing resembling the ancient Near Eastern law collections survive from Egypt. The same is true of China at a rather later date, where the codes deal almost exclusively with penal and administrative matters. That is not to say that regulation did not exist.[50] Indeed, the evidence for the collection of rules, of legal formulae and so on is abundant in both Egypt and China. The ownership of real property extends deep into the Egyptian past.[51] The property recording function of the state and land surveying is known from ancient Egypt, and private agreements appear to have been registered by the early first millennium BCE, a function perhaps related to the state collection of a sale tax.[52]

The legal treatment of property in India was quite highly developed. On the one hand, beginning from around the third century BCE, we get the first of what would become an extensive body of normative texts on *dharma*: an ethico-legal ideal embracing both law and piety (a Greek translation of an edict of the emperor Aśoka rendered *dharma* as he used it with the word *eusebeia*).[53] In the earliest of these works, the *Āpastamba Dharmasūtra*, only

---

46 Game 2008. 47 For a survey of Greek law, see Macdowell 2009. 48 Mackil 2013.
49 Mackil 2013; a different view is expressed by Sisov 2021a and Sisov 2021b. Property claims in the Greek world more broadly are treated by Mackil 2017.
50 For a survey of ancient Near Eastern 'law collections', see Roth 1997. On the problem of 'codes' in Egypt, see Martin (2020–21).
51 See the survey by VerSteeg 2002: 99–123, with the literature cited therein.
52 Muhs 2005: 19. 53 Norman 1972. See also Chapter 6, this volume.

a brief last section deals with public and private law, though in later dharmasūtras, this material is dealt with in different places in the text. The classical verse dharmaśāstras, beginning with the *Mānava Dharmaśāstra* (Laws of Manu, c. 200 CE) and *Yājñavalkya Dharmaśāstra* (c. fifth century CE), give much more prominence to these matters, and the *Nārada Smṛti* is wholly given over to them. The source of this 'secular' legal science is a tradition otherwise known only from a single unique treatise: Kauṭilya's *Arthaśāstra*, a work on statecraft and polity probably composed around the beginning of the Common Era and redacted under the influence of Dharmaśāstra between the second and fourth centuries.[54] Property is one of the major concerns of these works, discussed especially in the contexts of property disputes and inheritance.

The other major source for ancient Indian property law is epigraphic. Inscriptions on stone and on metal plates were commonly used, at least from the second century CE onward, to record religious endowment of land and other property. From the fourth century CE, there are also records of land sales, and eventually (in later inscriptions) references made to property disputes and transactions. Other sorts of records, made on perishable materials, have not survived. Although these inscriptions deal only with a narrow range of matters, involving mostly elite or religious parties, they do provide material to contrast with the treatment of property in the normative and scholastic works.

State and Property

'The state' is an important consideration in all premodern legal systems in assigning and in protecting rights, although the states under consideration here differ radically in size, structure and social structure.[55] It is still common to suggest that in Asia (from China and India to Mesopotamia) and in Egypt, the ruler owned all of the land, whence all other personal rights derived. There is a long theoretical pedigree here on the concept of 'Oriental Despotism' and the 'Asiatic Mode of Production' that can be traced in European intellectual history from Montesquieu to Marx and beyond. As noted above, in Egyptian and Indian thought the ruler as absolute owner was more an ideological claim, tied to rituals of kingship, than a practical reality.[56] Both normative texts and epigraphy in India attest to robust practices of

---

54 McClish 2019b.
55 On the role of the state, see Bang and Scheidel 2013 and Chapter 5, this volume.
56 For Egypt see Manning 2010. On India see Lubin 2018b.

private and public landownership, with a wide variety of methods of recognizing and transferring land rights. Nonetheless, land survey records and taxation records do suggest careful management of local conditions. This is also quite clear already in records from the Qin state in China.[57]

The role of the state to define, to determine limits and to set and collect taxation of agricultural production and the rules that governed the transfer of rights is a crucial aspect in premodern legal regimes. In many cases the state was the source of property rights: the grants of land to *kleruchs* – a tenant farmer subject to military call up, in Egypt – or to Roman citizens are good examples.[58] There were enormous differences between premodern states and in certain cases considerable development within legal institutions. For instance, the ancient Egyptian state, through the office of what is typically called the 'vizier', was responsible for the administration of justice, which included the registration of real property and related transactions.[59] Such registration was related to the state's interest in the survey and taxation of agricultural production. In India and in the ancient Near East, as we shall see in the following discussion on 'enforcement of rights and recording of title', religious institutions played an important administrative role. In classical Greece it was the city (*polis*) that held the main administrative institutions.

Enforcement of Rights and Recording of Title

Official land surveys and registration seem to have been a common feature across ancient societies, albeit with variable specific features, practices and changes over time. One recent overview of the Greek evidence concludes: 'Greek cities thus appear to have been concerned about control over real property transactions and to have developed systems for the keeping of archival records on perishable material to this effect.'[60] The Roman practice of centuriation began in the third century BCE, whereby a land survey laid out square plots of land within a larger bounded section of farmland and ownership was assigned. This was an important institution for establishing property rights in new areas under Roman control.[61] The names of the new owners and the location and the size of the plot were recorded by surveyors. The practice of land survey can be traced back to the ancient Egyptian practice of measuring fields (for which the Greeks used the term *geometria*); it is still found in demotic Egyptian land sales of the Ptolemaic and Roman periods, in which sold property is recorded to have been located in a specific area and the

---

57 Pines, von Falkenhausen, Shelach and Yates 2014.   58 Jakab 2015.
59 Van den Boorn 1988.   60 Faraguna 2015.   61 Gargola 2012; Jakab 2015: 114–17.

boundaries of neighbouring plots to the south, north, east and west are named – almost universally in that order.[62]

In India, almost all surviving ancient property records are religious endowments to members of the Brahmin priestly and scholastic elite, or to monastics, or to religious institutions such as temples. These endowments conferred not just beneficial possession of the properties themselves, but also exemption from what we understand to have been the usual prerogatives of the state over private property (including stipulated taxes and other financial obligations), and authority over those residing and providing labour or services in the lands thus granted. All of these special provisions imply the existence of private property rights and practices for which records copied onto metal or stone were simply not deemed necessary. In Late Antiquity and beyond, examples of land deeds and conveyances of this sort start to appear – beginning with land sales prefatory to and thus embedded within religious endowments from the fifth to seventh centuries CE in Bengal.[63]

Private transactions in ancient Egypt, on the other hand, were in the first instance guaranteed by the parties to the contract and enforced per community.[64] For example, in early demotic Egyptian land sale contracts a scribal tradition developed whereby there were witnesses to the transaction in which the seller of the property guaranteed to the buyer that the title was clear and would be defended by the seller. In the contract boilerplate in demotic Egyptian sale contracts, the burden of guaranteeing clear title – and a promise, by oath, to expel any third party who makes a subsequent claim on the property being sold – is explicitly the seller's:

> I have no claim at all with respect to it (sc. the sold property). No one in the world, myself included, may excise control over it except you from this day forward. The one who will come against you concerning it in my name or in the name of anyone else- – I shall expel him from you and I will cause it to be clear for you in the courthouse.[65]

The Ptolemaic state registered agreements as well as real property and tracked the ownership of livestock. In Roman Egypt, the 'property archive' (*bibliotheke enktesion*) was established, serving as a public records office in each district administrative centre (*nome*) for the registering of private property.[66] Such registers were concerned above all with land and slaves, with tracking

---

62 South, the source of the Nile flood, was 'up' in Egyptian geography.
63 Lubin 2018a: 53–61.   64 On contracts more generally, see Chapter 11, this volume.
65 P. Tsenhor 10 (Thebes, 510 BCE); for the publication of the text, part of a private archive of a woman from the Persian period, see Pestman 1994.
66 Lerouxel 2015; Jördens 2016.

changes in ownership, and liens on property. Private parties were required to declare their property and liens within six months of acquisition – as well as the origin of the property. The practice appears to have parallels in other Roman provinces.

A famous fragment of Theophrastus shows that each community in classical Greece took differing approaches to the issue of publicizing and registering sales of land (Theoph. *fr.* 21 [= Stobaeus 4.2.20]). At Athens there existed the practice of providing advance written notification of a sale, and the buyer might pay a tax of 1 per cent (*hekatoste*) as a kind of registration fee.[67] As Theophrastus says: 'Some say that there should be advance written notification with a magistrate no fewer than sixty days before as at Athens and that the buyer should deposit one percent of the price so that whoever wishes to may raise a protest and lodge an objection and so that it may be clear by virtue of the payment who is the legal purchaser.' Any buyer who wished to have secure title would want to make sure that there were no outstanding claims on the land or others who contested the seller's ownership. For this reason, the seller would publicize the sale sixty days before to give others a chance to come forward and lodge an objection. If there were no rival claims, the buyer had some assurance that his title to his purchase would be secure. This would reduce transaction costs for the buyer, who would not have to collect information about the seller's title. Recent research in law and economics has noted that one of the greatest obstacles to market exchange is the problem of asymmetrical information where one party has knowledge which the other lacks.[68] If buyers do not have the assurance that the seller has good title to the land he is offering, the buyer will be less inclined to purchase or insist on a lower price to compensate for the risk he incurs. This procedure served to correct the imbalance of information and thereby to facilitate market exchange.

Even in cases where there were no written records, the Athenian legal system provided another means for owners to prove title. In Athenian law, the contract of sale imposed the duty of warranty of title on all sellers.[69] This meant that if one sold property to another person, then later a third party claimed that the property belonged to him and that the seller did not have title, the seller was required to support the buyer in court. If he failed to perform his duty, he could be sued for damages by a special private action

---

67 Harris 2016b.
68 Frier and Kehoe 2007: 120, note 22 citing Akerlof 1970 and Furubotn and Richter 1998.
69 For the duty of warranty of title in the law of sale, see Pringsheim 1950: 429–72. See further on Greek sale, Game 2008.

called the *dike bebaioseos*.[70] Even though there were many written records, much of the information about ownership still resided in the memory of local inhabitants. The Athenian legal system was, however, willing to accept this oral evidence in court and gave owners a legal mechanism to ensure that sellers provide the necessary information to protect their title. The purpose of the written records of sales may not have been so much to prove the title of owners but to record the name of the seller so that he could not evade his legal duty to warrant the sale for the buyer. This duty of the seller was widely recognized throughout the Greek world; Athens was not unusual in this regard.[71]

Athens was not the only city that kept written records of sales and contracts in public archives. On the Aegean island of Tenos, the *Astynomoi* kept a record of sales and dowries dated by an eponymous archon and the month (IG xii.5.872–77, late fourth century BCE). One of these inscriptions contains an apparently complete record of forty-seven real property transactions for one year (IG xii.5.872).[72] The records include not only regular sales but also a few transactions involving real security, which are described as sales (IG xii.5.872, lines 74–75, 113–19). This was clearly for the benefit of the owners, who could prove that the lien on the property had been removed. The information for each transaction is quite detailed. There is (1) the name of the buyer identified by patronymic and deme (in the case of a woman, followed by the name of her tutor); (2) the name of the seller identified by patronymic and deme; (3) the verb 'bought'; 4) a description of the property; (5) location of the property (reference to one of the quarters of the city or to the deme in the countryside, to neighbours or other geographical markers); and (6) names of guarantors (*prateres* or *bebaiotai*, usually one or two, but in some cases as any as ten). In some instances there is additional information, such as the name of the previous owner, which would show that the seller had good title when he sold.[73] The description of the property can be as brief as one word: 'house' (οἰκία) or 'field' (χωρίον). Occasionally, however, one finds more details such as information about roof tiles, towers, doors, viaducts, gardens and enclosures.[74] In the Roman world, the practice of centuriation of newly taken land created a rudimentary form of registration

---

70 Pollux 8.34–35, Harpocration *s.v.* βεβαιώσεως. Cf. Isaeus 10.24. In some cases, a guarantor might be named who was not the seller. See Pringsheim 1950: 437–39.
71 See Pringsheim 1950: 429–72.
72 See in general Etienne 1990: 50–84. For a good summary, see Faraguna 2000: 87–92; 2015; and Harris 2016b.
73 See Étienne 1990: 55–57.
74 For the terms used to describe properties and their contents, see Étienne 1990: 25–27.

of ownership in the regions where it had taken place. Later, census records came to give not only the name of those in the empire, but since the individuals were identified also by the land they occupied, defined by reference to their neighbours, the census could function as a sort of reference point for the time being; but transfer of land by the owner did not require registration, so that the data would gradually become outdated until the next census came along. Such information was not so much valuable to the owners as evidence of their rights, as it was of value to the state in determining who was liable to pay the property tax.

Sanskrit scholastic texts enjoined upon the ruler the responsibility to recognize and protect private property as part of the 'dharma of a king'. The oldest such work, the *Āpastamba Dharmasūtra*, makes this a basic criterion of fulfilling the kingly function: 'That king [may be said] to provide protection in whose realm – whether in village or in forest – no fear of robbery is known' (*kṣemakṛd rājā yasya viṣaye grāme 'raṇye vā taskarabhayaṃ na vidyate*, ĀpDh 2.25.15). Moreover, the king was supposed to recover and restore stolen property, or else to compensate the victim, and such stipulations sometimes appear in later land-grant and tax-assessment documents (ĀpDh 2.26.6–7 and GDh 10.46–48).[75] The same works say that the king should safeguard the property of minors 'until they reach the age of legal competency or complete their Vedic studies' (*rakṣyaṃ bāla-dhanam ā vyavahāraprāpaṇāt samāvṛtter vā*, GDh 10.48).[76] The *Arthaśāstra* puts this obligation on village elders, who 'should make the property of [unprotected] minors increase in value until they reach the legal age, as also the property of a temple' (*bāladravyaṃ grāmavṛddhā vardhayeyur ā vyavahāraprāpaṇāt, devadravyaṃ ca*, KAŚ 2.1.27).

On the other hand, the legal literature recognized a rule of escheat, whereby the state could appropriate the property of those who die without offspring (once all funeral expenses and a maintenance for the widow had been provided). This privilege was subject to exemptions. A general one was applicable (in theory, at least) to Brahmins, or perhaps only to 'learned Brahmins' (*śrotriya*), whose property should go to other learned Brahmins: 'The king may take a property that has no heir, excluding what is required for the maintenance of the wife and for funeral expenses, with the exception of property belonging to Vedic scholars. He should present that to experts in the

---

75 ĀpDh limits the king's liability to thefts occurring within a perimeter of a *yojana* (9 miles) around a town and a *krośa* (2.25 miles) around a village.
76 We do not have records of whether such obligations ever formed the basis of formal complaints; in any case, the king could certainly not be taken to court.

triple Veda' (*adāyādakaṁ rājā haret strīvṛtti-pretakārya-varjam, anyatra śrotriya-dravyāt | tat traivedyebhyaḥ prayacchet, KĀŚ* 3.5.28–29).[77] A further special exemption was commonly granted as one of a list of stipulated immunities, conferred with other property rights, in religious endowments; or more rarely stipulated in charters (*sthiti-patra, vyavasthā-patra*) granted to particular social groups.[78]

Other common exemptions and immunities found in ancient Indian sources include exemption from paying taxes to the state – for example, one-sixth of agricultural produce and fixed shares of other production, duties on trade and compulsory labor (*viṣṭi*) – as well as exemptions from providing access and amenities to government officers or salt-mining.[79] Tax concessions could be made to encourage economic and infrastructure development, for example the building or restoration of reservoirs and dams, crucial for the improvement of dry fields for 'wet' cultivation. Beneficiaries could sell access to the water for a share of produce, and retained rights to sell or mortgage their land (*KĀŚ* 3.9.33–35).

The most visible evidence of state involvement in the epigraphic record, though, are land grants, most commonly in favour of religious beneficiaries, who received revenues that otherwise would have been paid into the state treasury. The earliest example of a religious grant is one by the emperor Aśoka, who had inscribed at the Buddha's birthplace: 'Considering that the Lord was born here, [Aśoka 'Beloved of the Gods'] made the village of Lumbinī tax-free' (*hida bhagavataṁ jate ti luṁminigāme ubbalike kaṭe aṭhabhāgiye ca*).[80] This grant was made not to a religious institution per se, but simply to the village itself; although it should be noted that, in the following centuries, kings dedicated rock-cut dwellings and shrines for Buddhist, Jain, Ajivika and Brahmin practitioners.

Later grants by the Sātavāhanas, Kṣaharātas, Śālaṅkāyanas, Pallavas and Guptas were made to Buddhist and Jain monastic communities, or to create Brahmin settlements called *agrahāra* (first portion, prime parcel). Such grants, made either by rulers or their family directly, or by others with their consent (on account of the loss of tax revenue), had the stated purpose of rewarding and supporting religious activity (ritual performance, training and scholarly activity), and for generating merit for the donor or his family. Inscriptions on

---

77 Cf. *MDh* 9.189: 'The king must never take the property of a Brahmin – that is the rule; but, in the absence of any heir, the king may take the property of persons belonging to the other classes' (*ahāryaṃ brāhmaṇadravyaṃ rājñā nityam iti sthitiḥ | itareṣāṃ tu varṇānāṃ sarvābhāve haren nṛpaḥ*) (trans. Olivelle).
78 Lubin 2015: 230–43.   79 Lubin 2018b.   80 Lubin 2018b: 819, n. 50.

stone or copperplates served as permanent copies of deeds of gift, for use in the future to confirm the beneficiaries' rights. In such cases, the property itself was treated as a permanent capital endowment (*akṣaya-nīvi*) yielding tax-exempt revenue; or else the *nīvi* consisted of a cash donation for investment (for example, through lending) yielding tax-exempt revenue; or else the property was used to secure cash for investment (again, for example, through lending), with interest providing the revenue.[81] We have surviving records of cases in which such an endowed property was subsequently reassigned, and the prior beneficiary petitioned to receive (and was granted) a new benefice.[82]

Kauṭilya makes it clear that besides these religious endowments, secular grants were also made:

- [The king] should present Brāhmaṇa land grants (*brahmadeyas*) exempt from fines and taxes to the officiating priest, teacher, Chaplain, and Vedic scholars, gifts that are inherited by heirs of equal competence.
- To superintendents, accountants, and the like, as also to revenue officers, county supervisors, elephant trainers, physicians, horse trainers, and couriers, he should present gifts that cannot be sold or mortgaged.
- He should give cultivated land to taxpayers for as long as they live, and uncultivated lands, made exempt from taxes, to those who would cultivate them.
- He should seize lands from those who do not cultivate them and give them to others.
- Alternatively, village servants or traders should cultivate them; or else, those who have not cultivated them should compensate the losses.[83]

These secular grants differed from religious endowments in that they could not be alienated or inherited.

Patterns of landholding changed significantly during the Warring States period in China (464–221 BCE), with the dissolution of the aristocratic lineages and the concentration of power in the hands of the ruler. Land was a resource held ('owned') by the state (ruler) and distributed in a systematic way, in defined portions, to individual peasant families for cultivation. This was an acceleration of a practice already commenced during the Spring and Autumn

---

81 Schopen 1994: 532–41 and Schopen 1997: 264–67.   82 Griffiths 2015: 22–27.
83 KAŚ 2.1.7–12: *ṛtvigācāryapurohitaśrotriyebhyo brchmadeyāny adaṇḍakarāṇy abhirūpadāyādakāni prayacchet, adhyakṣasaṁkhyāyakādibhyo gopasthānikānīkasthacikitsakāśvadamakajaṅgh ākārikebhyaś ca vikrayādhānavarjāni* || *karadebhyaḥ kṛtakṣetrāṇy aikapuruṣikāṇi prayacchet* || *akṛtāni kartṛbhyo nādeyāni* || *akṛṣatām āchidyānyebhyaḥ prayacchet* || *grāmabhṛtakavaidehakā vā kṛṣeyuḥ* || *akṛṣanto vāvahīnaṁ dadyuḥ* || (trans. Olivelle).

period. The best-known example is probably that constituted by Lord Shang's reform, in Qin, in the middle of the fourth century BCE. The effect of these reforms was to assign defined portions of land to individual families consisting of an adult male, his wife and young children. Adult sons were required to establish their own families and form separate households. The precise rights to inherit in this system of landholding, whether those retained by the state or those conferred on the individual family, are unclear. It is uncertain both whether the land was inheritable and whether the cultivating family had the right to sell. (On these and other issues concerning rights to land in early China, one is tempted to say that there are as many different opinions as writers.) Nor was the system under which land was allocated by the state to individual families the only type of landholding in this period. To be sure, there were remnants of large land aggregations under the control of lineages who retained the right to dispose of the land by sale or otherwise. During the Han period (206 BCE–220 CE), there were some abortive attempts on the part of the government to regulate the distribution of land by redressing the imbalance between the holdings of the rich and the poor. The issue of the equitable distribution of land was inherited and to some extent solved by later dynasties.

In the Three Kingdoms (Wei), Jin and Southern Dynasties (220–580 CE), we see regulations introduced by different governments to achieve any of the following three objectives: increased efficiency in the cultivation of land, limitation on the size of great estates and the provision of sufficient land for the support of individual families.[84] The first objective was a priority of the (Three Kingdoms) Wei (220–65 CE) government which established 'agricultural colonies' farmed by civilians – there were also military farming settlements in garrison areas – to whom, as individual heads of families, a certain amount of land was allotted. The objective was to produce grain for the army. The land remained in the 'ownership' of the state, the colonists being tenants farming the land under certain conditions. Half the produce was paid to the government as rent, being the supplies for the army. The land might not be sold and probably was not inheritable. The Wei agricultural colonies did not survive into the Jin period (265–420 CE), where the policy of the government was directed more at the regulation of land distribution throughout the country than the establishment of special colonies. The Jin introduced a scheme directed both at limiting the size of landholdings and the providing of land to individual families for their support. Thus, the law

---

84 Crowell 1979: chapters 4–6.

regulated the amount of land that nobles might hold in their fiefs; the amount of land that an official might be allocated (depending on his grade) and the amount that should be assigned to individual households (different amounts being assigned to men and women). It is unclear whether the land assigned to commoners might be inherited or disposed of by sale and the like, or whether it reverted to the government on death or inability to cultivate. While some serious effort was made to implement this land policy, it does not seem to have been entirely effective. It did not survive the collapse of the Western Jin in 316 CE. Successive governments were concerned mainly with the problem of controlling the wrongful expropriation by private persons of 'hill and marsh land', open to the public for the gathering of firewood and the catching of fish. During the Southern Dynasties (386–530 CE), there does not seem to have been any system of allotment of land to commoners resembling that attempted during the Western Jin. From time to time, grants of public land were made to the poor. By the end of this period, it is likely that all land which was not recognised as public, belonging to the government or emperor, was under the full control of the private households occupying and cultivating it, whether noble, official or commoner. Thus, such land was not only inheritable but might freely be alienated by sale or gift.

During the Northern Dynasties (386–589 CE), we see evidence of much stricter and more extreme control of land by the state than was apparent under the Southern Dynasties.[85] Essentially, the government sought to secure an equitable distribution of land among the people, both to provide them with a secure livelihood and to establish a sound tax base. The policy of the Northern Wei (386–584 CE) government was directed in the main towards a large-scale resettlement of the people and redistribution of land, though large private estates certainly continued to exist unaffected by the changes. From the establishment of the state at the end of the fourth century and throughout the fifth century, there were a number of resettlements ordered by the government, especially to bring people to the capital. Land was granted according to the number of individuals within the family, although we do not have details of specific amounts or the conditions under which the grant was made.

The principal reform introduced by the Northern Wei government was the so-called 'equal allotment' (*zhuntian*) system of land distribution. Following the lines of the earlier (Three Kingdoms) Wei and Western Jin experiments, this reform, on its face and in the areas to which it applied (such

---

85 Crowell 1979: chapter 7; Twitchett 1970: chapter 1.

as the capital), was designed to secure to each family a reasonable amount of land for cultivation. On the whole it appears to have been an effective system, properly implemented. The imperial decree of 486 CE, which introduced the *zhuntian* system, established the following three main points: first, land was divided into two main categories: 'open' land to be used for growing crops and 'mulberry' land to be used for the planting of mulberry trees and the production of silk; second, each family was to receive in principle a certain amount of both types of land in respect of each adult male, married woman, male or female sale, and ox (up to four) in the household; and third, the right to the 'open' land was not made hereditary or alienable: when an individual attained the age of seventy or died, their personal allocation of 'open' land was to be returned to the government. 'Mulberry' land, on the other hand, was granted on a hereditary basis, though it was to be returned to the government if the stipulated number of trees had not been planted within three years. Although inheritable, it does not seem that 'mulberry' land was normally alienable. The rules established in the decree of 486 CE applied only to commoners. Officials were subject to a different regime under which the land granted to them counted as their salary, to be transferred to their successors. However, by the end of the Northern Wei it seems that such grants to an official had become hereditary.

Northern Wei thus had two radically different systems of landholding. One was that constituted by the decree of 486 CE. Under this system land was granted to commoners upon terms that some was to revert to the state, some to pass to the grantee's heirs but none was to be freely alienable. The other system was that which existed before the introduction of the 'equal allotment' scheme and continued to survive along with the latter. Under this system land was held at the full disposal of the families occupying it and might be inherited, sold or sought in the courts under a claim of rightful possession.

The Northern Wei pattern of landholding continued with modifications in its successor regimes (Western Wei / Northern Zhou and Eastern Wei / Northern Qi). The Sui and Tang dynasties inherited the principles of landholding developed under the Northern Dynasties. Tang regulations, for example, divided land into two categories: 'personal share land' (*kou fen tian*) that reverted to the state when the grantee attained the age of sixty or died; and 'land held in perpetuity' (*yong ye*), which was heritable. The amount which each individual was entitled to receive depended upon age, sex and status. Nobles and officials received grants of 'land in perpetuity', as well as land for the support of their office. The bulk of the land received by commoners was 'personal share land', though some 'land in perpetuity' was also allocated. In principle neither type of land might be sold, though certain very limited exceptions were allowed.

When we consider the schemes of land distribution drafted by the Northern Dynasties, the Sui (589–618 CE) and the Tang (619–906 CE), it seems clear that they contain a strong 'ideal' element: that is, they stem from the desire of the legislators to devise a scheme that will ensure that all persons within the empire have enough land for cultivation both to support their families and to furnish taxes to the state. At the same time, land was not to be freely alienable – although some portion of the grant might be inherited. This principle was designed to ensure that peasants might not be deprived of their land through pressure from powerful families and concomitantly to prevent the latter from building up large estates at the expense of the former. However, we must raise the related, practical questions: how far were these schemes capable of initial implementation and to what extent was the state successful in maintaining the effectiveness of the schemes over a period of time? We do know from the excavated Dunhuang family registers that the Tang scheme was implemented in remote areas to a degree that might not have been expected.[86] Equally, we have to accept that the schemes of the earlier dynasties were capable of implementation to some, even a considerable, extent. This said, it has to remain doubtful whether the state was able to maintain effective implementation over a long period of time. In particular, it appears unlikely that it was able to enforce the prohibition on buying and selling land. Economic pressures under which the rich wanted to acquire more land and the poor to dispose of such land as they had would have been difficult to resist, even though the courts may not have recognized the legality of such transactions.

Apart from the introduction of centuriation in the third century BCE, the Roman state was more concerned with piecemeal reforms than fundamental changes. These piecemeal changes did little to alter the fundamental framework of the Republican (statute) law. One of the first epigraphically attested acts of legislation in the Republic, the *lex agraria* of 111 BCE, made changes to the pre-existing system of centuriation. The *Senatusconsultum de Aquaeductis* (10 BCE) dealt with the construction of aqueducts; here, perhaps more than anywhere, we get a sense of a form of eminent domain, as there had to be a right to force landowners to sell their land if the aqueducts were to go in straight lines. During the later Roman empire, the emperor Theodosius II

---

86 On the 'Dunhuang Texts', see Doumy 2021.

enacted that those taking deserted agricultural land and cultivating it for two years would become owners. But the most important changes to the operation of property rights were brought about by the (urban) praetors, who were able to introduce remedies in order to give rights which cut across rights which had existed as part of the civil law. Mention has already been made of the *actio publiciana*, giving protection to the person who had received a *res mancipi* by informal means; this was achieved by introducing a fiction that the requisite period for *usucapio* had passed (which would have resulted in the transferee becoming true owner provided the other conditions for *usucapio* had been met). A similar fiction assured proprietary protection to foreigners. Their introduction of the possessory interdicts (around 200 BCE) triggered a major change in the operation of property rights by giving an additional layer of protection to possessors. They introduced what was in effect a parallel system of inheritance to that recognized by the Roman civil law, by the granting of remedies to people who would not be recognized as having a claim at civil law. We cannot see any consistent policy thinking behind these praetorian innovations: they were rather ad hoc changes which had a substantial destabilizing effect on the pre-existing system.

In most cases the state could seize land, but it was generally limited in practice. For example, the – at times – very complex political tensions between Greek city states and individual property claims, especially around the issue of returning exiles and their property claims, seem to have evolved under the pressures of the interests of individuals in the context of unstable political regimes.[87] In sum, evidence for record-keeping of property ownership is well documented in Egypt, the Near East, India, China, Greece and in the Roman world, with 'the property archive' beginning to appear in the Egyptian record by the third quarter of the first century CE.[88]

Objects of Ownership

Property in Land

As we have seen already, the ancient documentary record shows a wide range of tenure conditions.[89] Agricultural production and distribution were at the heart of the civilizations treated in these volumes and so agricultural land in all premodern societies was the most important form of property. Who owned the land; who worked it; and what the relationship was between labour, the control of labour and production were three key components of

---

87 Mackil 2021.   88 Jördens 2016; Lerouxel 2016.   89 Libecap 1986: 235.

all premodern economies. The existence of private land in the ancient world has been much debated. Although in monarchic systems a theory of the king owning all land was prominent, as a practical matter land was often in private hands and could be conveyed by private instrument.[90] In Egypt temples held large estates by which the cult was maintained; but in fact, land survey records reveal how inter-nested rights to land were in these 'sacred domains'. Soldiers and those who served the temple had access to land nominally located within these domains and the land could be privately held by families and bought and sold.[91] In Ptolemaic period Egypt, soldiers were given plots of land according to their rank. Such was a special category of real property and tied to a soldier's service. The granting of land to soldiers was also common in the Near East. The land was subject to rent and given as a lifetime grant. Gradually the grants became conveyable to children, and by the late second century BCE the grants became private property and fully conveyable. Those who served temples, who were the major holders of agricultural land, also had access to land. Minor personnel such as herdsmen appear as sellers of plots of temple land in the Ptolemaic period. Acquisition by public auction was a new feature of the Ptolemaic period in Egypt. It appears to have been used to reassign land that had become abandoned. The period after major social unrest throughout Egypt (207–186 BCE) is the best documented for the auction of land.

Neo-Babylonian (626–539 BCE) records provide the most extensive evidence for property and the contracting for property rights in the ancient Near East.[92] Those attached to temples, the 'prebendary class' in Jursa's formulation, ranged from high-ranking temple staff to traders, and the entrepreneurial class, with again a wide range of social statuses, were landowning classes and were involved extensively in the leasing of privately owned land.[93] Temples – as in Egypt – with their permanence and their recording functions, also played an important role in guaranteeing property rights. Stones known as *kudurrus* documented grants of land, in Babylonian, roughly between the fourteenth and seventh centuries BCE; these were deposited in temples to guarantee the entitlement to and the inter-generational transfer of private property rights.[94]

Indian law too, at least in Late Antiquity, formally distinguished between moveable (*jaṅgama*) and immovable (*sthāvara*) property.[95] Immovable property consisted of fields, both 'dry' (dependent on rain) and 'wet' (irrigated);

---

90 Manning 2003a; Monson 2012.
91 Manning 2003a; Christensen, Thompson and Vandorpe 2017.
92 Surveyed in Oelsner, Wells and Wunsch 2003; Jursa 2010.   93 Jursa 2009: 229–32.
94 Slanski 2003a.   95 *NSm* 8.2, cf. 1.24; *KātSm* 516; and *BṛSm* 1.6.14, 1.18.1.

houses; and various other improvements such as water channels, dams, reservoirs, gardens and the like. Ownership in earliest times depended mainly on customary recognition of possession and transfers executed before witnesses; however, as formal legal institutions and the official use of writing began to develop, probably during the middle of the Maurya period (late fourth or third century BCE), ownership, especially of property in land, began to generate documentary records, especially in transfers by gift and, eventually, by sale. The Dharmaśāstra literature provides models for such documents and for their use in adjudicating lawsuits. The Buddhist scriptures and some literary works provide illustrative references to some aspects of property law as well.[96] Besides full ownership – with rights of beneficial use, exclusion, conveyance and heritability – various limited types of land-rights are known, including mortgage or pledge (*ādhi*; both utusfructuary, *bhogya*, and possessory, *gopya*), lease (*prakraya, avakraya*) and tenancy.

In Han period China (206 BCE–220 CE), we have more information than that available for earlier periods.[97] In the first place, a fundamental distinction was recognized between two categories of land: 'government or state land' and 'private land'. Government land comprised three subcategories: (i) the imperial palaces together with the imperial parks and pleasure grounds; (ii) land belonging to the emperor personally; and (iii) land belonging to the government. Most attention in the sources is paid to the second subcategory: land owned personally by the emperor. The emperor might retain control of these lands by having them cultivated by slaves; he might lease them to private individuals as tenants under an arrangement by which the tenant paid a fixed rent but otherwise was entitled to the produce; or he might make gifts of land to favoured individuals; or make grants of land to the poor and dispossessed. In the case of such gifts or grants, the land ceased to belong to the category of 'state of government land' and fell into that of 'private land'.

The category of 'private land' was constituted by land in the possession of private individuals in their own right (i.e. not as tenants). Heads of families were required to register the amount of land held by the household. Taxes were assessed on the basis of the land so registered. Registration constituted proof of the right to dispose of the land by sale or gift (it was clearly inheritable). The sources show that from the beginning of the Han period the sale of 'private land' was widespread. One problem concerns the identification of the person with the authority to dispose of the land. Although the evidence is

---

96 On the 'Buddhist Scriptures' see Schopen 1994, 1997.
97 Crowell 1979, chapter 3; Hsu 1980; Vandermeersch 1978: 39–56.

not entirely consistent, it seems that, while the head of the household might act on their own responsibility, it would be wise to obtain the consent of other members of the family (with an expectation of inheritance). Otherwise, there was a risk that the transaction would be contested in the courts.

Land in and around Rome was in principle capable of full private ownership. In the provinces, however, it was said to be the property of the Roman people or the emperor. Here, private ownership was impossible. Holders of land were 'merely' possessors, but since they had full possessory protection their position would have been barely distinguishable from Roman owners. Some aspects of property law could not apply to them, such as gaining ownership by long possession (*usucapio*). These problems were dealt with by surrogate institutions such as *longi temporis praescriptio*, where the rights of a holder of provincial land would be expunged if another person had possessed the land for ten or twenty years.

Other Real Property

Other objects of private ownership in Egypt included houses, gardens, vineyards, livestock, shops, baths, beehives and slaves.[98] These are well documented elsewhere as well. The conveyance of other specialized property rights, such as incomes from priesthoods, is well known in Egypt and the Near East. Funerary priests known as *choachytes* (water pourers), for example, were organized as family businesses and conveyed rights attached to their priestly function through families.[99] They also made formal written agreements of association that afforded certain protections as a group. Their property right to control particular tombs and the mummified bodies of people, as well as the income streams collected on the funerary rights were bought, sold, leased and donated by gift shares by private contract.[100] Finally, it is worth noting here that hydraulic resources could be the subject of both public and private ownership in Roman law.[101]

Moveable Property (and Slavery)

In India, moveable property included primarily livestock, commodities, merchandise, jewellery and enslaved people. In all periods in China, there seems no doubt that moveables (e.g. valuables, jewellery, cattle, slaves) were 'owned' by

---

98 Taubenschlag 1955: 232–39. For a recent survey of sale in the papyri, see Keenan, Manning and Yiftach-Firanko 2014: 276–338.
99 For a seventh-century BCE choachyte archive, see Donker van Heel 2021.
100 Muhs 2016: 243–45. On the income of such priests, see Martin 2009: 59–66.
101 Bruun 2015.

individuals, were inheritable and might be bought and sold, given away, exchanged, etc. Women (wives) might 'own' moveables such as their personal jewellery and such moveables as cattle or slaves that constituted part of their dowry. Moveables in the possession of sons and daughters were technically 'owned' by their father or senior male of the household. The sale of important and valuable moveables, especially cattle and slaves, was subject to special rules.[102]

Roman law made no formal distinction between land and moveable property. The category of *res mancipi*, as has been seen, included Italic land, slaves and cattle. It may be that in very early law, before the historical record, these things were seen to be the object of a special type of ownership, but as early as we can see with any clarity their only special characteristic was that, in theory, they required a more formal conveyance. The sale of moveable property is well documented in Roman Egypt, less so in earlier periods, although there can be little doubt that such transactions occurred earlier. The sale of moveable property involved mainly livestock and likely reflects the fact that animal sales were the most common type of sale of moveable property in Egypt. Donkey, horse and cow sales occur in surviving texts most often.[103] Other objects of sale documented in Egyptian papyri include looms, furniture and even wood. Interestingly in Egyptian and Near Eastern contracts, the sale of moveables was usually constructed from the seller's perspective: 'I have sold you . . .'.

All premodern societies, including nomadic ones, had some form of slavery, but the form and types of bound labour, and the location of slave labour within the productive sectors of these societies varied widely.[104] In most cases, slaves originated from outside ethnic groups. In India, slaves had to be from a caste below the owner; thus, the highest caste, Brahmins, could never be slaves, at least theoretically. In all Mediterranean systems, slaves are found in agricultural labour, mining and other unskilled settings like factory work, and in the domestic context. Definitions of slavery, and the boundary between fully slave and dependent worker can be difficult to discern, in part because of the lack of evidence and in part by the nature of our evidence that gives us several vantage points. Ancient categories were often fluid between the various kinds of dependent labour and slavery.[105]

---

102 The later history of real property in China is discussed by Zhang 2011.
103 Bagnall 2014: 305.
104 For an overview of ancient Near Eastern and Bronze Age Aegean slavery, see Steinkeller and Hudson 2015. For further discussion on slavery, see Chapter 8, this volume.
105 On Greek categories see Vlassopoulos 2009.

In the ancient Near East, as in Egypt, a wide range of labour is documented from fully free to chattel slavery. The terminology is complex and it is challenging to fully elucidate the nature of the institution. Short-term forced or corvée labour was used in canal maintenance; agricultural labour is also known and there is evidence to suggest that small numbers of enslaved people belonged to most households. We can identify three primary modes of enslavement: war captives, debt slavery and self-dedication to a temple, the last being a method of seeking protection and in many cases a means by which to gain training as an apprentice in a trade.[106] Marriage between free persons and slaves existed, and the status of the child was free. In the Laws of Hammurabi (1750 BCE), wrongs against slaves are recognized, but lower penalties are imposed than on wrongs against higher-status individuals. Slave status could be contested in a court of law and slaves had the right to marry. Privately owned slaves appear in a variety of functions, including money lending.[107] As elsewhere, by the seventh century BCE there is better documentation. In ancient Israel a similar pattern appears. Reforms documented in Deuteronomy include better treatment of slaves and the banning of the return of escaped slaves.[108]

With respect to the evidence from ancient Greece, masters already had all the standard property rights over enslaved people in the Homeric period.[109] Slaveholding is well attested in the Homeric poems and appears to have been as extensive as it was in later classical antiquity. The right to kill one's slaves, the right to exercise power over slave's children and the right to the capital from the slave of one's slaves are mentioned in Homer. All of this is suggestive of the deep history of slavery in Greek societies.[110] The spread of Greek chattel slavery into the Hellenistic kingdoms was an important trend after 300 BCE, although – as we have seen – it was also well established in places like Babylonia.[111] Slave markets probably grew in activity – Delos was the key node during the second century BCE with growing Roman demand in the wake of the crushing defeat of Carthage and Corinth.[112] In some parts of the Hellenistic world, we encounter slaves in large factory settings (*ergasteria*), mainly, it appears, making military equipment in urban regions such as Pergamum and Miletos.[113]

Greeks moving east to serve the new kings of the Hellenistic states, primarily as soldiers, brought the tradition of household slaves with them.

---

106 See Chapter 8, this volume.
107 On the status and function of slaves in first-millennium BCE Babylon, see Baker 2001.
108 Snell 2011 provides a summary of the Near Eastern, Egyptian, Israelite and Hittite material.
109 Harris 2012b.   110 Harris 2012b.   111 Thompson 2011; Lewis 2018.
112 Andreau and Descat 2011: 212–13.   113 Andreau and Descat 2011: 210–11.

And it is here, in the houses of Greek immigrants, whence most of the evidence for household slavery derives.[114] It is difficult to know what world Egyptian wisdom literature sayings such as 'Do not neglect to acquire a manservant and a maidservant when you are able' reflects.[115] We also move into more documentary evidence and less literary material.[116] Slavery is documented on large estates in Egypt (Zenon papyri), working as weavers on the estates, but also as agents for the estate manager, in households. House-born slaves had to be registered as part of the normal routine of household surveys.[117] They appear in the census returns.[118] Some of the extant slave sales in the Greek papyri from Egypt provide a good amount of detail on the origins of slaves, through sale at auctions and state regulation of them. Child exposure, especially of girls, is also recorded as a source of slaves; as is war and piracy – intertwined activities and a near constant in the Hellenistic period. Debt-slavery, an ancient institution, continued to some extent. Manumission by testament was the 'regular form of manumission'.[119]

The Indian legal literature distinguishes a number of ways of becoming a slave: by birth to slave, through capture in war, through sale or pledge (by self for sustenance, or by parent), by consequence of debt or as a punishment (KAŚ 3.13; MDh 8.415). In most of these cases, slaves should be able to redeem themselves, even recovering their free Ārya status, through repayment (whether in cash or in labour) according to fixed terms (KAŚ 3.13.15–21). Owners were prohibited from or penalized for engaging in certain forms of abuse, including compelling slave to engage in degrading work. Participation in the sale or pledge of a minor Ārya is punishable (KAŚ 3.13.1); as is resale (or repledging) by someone who has redeemed a slave (KAŚ 3.13.25).

Slaves in China – never the whole population as thought by Chinese Marxist historians – were a relatively small specific group constituted by capture in war, conviction of a serious offence (where relatives of the principal offender were subject to enslavement) or sale of children or even of oneself in times of poverty.[120] Slaves as such have to be distinguished from 'bondsmen': a servile group made up broadly of 'service households' attached to the government, performing various kinds of labour; and also from

---

114 Thompson 2011: 209–10.
115 *Wisdom of Onchsheshonqy* 7/17, a late Ptolemaic text but to a large extent reflecting earlier traditions, see Ryholt 2000.
116 Keenan, Manning and Yiftach-Firanko 2014: 442–69 for a survey.
117 See Keenan, Manning and Yiftach-Firanko 2014: 450–51.
118 Clarysse and Thompson 2006. 119 Thompson 2011: 205.
120 Yates 2001: 295–96, with remarks on the Qin laws on moveable property. For slavery in China in general, see also Wilbur 1943.

'personal retainers' who were attached to private persons, often as serfs to work the land. Both these statuses: 'service household' and 'personal retainer', once established, were hereditary – but the former was constituted by capture in war or conviction on the ground of an offence, while the latter was constituted by private agreement between the dependent and his master.

The hereditary classes of slaves and servile persons constituted groups strictly delimited from the ordinary, free population. Class separation was maintained by laws prohibiting marriage between free persons and slaves of members of 'service households', but not between free persons and personal retainers. The standard view that slaves could become permanently private property is that they might be bought and sold like cattle (according to Qin laws of the third century BCE). But recent analysis by Yates suggests that slaves were in fact distinguished from both moveable and immovable property, and they could be recorded in household registers.[121] If a commoner lacked an heir, the longest-serving slave could be manumitted and made heir. Slaves were punished in a similar way to children who did not show filial piety. The Tang Code itself established a special procedure for the sale of slaves, horses and cattle, camels, mules and donkeys (article 422). A 'personal retainer', on the other hand, worked at the direction of their masters but might not be bought or sold. The criminal law treated slaves and servile persons differently from free persons. For example, the killing or injury of a slave or personal retainer was treated as less serious than the killing or injury of a free person. Conversely, the killing or injury of a free person by a slave or 'personal retainer' was treated as less serious than the killing or injury of a free person by another free person. There was still a difference in the degree of leniency or severity drawn between slave and 'personal retainer'.

Roman law drew a sharp distinction between slaves and free persons, though the boundary between the two classes could be viewed – from the viewpoint of the Roman jurist at least – as porous: a free person might be enslaved, for example, as a punishment for a major crime, or a slave could be manumitted. There were also intermediate statuses. Hence slaves who had been freed informally and not by an appropriate civil-law method came to be treated as free while they lived, but they died as slaves – so that their erstwhile owner inherited their property. Freedmen, slaves who had been properly freed, owed obligations to their previous owner who had some limited right to inherit from them on death. In the later Empire *coloni*: free people who

---

121 Yates 2014b.

were nonetheless tied to the land they were farming, were in many respects in a quasi-servile position.[122]

Restrictions on Ownership

Mines and quarries were typically monopolized by the king, or other sovereign, in all periods and across all ancient traditions. In classical Athenian law, for example, private individuals were forbidden from owning silver mines which had to be leased from the state.[123] Similarly, normative works within the Indian jurisprudential tradition – like Kauṭiya's *Arthaśāstra* and the Dharmaśāstras – asserted that, in principle, kings had a claim to the majority share of unclaimed buried treasure and to other valuable natural resources discovered in the ground.[124] Mines (inter alia gold, silver, jewels) were a monopoly but could be leased to private persons (*KAŚ* 2.12.22).[125]

In Athens and in other Greek communities, foreigners could not own land unless they were granted this privilege.[126] In Rome only citizens could, in theory, own property, but the praetor gave a normal proprietary remedy, the *vindicatio*, to foreigners by the insertion of a fiction that the claimant was a citizen.

In Egypt, agricultural land was often under the joint control of a family. In such cases others with rights to the property had to agree to a sale. Co-heirs were required to agree to any transfer of family property. Auctions of land from the Ptolemaic period show that such purchases were often accomplished by groups of persons. We do not know how such common interests were subsequently divided. In some gifts, the donor could specify that the land could only be subsequently sold to other family members. Women and children had limited authority over family assets but were generally understood to be able to earn and own in their own right; at Athens, for example, women and children were not allowed to conduct transactions worth more than a *medimnus* of barley.[127]

Common Property

Ostrom's general survey of private and common property makes the important distinction between open-access and common property rights, the latter being a dominant mode of ownership by household and other

---

122 For Egypt see Haug 2014. See also Chapter 8, this volume.
123 On laws about mines in Attica, see MacDowell 2006.
124 Some residual rights to certain kinds of property – what is underground (treasure trove, minerals, etc.), and certain monopoly items such as salt and liquor; and common property such as grazing grounds were retained by the king: *KAŚ* 4.1.52–53; MDh 8.35–40.
125 Olivelle 2013: 44.   126 See Harris 2016b: 144.
127 Isaeus 10.10. On women's property rights, see Schaps 1979 and van Bremen 1996.

groups.[128] Many types of property were co-owned in ancient Egypt; land, houses, priestly offices could all be shared through inheritance and between co-heirs. Such shares could be conveyed or leased. Group purchase of land through a public auction are known from the Ptolemaic period (e.g. P. Hausw. Manning 16, Edfu, 221/220 BCE). Pasture land was under stricter control by the state, but grazing rights could be sold.[129] Athenian law recognized both common property and public, city-owned property such as roads and marketplaces; pasture land was controlled by cities, but also by the demes and certain shrines.[130] Citizens, as well as foreigners, in ancient Athens were given access to graze their flocks – as individuals or as a collective.[131]

An Indian precept ordains that, in general, 'there shall be no taxes on what is obtained from rivers, thickets, forests, cremation places, and mountains' (VDh 19.26), although those who earn a living thereby may be subject to some levy. This appears to recognize a notion of the commons. Rulers had the option to set aside forested land for purposes of the state. Kauṭilya's Arthaśāstra (KAŚ 2.2.3–11) indicates that forests were an important resource of the Indian kingdoms. It calls for the establishment of forest preserves for various purposes: elephant preserves (hastivana); game preserves (mṛgavana); preserves for gathering forest produce (kupyavana) – all of which had economic and strategic value. Elephants, for example, were prized for military deployment. Kauṭilya also, however, recommends the creation of sanctuaries where wildlife was protected (abhayavana) – 'where all the animals are treated as guests' – no doubt as a merit-making act in accordance with the religious virtue of harmlessness (ahiṃsā). Special protections are prescribed to prevent harm to such animals, even when they stray into cultivated fields.[132] Forests could also be cleared by royal order to open up new land for agricultural exploitation.

Roman law recognized the air, the sea and the shore as not purely private; some jurists described them as public, others as *res communes*, common. Rivers were a problem: the riverbed was in private ownership, but the river itself was common. In reality, this meant that there was a free right of navigation.

Who Can Hold Property Rights?

As already noted, in Egypt and the ancient Near East large temples, formally an administrative part of the state, controlled portfolios of land and attached labour and were important in land administration, record-keeping and the

---

128 Ostrom 1990.   129 Monson 2012.   130 Harris 2020.   131 Bresson 2016a: 139.
132 KAŚ 2.26.1 and 3.10.30–31. See Olivelle 2016b.

like. Those in state service, including military, received land in exchange for this service. Women also held property rights and were frequently involved in the buying and selling of land.[133]

Over time, across the evidence from ancient India, more and more non-Brahmin – non-religious parties – appear in records of private property (donations, transfers, disputes, etc.). This is due partly to the increasing preservation of records of private land records, but it is also evident that an ever-wider range of social actors came to participate in transactions such as religious donations and had recourse, even in private property matters, to the use of legal mechanisms and legal instruments that had earlier been the preserve mainly of elites.[134] The exemptions associated with the earliest religious endowments (made by the Sātavāhana kings of western India, beginning with Gautamīputra Sātakarṇi, early second century CE) included stipulations that the property was not to be entered by royal officers, not to be interfered with by district officials, not to be dug for salt, etc. Other early grants mention, without enumerating, a set of 'eighteen types of exemption'; in later records, produced as far afield as Indonesia, these exemptions proliferate.[135] Some of these exemptions show up as stipulated privileges exacted from rulers by guilds or other parties, and recorded in charters recognizing their customary norms. Early examples are the long Charter of Viṣṇuṣeṇa charter of 592 CE (for a merchant group in western India) and the early eighth-century CE Anjaneri plates and the Porigere charter issued to the inhabitants of municipalities in western and southern India respectively.[136] These are rare surviving examples of a principle, invoked in Sanskrit legal treatises, whereby rulers should acknowledge the customary norms current among their subjects – even when these curtail certain prerogatives of rulers.[137]

Concepts: Ownership and Possessions

Characteristics of Property Rights

Legal redress for what we might term 'forcible dispossession', such as theft and trespass, is well documented in the Egyptian, Greek and Mesopotamian tradition.[138] The legal concept is implied in the Middle Kingdom (c. 2000 BCE) Egyptian story *The Tale of the Eloquent Peasant*.[139] In ancient Greece,

---

133 Manning 2003a: 218.   134 Lubin 2018b.   135 Lubin 2018a: 48–53.
136 For the Charter of Viṣṇuṣeṇa, see Wiese and Das 2019 and Lubin 2015.
137 Lubin 2015: 230–43. For the Anjaneri plates: Vishnu Mirashi 1955: 154–59.
138 On theft more generally see Chapter 9, this volume.   139 Shupak 1992.

moreover, degrees of seriousness of the crime were evaluated based, inter alia, on the value of the stolen property.[140] The right to exclude others from privately held property is clearly expressed in the boilerplate language of sale documents from Egypt:

> I have no right, no law suit, nothing at all with respect to you in their (plots of land) name from today onward. No one shall be able to exercise control over them except you. Anyone who shall come against you concerning (the plots) to take them from you, to take any part of (the plots) from you saying 'they are not yours', in my name, or in anyone else's name, I shall expel them from you concerning (the plots).
> (P. Hausw. Manning 8, sale of plots of land, Edfu, 240 BCE)

In a case when title to property was disputed, there was a legal procedure that stretched over three years to establish clear title (see discussion below).

Private property – principally land, houses and livestock – could be permanently conveyed by a number of different legal mechanisms (including sale); it could also be temporarily leased, pledged or exchanged. This is an early feature of the written evidence from Egypt, the Near East and China. By the seventh century BCE, Egypt developed private contracts of sale and lease, and so-called marriage contracts that were in fact written agreements by the husband to guarantee that any children from the marriage would inherit the man's property.[141] In Egypt women as well as men appear as parties to private sales of land. While there were earlier forms of contracts, and a different tradition was preserved in Thebes in southern Egypt in a script known as 'Abnormal Hieratic', the demotic Egyptian language tradition and script took over the more ancient script in the south by the sixth century BCE. Contract language became more elaborate, with more extensive boilerplate language, by the end of the fourth century BCE.[142] Egyptian contracts were always conceived as verbal agreements ('Party A has declared to Party B . . .'). There were two basic types of private contract for conveyance: the 'writing for money' and the 'cession'. Both contracts were used together for the real sale, one stating that the purchase price had been received. Unlike most Greek sales, the purchase price is not mentioned in Egyptian contracts.[143] The writing for money also noted the location of the property being sold with specific boundaries, a statement of clear title and a promise by the vendor that the property rights being sold would be defended by them on behalf of

---

140 Cohen 1984.   141 Lüddeckens 1960; Pestman 1961; Smith 1995; Martin 1995.
142 Keenan, Manning and Yiftach-Firanko 2014.
143 For some exceptions in Greek practice, concerned with regional variation at Amphipolis, see Hatzopoulos 1991.

the buyer. A list of (usually) sixteen names appears on the verso of the sale, witnesses to the agreement. Cession contracts were similar in form but stressed that the purchaser of the property had sole rights to the property. Again, the seller guaranteed to defend the property rights being conveyed, and the document contained the names of sixteen witnesses listed on the verso of the contract. Such Egyptian contracts persisted, at least in the Fayyum region where evidence is preserved, until the second century CE. Loan contracts and leases are also known – beginning in the seventh century BCE. The mortgage was developed by the third century BCE.

There is a debate about the contract of sale in Greek Law. Pringsheim believed that ownership passed only when the full price was paid.[144] This, however, appears to be contradicted by the existence of credit sales, in which ownership passed to the buyer, who still owed the seller part of the price (see SEG 33: 175), which may indicate that the buyer gained ownership when the object entered his physical possession. The contract of sale created both a warranty of title and a warranty against latent defects for the seller. If the buyer discovered a defect after the sale he could return the defective object and demand the return of the price paid.

India's Sanskrit legal treatises prescribe the making of deeds recording land ownership and transfers, though very few have survived from the classical or early medieval periods due to the fact that they were normally written on perishable material such as cloth or palm leaf, which could not survive the rigours of India's monsoon climate.

Modes of Acquisition

State grants, purchase and inheritance were the main forms of acquiring property in Egypt and the ancient Near East. The Ptolemies, in the third century BCE, introduced the public auction to Egypt – by which land, among other things, could be purchased. Legal title to property in Egypt was in the first instance documented and could be asserted by the possession of valid prior agreements relating to the property. Such texts relating to the property were required to be turned over to the new owner at the time of sale, as stated in this demotic Egyptian sale of land:

> To you belong their documents, their titles in any place in which they are. Every document that has been drawn up regarding them and every document that has been drawn up for me regarding them and (every) document

[144] Pringsheim 1950. See Chapter 11, this volume.

by virtue of which I am entitled in respect of them, they belong to you and the rights conferred by them. To you belongs that by virtue of which I am entitled in respect of them.[145]

In the first instance, it was the seller that had a duty to defend the title of the property being sold against all other claimants. Egyptian law developed a procedure to assert claim to real property that did not have clear title. Legal title to land could be acquired by a process that the Egyptians called 'making a public protest', whose root meaning is something like 'to make a valuation' or 'price'. This procedure for asserting claim to land by 'long possession' is well described in the so-called Hermopolis legal compendium (P. Mattha, 2/16 and passim) of the third century BCE. The party asserting the property claim was required to publicize their claim in three successive years.[146] In the absence of any claim that arose, the possession of the land ripened into legal ownership.

In ancient Athens, claims over property were asserted by a process called *diadikasia*, a type of jury trial to assert claims; a regular case (*dike*) could also be brought to make a property claim on property (*dike ousias*).[147] As noted above, women at Athens were restricted in conveying their property, as were male office-holders.[148]

In India, the male head of household – together with his wife, according to the older sources – normally had authority over family property: 'Sons who have a father – whose father and mother are still there – are without power (*anīśvarāḥ*)' (*KAŚ* 3.5.1). Hence a son could not alienate such property, although he could dispose of what he earned by his own industry (*svayamarjita*), unless it was earned using family property as capital (*KAŚ* 3.5.3). A husband could make use of his wife's *strīdhana*, but only in an emergency. A widow could have a claim to her husband's estate but only a life-interest, for her own maintenance.[149]

As already implied above, the most useful general analytic model for Chinese property is probably that represented by the co-existence of multiple rights to land – whether those of the state/ruler and the principal aristocratic lineages, or those of the lineages and their sub-lineages, or those of the state/ruler and the individual household. The model bears comparison with ancient Egyptian practice. In all cases the holder of the primary right is the senior male in the lineage, sub-lineage or household, but other members of the relevant group tend to have what may be termed secondary rights with respect to cultivation or

---

145 P. BM Andrews 28, Thebes, 208 BCE; see Keenan, Manning and Yiftach-Firanko 2014: 281.
146 Muhs 2002.   147 MacDowell 1978: 146.   148 MacDowell 1978: 134.
149 Lubin 2018b.

alienation. Different aspects of this model are relevant at different periods, but, given the sparse sources, we cannot be sure that the version of the model applicable to any particular period in itself provides a full picture of rights to land within society at that time.

The transfer of property in Roman law required a conveyance, not simply a contract. Sale or gift, therefore, did not transfer ownership until the requisite conveyance took place. *Res mancipi* (Italic land, slaves, cattle) required a *mancipatio*, an elaborate formality with witnesses, or *cessio in iure*, effectively a collusive lawsuit leading to a magistrate adjudging the property to the transferee. *Res nec mancipi* could be transferred by simple delivery with the requisite intention to transfer ownership. Over time, these forms were attenuated. Probably in the middle of the first century BCE, the praetors introduced a remedy to protect the person who had received a *res mancipi* by *traditio*, the *actio publiciana*, and a defence to a proprietary claim by the transferor, who remained the true owner as a matter of civil law. Such a person did not have the rights of an owner – he could not free a slave, for example – but by the time of Justinian Byzantine lawyers writing in Greek saw this as a form of ownership: *despotikos bonitarios*. Modern commentators refer to it as 'bonitary ownership'. In practice, it meant that for most purposes the cumbersome *mancipatio* was unnecessary. *Traditio* too was attenuated. Where property was too heavy to pick up and hand over, the transferor might indicate to the transferee with words of transfer, and analogously the boundaries of land could be pointed out from a hill or high tower; where the transferee had control of the property already, as a borrower, *traditio* could be effected by simple words of transfer. From around the third century CE, the reverse of this might be effective, the transferor by appropriate language changing his own status from owner to borrower; handing over the keys to a warehouse was sufficient to transfer the intended property in the warehouse, and in later law handing over a document representing land served to transfer the land itself.

Roman ownership could be created by long possession, *usucapio*, provided certain other conditions were satisfied. The requisite period was two years for land, one year for moveables – perhaps already by the Twelve Tables. This was increased by Justinian to three years for moveables and ten or twenty years for land (adopting the *longi temporis praescriptio* applicable to provincial land). Ownership of property which had no owner, such as wild animals, could be obtained by a simple taking, though what constituted taking might be controversial. In the same way land which had no owner, such as an island springing up in the sea, would fall into the ownership of the first occupier.

Turning, finally, to inheritance as a mode of acquisition, we can begin by noting that property rights and inheritance rights were deeply connected across the ancient world. Egypt had a partible inheritance system; all children generally had an expectation to inherit a share of property from both parents.[150] It was legally permissible, however, for the testator to determine the shares and, in some cases, to assign all property to one child.[151] The eldest son had special responsibility, including the management of family property after the death of his parents and their burial and received an extra share (Hermopolis legal compendium, P. Mattha 8, 30). Pro forma wills were not commonly used. The standard means of inter-generational conveyance was a 'bequests by sale' used during the lifetime of the testator.[152] Disputes when children of several marriages were involved must have been common.[153] In the case of childlessness, the property went to brothers and sisters.[154] In theory, the eldest son received an extra share because of his responsibility of burying his parents.

The inheritance system in the ancient Near East, like Egypt, was a partible inheritance system; sons divided the family estate equally with the eldest son receiving a double share.[155] There was a preference for keeping family land undivided. In the case of children from two marriages, as in Egypt (e.g. the Asyut dispute) the estate was divided two-thirds for the children of the first marriage to one-third for the children of the second. Like Egypt, the testaments were used only in exceptional cases in the ancient Near East.

Our knowledge of inheritance law in ancient India derives only from scholastic works; no documentary evidence survives. There appears to have been no testamentary law or use of wills. In the view of the Brahmin theorists, inheritance was closely aligned with the *sapiṇḍa* relation. Indian funerary and ancestor rites required the senior male of a household to offer food (*piṇḍa*) to three generations of direct ascendents, to ensure their welfare in the afterlife – and the same responsibility was inherited by sons, along with the father's property (and debts).[156] Thus the property was in a sense inherited so as to subserve this ritual obligation.

The classical *Dharma* codes recognize three ways of dividing an estate: in equal parts (*GDh* 28.1; *BDh* 2.3.3; *MDh* 9.104; and *YDh* 2.117); by right of

---

150 Pestman 1969: 1987. A broad treatment of Egyptian inheritance law is provided by Versteeg 2002: 137–49 and Lippert 2008: 15–18 and 119–27.
151 Pestman 1969: 67–68.   152 Pestman 1969: 63–66; Clarysse 2014: 202.
153 Pestman 1969, and the Asyut dispute discussed herein.
154 Pestman 1969: 68, with the Hermopolis legal compendium (P. Mattha) 9, 1–9.
155 Oelsner, Wells and Wunsch 2003: 939.   156 Rocher 1992.

primogeniture, whereby the eldest son inherits the whole estate and his siblings live as dependents, as they all did under their father while he lived (GDh 28.3; MDh 9.105); or by unequal shares, with the eldest son receiving a larger or better share, and younger sons receiving progressively less (GDh 28.5–28.7, 9, 11–17; BDh 2.3.4, 6; MDh 9.112, 114; NSm 13.13; ViDh 18.37). The sons of a deceased son would divide (*per stirpes*) the share that would have been their father's. A head of household might, if he wished (YDh 2.114), divide his estate between heirs while he still lived, provided that his wives were no longer capable of bearing further children. In later times, there was much discussion among the commentators about whether sons themselves could initiate such a succession.

The Indian scholastic literature was quite unsettled on the question of inheritance by ascendants and collaterals. The property of a man without offspring might go to his father or to his brothers (MDh 9.185; YDh 2.135), or to his mother or maternal grandmother (MDh 9.217). Viṣṇu Dharmaśāstra (17.4–9; cf. YDh 2.135) gives precedence to wife and daughters, followed by father, mother, brothers and brothers' sons. Brothers inherit according to complex rules depending on the caste status of their mothers (if different) and whether they have divided family property or remain 'undivided'. In the absence of *sapiṇḍas*, a broader net is cast that can assign rights to less close relatives, classed as *sakulya* (MDh 9.187) or *bandhu* (ViDh 17.10–17.11). After all blood relations come 'spiritual' relations such as teacher (*ācārya*), fellow students (*sabrahmacārin*) or pupils (ĀpDh 2.14.3; VDh 17.82; BDh 1.11.13; MDh 9.187; ViDh 17.12).

Although it is sometimes asserted in the ancient texts that 'wives shall not own property; whatever they acquire becomes the property of the man to whom they belong' (MDh 8.416), this seems not to have been more than toothless rhetoric. When actually addressing pragmatic questions related to property, these same works often acknowledge that women could own property (called *strīdhana*, 'woman's wealth'), and that such property could be inherited. This could include gifts that she receives during the marriage rites, subsequent gifts from her husband or natal family and assets acquired as inheritance.

In spite of a Vedic maxim asserting that women do not receive inheritance (*Taittirīya-Saṃhitā* 6.5.8.2, quoted in BDh 2.3.46), other Dharmaśāstras affirm that, in the absence of male issue, a wife has the best claim to her husband's assets (BṛSm 26.92–94), followed by his daughters, his father and his mother, in order (ViDh 17.4–7), or even daughters before wife (NSm 13.47). Yājñavalkya proposes that just as sons divide their father's property, daughters divide their mother's (YDh 2.145; ViDh 17.19–20; cf. MDh 9.195–196). Authorities diverge on the disposition of a woman's own property. Gautama, an early voice, has it go to unmarried or indigent daughters (*GDh* 28.24; *YDh* 2.117 makes it a general principle). Manu rather gives brothers and sisters equal shares of their mother's property (*MDh* 9.192). If a woman dies without daughters, some authorities make her husband (if the marriage was of a pure sort) or her father (if not) the next to inherit. Even if she does not inherit from her husband, a widow should receive support from his property so long as she lives. Disabilities – whether physical (blindness, incurable diseases), mental (insanity), or social (excommunication from caste) – are an impediment both to inheritance and to its ritual corollary: the performance of ancestor offerings.[157]

Most of our information on the inheritance of property in early China comes from the Han and Tang dynasties. Inheritable property comprised land (except that excluded from inheritance under the terms of its allocation), slaves, cattle and valuables in general. Such property might pass either under rules of intestacy or by will. In both cases the beneficiaries were normally family members or relatives.

With respect to intestate succession under the Han, such property as had not already been divided between children in the lifetime of the parents passed on the death of the head of the household to the person designated in the statutes as successor. The laws of 186 BCE provided that even the widow or a daughter might succeed as head of the household, for a case in which the deceased had no natural successor (son).[158] The new head acquired responsibility for the management of the family property and controlled the way in which it was distributed among members of the household. The position in Tang law was less flexible. The order of succession started with the eldest son of the wife and then took in other male members of the family, but not females. Furthermore, no distribution of family property was permitted in the lifetime of the father or other head of household (practice, of course, may well have been different). On his death, it was to be divided equally between sons (daughters on marriage had already received their portion as dowry). Should there be no sons or other male descendants, the property might pass to daughters.

With respect to testate succession, the Han laws of 186 BCE laid down the rules for the making of a valid will for the disposition of land, houses, slaves and other property. There was general freedom to make a will, but the

---

157 Rocher 2017.
158 For intestate and testate succession in the Han period, see Barbieri-Low and Yates 2015.

testator's intention had to be recorded in writing and stated in the presence of a local official. Although no restriction was placed in the statute on the class of beneficiary, it is probable that wills were used primarily to distribute property among family members. A will of 5 CE made by a female head of household shows the possibilities available to a testator.[159] It noted that two sons had already received fields, that two daughters, being poor, had been given fields, but that one son, who had left home at the age of fifteen, had been sentenced to penal servitude and was now left with nothing. Accordingly, the fields originally given to the daughters, but now returned by them, were to be given to this son on condition that they should not be sold to anyone else. The freedom of testamentary power bestowed by the Han law was severely circumscribed in Tang law. The latter contemplates the making of a will only where a household has no heirs (although examples of surviving wills show that this was not always followed in practice). Extant wills either confirm the distribution of property prescribed by the law (equal division between sons) or, where there were no sons, made bequests to other relatives, including females, or even monasteries.

Most of the evidence about inheritance in ancient Greece comes from three communities: classical Athens, Sparta and Gortyn. At Athens, there were four main principles behind the laws about inheritance: universal succession, partible inheritance, the priority of descendants over collaterals and the preference given to males over females.[160] Wives did not inherit the property of their husbands but could receive gifts in a will, such as a dowry for remarriage. In universal succession (as in Roman law), the person who inherits (*kleronomos*) takes over all the rights and duties of the deceased. This meant that he not only has the right to the property of the deceased, but the obligation to pay all debts even if they exceed the value of the assets. The Athenians did not invent the expedient of the *heres necessarius* for a *damnosa hereditas* (insolvent estate) – see the discussion on Roman law below. The heir was required to carry out the funeral and perform commemorative ceremonies at the tomb. The heir was also responsible for paying any gifts specified in the will and thus combined the modern roles of heir and executor. On the other hand, we do not know how beneficiaries could enforce the provisions of a will if the heir did not carry them out. The order of succession was sons, daughters, grandsons, granddaughters, brothers and children of brothers, sisters and children of sisters, and finally cousins. The most remote relatives entitled to inherit were 'sons of cousins' (Isaeus 11.1–2; Dem. 43.5)

---

159 Hinsch 1998.   160 Vérilhac and Vial 1998.

though there was some dispute about whether this meant second cousins or cousins once removed. If there were several relatives in the same degree, each inherited an equal share (partible inheritance) though an elder son might have first choice when assets were divided. If a woman inherited, she became an *epikleros*. If she was married or unmarried, the nearest male relative could claim her in marriage (even if this meant that she divorced her husband). If a man did not have legitimate male children, he could either adopt an heir during this lifetime and introduce him to his phratry or appoint an heir in his will. If his children were under age when their father died, he could appoint an *epitropos* (guardian) to manage the estate until they became adults and could have the estate leased in return for rent and adequate security (*apotimema*).[161] Normally the heir asserted his claim by entering into the property and performing the rites of burial, but if there were several claimants, a decision would be made through the procedure of *diadikasia*. The rules at Sparta and at Gortyn were basically similar with one major exception: if there were both sons and daughters, the daughters inherited a share equal to half of that of her brothers.[162]

From as early as the Twelve Tables, Roman law recognized both intestate and testate succession – but it is likely that intestate represents the older strand. This was by far and away the most complicated part of the law, forming much the largest part of the law of things in Gaius' *Institutes*. The original structure of intestate succession is still visible during the Roman empire, though by then it had undergone some changes and been heavily supplemented by praetorian innovations. Of central importance was that, in any family, property was held by the eldest surviving male ancestor: the *paterfamilias*. It followed that issues of transmission of property on death would only arise in the case of a *paterfamilias*. It followed, too, that there could be no question of inheritance by a father or other male ancestor, since by definition none could exist (though the father of an emancipated son was an exception to this). If the deceased *paterfamilias* had (unemancipated) children (described as *sui heredes*), they would come out of paternal power as a result of his death and would jointly inherit his property and obligations, in particular the religious obligation to continue the family cult. Their inheritance would constitute a form of undivided ownership, *ercto no cito*, until steps were taken to divide it up by an *actio familiae erciscundae*. A woman could have no children through the male line, and so could have no *sui heredes*. In the absence of *sui heredes*, the inheritance passed to the nearest

---

161 See Harris 2006a: 207–40.   162 Bresson 2016b.

relative through the female line: the *proximus agnatus*. Collateral ascendants as well as descendants could inherit, and at first there seems to have been no rule excluding women, but in the late Republic or early Empire the rule had shifted so that the only women who could inherit were the sisters of the deceased. Failing even agnates, early law passed the inheritance to the gens; such gentile succession survived until the first century BCE but disappeared in the course of that century. Praetorian intervention, probably originating in the late Republic, expanded the range of family members who might inherit – it was probably this that finally ended gentile succession – so that emancipated children ranked alongside the unemancipated *sui heredes*, for example. This created a degree of conflict between the heirs under the civil law and the heirs under praetorian rules. In principle the civil law heir(s) prevailed, but the praetorian law heir(s) could gain the inheritance unless and until the civil law heir(s) brought an action to displace them.

Testate succession was already in place by the Twelve Tables. In early law the will might be made before the *comitia calata*, a Republican representative assembly presided over by a pontiff; and a will of a soldier on campaign might be made formally before other soldiers. These were obsolete by the end of the Republic. Another early form, which survived through the Empire was the mancipatory will. This may originally have been a straightforward transfer to the designated heir during the lifetime of the deceased – and so hardly a form of inheritance at all – but it later took the form of a transfer of a document, with attendant formalities, which would automatically take effect on the transferor's death. These forms were cumbersome, and by the start of the Empire the praetors had come to give force to a written will with seven witnesses. However, until the middle of the second century CE such an 'informal' will could be defeated by the heir(s) entitled on intestacy, the will not being valid at civil law. By the time of Justinian, this was given recognition as the principal valid form of will, provided it had been signed by the testator, though alongside this, other forms had also been recognized. The main function of the will was to appoint an heir; however, since the designated heir might not accept, it was common to name substitutes, finishing with someone who could not refuse. This was typically a slave of the deceased who was freed by the will and named heir; detailed rules allowed a technical separation to be made between the assets of the heir and the assets of the inheritance, designed to deal with problems of insolvency either of the testator or of the heir.

Roman law placed restrictions on who might be an heir, but these restrictions could be avoided by the use of *fideicommissa*: instructions to the designated heir to transfer the inheritance to another person. At first these instructions were binding in honour only, hence their name, but from the start of the Empire they could be enforced.[163] As well as dealing with the inheritance itself, a Roman will might contain legacies of different forms. A number of statutes in the second half of the Republic, culminating in the *lex Falcidia* of 40 BCE, placed restrictions on the size of legacies; the final form was that at least one-quarter of the net value of the estate had to remain with the heir. *Fideicommissa* could be used to avoid some restrictions on legacies, but in time the rules of *fideicommissa* and the rules of legacies fell into line with each other.

Restrictions on Property Rights ('Servitudes')

The right to an 'ancient light' – an easement and, apparently, a feature of demotic Egyptian law, but also documented much earlier as well – was concerned with a prior structure with a window that a neighbour could not block and is mentioned in a demotic building contract dated 290 BCE from Thebes.[164] Provisions in the so-called legal compendium of Hermopolis (P. Mattha), a third-century BCE text but with some sections that originally date earlier, concerned duties to avoid causing water to drain onto a neighbour's plot or building too close to a property line. The Hermopolis legal compendium from Egypt also recognizes the right of access to private land via a 'royal road'. Some later contracts from Egypt similarly provide a clause of 'entrance and exit' to property – common exits to property are also mentioned.[165] By the beginning of the Common Era in India, we find comparable textual provisions for eminent domain and setback requirements: 'Land must be surrendered for the road in a field through which a road runs, as also space for turning [a cart]. Between newly built houses and highways one should allow a passage three feet wide.'[166]

Right of way, on land and over water, was well known in Greek and Roman law. Already at the time of the Twelve Tables, Roman law recognized rights of way over another's land and the right to channel water (*aquaeductus*). Justinian's *Digest* shows various types of these rights, each with its own detailed rules, no doubt reflecting differences in agricultural

---

163 On the development of *fideicommissa* (trusts) in Roman law, see Johnston 1988.
164 P. BM Glanville 10524 = Glanville 1939: 19–27. Cf. VerSteeg 2002: 111.
165 E.g. P. Mich. 5 520 (18 CE, Fayyum), a demotic Egyptian contract with Greek subscription for the partial sale of a vacant plot. See Allam 2011.
166 *VDh* 16.11–12; Lubin 2018b.

practice; these were known as rustic praedial servitudes. There were also urban praedial servitudes, such as the right to build higher or the right to prevent a neighbour building higher. These would come about by the agreement of the parties, and they continued to apply if either plot of land was sold; they complemented, and existed against the background of, municipal regulations limiting the height of buildings.

Disputes over Property: Some Illustrative Cases

With respect to evidence from ancient India, Kauṭilya provides the oldest sustained account of property rights – including obligations towards neighbours (KAŚ 3.8–10). His list of limitations on property rights – setbacks on houses, water-channels, sheds, stables, fireplaces and the like – gives an indication of specific areas over which disputes concerning property might arise. Kauṭilya details fines for damage to neighbouring property, in addition to negligent waste caused by those who lease property or hold it as pledge. Indian jurisprudence also attempted to mitigate property disputes before they arose by requiring that sales of land were to be made 'in the presence of the community' more specifically, before witnesses such as local elders and neighbouring property owners (MDh 8.201). Kauṭilya even provides a formula for ranking potential buyers, with relatives having priority, followed by neighbours, creditors, then outsiders. All boundaries had to be clearly described and marked; if markers were subsequently lost or destroyed, the king could define new ones (KAŚ 3.9.14).

Disputes, when they inevitably arose, were to be settled in the presence of neighbouring property owners or municipal council members. Written documents (likhita, āgama), witnesses (sākṣin) or possession (bhukti, bhoga, lit. 'enjoyment') were the criteria accepted as proof of prior ownership (dhana-svīkaraṇam pūrvam, VDh 16.10; cf. NSm 1.65), with a general preference for documentation (or at least witnesses) over mere possession (as in MDh 8.200). As noted in Chapter 7 in this volume, across the Indian legal literature we can detect a shift over time towards favouring documents over witnesses in resolving disputes. Possession, however, did carry weight, and in the case of inherited property for which there was no deed of title it could be sufficient proof of ownership (NSm 1.77–78). There was even a principle of adverse possession giving rise to legal ownership: 'When an owner looks on silently as something is being enjoyed by others in his presence for ten years, he is not entitled to recover it' (MDh 8.147–9). This, of course, did not apply in cases in which the original owner was unable to assert his right – for example, on

Disputes over Property: Some Illustrative Cases

account of being a minor, or incapacitated – or when the rival claimant was holding the property by virtue of a contractual or goodwill arrangement.[167] If a case arose where neither party to a dispute could show clear title (or other proof of ownership), it could be forfeit to the king or apportioned at his discretion.[168]

Egyptian trial records of family disputes over landownership, dating to the middle of the second century BCE, provide an even greater wealth of detail concerning the interaction of the state and local legal institutions.[169] We shall conclude this section by focusing on the trial record of just one of these disputes, from Asyut (Middle Egypt). Three aspects of this dispute are important in understanding the relationship between the Ptolemaic bureaucracy and local law and how Egyptian law adjudicated 'divided interest' claims: first, the local dispute over control of family land, and the subsequent complaint brought by the wife of one of the parties to the dispute, was initiated as a petition written in Egyptian (presumably at some later stage translated into Greek) and addressed to Ptolemaic officials, and both the *epistates* and the *stratêgos* were involved; second, the dispute was eventually turned over by these Greek officials to the local Egyptian court to find the facts and adjudicate the dispute – this local court had an official representative of the state the *eisagogeus*, present; finally, the proceedings of the trial and the decision of the judges were recorded in full. The surviving text is in fact a copy of the trial proceeding, as is stated in the first line.[170] That implies that more than one copy was written. It documents both parties' oral responses to their written pleadings to Ptolemaic officials and marked, in theory, the resolution of the family dispute. As we shall see below, that dispute went back to a division of family property by a dying man to his two sons by different wives: the plaintiff was the wife of the oldest son, and the defendant was the younger son. The fact that we have before us a complete record of a trial proceeding and the decision of the judges with their legal reasoning

---

167 For a theoretical treatment of the issue, see Arruñada 2012.
168 *MDh* 3.9.17–18; cf. Medhātithi with reference to the *MDh* 8.265 on the ideal of fairness and utility in such decisions.
169 A new study by Baetens and Depauw 2015 offers good analysis and some differences from my own interpretation. The Erbstreit archive dating to the second century BCE from Pathyris (Upper Egypt) offers comparably rich material for a legal dispute, and a series of trials, over inherited land. See Vandorpe and Waebens 2009: 114–22.
170 P. BM 10591 (recto), trial between Cratianch and Tefhape, Siut (Asyut), 170 BCE. It is not certain why we have a copy of the trial proceeding. Was it issued to the winning party or to an advocate at their request? Some third-century BCE Greek proceedings of trials from Krokodilopolis (Fayyum) were recorded in two copies; see Modrzejewski 2011:123, n. 39.

behind their judgment is important enough.[171] I will not be able to resolve here whether such bureaucratic reporting of a trial is a new feature of the Ptolemaic bureaucracy, or a continuation from earlier times.

The trial itself – the second occasion when an attempt at a legal resolution was made – took place at Asyut, before the priest-judges of the temple of Wepwawet, the local *laokritai* court as it was called in the Ptolemaic administration – under whose authority the final resolution (in theory) of the dispute fell. The parties to the suit were associated with the temple, and the land in dispute was located within the temple estate. Despite the written petitions to Ptolemaic officials to have the dispute resolved by them, the case was turned over to the local temple to decide. The trial occurred in June 170 BCE, some sixteen years after the Ptolemies put down the most serious revolt against their rule in Egypt: the revolt in the Thebaid, 205–186 BCE, and just months before the first invasion of Egypt by Antiochus IV.[172] In the aftermath of the great Theban revolt, the Ptolemaic bureaucratic system appears to have gained an even tighter control of the region. It was a period when many scholars have thought that the Ptolemaic state was in full decline, economically, culturally and otherwise. And there is much to show that in terms of international politics this was the case. And yet this trial, as we shall demonstrate in the following discussion, implies something else important about state institutions.[173]

The trial presumably took place in front of the main temple gate, the traditional location of trials in Egyptian law. The court was composed of three priests and an 'introducer' (*eisagogeus*): a Ptolemaic official who introduced the case before the judges and acted as an official representative of the state.[174] The two parties appeared before the court, and the plaintiff, Chratianch, began with her main claim that all the land belongs to her and, through her, to her children. To support this claim, she cited a passage from what is termed the 'law of year 21' concerning the rights of children of a first marriage to inherit. The plaintiff also claimed that her husband was forced to cede one-third of the land. Tefhape, the defendant, then responded, at length,

---

[171] For earlier records of trials, see Modrzejewski 2011: 123–28.   [172] Veïsse 2004.
[173] On Egypt in this period of supposed decline, see Gorre and Wackenier 2020.
[174] The official has a Greek name, but by no means is it clear in the second-century BCE context that this official was ethnically Greek. The Greek word for the institution tells, us, however, that the person is functioning within the Ptolemaic state system in an official capacity. Whether this function has an ancient precedent in Egypt is debatable; to be sure, however, the role of the *eisagogeus* in Greek law was to introduce into court particular cases having to do with marketplace transactions, and it could also adjudicate cases involving small amounts of money themselves. See Bresson 2016a: 247–48.

denying the claims and producing documents proving his claim. The plaintiff then responded, and there was a second response by the defendant. The document records that the pleadings were then read out by a scribe in front of the parties. The judges asked each party if they agreed to what they have said. Then documents were produced that supported each party's claims. The judges summarized the main legal points of each argument, and quoted the 'law of year 21', the same law cited by the plaintiff. Importantly, however, the judges cited a fuller version of the law, observing that the children of a first marriage have priority to the father's property *unless they have agreed to assigning shares to other siblings*. And that was what happened in this case. Chratianch's husband had agreed to the cession of one-third of the land to his half-brother and she had, we learn, also agreed.[175] The judges found for the defendant on this basis, and affirmed their decision with their signatures at the end of the document, along with the signature of the scribe of the judges, perhaps the author of the document itself. In sum, the response of the Ptolemaic officials; the orderliness of the trial itself; the precise citation of the controlling law; and the introduction of supporting documentation of ownership show a well-functioning bureaucratic system: petitions written in the Egyptian language were heard before Greek-speaking officials and provide evidence for some new developments in Egyptian legal institutions. Crucially, the trial also demonstrates that the Ptolemies protected private claims to land.

Conclusion

The idea of property is an ancient one. The written evidence for the private ownership and the conveyance of various kinds of property, including slaves, is among the earliest documentation from the ancient Near East. Basic contract types (sale, loan, pledge and so on) from the ancient world will be familiar to modern legal scholars. The institution of slavery, in contrast, stands out as something shocking to modern sensibilities and certainly outside the boundaries of modern property systems (at least in theory). Yet, while we cannot draw a single line of development from Sumerian to Roman and Indian law, the richness and the creativity of premodern property systems – the literate classes who created juristic categories and wrote contracts, for example, in addition to the systemized legal rules that appear in the Hermopolis legal compendium from Egypt and the later Roman legal

---

175 Pestman 1961: 135.

codes – are things that are deeply engrained in modern legal systems. Yet the extensive boilerplate language of a demotic Egyptian land sale or the resolution of the property dispute from Asyut make for good reading not because these documents appear 'modern' to our eyes, but the reverse. These are merely two examples among many one could select to show us that modern property law has a very deep history, and this historical experience can still inform how we can better solve contemporary issues around property rights.

The societies treated here were all fundamentally agrarian, although the growth of cities during the first millennium BCE surely brought significant changes. It is not surprising that land, slaves, houses and animals were the subject of much of the ancient documentation. Formal distinctions between possession and ownership existed, and this was an important development in premodern economies. 'New Institutional Economics' suggests that the ability to lend and borrow assets and to defend private property interests underpin economic performance, that is, real growth, and provide the necessary incentives for the use of resources.[176] The logical conclusion is that we should observe real growth in the ancient world. Indeed, some cases – Greece, that is Athens in particular, and the early Roman empire being the most developed cases at the moment – provide concrete evidence of some real growth from 800–300 BCE on the basis of property registration and more equal distribution of wealth among citizens.[177] Elsewhere, given the nature of the evidence, including our lack of precise demographic figures, it is harder to demonstrate real growth. It may well be there, but we should keep in mind that even during the height of the Roman empire, real growth was limited by modern standards.[178] Here again it is worth remembering that we are dealing with substantially different environments (and different drivers of climate change) in Italy, Greece, Egypt, Mesopotamia, India and China. Climate variability and disease are additional factors in the economic performance of premodern societies that should be taken into account in future work.[179]

---

176 Alston and Mueller 2008.   177 Harris 2016b; Bresson 2016a: 199–222.
178 Saller 2005; Manning 2018: 216–27.   179 Harper 2021.

11

Commerce and Contracts

Lead Author: DAVID IBBETSON

Contributors: ERNEST CALDWELL, EDWARD HARRIS,
GEOFFREY MACCORMACK, JOSEPH G. MANNING
AND PATRICK OLIVELLE

Introduction

In developed Roman law, personal obligations were divided into obligations *dare*, obligations to transfer, and obligations *facere*, obligations to make or do something. This division reflects the main forms of economic activity: transferring property, be it land or moveable property, by gift, exchange or sale; and performing some service, for example through employment or manufacture. It is very likely that these forms of economic activity would have existed, in at least a rudimentary form, from an early period, though without leaving any trace in the archaeological record. The need for seasonal labour in agriculture surely caused a shift away from a purely domestic workforce. Remnants of what might have been an ownership inscription on a potsherd will in themselves tell us nothing about how the putative owner became owner, nor will the existence of a manufactured pot tell us very much about the economics of how the pot was created.

Urbanisation in southern Mesopotamia in the fourth millennium BCE brought about a measure of social stratification and in its wake the possibility of greater organization of the means of production. Engraved stones from Uruk show groups of (female) workers engaged in textile production; mass-produced pottery similarly points to economic organization.[1] A tablet from Ur in the third millennium gives wage rates for a substantial force of agricultural labourers, probably employed by a temple, pointing beyond doubt to the operation of wage labour by this time.[2] Wage labour is similarly evidenced in Old Kingdom Egypt: a surviving document testifies to an understanding between a tomb builder and his workers that they will receive payment in kind for their labour.[3] At the

1 Parker 2012: 19.   2 Quoted by Postgate 1994: 227.   3 Jasnow 2003a: 129, 130.

start of the second millennium BCE, the Laws of Lipit-Ishtar specify the rate for hiring oxen as well as penalties for various injuries to a hired ox, and the penalty where a hired boat is destroyed when the hirer deviates from the agreed route;[4] and around 1800 BCE the so-called Laws about Rented Oxen from Nippur presumably show that renting was a common practice.[5]

While localized trade will leave little trace, archaeological evidence of commodities at a distance from their source may indicate that long-distance trade was taking place. Perhaps the earliest evidence suggestive of trade dates from the Upper Palaeolithic (c. 12,000 BCE) in southeastern Poland, where flints are found over 100 miles from their source.[6] In the eleventh millennium BCE, obsidian from the island of Melos was finding its way into southern Greece, some 80 miles away by sea, though we cannot tell whether the users had voyaged to obtain it or the islanders had carried it to Greece. By the eighth millennium obsidian from Turkey was being carried over 500 miles from its source, and by the sixth millennium obsidian from Sardinia was making its way around the western Mediterranean.[7] The importance of obsidian in the making of stone tools raises the supposition that it was being deliberately traded and was not simply the object of multiple gift exchanges cementing relationships between groups of people. In the same way, the geographical spread of pottery of defined types over considerable distances in the ancient Near East points to the existence of trade, or at the very least cultural contact, by the seventh millennium. By the time we find law codes, from the end of the third millennium BCE, international trade is routinely recognized: the prologue to the Laws of Ur-Namma refers to ship masters having control of maritime trade.[8]

The existence of trade does not in itself point to the existence of merchants as intermediaries between producer and consumer. Merchants are referred to in the Laws of Eshnunna;[9] very slightly later the Laws of Hammurabi provide for compensation for a merchant who redeems a captive and helps him to return home, deals with loans by and pledges to merchants, and recognizes factors acting on behalf of merchants.[10] From about the same time, there is evidence of merchants in Egypt[11] and in the Hittite Laws.[12]

---

4 Laws of Lipit-Ishtar, par. a (Roth 1997: 26), pars. 34–37 (Roth 1997: 33), par. 5 (Roth 1997: 27).
5 Roth 1997: 40.   6 Wisniewski Crahcarz and Standzikowski 2020.
7 Parker 2012: 16.   8 Roth 1997: 15.
9 Laws of Eshnunna par. 15 (Roth 1997: 61): A merchant or a woman innkeeper will not accept silver, grain, wool, oil or anything else from a male or female slave.
10 Laws of Hammurabi par. 32 (Roth 1997: 87), 49–52 (Roth 1997: 90–91), 100–107 (Roth 1997: 99–101).
11 Jasnow 2003a: 129.   12 Hittite Laws, 5 (Hoffner 1997: 19).

Introduction

Other long-distance trade routes developed around the Mediterranean: inland from Egypt along the Nile into Africa; and by sea in the first millennium BCE from Phoenicia (modern Lebanon) in the east through the whole Mediterranean and down the coast of West Africa as far as modern-day Mauritania. Perhaps as early as the fifth millennium BCE, jade was being taken from Khotan in central Asia eastward into China;[13] by the fourth century BCE, there is evidence of goods from the Mediterranean reaching Gansu in China,[14] and by the end of the Roman Republic Chinese silk was reaching Rome.[15] Such long-distance trade cannot have been the result of direct contacts but depended on intermediate markets, revealing sophisticated commercial networks between East Asia and Europe.

The other type of transaction of which we have early evidence is the sale of land. Such sales are attested from the middle of the third millennium BCE from Egypt and Mesopotamia by documents inscribed on stone.[16] Even in India, from which we have little epigraphical evidence, stones memorialize sales of land, though direct evidence of land sales is sparse.[17] It is easy to see why transactions of this sort should leave evidence: the transfer of land would be expected to alter the identity of its holder in perpetuity, long after the memories of witnesses had been lost. For the same reason, it may be supposed, a substantial number of sealed land grants (if not strictly sales) have survived from the Hittite kingdom in the middle of the second millennium BCE,[18] as well as boundary markers recording security transactions, *horoi*, from Greece in the fourth century BCE.[19]

The evidence of transactions' existence does not entail that there were structures to give these transactions legal effect. Trade might take the form of immediate exchanges, or gifts in the expectation of a counter-gift at some unspecified time; it may be that it was through such mutual gifts aiming to cement diplomatic relations that elite goods passed from place to place in the ancient Near East. But such a model of exchange would not easily underpin employment relationships, for example, and the Egyptian document referred to above may suggest that the workers were simply trusting their employers. In time, though, mechanisms developed whose function was to ensure that another person acts in a particular way, or refrains from acting, in the future. We may refer to these generically as 'contracts'.

---

13 Wood 2002: 26.   14 Sun 2009: 7.   15 Hildebrandt 2017: 1.
16 Jasnow 2003a: 128; Wilcke 2003: 166.   17 Lubin 2018b: 832.   18 Easton 1981: 3.
19 Harris 2006, 2013.

Terminology: A Caveat

It is important to note in passing from the start that there is considerable terminological instability in the common English translations of the original terms. We read, for example, that the Chinese *yüeh*, which is commonly translated as 'contract', 'does not merely mean "promise" or "agreement", but "covenant"',[20] without any explanation being given of what the author means by the English terms. In the same way, the Hebrew *berith* is invariably translated as 'covenant', treated as an equivalent of the Latin *foedus* found in the Vulgate,[21] whereas it is in truth only an approximation of this. In the classical Indian texts, what we would treat as contracts fall under the heading *vyavahara*, commonly translated as 'transactions', where they are placed alongside the wrongs of theft and assault; and the subgroup 'cononventions' refers to the rules governing heretics, corporate bodies and the like (*NSm* 10.1 and *KAŚ* 3.62). It is best to avoid excessively sophisticated nuance, though at the same time we need to bear in mind that there will inevitably be nuanced differences between, and possibly also within, the different systems.

Philologically, a number of the nouns used to refer to what we treat as contracts have roots which relate to the idea of binding, harnessing or tying. This is the case with the Akkadian *riksu*, used in all periods for 'contract', the Hittite *ishiul*, the Hebrew *berith*,[22] the Egyptian *'rq* (for oath-swearing)[23] and the Chinese *yüeh*.[24] The early Roman *nexum* fits the same pattern, related to the verb *nectere*, essentially a voluntary transaction under which one person came into the servitude of another;[25] and from around the first century BCE the general noun *obligatio*, cognate with the verb *ligare* meaning tie, had a particular affinity with contracts.[26] The idea is given concrete representation in Livy's description of the events of 321 BCE, when two Roman generals, Postumius and Venturius, were led off naked and bound after they had made an oath to the Samnites which the Roman Senate had refused to ratify (Liv. 9.10.6). These may give us some pointers to the origins of the general word in some languages, and the connotation of binding may still have been present in later usage, as where

---

20 Hulsewé 1978b: 12; MacCormack 2014: 1, 7–11, 13–15.   21 For example, Deut 29.1.
22 Botterwick and Ringgren 1977: 253–79.   23 Wilson 1948: 129, 130.
24 Hulsewé 1978b: 12.
25 Ernout and Meillet 1994: 435; Jolowicz and Nicholas 1972: 164–66. The precise nature of the institution is controversial.
26 For example, Justinian, *Digest* 2.14.1.3, where *obligatio* appears as a synonym for *contractus*.

Justinian's *Institutes* 3.13 pr. define *obligatio* as a *vinculum iuris*. The binding here is metaphorical, though the Romans' institution of *nexum* might once have involved a physical binding in chains.

The Sanskrit *rna* may point towards a rather different thinking in classical Indian law. Traditionally, the first of the titles of law was the non-payment of debt, whose non-legal focus was on the congenital duties owed by the brahmin: of Vedic study, of sacrifice to the gods and of the fathering of children.[27] Hence it has been said that '[T]his theory of spiritual debts being already in the air, the same sanctity came gradually to be transferred to one's promises to repay monetary debts and carry out other secular engagements.'[28] Although different from the metaphor of physical tying, this indicates a similar extension: from the spiritual duty to the secular debt. But this is not ubiquitous; other linguistic forms exist without this connotation, such as the Latin *contractus* or *conventio* or the Greek *homologia* or *synallagma*, stressing the coming together of two parties.

'Contracts' between States: Treaties

Although untypical in that legal enforcement is wholly un-envisaged, treaties constitute an example of agreements intended to ensure (or to attempt to ensure, or to purport to ensure) future conduct.[29] Such treaties are found as early as the middle of the third millennium BCE, such as that fixing the disputed boundary between Lagash and Umma in Sumeria.[30] The largest corpus of such treaties from the ancient Near East are from the Hittite archive in central Anatolia.[31] The majority of these are unequal vassalage treaties imposed by the Hittites on client states. Although there is some variation in their content, their structure is constant: a nominally historical prologue and the terms of the relationship are invariably followed by a long list of divine witnesses, sometimes referred to as the thousand gods, called upon to witness the oath of the subordinate party; should the subordinate fail to observe the terms of the oath, the divine witnesses will inflict some punishment, for example:

> And if you, Manapa-Tarhunta, together with the people of the land of the Seha River and the land of Appawiya, do not observe these words, and in the

---

27 Davis 2010: 71–72.   28 Kane (1962–75), vol. III: 416.
29 Bederman 2001: Chapter 5. On 'interstate' treaties, see further Chapter 4, this volume.
30 Sollberger 1956: 9.   31 Translations in Beckman 1999.

future, to the first and second generation, you turn away, or you alter these words of the tablet – whatever is contained on this tablet, then these oath gods shall eradicate you, together with your person, your wives, your sons, your grandsons, your household, your land, your infantry, your horses, your chariots, and together with your possessions from the Dark Earth.[32]

Finally, there would be a clause to the effect that the gods would pour blessings on the subordinate if the terms of the treaty were observed.

These curse clauses, written from the Hittite point of view, take the form of threats that the oath gods will destroy the subordinate. Where the counterpart of the treaty survives, however, and the treaty is worded from the standpoint of the subordinate, it is rather different, the subordinate bringing down a curse on himself:

> If I, Prince Shattiwaza, and the Hurrians do not observe the words of this treaty and of the oath, let me, Shattizawa, together with my other wife, and us Hurrians, together with our wives, together with our sons, and together with our land – as a fir tree when it is felled has no more shoots, like this fir tree let me, Shattizawa, together with any other wife whom I might take, and us Hurrians, together with our lands, and together with our sons, like this fir tree have no progeny.[33]

These treaties are straightforwardly one-sided, imposed by the Hittites on their clients; they might even make explicit that they are not reciprocal.[34] Some treaties, though, were parity treaties between equals. An Akkadian version of one treaty, for example, records that the parties each swore an oath to the other.[35] The most important, and the best known, of such parity treatises is that between the Hittite Hattusili III and the Egyptian Rameses II, of which we have both the Hittite text and the Egyptian, dating from 1258 BCE.[36] Although transparently bilateral, its form is very similar to the vassal treaties, with the thousand gods of Egypt and the thousand gods of Hatti called upon as witnesses and the curse clause only slightly less menacing than in the vassal treaties, that the gods will destroy the house, the land and the servants of the ruler breaking the treaty.[37]

---

32 Treaty between Mursili II of Hatti and Manaha-Tarhunta of the Land of the Seha River, Beckman 1999: 86 (editorial material omitted).
33 Beckman 1999: 53.
34 For example, Beckman 1999: 91: 'These words are by no means reciprocal. They issue from Hatti.'
35 Beckman 1999: 18.
36 Hittite text in Beckman 1999: 98; Egyptian text in Pritchard 1969: 199.
37 Only known from the Egyptian text: Pritchard 1969: 201 (Hittite text broken at this point).

At the heart of the transactions to which these treaties testify are the oaths sworn by one or both of the parties. Significantly, the oaths themselves do not appear in the treaties, only the consequences of their breach. It is very likely that they were oral, for the oath gods are commonly called upon to be present and to listen to their making. The degree and form of ceremonial accompanying the oath would almost certainly depend on the culture of the parties, commonly involving animal sacrifices; but whatever the form it would embody the parties (or just the subordinate party), calling down the curse on themselves and commonly their family and land, as we see reflected in the treaty.[38]

The Lagash-Umma treaty mentioned above (from the standpoint of the subordinate party) contains a curse clause similar to that of the Hittite treaties of a millennium later:

> For ever and evermore I shall not transgress the territory of the
>   god Ningirsu
> I shall not shift the course of its irrigation channels and canals.
> I shall not rip out its monuments.
> Whenever I do transgress may the great battle-net of Enlil, king of heaven
>   and earth, by which I have sworn, descend on Gisa (Umma)[39]

The same focus on oaths is found in treaties from Babylon, Assyria and Greece.[40] This was so in Rome too; Livy describes the ceremony of ratification of the seventh-century BCE treaty between Rome and Alba, involving the slaying of a sacrificial animal coupled with an oath:

> If they [the Romans] are the first to violate any of [the terms] deliberately and by general consent, then on that day, O Jupiter, do thou strike down the Roman people, as I shall strike down this pig; and do thou strike them all the more as thy power and strength are greater! ... In like manner the Albans pronounced their own forms and their own oath, by the mouth of their own dictator and priests (1.24).[41]

This practice may have continued into the Roman empire.[42] Gaius, *Institutes* 3.94 (secondcentury CE), however, refers simply to the exchange of question and answer in the form *spondesne – spondeo*, as in private-law contracts, remarking that on the breach of such treaties recourse is had to war rather than law.

---

38 Bederman 2001: 62–65.   39 Frayne 2016: 133.
40 Bederman 2001: 142, 143, 173–74 Sommerstein and Torrance 2014.
41 To the same effect, Liv. 9.5.3.   42 Watson 1993: 85, n. 13.

But it is not only in this cultural context that the phenomenon is found. It is present in India too: the *Arthaśāstra* of Kautilya compares the relative strength of making a peace pact by oath or by taking hostages:

> Truth or oath constitutes an unstable pact. A surety or a hostage constitutes a stable pact,' so state the teachers. 'No,' says Kautilya. 'Truth or oath constitutes a stable pact here and in the hereafter, while a surety or a hostage, depending on strength, is of use only here.'[43]

Kautilya proceeds to describe the form of the curse attached to the oath:

> In case it [a peace pact] is transgressed, they touched with an oath the following: fire, water, a furrow, a clod from a rampart, the shoulder of an elephant, the back of a horse, the seat of a chariot, a weapon, a gem, seeds, perfume, poison, gold, and money, saying: 'May these kill or abandon the man who breaks his oath.'[44]

The presence of the Indian gods Mitra and Varuna in a Hittite treaty, too, may perhaps indicate some knowledge of oath-taking in Indian practice as early as the middle of the second millennium BCE.[45] Too much weight, however, cannot be placed on this: it may simply indicate that the names of these foreign gods were known.

The identical practice is found in China, well evidenced by a formal agreement, a *meng*, which can be dated to 631 BCE (Zhou dynasty); the curse clause here is reminiscent of the same clauses in the ancient Near East:

> Should anyone abrogate this agreement, may the Gods and Spirits strike him dead, bring about the downfall of his people so that (his heirs) might not enjoy the government of the State. Down to the fourth generation, may none, old or young, survive.[46]

The pre-Confucian *Book of Documents*, reproducing a form found in some very ancient Chinese documents, conjoins *meng* with *zu*, curse.[47] This points to heavenly punishment for breaking the oath, though it might be referring to interpersonal oaths as opposed to interstate ones.[48] As elsewhere, the oath in these treaties would be spoken and would be accompanied by some ritual, including animal sacrifice, the agreement being sanctified by the burial of the document together with the sacrificed animal.[49]

---

43 *KAŚ* 7.17 (Olivelle 2013: 323).   44 Olivelle 2013: 323.   45 Beckman 1999: 47.
46 Quoted in Dobson 1968: 269, 274.
47 Legge 1879: 582, translating as 'treaties and covenants'.
48 Cf. Dobson 1968: 260 ('private compacts').   49 Dobson 1968: 271.

Oaths in Interpersonal Agreements

The operative mechanism in these treaties was the oath. It is telling that the ancient Near Eastern form in which it appears from the standpoint of the dominant party – the gods 'will' (not 'are asked to') bring down disastrous misfortune on the oath-breaker – indicates that it was seen to be self-executing. Exactly the same would be true two millennia later, in medieval Europe.

The oath might sometimes be used outside the context of interstate relations; it is only in India that there is no evidence of this.[50] This may simply be the result of the lack of surviving evidence, but since oaths are frequently referred to in the Dharmaśāstra in the context of legal process, the failure to refer to them in contractual contexts is telling. In Egypt it is found where one person swears fealty to another with the oath of the God and a self-curse as is found in treaties,[51] as well as in commercial contexts (typically an oath to repay double for the breach of a sale or loan).[52] In the latter context the use of the verb 'rq, 'swear', is especially attested in the late Empire (though this may, again, be because of the chance survival and discovery of examples).[53] It is found in Hittite Anatolia in the oath sworn by soldiers and fealty oaths,[54] though perhaps not in other private settings (so far as can be judged from the scanty evidence). As in Anatolia, the Hebrew *berith* (2 Kings 11.4) and the Chinese *meng* was used to bring about a relationship of fealty between individuals – where the parallel with vassalage treaties was transparent – but there is little evidence of its use in other private contracts. In Greece the oath was used especially when putting an end to previous disputes (whether by private compact or arbitration) and in analogous situations.[55] In Mesopotamia, as late as the Neo-Babylonian period in the first millennium BCE, oaths of loyalty and oaths of office are found (though the former only rarely, no doubt because of the lack of excavation of royal archives from this period).[56] But here promissory oaths, sworn in the name of Gods and sometimes of the king, are used more generally: oaths to pay money by a certain date, to deliver goods, that goods sold are of a certain quality, that a boat will not deviate from its prescribed route, to observe an arbitration award and so on.[57]

---

50 Kane 1962–75, vol. III: 158–60.   51 Wilson 1948: 142 text 80, 81 (without self-curse).
52 Wilson 1948: 143–46, texts 90–93, 97–102   53 Wilson 1948: 152, Table 2.
54 Miller 2013.   55 Sommerstein and Torrance 2014.   56 Sandowicz 2012: 81–86.
57 Examples in Sandowicz 2012; see 39–75 for the gods and kings in whose name oaths are sworn.

The position in Rome is more complex. There is clear evidence of the continued use of oaths in the empire when a freed slave swore to perform services for his former master, the *iusiurandum liberti*, though it came to be substantially secular;[58] this was a special case, with clear parallels to the fealty oaths found elsewhere. More generally there was the *stipulatio*, a formal agreement embodied in an oral question and answer using congruent verbs. One of these pairs of words was *spondesne – spondeo*, which Gaius (*Institutes* 3.94) links to treaty practice when saying that it could only be used by foreigners when making peace with the people of Rome, a linkage visible too with the *sponsio* by which a party defeated in war would sue for peace.[59] Three other pairs of words (*promittisne – promitto, fidepromittisne – fidepromitto, fideiubesne – fideiubeo*) point to Fides, the goddess of trust.[60] This probably suggests that originally there might have been an oath by Fides, though any such connotation had disappeared before the Empire, by which time two very general words (*dare* 'give', and *facere* 'make' or 'do') had been added to the permissible words, probably only as examples rather than as a closed list.[61]

Another early feature of what will later be seen as contract is the imitation of the creation of a family relationship. The interstate relations testified to by the El-Amarna letters of the fourteenth century BCE are very commonly formulated in terms of brotherhood or father–son relations, no doubt depending on whether the pact was between equals or involved vassalage;[62] one letter refers specifically to an arrangement that the parties would become blood relations.[63] Most commonly, the creation of the artificial family link is symbolized by the intermingling of blood. This is clearly the case of the Chinese *meng*. Indispensable to it was a ritual smearing of the lips of the parties to a compact with the blood of one of them. This, it is said, 'derives, one may suppose, from a blood-brother pact binding otherwise unrelated parties in the solemn obligations of kinship'.[64] Tacitus speaks of a similar custom among Parthians entering into treaties, and Herodotus testifies to Scythians' solemn drinking of blood mixed with wine.[65] Frequently, the blood itself is actually replaced by wine. The equivalence is made explicit in a Hittite text, associated with the

---

58 Chevrier 1921: 89–256. 59 Chevrier 1921: 57–73.
60 For the equivalence of *promissio* and *fides*: Chevrier 1921: 82–89 and Lombardi 1961: 116–18.
61 Riccobono 1957. 62 Rainey 2015. 63 Rainey 2015: 331, letter EA 32.
64 Dobson 1968: 272.
65 Tac. *Ann.* 12.47; Herodotus 4.70 and see also 3.8 ('Arabians' smearing seven stones with their blood).

military oath. After wine had been poured onto the ground in front of the soldiers, the words were uttered:

> This is not wine, it is your blood. And as the Earth has swallowed it, so may the Earth in the same way swallow your blood and [. . . if you betray your oath.[66]

Similarly in Hebrew, wine might be termed 'blood of the grape' (Gen 49.11), and in later Rabbinic Judaism the equivalence is stressed by the requirement that the Passover wine be red;[67] and the covenant between God and Abraham, mirroring Hittite and later treaty practice, was explicitly a blood covenant.[68] There are occasional references to wine in contractual situations in Mesopotamia as well as anointing with oil,[69] and the same word, *kirrum*, is used to describe the beer drunk in both marriage ceremonies and commercial settings;[70] these may be symbolic substitutes for blood, though it is perhaps more likely that they are components of feasting. Later Chinese sale contracts, with none of the ceremonial of the *meng*, frequently testify to the provision of wine, and it is probable that the drinking of wine, whether by the parties or witnesses, is a derivation or transference from the intermingling of blood.[71] A similar process of development could explain the widespread use of libations to mark the making of agreements elsewhere: in Greece and Rome libations of wine marked the making of oaths in very early times, with a linguistic continuation into the later Roman form of the *stipulatio* using the verb *spondere*.[72] Another explicitly quasi-familial form is testified to in Roman law. In early law – we cannot tell how early – it was possible for Roman citizens to employ legal means to enter into a relationship, essentially a form of partnership, mirroring the *ercto non cito*, or undivided ownership of coheirs (Gaius, *Institutes* 3.154b). The same may have been true in Mesopotamia, where the Old Babylonian parallels between partnerships and the relationship between brothers or co-heirs are explicit.[73]

Paralleling this is what can perhaps be seen in terms of an extension of the person undertaking an obligation. In Mesopotamia, it was common to seal a document by impressing in the wet clay of the tablet either one's finger nail or the hem of one's garment. Such impressions could hardly serve to identify the individual but must rather have had a symbolic significance, probably of

---

66 Quoted by Beckman 2011: 96.   67 Daube 2000: 453.
68 Zechariah 9.11. For the relationship with treaty practice, see Botterwick and Ringgren 1977: 266–69.
69 Malul 1988: 346, 175–76.   70 Greengus 1966: 62–66.
71 Scogin 1990: 1383–84; Hulsewé 1978b: 27.   72 Gernet 1982: 54–56.
73 Westbrook 2003c: 411.

the personality, arguably taking on personal responsibility for the performance of the obligation.[74] The reverse of sealing with the hem of the garment can be seen in the plucking of the hem, a way of symbolizing divorce, drawing or brushing the hem symbolizing the discharging of a debt, and the plucking of a person's hem as a way of making a claim.[75]

One step removed from this is the Mesopotamian practice, traceable back to the pre-Sargonic period,[76] of marking the transfer of land by a ceremonial feast.[77] It may be that this marked the acceptance of the transferee into the family of the transferor, or imitated such an acceptance; but since the witnesses are invariably described as partakers in the feast, unless these were not purely witnesses but also members of the seller's extended family, it is perhaps more likely that the meal was a way of formalizing and memorializing the transfer, guarding against calling the transfer into question in the future.

The Use of Writing

Unsurprisingly, every legal system whose traces survive used written documents, if only as a way of memorializing what had occurred when witnesses might no longer be available or reliable or of setting down complex terms with a degree of certainty. Whether copies of these documents have survived depends a great deal on the perishability of the material on which they were written and whether the climatic and other conditions were conducive to their preservation. Thus, although there is clear evidence of the widespread use of documents in early Han China, from about 200 BCE, only a handful have survived; they seem typically to have been written on wood, and some of those which have survived have done so because they were on bricks buried in graves and designed to look like wood.[78] More have survived from a later period in caves in the deserts of northwestern China, emanating from trade along the Silk Road; those from the ancient oasis town of Dunhuang discovered in the early twentieth century are only now being edited as part of a major international project, while those from the oasis of Turfan some 800 kilometres distant are still being excavated.[79] Related to the Silk Road trade, too, there are a smattering of surviving documents from elsewhere in central

---

74 Postgate 1994: 61 at fn. 524. Malul 1988: 299–309.
75 Malul 1988: 153–59, 197–208, 332–37, 422–31.   76 Wilcke 2003: 166.
77 Malul 1988: 346–78.   78 Hulsewé 1978b.
79 The International Dunhuang Project, http://idp.bl.uk/ (accessed 16/08/2022); Turfanforschung of the Brandenburgische Akademie der Wissenschaften, http://turfan.bbaw.de/projekt-en (accessed 16/08/2022). See Yamamoto and Ikeda 1987 (for contracts edited by 1987).

The Use of Writing

Asia.[80] Nothing survives from Hittite Anatolia, which also probably employed wood, though allusive references in the laws proves that they were used.[81] The same is true of ancient Israel, though Old Testament texts make it clear that they were used.[82] Greek law similarly provides clear evidence of their use.[83] Very few survive from Roman law, except from Egypt: they were typically written on wood coated with wax, where the wax has melted or rotted away and the wood has only survived, with traces of the scratches which have come through the wax, when anaerobic conditions have preserved it. By contrast, there are many thousands of contract documents from the ancient Near East where they were inscribed on clay tablets – more than a thousand have been edited from Sumeria in the third millennium BCE – and they are found in Egypt as early as the Old Kingdom where papyri have been preserved in deserts.[84] Comparisons are therefore slightly problematic.

Mesopotamia

The largest amount of surviving evidence, by far, comes from Mesopotamia.[85] This evidence covers a great variety of contracts, the documents invariably recording the names of the parties and witnesses as well as the unilateral or bilateral obligations undertaken. Two further features are important. First, the documents commonly refer to matters such as the swearing of an oath or an act done by the parties; secondly, they are written in the past tense, recording something that has already happened. Together they strongly suggest that the document itself was not what generated the obligation(s), but the antecedent transaction. In general, in case of dispute the witnesses to the document would be called upon to authenticate it, and therefore to prove the underlying transaction, though some Old Assyrian texts refer to the production of witnesses *or* tablets,[86] suggesting that the document might have been enough in itself.

So far as the physical format of the documents is concerned, they were inscribed on clay tablets. It was common (though seemingly not invariable) for the tablet to be enclosed in a clay envelope, itself inscribed with a summary of the terms. In case of dispute the envelope would be broken and the tablet itself examined. The evidence, however, suggests that from the

---

80 Lerner and Sims-Williams 2011. 81 Haase 2003: 641. 82 Frymer-Kenski 2003: 1020.
83 Prignitz 2014, 2022.   84 Westbrook, 2003a: 127.
85 We rely largely on Renger 1977, supplemented by Ameri, Costello, Jamison and Scott 2018: 11–124.
86 Veenhof 2003: 445; cf. Laws of Hammurabi par. 7 (Roth 1997: 82), a provision on theft, seeming to allow witnesses or a contract to substantiate a sale; cf. too par. 122 (Roth 1997: 104).

Neo-Babylonian period (second half of the first millennium BCE) the envelope system was abandoned; instead, duplicate tablets were produced.[87]

The tablets were frequently sealed by the parties and/or the witnesses; commonly, though not always, the document itself referred to the fact of sealing. The seals might be on the document itself or on the envelope. Sometimes a party or witness might impress the hem of his garment or his fingernail into the wet clay 'instead of his seal', indicating just how ubiquitous was the practice of sealing. Moreover, the use of the hem or fingernail clearly shows that the function of sealing was not identificatory, and sometimes the document even specifies that another person's seal had been used. It was the fact of sealing that was important – like an illiterate medieval person making a cross instead of a signature – indicating an acceptance of a binding obligation or of the status of witness. A person might deny that a seal was his,[88] presumably denying thereby that he had accepted the alleged obligation.

Anatolia

The practice of writing on wood has meant that no private contracts from the Hittite kingdom have survived. A small number of land grants made by the king are attested,[89] sealed with the king's seal, and this has led to the suggestion that private contracts for the sale of land would similarly have been drawn up in documentary form and sealed.[90] But there is no direct evidence of this, and the texts of the Hittite Laws which refer to contracts give no hint as to whether they would be written or oral.

Egypt

There is very considerable evidence of written documents, mostly on papyrus, from Egypt, especially from the New Kingdom onwards;[91] and even after Egypt came under the domination of Persians and then Greeks in the first millennium BCE, demotic Egyptian law continued to apply to Egyptians until probably the latter part of the second century CE.[92] Documents on papyrus, sometimes very lengthy ones, were rolled and sealed, though they were evidence of oral agreements which had taken place rather than being contracts in themselves.[93] From the third century

---

87 Cf Neo-Babylonian Laws par. 5 (Roth 1997: 145), with the commentary of Driver and Miles 1952–55: 325–26.
88 Renger 1977: 79, n. 85.   89 Haase 2003: 639.   90 Haase 2003: 639, 642.
91 Jasnow 2003c: 336; see Keenan, Manning and Yiftach-Firanko 2014: esp. 31–95.
92 Manning 2003b: 820–21.
93 Manning 2003b: 843. See, however, Pliny, *Historia Naturalis*, 33.21, contrasting the Roman use of sealing rings with the Egyptian practice of relying simply on writing.

BCE until perhaps the turn of the millennia, many of the Egyptian documents follow the Hellenistic double-document form: the contract is written out twice on a single sheet, the top half then being rolled and sealed close leaving the bottom half open. This gradually degenerated and finally disappeared as the deposit of the whole document in an official registry became more normal.

From the first half of the first millennium BCE, a system of registration of private agreements is found, probably linked to the sales tax. This system expanded during the latter part of the first millennium, and in 146 BCE there was an order requiring demotic contracts written by a temple scribe to be registered in the state registry with a Greek summary, Greek being the administrative language of Egypt by this time, on pain of invalidity.[94] The registration system was greatly expanded and reformed in the Roman period, particularly through an Edict of the prefect M Mettius Rufus of 89 CE establishing a 'property record office' in Alexandria.[95]

There are no surviving law codes as are found in Mesopotamia and Anatolia, but the Ptolemaic text known as the *Zivilprozessordnung* indicates which written documents could be used as evidence and the burden of proof when a document's status was doubtful.[96]

India

There is no direct evidence of written contracts in India, and although there are some surviving seals, from the as early as the Harappan culture in the Indus valley,[97] there is no reason to associate these with contractual documents. It is clear from the sastric texts from the early centuries CE that documents might be used as evidence of a transaction. In the title 'Non-payment of Debts' in the *Manava Dharmaśāstra* it is said at the start that the liability may be evidenced by document or witnesses, but the rest of the title is concerned solely with witnesses.[98] After the fourth-century CE documents become more routine.[99] Thus, in the *Yājñavakya Dharmaśāstra* (c. 400 CE, probably), it is said that once a contract has been concluded, by mutual agreement a document might be drawn up in which the debtor acknowledges his debt in his own hand and the witnesses write that they have witnessed.[100] That said, although there is a stress

---

94 Pestman 1985a: 17; Muhs 2016: 229–30.
95 See Keenan, Manning and Yiftach-Firanko 2014: 69–71.   96 Depauw 1997: 114.
97 Parpola 2018: 127–43.
98 *MDh* 8.53–8.57 (Olivelle 2005a: 169). See also *KAŚ* 3.1.19 (Olivelle 2013: 180), referring to a litigant who says he will produce a document but fails to do so.
99 Olivelle and Davis 2017: 292; Olivelle 2019a: xiii.
100 *YDh* 18.86–97 (Olivelle 2019a): 142–45.

on documents, there is no reason to believe that debts contracted purely orally were unenforceable; the later *Nārada Smṛti* states that evidence can consist either of witnesses or a document (*NSm* 1.3), though adding later that the document is superior to witnesses (*NSm* 1.125).[101]

China

It is not easy to speak with any certainty about Chinese law.[102] On the one hand, the formal legal sources, from the so-called *Statutes of the Second Year* collected in 186 BCE[103] to the Tang Code of the seventh century CE[104] are concerned with penal and administrative matters; contract disputes were not the concern of the emperor and were dealt with locally, seemingly applying customary norms; what we know of litigation was more concerned with the establishment of facts than the application of rules.[105] On the other, climatic conditions in most of China were not conducive to the preservation of documents; survival of perishable material was far easier after Chinese power had extended westwards to the edge of the desert. Some of the contracts which have so far been discovered are in a bewildering variety of languages and scripts, mostly central Asian, reflecting non-Chinese drafting practices, though those written in Chinese closely mirror contractual documents from the Chinese heartland.[106]

The scant evidence does, however, allow us to say something about the earlier period, relying on references in historical texts, statements by commentators and archaeological evidence.[107] The historical texts show that documents were in use by 200 BCE; and a commentator of the second century CE refers to 'long contracts' being used in sales of slaves, horses and cattle, while 'short contracts' were used for the sale of arms and other valuable goods, inferentially suggesting that documents were not normally used for still smaller contracts. The same commentator describes the making of double copies of contract documents, each party getting one part.[108] Most of the early documents which have been found relate to the sale of land for graves, which have survived because they were buried in the tomb.[109] They record executed transactions, whose only forward-looking obligation is not to dispute the sale. They are obviously atypical, though their form appears to

---

101 See generally, Kane 1962–75, vol. III: 308–16.
102 See the remarks of Hulsewé 1986: 541–42.   103 Barbieri-Low and Yates 2015.
104 Johnson 1997.   105 Zhaoyang 2022.
106 Hansen 1995: 17–46; Hitch 2009: 20–36 (including later evidence); and see further below.
107 Hulsewé 1978b: 11, 15.   108 Hulsewé 1978b: 16.
109 Cf. the practice of burying documents recording *meng* (see above).

reflect normal contracts (examples survive of credit sales of land, sales of clothing and a parody of the sale of a slave); they name buyer and seller, identify the land sold and the price, adding commonly a guarantee against eviction (perhaps including eviction by the relatives of the seller), finishing with a list of bystanders (who were presumably witnesses) and a statement that wine was drunk by all present.[110] The document itself would not have been sealed, but it might be rolled and tied with a tag sealed with an impression on soft clay.[111] The *Statutes of the Second Year* explicitly penalized the falsification or loss of contract documents and the forgery of or tampering with seals.[112] The document itself was clearly evidentiary, testifying to an oral or ritual transaction, but it may have been a necessary formality to allow the state accurately to assess property taxes.[113]

There is substantially more evidence after the third or fourth century CE, largely the result of documents unearthed at Turfan, in Xinjiang.[114] As in the earlier period, the documents (typically written on paper) record the names of the parties, the details of the transaction and the names of the witnesses. A land sale contract from 542, for example, continues:

> The buyer and seller reached an agreement and then drew up a contract. Once the contract is drawn up, neither party can cancel the agreement. Should one party cancel the agreement he must pay a fine in rugs to the party who does not cancel. Commoners have private agreements they are obliged to fulfil. The buyer and seller each sign their names to show good faith, and they divide the cost of the wine.[115]

Typical, and noteworthy, is the clause about commoners' private agreements, differentiating them from contracts by officials; the fact that the document is drawn up after the agreement has been made but only becomes binding once the writing is completed; the fine for withdrawing once the contract is binding;[116] and the drinking of wine. The contract might specify that ownership of property sold would pass at some point in the future. Documents recording sales of property other than land are evidenced, sometimes relatively low-value contracts such as the sale of a shirt or the

---

110 Hulsewé 1978b: 17–27.
111 Tokyo National Museum 1998; cf. www.tnm.jp/modules/r_free_page/index.php?id=524&lang=en (accessed 11/09/2022).
112 'Statute on Assault', sections 9–11, quoted from Barbieri-Low and Yates 2015: 395.
113 Hulsewé 1978b: 34.   114 Yamamoto and Okida 1987: 10; Hansen 1995: 17–46.
115 Translation by Hansen 1995: 24–25. Cf. the similar contract from near modern Beijing, dated 507 CE (Hansen 1995: 26–27).
116 Compare a sale contract of 638 CE, providing that the person withdrawing should pay double to the other party (Hansen 1995: 28–29).

loan of a gown,[117] but there is no reason to suppose that all small contracts required writing. More valuable sale contracts might have had such a requirement, for tax purposes; and sales in market of slaves, horses, cattle, mules and donkeys required a market certificate, in the absence of which the parties would suffer corporal punishment.[118]

Greece

Outside the Athenian stone *horoi*, evidencing land rights as a result of a sale or mortgage, we have comparatively little direct evidence of Greek written contracts from outside Egypt, where the climatic conditions have allowed the survival of documents written on papyrus, but indirect evidence from the Attic orators shows that writing was in use at least from the fourth century BCE. The earliest reference is attributed to Isocrates around 393 BCE,[119] and there are passing references in later speeches. However, a document was just one form of evidence to be ranged alongside witnesses. According to one speech of the later Hyperides, 'The law says that whatever agreements one man makes with another are binding', a proposition countered by the speaker's opponent not on the grounds that writing was needed but because they needed also to be just (*Against Athenogenes*, 3.13; Demosthenes, *Against Evergus and Mnesibulus*, 47.77). The one major exception to this was maritime contracts, which from some time in the middle of the fourth century were the objects of a special procedure, the *dike emporike*, and were required to be written.[120] Generally, however, it is likely that the use of documents grew as contracting parties became more familiar with them.

The evidence from Ptolemaic Egypt is of a different order. As well as documents in demotic, there are a very substantial number of documents in Greek.[121] Typically, at first, the agreement was drawn up as a double document, the earliest evidence dating from the late fourth century BCE. The text of the agreement was written twice, in full, on a single sheet of papyrus. The top half was then rolled, tied and sealed by the parties and six witnesses; the bottom half was left open, able to be read, and if this open text was for some reason disputed the closed text could be unsealed and compared with it.[122] The document was then kept by one of the witnesses. Although most of the evidence for the use of these double documents is Egyptian, there is no good

---

117 Hansen 1995: 34.   118 Tang Code, article 422 (Johnson 1997: 485).
119 Isocrates, *Trapeziticus*, 17.20.   120 Harris 2015c.
121 Keenan, Manning and Yiftach-Firanko 2014: esp. 35–46.
122 Illustration in Meyer 2004: 189.

reason to doubt that they were used elsewhere in the Hellenistic world, the earliest non-Egyptian text in this form coming from Kurdistan early in the first century BCE. Late in the third century BCE, there developed a practice of depositing the document in the archives; over time this caused the double form to die away, as deposition and after 125 BCE registration guaranteed authenticity.[123] Alongside the double document, agreements could be embodied in the form of a letter from debtor to creditor, originally written by the debtor personally. There were no witnesses, nor was a copy deposited or registered. The second-century Roman lawyer Gaius refers to these two forms of Greek contracts that seem to be written (*litterarum obligatio fieri videtur*) in his *Institutes* (3.134): the syngraph, sealed, witnessed and registered; and the chirograph in letter form.

Rome

If we were to rely solely on the texts found in Justinian's *Corpus Iuris*, we would be led to believe that Roman contract law was little concerned with writing. As noted above, the formal *stipulatio* was constituted by an apparently oral question and answer which continued to bear the marks of an origin in oath-taking; so central was the orality that we are told it could not be used by the deaf and those unable to speak.[124] Informal contracts, such as sale, depended solely on the agreement of the parties, which might be brought about by letter but whose paradigm was clearly oral; it was only under Justinian that special rules relating to written sales were introduced.[125] Gaius' *Institutes* gives a very marginal situation in which writing did indeed generate the obligation, entries in the account book of a Roman *paterfamilias*, but this was soon obsolete, and the Greek version of Justinian's *Institutes* contents itself with saying that if you seek diligently you will find another (very marginal) situation of a written contract.[126]

The reality was different. Already at the end of the Republic, Cicero was able to describe the *stipulatio* as a written agreement (Cic. *Top.* 26.96),[127] so we may be sure that the use of written evidence was common; it became increasingly common in the empire, so much so that a rescript of Antoninus Pius deals with the conflict between the oral terms of an

---

123 Yiftach-Firanko 2008: 203.
124 Justinian, *Digest* 44.7.1.15 (Gaius) and 45.1.1 pr. (Ulpian). Similarly, Gaius, *Institutes* 3.105 and Justinian, *Inst.* 3.19.7.
125 de Zulueta 1945: 20–22; Justinian, *Cod.* 4.21.17 (528 CE).
126 Gaius *Institutes* .3.128; Theophilus, *Paraphrase* 3.22 (cf. Justinian, *Inst.* 3.21).
127 Also Cic. *Part. or.* 37.130 and the anonymous *Rhet. Her.* II.IX 13–14. See Ibbetson 2020: 99.

agreement and the written instrument.[128] That said, it was probably never the case that the documentary form entirely supplanted the theoretically oral form; it was simply that the writing was near-conclusive evidence that the oral interchange had occurred.

Direct evidence of contracts in writing survives from two principal sources. First of all, several caches of documents, totalling more than 400, have been excavated from Pompeii and the surrounding area; all these date from the first century CE. Secondly, many papyri have been found in the deserts of Egypt; from 212 CE, when all free people in the Roman empire were granted citizenship, these were governed by Roman law, though with provincial variants. The Italian and Egyptian forms, if we may so designate them, were very different. Those from Roman Italy took the form of wooden tablets coated with wax. Some took the form of diptychs, two tablets hinged together, with the writing protected on the interior; but, especially after the middle of the first century, the triptych form predominated, with the text written on two tablets which were then folded over, tied closed with a string and sealed, with the third tablet of the triptych folded over the first two and with a copy of the agreement written on the outside.[129] This form was not purely Italian; it is evidenced equally from a small cache of second-century documents found in a mine in Roman Dacia (Transilvania), as well as from fragmentary evidence from Britain and Switzerland.[130]

Classical and postclassical Roman law, especially in the eastern part of the empire, reveals a greater tendency towards the use of writing. The formal *stipulatio* remained stubbornly oral in legal theory, at the same time as its rules developed to accommodate the fact that it was increasingly proved by written documents; in 531 CE Justinian emphasized that a document stating that the parties had met together and exchanged question and promise should be taken as proof of the fact unless the party who made the 'shameless allegation' that they had not met could prove 'by the most manifest proofs' that they had been in different cities for the whole of the day in question and so could not possibly have met.[131] Further evidence of the role of writing by this time is provided by a constitution of 528 CE providing that where it had been agreed that a contract of sale would be put in writing, the normal rule that it became binding at the moment of agreement did not apply, bindingness arising only when it had been written and signed by the parties or, if it

---

[128] Justinian, *Cod.* 4.32.1.   [129] Meyer 2004: 125–68.
[130] Polay 1980 (see Bruns, *Fontes*: 419); Meyer 2004: 177–78.
[131] Justinian, *Cod.* 8.38.14, reproduced in a slightly different form in Justinian, *Inst.* 3.19.12. See van Oven 1958 and Ibbetson 2020.

had been drawn up by a notary, the writing was formally complete.[132] Diplomatic evidence of contractual forms can only be based on Egyptian evidence, the source of the vast majority of contractual papyri. These were increasingly in the chirograph form, documents which were superficially epistolary, written by one of the parties and recording their agreement.[133] In general they conformed to Roman law norms, though there was room for variation to reflect local practice.[134]

The Contract of Sale

Little purpose would be served by enumerating the types of contract found in different legal systems. Too much would depend on what contracts were reduced to writing, what contracts were expected to have long-term consequences and so were worth retaining, and the sheer capriciousness of survival rates. For what it is worth, from the ancient Near East, from where we have a sufficiently large number of surviving documents for the listing to have value, we can identify sale and exchange, hire, deposit, loan, pledge, suretyship and partnership;[135] but this tells us nothing about the types of contract which were not reduced to writing. Perhaps a better sense of what might have been recognized as typical contractual situations can be gained from those systems in which lists are given. In India, for example, there is evidence from the dharmaśāstra, culminating in the *Nārada Smṛti*, where the titles of law list nonpayment of debts, deposits, partnership, (resumption of) gifts, (breaches of) contracts for services, non-payment of wages and sale.[136] By the middle of the second century CE, Roman law could list loans of fungibles, loans for use, deposits, pledge, sale, *locatio conductio* (encompassing leases of land, the hire of moveable property, employment relationships, carriage of goods, the performance of a service and other similar relationships), partnership and the gratuitous performance of a service for another, as well as the formal *stipulatio* which allowed the creation in legal form of any relationship that was not immoral or illegal and was especially important in the creation of suretyship.

One form of contract, sale, is common in every system, sufficiently so that we can usefully compare both the general structure and the detail across time and space. One problem is that many documents, perhaps most, provide evidence of executed contracts, where both the price has been paid and the

---

132 Justinian, *Cod.* 4.21.17; Justinian, *Inst.* 3.23 pr.
133 Keenan, Manning and Yiftach-Firanko 2014: 84–89.   134 Taubenschlag 1955.
135 Westbrook 2003a: 68.
136 *NSm* (Lariviere 1989: 273–368). Cf. *KAŚ*, 3.11–3.16 (Olivelle 2013: 202–16).

object sold delivered, and this has sometimes led scholars to suppose that sale was always such an executed contract. But this is not a necessary conclusion: documents evidencing a sale, especially of land, might have been retained as indicia of the rights of the buyer, and even where the sale had been executed there might commonly have been contingent obligations of future performance, for example to pay a penalty if the object sold should be reclaimed by the true owner where it was not the seller's to dispose of.

In the ancient Near East the standard form of contract, though there were some variations in detail, simply specified the thing sold, the price paid and the witnesses; very occasionally it can be seen that either the price was to be paid or the property delivered in the future.[137] The documentary record provides very clear evidence of the sale of land, of slaves and of certain farm animals (cattle, oxen, donkeys), and it may be that these required a particular formality. Most documents were written from the standpoint of the buyer, but in Old and Middle Assyrian texts, followed by Neo-Babylonian, sales of land were written from the standpoint of the seller.[138] Alongside this core there might be additional obligations. It was possible that the seller might renege on the sale, and already in the Early Dynastic period this might be subject to punishment; the making of the contract could be symbolized by driving a nail into the wall, with it sometimes being made explicit that a nail would be driven into the mouth of the seller if he went back on the agreement.[139] Neo-Sumerian contracts point to the seller's guarantee against eviction here being strengthened by an oath, with the penalty, sometimes repayment of double the price, being specified in the oath.[140] In the eighteenth century BCE, the Babylonian Laws of Hammurabi deal with this type of guarantee in the context of the sale of slaves: if a third party makes a claim, the seller must defend the buyer.[141] Clauses to this effect are found in contracts for the sale of slaves or other property from about this time.[142] The fact that there is nothing in the Laws to say what penalty, if any, should be paid by the seller to the buyer if he does not successfully defend the buyer's title may suggest that the only obligation envisaged was to return the price, as was the case where a man had bought stolen goods from a thief.[143] However, we also find contractual clauses requiring the payment of double the price in the

---

137 For example Lafont and Westbrook 2003: 210–11 (Neo-Sumerian).
138 Oelsner, Wells and Wunsch 2003: 943.
139 Wilcke 2003: 169 and Slanski 2003b: 509 (Middle Babylonian), both in the context of the sale of slaves.
140 Lafont and Westbrook 2003: 210.   141 Laws of Hammurabi, par. 279 (Roth 1997: 132).
142 Driver and Miles 1952–55, vol. I: 479–81.
143 Laws of Hammurabi, par. 9 (Roth 1997: 82).

event of eviction by a third party with a paramount claim.[144] By the Middle Assyrian period, continued into the Neo-Babylonian, there is a differentiation between sales of land and sales of moveables: in the former the sale was publicized to allow those with claims on the property to come forward and if they did not do so their claims were barred, while in sales of moveables, typically slaves and animals, there was a guarantee against eviction typically requiring the seller to refund the price which had been paid.[145] As well as guarantees against eviction or a requirement that the seller defend the buyer's title, there is some evidence of obligations relating to the quality of the property sold. The Laws of Hammurabi, for example, specify that if a slave is sold and it emerges within a month that the slave is suffering from epilepsy, the price paid will be returned to the buyer.[146] Clauses guaranteeing against defects are unusual compared with guarantees against eviction, presumably because buyers could invariably satisfy themselves of the quality of the property they were buying. Epilepsy, as in the Code of Hammurabi, would be something that was not immediately discoverable by the buyer and hence atypical.

It is difficult to say much with certainty about Greek law: the direct evidence is sparse we cannot assume that the rules and practices of every polis were the same, though warranties of title and guarantees against latent fefects were comon.[147] It is likely that the paradigm was the cash sale with payment and delivery being simultaneous and ownership in the thing sold passing on payment of the price. Functionally, credit sale was made possible by treating the unpaid price as if it were a loan from the seller. The philosopher Theophrastus (fourth century BCE) refers to places where sales of land must be pre-announced to enable those claiming rights in the land to bring them forward, equivalent to first-millennium Assyrian and Babylonian practice.[148] In the same fragment Theophrastus refers to the giving of *arrabon*, 'earnest', as a way of firming the sale and justifying the buyer's taking possession (though ownership would pass only on payment of the full price).[149] If the buyer did not proceed with the purchase the *arrabon* was forfeited, though it is wholly unclear whether any liability attached to the

---

144 Slanski 2003b: 509.
145 Middle Assyrian Laws, C+G par. C4 (fragmentary) (Roth 1997: 183).
146 Laws of Hammurabi, par. 278 (Roth 1997: 132).
147 See in particular Pringsheim 1950; for criticisms of Pringsheim see, in particular, Finley 1951 and Millett 1990; all summarized in Todd 1993: 255–57.
148 Theoph., *fr.* 21(1) (Szegedy-Maszak 1981: 58–73).
149 Theoph., *fr.* 21(4) and 21(6). The term *arrabon* is etymologically related to Semitic *erabon*, representing a form of personal or real security, but there is no demonstrable juridical connection. See Pringsheim 1950: 333–429.

defaulting seller. An Egyptian document of 257 BCE, in Greek, testifies clearly to the practical use of *arrabon* to make the agreement to sell binding before the payment of the price.[150] Supplementing this core there would commonly be a clause guaranteeing the buyer against eviction, typically requiring the buyer or some other person to defend the buyer's title (though this might not have been necessary where the intended sale had been publicized in advance).[151] At first, it is likely that the guarantee would be given by a third party, probably the person from whom the seller had derived his title, but in time it became the buyer himself. The Cretan Law of Gortyn (mid-fifth century BCE) laid down that the seller who could not defend the buyer's title should pay back to the buyer double the sale price together with any additional loss which had been suffered by the buyer;[152] the amount of the penalty might vary from contract to contract. There is little evidence before the spread of Roman law of warranties of quality, except in the sale of slaves.[153] Plato tells of a rule in Athens that the seller of a slave in the marketplace must disclose any mental or physical disease of the slave that would not be obvious to the buyer, and in the event that any undisclosed defect appeared within six months (twelve in the case of epilepsy) the seller would have to refund the price, or double the price if the seller was a professional slave dealer.[154]

The evidentiary basis of Roman law is very different from that of the ancient Near East and Greece, juristic writings rather than contractual documents, but the structure of the contract of sale is almost identical.[155] The principal distinction is that the focus of classical Roman law was the purely executory contract, where neither the price had been paid nor the property delivered. This is explicable by the different focus of the evidence: this is the analytically problematic case even if the wholly or partly executed contract might have been far commoner in practice. It did not matter how the agreement was made, though in Justinianic law it was laid down that if the parties had agreed that the contract would be put in writing it only became binding when the writing was drawn up;[156] in classical law, the giving of earnest, *arra*, was no more than evidence that the contract had been made.[157] The core of the Roman contract was the agreement to hand over property in exchange for money: the obligation of the buyer was to pay the

---

150 Keenan, Manning and Yiftach-Firanko 2014: 300–301.   151 Pringsheim 1950: 429–72.
152 Gortyn, VI.22, 42 and IX.13 (Gagarin and Perlman 2016).
153 Pringsheim 1950: 472–93.
154 Pl. *Laws* 916. To the same effect Hyperides, *Against Athenogenes*, 3.15.
155 de Zulueta 1945.   156 Justinian, *Cod.* 4.21.17.   157 Gaius, *Institutes* 3.139.

price, that of the seller to hand over the property; the sale agreement itself did not transfer ownership to the purchaser, though the risk of accidental loss or damage passed to him, as did the right to receive the fruits of the property (such as the young of an animal which had been sold). Alongside this core we find two contingent obligations. First was the duty of the seller to guarantee against eviction where the seller who had performed his core obligation of delivery had not made the buyer owner and the true owner had claimed the property. In early law, where *res mancipi* (Italic land, slaves or beasts of burden) had been delivered pursuant to a formal *mancipatio*,[158] the buyer was able to claim double the price paid by an *actio auctoritatis*.[159] As noted above, in the later Republic the practice developed of making a formal promise by *stipulatio* to compensate the disappointed buyer, typically to repay double the price for important contracts (mirroring the *actio auctoritatis*) and to compensate for loss in the case of less important contracts. In time, it was seen as contrary to good faith not to give the customary *stipulatio*, and by the time of Justinian this was implied in the sale itself.[160] The second contingent obligation was to guarantee against latent defects. As with the guarantee against eviction, the earliest form was associated with *mancipatio*: the actio *de modo agri* where the dimensions of land had been overstated. More generally, the recognition of the purely consensual contract of sale in the later Republic imposed liability on the seller who was aware of a latent defect in the property sold but did not disclose it to the buyer, or who made a statement about the property which turned out to be untrue. This was supplemented by the *Edict of the Curule Aediles* requiring sellers of slaves (and later draft animals) in the market to disclose defects and guarantee that there were none that were undisclosed: if any emerged the buyer was given an *actio redhibitoria* to rescind the sale or an *actio quanti minoris* for the difference between the value which the thing should have had and its actual value.[161] The juristic focus of the texts meant it was possible to make explicit that a range of subsidiary clauses were possible, such as allowing the buyer to renege on the contract if the price was not paid by a certain time or a better offer had been received for the property.[162]

As the Roman Empire, and Roman law, spread, there was something of an intermingling of Greek and Roman law. In Egypt, for example, the Roman model of purely consensual sale appeared in legal practice alongside or in place of the Greco-Egyptian system of registration or notarization, and sales

---

158 See Jolowicz and Nicholas 1972: 143–49.   159 Buckland 1963: 489.
160 de Zulueta 1945: 43–46.   161 de Zulueta 1945: 46–47.   162 de Zulueta, 1945: 55–59.

of slaves and animals use a mixture of Roman and Greco-Egyptian forms.[163] So far as warranties of quality were concerned, Greek and Roman law alike had regulated the sale of slaves, but while Roman law had been extended to the sale of animals Greek notaries typically excluded any such warranty until perhaps the fourth century CE.[164] The interplay of Greek and Roman rules is very clear in the function of earnest, *arrabon* or *arra*. The classical Roman rule was that the *arra* was simply a token marking the making of the contract, whereas for the Greeks it was a money payment forfeited by the buyer in the event of non-payment of the price. In the second century CE, the Greek rule was regularized: the defaulting buyer would forfeit the *arrabon*, the defaulting seller would be required to restore it twofold.[165] Justinian's law, rather inelegantly, united the two forms.[166] The *arra* was still evidence that the agreement had been made, but a term of the contract – whether expressly agreed or not – permitted the buyer to withdraw on forfeiture of the earnest and the seller to withdraw on the repayment of double. The effect of this was to replicate the Greek rule at the same time as integrating it within a Roman matrix.

India does not provide any useful archaeological evidence of sales, but the references in the Dharmaśāstra enable us to piece together the legal structure of the contract. The earliest treatment of the subject is found in the *Arthaśāstra* of Kautilya, whose original text can be dated between the middle of the first century BCE and the middle of the first century CE.[167] All sales are subject to the general rules of transactions: subject to certain exceptions they should be carried out openly by persons with full mental capacity observing all necessary formalities.[168] Special conditions of publicity were required for the sale of immovables, by auction; the fact that the seller was free to sell the property again if the purchaser did not turn up points towards the agreement itself generating at least provisional obligations before the price was paid.[169] In any sale, the seller who failed to deliver the property sold in due time or the buyer who refused to accept it would be fined unless the default was due to 'defect, disaster or unacceptability', circumstances generally excusing contractual non-performance.[170] Certain classes of seller were given a right to cancel the sale within a period of between one and seven days, presumably qualifying the

---

163 Taubenschlag 1955: 247, 250–54.   164 Pringsheim 1950: 487.
165 Taubenschlag 1955: 310.   166 Justinian, *Cod.* 4.21.17 (528 CE); Justinian, *Inst.* 3.23 pr.
167 Olivelle 2013: 28.   168 KAŚ 3.1 (Olivelle 2013: 179–80).
169 KAŚ 3.9 (Olivelle 2013: 196–97).
170 KAŚ 3.15.1–3, 9–10 (Olivelle 2013: 212, 213). For the interpretation of the excusing conditions, see Olivelle 2013: 617.

prohibition on non-delivery.[171] As a general principle, the seller of an article should be able to prove his ownership of it;[172] however, proof of ownership might involve no more than showing that it had been bought apparently legitimately, and if a true owner should claim the property after the sale, the purchase price should be refunded to the buyer and the property restored to the true owner, with the possibility that the original seller (or someone along the chain of sellers leading up to him) would be penalized for theft.[173] Sales of slaves and animals were subject to rules relating to their fitness for purpose: the seller who described a slave or animal as lively, healthy or well-disposed when it was in fact sluggish, sick or ill-disposed would be fined and the buyer could revoke the sale within three fortnights in the case of an animal and one year in the case of a slave.[174] The treatment of sale in the slightly later *Manava Dharmaśāstra* (probably second century CE) is abbreviated and very likely derived from the *Arthaśāstra*; the only relevant difference is that both buyer and seller were permitted to renege on the sale without penalty within ten days.[175] Probably a century or so later, the treatment of sale in the *Nārada Smṛti* and *Yājñavakya Smṛti* is built on a substrate of the *Arthaśāstra*, but with some marked changes. The distinction between moveable and immoveable property is retained, though no significant consequence flows from it.[176] There is no provision allowing the seller to withdraw from the sale, but the buyer might do within three days, though forfeiting part of the price after the first day.[177] The duty of the seller is to transfer the property, with the risk of accidental loss or damage falling on him;[178] and unlike in the *Arthaśāstra*, the failure to deliver necessitates compensation to the buyer rather than a fine.[179] Similarly, if the seller transfers the property to someone other than the buyer he is required to repay to the buyer double the price as well as paying a fine.[180] The same compensation and fine is due if the property does not match the description previously given to it.[181] Generally, though, it is for the buyer to examine the property before buying it, and after he has done so he cannot return it to the seller; for certain things a time period is allowed after the sale for the buyer to assure himself of the quality of the property.[182]

---

171 KAŚ 3.15.5–8 (Olivelle 2013: 212–13).   172 KAŚ 3.1.15, 3.16.17–18 (Olivelle 2013: 180, 214).
173 KAŚ 3.16.10–28 (Olivelle 2013: 214–15).   174 KAŚ 3.15.16–18 (Olivelle 2013: 213).
175 MDh 6.222 (Olivelle 2005a: 179).   176 NSm 8.2 (Lariviere 2003: 361).
177 NSm 9.3 (Lariviere 2003: 365).
178 NSm 8.6 (Lariviere 2003: 362); YDh 2.261 (Olivelle 2019a: 197).
179 NSm 8.4–5 (Lariviere 2003: 361–62); YDh 2.259 (Olivelle 2019a: 197).
180 NSm. 8.8 (Lariviere 2003: 362); YDh 2.262 (Olivelle 2019a: 199).
181 NSm 8.7 (Lariviere 2003: 362) YDh 2.262 (Olivelle 2019a: 199).
182 NSm 9.4–5 (Lariviere 2003: 365); YDh 2.181 (Olivelle 2019a: 173).

The evidence from China is relatively sparse: although there might have been statutes or ordinances these have not survived, the principal collections of statutes from the early second century BCE to the Tang Code of the seventh century CE are concerned primarily with criminal and administrative matters; and it is only from the fifth or sixth century CE that substantial numbers of sale documents in Chinese survive from Turfan on the western borders.[183] The silence of the major codes is unsurprising, as civil cases were within the localized jurisdiction of the district bailiff, rather than forming a part of the system of prosecutions which had the emperor at its apex.[184] There is clear evidence from inscriptions of private sales or exchanges occurring before the tenth century BCE,[185] but it is not until much later that we can talk about the typical form of sale contracts, and even then we need to bear in mind that small contracts would rarely have been evidenced in writing and hence have left no trace in the written record. By the sixth century CE, typicality can be described. In the sale of land, the buyer and the seller are identified as well as the land and the price; there is a provision for adjusting the price if the dimensions of the land are less than described, as well as a prohibition of reneging on the sale, often with a penalty of repayment of double the price; the contract would generally specify that if a third party came along and claimed the land it was the duty of the seller to defend the claim and would end with a list of witnesses and a statement that wine had been shared.[186] A typical contract for the sale of a slave would be very similar, except that there was no provision allowing adjustment of the price mirroring that in land sales.[187] Considerably earlier than this, the few extant documents concerning the sale of land reflect this later typical form,[188] and it may therefore be that this written form was already normal in the Han period. While there is little direct evidence about sale in the Tang Code of the early seventh century, some information can be gleaned indirectly. Most importantly, article 422 of the Code provides that sales of slaves, horses, cattle, camels, mules and donkeys required a market certificate to be drawn up within three days, subject to a penalty of thirty blows with the light stick; the article continues by providing:

---

183 Yamamoto and Ikeda 1987: 10.   184 Zhaoyang 2022: 68–79.
185 MacCormack 2014.
186 Yamamoto and Ikeda 1987: 18–19; examples with English translations in Hansen 1995: 24–33.
187 Yamamoto and Ikeda 1987: 19.
188 Hulsewé 1978b; note especially the guarantee against eviction in a document of 184 CE described at 33.

After the certificate is drawn up, if within three days a previous sickness is disclosed, it is allowed to cancel the sale. Where there is no sickness, but either party attempts to cheat the other, the sale shall be considered to have been made according to the law. Violations are punished by forty blows with the light stick.[189]

Generalized Conceptions of 'Contract'

All of the legal systems under examination recognized types of contract and provided legal mechanisms for their enforcement or to penalize their breach. Whether there lay behind them any generalized conception of 'contract' is more problematic. Greece and Rome provide the clearest evidence of this, though there are shadowy general principles in India and perhaps also China.

From the fourth century BCE, orators' speeches testify to an Athenian law that agreements voluntarily entered into should be upheld.[190] The common word for 'agreement', *homologia*, clearly points to a meeting of the minds of the parties.[191] A text of Hyperides is very telling. The orator is described as saying that his opponent will refer to the law that agreements are binding, but this is countered not by denying that there was any such law but by saying that it does not apply to agreements which are unjust.[192] Against the background of this law, specific examples are found of contracts which the Athenians did not recognise as legal.[193] Alongside this, account must be taken of the Aristotelian idea of *synallagma*, justice in exchange, an aspect of his corrective justice, applicable to both voluntary and involuntary transactions (*Nicomachean Ethics*, V.2.13 1131a). When applied to contracts, the paradigm of voluntary transactions, Aristotle is not clear whether the equality of exchange is to be measured objectively or subjectively. If the latter, which is more likely, his theory underpins the enforcement of voluntary agreements on the supposition that agents who had acted voluntarily would have accurately valued their own interests.[194]

The first Roman stirrings of any generalized thinking about 'contract' are visible in the thought of Quintus Mucius Scaevola at the start of the first century BCE,[195] distinguishing between the *nexum* as a source of obligation

---

189 Art. 422.2 (Johnson 1997: 485); see MacCormack 1985: 33–35.
190 Very clearly, Dem. 56 (*Against Dionysodorus*), 2. See too Pl. *Symp*. 196c.
191 Harris 2018b: 234–36, criticizing earlier analyses.
192 Hyperides, *Against Athenogenes*, 13; See, too, to the same effect, Pl. *Symp*., 196c and Arist., *Rhetoric* 1375b.
193 Dimopoulou 2014: 265–73. 194 Despotopoulos 1968; Murphy 2002.
195 Schiavone 2012: 202–3 and 210–14, placing the generalization of contract at the heart of the scientific development of Roman law.

and the *mancipatio* as a property transfer; before this there may have been little more than a list of typical transactions which would give rise to actions, with the possibility of petitioning for a remedy outside these cases.[196] The first true anchor point for future development was the thinking of the early imperial Labeo, reported by Ulpian as identifying voluntary exchange, the Greek *synallagma*, as the unifying element in non-formal contracts: 'A contract, however, is something which involves an obligation on both sides, which the Greeks call *synallagma*, such as purchase or sale, hire or partnership.'[197] For Labeo, therefore, the formal *stipulatio* which involved an obligation on only one party was not a contract. Pedius, a jurist of the early second century CE, brought agreement to the fore, bringing the *stipulatio* into the general conception. Again, as reported by Ulpian:

> Moreover, so true is it that the word '*consensus*' has a general significance that Pedius elegantly says that there is no contract, no obligation, which does not include agreement, whether it is achieved by the handing over of something or by the use of certain words. In fact, even a *stipulatio*, which is made by the use of certain words, is void unless there is agreement.[198]

This is reflected in Gaius' *Institutes* a few decades later, where the general category of contracts included both formal and informal agreements.[199] From here it became canonical in the Roman taxonomy. This essentialism had three negative consequences. First, it meant that unilateral oaths or promises, where there was not even the appearance of agreement as there was in the *stipulatio*, were marginalized, being treated outside the law of contract.[200] Secondly, even if *consensus* was at the base of all contractual liability, it did not follow that all agreements were contracts. Ulpian grappled with this, saying that there need also be a *causa*, though the meaning of this is obscure.[201] Later law did extend actionability to otherwise unenforceable reciprocal agreements which had been performed on one side, the so-called innominate contracts; but there remained the category of bare pacts which were not actionable. Thirdly – and much later – it has affected the (English) language of the historiography and theorization of the language of contract law, with such words as 'contract', 'promise' and 'agreement' being used almost

---

196 Fiori 2016: 585–89.
197 Justinian, *Digest* 50.16.19 (Contractum autem ultro citroque obligationem, quod graeci sunallagma vocant, veluti emptionem venditionem, locationem conductionem, societatem); Schiavone 2012: 325–37.
198 Justinian, *Digest* 2.14.1.3.   199 Gaius, *Institutes* 3.89.
200 Buckland 1963: 457 n. 11 (*pollicitatio*).
201 Justinian, *Digest* 2.14.7, esp. 2.14.7.4. The better view is that *causa* here refers to something or performance given or done in exchange for an undertaking.

interchangeably without any sharp definition. Roman law went further. The basic framework of the *Institutes* divided informal contracts into those which were binding simply because of the making of the agreement and those whose bindingness depended on property having been delivered, conventionally described as consensual and real respectively. While this had a structural function in Roman law after Gaius' *Institutes*, it should not be seen as fundamental to its system of contracts. Moreover, the Roman system of actions recognized that some contracts (such as sale) depended on good faith, whereas other types of contract (such as a loan of money) entailed a strict obligation; but this distinction should not be taken too far, since from the middle of the first century BCE it was possible to counter an action based on a strict obligation with a defence, an *exceptio doli*, that it would be unjust to enforce the obligation. Moreover, the stress on consensus allowed the law to focus on the voluntariness of the parties' acts,[202] refusing to enforce contracts by those with impaired capacity.

Indian law was more granular, listing the grounds for litigation without any clear conceptual generalization. More or less the same lists are found in the *Arthaśāstra*, the *Manava Dharmaśāstra*, the *Nārada Smṛti* and the *Yājñavakya Smṛti*, though in different orders. The list in the *Manava Dharmaśāstra* is typical:

> Non-payment of debts; deposits; sale without ownership; partnerships; non-delivery of gifts; non-payment of wages; breach of contract;[203] cancellation of a sale or purchase; disputes between owners and herdsmen; the law on boundary disputes; verbal assault; physical assault; theft; violence; sexual crimes against women; law concerning husband and wife; partition of inheritance; gambling and betting.[204]

It is a disparate list, without any clear generalization.[205] However, the opening section of Book 3 of the *Arthaśāstra* does point to some underlying idea.[206] After specifying that transactions should normally be made openly and listing the class of people incapable of entering into legally valid arrangements, it specifies that transactions entered into openly by a person with full capacity might still not be valid: 'Even in such cases transactions executed by

---

202 Quintilian, *Institutiones Oratoriae* 7.6.1.
203 A narrow class of situations where a man has entered into a contract on behalf of a corporate entity truthfully but then breaks it out of greed; *MDh* 8.219 (Olivelle 2005a: 179 with note at 317).
204 *MDh*, 8.4–7 (Olivelle 2005a: 167).
205 For the parallels, see Kane 1962–75, vol. III: 248–49.
206 *KAŚ* 3.1.1–16 (Olivelle 2013: 179–80).

a person who is enraged, deeply afflicted, intoxicated, insane, or under someone else's control shall not be valid.'[207]

The Chinese evidence for the existence of any general principle is the most equivocal, unsurprisingly so given the lack of concern with civil law in the surviving Qin/Han and Tang codes. What can be seen is the crystallization of the word *yüeh* with the meaning of agreement; but it would be going too far to deduce from this any principle that all agreements should prima facie create binding obligations.[208]

Conclusion: An Economy of Ideas?

A final issue which needs to be addressed in this chapter is the extent to which ideas might have passed from one culture to another, even over long distances. The physical form of contractual documents points to the possibility that there might have been some influence. Some similarities can undoubtedly be put down to independent adoptions of similar practices: the Chinese scribe breaking a brick in two, one half for each party to an agreement, might have been doing something like what a contemporary Babylonian scribe was doing when he made two copies of a document; but we would not even want to conjecture that one had borrowed an obvious idea from the other. But when contracts on wooden diptychs are found not only in the Roman empire but also in Gandhara (now northwest Pakistan) or in a slightly different form in Khotan, in all cases with the text of the contract sealed inside and a summary written on the outside, it is hard not to see some practice spreading along the Silk Road through central Asia.[209] In the same way, when the Greek 'double document' form is found in Bactrian contracts from what is now northern Afghanistan, cultural diffusion along merchant routes is extremely likely.[210]

So far as substantive rules and practices are concerned, some similarities, such as the use of seals (as noted above), can plausibly be explained as independent developments responding to the need for some means of identification replacing or supplementing the signature, thumb print or other personal identifier. That said, their employment in long-distance trade could have stabilized their usage. Other common features are so widespread and so

[207] KAŚ 3.1.13 (Olivelle 2013: 180).   [208] MacCormack 2014: 13–15.
[209] Zang Zhang (personal communication); Burrow 1940. The same document may have a seal in Chinese characters and a seal showing a Greek-influenced head: http://idp.bl.uk/4DCGI/education/silk_road/pages/khot047.html (accessed 16/08/2022).
[210] Sims-Williams 2012.

fundamental that it is improbable that they had come about by diffusion from one developed system to another. The mixing of blood or the sharing of wine as a blood substitute (as discussed above) is perhaps the best example of this. Whether this arose independently in different places or is a reflection of a very deep-seated cultural practice goes beyond the evidence to resolve. As we have seen, the same is true of the marking out of certain property, essentially slaves and domestic animals, as requiring a particular form for their sale. The presence of very similar rules for the magisterial regulation of the quality of goods sold in the market in Greece, Rome and China cannot be so easily explained. That the Roman rules were derived from Greece is abundantly likely, but that these rules in their turn shaped the law in Tang China must remain an unproved conjecture.[211] However, the ubiquity of long-distance trade in slaves by the time of the Tang Code, and perhaps long before, renders it a not improbable conjecture.

211 MacCormack 1985: 35, n. 70.

12

Conclusion

CAROLINE HUMFRESS

Introduction: Thinking Historically about 'Ancient Law'

Everything is to be found in the *Corpus Iuris*.[1]

According to the medieval jurist Accursius (c. 1181–c. 1289 CE), all things are to be found within Emperor Justinian's sixth-century CE Roman lawbooks. As the chapters of the *Cambridge Comparative History of Ancient Law* (*CCHAL*) have shown, however, there is a wealth of ancient law to be discovered beyond the texts of Rome. To understand Accursius' claim accurately, we would have to contextualize it within the complex scholastic structures of the medieval *ius commune* – which is not our objective here. Suffice to say that the 'learned law' of the medieval and early modern *ius commune* tradition – in particular the doctrine of Roman law as *ratio scripta* (written reason), which Accursius himself helped to crystallize – continues to cast a long shadow over European – and global – legal history today.[2] That legal authority itself should be text-based and rational – amenable to human reasoning – tends to be understood within the Western legal tradition as an inheritance specifically from ancient Rome:

> In the past, the civilian tradition gave an order and system to a chthonic world. The Roman revolution was to create a secular law with written rules and written legal literature, a formalist procedure, and rational decision-making (albeit essentially casuistic) ... This civil law tradition emerges from

---

[1] Accurius, *Gl. notitia ad D.* 1.1.10: *omnia in corpore iuris inveniuntur*, quoted from Giuliani 2019: 37.
[2] See Winkel 2020 and Duve 2018.

Introduction: Thinking Historically about 'Ancient Law'

a gradual process in which the historical roots have been re-worked over various periods of time and in different countries. As a result, it has come to acquire a cumulation of features, many of which are common to the Western legal tradition. In the medieval revival, it dominated the chthonic ideas and provided a legal canvas larger than a local area, a network of ideas and discussions.[3]

In terms of this specific framing of the Western legal tradition, the medieval *ius commune* – which included the learned law of Romanists and Canonists – 'dominated the chthonic ideas' (the predominately oral law of small, bounded, communities across medieval Europe), which led, in turn, to the development of a written, textualized, legal canvas that stretched beyond the local and into the modern era. What the civil law tradition had done for the European Middle Ages, Roman law was also said to have done for the ancient world and, it was hoped, could do again, in a revived form, for a new, reconstructed, Europe – or so leading early- and mid-twentieth-century legal comparativists argued.[4]

In a series of publications stretching from his inaugural lecture at the University of Vienna in 1904 through to studies completed at Munich in the early 1930s, Leopold Wenger (1874–1953) famously argued for a new discipline of 'ancient legal history' (*antike Rechtsgeschichte*).[5] According to Wenger, ancient Roman law functioned as a melting pot for ancient Mediterranean law. Hence the study of Roman law could contribute to the understanding of non-Roman ancient law and vice versa: research into ancient Egyptian papyri, Greek law codes and cuneiform texts could advance Roman legal science, at the same time as the study of Roman jurisprudence could contribute to scientific knowledge about ancient Near Eastern law. Wenger's *antike Rechtsgeschichte* was partly intended as a move away from the private-law-focused, doctrinal or 'dogmatic', study of Roman law that had dominated nineteenth- and early twentieth-century ('modern') European legal studies and nation-state building alike. As Ulrike Babusiaux states: 'In Europe, the study of Roman law has a longstanding tradition as an analysis of the legal foundations of one's own codification of private law.'[6] Wenger's *antike Rechtsgeschichte*, however, was also a product of its time in the sense that

---

3 Bell 2006: 130, summarizing Patrick Glenn's view of the civil law tradition.
4 For discussion see Osler 1997 and Zimmermann 2015: esp. 470, on the recreation of 'a European scholarship of private law'.
5 Wenger 1905 and Wenger 1953: esp. 1–45. See Höbenreich 1992 for further discussion.
6 Babusiaux 2016: 6. See also Zimmermann 2001: 13 on 'Roman law as the basis for a contemporary theory of private law', arguing (implicitly) against Roman law's modern 'descent into history'.

fundamental primary sources for the study of non-Roman ancient law(s) had only been recently discovered.[7] Early scholars of non-Roman ancient law tended to have been scholars of Roman law first; hence, whilst these scholars did not subscribe to Wenger's theory of an ancient legal history (singular): 'Early twentieth-century scholars of newly discovered cuneiform texts ... tended to read the Near Eastern material "through the prism" of their Roman law training. Their work sought to determine how Babylonian law resembled or differed from Roman law, with the ulterior motive, sometimes unconscious, of highlighting the qualities of the latter in contrast to the deficiencies of the former.'[8] This 'tendency to attract Near Eastern law into the Roman matrix', as Démare-Lafont notes, 'has lost ground as our knowledge of legal practices of the ancient Near East has increased, but the relevance of the comparison is still a matter of debate'.[9] A similar observation could be made of the recent trend for comparative studies between ancient Greek law and Roman law or Jewish (rabbinic) law and Roman law, or indeed ancient China and Rome.

Expanding the comparative framework of ancient law, however, does not necessarily lead to a broadening of intellectual horizons. 'One of the colonialist techniques of modern anthropology was the presumption that ancient law reflects a primitive stage in human and legal development.'[10] During the late nineteenth century, comparative legal history was developed as one instrument of domination among many in the colonial administrator's toolbox: 'to study comparative legal history was to study the evolution of 'civilization' itself'.[11] Whether the linear-development framework was evolutionary (from ancient / primitive to modern / advanced) or historicist (explaining the complexity of the present by studying the processes through which it came about), ancient law was fashioned as a primitive, static, or even ahistorical, law – with the regular exception of classical, doctrinal, Roman law as a harbinger of 'the modern'.[12] If, however, we reject a general sense of Rome as the dynamic melting pot or lodestar of an ancient law focused

---

7 Egyptian papyri: from the late 1870s; Gortyn law code: 1884; *Codex Hammurabi*: 1902. Paul Koschaker's seminal *Babylonisch-Assyrisches Bürgschaftsrecht* was published in 1911, seven years after Wenger's inaugural Vienna lecture.
8 Démare-Lafont 2015b: xv–xx at xv, referring to Josef Kohler, Paulo Koschaker and Mariano San Nicolò.
9 Démare-Lafont 2015b: xv.
10 Wimpfheimer 2019: 72. See further Tuori 2015 and more generally, Ruskola 2013.
11 Goodale 2017: 9. For concrete examples see Adluri and Bagchee 2014.
12 Compare the portrayal of Roman legal development in Gans' Hegelian-influenced *Historical Development of Inheritance Law* (*Erbrecht in weltgeschichtlicher Entwicklung*, 1824–35) and Maine 1861.

Introduction: Thinking Historically about 'Ancient Law'

predominately on the Mediterranean – as we have consciously attempted to do throughout these volumes – where does a comparative approach to ancient legal history take us?

The first point to note is the scale of historical time covered by the *CCHAL* project. As Raymond Westbrook and others have argued, legal history does not begin with classical Greek and Roman antiquity.[13] The written primary source material included in *CCHAL* covers roughly three and a half millennia, from the earliest, very fragmentary, 'proto-cuneiform' tablets from Uruk III (3200–3000 BCE) to the Tang Code of 652 CE. As Chapter 10 of this volume argues, with specific reference to the concept of property, archaeological and material evidence pushes our legal timescale back further: 'By the time we get to our first written legal documentation discussed in this volume, the concept of property, of ownership and of property rights had evolved ... for more than 7,000 years.' In terms of ancient Near Eastern civilizations alone, 'the timespan from the late fourth to the late first millennium BCE is equal to, or even longer than, the rest of history, from the collapse of the Near Eastern cultures to our own time'.[14] Thinking historically about ancient law thus necessitates thinking about change and continuity *through* time and across multiple, changing, broader contexts. For example, the fact that ancient Near Eastern cuneiform traditions remained alive after the conquest of Alexander (331 BCE), through the period of Hellenistic rule (331–141 BCE) and well into the Parthian period (141 BCE–225 BCE), does not imply a single, static, legal tradition, but rather a living legal tradition, in which normative ideas and practices from the past were continually being reinterpreted and redeployed across new political, social and institutional contexts.

The second point to stress is the complexity of the ancient geographical and socioeconomic landscapes – plural – encompassed by the *CCHAL* project. This complexity is exposed, for example, by taking into account stark contrasts and variabilities in geomorphology, natural environments and climate – especially in terms of their impact on the organisation and governance of premodern societies. Complexity is also revealed across different forms of socioeconomic organisation (agricultural, nomadic, urban – not necessarily to be understood as discrete categories) and political organization (different types and scales of state formations). Long-distance interconnectivity, including interactions across and between the Mediterranean, Mesopotamia, Arabia, India, East Asia and beyond, is a further, fundamental, component of analysis, as demonstrated especially in Chapter 4 (this volume) with

---

13 Démare-Lafont 2015b: xviii.   14 Liverani 2020: 11.

reference to interstate relations and Chapter 11 with reference to contracts and the activity of contracting.

A more detailed legal topography would go beyond the heuristic ancient Eurasian traditions or 'systems' introduced in Chapter 1 – framing the analysis in terms of regional and other geographical sub-units, critiquing perceived divisions and boundaries.[15] To take one example: as explained in Chapter 1 and referred to throughout, major recent archaeological finds have yielded substantial new material relating to early Chinese law and legal practice – yet what we today refer to as 'China' accounts for only part of the Asian continent. 'If Asian law simply means Chinese law, this leaves a huge gap in the map between Istanbul (30°E) and Dunhuang (105°E)'; it also excludes mainland Southeast Asia and island Southeast Asia.[16] As noted in Chapter 8 of this volume – with specific reference to Buddhist, Jaina and Ājīvika mendicant orders, as well as Brahmin priestly and scholastic communities – ancient Tibetan (Central Asia) and Pali (Southeast Asia) Buddhist traditions developed elaborate legal codes and apparatus for internal self-governance. More broadly, as Huxley argues, most parts of Eurasia share a commitment to written law that was rarely matched in

> Africa or the Americas and never in Oceania or Antarctica. Written law has spread across Eurasia in all directions from the city of Uruk in Iraq. Spreading west, it flowered in the third century CE along the Tiber, forming the roots of Europe's legal tradition. Spreading east, it flowered along the Ganges during the last three centuries BCE, and along the Mekong and Irrawadi a millennium later. Since some Babylonian astronomical observations are preserved in the Chinese tradition, it is not beyond possibility that Mesopotamian written law influenced north China.[17]

Two further key questions for future research emerge: first, 'how does this Eurasian preference for written law tie in with Eurasia's distinctive crops, livestock, diseases and technology?'[18] Second, and more broadly, to what extent does this ancient Eurasian preference for written law underpin the idea of Europe as the 'preferred spatial frame of analysis' for legal history, right up until at least the end of the twentieth century?[19]

---

15 As Démare-Lafont 2015b: xvi explains, Raymond Westbrook 'considered antiquity as a geographic whole and sought in the Mediterranean world the signs of a Near Eastern legacy', arguing (1) there was a common Near Eastern tradition, including both Mesopotamian and biblical law; (2) that part of this tradition spread to Greek and Roman spheres; and (3) that contacts and exchanges were to be expected. For further discussion of the 'Westbrook thesis', see Chapter 6, this volume.
16 Huxley 2006: 160, critiquing Glenn's single category of 'Asian Law'.
17 Huxley 2006: 163.   18 Huxley 2006: 163.   19 Quotations from Duve 2018: 117.

Introduction: Thinking Historically about 'Ancient Law'

The comparative history of ancient law can thus be conceptualized as a pan-Eurasian research field, developed through collaborative work that draws upon numerous specialist traditions and technical expertise.[20] As to be expected, the thematic chapters of the *CCHAL* volume reveal some basic shared ideas, principles and procedures (see the more detailed discussion below), but not enough to warrant approaching 'ancient law' as a unified subject for either historical or legal inquiry. Via its relatively extended historical timeframe, the Eurasian focus and the working methods of the *CCHAL* project work to de-centre and contextualize ancient Roman legal categories and doctrines: Roman categories and doctrines which might otherwise be taken as the start-point for all comparands when thinking about 'ancient law'. For example, using ancient Indian material as our starting point for comparisons across ancient Near Eastern, Greek, Roman, Egyptian and Chinese traditions, as in Chapter 5 ('Law and the State'), Chapter 7 ('Legal Procedure') and Chapter 8 ('Status and Family'), not only showcases the sophistication of Brahmanical legal thinking but also pinpoints those ideas and concepts that do not feature as part of Roman (or Near Eastern, Greek, Chinese, etc.) ideas and practices.

What, then, of the 'ineradicable singularity' of Rome? Should Rome be understood as unique in relation to the rest of the ancient world?

> the Roman situation achieved an ineradicable singularity. It would be the only one in the ancient world where the production of rules of social behaviour – the creation of *ius* in the still archaic sense of the term – once it began to break away in a more definitive manner from the domain of religion, would not be entirely integrated within the model of politics and legislation, as in Greece, where the presence of statutes as forms of political command would soon become the mark of the fully achieved and complete secularization of the urban societies. Instead, it would remain in the hands of a restricted circle of wise men, who would build around it a technical and exclusive body of knowledge, which would be distinguished at a fairly early point from both religious and political experience.[21]

A key aspect of Rome's 'ineradicable singularity' seems to lie here with the Roman jurists and the technical, specifically 'legal' – not 'religious', not 'political' – body of knowledge that they produced. Rather than arguing

---

20 Recent examples focused mainly on Near Eastern (including biblical), Greek and Roman traditions: Faraguna 2013; Nowicki 2016; Pfeifer and Grotkamp 2017; and Etxabe 2019.
21 Schiavone 2012: 57. See also Schiavone 2012: 3, 'Law is a social and mental form that has invaded modernity, quickly becoming an essential component of our lives – and it is a form invented by the ancient Romans.'

that a comparative analysis of ancient law needs to go beyond such a legal dogmatic view, the more important counter-argument revealed by our comparative history of (Eurasian) ancient law is that Rome was *not* alone in developing a specifically 'legal' body of knowledge. The real challenge thus lies in defining and comparing the multiple, complex gradations that work to distinguish 'specifically legal' bodies of knowledge from 'religious and political experience' within and across diverse bodies of ancient source material.[22] It is to this point that we turn now.

Mapping the Ancient Legal Cosmos

Let him not become vexed or easily deceived by the pronouncements of hypocrites, crooks, infidels and fools. *Dharma* and *adharma* do not go around saying: 'Here we are!' Nor do gods and Gandharvas, or the ancestors declare: 'This is *dharma*. This is *adharma*.'[23]

According to the *Dharmaśāstra* of Āpastamba (probably third to early second century BCE), *dharma* and *adharma* do not identify themselves; nor are they defined for us by gods, minor deities or ancestors. Within the very different expert tradition of rabbinic literature (third to seventh century CE), the sages would have disagreed with Āpastamba's statement: (the Hebrew) God declares his commandments. Nonetheless, within late antique rabbinic traditions it still fell to expert human interpreters to state 'this is *Halakhah*, this is (all that is) not *Halakhah*'.[24] This idea, that making sense of law is a specifically *human* endeavour, is found across ancient societies and time periods from Indian Dharmaśāstras to archaic Greek legends and Roman imperial law codes.[25] Whether law is understood as unauthored and part of the cosmos itself (as in Hindu tradition and ancient Chinese Yellow Emperor or *Huang-Lao* thought), or understood as commanded by god(s), laid down by human rulers, or agreed between citizens, it must be identified and interpreted using *human* faculties and senses.

In Plato's *Symposium* (c. 385 BCE) written law is presented as one aspect of an all-too-human desire to overcome death: the goal of *eros* (erotic passion) is

---

22 For more detailed discussion see Chapter 3 ('Legal Science'), Chapter 5 ('Law and the State') and Chapter 6 ('Law and Religion'), this volume.
23 *ApDh* 1.20.6, Olivelle 2017a: 52–53.
24 On Jewish divine law as 'positive law' (an act of divine will), see Hayes 2015.
25 On archaic Greek legends see Szegedy-Maszak 1978: 208: 'It is striking how forcefully the [Greek] legends assert that law is a human endeavour.' On Roman imperial lawbooks see *Const. Omnem*, parallel Latin text and English translation in Justinian, *Digest*, ed. and trans. Watson et al., vol. I: l–lv.

not necessarily biological reproduction, some humans aim instead at a superior 'pregnancy of the soul' – a pregnancy that seeks to give birth to enduring works of art, such as the customs and laws crafted by the Spartan Lycurgus and Athenian Solon (208e–209e). The *Symposium* thus envisages 'the attainment of a degree of immortality through creating a law code'.[26] Plato's striking idea of erotic desire motivating the production of undying laws and customs underscores a broader connection, found across all ancient traditions, which links human creativity to the crafting of rightly ordered selves, households, cities, kingdoms and empires. According to Szegedy-Maszak's analysis of legends of ancient Greek lawgivers, for example, whether the lawgivers (*nomothetai*) are inspired by a god or not, the initial situation is invariably portrayed as crisis (either *stasis*, 'an active internecine conflict', or a 'sense of tension' created by 'colonial enterprise' in the colonies of Magna Graecia), which allows the legends' narrative momentum to be 'provided by the state's progress from lack to final acceptance of a code, that is from *anomia* to *eunomia*'.[27] Human creativity overcomes lawlessness (understood by some early Greek thinkers to include a cosmic lack of law and order) through the construction of well-ordered human associations.[28] *Eunomia*, good or 'lawful' order, in turn requires ordered behaviour, each in their right place – what we might term an ancient constitutional imaginary.

Ancient didactic wisdom literature should be understood as belonging to this same ancient constitutional imaginary, rather than being separated out from 'legal literature' as a qualitatively different sphere of intellectual activity. As some modern scholars of ancient Near Eastern law have argued, the scholasticism that underpins ancient Mesopotamian wisdom literature is the same type of intellectual method that gives authority to ancient Mesopotamian law collections.[29] Mesopotamian wisdom literature and law collections alike were used to teach students how to think in a rightly ordered way. As Don Davis puts it with reference to Hindu tradition, ethical expertise (including wisdom traditions) and legal expertise functioned 'as shared "jurisprudential regimes" for decision-making'.[30]

The science of *dharma* (*dharmaśāstra*) – the primary discipline devoted to jurisprudential reflection within the Brahmanical scholastic tradition – ordered a vast body of precepts into a Brahmanical model of 'right' conduct (Chapters 1 and 3, this volume). Fashioned gradually out of disparate

---

26 Sedley 2017: 334.   27 Szegedy-Maszak 1978: 201–2.
28 Compare Chapter 4 (this volume) on war and conflict being the normal state in international affairs, as opposed to peace and order.
29 Démare-Lafont 2015b: xviii.   30 Davis 2006: 287–88.

elements roughly during the centuries between the two Candraguptas (the founders of the Maurya and Gupta dynasties)', Dharmaśāstra was an elite, intellectual, project which aimed at defining 'a holistic vision of society, and the life well lived therein'.[31] Ancient Indian law as we know it is thus primarily a scholars' law, comparable in this respect to Roman and Rabbinic traditions (Chapter 3).

Within the Brahmanical tradition, 'law as *dharma* had no territorial or even temporal limits, and its epistemic sources, therefore, had to be universally applicable and recognized'.[32] Hence the importance, within Dharmaśāstra, of explicit discussions concerning how we come to know *dharma* and the sources of *dharma*. In this sense, (modern) categorizations of the science of *dharma* as 'religious', in contrast with the 'secularity' of Roman law, set up a false dichotomy. The more telling question, perhaps, is why the extant body of Roman jurisprudence does not feature more explicit, extended, discussions of how we come to know *ius* and the sources of *ius*. In sum, as Chapter 3 argues, law was considered as a specific field of knowledge, distinguishable from but related to others, across ancient Near Eastern, Chinese, Indian, Greek, Roman and late antique (Jewish) rabbinic traditions.

Jurisprudential literature from ancient India can, in fact, be classified according to three expert traditions: the science of *dharma* (*dharmaśāstra*), the science of 'statecraft' and Vedic exegesis. As Mark McLish explains, there were two approaches to the science of 'statecraft' in ancient India: an 'expert tradition on governance' (*nīti*; *arthaśāstra*) and a tradition of 'the law(s) for kings' (*rājadharma*).[33]

> Although both address the 'public functions of the king', the former is characterized by its singular commitment to the techniques of statecraft that will bring worldly success to the king, while the latter conceptualizes all of this within the soteriological framework of the 'Whole Duty of the king', strongly shaped 'by the ideal of the highest good of this individual'.[34]

Crucially, the (former) expert tradition on governance (*nīti*) did not evolve out of the (latter) *dharma* tradition: 'on the whole, we have clear evidence of a continuous and coherent tradition of technical rules for statecraft'.[35] According to Kauṭilya's *Arthaśāstra* (probably first century BCE to first

---

31 Lubin 2017: 179. See also Davis 2017: 3–4. 32 Olivelle 2017a: 19.
33 McClish 2017a: 257.
34 McClish 2017a: 257. See also Chapter 9, this volume.
35 McLish 2017a: 258 and 261–62, also suggesting a wider context for this statecraft tradition 'given ... that monarchies and empires had existed in South Asia already for many centuries'.

century CE), the techniques of statecraft encompass domestic administration: the duties of the king in 'settling the land', 'building fortified cities', providing for law and order through detailed bureaucratic and legal provisions and the ability to eradicate 'thorns' (which demands the surveillance of artisans' and traders' activities; 'remedial measures against disasters'; 'surveillance of people with secret income'; and detecting, investigating and punishing criminal behaviour, including sexual offences). Kauṭilya's techniques of statecraft also cover international relations: the duties of the king in relation to foreign policy and relations with various other types of polities; 'calamities to the state'; warfare and sieges etc., in addition to skills in the employment of 'esoteric [occult] practices' across both domestic and international spheres.[36] Here it is the king, rather than the ancient Greek lawgiver (or *demos*), who is expected to craft 'good' order by applying the techniques of law and statecraft, but it is once again human faculties and senses that are called upon to do the crafting. The idea of right-ordering *as legality* was not unique to Roman jurisprudence.[37]

Ordering Ancient Association(s): Ethics, Law and Statecraft

> The Grandee [Secretary] said: 'Edicts are the means to teach the people, and laws are the means to control wrongdoers. If edicts are severe then the people will be cautious, and if laws are applied then wrongdoing will be forbidden. If a net is loose, then animals will escape from it. So, too, if the law is loose then the guilty will slip away. If the guilty slip away, then the people will indulge themselves and casually violate prohibitions. If one is not resolute in one's prohibitions, cowards will get lucky'.[38]

The *Discourses on Salt and Iron* portray a number of Han dynasty government representatives engaging in an imperially sponsored debate, with 'classically trained [Confucian] scholars', over government control of salt and iron production (81 BCE). In the quotation above, from chapter 55 of the text, 'the Grandee [Secretary]' – possibly to be identified as the first-century BCE Grandee Secretary Sang Hongyang – compares penal laws to nets that must be held tight if the people are to be controlled. The Grandee [Secretary]'s interlocutor, the 'classically trained scholar' or 'literati', agrees that penal laws

---

36 Olivelle 2013: 63–434.   37 Contra Schiavone 2012: 449.
38 '"Punishment and Virtue" (*Xingde*), chapter 55 of the *Discourses on Salt and Iron* (*Yantielun*), 81 BCE)', quoted from Csikszentmihalyi 2006: 38. For background on government control of 'the profits of salt and iron' under the Han dynasty, see Loewe 2011: 102.

are necessary but they must be simple and few: 'Therefore when a true king administers laws, the true king makes them as clear as the sun and moon so the people are never confused; he makes them as wide as a highway so the people are never misled'; the failure of the previous Qin dynasty, continues the scholar, 'was not because their web was loose and the guilty passed through, but rather because ritual and social obligations were abandoned and punishments and laws were unrestricted'.[39] 'Laws', the scholar concludes, 'are administered based on human dispositions; they are not made to create guilt and entrap people so they fall into danger'.[40] This first-century BCE debate does not oppose ethics to law, rather the disagreement is carefully framed in terms of how, exactly, the lawgiver should expect edicts and penal laws to teach ethical values and ensure 'right' (cosmic, ethical, political, etc.) ordering. For the 'classically trained scholar', reforming people's morals in order to reduce lawsuits was a specifically legal (and cosmic, ethical, political, etc.) ideal.

All ancient states used legal techniques to make people and things 'legible'. These techniques range from the registration and tabulation of individuals at village level, through to the creation and maintenance of sophisticated property archives in urban centres. The late Roman bureaucracy even distinguished between the type of script to be used in communications sent from the provinces (commonly used letters, *litterae communes*) and communications sent from the central, imperial (Palatine) bureaus ('celestial letters', *litterae caelestes*).[41] Writing and record-keeping were equally central to the administration of the (ancient Indian) Kauṭilyan state: 'every administrator was required to keep written records of their activities and present them to the central authority; even wardens of elephant forests were expected to keep records of their elephant census'.[42] Official record-keeping in relation to taxation regimes also appears to have been a near-universal phenomenon. Premodern states played a fundamental role in defining – and collecting – taxes on agricultural (and to a lesser extent, mercantile) production, in addition to delineating 'enabling' rules that governed transfers of rights, obligations, privileges and exceptions.[43] Official land surveys and registration, in particular, appear as a common feature across ancient societies – as do various state schemes for standardizing weights, measures and units of time, all of which underpinned 'public' and 'private' legal processes and transactions alike.

---

39 Csikszentmihalyi 2006: 39. 40 Csikszentmihalyi 2006: 43.
41 *Theod. Cod.* 19.19.3 (Edict of Valentinian I and Valens, 367 CE). 42 Olivelle 2017b: 292.
43 See Chapters 5 and 10, this volume.

Private disputes and criminal punishment are two areas in which ancient states used legal techniques intensively.[44] As always in the field of ancient law, however, conclusions drawn from identifying patterns across the extant evidence can be misleading. For example, as discussed above, early Chinese states 'seem to espouse a positive belief that by writing down laws and making them publicly known, they can provide a visible, written standard of conduct for all levels of society'.[45] Given the focus of the early dynastic codes on administrative and penal measures (which included detailed penalties for 'deviant' conduct relating to 'civil' matters such as marriage, divorce, loans, bailment, etc.), traditional views of early Chinese law tend to stress the extent to which it was 'informed by the rationality of state and directed at social control'.[46] The discovery of new caches of bamboo strip manuscripts, however, suggests a widespread use of legal instruments to order private affairs, in addition to various kinds of private dispute resolution – for example, case reports preserved in the Han period – Juyan strips refer to the settlement of 'civil' disputes (debts, compensation, transactions, inheritances) by district bailiffs.[47] The similarity of language in legal documents found across the Chinese empires and dynasties suggests that parties employed scribes, who followed standard models for written documents.[48] Conversely, for Rome, it is the civil law – specifically the rules that governed private citizens – which is more visible in the historical record (to a large extent due to the importance of Roman jurisprudence within the later civilian law tradition), with the late Republican and early imperial statutes and *leges* that undeniably shaped Roman legal development being relatively neglected (as argued by Dario Mantovani).[49]

'In all cases examined, law is used to enhance the legitimacy of state power.'[50] State power, however, was not universally understood as the source of all law.[51]

Reading these statements alongside each other leads to two fundamental insights about ancient legal history: firstly, for every time and place covered in these volumes, numerous different kinds of legal orderings existed at levels not controlled by the state. Secondly, some ancient states carved out space for these non-state legal orderings, in addition to seeking to control them – thereby developing a distinctive set of normative ideas and practices relating

---

44 As argued in Chapter 5, this volume.   45 Caldwell 2014: 30.
46 Watson 2019: abstract.
47 Zhang 2022: 11.   48 Chapter 2, this volume.
49 See Chapter 3, this volume, for discussion.   50 Chapter 9, this volume.
51 Chapter 5, this volume.

to the (modern) concept of jurisdiction. Ancient law was not just the language of state, it was also the language of a much broader range of different kinds of ancient communities, associations and networks.[52]

Recent scholarship suggests that virtually all ancient 'private associations' shared the aim of producing good order, usually understood in a physical, concrete, sense, as ordered behaviour or 'decency'. Hence, as Gabrielson and Paganini state with reference to Greco-Roman 'associative phenomenon', a 'secure indication of the existence of a formal guild or association is the evidence of a lex or νόμος'.[53] The 'good order' of the Greco-Roman association, its lex or νόμος, is often framed in the source material as a reflection of – and participation in – civic (and from the Hellenistic era onwards, imperial) 'good order' and, by extension, cosmic good order too. Hence the laws of ancient Greek city states and Rome carve out space for 'private associations' and their customs and laws, whilst simultaneously seeking to define and limit a specific range of permissible behaviours and practices. The writers of ancient Dharmaśāstras also acknowledged numerous domains of law that, as Patrick Olivelle puts it, did not have to be recognized by the king to be valid.[54] Kauṭilya's Arthaśāstra portrays law as not one, but multiple; whilst the Nārada Smṛti lists five venues of litigation, 'each latter one superior to the former': families, guilds, assemblies, appointed judge and the king (NSm1.7). Both the Arthaśāstra and the Nārada Smṛti thus depict a juristic conception of jurisdiction, at the same time as acknowledging the co-existence of multiple types of ancient legal orderings.

Conclusion: What Is 'Ancient' about 'Ancient Law'?

What, in the final analysis, makes a legal tradition 'ancient'? The obvious answer is that ancient legal traditions are not 'modern', which leaves us instead with the challenge of attempting to define what is 'modern' about 'modern law'.[55] In this concluding section, I will limit myself to highlighting two points of contrast and comparison for future research: ancient

---

52 Ancient trade networks offer particularly rich examples: 'Nearly all sources of the Old Assyrian period [20,000 cunieform texts] stem from the commercial quarter (kārum) of the ancient Anatolian city of Kaniš, the administrative centre of a network of Assyrian trading colonies in Anatolia, dating to ca. 1950–1840' (Veenhof 2003: 431). See further Chapter 11, this volume.
53 Carrié 2002; Gabrielsen and Thomsen 2015; Venticinque 2016; Wiese and Das 2019; Gabrielsen and Paganini 2021; Noreña 2021; and Eckhardt 2021.
54 Personal communication.
55 For a classic statement of the broader context, see Latour 1983.

Conclusion: What Is 'Ancient' about 'Ancient Law'?

conceptions (plural) of 'state legality' and ancient conceptions (plural) of 'the legal subject'.

A key tenet of nineteenth-century liberalism was the submission of the (nation-)state to law. As William Twining notes: 'the near monopoly of coercive power by a centralized bureaucratic state is a modern exception'.[56] Modern regulatory states and welfare states, moreover, are defined by, operated through and constrained by, masses of statutory and administratively created legal rules. Since the early 1980s neoliberal network governance – 'reinventing government to steer rather than to row' – has contributed to an existing system of regulatory capitalism, with privatization leading to further growth in both state and non-state regulation (what has been termed 'the rise of the audit society').[57] All of these 'modern' – liberal and neoliberal – conceptions of state legality are fundamentally different from the conceptions and practices of state legality that we find in ancient source material.

There are instructive comparisons to be made, of course, between ancient and modern 'rule of law' values.[58] To cite just one example, Athenian judges were bound by the 'heliastic oath' to judge according to the laws and the decrees of the city.[59] The administration of justice in the Greek world, however, was 'based on citizen involvement rather than expertise'.[60] As David Cohen argues:

> It was essential to the notion of the 'radical democracy' that 'the laws' were the property of the people, of the *dēmos* whose rule was instantiated in the very name *dēmokratía*. What Athenian democratic ideologues implicitly understood was that the 'rule of law' is a legal fiction. 'Laws' do not rule but certain institutions may be empowered with ensuring the primacy of the law over arbitrary decisions . . . But because those institutions are composed of human beings, the issue is who controls the creation and operation of those institutions and who is entitled to participate in them.[61]

In this respect, the ancient Athenian 'rule of law' needs to be contextualized within a broader civic ideology that sought to tame the competitive and agonistic nature of ancient states. The crucial issue – between states and within states – was whether laws could constrain the strong.[62]

A fundamental ancient ideology of law and justice, recorded in both material and textual evidence from ancient Mesopotamia onwards, is that

---

56 Twining 2021: 42.   57 Power 1999.
58 Harris 2006a and 2006b; Canevaro 2017; and Forsdyke 2018.   59 Canevaro 2019.
60 Rhodes 2015: 138 and 139.
61 Cohen 2015: 170, 170, see Harris 2013 for counter-arguments.
62 See Chapters 4 and 5, this volume; also Gagarin 2008a: 72–76, on written law and 'aristocratic inter-lineage competition'.

the strong – gods, kings and judges – should protect the weak. 'The protection of widow, orphan, and the poor was the common policy of the ancient Near East ... From the earliest times on a strong king promulgated stipulations in connection with protection of this group. Such protection was seen as a virtue of gods, kings and judges.'[63] This ideology, of course, appears repeatedly in legal inscriptions and in didactic wisdom literature precisely because: 'In bad times, in times of decay, the protection of widow, orphan, and the poor was neglected. Widows, orphans, and the poor were sold as credit-slaves and kept in a state of slavery for a lifetime.'[64] Ancient Near Eastern debt-release decrees (with evidence dating from 2400 BCE onwards) can be viewed as another aspect of the same fundamental ancient ideology:

> Debt-release decrees are the clearest example of legislation as we would understand it today, issuing directly from a sovereign and applied by the courts. Their limitation from a modern point of view is in their duration. Being for the most part retrospective in effect, they did not do what legislation most typically seeks to achieve, namely establish norms to control conduct in projected future situations.[65]

Debt-release measures are recorded, in numerous different forms, in legal and documentary evidence from ancient Egypt, Greece (where some evidence portrays cancellation of debts as the act of a tyrant), Rome, India and China. As Blok and Krul note: 'Debts were a structural factor in the lives of peasants throughout the ancient world.'[66]

The idea that the 'haves' should contribute to the welfare of the 'have nots' also underpins ancient private property regimes, for example in classical Athens: 'Insofar as property owners were still obligated to use some of their wealth for the good of their *polis*, in the form of liturgies, *eisphorai*, and acts of euergetism, the notion of property that underpinned the evolving laws governing ownership remained distant from the modern individual notion of a right.'[67] Ancient private property regimes, in other words, were dependent on ancient conceptions of 'the legal subject'.

Chapter 8 surveys a range of different 'status-clusters of rights and obligations', identifying fundamental differences in how ancient legal systems defined legal subjects at the level of polity.[68] Most strikingly, a clearly distinct

---

63 Fensham 1962: 129. 64 Fensham 1962: 129.
65 Westbrook 2003b: 16, also noting the schemes for the release of debts, land and slaves in the future, at seven- and fifty-year intervals, at Lev 25:8–16, 23–54 and Deut 15:1–2.
66 Blok and Krul 2017: 607. 67 Mackil 2021: 208, see further Chapter 10 above.
68 Quoted text from Galanter 1966: 154.

Conclusion: What Is 'Ancient' about 'Ancient Law'?

status of (legal) citizenship appears as a peculiarity limited to Greece and Rome.[69] In classical Athens:

> citizenship was thought of as 'having a share in the city' ... What seems quite clear is that 'to have a share' (*metechien*) in its essence meant participating in civic institutions. At its core, the polis is a partnership/community (*koinonia*) of those qualified to 'have a share' ... What those shares were, or how equal they were, varied and was defined by the constitution (politeia) of each Greek *polis* – democracy, oligarchy, monarchy, tyranny, or aristocracy, What is without question at Athens is that foreigners, permanent alien residents, and slaves did not qualify 'to have a share'.[70]

As discussed in Chapter 8, Classical Sanskrit texts and early epigraphy from India give little indication of a formal status precisely corresponding to 'the citizen': 'All these sources look to the transregional macro-statuses, such as the four "estates" (*varṇa*s).' Moreover, 'the defence of class and caste may be one of the defining features of the Hinduism imagined in Dharmaśāstra'.[71] Again, as highlighted throughout Chapter 8, the category of 'status' provides a stronger comparative framework for analysis across ancient legal traditions, but we need to look 'beyond the formal status categories of any one system, in order to consider their relation to social structures and institutions and the interplay between diverse forms of status in the actual working of law'.[72]

Unfree status is a constant across all ancient societies, visible in both legal and extra-legal evidence in numerous different forms, from enslaved persons to labourers 'tied to the land'. One factor that emerges clearly from comparative research is the legal, socioeconomic, etc. complexities of unfree statuses and unfree labour across specific times, places and contexts.[73] Debt-release measures feature heavily in ancient ideologies, but daily realties were structured by harsh measures of debt enforcement and other forms of violence. As Brent Shaw states: 'instruments of credit and debt were the hard enforcers of the subaltern ... Here, too, the instruments of force and coercion were vitally connected with slavery.'[74]

What is ancient about ancient law? Perhaps, ultimately, it is time to reshape our scale of analysis. Twentieth-century proponents of the idea of 'an Axial Age' argued for the recognition of a 'global historical turning point

---

69 Chapter 8, this volume: 'Elsewhere, formal legal criteria of citizenship were not formalized to the same extent; instead, legal sources adopt and give legal force to an originally more "vernacular" distinction between native and foreigner, often framed partly in geographic and partly in ethnic terms.'
70 Cohen 2015: 175, quoting Patterson 2005: 279.   71 Davis 2017: 9.
72 Chapter 8, this volume.   73 Chapter 8, this volume.
74 Shaw 2022: xix, referring to no. 3 ff. of the 'so-called Twelve Tables of c. 450 BCE'.

toward modernity' between 800 and 200 BCE, citing as their evidence: 'an "axial" or "pivotal" transformation in the relationship between rulers and ruled and laws and customs, together with the emergence of a new form of moralizing religion and ideology, as manifested in Buddhism, Confucianism, Hinduism, Judaism, Platonism, and Zoroastrianism'.[75] More recent 'big data' approaches, however, have begun to 'undercut the notion of a specific "age" of axiality limited to a specific geo-temporal localization' through the incorporation of new evidence from ancient societies in Southeast Asia, Polynesia, West Africa, and North and South America.[76] Our hope is that the *Cambridge Comparative History of Ancient Law* will, in turn, open the way for a similar broadening of specific geo-temporal horizons, beyond the history of early law across Eurasia contained in this volume, towards a more global conception of ancient law.

75 Mullins et al. 2018: 596–97.   76 Hoyer and Reddish 2019.

Bibliography

Primary Sources

Aeschines, *Against Timarchus*: Carey, J. (trans.) (2021) 'Aeschines I. Against Timarchus', in Gagarin, M. (ed.), *Speeches from Athenian Law*. Austin, TX.: 188–243.
Aeschylus, *Oresteia*: Collard, C. (trans.) (2002) *Aeschylus Oresteia*. Oxford.
  Fragments: Mette, H. J. (ed.) (1959) *Die Fragmente der Tragödien des Aischylos*. Berlin.
Alalakh Tablets: Wiseman, D. J. (ed.) (1953) *The Alalakh Tablets*. Ankara.
Ammiṣaduqa, *Edict*: Finkelstein, J. J. (1969) 'The Edict of Ammiṣaduqa: A New Text', *Revue d'assyriologie et d'archéologie orientale* 63.1 (1969): 45–64.
Andocides, *Speeches*: Maidment, K. J. (trans.) (1941) *Minor Attic Orators. Volume I: Antiphon. Andocides*. Cambridge, MA: 325–583.
Antiphon, *Speeches*: Maidment, K. J. (trans.) (1941) *Minor Attic Orators. Volume I: Antiphon. Andocides*. Cambridge, MA: 8–312.
Āpastamba *Dharmasūtras*: Olivelle, P. (ed. and trans.) (2000) .*Dharmasūtras: The Law Codes of Āpastamba, Gautama, Baudhāyana and Vasiṣṭha*. Delhi: 20–115.
Aristides, P. Aelius: Behr, Charles A. (ed.) (1981) *P. Aelius Aristides: The Complete Works*. 2 vols. Leiden.
Aristophanes, *Thesmophoriazusae [Women at the Thesmophoria]*: Halliwell, S. (trans.) (2015) *Aristophanes: Clouds, Women at the Thesmophoria, Frogs*. Oxford.
Aristotle, *Rhetoric* : Kassel, R. (ed.) (1976) *Aristotelis Ars rhetorica*. Berlin.
  Nicomachean Ethics: Susemihl, F. and Apelt, O. (eds.) (1912) *Aristotelis Ethica Nicomachea*. 3rd ed. Leipzig.
  Politics: Dreizehnter, A. (ed.) (1970) *Aristoteles' Politik*. Munich.
  Prior Analytics: Ross, W. D. (ed.) (1951) *Aristotle's Prior and Posterior Analytics*. Oxford.
Ashoka, *Edicts* : Hultzsch, E. (ed. and trans.) (1925/1969) *Corpus Inscriptionum Indicarum*. Vol. I: *Inscriptions of Aśoka*. New ed. Oxford (repr. Delhi).
Athenaion politeia: Chambers, M. (ed.) (1994) *Aristoteles: AΘHNAIΩN ΠΟΛΙΤΕΙΑ*. 2nd ed. Stuttgart.
Augustus, *Res Gestae* : Brunt, P. A. and Moore, J. M. (trans.) (1969) *Res Gestae Divi Augusti*. Oxford.
Aulus Gellius, *Attic Nights*: Rolfe, John C. (ed. and trans.) (1927) *Aulus Gellius: Attic Nights, Books I–V*. Cambridge, MA.
Baudhāyana *Dharmasūtras*: Olivelle, P. (trans.) (2000) *Dharmasūtras: The Law Codes of Āpastamba, Gautama, Baudhāyana and Vasiṣṭha*. Delhi: 191–345.
Bṛhaspati *Smṛti*: Jolly, J. (1889) *The Minor Law-Books: Part I, Nārada. Bṛhaspati*. Oxford. Reconstructed ed.: Rangaswami Aiyangar, K. V. (1942). *Bṛhaspati-Smṛti (Reconstructed)*. Baroda.

Choachyte Petebaste, archive of: Donker van Heel, K. (ed.) (2021) *The Archive of the Theban Choachyte Petebaste son of Peteamunip (Floruit 7th Century* BCE*)*. Leiden.
Cicero, *Epistulae ad Atticum*: Shackleton Bailey, D. R. (ed. and trans.) (1999) *Letters to Atticus*. 5 vols. Cambridge, MA.
  Pro Balbo: Gardner R. (trans.) (1958) Cicero. *Pro Caelio. De Provinciis Consularibus. Pro Balbo*. Cambridge MA: 626–717.
  Brutus: Douglas, A. E. (ed.) (1966). *M. Tulli Ciceronis Brutus*. Oxford.
  In Catilinam: Macdonald, C. (trans.) (1976. Cicero. *In Catilinam 1–4. Pro Murena. Pro Sulla. Pro Flacco*. Cambridge, MA: 32–168.
  De legibus: Powell, J. G. F. (ed.) (2006) *M. Tulli Ciceronis De re publica, De legibus, Cato maior de senectute, Laelius de amicitia*. Oxford: 155–266.
  De officiis: Winterbottom, M. (ed.) (1994) *M. Tulli Ciceronis De officiis*. Oxford.
  De oratore: Wilkins, A. S. (ed.) (1902) *M. Tullius Cicero: De Oratore*. Oxford.
  De republica: Powell, J. G. F. (ed.) (2006) *M. Tulli Ciceronis De re publica, De legibus, Cato maior de senectute, Laelius de amicitia*. Oxford: 1–154.
  In Verrem: Greenwood, L. H. G. (trans.) (2014) *The Verrine Orations*. 2 vols. (rev. ed.). Cambridge, MA.
  Partitiones oratoriae: Rackham, H. (trans.) (1942) Cicero. *On the Orator: Book 3. On Fate. Stoic Paradoxes. Divisions of Oratory*. Cambridge, MA: 310–422.
  Topica: Reinhardt, T. (ed. and trans.) (2003) *Topica*. Oxford.
Confucius, *Liji*: Lau, D. C. and Chen, Fong Ching (ed.) (1992) *Liji Zhuzi Suoyin* 《禮記逐字索引》. Taiwan.
Consultatio veteris cuiusdam iurisconsulti [*Consultation with an ancient jurisconsult*]: Krüger, P. (1890) 'Consultatio veteris cuiusdam iurisconsulti', in *Collectio Librorum Iuris Anteiustiniani* III, ed. P. Krüger. Berlin: 199–220.
Demosthenes, *Against Leptines* [Dem. 20]: Harris, E. M. (ed. and trans.) (2008) *Demosthenes, Speeches 20–22*. Austin, TX.
Demosthenes, *Against Meidias* [Dem. 21]: Harris, E. M. (ed. and trans.) (2008) *Demosthenes, Speeches 20–22*. Austin, TX.
Demosthenes, *Against Timocrates* [Dem. 24]: Harris, E. M. (ed. and trans.) (2018) *Demosthenes, Speeches 23–26*. Austin, TX.
Demosthenes, *Against Neaera* [Dem. 59]: Bers, V. (ed. and trans.) (2003)*Demosthenes, Speeches 50–59*. Austin, TX.
Dio Chrysostom, *Speeches*: Cohoon, J. W. (ed. and trans.) (1932–51) *Dio Chrysostom*. 5 vols. London.
Diodorus Siculus, *Bibliotheca Historica*: Oldfather, C. H. et al. (trans.) (1933–67)*Diodorus Siculus. Library of History*. 12 vols. Cambridge, MA.
Dionysius of Halicarnassus, *Rhōmaïke archaiologia*: Cary, E. (ed.) (1937–50)*Dionysius of Halicarnassus. Roman Antiquities*. 7 vols. Cambridge, MA.
Duties of the Vizier: Van den Boorn, G. P. F. (ed. and trans.) (1988) *The Duties of the Vizier: Civil Administration in the Early New Kingdom*. London.
Ernian lüling [二年]: Zhangjiashan ersiqihao Hanmu zhujian zhengli xiaozu [張家山二四七號 漢墓竹簡整理 小組] (2006). Zhangjiashan Hanmu zhujian (ersiqihao mu): Shiwen xiuding ben [張家 山漢墓竹簡(二四七號墓):釋文修訂本]. Beijing.
Eshnunna, Laws of: Roth, M. T. (ed. and trans.) (1997) *Law Collections from Mesopotamia and Asia Minor*. 2nd ed. Atlanta: 57–70.

Bibliography

Euripides' *Hippolytos*: Kovacs, D. (ed. and trans.) (1995) *Euripides: Children of Heracles. Hippolytus. Andromache. Hecuba*. Cambridge, MA: 124–266.

Gaius *Institutes*: Seckel, E. and Kübler, B. (eds.) (1939) *Gai Institutiones*. 8th ed. Leipzig.

Gautama Dharmasūtra: Olivelle, P. (2000) *Dharmasūtras: The Law Codes of Āpastamba, Gautama, Baudhāyana and Vasiṣṭha*. Delhi: 116–90.

Gortyn, Laws ['Code']: Willetts, R. (1967) *The Code of Gortyn*. Berlin.

Hammurabi, Laws of: Roth, M. T. (ed. and trans.) (1997) *Law Collections from Mesopotamia and Asia Minor*. 2nd ed. Atlanta: 71–142.

Han shu [*History of the Former Han Dynasty*]: Pan Ku (ed.) (1975) *Han shu*. Beijing.

Herodotus, *Histories*: Wilson, N. G. (ed.) (2015) *Herodoti Historiae*. 2 vols. Oxford.

Hesiod, *Works and Days*: Most, G. W. (2018) *Hesiod: Theogony. Works and Days. Testimonia*. Cambridge, MA: 86–155

Hesiod, *Theogony*: Most, G. W. (2018) *Hesiod: Theogony. Works and Days. Testimonia*. Cambridge, MA: 2–85.

Hittite, Laws : Roth, M. T. (ed. and trans.) (1997) *Law Collections from Mesopotamia and Asia Minor*. 2nd ed. Ed. Piotr Michalowski, with a contribution from H. A. Hoffner. Atlanta.

Homer, *Iliad*: Monro, D. B. and Allen, T. W. (1920) *Homeri Opera*. Vols. I and II. Oxford. *Odyssey*: Monro, D. B. and Allen, T. W. (1922) *Homeri Opera*. Vols. III and IV. Oxford.

Hyperides, *Against Athenogenes*: Burtt, J. O. (trans.) (1954) *Minor Attic Orators*. Vol. II: *Lycurgus. Dinarchus. Demades. Hyperides*. Cambridge, MA: 430–61.

Isaeus, *Speeches*: Forster, E. S. (trans.) (1927) *Isaeus*. Cambridge, MA.

Isocrates, *Speeches*: Van Hook, La Rue (trans.) (1945) *Isocrates: Evagoras. Helen. Busiris. Plataicus. Concerning the Team of Horses. Trapeziticus. Against Callimachus. Aegineticus. Against Lochites. Against Euthynus. Letters*. Vol. III. Cambridge, MA.

Jerome, *Life of Paul of Thebes*: Leclerc, P., Morales, E. M. and de Vogüé, A. (eds. and trans.) (2007) *Jerome: Trois vies de moines: Paul, Malchus, Hilarion*. Paris: 142–83.

Jin shu (*History of the Jin Dynasty*): Heuser, R. (ed. and trans.) (1987) *Das Rechtskapitel im Jin-shu. Ein Beitrag zur Kenntnis des Rechts im frühen chinesischen Kaiserreich*. Munich.

Jiu Tangshu (Old History of the Tang Dynasty). Xu, Liu (ed.) (1975) *Jiu Tangshu*. Beijing.

Jiuzhao lükao (Investigations into the Laws of Various Dynasties): Cheng Shude (ed.) (1988). Beijing.

Justinian, *Digest*: Mommsen, T. (ed.) (1911) *Corpus Iuris Civilis*. Vol. I. 12th ed. Berlin; Watson A. et al. (trans.) (1985) *The Digest of Justinian*. 4 vols. Philadelphia.

Justinian, *Codex repetitae praelectionis*: Frier, B. W. et al. (ed. and trans.) (2016) *The Codex of Justinian: A New Annotated Translation with Parallel Latin and Greek Text*. 2 vols. Cambridge.

Justinian, *Institutes*: Krüger, P. (ed.) (1911) *Corpus Iuris Civilis*. Vol. I. 12th ed. Berlin; Birks, P. and McLeod, G. (eds. and trans.) (1987). *Justinian's Institutes*. London.

Kalachuri-Chedi Era Inscriptions: Mirashi, V. V. (ed.) (1955) *Corpus Inscriptionum Indicarum*. Vol. IV: *Inscriptions of the Kalachuri-Chedi Era, Part I*. Ootacamund.

Kātyāyana Smṛti: Kane, P. V. (trans.) (1933 repr.) *Kātyāyana-smṛti (Sāra-uddhāraḥ) on Vyavahāra, Text (Reconstructed)*. Bombay.

Kauṭilya, *Arthaśāstra* : Olivelle, P. (trans.) (2013) *King, Governance, and Law in Ancient India: Kauṭilya's Arthaśāstra*. Oxford.

Kangle, R. P. (1960) *The Kauṭilīya Arthaśāstra: Part I. A Critical Edition with a Glossary*. 2nd ed. (1972) Bombay.
Lex Irnitana: Crawford, M. H. and González, J. (trans. and ed.) (1986) 'The *Lex Irnitana*: A New Copy of the Flavian Municipal Law', *Journal of Roman Studies* 76: 147–253.
Libanius, *Letters*: Foerster, R. (1921–22) *Libanii Opera*. Vol. X: *Epistulae 1–839* and Vol. XI: *Epistulae 840–1544 una cum pseudepigraphicis et Basilii cum Libanio commercio epistolico: Fragmenta*. Leipzig.
Liji (Book of Rites): Legge, J. (ed.) (1967) *Li Chi: Book of Rites*. 2 vols. New York.
Livy, *Ab urbe condita*: Conway, R. S. et al (1920–99) *Titi Livi. Ab Urbe Condita*. 6 vols. Oxford.
Lipit-Ishtar, Laws of: Roth, M. T. (ed. and trans.) (1997) *Law Collections from Mesopotamia and Asia Minor*. 2nd ed. Atlanta: 23–35.
Lü Buwei, *Annals (Lüshi chunqiu)*: Knoblock, J. and Riegel, J. (eds.) (2000) *The Annals of Lü Buwei*. Stanford.
Lysias, *Speeches*: Lamb, W. R. M. (ed.) (1930) *Lysias*. Cambridge, MA.
Mahābhārata: Sukthankar, V. S. et al. (eds.) (1927–59) *Mahābhārata*. 19 vols. Poona.
Manu, Law Code. *Mānava Dharmaśāstra*. Olivelle, P. (trans. and ed.) (2005) *Manu's Code of Law: A Critical Edition and Translation of the Mānava-Dharmaśāstra*. Oxford.
Mṛcchakaṭika ['The Little Clay Cart'] by Śūdraka. Acharya, D. (ed.) (2009) *Mṛcchakaṭika*. New York.
Menander, *Fragments*: Arnott, W. G. (ed. and trans.) (2000) *Menander: Samia. Sikyonioi. Synaristosai. Phasma . Unidentified Fragments*. Vol. III. Cambridge, MA: 607–14.
Mishnah: Cohen, S. J. D., Goldenberg, R. and Lapin, H. (ed. and trans.) (2022) *The Oxford Annotated Mishnah: A New Translation of the Mishnah*. Oxford.
Nārada Smṛti: Lariviere, R. W. (ed.) (2003) *The Nāradasmṛti*. Delhi.
Osorkon, Chronicle of: Caminos, R. A. (trans.) (1958) *The Chronicle of Prince Osorkon*. Rome.
Pañcatantra: Olivelle, P. (ed. and trans.) (2006) *Pañcatantra: The Book of India's Folk Wisdom*. New York.
Pāṇini, *Aṣṭādhyāyī (Grammar)*: Vasu, S. C. (ed. and trans.) (1962 repr.) *Pāṇini, Aṣṭādhyāyī*. Delhi.
Philostratus, *Life of Apollonius*: Jones, C. P. (ed. and trans.) (2005) *Philostratus, Apollonius of Tyana*. Vols. I and II. Cambridge, MA.
Pindar, *Olympian Odes*: Race, W. H. (ed. and trans.) (1997) *Pindar. Olympian Odes. Pythian Odes*. Cambridge, MA: 44–215.
Plato, *Apology*: Emlyn-Jones, C. and Preddy, W. (ed. and trans.) (2017)*Plato: Euthyphro. Apology. Crito. Phaedo*. Cambridge, MA: 106–195.
  Euthyphro: Emlyn-Jones, C. and Preddy, W. (ed. and trans.) (2017) *Plato: Euthyphro. Apology. Crito. Phaedo*. Cambridge MA: 20–85.
  Laws: Bury, R.G. (trans.) (1926) *Plato: Laws*. Vols. I and II. Cambridge, MA.
  Symposium: Lamb, W. R. M. (trans.) (1925) *Plato; Lysis. Symposium. Gorgias*. Cambridge, MA: 73–246.
  Republic: Emlyn-Jones, C. and Preddy, W. (ed. and trans.) (2013) *Plato: Republic*. Vols. I and II. Cambridge, MA.
Pliny the Elder, *Natural History*: Mayhoff, C. (ed.) (1899–1909) *C. Plini Secundi naturalis historiae libri vii*. Leipzig.

Bibliography

Pliny the Younger, *Letters*: Mynors, R. A. B. (ed.) (1966) *C. Plini Caecili Secundi Epistularum libri decem*. Oxford.
Plutarch, *Lives*: Ziegler, K. (ed.) (1993)*Plutarchus: Vitae parallelae*. 2nd ed. with corr. H. Gärtner. 3 vols. Stuttgart.
Pollux, Julius, *Onomasticon*: Bethe, E. (1900–67) *Pollucis Onomasticon*. 3 vols. Leipzig.
Polybius, *Histories*: Dindorf, L. and Büttner-Wobst, T. (eds.) (1889–1905) *Polybios: Historiae*. Leipzig.
Ps-Asconius, *Commentary on the Verrines*: Strangl, T. (ed.) (1909) *Pseudoasconiana: Textgestaltung und Sprache der anonymen Scholien zu Cicero vier ersten Verrinen*. Paderborn.
Pūrva-Mīmāṃsā-Sūtra: Sandal, M. L. (ed. and trans.) (1923) *The Mimamsa sutra of Jaimini*. Allahabad.
Ṛgveda: Jamison, S. W. and Brereton, J. (trans.) (2014) *The Rigveda: The Earliest Religious Poetry of India*. 3 vols. Oxford.
Quintilian, *Declamationes maiores*: Stramaglia, A. and Winterbottom, M. (ed. and trans.) (2021) *The Major Declamations*. 3 vols. Cambridge, MA.
  Declamationes minores: Shackleton Bailey, D. R. (ed. and trans.) (2006)*The Lesser Declamations*. 2 vols. Cambridge, MA.
  Rhetorica ad Herennium: Caplan, H. (trans.) (1954) *[Cicero] Rhetorica ad Herennium*. Cambridge, MA.
Scholia Sinaitica: Riccobono, S. (ed.) (1898) 'Scholia Sinaitica ad Ulpiani Libros ad Sabinum', *Bullettino Istituto di Diritto Romano* 9: 217–300.
Seneca, *On Clemency*: Malaspina, E. (ed.) (2016) *L. Annaeus Seneca: De clementia libri duo*. Berlin.
Shang Yang, *Shangjunshu [Book of Lord Shang]*: Duyvendak, J. J. L. (trans.) (1963) *The Book of Lord Shang: A Classic of the Chinese School of Law*. Chicago.
Solon, *Laws of*: Leão, D. F. and P. J. Rhodes (ed. and trans.) (2015) *The Laws of Solon: A New Edition with Introduction, Translation and Commentary*. New York.
Sophocles *Antigone*: Lloyd-Jones, H. (ed. and trans.) (1994) *Sophocles*: Antigone. The Women of Trachis. Philoctetes. Oedipus at Colonus. Cambridge, MA: 1–128.
  Oedipus Tyrannus: Lloyd-Jones, H. (ed. and trans.) (1994) *Sophocles*: Ajax. Electra. Oedipus Tyrannus. Cambridge, MA: 323–483.
Strabo, *Geography*: Radt, S. (ed. and trans.) (2002–2011) *Strabons Geographika*. Göttingen.
Suetonius, *Life of Julius Caesar*: Ihm, M. (ed.) (1907) *C. Suetoni Tranquilli de Vita Caesarum libri VIII*. Leipzig.
Tacitus, *Annales*: Borzsák, S. (ed.) (1992) *Cornelii Taciti libri qui supersunt I: Ab excessu Divi Augusti libri I–VI*. Leipzig.
Tale of the Eloquent Peasant: Shupak, N. (1992) 'A New Source for the Study of the Judiciary and Law of Ancient Egypt: "The Tale of the Eloquent Peasant"', *Journal of Near Eastern Studies* 51.1: 1–18.
Talmud Yerushalmi (The Jerusalem Talmud): Guggenheimer, H. W. (ed. and trans.) (2000–15) *Jerusalem Talmud: Edition, Translation, and Commentary*. 18 vols. Berlin.
Tang Code (*Tanglüshuyi*): Johnson, W. (ed.) (1979) *The T'ang Code*. Princeton, NJ.
Tefhape, Archive of: Thompson, H. (1934) *A Family Archive from Siut: From Papyri in the British Museum*. Oxford.

Tertullian, *Apology*: Glover, T. R. and Rendall, G. H. (trans.) (1931) *Tertullian*, Apology. De Spectaculis. *Minucius Felix*: Octavius. Cambridge, MA: 2–229.

Theodosius II, law code: Mommsen, T., Krüger, P. and Meyer, P. M. (eds.) (1905) *Theodosiani libri XVI cum Constitutionibus Sirmondianis et Leges Novellae ad Theodosianum Pertinentes*. 2 vols. Berlin; Pharr, C. et al. (trans.) (1952) *The Theodosian Code and Novels and the Sirmondian Constitutions*. Philadelphia.

Theognis, *Elegaic poems*: Gerber, D. E. (ed. and trans.) (1999). *Tyrtaeus, Solon, Theognis, Mimnermus. Greek Elegiac Poetry: From the Seventh to the Fifth Centuries BC*. Cambridge, MA: 166–385.

Theophrastus, *Characters*: Diggle, J. (ed.) (2022) *Theophrastus Characters*. Cambridge.

Theophrastus, *Nomoi*: Szegedy-Maszak, A. (ed.) (1981) *The Nomoi of Theophrastus*. New York.

Thucydides: Warner, R. (trans.) (1954) *Thucydides: History of the Peloponnesian War*. London.

Twelve Tables: Crawford, M. H. (ed. and trans.) (1996) *Roman Statutes*. Vol. II. London: 555–721.

Ur-Namma, Laws of: Roth, M. T. (ed. and trans.) (1997) *Law Collections from Mesopotamia and Asia Minor*. 2nd ed. Atlanta: 13–22.

Valerius Maximus, *Facta et Dicta Memorabilia*: Shackleton Bailey, D. R. (2000) *Valerius Maximus: Memorable Doings and Sayings*. Vols. I and II. Cambridge, MA.

Vaiṣṇava Dharmaśāstra: Olivelle, P. (ed. and trans.) (2009) *The Law Code of Viṣṇu: A Critical Edition and Annotated Translation of the Vaiṣṇava-Dharmaśāstra*. Cambridge, MA.

Vasiṣṭha Dharmasūtra: Olivelle, P. (2000) *Dharmasūtras: The Law Codes of Āpastamba, Gautama, Baudhāyana and Vasiṣṭha*. Delhi: 346–463.

Vergil, *Aeneid*: Rushton Fairclough, H. and Goold, G. P. (1916 and 1918)*Virgil: Eclogues. Georgics. Aeneid, Books 1–6* [Vol. I] and *Virgil. Aeneid, Books 7–12. Appendix Vergiliana* [Vol. II]. Cambridge, MA.

Viṣṇusena, Charter of: Wiese, H. and Das, S. (ed. and trans.) (2019) *The Charter of Viṣṇuṣena*. Halle an der Saale.

Xenophon, *Hellenica*: Brownson, C. L. (trans.) (1918 and 1921) *Xenophon: Hellenica*, Vol. I: *Books 1–4; Xenophon: Hellenica*, Vol. II: *Books 5–7*. Cambridge, MA.

Xenophon, *Memorabilia*: Marchant, E. C. and Todd, O. J, rev. by Henderson, J. (2013) *Xenophon*: Memorabilia. Oeconomicus. Symposium. Apology. Cambridge, MA: 8–380.

Xin Tangshu [juan 56]: Bünger, K. (1946, 1996, repr.) *Quellen zur Rechtsgeschichte der T'ang-Zeit*. Peking.

Yājñavalkya Dharmaśāstra: Olivelle, P. (ed. and trans.) (2019) *Yājñavalkya: A Treatise on Dharma*. Cambridge, MA.

Zhouli (Rites of Zhou): Nylan, M. (trans.) (2001) *The Five 'Confucian' Classics*. New Haven: 168–202.

Zuo zhuan (Annals of the Spring and Autumn): Durrant, S. , Li, W. and Schaberg, D. (trans.) (2016). *Zuo Tradition. Zuozhuan* 左傳: *Commentary on the 'Spring and Autumn Annals'*. 3 vols. Seattle.

Secondary Sources

Abbot, F. F. and Johnson, A. C. (1926) *Municipal Administration in the Roman Empire*. Princeton NJ.
Abromson, M. S. (2008) *Ethnic Identity on Tang China*. Philadelphia.
Abusch, T. (2015) *The Witchcraft Series Maqlû*. Atlanta.
Abusch, T. and Schwemer, D. (2011) *Corpus of Mesopotamian Anti-Witchcraft Rituals*. Leiden.
Acharya, D. (ed.) (2009) *Mṛcchakaṭika: The Little Clay Cart by Śūdraka*. New York.
Adluri, V. and Bagchee, J. (2014) *The Nay Science: A History of German Indology*. Oxford.
Ager, S. L. (1996) *Interstate Arbitrations in the Greek World, 337–90 BC*. Berkeley.
  (2013) 'Interstate Governance: Arbitration and Peacekeeping', in *A Companion to Ancient Greek Government*, ed. H. Beck. Chichester: 497–511.
Aiyangar, K. V. Rangaswami. (1941a) *Bṛhaspatismṛti (Reconstructed)*. Gaekwad's Oriental Series 85. Baroda. (1941b) *Rajadharma*. Adyar.
Akerlof, G. (1970) 'The Market for "Lemons": Quality Uncertainty and the Market Mechanism', *The Quarterly Journal of Economics* 84: 488–500.
Alchian, A. A. (1977) *Economic Forces at Work*. Indianapolis.
Allam, S. (2008) 'Regarding the Eisagogeus at Ptolemaic Law Courts', *Journal of Egyptian History* 1.1: 3–19.
  (2011) 'On the Right of Way in Ancient Egypt (Entry to and Exit from an Estate εἴσοδος καὶ ἔξοδος', *Journal of Egyptian Archaeology* 97: 203–6.
Allan, K. (2012) *Explorations in Classical Sociological Theory: Seeing the Social World*. 3rd ed. Los Angeles.
Allen, D. S. (2000) *The World of Prometheus: The Politics of Punishing in Democratic Athens*. Princeton, NJ.
Allsen, T. (2006) *The Royal Hunt in Eurasian History*. Philadelphia.
Alexander, P. S. (1984) 'The Rabbinic Hermeneutical Rules and the Problem of the Definition of Midrash', *Proceedings of the Irish Biblical Association* 8: 97–125.
Alonso, V. (2007) 'War, Peace, and International Law in Ancient Greece', in *War and Peace in the Ancient World*, ed. K. A. Raaflaub. Malden, MA and Oxford: 206–25.
Alston, L. J. and Mueller, B. (2008) 'Property Rights and the State', in *Handbook of New Institutional Economics*, ed. C. Ménard and M. M. Shirley. Berlin: 573–90.
Altman, A. (2012) *Tracing the Earliest Recorded Concepts of International Law: The Ancient Near East (2500–330 BCE)*. Leiden.
Ameri, M., Costello, S. K., Jamison, G. and Scott, S. (eds.) (2018) *Seals and Sealing in the Ancient World*. Cambridge.
Amunátegui Perelló, C. F. (2014) 'On Supernatural Law: About the Origins of Human Rights and Natural Law in Antiquity', *Fundamina* 20.1: 15–26.
Anderson, G. (2005) 'Before *Turannoi* were Tyrants: Rethinking a Chapter of Early Greek History', *Classical Antiquity* 24: 173–222.
  (2009) 'The Personality of the Greek State', *Journal of Hellenic Studies* 129: 1–22.
Ando, C. (2006) 'Introduction: Religion and Law in Classical and Christian Rome', in *Religion and Law in Classical and Christian Rome*, eds. C. Ando and J. Rüpke. Stuttgart: 7–13.
  (2011) *Law, Language, and Empire in the Roman Tradition*. Philadelphia.

(2012) *Imperial Rome, AD 193–284: The Critical Century*. Edinburgh.
(2014) 'Pluralism and Empire: From Rome to Robert Cover', *Critical Analysis of Law* 1: 1–22.
(2023) 'Empire, Status, and the Law', *American Journal of Legal History* 63.2: 66–81.
Ando, C. and Richardson, S. (eds.) (2017) *Ancient States and Infrastructural Power: Europe, Asia, and America*. Philadelphia.
Andreau, J. and Descat, R. (2011) *The Slave in Greece and Rome*, trans. M. Leopold. Madison, WI and London.
Arruñada, B. (2012) *Institutional Foundations of Impersonal Exchange: Theory and Policy of Contractual Registries*. Chicago.
Assman, J. (2001) *Ma'at: Gerechtigkeit und Unsterblichkeit im alten Ägypten*. Munich.
Bablitz, L. (2007) *Actors and Audience in the Roman Courtroom*. London and New York.
Bablitz, L. (2016) 'Roman Courts and Private Arbitration', in *The Oxford Handbook of Roman Law and Society*, ed. P. J. du Plessis, C. Ando and K. Tuori. Oxford: 234–44.
Babusiaux, U. (2016) 'The Future of Legal History: Roman Law', *American Journal of Legal History* 56: 6–11.
Bacher, W. (1905) *Die Exegetische Terminologie der Jüdischen Traditionsliteratur*. 2 vols. Leipzig.
Badian, E. (1996/2006), 'Amicitia', *Der Neue Pauly* 1: coll. 590–91 (English edition in *Brill's New Pauly* (online version) 2006).
Baetens, G. and Depauw, M. (2015) 'The Legal Advice of Totoes in the Siut Archive (P. BM 10591, Verso, Col. I–III) ', *Journal of Egyptian Archaeology* 101: 197–215.
Bagnall, R. S. (1993) *Egypt in Late Antiquity*. Princeton, NJ.
  (ed.) (2009) *The Oxford Handbook of Papyrology*. Oxford.
  (2014) 'Sales of Moveables', in Keenan, Manning and Yiftach-Firanko (2014): 304–14.
Baker, H. D. (2001) 'Degrees of Freedom: Slavery in Mid-first Millennium BC Babylonia', *World Archaeology* 33: 18–26.
Balazs, É. (1954) *Le traité juridique du 'Souei-Chou'*. Leiden.
Baltrusch, E. (2008) *Außenpolitik, Bünde und Reichsbildung in der Antike*. Munich.
Bang, P. F. and Scheidel, W. (eds.) (2013) *The Oxford Handbook of the State in the Ancient Near East and Mediterranean*. Oxford.
Barbieri-Low, A. J. (2007) *Artisans in Early Imperial China*. Seattle.
Barbieri-Low, A. J. and Yates, R. D. S. (ed. and trans.) (2015) *Law, State, and Society in Early Imperial China: A Study with Critical Edition and Translation of the Legal Texts from Zhangjiashan Tomb no. 247*. 2 vols. Leiden.
Barmash, P. (2020) *The Laws of Hammurabi: At the Confluence of Royal and Scribal Traditions*. New York.
Baron, J. B. (2014) 'Rescuing the Bundle-of-Rights Metaphor in Property Law', *University of Cincinnati Law Review* 82.1: 57–101.
Bartlett, R. (2013) *Why Can the Dead Do Such Great Things? Saints and Worshippers from the Martyrs to the Reformation*. Princeton, NJ.
Barton, C. A. (2007) 'The Price of Peace in Ancient Rome', in *War and Peace in the Ancient World*, ed. K. A. Raaflaub. Malden, MA: 245–55.
Bauslaugh, R. A. (1991) *The Concept of Neutrality in Classical Greece*. Berkeley.
Beard, M. (1987) 'A Complex of Times: No More Sheep on Romulus' Birthday', *Proceedings of the Cambridge Philological Society* 33: 1–15.

(1990) 'Priesthood in the Roman Republic', In *Pagan Priests: Religion and Power in the Ancient World*, ed. M. Beard and J. North. Ithaca, NY: 19–48.

Beaulieu, P.-A. (1992) 'New Light on Secret Knowledge in Late Babylonian Culture', *Zeitschrift für Assyriologie und vorderasiatische Archäologie* 82: 98–111.

(2000) *Legal and Administrative Texts from the Reign of Nabonidus*. Yale Oriental Series (YOS) 19. New Haven.

(2007) 'Late Babylonian intellectual life', in *The Babylonian World*, ed. G. Leick. London: 473–84.

Beck, H. (1997) *Polis und Koinon*. Stuttgart.

Beckman, G. (1999) *Hittite Diplomatic Texts*. 2nd ed. Society of Biblical Literature. Writing from the Ancient World, 7. Atlanta.

(2011) 'Blood in Hittite Ritual', *Journal of Cuneiform Studies* 63: 95–102.

Bederman, D. J. (2001) *International Law in Antiquity*. Cambridge.

Behr, C. A. (ed.) (1981) *P. Aelius Aristides: The Complete Works*. 2 vols. Leiden.

Bell, J. (2006) 'Chapter Five: Civil Law Tradition', in 'A Fresh Start for Comparative Legal Studies? A Collective Review of Patrick Glenn's *Legal Traditions of the World*, 2nd Edition' (ed. N. H. D. Foster), *Journal of Comparative Law* 1.1: 100–199 (130–39).

Bellah, R. N. (2011) *Religion in Human Evolution: From the Paleolithic to the Axial Age*. Cambridge, MA.

Bellodi Ansaloni, A. (1998) *Ricerche sulla contumacia nelle cognitiones extra ordinem*. Milan.

Bender, D. R. (1967) 'A Refinement of the Concept of Household: Families, Co-Residence, and Domestic Functions', *American Anthropologist*, n.s. 69.5: 493–504.

Bendlin, A. (2007) 'Purity and Pollution', in *The Blackwell Companion to Greek Religion*, ed. D. Ogden. Oxford: 178–89.

Benn, C. (2002) *Daily Life in Traditional China: The Tang Dynasty*. Westport, CT.

Berger, P. L. (1967) *The Sacred Canopy: Elements of a Sociological Theory of Religion*. Garden City, NY.

Bernstein, M. and Koyfman, S. (2005) 'The Interpretation of Biblical Law in the Dead Sea Scrolls: Forms and Methods', in *Biblical Interpretation at Qumran*, ed. M. Henze. Grand Rapids, MI: 448–475.

Bielenstein, H. (1980) *The Bureaucracy of Han Times*. Cambridge.

Birks, P. (1985) 'The Roman Law Concept of Dominium and the Idea of Absolute Ownership', *Acta Juridica*: 1–38.

Blanshard, A. J. L. (2004) 'Depicting Democracy: An Exploration of Art and Text in the Law of Eukrates', *Journal of Hellenic Studies* 124: 1–15.

Bloch, J. (1950). *Les inscriptions d'Asoka*. Paris.

Blok, J. and Krul, J. (2017). 'Debt and Its Aftermath: The Near Eastern Background to Solon's *Seisachtheia*', *Hesperia: The Journal of the American School of Classical Studies at Athens* 86.4: 607–43.

Bodde, D. (1982) 'Forensic Medicine in Pre-Imperial China', *Journal of the American Oriental Society* 102: 1–15.

(1986) 'The State and Empire of Ch'in', in *The Cambridge History of China*, Vol. I: *The Ch'in and Han Empires 221 BC–AD 220*, ed. D. Twitchett and M. Loewe. Cambridge: 20–102.

Bodde, D. and Morris, C. (1967) *Law in Imperial China*. Philadelphia.

Bodnaruk, M. (2022) 'Late Antique Slavery in Epigraphic Evidence', in *Slavery in the Late Antique World, 150–700 CE*, ed. C. L. de Wet, M. Kahlos and V. Vuolanto. Cambridge: 224–50.

Boegehold, A. L. (1995) *The Lawcourts at Athens*. Princeton, NJ.

Bond, J. (2003) 'International Intersectionality: A Theoretical and Pragmatic Exploration of Women's International Human Rights Violations', *Emory Law Journal* 52: 71–186.

(2014) 'Altering Infamy: Status, Violence, and Civic Exclusion in Late Antiquity', *Classical Antiquity* 33.1: 1–30.

(2016) *Trade and Taboo: Disreputable Professions in the Roman Mediterranean*. Ann Arbor, MI.

Bonnechere, P. (2010) 'Oracles and Greek Mentalities: The Mantic Confirmations of Mantic Revelations', in *Myths, Martyrs, and Modernity*, ed. J. Dijkstra, J. Kroesen and Y. Kuiper. Leiden: 115–33.

(2013) 'The Religious Management of the *Polis*: Oracles and Political Decision-Making', in *A Companion to Ancient Greek Government*, ed. H. Beck. Chichester: 366–81.

Bottéro, J. (1987) *Mésopotamie: L'écriture, la raison et les dieux*. Paris.

(1992a) *Mesopotamia: Writing, Reasoning, and the Gods*, trans. Z. Bahrani and M. van de Mieroop. Chicago.

(1992b) 'The "Code" of Ḥammurabi', in *Mesopotamia: Writing, Reasoning, and the Gods*, trans. Z. Bahrani and M. van de Mieroop. Chicago: 156–84.

Botterwick, G. J. and Ringgren, H. (1977) *Theological Dictionary of the Old Testament*. Vol. II. Grand Rapids, MI.

Bourgon, J. (1999) 'Le role des schemas divinatoires dans la codification du droit chinois: À propos du Commentaire des code des Jin par Zhang Fei', *Extrême-Orient Extrême Occident* 21: 131–44.

Bovati, P. (1994) *Re-establishing Justice: Legal Terms, Concepts and Procedures in the Hebrew Bible*, tran. M. J. Smith. JSOTSup 105. Sheffield.

Bowles, S. and Choi J.-K. (2013) 'Coevolution of Farming and Private Property during the Early Holocene', *Proceedings of the National Academy of Science USA* 110.22: 8830–35.

Boyer, G. (1954) 'Sur quelques exemples de la fiction dans l'ancien droit oriental', *Revue internationale des droits de l'Antiquité* 3e série 1: 73–100.

Bresson, A. (2016a) *The Making of the Ancient Greek Economy: Institutions, Markets, and Growth in the City-States*, trans. S. Rendall. Princeton, NJ.

(2016b) 'Women and Inheritance in Ancient Sparta: The Gortynian Connection', *Studi Ellenistici* 30: 9–68.

Brick, D. (2012) 'Social and Soteriological Aspects of Sin and Penance in Medieval Hindu Law', in *Sin and Sinners: Perspectives from Asian Religions*, ed. P. Granoff and K. Shinohara. Leiden: 9–30.

(2014) 'The Widow-Ascetic under Hindu Law', *Indo-Iranian Journal* 57.4: 353–83.

(2023) *Widows under Hindu Law*. Oxford.

Brisch, N. (ed.) (2012) *Religion and Power: Divine Kingship in the Ancient World and Beyond*. Chicago.

Broekman, G. (2008) 'The Chronicle of Prince Osorkon and Its Historical Context', *Journal of Egyptian History* 1.2: 209–34.

Brosius, M. (ed.) (2003) *Ancient Archives and Archival Traditions: Concepts of Record-Keeping in the Ancient World*. Oxford.

Broughton, T. R. S. (1951–60) *The Magistrates of the Roman Republic*. 3 vols. New York.
Browne, G. M. (1987) 'The Sortes Astrampsychi and the Egyptian Oracle', in *Texte und Textkritik: Eine Aufsatzsammlung*, ed. J. Dummer. Berlin: 67–71.
Brown, M. and Sanft, C. (2011) 'Categories of Legal Reasoning in Early Imperial China: The Meaning of Fa in Received Texts', *Oriens Extremus* 50: 283–306.
Bruun, C. (2015) 'Water Use and Productivity in Roman Agriculture: Selling, Sharing, Servitudes', in *Ownership and Exploitation of Land and Natural Resources in the Roman World*, ed. P. Erdkamp, K. Verboven and A. Zuiderhoek. Oxford: 132–49.
Bryen. A. Z. (2012) 'Judging Empire: Courts and Culture in Rome's Eastern Provinces', *Law and History Review* 30: 771–811.
  (2013) *Violence in Roman Egypt: A Study in Legal Interpretation*. Philadelphia.
  (2014) 'Martyrdom, Rhetoric, and the Politics of Judicial Procedure', *Classical Antiquity* 33: 243–80.
  (2016) 'Crimes against the Individual: Violence and Sexual Crimes', in *The Oxford Handbook of Roman Law and Society*, ed. P. J. du Plessis, C. Ando and K. Tuori. Oxford: 322–32.
  (2018) 'Labeo's *iniuria*: Violence and Politics in the Age of Augustus', *Chiron* 48: 17–52.
Buckland, W. W. (1963) *Textbook of Roman Law: From Augustus to Justinian*. 3rd ed. rev. P. Stein. Cambridge.
Bünger, K. (1996) *Quellen zur Rechtsgeschichte der T'ang-Zeit. Neue, erweiterte Ausgabe mit einen Vorwort von Denis Twitchett*. Institut Monumenta Serica. Nettetal.
Burrow, T. (1940) *A Translation of the Kharosthi Documents from Chinese Turkestan*. London.
Bushala, E. (1968) 'Torture of Non-citizens in Homicide Investigations', *Greek, Roman, and Byzantine Studies* 9: 61–68.
Caldwell, E. (2014) 'Social Change and Written Law on Early Chinese Legal Thought', *Law and History Review* 32: 1–30.
  (2018) *Writing Chinese Laws: The Form and Function of Legal Statutes Found in the Qin Shuihudi Corpus*. London and New York.
Canepa, M. (2018) 'Sasanian Iran and the projection of power in Late Antique Eurasia: Competing Cosmologies and Topographies of Power', in *Empires and Exchanges in Eurasian Late Antiquity: Rome, China, Iran, and the Steppe, ca. 250–750*, ed. N. Di Cosmo and M. Maas. Cambridge: 54–69.
Canevaro, M. (2013) '*Nomothesia* in Classical Athens: What Sources Should We Believe?', *Classical Quarterly* 63: 139–60.
  (2016) 'The Procedure of Demosthenes against Leptines: How to Repeal (and Replace) an Existing Law', *Journal of Hellenic Studies* 136: 39–58.
  (2017) 'The Rule of Law as the Measure of Political Legitimacy in the Greek City States', *Hague Journal on the Rule of Law* 9: 211–36.
  (2019) 'Athenian Constitutionalism: Nomothesia and Judicial Review', in *Symposion 2017: Vorträge zur griechischen und hellenistischen Rechtsgeschichte*, ed. G. Thür and U. Yiftach-Firanko. Vienna: 65–98.
Cantarella, E. (1991) *I supplizi capitali in Grecia e a Roma*. Milan.
  (2002) 'Marriage and Sexuality in Republican Rome: A Roman Conjugal Love Story', in *The Sleep of Reason: Erotic Experience and Sexual Ethics in Ancient Greece and Rome*, ed. M. C. Nussbaum and J. Sihvola. Chicago: 269–82.
  (2005) 'Gender, Sexuality and Law', in Gagarin and Cohen (2005): 236–53.

(2016) 'Women and Patriarchy in Roman Law', in *The Oxford Handbook of Roman Law and Society*, ed. P. J. du Plessis, C. Ando and K. Tuori. Oxford: 419–31.
Capogrossi Colognesi, L. (2015) *Law and Power in the Making of the Roman Commonwealth*. Cambridge.
Carawan, E. (2007) 'Oath and Contract', in Horkos: The Oath in Greek Society, ed. A. Sommerstein and J. Fletcher. Exeter: 73–80.
Carbon, J.-M., and E. M. Harris. (2024) 'Policing Sanctuaries in Ancient Greece' in *The Logistics of Sanctuaries*. ed. J. Barringer, G. Ekroth and D. Scahill. Leiden: forthcoming.
Cardascia, G. (1995) 'L'ordalie fluviale dans la Mésopotamie ancienne', *Méditerranées* 3: 269–88.
Carey, C. (1994) '"Artless" Proofs in Aristotle and the Orators', *Bulletin of the Institute of Classical Studies* 39: 95–106.
Carrié, J.-M. (2002) 'Les associations professionnelles à l'époque tardive: Entre munus et Convivialité', in *Humana Sapit*, ed. J.-M. Carrié and R. Lizzi Testa. Turnhout: 309–32.
Cartledge, P. (2002a) *The Greeks: A Portrait of Self and Others*. 2nd ed. Oxford.
  (2002b) 'The Origins and Organisation of the Peloponnesian League', in *Sparta*, ed. M. Whitby. New York: 223–30.
  (2018) 'The Spartan Contribution to Greek Citizenship Theory', in *Defining Citizenship in Archaic Greece*, ed. A. Duplouy and R. W. Brock. Oxford: 179–88.
Champlin, E. (1991) *Final Judgments: Duty and Emotion in Roman Wills, 200 BC–AD 250*. Berkeley and Los Angeles.
Chang, W. (2000) 'Foreword', in *The Limits of the Rule of Law in China*, ed. K. G. Turner, J. V. Feinerman and R Kent Guy. Seattle and London: vii.
Chaniotis, A. (1995) '"Tempeljustiz" im kaiserzeitlichen Kleinasien: Rechtliche Aspekte der Sühninschriften Lydiens und Phrygiens', in *Symposium 1995: Vorträge zur griechishen und hellenistichen Rechtsgeschichte (Korfu, 1–5 September 1995)*, ed. G. Thür and J. Velissaropoulos-Karakostas, Cologne: 353–84.
  (1996) *Die Verträge zwischen kretischen Poleis in der hellenistischen Zeit*. Stuttgart.
  (2004) 'Justifying Territorial Claims in Classical and Hellenistic Greece: The Beginnings of International Law', in *The Law and the Courts in Ancient Greece*, ed. E. M. Harris and L. Rubinstein. London: 185–213.
Charpin, D. (1990) 'Les édits de "restauration" des rois babyloniens et leur application', in *Du pouvoir dans l'Antiquité: Mots et réalités*, ed. Claude Nicolet. Paris: 13–24.
  (1993a) 'qabbâ'um, "délateur"?', *Nouvelles assyriologiques brèves et utilitaires* 1 (March): 19–20.
  (1993b) 'À propos des contrats d'embauche pour la moisson', *Nouvelles assyriologiques brèves et utilitaires*, 2 (June): 49.
  (2000) 'Les prêteurs et le palais: Les édits de *mîšarum* des rois de Babylone et leurs traces dans les archives privées', in *Interdependency of Institutions and Private Entrepreneurs: Proceedings of the Second MOS Symposium (Leiden, 1998)*, ed. A. C. V. M. Bongenaar. Publications de l'Institut Historique et Archéologique Néerlandais de Stamboul 87. Leiden: 185–211.
  (2005) 'Le statut des codes de lois des souverains babyloniens', in *Le législateur et la loi dans l'Antiquité: Hommage à Françoise Ruzé*, ed. P. Sineux. Caen: 93–108.
  (2010) *Writing, Law, and Kingship in Old Babylonian Mesopotamia*. Chicago.
  (2012) *Hammurabi of Babylon*. London, New York.

(2016) 'Chroniques bibliographiques 18: Les débuts des relations diplomatiques au Proche-Orient ancien', *Revue d'assyriologie et d'archéologie orientale* 110.1: 127–86.

(2019) *'Tu es de mon sang': Les alliances dans le Proche-Orient ancien.* Paris.

(2022) 'La gestuelle de l'alliance à l'époque paléo-babylonienne: Textes et images', in *'A Community of Peoples': Studies on Society and Politics in the Bible and Ancient Near East in Honor of Daniel Fleming*, ed. M. Leonard-Fleckman, L. A. S. Monroe, M. J. Stahl and D. R. Johnson. Harvard Semitic Studies 69. Leiden: 6–29.

Charpin, D. and Durand, J.-M. (1997) 'Aššur avant l'assyrie', *Mari, Annales de recherches interdisciplinaires* 8: 367–92.

Chavalas, M. (2020) 'The Ancient Near East and Biblical Scholarship: Recently Uncovered Archives from the Cunieform World', in *A Companion to the Ancient Near East*, 2nd ed., ed. D. C. Snell. Hoboken, NJ: 455–70.

Cheng, S. (1988) *Jiuzhao lükao* [Investigations into the Laws of Various Dynasties]. Beijing.

Chevrier, M. (1921) *Du serment promissoire en droit romain.* Dijon.

Christ, M. R. (1998) *The Litigious Athenian.* Baltimore.

Christensen, T., Thompson, D. and Vandorpe, K. (eds. and trans.) (2017) *Land and Taxes in Ptolemaic Egypt: An Edition, Translation and Commentary for the Edfu Land Survey (P. Haun. IV 70).* Cambridge.

Ch'ü, T. (1980) *Law and Society in Traditional China.* Westport, CT.

Civil, M. (2011) 'The Law Collection of Ur-Namma', in *Cuneiform Royal Inscriptions and Related Texts in the Schøyen Collection*, ed. A. George. Bethesda: 221–86.

Clarysse, W. (2014) 'Deeds of Last Will: Demotic, Greek, and Latin', in Keenan, Manning and Yiftach-Firanko (2014): 202–13.

(2019) 'Ethnic Identity: Egyptians, Greeks and Romans', in *A Companion to Greco-Roman and Late Antique Egypt*, ed. K. Vandorpe. Hoboken, NJ: 219–314.

Clarysse, W. and Thompson, D. J. (2006) *Counting the People in Hellenistic Egypt.* 2 vols. Cambridge.

Cohen, B. (2018) *Jewish and Roman Law.* Vol. I: *A Comparative Study.* Piscataway, NJ.

Cohen, D. J. (1984) *Theft in Athenian Law.* Münchener Beiträge zur Papyrusforschung und antiken Rechtsgeschichte 74. Munich.

(1995) *Law, Violence and Community in Classical Athens.* Cambridge.

(2003) 'Writing, Law, and Legal Practice in the Athenian Courts', in *Written Texts and the Rise of Literate Culture in Ancient Greece*, ed. H. Yunis. Cambridge: 78–96.

(2005) 'Crime, Punishment, and the Rule of Law in Classical Athens,' in Gagarin and Cohen (2005): 211–35.

(2015) 'Tyranny or the Rule of Law? Democratic Participation in Legal Institutions in Athens', in *A Companion to Greek Democracy and the Roman Republic*, ed. D. Hammer. Chichester: 167–78.

Cohen, R. (2000) 'Intelligence in the Amarna Letters', in *Amarna Diplomacy? The Beginnings of International Relations*, ed. R. Cohen and R. Westbrook. Baltimore: 85–98.

Cohen, R. and Westbrook R. (eds.) (2000) *Amarna Diplomacy? The Beginnings of International Relations.* Baltimore.

Cohen, S. J. D. (1981a) 'Epigraphical Rabbis', *Jewish Quarterly Review* 72: 1–17.

(1981b) 'Patriarchs and Scholarchs', *Proceedings of the American Academy of Jewish Research* 48: 57–85.

(1987) *From the Maccabees to the Mishnah.* Louisville.

Cohen, Y. and Kedar, S. (2011) 'Teacher–Student Relationships: Two Case Studies', in *The Oxford Handbook of Cuneiform Culture*, ed. K. Radner and E. Robson. Oxford: 229–47.

Connolly, S. (2010) *Lives behind the Laws: The World of the Codex Hermogenianus*. Bloomington.

Cooley, A. E. (ed. and trans.) (2009) *Res Gestae Divi Augusti: Text, Translation, and Commentary*. Cambridge.

Coppens, F. (2021) 'The Ptolemaic Basileus and the Roman Emperor Slaying the Enemies of Egypt', in *Continuity, Discontinuity and Change: Perspectives from the New Kingdom to the Roman Era*, ed. F. Coppens. Prague: 405–89.

Corcoran, S. (2014) 'State Correspondence in the Roman Empire: Imperial Communication from Augustus to Justinian', in *State Correspondence in the Ancient World*, ed. K. Radner. Oxford: 172–209.

Corey Brennan, T. (2000) *The Praetorship in the Roman Republic*. Vol. II. Oxford.

Cotterrell, R. (2008) 'Transnational Communities and the Concept of Law', *Ratio Juris* 21.1: 1–18.

(2014) 'A Concept of Law for Global Legal Pluralism?', in *Concepts of Law. Comparative, Jurisprudential, and Social Science Perspectives*, ed. S. P. Donlan and L. Heckendorn Urscheler. London: 193–208.

Cotton, H. M. (1998) 'The Rabbis and the Documents', in *Jews in a Graeco-Roman World*, ed. M. Goodman. Oxford: 167–79.

Cotton, H. M. and Yardeni, A. (eds.) (1997) *Aramaic, Hebrew and Greek Documentary Texts from Nahal Hever and Other Sites*. Discoveries in the Judaean Desert 27. Oxford.

Cox, R. (2017) 'Expanding the History of the Just War: The Ethics of War in Ancient Egypt', *International Studies Quarterly* 61.2: 371–84.

Crawford, M. H. (ed.) (1996) *Roman Statutes*. 2 vols. Bulletin of the Institute of Classical Studies, Supplement 64. London.

Creel, H. G. (1970) *The Origins of Statecraft in China*. Vol. I: *The Western Chou Empire*. Chicago.

Crenshaw, K. W. (1989) 'Demarginalizing the Intersection of Race and Sex: A Black Feminist Critique of Antidiscrimination Doctrine, Feminist Theory and Antiracist Politics', *University of Chicago Legal Forum* 1989.1: 139–67.

Crook, J. A. (1967) *Law and Life of Rome*. Ithaca and London.

(1995) *Legal Advocacy in the Roman World*. London.

Cross, M. K. D. (2013) 'Rethinking Epistemic Communities Twenty Years Later', *Review of International Studies* 39: 137–60.

Crowell, W. G. (1979) 'Government Land Policies and Systems in Early Imperial China', Doctoral dissertation, University of Washington.

Crowther, C. (2007) 'Foreign Judges and Regional Variations in Hellenistic Asia Minor', in *Regionalism in Hellenistic and Roman Asia Minor*, ed. H. Elton and G. Reger. Bordeaux: 53–60.

Csikszentmihalyi, M. (ed. and trans.) (2006) *Readings in Han Chinese Thought*. Indianapolis.

Czajkowski, K. (2017) *Localized Law: The Babatha and Salome Komaise Archives*. Oxford Studies in Roman Society and Law. Oxford and New York.

Dahlheim W. (1968) *Struktur und Entwicklung des römischen Völkerrechts im dritten und zweiten Jahrhundert v. Chr.* Munich.

Dalby, M. (1981) 'Revenge and the Law in Traditional China', *American Journal of Legal History* 25: 267–307.

Daube, D. (1969) *Roman Law: Linguistic, Social, and Philosophical Aspects*. Edinburgh.

(1991; original 1951) 'Ne quid infamandi causa fiat: The Roman Law of Defamation', in *Collected Studies in Roman Law*, ed. D. Cohen and D. Simon. Frankfurt: 465–500.

(2000) 'Wine in the Bible', in *Collected Works of David Daube*, Vol. II, ed. C. Carmichael. Berkeley: 453–62.

David, J.-M. (2019) *Au service de l'honneur: Les appariteurs de magistrats romains*, Paris.

Davidson, J. N. (1997) *Courtesans & Fishcackes: The Consuming Passions of Classical Athens*. Hammersmith.

Davis, D. R. Jr (2006) 'A Realist View of Hindu Law', *Ratio Juris* 19.3: 287–313.

(2010) *The Spirit of Hindu Law*. Cambridge.

(2014) 'Responsa in Hindu Law: Consultation and Lawmaking in Medieval India', *Oxford Journal of Law and Religion*: 1–19.

(2017) 'Introduction', in Olivelle and Davis (2017): 1–11.

de Angelis, F. (ed.) (2010) *Spaces of Justice in the Roman World*. Leiden.

Debourse, C. (2022) *Of Priests and Kings: The Babylonian New Year Festival in the Last Age of Cuneiform Culture*. Leiden.

de Crespigny, R. (1981) 'Inspection and Surveillance Officials under the Two Han Dynasties', in *State and Law in East Asia, Festscrift für Karl Bünger*, ed. D. Eikemeir and H. Franke. Wiesbaden: 40–79.

(2007) *A Biographical Dictionary of Later Han to the Three Kingdoms (23–220 AD)*. Leiden.

(2018) *Emperor Han and Emperor Ling: Being the Chronicle of Later Han for the years 157 to 180 AD as Recorded in Chapters 54 to 59 of the Zizhi Tongjian of Sima Guang*. Online edition: https://openresearch-repository.anu.edu.au/handle/1885/42048 (accessed 19/09/2022).

Démare-Lafont, S. (1997) 'La procédure par serment au Proche-Orient ancien', in *Jurer et maudire: Pratiques politiques et usages juridiques du serment dans le Proche-Orient ancien*, ed. S. (Démare-)Lafont. Paris: 185–98.

(1999a) 'Le juge biblique', in *La conscience du juge*, ed. J.-M. Carbasse and L. Depambour-Tarride. Paris: 19–48.

(1999b) *Femmes, droit et justice dans l'Antiquité orientale: Contribution à l'étude du droit pénal au Proche-Orient ancien*. Orbis Biblicus et Orientalis 165. Fribourg-Göttingen.

(2000a) 'Codification et subsidiarité dans les droits du Proche-Orient ancien', in *La Codification des lois dans l'antiquité*, ed. E. Lévy. Paris: 49–64.

(2000b) 'Considérations sur la pratique judiciaire en Mésopotamie', in *Rendre la justice en Mésopotamie: Archives judiciaires du Proche-Orient ancien (IIIe–Ier millénaires avant J.-C.)*, ed. F. Joannès. Saint-Denis: 15–34.

(2003) 'Middle Assyrian Period', in Westbrook (2003a): 521–64.

(2007) 'Les droits sans doctrine: Réflexions autour d'une absence dans le monde cunéiforme', in *L'autorité de la doctrine, Actes de la Journée d'études du 23 septembre 2005 organisée par l'IHD et l'Ecole doctorale d'histoire du droit de Paris II*, ed. G. Leyte. *Revue d'histoire des Facultés de droit et de la science juridique* 27: 407–24.

(2011) 'The Status of Women in the Legal Texts of the Ancient Near East', in *Torah*, ed. I. Fischer, M. N. Puerto, A. Taschl-Erber, and J. Økland. Atlanta: 109–32.

(2012) 'Le Marriage Babylonien: Une approche historiographique', *Zeitschrift für Altorientalische und Biblische Rechtsgeschichte* 18: 175–90.
(2015a) 'Les inégalités sociales en Mésopotamie: Quelques précautions de vocabulaire', *Droit et cultures* 69: 75–87.
(2015b) 'Introduction: Raymond Westbrook and the Ends of the Earth', in *Ex oriente lex: Near Eastern Influences on Ancient Greek and Roman Law*, ed. R. Westbrook, D. Lyons and K. Raaflaub. Baltimore: xv–xx.
(2016–17) 'Adoption and Apprenticeship in the Old Babylonian Period', *Journal of the Ancient Near Eastern Society 'Ex Oriente Lux'* 46: 45–57.
Démare-Lafont, S. and Fleming, D. (eds.) (2023) *Judicial Decisions in the Ancient Near East.* Writings from the Ancient World 43. Atlanta.
Deng, X. (2012) 'Women in Turfan during the Sixth to Eighth Centuries: A Look at Their Activities Outside the Home', in *The Silk Road. Key Papers. Part I: The Pre-Islamic Period*, ed. V. Hansen. Leiden: 448–68.
Depauw, M. (1997) *Companion to Demotic Studies*. Brussels.
Dercksen, J. G. (2004) *Old Assyrian Institutions*. Publications de l'Institut Historique et Archéologique Néerlandais de Stamboul 98. Leiden.
Derrett, J. D. M. (1973) *Dharmaśāstra and Juridical Literature*. Wiesbaden.
Despotopoulos, C. (1968) 'La notion de Synallagma chez Aristote', *Archives de philosophie du droit* 13: 115–27.
des Retours, R. (1947) *Traité des fonctionnaires et traité de l'armée*. Vol. I. Leiden.
Detienne, M. (2008) *Comparing the Incomparable*. Stanford, CA.
de Zulueta, F. (1945) *The Roman Law of Sale*. Oxford.
Dhammika, S. (1993) *Edicts of King Asoka*. Kandy. Online edition: www.cs.colostate.edu/~malaiya/ashoka.html (accessed 19/09/2022).
Dignas, B. (2002) *Economy of the Sacred in Hellenistic and Roman Asia Minor*. Oxford.
Dillon, J. N. (2012) *The Justice of Constantine: Law, Communication, and Control*. Ann Arbor, MI.
Dimopoulou, A. (2014) 'Άκυρου έστω: Legal Invalidity in Greek Inscriptions', in *Symposion 2013*, ed. M. Gagarin and A. Lanni. Vienna: 249–75.
Dobson, W. A. C. (1968) 'Some Legal Instruments of Ancient China', in *Wen-lin*, ed. Chow Tse-tsung. Madison: 268–82.
Doerfler, M. (2013) 'Law and Order: Monastic Formation, Episcopal Authority and Conceptions of Justice in Late Antiquity', PhD thesis, Duke University.
Dombradi, E. (1996) *Die Darstellung des Rechtsaustrags in den altbabylonischen Prozessurkunden*. 2 vols. Stuttgart.
Donker van Heel, K. (2021) *The Archive of the Theban Choachyte Petebaste Son of Peteamunip (Floruit 7th Century BCE)*. Leiden.
Donlan, S. P. and Heckendorn Urscheler, L. (eds.) (2014) *Concepts of Law: Comparative, Jurisprudential, and Social Science Perspectives*. London.
Dougherty, R. P. (1923) *The Shirkûtu of Babylonian Deities*. New Haven.
Doumy, M (2021) 'Dunhuang Texts', in *Oxford Research Encyclopedia of Religion*. Online edition: https://oxfordre.com/religion/view/10.1093/acrefore/9780199340378.001.0001/acrefore-9780199340378-e-771 (accessed 04/07/2022).
Driver, G. R. and Miles, J. C. (eds. and trans.) (1935) *The Assyrian Laws*. Oxford.
(eds. and trans.) (1952–55) *The Babylonian Laws*. Oxford.

Dubber, M. (ed.) (2014) *Foundational Texts in Modern Criminal Law*. Oxford.
Dubs, H. H. (ed.) (1954) *The History of the Former Han Dynasty, by Pan Ku*. Vol. II. Baltimore.
Dull, J. (1966) 'A Historical Introduction to the Apocryphal (Ch'an-Wei) Texts of the Han Dynasty', PhD thesis, University of Washington.
du Plessis, P. J. (2012) *Studying Roman Law*. London.
  (2015). 'Property', in Johnston (2015): 175–98.
Durand, J.-M. (1988) 'L'ordalie', in *Archives épistolaires de Mari* I.1, ed. J.-M. Durand. Paris: 509–39.
Durand, J.-M. (1997). *Les Documents épistolaires du palais de Mari*. Vol. I. Littératures anciennes du Proche-Orient 16. Paris.
Durand, J.-M. (2000). *Les Documents épistolaires du palais de Mari*, Vol. II. Littératures anciennes du Proche-Orient 18. Paris.
Dutton, M. R. (1992) *Policing and Punishment in China: From Patriarchy to 'the People'*. Cambridge.
Duve, T. (2018) 'Global Legal History: Setting Europe in Perspective', in *The Oxford Handbook of European Legal History*, ed. H. Pihlajamäki, M. D. Dubber and M. Godfrey. Oxford: 115–39.
  (2020) 'What Is Global Legal History?', *Comparative Legal History* 8.2: 73–115.
  (2022) 'Legal Traditions', in *The Oxford Handbook of Law and Anthropology*, ed. M.-C. Foblets, M. Goodale, M. Sapignoli and O. Zenker. Oxford: 352–67.
Duyvendak, J. J. L. (ed.) (1963) *The Book of Lord Shang: A Classic of the Chinese School of Law*. London.
Easton, D. F. (1981) 'Hittite Land Donations and Tabarna Seals', *Journal of Cuneiform Studies* 33: 3–43.
Eckhardt, B. (2021) *Romanisierung und Verbrüderung: Das Vereinswesen im römischen Reich*. Berlin and Boston.
Economou, E. M. L. and Kyriazis, N. C. (2017) 'The emergence and the evolution of property rights in ancient Greece', *Journal of Institutional Economics* 13: 53–77.
Edel, E. (1994) *Die ägyptisch-hethitische Korrespondenz aus Boghazköy*. 2 vols. Opladen.
Eidinow, E. (2007) *Oracles, Curses and Risk among the Ancient Greeks*. Oxford.
El-Aguizy, O. (1989) 'A Demotic Deed of "Not Hindering" from Sharunah', *Bulletin de l'Institut français d'archéologie orientale* 89: 89–99.
Ellickson, R. C. (1993) 'Property in Land', *The Yale Law Journal* 102.6: 1315–400.
Ellickson, R. C. and Thorland, C. D. (1995) 'Ancient Land Law: Mesopotamia, Egypt, Israel', *Chicago-Kent Law Review* 71.1: 321–411.
Ellickson, R. C., Rose, C. M. and Smith, H. E. (eds.) (2014) *Perspectives on Property Law*. 4th ed. New York.
Elon, M. (1994) *Jewish Law: History, Sources, Principles*. 4 vols. Trans. Bernard Auerbach and Melvin Sykes. Jerusalem and Philadelphia.
Epstein, J. N. (1964) *Introduction to the Text of the Mishna* [Hebrew]. 2 vols. Jerusalem (1948). 2nd ed. 1964.
Epstein, R. A. (2016) 'The Economic Structure of Roman Property Law', in *The Oxford Handbook of Roman Law and Society*, ed. P. J. du Plessis, C. Ando and K. Tuori. Oxford: 513–23.
Ernout, A. and Meillet, A. (1994) *Dictionnaire étymologique de la langue latine: Histoire des mots*. 4th repr. ed. J. André. Paris.

Esu, A. (2021) 'Adeia in Fifth-Century Athens', *Journal of Hellenic Studies* 141: 153–78.
Étienne, R. (1990) *Tenos II: Tenos et les Cyclades du milieu du IVe siecle av J.-C. au milieu du IIIe siecle ap. J.-C.* Paris.
Eyre, C. (2004) 'Judgement to the Satisfaction of All', *La Fonction de juger: Égypte ancienne et Mésopotamie. Droit et cultures: Revue semestrielle d'anthropologie et d'histoire* 47.1: 91–107.
Etxabe, J. (ed.) (2019) *A Cultural History of Law in Antiquity*. London and New York.
Fahrner, M. (2020) 'Aufsatz: Die Sicherheit im Staatsschutzstrafrecht', *Zeitschrift für die gesamte Strafrechtswissenschaft* 132.1: 84–101.
Faraguna, M. (2000) 'A proposito degli archivi nel mondo greco: Terra e registrazioni fondiarie', *Chiron* 30: 65–115.
  (ed.) (2013) *Archives and Archival Documents in Ancient Societies*. Trieste.
  (2015) 'Archives, Documents, and Legal Practices in the Greek Polis', in *The Oxford Handbook of Ancient Greek Law*, ed. E. Harris and M. Canevaro. Online edition: https://doi.org/10.1093/oxfordhb/9780199599257.013.14 (accessed 01/09/2022).
Farber, W. (1995) 'Witchcraft, magic, and divination in ancient Mesopotamia', in *Civilizations of the Ancient Near East*, ed. J. M. Sasson. New York: 1895–909.
Feigin, S. I. (1979) *Legal and Administrative Texts of the Reign of Šamšu-Iluna*. Yale Oriental Series (YOS) 12. New Haven.
Fensham, F. C. (1962) 'Widow, Orphan, and the Poor in Ancient Near Eastern Legal and Wisdom Literature', *Journal of Near Eastern Studies* 21.2: 129–39.
Figueira, Th. and Jensen, S. R. (2013) 'Governing Interstate Alliances', in *A Companion to Ancient Greek Government*, ed. H. Beck. Chichester: 480–96.
Figulla, H. H. (1967) *Old-Babylonian nadītu Records*. CT 47. London.
Fine, J. V. A. (1951) *Horoi: Studies in Mortgage, Real Security and Land Tenure in Ancient Athens*. Athens.
Finkelstein, J. J. (1961) 'Ammiṣaduqa's Edict and the Babylonian "Law Codes"', *Journal of Cuneiform Studies* 15: 91–104.
Finley, M. (1951) 'Some Considerations of Greek Law', *Seminar* 9: 72–102.
  (1981) *Economy and Society in Ancient Greece*, ed. B. D. Shaw and R. P. Saller. London.
Fiori, R. (2016) 'Contracts, Commerce and Roman Society', in *The Oxford Handbook of Roman Law and Society*, ed. P. J. du Plessis, C. Ando and K. Tuori. Oxford: 581–95.
Fishbane, M. (1985) *Biblical Interpretation in Ancient Israel*. Oxford.
Fitzgerald, J. (trans.) (2004) *The Mahābhārata*. Vol. VII: *11: The Book of the Women, 12: The Book of Peace, Part 1*. Chicago.
Fleming, D. (1992) 'A Limited Kingship: Late Bronze Age Emar in Ancient Syria', *Ugarit Forschungen* 24: 59–71.
Flower, H. I. (2010) *Roman Republics*. Princeton, NJ.
Flynn, S. W. (2018) *Children in Ancient Israel: The Hebrew Bible and Mesopotamia in Comparative Perspective*. Oxford.
Fonrobert, Ch. and Jaffee, M. (2007) 'Introduction', in *The Cambridge Companion to the Talmud and Rabbinic Literature*, ed. C. Fonrobert and M. Jaffee. Cambridge: 1–14.
Forsdyke, S. (2018) 'Ancient and Modern Conceptions of the Rule of Law', in *Ancient Greek History and the Contemporary Social Sciences*, ed. M. Canevaro, A. Erskine, B. Gray and J. Ober. Edinburgh: 184–212.
Foxhall, L. (1989) 'Household, Gender and Property in Classical Athens', *Classical Quarterly* 39.1: 22–44.

Fraade, S. D. (1991) *From Tradition to Commentary: Torah and Its Interpretation in the Midrash Sifre Deuteronomy*. Albany, NY.
  (1998) 'Looking for Legal Midrash at Qumran', in *Biblical Perspectives: Early Use and Interpretation of the Bible in Light of the Dead Sea Scrolls. Proceedings of the First International Symposium of the Orion Center for the Study of the Dead Sea Scrolls and Associated Literature, 12–14 May, 1996*, ed. M. E. Stone and E. G. Chazon. Leiden: 59–79.
Fraenkel, Y. (1991) *Darkei Ha'aggadah wehamidrash*. 2 vols. Givatayyim.
Frankfurter, D. (1998) *Religion in Roman Egypt*. Princeton, NJ.
  (2018) *Christianizing Egypt: Syncretism and Local Worlds in Late Antiquity*. Princeton, NJ.
Frayne, D. (2016) *Royal Inscriptions of Mesopotamia: Presargonic Period, Early Periods*. Toronto.
Fressura, M. and Mantovani, D. (2018) 'P.Vindob. L 59+92: Frammenti delle Institutiones di Elio Marciano', *Athenaeum* 105: 619–90.
Friedman, M. A. (1996) 'Babatha's *ketubba*: Some Preliminary Observations', *Israel Exploration Journal* 46: 55–76.
Frier, B. W. and Kehoe, D. P. (2007) 'Law and Economic Institutions', in *The Cambridge Economic History of the Greco-Roman World*, ed. W. Scheidel, I. Morris and R. Saller. Cambridge: 113–43.
Frier, B. W., and McGinn, T. A. J. (eds.) (2004) *A Casebook on Roman Family Law*. American Philological Association Classical Resources Series 5. Oxford.
Frymer-Kensky, T. (1977) 'The Judicial Ordeal in the Ancient Near East', PhD thesis, Yale University.
  (2003) 'Israel', in Westbrook (2003a): 974–1046.
Fuhrmann, M. (1960) *Das systematische Lehrbuch: Ein Beitrag zur Geschichte der Wissenschaft in der Antike*. Göttingen.
Funke, P. (ed.) (2012) *Greek Federal States and Their Sanctuaries*. Stuttgart.
  (2013) 'Greek Amhiktyonies: An Experiment in Transregional Governance', in *A Companion to Ancient Greek Government*, ed. H. Beck. Chichester: 451–65.
Furubotn, E. G. and Richter, R. (1998) *Institutions and Economic Theory: The Contribution of the New Institutional Economics*. Ann Arbor, MI.
Gabrielsen, V. and Paganini, M. C. D. (eds.) (2021) *Private Associations in the Ancient Greek World: Regulations and the Creation of Group Identity*. Cambridge and New York.
Gabrielsen, V. and Thomsen, C. A. (eds.) (2015) *Private Associations and the Public Sphere*. Copenhagen.
Gagarin, M. (1984) 'The Testimony of Witnesses in the Gortyn Laws', *Greek, Roman, and Byzantine Studies* 25.4: 345–49.
  (1996) 'The Torture of Slaves in Athenian Law', *Classical Philology* 91: 1–18.
  (2005a) 'The Unity of Greek Law', in Gagarin and Cohen (2005): 29–40.
  (2005b) 'Early Greek Law', in Gagarin and Cohen (2005): 82–94.
  (2007) 'Litigants' Oaths in Athenian Law', in *Horkos: The Oath in Greek Society*, ed. A. Sommerstein and J. Fletcher. Bristol: 39–47.
  (2008a) *Writing Greek Law*. Cambridge.
  (2008b) 'Women and Property at Gortyn', *Dike: Rivista di storia del diritto greco ed ellenistico* 11: 5–25.
  (2010) 'Serfs and Slaves at Gortyn', *Zeitschrift der Savigny-Stiftung für Rechtsgeschichte, Romanistische Abteilung* 127: 14–31.

(2011) *Speeches from Athenian Law*. Austin, TX.
(2012) 'Women's Property at Gortyn', *Dike: Rivista di storia del diritto greco ed ellenistico* 15: 73–92.
(2013) 'Law and Religion in Early Greece', in *Law and Religion in the Eastern Mediterranean: From Antiquity to Early Islam*, ed. A. C. Hagedorn and R. G. Kratz. Oxford: 59–78.
(2020) *Democratic Law in Classical Athens*. New York.
Gagarin, M. and Cohen, D. (eds.) (2005) *The Cambridge Companion to Ancient Greek Law*. Cambridge.
Gagarin, M. and Perlman, P. (eds. and trans.) (2016) *The Laws of Ancient Crete c. 650–400 BCE*. Oxford.
Gager, J. (ed.) (1992) *Curse Tablets and Binding Spells from the Ancient World*. New York.
Gagliardi, L. (2008) 'Zur Figur des iudex privatus im römischen Zivilprozess. Eine historisch-soziologische Untersuchung auf der Grundlage literarischer Quellen', *Revue internationale des droits de l'Antiquité* 55: 241–66.
Gagos, T. and Van Minnen, P. (1994) *Settling a Dispute: Towards a Legal Anthropology of Late Antique Egypt*. Ann Arbor, MI.
Galanter, M. (1966) 'The Modernization of Law', in *Modernization: The Dynamics of Growth*, ed. M. Weiner. New York: 153–65.
Galiani, S. and Sened, I. (eds.) (2014) *Institutions, Property Rights and Economic Growth. The Legacy of Douglass North*. Cambridge.
Galsterer, H. (1998/2006) 'Foedus', *Der Neue Pauly* 4: coll. 580–81 (English edition in *Brill's New Pauly* (online version) 2006).
Game, J. (2008) *Actes de Ventes dans le monde grec: Témoignages épigraphiques des Ventes immobilières*. Lyons.
Gans, E. (1824–35) *Erbrecht in weltgeschichtlicher Entwicklung*. 4 vols. Berlin.
Gardiner, J. F. (1993) *Being a Roman Citizen*. London.
Gargola, D. J. (2012) 'Centuriation', in *The Encyclopedia of Ancient History*, ed. R. S. Bagnall, K. Brodersen, C. B. Champion, A. Erskine and S. R. Huebner. Online edition: https://onlinelibrary.wiley.com/doi/abs/10.1002/9781444338386.wbeah20028 (accessed 19/09/2022).
Garnsey, P. (1970) *Social Status and Legal Privilege in the Roman Empire*. Oxford.
(2007) *Thinking about Property: From Antiquity to the Age of Revolution*. Cambridge.
Gaurier, D. (1992) 'Responsabilité morale en Chine ancienne: Le Fils du Ciel et le Mandat Céleste', *Revue internationale des droits de l'Antiquité* 39: 27–54.
Gauthier, P. (1972) *Symbola: Les étrangers et la justice dans les cités grecques*. Nancy.
Gelb, I. (1979) 'Household and Family in Early Mesopotamia', in *State and Temple Economy in the Ancient Near East*, ed. E. Lipinski. Leuven: 1–99.
Gelb, I. J., Steinkeller, P. and Whiting, R. M. Jr (1991) *Earliest Land Tenure Systems in the Near East: Ancient Kudurrus*. Chicago.
Geller, M. J. (2016) *Healing Magic and Evil Demons: Canonical Udug-hul Incantations*. Berlin.
George, A. R. (ed.) (2011) *Cuneiform Royal Inscriptions and Related Texts in the Schøyen Collection*, with contributions by M. Civil, K. Richard Walters Jr, P. Steinkeller and F. Vallet. Cornell University Studies in Assyriology and Sumerology, 17. University Park, PA.
Gerardi, P. (1986) 'Declaring War in Mesopotamia', *Archiv für Orientforschung* 33: 30–38.

Gernet, L. (1982) *Droit et institutions en Grèce antique*. Paris.
  (1981) 'Law and Prelaw in Ancient Greece', in *The Anthropology of Ancient Greece*, trans. J. Hamilton and B. Nagy. Baltimore: 143–215.
Gesundheit, S. (2012) *Three Times a Year: Studies on Festival Legislation in the Pentateuch*. Tübingen.
Giovannini, A. (2007) *Les relations entre États dans la Grèce antique: Du temps d'Homère à l'intervention romaine (ca. 700 – 200 av. J.-C.)*. Stuttgart.
Gintis, H. (2007) 'The evolution of private property', *Journal of Economic Behavior & Organization* 64: 1–16.
Giuliani, A. (2019) 'What Is Comparative Legal History? Legal Historiography and the Revolt against Formalism, 1930–60', in *Comparative Legal History*, ed. A. M. Moréteau and K. A. Modéer. Cheltenham: 30–77.
Glackin, S. N. (2014) 'Back to Bundles: Deflating Property Rights, Again', *Legal Theory* 20.1: 1–24.
Glanville, S. R. K. (1939) *A Theban Archive of the Reign of Ptolemy I Soter*. Catalogue of Demotic Papyri in the British Museum, vol. 1. London.
Gleason, M. W. (1999) 'Truth Contests and Talking Corpses', in *Constructions of the Classical Body*, ed. J. I. Porter. Ann Arbor, MI: 287–313.
Glenn, P. (2014) *Legal Traditions of the World*. 5th ed. Oxford.
Goldberg, A. (1987) 'Die Schrift der rabbinische Schriftausleger', *Frankfurter Judaistische Beiträge* 15: 1–15.
  (1990) 'The Rabbinic View of Scripture', in *A Tribute to Geza Vermes: Essays on Jewish and Christian Literature and History*, ed. P. R. Davies and R. T. White. Sheffield: 153–66.
Goldin, P. R. (2011) 'Persistent Misconceptions about Chinese "Legalism"', *Journal of Chinese Philosophy* 38.1: 88–104.
Goodale, M. (2017) *Anthropology and Law: A Critical Introduction*. New York.
Goodblatt, D. M. (1975) *Rabbinic Instruction in Sasanian Babylonia*. Leiden.
  (1994) *The Monarchic Principle: Studies in Jewish Self-Government in Antiquity*. Tübingen.
  (2008) 'The History of the Babylonian Academies', in *Cambridge History of Judaism*, Vol. IV: *The Late Roman-Rabbinic Period*, ed. S. Katz. Cambridge: 821–39.
Goodman, M. (1983) *State and Society in Roman Galilee AD 132–212*. Totowa.
Goody, J. (1990) *The Oriental, the Ancient and the Primitive: Systems of Marriage and the Family in the Ppre-industrial Societies of Eurasia*. Cambridge.
Gorre, G. and Wackenier, S. (eds.) (2020) *Quand la Fortune du Royaume ne depend pas de la Vertu du Prince: Un Renforcement de la Monarchie lagide de Ptolémée VI à Ptolémée X (169–88 av. J.-C.)?* Studia Hellenistica 59. Leuven.
Gradel, I. (2004) *Emperor Worship and Roman Religion*. Oxford.
Gray, B. (2015) *Stasis and Stability: Exile, the Polis, and Political Thought, c. 404–146 BC*. Oxford.
Green, M. (1979) 'Wenamun's Demand for Compensation', *Zeitschrift für Sprache und Altertumskunde* 106: 116–20.
Greengus, S. (1966) 'Old Babylonian Marriage Ceremonies and Rites', *Journal of Cuneiform Studies* 20: 55–72.
Greenidge, A. H. J. (1894) *Infamia: Its Place in Roman Public and Private Law*. Oxford.

Griffiths, A. (2015) 'New Documents for the Early History of Puṇḍravardhana: Copperplate Inscriptions from the Late Gupta and Early Post-Gupta Periods', *Pratna Samiksha*, NS 6: 15–38.

Griffiths, J. (1986) 'What Is Legal Pluralism?', *Journal of Legal Pluralism and Unofficial Law* 24: 1–55.

Gruen, E. (1982) 'Greek Πίστις and Roman *Fides*', *Athenaeum* 60: 50–68.

Guarducci, M. (ed.) (1935–50) *Inscriptiones Creticae*. Rome.

Guozhong, L. (2016) *Introduction to the Tsinghua Bamboo-Strip Manuscripts*, trans. C. J. Foster and W. N. French. Leiden.

Gunderson, E. (ed.) 2009) *The Cambridge Companion to Ancient Rhetoric*. Cambridge.

Gvaryahu, A. (2017) 'Twisting Words: Does Halakah Really Circumvent Scripture?', *Journal of Jewish Studies* 68: 260–83.

Haase, R. (2003) 'The Hittite Kingdom', in Westbrook (2003a): 619–56.

Haensch, R. (2015) 'From Free to Fee? Judicial Fees and Other Litigation Costs during the High Empire and Late Antiquity', in *Law and Transaction Costs in the Ancient Economy*, ed. D. Kehoe, M. Ratzan and U. Yiftach. Ann Arbor, MI: 253–72.

Halbertal, M. (1998) 'Coexisting with the Enemy: Jews and Pagans in the Mishna', in *Tolerance and Intolerance in Early Judaism and Christianity*, ed. G. Stanton and G. Stroumsa. Cambridge: 159–72.

Halivni, D. W. (1986) *Midrash, Mishna, and Gemara: The Jewish Predilection for Justified Law*. Cambridge, MA.

Hansen, M. H. (1976a) *Apagoge, endeixis and ephegesis against kakourgoi, atimoi and pheugontes: A Study in the Athenian Administration of Justice in the Fourth Century BC*. Odense.

(1976b) 'How Many Athenians Attended the Ecclesia?', *Greek, Roman, and Byzantine Studies* 17: 115–34.

(1991) *The Athenian Democracy in the Age of Demosthenes*. Oxford.

(2018) 'Oral Law in Ancient Greece?', in *Ancient Greek Law in the Twenty-First Century*, ed. Paula Perlman. Austin, TX: 172–92.

Hansen, V. (1995) *Negotiating Daily Life in Traditional China: How Ordinary People Used Contracts 600–1400*. New Haven and London.

(2021) 'Silk Road Cities and Their Co-existing Legal Traditions', in *Research Handbook on International Law and Cities*, ed. H. P. Aust and J. E. Nijman. Cheltenham and Northampton, MA: 17–28.

Hanson, A. E. (ed.) (1976) *Collectanea Papyrologica: Texts Published in Honor of H. C. Youtie*. Bonn.

Hardwick, L. (2000) 'Concepts of Peace', in *Experiencing Rome: Culture, Identity and Power in the Roman Empire*, ed. J. Huskinson. London: 335–68.

Harker, A. (2008) *Loyalty and Dissidence in Roman Egypt: The Case of the* Acta Alexandrinorum. Cambridge.

Harper, K. (2016) *Slavery in the Late Roman World, AD 275–425*. Cambridge.

(2021) *Plagues upon the Earth: Disease and the Course of Human History*. Princeton, NJ.

Harries, J. (2007) *Law and Crime in the Roman World*. Cambridge.

Harris, E. M. (1995) *Aeschines and Athenian Politics*. Oxford.

(2004) 'Antigone the Lawyer, or the Ambiguities of Nomos', in *The Law and the Courts in Ancient Greece*, ed. E. M. Harris and L. Rubinstein. London: 19–56.

(2006a) *Democracy and the Rule of Law in Classical Athens: Essays on Law, Society and Politics*. Cambridge.
(2006b) 'The Rule of Law in Athenian Democracy: Reflections on the Judicial Oath', *Dike: Rivista di storia del diritto greco ed ellenistico* 9: 157–81.
(ed.) (2008) *Demosthenes, Speeches 20–22*. Austin, TX.
(2010) 'Introduction', in *Law and Drama in Ancient Greece*, ed. E. M. Harris, D. Leao and P. J. Rhodes. London: 1–24
(2012a) 'Sophocles and Athenian law', in *A Companion to Sophocles*, ed. K. Ormand. Oxford: 287–300.
(2012b) 'Homer, Hesiod, and the "Origins" of Greek Slavery', *Revue des études anciennes* 114.2: 345–66.
(2013a) 'The Plaint in Athenian Law and Legal Procedure', in *Archives and Archival Documents in Ancient Societies*, ed. M. Faraguna. Trieste: 143–62.
(2013b) *The Rule of Law in Action in Democratic Athens*. Oxford.
(2013–14) 'The Authenticity of the Document at Andocides *on the Mysteries* 96–98', Τεκμήρια 12: 121–53.
(2015a) 'The Family, the Community and Murder: The Role of Pollution in Athenian Homicide Law', in *Public and Private in Ancient Mediterranean Law and Religion*, ed. C. Ando and J. Rüpke. Berlin: 11–35.
(2015b) 'Toward a Typology of Greek Regulations about Religious Matters: A Legal Approach', *Kernos* 28: 53–83.
(2015c) 'The Meaning of the Legal Term *Symbolaion*, the Law about *Dikai Emporikai* and the Role of the *Paragraphe* Procedure', *Dike: Rivista di storia del diritto greco ed ellenistico* 18: 7–36.
(2016a) 'From Democracy to the Rule of Law? Constitutional Change in Athens during the Fifth and Fourth Centuries BCE', in *Die Athenische Demokratie im 4. Jahrhundert: Zwischen Modernisierung und Tradition*, ed. C. Tiersche. Stuttgart: 73–87.
(2016b) 'The Legal Foundations of Economic Growth in Ancient Greece: The Role of Property Records', in *The Economy of Ancient Greece: Markets, Households, and City-States*, ed. E. Harris, D. Lewis and M. Woolmer. Cambridge: 116–48.
(2018a) 'The Athenian View of an Athenian Trial', in *The Use and Abuse of Law in the Athenian Courts*, ed. C. Carey, I. Giannadaki and B. Griffith-Williams. Leiden: 42–74.
(2018b) 'Some Recent Developments in the Study of Ancient Greek Law', *Journal of Ancient Civilizations* 33: 187–226.
(2020) 'The Rule of Law and Economic Growth in Ancient Greece', in *The Oxford Handbook of Ancient Greek Law*, ed. E. M. Harris and M. Canevaro. Online edition: https://doi.org/10.1093/oxfordhb/9780199599257.013.6 (accessed 1 Sept. 2022).
(2021) 'Ownership and Property, Greek', in *Oxford Classical Dictionary*, ed. S. Goldberg and T. Whitmarsh. Online edition: https://doi.org/10.1093/acrefore/9780199381135.013.8594 (accessed 19/09/2022).
Harris, E. M. and Rubinstein, L. (eds.) (2004) *The Law and the Courts in Ancient Greece*. London.
Harris, E. M. and Thür, G. (eds.) (2008) *Akten des Gesellschaft für griechische und hellenistische Rechtsgeschichte, Symposion 2007*. Vienna.
Harrison, A. R. W. (1968) *The Law of Athens*. Vol. I: *The Family and Property*. Oxford.
(1971) *The Law of Athens*. Vol. II: *Procedure*. Oxford.

Hart, H. L. A. (1961) *The Concept of Law*. 3rd ed. with an Introduction by Leslie Green, 2012. Oxford.
Hatzopoulos, M. B. (1991) *Actes de Vente d'Amphipolis*. Melethmata 14. Athens.
Harvey, D. (1990) 'Sykophancy and the Sykophancy: Vexatious Redefinition', in *Nomos: Essays in Athenian Law, Politics and Society*, ed. P. Cartledge, P. Millett and S. Todd. Cambridge: 103–21.
Haug, B. (2014) 'Dependent Labor: The Case of the *enapographai geôrgoi*', in Keenan, Manning and Yiftach-Firanko (2014): 430–41.
Hayes, C. (2015) *What's Divine about Divine Law? Early Perspectives*. Princeton, NJ.
    (2017) 'Law in Classical Rabbinic Judaism', in *Cambridge Companion to Judaism and Law*, ed. C. Hayes. Cambridge: 76–127.
Heinemann, Y. (1970) *Darkhei ha'aggadah*. 3rd ed. Givatayim.
Herman, G. (2006) *Morality and Behaviour in Democratic Athens: A Social History*. Cambridge.
Heuser, R. (1987) *Das Rechtskapitel im Jin-Shu. Ein Beitrag zur Kenntnis des Rechts im frühen chinesischen Kaiserreich*. Munich.
Heyde, D. (1981) 'Du Yu – eine Biographie aus den Gründungsjahren der Jin-Dynastie', *Altorientalische Forschungen* 8: 299-322.
Hezser, C. (1997) *The Social Structure of the Rabbinic Movement in Roman Palestine*. Tübingen.
    (2022) 'What Was Jewish about Jewish Slavery in Late Antiquity?', in *Slavery in the Late Antique World, 150–700 CE*, ed. C. L. de Wet, M. Kahlos and V. Vuolanto. Cambridge: 129–48.
Hildebrandt, B. (2017) 'Silk on the Silk Roads: Exchange between East and West in Antiquity', in *Trade and Exchange along the Silk Roads between Rome and China in Antiquity*, ed. B Hildebrandt. Oxford: 11–25.
Hillner, J. (2015) *Prison, Punishment, and Penance in Late Antiquity*. Cambridge.
Hinsch, B. (1998) 'Women, Kinship and Property as Seen in a Han Dynasty Will', *T'oung Pao*, 2nd ser. 84: 1–20.
Hipp, K. (2021) '"For Each Runaway Assyrian Fugitive, Let Me Replace Him One Hundred-Fold": Fugitives/Runaways in the Neo-Assyrian Empire', in *Law and (Dis)Order in the Ancient Near East: Proceedings of the 59th Rencontre Assyriologique Internationale Held at Ghent, Belgium, 15-19 July 2013*, ed. K. De Graef and A. Goddeeris. University Park, PA: 136–43.
Hirschfeld, H. S. (1840) *Halachische Exegese: Ein Beitrag zur Geschichte der Exegese und zur Methodologie des Talmuds*. Berlin.
Hitch, D. (2009) *The Special Status of Turfan*. Sino Platonic Papers 186. Philadelphia.
Ho, N. P. (2016) 'A Confucian Theory of Property', *Tsinghua China Law Review* 9.1. Peking University School of Transnational Law Research Paper No. 17. Online edition: https://ssrn.com/abstract=2767275 (accessed 03/07/2022).
    (2019) 'A Look into Traditional Chinese Administrative Law and Bureaucracy: Feeding the Emperor in Tang Dynasty China', *University of Pennsylvania Asian Law Review* 15: 125–71.
Höbenreich, E. (1992) 'À propos 'Antike Rechtsgeschichte': Einige Bemerkungen zur Polemik zwischen Ludwig Mitteis und Leopold Wenger', *Zeitschrift der Savigny-Stiftung für Rechtsgeschichte. Romanistische Abteilung* 109.1: 547–62.
Hölbl, G. (2001) *A History of the Ptolemaic Empire*. London.

Hodkinson, S. (2000) *Property and Wealth in Classical Sparta*. London.
  (2009) 'Was Sparta an Exceptional Polis?' in *Sparta: Comparative Approaches*, ed. S. Hodkinson. Swansea: 417–72.
Hoffner, H. A. (ed.) (1997) *The Laws of the Hittites: A Critical Edition*. Documenta et Monumenta Orientis Antiqui 23. Leiden.
Hohfeld, W. N. (1913) 'Some Fundamental Legal Conceptions as Applied in Legal Reasoning', *Yale Law Journal* 23: 16–59.
  (1917) 'Legal Conceptions as Applied in Judicial Reasoning', *Yale Law Journal* 26: 710–70.
Hölkeskamp, K.-J. (1999) *Schiedsrichter, Gesetzgeber und Gesetzgebung im archaischen Griechenland*. Stuttgart.
  (2000) '*Fides – deditio in fidem – dextra data et accepta*: Recht, Religion und Ritual in Rom', in *The Roman Middle Republic: Politics, Religion, and Historiography c. 400–133 BC. Papers from a Conference at the Institutum Romanum Finlandiae, September 11–12, 1998*, ed. C. Bruun. Rome: 223–49.
Holtz, S. E. (2008) 'The Career of a Neo-Babylonian Court Scribe', in *Journal of Cuneiform Studies* 60: 81–85.
  (2009) *Neo-Babylonian Court Procedure*. CM 38. Leiden.
Honigman, S. (2016) 'The Ptolemaic and Roman Definitions of Social Categories and the Evolution of Judean Communal Identity in Egypt', in *Jewish and Christian Communal Identities in the Roman World*, ed. Y. Furstenberg. Leiden: 23–74.
  (2019) 'Ethnic Minority Groups', in *A Companion to Greco-Roman and Late Antique Egypt*, ed. K. Vandorpe. Hoboken, NJ: 315–25.
Honoré, A. M. (1961) 'Ownership', in *Oxford Essays in Jurisprudence*, ed. A. G. Guest. Oxford: 107–47.
  (1998) *Law in the Crisis of Empire 379–455 AD: The Theodosian Dynasty and Its Quaestors*. Oxford.
Horsch, P. (2004) 'From Creation Myth to World Law: The Early History of Dharma' (trans. J. L. Whitaker), *Journal of Indian Philosophy* 32: 423–48. Originally published as 'Vom Schöpfungsmythos zum Weltgesetz', *Asiatische Studien: Zeitschrift der Schweizerischen Gesellschaft für Asiankunde* (1967) 21: 31–61.
Hoyer, D. and Reddish, J. (eds.) (2019) *Seshat History of the Axial Age*. Chaplin, CT.
Hoyos, D. B. (1998) *Unplanned Wars: The Origins of the First and Second Punic Wars*. Berlin and New York.
Hsing, I-tien (2014) 'Qin-Han Census and Tax and Corvée Administration: Notes on Newly Discovered Materials', in Pines, von Falkenhausen, Shelach and Yates (2014): 155–86.
Hsu, C-Y. (1980) *Han Agriculture. The formation of Early Chinese Agrarian Policy (206 BC–AD 220)*. Seattle.
  (1999) 'The Spring and Autumn Period', in *The Cambridge History of Ancient China: From the Origins of Civilization to 221 BC*, Vol. I, ed. M. Loewe and E. L. Shaughnessy. Cambridge: 545–86.
Huebner, S. (2013) 'Adoption and Fosterage in the Ancient Eastern Mediterranean', in *The Oxford Handbook of Childhood and Education in the Classical World*, ed. J. Evans Grubbs and T. Parkin : Oxford: 510–31.

Hulsewé, A. F. P. (ed. and trans.) (1955) *Remnants of Han Law*. Vol. I: *Introductory Studies and an Annotated Translation of Chapters 22 and 23 of the History of the Former Han Dynasty*. Leiden.
  (1978a) 'The Ch'in Documents Discovered in Hupei in 1975', *T'oung Pao* 64: 175–217.
  (1978b) 'Contracts of the Han Period', in *Il Diritto in Cina*, ed. L. Lanciotti. Florence: 11–35.
  (1979) 'A Lawsuit of AD 28', in *Studia Sino-Mongolica: Festschrift für Herbert Franke*, ed. Wolfgang Bauer. Wiesbaden: 23–34.
  (ed. and tr.) (1985a) *Remnants of Ch'in Law: An Annotated Translation of the Ch'in legal and Administrative Rules of the Third Century BC Discovered in Yün-meng Prefecture, Hu-pei Province, in 1975*. Leiden.
  (1985b) 'The Influence of the "Legalist" Government of Qin on the Economy as Reflected in the Texts Discovered in Yunmeng County', in *The Scope of State Power in China*, ed. S. R. Schram. London: 215–18.
  (1986) 'Chin and Han Law', in *The Cambridge History of China*, Vol. I: *The Ch'in and Han Empires 221 BC–AD 220*, ed. D. Twitchett and M. Loewe. Cambridge: 520–44.
  (1987) 'The Functions of the Commandant of Justice during the Han Period', in *Chinese Ideas about Nature and Society. Studies in Honor of Derk Bodde*, ed. C. Le Blanc and S. Blader. Hong Kong: 249–64.
  (1988) 'The Wide Scope of Tao "Theft" in Ch'in-Han Law', *Early China* 13: 166–200.
Hultzsch, E. (ed.) (1925) *Corpus inscriptionum Indicarum*. Vol. I: *Inscriptions of Aśoka*. New ed. Oxford.
Humbert, M. (2018) *La loi des XII Tables: Édition et commentaire*. Rome.
Humfress, C. (2007a) 'Law and Justice in the Later Roman Empire', in *A. H. M. Jones and the Later Roman Empire*, ed. D. M. Gwynn. Leiden: 121–42.
  (2007b) *Orthodoxy and the Courts in Late Antiquity*. Oxford.
  (2011) 'Bishops and Lawcourts in Late Antiquity: How Not to Make Sense of the Legal Evidence', *Journal of Early Christian Studies* 19.3: 375–400.
  (2013) 'Laws' Empire: Roman Universalism and Legal Practice', in *New Frontiers: Law and Society in the Roman World*, ed. P. J. du Plessis. Edinburgh: 73–101.
Hundley, M. B. (2011) *Keeping Heaven on Earth: Safeguarding the Divine Presence in the Priestly Tabernacle*. Tübingen.
Hunt, P. (2018) 'Ancient Greece as a "Slave Society"', in *What Is a Slave Society? The Practice of Slavery in Global Perspective*, ed. N. Lenski and C. M. Cameron. Cambridge: 61–85.
Hunter, V. J. (1997) 'The Prison of Athens: A Comparative Perspective', *Phoenix* 51: 296–326.
  (2000) 'Introduction: Status Distinctions in Athenian Law', in *Law and Social Status in Classical Athens*, ed. V. J. Hunter and J. C. Edmondson. Oxford: 1–29.
Hurowitz, V. A. (2011) 'What Was Codex Hammurabi, and What Did It Become?', *Maarav* 18: 89–100.
Hurvitz, L. (ed. and trans.) (1956) *Wei Shou, Treatise on Buddhism and Taoism: An English Translation of the Original Chinese Text of Wei-shu CXIV and the Japanese Annotation of Tsukamoto Zenryū*. Kyoto.
Huxley, A. (2006) 'Buddhist Law, Asian Law, Eurasian Law', in 'A Fresh Start for Comparative Legal Studies? A Collective Review of Patrick Glenn's *Legal Traditions*

of the World, 2nd Edition' (ed. N. H. D. Foster), *Journal of Comparative Law* 1.1: 100–199 (158–64).

Ibbetson, D. (2020) 'Writing, Speaking and the Roman Stipulatio', in *Principle and Pragmatism in Roman Law*, ed. B. Spagnolo and J. Sampson. Oxford: 99–115.

Ilan, T. (1995) *Jewish Women in Greco-Roman Palestine: An Inquiry into Image and Status*. Tübingen.

Irwin, E. (2005) *Solon and Early Greek Poetry: The Politics of Exhortation*. Cambridge.

Jacobs, M. (1995) *Die Institution des jüdischen Patriarchen. Eine quellen- und traditionskritische Studie zur Geschichte der Juden in der Spätantike*. Tübingen.

Jakab, É. (2015) 'Property Rights in Ancient Rome', in *Ownership and Exploitation of Land and Natural Resources in the Roman World*, ed. P. Erdkamp, K. Verboven and A. Zuiderhoek. Oxford: 107–31.

Jamison, S. (2017) 'Women: *Strīdharma*', in Olivelle and Davis (2017): 137–50.

Janko, R. (1987) *Aristotle* Poetics *I with* The Tractatus Coislinianus, *A Hypothetical Reconstruction of* Poetics *II, The Fragments of the* On Poets. Indianapolis.

Janssen, C. (1991) 'Samsu-iluna and the Hungry naditums', *Northern Akkadian Project Reports* 5: 3–40.

Jas, R. (1996) *Neo-Assyrian Judicial Procedures*. State Archives of Assyria Studies 5. Helsinki.

Jasnow, R. (2003a) 'Old Kingdom and First Intermediate Period', in Westbrook (2003a): 93–140.

(2003b) 'Middle Kingdom and Second Intermediate Period', in Westbrook (2003a): 255–88.

(2003c) 'New Kingdom', in Westbrook (2003a): 289–359.

Jehne, M. (1994) *Koine Eirene*. Stuttgart.

Jenner, W. F. L. (1981) *Memories of Loyang: Yang Hsüan-Chih and the Lost Capital (493–534)*. Oxford.

Jha, G. (trans.) (1924) *Manu-Smṛti: The Laws of Manu with the Bhāṣya of Medhāthiti*. Vol. IV, Part I. Calcutta.

Joannès, F. (1997) 'La pratique du serment à l'époque néo-babylonienne', in *Jurer et maudire: Pratiques politiques et usages juridiques du serment dans le Proche-Orient ancien*, ed. S. Démare-Lafont. Paris: 163–74.

(2000a) 'Les textes judiciaires néo-babyloniens', in *Rendre la justice en Mésopotamie: Archives judiciaires du Proche-Orient ancien (IIIe–Ier millénaires avant J.-C.)*, ed. F. Joannès. Saint-Denis: 201–39.

(2000b) 'Une chronique judiciaire d'époque hellénistique et le châtiment des sacrileges à Babylone', in *Assyriologica et Semitica: Festschrift für Joachim Oelsner*, ed. J. Marzahn, H. Neumann and A. Fuchs. Münster: 193–211.

Johnson, A. C., Coleman-Norton, P. R. and Bourne, F. C. (eds.) (1961) *Ancient Roman Statutes*. Austin, TX.

Johnson, D. (2020) *Sovereign Authority and the Elaboration of Law in the Bible and the Ancient Near East*. Forschungen zum Alten Testament 2, Reihe 122. Tübingen.

Johnson, W. (1979) *The T'ang Code*. Vol. I: *General Principles*. Princeton, NJ.

(1987) 'The Concept of Doubt in T'ang Criminal Law', in *Chinese Ideas about Nature and Society: Studies in Honor of Derk Bodde*, ed. C. Le Blanc and S. Blader. Hong Kong: 271–79.

(1997) *The T'ang Code*. Vol. II: *Specific Articles*. Princeton, NJ.

Bibliography

Johnson, W. and Twitchett, D. (1993) 'Criminal Procedure in T'ang China', *Asia Major* 6.2: 113–46.

Johnston, D. (1988) *The Roman Law of Trusts*. Oxford.

(1997) 'The General Influence of Roman Institutions of State and Public Law', in *The Civilian Tradition and Scots Law*, ed. D. L. C. Miller and R. Zimmermann. Berlin: 87–101.

(ed.) (2015) *The Cambridge Companion to Roman Law*. Cambridge.

(2022) *Roman Law in Context*. 2nd ed. Cambridge.

Jolowicz H. F. and Nicholas, B. (1972) *Historical Introduction to the Study of Roman Law*. Cambridge.

Jones, C. P. (1987) 'Stigma: Tattooing and Branding in Greco-Roman Antiquity', *Journal of Roman Studies* 77: 139–55.

(2007) 'Juristes romains dans l'Orient grec', *Comptes rendus des séances de l'Académie des Inscriptions et Belles-Lettres* 151: 1331–59.

Jones, G. (1984) *A History of the Vikings*. Oxford.

Jones, J. W. (1956) *Law and Legal Theory of the Greeks: An Introduction*. Oxford.

Jördens, A. (2010) 'Öffentliche Archive und römische Rechtspolitik,' in *Tradition and Transformation: Egypt under Roman Rule*, ed. K. Lembke, M. Minas-Nerpel and S. Pfeiffer. Leiden: 159–79.

(2016) 'Possession and provincial practice', in *The Oxford Handbook of Roman Law and Society*, ed. P. J. du Plessis, C. Ando and K. Tuori. Oxford: 553–65.

Jursa, M. (1997) '"Als König Abi-ešuh gerechte Ordnung hergestellt hat": eine bemerkenswerte altbabylonische Prozeßurkunde', *Revue d'assyriologie et d'archéologie orientale* 91: 135–45.

(2009) 'The Babylonian economy in the first millennium BC', in *The Babylonian World*, ed. Gwendolyn Leick. New York: 224–35.

(2010) *Aspects of the Economic History of Babylonia in the First Millennium BC: Economic Geography, Economic Mentalities, Agriculture, the Use of Money and the Problem of Economic Growth*. Münster.

Kalinowski, M. (2010) 'Divination and Astrology: Received Texts and Excavated manuscripts', in *China's Early Empires: A Re-appraisal*, ed. M. Nylan and M. Loewe. Cambridge: 339–66.

Kalmin, R. (1989) *The Redaction of the Babylonian Talmud: Amoraic or Saboraic?* Cincinnati.

(2001) 'Rabbinic Literature of Late Antiquity as a Source for Historical Study', in *Where We Stand, Issues and Debates in the Study of Ancient Judaism*, Vol. II, ed. J. Neusner and A. Avery-Peck. Leiden: 187–200.

Kamen, D. (2013) *Status in Classical Athens*. Princeton, NJ and Oxford.

Kane, P. V. (1962–75) *History of Dharmaśāstra*. 5 vols. Poona.

Kantor, G. (2013) 'Law in Roman Phrygia: Rules and Jurisdictions', in *Roman Phrygia: Culture and Society*, ed. P. Thonemann. Cambridge: 143–66.

(2015) 'Greek Law under the Romans', in *The Oxford Handbook of Ancient Greek Law*, ed. E. M. Harris and M. Canevaro. Online edition: https://doi.org/10.1093/oxfordhb/9780199599257.013.25 (accessed 19/9/2022).

(2021) 'Citizenships and Jurisdictions: The Greek City Perspective', in *Roman and Local Citizenship in the Long Second Century* CE, ed. C. Ando and M. Lavan. Oxford: 231–54.

Karlgren, B. (1950) *The Book of Documents*. Repr. from the Bulletin of the Museum of Far Eastern Antiquities 22. Stockholm.

Kaser, M. (1967) 'The Changing Face of Roman Litigation', *Irish Jurist* 2: 129–43.

Kasher, R. (1990) 'The Interpretation of Scripture in Rabbinic Literature', in *Mikra: Text, Translation, Reading and Interpretation of the Hebrew Bible in Ancient Judaism and Early Christianity*, ed. M. J. Mulder. Assen and Maastricht: 547–94.

Kaster, R. A. (1997) *Guardians of Language. The Grammarian and Society in Late Antiquity*, Berkeley.

Keenan, J. G., Manning, J. G. and Yiftach-Firanko, U. (eds.) (2014) *Law and Legal Practice in Egypt from Alexander to the Arab Conquest: A Selection of Papyrological Sources in Translation, with Introductions and Commentary*. Cambridge.

Kehoe, D. (2007) *Law and the Rural Economy in the Roman Empire*. Ann Arbor, MI.

Kehoe, D., Ratzan, D. M. and Yiftach, U. (eds.) (2015) *Law and Transaction Costs in the Ancient Economy*. Ann Arbor, MI.

Kelly, B. (2010) *Petitions, Litigation, and Social Control in Roman Egypt*. Oxford.

Kelly, G. (2018) 'Ammianus, Valens and Antioch', in *Antioch II: The Many Faces of Antioch – Intellectual Exchange and Religious Diversity*, CE 350–450, ed. S.-P. Bergjan and S. Elm. Tübingen: 137–62.

Kitchen, K. A. and Lawrence, P. J. N. (2012) *Treaty, Law and Covenant in the Ancient Near East*. 3 vols. Wiesbaden.

Kitz, A. M. (2014) *Cursed Are You: The Phenomenology of Cursing in Cuneiform and Hebrew Texts*. Winona Lake, IN.

Klawans, J. (2001) 'Pure Violence: Sacrifice and Defilement in Ancient Israel', *Harvard Theological Review* 94: 133–55.

Knoblock, J. and Riegel, J. (eds.) (2000) *The Annals of Lü Buwei*. Stanford.

Koch, C. (2008) *Vertrag, Treueid und Bund: Studien zur Rezeption des altorientalischen Vertragsrechts im Deuteronomium und zur Ausbildung der Bundestheologie im Alten Testament*. Berlin.

Korolkov, M. (2011) 'Arguing about the Law: Interrogation Procedure under the Qin and Former Han Dynasties', *Études chinoises* 30: 37–71.

(2017) 'Legal Process Unearthed: A New Source of Legal History of Early Imperial China', *Journal of the American Oriental Society* 137.2: 383–91.

Kränzlein, A. (1963) *Eigentum und Besitz in griechischen Recht des fünften und vierten Jahrhunderts v. Chr*. Berlin.

Kraus, F. R. (1960) 'Ein zentrales Problem des altmesopotamischen Rechtes: was ist der Codex Hammu-rabi?', *Genava* 8: 283–96.

(1984) *Königliche Verfügungen in altbabylonischer Zeit*. Leiden.

Krause, J-U. (1996) *Gefängnisse im römischen Reich*. Stuttgart.

Kroll, E. (2010) 'A Logical Approach to Law', PhD thesis, University of Chicago.

Kuefler, M. (2007) 'The Marriage Revolution in Late Antiquity: The Theodosian Code and Later Roman Marriage Law', *Journal of Family History* 32.4: 343–70.

Kugler, K. A. (2022) *Resolving Disputes in Second Century* BCE *Herakleopolis*. Leiden.

Kunkel, W. (1967) *Herkunft und soziale Stellung der römischen Juristen*. Weimar (repr. 2001).

Laes, C. and Strubbe, J. (2014) *Youth in the Roman Empire: The Young and the Restless Years?* Cambridge.

Lafont, B. (1997) 'Serments politiques et serments judiciaires à l'époque sumérienne: quelques données nouvelles', in *Jurer et maudire: Pratiques politiques et usages juridiques du serment au Proche-Orient ancien*, ed. S. [Démare-]Lafont. Paris: 31–48.

(2001a) 'Relations internationales, alliances et diplomatie au temps des royaumes amorrites. Essai de synthèse', in *Amurru. 2, Mari, Ebla et les Hourrites: dix ans de travaux. Deuxime partie: Actes du colloque international (Paris, mai 1993)*, ed. J.-M. Durand and D. Charpin. Paris: 213-328.

(2001b) 'International Relations in the Ancient Near East: The Birth of a Complete Diplomatic System', *Diplomacy and Statecraft* 12: 39–60.

(2022) 'La conclusion des alliances diplomatiques au temps des rois de Mari: un dossier qui reste ouvert', in *'A Community of Peoples': Studies on Society and Politics in the Bible and Ancient Near East in Honor of Daniel Fleming*, ed. M. Leonard-Fleckman, L. A. S. Monroe, M. J. Stahl and D. R. Johnson. Harvard Semitic Studies 69. Leiden: 196-211.

Lafont, B. and Westbrook, R. (2003) 'Neo-Sumerian Period (Ur III)', in Westbrook (2003a): 183–226.

Lamb, W. R. M. (ed.) (1930) *Lysias*. Cambridge, MA.

Lanfranchi, G. B., Ponchia S. and Rollinger, R. (eds.) (2022) *Making Peace in the Ancient World: Proceedings of the 7th Melammu Workshop Padova, 5-7 November 2018*. Melammu Workshops and Monographs 5. Münster.

Lanni, A. (2006) *Law and Justice in the Courts of Classical Athens*. Cambridge.

(2010) 'The Expressive Effect of Athenian Prostitution Laws', *Classical Antiquity* 29: 45–67.

(2016) *Law and Order in Ancient Athens*. Cambridge.

Lapin, H. (1995) *Early Rabbinic Civil Law and the Social History of Roman Galilee: A Study of Mishna Tractate Baba ' Meṣi 'a '*. Atlanta.

(1996) 'Jewish and Christian Academies in Roman Palestine: Some Preliminary Observations', in *Caesarea Maritima: A Retrospective after Two Millenia*, ed. A. Raban and K. G. Holum. Leiden: 496–512.

(1999) 'Rabbis and Cities: The Literary Evidence', *Journal of Jewish Studies* 50: 187–207.

(2008) 'Origins and Development of the Rabbinic Movement in the Land of Israel', in *Cambridge History of Judaism*, Vol. IV: *The Late Roman-Rabbinic Period*, ed. S. Katz. Cambridge: 206–29.

Lariviere, R. W. (1981a) *The Divyatattva of Raghunandana Bhaṭṭācārya: Ordeals in Classical Hindu Law*. New Delhi.

(1981b) 'The Judicial Wager in Hindu Law', *Annals of the Bhandarkar Oriental Research Institute* 62: 135–45.

(1989) *The Nāradasmṛti*. 2 vols. Philadelphia. (Repr. in one volume: Delhi, 2003.)

(2004) 'Dharmaśāstra, Custom, "Real Law" and "Apocryphal" Smṛtis', *Journal of Indian Philosophy* 32.5–6: 611–27.

Larsen, J. A. O. (1968) *Greek Federal States: Their Institutions and History*. Oxford.

Latour, B. (1983) *We Have Never Been Modern*. Boston, NJ.

Latte, K. (1920) *Heiliges Recht: Untersuchungen zur Geschichte der sakralen Rechtsformen in Griechenland*. Tübingen.

Lau, U. (2005) 'The Scope of Private Jurisdiction in Early Imperial China: The Evidence of Newly Excavated Legal Documents', *Asiatische Studien* 59: 333–52.

Bibliography

Lau, U. and Lüdke, M. (2012) *Exemplarische Rechtsfällen vom Beginn der Han-dynastie. Eine kommentierte Übersetzung des Zouyanshu aus Zhangjiashan/Provinz Hubei*. Tokyo.

Lau, U. and Staack, T. (eds. and trans.) (2016) *Legal Practice in the Formative Stages of the Chinese Empire: An Annotated Translation of the Exemplary Qin Criminal Cases from the Yuelu Academy Collection*. Leiden.

Lavan, M. (2013) *Slaves to Rome: Paradigms of Empire in Roman Culture*. Cambridge.

Leão, D. F. and Rhodes, P. J. (eds. and trans.) (2015) *The Laws of Solon: A New Edition with Introduction, Translation, and Commentary*. London.

Le Blanc, C. and Blader, S. (eds.) (1987) *Chinese Ideas about Nature and Society. Studies in Honor of Derk Bodde*. Hong Kong.

Leduc, C. (1991) 'Comment la donner en mariage? La mariée en pays grec (IXe–IVe s. av. J.-C.),' in *Histoire des femmes I: L'antiquité*, ed. P. Schmitt Pantel. Paris: 259–316.

Legge, J. (trans.) (1879) *The Sacred Books of China: The Texts of Confucianism. Part 1, the Shu King, the Religious Portions of the Shih King, the Hsiao King*. Oxford.

 (trans.) (1887) *The Chinese Classics. Part I: Confucius*. New York.

 (trans.) (1960) *The Chinese Classics. Vol. III: The Shoo King; Or, the Book of Historical Documents*. Hong Kong. (Repr. of 1893–4, 2nd ed.).

 (ed.) (1967) *Li Chi: Book of Rites*. 2 vols. New Hyde Park, NY. (Repr. of 1885 ed.).

Lehne, C. (2014) 'Die Stellung der Juristen im Formularverfahren', *Zeitschrift der Savigny Stiftung für Rechtsgeschichte, Romanistische Abteilung* 131: 261–312.

 (2016) 'Jurists in the Shadows: The Everyday Business of the Jurists of Cicero's Time', in *Cicero's Law: Rethinking Roman Law of the Late Republic*, ed. P. Du Plessis. Edinburgh: 88–99.

Lendon, J. A. (1997) *Empire of Honor: The Art of Government in the Roman World*. Oxford.

Lenzi, A. (2008) *Secrecy and the Gods: Secret Knowledge in Ancient Mesopotamia and Biblical Israel*. Helsinki.

Lerouxel, F. (2015) 'The βιβλιοθήκη ἐγκτήσεων and Transaction Costs in the Credit Market of Roman Egypt (30 BCE–ca. 170 CE)', in *Law and Transaction Costs in the Ancient Economy*, ed. D. Kehoe, D. M. Ratzan and U. Yiftach. Ann Arbor, MI: 162–84.

 (2016) *Le marché du crédit dans le monde romain (Égypte et Campanie)*. Rome.

Lerner, J. and Sims-Williams, N. (eds. and trans.) (2011) *Seals, Sealings and Tokens from Bactria to Gandhara: 4th to 8th Century CE*. Vienna.

Letsas, G. (2023) 'Offences against Status', *Oxford Journal of Legal Studies* 20: 1–28.

Letteney, M. and Larsen, M. (forthcoming). *Ancient Mediterranean Incarceration*. Oakland.

Levine, L. I. (1989) *The Rabbinic Class of Roman Palestine in Late Antiquity*. Jerusalem.

 (2008) *The Ancient Synagogue: The First Thousand Years*. New Haven.

Levinson, B. M. (1997) *Deuteronomy and the Hermeneutics of Legal Innovation*. Oxford.

 (2008) *Legal Revision and Religious Renewal in Ancient Israel*. Cambridge.

Levmore, S. (2002) 'Two Stories about the Evolution of Property Rights', *Journal of Legal Studies* 31: 421–51.

Lévy, E. (ed.) (2000) *La codification des lois dans l'antiquité: Actes du Colloque de Strasbourg 27–29 novembre 1997*. Strasbourg.

Lewis, A. (2015) 'Slavery, Family, and Status', in Johnston (2015): 151–74.

Lewis, D. (2013) 'Slave Marriages in the Laws of Gortyn: A Matter of Rights?', *Historia* 62.4: 390–416.

Lewis, D. M. (2018) *Greek Slave Systems in Their Eastern Mediterranean Context c. 800–146 BC*. Oxford.

Lewis, M. E. (1990) *Sanctioned Violence in Early China*. Albany, NY.

(2007) *The Early Chinese Empires: Qin and Han*. Cambridge, MA.

(2009) *China's Cosmopolitan Empire: The Tang Dynasty*. Cambridge.

Lewis, N. (2000) 'Judiciary Routines in Roman Egypt', *Bulletin of the American Society of Papyrologists* 37: 83–93.

Li, F. *Early China* (2013) *A Social and Cultural History*. Cambridge.

(2008) *Bureaucracy and the State in Early China: Governing the Western Zhou*. Cambridge.

Li, J. (1996) *Chinese Civilization in the Making, 1766–221 BC*. London.

Li, S. (2018) *The Constitution of Ancient China*, trans. D. A. Bell and Zhang Yongle. Princeton, NJ.

Liao, W. K. (ed.) (1939; 1958) *The Complete Works of Han Fei Tzu: A Classic of Chinese Political Science*. 2 vols. London.

Libecap, G. D. (1986) 'Property Rights in Economic History: Implications for Research', *Explorations in Economic History* 23: 227–52.

(1989) *Contracting for Property Rights*. Cambridge.

Lichtheim, M. (1980) *Ancient Egyptian Literature: A Book of Readings*. Berkeley.

(2006) *Ancient Egyptian Literature*. Vol. I: *The Old and Middle Kingdoms*. Berkeley.

Liebermann, S. (1968) *Sifre Zutta (The Midrash of Lydda)*. New York.

Liebs, D. (1987) *Die Jurisprudenz im spätantiken Italien (260–640 n. Chr.)*. Berlin.

(2002a) *Römische Jurisprudenz in Gallien (2. bis 8. Jahrhundert)*. Berlin.

(2002b) 'Rechtskunde im römischen Kaiserreich. Rom und die Provinzen', in *Iurisprudentia universalis: Festschrift für Theo Mayer-Maly zum 70. Geburtstag*, ed. Martin J. Schermaier et al. Cologne: 383-407.

(2005) *Römische Jurisprudenz in Africa*. Berlin.

(2019) 'Der Beruf des Juristen in der Spätantike', in *Atti dell'Accademia romanistica costantiniana XXIII*. Napoli: 141-182.

Linderski, J. (1986) 'The Augural Law', in *Aufstieg und Niedergang der römischen Welt*, ed. H. Temporini and W. Haase. Berlin: 2146–312.

Lingat, R. (1962) 'Les quatre pieds du procès', *Journal Asiatique* 250.4: 489–503.

(1973) *The Classical Law of India*, trans. J. D. M. Derrett. Berkeley.

Lintott, A. W. (1999) *The Constitution of the Roman Republic*. Oxford.

Lion, B. (2012) 'Assemblies: Ancient Near East', in *The Encyclopedia of Ancient History*, ed. R. S. Bagnall, K. Brodersen, C. B. Champion, A. Erskine and S. R. Huebner. Online edition: https://doi.org/10.1002/9781444338386.wbeah01019 (accessed 19/09/2022).

Lippert, S. (2004) *Ein demotisches juristisches Lehrbuch: Untersuchungen zu Papyrus Berlin P 23757 rto*. Wiesbaden.

(2008) *Einführung in die Altägyptische Rechtsgeschichte*. Berlin.

Liu, Y. (1998) *Origins of Chinese Law: Penal and Administrative Law in Its Early Development*. Hong Kong.

Liverani, M. (2000) 'The Great Powers' Club' in R. Cohen and R. Westbrook, ed. *Amarna Diplomacy. The Beginnings of International Relations*. Baltimore-London: 15–27.

Liverani, M. (2001) *International Relations in the Ancient Near East, 1600–1100 BC*. Basingstoke and New York.

(2020) 'A History of the Ancient Near East', in *A Companion to the Ancient Near East*, ed. D. C. Snell. Hoboken, NJ: 11–26.
Lobban, M. (2014) 'Sociology, History and the "Internal" Study of Law', in *Law, Society and Community: Socio-Legal Essays in Honour of Roger Cotterrell*, ed. R. Nobles and D. Schiff. Farnham: 39–60.
  (2016) *A Treatise of Legal Philosophy and General Jurisprudence*. Vol. VIII: *A History of the Philosophy of Law in the Common Law World 1600–1900*: Dordrecht.
Loewe, M. (1994) *Divination, Mythology and Monarchy in Han China*. Cambridge.
  (2004) *The Men Who Governed Han China*. Leiden.
  (2006) *The Government of the Qin and Han Empires: 221 BCE–220 CE*. Indianapolis.
  (2009) 'Dong Zhongshu as Consultant', *Asia Major* 22.1: 163–82.
  (2011) *Dong Zhongshu, a 'Confucian' Heritage and the Chunqiu fanlu*. Leiden.
Loewe, M. and Shaughnessy, E. L. (eds.) (1999) *The Cambridge History of Ancient China: From the Origins of Civilization to 221 BC*. Cambridge.
Lombardi, L. (1961) *Dalla Fides alla Bona Fides*. Milan.
Long, A. A. (2005) 'Law and Nature in Greek Thought', in Gagarin and Cohen (2005): 412–30.
Lonis, R. (1979) *Guerre et religion en Grèce à l'époque classique: Recherches sur les rites, les dieux, l'idéologie de la victoire*. Paris.
Lonis, R. (2007) *La cité dans le monde grec: Structures, fonctionnement, contradictions*. 2nd ed. Paris.
Low, P. A. (2007) *Interstate Relations in Classical Greece: Morality and Power*. Cambridge.
Lubin, T. (2005) 'The Transmission, Patronage, and Prestige of Brahmanical Piety from the Mauryas to the Guptas', in *Boundaries, Dynamics, and Construction of Traditions in South Asia*, ed. F. Squarcini. Florence: 77–103.
  (2007) 'Punishment and Expiation: Overlapping Domains in Brahmanical Law', *Indologica Taurinensia* 33: 93–122.
  (2015) 'Writing and the Recognition of Customary Law in Premodern India and Java', *Journal of the American Oriental Society* 135.2: 225–59.
  (2017) 'Daily Duties: āhnika', in Olivelle and Davis (2017): 179–88.
  (2018a) 'Towards a South Asian Diplomatics: Cosmopolitan Norms and Regional Idioms in the Use of Documents', in *Studies in Historical Documents from Nepal and India*, ed. S. Cubelic, A. Michaels and A. Zotter. Heidelberg: 37–84.
  (2018b) 'The Theory and Practice of Property in Premodern South Asia: Disparities and Convergences', *Journal of the Economic and Social History of the Orient* 61.5–6: 803–50.
  (2022) 'Dignity and Status in Ancient and Medieval India', in *Human Dignity in Asia: Dialogue between Law and Culture*, ed. J. C.-S. Hsu. Cambridge: 285–307.
  (2023) 'Religious Endowments in Ancient India and the Institutionalization of Brahmin Caste Status', *American Journal of Legal History* 63.2: 97–114.
Lubin, T., Davis D.R. Jr and Krishnan, J. K. (eds.) (2010) *Hinduism and Law: An Introduction*. Cambridge.
Lüddeckens, E. (1960) *Ägyptische Eheverträge*. Wiesbaden.
Lupu, E. (2009) *Greek Sacred Law A Collection of New Documents*. 2nd ed. with a Postscript. Leiden.
Ma, D. and van Zanden, J. L. (eds.) (2011) *Law and Long-Term Economic Change: A Eurasian Perspective*. Stanford.

Ma, J. (2009) 'Empire, Statuses, and Realities', in Ma, Papazarkadas and Parker (2009): 125–48.
Ma, J., Papazarkadas, N. and Parker, R. (eds.) (2009) *Interpreting the Athenian Empire*. London.
MacCormack, G. (1985) 'The Law of Contract in China under the T'ang and Sung Dynasties', *Revue internationale des droits de l'Antiquité* 32: 17–68.
  (1989) 'Natural Law and Cosmic Harmony in Traditional Chinese Thought', *Ratio Iuris* 2: 254–73.
  (1990) *Traditional Chinese Penal Law*. Edinburgh.
  (1995) 'Was the Ordeal Known in Ancient China?' *Revue internationale des droits de l'Antiquité* 52: 71–93.
  (1996) *The Spirit of Traditional Chinese Law*. Athens, GA.
  (2001) 'Mythology and the Origin of Law in Early Chinese Thought', *Journal of Asian Legal History* 1: 1–23.
  (2004) 'The Transmission of Penal Law (*lü*) from the Han to the T'ang: A Contribution to the Study of the Early History of Codification in China', *Revue internationale des droits de l'Antiquité* 51: 47–83.
  (2006a) 'The Legalist School and its Influence upon Traditional Chinese Law', *Archiv für Rechts-und Sozialphilosophie* 92: 59–81.
  (2006b) 'Filial Piety (*xiao*) and the Family in Pre-*Tang* Law', *Revue internationale des droits de l'Antiquité* 53: 55–83.
  (2007) 'On the Relationship between Law and Religion in Early China: Some Issues', *xingda lishi xuebao* 18: 1–20.
  (2008) 'A Reassessment of the "Confucianization of the Law" from the Han to the T'ang', in *New Perspectives on Chinese History: The Formation and Transformation of Chinese Legal Culture*, ed. Nap-yin Lau. Taiwan: 397–442.
  (2013a) *Traditional Chinese Penal Law*. London.
  (2013b) 'Natural Law in Traditional China', *Journal of Comparative Law* 8.2: 104–26.
  (2014) '"Agreement", "Contract" and "Debt" in Early Chinese Law', *Comparative Legal History* 2–1: 1–29.
MacCoull, L. (1988) *Dioscorus of Aphrodito: His Work and His World*. Berkeley.
MacDowell, D. M. (1978) *The Law in Classical Athens*. Ithaca.
  (1986) *Spartan Law*. Edinburgh.
  (1990) *Jurisdiction in the Workmen's Community of Deir el-Medina*. Leiden.
  (2006) 'Mining Cases in Athenian Law', in *Symposium 2003: Vorträge zur griechischen und hellenistischen Rechtsgeschichte*, ed. H. A. Rupprecht. Vienna: 121–31.
  (2008) 'The Athenian Penalty of Epobolia', in *Akten des Gesellschaft für griechische und hellenistische Rechtsgeschichte*, eds. E. Harris and G. Thür. Vienna: 87–94.
  (2009). *Demosthenes the Orator*. Oxford.
Mackil, E. (2013) *Creating a Common Polity: Religion, Economy, and Politics in the Making of the Greek Koinon*. Berkeley.
Mackil, E. (2017) 'Property Claims and State Formation in the Archaic Greek World', in *Ancient States and Infrastructural Power: Europe, Asia, and America*, ed. S. Richardson and C. Ando. Philadelphia: 63–90.

(2021) 'Confiscation, Exile, and Return: The Property Problem and its Legal Solutions', in *Symposion 2019: Vorträge zur Griechischen und hellenistischen Rechtsgeschichte*, ed. K. Harter-Uibopuu and W. Riess. Vienna: 185–212.

Maffi, A. (2005) 'Family and Property Law', in Gagarin and Cohen (2005): 254–66.

Magdalene, F. R. (2007) *On the Scales of Righteousness: Neo-Babylonian Trial Law and the Book of Job*. Providence, RI.

(2011) 'Legal Science Then and Now: Theory and Method in the Work of Raymond Westbrook', *Maarav* 18: 17–53.

Magdalene, F. R., Wells, B. and Wunsch, C. (2019) *Fault, Responsibility, and Administrative Law in Late Babylonian Legal Texts*. University Park, PA.

Magnetto, A. (2015) 'Interstate Arbitration and Foreign Judges', in *The Oxford Handbook of Ancient Greek Law*, ed. E. Harris and M. Canevaro. Online edition: https://doi.org/10.1093/oxfordhb/9780199599257.013.20 (accessed 01/09/ 2022).

Maine, H. S. (1861) *Ancient Law*. London.

Malay, H. and Petzl, G. (ed. and trans.) (2017) *New Religious Texts from Lydia*. Vienna.

Malul, M. (1988) *Studies in Mesopotamian Legal Symbolism*. Kevelaer.

Manning, J. G. (1995) 'Demotic Egyptian Instruments of Transfer as Evidence for Private Ownership of Real Property', *Chicago-Kent Law Review* 71: 237–68.

(2003a) *Land and Power in Ptolemaic Egypt: The Structure of Land Tenure*. Cambridge.

(2003b) 'Demotic Law', in Westbrook (2003a): 819–62.

(2010) *The Last Pharaohs: Egypt under the Ptolemies 305–30 BC*. Princeton, NJ.

(2012) 'The Representation of Justice in Ancient Egypt', *Yale Journal of Law and Humanities* 24.1: 111–18.

(2018) *The Open Sea: Economic Life of the Ancient Mediterranean World from the Iron Age to the Rise of Rome*. Princeton, NJ.

Mantovani, D. (2007) 'I giuristi, il retore e le api. Ius controversum e natura nella Declamatio maior XIII', in *Testi e problemi del giusnaturalismo romano*, ed. D. Mantovani and A. Schiavone. Pavia: 323–85.

(2016) 'More than Codes: Roman Ways of Organizing and Giving Access to Legal Information', in *The Oxford Handbook of Roman Law and Society*, ed. P. J. du Plessis, C. Ando and K. Tuori. Oxford: 23–42.

(2018a) *Les juristes écrivains de la Rome antique: Les œuvres des juristes comme littérature*. Paris.

(2018b) *Legum multitudo: Die Bedeutung der Gesetze im römischen Privatrecht*, trans. U. Babusiaux. Berlin.

(2020) 'Sulle tracce dei *rescripta* richiesti da privati nella tarda antichità', *Tesserae iuris* 1: 9–46.

Marek, C. (1984) *Die Proxenie*. Frankfurt am Main.

Martin, C. (2012) *A Critical Introduction to the Study of Religion*. London and New York.

Martin, C. J. (1995) 'Marriage, Wills, Leases of Land: Some Notes on the Formulae of Demotic Contracts', in *Legal Documents of the Hellenistic World: Papers from a Seminar*, ed. M. J. Geller and H. Maehler. London: 58–78.

(2009) *Demotic Papyri from the Memphite Necropolis in the Collections of the National Museum of Antiquities in Leiden, the British Museum and the Hermitage Museum*. Turnhout.

(2019) 'A Persian Estate in Egypt: Early Demotic Papyri in the British Museum', in *New Approaches in Demotic Studies: Acts of the 13th International Conference of Demotic Studies*, ed. F. Naether. Berlin: 175–95.

(2020–21) 'The Demotic Legal Manuals – Or Codes – Or Coutumiers – Or Commentaries – Or Case Laws? Does Modern Terminology Help or Hinder Us in Interpreting These Texts?' *Revue internationale des droits de l'Antiquité* 67–68: 249–90.

McClish, M. (2014) 'The Dependence of Manu's Seventh Chapter on Kauṭilya's Arthaśāstra', *Journal of the American Oriental Society* 134.2: 241–62.

(2017a) 'King, *rājadharma*', in Olivelle and Davis (2017): 257–72.

(2017b) 'Punishment: *daṇḍa*', in Olivelle and Davis (2017): 273–82.

(2017c) 'Titles of Law: *vyavahārapada*', in Olivelle and Davis (2017): 299–312.

(2019a) 'From Law to *Dharma*: State Law and Sacred Duty in Ancient India', *Journal of Law and Religion* 34.2: 284–309.

(2019b) *The History of the* Arthaśāstra: *Sovereignty and Sacred Law in Ancient India*. Cambridge.

McClish, M. and Olivelle, P. (eds. and trans.) (2012) *The* Arthaśāstra: *Selections from the Classic Indian Work on Statecraft*. Indianapolis and Cambridge.

McDowell, A. G. (1990) *Jurisdiction in the Workmen's Community of Deir El-Medîna*. Leiden.

McInerney, J. (2013) '*Polis* and *koinon*: Federal Government in Greece', in *A Companion to Ancient Greek Government*, ed. H. Beck. Chichester: 466–79.

McNeal, R. (2012) *Conquer and Govern: Early Chinese Military Texts from the Yizhou shu*. Honolulu.

Meier, S. A. (2000) 'Diplomacy and International Marriages', in *Amarna Diplomacy? The Beginnings of International Relations*, ed. R. Cohen and R. Westbrook. Baltimore: 165–73.

Meiggs, R. and Lewis, D. (ed. and trans.) (1969) *A Selection of Greek Historical Inscriptions to the End of the Fifth Century BC*. Oxford.

Menski, W. (2006) *Comparative Law in a Global Context*. 2nd ed. Cambridge.

Merrill, T. W. (2001) 'What Happened to Property in Law and Economics?', *The Yale Law Journal* 111: 357–98.

Merrill, T. W. and Smith, H. E. (2012) *Property: Principles and Policies*. 2nd ed. New York.

Merryman, J. H. and Pérez-Perdomo, R. (2018) *The Civil Law Tradition*. 4th ed. Stanford.

Metzger, E. (2015) 'Litigation', in Johnston (2015): 272–300.

Meyer, E. A. (2004) *Legitimacy and Law in the Roman World: Tabulae in Roman Belief and Practice*. Cambridge.

(2023) 'Metics and Freedmen: Conflicts of Social and Juridical Status in the Classical and Hellenistic Greek World', *American Journal of Legal History* 63.2: 82–96.

Michel, C. (2000) 'Les litiges commerciaux paléo-assyriens', in *Rendre la justice en Mésopotamie: Archives judiciaires du Proche-Orient ancien (IIIe–Ier millénaires avant J.-C.)*, ed. F. Joannès. Paris: 113–39.

(2006) 'Bigamie chez Assyriens au debut du IIe millenaire avant J.-C.', *Revue historique de droit français et étranger* 84: 155–76.

(2008) 'Les Assyriens et leurs femmes anatoliennes', in *Anatolia and the Jazira during the Old Assyrian Period*, ed. J. G. Dercksen. Old Assyrian Archives Studies 3. Leiden: 209–29.

(2020) *Women of Assur and Kanesh: Texts from the Archives of Assyrian Merchants*. Atlanta.

(2023) 'Old Assyrian Legal Cases' in S. Démare-Lafont and D. Fleming (eds.), *Judicial Decisions in the Ancient Near East*. Writings from the Ancient World 43. Atlanta: 223–296.

Micolier, G. (1932) *Pécule et capacité patrimoniale: Étude sur le pécule, dit profectice, depuis l'édit 'de peculio' jusqu'à la fin de l'époque classique*. Lyon.

Millar, F. (1992) *The Emperor in the Roman World (31 BC–AD 337)*. London.

(2004) 'Condemnation to Hard Labour in the Roman Empire, from the Julio-Claudians to Constantine', in *Rome, the Greek World, and the East*, Vol. II: *Government, Society, and Culture in the Roman Empire*, ed. H. Cotton and G. M. Rogers. Chapel Hill: 120–50.

(2006) *A Greek Roman Empire. Power and Belief under Theodosius II*. Berkeley.

Miller, J. (2013) *Royal Hittite Instructions and Related Administrative Texts*. Atlanta.

Miller, W. I. (2006) *Eye for an Eye*. Cambridge.

Millett, P. (1990) 'Sale, Credit and Exchange in Athenian Law and Society', in *Nomos: Essays in Athenian Law, Politics and Society*, ed. P. Cartledge, P. Millett and S. Todd. Cambridge: 167–94.

Milstein, S. J. (2021) *Making a Case: The Practical Roots of Biblical Law*. Oxford.

Minakshi, C. (1938) *Administration and Social Life under the Pallavas*. Madras.

Mirashi, V. V. (ed.) (1955) *Corpus Inscriptionum Indicarum*, Vol. IV: *Inscriptions of the Kalachuri-Chedi Era, Part I*. Ootacamund.

Mirhady, D. C. (1996) 'Torture and Rhetoric in Athens', *Journal of Hellenic Studies* 116: 119–31.

Mitchell, S. (1976) 'Requisitioned Transport in the Roman Empire: A New Inscription from Pisidia', *Journal of Roman Studies* 66: 106–31.

Mitteis, L. (1891) *Reichsrecht und Volksrecht in den östlichen Provinzen des römischen Kaiserreichs. Mit Beitragen zur Kenntniss der griechischen Rechts und der spatrömischen Rechtsentwicklung*. Lepizig.

Modrzejewski, J. M. (2011) *Droit et justice dans le monde grec et hellénistique*. Warsaw.

Monson, A. (2012) *Agriculture and Taxation in Early Ptolemaic Egypt. Demotic Land Surveys and Accounts (P. Agri.)*. Bonn.

Moore, S. F. (1986) 'Legal Systems of the World: An Introductory Guide to Classifications, Typological Interpretations, and Bibliographical Resources', in *Law and the Social Sciences*, ed. L. Lipson and S. Wheeler. New York: 11–62.

Morrow, G. R. (1960) *Plato's Cretan City: A Historical Interpretation of the Laws*. Princeton, NJ.

Mosley, D. J. (1973) *Envoys and Diplomacy in Ancient Greece*. Wiesbaden.

Mouritsen, H. (2011) *The Freedman in the Roman World*. Cambridge

Muhs, B. P. (2002) 'Clear Title, Public Protests and P. Brux Dem. 4', in *Acts of the Seventh International Conference of Demotic Studies, Copenhagen, 23-27 August 1999*, ed. K. Ryholt. Copenhagen: 259–72.

(2005) *Tax Receipts, Taxpayers, and Taxes in Early Ptolemaic Thebes*. Oriental Institute Publications 126. Chicago.

(2016) *The Ancient Egyptian Economy*. Cambridge.

Müller, G. G. W. (2012) 'Archive, Familien und geographischer Horizont', in *The Nuzi Workshop at the 55th Rencontre Assyriologique Internationale (July 2009, Paris)*, ed. P. Abrahami and B. Lion. Bethesda: 187–203.

Mullins, D. A. et al. (2018). 'A Systematic Assessment of "Axial Age" Proposals Using Global Comparative Historical Evidence', *American Sociological Review* 83.3: 596–626.

Murphy, J. (2002) 'Equality in Exchange', *American Journal of Jurisprudence* 47: 85–121.

Musurillo, H. (ed.) (1954) *The Acts of the Pagan Martyrs: Acta Alexandrinorum*. Oxford.

Na'aman, N. (2008) 'Sojourners and Levites in the Kingdom of Judah in the Seventh Century BCE', *Zeitschrift für Altorientalische und Biblische Rechtsgeschichte* 14: 237–79.

Naiden, F. S. (2013) 'Gods, Kings, and Lawgivers', in *Law and Religion in the Eastern Mediterranean: from Antiquity to Early Islam*, ed. A. C. Hagedorn and R. G. Kratz. New York and Oxford: 79–104.

Neumann, H. (2003) 'Recht im antiken Mesopotamien', in *Die Rechtskulturen der Antike: Vom Alten Orient bis zum Römischen Reich*, ed. U. Manthe. Munich: 55–122.

(2006–2008) 'Richter. A. Mesopotamien', *Reallexikon der Assyriologie* 11: 346–51.

Ng, P. (2020) 'History of Aristocratic Families in Tang China, Part 1: The Struggle to Adapt', *Journal of Asian History* 54.2 (2020): 211–60.

Nicholas, B. (1962). *An Introduction to Roman Law*. Rev. ed. 2008. Oxford.

Nikam N. A. and McKeon, R. (1959) *The Edicts of Aśoka*. Chicago.

Noreña, C. (2012) 'The Ethics of Autocracy in the Roman World', in *A Companion to Greek and Roman Political Thought*, ed. R. K. Balot. Chichester: 266–79.

(2021) 'Private Associations and Urban Experience in the Han and Roman Empires', in *Rulers and Ruled in Ancient Greece, Rome, and China*, eds. H. Beck and G. Vankeerberghen. Cambridge: 101–30.

Norman, K. R. (1972) 'Notes on the Greek Version of Aśoka's Twelfth and Thirteenth Rock Edicts', *Journal of the Royal Asiatic Society of Great Britain and Ireland* 2: 111–18.

North, D. C. (1981) *Structure and Change in Economic History*. New York.

(1990) *Institutions, Institutional Change and Economic Performance*. Cambridge.

North, D. C. and Thomas, R. P. (1973) *The Rise of the Western World: A New Economic History*. Cambridge.

North, D. C., Wallis, J. J. and Weingast, B. R. (2009) *Violence and Social Orders: A Conceptual Framework for Interpreting Recorded Human History*. Cambridge.

Novak, W. J. (2015) 'Beyond Max Weber: The Need for a Democratic (not Aristocratic) Theory of the Modern State', *The Toqueville Review* 36: 43–91.

Nowicki, S. (ed.) (2016) *'They Called Me to Destroy the Wicked and the Evil': Selected Essays on Crime and Punishment in Antiquity*. Münster.

Núñez Vaquero, Á. (2013) 'Five Models of Legal Science', *Revus* 19: 53–81.

Ober, J. (1990) *Mass and Elite in Democratic Athens: Rhetoric, Ideology, and the Power of the People*. Princeton, NJ.

Oded, B. (1979) *Mass Deportations and Deportees in the Neo-Assyrian Empire*. Wiesbaden.

(1992) *War, Peace and Empire: Justifications for War in Assyrian Royal Inscriptions*. Wiesbaden.

Oelsner, J. (2022) *Der Kodex Ḥammu-rāpi: Textkritische Ausgabe und Übersetzung*. Münster.

Oelsner, J., Wells, B. and Wunsch, C. (2003) 'Neo-Babylonian Period', in Westbrook (2003a): 911–74.

Ogilvie, S. (2021) *The European Guilds: An Economic Analysis*. Princeton, NJ.

Olabarria, L. (2020) *Kinship and Family in Ancient Egypt. Archaeology and Anthropology in Dialogue*. Cambridge.

Olberding, G. P. (2022) *Designing Boundaries in Early China: The Composition of Sovereign Space*. Cambridge.

Olivelle, P. (ed. and trans.) (1997) *Pañcatantra: The Book of India's Folk Wisdom*. Oxford.

(ed. and trans.) (2000) *The Dharmasūtras of Āpastamba, Gautama, Baudhāyana, and Vasiṣṭha*. Delhi.

(trans.) (2004a) *The Law Code of Manu: A New Translation Based on the Critical Edition*. Oxford.

(2004b) 'The Semantic History of *Dharma*: The Middle and Late Vedic Periods', *Dharma: Studies in Its Semantic, Cultural, and Religious History* (ed. P. Olivelle). Special issue of *Journal of Indian Philosophy* 32: 491–511.

(ed. and trans.) (2005a) *Manu's Code of Law: A Critical Edition and Translation of the Mānava-Dharmaśāstra*. Oxford.

(2005b) 'Power of Words: The Ascetic Appropriation and the Semantic Evolution of *Dharma*', repr. in *Language, Texts, and Society: Explorations in Ancient Indian Culture and Religion*, ed. P. Olivelle. Florence: 120–35.

(ed. and trans.) (2009) *Viṣṇu's Code of Law: A Critical Edition and Translation of the Vaiṣṇava-Dharmaśāstra*. Harvard Oriental Series, No. 73. Cambridge, MA.

(2010) 'Dharmaśāstra: A Literary History', in Lubin, Davis and Krishnan (2010): 28–57.

(2011) 'War and Peace: Semantics of Saṃdhi and Vigraha in the Arthaśāstra', in *Pūrvāparaprajñābhinandanam – East and West, Past and Present: Indological and Other Essays in Honour of Klaus Karttunen*, ed. B. Tikkanen and A. M. Butters. Studia Orientalia 110. Helsinki: 131–39.

(2012a) 'Patañjali and the Beginnings of Dharmaśāstra: An Alternate Social History of Early Dharmasūtra Production', in *Aux dabords de la clairière*, ed. C. Guenzi and S. d'Intino. Paris: 117–33.

(2012b) 'Kaṇṭakaśodhana: Courts of Criminal Justice in Ancient India', in *Devadattīyam: Johannes Bronkhorst Felicitation Volume*, ed. F. Voegeli, V. Eltschinger, D. Feller, M. P. Candotti, B. Diaconescu and M. Kulkarni. Bern: 629–42.

(2013) *King, Governance, and Law in Ancient India: Kauṭilya's* Arthaśāstra. Oxford.

(2016a) *A Dharma Reader: Classical Indian Law*. Historical Sourcebooks in Classical Indian Thought. New York.

(2016b) 'Economy, Ecology, and National Defense in Kauṭilya's *Arthaśāstra*', in *Indigenous Historical Knowledge: Kauṭilya and His Vocabulary*, ed. P. K. Gautam, S. Mishra and A. Gupta. New Delhi: 3–15.

(ed. and trans.) (2017a) *A Dharma Reader: Classical Indian Law*. New York.

(2017b) 'Legal Procedure, *vyavahāra*', in Olivelle and Davis (2017): 283–98.

(2017c) 'The Medical Profession in Ancient India: Its Social, Religious, and Legal Status', *eJournal of Indian Medicine* 9: 1–21.

(ed. and trans.) (2019a) *Yajnavalkya: A Treatise on Dharma*. Cambridge, MA.

(2019b) *Grhastha: The Householder in Ancient Indian Religious Culture*. Oxford.

(2023) *Ashoka: Portrait of a Philosopher King*. Delhi.

Olivelle P., Brick, D. and McClish, M. (eds.) (2015) *A Sanskrit Dictionary of Law and Statecraft*. Delhi.

Olivelle, P. and Davis, D. R. (eds.) (2017) *The Oxford History of Hinduism: Hindu Law: A New History of Dharmaśāstra*. Oxford.

Olivelle, P. and McClish, M. (2015) 'The Four Feet of Legal Procedure and the Origins of Jurisprudence in Ancient India', *Journal of the American Oriental Society* 135.1: 33-47.

Oliver, L. (2011) *The Body Legal in Barbarian Law*. Toronto and London.

On, I. (1973) 'T'ang Household Registers and Related Documents', in *Perspectives on the T'ang*, ed. A. F. Wright and D. Twitchett. New Haven: 121–50.

Osborne, R. (1985) 'Law in Action in Classical Athens', *Journal of Hellenic Studies* 105: 40–58.

　(1990) 'Vexatious Litigation in Classical Athens: Sycophancy and the Sykophant', in *Nomos: Essays in Athenian Law, Politics and Society*, ed. P. Cartledge, P. Millett and S. Todd. Cambridge: 83–102.

　(1999) 'Private and Common Property Rights', in *Encyclopedia of Law and Economics*, ed. B. Bouckaert and G. De Geest. Cheltenham: 332–79.

　(2000) 'Religion, Imperial Politics, and the Offering of Freedom to Slaves', in *Law and Social Status in Classical Athens*, ed. V. J. Hunter and J. Edmondson. Oxford: 75–92.

　(2011) *History Written on the Classical Greek Body*. Cambridge.

Osborne, R. and Rhodes, P. J. (eds.) (2018) *Greek Historical Inscriptions 478–404 BC*. Oxford.

Osler, D. (1997) 'The Myth of European History', *Rechtshistorisches Journal* 16: 393–410.

Ostrom, E. (1990) *Governing the Commons: The Evolution of Institution for Collective Action*. Cambridge.

Ostrom, E. and Hess, C. (2007) 'Property and Common Property Rights'. Online edition: http://ssrn.com/abstract=1304699 (accessed 19/9/2022).

Otto, E. (2002) *Gottes Recht als Menschenrecht: Rechts- und literaturhistorische Studien zum Deuteronomium*. Wiesbaden.

Papazarkadas, N. (2011) *Sacred and Public Land in Ancient Athens*. Oxford.

Pardee, D. (1998) 'Les documents d'Arslan Tash: authentiques ou faux?', *Syria* 75: 15–54.

Parker, P. (ed.) (2012) *The Great Trade Routes*. Annapolis.

Parker, R. (1983) *Miasma: Pollution and Purification in Early Greek Religion*. Oxford.

　(2000) 'Greek States and Greek Oracles', in *Oxford Readings in Greek Religion*, ed. R. Buxton. Oxford: 76–108.

　(2004) 'What Are Sacred Laws?', in *The Law and the Courts in Ancient Greece*, ed. E. M. Harris and L. Rubinstein. London: 57–70.

　(2005) 'Law and Religion', in Gagarin and Cohen (2005): 61–81.

Parkinson, R. B. (1991) *The Tale of the Eloquent Peasant*. Oxford.

　(2012) *The Tale of the Eloquent Peasant: A Reader's Commentary*. Hamburg.

Parpola, A. (2018) 'Indus Seals and Glyptic Studies: An Overview', in Ameri, Costello, Jamison and Scott (2018): 127–43.

Patterson, C. (2005) 'Athenian Citizenship Law', in *The Cambridge Companion to Ancient Greek Law*, ed. M. Gagarin and D. Cohen. Cambridge: 267–89.

　(2009) 'Status: Ancient Greek Law', in *The Oxford International Encyclopedia of Legal History*, Vol. V, ed. S. N. Katz. Oxford: 354–58.

Patterson, O. (1982) *Slavery and Social Death: A Comparative Study*. Cambridge, MA.

　(2008) 'Freedom, Slavery, and the Modern Construction of Rights', in *The Cultural Values of Europe*, ed. H. Joas and K. Wiegandt. Liverpool: 115–51.

Paulus, S. (2015) 'Ordal statt Eid: das Beweisverfahren in mittelbabylonischer Zeit', in *Prozessrecht und Eid: Recht und Rechtsfindung in antiken Kulturen*, ed. H. Barta, M. Lang and R. Rollinger. Wiesbaden: 207–25.

Peachin, M. (2015) 'Augustus' Emergent Judicial Powers, the "Crimen Maiestatis," and the Second Cyrene Edict', in *Il princeps romano: autocrate o magistrato? Fattori giuridici e fattori sociali del potere imperiale da Augusto a Commodo*, ed. J.-L. Ferrary and J. Scheid. Pavia: 497–554.

Pébarthe, C. (2006) *Cité, démocratie et écriture: Histoire de l'alphabétisation d'Athènes à l'époque classique*. Paris.

Pecorella Longo C. (2004) 'Il condono della pena in Atene in età classica', *Dike: Rivista di storia del diritto greco ed ellenistico* 7: 85–111.

Peerenboom, R. P. (1993) *Law and Morality in Ancient China: The Silk Manuscripts of Huang-Lao*. New York.

Pestman, P. W. (1961) *Marriage and Matrimonial Property in Ancient Egypt: A Contribution to Establishing the Legal Position of the Poman*. Leiden.

(1969) 'The Law of Succession in Ancient Egypt', in *Essays on Oriental Laws of Succession*, ed. M. David, F. R. Kraus and P. W. Pestman. Leiden: 58–77.

(1985a) 'Registration of Demotic Contracts in Egypt', in *Satura Robert Feenstra Oblata*, ed. J. A. Ankum, J. E. Spruit and F.B. J. Wubbe. Fribourg: 17–25.

(1985b) 'The Competence of Greek and Egyptian Tribunals according to the Decree of 118 BC', *Bulletin of the American Society of Papyrologists* 22.1–4: 265–69.

(1987) '"Inheriting" in the Archive of the Theban Choachytes (2nd Cent. BC)', in *Aspects of Demotic Lexicography*, ed. S. P. Vleeming. Leuven: 57–73.

(1994) *Les papyrus démotiques de Tsenhor (P. Tsenhor): Les Archives privées d'une Femme égyptienne du Temps de Darius Ier*. Leuven.

Pfeifer, G. and Grotkamp, N. (eds.) (2017) *Außergerichtliche Konfiktlösung in der Antike. Beispiele aus drei Jahrtausenden*. Frankfurt.

Pfeiffer, R. H. (1932) *Excavations at Nuzi*, Vol. II: *The Archives of Shilwateshup, Son of the King*. Cambridge, MA.

Pfoh, E. (2019) 'Assessing Foreignness and Politics in the Late Bronze Agew', in *A Stranger in the House – the Crossroads III: Proceedings of an International Conference on Foreigners in Ancient Egyptian and Near Eastern Societies of the Bronze Age held in Prague, September 10–13, 2018*, ed. J. Mynářová, M. Kilani and S. Alivernin. Prague: 257–67.

Phang, S. E. (2008) *Roman Military Service: Ideologies of Discipline in the Late Republic and Early Empire*. Cambridge.

Phillipson, C. (1911) *The International Law and Custom of Ancient Greece and Rome*. London.

Piccirilli, L. (2002) *L'invenzione della diplomazia nella Grecia antica*. Rome.

Pina Polo F. (2011) *The Consul at Rome: The Civil Functions of the Consul in the Roman Republic*. Cambridge.

(2016) 'SPQR: Institutions and Popular Participation in the Roman Republic', in *The Oxford Handbook of Roman Law and Society*, ed. P. J. du Plessis, C. Ando and K. Tuori. Oxford: 85–97.

Pines, Y., von Falkenhausen, L., Shelach, G. and Yates, R. D. S. (eds.) (2014) *Birth of an Empire: The State of Qin Revisited*. Berkeley.

Polay, E. (1980) *The Contracts in the Triptychs Found in Transilvania and Their Hellenistic Features*. Studia Historica Academiae Scientiarum Hungaricae, no 133. Budapest.

Poo, Mu-chou. (2014) 'Religion and Religious life of the Qin', in Pines, von Falkenhausen, Shelach and Yates (2014): 187–205.

Porten, B. et al. (ed. and trans.) (1996) *The Elephantine Papyri in English: Three Millennia of Cross-Cultural Continuity and Change*. Leiden.
Posner, E. (1972) *Archives in the Ancient World*. Cambridge, MA.
Postgate, J. N. (1994) *Early Mesopotamia: Society and Economy at the Dawn of History*. London.
Powell, J. and Paterson, J. (eds.)(2004) *Cicero the Advocate*. Oxford.
Power, M. (1999) *The Audit Society: Rituals of Verification*. Oxford.
Prignitz, S. (2014, 2022) *Bauurkunden und Bauprogramm von Epidauros (400–350)*. Munich.
Pringsheim, F. (1950) *The Greek Law of Sale*. Weimar.
Pritchard, J. B. (ed.) (1969) *Ancient Near Eastern Texts Relating to the Old Testament*. 3rd ed. Princeton, NJ.
Purcell, N. (2014) '"No Two Characters Seem More Inconsistent Than Those of Trader and Sovereign' (Adam Smith, *The Wealth of Nations*, V, 2, 1): The Problem of Roman Imperial Estates', in *Beyond Vagnari: New Themes in the Study of Roman South Italy*, ed. A. M. Small. Bari: 265–75.
Qiang F. (2013) *Chinese Complaint Systems: Natural Resistance*. London.
Quack, J.F. (2016). 'Translating the realities of cult: the case of the book of the temple,' in *Greco-Egyptian Interactions: Literature, Translation, and Culture, 500 BCE–300 CE*, ed. I. Rutherford. Oxford: 267–286.
Queen, S. A. (1996) *From Chronicle to Canon: The Hermeneutics of the Spring and Autumn according to Tung Chung-shu*. Cambridge.
Raaflaub, K. A. (ed.) (2007) *War and Peace in the Ancient World*. Malden, MA and Oxford.
Rackham, H. (ed.) (1934) *Aristotle: The Nicomachean Ethics*. Cambridge, MA.
Radner, K. (2005) 'The Reciprocal Relationship between Judge and Society in the Neo-Assyrian Period', *Maarav* 12: 41–68.
Ragionieri, R. (2000) 'The Amarna Age: An International Society in the Making', in *Amarna Diplomacy? The Beginnings of International Relations*, ed. R. Cohen and R. Westbrook. Baltimore: 42–53.
Rainey, A. F. (2015) *The El-Amarna Correspondence*. Leiden.
Ray, J. D. (1981) 'Ancient Egypt', in *Divination and Oracles*, ed. M. Loewe and C. Blacker. London: 176–90.
Rea, J. (1977) 'A New Version of P. Yale Inv. 299', *Zeitschrift für Papyrologie und Epigraphik* 27: 151–56.
Reid, A. (1983) '"Closed" and "Open" Slave Systems in Pre-Colonial Southeast Asia', in *Slavery, Bondage and Dependency in Southeast Asia*, ed. A. Reid. New York: 156–81.
Renger, J. (1977) 'Legal Aspects of Seals in Ancient Mesopotamia', in *Seals and Sealing in the Ancient Near East*, ed. M. Gibson and R. D. Biggs. Bibliotheca Mesopotamica 6. Malibu: 75–88.
Rhodes, P. J. (1981) *A Commentary on the Aristotelian Athenaion Politeia*. Oxford.
  (trans.) (1984) *Aristotle, The Athenian Constitution*. Harmondsworth.
  (2004) 'Keeping to the Point', in Harris and Rubinstein (2004): 137–58.
  (2015) 'The Congruence of Power: Ruling and Being Ruled in Greek Participatory Communities', in *A Companion to Greek Democracy and the Roman Republic*, ed. D. Hammer. Chichester: 131–45.
Rhodes, P. J. and Osborne, R. (2003) *Greek Historical Inscriptions 404–323 BC*. Oxford.
Riccobono, S. (1957) *Stipulatio and the Theory of Contract*. Amsterdam.

Richards, J. (2002) 'Text and Context in late Old Kingdom Egypt: The Archaeology and Historiography of Weni the Elder', *Journal of the American Research Centre in Egypt* 39: 75–102.

Richardson, S. (2012) 'Early Mesopotamia: The Presumptive State', *Past & Present* 215: 3–49.

(2017) 'Before Things Worked: A "Low Power" Model of Early Mesopotamia', in *Ancient States and Infrastructural Power: Europe, Asia, and America*, ed. C. Ando and S. Richardson. Philadelphia: 17–62.

(2019) 'Walking Capital: The Economic Function and Social Location of Babylonian Servitude', *Journal of Global Slavery* 4.3: 285–342.

Ries, G. (1999) 'Zur Strafbarkeit des Meineids im Recht des Alten Orients', in *Festschrift für Dieter Medicus zum 70. Geburtstag*, ed. V. Beuthien. Cologne: 457–68.

Riggsby, A. M. (1999) *Crime and Community in Ciceronian Rome*. Austin, TX.

(2010) *Roman Law and the Legal World of the Romans*. Cambridge.

Rilinger, R. (1988) *Honestiores/Humiliores: Zu einer sozialen Dichotomie im Strafrecht der römischen Kaiserzeit*. Munich.

Robinson, O. F. (2007) *Penal Practice and Penal Policy in Ancient Rome*. London and New York.

Rocher, L. (1968/69) 'Lawyers' in Classical Hindu Law', *Law & Society Review* 3.2/3: 383–402.

(1989) 'Caritram pustakaraṇe', *Indologica Taurinensia* 7: 345–50.

(1992) 'Inheritance and śrāddha: The Principle of "Spiritual Benefit"', in *Ritual, State and History in South Asia*, ed. A. W. Van den Hoek and M. S. Oort. Leiden: 637–49.

(2012) *Studies in Hindu Law and Dharmaśāstra*, ed. D. R. Davis, Jr. London, New York and Dehli.

(2017) 'Inheritance: *dāyabhāga*', in Olivelle and Davis (2017): 164–78.

Rodriguez, C. (2010) 'Les *Acta Isidori*: Un procès pénal devant l'Empereur Claude', *Revue historique de droit français et étranger* 88: 1–41.

Rolfe, J. C. (ed.) (1927) *Aulus Gellius: Attic Nights, Books I–V*. Cambridge, MA.

Roller, M. B. (2001) *Constructing Autocracy: Aristocrats and Emperors in Julio-Claudian Rome*. Princeton, NJ.

Rose, C. M. (1990) 'Property as Storytelling: Perspectives from Game Theory, Narrative Theory, Feminist Theory', *Yale Journal of Law and Humanities* 2: 37–57. (Repr. in Ellickson, Rose and Smith (2014): 16–28.)

Rosenstein, R. (2007) 'War and Peace, Fear and Reconciliation at Rome', in Raaflaub (2007): 226–44.

Rossi, C. (2004) *Architecture and Mathematics in Ancient Egypt*. Cambridge.

Roth, M. T. (1979) 'Scholastic Tradition and Mesopotamian Law: A Study of FLP 1287, a Prism in the Collection of the Free Library of Philadelphia', PhD thesis, University of Pennsylvania.

(1988) '"She Will Die by the Iron Dagger": Adultery and Neo-Babylonian Marriage', *Journal of the Economic and Social History of the Orient* 31: 186–206.

(1995) 'Mesopotamian Legal Traditions and the Laws of Hammurabi', *Chicago Kent Law Review* 71: 13–39.

(ed. and trans.) (1997) *Law Collections from Mesopotamia and Asia Minor*. 2nd ed. Atlanta.

(1998) 'Gender and Law: A Case Study from Ancient Mesopotamia', in *Gender and Law in the Hebrew Bible and the Ancient Near East*, ed. B. Levinson, T. Frymer-Kensky and V. H. Matthews. Sheffield: 173–84.

(2000) 'The Law Collection of King Hammurabi: Toward an Understanding of Codification and Text', in *La Codification des lois dans l'antiquité*, ed. E. Lévy. Paris: 9–31.

(2013a) 'Women and Law', in *Women in the Ancient Near East*, ed. M. Chavalas. London and New York: 144–74.

(2013b) 'On *mār awīlim* in the Old Babylonian Law Collections', *Journal of Near Eastern Studies* 72.2: 267–72.

Rubenstein, J. (2001) 'The Rise of the Babylonian Rabbinic Academy: A Reexamination of the Talmudic Evidence', *Jewish Studies: An Internet Journal* 1: https://jewish-faculty.biu.ac.il/en/node/1042 (accessed 17/06/2022).

(2007) 'Social and Institutional Settings of Rabbinic Literature', in *Cambridge Companion to the Talmud and Rabbinic Literature*, ed. C. Fonrobert and M. Jaffee. Cambridge: 58–74.

Rubinstein, L. (1993) *Adoption in IV. Century Athens*. Copenhagen.

(2000) *Litigation and Cooperation: Supporting Speakers in the Courts of Classical Athens*. Stuttgart.

(2005) 'Differentiated Rhetorical Strategies in the Athenian Courts', in Gagarin and Cohen (2005): 129–45.

(2007) '"*Arai*" in Greek Laws in the Classical and Hellenistic Periods: Deterrence or Concession to Tradition?' in *Symposion 2005*, ed. E. Cantarella. Vienna: 269–86.

Rüfner, T. (2016) 'Imperial *Cognitio* Process', in *The Oxford Handbook of Roman Law and Society*, ed. P. J. du Plessis, C. Ando and K. Tuori. Oxford: 257–69.

Rüpke, J. (2006) 'Religion in *Lex Ursonensis*', in *Religion and Law in Classical and Christian Rome*, ed. C. Ando and J. Rüpke. Stuttgart: 34–46.

(2007) *Religion of the Romans*. Cambridge and Malden, MA.

(2011) 'History', in *The Routledge Handbook of Research Methods in the Study of Religion*, ed. S. Engler and M. Stausberg. London: 285–309.

(2014) 'Historicizing Religion: Varro's *Antiquitates* and the History of Religion in the Late Roman Republic', *History of Religions* 53: 246–68.

Ruschenbusch, E. (ed) (1966) *Solōnos nomoi: Die Fragmente des solonischen Gesetzeswerkes mit einer Text- und Überlieferungsgeschichte*. Wiesbaden.

Ruskola, T. (2012) 'The East Asian Legal Tradition', in *The Cambridge Companion to Comparative Law*, ed. M. Bussani and U. Mattei. Cambridge: 257–77.

(2013) *Legal Orientalism, China, the United States, and Modern Law*. Cambridge.

Ryholt, K. (2000) 'A New Version of the Introduction to the Teachings of "Onch-Sheshonqy"', in *A Miscellany of Demotic Texts and Studies*, ed. P. J. Frandsen and K. Ryholt. Copenhagen: 113–40.

Said, R. (1993) *The River Nile: Geology, Hydrology, Utilization*. Oxford.

Saller, R. P. (1994) *Patriarchy, Property and Death in the Roman Family*. Cambridge.

(1999) 'Pater Familias, Mater Familias, and the Gendered Semantics of the Roman Household', *Classical Philology* 94.2: 182–97.

(2005) 'Framing the Debate over Growth in the Ancient Economy', in *The Ancient Economy. Evidence and Models*, ed. J. G. Manning and I. Morris. Stanford: 223–38.

Salomon, R. (1998) 'Two New Kharoṣṭhī Documents from Central Asia', *Central Asiatic Journal* 32.1–2: 98–108.
Samely, A. (1990) 'What Scripture Does Not Say: Interpretation through Contrast in Tagum Pseudo-Jonathan', in *Die Alttestamentliche Botschaft als Wegweisung: Festschrift für Heinz Reinalt*, ed. J. Zmijewski. Stuttgart: 253–83.
  (1991) 'Between Scripture and Its Rewording: Towards a Classification of Rabbinic Exegesis', *Journal of Jewish Studies* 42: 39–67.
  (1992) 'Scripture's Implicature: The Midrashic Assumptions of Relevance and Consistency', *Journal of Semitic Studies* 36: 167–205.
  (1995) 'Stressing Scripture's Words: Semantic Contrast as a Midrashic Technique in the Mishna', *Journal of Jewish Studies* 46: 196–229.
  (1999) 'Scripture's Segments and Topicality in Rabbinic Discourse and the Pentateuch Tar-gum', *Journal of the Aramaic Bible* 1: 87–123.
  (2000) 'Delaying the Progress from Case to Case: Redundancy in the Halakic Discourse of the Mishna', in *Jewish Ways of Reading the Bible*, ed. G. Brooke. Oxford: 99–132.
  (2002) *Rabbinic Interpretation of Scripture in the Mishnah*. Oxford.
  (2017) 'Educational Features in Ancient Jewish Literature: An Overview of Unknowns', in *Jewish Education from Antiquity to the Middle Ages: Studies in Honour of Philip S. Alexander*, ed. G. Brooke and R. Smithuis. Leiden: 147–200.
Sandowicz, M. (2012) *Oaths and Curses: A Study in Neo- and Late Babylonian Legal Formulary*. AOAT 398. Münster.
Sanft, C. (2005) 'Six of One, Two Dozen of the Other: The Abatement of Mutilating Penalties under Han Emperor Wen', *Asia Major* 18: 79–100.
  (2008–2009) 'Edict of Monthly Ordinances for the Four Seasons in Fifty Articles from 5 CE Introduction to the Wall Inscription Discovered at Xuanguanzhi, with Annotated Translation', *Early China* 32: 178–208.
Sankararama Sastri, C. (1926) *Fictions in the Development of the Hindu Law Texts*. Madras.
Satlow, M. (2001) *Jewish Marriage in Antiquity*. Princeton, NJ.
  (2010) 'Marriage and Divorce', in *The Oxford Handbook of Jewish Daily Life in Roman Palestine*, ed. C. Hezser. Oxford: 344–59.
Saunders, T. J. (1994) *Plato's Penal Code: Tradition, Controversy, and Reform in Greek Penology*. Oxford.
Sawyer, R. D. (1993) *The Seven Military Classics of Ancient China*. Boulder, San Francisco and Oxford.
Schafer, E. H. (1963) *The Golden Peaches of Samarkand: A Study of T'ang Exotics*. Berkeley.
Schaps, D. M. (1979) *Economic Rights of Women in Ancient Greece*. Edinburgh.
Scharfe, H. (1989) *The State in Indian Tradition*. Leiden.
  (1993) *Investigations in Kauṭilya's Manual of Political Science*. 2nd ed. Wiesbaden.
  (2002) *Education in Ancient India*. Leiden.
Scheid, J. (2003) *An Introduction to Roman Religion*, trans. J. Lloyd. Bloomington
  (2005) *Quand faire, c'est croire. Les rites sacrificiels des Romains*. Paris.
Scheidel, W. (2013) 'Studying the State', in *The Oxford Handbook of the State in the Ancient Near East and Mediterranean*, ed. P. F. Bang and W. Scheidel. Oxford: 5–57.
  (2017) 'Slavery and Forced Labour in Early China and the Roman World', in *Eurasian Empires in Antiquity and the Early Middle Ages: Contact and Exchange between the Graeco-*

Roman World, Inner Asia and China, ed. H. Kim, F. Vervaet and S. Adali. Cambridge: 110–32.

Scheuble-Reiter, S. and Bussi, S. (2019) 'Social Identity and Upward Mobility: Elite Groups, Lower Classes, and Slaves', in *A Companion to Greco-Roman and Late Antique Egypt*, ed. K. Vandorpe. Hoboken, NJ: 283–98.

Schiavone, A. (2012) *The Invention of Law in the West*, trans. J. Carden and A. Shugaar. Cambridge, MA.

Schiller, A. A. (1978) *Roman Law: Mechanisms of Development*. The Hague.

Schmidt, K. I. (2017) 'Henry Maine's "Modern Law": From Status to Contract and Back Again?', *American Journal of Comparative Law* 65: 145–86.

Schneider, T. J. (2011) *An Introduction to Mesopotamian Religion*. Grand Rapids, MI.

Schofer, J. (2005) *The Making of a Sage: A Study in Rabbinic Ethics*. Madison, WI.

Schopen, G. (1994) 'Doing Business for the Lord: Lending on Interest and Written Loan Contracts in the *Mūlasarvāstivāda-Vinaya*', *Journal of the American Oriental Society* 114.4: 527–54.

(1997) 'The Buddha as an Owner of Property and Permanent Resident in Medieval Indian Monasteries', in *Stones, Bones, and Buddhist Monks: Collected Papers on the Archaeology, Epigraphy, and Texts of Monastic Buddhism in India*, ed. G. Schopen. Honolulu: 258–89.

Schwartz, B. J. (2009) 'Introduction: The Strata of the Priestly Writings and the Revised Relative Dating of P and H', in *The Strata of the Priestly Writings*, ed. S. Shectman and J. S. Baden. Zurich: 1–12.

Schwartz, S. (2001) *Imperialism and Jewish Society, 200 BCE to 640 CE*. Princeton, NJ.

(2007) 'Political Geography of Rabbinic Texts', in *The Cambridge Companion to the Talmud and Rabbinic Literature*, ed. C. Fonrobert and M. Jaffee. Cambridge: 75–96.

Scogin, H. T. (1990) 'Between Heaven and Man: Contract and State in Han Dynasty China', *Southern California Law Review* 63: 1325–404.

Scullion, S. (2007) 'Festivals', in *A Companion to Greek Religion*, ed. D. Ogden. Malden, MA and Oxford: 190–203.

Scurlock, J. (2003) 'Ancient Mesopotamian Medicine', in *A Companion to the Ancient Near East*, ed. D. C. Snell. Oxford: 302–15.

(2006) *Magico-Medical Means of Treating Ghost-Induced Illnesses in Ancient Mesopotamia*. Leiden.

Sedley, D. (2017) 'Becoming Godlike', in *The Cambridge Companion to Ancient Ethics*, ed. C. Bobonich. Cambridge: 319–37.

Segre, M. (ed.) (1993) *Iscrizioni di Cos*. Rome.

Shaw, B. D. (1984) 'Bandits in the Roman Empire', *Past & Present* 105: 3–52.

(1993) 'The Passion of Perpetua', *Past & Present* 139: 3–45.

(2003) 'Judicial Nightmares and Christian Memory', *Journal of Early Christian Studies* 11.4: 533–63.

(2022) 'What Is This History to Be?', in *Ancient History from Below: Subaltern Experiences and Actions in Context*, ed. C. Courrier and J. C. Magalhaes de Oliveira. Abingdon, Oxford and New York: x–xxv.

Shear, T. L. (1971) 'The Athenian Agora: Excavations of 1970', *Hespera* 40: 241–79.

Shupak, N. (1992) 'A New Source for the Study of the Judiciary and Law of Ancient Egypt: "The Tale of the Eloquent Peasant"', *Journal of Near Eastern Studies* 51.1: 1–18.

Sickinger, J. P. (1999) *Public Records and Archives in Classical Athens*. Chapel Hill.
Sigurdsson, G. (2004) *The Medieval Icelandic Saga and Oral Tradition: A Discourse on Method*. Cambridge, MA. (Icelandic original published in 2002.)
Sims-Williams, N. (ed. and trans.) (2012) *Bactrian Documents from Northern Afghanistan. 1, Legal and Economic Documents*. Oxford.
Sippel, B. (2020) *Gottesdiener und Kamelzüchter: Das Alltags- und Sozialleben der Sobek-Priester im kaiserzeitlichen Fayum*. Wiesbaden.
   (2022) 'Temples in Decline? The Egyptian Priesthood under Roman Rule', in *Proceedings of the 29th International Congress of Papyrology*, Vol. II, ed. M. Capasso, P. Davoli and N. Pellé. Lecce: 905–14.
Sisov, S. K. (2021a) 'Federal Citizenship and the Right of ΕΓΚΤΗΣΙΣ in the Achaian *Koinon*', *Zeitschrift für Papyrologie und Epigraphik* 217: 105–18.
   (2021b) 'Federal Citizenship and the Right of ΕΓΚΤΗΣΙΣ in the Aitolian *Koinon*', *Zeitschrift für Papyrologie und Epigraphik* 217: 119–27.
Sizgorich, T. (2009) *Violence and Belief in Late Antiquity: Militant Devotion in Christianity and Islam*. Philadelphia.
Skosey, L. A. (1996) 'The Legal System and Legal Tradition of the Western Zhou ca. 1045–771 BCE', PhD thesis, University of Chicago.
Slanski, K. E. (2003a) *The Babylonian Entitlement Narûs (Kudurrus): A Study in Their Form and Function*. Boston.
   (2003b) 'Middle Babylonian Period', in Westbrook (2003a): 485–520.
Smith, H. E. (2000) 'Semicommon Property Rights and Scattering in the Open Fields', *Journal of Legal Studies* 29.1: 131–69.
   (2017) 'Economics of Property Law', in *The Oxford Handbook of Law and Economics. Vol. 2. Private and Commercial Law*, ed. F. Parisi. Oxford. Online edition: https://doi.org/10.1093/oxfordhb/9780199684205.013.007 (accessed 15 Sept. 2022).
Smith, H. S. (1995) 'Marriage and the Family in Ancient Egypt. I. Marriage and Family Law', in *Legal Documents of the Hellenistic World: Papers from a Seminar*, ed. M. J. Geller and H. Maehler. London: 46–57.
Smith, R. R. R. (2002) 'The Statue Monument of Oecumenius: A New Portrait of a Late Antique Governor from Aphrodisias', *Journal of Roman Studies* 92: 134–56.
Snell, D. C. (2011) 'Slavery in the Ancient Near East', in *The Cambridge World History of Slavery*, Vol. I, ed. K. Bradley and P. Cartledge. Cambridge: 4–21.
Sokolowski, F. (ed.) (1955) *Lois sacrées d'Asie Mineure*. Paris.
   (ed.) (1962) *Lois sacrées des cités grecques: Supplement*. Paris.
   (ed.) (1969) *Lois sacrées des cités grecques*. Paris.
Sollberger, E. (1956) *Corpus des Inscriptions Royales Présargoniques de Lagas*. Geneva.
Sommerstein, A. H. (2013) 'The Judicial Sphere', in *Oath and State in Ancient Greece*, ed. A. Sommerstein and A. Baylis. Berlin: 57–119.
Sommerstein, A. H., and I. C. Torrance (eds.) (2014) *Oaths and Swearing in Ancient Greece*. Berlin.
Stackert, J. (2007) *Rewriting the Torah: Literary Revision in Deuteronomy and the Holiness Legislation*. Tübingen.
Stein, P. (1995) 'Interpretation and Legal Reasoning in Roman Law', *Chicago-Kent Law Review* 70: 1539–56.
   (1999) *Roman Law in European History*. Cambridge.

Steinkeller, P. and Hudson, M. (eds.) (2015) *Labour in the Ancient World*. Dresden.
Stol, M. (1998) 'The Care of the Elderly in Mesopotamia in the Old Babylonian Period', in *The Care of the Elderly in the Ancient Near East*, ed. M. Stol and S. P. Vleeming. Leiden: 59–118.
  (2000) *Birth in Babylonia and the Bible: Its Mediterranean Setting*. Cuneiform Monographs 14. Groningen.
  (2016) *Women in the Ancient Near East*. Boston and Berlin.
Strack, H. L. and Stemberger, G. (1996) *Introduction to Talmud and Midrash*. 2nd ed. Minneapolis.
Straumann, B. (2016) *Crisis and Constitutlonalism: Roman Political Thought from the Fall of the Republic to the Age of Revolution*. Oxford.
Stroh, W. (2004) 'De Domo Sua: Legal Problem and Structure', in Powell and Paterson (2004): 313–70.
Sun, Z. J. (2009) 'Life and Afterlife in Early Imperial China', *American Journal of Archaeology* 113.3: 1–9.
Syme, R. (1952; orig. 1939) *The Roman Revolution*. Oxford.
Szegedy-Maszak, A. (1978) 'Legends of the Greek Lawgivers', *Greek, Roman and Byzantine Studies* 19: 199–209.
  (1981) *The Nomoi of Theophrastus*. New York.
Tabory, J. (2006) 'Jewish Festivals in Late Antiquity', in *The Cambridge History of Judaism*, Vol. IV: *The Late Roman-Rabbinic Period*, ed. S. Katz. Cambridge: 556–72.
Talamanca, M. (2000-2001) 'I clienti di Q. Cervidio Scaevola', in *Bullettino dell'Istituto di diritto romano* 103–4: 483–699.
Tamanaha, B. Z. (2001) *General Jurisprudence of Law and Society*. Oxford.
  (2008) 'Understanding Legal Pluralism: Past to Present, Local to Global', *Sydney Law Review* 30: 375–411.
Tambiah, S. J. (1976) *World Conqueror & World Renouncer: A Study of Buddhism and Polity in Thailand against a Historical Background*. Cambridge.
Tate, J. C., de Lima Lopes, J. R. and Botero-Bernal, A. (eds.) (2019) *Global Legal History: A Comparative Law Perspective*. London.
Taubenschlag, R. (1955) *The Law of Greco-Roman Egypt in the Light of the Papyri*. 2nd rev. ed. Warsaw.
Taylor, T. S. (2016) 'Social Status, Legal Status and Legal Privilege', in *The Oxford Handbook of Roman Law and Society*, ed. P. J. du Plessis, C. Ando and K. Tuori. Oxford: 349–61.
Tcherikover, V. (ed.) (1957–64) *Corpus Papyrorum Judaicarum*. 3 vols. Cambridge, MA.
Teeter, D. A. (2014) *Scribal Laws: Exegetical Variation in the Textual Transmission of Biblical Law in the Late Second Temple Period*. Tübingen.
Teeter, E. (2020) 'Ritual and Worship in Ancient Egypt', in *The Oxford Handbook of Ritual and Worship in the Hebrew Bible*, ed. S. E. Balentine. Oxford: 19–35.
Terrenato, N. (2019) *The Early Roman Expansion into Italy: Elite Negotiation and Family Agendas*. Cambridge.
Thomas, P. (2014) 'Ars aequi et boni, legal argumentation and the correct legal solution', *Zeitschrift der Savigny-Stiftung für Rechtsgeschichte, Romanistische Abteilung* 131: 41–59.

Thomas, R. (1994) 'Law and the Lawgiver in Athenian Democracy', in *Ritual, Finance, Politics: Athenian Democratic Accounts Presented to David Lewis*, ed. R. Osborne and S. Hornblower. Oxford: 119–34.

Thomas, Y. (2011) *Les Opérations du droit*. Paris.

Thompson, D. J. (1999) 'New and Old in the Ptolemaic Fayyum', in *Agriculture in Egypt. From Pharaonic to Modern Times*, ed. A. K. Bowman and E. Rogan. Oxford: 123–38.

  (2011) 'Slavery in the Hellenistic World', in *The Cambridge World History of Slavery*, Vol. I: *The Ancient Mediterranean World*, ed. K. Bradley and P. Cartledge. Cambridge: 194–213.

Thompson, H. (1934) *A Family Archive from Siut, from Papyri in the British Museum Including an Account of a Trial before the Laocritae in the Year BC 170*. Oxford.

Todd, S. C. (1993) *The Shape of Athenian Law*. Oxford.

  (1994) 'Status and Contract in Fourth-Century Athens', in *Symposion 1993: Vorträge zur griechischen und hellenistischen Rechtsgeschichte*, ed. G. Thür. Cologne: 125–40.

  (1996) 'Lysias against Nikomachos: The Fate of the Expert in Athenian Law', in *Greek Law in its Political Setting*, ed. L. Foxhall and A. Lewis. Oxford: 101–31.

  (2000) 'How to Execute People in Classical Athens', in *Law and Social Status in Classical Athens*, ed. V. J. Hunter and J. Edmondson. New York: 31–51.

Tokyo National Museum (1998) *Illustrated Catalogue of Tokyo National Museum Clay Seals*. Tokyo.

Tomlin, R. (2010) 'Cursing a Thief in Iberia and Britain', in *Magical Practice in the Latin West*, ed. R. Gordon and F. M Simón. Leiden: 245–73.

Tongzu, Qu [T'ung-tsu Ch'ü] (1980) *Law and Society in Traditional China*. Westport, CT.

Treggiari, S. (1991) *Roman Marriage: Iusti Coniuges from the Time of Cicero to the Time of Ulpian*. Oxford.

  (2019) *Servilia and Her Family*. Oxford.

Tritle, L. A. (2007) '"Laughing for Joy": War and Peace among the Greeks', in Raaflaub (2007): 172–90.

Tuori, K. (2015) *Lawyers and Savages: Ancient History and Legal Realism in the Making of Legal Anthropology*. Abingdon-on-Thames.

  (2016) *The Emperor of Law: The Emergence of Roman Imperial Adjudication*. Oxford.

Tuplin, C. (1987) 'The Leuctra Campaign: Some Outstanding Problems', *Klio* 69: 72–107.

Turner, K. (1989) 'The Theory of Law in the Ching-fa', *Early China* 14: 55–76.

  (1993) 'War, Punishment, and the Law of Nature in Early Chinese Concepts of the State', *Harvard Journal of Asiatic Studies* 53.2: 291–96.

Twining, W. (2009) *General Jurisprudence: Understanding Law from a Global Perspective*. Cambridge.

  (2010) 'Normative and Legal Pluralism: A Global Perspective', *Duke Journal of Comparative & International Law* 20.3: 473–518.

  (2021) 'Normative and Legal Pluralism: A Global Perspective', in *The Oxford Handbook of Transnational Law*, ed. P. Zumbansen. Oxford: 31–66.

Twitchett, D. C. (1970) *Financial Administration under the T'ang Dynasty*. 2nd ed. Cambridge.

Urbach, E. (1968) 'The Talmudic Sage: Character and Authority', *Journal of World History* 11: 116–47.

Urman, D. (1995) 'The House of Assembly and the House of Study: Are They One and the Same?', in *Ancient Synagogues: Historical Analysis and Archaeological Discovery*, ed. D. Urman and P. V. M. Flesher. Leiden: 232–55.

Usher, S. (1999) *Greek Oratory: Tradition and Originality*. Oxford.

Valerio, M. (2019) 'The Egyptians' Ambivalent Relationship with Foreigners: The Case of the Prisoners of War in the New Kingdom', in *A Stranger in the House – the Crossroads III: Proceedings of an International Conference on Foreigners in Ancient Egyptian and Near Eastern Societies of the Bronze Age held in Prague, September 10–13, 2018*, ed. J. Mynářová, M. Kilani and S. Alivernin. Prague: 371–85.

Van Brennan, R. (1996) *The Limits of Participation: Women and Civic Life in the Greek East in the Hellenistic and Roman Periods*. Amsterdam.

Van den Boorn, G. (1985) 'Wdc-ryt and Justice at the Gate', *Journal of Near Eastern Studies* 44: 1–25.

(1988) *The Duties of the Vizier: Civil Administration in the Early New Kingdom*. London.

Van De Mieroop, M. (2015) *Philosophy before the Greeks: The Pursuit of Truth in Ancient Babylonia*. Princeton, NJ.

(2022) 'Making Peace in the Ancient Near East', in *Making Peace in the Ancient World: Proceedings of the Seventh Melammu Workshop Padova, 5–7 November 2018*, ed. G. B. Lanfranchi, S. Ponchia and R. Rollinger. Melammu Workshops and Monographs 5. Münster: 19–30.

Vandermeersch, L. (1978) *Le Statut des terres en Chine à l'époque des Han*, in *Il diritto in Cina*, ed. L. Lanciotti. Firenze.

Vandorpe, K. and Waebens, S. (2009) *Reconstructing Pathyris' Archives: A Multicultural Community in Hellenistic Egypt*. Brussels.

van Gulik, R. H. (1956) *T'ang-Yin-Pi-Shih' Parallel Cases from under the Pear Tree: A 13th Century Manual of Jurisprudence and Detection*. Leiden.

van Heel, K. D. (2021) *The Archive of the Theban Choachyte Petebaste Son of Peteamunip (Floruit 7th Century BCE)*. Papyrologica Lugduno-Batava 38. Leiden.

van Oven, J. C. (1958) 'La Stipulation, a-t-elle Dégénerée?', *Tijdschrift voor Rechtsgeschiedenis* 26: 409–36.

Veenhof, K. R. (1991) 'Private Summons and Arbitration among the Old Assyrian Traders', in *Studies Dedicated to H.I.H. Prince Takahito Mikasa on the Occasion of His Seventy-Fifth Birthday*, ed. M. Mori, H. Ogawa and M. Yoshikawa. Wiesbaden: 437–59.

(1995) 'In Accordance with the Words of the Stele: Evidence for Old Assyrian Legislation', *Chicago-Kent Law Review* 70: 1717–44.

(1998) 'Old Assyrian and Ancient Anatolian Evidence for the Care of the Elderly', in *The Care of the Elderly in the Ancient Near East*, ed. M. Stol and S. P. Vleeming. Leiden: 119–51.

(2003) 'Mesopotamia: Old Assyrian Period', in Westbrook (2003a): 431–83.

(2007) 'Sisterly Advice on an Endangered Marriage in an Old Assyrian Letter', in *Studies Presented to Robert D. Biggs*, ed. M. Roth, W. Farber, M. W. Stolper and P. von Bechtolsheim. Chicago: 285–304.

Veïsse, A-E. (2004) *Les 'révoltes égyptiennes': Recherches sur les troubles intérieurs en Égypte du règne de Ptolémée III à la conquête romaine*. Leuven and Paris.

Venkayya, V. (1904–5) 'Two Inscriptions at Uttaramallūr', in *Annual Report of the Archaeological Survey of India, 1904–5*. Calcutta: 131–45.

Venticinque, P. F. (2016) *Honor among Thieves: Craftsment, Merchants, Associations in Roman and Late Roman Egypt.* Ann Arbor, MI.

Vérilhac, A. M. and Vial, C. (eds.) (1998) *Le mariage grec du VI siècle à l'époque d'Auguste.* BCH Supplement 32. Athens.

Versteeg, R. (1988–89) 'From Status to Contract: A Contextual Analysis of Maine's Famous Dictum', *Whittier Law Review* 10: 669–81.

  (2002) *Law in Ancient Egypt.* Durham, NC.

  (2021) 'Ancient Egypt and Laws Relating to the Status of Women', *Women & Criminal Justice.* Online publication: https://doi.org/10.1080/08974454.2021.2004971 (accessed 29/09/2022).

Villard, P. (2000) 'Les textes judiciaires néo-assyriens', in *Rendre la justice en Mésopotamie: Archives judiciaires du Proche-Orient ancien (IIIe-Ier millénaires avant J.-C.)*, ed. F. Joannès. Paris: 171–200.

  (2023) 'Neo-Assyrian Judicial Decisions' in S. Démare-Lafont and D. Fleming (eds.), *Judicial Decisions in the Ancient Near East.* Writings from the Ancient World 43. Atlanta: 429–483.

Vinson, S. (2018) *The Craft of a Good Scribe: History, Narrative and Meaning in the First Tale of Setne Khaemwas.* Leiden.

Viswanatha, S. V. (1925) *International Law in Ancient India.* London, New York and Toronto.

Vlassopoulos, K. (2009) 'Slavery, Freedom and Citizenship in Classical Athens: Beyond a Legalistic Approach', *European Review of History: Revue européenne d'histoire* 16.3: 347–63.

Vleeming, S. (1989) 'Strijd om het erfdeel van Tefhape', in *Familiearchieven uit het land van Pharao*, ed. P. W. Pestman. Louvain: 30–45.

von Dassow, E. 2014. 'Awīlum and Muškēnum in the Age of Hammurabi', in *La famille dans le Proche-Orient ancien*, ed. L. Marti. Winona Lake: 291–308.

von Jhering, R. (1919, [1893]) *Law as a Means to an End*, trans. I. Husik. Boston.

Wacher, J. (2013) *The Roman World.* 2nd ed. London.

Waerzeggers, C. (2020) 'Changing Marriage Practices in Babylonia from the Late Assyrian to the Persian Period', *Journal of Ancient Near Eastern History* 7.2: 101–31.

Wallacker, B. (1985) 'The Spring and Autumn Annals as a Source of Law in Han China', *Journal of Chinese Studies* 2: 59–72.

  (1986) 'Chang Fei's Preface to the Chin Code of Laws', *T'oung Pao* 72: 229–68.

Waldron, J. (2020) 'Property and Ownership', in *The Stanford Encyclopedia of Philosophy* (Summer 2020 Edition), ed. E. N. Zalta. Online edition: https://plato.stanford.edu/archives/sum2020/entries/property/ (accessed 19/9/2022).

Walzer, M., Lorberbaum, M. and Zohar, N. J. (eds.) (2003) *The Jewish Political Tradition.* Vol. II: *Membership.* New Haven.

Wang, A. (2000) *Cosmology and Political Culture in Early China.* Cambridge.

Waterfield, R. (ed.) (1998) *Herodotus: The Histories.* Oxford.

Watson, A. (1993) *International Law in Archaic Rome.* Baltimore.

Watson, B. (1961) *Records of the Grand Historian of China: Translated from the Shih-chi of Ssu-ma Ch'ien.* Vol. I: *Early Years of the Han Dynasty, 209–141 BC.* New York.

Watson, J. (2019) 'Paperwork before Paper: Law and Materiality in China's Early Empires (221 BCE–220 CE)', PhD thesis, University of California Berkeley.

Watson, J. L. (1980) *Asian and African Systems of Slavery*. Berkeley and Los Angeles.

Weber, M. (1946) 'Politics as a Vocation', in *From Max Weber: Essays in Sociology*, ed. H. H. Gerth and C. W. Mills. New York: 77–128.

(1978 [1922]) *Economy and Society: An Outline of Interpretive Sociology*. Berkeley.

(1992 [1919]) *Politik als Beruf*. Ditzingen.

Weinfeld, M. (1982) '"Justice and Righteousness" in Israel against the Background of "Social Reforms" in the Ancient Near East', in *Mesopotamien und seine Nachbarn: politische und kulturelle Wechselbeziehungen im Alten Vorderasien vom 4. bis 1. Jahrtausend v. Chr.*, Vol. II, ed. H. J. Nissen and J. Renger. Berlin: 491–519.

Weld, S. (1999) 'Chu Law in Action: Legal Documents from Tomb 2 at Baoshan', in *Defining Chu: Image and Reality in Ancient China*, ed. C. A. Cook and J. S. Major. Honolulu: 77–97.

(2003) 'Grave Matters: Warring States Law and Philosophy', in *Understanding China's Legal System. Essays in Honor of Jerome A. Cohen*, ed. C. S. Hsu. New York: 122–79.

Wells, B. (2004) *The Law of Testimony in the Pentateuchal Codes*. Beihefte zur Zeitschrift für altorientalische und biblische Rechtsgeschichte 4. Wiesbaden.

(2008a) 'What Is Biblical Law? A Look at Pentateuchal Rules and Near Eastern Practice', *Catholic Biblical Quarterly* 70: 223–43.

(2008b) 'The Cultic versus the Forensic: Judahite and Mesopotamian Judicial Procedures in the First Millennium BCE', *Journal of the American Oriental Society* 128: 205–32.

(2020) 'Law and Practice', in *A Companion to the Ancient Near East*, 2nd ed., ed. D. C. Snell. Malden, MA: 165–80.

Wells, B., Magdalene, F. R. and Wunsch, C. (2010) 'The Assertory Oath in Neo-Babylonian and Persian Administrative Texts', *Revue internationale des droits de l'Antiquité* 57: 13–29.

Wendt, H. (2016) *At the Temple Gates: The Religion of Freelance Experts in the Roman Empire*. New York and Oxford.

Wenger, L. (1905) *Römische und antike Rechtsgeschichte. Akademische Antrittsvorlesung an der Universität Wien gehalten am 26. Oktober 1904*. Graz.

(1953) *Die Quellen des Römischen Rechts*. Vienna.

West, E. G. (2003) 'Property Rights in the History of Economic Thought: From Locke to J. S. Mill', in *Property Rights. Cooperation, Conflict, and Law*, ed. T. L. Anderson and F. S. McChesney. Princeton, NJ: 20–42.

Westbrook, R. (1985) 'Biblical and Cuneiform Law Codes', in *Revue Biblique* 92: 247–265. Repr. in *Law from the Tigris to the Tiber: The Writings of Raymond Westbrook*, Vol. I: *The Shared Tradition*, ed. B. Wells and F. Rachel Magdalene. Winona Lake, IN: 3–20.

(1988) *Old Babylonian Marriage Law*. Horn, Austria.

(1989) 'Cuneiform Law Codes and the Origins of Legislation', in *Zeitschrift für Assyriologie* 79: 201–22. (Repr. in *Law from the Tigris to the Tiber: The Writings of Raymond Westbrook*, Vol. I: *The Shared Tradition*, ed. B. Wells and F. Rachel Magdalene, Winona Lake, IN: 73–95.)

(1995) 'Social Justice in the Ancient Near East', in *Social Justice in the Ancient World*, ed. K. D. Irani and M. Silver. Westport, CT: 149–63.

(1998a) 'The Female Slave', in *Gender and Law*, ed. V. Matthews. Sheffield: 214–38.

(1998b) 'Legal Aspects of Care of the Elderly in the Ancient Near East: Conclusion', in *The Care of the Elderly in the Ancient Near East*, ed. M. Stol and S. P. Vleeming. Leiden: 241–50.
(2000) 'International Law in the Amarna Age', in *Amarna Diplomacy? The Beginnings of International Relations*, ed. R. Cohen and R. Westbrook. Baltimore: 29–41.
(2001) 'Social Justice and Creative Jurisprudence in Late Bronze Age Syria', *Journal of the Economic and Social History of the Orient* 44: 22–43.
(ed.) (2003a) *A History of Ancient Near Eastern Law*. 2 vols. Leiden.
(2003b) 'The Character of Ancient Near Eastern Law', in Westbrook (2003a): 1–90.
(2003c) 'Old Babylonian Period', in Westbrook (2003a): 361–430.
(2003d) 'Emar and Vicinity', in Westbrook (2003a): 657–92.
(2005) 'Judges in the Cuneiform Sources', *Maarav* 12: 27–39.
(2006a) 'Reflections on the Law of Homicide in the Ancient World', *Maarav* 13: 145–74.
(2006b) 'Witchcraft and the Law in the Ancient Near East', in *Recht gestern und heute: Festschrift zum 85. Geburtstag von Richard Haase*, ed. J. Hengstl and U. Sick. Wiesbaden: 45–52.
(2007) 'The Trial of Jeremiah', in *Reading the Law: Studies in Honour of Gordon J. Wenham*, ed. J. G. McConville and K. Möller. New York: 95–107.
Westbrook, R. and Wells, B. (2009) *Everyday Law in Biblical Israel*. Louisville, KY.
Westermann, W. L. (1955) *The Slave Systems of Greek and Roman Antiquity*. Philadelphia.
Wewers, G. A. (1984) *Probleme der Bavot-Traktate: Ein redaktionskritischer und theologischer Beitrag zum Talmud Yerushalmi*. Tübingen.
Wezler, A. (2004) 'Dharma in the Veda and the Dharmaśāstras', *Journal of Indian Philosophy* 32.5/6: 629–54.
Whitman, J. Q. (1990) *The Legacy of Roman Law in the German Romantic Era: Historical Vision and Legal Change*. Princeton, NJ.
(1995–96) 'At the Origins of Law and the State: Supervision of Violence, Mutilation of Bodies, or Setting of Prices?', *Chicago-Kent Law Review* 71: 41–84.
(2002) 'Au origines du "monopole de la violence"', in *De la société à la sociologie*, ed. C. Colliot-Thélène and J.-F. Kervégan. Lyon: 71–91.
(2012) *The Verdict of Battle: The Law of Victory and the Making of Modern War*. Cambridge, MA.
Whitmarsh, T. (2015) *Battling the Gods: Atheism in the Ancient World*. New York.
Wiater, N. (2022) 'The Empire Becomes a Body: Power, Space and Movement in Polybius' Histories', in *Late Hellenistic Greek Literature in Dialogue*, ed. J. König and N. Wiater. Cambridge: 36–68.
Wibier, M. (2014) 'The Topography of the Law Book', in *The Roman Paratext: Frame, Texts, Readers*, ed. L. Jansen. Cambridge: 56–72.
Wieacker, F. (1988) *Römische Rechtsgeschichte: Quellenkunde, Rechtsbildung, Jurisprudenz und Rechtsliteratur. Erster Abschnitt: Einleitung, Quellenkunde, Frühzeit und Republik*. Munich.
Wieling, H. (2000) 'Assessoren in der Spätantike', in *Timai (Festschrift für) I. Triantaphyllopoulos*. Athens: 339–56.
Wiese, H. and Das, S. (2019) *The Charter of Viṣṇuṣena*. Halle an der Saale.
Wilbur, C. M. (1943) *Slavery in China during the Former Han Dynasty 206 BC –AD 25*. Chicago.
Wilcke, C. (2003) 'Early Dynastic and Sargonic Periods', in Westbrook (2003a): 141–82.

(2007) *Early Ancient Near Eastern Law: A History of Its Beginnings – the Early Dynastic and Sargonic Periods*. Winona Lake, IN.

Wilcken, U. (ed.) (1977) *Urkunden der Ptolemäerzeit (ältere Funde)*. 2 vols. Berlin.

Wilhelm, G. (1995) 'Ein neuer Text zum Ordal in Nuzi (*JEN* 659 + SMN 1651)', in *General Studies*, ed. D. I. Owen. Winona Lake, IN: 71–74.

Willis, M. D. (2009) *The Archaeology of Hindu Ritual: Temples and the Establishment of the Gods*. Cambridge.

Wilson, J. A. (1948) 'The Oath in Ancient Egypt', *Journal of Near Eastern Studies* 7: 129–56.

Wimpfheimer, B. (2019) 'Codes', in *A Cultural History of Law in Antiquity*, ed. J. Etxabe. London and New York: 59–74.

Winkel, L. (2020) 'The Method of Comparative Law Reconsidered in the Light of Legal Epistemology and the Reception of Roman Law', in *Comparative Law – Mixes, Movements, and Metaphors*, ed. S. P. Donlan and J. Mair. London: 158–70.

Wisniewski, T., Crahcarz, M. and Standzikowski, K. (eds.) (2020) 'Turonian Flint Economy in the Easternmost Magdalenian: New Data from Stare Baraki, Site 1 (Eastern Poland)', *Archaeological and Anthropological Sciences* 12.281: 1–24.

Wohl, V. (2010) *Law's Cosmos: Juridical Discourse in Athenian Forensic Oratory*. Cambridge.

Wöhrle, J. (2021) 'The Priestly Writing(s): Scope and Nature', in *The Oxford Handbook of the Pentateuch*, ed. J. S. Baden and J. Stackert. Oxford: 255–75.

Wolff, H-J. (1960) 'Plurality of laws in Ptolemaic Egypt', *Revue international des droits de l'Antiquité* 7: 191–223.

(1962) *Das Justizwesen der Ptolemäer*. Münchener Beiträge zur Papyrusforschung und antiken Rechtsgeschichte 44. Munich.

Wright, A. F. (1979) 'The Sui Dynasty (581–617)', in *The Cambridge History of China*, ed. D. C. Twitchett. Cambridge: 48–149.

Wright, C. J. H. (1990) *God's People in God's Land: Family, Land, and Property in the Old Testament*. Grand Rapids, MI.

Wright, D. P. (2009) *Inventing God's Law: How the Covenant Code of the Bible Used and Revised the Laws of Hammurabi*. Oxford.

Wood, F. (2002) *The Silk Road*. Berkeley.

Wunsch, C. (2020) 'Grundzüge des Babylonischen Erbrechts in Neubabylonischer und Frühachämenidischer Zeit', in *Altorientalische Studien zu Ehren von Konrad Volk* 17, ed. J. Baldwin and J. Matuszak. Munich: 453–509.

Yadin, I. A. (2004) *Scripture as Logos: Rabbi Ishmael and the Origins of Midrash*. Philadelphia.

Yamamoto, T. and Ikeda, O. (eds.) (1987) *Tun-huang and Turfan Documents, Concerning Social and Economic History: Contracts* (A). Tokyo.

Yates, R. D. S. (1994) 'The Yin-Yang Texts from Yinqueshan: An Introduction and Partial Reconstruction, with Notes on Their Significance in Relation to Huang-Lao Daoism', *Early China* 19: 75–144.

(1995) 'State Control of Bureaucrats under the Qin: Techniques and Procedures', *Early China* 20: 331–65.

(1997) (ed.) *Five Lost Classics: Tao, Huang-Lao, Yin-Yang in Han China*. New York.

(2001) 'Slavery in Early China: A Socio-Cultural Approach', *Journal of East Asian Archaeology* 3.1–2: 283–331.

(2012–13) 'The Qin Slips and Boards from Well No. 1, Liye, Hunan: A Brief Introduction to the Qin Qianling County Archives', *Early China* 35–36: 291–329.

(2014a) 'Introduction: The Empire of the Scribes', in Pines, von Falkenhausen, Shelach and Yates (2014): 141–53.
(2014b) 'The Changing Status of Slaves in the Qin-Han Transition', in Pines, von Falkenhausen, Shelach and Yates (2014): 206–23.
(2021) 'Female Commoners and the Law in Early Imperial China: Evidence from Recently Recovered Documents with Some Comparisons with Classical Rome', in *Rulers and Ruled in Ancient Greece, Rome and China*, ed. H. Beck and G. Vankeerberghen. Cambridge: 156–92.
Yiftach-Firanko, Y. (2008) 'Who Killed the Double Document in Ptolemaic Egypt?', *Archiv für Papyrusforschung* 54: 203–18.
Yü, Y.-S. (1986) 'Han Foreign Relations', in *The Cambridge History of China*, Vol. I: *The Ch'in and Han Empires 221 BC–AD 220*, ed. D. Twitchett and M. Loewe. Cambridge: 377–462.
Yunis, H. (2005) 'The Rhetoric of Law in Fourth-Century Athens', in Gagarin and Cohen (2005): 191–208.
Zaccagnini, C. (2000) 'The Interdependence of the Great Powers', in *Amarna Diplomacy? The Beginnings of International Relations*, ed. R. Cohen and R. Westbrook. Baltimore: 141–53.
(2003) 'Nuzi', in Westbrook (2003a): 565–617.
Zangani, F. (2019) 'Foreign-Indigenous Interactions in the Late Bronze Age Levant: Tuthmosid Imperialism and the Origin of the Amarna Diplomatic System', in *A Stranger in the House – the Crossroads III: Proceedings of an International Conference on Foreigners in Ancient Egyptian and Near Eastern Societies of the Bronze Age Held in Prague, September 10–13, 2018*, ed. J. Mynářová, M. Kilani and S. Alivernini. Prague: 405–23.
Zhang, T. (2011) 'Property Rights in Land, Agricultural Capitalism, and the Relative Decline of Pre-Industrial China', *San Diego International Law Journal* 13: 129–99.
Zhang, Z. (2008) 'A Note on Civil Cases in Early China', *Journal of the American Oriental Society* 128.1: 121–30.
(2010) 'Civil Laws and Civil Justice in Early China', PhD thesis, University of California, Berkeley.
(2011) 'The Legal Concept of Zhi: The Emphasis of Verification in Early China', *Monumenta Serica* 59: 1–16.
(2022) *A History of Civil Law in Early China: Cases, Statutes, and Beyond*. Leiden.
Zimmermann, R. (2001) *Roman Law, Contemporary Law, European Law*. Oxford.
(2015) 'Roman Law in the Modern World', in Johnston (2015): 452–80.

Index

Introductory Note
References such as '178–79' indicate (not necessarily continuous) discussion of a topic across a range of pages. Wherever possible in the case of topics with many references, these have been divided into sub-topics or only the most significant discussions of the topic are listed. Because the entire work is about 'ancient law', the use of this term (and certain others which occur constantly throughout the book) as an entry point has been restricted. Information will be found under the corresponding detailed topics. Cross-references such as '*see also* individual civilizations' direct the reader to entries in a category (e.g. in this case 'China') rather than a specific 'individual civilizations' entry.

abominations, 455–56, 465
  ten, 287, 327, 455–56
abortion, 205, 292, 408, 441–42
Abraham, 129, 433, 575
absolute morality, 139–40
absolute rights, 521
abuses, 210–11, 213, 289, 305, 354–55, 521, 544
accusations, 56–59, 61, 62–63, 299, 303, 304, 326–28, 330–32, 374, 506–7
  false, 205, 305, 359–61, 362
  formal, 23, 60
accusers, 317–18, 319, 326, 331–32, 334–36, 337, 339, 343, 360, 362
  false, 360–61
Achilles, shield of, 15, 24, 79, 188, 209, 216, 335
adharma, 604
adhikaraṇa (court), 320
adikema (injustice), 176
adjudication, 12, 33, 73, 303, 368, 410, 437, 497
  rules, 303
administration, 27, 29–30, 41–42, 45, 62, 67, 88, 212, 221, 251
  imperial, 61, 104
  of justice, xiv, 68, 74, 75, 79, 87, 99, 103, 307, 313
  provincial, 314, 497, 513
  temples, 50, 248, 250
administrative bodies, 87, 150, 155

administrative control, 161
administrative laws/regulations/statutes, 14, 75, 88, 120, 205, 222, 373, 389, 394, 456
administrative rules, 42, 87, 122
administrators, 57, 228, 279, 323, 608
  grand, 363, 372
adoptees, 47, 428, 431
adoption, 7, 11, 34, 47, 53, 86, 424, 428–29, 430–31, 437
adsessores (assistants), 99, 103, 318, 364
adulterers, 96, 420–21, 441, 484, 508
adultery, 205, 295, 322, 329, 339, 384, 408, 441, 501, 508
advisers, 99, 103, 196, 212, 316, 318, 364
advisory councils, 89, 318, 364
aediles, 451–53, 589
Aelius Marcianus, 117
aequitas (equity), 70, 134, 137–38, 183, 201, 242, 378
Aeschylus, 68, 80, 275, 477
Agamemnon, 209, 216
agreements, 50–52, 160, 164–68, 206, 232–33, 418–19, 424–25, 581–85, 586–88, 593–96
  commercial, 148, 168
  formal, 369, 572, 574
  interpersonal, 573
  private, 214, 425, 525, 545, 579, 581
  written, 425, 541, 549, 583

Index

agricultural land, 81, 523, 538–39, 546
agriculture, 512, 565
Aiakeion, 44
Ājīvika mendicant order, 438, 602
Akhenaten, 249
Akkadian, 157, 223, 385, 397, 570
Alexander the Great, 17, 29, 175, 257, 601
Alexandria, 37, 108, 192, 387–88, 394, 399, 441, 513, 579
aliens, 377, 390, 416, 488, 510
   resident, 379, 381
   unassimilable, 395
alliances, 147, 155, 158–59, 161–64, 166–68, 175, 179
   equal, 160, 168
   hegemonic, 162–63, 174
   marriage, 157, 390
   unequal, 159–60
allies, 71, 157–58, 160, 170–71, 174, 175–77, 178–79, 265, 460
ambassadors, 150, 153, 167, 189
amicitia (friendship), 164, 167, 191
amicus populi Romani, 167
Amoraic period, 79, 93–94, 106, 112–13
Amun, 249, 257, 273
Anatolia, 5, 8, 420, 573, 579
   central, 8, 569
ancestors, 147, 172, 227, 253, 257, 328, 427, 429, 454, 604
   male, 519, 557
   rites, 429, 431, 553
animals, 49, 52, 294, 296–97, 479, 511, 547, 587, 589, 591
   draft, 137, 589
   farm, 341, 586
   sacrificial, 264, 266, 285, 571–72
   wild, 132, 479, 552
Antigone, 143, 210
Antinoopolis, 387–88, 395
Antioch, 318, 356
Antiphon, 62, 96
Antoninus Pius, emperor, 103, 356, 583
antyaja (lowest born), 389
Āpastamba-Dharmasūtra, 76, 89, 111, 411, 525, 531
apauruṣeya (not of human origin), 238
apetairos, 382, 441
Aphrodisias, 101, 104
Apollo, 42, 115, 162, 174–75, 283
apostates, 247, 384
apparitores, 100
appeals, 27, 56–57, 61, 62–63, 142, 143, 222–23, 370, 371, 373, 508
   in legal procedure, 370–74

apprenticeship, 416, 431–32
aqueducts, 43, 537
Aramaic language, 41, 47, 106, 112–14, 422
arbitration, 164, 168–69, 174, 180, 213, 216, 219–20, 338, 368, 573
   private, 216, 319
arbitrators, 130, 168, 216, 310, 338, 370
   formal, 366, 370
   public, 317, 338
archaeological evidence, 10, 105, 248, 566, 580, 590
archives, 22–23, 47, 52, 58, 148, 583
   property, 528, 608
   public/official, 48, 51, 53, 497, 530
   royal, 26, 58, 207, 573
archons, 80, 96, 264, 530
Ardhamāgadhī, 10
Areopagus, 68, 96–97, 115, 130, 264, 317, 325, 383, 460
Aristides, Aelius, 504
aristocracy, 147, 191, 385, 447, 463–64, 478, 613
   warrior, 147, 172
aristocrats, 85, 99, 145, 172–73, 454, 459
Aristophanes, 68, 96, 259, 264, 408, 460, 461
Aristotle, 4, 16, 68, 142–43, 464, 481–82, 487, 515, 516, 593
   Rhetoric, 69, 97, 129–30
armies, 173–74, 264, 383, 454, 469, 534
artha (politics and statecraft), 11, 244–45, 301
Arthaśāstra
   commerce and contracts, 572, 590–91, 595
   crime, redress, and social control, 502
   law and state, 207, 216–17, 225
   law as text, 32, 70
   legal procedure, 311, 351, 353
   legal science, 76, 91, 111
   property, 517, 526, 531, 547
   status and family, 389, 392, 404, 411, 413, 427, 438, 442–44
   tradition, 11, 91
   war, peace and interstate relations, 147, 157–58, 159, 171–72, 178
artless proofs, 129, 135
Āryas, 381, 389–90, 402, 544
Asahaya, 286–87
Asclepius, 265
   priesthood of, 283
asebeia (impiety), 251, 289
Asia Minor, 101, 162, 205, 283, 448
āšipu-priest, 299

671

Index

Aśoka
    crime, redress, and social control, 490–91
    edicts, 41, 55
    law and religion, 244, 249–50
    law and state, 195, 217–18
    law as text, 21, 26–27
    property, 525, 532
    status and family, 393
    see also India.
assassins, 493
assault, 58, 324, 336, 339, 343, 476, 480, 495, 497, 501
    physical, 329, 390, 499, 501–3, 595
    verbal, 329, 390, 499, 595
assemblies, 35, 89, 95, 98, 130, 201–2, 205, 216, 264, 490–91
    Athenian, 95, 97, 239, 264–65, 371, 408
    legal *(pariṣad)*, 89
    local, 183, 223, 259, 517
    popular, 29, 134, 175, 188, 452
assessors, 90, 101, 124, 216, 312, 336, 362, 365, 384, 389
assets, 405, 411, 554, 556–57, 558
Aššur, 183, 205, 386, 420
Assyria, 157, 236, 260–61, 408, 420, 442, 571
    contracts, 404, 420
    kings, 261
    Middle Assyria, 8, 40, 91, 270, 299, 386
    Neo-Assyrian period, 298, 315–16, 350, 385
Assyrians, 170, 179, 233, 386, 420
Asyut, 317, 366, 367, 553, 561–62, 564
Athena, 80, 239, 265, 275, 282, 283, 477
Athenians, 50, 95, 96, 175, 199, 210, 216, 251–53, 265, 460–61
Athens, 16, 612–13
    Assembly, 95, 97, 239, 264–65, 371, 408
    cases, 16, 325
    citizens, 95, 381
    commerce and contracts, 588, 593
    courts, 95, 97, 215
    crime, redress and social control, 458–59, 460, 464, 468, 472, 474–78, 483, 489–90, 495, 500
    democracy, 188, 459, 489, 508
    democratic, 163, 458
    empire, 265, 460
    law and religion, 235, 239, 252–53, 258–59, 264–65, 275, 288, 293, 302
    law and state, 199, 209–10, 215–16
    law as text, 21–23, 40, 43–44, 50, 54, 60–62, 63–64, 65, 69, 71
    legal procedure, 311, 317, 325, 337, 340, 344, 346, 355–56, 361, 366–67
    legal science, 79, 80, 94–97, 114
    property, 514, 518, 522, 525, 529–30, 546–47, 551, 556, 564
    status and family, 380, 381–82, 383, 397–98, 408–9, 412, 415, 422, 434
    war, peace and interstate relations, 146, 163–64, 174
atimia, partial, 361
attorneys, 338–39
auctions of land, 539, 546
audience halls, 320, 321
audiences, 22–24, 36, 53, 62, 66, 106, 151, 323
Augustine, Bishop of Hippo, 284, 350
Augustus, emperor, 98, 100, 103, 116, 119, 164, 176–77, 190, 254, 356
authoritative rules, 20, 23, 199
authorities
    central, 22, 310, 608
    divine, 34, 286
    higher, 3, 57–58, 322, 372, 374
    human, 200, 268
    local, 60, 213, 314, 371–72, 465, 474
    public, 23, 206, 437
    state, 35, 193, 210, 438, 440, 447, 454, 501
    supreme legal, 215, 219
authority, 78–79, 92–93, 197–200, 222–23, 234–36, 276–77, 301–2, 310–13, 363–64, 417
    jurisdictional, 204, 310, 322, 323, 332
    ultimate, 140
autopsies, 91, 351, 353
awīlu/amīlu, 385

Babylon, 3, 8–9, 600
    commerce and contracts, 571, 586
    law and religion, 231–33, 235, 236–37, 254, 256
    law and state, 200
    law as text, 41
    legal procedure, 315, 321
    legal science, 78–79, 93–94, 106, 113, 141
    Neo-Babylonian period *see* Neo-Babylonian period
    Old Babylonian period, 148, 200, 316, 330, 360, 366, 397, 404, 414, 419–21
    property, 513, 524, 539, 543
    status and family, 404, 421, 429–31, 432
    war, peace and interstate relations, 157
    see also Eshnunna; Laws of Hammurabi.
Babylonian Talmud *(Bavli)*, 92, 106, 113–14
bad acts, 482, 486, 493–94, 496
bailiffs, 87, 197, 224, 258, 329–30, 360
    district, 592, 609
bamboo, 48, 51
    strips/slips, 26, 38, 48, 58, 61, 65, 401, 609

672

Baoshan, 58
Baraita texts, 112
barristers, 83, 89
Bavli (Babylonian Talmud), 92, 106, 113–14
beatings, 305, 320, 354, 473
behaviour
　human, 86, 140, 186, 245
　normative, 198, 447–48
　proper, 225, 245, 251
'being theft', 121
beliefs, 227, 235, 238, 240, 246–48, 253, 287, 291, 293, 300
Bēl-kāṣir, 291
Bellah, Robert, 233–34
bellum iustum (just war), 169, 176, 178
belly-slaves, 402
Bēlšunu, 343
beneficiaries, 438, 532–33, 555–56
Bentham, Jeremy, 416
Berytus, 102, 104, 108
bestiality, 284, 295–96
betrothal, 419, 421, 425
　gifts, 425
betting, 194, 329, 499, 595
biblical laws, 128, 255, 268, 278, 295
biblical texts/literature, 10, 92, 114, 142, 232, 236, 247–48, 255, 296
biological parents, 414, 428
birth, 80, 292–93, 378, 381, 382, 385, 404, 408–9, 419, 420
blood, 80, 123, 160, 176, 296, 348, 357, 436, 574–75, 597
　covenants, 160, 273, 575
　relations, 144, 554, 574
bloodshed, 80, 225, 293
board of punishments, 313–14
boilerplate language, 549, 564
Boiotian league, 163
bonitary ownership, 552
boundary disputes, 5, 274, 328, 344, 413, 499, 595
Brāhmaṇas, 312, 357, 457
Brahmins, 10–11, 12
　class, 195, 426, 457
　commerce and contracts, 569
　communities, 32, 90
　crime, redress and social control, 457–58, 492
　law and religion, 244, 273, 280–81, 286, 297
　law and state, 208
　law as text, 23, 31, 49
　learned, 208, 531
　legal procedure, 347, 353

legal science, 76
　property, 528, 531, 542
　status and family, 385, 389, 392–93, 401, 410, 438, 442
　war, peace and interstate relations, 172
breach of contract, 328, 336, 495, 497, 499, 595
'bribe-devouring kings', 16, 209
brides, 418–20, 421, 423, 426, 434
　wealth, 47, 411, 427
bronze, 5, 28–29, 137, 152
　inscriptions, 329, 339, 509
　Late Bronze Age, 148, 156, 271, 305, 349, 366
　Middle Bronze Age, 236
　vessels, 48, 57
brothers, 401, 407, 422, 429, 430–31, 432–33, 436, 553, 554–55, 556–57
　father's brothers, 433–34, 466
Buddhism, 10–11, 28, 49, 244, 249–50, 281, 438–39, 532, 602, 614
Buddhist monks, 151, 281
burden of proof, 123, 334, 336–37, 341, 357, 362, 579
bureaucracy
　imperial, 57, 103
　state, 193, 322, 374
bureaucratic procedures, 309, 338
bureaucratic state, 30, 38, 197, 391–92, 435, 495, 611
bureaucrats, 145, 374, 456
　imperial, 266, 323
business transactions, 231, 292, 397
buyers, 44, 45, 49, 132, 282–83, 520, 528–30, 550, 581, 586–92
　title, 586–88

Caesar, Julius, 177, 260
calendars, 288, 511
　holy days and festivals, 254–60
Cambodia, 34
campaigns, 172–75, 253, 454, 510, 558
caṇḍālas, 389
capital offences/cases, 221, 285, 287–88, 326–27, 392, 411, 414, 455, 458, 465
capital punishment, 150, 155, 221, 222, 314, 442, 446, 472, 492, *see also* death, penalty/punishment
capitis deminutio maxima, 475
Caracalla, emperor, 318, 413
careers, 78, 87, 103–4, 264
　political, 62, 99, 107, 452
Carthage, 101, 108, 154, 167, 543
Carthaginians, 167
cases, private, 56, 194, 317, 319, 324, 328, 338, 366, 375

673

castes, 12, 214, 243, 278, 325, 342, 352, 389–90, 392–93, 396
  loss of status, 390, 401
  see also individual castes.
casuistic form, 9, 42, 125
cattle, 45, 49, 52, 290, 541–42, 545, 552, 555, 580, 582
censorate, 313–14
central government, 87, 313–14, 330, 364, 371–72, 439, 474
centuriation, 527, 530, 537
centurions, 221
certificates, 52, 413, 593
  market, 49, 52, 582, 592
chaos, 146, 149, 171, 231, 238, 243, 246
Charter of Viṣṇuṣeṇa, 35, 41, 195, 390, 438
charters, 41, 192, 214, 259, 390, 532, 548
chief judges, 123, 216, 300, 316, 365
childbirth, 292, 294
children, 270, 404–6, 407–10, 414–17, 422–25, 428–29, 431–34, 507–8, 553–54, 556–57
  female, 295, 435
  male, 295, 405, 430
  see also daughters; minors; sons
China, 4, 13–15, 612
  commerce and contracts, 567, 572, 576, 580, 592, 593, 597
  crime, redress and social control, 459, 465, 468, 470, 474, 476, 495, 505–6
  imperial, 139, 196, 211, 339, 442, 466
  law and religion, 238–39, 251, 258, 263, 268, 281, 287–88
  law and state, 181–82, 196–97, 204, 214, 224, 227
  law as text, 21, 22, 24–26, 30, 36–37, 41, 42, 51–52, 62–66, 69–70
  legal procedure, 319, 320, 322, 337, 348, 352, 354, 359–60, 362, 367–68
  legal science, 75, 83, 108, 119, 145
  'Mandate of Heaven', 185, 227, 251
  Northern Dynasties, 455, 535–37
  pre-Tang period, 54, 372–73
  property, 513–14, 516, 524–27, 533, 538, 541, 544, 549, 564
  society, 465, 486, 507
  Southern Dynasties, 372, 373, 534–35
  Spring and Autumn period, 147, 168, 172, 178, 182, 329, 533
  status and family, 397, 400, 411, 415, 417, 425–26, 429, 435, 439, 442
  traditions, 140, 602–3
  war, peace and interstate relations, 146–47, 151, 155, 159–61, 167, 179

Warring States period, 84–86, 120, 173, 197, 211, 238, 313, 339, 465, 533
  see also individual dynasties/periods
Christianity, 94, 253, 266, 297
Christians, 228, 249, 276, 302, 425, 462, 472
  punishments, 462
  saints, 272, 350
Chu, 58, 61, 120, 273, 313, 348, see also China
Cicero, 5
  commerce and contracts, 583
  crime, redress and social control, 454–55, 487
  law and religion, 290
  law and state, 201
  law as text, 59, 62, 63, 69–70
  legal procedure, 308, 341, 369
  legal science, 82–83, 99, 117, 134, 135, 138, 143
  status and family, 383
  war, peace and interstate relations, 176
citizenry, 248, 459, 508
citizens, 152, 162–63, 202–3, 325, 340, 379–80, 381–83, 387, 453, 546–47
  adult male, 325, 344
  Athens, 95, 381
  free, 382–83, 398, 406, 444
  status, 408, 444, 446
citizenship, 162, 165–66, 374, 377–78, 380, 382, 385–88, 398, 399, 613
  equal, 162, 382
  extensions, 100, 102, 410
city states, 147–48, 152, 155, 161–64, 169–70, 174–76, 306–7, 311, 518, 525
civic communities, 189, 482, 488
civic rights, 361, 401, 474
civil cases, 110, 120, 271, 324, 326, 345, 368, 495, 592
civil complaints, 327, 330, 360
civil disputes, 195–96, 212–13, 278, 304, 353, 486, 492, 609
civil law, 15, 78, 144, 205, 309, 422, 538, 552, 558, 596
  heirs, 558
  tradition, 598–99
civil litigation/lawsuits, 111, 219, 313, 319, 327, 329, 368
civil procedure, 81, 308–9, 321
civil proceedings, 329–30, 333
civil rights, 162, 403
claimants, 42, 369, 520, 546, 551, 557, 561
clans, 214, 378, 435
classes, social, 90, 312, 357, 374, 400, 424
classically trained scholars, 607–8
classifications, 12, 111, 138, 287, 304, 333, 388, 395, 406, 483–84

674

Index

clay tablets, 8, 23, 25, 30, 46–47, 51, 428, 577
Cleomenes, 226
Clisthenes, 235, 239
codes, 3, 8–9, 14–15, 602, 605
   commerce and contracts, 566, 592
   crime, redress and social control, 455–56, 465, 476, 510
   law and religion, 251, 253, 258, 273, 274, 287, 288, 291, 297
   law and state, 188, 193–96, 199–201, 204, 206–8
   law as text, 24, 30–32, 37–40, 43, 58, 65
   legal procedure, 304, 306, 327, 343, 345, 360, 373
   legal science, 77, 87, 88, 94, 97, 109, 121, 122, 124, 127
   penal, 42, 87, 187, 196
   property, 564
   status and family, 410, 426, 437, 438
   war, peace and interstate relations, 154
   see also law collections and individual codes.
Codex Gregorianus, 119
Codex Hermogenianus, 119
Codex Theodosianus, 19
codification, 38, 39–41, 73, 201, 447, 599
cognitio, 309, 318, 326
   extra ordinem, 309, 318, 326
co-heirs, 546–47, 575
collections
   authoritative, 40, 65, 307
   of cases, 110–11
   law, 26, 30, 42–43, 77–78, 111–12, 118–19, 122, 125–26, 200, 205
      see also codes.
   of rules, 24, 525
collective liability, 122, 400, 466
colleges, 64, 105, 283
   of priests, 81, 178, 189
coloni (tenant cultivators), 399
colonies, 162, 259, 605
commandants of justice, 187, 363
commanderies, 87, 122, 263, 322, 363, 371–72
commentaries, 4, 10, 15, 23, 39, 64–66, 87–88, 109–10, 114, 116–17
   audience and use, 66
   emergence, 64–65
   production, 65–66
   shuyi, 65, 87, 121, 354, 360
   as source materials, 4
   see also individual works.
commentators, 286, 481, 554, 580
common law, 65, 83, 143

common property, 546–47
commoners, 385, 391–92, 467, 469, 499–500, 535, 536–37, 545, 581, 588
communities, 16, 28, 33, 41, 45–46, 79, 165–66, 203, 306, 487–89
   Brahmin, 32, 90
   civic, 189, 482, 488
   epistemic, 74, 98, 145
   Jewish, 41, 79, 417, 422
   members, 306, 446–47
   political, 28, 200, 209, 451, 500
compensation, 63, 368, 375, 442, 476, 477, 493, 495–96, 503, 591
   private, 494, 495
competition, 146, 210, 247, 458, 490
complaints, 58, 63, 213, 274, 372, 394, 483, 490, 492, 497
   civil, 327, 330, 360
concubinage, 404, 424
concubines, 160, 404, 419, 426, 433, 436, 508
   sons, 433, 436
conduct, 20, 37, 82, 160, 186, 209, 211, 226–27, 304–5, 330
   human, 140, 186
   proper, 21, 24
   rules of, 42, 141
confederacies, 159, 161
confessions, 57, 120, 354–55, 362–63, 365
confiscation of property, 269, 289, 361, 369
conflicts, 147, 152–53, 156, 158, 164, 165, 168–70, 176, 179, 210
   management, 147, 168
   military, 165
Confucianism, 15, 88, 139, 197, 614
consensus, 137, 220, 411, 482, 595
   social, 461, 482, 483
   strong, 477, 483
consent, 165, 421, 424, 426, 489, 516, 532, 541, 571
consiliarii (advisers), 318
consilium (group of advisers), 99, 212
consociations, 159
Constantine, emperor, 103, 228, 321, 384, 399, 413, 472, 490
Constantinople, 23, 36, 108
constitutional frameworks, 183–93
constitutional law, 94, 97, 183, 185, 188, 190, 193, 230
constitutions, 119, 132, 163, 184, 192, 310, 311, 584, 613
   imperial, 19, 40, 98, 117, 119, 134, 136, 338, 344, 367
consuls, 35, 98, 106–7, 116, 117, 152, 154, 165, 220, 454

675

consultations, 35, 37, 90, 94, 131, 164, 168, 239, 261, 264
contests, 146, 159, 172, 174, 182, 205
contracts, xiv, 2, 5, 7, 16, 19, 602
   Assyrian, 404, 420
   breach, 328, 336, 495, 497, 499, 595
   commerce, 565, 567–69, 574, 577–82, 584–86, 588–90, 592–95, 596
   crime, redress and social control, 494, 497
   demotic, 579
   Egyptian, 549–50
   executed, 585–86, 588
   Greek, 50, 583
   law and religion, 232, 245, 267, 283, 301–2
   law and state, 194, 197, 205–6, 229
   law as text, 23, 30, 40, 44–45, 48–49, 50–54, 63–64, 69, 70–71
   law of contract, 79, 594
   legal procedure, 327, 337, 345–47, 368
   legal science, 87, 108, 111, 119, 121, 129, 144
   maritime, 50, 582
   marriage, 48, 51, 419, 422, 433, 549
   private, 165, 386, 514, 519, 541, 549, 573, 578
   property, 518, 522, 528, 530, 549–50, 552, 559, 563
   of sale, 52–53, 133, 137, 529, 550, 582, 584–85, 588, 592
   status and family, 396, 405–6, 408, 414–15, 416, 419, 420–21, 428, 431–32, 443
   war, peace and interstate relations, 165
   written, 46, 48, 50, 55, 386, 421, 579, 582, 583
contractual arrangements, 414, 421, 443
contractual documents, 8, 577, 579–81, 588
contractual penalties, 421, 425
control
   direct, 93, 434
   political, 17, 165, 483
   social, xiv, 2, 446–511
conventions, 6, 41, 55, 153, 193–94, 396, 443, 568
convictions, 60–61, 343, 355, 360, 365, 372, 400, 452, 544–45
convicts, 326–27
copper
   payments, 392, 413, 465
   plates, 49, 533
corporal punishments, 324, 395, 402, 442, 471, 472, 582
corporate persons, 460–61
corpses, 293, 294–95, 296, 352, 519
Corpus Iuris Civilis, 19, 308, 409
corrective justice, 480–81, 593
cosmic justifications, 485–86, 488

cosmic order, 183, 234, 238, 243–44, 300, 487
cosmos, 139–40, 198, 235, 237, 486, 604
costs, 158, 319, 581
councils
   advisory, 89, 318, 364
   guild, 390
   local, 315, 395
counties, 221, 373, 466
court proceedings, 59, 102, 123, 312–13, 320, 347, 368
   preliminary, 324–41
courthouses/rooms, 91, 212, 312, 319–20, 528
courts
   cases, 21, 63, 194, 210, 246, 303–4, 312, 316
   constitution, 310–23
   costs, 319, 326
   deliberations, 123, 361–64
   fees, 319, 369
   fines, 319, 326
   officials/officers, 224, 286, 311–12, 316, 319, 329, 357–58, 361, 367, 370
   personnel, 303, 310–19, 328
   procedures, 69, 304
   see also individual civilizations and courts.
covenants, 348, 381, 568, 575
   Israelite, 232–33
credit sales, 550, 581, 587
Crete, 16, 115, 274, 307, 317, 588, see also Gortyn
crime scenes, 304, 351–53
crime(s), 284, 285, 351, 352–53, 355–56, 360–61, 390–91, 446–511
   against the gods and the sacred, 284–92
   making sense of, 480–92
   processes of marking off, 448–68
   sexual, 194, 329, 499, 595
   see also bestiality; incest; rape.
   see also under individual civilizations and offences.
crimen maiestatis (treason), 361
criminal cases, 320, 321, 324, 326, 344, 345, 351–52, 353, 362, 372
criminal courts, 91, 195
criminal law, 391, 450–51, 457–58, 477, 481–83, 486–87, 491, 502–3, 505, 509
   system, 194
   see also under individual civilizations.
criminal offences, 327, 334, 466
criminal procedures, 82, 483, 493
criminal proceedings, 326, 330, 365, 368
criminal prohibitions, 480, 482, 485, 487, 489, 502, 509
criminal prosecutions, 215, 360
criminal punishments, 224, 609

criminal records, 334, 343
criminal trials, 205, 321
criminals, 61, 471–72
Crito, 95, 97
crops, 177, 260, 463, 523, 536, 602
crown, 223, 236, 262, 280, 460
cultic procedures/rituals, 234, 276, 278, 302
cultivation, 532, 533–34, 536, 537, 551
cults, 249, 253–54, 286, 294, 299, 509, 539
    ancestral, 173, 178
cuneiform texts, 599–600
curators, 412, 415, 435
curse clauses, 570–72
curses, 210, 264, 297–98, 300, 340, 350
customary laws, 12, 112, 141, 195, 205, 206–7, 238, 517
customary norms/practices/rules, 14–15, 21, 77, 197, 230, 379, 381, 390, 437, 548

Dalmatia, 101
damages, 281, 289–90, 366, 369, 476–77, 487, 493, 497, 589, 591
    punitive, 471, 476
dānapratibhū (surety for appearance), 334
daṇḍa (staff/scepter), 184, 216, 486
dang, 120–21
Dao, 85–86, 140, 238, 245
Daoist priests, 439
darśanapratibhū (surety for appearance), 334
daughters, 407, 420, 421, 423, 428, 430–31, 432–34, 436–37, 441, 554–57
    of Zelophehad, 433
    see also children.
death, 80, 150, 254–55, 284–85, 295–96, 351–53, 358–59, 372–73, 436–37, 472–75
    penalty/sentences, 14, 86, 217, 247, 252, 284, 299, 359, 465, 472–73
death, penalty/sentences
see also capital punishment.
debt
    non-payment, 13, 328, 499, 569, 579, 585, 595
    slavery, 262, 396–97, 543, 544
debtors, 123, 137, 386, 474, 579, 583
    public, 60, 381
debt-release decrees, 111, 612
debts, 60–61, 257, 258, 262, 327, 345–46, 396–97, 499, 579–80, 612–13
Decius, emperor, 249, 487
declarations, 158, 170, 176, 237, 268
    solemn *(shi)*, 172, 329, 348
    of war, 170–71, 175–76, 178
decrees, 25–28, 34–36, 70–71, 195, 201–2, 242, 265–66, 281–83, 286, 536

debt-release, 111, 612
imperial, 373, 536
deductive reasoning, 78, 123, 134, 357
deeds, 23, 44, 49, 53, 55, 205, 345, 432, 483, 533
defecation, 292, 296
defences, 18, 95, 161, 176–77, 252, 333, 505, 508, 552, 595
defendants, 62–63, 271–73, 307–8, 317–18, 327–39, 350–52, 357, 365, 366–68, 561–63
Deioces, 448–50
Deir el-Medina, 306, 316, 408
deities, 10, 50, 125, 232, 236, 249, 251, 284, 290, 462–63, *see also* gods and individual deities
delegates/delegations, 152–54, 169, 192, 221–22, 309, 312, 323, 338
Delian League, 146, 163
Delos, 163, 265, 543
Delphi, 162, 174–75, 239
    oracle, 94, 175, 239, 265
demes, 289–90, 318, 331, 530, 547
democracies, 97, 147, 163, 459–61, 613
    Athens, 188, 459, 489, 508
Demos, 459–60, 607
Demosthenes, 5, 130, 289, 340, 476, 489, 496, 525
demotic, 41, 48, 519, 524, 527, 549, 550, 559, 564
    contracts, 579
dependency, 159, 378, 396, 410, 414, 445
dependents, 222, 278, 325, 379, 395, 416–17, 542, 554
descendants, 99, 361, 417, 428, 436, 460, 556, 558
    male, 429, 436–37, 555
descriptions of trials, 5–6, 9
deserts, 327, 576–77, 584
Deuteronomic Code, 10, 92, 126
Deuteronomy, 142, 247, 262, 277, 430, 543
Dhamma regulations, 491
dharma, 11–13, 604, 605–6, 613
    law and religion, 238, 243–45, 250, 286, 301
    law and state, 184–85, 195–96, 206–8, 217, 225–26
    law as text, 21, 34, 35, 69, 70
    legal science, 76, 89–90, 104, 140–41, 145
    property, 525
    protecting, 225, 244
    rules of, 70, 141, 195
    science of *see* Dharmaśāstras.
    sources of, 76, 140
    status and family, 389, 393
    war, peace and interstate relations, 171
dharmādhikaraṇa, 320
dharma-king, 226

dharmapāṭhaka (preceptor of *dharma*), 89
dharmapravaktṛ (expounder of *dharma*), 89
dharmarāja (dharma-king), 226
Dharmaśāstras, 11–12, 613
   commerce and contracts, 573, 585, 590
   crime, redress and social control, 499–501
   law and religion, 238, 263, 286
   law and state, 195
   law as text, 31–32, 34–35, 43, 49, 70
   legal procedure, 312, 351
   legal science, 76, 90, 105, 111, 140
   Manu, 457–58, 501
   see also Manu.
   property, 526, 546, 554
   status and family, 380–81, 389, 392, 401–2, 407, 411, 427, 430, 437, 438
   texts, 281, 438
   tradition, 4, 76, 91, 280, 429
   war, peace and interstate relations, 172
Dharmasūtras, 11, 31, 111, 427, 526
   Āpastamba-Dharmasūtra, 76, 89, 111, 411, 525, 531
dharmavid (expert in *dharma*), 89
dikastai (judges/jurors), 95, 215, 317, 321
Dike, 246
Diocletian, emperor, 100, 102, 118–19, 384
Dionysius of Halicarnassus, 81, 164–65
diplomacy, 41, 148, 149, 155–68, 180
diplomatic immunity, 148, 152, 155
diplomatic relations, 147, 155–56, 567
diplomats, 148, 150, 154–55, *see also* emissaries; envoys,
disabilities, 388, 412, 415–16, 475, 555
   physical, 325, 378
disagreements, 22, 164, 241, 364, 608
disciples, 78, 93, 105–6
discretion, 212, 217, 333, 364, 383, 443, 497–98, 561
diseases, 80, 415, 426, 555, 564, 588, 602
dispositions, 141, 417, 430, 434, 516, 555, 608
   of land, 49, 555
   of property by will, 136, 436
dispositive oath, 269, 271, 274, 276
disputants, 93, 213, 216, 338, 349, 369
disputes, 8–9, 77–78, 197–99, 207–8, 213–14, 219–20, 303, 310–11, 322–23, 560–62
   boundary, 5, 274, 328, 344, 413, 499, 595
   civil, 195–96, 212–13, 278, 304, 353, 486, 492, 609
   legal, 168, 275, 314–15, 438
   private, 14, 40, 48, 204, 224, 306, 351, 369, 609
   property, 271, 526, 560, 564
   resolution/settlement, 15–16, 24–25, 164, 169, 224–25, 275–77, 310, 311, 327–28, 368–69

settled, 12, 24, 211, 212, 370, 487
disrepute, 384–85, 456, 500
district courts, 49, 323
district magistrates, 330
disturbances, 86, 245
divergences, 145, 229, 280, 377
divination, 261, 265, 287, 483
   experts, 124, 261
divine court, 299, 301, 306, 314
divine mandates, 231, 237, 239, 262
divine punishments, 262, 274, 277, 292
divine will, 142, 183–84, 235–36
divine witnesses, 50, 569
divorce, 307, 350, 403, 420–23, 424–26, 427, 434, 609
djadjat (court), 316
documentary evidence, 207, 314, 342–43, 355, 524, 544, 553, 612
documentary forms, 5, 578, 584, 596
documentary records, 4, 46, 381, 538, 540, 586
documents.
   caches, 13, 584
   contractual, 8, 577, 579–81, 588
   creation, 45, 52
   double, 582–83
   emergence, 44–51
   as evidence in legal proceedings, 344–47
   excavated, 363, 468
   forged, 343, 346, 375
   formal, 167
   legal, 23, 47, 49, 58, 61, 70, 342, 345, 347, 352
   loan, 53
   non-legal, 67, 70–71
   official, 55, 285
   production, 51–53
   recording verdicts, 367
   sale, 549, 592
   special features, 53–56
   surviving/extant, 15, 47, 320, 576, 585, 592
   use, 17, 45, 576, 582
   written, 17, 27, 44–47, 50–52, 54, 60, 346, 576, 578–79, 584
   see also Introductory Note.
Dong Zhongshu, 86, 88, 110
'doubtful' cases, 314, 363–64
dowries, 47, 405, 408, 419, 421–23, 424, 432–33, 434, 436, 555–56
Draco, 24, 28–30
Dreros, 16, 28, 35, 115
Dunhuang, 576, 602
durable materials, 33, 35, 52, 61
duties of officials, 75, 122, 185, 196, 266, 313, 395

Index

"Duties of the Vizier", 40, 71, 386
dynasties *see* individual dynasties

Eanna temple, 291, 335
earth, 102, 165, 251, 296, 358, 504, 571, 575
Ecbatana, 449
'ecclesial polities', 380–81
Edfu, 547, 549
edicts, 18, 607–8
   Aśoka, 41, 55
   commerce and contracts, 579, 589
   crime, redress and social control, 483, 497
   imperial, 19, 42–43, 86, 196, 363, 439, 457
   law and religion, 242, 262
   law and state, 192, 195–96, 201, 204, 205, 207, 219, 228
   law as text, 23, 25–27, 29–30
   legal procedure, 305, 321
   legal science, 86, 98, 99, 101, 109, 116–17, 119, 136
   praetors, 29, 35, 43, 136, 307
   property, 525
   royal, 25, 207–8
   status and family, 393, 394, 413, 435, 438
Egypt, 5, 8, 16–17, 612
   Asyut, 317, 366, 367, 553, 561, 562, 564
   commerce and contracts, 566–67, 570, 573, 577–79, 582, 584, 589
   contracts, 549–50
   courts, 17, 41, 156, 387
   crime, redress and social control, 483, 488
   documents, 567, 579, 588
   Elephantine, 255, 273
   gods, 331, 570
   Greco-Roman *see* Greco-Roman Egypt.
   king, 248–49
   language, 48, 549, 563
   see also demotic.
   law and religion, 237, 248–49, 255–57, 260, 262, 272–74, 279, 285, 297, 300
   law and state, 192, 221
   law as text, 19, 22, 29–30, 37, 47–48, 50–51, 59, 67, 68, 70–72
   legal procedure, 306, 311, 314, 316, 321, 331, 339, 343, 355, 366
   Middle Kingdom, 47, 68, 156, 297, 306, 316, 386, 548
   New Kingdom, 30, 47, 70–71, 149, 171, 272, 280, 306, 316, 386
   Old Kingdom, 25, 59, 67, 300, 306, 515, 565, 577
   papyri, 101, 346, 542, 599
   Pharaonic, 297, 386, 408, 423
   practices, 430, 527, 551
   prefects, 273, 311, 399, 483
   property, 512–16, 522–27, 538–39, 541–43, 546–47, 549, 550–51, 553, 559, 561–64
   Ptolemaic *see* Greco-Roman Egypt.
   status and family, 386–88, 394–95, 399, 409, 422–23, 433, 439, 443
   war, peace and interstate relations, 149, 156–57, 169, 170–71
Egyptians, 17, 41, 149, 237, 249, 300, 386–88, 399, 413, 551
elders, 15, 79, 188, 222, 295, 306–7, 413, 415, 435–36, 467
   town, 125, 277
Elephantine, 255, 273
elephants, 479, 547, 572
Eleusis, 265
elite families, 278, 450
elites, 48, 70, 386, 408, 409, 433, 438, 445, 471, 475
   local, 101, 221
Emar, 183, 366
emissaries, 151, 171, 372, *see also* diplomats; envoys
emperors, 102–3, 187, 190–91, 202, 219–22, 228, 370–74, 455–57, 540–41, *see also* individual names
employment relationships, 567, 585
endowments, 50, 411, 421, 438, 528, 533
   religious, 526, 528, 532, 533
enemies, 149, 154, 156, 157–58, 170–71, 173, 175–79, 334, 342, 344
enforcement, 97, 196, 247, 251, 332, 368–69, 375, 448, 453, 593
   property rights, 513
   religious practices, 247–54
   verdicts, 368–70
enforcers, 160, 168, 453, 459
enjoyment, 259, 341, 517–19, 560
Enmetena, 262
enslaved persons, 144, 353, 358, 374, 379, 396, 399, 403, 464, 541–43, *see also* slaves
enslavement, 177, 392, 396–97, 400, 402, 404, 421, 475, 543, 544, *see also* slavery
envoys, 148–49, 150–52, 153–54, 155, 168, 175–76, 180, 329, *see also* diplomats; emissaries
epistemic communities, 74, 98, 145
epistemology, 12, 76
equal citizenship, 162, 382
equality, 12, 84, 163, 164, 167–68, 310, 378, 384, 593
equestrians, 100–1, 103, 107, 383, 388, 454, 458

679

equites, 100
equity, 70, 134, 183, 201, 242, 378
Eratosthenes, 95–96, 508
Esarhaddon, king, 261
Eshnunna, 8, 112, 125, 352, 566
estates, 42, 47, 403, 408, 432, 434–35, 437, 553–54, 557, 559
  fathers, 137, 405
  large, 429, 537, 539, 544
ethics, 4, 75, 140, 183, 192, 206, 607–8
Eumenides, 68, 80
eunomia, 246
Euphiletos, 95–96
Euthyphro, 80
eviction, 581, 586–88, 589
evidence
  archaeological, 10, 105, 248, 566, 580, 590
  best, 16, 217, 236, 393
  clear, 17, 174, 186, 197, 279, 281, 574, 576, 586, 592
  direct, 16, 36, 40, 99, 206, 516, 578–79, 582, 587, 592
  documentary, 207, 314, 342–43, 355, 524, 544, 553, 612
  forensic investigation, 351–53
  human, 347
  inscriptional *see* inscriptions.
  in legal procedure, 341–56
  oaths and ordeals, 347–50
  presentation and evaluation, 356–64
  prima facie, 51, 341, 517
  rules, 339, 343, 355
  slave, 346, 484
  surviving/extant, 2, 16, 18, 41, 60–61, 63, 89, 108, 573, 577
  textual, 119, 299, 611
  torture for evidentiary purposes, 353–56, 374
  war, peace and interstate relations, 149, 151, 155
  witnesses, 342–44, 359–60
  see also testimony.
  written, xiv, 3, 7, 121, 196–97, 346, 549, 563, 583
  see also Introductory Note.
evidentiary purposes, 49, 51–52, 353–56, 374
evidentiary stage, 337–38
examinations, 26, 87, 187, 231, 261, 304, 330, 351, 352–54, 593
executions, 187, 342, 345, 359, 360, 368, 369, 471, 472, 474–75 *see also* capital punishment; death, penalty/sentences.
Exegetes, 80
exemptions, 55, 148, 150, 353, 356, 392, 394, 531–32, 533, 548

exile, 287, 289–90, 293–94, 295, 373, 411, 465, 467, 470–72, 474–75
expert traditions, 604, 606
expertise, xi, xii, 74, 76, 82, 89, 95, 97, 108, 114
  legal, 9, 74–75, 80, 96, 145, 309, 311, 340, 455, 605
experts, xii, 2, 4, 74–75, 76, 78, 89, 92, 98–99, 195
  divination, 124, 261
  legal *see* legal experts.
  religious/ritual, 76, 265–66
expiations, 13, 76, 390, 485–87
eyewitnesses, 299

fajia (legalist school), 84
false accusations, 205, 305, 359–61, 362
false accusers, 360–61
false testimony/witness, 357, 358–61, 371, 375, 477, 480
families, 47–49, 211–14, 370, 376–445, 505–6
  disputes, 561
  elite, 278, 450
  estates, 430, 553
  extended, 214, 435, 576
  five families *(wujia)*, 466–67
  land, 553, 561
family property, 206, 417, 432–37, 519, 546, 551, 553, 555, 561
family status, 416–37
fathers, 157–59, 212–13, 407–8, 423–24, 431–32, 433–34, 504–5, 551, 554–55, 557
  brothers (paternal uncles), 433–34, 466
  estates, 137, 405
  property, 433, 553, 554, 563
  see also parents.
fealty oaths, 573–74
fees, 316, 319, 339, 367
Feishi, 172–73
'female son', 430–31
females, 412, 555–56
  children, 295
  slaves, 298, 397, 401–3, 404–6
  see also women.
festivals, 42, 152, 174, 253–60, 265, 473, 488
  of booths, 255–56
  of unleavened bread, 255–56
  religious, 152, 239, 253, 257, 263, 288
fetuses, 500
fictions, 135, 191, 195, 257, 355, 408, 416–17, 430, 445, 538
Fides, 574
filial piety, 227, 327, 455, 469, 505, 545
financial obligations, 383, 421, 528

fines, 319, 324, 326, 365–66, 368–69, 370–71, 438, 441, 473–74, 476
fire, 171, 255, 273, 290, 296, 347–48, 457, 462, 572
firemen, 131
five families *(wujia)*, 466–67
foedus (treaty), 164–65
food, 14, 148, 287, 295–96, 553
force of law, 23, 29
foreign judges, 71, 169
foreign polities, 149, 156
foreign powers, 151, 158, 236
foreign traders, 150–51, 153
foreigners, 115, 148, 149–51, 153, 308, 325, 379–80, 381, 389, 546–47
forensic investigations, 91, 351–53, 362
forensic speeches, 6, 16, 23, 61–62, 65, 82
forests, 531, 547
forged documents, 343, 346, 375
formal requirements, 52, 54, 346, 435
formal statuses, 377, 388, 613
formulae, 18, 55, 122, 142, 219–20, 283, 308, 328, 332, 333
formulary procedures, 221, 321, 328, 332, 366, 369–70
formulary systems, 18, 308, 318, 333, 338, 350
Forty, the, 317
forums, 29, 35, 223, 326, 379, 390
fraud, 53, 121, 205, 345
free citizens, 382–83, 398, 406, 444
free persons, 149, 325, 356, 382–83, 397–98, 399–400, 403, 473, 476, 545
free women, 403–4, 405
freedmen/freed slaves, 101, 213, 382, 396–99, 424, 497, 500, 545
freedom, 105, 134, 136, 144, 203, 325, 332, 382, 396–98, 404–5
friendship, 152, 157, 165, 167, 191
  guest, 152, 450
funeral rites, 81, 385

Gaius, 100, 107, 135–36, 143, 350, 409, 417, 424, 574, 575
  Institutes, 18, 66, 423, 518, 525, 557, 571, 583, 594–95
gambling, 150, 194, 329, 499, 595
games, 152, 153, 174, 259, 452
Gaozi, emperor, 211
gardens, 43, 472, 530, 540, 541
Gauls, 154, 177
Gautama, 89, 555
gender statuses, 407
general principles, 21, 38–39, 42, 121, 122, 326, 336, 591, 593, 596

Geneva conventions, 170, 177
Gentiles, 381, 403, 488
  succession, 558
gestures, 7, 123, 159, 308, 420
Gewaltsamkeit (violence), 502–3
ghaṭikāsthāna, 90
gifts
  betrothal, 425
  bridal, 418–19
  commerce and contracts, 565, 567, 585
  exchange of, 157, 168
  law and religion, 290
  law and state, 194, 217, 226
  law as text, 27, 49
  legal science, 113, 123
  non-delivery of, 328, 499, 595
  property, 521, 533, 535, 540, 546, 552, 554, 556
  status and family, 401–3, 408, 411, 424
  war, peace and interstate relations, 154, 159–61
girls, 325, 412, 422, 424–25, 429, 508, 544, *see also* females
Gnomon of the Idios Logos, 297, 388
gods, 183–84, 235–43, 251–54, 259–61, 264–69, 271–72, 283–87, 298–300, 462, 569–70
  Greek, 259
  oaths, 570–71
  of Egypt, 331, 570
  see also deities and individual gods/goddesses.
goods, 122, 132, 175, 405, 471, 475, 567, 573, 580, 585
  stolen, 337, 351, 353, 586
Gortyn, 3
  commerce and contracts, 588
  law and religion, 274
  law and state, 199
  law as text, 21, 40, 56
  legal procedure, 307, 311, 317, 340, 350, 361, 371
  legal science, 115
  property, 556–57
  status and family, 394, 397–98, 404, 409, 412, 422, 428, 434, 441, 444
governance, 28, 181, 193, 230, 263, 265–66, 311, 503, 601, 606
  religion, 260–66
  state, 234, 248
government officials, 91, 262, 305, 315, 316, 324, 368
governors, 25, 27, 87, 192, 217, 221–22, 315, 318, 497, 498
  provincial, 93, 99, 103, 117, 318, 323, 369, 498

681

grain, 12, 43–44, 122, 260, 399, 523, 534
grand administrators, 363, 372
grandsons, 157, 229, 436, 466, 556, 570
grants, 27, 55–56, 277, 282–83, 408, 412, 516, 532, 535–37, 539–40
  land, 516, 527, 532, 540, 578
  secular, 533
Great Powers' club, 147, 157
Greco-Roman Egypt, 17, 610
  commerce and contracts, 582
  crime, redress, and social control, 473, 496
  law and religion, 248, 257, 300
  law and state, 191, 221
  law as text, 41, 47–48, 51–52, 53–54, 60, 67, 69, 70
  legal procedure, 331, 367, 371
  property, 514, 516, 523, 528, 539, 542, 546–47, 562
  status and family, 385–87, 394, 408, 409, 412, 423, 424, 429, 439–41
Greece / Greek city states, 2, 12, 15–17, 600, 603, 610, 611–13
  commerce and contracts, 50, 566–67, 571, 573, 577, 583, 587–88, 589–90, 593, 597
  courts, 17, 41, 272
  crime, redress and social control, 464, 472–73, 474–75, 487, 509
  documents, 48
  Hellenistic period *see* Hellenistic period.
  law and religion, 239, 241, 251, 258–59, 264, 270, 274, 282, 288–94
  law and state, 181, 187–88, 198–200, 201, 204, 209–10, 214–15, 225–26
  law as text, 22–23, 24–25, 28–30, 33, 35, 36, 40–41, 50, 51, 69–71
  legal procedure, 317, 321, 335, 337, 339, 344, 350, 355, 357–58, 361
  legal science, 80, 83, 94, 95–97, 114–15, 145
  material, 79–80, 209
  officials, 279, 561
  polis, 79, 210, 387, 613
  property, 513–14, 518, 522, 524–25, 527, 529–30, 548–50, 556, 559, 564
  slaves, 398
  status and family, 381, 387–88, 394, 397–98, 412, 422, 441
  war, peace and interstate relations, 146–47, 152–53, 155, 161, 162–64, 168, 169, 174, 177, 179–80
  see also individual states.
Greek-Macedonian dynasty, 17, 29

grooms, 418–19, 421, 425, 434
gu poison, 288
guarantees, 148, 153, 164, 178, 335, 347, 350, 581, 586–88, 589
guarantors, 52, 54, 334–35, 530
guardians, 131, 133, 223, 270, 407, 408–9, 412, 434, 497, 557
guest friendship, 152, 450
guilds, 35, 208, 214, 260, 311, 322, 326, 347, 370, 438
guilt, 298, 299, 333, 334, 336–37, 347, 349–51, 354–55, 375, 607–8
guilty parties, 349, 390, 471
Guptas, 11, 27, 250, 342, 532, 606, *see also* India

Hadrian, emperor, 19, 119, 132
hair, 171, 296
halakha ('religious law'), 79, 105, 112–13, 129, 380, 604
Halicarnassus, 164–65, 448
halitzah (release), 430
Hammurabi *see also* Laws of Hammurabi.
Han, 13–15, 607, 609
  commerce and contracts, 576, 592, 596
  crime, redress and social control, 455–56, 465, 467–68, 473, 505, 506
  law and religion, 251, 258, 263–64, 287–88
  law and state, 185, 187, 197, 211, 222, 227
  law as text, 42, 48–49, 54, 58, 61, 64–65, 69, 72
  legal procedure, 305, 313–14, 326–27, 330, 348, 354, 359–60, 362–63, 368, 371–73
  legal science, 84, 85–88, 108–10, 120, 122, 139
  property, 534, 540, 555–56
  status and family, 391–92, 400, 413, 426, 429, 435–36, 439
  war, peace and interstate relations, 147, 160–61
  see also China.
Han Fei, 85
Hannibal, 154, 166, 167, 176
hardships, 406, 469
harmony, 139, 224, 243, 245, 251, 486, 510
Hatti, 157, 570
heads of households, 325, 327, 395, 417–18, 465, 468, 554, 555
heaven, 75, 86, 140, 165, 173, 185–86, 218, 227, 251, 288
  Mandate of Heaven, 185, 227, 251
  see also Tian
Hebrew, 8, 113, 604

Bible, 8, 10, 128–29, 232–33, 245, 248, 294, 296, 298, 433
hegemons, 160
heiresses, 433–35
heirs, 403, 404–5, 418, 429, 430–31, 432–35, 437, 516–17, 545, 556–59
   civil law, 558
   male, 49, 430
   unusual, 47
Heka, 300
Hellenika Oxyrhynchia, 163
Hellenistic period, 23, 51, 152, 162, 263, 272, 279, 282, 355, 523–25
   monarchs, 164, 169, 174
   states, 146–47, 543
helots, 382, 398, 401
Hephaistos, 15, 209
Heqing Code, 15
Hermes, 152, 215
Hermopolis legal compendium/code, 40, 306, 515, 551, 553, 559, 563
Herodotus, 67, 94, 142, 239, 449–50, 461, 574
Hesiod, 15, 209, 246, 306
hierarchical relationships, 196, 420, 501
hierarchical societies, 386, 394, 442
hierarchy, 85, 205, 207–8, 245, 314–15, 371, 379, 426, 433, 456
   social, 406, 501, 510
hieroglyphic, 25
high priests, 92, 243, 254, 278, 285, 295
high ranking officials, 87, 360
higher courts, 314, 323, 370–71
higher law, 139–40, 186, 227, 440
hīnavādin, 328
Hindu law, 90, 238
Hindu temples, 250, 280
Hindu traditions, 140, 238, 243, 287, 605
Hinduism, 244, 249, 613–14
historical records, 12, 35, 90, 542, 609
Hittite Kingdom, 200, 295, 567, 578
Hittite laws, 9, 25, 200, 296, 566, 578
Hittite treaties, 571–72
Hittites, 8, 233, 295, 569–70, 575
holy water, 347–48
Homer, 15, 24, 79, 154, 174, 259, 306, 543
homes, 48, 90, 99, 106, 108, 132, 155, 472, 479, 508
   marital, 407, 411
homicide, 28, 58, 80, 205, 209, 293, 295, 317, 505, 508
   cases/trials, 80, 96, 111, 129–30, 293, 325, 364
   involuntary, 293–94, 508
   see also murder.

horkiōtera (more oath-worthy), 274
horsemen, 100
horses, 52, 148, 151, 263, 542, 545, 570, 572, 580, 582
hospitality rules and customs, 148–55
host countries, 148–49, 155
hostages, 158, 161, 164, 168, 572
hostilities, 153, 158, 171, *see also* war
households, 605
   commerce and contracts, 570
   crime, redress and social control, 466, 468, 507
   head of, 325, 327, 395, 417–18, 465, 468, 554, 555
   law and religion, 260, 263
   legal procedure, 326, 348
   legal science, 96, 137
   property, 516, 535–36, 540–43, 544, 546, 551, 553, 555–56
   registers, 466, 468, 545
   separate, 435–36, 455, 534
   service, 400, 544–45
   status and family, 379, 382, 397, 400, 404, 414, 416–18, 423, 435–36
Huang-Lao thought, 238, 604
hubris, 130
human behaviour/conduct, 86, 140, 186, 245
human corpses, 294–95, 296
human evidence, 347
human rights, 144, 148, 443
Hurrians, 156, 570
husbands, 270, 404–5, 407–8, 410–11, 418–22, 423–25, 426–27, 432–34, 554–55, 556–57
Hyksos, 156, 171
Hypereides, 96
Hyperides, 582, 593

Iliad, 15, 24, 68, 79, 187–88, 209, 216, 246, 335
immovable property, 499, 518, 539, 545 *see also* real estate/property
immunities, 148, 155, 391, 438, 440, 442, 507, 532
   diplomatic, 148, 152, 155
impartiality, 99, 219, 246, 310
imperial agents, 103, 490
imperial bureaucracy, 57, 103
imperial chancery, 102
imperial China, 139, 196, 211, 339, 442, 466
   see also China
imperial constitutions, 19, 40, 98, 117, 119, 134, 136, 338, 344, 367
imperial edicts, 19, 42–43, 86, 196, 363, 439, 457
imperial laws, 213, 240
imperial legislation, 203, 439

683

imperial magistrates, 39, 311, 318, 323, 338, 347, 367, 370
imperial officials, 104, 203, 323, 373
imperial polities, 214, 385
imperial power, 103, 190, 315
imperial properties, 457, 490
imperial Rome see Rome.
imperial statutes, 64, 99
impiety, 62, 251, 289, 509
impurity, 294–95, 296
incentives, 282, 396, 446–47, 463, 469, 477, 511
   negative, 446–47, 469, 477, 491, 509
incest, 143, 205, 284, 295–96, 408, 425, 455
India, 2, 10–13, 601, 606, 608, 612–13
   commerce and contracts, 567, 572, 573, 579, 585, 590, 593, 595
   crime, redress and social control, 471
   judges, 123, 358
   jurisprudence, 304, 311, 333, 336, 341, 347, 368, 423, 560
   law and religion, 237–38, 244–45, 249, 257, 263, 273, 281, 285–86, 291–92, 297
   law and state, 184, 193, 204, 214, 224–25
   law as text, 21, 23–24, 26, 34, 41, 50, 51, 53, 55, 69–70
   legal procedure, 312, 314, 320, 322–25, 334, 337–39, 341–45, 356, 359, 360
   legal science, 76, 82–83, 89, 90, 104, 111, 117, 141, 145
   material, xii, 31, 76, 105, 206, 327, 410, 603
   property, 517, 525–28, 538, 539, 541–42, 548, 551, 553, 559–60, 563–64
   sources, xii, 312, 319, 342, 358, 375, 389, 413, 431, 532
   status and family, 379, 380, 385, 388, 390–91, 400, 429, 430, 437, 438
   system, 326, 329, 335, 365, 367, 370
   texts, 12, 328, 335, 359
   traditions, 35, 114, 336, 353
   war, peace and interstate relations, 146–47, 150, 155, 158, 168, 178, 180
   western, 35, 390, 438, 548
   see also individual dynasties
indictments, 60, 62, 318, 362, 459, 493
Indonesia, 34, 548
inductive reasoning, 77, 135
Indus Valley, xiv, 579
inferences, 77, 123, 134–35, 138, 141
inferior states, 159–61
inheritance, 401, 405, 406–7, 432–35
   commerce and contracts, 595
   crime, redress and social control, , 499

law and religion, 245, 278
law and state, 194, 196, 205, 209
law as text, 47, 48, 53, 68–69
legal procedure, 329, 345, 369
legal science, 80, 120
partition, 329, 499, 595
property, 513, 515, 526, 538, 541, 547, 550, 553–55, 556–59
rules, 433, 524
systems, 553
injured parties, 97, 215, 476, 483–84, 496
injuries, 88, 398, 403, 441, 442, 476, 484, 499, 500–1, 545
injustice, 176, 186, 300, 314, 372–73, 486, 503
innocence, 15, 63, 228, 270, 295, 347, 349–51, 362, 419, 463
inquiries, 2, 36, 65, 230, 309, 317, 341, 362
inscriptions, 13, 17
   boundary, 111
   bronze, 329, 339, 509
   commerce and contracts, 592
   crime, redress and social control, 460, 490, 495
   law and religion, 249, 282, 292
   law as text, 21, 27, 34, 36, 49–50
   legal, 55, 612
   legal procedure, 317, 318
   legal science, 86, 100, 104–5, 115
   property, 516, 526, 530, 532
   status and family, 390, 392, 410, 440
   stone, 203, 259
inspectors, 372
Institutes of Gaius, 18, 66, 423, 518, 525, 557, 571, 583, 594–95
institutional witness, 224
Institutiones, 107, 117
institutions, 2, 611, 613
   crime, redress and social control, 447, 449–50, 453, 459
   law and religion, 249–50
   law and state, 190
   law as text, 21, 23, 49, 66
   legal, xiii, 13, 67, 136–37, 193, 293, 306, 512, 527
   legal procedure, 306, 355, 372–73
   legal science, 75, 90–91, 104–5
   property, 543, 563
   religious, 81, 527–28, 532
   state, 181, 190, 448, 562
   status and family, 376–77, 379, 385, 417
   war, peace and interstate relations, 152, 155, 163
instructional materials, 67, 71
international court, 168

international laws, 148, 179, 227
interpersonal violence, 209, 476, 497, 500
interpreters, 128, 240, 481
interrogations, 58, 63, 120, 305, 339, 343, 345, 352, 355–57, 362–63
interrogators, 312, 354
interstate relations, xiv, 146, 147–48, 157–58, 179–80, 573, 574, 602
  arbitration, meditation and Common-Peace experiment, 168–69
  states declaring war and just wars, 169–79
  states forming alliances and pursuing diplomacy, 155–68
intestate succession, 435, 555, 557
investigations, 47, 120, 185, 313–14, 330, 351, 352, 360, 362, 364
  forensic, 91, 351–53, 362
investigators, 351
involuntary homicide, 293–94, 508
Irikagina, 262, 305
Isaeus, 6, 96, 408, 556
Israel
  commerce and contracts, 577
  law and religion, 232–33, 236, 241–42, 247–48, 262, 292, 294
  legal procedure, 350
  legal science, 78
  people, 233, 236
  property, 543
  status and family, 403
  Tannaitic period, 78, 92–93, 105, 113
Israelites, 232–33, 255, 297 see also Jews
Italic land, 519, 542, 552, 589
Iulianus, Salvius, 100
iuris peritus nobilissimus ex Africa, 100
iuris studiosus, 100–1
iurisdictio see jurisdiction.
ius (law), 21, 81, 99, 117, 189, 307, 603, 606
ius civile (law of the city), 81–82, 98
ius dicere (declare what is law), 220, 323
ius gentium (laws observed among all peoples), 143, 154, 417
ius naturale (natural law), 143–44
ius personarum (law of persons), 377
ius pontificium, 81–82

Jain, 10–11, 49, 172, 532
Jaina, 438, 602
jayapatra (victory-document), 336, 367
Jehoshaphat, 92, 245
Jeremiah, 112
Jerusalem, 105–6, 113, 248, 262, 277
jewellery, 541–42

Jewish communities, 41, 79, 417, 422
Jewish laws, 10, 381, 422
Jewish marriage, 422
Jewish slaves, 403
Jews, 256, 268, 295, 381, 388, 422, 488 see also Israelites
Jin, 15, 38, 65, 87, 109, 288, 329, 373, 425, 534
  code, 4, 15, 87, 109
  Western, 535
  see also China.
Josiah, king, 92, 248
Jove, 350, 361
Judah, 92, 232, 236, 247–48, 262
Judaism, 79, 94, 253, 488, 614
Judean kings, 92, 245, 262
judges, 19, 611–12
  chief, 123, 216, 300, 316, 365
  crime, redress and social control, 481, 498
  foreign, 71, 169
  law and religion, 243, 246, 269–71, 272–74, 276–79, 280–81, 289, 299
  law and state, 187, 206, 208, 216, 219–23, 228
  law as text, 27, 42, 50, 58–59, 60–63, 66
  legal procedure, 307–12, 315–18, 329–30, 337–38, 348–50, 357, 361–63, 365–67, 370–71, 374–75
  legal science, 77, 78, 80, 82, 83, 90–92, 99, 120–21, 123–25, 133
  professional, 91, 205, 222, 312, 315
  property, 516, 561–63
  royal, 208, 315
  status and family, 383, 389, 392, 408, 414–15, 443
judgments, 24–25, 221, 317, 336, 338, 364, 366–67, 368–70, 471, 473 see also rulings
judicial activities, 101, 219, 223
judicial authority, 168, 216, 277, 279–80, 311–12, 313, 315, 320
judicial functions, 78, 92, 221, 280, 310, 313, 319
judicial oaths, 269–77, 279, 317, 349
judicial officers, 218
judicial officials, 64, 92, 351, 354, 505
judicial opinions, 64–66
  audience and use, 66
  emergence, 64–65
  production, 65–66
  see also commentaries.
judicial oracles, 269–77
judicial ordeals, 269–77
judicial panels, 112, 281, 315, 364
judicial powers, 219, 311, 313
judicial practices, 27, 273, 280
judicial proceedings, 88, 357, 361

Index

judicial records, 61, 313
judicial responsibilities, 313, 315, 362
judicial systems, 68, 221, 305, 314
juries, 62, 68, 80, 96–97, 130, 337, 340, 356, 361, 366
   system, 311, 317, 361
jurisdiction, 211–13, 214, 216, 220, 277, 279–80, 322, 323, 326, 391, 610
   domestic, 222, 431
   and legal procedure, 322–23
   states within greater legal environment, 204–15
jurisdictional authority, 204, 310, 322, 323, 332
jurisprudence, 76, 89, 91, 117, 223, 304, 445, 447, 454, 481
   Indian, 304, 311, 333, 336, 341, 347, 368, 433, 560
   Roman, 82, 189, 323, 377, 382, 599, 606, 607, 609
juristic literature, 102, 117, 118
jurists, 18–19, 64–66, 75, 82–83, 98–104, 106–8, 116–19, 131–38, 143–44, 493–94
   minor, 100–1
   Roman, 82–83, 98, 100, 131–32, 133–34, 135–36, 138, 144–45, 415, 493–94
jurors, 62, 97, 251, 307, 317, 350, 364, 374, 381, 408
just war (*bellum iustum*), 169, 176, 178
justice
   administration, xiv, 68, 74, 75, 79, 87, 99, 103, 307, 313
   commandant of, 187, 363
   corrective, 480–81, 593
   ministries of, 87, 313–14, 363
   miscarriages, 90, 312, 358, 365
   plaintiffs and access to justice, 324–27
   religious concepts of, 242–47
   social, 70, 225, 386
   systems, 141, 198, 303, 374, 497
   term, 21
   see also Introductory Note.
justifications, 113, 138, 141, 171, 173, 371
   civic, 487–89
   cosmic, 485–86, 488
   of prohibitions, 485, 488
Justinian, emperor, 18, 19
   commerce and contracts, 583–84, 589–90
   Corpus Iuris Civilis, 19, 308, 409
   crime, redress and social control, 19
   Digest, 18, 66, 98–99, 101, 119, 240–41, 336, 344, 415, 493
   law and religion, 240–41
   law as text, 23, 37, 40, 66
   legal procedure, 336, 338, 342, 346, 369

legal science, 101–3, 107–8, 116, 118–19, 132, 136, 138
property, 552, 558
status and family, 384, 395, 415

Karnak, 48, 249, 257
Kātyāyana, 76, 304
Kauṭilya, 385, 389, 393–94, 401–2, 411, 413, 560, 572, 606–7, 608
   Arthaśāstra, 32 *see Arthaśāstra*
kāyastha (scribe), 345
Khotan, 567, 596
kings, 182–85, 194–96, 216–17, 224–26, 241–45, 260–63, 279–81, 314–16, 448–50, 457–58
   bribe-devouring, 16, 209
   'king of justice', 200, 229, 237
   see also monarchs and individual kings.
kingship, 183, 241, 457, 526
knowledge, legal *see* legal knowledge.
koine eirene (common peace), 169
koinon (confederation), 163, 525
Kṣatriyas, 12, 312, 357

Labeo, M. Antistius, 106, 143, 493–94, 594
labour, 327, 400, 403, 451, 472, 481, 528, 538, 543, 544
   agricultural, 542–43, 565
   corvée, 490, 543
labourers, 80, 161, 167, 613
Lagash, 569, 571
lajūkas, 217
land, 17
   agricultural, 81, 523, 538–39, 546
   amounts, 534–36, 540
   auctions, 539, 546
   commerce and contracts, 565, 567, 569–71, 576, 581, 586, 587, 589, 592
   crime, redress and social control, 468, 479, 488, 497, 504, 511
   disposition, 49, 555
   distribution, 514, 534–35, 537
   grants, 516, 527, 532, 540, 578
   Italic, 519, 542, 552, 589
law and religion, 231, 236–37, 242, 247–48, 249, 260–61, 265, 280, 290, 295
law and state, 183, 196, 229
law as text, 47, 49, 51
legal procedure, 306, 345, 358
legal science, 78, 132, 137
mulberry, 536
ownership, 45, 497, 518, 525, 561
pasture, 547
personal share, 536–37

plots, 206, 549, 560
private, 516, 539, 540, 559
property, 513–17, 518, 521–23, 525–26, 527–29, 530–32, 533–42, 545–48, 550–52, 562–64
provincial, 541, 552
public, 440, 535
registry, 51
rights, 393, 582
sale of, 49, 345, 526, 560, 567, 578, 580, 586–87, 592
sanctuary, 290
status and family, 382, 385, 395, 397–400, 402–3, 434–35
surveys, 223, 527, 539
transactions, 14, 45
transfers, 19, 25, 345, 531, 567, 576
war, peace and interstate relations, 152, 158
land-grants, 49, 531
landholdings, 439, 516, 533–34, 536
landlords, 395, 399, 504
landowners, 45, 132, 399, 537
language, 7, 41, 44, 54–55, 110, 112, 234, 478, 594, 609–10
boilerplate, 549, 564
see also individual languages
Late Antiquity, 102–3, 118, 245, 249, 384, 399, 440, 474, 528, 539
Late Bronze Age, 148, 156, 271, 305, 349, 366
Latin, 41, 101, 104, 112, 153, 165, 318, 383, 430
law as text, xiv, 20–72
audience and use, 36–37, 62–63
commentaries see commentaries.
documents, 44–56
historical accounts and reports, 67–68
instructional materials, 67, 71
judicial opinions, 64–66
literature, 68–69
non-legal documents, 70–71
procedural records, 56–64
secondary legal texts, 66–72
visual texts, 71
law codes see codes.
law collections, 605
Babylonian, 420
commerce and contracts, 592
crime, redress and social control, 500
law and religion, 237, 248, 261, 299
law and state, 183, 200, 205, 224
law as text, 21, 23, 26, 30, 38, 40, 42–43, 70
legal science, 75, 77–78, 91, 111–12, 118–19, 122, 125–26, 141
Mesopotamian, 404–5, 605
status and family, 419, 431, 441
Sumerian, 40
see also codes.
law of the city (*ius civile*), 81–82, 98
law schools, xv, 15, 66, 102
lawbocks, 34, 430, 442, 598
lawcourts, 95
lawgivers, 35, 94, 96–98, 199, 236, 239, 241, 489, 605, 608
ancient Greek, 605, 607
intentions, 94–96
nomothetai, 35, 95, 98, 130, 199
lawmakers, 3, 95, 199, 236
laws
emergence, 24–34
production, 34–36
special features, 37–44
statutory, 77, 135–37, 426
see also Introductory Note
Laws of Eshnunna, 8, 112, 125, 352, 566
Laws of Hammurabi, 10
commerce and contracts, 566, 587
crime, redress and social control, 499, 504
law and religion, 237, 260, 299
law as text, 40, 44, 71
legal procedure, 360–61
legal science, 112, 125
property, 543
status and family, 385, 404–5, 414, 428, 431–32, 441
Laws of Lipit-Ishtar, 112, 125, 404–5, 407, 414, 431, 442
laws of nature, 142–43
Laws of Ur-Namma, 26, 30, 112, 298, 404, 405, 566
lawsuits, 4–5, 197–98, 310–11, 312–13, 324–25, 334, 335–36, 347–48, 387, 389
civil, 111, 313, 319, 368
lawyers, xii, xiii, 1, 37, 54, 71, 89, 101, 107, 338–39
leagues, 162, 163, 168, 174, 525
legal authorities, 65, 92, 194, 196, 205, 207, 215, 230, 235, 280–81
and religion, 235–47
highest, 65, 110
legal capacity, 137, 144, 344, 381, 407, 412, 424, 435, 443
legal codes see codes.
legal collections see law collections.
legal commentaries see commentaries.
legal contexts, 6, 21, 68, 234, 266–68, 275, 293, 300, 491
legal cultures, 8, 16, 198, 443
legal education, 66, 89, 92, 104–5, 107–8, 318, 364

687

legal enforcement *see* enforcement.
legal expertise, 9, 74–75, 80, 96, 145, 309, 311, 340, 455, 605
legal experts, 9, 37, 66, 73–74, 76, 80, 124, 131, 145, 364
   legal science, 83–104
   private, 84, 88, 119
legal fictions *see* fictions.
legal forms, 9, 104, 126, 585
legal history, 443, 599–600, 601, 609
   comparative, xiii, 600
legal institutions, xiii, 13, 67, 136–37, 193, 293, 306, 512, 527
legal interpretations, 127–28
legal knowledge, 18, 73, 74, 82–83, 87–88, 91, 96, 99, 103, 106, 108
   emergence, 108, 114
   legal science, 75–83
legal literature, 108–19, 125, 140, 145, 598, 605
legal materials, xiv, 8, 12, 32, 65
legal norms, 69, 73, 81–82
legal penalties, 383, 440
   status as a factor, 440–43
legal practices, 31–32, 34, 108, 234, 238, 240, 379, 381, 600, 602
legal procedure, xii, 12–13, 18, 70–71, 111, 303–75
   appeals, 370–74
   assigning the burden of proof and disclosing evidence to the court, 336–38
   constitution of the court, 310–23
   court deliberations, 123, 361–64
   enforcement of the verdict, 368–70
   evidence, 341–56
   jurisdiction, 322–23
   legal representation, 89, 338–41, 374
   legal space, 245, 310, 319–22, 451
   plaint and summons, 327–32
   plaintiffs and access to justice, 324–27
   plea *see* pleas.
   preliminary court proceedings, 324–41
   presentation and evaluation of evidence, 356–64
   punishment for perjury, 358–61
   sureties and wagers, 334–35
   verdicts in, 364–70
legal proceedings *see* proceedings.
legal processes, 6, 10, 19, 32, 57, 390, 429, 445, 477, 573
legal reasoning, 119–39
legal representation, 89, 338–41, 374
legal science, xiv, 16, 73–145
   law and nature, 139–44

legal experts, 83–104
legal knowledge, 75–83
legal literature, 108–19
legal reasoning, 119–39
legal training, 104–8
legal space, 245, 310, 319–22, 451
legal status, 377, 379, 385, 389–90, 406, 407–8, 437, 443–44, 485
legal systems, 4–5, 16–17, 44, 71–72, 214–16, 322–25, 335–36, 341–42, 353, 379–81
   state, 215–24
legal terms, 65, 242, 377, 492
legal texts, 20, 23, 25, 60, 70, 140–41, 298, 299, 361, 363
   secondary, 23, 65–72
legal traditions, xii–xiii, 34, 112–13, 119, 207, 340, 377, 601–2, 610, 613
   Western, 598–99
legal training, 79, 87, 92, 104–8, 312
   formal, 105, 315, 340
legal transactions, 9, 23, 70, 119, 137, 266, 325, 342, 385, 415
legal treatises, 60, 89–91, 354, 548
legalists, 14, 84–85, 186–87, 197, 462, 465
legality, 130, 188, 190, 191, 306, 537
   state, 611
legis actio (form of action), 58, 335
legislation, 13–15, 16–19, 29–30, 34–35, 75, 77, 190–91, 201–4, 482, 612
   acts of, 9, 221, 537
   imperial, 203, 439
   Roman, 33, 111, 201
   royal, 17, 200
   see also codes; law as text; statutes
legislative power, 182, 230
   over law, 193–204
legislators, 28, 38, 130, 132, 135, 136, 280, 354, 537
legitimacy, 182, 185, 188, 190, 193, 197–200, 224, 225, 226, 227, 228, 229, 469–70, 478, 506
   and law, 224–29
lekhaka (scribe), 345
leniency, 177–78, 179, 506, 545
'levirate marriage', 429–30
Leviticus, 256, 262
lex (statute), 21, 135–36, 201–2, 610
lex Cornelia, 493
liability, 8–9, 121, 401, 414, 426, 466–67, 522, 579, 587, 589
   collective, 122, 400, 466
   of officials, 122, 467
   strict, 465, 467
Liang dynasty, 88, 109
libertus see freedmen.

limitations, 5, 12, 188, 193, 322–23, 376, 407, 411, 417, 489–90
lineages, 192, 212, 345, 352, 381, 389–90, 449, 516, 534, 551
ling (ordinances), 14, 42–43, 122, 196, 373
Lipit-Ishtar, 237, 407, 414, 566
literacy, 4, 22, 28, 36–37, 51, 344–45
literary texts, 13, 35, 68–69, 79, 306
literati, 607
literature, 9, 11, 68–69, 70, 77, 99, 117, 124, 247–48, 273, 492
  biblical, 142, 248
  juristic, 102, 117, 118
  legal, 108–19, 125, 140, 145, 598, 605
  rabbinic, 92, 105, 256, 268, 421, 604
litigants/litigating parties, 56–57, 61–62, 275–76, 306–8, 334–35, 336–41, 346–47, 357–58, 361–62, 367–70
litigation
  civil, 111, 219, 313, 319, 327, 329, 368
  private, 56, 194, 317, 319, 324, 328, 338, 366, 375
livestock, 174, 517, 519, 528, 541–42, 549, 602
Livy, 67, 81, 164, 568, 571
loan documents, 53
loans, 47–48, 123, 334, 342, 345–46, 563, 566, 582, 585, 587
local assemblies, 183, 223, 259, 517
local authorities/government, 60, 213, 314, 371–72, 465, 474
local councils, 315, 395
local courts, 87, 277, 314, 316, 328, 561
local elites, 101, 221
local laws, 35, 108, 195, 561
local rules, 35, 116, 153, 229
logographers *logographoi*, 60, 61, 63, 340–41, 346, 364
long possession (*usucapio*), 538, 541, 551, 552
losing parties, 81, 268, 319, 365–66, 368, 486
lower courts, 208, 322, 368, 375
lü (statutes), 14, 42–43, 109, 196
Lycurgus, 94, 239
Lysias, 95, 130, 270, 525

ma'at (justice), 21, 72, 386
Macedonia, 153, 161, 175
Macedonian dynasty, 17, 29
Maecianus, Lucius Volusius, 103–4
magic, 287, 288, 298–301, 356
  harmful, 297–99
  sympathetic, 471, 510
  see also sorcery; witchcraft
magical practices, 300, 455

magistrates, 99, 117–18, 119–20, 188–89, 201–2, 221–23, 283–84, 318, 320–21, 452
  imperial, 39, 311, 318, 323, 338, 347, 367, 370
  presiding, 331, 333
  Roman, 191, 364, 369, 453
Mahābhārata, 11, 185
Mahamatras, 218
maiestas (superiority), 174, 203, 254, 391, 453, 484–85, 501
male children, 295, 405, 430, 434 *see also* sons
male descendants, 429, 436–37, 555
male slaves, 298, 405
management, 14, 514, 521, 523, 527, 553, 555
  conflicts, 147, 168
Mānava Dharmaśāstra, 3, 11, 385, 401–2, 526, 579, 591, 595
Mancinus, Aulus Hostilius, 451–53, 455
'Mandate of Heaven', 185, 227, 251
mandates, divine, 231, 237, 239, 262
Manilia, 451–53
Manu, 11
  crime, redress, and social control, 457–58, 499, 501–2
  Dharmaśāstra, 457–58, 501
  law and religion, 291, 296–97
  law and state, 184–85
  law as text, 20
  legal procedure, 359
  legal science, 76, 89–90, 111, 123
  property, 526, 555
  status and family, 427, 437
  see also India.
manumission, 134, 396, 399–400, 402, 404, 544
Marcus Aurelius, emperor, 356
Marduk, 254
Mari, 148, 157, 385, 419
maritime cases, 325
maritime contracts, 50, 582
market certificates, 49, 52, 582, 592
marketplaces, 29, 278, 346, 474, 510, 518, 547
marriage, 11, 609
  alliances, 157, 390
  contracts, 48, 51, 419, 422, 433, 549
  crime, redress and social control, 499
  first, 553, 562–63
  Jewish, 422
  law and religion, 273
  law and state, 196, 205, 208
  law as text, 47, 53, 68
  legal *see conubium; justae nuptiae*
  legal procedure, 325
  legal science, 79, 113, 120
levirate, 429–30

marriage (cont.)
  property, 543, 549, 553, 555, 557
  status and family, 390, 396, 398, 403–6, 408, 417–27, 430, 437
  treaty system, 160–61
  war, peace and interstate relations, 157
materials
  durable, 33, 35, 52, 61
  Greek, 79–80, 209
  instructional, 67, 71
  legal, xiv, 8, 12, 32, 65
  Near Eastern, 77, 82, 142, 316, 338, 355, 371, 600
Mauryas, 10–11, 606 *see also* India
maxims, 70, 401, 426–27
Medes, 448–49
mediation, 164, 168, 214, 243, 338, 437
Megasthenes, 150, 393
Meidias, 496
Memorabilia, Xenophon, 97
Memphis, 249, 257, 280
meng (oath/blood covenant), 120, 160, 273–74, 348–49, 572, 575
merchants, 45, 148, 151, 153, 154, 312, 315, 386, 390, 566
Mesopotamia, 5, 8, 12, 601, 611
  commerce and contracts, 565, 567, 573, 575, 577, 579
  kings, 242, 262
  see also individual names
  law collections, 404–5, 605
  law and religion, 233, 236, 241–42, 254, 269, 278–79, 291, 302
  law and state, 181, 183–84, 200–1, 205, 222, 224–25, 229
  law as text, 21, 41, 46–47, 51–53, 60, 62, 64, 66, 71
  law collections, 404–5, 605
  legal procedure, 364
  legal science, 91
  property, 515, 526, 564
  sources, 414, 416
  southern, 91, 302, 515, 565
  status and family, 397, 407, 431–32, 434, 445
  war, peace and interstate relations, 157
messengers, 148–49, 154, 157, 329, 449
Middle Bronze Age, 236
Middle Kingdom period, 47, 68, 156, 297, 306, 316, 386, 548
military conflicts, 165
military office, 391–95
mines, 462, 472, 474, 475, 546
ministers, 86, 187, 197, 221, 280, 313, 349, 393–94

chief, 14, 329
ministries of justice, 87, 313–14, 363
minors, 100, 325, 402, 407, 412–13, 518, 531
  property, 518, 531
  see also children
misbehaviour, 69, 288, 420, 456
miscarriages of justice, 90, 312, 358, 365
misconduct, 32, 185, 310, 316, 385, 394, 485
Mishnah, 10, 93, 112–14, 127, 255, 256
mistresses, 298, 404, 420
mitra (allies), 158, 572
modern scholars, 43, 67, 138, 177, 199, 342, 400, 418, 507, 605
mokṣa, 307 *see* divorce.
monarchs, 35, 182, 188, 232, 236, 248, 449, 498
  Hellenistic, 164, 169, 174
  see also kings and individual names
monarchy, 35, 147, 162, 181–82, 190, 192, 201, 213, 220, 232
monetary penalties, 439, 441, 442, 484
money, 131–33, 364, 365–66, 402–3, 475–76, 508, 511, 520, 572, 573
  payment, 403, 590
monks, 11, 155, 281, 440
  Buddhist, 151, 281
monopolies, 192, 502–3, 506, 517, 546, 611
  pontifical, 18, 99, 240
monopolization of violence, 501–10
moon, 55, 85, 245, 254, 257, 288, 608
morality, 11, 70, 85, 243, 391, 393
  absolute, 139–40
Moses, 92, 113, 114, 126, 142, 236, 284–85, 433
mothers, 68, 80, 158, 405, 408, 436, 437, 441, 551, 554–55 *see also* parents
moveables, 290, 341, 402, 517, 541–42, 552
  sales of, 587
  see also cattle; slaves
mulberry land, 536
murder, 80, 329, 339, 353, 455, 477, 480, 497, 504
  see also homicide
murderers, 138, 352
mutilations, 72, 392, 413, 470, 473, 476

*nagalaviyohālaka*s (judicial officers of the city), 217–18
nāgîd (governor), 92
nails, 296, 586
Nārada (codes), 32, 111, 304, 457
Nārada Smṛti, 90, 286, 427, 526, 610
Naram-Sin, 229, 260
narrative texts, 90, 129
Nasica, P. Scipio, 454–55
natural ascriptive statuses, 406–16

natural law, 22, 139–41, 142–44, 154, 180
natural phenomena, 85, 140–41
natural sons, 42, 50
Naukratis, 387–88, 394
Near Eastern courts, 323, 366, 368
Near Eastern law, 8–10, 124, 183, 525, 599–600, 605 *see also* individual civilisations
Near Eastern material, 77, 82, 142, 316, 338, 355, 371, 600
negative incentives, 446–47, 469, 477, 491, 509
negotiations, peace, 154, 178
neighbouring property, 520, 560
neighbours, 45, 81, 176, 344, 382, 448, 467, 505, 530–31, 559–60
Neo-Babylonian period, 8
 commerce and contracts, 573, 578, 586–87
 law and religion, 271, 278–79
 legal procedure, 315–16, 320, 331, 343, 349–50, 352, 355, 361, 364, 366
 legal science, 78, 91
 property, 515, 539
 status and family, 431–32
Nergal-ina-tēši-ēṭer, 335
Nero, emperor, 254, 472
neutrality, 170, 179
New Kingdom, 30, 47, 70–71, 149, 171, 272, 280, 306, 316, 386
Nippur Homicide Trial, 111, 364
nirṇaya (verdict), 365
nitya (eternal), 238
niyoga (appointment), 430
niyukta. ('appointed' witnesses), 337
nobiles (aristocrats), 454
nobles, 329, 339, 385, 391–92, 495, 535, 536
nomothetai (lawgivers), 35, 95, 98, 130, 199
non-aggression pacts, 158
non-capital offences, 392, 413–14
non-dispositive oaths, 271
non-elites, 386, 471
non-Jews, 381, 403 *see also* Gentiles
non-legal documents, 67, 70–71
non-payment
 of debts, 13, 328, 499, 569, 579, 585, 595
 of wages, 328, 499, 585, 595
non-state laws, 209–10
normative behaviour, 198, 447–48
normative principles, 137
normative rules, 10, 31–32, 103, 136, 138, 179
normative systems, 4, 191
normative texts, 6, 136, 380, 457, 525, 526
norms, 1, 4, 98–99, 136–38, 195–98, 204, 206, 208, 235, 238

behavioural, 235, 447
customary, 14–15, 21, 77, 197, 230, 379, 381, 390, 437, 548
ethical, 16, 410
legal, 69, 73, 81
shaping state power, 183–93
Northern Dynasties, 455, 535–37
Northern Qi, 314, 455, 536 *see also* China
Northern Wei, 281, 288, 372–73, 425–26, 472, 505, 535–36 *see also* China
notaries, 37, 51, 53–54, 61, 346, 585
Nuzi, 223, 271, 305, 316, 331, 339, 349, 366

oaths, 8, 18
 as evidence, 347–50
 broken, 168, 350
 commerce and contracts, 568–75, 577, 586
 dispositive, 269, 271, 274, 276
 fealty, 573–74
 gods, 570–71
 judicial, 269, 271–72, 279, 317, 349
 law and religion, 267–76, 278–79, 287, 291, 301
 law and state, 209, 224
 law as text, 42
 legal procedure, 306–7, 329, 341–42, 346–47, 348–50, 357–59, 360–61, 366, 368
 legal science, 81, 129
 meng, 120, 160, 273–74, 348–49, 572, 575
 non-dispositive, 271
 promissory, 266–68, 573
 property, 520, 528
 use, 120, 180, 301, 574
 war, peace and interstate relations, 155–56, 160, 161–64, 167, 168, 172
objects of ownership, 538–46
oblates, 278, 291–92, 397
obligatio, 569
obligations, 14, 608, 612
 commerce and contracts, 565, 575–76, 577, 583, 586–87, 588, 593–95
 contingent, 586, 589
 crime, redress, and social control, 467, 505
 financial, 383, 421, 528
 law and religion, 243, 262, 267, 280, 389, 557
 law and state, 226
 law as text, 47, 49
 legal procedure, 357
 property, 517, 518, 531, 545, 556, 557, 560
 ritual, 426, 553
 status and family, 379, 381–82, 383, 412, 415, 430, 431, 435

691

obligations (cont.)
  strict, 595
  war, peace and interstate relations, 160–61
observance, 13, 255, 256–58, 380
occupations, 205, 315, 352, 389
Oecumenius, 104
offences, 14
  capital, 221, 285, 287–88, 326–27, 392, 411, 414, 455, 458, 465
  crime, redress and social control, 449, 455–56, 465–67, 474, 483–84, 486–87, 506–7
  criminal, 327, 334, 466
  grave, 251, 507
  law and religion, 245, 264, 281–82, 285–86, 287, 288–89, 291, 301
  law and state, 196
  law as text, 38–39
  legal procedure, 313, 324, 326–27, 330, 359–60, 361–64, 365, 373
  legal science, 75, 85, 97, 120–22
  non-capital, 392, 413–14
  property, 544–45
  punishable, 287, 391, 425–26
  religious, 264, 287, 288
  status and family, 391, 400, 411, 413–14, 436, 439, 442
  war, peace and interstate relations, 173
offenders, 288, 314, 320, 363, 368, 373–74, 472, 476, 486, 489
officers, 28, 56, 151, 218, 223, 330, 362, 372, 393
  judicial, 218
official statuses, 221, 391, 393, 443, 453
officials, 29–30, 35–37, 87, 109–10, 211–12, 215–17, 263–64, 313–16, 390–94, 465
  administrative, 315–16
  duties of, 75, 122, 185, 196, 266, 313, 395
  government, 91, 262, 305, 315, 316, 324, 368
  Greek, 279, 561
  high-ranking, 87, 360
  imperial, 104, 203, 323, 373
  judicial, 64, 92, 351, 354, 505
  local, 14, 125, 150, 277, 289, 323, 330, 368, 371
  low ranking, 87, 392
  provincial, 192, 364
  Ptolemaic, 561–62, 563
  public, 37, 305, 474
  religious, 234, 259, 277, 281, 289, 315
  state, 14, 185, 192, 240, 249, 280, 281, 287, 454, 457
offspring, 396, 402, 403–4, 406, 418, 419–20, 426, 429, 437, 531
Old Kingdom period, 25, 59, 67, 300, 306, 515, 565, 577

oligarchic society, 498
oligarchy, 147, 452, 613
Olympia, 152, 174
Olympic games, 153
omens, 75, 124, 174–75, 261, 264, 456
opinions, 64 *see* judicial opinions.
oracles, 70, 174–75, 178, 239, 243, 264–65, 269, 272–73, 276, 306
  judicial, 269–77
oral agreements, 47, 48, 155, 578
oral laws, 22, 24, 599
oral rules, 24, 33
orator, 82, 153
orators, 83, 96, 99, 138, 290, 593
  Attic, 317, 582
oratory, 75, 76, 82, 364
ordeals, 120, 287, 306, 341, 362, 366
  as evidence, 347–50
  judicial, 269–77
  river, 42, 269, 270–71, 299, 349
order, religious concepts of, 242–47
ordinances, 14, 27, 42, 122, 142, 363, 488, 592
Oropos, 289–90
orphans, 200, 243, 612
orthodoxy, 94
ostraca, 51, 272
outrage, 246, 484, 489
owners, 132–33, 396–98, 402, 405, 493, 499, 516–19, 521–23, 529–31, 552
  erstwhile, 131, 545
  true, 538, 552, 586, 589, 591
ownership, 278, 499, 512–13, 515, 517–19, 521, 524–25, 527–29, 540–42, 550
  land, 45, 497, 518, 525, 561
  objects, 538–46
  private, 518, 523, 541, 547, 563
  proof of, 341, 517–18, 560–61, 591
  restrictions, 546–48
  rights, 403, 521
  undivided, 557, 575

pacts, 158–59, 425, 574
  non-aggression, 158
Palestine, 79, 93–94, 106, 113, 114
  Roman, 78, 430
Pāli, 10
Pallava dynasty, 55
Papias, Aelius Aurelius Ammianos, 101
papyri, 5, 17, 19
  commerce and contracts, 577–78, 582, 584
  crime, redress, and social control, 473
  Egypt, 101, 346, 542, 599

law and religion, 272
law as text, 23, 25, 47, 50, 51, 61
legal procedure, 311
legal science, 100, 118
property, 523
status and family, 413, 421, 439
parents, 325, 326–27, 414, 423, 425, 431–32, 433, 436–37, 506–7, 553
  aged, 412
  biological, 414, 428
  see also fathers; mothers
pariṣad, 89–90, 280
parity treaties, 155, 267, 570
Parthians, 93, 164–65, 574
partial *atimia*, 361
parties
  accusing, 337, 343
  aggrieved, 200, 206
  guilty, 349, 390, 471
  injured, 97, 215, 476, 483–84, 496
  private, 82, 99, 193, 451, 529
  subordinate, 569–71
  third *see* third parties.
partition of inheritance, 329, 499, 595
partnerships, 13, 47, 158–59, 164, 194, 499, 575, 585, 594, 595
  strategic, 158–59
Passover (*pesaḥ*), 255–56, 488
paterfamilias (senior male ascendant), 212, 395, 409, 412, 417, 423–24, 518–19, 522, 557, 583
paternal power, 395, 409, 417, 424, 557
patricians, 201, 240, 265, 383, 423–24
patrons, 51, 152, 167, 189, 213, 237, 399, 463, 497, 500
  deity, 254, 261
patronus, 82, 340
patronymics, 318, 331, 387, 530
Paulus, Iulius, 100, 101, 116
payments, 54, 334, 341, 345, 413, 415, 421–22, 465, 475–76, 586–88
  copper, 392, 413, 465
peace, xiv, 17, 146–80
  arbitrations, meditation and Common-Peace experiment, 168–69
  hospitality rules and customs, 148–55
  negotiations, 154, 178
  pacts, 572
  states forming alliances and pursuing diplomacy, 155–68
Pedius, 594
peers, 223, 340, 382, 441, 449, 454
Peiraieus, 290

Peloponnesian War, 174–75
penal codes, 42, 87, 187, 196
penal laws, 14–15, 38, 42, 466, 607–8
penal rules, 38, 122, 227
penal servitude, 288, 359, 368, 373, 470, 472, 474, 556
penal statutes, 75, 120, 122, 455–56
penalties, 319, 335, 368–69, 390, 440–41, 474–77, 489–90, 566, 586, 591–92
  contractual, 421, 425
  death *see* death, penalty/sentences.
  legal, 383, 440
  monetary, 439, 441, 442, 484
  see also punishments
penances, 11, 13, 258, 297, 485–86
Pentateuch, 10, 232
Pergamum, 283, 543
Pericles, 97, 408
perjury, 57, 270, 374
  punishments for, 358–61
Persians, 163, 175, 315, 430, 523, 578
personal property, 437, 460
personal retainers, 327, 395, 400, 545
personal status, 2, 205, 376–77, 378–79, 382, 386, 418, 441, 443, 445
personal surety, 335
personnel, 20, 223, 310, 315, 513
pesaḥ (Passover), 255–56, 488
petitioners, 62, 272, 374, 413
petitions, 27, 29, 59–60, 62–63, 101–3, 371, 373, 386, 388, 439–40
  oral, 327, 331
  written, 59, 331, 562
Petronius, 107
pharaohs, 146, 149, 155–57, 170–71, 262–63, 280
Philip II of Macedonia, 153, 161, 175
Philo, 399
philosophers, 84, 85, 153, 481
physical assault, 329, 390, 499, 501–3, 595
piety, filial, 227, 327, 455, 469, 505, 545
pigs, 9, 290, 292, 296, 571
plaintiffs, 95–97, 271, 308, 325, 326, 327–33, 336–37, 338–39, 357, 366–68, 561–63
  and access to justice, 324–27
  Roman, 58, 326
plaints, 69, 123, 304, 333–34, 336, 357, 365, 367
  and summonses, 327–32
  valid, 328, 330
Plato, 69, 97, 142–43, 200, 252–53, 293, 366, 481, 487, 515
  Crito, 95, 97

693

Platonism, 614
pleadings, 56–57, 59, 63, 307, 310, 333, 367, 563
pleas, 63, 69, 115, 123, 304, 327–29, 333–34, 336, 357, 367
  special, 123, 334, 336
plebeians, 135, 201, 424
pledges, 123, 342, 386, 402, 540, 544, 560, 563, 566, 585
Pliny, 70, 308, 479
plots of land, 206, 549, 560
poets, 246, 253, 504
poison, 288, 347–48, 480, 493, 497, 572
poisoners, 493
polis (city), 16, 28, 33, 182, 209, 258, 366, 444, 496, 612–13
political agendas, 57, 202
political anthropology, 143–44
political authorities, 79, 93, 97, 183, 223, 284, 452, 486
political careers, 62, 99, 107, 452
political communities, 28, 200, 209, 451, 500
political control, 17, 165, 483
political experience, 603–4
political formations, 159, 182, 199
political influence, 200, 244
political offices, 188, 193
political power, 117, 182–84, 193, 281, 457, 510
political practices, 189, 223
political science, 70, 76, 91, 111, 114, 311 see also Arthaśāstra
political stability, 147, 155–57, 451
political statuses, 386, 388, 454
political theories, 179, 486, 488
politics, 11, 75, 243, 252, 450, 498, 603
polities, 146–47, 152, 157, 160, 164, 167, 179, 182, 379–80, 416
  ecclesial, 380–81
  foreign, 149, 156
  imperial, 214, 385
  status within, 379–91
pollution, 256, 463
  and purity, 292–97
Pompeii, 584
Pomponius, Sextus, 107, 116, 395
pontiffs, 18, 81–82, 83, 240, 558
pontifical monopoly, 18, 99, 240
pontifices, 64, 81, 240
possession, 287–88, 341, 343, 351, 353, 515, 517–19, 540–42, 550–51, 560
power
  coercive, 368, 611
  imperial, 103, 190, 315
  legislative *see* legislative power.

paternal, 395, 409, 417, 424, 557
political, 117, 182–84, 193, 281, 457, 510
ruling, 191–93, 230
state, 184, 188–89, 193, 199, 219, 447, 450, 490, 491, 609
prādvivāka (judge), 90, 217, 312
praecones, 100
praefectus praetorio, 104
praetorian rules, 558
praetors, 18, 116, 219–21, 308–9, 332, 493, 498, 546, 552, 558
  court, 220, 493
  edict, 29, 35, 43, 136, 307
  urban, 213, 307–8, 369, 435, 498
Prakrit, 55
prāṅnyāya (prior judgment), 334, 336, 367
pratibhū (surety), 334
prativādin (substitute), 329, 338
prāyaścitta (penance), 12–13, 486
prayers, 243, 264, 292, 295, 300, 415
prebendaries, 278
prebends, 278
precedents, 14, 75, 108–9, 110, 114, 129, 192, 203, 237, 363
prefects, 60, 103, 221, 273, 399, 467, 483, 579
  of Egypt, 273, 311, 399, 483
prefectures, 104, 263, 363, 371–73
preliminary court proceedings, 324–41
premodern societies, 513, 538, 542, 564, 601
prescribed punishments, 21, 264, 392
prescriptive statements, 137
presiding magistrates, 331, 333
prestige, 99, 107, 154, 166–67, 378
'presumptive' states, 448
prices, 54, 58, 153, 476, 477, 520, 529, 550–51, 581, 585–92
  purchase, 267, 520, 549, 591
priestesses, 47, 276, 282, 283, 428
priesthoods, 176, 189, 240, 282–83, 429, 541
Priestly Writings, 256, 277, 284, 294
priests, 240, 249, 265–66, 272, 277–84 289, 294–96, 297–98, 316–17, 335
  āśipu, 299
  colleges of, 81, 189
  Daoist, 439
  Elected, 283
  high, 92, 243, 254, 278, 285, 295
prima facie evidence, 51, 341, 517
principal legal traditions, 8–19
  China, 13–15
  Greece, 15–17
  India, 10–13

Near East, 8–10
Rome, 17–19
Principate, 100, 106, 116, 190, 317–18, 323, 356, 370, 383, 498
  early, 136, 309, 340
'principle terms', 137
prior judgment *(prāṅnyāya)*, 334, 336, 367
prisoners, 27, 152, 354, 397, 445, 474, 490
prisons, 27, 217, 320, 369, 372, 392, 411, 413, 474
private actors, 224
private agreements, 214, 425, 525, 545, 579, 581
private cases/litigation, 56, 194, 317, 319, 324, 328, 338, 366, 375
private contracts, 165, 386, 514, 519, 541, 549, 573, 578
private courts, 208, 217
private disputes, 14, 40, 48, 204, 224, 306, 351, 369, 609
private groups, 207, 448
private individuals/persons, 99, 152, 155, 303, 304, 310, 311, 495, 540, 545–46
private land, 516, 539, 540, 559
private law, 14–15, 98, 136, 207, 212, 409, 412, 417, 518, 526
private legal experts, 84, 88, 119
private ownership, 518, 523, 541, 547, 563
private parties, 82, 99, 193, 451, 529
private property, 446, 451, 512, 515, 516, 523–24, 528, 531, 545, 548–49
  rights, 519, 523, 528, 539
private sales, 523, 549, 592
private transactions, 14, 48, 480, 494, 496
privileges, 49, 282–83, 376, 378, 386, 391–92, 411–13, 440, 453–54, 465
  legal, 383–85, 413
  special, 207, 381, 394, 412, 416, 440
procedural law *see* legal procedure
procedural records, 23, 44, 56–64
  audience and use, 62–63
  emergence, 56–61
  production, 61
  special features, 63–64
procedural rules, 32, 57, 188, 306, 308, 333
  see also legal procedure
procedural texts, 59–60, 62–63
procedure
  bureaucratic, 309, 338
  civil, 81, 308–9, 321
  criminal, 82, 483, 493
  cultic, 234, 276, 278, 302
  legal *see* legal procedure

rules, 42, 195, 304, 306
  special, 522, 545, 582
proceedings
  appeals, 370–74
  civil, 329–30, 333
  criminal, 326, 330, 365, 368
  judicial, 88, 357, 361
  verdict, 364–70
procuratores a libellis (agents in charge of responses to petitions addressed to the emperor), 102–3
professional associations, 437–40
professional judges, 91, 205, 222, 312, 315
prohibitions, 42, 278, 287–88, 326, 451, 477–79, 481–83, 487, 506–7, 509–10
  justification, 485, 488
  religious, 478, 479, 509
promissory oaths, 266–68, 573
proof, 123, 129, 328, 334, 336–37, 341–42, 357, 362, 579, 584
  artless, 129, 135
  burden of, 123, 334, 336–37, 341, 357, 362, 579
  of ownership, 341, 517–18, 560–61, 591
property, 512–64
  archives, 528, 608
  claims, 538, 551
  commerce and contracts, 565, 581, 585–87, 588–89, 590–91, 595, 597
  common, 546–47
  confiscation, 269, 289, 361, 369
  crime, redress and social control, 450, 455, 459, 460, 463, 497–99, 502, 504
  disposal by will, 136, 436
  disputes, 271, 526, 560, 564
  family, 206, 417, 432–37, 519, 546, 551, 553, 555, 561
  fathers, 433, 553, 554, 563
  history, 512–21
  immovable, 499, 518, 539, 545
    see also real estate/property
  law and religion, 242, 258, 289, 290
  law and state, 197, 205–6, 209, 212–13
  law as text, 43, 46, 52–53, 55, 58, 60, 69
  legal procedure, 307, 327, 341, 350, 351, 360, 366, 369
  legal science, 81, 121–22, 131–33, 144
  minors, 518, 531
  modern theories, 521–24
  moveable *see* moveables.
  neighbouring, 520, 560
  ownership *see* ownership.
  personal, 437, 460
  public, 440, 513

property (cont.)
  real *see also* property, immovable; real estate/property
    rights, 515–17, 519–23, 527, 531, 533, 534, 538, 540–41, 550–52, 554
      enforcement, 512–13, 515, 519, 521–22, 524–25, 527, 539, 547–48, 549–50, 559–60
      history, 512–14
      operation, 538
      private, 519, 523, 528, 539
    sold, 527–28
    sources, 524–26
    and state, 526–38
    status and family, 397–98, 401–3, 408–11, 412, 416–17, 419, 422–23, 424, 430, 433–37
    taxes, 531, 581
    transactions, 48, 49, 526–28, 530, 537, 541, 542, 548
    transfers, 5, 7, 445, 552, 594
    war, peace and interstate relations, 150, 177
prosecutions, 95, 199, 215, 252, 289, 305, 314, 324, 337, 340
prosecutors, 215, 476, 484
prostitutes, 384, 407–8, 442
provinces, 100–2, 107, 191–92, 213, 221, 222, 318, 323, 364, 525
provincial administrations, 314, 497, 513
provincial governors, 93, 99, 103, 117, 318, 323, 369, 498
provincial land, 541, 552
Ptolemaic officials, 561–62, 563
Ptolemaic peiod *see* Greco-Roman Egypt
Ptolemais, 387–88, 394
Ptolemies, 17, 29, 550, 562, 563
public authorities, 23, 206, 437
public cases, 61, 319, 337
public land, 440, 535
public law, 81, 190, 234, 240, 283, 323
public office(s), 104, 377, 384, 391–95, 459, 474
public property, 440, 513
public records, 47, 50, 51, 528
punishments, 13, 38–39, 42, 84–86, 120–22, 285–87, 359, 360, 361, 462, 463, 465–81
  board of, 313–14
  capital, 150, 155, 221, 222, 314, 442, 446, 472, 492
  see also death, penalty/sentences
  of Christians, 462
  corporal, 324, 395, 402, 442, 471, 472, 582
  divine, 262, 274, 277, 292
  of exile, 465, 467
  lesser, 360, 466
  mutilating *see* mutilations
  for perjury, 358–61
  prescribed, 21, 264, 392
  severity, 381, 442
  see also penalties
punitive damages, 471, 476
pupils, 105, 253, 401–2
purchase prices, 267, 520, 549, 591
purchasers, 49, 52, 283, 520, 550, 589, 590
purchases, 396, 397, 401–2, 499, 529, 546, 550, 587, 594, 595
purification, 80, 265, 282, 295, 296–97, 463
  rituals, 292–93, 296
purity, 113, 208, 282
  and pollution, 292–97

Qi, Northern, 314, 455, 536
Qin, 13–14, 608
  crime, redress and social control, 456, 465–66, 467–68, 473, 495, 506
  law and religion, 258, 287
  law and state, 211, 227
  law as text, 26, 38, 61, 64
  legal procedure, 304–5, 313, 326, 330, 348, 352, 359
  legal science, 85, 87–88, 109, 121
  property, 527, 534, 545
  status and family, 391, 400, 426
  see also China
qualifications, 74, 190, 211, 222, 315, 342–44, 374
Quintilian, 69, 82

rabbinic hermeneutics, 126–27
rabbinic interpretation, 127, 129
rabbinic law, 79, 105, 112–13, 271, 278, 285, 295, 380, 422
rabbinic literature, 92, 105, 256, 268, 421, 604
rabbinic movement, 78–79
rabbinic sages, 79, 106, 113
rabbinic tradition, 94, 606
rabbis, 92–93, 106, 114, 126–28, 129, 255, 256–57, 278, 285, 402–3
Rāmāyaṇa, 11
rape, 96, 177, 205, 324, 398, 401, 408, 419, 426, 441, *see also* sexual crimes
rationalization, 456, 470, 482–83, 487
real estate/property, 132, 341, 397, 408–9, 517–18, 525, 527, 528, 539, 541 *see also* immovable property
realists, 225
reasoning, 6, 111–12, 119–39, 143–45

Index

deductive, 78, 123, 134, 357
inductive, 77, 135
rebels, 170, 285
receipts, 23, 44, 53, 345, 520
recipients, 55, 239, 393, 516–17
recitations, 291–92, 299, 300
records
  of cases/trials, 5–6, 9, 56, 58, 60–61, 63, 111, 276, 367, 368
  documentary, 4, 381, 538, 540, 586
  historical, 12, 35, 90, 542, 609
  judicial, 61, 313
  procedural *see* procedural records
  public, 47, 50, 51, 528
  tax, 346, 399
redress, xiv, 69, 320, 324, 329, 394, 446–511
referral, system of, 363–64
reforms, 247, 262, 534, 535, 543
registration, 435, 465–66, 497, 527, 530–31, 540, 579, 589, 608
regularities, 85, 141–42
regulation(s), 83, 85, 282, 289, 294, 297, 393, 395, 451–52, 534
  administrative, 14, 75, 120, 205, 456
  Dhamma, 491
  internal, 32, 437
  legal, 132, 279
  sanctuary, 282
  state, 13, 239, 544
Rekh-mi-rē, 22, 72
relatives, 27, 121, 214, 392, 400, 402, 442, 466, 507, 555–57
  close, 434, 436, 455, 554
  male, 411, 422, 430
  see also families; family members
release, 86, 137, 152, 403, 427, 430, 490
religion, 75–76, 80–82, 231–32, 233–35, 237–38, 240, 249–50, 252–53, 266, 300–2
  governance, 260–66
  and legal authority, 235–47
  and state, 247–66
  and wrongdoing, 284–301
  see also individual religions
religious activities, 147, 172, 248, 253, 281, 284, 532
religious authorities, 93, 312, 380, 444
religious beliefs, 10, 231, 245, 276
religious duties, 11, 264, 280, 454
religious endowments, 526, 528, 532, 533
religious experts, 76, 265–66
religious festivals, 152, 239, 253, 257, 263, 288
religious groups, 49, 209, 393, 440
religious institutions, 81, 527–28, 532

religious laws, 32, 79, 239
religious legitimation of law, 235–42
religious obligations, 280, 389, 557
religious offences, 264, 287, 288
religious officials, 234, 259, 289, 315
  and the law, 277–84
religious orders, 150, 229, 439
religious practices, 93, 234, 286
  enforcement, 247–54
religious prohibitions, 478, 479, 509
religious rituals, 234, 302
  in legal contexts, 266–77
religious specialists, 238, 264
religious texts, 4, 127, 234, 331
reports, 5–6, 58, 67–68
Republican Rome
  commerce and contracts, 583, 589
  crime, redress and social control, 454, 458, 464, 471, 478, 484, 498
  law and religion, 265–66, 275
  law and state, 189–90, 201–2, 219–20, 227
  law as text, 29, 54, 59, 63
  legal procedure, 307, 309, 322, 328
  legal science, 99, 106
  property, 537, 558–59
  status and family, 384, 394, 424
  war, peace and interstate relations, 146, 164, 166–67, 178
Res Gestae, 176
res mancipi, 538, 542, 552, 589
res publica (Roman state), 189
res religiosa (sacred thing), 290, 518
rescripts, 23, 29–30, 62, 77, 102–3, 119, 200–1, 205, 369, 384
reservoirs, 43, 532, 540
resolutions, 2, 7, 13–14, 71, 120, 124, 176, 197–98, 561, 564
responsa, 90, 99–100, 106–7
responsibilities, 215, 217, 264, 269, 279–80, 282, 313, 316, 397–98, 553
  judicial, 313, 315, 362
restitution, 176, 419, 447, 470, 487
restrictions, 40, 291–92, 325–26, 344, 374, 424, 523, 556, 558–59
  legal, 407, 409, 432
  ownership, 546–48
retainers, personal, 327, 395, 400, 545
revenge, 252, 361, 494, 505
revenue, 316, 383
  tax, 516, 532–33
Rhetoric, Aristotle, 69, 97, 130
Richardson, Seth, 448
righteousness, 21, 206, 229, 242–43

697

rights, 608, 612
  absolute, 521
  civic, 361, 401, 474
  civil, 162, 403
  commerce and contracts, 586
  crime, redress and social control, 451, 460, 475
  human, 144, 148, 443
  land, 393, 582
  law and religion, 246, 262, 278
  law as text, 35, 49, 55
  legal procedure, 307, 361
  ownership, 403, 521
  property, 515–17, 519–23, 527, 531, 533, 534, 538, 540–41, 550–52, 554
  status and family, 397–98, 404, 406–8, 409, 414, 418, 421, 423, 428, 433
  to use violence, 453, 506–9
  war, peace and interstate relations, 154
risks, 5, 269, 277, 286, 291, 444, 483–84, 505
  of accidental loss or damage, 589, 591
rites, 186, 253, 258, 263, 292, 296, 392, 418, 423, 427
  ancestor, 429, 431, 553
  funeral, 81, 385
  Vedic, 280, 285
ritual obligations, 426, 553
ritual performances, 240, 259, 532
rituals, 7, 10, 11, 14, 608
  classics, 110, 186, 415, 425, 429
  commerce and contracts, 572
  crime, redress and social control, 510
  cultic, 234, 278
  forms, 7
  law and religion, 243–44, 254, 256–58, 259–61, 280, 282, 283, 291–92, 295–96, 298–99
  law and state, 183, 226
  law as text, 70
  legal procedure, 312, 348, 366
  legal science, 80, 140
  property, 526
  purification, 292–93, 296
  ritual forms as source materials, 7
  status and family, 380
  war, peace and interstate relations, 156, 171, 176, 178
river ordeals, 42, 269, 270–71, 299, 349
rivers, 269, 349, 547
Rock Edicts, 393, 491
role-statuses, 378
Roman Egypt *see* Greco-Roman Egypt.
Roman Palestine, 78, 430

Rome, xii, 2, 17–19, 598–600, 603–4, 606, 609, 612–13
  citizens, 135, 383, 417, 424, 453, 454, 485, 487, 518, 527
  cognitio, 309, 318, 326
  commerce and contracts, 571, 574, 575–77, 584–85, 589–90, 595, 597, 600, 603–4, 612–13
  crime, redress and social control, 446, 453, 459, 468, 472–74, 482, 498, 504
  emperors, 245, 459, 464
  see also individual names.
  envoys, 153, 176
  governors, 192, 203, 221, 321, 394, 483
  jurisprudence, 82, 189, 323, 377, 382, 599, 606, 607, 609
  jurists, 82–83, 98, 100, 131–32, 133–34, 135–36, 138, 144–45, 415, 493–94
  law and religion, 189, 240–41, 245, 253–54, 259–60, 265–67, 283, 290, 292, 302
  law and state, 181, 189–91, 203–4, 212–13, 219, 221, 225, 321, 453–54, 496
  law as text, 19, 22, 24–25, 28–30, 40–41, 43–45, 51, 64, 68, 69–71
  legal procedure, 307–9, 317–18, 324–26, 332–33, 337–38, 339–40, 350, 356–57, 366–67, 369–70
  legal science, 81, 82–83, 98–102, 106–8, 116, 118
  legislation, 33, 111, 201
  magistrates, 191, 364, 369, 453
  officials, 192, 221, 399
  plaintiffs, 58, 326
  praetors *see* praetors
  Principate, 100, 106, 116, 190, 317–18, 323, 356, 370, 383, 498
  early, 136, 309, 340
  property, 513–14, 518–19, 522–24, 525, 541–42, 545–47, 552, 556–57, 558–59
  provinces, 19, 309, 395, 482, 514, 529
  Republican *see* Republican Rome
  Senate, 29, 35–36, 134, 136, 169, 176–77, 190–91, 201–2, 253–54, 266
  society, 154, 254, 396
  status and family, 377, 380, 383, 397, 409–10, 417–18, 423–24, 435, 444–45
  system, 417, 496, 524, 595
  tradition, 90, 117, 178
  Twelve Tables, 35–36, 43, 58, 307, 462
  war, peace and interstate relations, 147, 154, 165–69, 176–77, 178
royal administration, 29–30, 248, 261, 268, 276, 316, 368

698

Index

royal courts, 185, 193, 195, 207, 223, 261, 311, 316, 326, 329
royal edicts, 25, 207–8
royal judges, 208, 315
Rufus, Servius Sulpicius, 106, 116
rule of law, 20, 201, 205, 206, 305, 611
rulers *see* individual names, dynasties and civilizations.
ruling classes, 41, 172, 451, 454, 458–59, 510
ruling power, 191–93, 230
rulings, 14, 21, 77, 79, 88, 125, 141, 208, 220, 433, *see also* judgments

Sabbath, 255
  laws, 129, 284
sabhā (courthouse), 216, 320
sabhyas (assessors), 90–91, 124, 216–17, 312, 362, 365
Sabinus, Masurius, 106–7, 116
šābuʿôt (festival of weeks), 256
sacer, 290, 463, 475
sacra, 283
sacramentum, 81
sacred laws, 282, 289
sacred space, 289, 292–93, 294
sacrifices
  animals, 285, 572
  commerce and contracts, 569
  crime, redress and social control, 487
  five great, 257, 263, 287
  law and religion, 256–60, 263–64, 265, 273, 279, 281–82, 284–86, 287, 289–90, 293–95
  law as text, 40
  legal procedure, 348–49
  pagan, 249
  state, 263–64, 287, 457
  status and family, 429
  war, peace and interstate relations, 154, 155, 160, 172–73, 175, 178
sages, 78–79, 90, 92–93, 105, 112, 140, 604
sales, 44–47, 282–83, 499, 529–30, 534–35, 540–42, 544, 549–50, 580–82, 583–97
  contracts, 52–53, 133, 137, 529, 550, 582, 584–85, 588, 592
  credit, 550, 581, 587
  documents, 549, 592
  of land, 49, 345, 526, 560, 567, 578, 580, 586–87, 592
  of moveables, 587
  private, 523, 549, 592
  slaves, 49, 52, 137, 545, 580, 586, 588, 590, 592
sāmanta (allies), 158

samavāya (consociation), 158–59
Samsu-iluna, 205, 428
sanctuaries, 149, 152, 162, 257, 265, 282–83, 289, 297, 547
  land, 290
  regulations, 282
Sanskrit, 10, 34, 55, 69, 427, 492, 548
Sardinia, 153, 566
Sastra, 286–87
Scaevola, Cervidius, 100, 131
Scaevola, Quintus Mucius, 116, 131–33, 593
scepters, 184
scholars, 31–32, 36, 65–66, 110, 232, 280–81, 290–93, 355, 600, 607–8
  biblical, 126, 294
  classically trained, 607–8
  modern, 43, 67, 138, 177, 199, 342, 400, 418, 507, 605
schools, 6, 62, 68, 84, 85–86, 102, 104–5, 107–8, 118, 187
  law, xv, 15, 66, 102
Scipio Nasica, P., 454–55
scribes
  law and religion, 241, 261, 278, 291–92
  law as text, 34, 37, 48, 51–54, 61
  legal, 26, 61
  legal procedure, 312–13, 315–16, 329, 345–46, 358, 366, 367
  legal science, 77–78, 87, 88, 91–92, 109, 111–12, 124, 125, 145
  professional, 345
  property, 520, 563
scriptural laws, 128–29
scriptures, 127–29, 195
sea, 151, 163, 519, 547, 552, 566–67
seals, 575, 578, 581, 596
Second Roman–Carthaginian War, 154, 167, 176
secondary texts, 23–25, 65–67, 72
secular laws, 239, 598
sefu (bailiff), 87, 197, 258, 330, 360
Seleucus Nicator, 150, 393
self-defence, 143, 171, 178, 502
sellers, 45, 403, 520, 528–30, 539, 550–51, 576, 581, 586–92
Senate, 35–36, 99, 134, 136, 176–77, 190–91, 201–2, 253–54, 259, 266
senators, 178, 266, 388, 452, 454, 458, 464, 475, 500
Septimius Severus, emperor, 395, 413
servants, 172, 254, 296, 338, 379, 395, 402, 466, 515, 570
service households, 400, 544–45

699

Index

servile persons, 400, 545
servitude, 403, 559, 568
   penal, 288, 359, 368, 373, 470, 472, 474, 556
   status, 395–406
settlement, disputes *see* disputes, resolution/settlement.
sex, 80, 259, 292, 296–97, 404, 406, 419, 441, 443, 445
sexual crimes, 194, 329, 499, 595 *see also* bestiality; incest; rape
Shamash, sun-god, 261, 504
Shang shu, 172–73
Shang Yang, 85, 469–70, 478, 534
Shang, , 13, 26, 160, 173, 211 *see also* China
Shangjunshu, 85
shanyu, 161
Shattizawa, 570
shi, 42, 88, 172, 329, 348, 400
shield of Achilles, 15, 24, 79, 188, 209, 216, 335
shrines, 239, 240, 256, 272, 275, 292–94, 350, 532, 547
shuyi (commentary), 65, 87, 121, 354, 360
Sicily, 153, 175, 215
signatures, 54, 56, 111, 366, 367, 563, 578, 596
Silk Road, 576, 596
silver, 335, 421, 441, 449, 499–500, 546
sins, 76, 256–57, 285, 297, 359, 401, 485–87
Sippar, 205, 405
sisters, 157, 246, 420, 466, 553, 555, 556, 558
slave status, 389, 396, 403, 405, 406, 543
slave-husbands, 404, 405
slavery, 144, 395–406, 417, 420, 464, 541–44, 612–13
slaves, 398, 613
   commerce and contracts, 581–82, 586–87, 588–91, 592, 597
   crime, redress and social control, 464, 466, 468, 473, 475–76, 480, 493, 499, 500, 506–7
   evidence, 346, 484
   female, 298, 397, 401–3, 404–6
   freed, 382, 397–99
   Jewish, 403
   law and religion, 260, 262, 278, 298
   law and state, 189, 212–13
   law as text, 45–47, 49, 52, 69
   legal procedure, 307, 325–26, 341, 346, 355–56, 374
   legal science, 125, 134
   male, 298, 405
   property, 517, 519, 522, 528, 540, 541–45, 552, 555, 558, 563–64
   sale, 49, 52, 137, 545, 580, 586, 588, 590, 592
   status and family, 379, 381, 382–84, 385–86, 395–406, 408, 414–15, 417, 422, 441
   testimony, 343, 346, 398
   war, peace and interstate relations, 149
slave-wives, 404
social classes, 90, 312, 357, 374, 400, 424
social control, xiv, 2, 446–511
social hierarchy, 406, 501, 510
social justice, 70, 225, 386
social practices, 18, 98, 206
social status, 13, 344, 379–80, 386, 390, 392, 394, 437, 441, 443–44
societas (partnership), 164, 167
Socrates, 62, 95, 252–53, 366
soldiers, 150, 153, 158, 161, 171–72, 394, 539, 558, 573, 575
solemn declarations (*shi*), 172, 329, 348
solicitors, 89
Solomon, king, 24, 243
Solon, 28–30, 35, 40, 50, 60, 94–95, 239, 246, 381
   laws, 68, 115
Song dynasty, 110
sons
   adopted, 42, 428
   commerce and contracts, 570
   of concubines, 433, 436
   crime, redress and social control, 457, 466, 469, 497, 505
   elder, 431, 557
   eldest, 423, 432, 436, 553–54, 555
   'female', 430–31
   firstborn, 433
   law and religion, 249, 254, 270, 275
   law and state, 184
   law as text, 42, 47
   legal procedure, 325
   legal science, 106–7, 139
   natural, 42, 50
   property, 522, 542, 551, 553–57, 561
   status and family, 400, 401, 405, 407–8, 410–11, 425–26, 428–30, 431–32, 434, 435–37
   see also children
sorcery, 287, 297–301 *see also* magic; witchcraft
source materials, 158, 229, 423, 610
   commentaries, 4
   documentary records, 4
   model forensic speeches *see* forensic speeches.
   normative texts, 3
   portrayals of legal processes, 6
   property, 524–26
   records of cases, 5–6, 9, 56, 58, 60–61, 63, 111, 276, 367, 368

Index

reports, 5–6, 58, 67–68
ritual forms, 7
types, 3–7
Southeast Asia, 34, 182, 381, 438, 614
sovereigns, 159, 183, 213, 379, 444, 469, 501, 546, 612
sovereignty, 159, 172, 448
Sparta
  helots, 382, 398, 401
  law and religion, 239
  law and state, 188, 226
  law as text, 21
  legal procedure, 306
  legal science, 94
  property, 556–57
  status and family, 382, 398, 401, 404, 422, 428, 434
  war, peace and interstate relations, 164, 174
Spartans, 153, 175, 188, 382
Spartiates, 382, 398, 422
speakers, 79, 96–97, 129–30, 165, 215, 264, 268, 270, 340
  in Athenian courts, 95, 97, 215
special pleas, 123, 334, 336
specialists, xi–xii, 66, 94, 105, 346
  legal, 87, 94, 114
  religious, 238, 264
'Speech at Fe', 172–73
speeches, forensic, 6, 16, 23, 61–62, 65, 82
spouses, 293, 325, 405, 418, 421–22, 424, 427, 431, 435 *see also* husbands; wives
Spring and Autumn period, 147, 168, 172, 178, 182, 329, 533
state actors, 453, 460, 511
state and property, 526–38
state authority, 35, 210, 438, 440, 447, 454, 501
  over law, 193–204
state bureaucracy, 193, 322, 374
state claims, 215, 448, 494–95
state courts, 93, 207–8, 217, 310, 336, 439
state governance, 234, 248
state institutions, 181, 190, 448, 562
state involvement, 230, 532
state law, 79, 181, 188, 193, 196–97, 204, 206–10, 215, 301, 492
state legal systems, 215–24
state legality, 611
state officials, 14, 185, 192, 240, 249, 280, 281, 287, 454, 457
state power, 184, 188–89, 193, 199, 219, 447, 450, 490, 491, 609
state religion, 247–49
state sacrifices, 263–64, 287, 457

state violence, 479–80
statecraft, 11, 184–85, 448, 477, 479, 480, 496, 501–10, 606–7
  practices, 451, 497, 499
  process, 450, 505
  processes of marking off, 448–68
  techniques, 481, 606–7
statues, 170, 215, 272, 281, 290, 462
  divine, 269, 279
status, 376–445
  distinctions, 378, 406, 416, 443, 444
  as a factor in legal penalties, 440–43
  family, 416–37
  formal, 377, 388, 613
  official, 221, 391, 393, 443, 453
  personal, 2, 205, 376–77, 378–79, 382, 386, 418, 441, 443, 445
  putatively natural ascriptive, 406–16
  slavery or servitude, 395–406
  special, 204, 260, 394, 440
  within polity, 379–91
status civitatis, 377
status familiae, 377
status libertatis, 377
statutes, 14–15, 603
  commerce and contracts, 592
  crime, redress and social control, 446
  imperial, 64, 99
  law and religion, 246, 288
  law and state, 194, 196, 201, 208
  law as text, 21, 23, 35, 37, 41, 42–43, 64
  legal procedure, 308–9, 327, 331, 354, 359–60, 363, 373
  legal science, 74–75, 98, 108–9, 120–22, 130, 132, 134–36, 140, 142, 145
  penal, 75, 120, 122, 455–56
  property, 537, 555–56, 559
  relevant, 120, 327, 359, 363
  status and family, 394
statutory law, 77, 135–37, 426
stelae, 25, 70
stipulatio, 335, 574, 575, 594
  customary, 589
  formal, 583–85, 589, 594
stipulations, 49, 233, 279, 425–26, 531, 548
Stoic philosophy, 176, 178
stolen goods, 337, 351, 353, 586
stone, 16, 23, 25, 28–29, 36, 452, 526, 528, 533, 539
  inscriptions, 203, 259
strangulation, 39, 288, 472
strict liability, 465, 467
strīdhana (women's wealth), 411, 554
'striking the drum', 373

subordinate parties, 569–71
subordination treaties, 155, 167
substantive law/rules, 6, 8, 11, 13, 19, 79, 111, 185, 303, 307
substitutes, 89, 278, 329, 338–39, 349
succession, 78, 81, 374, 409, 423, 432, 436, 518, 554, 555–56
  intestate, 435, 555, 557
  testate, 555, 557–58
Śūdras, 291, 400–1, 437, 458
Sui dynasty, 15, 314, 372–73, 455, 536–37 *see also* China
Sumeria, 8–9, 25–26, 40–41, 223–24, 385, 397, 563, 569, 577
  Neo-Sumerian period, 316, 366, 397, 586
sumptuary laws, 391
sun, 72, 85, 245, 249, 288, 296, 608
superiority (*maiestas*), 174, 203, 391, 453
superiors, 57, 63, 85, 281, 345, 371, 391, 442, 465, 467
supreme courts, 87, 109, 313–14, 363, 373
sureties, 152, 334–35, 350, 368, 572
surnames, 425, 429
surveys, land, 527, 608
synallagma (justice in exchange), 569, 593–94
synegoroi (fellow-speakers), 95
Syria, 46, 104, 107–8, 233, 252, 385, 408, 421

tablets, 29, 91, 242, 291, 299, 565, 570, 575, 577–78, 584
Tacitus, 67, 136, 574
Talmud, 105, 112–14, 127, 278, 380–81, 403, 488
Tang, 15
  Code, 15, 49, 121, 122, 287–88, 327, 330, 360, 425–26, 455–56
  commerce and contracts, 580, 592, 596–97
  crime, redress and social control, 455–56, 466, 474, 505
  early, 468
  law and religion, 263–64, 281, 287–88
  law as text, 42, 49, 52, 54, 65
  legal procedure, 305, 314, 320, 327, 330, 334, 354, 360, 364, 372–73
  legal science, 87, 109–11, 121, 122, 139
  Penal Code, 39–40, 65
  property, 536–37, 545, 555–56
  status and family, 391–92, 411, 413, 415, 425–26, 436, 439
  statutes, 362–63
  war, peace and interstate relations, 151, 161 *see also* China
Tanglüshuyi, 38–39
Tannaitic period, 78–79, 92–94, 105, 113

tax records, 346, 399
tax revenue, 516, 532–33
taxes, 43–45, 207, 388, 389, 466, 468, 516–17, 527, 529, 533
  property, 531, 581
teachers, 79, 89, 104–8, 413, 455, 533, 554, 572
Tefhape, 343, 562
temple courts, 271, 279, 280
temple estates, 386, 513–14, 515, 520, 562
temple officials/personnel, 91, 268, 278–79, 291, 296, 320, 323
temples
  administration, 50, 248, 250
  commerce and contracts, commerce and contracts, 565
  crime, redress, and social control, 492, 504
  Eanna, 291, 335
  gates, 272, 276, 280, 320
  Hindu, 250, 280
  law and religion, 248–50, 256, 266, 268, 271–73, 278–81, 285–86, 290, 291, 295–96
  law as text, 28, 30, 47–48, 50, 72
  legal procedure, 314–15, 319–21, 323, 335, 343, 349–50
  local, 280, 317, 523, 562
  property, 514–15, 518, 523, 528, 531, 539, 543, 562
  status and family, 385, 387, 397, 430, 439
  walls, 70, 171
  war, peace and interstate relations, 150, 162, 175–76
'ten abominations', 287, 327, 455–56
tenants, 399, 513, 527, 534, 540
territorial states, 148, 155, 170
territories, 22, 25, 147, 150–51, 153, 203–4, 211, 322, 448, 450
  enemy, 148, 152, 176
Tertullian, 462, 464
Testa, C. Trebatius, 138
testaments, 108, 137, 344, 346, 430, 544, 553
testate succession, 555, 557–58
testatio, 344
testators, 47, 50, 53, 432, 433, 435, 437, 553, 556, 558
testimony, 56, 57, 60, 307, 337, 342–43, 346, 354–55, 357–60, 362
  false, 357, 358–61, 371, 375, 477, 480
  slave, 343, 346, 398
  see also evidence; witnesses
texts *see* law as text
Thebes, 22, 59, 72, 163–64, 226, 249, 273, 280, 285, 306
theft, 13

commerce and contracts, 568, 591, 595
crime, redress and social control, 467, 471, 476–77, 480, 495, 497, 499, 501, 503
law and religion, 245, 281, 287, 289
law and state, 194, 205
legal procedure, 329, 336, 339, 343, 351–52, 360
legal science, 121–22
objects, 287
property, 548
status and family, 401, 440
temple property, 279, 323
Theodosius II, emperor, 37, 40, 119, 338, 384, 537
Theophrastus, 97, 529
things of the king, 92, 245, 301
things of Yahweh, 92, 245, 301
third parties
  commerce and contracts, 586–88, 592
  crime, redress, and social control, 458, 484
  law and state, 215
  law as text, 52–53
  legal procedure, 333, 334–35
  legal science, 97
  property, 528–29
  status and family, 403, 418
  war, peace and interstate relations, 164, 168–69, 180
Thoth, 257, 300, 474
Thucydides, 67, 174
Tian (heaven), 86, 140
Tiberius, emperor, 107, 254, 384, 497
timesis (evaluation), 369, 476
tingwei (coomandant of the court), 87, 314
title, 517–18, 520
  buyers, 586–88
  recording, 527–38
titles (of persons), 55, 123, 167, 190–91, 211, 243, 315–16, 385, 386, 436
Topica, 138
Torah, 79, 114, 126, 387
tort law, 495, 499, 501
torts, 81, 396, 403, 491, 493–501
torture, 129, 218, 304–5, 358, 363, 366, 383, 413, 484
  for evidentiary purposes, 353–56, 374
  judicial, 354, 398
Tosefta, 112–13
town elders, 125, 277
tractates, 113–14, 255, 256
trade, 116, 151, 399, 446, 532, 566, 567, 576
  long-distance, 566–67, 596–97
traders, 35, 151, 223, 312, 362, 437, 533, 539, 607

foreign, 150–51, 153
trades, 399, 543
shameful, 464
traditions, xi, 11–12, 17–18, 599, 604, 606
  crime, redress and social control, 465, 502
  law and religion, 238, 240, 241, 282, 286, 288
  law and state, 182–84, 189, 193, 196, 203, 224, 228, 229–30
  law as text, 22, 23, 29–30, 35–36
  legal procedure, 311, 339
  legal science, 73–74, 76, 78, 105, 112–13, 140–41
  literary, 111, 114
  property, 515, 526, 543, 549
  status and family, 377, 396, 406, 416, 426–27, 444
  textual, 75, 76, 81, 312
transactions, 5, 7, 9, 18, 608–9
  commerce and contracts, 567–68, 571, 577, 579, 581, 590, 594, 595
  crime, redress and social control, 447, 480, 497, 498–99
  involuntary, 480–81, 593
  land, 14, 45
  law and religion, 262, 290
  law and state, 194, 196–97, 220
  law as text, 44–47, 49–50, 51–52, 54
  legal, 9, 23, 70, 119, 137, 266, 325, 342, 385, 415
  legal procedure, 303, 342, 344–45
  legal science, 116, 123
  private, 14, 48, 480, 494, 496
  property, 526–27, 528, 530, 537, 541, 542, 548
  status and family, 409, 413, 427
transferees, 538, 552, 576
transferors, 552, 576
transfers
  land, 19, 25, 345, 531, 567, 576
  property, 5, 7, 445, 552, 594
transregional macro-statuses, 388, 613
treason, 62, 216, 254, 339, 361, 381, 469
treaties, 71, 149, 153, 154–56, 158–60, 164, 165–68, 169, 232–33, 569–73
  Hittite, 571–72
  parity, 155, 267, 570
  practice, 574–75
  subordination, 155, 167
  vassal, 232–33, 570
  see also foedus.
treatises, 11, 60, 70, 76, 89–91, 97, 109, 111, 147, 194
trial records, 9, 56, 60–61, 63, 111, 276, 317, 330, 367, 368
trial scenes, 6, 24, 68, 335

trials, 9
  crime, redress, and social control, 455, 458, 463, 484, 492
  criminal, 205, 321
  descriptions, 5–6, 9
    see also trail records.
  homicide, 111, 129, 293, 364
  law and religion, 246, 251, 268–69, 271, 274, 275–76, 277, 279, 281, 300–2
  law and state, 185, 216, 219, 222
  law as text, 32, 43, 47–48, 56–58, 59, 60–62, 69
  legal procedure, 304–8, 317–18, 330–31, 333–35, 337–38, 343–44, 349–50, 355–56, 357–58, 367–69
  legal science, 112, 120
  Nippur Homicide, 111, 364
  property, 561–63
  status and family, 383, 396, 408, 415
  war, peace and interstate relations, 168–69
tribes, 160–61, 163, 172, 188, 289, 322, 379
tribunals, 208, 217, 279, 484
tribunes, 165, 201–2, 452
tribute, 151, 156, 160–61, 167, 265, 460
Turfan, 327, 576, 581, 592
tutors, 409, 435, 530
Twelve Tables, 35–36, 43, 58, 307, 462
typologies, xii, 477, 481
tyranny, 147, 460–61, 489, 613
tyrants, 97, 199, 225, 247, 252, 449, 450

udara-dāsa ('belly-slave'), 402
udāsīna (uninvolved), 179
Ulpian, 100, 104, 107, 116–17, 144, 202, 240, 283, 493–94, 594
Umma, 569, 571
uncles see fathers, brothers.
unequal alliances, 159–60
unfree status, 381, 395, 444, 613
uniformity, 27, 52, 54, 64, 179, 217, 219, 306, 364
universe, 86, 139–40, 237–38, 245, 251, 447, 486, 491, 497
unleavened bread, 255–56, 488
unwritten law, 143, 187, 198, 209, 239
Upaniṣads, 10
urban praetors, 213, 307–8, 369, 435, 498
urination, 296
Ur-Namma, laws of, 26, 30, 112, 298, 404, 405, 566
Uruk, 46, 565, 601, 602

usucapio (long possession), 538, 541, 551, 552
uttarasākṣin (secondary witnesses), 343

vades (guarantors), 335
vadimonium (personal surety), 335
Vaiśya, 312, 357
varṇas (castes), 12, 388–90, 392–93, 400, 613
vassal treaties, 232–33, 570
vassals, 156–57, 161, 184, 232–33, 268
Vedas, 10, 76, 140, 141, 195, 238, 291
Vedic rites, 280, 285
Vedic scholars, 531, 533
veracity, 269, 336, 357, 362
verbal assault, 329, 390, 499, 595
verdicts, 56–58, 59–61, 62–63, 272–73, 276–77, 279, 303–4, 356–57, 364, 365, 366, 367, 368, 369, 370, 371, 375
  documents recording, 367
  enforcement, 368–70
  in legal procedure, 364–70.
  see also judgments; rulings.
Vestal Virgins, 454
villages, 87, 310–11, 312, 316, 319, 322, 437, 439, 531, 532
violence, 173, 184, 454, 456, 464, 473, 479–80, 499–505, 506–7, 509–10
  monopolization of, 501–10
  rights to use, 453, 506–9
  use of, 489
  see also sāhasa
virgins, 339, 414, 419–20, 426, 430, 454
vis publica (political violence), 484–85
Viṣṇuṣeṇa, Charter of, 35, 41, 195, 390, 438
viziers, 23, 30, 72, 280, 527
  'Duties of the Vizier', 40, 71, 386
voluntary associations, 437–40
vyavahāra (transactional law), 12, 21, 193–94, 207, 304, 365, 427
vyavahārapada (titles of law), 111, 194, 328

wagers, 334–35, 365, 486
wages, 319, 328, 365, 368, 499, 585, 595
  non-payment, 328, 499, 585, 595
war, 146–80, 478–79, 544–45
  arbitration, meditation and Common-Peace experiment, 168–69
  declarations of, 170–71, 175–76, 178
  hospitality rules and customs, 148–55
  states declaring wars and just wars, 169–79

states forming alliances and pursuing diplomacy, 155–68
see also individual wars
warranties, 550, 588, 590
Warring States period, 84–86, 120, 173, 197, 211, 238, 313, 339, 465, 533
wartime, 170, 178
Wasps, 68, 96
water, 269, 273, 296, 320, 347–48, 514, 523, 532, 559, 572
supply, 44, 162
wax, 577, 584
wealth, 137, 158, 191, 246, 341, 352, 381, 401, 561, 564
bride, 47, 411, 427
women's wealth (*strīdhana*), 411, 554
Weber, Max, 502–3, 506–7
Wei, 15, 38, 88, 109, 373, 505, 534–36
Northern, 281, 288, 372–73, 425–26, 472, 505, 535–36
see also China.
wei dao (being theft), 121–22
Wen, emperor, 473
Western Zhou
crime, redress and social control, 473, 495
law and state, 182, 185, 211, 227
law as text, 26, 48, 58
legal procedure, 313, 329, 339, 348, 362
property, 13, 516
status and family, 391
war, peace and interstate relations, 147, 160, 172
see also China.
widows, 405, 407–8, 410, 419, 427, 430, 436, 437, 555, 612
wills, 5, 14, 23, 44, 50–51, 53, 346–47, 408, 553, 556
extant, 556
written, 49–50, 432
wine, 574–75, 581, 592, 597
winning parties, 268, 366–67
wisdom, 92, 141–42, 237
witchcraft, 288, 298 *see also* magic; sorcery
witness testimony *see* testimony.
witnesses, 52–53, 54, 56–57, 63–64, 123, 273–74, 331, 341–46, 355–63, 575–83
divine, 50, 569
evidence, 342–44, 359–60
false, 360, 477, 480
names, 52, 54, 273, 520
wives, 270–71, 404–5, 407–8, 418–21, 423–24, 426, 508, 554–56, 561, 570 *see also* spouses

women
commerce and contracts, 595
crime, redress and social control, 499–500, 509
free, 403–4, 405
law and religion, 253, 270, 275, 288, 292, 294, 296, 298–99
law and state, 194, 225
legal procedure, 325, 327, 329, 338, 342–43, 347, 350, 353, 374
legal science, 125, 128
pregnant, 125, 411
property, 524, 530, 535, 542, 546–48, 551, 554–55, 557, 558
status and family, 386, 401–2, 407–11, 419–25, 427, 432–33, 434, 436, 438, 441
war, peace and interstate relations, 172, 177
workers, 14, 565, 567
written agreements, 425, 541, 549, 583
written collections of laws, 30, 237, 261
written contracts, 46, 48, 50, 55, 386, 421, 579, 582, 583
written documents, 17, 27, 44–47, 50–52, 54, 60, 346, 576, 578–79, 584
written evidence, xiv, 3, 7, 121, 196–97, 346, 549, 563, 583
written laws, 15–16, 22, 33–34, 36, 48, 187, 239, 305–6, 602, 604
written petitions, 59, 331, 562
written texts, 22–23, 33, 71
wrongdoers, 170, 175–76, 215, 293, 458, 495, 607
wrongs, 279, 284, 481, 494, 543, 568
private, 59, 494
public, 489
Wu, emperor, 88, 372
Wudi, emperor, 161
wu jia (five families), 466–67

xenia (guest friendship), 152
Xiongnu, 161
Xuan, emperor, 507

Yahweh, 78, 125, 232–33, 236, 247–48, 255–56, 278, 284–85, 294–95
exclusive worship, 248
things of, 92, 245, 301
Yājñavalkya, 32, 90, 111, 185, 208, 304, 345, 486, 526, 554

Yarushalmi, 106, 113–14
Yehuda Ha-Nasi, 93, 113
yu dao tong fa (by the same law as theft), 121–22

Zai Fadu, 88
Zelophehad, daughters of, 433
Zēria, 335
Zeus, 16, 80, 174–75, 187, 246, 504
Zhang Fei, 4, 87, 109
Zheng Xuan, 88, 109, 339
Zhou, 160, 172, 211, 251, 392, 572
  king, 173, 211, 495
  princes, 172–73
  royal house, 160
  Western *see* Western Zhou.
  see also China.
Zoroastrianism, 614
Zouyanshu, 110, 363
Zuozhuan, 172